Contemporary Theatre, Film and Television

ISSN 0749-064X

Contemporary Theatre, Film and Television

A Biographical Guide Featuring Performers, Directors, Writers, Producers, Designers, Managers, Choreographers, Technicians, Composers, Executives, Dancers, and Critics in the United States, Canada, Great Britain and the World

Thomas Riggs, Editor

Volume 79

THOMSON

GALE

Detroit • New York • San Francisco • New Haven, Conn. • Waterville, Maine • London

Contemporary Theatre, Film & Television, Vol. 79

Editor
Thomas Riggs

CTFT Staff
Erika Fredrickson, Mariko Fujinaka, Annette Petrusso, Susan Risland, Lisa Sherwin, Arlene True, Andrea Votava, Pam Zuber

Project Editor
Michael J. Tyrkus

Editorial Support Services
Ryan Cartmill

Composition and Electronic Capture
Gary Oudersluys

Manufacturing
Drew Kalasky

LIBRARY OF CONGRESS CATALOG CARD NUMBER 84-649371

ISBN-13: 978-0-7876-9052-6
ISBN-10: 0-7876-9052-X
ISSN: 0749-064X

This title is also available as an e-book.
ISBN-13: 978-1-4144-3283-0, ISBN-10: 1-4144-3283-6
Contact your Thomson Gale sales representative for ordering information.

Printed in the United States of America
10 9 8 7 6 5 4 3 2 1

Contents

Preface.. vii

Biographies... 1

Cumulative Index 347
    (Including references to *Who's Who in the Theatre* and
    Who Was Who in the Theatre)

Preface

Provides Broad, Single-Source Coverage in the Entertainment Field

Contemporary Theatre, Film and Television (*CTFT*) is a biographical reference series designed to provide students, educators, researchers, librarians, and general readers with information on a wide range of entertainment figures. Unlike single-volume reference works that focus on a limited number of artists or on a specific segment of the entertainment field, *CTFT* is an ongoing publication that includes entries on individuals active in the theatre, film, and television industries. Before the publication of *CTFT*, information-seekers had no choice but to consult several different sources in order to locate the in-depth biographical and credit data that makes *CTFT*'s one-stop coverage the most comprehensive available about the lives and work of performing arts professionals.

Scope

CTFT covers not only performers, directors, writers, and producers, but also behind-the-scenes specialists such as designers, managers, choreographers, technicians, composers, executives, dancers, and critics from the United States, Canada, Great Britain, and the world. With 254 entries in *CTFT 79*, the series now provides biographies on approximately 22,649 people involved in all aspects of theatre, film, and television.

CTFT gives primary emphasis to people who are currently active. New entries are prepared on major stars as well as those who are just beginning to win acclaim for their work. *CTFT* also includes entries on personalities who have died but whose work commands lasting interest.

Compilation Methods

CTFT editors identify candidates for inclusion in the series by consulting biographical dictionaries, industry directories, entertainment annuals, trade and general interest periodicals, newspapers, and online databases. Additionally, the editors of *CTFT* maintain regular contact with industry advisors and professionals who routinely suggest new candidates for inclusion in the series. Entries are compiled from published biographical sources which are believed to be reliable, but have not been verified for this edition by the listee or their agents.

Revised Entries

To ensure *CTFT*'s timeliness and comprehensiveness, entries from previous volumes, as well as from Gale's *Who's Who in the Theatre*, are updated for individuals who have been active enough to require revision of their earlier biographies. Such individuals will merit revised entries as often as there is substantial new information to provide. Obituary notices for deceased entertainment personalities already listed in *CTFT* are also published.

Accessible Format Makes Data Easy to Locate

CTFT entries, modeled after those in Gale's highly regarded *Contemporary Authors* series, are written in a clear, readable style designed to help users focus quickly on specific facts. The following is a summary of the information found in *CTFT* sketches:

- *ENTRY HEADING:* the form of the name by which the listee is best known.

- *PERSONAL:* full or original name; dates and places of birth and death; family data; colleges attended, degrees earned, and professional training; political and religious affiliations when known; avocational interests.

- *ADDRESSES:* home, office, agent, publicist and/or manager addresses.

- *CAREER:* tagline indicating principal areas of entertainment work; resume of career positions and other vocational achievements; military service.

- *MEMBER:* memberships and offices held in professional, union, civic, and social organizations.

- *AWARDS, HONORS:* theatre, film, and television awards and nominations; literary and civic awards; honorary degrees.

- *CREDITS:* comprehensive title-by-title listings of theatre, film, and television appearance and work credits, including roles and production data as well as debut and genre information.

- *RECORDINGS:* album, single song, video, and taped reading releases; recording labels and dates when available.

- *WRITINGS:* title-by-title listing of plays, screenplays, scripts, and musical compositions along with production information; books, including autobiographies, and other publications.

- *ADAPTATIONS:* a list of films, plays, and other media which have been adapted from the listee's work.

- *SIDELIGHTS:* favorite roles; portions of agent-prepared biographies or personal statements from the listee when available.

- *OTHER SOURCES:* books, periodicals, and internet sites where interviews or feature stories can be found.

Access Thousands of Entries Using *CTFT*'s Cumulative Index

Each volume of *CTFT* contains a cumulative index to the entire series. As an added feature, this index also includes references to all seventeen editions of *Who's Who in the Theatre* and to the four-volume compilation *Who Was Who in the Theatre.*

Available in Electronic Format

Online. Recent volumes of *CTFT* are available online as part of the Gale Biographies (GALBIO) database accessible through LEXIS-NEXIS. For more information, contact LEXIS-NEXIS, P.O. Box 933, Dayton, OH 45401-0933; phone (937) 865-6800, toll-free: 800-543-6862.

Suggestions Are Welcome

Contemporary Theatre, Film and Television is intended to serve as a useful reference tool for a wide audience, so comments about any aspect of this work are encouraged. Suggestions of entertainment professionals to include in future volumes are also welcome. Send comments and suggestions to: The Editor, *Contemporary Theatre, Film and Television,* Thomson Gale, 27500 Drake Rd., Farmington Hills, MI 48331-3535; or feel free to call toll-free at 1-800-877-GALE.

Contemporary Theatre, Film and Television

ACKERMAN, Robert Allan 1945–

PERSONAL

Born 1945, in Brooklyn, New York, NY.

Addresses: *Agent*—International Creative Management, 10250 Constellation Way, Ninth Floor, Los Angeles, CA 90067.

Career: Director and producer. Directed productions at the Yale Repertory Theatre, New Haven, CT; the Eugene O'Neill Playwrights Conference, Waterford, CT; and the Haifa Municipal Theatre, Haifa, Israel.

Member: Directors Guild of America.

Awards, Honors: Obie Award, direction, *Village Voice*, 1978, for *A Prayer for My Daughter;* Outer Critics Circle Award, best director, and Drama Desk Award nomination, outstanding director of a play, both 1983, for *Extremities;* Outer Critics Circle Award, 1983, for *Slab Boys;* Emmy Award nominations, outstanding directing for a miniseries, movie, or a special, and (with others) outstanding miniseries, both 2001, and Directors Guild of America Award nomination, outstanding directorial achievement in movies for television, 2003, all for *Life with Judy Garland: Me and My Shadows;* Emmy Award nomination, outstanding directing for a miniseries, movie, or a dramatic special, 2003, for *The Roman Spring of Mrs. Stone;* Emmy Award nomination, outstanding made for television movie, 2003, and Television Producer of the Year Award in Longform, PGA Golden Laurel awards, 2004, both with others, both for *My House in Umbria;* Emmy Award nominations (with others), outstanding made for television movie, 2004, for *The Reagans.*

CREDITS

Film Work:
Director, *Safe Passage* (also known as *Duygu gecidi, Halalhirre varva, Loin des yeux, pres du coeur, Ritrovarsi,* and *Tensa espera*), New Line Cinema, 1994.
Director and producer, *The Ramen Girl,* c. 2007.

Television Work; Miniseries:
Director, *Night Sins* (also known as *El pecado, Night Sins—Der Moerder ist unter uns, Pecados da noite, Pitkaen yon varjot,* and *Puzzle criminel*), CBS, 1997.
Director and co–executive producer, *Life with Judy Garland: Me and My Shadows* (also known as *Me & My Shadows, I skuggan av Judy Garland, Judy Garland, la vie d'une etoile, Judy Garland: L'ombre d'une etoile, Legenden Judy Garland,* and *Taehtitarina: Judy Garland*), ABC, 2001.

Television Work; Movies:
Director, *Mrs. Cage,* PBS, 1992.
Director, *David's Mother,* CBS, 1994.
Director, *Radiant City,* ABC, 1996.
Director and executive producer, *Suddenly,* ABC, 1996.
Director and co–executive producer, *The Reef* (also known as *Passion's Way* and *Das Riff*), CBS, 1997.
Director, *Outrage,* ABC, 1998.
Director, *Double Platinum* (also known as *Double platine, Double Platinum—Doppel Platin!, Duo de platino,* and *Kaksi taehteae*), ABC, 1999.
Director, *Forget Me Never* (also known as *Au coeur du labyrinthe*), CBS, 1999.
Director, *Baby* (also known as *Baby—Glueck auf Zeit, Hasta que vuelva, Sophie, Un intrus la famille,* and *Utracone dziecko*), TNT, 2000.
Director and co–executive producer, *The Reagans,* Showtime, 2003.
Director, *The Roman Springs of Mrs. Stone* (also known as *Tennessee Williams' "The Roman Springs of Mrs. Stone"*), Showtime, 2003.

Executive producer, *My House in Umbria* (also known as *La mia casa in Umbria*), HBO, 2003.

Television Director; Episodic:
Directed episodes of *Nothing Sacred* (also known as *Priesthood, Ei mitaeaen pyhaeae, Ein Ganz normaler Heiliger,* and *Une sacree vie*), ABC.

Television Work; Pilots:
Director and executive producer for the project *Filthy Gorgeous,* Showtime.

Stage Director:
Ionescopade, Theatre Four, New York City, 1974.
Joe's Opera, Musical Theatre Lab, St. Clement's Church Theatre, New York City, 1975.
Memphis Is Gone, St. Clement's Church Theatre, 1977.
A Prayer for My Daughter, New York Shakespeare Festival, Public Theater, New York City, 1977–78.
Broadway, Wilbur Theatre, Boston, MA, 1978.
A Christmas Carol: Scrooge and Marley, Center Stage, Baltimore, MD, 1978.
Fathers and Sons, New York Shakespeare Festival, Public Theater, 1978.
Taken in Marriage, New York Shakespeare Festival, Public Theater, 1979.
Bent, New Apollo Theatre, New York City, 1979–80.
The Front Page, Williamstown Theatre Festival, Main Stage, Williamstown, MA, 1980.
Salt Lake City Skyline, New York Shakespeare Festival, Public Theater, 1980.
Arms and the Man, Williamstown Theatre Festival, Main Stage, 1981.
Family Devotions, New York Shakespeare Festival, Public Theater, 1981.
Holiday, Center Theatre Group, Ahmanson Theatre, Los Angeles, 1981.
Extremities, Westside Arts Center, Cheryl Crawford Theatre, New York City, 1982, then Los Angeles Public Theatre, Los Angeles, 1983.
Slab Boys, Playhouse Theatre, New York City, 1983.
Legs Diamond (musical), Mark Hellinger Theatre, New York City, 1988–89.
A Madhouse in Goa, Lyric Hammersmith Theatre, London, 1989.
Burn This, Lyric Theatre, London, beginning 1990.
Salome, Circle in the Square Theatre, New York City, 1992.
Scenes from an Execution, Mark Taper Forum, Los Angeles, 1993.

Also directed productions of *Flesh and Blood, The Mystery of the Rose Bouquet, Torch Song Trilogy,* and *When She Danced,* all in London.

Stage Appearances:
The judge and Steve Frager, *An Ordinary Man,* Cherry Lane Theatre, New York City, 1968.

WRITINGS

Writings for the Stage:
Author of concept, *Ionescopade* (based on the work of Eugene Ionesco), Theatre Four, New York City, 1974.
Tabletop, American Place Theatre, New York City, 2000.

ADLER, Charles 1957–
(Charlie Adler)

PERSONAL

Born February 20, 1957, in Brooklyn, NY. *Avocational Interests:* Animals.

Addresses: *Agent*—Innovative Artists, 1505 10th St., Santa Monica, CA 90401; (voice) Arlene Thornton and Associates, Inc., 12711 Ventura Blvd., Suite 490, Studio City, CA 91604.

Career: Actor, voice artist, voice director, director, and writer. Performed with the improvisation group the Proposition. Nickelodeon Television Network, appeared in *Johnnie Talk* (short comedy spots), 2003; appeared in hundreds of commercials for McDonald's restaurants, Coca–Cola soft drinks, Beck's beer, and other products. Also works as an artist; formerly worked as remedial reading teacher, church janitor and caretaker, house painter and renovator, and nude model.

Awards, Honors: Annie Award nomination, outstanding individual achievement for voice acting in an animated television production, International Animated Film Society, 1999, for *Cow and Chicken;* named "Voice of the Decade" by *Animation World News;* Helen Hayes Award nomination, best actor, Washington Theatre Awards Society, for *Torch Song Trilogy;* DramaLogue Award, best actor, for *There Used to Be Fireflies.*

CREDITS

Film Appearances:
(As Charlie Adler) Voice of Popo, *Rainbow Brite and the Star Stealer* (animated), Warner Bros., 1985.
Voices of Spike and woodland creature, *My Little Pony: The Movie* (animated), De Laurentiis Entertainment Group, 1986.
Voice of Silverbolt, *Transformers: Five Faces of Darkness* (animated), 1986.

Voice of chimp, *Project X,* 1987.

(As Charlie Adler) Voice of Low Light, *G.I. Joe: The Movie* (animated; also known as *Action Force: The Movie*), 1987.

(As Charlie Adler) Voices of Deputy Fuzz and Tex Hex, *Bravestarr* (animated; also known as *Bravestarr: The Legend*), Taurus Entertainment, 1988.

(As Charlie Adler) Voices of weasels, pig driver, peasant, and man in street, *The Prince and the Pauper* (animated; also known as *Mickey's "The Prince and the Pauper"*), Buena Vista, 1990.

(As Charlie Adler) Voice of Arab, *DuckTales: The Movie—Treasure of the Lost Lamp* (also known as *La bande a picsou: le tresor de la lampe perdue*), Buena Vista, 1990.

Voice of Buster J. Bunny, *Tiny Toon Adventures: How I Spent My Vacation* (animated; also known as *How I Spent My Vacation*), Warner Bros. Home Video, 1992.

Voice of Nails, *Cool World* (animated), Paramount, 1992.

Voices of Gazeem, melon merchant, and nuts merchant, *Aladdin* (animated), 1992.

Voice of Waggs, *Once Upon a Forest* (animated), Twentieth Century–Fox, 1993.

Voices of Cow, Chicken, and the Devil, *No Smoking!,* 1995.

Voices of Loki and others, *Siegfried & Roy: Masters of the Impossible,* Twentieth Century–Fox Home Entertainment, 1996.

Voice of Agent the Snake, *Rusty: A Dog's Tale* (also known as *Rusty: The Great Rescue*) 1997.

Voices of Hamburglar, a McNugget, and McSplorer, *The Wacky Adventures of Ronald McDonald: Scared Silly,* 1998.

Voice of United Express driver, *The Rugrats Movie* (animated), Paramount, 1998.

Voice of Mechanicles, *Aladdin's Arabian Adventures: Creatures of Invention* (animated), 1998.

(As Charlie Adler) Voice of inspector, *Rugrats in Paris: The Movie* (animated; also known as *Rugrats in Paris: The Movie—Rugrats II* and *Rugrats in Paris—Der Film*), Paramount, 2000.

Cindy, *No Prom for Cindy* (short film), 2002.

(As Charlie Adler) Voices of Templeton and Lurvy, *Charlotte's Web 2: Wilbur's Great Adventure* (animated), Paramount, 2003.

Voice of Grammy, *Tom and Jerry: The Fast and the Furry* (animated), Warner Home Video, 2004.

Film Director:
No Prom for Cindy (short film), 2002.

Animated Film Work; Additional Voices:
The Chipmunk Adventure, Samuel Goldwyn Company, 1987.

The Little Mermaid, Buena Vista, 1989.

The Rescuers Down Under, 1990.

(As Charlie Adler) *Aladdin,* Buena Vista, 1992.

The Flintstones Christmas in Bedrock, 1996.

Film Voice Director:
(As Charlie Adler) *The Wacky Adventures of Ronald McDonald: Scared Silly,* 1998.

The Rugrats Movie (animated), Paramount, 1998.

Rugrats in Paris: The Movie (animated; also known as *Rugrats in Paris: The Movie—Rugrats II* and *Rugrats in Paris—Der Film*), Paramount, 2000.

(As Charlie Adler) *The Wild Thornberrys Movie* (animated), Paramount, 2002.

Rugrats Go Wild (animated), Paramount, 2003.

Television Appearances; Animated Series:
Voice of young Smurf, *The Smurfs* (also known as *Smurfs' Adventures*), NBC, 1981.

Voices of Silverbolt, Duros, Triggerhappy, and Vorath, *Transformers* (also known as *Super God Robot Force, Transformers: Generation, Transformers: 2010,* and *Tatakae! Cho robot semeitai Transformers*), syndicated, 1984.

Voice of Low Light, *G.I. Joe* (also known as *Action Force* and *Chijo saikyo no Expert Team G.I. Joe*), syndicated, 1984.

Voice of Rowdy Roddy Piper in animated segments, *Rock 'n' Wrestling* (also known as *Hulk Hogan's "Rock 'n' Wrestling"*), CBS, 1985.

Voice of Natural "Nat" Smurf, *The Smurfs* (also known as *Smurfs' Adventures*), NBC, 1985–90.

Voices of Eric Raymond, Tech Rat, Johnny Walken, and others, *Jem!* (also known as *Jem and the Holograms;* broadcast in England as *Jem: The Movie*), syndicated, between 1985 and 1988.

Voices of Captain "Cavey" Caveman, Jr., and Mr. Bad, *The Flintstone Kids,* 1986.

Voice of Spike, a recurring role, *My Little Pony and Friends,* syndicated, 1986–87.

Voices of Rafael and others, *The Real Ghost Busters,* 1986–89, broadcast as *Slimer! and the Real Ghostbusters,* syndicated, 1988.

Voice of Kreeg, *Sky Commanders,* 1987.

Voice, *The Little Wizards,* 1987.

Voices of Deputy Fuzz and Tex Hex, recurring roles, *BraveStarr,* 1987–88.

Voice of Grouchy Bear, *The Adventures of Raggedy Ann and Andy,* CBS, 1988.

Voices of Pinky Dalton, pig, television announcer from Bit–2 News, and others, *The Good, the Bad and Huckleberry Hound,* 1988.

Voice of Hammerhead, *Dino–Riders,* syndicated, 1988.

(As Charlie Adler) Voice of Cowardly Lion, *The Wizard of Oz,* ABC, 1990.

Voices of Buster J. Bunny and Roderick Rat, *Tiny Toon Adventures* (also known as *Steven Spielberg Presents ... "Tiny Toon Adventures"*), Fox, 1990–93.

Voice, *Gravedale High* (also known as *Rick Moranis in "Gravedale High"*), NBC, 1990.

Voices of Count Catula and Igor, Jr., *Wake, Rattle & Roll,* 1990.

Voice, *Bobby's World,* 1990.

Voice, *Yo! Yogi,* 1991.

Voice, *ProStars,* 1991.

Voice of Jammet, *Capitol Critters,* ABC, 1992.

Voice of Sput, *Eek! the Cat* (also known as *Eek! and the Terrible Thunderlizards* and *Eek!stravaganza*), Fox, 1992.

Voice of Buster J. Bunny, *The Plucky Duck Show,* 1992.

Voices, *Super Dave: Daredevil for Hire,* 1992.

Voices of Mr. Doodles and others, *Bonkers* (also known as *Disney's "Bonkers"*), syndicated, 1993.

Voices of Steamer, Mojo, and Big Red, *Cro,* 1993.

Voices of Ed Bighead, Bev Bighead, and others, *Rocko's Modern Life,* Nickelodeon, 1993–96.

Voice of Snively, a recurring role, *Sonic the Hedgehog,* ABC and syndicated, 1993–94.

Voice, *Droophy: Master Detective,* Fox, 1993.

Voices of Chance Furlong, T–Bone, Dr. Viper, and others, *Swat Kats: The Radical Squadron,* syndicated, 1993.

Voice of Mechanikles, *Aladdin* (also known as *Disney's "Aladdin"*), CBS and syndicated, 1994.

Voice of groom, *Marsupilami,* 1994.

Voice, *What–a–Mess,* 1995.

Voice of Felix the Cat, *The Twisted Tales of Felix the Cat,* 1995.

Voice of Chafe, *Schnookums and Meat Funny Cartoon Show,* syndicated, 1995.

Voice of Pete, *The Mask,* 1995.

Multiple voices, *Timon and Pumbaa,* 1995.

Voice of Professor Monkey–for–a–Head, a recurring role, *Earthworm Jim,* The WB, 1995–96.

Voices of Eaton, Miguel, and bug number one, *Santo Bugito,* CBS, 1996.

Voices of Dr. Maston and Jake Dragonn, *Project G.e.e.K.e.R.,* CBS, 1996.

Voices of Dr. Droid, Otto Maton, and others, *Mighty Ducks* (also known as *Disney's "Mighty Ducks"* and *Mighty Ducks: The Animated Series*), ABC and syndicated, 1996.

(As Charlie Adler) Voice of Ned, *Jungle Cubs,* ABC, 1996.

Voices of Cow, Chicken, I. B. Red Guy, Cousin Boneless, I. R. Baboon, and others, *Cow and Chicken,* Cartoon Network, 1997, broadcast as part of *Cartoon Cartoon Fridays* (also known as *Cartoon Network's Fridays, CCF,* and *Fridays*), 2000.

(As Charlie Adler) Voice of Candy Caramella, *Space Goofs* (also known as *Home to Rent, Stupid Invaders,* and *Les zinzins de l'espace*), Fox, 1997.

Voice, *Channel Umptee–3,* The WB, 1997.

Voice of I. R. Baboon, a recurring role, *I Am Weasel,* Cartoon Network, 1997.

Toonsylvania (also known as *Steven Spielberg Presents "Toonsylvania"*), Fox, 1998.

Voice, *Mad Jack the Pirate,* 1998.

Voices of Patrick Winks and Mr. Hornsby, *Jakers! The Adventures of Piggley Winks,* PBS, 2003–2006.

Voice of Gormel, *Dave the Barbarian,* 2004.

Voice of Mr. Whiskers, *Brandy & Mr. Whiskers,* Disney Channel, 2004–2006.

Voices of Dink and Flip, *Pet Alien,* 2005.

Voice of Savo, *Danger Rangers,* 2005.

(As Charlie Adler) Voice of Optimatus, *Loonatics Unleashed,* CW Network, beginning 2005.

Voices of principal of Katana, principal of Shuriken, Tetsuo Matsura, and Vladmir Keltawa, *Shuriken School* (anime), 2006.

Also appeared briefly in the live–action series *The Redd Foxx Show;* some sources also cite appearance in multiple roles in a series titled *Then and Now,* PBS.

Television Appearances; Animated Movies:

Voices of Quark and Zappy, *Rockin' with Judy Jetson,* 1988.

Voice of Rocky, *Hollyrock–a–Bye Baby,* ABC, 1993.

Voice of Buster Bunny, *Tiny Toons Spring Break,* 1994.

Christopher Bear, *The Bears Who Saved Christmas,* 1994.

Voices of captain and first royal guard, *Scooby Doo in Arabian Nights* (also known as *Arabian Nights* and *Scooby Doo's Arabian Nights*), 1994.

Voices of proctor and first man, *The Happy Elf,* NBC, 2005.

Television Appearances; Specials:

Voice, *'Tis the Season to Be Smurfy* (animated), 1987.

Voice, *The Monster Bed,* 1989.

Voice of Willard, *Blondie and Dagwood's "Second Wedding Workout"* (animated), 1989.

Voice of Buster J. Bunny, *It's a Wonderful Tiny Toons Christmas Special* (animated), 1992.

Voice, *Eek! the Cat Christmas Special* (animated), 1993.

Voices of Quarry and the postman, *A Flintstone Family Christmas* (animated), 1993.

Voice of street pig and Dad Funnybunny, *"P. J.'s Unfunnybunny Christmas"* (animated), *ABC Weekend Specials,* ABC, 1994.

(As Charlie Adler) Voice of Smokey, *"The Third Pig," Tales from the Crypt* (also known as *HBO's "Tales from the Crypt"*), HBO, 1996.

Voice of B–movie mad scientist, *The Rugrats: All Growed Up* (animated), Nickelodeon, 2001.

Voice of Professor Spooky, *A Rugrats Kwanzaa* (animated), Nickelodeon, 2001.

Television Appearances; Animated Pilots:

Voice of Patton, *Hound Town,* NBC, 1989.

(As Charlie Adler) Voices of second man, Mortiche, and waiter, *Hillbilly Blue,* 1995.

Television Appearances; Animated Episodes:

Voice of greed monster, *"The Greed Monster," Yogi's Treasure Hunt,* 1985.

Voices of Filler Brushbill and Pluck, "Much Ado about Scrooge," *DuckTales* (also known as *Disney's "DuckTales"*), 1987.

Voices of Bat–Bat and others, "Night of the Bat–Bat/Scrap–Happy," *Mighty Mouse, the New Adventures,* 1987.

Voices of Bat–Bat and others, "Bat with a Golden Tongue/Mundane Voyage," *Mighty Mouse, the New Adventures,* 1988.

Voices of Mad Dog and others, "A Bad Reflection on You: Part 2," *Tale Spin,* syndicated, 1990.

Voice of Mad Dog, "Plunder & Lightning," *Tale Spin,* syndicated, 1990.

Voices of Mad Dog and others, "From here to Machinary," *Tale Spin,* syndicated, 1990.

Voice of Mad Dog, "Random of the Red Chimp, *Tale Spin,* syndicated, 1991.

Voice of Colonel Trenchrot, "Apes of Wrath," *Darkwing Duck,* ABC and syndicated, 1991.

Voice of newscaster, "Fraudcast News," *Darkwing Duck,* ABC and syndicated, 1992.

Voice of Ernie, "The Brain Suckers Cometh!," *Mighty Max,* 1993.

Voice of Corroder Cody, "A Mouse and His Motorcycle," *Biker Mice from Mars,* 1993.

Voice of first squid, "Tail of Two Crabs," *The Little Mermaid,* 1993.

Voice, "Gland of Opportunity," *Duckman: Private Dick/Family Man,* USA Network, 1994.

Voice of Ickis, "Curse of the Krumm/Krumm Goes Hollywood," *Aaahh!!! Real Monsters,* Nickelodeon, 1994.

Voice of Ickis, "Monster Make–over/Airplane, a Wing and a Scare," *Aaahh!!! Real Monsters,* Nickelodeon, 1994.

Voice, "Days of Whining and Neurosis," *Duckman: Private Dick/Family Man,* USA Network, 1995.

(As Charlie Adler) Voice of Mr. Adler, "Whiplash," *Beavis and Butt–Head,* 1995.

(As Charlie Adler) Voice of Mr. Adler, "Sexual Harassment," *Beavis and Butt–Head,* 1995.

Voice, "The Once and Future Duck," *Duckman: Private Dick/Family Man,* USA Network, 1996.

(As Charlie Adler) Voices of Rawlings and second robber, "The Ballad of Belle Bonnet," *The Real Adventures of Jonny Quest* (also known as *Jonny Quest: The Real Adventures*), Cartoon Network and syndicated, 1996.

Voice of Sarcastro, "The Tick vs. Education," *The Tick,* Fox, 1996.

Voice of Rocco, "Mano's Hands," *Spicy City,* 1997.

Voice of Zbig, "Tears of a Clone," *Spicy City,* 1997.

Voice, "Raven's Revenge," *Spicy City,* 1997.

Voice, "The Unseen," *Extreme Ghostbusters,* syndicated, 1997.

Voice of Ickis, "Ghost Story/Chucky's Complaint," *Rugrats,* Nickelodeon, 1999.

Voice of television announcer, "Love and Cheese/Weighing Harold," *Hey Arnold!,* 1999.

Voices of wrestlers, "Horse Sense," *The Wild Thornberrys,* 2000.

Voice, "My Name Is Robbie," *The Oblongs,* The WB, 2001.

Voice of snowman, "Big Trouble in Billy's Basement/Christmas Con Carne/Tickle Me Mandy," *Grim & Evil* (also known as *The Grim Adventures of Billy & Mandy*), Cartoon Network, 2002.

Voice of Junkman, "The Junkman Cometh," *The Adventures of Jimmy Neutron: Boy Genius,* Nickelodeon, 2004.

Voice of Junkman, "The League of Villains," *The Adventures of Jimmy Neutron: Boy Genius,* Nickelodeon, 2005.

Voice of bear, "Snake Eyes/Racing Slicks," *Camp Lazlo,* Cartoon Network, 2005.

Voices of Lubbermouth and zombie kid, "Happy Huggy Stuffy Bears/Secret Decoder Ring," *Grim & Evil* (also known as *The Grim Adventures of Billy & Mandy*), Cartoon Network, 2005.

(As Charlie Adler) Voice of director, "The Comet Cometh," *Loonatics Unleashed,* CW Network, 2005.

(As Charlie Adler) Voice of Prime Minister Ricobo, "Running from Office," *The Replacements,* Disney Channel, 2006.

Voice of Mano Negra, "Old Money," *El Tigre,* 2007.

Some sources cite appearances as a photographer in an episode of the live–action series *First & Ten* and guest on a Joan Rivers talk show.

Television Appearances; Other:

Voice of Stav the Taurine Troll, *The Little Troll Prince* (animated), 1985.

Voice of Low–Light, *G.I. Joe: Arise, Serpentor, Arise!* (animated; also known as *Action Force: Arise, Serpentor, Arise!*), 1986.

(As Charlie Adler) Voices of Sidney the Spider and others, *Christmas in Tattertown* (animated), 1987.

Voice of Dr. Mayhem, *Defenders of Dynatron City* (animated), 1992.

(As Charlie Adler) Voices of alien dad, alien grandpa, terrified man, and wimpy alien, *Gramps* (animated), 1992.

Television Voice Director; Animated Series:

Stressed Eric, NBC, 1998.

The Wild Thornberrys, Nickelodeon, 1998.

Rocket Power, Nickelodeon, 1999.

Stripperella (also known as *Stan Lee's "Stripperella"*), Spike, 2003.

Television Voice Director; Animated Specials:

(As Charlie Adler) *Rugrats: Still Babies after All These Years,* Nickelodeon, 2001.

Rugrats: All Growed Up, Nickelodeon, 2001.

All Grown Up: Dude, Where My Horse?, Nickelodeon, 2005.
Bratz Rock Angelz, Cartoon Network, 2005.

Television Voice Director; Animated Movies:
Rocket Power: Reggie's Big (Beach) Break, Nickelodeon, 2003.
The Happy Elf, NBC, 2005.

Television Voice Director; Animated Episodes:
Worked as voice director for episodes of *The Brothers Flubb; 100 Deeds for Eddie McDowd,* Nickelodeon; and *Rocket Power,* Nickelodeon.

Television Voice Director; Animated Pilots:
As Told by Ginger, Nickelodeon, 2000.

Also voice director for a pilot titled *Psycho Ferret.*

Television Additional Voices; Animated Series:
ABC Weekend Specials, ABC, 1977.
A Pup Named Scooby–Doo, ABC, 1988.
(As Charlie Adler) *Captain Planet and the Planeteers* (also known as *The New Adventures of Captain Planet*), TBS and syndicated, 1990.
Tom and Jerry Kids Show, 1990.
Potworth & Co. (also known as *Midnight Patrol*), 1990.
Darkwing Duck, ABC and syndicated, 1992.
The Little Clowns of Happy Town, 1992.
The Further Adventures of SuperTed, 1993.
Family Dog, 1993.
Spawn (also known as *Todd McFarlane's "Spawn"*), HBO, 1997.
The Secret Files of the Spy Dogs, Fox, 1998.

Television Additional Voices; Animated Movies:
Yogi the Easter Bear, syndicated, 1994.

Stage Appearances:
Appeared as master of ceremonies, *Cabaret* (musical); as Hero, *Dr. Zero;* in *Family Business,* Astor Place Theatre, New York City; in *God's Favorite;* as Zeppo Marx, *Minnie's Boys;* in *Once upon a Mattress;* in *There Used to Be Fireflies* (solo show); as Arnold, *Torch Song Trilogy,* Broadway production; and as Snoopy, *You're a Good Man, Charlie Brown.*

Major Tours:
Toured U.S. cities in his solo show *There Used to Be Fireflies;* as Arnold, *Torch Song Trilogy;* and in *Zoo Story.*

Stage Director:
Directed a production of *Rugrats,* Radio City Music Hall, New York City.

RECORDINGS

Video Games:
(As Charlie Adler) Voice, *Blazing Dragons,* 1996.
Voice of Ickis, *Nickelodeon 3D Movie Maker,* 1996.
Voice of Harold, *Fallout: A Post–Nuclear Role–Playing Game* (also known as *Fallout*), Interplay Productions, 1997.
Voices of Dr. Klin and T–Hoppy, *Clayfighter 63 1/3* (also known as *Clayfighter: Sculptor's Cut*), Interplay Productions, 1997.
Voice of Harold, *Fallout 2: A Postnuclear Role Playing Game* (also known as *Fallout 2*), Interplay Productions, 1998.
Voice of Ignus, *Planescape: Torment,* 1999.
Voices of Jumbeaux LaFeet and Mungle the Pirate Student, *Escape from Monkey Island,* Electronic Arts, 2000.
Voices of Kalah, Teos, Rielev, and Rejiek Hidesman, *Forgotten Realms: Baldur's Gate II—Shadows of Amn,* 2000.
(As Charlie Adler) Voice, *Sacrifice,* 2000.
Voice of Candy Caramella, *Stupid Invaders,* Ubi Soft Entertainment, 2001.
Voice of Ickis, *Nicktoons Racing,* Hasbro Interactive, 2001.
Voice of Gratis August Var, *Earth and Beyond,* Electronic Arts, 2002.
Voice of Coach Oleander, *Psychonauts,* Majesco Entertainment, 2005.
(Uncredited) Voice of Diddy Kong, *Mario Superstar Baseball,* Nintendo of America, 2005.
Voice of Redback Russ, *Ty the Tasmanian Tiger 3: Night of the Quinkan* (also known as *Ty 3: Night of the Quinkan*), Activision, 2005.

WRITINGS

Film:
No Prom for Cindy (short film), 2002.

Stage:
Author of the solo show *There Used to Be Fireflies.*

Television Episodes:
Wrote episodes of *Tiny Toon Adventures* (animated; also known as *Steven Spielberg Presents ... "Tiny Toon Adventures"*), Fox.

OTHER SOURCES

Periodicals:
Animation World, February 1, 2001.

Electronic:
Charles Adler Official Site, http://www.adler.what.cc, June 11, 2007.

ALDREDGE, Tom 1928–
(Thomas Aldredge)

PERSONAL

Full name, Thomas Ernest Aldredge; born February 28, 1928, in Dayton, OH; son of W. J. (an Air Force officer) and Lucienne Juliet (maiden name, Marcillat) Aldredge; married Theoni Athanasiou Vachlioti (a costume designer, wardrobe supervisor, and art director) December 10, 1953. *Education:* Attended University of Dayton, 1947–49; DePaul University, B.F.A., 1953; studied acting with Maurice Gnesin, Mary Agnes Doyle, and David Itkin. *Avocational Interests:* Sailing, boat design.

Career: Actor and director. Chicago Educational Television Association, producer and director, 1955–57.

Member: American Federation of Television and Radio Artists, Actors' Equity Association, and Screen Actors Guild.

Awards, Honors: Obie Award, distinguished performance, *Village Voice,* 1967, for *Measure for Measure* and *Stock Up On Pepper 'cause Turkey's Going to War;* Drama Desk Award, outstanding performance, and Antoinette Perry Award nomination, best actor in a play, both 1972, for *Sticks and Bones;* Antoinette Perry Award nomination, best supporting actor in a musical, 1975, for *Where's Charlie?;* Emmy Award, 1978, for "Henry Winkler Meets Shakespeare," *The CBS Festival of Lively Arts for Young People;* Drama Desk Award nomination, best actor in a play, 1979, for *On Golden Pond;* Antoinette Perry Award nomination, outstanding featured actor in a play, 1981, for *The Little Foxes;* Antoinette Perry Award nomination, best actor in a musical, 1994, for *Passion;* Drama Desk Award nomination, best actor in a play, 1995, for *Incommunicado;* Antoinette Perry Award nomination, best actor in a play, 2004, for *Twentieth Century;* Richard Serf Award, outstanding older character actor in a supporting role in a Broadway or off–Broadway production, Actors' Equity Association, 2004; Obie Award, for *The Premise;* career achievement award, DePaul University.

CREDITS

Stage Appearances:
Messenger, *Hamlet,* Goodman Memorial Theatre, Chicago, IL, 1950.

Bud Norton, *Personnel Appearance,* Crystal Palace Theatre, St. Louis, MO, 1950.
Jason, Tower Ranch Tenthouse Theatre, Rhinelander, WI, c. 1951.
The Corn Is Green, Tower Ranch Tenthouse Theatre, c. 1951.
Summer and Smoke, Tower Ranch Tenthouse Theatre, c. 1951.
The Play's the Thing, Tower Ranch Tenthouse Theatre, c. 1951.
Death of a Salesman, Tower Ranch Tenthouse Theatre, c. 1952.
The Hasty Heart, Tower Ranch Tenthouse Theatre, c. 1952.
Blood Wedding, Tower Ranch Tenthouse Theatre, c. 1952.
The Drunkard, Tower Ranch Tenthouse Theatre, c. 1952.
The Glass Menagerie, Tower Ranch Tenthouse Theatre, c. 1952.
Private Lives, Tower Ranch Tenthouse Theatre, c. 1952.
Tovarich, Tower Ranch Tenthouse Theatre, c. 1953.
Our Town, Tower Ranch Tenthouse Theatre, c. 1953.
The Little Foxes, Tower Ranch Tenthouse Theatre, c. 1953.
Laura, Tower Ranch Tenthouse Theatre, c. 1953.
Blithe Spirit, Tower Ranch Tenthouse Theatre, 1953.
Inherit the Wind, Tower Ranch Tenthouse Theatre, c. 1953.
Arms and the Man, Tower Ranch Tenthouse Theatre, 1954.
The Guardsman, Tower Ranch Tenthouse Theatre, 1954.
A Streetcar Named Desire, Tower Ranch Tenthouse Theatre, 1954.
The Heiress, Tower Ranch Tenthouse Theatre, 1954.
Shadow and Substance, Tower Ranch Tenthouse Theatre, 1954.
Here Today, Tower Ranch Tenthouse Theatre, 1954.
Saturday's Children, Tower Ranch Tenthouse Theatre, 1954.
The Rope, Tower Ranch Tenthouse Theatre, 1954.
The Moon Is Blue, Tower Ranch Tenthouse Theatre, 1954.
The Immoralist, Tower Ranch Tenthouse Theatre, 1954.
The Lady's Not for Burning, Tower Ranch Tenthouse Theatre, 1954.
I Am a Camera, Tower Ranch Tenthouse Theatre, 1955.
Sabrina Fair, Tower Ranch Tenthouse Theatre, 1955.
Mister Roberts, Tower Ranch Tenthouse Theatre, 1955.
The Rainmaker, Tower Ranch Tenthouse Theatre, 1955.
Cat on a Hot Tin Roof, Tower Ranch Tenthouse Theatre, 1955.
Will Success Spoil Rock Hudson, Tower Ranch Tenthouse Theatre, 1958.
Inherit the Wind, Tower Ranch Tenthouse Theatre, 1958.
No Time for Sergeants, Tower Ranch Tenthouse Theatre, 1958.

Teahouse of the August Moon, Tower Ranch Tenthouse Theatre, 1958.

A Member of the Wedding, Tower Ranch Tenthouse Theatre, 1958.

(New York debut) Messenger, *Electra,* Jan Hus Theatre, 1958.

Vladimir, *Waiting for Godot,* Crystal Palace Theatre, 1958.

(Broadway debut) Danny, *The Nervous Set,* Crystal Palace Theatre, then Henry Miller's Theatre, New York City, 1959.

Trinculo, *The Tempest,* East 74th Street Theatre, New York City, 1959.

David, *Between Two Thieves,* York Playhouse, New York City, 1960.

Dauphin, *Henry V,* New York Shakespeare Festival, Delacorte Theatre, Public Theatre, New York City, 1960.

(As Thomas Aldredge) *The Premise* (improvisational revue), Premise Theatre, New York City, 1960, then Shoreham Theatre, Washington, DC, 1962, later (London debut) Comedy Theatre, 1962, then Ivar Theatre, Los Angeles, 1964.

Boyet, *Love's Labour's Lost,* New York Shakespeare Festival, Delacorte Theatre, Public Theatre, 1965.

Nestor, *Troilus and Cressida,* New York Shakespeare Festival, Delacorte Theatre, Public Theatre, 1965.

Eugene Boyer, *UTBU* (also known as *Unhealthy to Be Unpleasant*), Helen Hayes Theatre, New York City, 1965–66.

Bernie, "The Mutilated," *Slapstick Tragedy* (double–bill), Longacre Theatre, New York City, 1966.

Angelo, *Measure for Measure,* New York Shakespeare Festival, Delacorte Theatre, Public Theatre, 1966.

A murderer and a citizen, *King Richard III,* New York Shakespeare Festival, Delacorte Theatre, Public Theatre, 1966.

Jack McClure, *The Butter and Egg Man,* Cherry Lane Theatre, New York City, 1966.

Peter Quince, *A Midsummer Night's Dream,* American Shakespeare Theatre, Stratford, CT, 1967.

Chorus member, *Antigone,* American Shakespeare Theatre, 1967.

Gratiano, *The Merchant of Venice,* American Shakespeare Theatre, 1967.

Macduff, *Macbeth,* American Shakespeare Theatre, 1967.

Gilbert, *Everything in the Garden,* Plymouth Theatre, New York City, 1967–68.

McKeating, *Stock Up On Pepper 'cause Turkey's Going to War,* Ellen Stewart Theatre, New York City, 1967.

Hamm, *Endgame,* Crystal Palace Theatre, 1968.

Wurz, *Ergo,* New York Shakespeare Festival, Anspacher Theatre, Public Theatre, New York City, 1968.

Tybalt, *Romeo and Juliet,* New York Shakespeare Festival, Delacorte Theatre, Public Theatre, 1968.

Sir Andrew Aguecheek, *Twelfth Night,* New York Shakespeare Festival, Delacorte Theatre, Public Theatre, 1968.

Emory, *The Boys in the Band,* Wyndham's Theatre, London, 1969.

Senator Logan, *Indians,* Brooks Atkinson Theatre, New York, 1969.

Victor Bard, *The Engagement Baby,* Helen Hayes Theatre, 1970.

William Detweiler, *How the Other Half Loves,* Royale Theatre, New York City, 1971.

Title role, *The Tale of Cymbeline,* New York Shakespeare Festival, Delacorte Theatre, Public Theatre, 1971.

Ozzie, *Sticks and Bones,* New York Shakespeare Festival, Anspacher Theatre, Public Theatre, 1971–72, then John Golden Theatre, New York City, 1972.

Second gravedigger, *Hamlet,* New York Shakespeare Festival, Delacorte Theatre, Public Theatre, 1972.

Calchas, *The Orphan,* New York Shakespeare Festival, Public Theatre, New York City, 1973.

Lear's fool, *King Lear,* New York Shakespeare Festival, Delacorte Theatre, Public Theatre, 1973.

James Cameron, *The Iceman Cometh,* Circle in the Square, New York City, 1973.

Mr. Spettigue, *Where's Charley?* (musical), Circle in the Square, 1974–75.

Shaughnessy, *The Leaf People,* New York Shakespeare Festival, Booth Theatre, New York City, 1975.

Will Somers, *Rex* (musical), Lunt–Fontanne Theatre, New York City, 1976.

Father, *Canadian Gothic/American Modern,* Phoenix Theatre, New York City, 1976.

Painter, *Vieux Carre,* St. James Theatre, New York City, 1977.

Archbishop of Rheims, *Saint Joan,* Circle in the Square, 1977–78.

Bill Blue, chairman, Harold, Mr. Stevens, and red-headed husband, *Stages,* Belasco Theatre, New York City, 1978.

Norman Thayer, Jr., *On Golden Pond,* New Apollo Theatre, New York City, 1979, then John Golden Theatre, 1979–80.

Love's Labour's Lost, Folger Theatre Group, Washington, DC, 1980–81.

Horace Giddens, *The Little Foxes,* Martin Beck Theatre, New York City, 1981.

Louis Puget, *The Black Angel,* Circle Repertory Theatre, New York City, 1982–83.

Harmon, *Actors and Actresses,* Hartman Theatre, Stamford, CT, 1983.

Old man, *Fool for Love,* Circle Repertory Theatre, then Douglas Fairbanks Theatre, New York City, 1983.

Sandy Castle, *Getting Along Famously,* Hudson Guild Theatre, New York City, 1984.

Marius, *The Road to Mecca,* Yale Repertory Theatre, New Haven, CT, 1984.

"Pa" Lester, *Tobacco Road,* Long Wharf Theatre, New Haven, CT, 1985.

Professor Henry Leeds, *Strange Interlude,* Nederlander Theatre, New York City, 1985.

The Imaginary Invalid, Hartman Theatre, 1985–86.

Luton Mears, *Neon Psalms,* American Place Theatre, New York City, 1986.

John of Gaunt, *Richard II,* New York Shakespeare Festival, Delacorte Theatre, Public Theatre, 1987.

Narrator and mysterious man, *Into the Woods,* Martin Beck Theatre, 1987–89.

Washington Irving, *Two Shakespearean Actors,* Cort Theatre, New York City, 1992.

John Frick, *The Last Yankee,* Manhattan Theatre Club Stage II, New York City, 1993.

Dr. Tambourri, *Passion* (musical), Plymouth Theatre, New York City, 1994.

Ezra Pound, *Incommunicado,* 1994.

Reverend Jeremiah Brown, *Inherit the Wind,* Royale Theatre, 1996.

Aegeon, *The Boys from Syracuse,* City Center Theatre, New York City, 1997.

The Road to Mecca, Long Wharf Theatre, 1997.

Stephen Hopkins, *1776* (musical), Roundabout Theatre Company, Criterion Center Stage Right Theatre, New York City, 1997, then George Gershwin Theatre, New York City, 1997–98.

The general, *La Terrasse,* Manhattan Theatre Club Stage II, 1999.

Lloyd McIlhenny, *The Time of the Cuckoo,* Mitzi E. Newhouse Theatre, New York City, 2000.

Muff Potter, *The Adventures of Tom Sawyer* (musical), Minskoff Theatre, New York City, 2001.

Giles Corey, *The Crucible,* Virginia Theatre, New York City, 2002.

Arthur "Cookie" Silverstein, *The 75th,* 2003.

Harvey Lustgarten, *The Vibrator,* George Street Playhouse, New Brunswick, NJ, 2003.

Matthew Clark, *Twentieth Century,* Roundabout Theatre Company, American Airlines Theatre, New York City, 2004.

Juror number nine, *Twelve Angry Men,* Roundabout Theatre Company, American Airlines Theatre, 2004–2005.

Matt Singer, *Two Lives,* George Street Playhouse, 2005.

Ziggy, *Mimi le Duck,* New World Stages Stage III, New York City, 2006.

Appeared in productions of *Colette* and *Wind;* also appeared in benefits and concert performances.

Stage Director:

The Fourposter, Tower Ranch Tenthouse Theatre, Rhinelander, WI, 1954.

Here Today, Tower Ranch Tenthouse Theatre, 1954.

Saturday's Children, Tower Ranch Tenthouse Theatre, 1954.

The Rope, Tower Ranch Tenthouse Theatre, 1954.

Arms and the Man, Tower Ranch Tenthouse Theatre, 1954.

The Guardsman, Tower Ranch Tenthouse Theatre, 1954.

A Streetcar Named Desire, Tower Ranch Tenthouse Theatre, 1954.

The Heiress, Tower Ranch Tenthouse Theatre, 1954.

Shadow and Substance, Tower Ranch Tenthouse Theatre, 1954.

Years Ago, Tower Ranch Tenthouse Theatre, 1954.

I Am a Camera, Tower Ranch Tenthouse Theatre, 1955.

Sabrina Fair, Tower Ranch Tenthouse Theatre, 1955.

Mister Roberts, Tower Ranch Tenthouse Theatre, 1955.

The Rainmaker, Tower Ranch Tenthouse Theatre, 1955.

A Member of the Wedding, Tower Ranch Tenthouse Theatre, 1958.

The Happiness Cage, Estelle R. Newman Theatre, Public Theatre, New York City, 1970.

Television Appearances; Series:

Host, *The Curious One,* Chicago Educational Television, 1956.

Matt Pearse, *Ryan's Hope,* ABC, 1980–82.

Mr./Mrs. Tony Nagro, *Search for Tomorrow,* CBS, 1984.

Hugh DeAngelis, a recurring role, *The Sopranos,* HBO, between 2000 and 2007.

Uncle Pete, *Damages,* FX Network, 2007.

Television Appearances; Movies:

Baron de Charlus, *Ten Blocks on the Camino Real,* PBS, 1966.

Nemith, "The Spy Who Returned from the Dead," *Wide World Mystery,* 1974.

Fred Eberhardt, *The Storyteller,* NBC, 1977.

Kelly O'Brien, *Nurse,* CBS, 1980.

Edward, *The Man that Corrupted Hadleyburg,* 1980.

Monsignor Nicholson, *The Gentleman Bandit* (also known as *The Bandit Priest*), CBS, 1981.

Judge Driscoll, *Pudd'nhead Wilson,* 1984.

Rappaport, *Seize the Day,* 1986.

Jefferson Davis, *A Special Friendship,* 1987.

Ivar, *O Pioneers!,* 1992.

Charlie Hugel, *Barbarians at the Gate,* HBO, 1993.

Jacob Hostetler, *Harvest of Fire,* CBS, 1996.

Spry old man, *Earthly Possessions,* HBO, 1999.

Television Appearances; Miniseries:

The Adams Chronicles, PBS, 1976.

Glendon Lane, *Doubletake,* 1985.

Justice Hugo Black, *Separate But Equal,* 1991.

Dr. Frederick Klenner, *In the Best of Families: Marriage, Pride & Madness* (also known as *Bitter Blood*), CBS, 1994.

Dr. Tambourri, *Passion,* PBS, 1996.

Television Appearances; Specials:

Sticks and Bones, CBS, 1972.

Fool, *King Lear,* PBS, 1974.

William Shakespeare, "Henry Winkler Meets William Shakespeare," *The CBS Festival of Lively Arts for Young People,* CBS, 1977.

Washington Irving and host, "Robbers, Rooftops and Witches," *CBS Library*, CBS, 1982.

Mazzini, *Heartbreak House*, PBS and Showtime, 1986.

Joseph "Joe" Miller/Joseph Hauptmann, "A Matter of Conscience," *CBS Schoolbreak Special*, CBS, 1989.

Older Edward, *Sensibility and Sense*, PBS, 1990.

Narrator and mysterious man, *Into the Woods*, PBS, 1990.

Lincoln and the War Within, 1992.

Sergeant Horace Trimble, *Andersonville*, 1996.

The 58th Annual Tony Awards (also known as *The 2004 Tony Awards*), CBS, 2004.

According to some sources, also appeared in *Seasons of Youth*, ABC; and *The Threepenny Opera*, PBS.

Television Appearances; Episodic:

Philip Lamareaux, "Good–bye Gator," *New York News*, CBS, 1995.

Mr. Leflin, "I've Grown Accustomed to His Face," *Now and Again*, ABC, 1999.

Stroke victim, "Young Men and Fire ...," *Third Watch*, NBC, 2000.

Retired properties clerk, "Amends," *Law & Order*, NBC, 2000.

"Enemy Within," *Law & Order: Criminal Intent* (also known as *Law & Order: CI*), NBC, 2001.

Senator Glenn Boulder, "The Senator," *Line of Fire*, ABC, 2004.

Film Appearances:

Wendover, *The Mouse on the Moon*, United Artists, 1963.

Jack Armstrong, *The Troublemaker*, Janus, 1964.

Adler, *Who Killed the Teddy Bear?*, Strand Releasing, 1965.

(Uncredited) Harold Lacey, *The Boston Strangler*, 1968.

Mr. Alfred, *The Rain People*, Warner Bros., 1969.

Medic, *The Happiness Cage* (also known as *The Demon Within* and *The Mind Snatchers*), Cinerama, 1972.

Ben Amed, *Countdown at Kusini* (also known as *Cool Red*), Columbia, 1976.

Jailer, *Full Moon High* (also known as *Moon High*), Orion, 1981.

Sid Hogenson, **batteries not included*, Universal, 1987.

The fake Captain Borg, *Brenda Starr*, Triumph Releasing, 1989.

Beth's father, *See You in the Morning*, 1989.

Mr. Guttman, *What about Bob?*, Buena Vista, 1991.

Ozzie, *Other People's Money* (also known as *Riqueza ajena*), Warner Bros., 1991.

Dr. Robinson, *The Adventures of Huck Finn* (also known as *The Adventures of Huckleberry Finn*), Buena Vista, 1993.

Grizzled old man, *The Stars Fell on Henrietta*, 1995.

Jake, *Lawn Dogs*, Strand Releasing, 1997.

Mr. Mann, *Commandments*, Gramercy, 1997.

Judge Marinacci, *Rounders*, Miramax, 1998.

Elijah Kinneson, *A Stranger in the Kingdom*, Kingdom Come Pictures, 1998.

Hank Land, *Message in a Bottle*, Warner Bros., 1999.

Lionel Pond, *Camouflage*, PM Entertainment Group, 1999.

Old man, *The American Astronaut*, Artistic License, 2001.

Herb Myerson, *Intolerable Cruelty*, Universal, 2003.

Blind man, *Cold Mountain*, Miramax, 2003.

Tony, *Wrigley* (short film), Oliver Refson Films, 2004.

Virginia' husband, *Twilight's Last Gleaming* (short film), Snow Mountain Productions, 2005.

Michael Rogan, *Game 6*, Kindred Media Group, 2006.

Carruthers's banker, *All the King's Men* (also known as *Das Spiel der macht*), Columbia, 2006.

ALEXANDER, Jace 1964–

PERSONAL

Full name, Jason Alexander; born April 7, 1964, in New York, NY; son of Robert (a stage director) and Jane (an actress) Alexander; married Maddie Corman (an actress), September 6, 1998; children: three. *Education:* Attended New York University; studied at American Film Institute, 1992–94.

Addresses: *Agent*—Jack Tantleff, William Morris Agency, 1 William Morris Pl., Beverly Hills, CA 90212. *Manager*—Ross Fineman, Fineman Entertainment, 9437 Santa Monica Blvd., Suite 206, Beverly Hills, CA 90210.

Career: Actor and director. Naked Angels (theatre company), New York City, founding member and director.

CREDITS

Television Director; Series:

Law & Order, NBC, multiple episodes, between 1994 and 2005.

Rescue Me, FX Network, multiple episodes, between 2004 and 2006.

Burn Notice, USA Network, 2007.

Television Director; Movies:

Jenifer (also known as *The Jenifer Estess Story*), CBS, 2001.

Carry Me Home, Showtime, 2004.

Television Director; Episodic:
"Hooves and Harlots," *Xena: Warrior Princess,* syndicated, 1995.
"The Damage Done," *Homicide: Life on the Street* (also known as *Homicide*), NBC 1996.
Players, NBC, 1997.
Crisis Center, 1997.
"It's My Party," *Ally McBeal,* Fox, 1998.
"Reasons to Believe," *The Practice,* ABC, 1998.
"History," *Third Watch,* NBC, 2000.
"The Self–Importance of Being Carlos," *Third Watch,* NBC, 2001.
"Lizzie's Nightmares," *Lizzie McGuire,* Disney Channel, 2001.
"The Old Head," *Prison Break* (also known as *Prison Break: Manhunt* and *Prison Break: On the Run*), Fox, 2005.
"Bluff," *Prison Break* (also known as *Prison Break: Manhunt* and *Prison Break: On the Run*), Fox, 2006.
"Failure to Communicate," *House M.D.* (also known as *House*), Fox, 2006.
"Nice Package," *Love Monkey,* CBS, 2006.
(And producer) "What Are the Odds?," *Six Degrees,* ABC, 2006.

Also directed episodes of *Arli$$,* HBO; *Early Edition,* CBS; *The Expert; M.Y.O.B.; New York Undercover* (also known as *Uptown Undercover*), Fox; *Now and Again,* CBS; *Phil of the Future,* Disney Channel; and *Queens Supreme,* CBS.

Television Director; Other:
Swift Justice (pilot), 1996.
IFP Gotham Awards, Bravo, 2001.

Television Appearances; Miniseries:
Dan, *George Washington,* CBS, 1984.
Carl Flynn, *Menendez: A Killing in Beverly Hills,* CBS, 1994.

Television Appearances; Movies:
Nick, *Open Admissions,* 1988.
Alex Twining, *When We Were Young* (also known as *That Magic Moment*), NBC, 1989.
Patrick Sixbury, *Follow Your Heart* (also known as *Walk Me to the Distance*), NBC, 1990.
Alan's father, *For Caroline,* Independent Film Channel, 2004.

Television Appearances; Specials:
Sole, *Roanoak,* PBS, 1986.
Intimate Portrait: Jane Alexander, Lifetime, 1999.

Television Appearances; Episodic:
"For What It's Worth," *Tour of Duty,* CBS, 1989.
Larry Philbert, "Deceit," *Law & Order,* NBC, 1996.

Film Appearances:
Hillard Elkins, *Matewan,* Cinecom, 1987.
Rat, the gang leader, *"Crocodile" Dundee II,* Paramount, 1988.
Dickie Kerr, *Eight Men Out,* Orion, 1988.
M. K./M. J., *High Score,* Royal, 1990.
Bobby, *City of Hope,* Samuel Goldwyn Company, 1991.
Stuart Stratland, Jr., *Mistress* (also known as *Hollywood Mistress*), Rainbow Releasing, 1992.
Creepy Cody, *Love and a .45,* Trimark Pictures, 1994.
Robber, *Clueless* (also known as *I Was a Teenage Teenager* and *No Worries*), Paramount, 1995.

Film Work:
Director, *Benders,* 1994.

Stage Appearances:
Junius Urban, *The Caine Mutiny Court–Martial,* Circle in the Square, New York City, 1983.
Gilley, *I'm Not Rappaport,* American Place Theatre (some sources cite Booth Theatre), New York City, 1985–88.
Man, *The Good Coach,* Workshop of the Players Art Theatre, New York City, 1989.
Pooch/Poochkov, *Heart of a Dog,* Classic Stage Company, East Thirteenth Street Theatre, New York City, 1989.
Lee Harvey Oswald, *Assassins* (musical), Playwrights Horizons Theatre, New York City, 1990–91.

Stage Director:
Snakebit, Grove Street Playhouse, New York City, 1998, then Century Center for the Performing Arts, New York City, 1999, and Hudson Guild Theatre, Hollywood, CA, 2000.
Once Around the Sun, Zipper Theatre, New York City, 2005.

Directed a production of *Home,* Ensemble Studio Theatre, New York City; also directed productions at Coast Theatre, Los Angeles, Mark Taper Forum, Los Angeles, and West Bank Cafe.

ALLEN, Krista 1971(?)–

PERSONAL

Full name, Krista J. Allen; born April 5, 1971 (some sources cite 1972), in Ventura, CA; raised in Houston, TX; daughter of Daldon Earl and Katherine Mary (maiden name, Raposa) Allen; married Julian Morritt (a production manager and director), September 14, 1996 (divorced, 1999); children: Jacob Nolan. *Education:* Attended Austin Community College, Austin, TX. *Avocational Interests:* Reading.

Addresses: *Agent*—Jordan Tilzer, ROAR, 9701 Wilshire Blvd., 8th Floor, Beverly Hills, CA 90212.

Career: Actress. Appeared in commercials as Budweiser Girl for Budweiser beer. SuperEXcellent (t–shirt brand; also known as Sex Brand), creator; previously worked as aerobics teacher and model. Volunteer for Children of the Night, Pediatric AIDS Foundation, People for the Ethical Treatment of Animals, and other charities.

CREDITS

Television Appearances; Series:
Shelley, *The Bold and the Beautiful* (also known as *Glamour* and *Top Models*), ABC, 1995.
Billie Reed, *Days of Our Lives* (also known as *Days* and *DOOL*), NBC, 1996–99.
Jenna Avid, *Baywatch Hawaii,* syndicated, 2000–2001.
Singer, *The Screaming Cocktail Hour,* 2004.
Herself, *Unscripted,* HBO, 2005.
Bridget Keller, *What About Brian,* ABC, 2006–2007.

Television Appearances; Pilots:
Dr. Katherine "K" Harrison (some sources cite role of K. Adjani), *Avalon: Beyond the Abyss,* UPN, 1999.
(Uncredited) Kristy Hopkins, *C.S.I.: Crime Scene Investigation* (also known as *C.S.I., CSI: Weekends, CSI: Las Vegas,* and *Les experts*), CBS, 2000.
Zero Effect, NBC, 2002.
Laurie Payne, *Head Cases,* Fox, 2005.
Felicity Vesco, *Business Class,* NBC, 2007.

Television Appearances; Episodic:
Sharon Grayson/Cora Jean Riggs, "Black and Blue," *Silk Stalkings,* USA Network, 1995.
Patty, "Bikini Patrol," *High Tide,* 1995.
Mrs. Fleisig, "One Mean Mother," *Deadly Games,* UPN, 1995.
Page Tanner, "Misdiagnosis Murder," *Diagnosis Murder,* CBS, 1996.
Crystal Clark, "Calendar Girl," *Married ... with Children,* Fox, 1996.
Patty, "A Three Hour Tour," *High Tide,* 1996.
Patty, "Sunspirit," *High Tide,* 1996.
Theresa Vanoni, "Takedown," *Pacific Blue,* 1996.
Ann Fairchild, "Just a Gigolo," *Pacific Blue,* 1999.
Maitreya and Jade Blue Cockburn, "First Person Shooter," *The X–Files,* Fox, 2000.
Jessica Macy, "Smuggler's Blues," *18 Wheels of Justice,* 2000.
To Tell the Truth, syndicated, 2000.

Krista, "Hard Choices," *Arli$$,* HBO, 2001.
Jesse, "Yeah Baby!," *Spin City,* ABC, 2001.
The oracle, "Charmed Again: Parts 1 & 2," *Charmed,* The WB, 2001.
The oracle, "Brain Drain," *Charmed,* The WB, 2001.
Kelsie Anders, "Comic Relief Pitcher," *Inside Schwartz,* NBC, 2001.
Kristy Hopkins, "I–15 Murders," *C.S.I.: Crime Scene Investigation* (also known as *C.S.I., CSI: Weekends, CSI: Las Vegas,* and *Les experts*), CBS, 2001.
Kristy Hopkins, "Boom," *C.S.I.: Crime Scene Investigation* (also known as *C.S.I., CSI: Weekends, CSI: Las Vegas,* and *Les experts*), CBS, 2001.
Mabel, "The One Where Joey Dates Rachel," *Friends,* NBC, 2002.
Melanie Stark, "Miss Fortune Teller," *Glory Days* (also known as *Demontown*), The WB, 2002.
Lorna Templeton, "Deadly Desire," *Mutant X,* syndicated, 2002.
Desiree Atkins, "Heat," *Smallville* (also known as *Smallville Beginnings* and *Smallville: Superman the Early Years*), The WB, 2002.
Herself, "Bartender Pours On the Charm," *Rendez–View,* syndicated, 2002.
Skyler "Sky" Chase, "Defense," *Fastlane,* Fox, 2003.
Skyler "Sky" Chase, "Offense," *Fastlane,* Fox, 2003.
The princess, "The Illusion of Majesty," *Andromeda* (also known as *Gene Roddenberry's "Andromeda"*), syndicated, 2003.
Mary Elizabeth, "The Last Temptation of Elliot," *Just Shoot Me!,* NBC, 2003.
Gloria, "Separation Anxiety," *The Lyon's Den,* NBC, 2003.
Liz Wright, "The Placeholder," *Frasier,* NBC, 2003.
Olivia Pearson, "Did You Check with the Captain of the Flying Monkeys?," *Two and a Half Men,* CBS, 2003.
The Late Late Show with Craig Kilborn (also known as *The Last Late Show*), CBS, 2003.
The New Tom Green Show, MTV, 2003.
Jennifer, "I'm Not with Her," *I'm With Her,* ABC, 2004.
Last Call with Carson Daly, NBC, 2004, 2005, 2006.
Teresa Telenko, "Mr. Monk Goes to Vegas," *Monk,* USA Network, 2005.
Lisa, "Take a Number," *Jake in Progress,* ABC, 2005.
Laurie Payne, "S(elf) Help," *Head Cases,* Fox, 2005.
Project Greenlight 3, Bravo, 2005.
Kathy Kelly, "Restaurant Row," *Out of Practice,* CBS, 2006.
Kaitlyn, "Freddie and the Hot Mom," *Freddie,* ABC, 2006.

Television Appearances; Movies:
Title role, *Emmanuelle: First Contact* (also known as *Emmanuelle in Space 1: First Contact*), 1994.
Title role, *Emmanuelle 2: A World of Desire* (also known as *Emmanuelle in Space 2: A World of Desire*), 1994.
Title role, *Emmanuelle 3: A Lesson in Love,* 1994.

Title role, *Emmanuelle 4: Concealed Fantasy,* 1994.
Title role, *Emmanuelle 5: A Time to Dream,* 1994.
Title role, *Emmanuelle 6: One Final Fling,* 1994.
Title role, *Emmanuelle 7: The Meaning of Love,* 1994.
Cali Goodwin, *Raven,* The Movie Channel, 1996.

Television Appearances; Other:
Scream Awards 2006, Spike, 2006.
Fast Cars and Superstars: The Gillette Young Guns Celebrity Race (miniseries), ABC, 2007.

Film Appearances:
Title role, *Emmanuelle, Queen of the Galaxy* (also known as *Emmanuelle in Space* and *Emmanuelle in Space: A World of Desire*), 1994.
Michelle, *Rolling Thunder,* 1995.
Busty woman on elevator, *Liar Liar,* Universal, 1997.
Second Mate Johnson, *Haunted Sea,* Concorde, 1997.
Jennifer, *Sunset Strip,* Twentieth Century–Fox, 2000.
Syd Deshaye, *Face Value,* New Concorde Home Entertainment, 2001.
Meg Peters, *Totally Blonde,* Panorama Entertainment/V Releasing, 2001.
Pretty woman, *Confessions of a Dangerous Mind* (also known as *Confessions d'un homme dangereux*), Miramax, 2002.
Stacy, *Anger Management,* Columbia, 2003.
Holographic woman, *Paycheck,* Paramount, 2003.
Lucinda, *Meet Market,* 2004, Cut Entertainment Group, 2007.
Tiara Benedette, *Shut Up and Kiss Me!,* American World Pictures, 2004.
Maddy, *Tony 'n' Tina's Wedding,* 2004.
Tuffy, *Feast,* Dimension Films/Weinstein Co., 2006.
Krista, *Strange Wilderness,* Twentieth Century–Fox, 2006.
Dr. Sara Thompson, *All Along,* Apprentice Productions, 2007.
Hannah, *The Third Nail,* Romar Entertainment, 2007.

Stage Appearances:
Eve, *Orgasms,* Canon Theatre, Beverly Hills, CA, 2003.

RECORDINGS

Videos:
Appeared in the music video "Little Too Late" by Toby Keith, 2006.

OTHER SOURCES

Periodicals:
Femme Fatales, January, 1997, pp. 48–53.
Perfect 10, October, 2000, pp. 90–93.
Premiere, May, 2003, p. 23.
Soap Opera Update, September 12, 2000, pp. 44–45.

Electronic:
Krista Allen Official Site, http://www.kristaallen.com, June 11, 2007.

AXELROD, Jack 1930–

PERSONAL

Born January 25, 1930, in Los Angeles, CA; son of Samuel Maier and Esther (maiden name, Rosenthal) Axelrod. *Education:* University of California, Berkeley, A.A., 1950, B.A., 1956. *Avocational Interests:* Early fountain pens, four wall handball.

Career: Actor and teacher. Pittsburgh Playhouse, Pittsburgh, PA, actor, 1957–58; Cooper Milliken AIA, Old Town, ME, architectural designer, 1958–64; Brandeis University, Waltham, MA, artist in residence, 1973–74; University of Wisconsin–Green Bay, visiting director, 1976; assistant professor at Pennsylvania State University, State College, PA, 1977–78, Temple University, Philadelphia, PA, 1979–81, and Boston University, Boston, MA, 1981–82; University of Michigan, Ann Arbor, MI, acting M.F.A. coordinator, 1982; California State University, Northridge, lecturer, 1986–90. *Military service:* U.S. Army, 1953–55, served as a corporal.

Member: Actors' Equity Association, Screen Actors Guild, American Federation of Television and Radio Artists.

CREDITS

Television Appearances; Series:
Victor Jerome, *General Hospital,* ABC, 1988–89.
Grandpa Eddie, a recurring role, *The Help,* The WB, 2004.

Television Appearances; Movies:
Harlan Crockett, *Not My Kid* (also known as *Com o meu filho nunca!, Ikke mitt barn, Nicht meine Tochter, Nicht unsere Tochter, Niemojedziecko, Pas mon enfant,* and *Sfida alla vita*), CBS, 1985.
Mario Columbard, *Love, Cheat & Steal,* Showtime, 1993.
Mr. Thompson, *Something to Sing About,* syndicated, 2000.
Sid, *Blowing Smoke,* 2004.
Elderly neighbor, *Christmas Do-Over,* ABC Family Channel, 2006.

Television Appearances; Specials:

Grandpa, *Comedy Central Thanxgiveaway: Home Fires* (also known as *Thanksgivaway 2001*), Comedy Central, 2001.

Television Appearances; Episodic:

Forensics man, "Lady in the Squad Room," *Kojak*, CBS, 1977.

Salesperson, "The Count of Monty Tasco," *Hill Street Blues*, NBC, 1984.

Charlie, "The Mothers," *Dynasty*, ABC, 1987.

Arnie Zimmer, "The Good Guys," *Knots Landing*, CBS, 1989.

Arnie Zimmer, "When Push Comes to Shove," *Knots Landing*, CBS, 1989.

Mr. Williams, "If I Were a Rich Man," *Night Court*, NBC, 1989.

Arnie Zimmer, "The Ripple Effect," *Knots Landing*, CBS, 1990.

Leon, "Rage before Beauty," *Murphy Brown*, CBS, 1992.

Bartender, "Lawyers, Beer and Money," *Dharma & Greg*, ABC, 1999.

Jacobus Blitzer, "Cliffhanger," *GvsE* (also known as *G vs. E*), USA Network, 1999, later known as *Good versus Evil*, Sci–Fi Channel.

Lodge member, "Frank's Tribute," *Everybody Loves Raymond* (also known as *Raymond, Alla aelskar Raymond, Alle elsker Raymond, Alle lieben Raymond, Kaikki rakastavat Raymondia, Svi vole Raymonda, Todo el mundo quiere a Raymond, Tothom estima en Raymond, Tout le monde aime Raymond,* and *Tutti amano Raymond*), CBS, 1999.

Organ grinder, "You Light Up My Union," *Boy Meets World* (also known as *Cory si restul lumii, Crescere che fatica, Das Leben und ich, De wereld om de hoek, Du store verden!, Et gutteliv, Incorigible Cory, Isojen poikien leikit, O mundo e dos jovens, O rapaz e o mundo,* and *Yo y el mundo*), ABC, 1999.

Elderly man, "The Mistake," *Gideon's Crossing*, ABC, 2000.

Second chorus member, "Muse," *Star Trek: Voyager* (also known as *Voyager*), syndicated, 2000.

Giovanni Donato, "Time Will Tell," *Alias*, ABC, 2001.

Mr. Kanter, "Seduced and Abandoned," *The Division* (also known as *Heart of the City*), Lifetime, 2001.

Mr. Jenkins, "Love Thy Neighbor," *In–Laws* (also known as *Meine Frau, ihr Vater und ich* and *Melkein sukua*), NBC, 2002.

Old Frasier, "The Devil & Dr. Phil," *Frasier* (also known as *Dr. Frasier Crane*), NBC, 2003.

Uncle Paddy, "Waking Uncle Paddy," *It's All Relative* (also known as *Absolut relativ, En svaefar foer mycket, Kaikki on suhteellista,* and *Todo es relativo*), ABC, 2003.

Electrolarynx (voicebox) man, "Cost Dad the Election," *My Name Is Earl* (also known as *Kovan onnen kundi* and *Me llamo Earl*), NBC, 2005.

Fake father, "Randy's Touchdown," *My Name Is Earl* (also known as *Kovan onnen kundi* and *Me llamo Earl*), NBC, 2005.

Old man, "Quit Smoking," *My Name Is Earl* (also known as *Kovan onnen kundi* and *Me llamo Earl*), NBC, 2005.

Sheldon, "Halloween," *Malcolm in the Middle* (also known as *Fighting in Underpants*), Fox, 2005.

Electrolarynx (voicebox) man, "Sticks & Stones," *My Name Is Earl* (also known as *Kovan onnen kundi* and *Me llamo Earl*), NBC, 2006.

Father O'Grady, "The Gang Exploits a Miracle," *It's Always Sunny in Philadelphia* (also known as *Sunny*), FX Channel, 2006.

Italian man, "My New Suit," *Scrubs*, NBC, 2006.

Very old man, "Don't Stand So Close to Me," *Grey's Anatomy* (also known as *Complications, Procedure, Surgeons, Under the Knife,* and *Grey's Anatomy—Die jungen Aerzte*), ABC, 2006.

Very old man, "Let the Angels Commit," *Grey's Anatomy* (also known as *Complications, Procedure, Surgeons, Under the Knife,* and *Grey's Anatomy—Die jungen Aerzte*), ABC, 2006.

Electrolarynx (voicebox) man, "Our 'Cops' Is On!," *My Name Is Earl* (also known as *Kovan onnen kundi* and *Me llamo Earl*), NBC, 2007.

Appeared as an elderly man in *Philly*, ABC; also appeared in *Jack & Jill* (also known as *Jack ja Jill, Jack og Jill,* and *Jack und Jill*), The WB.

Television Appearances; Pilots:

Hammer, Slammer and Slade, ABC, 1990.

Grandpa Eddie, *The Help*, The WB, 2004.

Stage Appearances:

Gandhi, Playhouse Theatre, New York City, 1970.

Robert, *Tug of War*, Roundabout Theatre Company, New York City, 1970–71.

Hedda Gabler, 1973.

The Miser, 1973.

Edouard Bacher, Menachem Ussishkin, first delegate, Russian general, and other roles, *Herzl*, Palace Theatre, New York City, 1976.

The Fantasticks (musical), 1978.

Waiting for Godot, 1978.

How the Other Half Loves, 1979.

Autumn Elegy, 1989.

I'm Not Rappaport, 1989.

Appeared in other productions, including productions of the Pittsburgh Playhouse, Pittsburgh, PA.

Film Appearances:

Arroyo, *Bananas*, United Artists, 1971.

Gus, *Through Thick and Thin* (short film), 1999.

AZZOPARDI, Mario 1950–

PERSONAL

Born in 1950, in Malta.

Addresses: *Agent*—Agency for the Performing Arts, 405 South Beverly Dr., Beverly Hills, CA 90212. *Manager*—Course Management, 15159 Greenleaf St., Sherman Oaks, CA 91403.

Career: Director and writer. Also a poet and literature teacher.

Awards, Honors: Gemini Award nomination, best direction in a dramatic program or series, Academy of Canadian Cinema and Television, 1986, for *Night Heat;* Gemini Award nomination, best direction in a dramatic or comedy series, 1995, for *Robocop;* Craft Award nomination, outstanding achievement in direction—feature film, Directors Guild of Canada, 2003, for *Savage Messiah.*

CREDITS

Film Director:
Gagga (also known as *The Cage*), 1971.
Deadline, 1979.
Nowhere to Hide, New Century Vista, 1987.
Divided Loyalties, 1989.
Savage Messiah (also known as *Moise: L'affaire roch theriault*), Christal Films, 2002.

Television Director; Movies:
Die Einzige zeugin, 1995.
Bone Daddy (also known as *Palmer's Bones* and *L'affaire Palmer*), HBO, 1998.
Profile of a Director, PBS, 1998.
Freefall (also known as *Angst ueber den wolken*), Fox Family Channel, 1999.
The Time Shifters (also known as *Thrill Seekers*), TBS, 1999.
On Hostile Ground, TBS, 2000.
Loves Music, Loves to Dance (also known as *Mary Higgins Clark's "Loves Music, Loves to Dance"*), Independent Television, 2001.
Stiletto Dance, HBO, 2001.
The Stork Derby (also known as *Course a la cigogne* and *La course aux enfant*), Lifetime, 2002.
Still Small Voices, Lifetime, 2006.
The Wives He Forgot, Lifetime, 2006.
Lie and Crimes, Lifetime, 2007.

Television Executive Producer; Movies:
The Stork Derby (also known as *Course a la cigogne* and *La course aux enfant*), Lifetime, 2002.

Television Director; Pilots:
Captain Power and the Soldiers of the Future, syndicated, 1987.
E.N.G., Lifetime, 1989.

Stargate SG–1, Showtime and syndicated, 1997.
Total Recall 2070 (also known as *Total Recall 2070: Machine Dreams*), Showtime, 1998.

Also directed *Counterstrike.*

Television Director; Specials:
Police File, ABC, 1994.

Television Director; Episodic:
The Littlest Hobo, CTV, 1979.
Night Heat, CBS, 1985–89.
Wiseguy, ABC, 1987.
"The Abyss," *Captain Power and the Soldiers of the Future,* syndicated, 1987.
"Shattered," *Captain Power and the Soldiers of the Future,* syndicated, 1987.
Booker (also known as *Booker, P.I.*), Fox, 1989.
Top Cops, 1989.
"Fairest of Them All," *In the Heat of the Night,* NBC, 1989.
"Lessons Learned," *In the Heat of the Night,* NBC, 1990.
The Flash, NBC, 1990.
E.N.G., Lifetime, 1990.
Sweating Bullets (also known as *Tropical Heat*), 1991.
"Survival Instinct," *Counterstrike* (also known as *Force de frappe*), 1991.
"Sanctuary," *In the Heat of the Night,* NBC, 1992.
Human Target, ABC, 1992.
Secret Service, 1992.
Highlander (also known as *Highlander: The Series*), syndicated, 1992.
"Marked Man," *Matrix,* USA Network, 1993.
Kung Fu: The Legend Continues, syndicated, 1993–95.
Viper, NBC, 1994.
Robocop (also known as *RoboCop: The Series*), syndicated, 1994.
M.A.N.T.I.S., ABC, 1994.
"Fever," *Sliders,* Fox, 1995.
"Summer of Love," *Sliders,* Fox, 1995.
The Outer Limits, Showtime and syndicated, 1995–2001.
"Man in the Mist," *Poltergeist: The Legacy,* Showtime, 1996.
Two, syndicated, 1996.
"Man in the Mist," *Poltergeist: The Legacy,* Showtime, 1996.
F/X: The Series, syndicated, 1996.
Dead Man's Gun, 1997.
"Blood Lines," *Stargate SG–1,* Showtime and syndicated, 1997.
"Brief Candle," *Stargate SG–1,* Showtime and syndicated, 1997.
"Children of the Gods," *Stargate SG–1,* Showtime and syndicated, 1997.
"Singularity," *Stargate SG–1,* Showtime and syndicated, 1997.

"Cor–ai," *Stargate SG–1,* Showtime and syndicated, 1998.

Total Recall 2070 (also known as *Total Recall: The Series*), Showtime, 1999.

"Contact," *Dinotopia* (also known as *"Dinotopia": The Series*), 2002.

"Car Wars," *Dinotopia* (also known as *"Dinotopia": The Series*), 2003.

Jeremiah, Showtime, 2004.

"Thirty Eight Minutes," *Stargate: Atlantis* (also known as *La porte d'Atlantis* and *Stargate: Atlantis*), Sci–Fi Channel, 2004.

"Suspicion," *Stargate: Atlantis* (also known as *La porte d'Atlantis* and *Stargate: Atlantis*), Sci–Fi Channel, 2004.

"Hot Zone," *Stargate: Atlantis* (also known as *La porte d'Atlantis* and *Stargate: Atlantis*), Sci–Fi Channel, 2004.

"Letters from Pegasus," *Stargate: Atlantis* (also known as *La porte d'Atlantis* and *Stargate: Atlantis*), Sci–Fi Channel, 2005.

"Open Your Eyes," *Angela's Eyes,* Lifetime, 2006.

Also directed *Beyond Reality.*

Television Appearances; Episodic:

Ferraro Benedetti, "Lucky," *The Littlest Hobo,* CTV, 1984.

Quintaro, "Freedom Dead," *Night Heat,* 1987.

The count, "Double Eagle," *Highlander* (also known as *Highlander: The Series*), 1995.

WRITINGS

Screenplays:

Gagga (also known as *The Cage*), 1971.

Deadline, 1979.

Television Movies:

Die Einzige zeugin, 1995.

Other:

Naked as Water (poetry), translated from Maltese by Grazio Falzon, University of Oklahoma Press (Norman), 1997.

OTHER SOURCES

Periodicals:

World Literature Today, winter, 1997, p. 197.

B

BACCARIN, Morena 1979–
(Monrena Baccarin)

PERSONAL

Born June 2, 1979, in Rio de Janeiro, Brazil; raised in New York, NY; daughter of Vera Setta (an actress). *Education:* Studied at the Juilliard School; also attended Fiorello H. LaGuardia High School of Music & Art and Performing Arts, New York City.

Addresses: *Agent*—International Creative Management, 10250 Constellation Way, Ninth Floor, Los Angeles, CA 90067. *Manager*—3 Arts Entertainment, 9460 Wilshire Blvd., Seventh Floor, Beverly Hills, CA 90212.

Career: Actress. Appeared in advertisements.

Awards, Honors: Best Actress Award, Wine Country Film Festival, 2001, for *Way Off–Broadway.*

CREDITS

Television Appearances; Series:
Inara Serra, *Firefly* (also known as *Firefly: The Series* and *Firefly—Der Aufbruch der Serenity*), Fox, 2002–2003.
Maggie Jones, *Still Life,* Fox, produced c. 2003 but never broadcast.
Adria, *Stargate SG–1* (also known as *La porte des etoiles* and *Stargaate SG–1*), Sci–Fi Channel, Showtime, and syndicated, beginning 2006.
Nurse Jessica Kivala, *Heartland,* TNT, beginning 2007.

Television Appearances; Movies:
Alice Carter, *Sands of Oblivion,* Sci–Fi Channel, 2007.

Television Appearances; Specials:
Herself, *Sci Fi Inside: "Serenity,"* Sci–Fi Channel, 2005.

Television Appearances; Episodic:
"Juilliard," *American Masters,* PBS, c. 2003.
Voice of the Black Canary, "The Cat and the Canary," *Justice League* (animated; also known as *JL, JLA, Justice League of America,* and *Justice League Unlimited*), Cartoon Network, 2005.
Voice of the Black Canary, "Double Date," *Justice League* (animated; also known as *JL, JLA, Justice League of America,* and *Justice League Unlimited*), Cartoon Network, 2005.
Herself, *The Film Programme* (also known as *Film 2005*), BBC, 2005.
Chloe, "Swarley," *How I Met Your Mother,* CBS, 2006.
Gia, "An Affair to Remember," *Kitchen Confidential,* Fox, 2006.
Lisa Cruz, "Christmas Party," *Justice,* Fox, 2006.
Maya Griffin, "The Cliffhanger," *The O.C.* (also known as *California Teens, Newport Beach, O.C., O.C., California, Orange County, A Narancsvidek, O.C.—Um estranho no paraiso,* and *Zycie na fali*), Fox, 2006.
Maya Griffin, "The Heavy Lifting," *The O.C.* (also known as *California Teens, Newport Beach, O.C., O.C., California, Orange County, A Narancsvidek, O.C.–Um estranho no paraiso,* and *Zycie na fali*), Fox, 2006.
Maya Griffin, "The Road Warrior," *The O.C.* (also known as *California Teens, Newport Beach, O.C., O.C., California, Orange County, A Narancsvidek, O.C.—Um estranho no paraiso,* and *Zycie na fali*), Fox, 2006.
Voice of the Black Canary, "Grudge Match," *Justice League* (animated; also known as *JL, JLA, Justice League of America,* and *Justice League Unlimited*), Cartoon Network, 2006.
Sara Samari, "The Burning Bedouin," *Las Vegas* (also known as *Casino Eye*), NBC, 2007.

Appeared as an extra in *Law & Order: Criminal Intent* (also known as *Law & Order: CI*), NBC.

Television Appearances; Pilots:

Maggie Jones, *Still Life,* Fox, 2003.

Nurse Jessica Kivala, *Heartland,* TNT, 2007.

Film Appearances:

(As Monrena Baccarin) Monica, *Perfume* (also known as *Dress to Kill*), Imagem, 2001.

Rebecca, *Way Off–Broadway,* Small Planet Pictures, 2001.

Girl in bar, *Roger Dodger,* Artisan Entertainment, 2002.

Inara Serra, *Serenity* (also known as *Firefly, Firefly: The Movie, Serenity—A luta pelo amanha, Serenity—Flucht in neue Welten,* and *Serenity—pogenemine uude maailma*), Universal, 2005.

Adria, *Stargate: The Ark of Truth,* Metro–Goldwyn–Mayer Home Entertainment, 2008.

Stage Appearances:

Servant and understudy, *The Seagull,* New York Shakespeare Festival, Public Theater, Delacorte Theater, New York City, 2001.

Appeared in other productions, including *The Importance of Being Earnest* and *Love's Labour's Lost.*

RECORDINGS

Videos:

Herself, *Here's How It Was: The Making of "Firefly"* (short), Twentieth Century–Fox, 2003.

Herself, *Serenity: The 10th Character* (short), 2003.

Herself, *Re–Lighting the Firefly* (short), 2005.

Herself, *Done the Impossible: The Fans' Tale of "Firefly" and "Serenity,"* Done the Impossible, 2006.

Herself, *A Filmmaker's Journey* (short), 2006.

BADALAMENTI, Angelo 1937–

(Andy Badale, Angelo Bagdelamenti)

PERSONAL

Born March 22, 1937, in Bensonhurst neighborhood, Brooklyn, NY; raised in New Jersey; married, wife's name Lonny, c. 1968; children: Danielle, Andre (a musician). *Education:* Attended University of Rochester and Manhattan School of Music; received master's degrees.

Addresses: *Manager*—Kraft–Engel Management, 15233 Ventura Blvd., Suite 200, Sherman Oaks, CA 91403.

Career: Composer, conductor, music director, orchestrator, music producer, lyricist, and musician. Composer of advertising jingles, including music for Opium and Obsession perfume commercials, and television theme music; arranger of musical pieces for recording artists, including George Benson, Paul McCartney, Liza Minelli, Melba Moore, and Mel Tillis; occasional songwriter with John Clifford, under the name Andy Badale. Also worked as a voice coach, a junior high school teacher in Brooklyn, NY, a pianist at resorts in the Catskill Mountains of New York State, and as an employee of a music publishing company.

Awards, Honors: Emmy Award nominations, outstanding achievement in music composition of a dramatic underscore for a television series, and outstanding achievement in main title theme music (with David Lynch), both 1990, for *Twin Peaks;* Emmy Award nomination (with Lynch), outstanding achievement in song music and lyrics, 1990, for "Into the Night," *Twin Peaks;* Grammy Award, best pop instrumental performance, National Academy of Recording Arts and Sciences, 1990, for "Twin Peaks Theme"; Grammy Award nomination, best instrumental composition written for a motion picture or for television, 1991, for soundtrack recording of *Twin Peaks;* Independent Spirit Award, best original score, Independent Features Project/West, and Saturn Award, best music, Academy of Science Fiction, Fantasy, and Horror Films, both 1993, for *Twin Peaks: Fire Walk with Me;* Cesar Award nomination, best music written for a film, Academie des Arts et Techniques du Cinema, 1996, for *La cite des enfants perdus;* Golden Globe Award nomination, best original score for a motion picture, Online Film Critics Society Award nomination, best original score, and Sierra Award nomination, best score, Las Vegas Film Critics Society, all 2000, for *The Straight Story;* Golden Globe Award nomination, best original score for a motion picture, American Film Institute Award nomination, composer of the year, nomination for Anthony Asquith Award for Film Music, British Academy of Film and Television Arts, Saturn Award nomination, best music, Chicago Film Critics Association Award nomination (with others), best original score, and Online Film Critics Society Award, best original score, all 2002, for *Mulholland Drive;* Cesar Award nomination, best music written for a film, and World Soundtrack Award, soundtrack composer of the year, both 2005, for *Un long dimanche de fiancailles;* Technical Excellence and Creativity Award nomination, Mix Foundation, 2007; won at least eight awards from American Society of Composers, Authors, and Publishers.

CREDITS

Film Work:

Music director and (uncredited) conductor, *Blue Velvet,* Di Laurentiis Entertainment Group, 1986.

Orchestrator and musical director, *Tough Guys Don't Dance* (also known as *Norman Mailer's "Tough Guys Don't Dance"*), Cannon, 1987.

Orchestrator, *Christmas Vacation* (also known as *National Lampoon's "Christmas Vacation"* and *National Lampoon's Winter Holiday*), 1989.

Orchestrator, *Wait Until Spring, Bandini* (also known as *Bandini,* John Fante's *"Wait Until Spring, Bandini," Aspetta primavera Bandini,* and *Le ragioni del cuore*), 1989.

Orchestrator, music director, and conductor, *Cousins* (also known as *A Touch of Infidelity*), Paramount, 1989.

Orchestral music producer, *Parents,* Vestron, 1989.

Orchestrator and keyboard performer, *Twin Peaks: Fire Walk with Me* (also known as *Twin Peaks*), New Line Cinema, 1992.

Orchestrator, music director, and conductor, *Lost Highway,* October Films, 1997.

Orchestrator, *Arlington Road,* Screen Gems, 1999.

Orchestrator and conductor of score, and arranger and producer of the song "Maya, Mayi Ma—The Celebration," *Holy Smoke,* Miramax, 1999.

Orchestrator and conductor, *The Straight Story* (also known as *Une histoire vraie*), Buena Vista, 1999.

Orchestrator and producer of the song "Beached," *The Beach,* Twentieth Century–Fox, 2000.

Music conductor, *Mulholland Drive* (also known as *Mulholland Dr.*), Universal Focus, 2001.

Orchestrator, *Secretary,* Lions Gate Films, 2002.

Score producer, *The Wicker Man,* Warner Bros., 2006.

Film Appearances:

(As Andy Badale) Piano player, *Blue Velvet,* Di Laurentiis Entertainment Group, 1986.

Luigi Castigliani, *Mulholland Drive* (also known as *Mulholland Dr.*), Universal Focus, 2001.

Television Work; Series:

Music orchestrator, director, conductor, and musician, *Twin Peaks,* ABC, 1990–91.

Music performer, *Parashat Ha–Shavua,* 2006.

Television Work; Specials:

Producer, *Industrial Symphony No. 1: The Dream of the Broken Hearted,* 1990.

Music conductor, *Hotel Room* (also known as *David Lynch's "Hotel Room"*), HBO, 1993.

Television Work; Other:

Music orchestrator, director, conductor, and musician, *Twin Peaks* (pilot), ABC, 1990–91.

Orchestrator and conductor of main theme music, *The Last Don* (also known as *Mario Puzo's "The Last Don"*), 1997.

Orchestrator, musician, and song producer, "Apple Tree," "Faded," and "She's Gone," *Julie Johnson* (movie), here! TV, 2001.

Television Appearances; Specials:

Musician, *Industrial Symphony No. 1: The Dream of the Broken Hearted,* 1990.

Jonathan Ross Presents for One Week Only: David Lynch, 1990.

Conductor of opening song, *Cerimonia d'inauguracio jocs olimpics Barcelona '92,* 1992.

Pretty As a Picture: The Art of David Lynch, 1997.

A Very Long Engagement: On the Set of a Romantic Epic, 2004.

Television Appearances; Episodic:

"David Lynch: Don't Look at Me," *Cinema, de notre temps,* 1989.

Pianist, premiere episode, *On the Air,* 1992.

"David Lynch Special," *Tracks,* 2007.

Television Appearances; Other:

Der Klang der bilder, 1995.

Stage Appearances:

Musician, *Industrial Symphony No. 1: The Dream of the Broken Hearted,* Brooklyn Academy of Music, Brooklyn, NY, 1990.

RECORDINGS

Videos:

Mysteries of Love, Metro–Goldwyn–Mayer/United Artists Home Entertainment, 2002.

Cabin Fever: Beneath the Skin, Lions Gate Films Home Entertainment, 2004.

Une annee au front, les coulisses de "Un long dimanche de fiancailles," Warner Bros., 2004.

Le son de Lynch, Nomad Films International, 2005.

Dark Water: Extraordinary Ensemble, Buena Vista Home Entertainment, 2005.

Albums as Musician or Conductor:

Blue Velvet (soundtrack recording), Varese Sarabande, 1986.

Cousins (soundtrack recording), Warner Bros., 1988.

Industrial Symphony No. 1: The Dream of the Broken Hearted (soundtrack recording), 1990.

(With David Lynch and Julee Cruise) *Floating into the Night,* 1990.

Twin Peaks (soundtrack recording), Warner Bros., 1991.

Twin Peaks: Fire Walk with Me (soundtrack recording), Warner Bros., 1992.

(With Tim Booth) *Booth and the Bad Angel,* 1996.

Lost Highway (soundtrack recording), 1997.

The Straight Story (soundtrack recording), Windham Hill, 1999.

Holy Smoke! (soundtrack recording), Milan, 1999.

The Beach, Sire, 2000.

Cabin Fever (soundtrack album), 2002.

Also recorded the albums *Andy Badale* and *The Nashville Beer Garden Band.* Badalamenti's film music has been included in numerous soundtrack recordings; many compositions have also been recorded by other artists.

Soundtrack Albums as Composer:

Weeds, 1987.

Nightmare on Elm Street 3: The Dream Warriors, Colosseum, 1987.

Comfort of Strangers, Cam Soundtrack, 1990.

The City of Lost Children, Point Music, 1996.

Arlington Road, Will, 1999.

A Very Long Engagement, WEA, 2004.

Dark Water, Hollywood, 2005.

Wicker Man, Silva Screen, 2006.

Albums as Producer:

Marianne Faithfull—A Secret Life, 1995.

WRITINGS

Film Music:

(As Andy Badale) *Law and Disorder,* Columbia, 1974.

(As Andy Badale) Score and title song lyrics, *Across the Great Divide,* Pacific International Enterprises, 1976.

(Including songs "Blue Star" and "Mysteries of Love") *Blue Velvet,* Di Laurentiis Entertainment Group, 1986.

A Nightmare on Elm Street Part III: Dream Warriors (also known as *A Nightmare on Elm Street Part III*), New Line Cinema, 1987.

(Including songs "You'll Come Back (You Always Do)" and "Real Man") *Tough Guys Don't Dance* (also known as *Norman Mailer's "Tough Guys Don't Dance"*), Cannon, 1987.

(Including song "Mysteries of Love") *Weeds,* Di Laurentiis Entertainment Group, 1987.

(Including song "I Love You for Today") *Cousins* (also known as *A Touch of Infidelity*), Paramount, 1989.

(With Jonathan Elias and Sherman Foote) *Parents,* Vestron, 1989.

Christmas Vacation (also known as *National Lampoon's "Christmas Vacation"* and *National Lampoon's Winter Holiday*), Warner Bros., 1989.

Wait Until Spring, Bandini (also known as *Bandini, John Fante's "Wait Until Spring, Bandini," Aspetta primavera Bandini,* and *Le ragioni del cuore*), Orion, 1989.

The Comfort of Strangers (also known as *Cortesie per gli ospiti*), Skouras, 1990.

(Including song "Up in Flames") *Wild at Heart* (also known as *David Lynch's "Wild at Heart"*), Samuel Goldwyn Films, 1990.

(Including songs "The Black Dog Runs at Night," "Falling," "Love Theme," "Moving through Time," "Questions in a World of Blue," "A Real Indication," "She

Would Die for Love," "Sycamore Trees" and "The Voice of Love") *Twin Peaks: Fire Walk with Me,* New Line Cinema, 1992.

Naked in New York, Fine Line, 1994.

(Including song "Who Will Take Your Dreams Away") *La cite des enfants perdus* (also known as *The City of Lost Children, La ciudad de los ninos perdidos, La ciutat dels nens perduts,* and *Die Stadt der verlorenen kinder*), 1995.

(Including theme music) *Invasion of Privacy,* Trimark Pictures, 1996.

Lost Highway, October Films, 1997.

The Blood Oranges, Trimark Pictures, 1997.

Arlington Road, Screen Gems, 1999.

The Straight Story (also known as *Une histoire vraie*), Buena Vista, 1999.

Holy Smoke!, Miramax, 1999.

(Including theme music) *The Story of a Bad Boy,* 1999.

(Including songs "Beached" and "Bloody Boy") *The Beach,* Twentieth Century–Fox, 2000.

A Piece of Eden, Film Acres, 2000.

Mulholland Drive (also known as *Mulholland Dr.*), Universal Focus, 2001.

Suspended Animation (also known as *Mayhem*), First Run Features, 2001.

Cet amour la (also known as *This Very Love*), 2001, subtitled version, New Yorker, 2003.

Rabbits, Davidlynch.com, 2002.

Mysteries of Love (documentary), Metro–Goldwyn–Mayer Home Entertainment, 2002.

Secretary, Lions Gate Films, 2002.

Darkened Room (short film), Davidlynch.com, 2002.

L'adversaire (also known as *The Adversary* and *El adversario*), Paradiso Home Entertainment, 2002.

Auto Focus, Sony Pictures, 2002.

Cabin Fever, Lions Gate Films, 2003.

Resistance, A–Film Distribution, 2003.

Indoor Fireworks (short film), Sleeve Monkey Film, 2003.

Push (short film), 2004.

Evilenko, Mikado, 2004.

Un long dimanche de fiancailles (also known as *A Very Long Engagement*), Warner Independent Pictures, 2004.

The Monster of Rostov, 2004.

NaPolA (also known as *Before the Fall, Before the Fall (Napola), Napola—Elite fuer den Fuehrer,* and *Napola: Hitler's Elite*), Picture This! Entertainment, 2005.

Dominion: Prequel to "The Exorcist" (also known as *Paul Schrader's "Exorcist:" The Original Prequel*), Warner Bros., 2005.

Dark Water, Buena Vista, 2005.

The Wicker Man, Warner Bros., 2006.

The Eye, Lions Gate Films, 2007.

Songs Featured in Films:

(As Andy Badale) *Gordon's War,* Twentieth Century–Fox, 1973.

"Fall in Love with Me," *The Very Thought of You,* Miramax, 1999.

"Who Will Take My Dreams Away?," *Girl on the Bridge,* Paramount Vantage, 1999.

"Sleep," *Son frere* (also known as *His Brother*), Strand Releasing, 2004.

"What You Want," *Take the Lead,* New Line Cinema, 2006.

Television Music; Series:

Score, theme music, and songs "Falling" and "The Nightingale," *Twin Peaks,* ABC, 1990–91.

On the Air, 1992.

(As Angelo Bagdelamenti) Main theme music, *Inside the Actors Studio,* Bravo, 1994.

Main title theme music, *The Profiler,* NBC, 1996–98.

Cracker (also known as *Cracker: Mind Over Murder* and *Fitz*), 1997.

According to some sources, also wrote songs for *Captain Kangaroo.*

Television Music; Specials:

(With David Lynch and Julee Cruise) *Industrial Symphony No. 1: The Dream of the Broken Hearted,* 1990.

Song "The Flaming Arrow," *Cerimonia d'inauguracio jocs olimpics Barcelona '92,* 1992.

Main theme music "Dark Spanish Symphony," *The Donner Party,* PBS, 1992.

Hotel Room (also known as *David Lynch's "Hotel Room"*), HBO, 1993.

A Very Long Engagement: On the Set of a Romantic Epic, 2004.

Inside the Actors Studio: 10th Anniversary Special, Bravo, 2004.

Television Music: Movies:

Witch Hunt, 1994.

Forever Mine, Starz!, 1999.

Julie Johnson, here! TV, 2001.

The Lathe of Heaven, Arts and Entertainment, 2002.

Theme music, *Undefeated,* HBO, 2003.

Theme music, *Frankenstein,* USA Network, 2004.

Television Music: Miniseries:

Main theme music, *The Last Don* (also known as *Mario Puzo's "The Last Don"*), 1997.

Les liaisons dangereuses (also known as *Dangerous Liaisons*), WE Network, 2003.

Television Music; Pilots:

Twin Peaks, ABC, 1990.

Television Music; Episodic:

Song "Dark Lolita," "De nye hjerter," *Arhundredets vidner,* 1998.

Video Music:

Les enfants de la cite perdue (also known as *Les enfants de la cite perdue. Visite sur le tournage du film de Caro & Jeunet: La cite des enfants perdus*), 1995.

Une annee au front, les coulisses de "Un long dimanche de fiancailles," Warner Bros., 2005.

Fahrenheit (video game; also known as *Indigo Prophecy*), Atari, 2005.

OTHER SOURCES

Books:

Contemporary Musicians, Volume 17, Gale, 1996.

Periodicals:

Billboard, June 22, 1996, p. 13.

Commerce, June 1, 2006, pp. 38–39, 74, 76.

Electronic:

Angelo Badalamenti Official Site, http://www.angelobadalamenti.com, June 11, 2007.

BAILEY, Steven W. 1971–
(Steve W. Bailey)

PERSONAL

Born July 1, 1971, in San Diego, CA; raised in WA; married Anneliese Boies (a special effects artist), June 1, 2002. *Education:* Graduated from the Advanced Training Program of the American Conservatory Theater, San Francisco, CA.

Addresses: *Agent*—Abrams Artists Agency, 9200 Sunset Blvd., Suite 1130, West Hollywood, CA 90069.

Career: Actor. Appeared in advertisements.

Member: Screen Actors Guild, American Federation of Television and Radio Artists, Actors' Equity Association.

CREDITS

Television Appearances; Series:

Steve Williams, *My Big Fat Obnoxious Fiance* (also known as *Minu vaega paks ja taeiesti talumatu peigmees*), Fox, 2004.

Joe, *Grey's Anatomy* (also known as *Complications, Procedure, Surgeons, Under the Knife,* and *Grey's Anatomy—Die jungen Aerzte*), ABC, beginning 2005.

Television Appearances; Specials:
Narrator, *Grey's Anatomy: Complications of the Heart,* ABC, 2006.
Narrator, *Grey's Anatomy: Straight to the Heart,* ABC, 2006.
Narrator, *Grey's Anatomy: Under Pressure,* ABC, 2006.

Appeared in archive footage in other programs.

Television Appearances; Episodic:
Ray, "Hide and Seek," *Nash Bridges* (also known as *Bridges*), CBS, 1999.
Danny, "Liar's Poker," *Nash Bridges* (also known as *Bridges*), CBS, 2000.
(As Steve W. Bailey) Phone man, "Psycho Therapy," *Becker,* CBS, 2001.
Ryan, "Carpe Noctem," *Angel* (also known as *Angel: The Series, Angel—Jaeger der Finsternis,* and *Skoteinos angelos*), The WB, 2001.
Cave demon, "Grave," *Buffy the Vampire Slayer* (also known as *BtVS, Buffy,* and *Buffy the Vampire Slayer: The Series*), UPN, 2002.
Cave demon, "Two to Go," *Buffy the Vampire Slayer* (also known as *BtVS, Buffy,* and *Buffy the Vampire Slayer: The Series*), UPN, 2002.
Cave demon, "Villains," *Buffy the Vampire Slayer* (also known as *BtVS, Buffy,* and *Buffy the Vampire Slayer: The Series*), UPN, 2002.
Vin, "Fagmalion Part 4: The Guy Who Loved Me," *Will & Grace,* NBC, 2003.
Himself, *Late Show with David Letterman* (also known as *The Late Show* and *Late Show Backstage*), CBS, 2004.
Himself, *The Tonight Show with Jay Leno,* NBC, 2004.
Jeremy, "If Tomorrow Never Comes," *Grey's Anatomy* (also known as *Complications, Procedure, Surgeons, Under the Knife,* and *Grey's Anatomy—Die jungen Aerzte*), ABC, 2005.
Jeremy, "Shake Your Groove Thing," *Grey's Anatomy* (also known as *Complications, Procedure, Surgeons, Under the Knife,* and *Grey's Anatomy—Die jungen Aerzte*), ABC, 2005.
Jeremy, "Winning a Battle, Losing the War," *Grey's Anatomy* (also known as *Complications, Procedure, Surgeons, Under the Knife,* and *Grey's Anatomy—Die jungen Aerzte*), ABC, 2005.
Himself, "On Location: Oprah on the Set of *Grey's Anatomy,*" *The Oprah Winfrey Show* (also known as *Oprah*), syndicated, 2006.

Appeared as a security guard, "Christina's First Day," *All That,* Nickelodeon; appeared as a motel clerk in "Back in the Bottle," an unaired episode of *The Court,* ABC.

Television Appearances; Pilots:
Rick, *Chestnut Hill,* NBC, 2001.

Film Appearances:
Walter, *Ultimate Reality,* WonderPhil Productions, 2002.
Brody, *Mix Tape,* Cr02Films, 2003.

Stage Appearances:
Appeared in various productions, including productions of the California Shakespeare Festival, the Utah Shakespearean Festival, and the American Conservatory Theater.

RECORDINGS

Video Games:
Voice of Cyrus, *Phantasmagoria* (also known as *Roberta Williams' "Phantasmagoria"*), Sierra On–Line, 1995.

OTHER SOURCES

Electronic:
Steven W. Bailey, http://www.stevenwbailey.com, May 12, 2007.

BALTES, Alan 1962–
(Alan Dakota)

PERSONAL

Full name, Alan Joseph Baltes; born August 5, 1962, in St. Paul, MN; son of Verna Mae Baltes; grandson of Roman Baltes (an animator). *Education:* Studied acting with Cliff Osmond.

Career: Actor. Appeared in advertisements. Motocross racer as a teenager. Also known as Alan Dakota.

Member: Screen Actors Guild (affiliated with the Casting Access Project and member of committees addressing affirmative action, diversity, and Native American issues), American Federation of Television and Radio Artists.

CREDITS

Television Appearances; Series:
Police cadet McDonald, *General Hospital,* ABC, 1983–88.
Detective Gibson, *Days of Our Lives* (also known as *Cruise of Deception: Days of Our Lives, Days, DOOL, Des jours et des vies, Horton–sagaen, I*

gode og onde dager, Los dias de nuestras vidas, Meres agapis, Paeivien viemaeae, Vaara baesta aar, Zeit der Sehnsucht, and *Zile din viata noastra*), NBC, 1985–96.

Television Appearances; Episodic:
Alex Haber, "Santa Clause Is Dead," *St. Elsewhere,* NBC, 1985.
Task force officer, "Secrets," *Cagney & Lacey,* CBS, 1987.
Band manager, "Sledge, Rattle 'n' Roll," *Sledge Hammer!* (also known as *Sledge Hammer: The Early Years*), ABC, 1988.
(Uncredited) Football player, "Poke High," *Married ... with Children* (also known as *Not the Cosbys*), Fox, 1988.
Jail guard, "Murder by Ten Count," *Trial by Jury,* syndicated, 1989.
Skydiving student, "Blind Date," *The Golden Girls* (also known as *Golden Girls, Miami Nice, Bnot Zahav, Cuori senza eta, Las chicas de oro, Les craquantes, Los anos dorados, Oereglanyok, Pantertanter,* and *Tyttoekullat*), NBC, 1989.
Billiards player, *Totally Hidden Video,* Fox, 1989.
Fire fighter, "Four Alarm Tony," *Who's the Boss?,* ABC, 1990.
Jason Fowler, "Where Echoes End," *Hunter,* NBC, 1990.
Waiter, "Murder in F Sharp," *Murder, She Wrote,* CBS, 1990.
Skydiving student, "Bloom Is Off the Rose," *The Golden Girls* (also known as *Golden Girls, Miami Nice, Bnot Zahav, Cuori senza eta, Las chicas de oro, Les craquantes, Los anos dorados, Oereglanyok, Pantertanter,* and *Tyttoekullat*), NBC, 1991.
Thought police, "Last Stand in Glen Brook," *Life Goes On* (also known as *Glenbrook*), ABC, 1991.
Waiter, "Tainted Lady," *Murder, She Wrote,* CBS, 1991.
Reporter, "Temptation Eyes—February 1, 1985," *Quantum Leap,* NBC, 1992.
I.R.S. agent, "Cold Shower," *L.A. Law,* NBC, 1993.
Police officer, "Hit and Run," *Baywatch* (also known as *Baywatch Hawaii* and *Baywatch Hawai'i*), syndicated, 1995.
Doctor, *Port Charles* (also known as *Port Charles: Desire, Port Charles: Fate, Port Charles: The Gift, Port Charles: Miracles Happen, Port Charles: Naked Eyes, Port Charles: Secrets, Port Charles: Superstitions, Port Charles: Surrender, Port Charles: Tainted Love, Port Charles: Tempted, Port Charles: Time in a Bottle,* and *Port Charles: Torn*), ABC, 1997, 1998, 2001.
Insomniac husband, *Running with Scissors,* c. 2000.
The ex–boyfriend, "Girls' Night Out," *The Geena Davis Show,* ABC, 2001.
(Uncredited) Dr. Levine, "Guilty," *Desperate Housewives,* ABC, 2004.
Marcus, "Raised by Another," *Lost,* ABC, 2004.

Television Appearances; Pilots:
Murder suspect, *Blind Justice* (also known as *Justicia ciega*), ABC, 2005.

Television Work; Episodic:
Stand–in, "The Judge Is Free," *Strip Mall,* Comedy Central, 2001.

Film Appearances:
(Uncredited) Driver, *To Live and Die in L.A.,* Metro–Goldwyn–Mayer/United Artists, 1985.
(Uncredited) Boarding school student, *Free Ride,* Galaxy International Releasing, 1986.
(Uncredited) Waiter, *Kazaam,* Buena Vista, 1996.

Film Work:
(Uncredited) Stunt driver, *To Live and Die in L.A.,* Metro–Goldwyn–Mayer/United Artists, 1985.

Stage Appearances:
Performed with the Los Angeles Repertory Company.

Stage Work:
Assistant producer for the American Indian Dance Theatre.

BANERJEE, Victor 1946–
(Victor Bannerjee)

PERSONAL

Born October 15, 1946, in Calcutta, India; married, wife's name, Maya; children: two daughters. *Education:* Received M.A. in comparative literature. *Avocational Interests:* Tennis, swimming, hockey, soccer.

Addresses: *Agent*—Scott Zimmerman, William Morris Agency, 151 El Camino Drive, Beverly Hills, CA 90212. *Publicist*—Rogers and Cowan Public Relations, 10000 Santa Monica Boulevard, Los Angeles, CA 90067.

Career: Actor. Founder and founding secretary of India's first Screen Extras Union.

Awards, Honors: National Board of Review Award, best actor, National Association of Theatre Owners of Texas Award, International Star of the Year, and United Motion Picture Association Award, all 1985, for *A Passage to India;* *Evening Standard* British Film Award, best actor, Film Award nomination, best actor, British Academy of Film and Television Arts, 1986, for *A Passage to India;* National Critics Association Award, best actor, for *Pratidan;* National Debate Champion Award, India.

CREDITS

Film Appearances:

(Debut) Prime Minister of Oudh Ali Naqi Khan, *Shatranj ke Khilari* (also known as *The Chess Players*), Connoisseur Films Ltd., 1977.

Georgie, Maharaja of Tasveer, *Hullabaloo Over Georgie and Bonnie's Pictures,* Contemporary Films Ltd./New Yorker, 1979.

Dhan Raj, *Kalyug* (also known as *The Machine Age*), 1981.

Jaipur Junction, 1982.

(As Victor Bannerjee), *Doosri Dulhan,* 1983.

Dr. Aziz, *A Passage to India,* Columbia, 1984.

Nikhilesh Choudhury, *Ghare Baire* (also known as *The Home and the World*), European Classics, 1984.

Ram Das, *Foreign Body,* Orion, 1986.

Hard to Be a God (also known as *Es Ist night leicht ein gott zu zein* and *E'Difficile essere un dio es*), Union Generale Cinematographique/Jugendfilm Verleigh/Titanus Distribuzione/Films du Volcan, 1989.

Elder son, *Mahaprithivi* (also known as *World Within, World Without*), 1992.

Mr. Singh, *Bitter Moon* (also known as *Lunes de fiel*), Fine Line, 1992.

Antarghaat, Arjoe, 2002.

Dr. Rjan, *Bhoot* (also known *Ghost*), Bodega, 2003.

Justice J. P. Chatterjee, *Joggers' Park,* Rainbow, 2003.

Peter the cheater, *Bow Barracks Forever,* Cinemawalla, 2004.

Yatna, 2005.

It Was Raining That Night, Columbia TriStar, 2005.

Navin Kapoor, *My Brother ... Nikhil,* Antiprod, 2005.

Hari Singh, *Amavas,* Shreya, 2005.

Sunny's father, *Home Delivery: Aapko ... Ghar Tak,* Sahara One, 2005.

Dadaji, *Ho Sakta Hai,* Ashco, 2006.

Gary, *The Bong Connection,* Moxie, 2006.

Mr. Bannerjee, *Ta Ra Rum Pum,* Yash Raj, 2007.

Apne, Glamour Entertainment, 2007.

Also appeared in *Arohan* (also known as *The Ascent*), 1982, and in *Madhurban, Tanaya, Pratidan, Prarthana,* and *Dui Prithri.*

Film Director:

An August Requiem, 1982.

Stage Appearances:

Made stage debut in *Pirates of Penzance.* Also appeared in productions of *Desert Song* and *Godspell.*

Stage Work:

Directed *An August Requiem,* 1981.

Television Appearances; Movies:

Georgie, *Hullabaloo Over Georgie and Bonnie's Pictures,* 1978.

Karpal Singh, *Dadah Is Death,* CBS, 1988.

Azad, *Bradford Riots,* Channel 4, 2006.

Television Appearances; Specials:

The lover, *Pikoor Diary* (also known as *Pikoo's Diary*), 1981.

"Subway Safari," *Travels,* PBS, 1989.

Television Appearances; Series:

Guananagari, *True Adventures of Christopher Columbus,* BBC, 1992.

Television Appearances; Episodic:

Judge, *Star Search,* syndicated, 1985.

BARBER, Gary

PERSONAL

Addresses: *Office*—Spyglass Entertainment Group, 10900 Wilshire Blvd., 10th Floor, Los Angeles, CA 90024.

Career: Producer. Price Waterhouse, worked as member of entertainment specialty group; Vestron International Group, president; Morgan Creek Productions, director, vice chair, and chief operating officer for several years; Morgan Creek International, president and chief operating officer; Spyglass Entertainment Group, Los Angeles, cofounder, cochair, and co–chief executive officer, 2000—. Los Angeles Police Department, member of executive committee of Crime Prevention Advisory Board; member of board of directors, Foundation of Motion Picture Pioneers and C.L.E. A.R. Foundation.

Member: Academy of Motion Pictures Arts and Sciences.

CREDITS

Film Executive Producer:

Midnight Crossing, Vestron, 1988.

Communion (also known as *Communion: A True Story*), New Line Cinema, 1989.

Howling V: The Rebirth, International Video Entertainment, 1989.

Co–executive producer, *Young Guns II* (also known as *Young Guns II: Blaze of Glory*), Twentieth Century–Fox, 1990.

Co–executive producer, *Pacific Heights,* Twentieth Century–Fox, 1990.
Robin Hood: Prince of Thieves, Warner Bros., 1991.
Freejack, Warner Bros., 1992.
White Sands, Warner Bros., 1992.
Stay Tuned, Warner Bros., 1992.
The Crush, Warner Bros., 1993.
True Romance (also known as *Breakaway*), Warner Bros., 1993.
Ace Ventura: Pet Detective, Warner Bros., 1994.
Chasers, Warner Bros., 1994.
Imaginary Crimes, Warner Bros., 1994.
Silent Fall, Warner Bros., 1994.
Trial by Jury, Warner Bros., 1994.
Major League II, Warner Bros., 1994.
Ace Ventura: When Nature Calls (also known as *Ace Ventura Goes to Africa*), Warner Bros., 1995.
Two if by Sea (also known as *Stolen Hearts*), Warner Bros., 1996.
Big Bully, Warner Bros., 1996.
Diabolique, Warner Bros., 1996.
Bad Moon, Warner Bros., 1996.
Wild America, Warner Bros., 1997.
Incognito, Warner Bros., 1997.
Major League: Back to the Minors (also known as *Major League III*), Warner Bros., 1998.
Wrongfully Accused (also known as *Leslie Nielsen ist sehr verdaechtig, Sehr Verdaechtig,* and *Unter falschem verdacht*), Warner Bros., 1998.
The King and I, Warner Bros., 1999.
Keeping the Faith, Buena Vista, 2000.
Unbreakable, Buena Vista, 2000.
Out Cold, Buena Vista, 2001.
Bruce Almighty, Universal, 2003.
1 Love (also known as *The Supreme Court*), Spyglass Entertainment Group, 2003.
Seabiscuit, Universal, 2003.
The Legend of Zorro (also known as *Z*), Columbia, 2005.
Memoirs of a Geisha, Columbia, 2005.
Eight Below (also known as *8 Below*), Buena Vista, 2006.
Stay Alive, Buena Vista, 2006.
Stick It, Buena Vista, 2006.

Film Producer:
Shanghai Noon, Buena Vista, 2000.
The Count of Monte Cristo (also known as *Alexandre Dumas' "The Count of Monte Cristo"*), Buena Vista, 2001.
Reign of Fire, Buena Vista, 2002.
Dragonfly (also known as *Im Zeichen der libelle*), Universal, 2002.
Abandon, Paramount, 2002.
The Recruit, Buena Vista, 2003.
Shanghai Knights, Buena Vista, 2003.
Connie and Carla, Universal, 2004.
Mr. 3000, Buena Vista, 2004.

The Pacifier (also known as *Gnome* and *Le pacificateur*), Buena Vista, 2005.
The Hitchhiker's Guide to the Galaxy, Buena Vista, 2005.
The Lookout, Miramax, 2006.
The Invisible, Hollywood Pictures, 2007.
Evan Almighty, Universal, 2007.
Underdog, Walt Disney, 2007.
Balls of Fury, Rogue Pictures, 2007.

Television Executive Producer; Series:
Ace Ventura: Pet Detective, 1996.
Miracles, ABC, 2003.

Television Executive Producer; Pilots:
Criminology 101 (also known as *Not a Clue*), CBS, 2003.
Weekends, NBC, 2004.

Television Executive Producer; Other:
The Rein–Deer Hunter (special), CBS, 1995.
The Ranch (movie), Showtime, 2004.

Video Game Executive Producer:
Ace Ventura, 1996.

BARRON, David

PERSONAL

Addresses: *Office*—Contagious Films, 14 Newburgh St., London W1 FRT England.

Career: Producer and production manager. Contagious Films, London, producer.

CREDITS

Film Work:
Location manager, *The French Lieutenant's Woman,* United Artists, 1981.
Location manager, *Giro City,* 1982.
Assistant director, *The Killing Fields,* Warner Bros., 1984.
Unit manager, *Legend* (also known as *Legend: Ultimate Edition*), Universal, 1985.
Production manager, *Revolution,* Warner Bros., 1985.
Production manager, *The Princess Bride* (also known as *The Bridges' Bride*), Twentieth Century–Fox, 1987.
Production supervisor, *The Lonely Passion of Judith Hearne,* Island, 1987.

Associate producer, *Hellbound: Hellraiser II* (also known as *Hellraiser II*), Anchor Bay Entertainment, 1988.

Production supervisor, *Strapless*, Miramax, 1989.

Production supervisor and associate producer, *Nightbreed* (also known as *Clive Barker's "Nightbreed"*), Twentieth Century–Fox, 1990.

Line producer, *The Muppet Christmas Carol*, Buena Vista, 1992.

Unit production manager and associate producer, *Frankenstein* (also known as *Mary Shelley's "Frankenstein"*), TriStar, 1994.

Producer, *In the Bleak Midwinter* (also known as *A Midwinter's Tale*), Sony Pictures Classics, 1995.

Producer, *Othello*, Columbia, 1995.

Producer, *Hamlet* (also known as *William Shakespeare's "Hamlet"*), Columbia, 1996.

Producer, *Siamese Cop*, 1998.

Executive producer, *Anno Domini* (short), 2000.

Producer, *Love's Labour's Lost* (also known as *Peines d'amour perdues*), Miramax, 2000.

Executive producer, *It Was an Accident*, Pathe, 2000.

Executive producer, *Possession*, USA Films, 2002.

Executive producer, *Harry Potter and the Chamber of Secrets* (also known as *Harry Potter und die kammer des schreckens*), Warner Bros., 2002.

Coproducer, *Sahara* (also known as *Sahara—Abenteuer in der wuste*), Paramount, 2005.

Executive producer, *Harry Potter and the Goblet of Fire* (also known as *Harry Potter and the Goblet of Fire: The IMAX Experience*), Warner Bros., 2005.

Producer, *Harry Potter and the Order of the Phoenix*, Warner Bros., 2007.

Producer, *Inbetween* (short) 2007.

Film Appearances:

Himself, *Preparing for the Yule Ball*, 2006.

Himself, *In Too Deep: The Second Task*, 2006.

Television Work; Miniseries:

Location manager, *Reilly: The Ace of Spies* (also known as *Reilly: Ace of Spies*), 1983.

Production supervisor, *The Storyteller: Greek Myths* (also known as *Jim Henson's "The Storyteller: Greek Myths"*), 1990.

Television Work; Movies:

Production supervisor, *A Murder of Quality*, 1991.

BARRY, Raymond J. 1939–
(Ray Barry, Raymond Barry, Raymond Berry)

PERSONAL

Born March 14, 1939, in Hempstead, NY; son of Raymond (in sales) and Barbara (an actress; maiden name, Duffy) Barry; married Robyn Mundell (an actress); children: Oona. *Education:* Brown University, B.A., philosophy; Yale University School of Drama, M.F.A.; studied acting with William Hickey and Kenneth MacMillan. *Religion:* Roman Catholicism.

Addresses: *Agent*—Metropolitan Talent Agency, 4500 Wilshire Blvd., Second Floor, Los Angeles, CA 90010. *Manager*—McGowan Management, 8733 West Sunset Blvd., Suite 103, West Hollywood, CA 90069.

Career: Actor and director. Actor with various theatrical companies, including the Living Theatre, beginning c. 1964, Joseph Chaikin's Open Theater, 1967–73, the New York Shakespeare Company and Joseph Papp's Public Theater, New York City, c. 1970–82, Richard Forman's Ontological–Hysterical Theatre, 1980–82, the Performance Garage, 1983, and the Theatre of the Ridiculous; worked as a director with the Quena Company, 1973–83, and the Street Theatre, 1975–80; worked as the director of Puerto Rican Writer's Workshop, 1974–76. Involved with workshops at penitentiaries; founder of a theatre company consisting of former criminal offenders.

Awards, Honors: Obie Award, performance, *Village Voice*, c. 1976, for *The Leaf People;* DramaLogue Award, 1987, for *Buried Child;* Los Angeles Drama Critics Circle Award, best lead performance, and *DramaLogue* Award, both 1990, for *Once in Doubt;* Independent Spirit Award nomination, best supporting male, Independent Feature Project/West, 2007, for *Steel City;* Obie Award, for *Molly's Dream.*

CREDITS

Stage Appearances:

Second prisoner, *The Brig*, Living Theatre, New York City, 1962.

Man Is Man, Masque Theatre, New York City, 1963.

(As Raymond Barry) *The Serpent* (also known as *The Serpent: A Ceremony*), Open Theater Ensemble, Washington Square Methodist Church, New York City, 1970.

(As Raymond Barry) *Terminal*, Open Theater Ensemble, Washington Square Methodist Church, 1970.

Clown, *Nightwalk*, Open Theater, New York City, c. 1972–73.

Man who hits himself, *Mutation Show*, Open Theater, New York City, c. 1973.

The Amerind, *The Last Days of British Honduras*, New York Shakespeare Festival, Public Theater, New York City, 1974.

Gitaucho (Meesho), *The Leaf People*, Booth Theatre, New York City, 1975.

Rory, *Fishing*, New York Shakespeare Festival, Public Theater, 1975.

A Movie Star Has to Star in Black and White, New York Shakespeare Festival, Public Theater, Martinson Hall, 1975.

Drum major, grandmother, and police officer, *Woyzeck,* Joseph Papp Public Theater, New York City, 1976.

Johnny "Baby Face" Flint, *Happy End* (musical), Martin Beck Theatre, New York City, 1977.

Masked man, dope king, king of Providence, and bank teller, *Landscape of the Body,* New York Shakespeare Festival, Public Theater, 1977.

Slater, *Curse of the Starving Class,* New York Shakespeare Festival, Public Theater, 1978.

(As Raymond Barry) Sergeant Smith, Lieutenant Edwards, Judge F. W. Charles, the bailiff, a guard, a sailor, and a member of the press, *Zoot Suit,* Winter Garden Theatre, New York City, 1979.

Dangerous man, *Penguin Touquet,* New York Shakespeare Festival, Public Theater, 1981.

Mike, *Soft Targets,* La MaMa Experimental Theatre Company, New York City, 1981.

Volker, *Hunting Scenes from Lower Bavaria,* Manhattan Theatre Club, New York City, 1981.

Transvestite agent, *Tourists and Refugees No. 2,* La MaMa Experimental Theatre Company, Winter Project, New York City, c. 1981.

Messenger, *Antigone,* New York Shakespeare Festival, Public Theater, 1982.

First strong man, *Egyptology: My Head Was a Sledgehammer,* New York Shakespeare Festival, Public Theater, 1983.

Once in Doubt, La MaMa Experimental Theatre Company, New York City, 1983 (some sources cite 1988), Cast at the Circle Theatre, 1989, People's Light and Theatre Company, Philadelphia, PA, 1989, Los Angeles Theatre Center, Los Angeles, 1989–90, Remains Theatre, Chicago, IL, 1992, and Odyssey Theatre, Los Angeles, 1999.

Hot Lunch Apostles, La MaMa Experimental Theatre Company, 1984.

Buried Child, South Coast Repertory Theatre, Costa Mesa, CA, 1986.

Mother'Son (also known as *Mother's Son*), Magic Theatre, Omaha, NE, 1993, MET Theatre, Los Angeles, 1994, Smokebrush Center for the Arts and Theater, Colorado Springs, CO, 1994, and Edinburgh Fringe Festival, Pleasance Theatre, Edinburgh, Scotland, 1995.

Back When Back Then, Smokebrush Center for the Arts and Theater, 1996, Theatre! Theatre!, Portland, OR, 1997, Northside Theatre, San Francisco, CA, 1997, Theatre for the New City, New York City, 1997, Palazzo Mundell, Santa Colomba, Italy, 2000, and Dublin Fringe Festival, Andrews Lane Theatre, Dublin, Ireland, 2000.

And Then I Did This, and Then I Did That, Theatre! Theatre!, 2003, then known as *Because I Said So,* Odyssey Theatre, Los Angeles, 2003, then known as *Foul Shots,* Theatre for the New City, 2004.

Ephraim Cabot, *Desire under the Elms,* American Repertory Theatre, Loeb Drama Center, Cambridge, MA, 2005.

Also appeared in other productions, including *Endgame* and *Masques,* both Open Theater; and in *Molly's Dream.* Appeared as a football player in *Picnic,* Brown University.

Major Tours:
While often billed as Raymond Barry, appeared as a man who hits himself, *Mutation Show,* as a clown, *Nightwalk,* and in *Endgame, Masques, The Serpent* (also known as *The Serpent: A Ceremony*), and *Terminal,* all productions of the Open Theater, in U.S., Canadian, European, and Far Eastern cities.

Film Appearances:
Herbert Fisk, *Between the Lines,* Midwest Films, 1977.

(As Ray Barry) *Richard III* cast member, *The Goodbye Girl* (also known as *Neil Simon's "The Goodbye Girl"*), Metro–Goldwyn–Mayer, 1977.

Edward Thoreau, *An Unmarried Woman,* Twentieth Century–Fox, 1978.

Detective Gleason, *You Better Watch Out* (also known as *Christmas Evil* and *Terror in Toyland*), 1980.

Athlete's father, *Insignificance* (also known as *She's the Bomb, Blahostka, Insignificance—Die verflixte Nacht, Insignificancia, Neinsemnatii, La signora in biano, Uma noite inesquecivel, Une nuit de reflexion,* and *Yhta tyhjaen kanssa*), Zenith Productions, 1985.

Louis Bukowski, *Year of the Dragon* (also known as *Chinatown bloder, Drakens aar, El ano del dragon, Im Jahr des Drachen, L'anne du dragon, L'anno del dragone, Lohikaeaermeen vuosi, Manhattan Massker, Manhattan Sur,* and *O ano do dragao*), Metro–Goldwyn–Mayer, 1985.

Hurley, *Out of Bounds,* Columbia, 1986.

Mr. Hatcher (Chloe's father), *Playing for Keeps,* Universal, 1986.

Captain Fred Gaffney, *Cop,* Atlantic Releasing, 1987.

Senator Kitteredge, *Three for the Road,* New Century/Vista Film Company, 1987.

Daddy, *Daddy's Boys,* Concorde Pictures, 1988.

Mr. Kovic, *Born on the Fourth of July* (also known as *Fodt den 4. juli, Foedd den fjaerde juli, Geboren am 4. Juli, Gennimenos tin 4i louliou, Nacido el cuatro de julio, Nascido a 4 de julho, Nascut el 4 de julio!, Nato il quattro luglio, Ne un quatre juillet, Syntynyt 4. heinaekuuta, Szueletett Julius 4–en,* and *Urodzony czwartego lipca*), Universal, 1989.

(As Raymond Barry) Petey, *December Bride* (also known as *Dezemberbraut, Joulukuun morsian, Novia de dezembro, La novia de diciembre,* and *Winterbraut*), MDWax/Courier Films, 1990.

Mark, *Nothing but Trouble* (also known as *Bara bekymmer, El gran lio, Git, Kaistapaeiden kaupunki, Masser af modgang, Nada alem de problemas, Nient'altro che guai, Tribunal fantome, Valkenvania,* and *Valkenvenia—Die wunderbare Welt des Wahnsinns*), Warner Bros., 1991.

Philip Claiborne, *K2* (also known as *K2: The Ultimate High*), Paramount, 1991.

Agent Frank Stewart, *Rapid Fire*, Twentieth Century–Fox, 1992.

Mark Harnish, *The Turning* (also known as *Pocahontas, Virginia*), Phaedra Cinema, 1992.

Captain Yardley, *Falling Down* (also known as *Chute libre, Falling Down—Ein ganz normaler Tag, L'enrage, Oesszeomlas, Pad, Prosti pad, Rankka paeivae, Um dia de furia, Um dia de raiva, Un dia de furia, Un giorno di ordinaria follia,* and *Upadek*), Warner Bros., 1993.

Kurt Hemphill, *Cool Runnings* (also known as *Rasta Rocket, Cool Runnings—Dabei sein ist alles, Cool runnings—Quattro sottozero, Elegidos para el triunfo, Jamaica abaixo de zero, Jeg veled, Kalde rumper, Kelkkajengi,* and *Les apprentis champions*), Buena Vista, 1993.

Lieutenant Huff, *The Ref* (also known as *Hostile Hostages*), Buena Vista, 1994.

Earl Delacroix, *Dead Man Walking*, Gramercy Pictures, 1995.

Man, *Headless Body in Topless Bar*, Northern Arts Entertainment, 1995.

Vice president, *Sudden Death* (also known as *Overtime, A rischio della vita, Aekkikuolema, Ani oeluem, Hirtelen halal, Ksafniki apeili, Mort subite, Morte subita, Muerte subita, Nagla smierc, Nenadna smrt, Sudden Death: muerte subita,* and *Suspense en prolongation*), Universal, 1995.

(As Raymond Barry) Rollie Wedge and Donnie Cayhall, *The Chamber*, Universal, 1996.

Agent Hoover, *Best Men*, Orion, 1997.

Chester Hoenicker, *Flubber* (also known as *The Absent Minded Professor, Disney's "Flubber: The Absent Minded Professor," Flubber—maailman mahtavin moenjae, Flubber—Un professore tra la nuvole, Flubber y el professor chiflado, O professor distraido, Plaxmol,* and *Raztreseni profesor*), Buena Vista, 1997.

Special agent Laurence Dobbins (FBI), *Mad City*, Warner Bros., 1997.

(Uncredited) Sheriff's father, *Return to Paradise* (also known as *All for One*), 1998.

Principal Edwards, *New Port South*, Buena Vista, c. 2000.

(As Raymond Barry) Carlie Nagle, *The Deep End*, Fox Searchlight Pictures, 2001.

Killian, *Recoil*, 2001.

Lou Jacobs, *Training Day* (also known as *Dan obuke, Dia de entrenamiento, Dia de treinamento, Jour de formation, Kikepzes, Training day: Dia de entrenamiento,* and *Treeningpaeev*), Warner Bros., 2001.

Walter Ohlinger, *Interview with the Assassin*, Magnolia Pictures, 2002.

Mr. Leezak, *Just Married* (also known as *Nouveaux maries, Oggi sposi ... niente sesso, Pour le meilleur et pour le rire, Recem–casados, Recien casados, Smekmaanaden,* and *Voll verheiratet*), Twentieth Century–Fox, 2003.

Stephen Figura, *The Tulse Luper Suitcases, Part 1: The Moab Story* (also known as *As maletas de Tulse Luper—Parte I: A historia de Moab, Las maletas de Tulse Luper: La historia de Moab,* and *Le valigie di Tulse Luper—La storia di Moab*), Laurenfilm, 2003.

Stephen Figura, *The Tulse Luper Suitcases, Part 2: Vaux to the Sea*, Kassander Film Company, 2004.

Himself, *Special Thanks to Roy London* (documentary), 2005.

Bullhorn Bob, *Little Children* (also known as *Apro titkok, Juegos secretos, Kryfes epithymies, Les enfants de choeur, Pecados intimos, Secretos intimos, Tutku oyunlari,* and *Vaeikesed lapsed*), New Line Cinema, 2006.

Harry, *Slumberland*, Baltazar Works, 2006.

Uncle Victor "Vic" Lee, *Steel City*, New Films International, 2006, Truly Indie, 2007.

(As Raymond Berry) Captain Bashore, *Plane Dead* (also known as *Flight of the Living Dead* and *Flight of the Living Dead: Outbreak on a Plane*), New Line Home Video, 2007.

Dr. Jack Everland, *The Yellow Wallpaper*, Nostromo Entertainment, 2007.

Dr. Joel Sheinbaum, *Seducing Spirits*, Pinnacle Media, 2007.

General Boyt, *The Dot Man*, Carter Films, 2007.

Mr. Young, *American Crude*, Sheffer/Kramer Productions, 2007.

Dmitri Debartolla, *Hotel California*, Alliance Group Entertainment, 2008.

Walk Hard (also known as *Walk Hard: The Dewey Cox Story*), Columbia, 2008.

Television Appearances; Series:

Lieutenant Marco Zaga, *The Oldest Rookie*, CBS, 1987–88.

Sam Haskell, *Four Corners* (also known as *Homestead*), CBS, 1998.

Frank Sweeney, *Hyperion Bay* (also known as *Kaukainen lahti*), The WB, 1998–99.

D'Wight Sloman, *Push, Nevada*, ABC, 2002.

Television Appearances; Miniseries:

Jack Lawn, *Drug Wars: The Camarena Story* (also known as *The Drug Wars: Camarena, A guerra das drogas, Agente speciale Kiki Camarena sfida ai narcos,* and *Das Camarena–Komplott*), NBC, 1990.

Television Appearances; Movies:

Tony, *Daddy, I Don't Like It Like This* (also known as *Daddy, I Don't Like It This Way Anymore*), CBS, 1978.

Sid, *The Face of Rage*, ABC, 1983.

Gerald McMurty, *Slow Burn*, Showtime, 1986.

Charles Templeton, *Between Love and Hate*, ABC, 1993.

Jack Graves, *Fugitive Nights: Danger in the Desert* (also known as *Fugitive Nights*), NBC, 1993.

Reverend Tucker, *Mystery Woman: Redemption,* The Hallmark Channel, 2006.

Television Appearances; Specials:
Sur Faces, PBS, 1977.
Cat in the Ghetto, 1981.

Also appeared in *Works of the Open Theater.*

Television Appearances; Episodic:
Stavros, *The Hamptons,* ABC, 1983.
Captain Ted Ronson, "J. Edgar's Ghost," *Scarecrow and Mrs. King,* CBS, 1985.
Gangster, "Ginger's Baby," *It's a Living* (also known as *Making a Living*), syndicated, 1987.
(As Ray Barry) "King of the Road," *Tales from the Crypt* (also known as *HBO's "Tales from the Crypt"*), HBO, 1992.
"Love on the Rox," *L.A. Law,* NBC, 1992.
Senator Richard Matheson, "Little Green Men," *The X–Files,* Fox, 1994.
Vince Connors, "No Strings Attached," *Melrose Place,* Fox, 1994.
"You Can't Tell a Crook by His Cover," *Frasier* (also known as *Dr. Frasier Crane*), NBC, 1994.
Senator Richard Matheson, "Nisei," *The X–Files,* Fox, 1995.
Senator Richard Matheson, "S.R. 819," *The X–Files,* Fox, 1999.
Dr. Philip Gerard, "The Accused Is Entitled," *CSI: Crime Scene Investigation* (also known as *C.S.I., CSI: Las Vegas, CSI: Weekends,* and *Les experts*), CBS, 2002.
Nathan Dubinsky, "Teddy C," *UC: Undercover* (also known as *Undercover*), NBC, 2002.
Sergeant Gil Thorn, "The Little Guy," *Dragnet* (also known as *L.A. Dragnet*), ABC, 2003.
Senator Reed, "The Frame," *Alias,* ABC, 2004.
Senator Reed, "Taken," *Alias,* ABC, 2004.
Robert Dolan, "Ghosts," *Law & Order* (also known as *Law & Order Prime*), NBC, 2005.

Appeared in other programs, including appearances as Sergeant Spinoli, *All My Children* (also known as *All My Children: The Summer of Seduction* and *La force du destin*), ABC; as Jenks, *As the World Turns,* CBS; as a gangster, *The Doctors,* NBC; as Sonny Lundstrom, *One Life to Live* (also known as *Between Heaven and Hell*), ABC; and as Sutar, *Texas,* NBC. Appeared in "Death Becomes Her" and "Defining Moments," both unaired episodes of *Wasteland* (also known as *wasteLAnd*), ABC. While billed as Raymond Barry, some sources cite an appearance as Mr. Lyon's friend in "The Sudden Storm," *Upstairs, Downstairs,* London Weekend Television, 1974, also broadcast on *Masterpiece Theatre* (also known as *ExxonMobil Masterpiece Theatre* and *Mobil Masterpiece Theatre*), PBS.

Television Appearances; Pilots:
Garrett, "King of the Road," *Two–Fisted Tales,* Fox, c. 1992.
Sam Connolly, *Wind on Water,* NBC, 1998.
The general, *The Captain,* CBS, 2007.

WRITINGS

Writings for the Stage:
Once in Doubt, La MaMa Experimental Theatre Company, New York City, 1983 (some sources cite 1988), Cast at the Circle Theatre, 1989, People's Light and Theatre Company, Philadelphia, PA, 1989, Los Angeles Theatre Center, Los Angeles, 1989–90, Remains Theatre, Chicago, IL, 1992, and Odyssey Theatre, Los Angeles, 1999.
Mother'Son (also known as *Mother's Son*), Magic Theatre, Omaha, NE, 1993, MET Theatre, Los Angeles, 1994, Smokebrush Center for the Arts and Theater, Colorado Springs, CO, 1994, Edinburgh Fringe Festival, Pleasance Theatre, Edinburgh, Scotland, 1995, and Open Fist Theatre, 2001, published in *Mother'Son and Other Plays* (compilation), 1996.
Back When Back Then, Smokebrush Center for the Arts and Theater, 1996, Theatre! Theatre!, Portland, OR, 1997, Northside Theatre, San Francisco, CA, 1997, Theatre for the New City, New York City, 1997, Palazzo Mundell, Santa Colomba, Italy, 2000, and Dublin Fringe Festival, Andrews Lane Theatre, Dublin, Ireland, 2000.
Pornographic Panorama, The Stark Raving Theatre Company, Theatre! Theatre!, 1999.
A Piece of Cake, The Stark Raving Theatre Company, Theatre! Theatre!, 2000.
And Then I Did This, and Then I Did That, Theatre! Theatre!, 2003, then known as *Because I Said So,* Odyssey Theatre, Los Angeles, 2003, then known as *Foul Shots,* Theatre for the New City, 2004.

OTHER SOURCES

Periodicals:
Entertainment Weekly, January 26, 1996, p. 43.

Electronic:
Raymond J. Barry, http://www.raymondjbarry.org, May 16, 2007.

BASSETT, Linda 1950–

PERSONAL

Born February 4, 1950, in Kent, England; father, a police officer; mother, a typist.

Career: Actress. Performer with and director of the Belgrade Theatre–in–Education Company, Coventry, England, 1977.

Awards, Honors: Valladolid International Film Festival Award, best actress, 1999, Film Award nomination, best performance by an actress in a leading role, British Academy of Film and Television Arts, 2000, and ALFS Award nomination, British Actress of the Year, London Film Critics Circle awards, 2000, all for *East Is East;* Theatrical Management Association (TMA) Award, best actress, 2004, for *Lucky Dog.*

CREDITS

Film Appearances:

Gertrude Stein, *Waiting for the Moon* (also known as *Warten auf den Mond*), Skouras Pictures, 1987.

Janet Swanton, *Paris by Night,* Cineplex Odeon Films, 1988.

Mrs. Miles, *Let Him Have It* (also known as *L'age de vivre*), 1991.

Sandra Matkin, *A Small Dance,* 1991.

Gwen, *A Village Affair,* 1994.

Madame Brontski, *Haunted,* October Films, 1995.

Doctor, *Indian Summer* (also known as *Alive and Kicking* and *Alive & Kicking*), First Look Pictures Releasing, 1996.

Mary's mother, *Mary Reilly,* TriStar, 1996.

Betty Stratton, *Oscar and Lucinda,* Fox Searchlight Pictures, 1997.

Ella Khan, *East Is East* (also known as *Fish & Chips, Aust er aust, El casamiento, Itae on itae, Oriente es oriente,* and *Tradicao e tradicao*), Channel Four Films, 1999, Miramax, 2000.

Nurse, *Beautiful People* (also known as *Ihminen ihmiselle, Oraioi anthropoi,* and *Underbara maenniskor*), Channel Four Films, 1999, Trimark Pictures, 2000.

Voice, *Lounge Act* (animated short film), 2000.

Anthea, *The Martins,* Icon Film Distribution, 2001.

Evelyn, *The Last Time* (short film), Zanita Films, 2002.

Nelly Boxall, *The Hours* (also known as *As horas, Az orak, The Hours—Von Ewigkeit zu Ewigkeit, Las horas, Les heures, Timmarna,* and *Tunnit*), Paramount, 2002.

Cora, *Calendar Girls* (also known as *As garotas do calendario, Chicas de calendario, Dziewczyny z kalendarza, Feluel semmi, Fetele din calendar, Kalender Girls, Kalenderflickorna, Kalendrituedrukud, Kalenteritytoet, Las chicas del calendario,* and *Ta koritsia tou imerologiou*), Buena Vista, 2003.

Auntie Vee, *Spivs,* Carnaby International, 2004.

Maggie, *Separate Lies,* Twentieth Century–Fox/Fox Searchlight Pictures, 2005.

Melanie (Mel), *Kinky Boots* (also known as *The Kinky Boot Factory* and *Pisando fuerte*), Harbour Pictures, 2005, Miramax, 2006.

Trolley lady, *Colour Me Kubrick: A True ... ish Story* (also known as *Color Me Kubrick, Colour Me Kubrick, Appelez–moi Kubrick, Kubrick menet,* and *Lege me Kubrick*), First Choice Films, 2005, Magnolia Pictures, 2007.

Doll, *Cass,* Optimum Releasing, 2008.

Television Appearances; Series:

Ellen, *No Bananas* (also known as *Unidos pela guerra*), BBC, 1996.

Carol–Anne Kumar, *Out of Hours* (also known as *Paeivystysvuoro*), BBC, 1998.

Maureen Tyler, *The Brief,* Independent Television (England), 2004–2005.

Television Appearances; Miniseries:

Rachel Lithgow, *Traffik* (also known as *Traffik, le sang du pavot*), Channel 4 (England), 1989, broadcast on *Masterpiece Theatre* (also known as *ExxonMobil Masterpiece Theatre* and *Mobil Masterpiece Theatre*), PBS, 1990.

Mary Thornton, *The Life and Crimes of William Palmer,* Yorkshire Television, 1998, broadcast on *Mystery!,* PBS, 1998.

Maryann Money, *Far from the Madding Crowd* (also known as *Thomas Hardy's "Far from the Madding Crowd"*), Granada Television, 1998, broadcast on *Masterpiece Theatre* (also known as *ExxonMobil Masterpiece Theatre* and *Mobil Masterpiece Theatre*), PBS, 1998.

Abby Potterson, *Our Mutual Friend* (also known as *"Our Mutual Friend"—By Charles Dickens* and *Um amigo comum*), BBC, 1998, broadcast on *Masterpiece Theatre* (also known as *ExxonMobil Masterpiece Theatre* and *Mobil Masterpiece Theatre*), PBS, 1999.

The housekeeper, *Don Quixote* (also known as *Don Quichotte* and *Don Quijote*), TNT, 2000.

Mrs. Jennings, *Sense and Sensibility,* BBC, 2007.

Television Appearances; Movies:

Leave to Remain, Channel 4 (England), 1988.

Virginia Lyddon, *News Hounds,* BBC, 1990.

Mother, *Loved Up,* BBC, 1995.

Tom's mother, *Losing It,* 2000.

Nurse Nina, *The Little Life,* BBC, 2003.

Monica Pringle, *The English Harem,* Independent Television (England), 2005.

Television Appearances; Specials:

Meg Crawford, "Making Waves," *Dramarama,* Independent Television (England), 1988.

Therapist, *Say Hello to the Real Dr. Snide,* Channel 4 (England), 1992.

Mrs. Spud, *Spoonface Steinberg,* BBC, 1998.

Television Appearances; Awards Presentations:

The British Comedy Awards 2003, Independent Television (England), 2003.

Television Appearances; Episodic:

Mrs. Sheridan, "In It for the Monet," *Boon,* Independent Television (England), 1989.

Shena Jackson, "Plato for Policemen," *The Bill,* Independent Television, 1990.

Shena Jackson, "Testimony," *The Bill,* Independent Television, 1990.

Eileen, "Babies," *Frank Stubbs Promotes* (also known as *Frank Stubbs*), Independent Television, 1994.

Janice, "Blue Heaven," *Love Hurts,* BBC, 1994.

Mrs. Cornish, "Nothing to Hide," *A Touch of Frost,* Independent Television, 1994.

Maud, *Bramwell* (also known as *Bramwell II*), Independent Television, 1995, broadcast on *Masterpiece Theatre* (also known as *ExxonMobil Masterpiece Theatre* and *Mobil Masterpiece Theatre*), PBS, c. 1996.

Miss Haddon (Queen's counsel), "Mute of Malice," *Kavanagh QC* (also known as *Kavanagh Q.C.*), Central Independent Television (England), 1997.

Peggy, "Trouble," *Dinnerladies,* BBC, 1999.

Beryl Palmer, "Burden of Proof," *Heartbeat* (also known as *Classic Heartbeat*), Independent Television, 2005.

Eileen Carnack, "The Animal Within," *Midsomer Murders,* Independent Television, BBC, and Arts and Entertainment, 2007.

Television Appearances; Pilots:

Iris Jennings, *The Peter Principle* (also known as *The Boss* and *Herra pankinjohtaja*), BBC, 1995.

Stage Appearances:

Shirley, Shona, Miss Cade, and Margaret, *Fen,* Joint Stock Theatre Group, London, and New York Shakespeare Festival, Public Theater, LuEsther Hall, New York City, both 1983.

Doctor, House, and first girl, *Woyceck,* Haymarket Studio Company, Liverpool, England, then Almeida Theatre, London, 1985.

Mrs. Smith, *The Bald Prima Donna,* Haymarket Studio Company, then Almeida Theatre, 1985.

Mother, June, and Flora, *Aunt Dan and Lemon,* Royal Court Theatre, London, beginning 1985, and New York Shakespeare Festival, Public Theater, 1985–86.

Marylou Baines, Mrs. Etherington, and Dolcie Star, *Serious Money,* Royal Court Theatre and New York Shakespeare Festival, Public Theater, Newman Theater, both 1987.

Leontine, *The Triumph of Love,* Almeida Theatre, 1999.

Five Kinds of Silence, Lyric Hammersmith Theatre, London, 2000.

Sue Webber, *Lucky Dog,* Royal Court Theatre, Jerwood Theatre Upstairs, London, 2004.

Oenon, *Phaedra,* Donmar Warehouse Theatre, London, 2006.

Appeared in *The Cherry Orchard, George Dandin,* and *Medea,* all Leicester Haymarket Studio, Leicester, England. Also appeared in other productions, including *Abel's Sister* and *East Is East.*

RECORDINGS

Videos:
Herself, *"Calendar Girls": Creating the Calendar* (short), 2004.

BATEMAN, Michael John 1947–
(Michael Bateman, Michael J. Bateman)

PERSONAL

Born January 14, 1947.

Career: Film editor and director. Worked as assistant film editor and associate film editor, dialog and vocal effects editor, sound designer and sound editor and supervisor, and as unit director and production manager, sometimes as Michael Bateman or Michael J. Bateman.

Awards, Honors: Leo Award nomination, best editing in a dramatic series, Motion Picture Arts and Sciences Foundation of British Columbia, 1999, for *Dead Man's Gun;* Leo Award nomination, best picture editing in a dramatic series, 2000, for "Three for the Road," *Nothing Too Good for a Cowboy;* Leo Award nomination, best picture editing in a dramatic series, 2001, for "Demons of the Night," *The Immortal;* Gemini Award nomination, best picture editing in a comedy, variety, or performing arts program or series, Academy of Canadian Cinema and Television, and Leo Award nomination, best picture editing for a feature–length drama, both 2002, for *The Overcoat;* Leo Award nomination, best editing, 2003, for *Flower & Garnet;* Leo Award nomination (with others), best overall sound documentary program and series, 2004, for *Linton Garner: I Never Said Goodbye.*

CREDITS

Film Editor:
Sahara, Metro–Goldwyn–Mayer, 1983.
Nomads, Atlantic Releasing, 1986.
(Uncredited) *Retribution,* Taurus Entertainment, 1988.
(As Michael Bateman) *Night Life* (also known as *Campus Spirits*), RCA/Columbia, 1989.
U.F.O., 1993.

Mi amigo, Azalea Film, 2002.
Flower & Garnet (also known as *Flower et Garnet*), Odeon Films, 2002.
Linton Garner: I Never Said Goodbye (documentary), 2003.
The Wild Guys, MVP Entertainment, 2004.
(As Michael J. Bateman) *Submerged,* Nu Image, 2005.
The Score, Screen Siren Pictures, 2005.

Film Director:
Lies like Truth, 2004.

Television Film Editor; Series:
L.A. Law, NBC, 1989.
Press Gang, ITV, multiple episodes, between 1990 and 1992.
Murder Most Horrid, BBC1, 1991.
My Good Friend, ITV, 1996.
Dead Man's Gun, Showtime, 1997–98.
Nothing Too Good for a Cowboy, CBC, 1998.
The Immortal, syndicated, 2000.
Tom Stone (also known as *Stone Undercover*), CBC, 2002.

Television Film Editor; Miniseries:
Berlin Break, 1992.
(Contributor) *Kingdom Hospital* (also known as *Stephen King's "Kingdom Hospital"*), ABC, 2004.

Television Film Editor; Movies:
Love Bites, BBC2, 1994.
The Rites of Mu, KLF, 1994.
To Hear Her Name, WTN, 1995.
Hostile Force (also known as *The Heist* and *Alarm fuer Security 13*), 1996.
Exception to the Rule (also known as *Nach gefaehrlichen regeln*), HBO, 1997.
(As Michael J. Bateman) *Profile for Murder,* Prism Entertainment Group, 1997.
Luna: Spirit of the Whale, 2007.

Television Film Editor; Specials:
Stand–up Samurais, 2001.
The Overcoat, CBC, 2001.

Television Film Editor; Episodic:
"Pandas," *Champions of the Wild,* 1998.
"Swift Foxes," *Champions of the Wild,* 1998.
"Family Reunion," *So Weird,* Disney Channel, 1999.
"Tulpa," *So Weird,* Disney Channel, 1999.

Television Film Editor; Other:
Shrinks, 1990.
Final Days of Planet Earth, Hallmark Channel, 2006.
A Girl like Me: The Gwen Araujo Story, Lifetime, 2006.

Television Director; Episodic:
"Home Is the Hero," *Nothing Too Good for a Cowboy,* CBC, 1999.
"The Oath," *Dead Man's Gun,* Showtime, 1999.
"The Seven Deadly Sins," *Dead Man's Gun,* Showtime, 1999.

BATES, Tyler

PERSONAL

Addresses: *Office*—Tyler Bates Music, Inc., 419 N. Larchmont Blvd., Suite 300, Los Angeles, CA 90004. *Agent*—Soundtrack Music Associates, 2229 Cloverfield Blvd., Santa Monica, CA 90405.

Career: Composer. Pet (a musical group), founder, producer, and member, through 1997; Roseland (a musical group), founder and producer; JBOT (a musical group), drummer. Managed stock trading firm in Chicago, IL, at the age of 19.

CREDITS

Film Work:
Orchestrator and guitar player, *What's the Worst That Could Happen?,* Metro–Goldwyn–Mayer, 2001.
Choral arranger, *300,* Warner Bros., 2006.
Score producer, *Slither,* 2006.

Film Appearances:
Himself, *The Story Behind Baadasssss!: The Birth of Black Cinema* (documentary), 2004.

Television Work; Movies:
Music engineer, *Not Like Us,* Showtime.

Television Work; Specials:
Recording engineer, *Montgomery Clift: The Hidden Star,* Arts and Entertainment, 1998.
Music engineer, *The Hustons: Hollywood's Maverick Dynasty,* Arts and Entertainment, 1998.

RECORDINGS

Albums:
Recorded (with Roseland) *Roseland;* also recorded an album with Pet.

WRITINGS

Film Scores:
Blue Flame, Silver Shadow, 1993.

Deep Down (also known as *Conversations in Public Places*), Imperial Entertainment, 1994.

Tammy and the T–Rex (also known as *Teenage T–Rex*), 1994.

Criminal Hearts, Libra Home Entertainment, 1995.

Not Like Us, Concorde Pictures, 1995.

Ballistic (also known as *Fist of Justice*), Imperial Entertainment, 1995.

The Last Time I Committed Suicide, New City Releasing, 1997.

Denial (also known as *Something About Sex*), A–Pix Entertainment, 1998.

Suicide, the Comedy (also known as *The Intervention*), Cargo Films, 1998.

Thicker Than Water, Palm Pictures, 1999.

Born Bad, Concorde Pictures, 1999.

Get Carter, Warner Bros., 2000.

Shriek If You Know What I Did Last Friday the Thirteenth, Lions Gate Films, 2000.

Kingdom Come, Fox Searchlight, 2001.

What's the Worst That Could Happen?, Metro–Goldwyn–Mayer, 2001.

Scene Stealers (documentary short), Metro–Goldwyn–Mayer Home Entertainment, 2002.

Lone Star State of Mind (also known as *Coyboys and Idiots*), Columbia TriStar, 2002.

Night at the Golden Eagle, Keystone Entertainment, 2002.

Love and a Bullet, TriStar, 2002.

City of Ghosts, Metro–Goldwyn–Mayer, 2002.

Half Past Dead (also known as *Halbtot—Half Past Dead*), Sony, 2002.

How to Get the Man's Foot Outta Your Ass (also known as *Baadasssss!, Badass,* and *Gettin' the Man's Foot Outta Your Baadasssss!*), Sony Pictures Classics, 2003.

You Got Served, Screen Gems, 2004.

Dawn of the Dead, Universal, 2004.

The Story Behind Baadasssss!: The Birth of Black Cinema (documentary short), Columbia TriStar Home Video, 2004.

The Devil's Rejects (also known as *TDR—The Devil's Rejects*), Lions Gate Films, 2005.

30 Days in Hell (documentary; also known as *30 Days in Hell: The Making of "The Devil's Rejects"*), Lions Gate Films Home Entertainment, 2005.

Slither, Universal, 2006.

See No Evil, Lions Gate Films, 2006.

300, Warner Bros., 2006.

Fake trailer segment "Werewolf Women of the SS," *Grindhouse* (also known as *Quentin Tarantino's "Death Proof"* and *Robert Rodriguez's "Plant Terror"*), Dimension Films, 2007.

Halloween, Dimension Films, 2007.

Resident Evil: Extinction, Screen Gems, 2007.

Day of the Dead, Millennium Films, 2007.

Film Additional Music:

(Uncredited) *Fall Time,* 1995.

Television Scores; Miniseries:

Gone But Not Forgotten (also known as *Phillip Margolin's "Gone But Not Forgotten"*), Lifetime, 2004.

Television Scores; Movies:

Not Like Us, Showtime, 1995.

Alien Avengers (also known as *Roger Corman Presents "Alien Avengers"* and *Welcome to Planet Earth*), Showtime, 1996.

Alien Avengers II (also known as *Aliens Among Us, Roger Corman "Alien Avengers II,"* and *Welcome Planet Earth II*), TMC, 1998.

Rated X, Showtime, 2000.

Strange Frequency, 2001.

Wasted, MTV, 2002.

The Dead Will Tell, CBS, 2004.

Television Title Sequence Title; Movies:

Not Like Us, Showtime, 1995.

Television Scores; Specials:

The Real Sex Xtra: Pornucopia: Going Down in the Valley, HBO, 2004.

Television Scores; Episodic:

American High, 2000.

Strange Frequency, VH1, 2001.

Military Diaries, 2002.

Black Sash, The WB, 2003.

Video Game Scores:

300: March to Glory, 2007.

OTHER SOURCES

Electronic:

Tyler Bates Website, http://www.tylerbates.com, July 20, 2007.

BECKEL, Graham 1949–

   (Graham S. Beckel)

PERSONAL

Born December 22, 1949, in Old Lyme, CT.

Addresses: *Agent*—Cunningham/Escott/Slevin & Doherty Talent Agency, 10635 Santa Monica Blvd., Suite 140, Los Angeles, CA 90025.

Career: Actor. Appeared in advertisements.

CREDITS

Film Appearances:
Eric, *Happy as the Grass Was Green* (also known as *The Grass Was Green* and *Hazel's People*), Martin, 1973.

Ford, *The Paper Chase,* Twentieth Century–Fox, 1973.

Roland, *The Money* (also known as *Atlantic City Jackpot*), Calliope, 1975.

Val, *C.H.U.D.* (also known as *C.H.U.D.—New Yorkin alamaailma, C.H.U.D.—Panik in Manhattan,* and *New Yorkin alamaailma*), New World Pictures, 1984.

Charlie Benson, *Marie* (also known as *Marie: A True Story*), Metro–Goldwyn–Mayer, 1985.

Richard Doolan, *Lost Angels* (also known as *The Road Home*), Orion, 1989.

Vinny Sklaroff, *True Believer* (also known as *Fighting Justice*), Columbia, 1989.

Les Bossetti, *Welcome Home, Roxy Carmichael,* Paramount, 1990.

Sheriff Pete Ricker, *Liebestraum* (also known as *Liebestraum—Atracao proibida, Pasiones prohibidas,* and *Todestraum—Der letzte Zeuge schweight*), Metro–Goldwyn–Mayer/Pathe, 1991.

John Taylor, *Jennifer Eight* (also known as *Jennifer 8, Gli occhi del delitto, Jennifer, det 8. offer, Jennifer 8—A proxima vitima, Jennifer 8: Est la prochaine,* and *Jennifer 8 ist die Naechste*), Paramount, 1992.

Bartender, *Leaving Las Vegas* (also known as *Adieu Las Vegas, Adios a Las Vegas, Adjo Las Vegas, Despedida em Las Vegas, Elveda Las Vegas, Farvael Las Vegas, Las Vegas, vegallomas, Liebe bis in den Tod, Morrer em Las Vegas, Via da Las Vegas,* and *Zbogom Las Vegas*), United Artists, 1995.

Detective sergeant Richard Alex "Dick" Stensland, *L.A. Confidential* (also known as *L.A. konfidensielt, L.A. konfidentiellt, L.A. prisne tajne, L.A. zaupno, Los Angeles al desnudo, Los Angeles—Cidade proibida, Los Angeles confidencial, Los Angeles interdite,* and *Poverljivo iz el eja*), Warner Bros., 1997.

Cutler, *Black Dog* (also known as *Alto riesgo, Black Dog—Estrada alucianante, Black Dog—kuoleman kilmetrit, Czarny pies, Duelo na estrada, Estrada alucinante,* and *Traquer*), Universal, 1998.

Man with dark glasses, *Bulworth* (also known as *Tribulations, Bulworth—Candidato em perigo, Bulworth—Il senatore, El senador Bulworth, Koko kansan Bulworth,* and *Politicamente incorreto*), Twentieth Century–Fox, 1998.

(Uncredited) *Fallen* (also known as *A queda, Daemon, Fallen—Trau keiner Seele!, Il tocco del male, Kadotettu, La chute de l'ange, Le temoin du mal, Letaszitva, Ondskans spaar, Poseidos,* and *Possuidos*), Warner Bros., 1998.

Arnold McCardle, *True Crime* (also known as *True Crimes, Crimenes verdaderos, Ein Wahres Verbrechen, Ejecucion inminente, Fino a prova contraria, Juge coupable, Oegonblicket foere tystnaden, Pahin rikos,* and *Um crime real*), Warner Bros., 1999.

Captain Rizzo, *Blue Streak* (also known as *Batsos diamanti, De ladro a poliziotto, De ladron a policia, Der Diamanten–Cop, Flic de haut vol, Flic ou voleur, Ladrao e policia, Libavomm, Pandur lopovskih navika, Timanttikyttae,* and *Um tira muito suspeito*), Sony Pictures Entertainment, 1999.

"Do It Again" man, *No Vacancy,* 1999.

Admiral Chester W. Nimitz, *Pearl Harbor* (also known as *Pearl Harbour*), Buena Vista, 2001.

Duffy, *Hardball* (also known as *Hard Ball*), Paramount, 2001.

Peltz, *Dark Blue* (also known as *4–29–92, The Plague Season, A face oculta de lei, Bleu sombre, Immagini sporche, Indagini sporche—Dark blue, Modri angeli, Tamno plava,* and *Tumesinine*), Metro–Goldwyn–Mayer, 2002.

Marvin, *Northfork,* Paramount Classics, 2003.

Mr. Miler, *Two Days* (also known as *Dois dias, Tempo esgotado,* and *2 paeivaeae*), American World Pictures, 2003.

L. D. Newsome, *Brokeback Mountain* (also known as *Brokeback Mountain—El secreto de la montana, Brokeback Mountai—En terreno vedado, El secreto de la montana, I segreti di Brokeback Mountain, Le secret de Brokeback Mountain, O segredo de Brokeback Mountain, Secreto en la montana, Souvenirs de Brokeback Mountain, To mystiko tou Brokeback Mountain,* and *Tul a baratsagon*), Focus Features, 2005.

Man of God (also known as *Rabbi*), Catchlight Films, 2005.

Frank, *The Astronaut Farmer,* Warner Bros., 2006.

Officer Stone, *Bachelor Party Vegas,* Sony Pictures Home Entertainment, 2006.

Joey's boss, *The Rat Thing,* Relentless Productions, 2007.

Television Appearances; Series:
Chris Morgan, *All My Children* (also known as *All My Children: The Summer of Seduction* and *La force du destin*), ABC, 1984.

Officer Jenkins, *Another World* (also known *Another World: Bay City*), NBC, 1984.

Steve Sullivan, *Cafe Americain,* NBC, 1993–94.

Television Appearances; Miniseries:
Detective Clever, *Seventh Avenue* (also known as *Septima avenida*), NBC, 1977.

Clayton Cullen, *Amerika* (also known as *Topeka, Kansas … U.S.S.R.* and *Miehitetty Amerikka*), ABC, 1987.

Jerry A. Whitworth, *Family of Spies* (also known as *Family of Spies: The Walker Spy Ring, Familia de espioes,* and *Spie allo specchio*), CBS, 1990.

Josiah B. Tulley, *Separate but Equal,* ABC, 1991.

Paul Wells, *The 70s* (also known as *Los 70* and *Os anos 70*), NBC, 2000.

Voice, *Empires: The Roman Empire in the First Century* (documentary; also known as *The Roman Empire in the First Century*), PBS, 2001.

Television Appearances; Movies:

Dan (the bartender), *Class of '63,* ABC, 1973.

Rich, *The Face of Rage,* ABC, 1983.

Ron Ziegler, *The Final Days* (also known as *Der Fall Nixon* and *Giorni di fuoco*), 1989.

Billy, *Rising Son* (also known as *Apa es fia, Aufbruch der Soehne, Droemmen om framgaang, Io e Charlie, Kapina, L'ecole de la vie,* and *Mi unica razon*), TNT, 1990.

Desperate Rescue: The Cathy Mahone Story (also known as *Ich will mein Kind!, La veritable histoire de Cathy Mahone, Nicht ohne mein Kind,* and *Tahdon lapseni takaisin*), NBC, 1992.

Detective Frank Kendall, *Murder of Innocence* (also known as *A outra face da inocencia, Demence criminelle, La senda de la locura, Mord aus Unschuld, Psychose meurtriere,* and *Sem ajuda possivel*), CBS, 1993.

Don Kelly, *Barbarians at the Gate* (also known as *Barbarzyncy u bram, Der Konzern, Kaos paa Wall Street, Les requins de la finance, Panico en Wall Street, Selvagens em Wall Street,* and *Sota poerssikadulla*), HBO, 1993.

Charlie, *Jane's House,* CBS, 1994.

Detective Ken Brodhagen, *The Disappearance of Vonnie,* CBS, 1994.

Ted, *The Other Mother: A Moment of Truth Movie,* NBC, 1995.

Sykes, *Lost in the Bermuda Triangle* (also known as *Reunion: Journey beyond the Bermuda Triangle*), UPN, 1998.

Detective Denver Dunn, *Just Ask My Children* (also known as *Best Intentions, Com a melhor das intencoes, Non coupable, Preguntale a mis hijos,* and *Une famille meurtrie*), Lifetime, 2001.

Clarence Hyde, *Point of Origin* (also known as *In the Heat of Fire*), HBO, 2002.

Randy Fogle, *The Pennsylvania Miners' Story* (also known as *Os mineiros da Pensilvania*), ABC, 2002.

Jerry, *Helter Skelter* (also known as *Helter Skelter–Le folie da Charles Manson*), CBS, 2004.

Television Appearances; Specials:

Vic Graham, *The Execution of Raymond Graham* (also known as *A execucao de Raymond Graham*), ABC, 1985.

Oscar, "O Pioneers!" (also known as "Terra di pionieri"), *Hallmark Hall of Fame,* CBS, 1992.

Terry Bidwell, *Partners,* Fox, c. 1993.

Colonel Jack Fisk, *Battlestar Galactica: Razor* (also known as *Untitled Battlestar Galactica TV Special*), Sci–Fi Channel, c. 2007.

Television Appearances; Episodic:

"Another Gypsy Queen," *Kojak* (also known as *Einsatz in Manhattan*), CBS, 1977.

Kevin Cates (South Beach Vice, also known as Lou Carlin), "Payback," *Miami Vice* (also known as *Gold Coast* and *Miami Unworthiness*), NBC, 1986.

Bill Davis, "The Kingdom of Money," *Crime Story,* NBC, 1987.

George Hershey, "Re–Entry," *The Equalizer,* CBS, 1987.

Maximillian Petrovsky, "The Color of Maddie," *Moonlighting,* ABC, 1988.

Sully, "Company Man," *Spenser: For Hire,* ABC, 1988.

Willie Kosar, "The Plane Mutiny," *L.A. Law,* NBC, 1989.

Mr. O'Brien, "Death in Brooklyn," *Brooklyn Bridge,* CBS, 1991.

Thomas Lesser, "Honi Soit Qui Mal y Pense," *Civil Wars,* ABC, 1991.

Joel Helms, "Burden of Proof," *The Practice,* ABC, 1998.

Joel Helms, "Truth and Consequences," *The Practice,* ABC, 1998.

Ron Rawlins (some sources cite Ray Rawlins), "Maybe It's You," *L.A. Doctors* (also known as *L.A. Docs, Kliniken, Kohtaloni Los Angeles,* and *Medicos de Los Angeles*), CBS, 1998.

Detective Douglas Majeski, "Humpty Dumpty," *Chicago Hope,* CBS, 1999.

"Pseudos, Sex and Sidebars," *Jack & Jill* (also known as *Jack ja Jill, Jack og Jill,* and *Jack und Jill*), The WB, 1999.

Detective Houtch, "The Stolen Diskette," *Snoops* (also known as *Eliittietsivaet, Snoops—Charmant und brandgefaehrlich,* and *Spie*), ABC, 2000.

Dr. Steve Califano, "Is There a Wise Man in the House?," *Gideon's Crossing,* ABC, 2000.

Dr. Steve Califano, "Dr. Cherry Must Be Stopped," *Gideon's Crossing,* ABC, 2001.

Dr. Steve Califano, "Filaments and Ligatures," *Gideon's Crossing,* ABC, 2001.

Mr. Feldman, "Heart and Soul," *Ally McBeal,* Fox, 2002.

"Down Came the Rain," *Strange World* (also known as *Geheimprojekt X—Dem Bosen auf der Spur* and *Tuntematon uhka*), Sci–Fi Channel, 2002.

Carl Williman, "Twilight," *Six Feet Under,* HBO, 2003.

Perkins, "Rash Decisions," *Strong Medicine,* Lifetime, 2003.

Police detective, "Frame of Mind," *Dragnet* (also known as *L.A. Dragnet*), ABC, 2004.

"Slam Dunk," *Crossing Jordan* (also known as *Untitled Tim Kring Project*), NBC, 2004.

Colonel Jack Fisk, "Pegasus," *Battlestar Galactica* (also known as *Galactica, Galactica—Estrella de combate,* and *Taisteluplaneetta Galactica*), Sci–Fi Channel, 2005.

McGloin's father, "Judas," *Wanted,* TNT, 2005.

"Rubbing One Out," *Wanted,* TNT, 2005.

Captain Bill Gibbard, "Mr. Monk, Private Eye," *Monk,* USA Network, 2006.

Captain Hendricks, "I Like to Watch," *CSI: Crime Scene Investigation* (also known as *C.S.I., CSI: Las Vegas, CSI: Weekends,* and *Les experts*), CBS, 2006.

Colonel Jack Fisk, "Black Market," *Battlestar Galactica* (also known as *Galactica, Galactica—Estrella de combate,* and *Taisteluplaneetta Galactica*), Sci–Fi Channel, 2006.

Colonel Jack Fisk, "Resurrection Ship: Parts 1 & 2," *Battlestar Galactica* (also known as *Galactica, Galactica—Estrella de combate,* and *Taisteluplaneetta Galactica*), Sci–Fi Channel, 2006.

Hal Sanders, "Six Months Ago," *Heroes,* NBC, 2006.

(As Graham S. Beckel) Jim Johnson, "Damage Case," *Grey's Anatomy* (also known as *Complications, Procedure, Surgeons, Under the Knife,* and *Grey's Anatomy—Die jungen Aerzte*), ABC, 2006.

Appeared in other programs, including an appearance as Jimmy in *Love, Sidney* (also known as *Alla aelskar Sidney*), NBC. Appeared in "Das Bootie," an unaired episode of *Total Security* (also known as *Os vigilantes* and *Taeyttae turvaa*), ABC.

Television Appearances; Pilots:

Ben Kagen, *Eyes,* ABC, 2005.

Captain Marco Settembrini, *Briar & Graves,* Fox, 2005.

Vernon Boudreau, *Raines,* NBC, 2007.

Stage Appearances:

Military aide to the king and understudies for the roles of Fortinbras's captain and the dumb show queen, *Hamlet,* New York Shakespeare Festival, Delacorte Theater, New York City, 1975.

Ah, Wilderness!, Stage West Theatre, West Springfield, MA, 1975.

Time Trial, New York Shakespeare Festival, Public Theater, New York City, 1975.

Skip Hampton, "Lu Ann Hampton Laverty Oberlander," and Skip Hampton, "The Last Meeting of the Knights of the White Magnolia," both part of *A Texas Trilogy,* John F. Kennedy Center for the Performing Arts, Washington, DC, 1976, then Broadhurst Theatre, New York City, 1976.

Rain, Hartford Stage Company, Hartford, CT, 1977.

Slick Jessup, *The Elusive Angel,* Marymount Manhattan Theatre, New York City, 1977, and New Dramatists, New York City, 1977–78.

Garrison, *Fathers and Sons,* New York Shakespeare Festival, Public Theater, 1978.

Amazing Grace, New Dramatists, 1978.

Dancin' to Calliope, New Dramatists, 1978.

Macbeth, Long Wharf Theatre, New Haven, CT, 1978.

Harold, *Father's Day,* American Place Theatre, New York City, 1979.

Larry, "Stops Along the Way," number five, "In Fireworks Lie Secret Codes," and understudy for the role of Paul, "Vivien" (all one–act plays), *The One–Act Play Festival,* Lincoln Center Theater Company, Mitzi E. Newhouse Theater, New York City, 1981.

The Woods, Center Stage Theatre, Baltimore, MD, 1981.

Last Looks, Center Stage Theatre, 1982.

Savages, Center Stage Theatre, 1982.

Sammy, *Flirtations,* T.O.M.I. Terrace Theatre, New York City, 1983.

Ed, *The Vampires,* Astor Place Theatre, New York City, 1984.

Boo, *The Marriage of Bette and Boo,* New York Shakespeare Festival, Public Theater, Newman Theatre, New York City, 1985.

Dad, *the dreamer examines his pillow,* Forty–Seventh Street Theatre, New York City, 1986.

Alfred Chamberlain, *Little Murders,* Second Stage Theatre, McGinn–Cazale Theatre, New York City, 1987.

Omar, *The Big Funk,* New York Shakespeare Festival, Joseph Papp Public Theater, Anspacher Theater, New York City, 1990.

Caliban, *The Tempest,* American Conservatory Theater, Geary Theater, San Francisco, CA, 1996.

RECORDINGS

Video Games:

Mad Jackson, *Of Light and Darkness,* 1998.

OTHER SOURCES

Periodicals:

Hollywood Reporter, April 5, 1991.

BELL, E. E. 1955–

PERSONAL

Born December 27, 1955.

Career: Actor. Appeared in television commercials, including MoneyGram stores and petopia.com. Played in The Whooligans (an Irish band), 1998.

CREDITS

Film Appearances:

Voice, *"A" gai waak* (also known as *"A" ji hua, Jackie Chan's Project A, Mark of the Dragon, Operazione pirati, Pirate Patrol,* and *Project A*), Buena Vista Home Video, 1983.

Umpire, *Don't Tell Mom the Babysitter's Dead,* Warner Bros., 1991.

Fragoso, *Eight Hundred Leagues Down the Amazon* (also known as *800 Leagues Down the Amazon* and *Jules Verne's "Eight Hundred Leagues Down the Amazon"*), Concorde Pictures, 1993.

Happy doctor, *Ice Cream Man,* A–Pix Entertainment, 1995.

Angry fan, *Forget Paris,* Columbia, 1995.

Reporter number one, *Air Force One* (also known as *AFO*), Sony, 1997.

Mailman, *Lewis & Clark & George,* 1997.

Mayor Bronch, *Grizzly Mountain,* Legacy Releasing Corp., 1997.

Ringer announcer, *My Giant,* Columbia, 1998.

Dwight, *Storm* (also known as *Storm Trackers*), New City Releasing, 1999.

Al, *Big Brother Trouble,* Mainline Releasing, 2000.

Duke, *Thank You, Good Night,* Roaring Leo Productions, 2001.

Norman, *I Am Stamos* (short), Red Navel Filmworks, 2004.

Beeman, *Herbie Fully Loaded,* Buena Vista, 2005.

Rick Lumet, *3 Wise Women,* 2005.

Tourist Dad, *The Heartbreak Kid,* Paramount, 2007.

Dan, *Kiss the Bride,* Regent Releasing, 2007.

Television Appearances; Series:

Jelly the Panda, *Xuxa,* syndicated, 1993.

Bob Rooney, a recurring character, *Married … with Children,* Fox, 1993–97.

Morgue attendant, *Sunset Beach,* NBC, 1998.

Television Appearances; Movies:

Desk clerk, *Murderous Vision,* USA Network, 1991.

Quirky Mart owner, *Black Widow Murders: The Blanche Taylor Moore Story,* NBC, 1993.

Officer Drake, *Moment of Truth: Cradle of Conspiracy* (also known as *Cradle of Conspiracy*), NBC, 1994.

Dwight, *Storm,* Fox Family, 1999.

The Babe, *61** (also known as *61*), HBO, 2001.

Television Appearances; Specials:

Stage hand, *Abbott and Costello Meet Jerry Seinfeld,* NBC, 1994.

Television Appearances; Pilots:

Ralph, *Herndon and Me,* ABC, 1983.

Donny, *Yesterday/Today,* NBC, 1992.

Television Appearances; Episodic:

Joe Blake, "Baseball Blues," *Diff'rent Strokes,* NBC, 1985.

Delivery man, "Always a Thief," *Murder, She Wrote,* CBS, 1990.

Bradley, "Bad Neighbor Sam," *Cheers,* NBC, 1990.

Bartender, *Can't Hurry Love,* CBS, 1995.

Walter, *Players,* NBC, 1997.

Auto show boss, "I Only Have Eyes for You," *Beverly Hills, 90210,* Fox, 1997.

Corpse, "Caroline and the Wayward Husband," *Caroline in the City* (also known as *Caroline*), NBC, 1997.

Drink guy, "Sex and Violence," *House Rules,* NBC, 1998.

Wendell, "Community Service," *One World,* NBC, 1998.

Mailman, "Ashes," *Brimstone,* Fox, 1998.

Roscoe, *Guys Like Us,* UPN, 1998.

Impound man, *Grown Ups,* UPN, 1999.

Barney, "Amanda Bynes/City High," *All That,* Nickelodeon, 2000.

Barney, *The Amanda Show,* Nickelodeon, 2000.

"Married.. with Children," *E! True Hollywood Story,* E! Entertainment Television, 2001.

Man, *That's Life,* CBS, 2001.

Advisor number two, "Two Cathedrals," *The West Wing,* NBC, 2001.

Department store Santa, "Answered Prayers," *JAG,* CBS, 2001.

Mr. Weatherwax, "Tanner," *Phil of the Future,* Disney Channel, 2004.

Motel resident, "Nickel and Dimed," *Without a Trace* (also known as *W.A.T.*), CBS, 2004.

Minister, "Let Go, Let Golf," *In Case of Emergency,* ABC, 2007.

Mystery man, "Stuff," *How I Met Your Mother,* CBS, 2007.

Also appeared in "Deadly Starfish (Pestar)," *Ultraman: The Ultimate Hero* (also known as *Ultraman Powered*); *Hollywood Squares.*

BEMIS, Cliff 1948–

PERSONAL

Full name, Clifford Oliver Bemis; born May 21, 1948, in Amherst, OH; son of Oliver Scott (a farmer and floral greenhouse business operator) and Olive Jeanette Bemis; married Sally Winter (marriage ended). *Education:* Studied music at Baldwin–Wallace College's Conservatory of Music. *Avocational Interests:* Skiing, hiking, backpacking, watching football, and motorcycles.

Addresses: *Agent*—Abrams Artists Agency, 9200 Sunset Blvd, Suite 1130, Los Angeles, CA 90069.

Career: Actor. Previously served as the spokesperson for IHOP restaurants; sang numerous commercial jingles.

Member: Screen Actors Guild, American Federation of Television and Radio Artists, Actors Equity Association.

CREDITS

Film Appearances:
Leroy, *Hell Comes to Frogtown*, New World Pictures, 1987.
Boat yard owner, *The Great Outdoors*, 1988.
Dwayne, *White Hot* (also known as *Crack in the Mirror*), Paul Entertainment, 1989.
Jeff, *Pink Cadillac*, Warner Bros., 1989.
Dirk Martin, *Modern Love*, 1990.
Barbecue dad, *The Naked Gun 2 ½: The Smell of Fear* (also known as *The Naked Gun 2 ½*), Paramount, 1991.
Gun lobbyist, *The Distinguished Gentleman*, Buena Vista, 1992.
Billy, *Deadly Exposure*, Kushner–Locke Company, 1993.
Detective John Marker, *Jack the Bear*, Twentieth Century–Fox, 1993.
Dance partner, *The Odd Couple II* (also known as *Neil Simon's "The Odd Couple II"*), Paramount, 1998.
Frank Capps, *My Beautiful Me* (short), 1998.
Desk cop, *World Trade Center*, Paramount, 2006.
Chief McGinnis, *Nancy Drew*, Warner Bros., 2007.

Television Appearances; Series:
Paul, *Newhart*, CBS, 1988–90.
Gary Beck, *Reunited*, UPN, 1998.

Television Appearances; Miniseries:
Louie, *The Secrets of Lake Success*, NBC, 1993.

Television Appearances; Movies:
The Ryan White Story, ABC, 1989.
Site foreman, *Heat Wave*, TNT, 1990.
The Whereabouts of Jenny, ABC, 1991.
Danny, *Men Don't Tell*, CBS, 1993.
Tom Fowler, *For My Daughter's Honor* (also known as *Indecent Seduction*), CBS, 1996.
Loomis, *"Murder, She Wrote": South by Southwest*, CBS, 1997.
Sam Morgan, *Au Pair II*, Fox Family, 2001.
Robert Tillman, *The Long Shot* (also known as *The Long Shot: Believe in Courage*), Hallmark Channel, 2004.

Television Appearances; Episodic:
"Marsha's Job," *Mr. Belvedere*, ABC, 1987.
"The Apartment," *Mr. Belvedere*, ABC, 1988.

Officer Fred, "Nineteen Again," *Who's the Boss?*, ABC, 1988.
"Coach of the Year," *21 Jump Street*, Fox, 1988.
Police officer, "Chinny Chin Chum," *Marblehead Manor*, syndicated, 1988.
Termite boss, "The Great Escape," *Married … with Children*, Fox, 1988.
Mr. Shaughnessy, "Cry Me a River of Oil," *Dallas*, CBS, 1989.
Stan Willis, "Danny," *Falcon Crest*, CBS, 1989.
"You Turned the Tables on me," *Jake and the Fatman*, CBS, 1990.
Dream On, HBO, 1990.
Sheriff Michaels, "A Hunting Will We Go—June 18, 1976," *Quantum Leap*, NBC, 1991.
Fred Tuttwyler, "A Thousand Sprinkles," *Sisters*, NBC, 1991.
Fred Tuttwyler, "Of Mice and Women," *Sisters*, NBC, 1991.
Fred Tuttwyler, "Strikes and Spares," *Sisters*, NBC, 1991.
Marvin, *Dear John*, NBC, 1991.
Mike, "The King of Beers," *Cheers*, NBC, 1992.
Uncle Henry, "A Presumption of Innocence," *Beverly Hills, 90210*, Fox, 1992.
Fred Tuttwyler, "Things Are Tough All Over," *Sisters*, NBC, 1993.
Jerry, *The Mommies*, NBC, 1993.
Dan, "Out of the Mouths of Babes," *Platypus Man*, UPN, 1995.
Enviro–man, "Buzz Off, Buzzard Boy," *Thunder Alley*, ABC, 1995.
Smiler lawyer, "Whine, Whine, Whine," *Lois & Clark: The New Adventures of Superman* (also kwon as *Lois & Clark* and *The New Adventures of Superman*), ABC, 1995.
Doug, "She's Having Our Baby: Part 2," *Coach*, ABC, 1995.
Doug, "Somebody's Baby," *Coach*, ABC, 1996.
Mr. Nicholson, "Family Secrets," *7th Heaven* (also known as *Seventh Heaven*), The WB, 1996.
Al's dad, "Requiem for a Chevyweight: Part 1," *Married … with Children*, Fox, 1996.
Merle, "The Hole," *Gun* (also known as *Robert Altman's "Gun"*), ABC, 1997.
Coach, "Taking One for the Team," *Arli$$*, HBO, 1999.
"Hostile Witness," *Pacific Blue*, USA Network, 1999.
"Safe at Home," *Providence*, NBC, 2000.
Stanton, "Black Widow," *The Huntress*, USA Network, 2001.
Bill, "Hot Streak," *Titus*, Fox, 2002.

Stage Appearances:
Jacques Brel Is Alive and Well and Living in Paris, Playhouse Square Association, Cleveland, OH, 1973–75.

Also appeared in *Wonderful Town* and *Promises, Promises*, Freud Playhouse, Los Angeles; *Cinderella*, The

Muny Theatre, St. Louis, MO; *Do Black Patent Leather Shoes Really Reflect Up?,* Kenley Players, Ohio; *Man of La Mancha, Sweeney Todd,* and *Tomfoolery,* Cleveland Playhouse, Cleveland, OH; *Tintypes,* San Francisco and Cleveland Playhouse; *A Funny Thing Happened on the Way to the Forum,* Playhouse Square Association; *Images.*

RECORDINGS

Albums:
Released *Christmas Eve.*

OTHER SOURCES

Electronic:
Cliff Bemis Website, http://www.cliffbemis.com, July 13, 2007.

BENDER, Jack

PERSONAL

Addresses: *Agent*—United Talent Agency, 9560 Wilshire Blvd., Suite 500, Beverly Hills, CA 90212.

Career: Director, producer, actor, and writer.

Awards, Honors: Emmy Award nomination, outstanding directing in a drama series, 1992, for "Seoul Mates," *Northern Exposure;* Emmy Award (with others), outstanding drama series, 2005, Golden Laurel Award (with others), 2006, and Golden Laurel Award nomination (with others), 2007, both television producer of the year in episodic category, Producers Guild of America, all for *Lost;* Emmy Award nomination, outstanding directing for a drama series, 2006, for "Live Together, Die Alone," *Lost.*

CREDITS

Television Producer; Series:
Supervising producer, *Jack and Mike,* 1986.
Co–executive producer, *Lost,* ABC, 2004–2005.
Executive producer, *Lost,* ABC, 2005—.

Television Director; Series:
Jack and Mike, 1986.
Judging Amy, CBS, multiple episodes, between 1999 and 2001.

Alias, ABC, multiple episodes, between 2001 and 2004.
The Lyon's Den, NBC, 2003.
Lost, ABC, multiple episodes, beginning 2004.

Television Director; Movies:
In Love with an Older Woman, 1982.
Two Kinds of Love, CBS, 1983.
Shattered Vows, NBC, 1984.
The Midnight Hour (also known as *In the Midnight Hour*), ABC, 1985.
Letting Go, USA Network, 1985.
Deadly Messages, ABC, 1985.
Side by Side, 1988.
Tricks of the Trade, CBS, 1988.
My Brother's Wife, 1989.
The Dreamer of Oz (also known as *The Dreamer of Oz: The L. Frank Baum Story*), CBS, 1990.
The Perfect Tribute, ABC, 1991.
Love Can Be Murder (also known as *Kindred Spirits*), NBC, 1992.
Armed and Innocent, CBS, 1994.
A Face to Die For (also known as *The Face*), NBC, 1996.
Sweet Dreams, NBC, 1996.
Friends 'til the End, NBC, 1997.
Killing Mr. Griffin (also known as *Killing Griffin*), NBC, 1997.
(And executive producer) *A Call to Remember,* Starz!, 1997.
(And executive producer) *The Tempest* (special), NBC, 1998.
My Little Assassin, Lifetime, 1999.
(And executive producer) *It Came from the Sky* (also known as *Les visiteurs impromtus*), Romance Classics, 1999.
The David Cassidy Story, NBC, 2000.
The Lone Ranger, The WB, 2003.

Television Director; Pilots:
High School, U.S.A., NBC, 1984.
The City, ABC, 1986.
Charlie, ABC, 1989.
Joan of Arcadia, CBS, 2003.

Television Director; Miniseries:
Gambler V: Playing for Keeps, CBS, 1994.
Family Album (also known as *Danielle Steel's "Family Album"*), NBC, 1994.
Nothing Lasts Forever (also known as *Sidney Sheldon's "Nothing Lasts Forever"*), CBS, 1995.

Television Director; Episodic:
Breaking Away, 1980.
The American Dream, 1981.
King's Crossing, CBS, 1982.

"A Tough Act to Follow," *Fame,* syndicated, 1982.
"Ending on a High Note," *Fame,* syndicated, 1983.
"Birthday Party," *The Paper Chase,* Showtime, 1983.
"Limits," *The Paper Chase,* Showtime, 1984.
"What Do People Do All Day?," *A Year in the Life,* 1987.
"Seoul Mates," *Northern Exposure,* CBS, 1991.
"Home and Away," *Beverly Hills, 90210,* Fox, 1992.
Angel Falls, 1993.
"Return to Plum Creek," *Ned Blessing: The Story of My Life and Times,* CBS, 1993.
"The Game Is Chicken," *Beverly Hills, 90210,* Fox, 1993.
"Sentenced to Life," *Beverly Hills, 90210,* Fox, 1995.
"Modus Operandi," *Profiler,* NBC, 1996.
"Old Acquantaince," *Profiler,* NBC, 1997.
"It Cuts Both Ways," *Profiler,* NBC, 1997.
"Cycle of Violence," *Profiler,* NBC, 1998.
"The Aretha Theory," *Felicity,* The WB, 2000.
"The Biggest Deal There Is," *Felicity,* The WB, 2000.
"The Anti–Natalie Intervention," *Felicity,* The WB, 2000.
"Chapter Two," *Boston Public,* Fox, 2000.
"The Ex–Files," *Ally McBeal,* Fox, 2001.
"Another Toothpick," *The Sopranos,* HBO, 2001.
"To Save Us All from Satan's Power," *The Sopranos,* HBO, 2001.
"The Weight," *The Sopranos,* HBO, 2002.
"Breathless," *Presidio Med,* CBS, 2003.
"Blackout," *Boomtown,* NBC, 2003.
"Insomnia," *Carnivale,* HBO, 2003.
"Alamogordo, N.M.," *Carnivale,* HBO, 2003.
"Mayham," *The Sopranos,* HBO, 2006.

Also directed episodes of *Eight Is Enough,* ABC; *Girls Club,* Fox; *I'll Fly Away,* NBC; and *That's Life,* CBS.

Television Producer; Episodic:
Co–executive producer, "Book of Virtues," *Girls Club,* Fox, 2002.

Television Appearances; Movies:
Jerry, *Savage* (also known as *The Savage File* and *Watch Dog*), NBC, 1973.
Wolpert, *Columbo: Publish or Perish,* NBC, 1974.
Joe Cordova, *Target Risk,* NBC, 1975.
McNaughton's Daughter (also known as *Try to Catch a Saint*), NBC, 1976.
Allcott, *Sergeant Matlovich vs. the U.S. Air Force,* NBC, 1978.

Television Appearances; Miniseries:
Musician in cafe, *Naomi and Wynonna: Love Can Build a Bridge* (also known as *Love Can Build a Bridge*), NBC, 1995.

Television Appearances; Specials:
Priest, "Lizzie Borden" segment, *Case Reopened,* 1999.

Television Appearances; Episodic:
Robert Loper, "Antennae of Death," *The F.B.I.,* 1970.
Paul Goodrow, "Mike's Hippie Friends Come to Visit" (some sources cite the episode "Now That You Know the Way, Let's Be Strangers"), *All in the Family,* CBS, 1971.
Jeff Dalton, "A Short Course in War," *The Mod Squad,* 1971.
Michael Lee, "More than Neighbors," *The Mary Tyler Moore Show* (also known as *Mary Tyler Moore*), CBS, 1972.
Paul Sanders, "The Crash of 29 Years Old," *The Bob Newhart Show,* CBS, 1973.
Bill, "Class of '77," *Here We Go Again,* 1973.
John Boyd, "N Is for Nightmare," *Owen Marshall, Counselor at Law,* 1973.
Joe, "The Killing Truth," *The F.B.I.,* 1973.
Earl Mowbray, "Speak No Evil," *Ironside* (also known as *The Raymond Burr Show*), NBC, 1974.
Sills, "Fair Fight," *Emergency!* (also known as *Emergency One* and *Emergencia*), NBC, 1976.
Restaurant owner, "The Women Strike," *Husbands, Wives & Lovers,* 1978.
Process server, "Things You Should Know Before and After," *A Year in the Life,* 1987.

Film Director:
Third farmer, *Hot Lead and Cold Feet,* 1978.
A Real Naked Lady, 1980.
Child's Play 3 (also known as *Child's Play 3: Look Who's Stalking*), Universal, 1991.
Lone Justice 2, Triboro Entertainment, 1995.

Film Appearances:
Tom, *The Barefoot Executive,* Buena Vista, 1970.
Arvin Wadlow, *$1,000,000 Duck* (also known as *The Million Dollar Duck*), Buena Vista, 1971.
Slither Ross, *Now You See Him, Now You Don't,* Buena Vista, 1972.

WRITINGS

Television Movies:
Lyricist, "Get Dead," *The Midnight Hour* (also known as *In the Midnight Hour*), ABC, 1985.
It Came from the Sky (also known as *Les visiteurs impromtus*), Romance Classics, 1999.

Television Episodes:
Writer for an episode of *The Paper Chase,* Showtime.

BENNETT, Jeff 1962–

(Jeff Bennet, Jeff Glen Bennet, Jeff Glenn Bennet, Jeff Glen Bennett, Jeff Glenn Bennett, Jess Bennett)

PERSONAL

Born October 2, 1962, in Burbank, CA.

Addresses: *Contact*—Suston, Barth and Vennari, 145 South Fairfax Ave., Suite 310, Los Angeles, CA 90036.

Career: Actor, voice artist, and singer. Appeared in radio commercial for Spring Broadband Director, c. 2000–01; also performer in promotional advertisements on television.

Awards, Honors: Annie Award nominations, best male voice actor in an animated television production, International Animated Film Society, 1995 and 1997, both for *Johnny Bravo;* DVD Premiere Award nomination (with others), best animated character performance, DVD Exclusive Awards, 2003, for *Tom and Jerry: The Magic Ring;* DVD Premiere Award nomination (with others), best original song, 2003, for "Imaginary Friend," *The Land before Time IX: Journey to the Big Water.*

CREDITS

Television Appearances; Animated Series:
Voices of Horace Boothroys (IQ) and Knick Knack, *James Bond Jr.,* syndicated, 1988.
Voice of Lord Maldon, *Prince Valiant* (also known as *The Legend of Prince Valiant*), The Family Channel, 1991.
Voice of Cowlarado Kid, *Wild West C.O.W.–Boys of Moo Mesa,* 1992–93.
Voices of H.A.R.D.A.C., Batcave computer, and others, *Batman* (also known as *The Adventures of Batman & Robin* and *Batman: The Animated Series*), Fox, 1992–93.
Voices of Jitters, Officer Dennis, Meenie, Roderick Lizard, and others *Bonkers,* syndicated, 1993.
Voices of Camembert and Mace, *Biker Mice from Mars,* syndicated, 1993.
(Sometimes credited as Jeff Glen Bennett) Voices of Baloney and others, *Animaniacs* (also known as *Steven Spielberg Presents "Animaniacs"*), Fox, then The WB, 1993–96.
Voice of Amin Doumoula, *Aladdin* (also known as *Disney's "Aladdin"*), CBS and syndicated, 1994.
Voices of Brooklyn, Owen Burnett, Magus, and others, *Gargoyles,* syndicated, 1994–96.

Voices of Maxwell Madison, Madison, Sr., Dr. Singh, and others, *Phantom 2040* (also known as *Phantom 2040: The Ghost Who Walks*), syndicated, 1994.
Voices of Pith Possum and Tex Tinstar, *Schnookums and the Meat Funny Cartoon Show,* syndicated, 1995.
Voices of Lord Bravery, cave guy, Candle Jack, the huntsman, and others *Freakazoid!,* The WB, multiple episodes, beginning 1995.
Narrator and voice of Peter Puppy, *Earthworm Jim,* The WB, 1995.
Voices of fish guy and others, *The Mask,* 1995.
Voices of Count Down, Duke Meerkat, Mr. Vam Pire-bat, Toucan Dan, and others, *Timon and Pumbaa,* 1995.
Voices of Christopher "Chris" and others (sometimes uncredited), *Pinky and the Brain,* The WB, 1995–98.
Voices of thug and others, *Gargoyles: The Goliath Chronicles,* ABC, 1996.
Voices of Orbitron and others, *Captain Simian & the Space Monkeys,* syndicated, 1996–97.
Voices of Duke L'Orange and others, *Mighty Ducks* (also known as *Disney's "Mighty Ducks"* and *Mighty Ducks: The Animated Series*), ABC and syndicated, 1996.
Voices of dad and others, *Dexter's Laboratory* (also known as *Dexter's Lab* and *Dexter de Shiyanshi*), Cartoon Network, between 1996 and 2002.
Voices of Roger Dearly, Lieutenant Pug, and Tibbs, *101 Dalmatians* (also known as *101 Dalmatians: The Series*), ABC, 1997.
Voice of Bud Buddiovitch, *Space Goofs* (also known as *Home to Rent, Stupid Invaders,* and *Les zinzins de l'espace*), Fox, 1997.
Voice of WGBS anchor Jack Ryder, a recurring role, *The New Batman Adventures* (also known as *Batman: Gotham Knights*), 1998.
Voice of Commander Shuta, *Invasion: America,* 1998.
Voices of Lucky Bob and Napoleon, *Histeria!,* The WB, 1998.
Voices of Johnny Bravo and others, *Johnny Bravo,* Cartoon Network, 1999–2004 (also broadcast as part of *Cartoon Cartoon Fridays;* also known as *Cartoon Network's Fridays, CCF,* and *Fridays*), beginning 2000.
Voices of Ace, Big Billy, Grobber, Pat Garrett, and others, *The Powerpuff Girls* (also known as *PPG* and *Youlide–Chui nu*), Cartoon Network, 1999.
Voice of Johnny Bravo, *JBVO,* 2000.
Voices of Mr. Hassenfeld, Mr. Higgenbotham, and others, *The Weekenders* (also known as *Disney's "The Weekenders"*), 2000.
Singing voice of Piglet, *The Book of Pooh,* Disney Channel, 2001.
Voices of Horace Horsecollar, Magical Mouse, Mr. Jollyland, and others, *House of Mouse,* ABC, 2001–2002.
Voice of Professor Archimedes Q. Porter, *The Legend of Tarzan* (also known as *Disney's "The Legend of Tarzan"*), 2001–2003.

Voice of coach/Principal Madman, *Whatever Happened to Robot Jones?,* Cartoon Network, 2002.

Miscellaneous voices, *Teamo Supremo* (also known as *Disney's "Teamo Supremo"*), ABC, 2002.

Voices of Mr. Boss, Mr. Fizz, Mr. Beatles, and others, *Codename: Kids Next Door,* Cartoon Network, between 2002 and 2006.

Voices of Ghost Car, narrator, and others, *Kim Possible* (also known as *Disney's "Kim Possible"*), Disney Channel, between 2002 and 2007.

Announcer and miscellaneous voices, *What's New, Scooby–Doo?,* The WB, between 2003 and 2005.

Voices of Dr. Jacques Von Haemsterviel and others, *Lilo & Stitch* (also known as *Lilo & Stitch: The Series*), Disney Channel, between 2003 and 2005.

Voices of narrator, Count Muerte, and others, *Duck Dodgers* (also known as *Duck Dodgers in the 24-1/2th Century*), Cartoon Network, between 2003 and 2005.

Voices of Clay Bailey and others, *Xiaolin Showdown,* The WB, between 2003 and 2006.

Voices of Barbarino and others, *The Adventures of Jimmy Neutron: Boy Genius,* Nickelodeon, between 2003 and 2006.

(As Jeff Bennett) Voices of storyteller, Popo, Twinkle, and others, *Dave the Barbarian* (also known as *Disney's "Dave the Barbarian"*), Disney Channel, 2004.

(As Jeff Glen Bennett) Announcer and voices of Bendy, Dad, farmer, father, Moose, and Mitch, *Foster's Home for Imaginary Friends,* Cartoon Network, 2004.

Voices of ring announcer, Cletus, Jody Viking, Loki, and others, *The Life and Times of Juniper Lee,* Cartoon Network, 2005.

Voices of Jake's father, hunt master, and others, *American Dragon: Jake Long,* Disney Channel, between 2005 and 2006.

Voice of Dr. Phineas Phibes, *Shaggy & Scooby–Doo: Get a Clue!,* CW Network, 2006.

Voice of Principal Luna and others, *Class of 3000,* Cartoon Network, 2006.

Voices of Conrad Fleem, Shelton Klutzberry, and others, *The Replacements,* Disney Channel, 2006–2007.

Voices of Raj the elephant, Samson the guinea pig, and others, *Camp Lazlo,* Cartoon Network, 2007.

Television Appearances; Animated Movies:

Voice of chief, *Short Pfuse,* 1995.

Voice of chief, *Pfish and Chip* (also known as *Blammo the Clown*), 1997.

Voices of Dexter's dad and Hero Dexter, *Dexter's Laboratory Ego Trip,* 1999.

Voices of Xavier the villain, club announcer, and pool waiter, *The Flintstones: On the Rocks,* Cartoon Network, 2001.

Voices of second gorlock and first brain, *Jimmy Neutron: Win, Lose, and Kaboom,* Nickelodeon, 2004.

Voice of Dr. Jacques Von Haemsterviel, *Lilo & Stitch,* Disney Channel, 2006.

Voices of Mr. Boss, Mr. Fizz, and Benedict Wigglestein, *Codename: Kids Next Door—Operation Z.E.R.O.* (also known as *Operation: Z.E.R.O.*), Cartoon Network, 2006.

Television Appearances; Animated Specials:

Voice of Schotzie, *A Pinky & the Brain Christmas Special,* 1995.

Voice of Ed Edwards, *Edith Ann's Christmas (Just Say Noel),* 1996.

Voice, *Night of the Headless Horseman,* Fox, 1999.

Voices of Juanito, first man, and policeman, *The Ugly Duck–Thing,* Nickelodeon, 2002.

Voice of Suavo, *The Groovenians,* Cartoon Network, 2002.

Voice of host (Johnny Bravo), *The 1st 13th Annual Fancy Anvil Award Show Program Special ... Live! ... in Stereo,* Cartoon Network, 2002.

Voice of second fairy agent, *The Jimmy Timmy Power Hour,* Nickelodeon, 2004.

Voice of Dr. Most, *The Jimmy Timmy Power Hour 2: When Nerds Collide,* Nickelodeon, 2006.

Television Appearances; Animated Pilots:

(As Jeff Glen Bennett) Voices of dad and bus driver, *My Freaky Family,* Cartoon Network, 2001.

Voices of Vex and Farmer Bill, *Imp, Inc.,* Cartoon Network, 2001.

Voice of Sparkles, *Major Flake,* Cartoon Network, 2001.

Television Appearances; Live–Action Episodes:

Mitchell Hunt, "Lost Resort," *Charles in Charge,* ABC, 1990.

Mayhem, "Valentine Day's Massacre," *Married ... with Children,* Fox, 1994.

First environmentalist, *Working,* c. 1998.

Television Appearances; Animated Episodes:

Voice of Kevin Costner, "Return of Batduck," *Tiny Toon Adventures* (also known as *Steven Spielberg Presents "Tiny Toon Adventures"*), Fox, 1992.

Voice of Eric, "Thingamajigger," *The Little Mermaid,* 1992.

Voices of Baron Dark, Joshua Steele, Lightstar, and Grimskull, "Long Live the King," *Skeleton Warriors,* CBS, 1994.

Voice of Gloog, "Love Stinks," *Bump in the Night,* ABC, 1994.

Voice of Gloog, "Love's Labor Bumped," *Bump in the Night,* ABC, 1994.

Voice of Prince Eric, "Scuttle," *The Little Mermaid,* 1994.

Voice of Thomas Edison, "Leonardo da Vinci and His Fightin' Genius Time Commandos!," *The Tick,* 1995.

(As Jeff Glen Bennett) Voice of Blitz, "Let's Hit the Road," *Road Rovers,* The WB, 1996.

Voice, "Honesty," *Adventures from the Book of Virtues* (also known as *The Book of Virtues*), PBS, 1996.

Voice, "Apocalypse Not," *Duckman: Private Dick/ Family Man,* USA Network, 1996.

Voice, "A Trophied Duck," *Duckman: Private Dick/ Family Man,* USA Network, 1996.

Voices of gun captain and diver number one, "The Darkest Fathoms," *The Real Adventures of Jonny Quest* (also known as *Jonny Quest: The Real Adventures*), Cartoon Network and syndicated, 1996.

Voices of Sonarman, medical officer, navigator, and crew member, "East of Zanzibar," *The Real Adventures of Jonny Quest* (also known as *Jonny Quest: The Real Adventures*), Cartoon Network and syndicated, 1996.

Voice of young doctor, "The Way of All Flesh," *Superman* (also known as *Superman: The Animated Series*), The WB, 1996.

Voice of Orbitron, "Splitzy's Choice," *Captain Simian & the Space Monkeys,* 1996.

Voice of Orbitron, "Invasion of the Banana Snatchers," *Captain Simian & the Space Monkeys,* 1996.

Voice of Aronus, "Planet of the Humans," *Captain Simian & the Space Monkeys,* 1997.

(As Jeff Glen Bennett) Voice, "Grease," *Extreme Ghostbusters,* syndicated, 1997.

Voice of Sam Bass, "An Army of Rogues," *The Legend of Calamity Jane,* The WB, 1997.

(As Jeff Glen Bennett) Voice of officer, "Vacant Lot," *The Wild Thornberrys,* Nickelodeon, 1998.

Voice of Baloney, "Gee, Your Hair Spells Terrific," *Pinky, Elmyra & the Brain,* 1998.

Voice of Baloney, "A Walk in the Park," *Pinky, Elmyra & the Brain,* 1999.

Voices of Craig Bean, Dieter Leiderhosen, and Sir Helpsalot, "Unhappy Campers," *Pepper Ann* (also known as *Disney's "Pepper Ann"*), ABC, 1999.

Voices of Craig Bean, Dieter Leiderhosen, Sir Helpsalot, and others "The Finale," *Pepper Ann* (also known as *Disney's "Pepper Ann"*), ABC, 1999.

Voices of Craig Bean, Dieter Leiderhosen, and Sir Helpsalot, "One of the Guys," *Pepper Ann* (also known as *Disney's "Pepper Ann"*), ABC, 1999.

(As Jeff Glen Bennett) Voices of two–dimensional man and Stewart Lowe, "Heroes," *Batman Beyond* (also known as *Batman of the Future*), The WB, 1999.

(As Jeff Glen Bennett) Voice of Buzzsaw, "Capitol Punishment," *Detention,* The WB, 1999.

Voice of Zookeeper, "Babel," *Batman Beyond* (also known as *Batman of the Future*), The WB, 2000.

Voices of Brain Pods and Dreadnaught Computer, "The Lightyear Factor," *Buzz Lightyear of Star Command,* UPN and syndicated, 2000.

Voices of Binipinardians, "Devolutionaries," *Buzz Lightyear of Star Command,* ABC, 2000.

Voice, "The Clipshow Wherein Dante and Randal Are Locked in the Freezer and Remember Some of the Great Moments in Their Lives," *Clerks: The Animated Series* (also known as *Clerks, Clerks: The Cartoon,* and *Clerks: Uncensored*), ABC, 2000.

(Uncredited) Voice of announcer in parody sequence, "If I'm Dyin' I'm Lyin'," *Family Guy* (also known as *Padre de familia*), 2000.

Voice, "Leonardo Leonardo Returns and Dante Has an Important Decision to Make," *Clerks: The Animated Series* (also known as *Clerks, Clerks: The Cartoon,* and *Clerks: Uncensored*), ABC, 2001.

Voice, "Kurtlas the Symbiotic Boy," *Lloyd in Space,* ABC, 2001.

Voice of Cody Koala, "Taffy Time," *The Zeta Project,* The WB, 2001.

Voice of Wesley Rank, "Snake Hunt," *Jackie Chan Adventures,* The WB, 2001.

Voices of announcer and Frankie, "She's Got Game," *The Proud Family,* Disney Channel, 2001.

Voice of Joseph, "Seven Days of Kwanzaa," *The Proud Family,* Disney Channel, 2001.

Voice of director, "Makeover," *The Proud Family,* Disney Channel, 2001.

Voices of townspeople, "Eli Whitney's Flesh Eating Mistake," *Time Squad,* Cartoon Network, 2001.

Voices of first Magister and policeman Magister, "The Chan Who Knew Too Much," *Jackie Chan Adventures,* The WB, 2002.

Voice of brain–eating meteor, "Little Rock of Horrors/ The Pie Who Loved Me/Dream a Little Dream," *Grim & Evil* (also known as *The Grim Adventures of Billy & Mandy*), Cartoon Network, 2002.

Voice of second man, "Chicken Jack," *Samurai Jack,* Cartoon Network, 2002.

Voice of Edison, "Spies vs. Spies," *Totally Spies!,* ABC Family Channel, 2002.

Voice of announcer, "Smackmania 6: Mongo vs. Mama's Boy," *The Proud Family,* Disney Channel, 2003.

Voice of Fadil, "The Dark Medjai," *The Mummy: The Animated Series* (also known as *The Mummy: Secrets of the Medjai*), The WB, 2003.

Voice of Fadil, "Trio," *The Mummy: The Animated Series* (also known as *The Mummy: Secrets of the Medjai*), The WB, 2003.

Voice of Drix, "An Out of Body Experience: Parts 1 & 2," *Ozzy & Drix,* The WB, 2003.

Voice of Robo–Ape Alfa, "Ape New World," *Super Robot Monkey Team Hyperforce Go!,* ABC Family Channel, 2004.

Voice of Zarek, "S–Force S.O.S.," *Megas XLR,* Cartoon Network, 2004.

(As Jeff Glen Bennett) Voices of Drallag and crew member, "Ice Ice Megas," *Megas XLR,* Cartoon Network, 2004.

(As Jeff Glen Bennett) Voice of Skalgar, "Universal Remote," *Megas XLR,* Cartoon Network, 2005.

Voices of anchorman, armadillo guy, and super spy, *Teen Titans,* Cartoon Network, 2005.

Voice of Ragdoll, "Ragdolls to Riches," *The Batman,* The WB, 2005.

Voice of Mahmood, "Stan of Arabia: Part 1," *American Dad,* Fox, 2005.

(As Jeff Glen Bennett) Voices of mayor, Tio, and Yankee, "Rube Job," *Stroker and Hoop,* Cartoon Network, 2005.

Voices of Gary and doctor, "Just Voodoo It," *Stroker and Hoop,* Cartoon Network, 2005.

Voices of Freddy, Steve, and guard, "How to Get Dead (Behind) in Advertising," *Stroker and Hoop,* Cartoon Network, 2005.

Voice of mayor, "Putting the 'Ass' in Assassin," *Stroker and Hoop,* Cartoon Network, 2005.

Voices of Mr. Two and Mr. Three, "Two Heads Are Not Better than One," *Brandy & Mr. Whiskers,* Disney Channel, 2005.

Voice of Tapir Leafrider, "Bad Brandy," *Brandy & Mr. Whiskers,* Disney Channel, 2005.

Voices of tracker and Mr. Puddington, "The Labyrinth," *W.I.T.C.H.,* ABC Family Channel, 2005.

Voices of tracker and usher, "Return of the Tracker," *W.I.T.C.H.,* ABC Family Channel, 2005.

Voice of Principal Pestrip, "The Candidate," *The Buzz on Maggie* (also known as *Disney's "The Buzz on Maggie"*), Disney Channel, 2005.

Voice of Principal Pestrip, "Lunchlady," *The Buzz on Maggie* (also known as *Disney's "The Buzz on Maggie"*), Disney Channel, 2005.

Voice of Principal Pestrip, "Pieface," *The Buzz on Maggie* (also known as *Disney's "The Buzz on Maggie"*), Disney Channel, 2005.

Voice of Principal Pestrip, "The Usual Insects," *The Buzz on Maggie* (also known as *Disney's "The Buzz on Maggie"*), Disney Channel, 2005.

Voice of Professor Zane, "Attack of the Fuzz Balls," *Loonatics Unleashed,* The WB, 2005.

Voices of Colonel Trench and Dr. Fidel Chroniker, "Time after Time," *Loonatics Unleashed,* CW Network, 2006.

Voice of D.A.V.E., "Gotham's Ultimate Criminal Mastermind," *The Batman,* The WB, 2006.

Voices of Ragdoll and killer moth, "Team Penguin," *The Batman,* CW Network, 2006.

Voice, "The Real," *The Boondocks,* Cartoon Network, 2006.

Voice of Rick Wilson, "Patriot Act," *Justice League* (also known as *JL*), Cartoon Network, 2006.

(As Jeff Glen Bennett) Voice of expert guy, "Riley Wuz Here," *The Boondocks,* Cartoon Network, 2006.

Voice of Zan–Tar, "Hornswiggle," *Random! Cartoons,* Nickelodeon, 2006.

Voice of man with yellow hat, "Curious George's Home for Pigeons: Out of Order," *Curious George,* PBS, 2006.

Voices of Brand–Something and Mash, "The British Invasion," *Biker Mice from Mars,* syndicated, 2006.

Voice of Frankie, "Boyz on da Run: Parts 1–3," *Shorty McShorts' Shorts,* Disney Channel, 2006.

Voice of Punky, "Mind the Kitty," *Random! Cartoons,* Nickelodeon, 2007.

Voice of Petrie, "The Mysterious Tooth Crisis," *The Land Before Time,* Cartoon Network, 2007.

Voice of Petrie, "The Brave Longneck Scheme," *The Land Before Time,* Cartoon Network, 2007.

Voice of Petrie, "Legend of the Story Speakers," *The Land Before Time,* Cartoon Network, 2007.

Narrator and voice of Clancy, premiere episode, *Saul of the Mole Men* (also known as *S.T.R.A.T.A.*), 2007.

(As Jeff Bennett) Narrator and voice of Clancy, "Blood Is Thicker than Water," *Saul of the Mole Men* (also known as *S.T.R.A.T.A.*), 2007.

Narrator and voice of Clancy, "Finger of Fate, or the Fateful Finger," *Saul of the Mole Men* (also known as *S.T.R.A.T.A.*), 2007.

Voices of Sergio and Senor Sinestro, "El Tigre," *El Tigre,* 2007.

Voices of Sergio and Senor Sinestro, "El Jefe," *El Tigre,* 2007.

Voices of Sergio and Senor Sinestro, "The Late Manny Rivera," *El Tigre,* 2007.

Also voices of Barberic, Niceman, and Mako the Shark, *Savage Dragon;* voices for *Sinbad;* miscellaneous voices, *The Sylvester and Tweety Mysteries,* The WB; voice, *What-a–Mess.*

Television Appearances; Other:
John Weider, *Marilyn & Bobby: Her Final Affair* (live–action movie), USA Network, 1993.

(As Jeff Bennett) (English version) Voice of Hachiro, *Afro Samurai* (anime miniseries; also known as *Afuro zamurai*), 2007.

Television Work; Animated Series; Additional Voices:
Where's Waldo? (also known as *Where's Wally?*), CBS, 1991–92.

Raw Toonage, CBS, 1992.

Marsupilami, CBS, 1994.

The Twisted Adventures of Felix the Cat (also known as *The Twisted Tales of Felix the Cat*), CBS, 1995.

Mickey Mouse Works (also known as *Disney's "Mickey-Mouse Works"*), ABC, 1999.

Television Work; Animated Episodes; Additional Voices:
Rugrats, Nickelodeon, 1991.

"Hercules and the Trojan War," *Hercules* (also known as *Disney's "Hercules"*), ABC and syndicated, 1998.

Additional voices for episodes of *Jungle Cubs* and *Waynehead,* The WB.

Film Appearances:
Eddie, *Friday the 13th Part VII: The New Blood,* Paramount, 1988.

Second trooper, *Cohen and Tate,* Hemdale, 1989.

Television man, *The Wacky Adventures of Ronald Mc-Donald: Scared Silly,* 1998.

Animated Film Appearances:

(English version) Voice of Gikuri, *Kaze no tani no Naushika* (anime; also known as *Nausicaa of the Valley of the Winds, Warriors of the Wind, Kaze no tani no Nausicaa,* and *Nausicaa*), 1984.

(English version) Voice of Kiki's father, *Kiki's Delivery Service* (anime; also known as *The Witch's Express Mail* and *Majo no takkyubin*), 1989.

Voice of the thief, *The Return of Jafar* (also known as *Aladdin 2*), Buena Vista Home Video, 1994.

Voices of Petrie and Ozzy, *The Land Before Time II: The Great Valley Adventure,* 1994.

Voices of Brooklyn, Magus, and Owen, *Gargoyles: The Heroes Awaken,* Buena Vista, 1994.

(As Jeff Glen Bennett) Voice, *Mortal Kombat: The Journey Begins,* 1995.

Voices of Petrie, Mutt, and Iguanadon, *Land Before Time III: The Time of Great Giving,* MCA Home Entertainment, 1995.

Voices of Elvis, Eustice, and first man, *Hillbilly Blue,* 1995.

Voice of Johnny Bravo, *Johnny Bravo,* 1995.

Voice of Jitters A. Dog, *Petal to the Metal,* 1995.

Voice of Roy, *Seigfried & Roy: Masters of the Impossible,* Twentieth Century–Fox, 1996.

Voices of Petrie and Ichy, *Land Before Time IV: Journey Through the Mists,* MCA Home Entertainment, 1996.

Voices of Axe and Poke, *Beauty and the Beast: The Enchanted Christmas* (also known as *Beauty and the Beast 2*), Walt Disney Home Video, 1997.

Voice of Duke D'Orange, *Mighty Ducks the Movie: The Face–Off,* Walt Disney Home Video, 1997.

Voices of Petri and Mr. Clubtail, *The Land Before Time V: The Mysterious Island,* Universal Pictures Home Video, 1997.

Voice of Johnny Bravo, *The Amazon Women,* 1997.

Voice of Petrie, *The Land Before Time VI: The Secret of Saurus Rock,* Universal Home Video, 1998.

Voices of Brooklyn and Owen Burnett, *Gargoyles: Brothers Betrayed,* 1998.

Voice of Brooklyn, *Gargoyles: The Force of Goliath,* 1998.

Voices of Brooklyn and Owen, *Gargoyles: The Hunted,* 1998.

(As Jeff Glen Bennett) Voices of Baloney and captain of the guard, *Wakko's Wish* (also known as *Steven Spielberg Presents "Animaniacs": Wakko's Wish*), 1999.

Voices of the colonel, mouse doctor, and mouse soldier, *The Nuttiest Nutcracker,* 1999.

(As Jeff Glen Bennett) Voice of elderly man, *Fractured Fairy Tales: The Phox, the Box & the Lox,* Universal, 1999.

Voices of father and Mortimer, *Mickey's "Once Upon a Christmas,"* Walt Disney Home Video, 1999.

(As Jeff Glenn Bennet) Voices of Petrie and spokes–dinosaur, *The Land Before Time VII: The Stone of Cold Fire,* 2000.

Voices of Bradley "Brad" Uppercrust III, unemployment lady, and Chuck the sportscaster, *An Extremely Goofy Movie,* Buena Vista, 2000.

Voice of Great Dane, *An American Tail: The Mystery of the Night Monster,* Universal, 2000.

(As Jeff Glen Bennett) Voice of Lester, *Scooby–Doo and the Alien Invaders,* Warner Bros. Home Video, 2000.

Voice of Levi, *Joseph: King of Dreams,* 2000.

Voices of Tramp, Jock, Trusty, and dogcatcher, *Lady and the Tramp II: Scamp's Adventure,* Buena Vista Home Video/Walt Disney Home Video, 2001.

Voices of Mr. Jollyland and others, *Mickey's Magical Christmas: Snowed In at the House of Mouse,* Buena Vista Home Video/Walt Disney Home Video, 2001.

Voice of Petrie, *The Land Before Time VIII: The Big Freeze* (also known as *The Land before Time: The Big Freeze*), Universal Studios Home Video, 2001.

(As Jess Bennett) Voice, *Disney's "Snow White and the Seven Dwarfs": Still the Fairest of Them All,* 2001.

Voice of Yak, *Balto II: Wolf Quest,* Universal Cartoon Studios, 2002.

(As Jeff Glen Bennett) Voice of Tom, *Tom and Jerry: The Magic Ring,* Warner Home Video, 2002.

Voice of Professor Archimedes W. Porter, *Tarzan & Jane,* Buena Vista Home Video, 2002.

Voice of salesman, "Mickey's Mechanical House" segment, *Mickey's House of Villains,* Walt Disney Home Entertainment, 2002.

Voice of Petrie, *The Land Before Time IX: Journey to the Big Water* (also known as *The Land before Time: Journey to Big Water*), Universal Studios Home Video, 2002.

Voices of Mr. Smee and pirates, *Return to Neverland,* Buena Vista, 2002.

(As Jeff Glen Bennett) Voices of Ace, Big Billy, Drubber, Baboon Kaboom, and others, *The Powerpuff Girls,* Warner Bros., 2002.

Voice of Foghorn Leghorn, *Cock–a–Doodle–Duel,* Warner Bros., 2003.

Voice of Daffy Duck, *Duck Dodgers in Attack of the Drones,* Warner Bros., 2003.

Voice of Jasper, *101 Dalmatians II: Patch's London Adventure,* Walt Disney Home Video, 2003.

(As Jeff Bennet) Voices of Jasper Ridgeway, Jack, and first lifeguard, *Scooby–Doo! And the Legend of the Vampire,* Warner Home Video, 2003.

Voice of Sam McKeane, *Atlantis: Milo's Return,* Buena Vista Home Video, 2003.

Voice of Dr. Jacques Von Haemsterviel, *Stitch! the Movie* (also known as *Disney's "Stitch! the Movie"*), Buena Vista Home Video, 2003.

Voice of Petrie, *The Land Before Time X: The Great Longneck Migration,* Universal, 2003.

(As Jeff Glenn Bennett) Voices of Yosemite Sam, Foghorn Leghorn, and Nasty Canasta, *Looney*

Tunes: Back in Action (also known as *Looney Tunes Back in Action: The Movie*), Warner Bros., 2003.

Voice of Sylvester, *Museum Scream,* Warner Bros., 2003.

Voice of Yosemite Sam, *Hare and Loathing in Las Vegas,* Warner Bros., 2004.

Voice of Petrie, *The Land Before Time XI: Invasion of the Tinysauruses,* Universal Studios Home Video, 2004.

Voices of Del Chillman, Sir Ian Locksley, and harpoon gunner, *Scooby–Doo and the Loch Ness Monster,* Warner Bros., 2004.

Voice of Beagle Boy, *Mickey, Donald, Goofy: The Three Musketeers,* Buena Vista, 2004.

Voices of elves, grouchy man, and Donner, *Mickey's "Twice Upon a Christmas,"* Buena Vista, 2004.

Voices of Jackie Legs and lounge singer, *Kangaroo Jack: G'Day,* Warner Home Video, 2004.

Voice of Dr. Gluckman, *Tom and Jerry Blast Off to Mars,* Warner Bros., 2005.

Voice of Steed, *Tom and Jerry: The Fast and the Furry,* Warner Home Video, 2005.

Voices of Arkham Asylum inmate and others, *The Batman vs. Dracula: The Animated Movie,* Warner Bros., 2005.

Voices of skinny old man, stout old man, Gollum–Rudy, and others, *The Emperor's New Groove 2: Kronk's New Groove,* Buena Vista Home Video, 2005.

Voice of Sylvester, *Executive Tweet,* Warner Bros., 2005.

Voice of Daffy Duck, *Badda Bugs,* Warner Bros., 2005.

Voice of Ivan, *Bongee Bear and the Kingdom of Rhythm,* Yankee Films, 2005.

Voice of Daffy Duck, *Duck Suped,* Warner Bros., 2005.

Voice of Daffy Duck, *Beach Bunny,* Warner Bros., 2005.

Voice of Yosemite Sam, *Deep Sea Bugs,* Warner Bros., 2005.

Voice of Daffy Duck, *Daffy Contractor,* Warner Bros., 2005.

Voice of Pepe Le Pew, *Dancing Pepe,* Warner Bros., 2005.

Voice of Daffy Duck, *Slacker Quacker,* Warner Bros., 2005.

Voice of salesman, *Curious George,* Universal, 2006.

Voice of Atka, *Brother Bear 2,* Buena Vista, 2006.

Voice of Petrie, *The Land Before Time XII: The Great Day of the Flyers,* Universal Studios Home Entertainment, 2006.

Voice of Reverend Vander Gelding, *Queer Duck: The Movie,* 2006.

Animated Film Work; Additional Voices:

Kurenai no buta (anime; also known as *Crimson Pig* and *Porco rosso*), 1992.

Batman: Mask of the Phantasm (also known as *Batman: The Animated Movie,* and *Batman: The Animated Movie—Mask of the Phantasm, Batman: Mask of*

the *Phantasm: The Animated Movie,* and *Mask of the Phantasm: Batman the Animated Movie*), Warner Bros., 1993.

(Uncredited) Singing voice, "The Morning Report," *The Lion King* (also known as *El rey leon*), Buena Vista Home Entertainment, 1993.

Pom Polo (anime), 1994.

Aladdin and the King of Thieves, Walt Disney Home Video, 1996.

Singing voice of centipede, *James and the Giant Peach,* 1996.

Belle's Magical World (also known as *Disney's "Belle's Magical World"*), Buena Vista Home Video, 1997.

Pocahontas II: Journey to a New World (also known as *Disney's "Pocahontas II: Journey to a New World"* and *Pocahontas: Journey to a New World*), Buena Vista Home Video, 1998.

(As Jeff Glen Bennett) *Tweety's High–Flying Adventure,* 2000.

The Jungle Book 2, Buena Vista, 2003.

The Lion King 1 ½ (also known as *The Lion King 3*), Buena Vista Home Video/Walt Disney Home Video, 2004.

Mulan II, Buena Vista Home Video, 2004.

The Fox and the Hound 2, Buena Vista, 2006.

TMNT (also known as *Teenage Mutant Ninja Turtles*) Warner Bros., 2007.

RECORDINGS

Video Games:

Voice of Gary the towel attendant, *Leisure Suit Larry 6: Shape Up or Slip Out!* (also known as *Larry 6*), 1993.

Voices of Sam, technical artist, Bruno, and others, *Gabriel Knight: Sins of the Fathers,* 1993.

Voice of Murph Winkie, *Stonekeep,* 1994.

Voices of Ad Avis, Bonehead, Dr. Cranium, and Igor, *Quest for Glory IV: Shadows of Darkness,* 1994.

Voice, *Blazing Dragons,* 1996.

(As Jeff Glen Bennett) Voices of Blub, Sir Eaton Scraps, Dendron, and others, *Someone's in the Kitchen!,* 1996.

Voice of Pumpkin, *Goosebumps: Escape from Horrorland,* 1996.

Voices of The Carecrow, Jim, Spike, Woof, outhouse guard, and robot maker, *Toonstruck,* 1996.

(As Jeff Glenn Bennett) Voices, *Star Trek: Starfleet Academy,* 1997.

Voice of Loxley, *Fallout* (also known as *Fallout: A Post–Nuclear Role–Playing Game*), Interplay Productions, 1997.

(As Jeff Glenn Bennett) Voices, *Clayfighter 63 1/3* (also known as *Clayfighter: Sculptor's Cut* and *Clayfighter 63 ½*), Interplay Productions, 1997.

Voices of Dream Knight, Drizzt, Quayle, and Xan, *Baldur's Gate,* Interplay Productions, 1998.

Voice of Baloney, *Animaniacs Game Pack,* 1998.

Voice of Mr. Peabody, *Rocky & Bullwinkle's Know–It–All Quiz Game,* 1998.

Voices of Xan, Drizzi Do'Urden, Saemon Havarian, and Gaelan Bayle, *Forgotten Realms: Baldur's Gate II—Shadows of Amn,* 2000.

(As Jeff Glen Bennett) Voice of Marco de Pollo, *Escape from Monkey Island,* Electronic Arts, 2000.

Voice of Jasper, *102 Dalmatians: Puppies to the Rescue,* 2000.

Voice, *Sacrifice,* 2000.

(As Jeff Glen Bennett) Voices of Brenn Tantor and first Abridon refugee, *Star Wars: Force Commander,* 2000.

Voices of Willy, Fred, and Danny, *Who Wants to Be a Millionaire CD–ROM: Sports Edition,* 2000.

(As Jeff Glenn Bennett) Voice of NOS 4A2, *Buzz Lightyear of Star Command* (also known as *Disney/Pixar's "Buzz Lightyear of Star Command"*), 2000.

(As Jeff Glenn Bennett) Voice, *Baldur's Gate II: Throne of Bhaal,* Bioware/Interplay Productions, 2000.

Miscellaneous voices, *Giants: Citizen Kabuto,* 2000.

(As Jeff Glen Bennet) Voices of Big Billy and Ace, *The Powerpuff Girls: Chemical X–Traction,* BAM! Entertainment, 2001.

(As Jeff Glenn Bennett) Voices of Jango Fett and clone trooper, *Star Wars: Galactic Battlegrounds,* LucasArts Entertainment, 2001.

Voice of Bud Buddiovitch, *Stupid Invaders,* Ubi Soft Entertainment, 2001.

Voice, *The Jungle Book: Rhythm 'n Groove,* Ubi Soft Entertainment, 2001.

Voice of imperial officer, *Star Wars: Rogue Squadron II—Rogue Leader* (also known as *Rogue Leader* and *Star Wars: Rogue Squadron*), LucasArts Entertainment, 2001.

Voice of Drizzi Do'Urden, *Forgotten Realms: Baldur's Gate—Dark Alliance,* Interplay Entertainment, 2001.

(As Jeff Glenn Bennett) Voices of Grubber, Big Billy, Ace, and others, *The PowerPuff Girls: Relish Rampage,* BAM! Entertainment, 2002.

Voices of clone, Dooku, Jango Fett, and troop transport captain, *Star Wars: Jedi Starfighter,* LucasArts Entertainment, 2002.

Voices of mayor of Halloweentown, Mr. Smee, and barrel, *Kingdom Hearts* (also known as *Kingudamu hatsu*), Square Electronic Arts, 2002.

Voices of Kyle Katarn and first storm trooper officer, *Star Wars: Jedi Knight II—Jedi Outcast,* LucasArts Entertainment, 2002.

(As Jeff Glenn Bennett) Voice, *Freelancer,* Microsoft, 2003.

Voice, *Extreme Skate Adventure* (also known as *Disney's "Extreme Skate Adventure"*), 2003.

Voice of Kyle Katarn, *Star Wars: Jedi Knight—Jedi Academy,* LucasArts Entertainment, 2003.

(As Jeff Glenn Bennett) Voices of first head, mummy, pins and needles, and others, *Tak and the Power of Juju,* Nickelodeon Productions, 2003.

Voice, *Looney Tunes: Back in Action,* 2003.

(As Jeff Glenn Bennett) Voice of Jonesy, mayor, and messenger, *Armed & Dangerous,* LucasArts Entertainment, 2003.

(As Jeff Glenn Bennett) Voice of Drizzi Do'Urden, *Forgotten Realms: Baldur's Gate—Dark Alliance II,* 2004.

Voices of Alan Disndale, Robert Zabrinski, Travis Sherman, and mercenaries, *Scooby–Doo! Mystery Mayhem,* THQ, 2004.

(As Jeff Glenn Bennett) Voices of Extor, Jack's father, priest, and others, *Samurai Jack: The Shadow of Aku,* Sega of America, 2004.

(As Jeff Glenn Bennett) Voices of Belly juju, caged juju, pins and needles, and J. B., *Tak 2: The Staff of Dreams,* THQ, 2004.

Voice, *Chicken Little,* Buena Vista Games, 2005.

Voices of Merlin, Lumiere, and barrel, *Kingdom Hearts II* (also known as *Kingudamu hatsu II*), Square Enix, 2005.

Voices of Cyril and Sparx's father, *The Legend of Spyro: A New Beginning,* 2006.

Voice of Clay, *Xiaolin Showdown,* Konami Digital Entertainment America, 2006.

OTHER SOURCES

Periodicals:

TV Guide, October 11, 2003, p. 20.

BERKOFF, Steven 1937–
(Stephen Berkoff)

PERSONAL

Original name, Leslie Steven Berks; born August 3, 1937, in Stepney, London, England; son of Alfred (a tailor) and Pauline (maiden name, Hyman) Berkoff; married Shelley Lee (a dancer and choreographer), August 21, 1976 (marriage ended). *Education:* Trained at Webber–Douglas Academy of Dramatic Arts, London, 1958–59, and Ecole Jacques Le Coq, Paris, 1965.

Addresses: *Office*—East Productions, 1 Keepier Wharf, 12 Narrow St., London E14 8DH, England. *Agent*—(film and television) Michael Hallett, Emptage Hallett, 24 Poland St., London W1F 8QL, England; (literary) Joanna Marston, Rosica Colin Ltd., 1 Clareville Grove Mews, London, SW7 5AH England.

Career: Actor, director, and writer. Worked with various repertory companies; London Theatre Group, London, founding member, director, and actor, 1968—; East Productions, affiliate; toured Israel, Europe, and the United States; appeared in commercials. Photographer, with work exhibited at Slaughterhouse Gallery, Pittsburgh, PA, 1992. Formerly worked as a cruise ship waiter and sales representative.

Awards, Honors: Los Angeles Drama Critics Circle Award, best directing, 1983; *L.A. Weekly* Theatre Award nomination, best performance, 1997, for *Massage;* Total Theatre Lifetime Achievement Award, Edinburgh Festival, 1997.

CREDITS

Stage Appearances:
Louis, *A View from the Bridge,* Empire Theatre, Finsbury Park, England, 1959.
Bellboy, *Oh Dad, Poor Dad,* Lyric Theatre, Hammersmith, England, 1961.
Gregor Samsa, *Metamorphosis,* London production, 1968, then Mark Taper Forum, Los Angeles, c. 1982.
Titorelli, *The Trial,* Dutch production, 1971.
Knock at the Manor Gate, London, 1972.
Miss Julie versus Expressionism, London, 1973.
Title role, *Agamemnon,* c. 1973.
Usher, *The Fall of the House of Usher,* Edinburgh, Scotland, 1974.
East, Edinburgh Festival, Edinburgh, Scotland, and London, 1975.
Decadence, Wyndham's Theatre, London, 1987.
Herod, *Salome,* National Theatre, London, 1989.
Titorelli, *The Trial,* National Theatre, 1990.
Title role, *Coriolanus,* West Yorkshire Playhouse, Leeds, England, 1995, then Mermaid Theatre, London, 1996.
Massage, Odyssey Theatre, Los Angeles, then Everyman Theatre, Liverpool, England, later Edinburgh Festival, 1997.
Shakespeare's Villains (solo show), Haymarket Theatre, London, 1998.
The Tell–Tale Heart and *Dog* (double–bill), Sadler's Well Theatre, London, 2000.
Shakespeare's Villains: A Masterclass in Evil (solo show), West End production, then New York Shakespeare Festival, Anspacher Theatre, Public Theatre, New York City, 2001.
Requiem for Ground Zero (solo reading), London, 2001.
One Man (solo show), Culture Project, New York City, 2002.
Berkoff Is Back, New York City, 2002.

Also appeared in *Arturo Ui; Hamlet; Macbeth;* and *Miss Julie* and *The Zoo Story* (double–bill); also presented a one–man show at Donmar Warehouse Theatre, London, 1985–86.

Major Tours:
Shakespeare's Villains (solo show), Connecticut cities, 2000, and international cities.
Requiem for Ground Zero (solo reading), beginning 2001.

Also appeared in touring production of *Shakespeare's Villains: A Masterclass in Evil* (solo show), international cities.

Stage Director:
The Zoo Story, Newcastle Upon Tyne, England, 1973.
Hamlet, Edinburgh Festival, Edinburgh, Scotland, 1979.
Greek, Croydon Warehouse, Croydon, England, then Actors Playhouse Theatre, New York City, 1983.
Kvetch, Garrick Theatre, London, 1986, then Westside Theatre Upstairs, New York City, 1987.
(And lighting director) *Coriolanus,* New York Shakespeare Festival, Anspacher Theatre, Public Theatre, New York City, 1988–89.
Salome, National Theatre, London, 1989.
Metamorphosis, Ethel Barrymore Theatre, New York City, 1989.
The Trial, National Theatre, 1990.
The Tragedy of Richard II, New York Shakespeare Festival, Anspacher Theatre, Public Theatre, 1994.
Coriolanus, West Yorkshire Playhouse, Leeds, England, 1995, then Mermaid Theatre, London, 1996.
Massage, Odyssey Theatre, Los Angeles, then Everyman Theatre, Liverpool, England, later Edinburgh Festival, 1997.
East, Vaudeville Theatre, London, 1999.
Shakespeare's Villains: A Masterclass in Evil (solo show), West End production, then New York Shakespeare Festival, Anspacher Theatre, Public Theatre, 2001.
One Man (solo show), Culture Project, New York City, 2002.
Berkoff Is Back, New York City, 2002.

Stage Director: Major Tours:
Director of touring productions of *Agamemnon; The Fall of the House of Usher; Hamlet; Macbeth;* and *Salome.*

Film Appearances:
(Uncredited) Extra, *The Sheriff of Fractured Jaw,* 1958.
(Uncredited) Extra, *I Was Monty's Double* (also known as *Hell, Heaven, or Hoboken*), 1958.
(Uncredited) *The Captain's Table* (also known as *Shenanigans*), 1959.
(Uncredited) British corporal, *The Devil's Disciple,* 1959.
(Uncredited) Medical student, *The Flesh and the Fiends* (also known as *The Fiendish Ghouls, Mania,* and *Psycho Killers*), 1960.
(Uncredited) Student on field trip, *Konga,* 1961.

John, *Prehistoric Women* (also known as *Slave Girls*), Twentieth Century–Fox, 1967.

Bertoli, *Vendetta for the Saint,* 1968.

Detective Constable Tom, *A Clockwork Orange* (also known as *Stanley Kubrick's "A Clockwork Orange"*), Warner Bros., 1971.

Pankratov, *Nicholas and Alexandra,* Columbia, 1971.

Lord Ludd, *Barry Lyndon,* Warner Bros., 1975.

(As Stephen Berkoff) Stephen, *The Passenger* (also known as *Profession: Reporter, Professione: Reporter,* and *El reportero*), Metro–Goldwyn–Mayer/United Artists, 1975.

Greasy fellow, *Joseph Andrews,* 1977.

Sagan, *Outland,* Warner Bros., 1981.

Ronnie Harrison, *McVicar,* Crown International, 1982.

General Orlov, *Octopussy,* Metro–Goldwyn–Mayer, 1983.

Victor Maitland, *Beverly Hills Cop,* Paramount, 1984.

Lieutenant Colonel Podovsky, *Rambo: First Blood, Part II,* TriStar, 1985.

Sergeant Jones, *Revolution,* Warner Bros., 1985.

Hugo Motherskille, *Underworld* (also known as *Transmutations*), Empire Entertainment, 1985.

The fanatic, *Absolute Beginners,* Orion, 1986.

Mr. Sharon, *Under the Cherry Moon,* Warner Bros., 1986.

Hugo Motherskille, *RawHeadRex,* 1986.

Streets of Yesterday, Perfect Features, 1989.

George Cornell, *The Krays* (also known as *The Kray Brothers* and *The Kray Twins*), Rank, 1990.

Steve, Les, and Helen's couturier, *Decadence,* 1994.

Colonel Ilya Kazak, *Fair Game,* 1995.

Klaus Reicher, *Flynn,* Beyond Distribution Sydney, 1996.

Vittorio DaSilva, *Love in Paris* (also known as *9 ½ Weeks II* and *Another 9 ½ Weeks*), Trimark Pictures, 1997.

Voices of Backhander and Reggie, *Doppelganger* (animated short film), 1997.

Sergeant Steinkampf, *Legionnaire,* Twentieth Century–Fox, 1998.

Mr. Kant, *Rancid Aluminum* (also known as *Rancid Aluminium*), 2000.

Magic Bob, *Beginner's Luck,* Guerilla Films, 2001.

Bokshu the Myth, Arjun Creations, 2002.

Jeff, *9 Dead Gay Guys,* Park Entertainment, 2003.

Surtayne, *Riders* (also known as *Steal, $teal, Team Riders,* and *Extreme inconduite*), Alliance Atlantis Communications, 2003.

The uncle, *Headrush,* Paradisio Home Entertainment, 2003.

Charlie Richardson, Sr., *Charlie,* Twentieth Century–Fox Home Entertainment, 2004.

Charles Besse, *Head in the Clouds* (also known as *Juegos de mujer*), Sony Pictures Classics, 2004.

Karaboulat, *Nyfes* (also known as *Brides*), Bristol Media International, 2004.

Lawrence Masters, *Naked in London,* London Film Syndicate, 2005.

Inquisitor, *The Headsman* (also known as *Shadow of the Sword* and *Henker*), Allegro Film, 2005.

Commandant Hoppe, *Forest of the Gods* (also known as *Dievu miskas*), MDC Films, 2005.

Voice of Herod, *It's a Boy!* (short film), 2005.

Ernst Hagemann, *The Flying Scotsman,* Metro–Goldwyn–Mayer, 2006.

Kurchatov, *The Half Life of Timofey Berezin,* Picturehouse Entertainment, 2006.

"Red" Jack Weinbaum, *The 10th Man* (short film), Baby Cow Productions/Leifer Brothers, 2006.

Oleg Rozhin, *Say It in Russian,* Imperia Entertainment, 2007.

Victims, Blue Spice Film/Carousel/Visionview, 2007.

General West, *The Dot Man,* Carter Films/Dot Man Films, 2007.

Film Director:

Decadence, 1994.

East, 2000.

Television Appearances; Miniseries:

Defense counsel, *An Enemy of the State,* BBC, 1965.

Karl Von Eiderfeld, *Sins,* CBS, 1986.

Adolf Hitler, *War and Remembrance,* ABC, 1988.

Girolamo Savonarola, *A Season of Giants* (also known as *Michelangelo: The Last Giant*), TNT, 1991.

Addison Leach, *Intruders,* 1992.

Potiphar, *In the Beginning,* NBC, 2000.

Himself, *Changing Stages,* PBS, 2000.

King Rua, *Attila* (also known as *Attila the Hun*), USA Network, 2001.

Meisling, *Hans Christian Andersen: My Life as a Fairy Tale,* Hallmark Channel, 2001.

Stilgar, *Children of Dune* (also known as *Frank Herbert's "Children of Dune," Dune—Bedrohung des imperiums, Dune—Der messias, Dune—Die kinder des wuestenplaneten,* and *Dune—Krieg um den wuestenplaneten*), Sci–Fi Channel, 2003.

John Roebling, "Brooklyn Bridge," *Seven Wonders of the Industrial World,* BBC, 2003.

Freddie Eccles, *Marple: By the Pricking of My Thumbs,* PBS, 2006.

Television Appearances; Specials:

Councillor, "Sir Jocelyn, the Minister Would Like a Word …," *The Wednesday Play,* BBC, 1965.

Private First Class Gutkowski, "The Pistol," *The Wednesday Play,* BBC, 1965.

Koslov, "Beloved Enemy," *Play for Today,* BBC1, 1981.

Mr. Samsa, *Metamorphosis,* BBC2, 1989.

The man, *The Tell–Tale Heart,* Bravo, 1991.

Stanley Kubrick: A Life in Pictures, Cinemax, 2001.

Attila: The Making of an Epic Miniseries, USA Network, 2001.

Voice of Aleister Crowley, *Masters of Darkness: Aleister Crowley—The Wickedest Man in the World,* Channel 4, 2002.

Multiple roles, *Shakespeare's Villains*, 2002.
Narrator, *Alive: Back to the Andes*, Channel 5, 2006.
Himself, *David Walliams: My Life with James Bond*, ITV, 2006.

Television Appearances; Movies:
Lucianus, *Hamlet* (also known as *Hamlet at Elsinore*), BBC, 1964.
Atoman, *Coming Out of the Ice*, CBS, 1982.
Jack McFarland, *Prisoner of Rio* (also known as *Wiezien Rio*), 1988.
Mayor, *Broken Morning*, London Weekend Television, 2003.

Television Appearances; Series:
Harry, *Silent Night*, Channel 4, 1990.
George Rolf, *NCS Manhunt*, BBC, 2002.

Television Appearances; Episodic:
Barman, "Love Bird," *Corrigan Blake*, BBC, 1963.
Sager, "The Gravediggers," *The Avengers*, ITV, 1965.
Police constable Archer, "The Informant, Part 1: Rough Justice," *Softly Softly* (also known as *Softly, Softly: Task Force*, BBC, 1967.
Dave Banks, "The Climber," *Dixon of Dock Green*, BBC, 1967.
Carlos, "The Iron Man," *The Champions*, NBC, 1968.
Captain Steve Minto, "The Cat with 10 Lives," *UFO*, syndicated, 1969.
Carl, "The Man Who Gambled with Life," *The Saint*, ITV, 1969.
Captain Steve Minto, "Destruction," *UFO*, syndicated, 1970.
Captain Steve Minto, "Mindbender," *UFO*, syndicated, 1971.
Krasnov, "A Man Called Quinn," *The Professionals*, ITV, 1983.
Club X, Channel 4, 1989.
The South Bank Show, 1989.
Dr. Paul Jorry, "Deadline," *Space Precinct*, syndicated, 1994.
Hagath, "Business as Usual," *Star Trek: Deep Space Nine* (also known as *Deep Space Nine*, *DS9*, and *Star Trek: DS9*), syndicated, 1997.
Himself, "Science," *Brass Eye* (also known as *Trip TV*), Channel 4, 1997.
Charles Sand/Carlo Giraldi, "In Between," *La Femme Nikita* (also known as *Nikita*), USA Network, 1998.
The mouth, "Mental Apparition Disorder," *Randall and Hopkirk (Deceased)*, BBC1, 2000.
Herman Grole, "Satan's Chimney," *Jonathan Creek*, PBS, 2001.
Guest panelist, *The Wright Stuff*, Channel 5, 2003.
Mr. Wiltshire, *Hotel Babylon*, BBC, 2006.
Ray Cook, "Bank Robbery," *New Tricks*, BBC, 2006.

Radio Appearances:
Title role, *Macbeth*, BBC4, 1996.
Master of ceremonies, *Cabaret*, BBC2, 1996.
Narrator, *An Actor's Tale*, BBC4, 1997.

RECORDINGS

Videos:
The fanatic in "Absolute Beginners" segment (in archive footage), *Bowie: The Video Collection*, 1993.
Inside "Octopussy," 2000.
The fanatic in "Absolute Beginners" segment (in archive footage), *Best of Bowie*, Ventura Distribution, 2002.
Voice of General Lente, *Killzone* (video game), Sony Computer Entertainment, 2004.

Audio Books:
Reader for *Metamorphosis, by Franz Kafka* and *The Trial, by Franz Kafka*, both Penguin Audiobooks.

Albums:
Singles include "The Mind of the Machine" by N–Trance.

WRITINGS

Original Plays:
Mr. Prufrock's Songs, London, 1974, revised as *Lunch*, produced in London, 1981.
East (verse play), Edinburgh Festival, Edinburgh, Scotland, and London, 1975, later Vaudeville Theatre, London, 1999.
Greek (verse play), London, 1980, later Croydon Warehouse Theatre, Croydon, England, then Actors Playhouse, New York City, 1983.
West (verse play), London, 1980.
Massage, Odyssey Theatre, Los Angeles, c. 1980, then Everyman Theatre, Liverpool, England, later Edinburgh Festival, 1997, published in 1987.
Lunch, 1983.
Harry's Christmas (solo show), London, 1985.
Kvetch, Garrick Theatre, London, 1986, then Westside Theatre Upstairs, New York City, 1987, published by Faber and Faber, 1986.
Acapulco, Los Angeles, 1986, then London, 1992.
Sink the Belgrano!, Mermaid Theatre, London, 1986, published by Faber and Faber, 1987.
Dog (solo show), 1993.
Actor (solo show), 1994.
Berkoff's Women, Du Maurier World Stage Festival, Factory Theatre, Toronto, Ontario, Canada, 2000.
Brighton Beach Scumbags, Lillian Theatre, Hollywood, CA, 2000.
Messiah: Scenes from a Crucifixion, Edinburgh Festival and Old Vic Theatre, London, 2000.
The Secret Love Life of Ophelia, 2001.
Shakespeare's Villains: A Masterclass in Evil (solo show), West End production, then New York Shakespeare Festival, Anspacher Theatre, Public Theatre, New York City, 2001.
Ritual in Blood, 2001.

Requiem for Ground Zero (solo verse reading), London, 2001, then other cities.
One Man (solo show), Culture Project, New York City, 2002.
Berkoff Is Back, New York City, 2002.
The Bow of Ulysses, 2002.
Sit and Shiver, Los Angeles, 2004.

Also author of *Dahling You Were Marvellous.*

Stage Adaptations:

In the Penal Colony (based on story by Franz Kafka), produced by London Theatre Group, London, 1968.
Metamorphosis (based on story by Kafka), produced in London, 1968, then Mark Taper Forum, Los Angeles, 1982, later Ethel Barrymore Theatre, New York City, 1989.
The Trial (based on story by Kafka), produced in the Netherlands, 1971, then London, 1973, and National Theatre, London, 1990.
Knock at the Manor Gate (based on story by Kafka), London, 1972.
Agamemnon (based on play by Aeschylus), produced c. 1973, published by Amber Lane Press, 1990.
Miss Julie versus Expressionism (based on play by August Strindberg), London, 1973.
The Fall of the House of Usher (based on story by Edgar Allan Poe), Edinburgh, Scotland, 1974, later London, 1975, published by Amber Lane Press, 1990.
The Tell–Tale Heart (based on story by Poe), London, 1985.
Salome, National Theatre, 1989, published by Faber and Faber, 1989.

Other writings include *Strum und Drang.*

Collected Plays:

East and Other Plays (includes *Agamemnon, East,* and *The Fall of the House of Usher*), J. Calder, 1977, Riverrun Press, 1982.
The Trial and *Metamorphosis,* Amber Lane Press, 1981.
Decadence and *Greek,* J. Calder, 1982, Riverrun Press, 1983.
West and Other Plays, Faber and Faber, 1985.
West, Lunch, Harry's Christmas, Grove Press, 1985.
Acapulco and *Kvetch,* Faber and Faber, 1986, Grove Press, 1987.
The Trial, Metamorphosis, In the Penal Colony: Three Theatre Adaptations from Franz Kafka, Amber Lane Press, 1988.
Decadence and Other Plays: East/West/Greek, Faber and Faber, 1989.
Collected Plays of Steven Berkoff, Volume I, Faber and Faber, 1994.
Plays of Berkoff, Volume 2, Faber and Faber, 1994.

Plays One, 2000.
Plays Three, Faber, 2000.

Television Specials:
West (based on his stage play), Channel 4, 1984.
Metamorphosis (based on his stage adaptation), BBC2, 1989.
The Tell–Tale Heart, Bravo, 1991.
Shakespeare's Villains, 2002.

Screenplays:
Greek (based on his stage play), 1990.
Decadence (based on his stage play), 1994.
East (based on his stage play), 2000.

Other:
Gross Intrusion and Other Stories, Quartet Books, 1977, Riverrun Press, 1979.
Steven Berkoff's America, Hutchinson, 1988.
A Prisoner in Rio (film journal), Hutchinson, 1989.
I Am Hamlet (production journal), Faber and Faber, 1989, Grove Press, 1990.
The Theatre of Steven Berkoff (photographic journal), Methuen, 1992.
Overview (travel writing), 1994.
Meditations on Metamorphosis, 1995.
Free Association (autobiography), London, England, 1996.
Graft: Tales of an Actor (fiction), Oberon Books, 1998.
Shopping in the Santa Monica Mall: The Journals of a Strolling Player, 2000.
Tough Acts: Memories of Working With ..., Robson Books, 2003.

Also wrote *Coriolanus in Deutschland,* Amber Lane Press.

OTHER SOURCES

Books:
Berkoff, Steven, *Steven Berkoff's America,* Hutchinson, 1988.
Berkoff, Steven, *A Prisoner in Rio* (film journal), Hutchinson, 1989.
Berkoff, Steven, *I Am Hamlet* (production journal), Faber and Faber, 1989, Grove Press, 1990.
Berkoff, Steven, *The Theatre of Steven Berkoff* (photographic journal), Methuen, 1992.
Berkoff, Steven, *Free Association* (autobiography), London, England, 1996.
Berkoff, Steven, *Shopping in the Santa Monica Mall: The Journals of a Strolling Player,* 2000.
Berkoff, Steven, *Tough Acts: Memories of Working With ...,* Robson Books, 2003.
Contemporary Dramatists, 6th edition, St. James Press, 1999.

Periodicals:
Economist, December 16, 1989, p. 89.

Electronic:
Steven Berkoff Official Site, http://www.stevenberkoff.
com, June 12, 2007.

BERRY, Raymond
    See BARRY, Raymond J.

BESSO, Claudia
    (Claudio Besso)

PERSONAL

Career: Actress.

CREDITS

Film Appearances:
Third woman on couch, *The Myth of the Male Orgasm,*
1993.
Jan Atkinson, *Marked Man* (also known as *Le guet–
apens*), Live Entertainment, 1995.
Secretaire, *Liste noire* (also known as *Black List*), 1995.
Lois, *Le sphinx,* 1995.
Model, *Twist of Fate* (also known as *Psychopath*), 1997.
Monica Bloom, *Afterglow,* Sony Pictures Classics,
1997.
Sherry, *Strip Search,* A–Pix Entertainment, 1997.
Femme au Hot–Dog, *Les Boys* (also known as *The
Boys*), CFP International, 1997.
Sunglasses woman, *Sublet* (also known as *Codename:
Jaguar*), Avalanche Home Entertainment, 1998.
Miss Brooks, *Provocateur* (also known as *Agent provo-
cateur*), 1998.
Laurie, *Blue Moon,* Castle Hill Productions, 2000.
Lucy Boxwell, *Achilles' Love,* Castle Hill Productions,
2000.
Angela, *Cafe Ole,* Equinox Entertainment, 2000.
(As Claudio Besso) Tracy Hunt, *Pressure Point* (also
known as *Back Road Justice* and *Backroad Justice*),
Velocity Pictures, 2001.
Florence Chadwick, *Heart: The Marilyn Bell Story* (also
known as *Marilyn Bell: Une histoire de coeur*),
2001.
Beth Locke, *$windle* (also known as *Swindle*), DEJ
Productions, 2002.
Woman in van, *Heartstrings* (short; also known as
Cordes et coeurs), Les Distributions Netima Ltee,
2002.
Susan Bunwell, *Abandon,* Paramount, 2002.

Chuck's mother, *Confessions of a Dangerous Mind* (also
known as *Confessions d'un homme dangereux*),
Miramax, 2002.
Lucy, *Horsie's Retreat,* 2005.
Additional voices, *Ice Age: The Meltdown* (animated;
also known as *Ice Age 2* and *Ice Age: The Melt-
down*), Twentieth Century–Fox, 2006.
Melony, *Jack and Jill vs. the World,* 2007.

Film Work:
Loop group, *People I Know,* Miramax, 2003.

Television Appearances; Series:
Chantel, *Metropia,* Omni, 2004.

Television Appearances; Miniseries:
Margie, *Bonanno: A Godfather's Story* (also known as
The Youngest Godfather), Showtime, 1999.
Vince's wife, *Il duce canadese* (also known as *Il duce
canadese: Le Mussolini canadien*), 2004.

Television Appearances; Movies:
Mai, *Twists of Terror* (also known as *Primal Scream*),
TMC, 1996.
Claire, receptionist, *Natural Enemy,* HBO, 1997.
Claire Powell, *Escape from Wildcat Canyon,* Showtime,
1998.
Model, *Twist of Fate,* Cinemax, 1999.
Lucille, *The Great Gatsby,* Arts and Entertainment,
2000.
Kimberly Touches, *Stiletto Dance,* HBO, 2001.
Personality number one, *Lathe of Heaven,* Arts and
Entertainment, 2002.
Juror number twelve, *Obsessed,* Lifetime, 2002.
CBS costumer, *Gleason* (also known as *Gleason: The
Jackie Gleason Story*), CBS, 2002.
Junior partner's wife, *Wall of Secrets* (also known as *Le
mur des secrets*), Lifetime, 2003.
Doria Palmieri, *The Reagans,* Showtime, 2003.
Laura Jackson, *Baby for Sale,* Lifetime, 2004.
Vanessa, *Tipping Point,* Lifetime, 2007.

Television Appearances; Specials:
Lisa Hall, *More Tears,* PBS, 1999.

Television Appearances; Episodic:
Nevila, "A Matter of Style," *The Hunger,* Showtime,
1997.
Marie Currie, *Cosby,* CBS, 1998.
Monica, "The Freak Show," *Sex and the City,* HBO,
1999.
Linda, "The Perfect Couple," *The Hunger,* Showtime,
2000.
Karen Bell, "Fool for Love," *Mutant X,* syndicated, 2001.
Annie, "Penelope and Her Suitors," *Bliss* (also known
as *Bliss II*), Oxygen, 2004.

Rachel, "Game, Set–up, Match," *Naked Josh* (also known as *Les lecons de Josh*), Showcase and Oxygen, 2004.

Additional voice, "Mutilation Ball," *Tripping the Rift*, Sci–Fi Channel, 2004.

Additional voice, "Miss Galaxy 5000," *Tripping the Rift*, Sci–Fi Channel, 2004.

Additional voice, "2001 Space Idiocies," *Tripping the Rift*, Sci–Fi Channel, 2004.

Yvette, "Hey Sister," *Instant Star*, CTV and The Nighttime Network for Teens, 2005.

Yvette, "Kiss Me Deadly," *Instant Star*, CTV and The Nighttime Network for Teens, 2005.

Yvette, "Won't Get Fooled Again," *Instant Star*, CTV and The Nighttime Network for Teens, 2005.

Kris Von Getz, "Mission La Roca: Parts 1 & 2," *Medical Investigation*, NBC, 2005.

Also appeared as Monique, "The Big Adjustment," *15/Love* (also known as *15/a*).

RECORDINGS

Video Games:

Voice, *Splinter Cell* (also known as *Tom Clancy's "Splinter Cell"*), Ubi Soft Entertainment, 2002.

Voice of comedian VO, *Myst IV: Revelation*, Ubi Soft Entertainment, 2004.

Voice, *Prince of Persia: Warrior Within*, Mastertronic Ltd., 2004.

Voice of Anna, *Splinter Cell: Chaos Theory*, 2005.

Voice of Milena, *Still Life*, The Adventure Company, 2005.

BEVERIDGE, Ryan

PERSONAL

Addresses: *Agent*—Soundtrack Music Associates, 2229 Cloverfield Blvd., Santa Monica, CA 90405.

Career: Composer, musician, and music assistant. Also wrote scores for trailers at the Sundance Film Festival, and the Sundance 25th Anniversary Documentary, Sundance Institute, and Delta In–Flight films.

CREDITS

Film Work:

Assistant for Stewart Copeland, *Very Bad Things*, Poly-Gram Films, 1998.

Music technical assistant, *Simpatico*, Fine Line Features, 1999.

Music assistant, *She's All That*, Miramax, 1999.

Music technical assistant, *More Dogs Than Bones*, Dream Entertainment, 2000.

Orchestrator, *Taboo*, Sony Pictures Video, 2002.

Percussion musician, *Dirty*, 2005.

Television Work; Movies:

Music editor, *Night of the Wolf*, Animal Planet, 2002.

WRITINGS

Film Scores:

Taboo, Sony Pictures Video, 2002.

Nightstalker, Smooth Pictures, 2002.

Valentine Man (short), 2004.

Race You to the Bottom, Regent Releasing, 2005.

The Wright Stuff (short), 2005.

L.A. Dicks, 2005.

Dirty, Silver Nitrate Releasing, 2005.

Gigi (short), First Look International, 2005.

Rampage: The Hillside Strangler Murders, Silver Nitrate Releasing, 2006.

Why He Skied (documentary), 2006.

Zyzzyx Rd., Regent Worldwide Sales, 2006.

Boy Culture, TLA Releasing, 2006.

Tiny Dancer (short), Fleaco Pix, 2006.

Easy Winners (short), 2006.

Fly Like Mercury, 2007.

Television Scores; Movies:

Frankenfish, Sci–Fi Channel, 2004.

Television Scores; Pilots:

Aces, The WB, 2002.

Television Scores; Episodic:

Brutally Normal, The WB, 2000.

Breaking News, Bravo, 2002.

"Strife," *Heist*, NBC, 2006.

"How Billy Got His Groove Back," *Heist*, NBC, 2006.

"Bury the Lead," *Heist*, NBC, 2006.

"Ladies and Gentleman … Sweaty Dynamite," *Heist*, NBC, 2006.

Video Game Scores:

Spyro: Year of the Dragon (also known as *Spyro the Dragon 3: Year of the Dragon*), 2000.

OTHER SOURCES

Electronic:

Ryan Beveridge Website, http://www.ryanbeveridge.com, July 20, 2007.

BHATIA, Amin

PERSONAL

Born in London, England.

Addresses: *Agent*—Soundtrack Music Associates, 2229 Cloverfield Blvd., Santa Monica, CA 90405.

Career: Composer. Winter Olympics, contributing musician and programmer, 1988; Q Sound Labs, composer and sound design for 3D audio presentations, 1991; CFNY 102.1 FM, Toronto, Ontario, Canada, special projects producer and sound designer (alternative format), 1993—; wrote music for numerous national advertising campaigns.

Member: Canadian Cinema and Television (board member); Guild of Canadian Film Composers (board member); Academy of Canadian Cinema and Television; Academy of Canadian Television and Radio Artists; Society of Composers and Lyricists.

Awards, Honors: Grand Prize, Roland International Synthesizer Competition, 1981; First Prize, Roland International Synthesizer Competition, 1982; AMPIA Award, best original score, Alberta Motion Picture Industry Association, 1986, for *Storm;* CLIO Awards of Excellence, 1985–90; Gemini Award nomination, best original music score for a program, Academy of Canadian Cinema and Television, 1997, for *Gridlock;* Gemini Award nomination, best original music score for a dramatic series, 1998, for *Once a Thief;* Golden Reel Award nomination, best sound editing in television—music, movies, and specials, Motion Picture Sound Editors, 2002, for *A Colder Kind of Death;* Gemini Award nomination (with Meiro Stamm), best original music score for an animated program or series, 2005, for *Franny's Feet;* Gemini Award (with Ari Posner), best original music score for an animated program or series, 2005, for *King;* Gemini Award, best original music score for a program or miniseries, 2005, for *In the Dark;* Emmy Award nomination (with Posner), outstanding original main title theme music, 2006, for *Get Ed.*

CREDITS

Film Work:
Musician, *Iron Eagle II* (also known as *L'aige de fer II* and *Iron Eagle II: The Battle Beyond the Flag*), TriStar, 1988.
Producer, *Jane Goodall's Wild Chimpanzees: The Making of the Music* (documentary short), SlingShot Entertainment, 2003.

Radio Work:
Sound designer, *Vanishing Point* and *Birdie French,* CBC, 1987–93.

RECORDINGS

Albums:
Interstellar Suite, Capitol/Cinema Records, 1987.

WRITINGS

Film Scores:
Storm (also known as *Turbulences*), Warner Home Video, 1987.
Primo Baby, 1988.
Iron Eagle II (also known as *L'aige de fer II* and *Iron Eagle II: The Battle Beyond the Flag*), TriStar, 1988.
Black Ice (also known as *A Passion for Murder*), Prism Pictures, 1992.
Cafe Romeo, Ascot Video, 1992.
Anything for Love (also known as *Just One of the Girls*), 1993.
Tomcat Dangerous Desires, Republic, 1993.
Gold Fever (documentary short), SK Films, 1999.
Jane Goodall's Wild Chimpanzees (documentary), IMAX, 2002.
Detention, Lions Gate Films Home Entertainment, 2003.
Rescue Heroes: The Movie (animated), 2003.
Jambo Kenya (documentary), 2005.

Television Scores; Movies:
Ordeal in the Arctic, ABC, 1993.
A Stranger in the Mirror, ABC, 1993.
Just One of the Girls, Fox, 1993.
Shock Treatment, 1995.
The Awakening (also known as *La force d'aimer* and *Harlequin's "The Awakening"*), CBS, 1995.
Gridlock (also known as *Gridlock—Die Falle* and *Obstruction*), NBC, 1996.
John Woo's "Once a Thief: Family Business," TMC, 1998.
John Woo's "Once a Thief: Brother Against Brother," TMC, 1998.
A Colder Kind of Death (also known as *Criminal Instinct: A Colder Kind of Death* and *Manipulation*), Lifetime, 2001.
The Wandering Soul Murders (also known as *Criminal Instinct: The Wandering Soul Murders* and *Sure les traces de Littleflower*), Lifetime, 2001.
Going Back (also known as *Freres de guerre* and *Under Heavy Fire*), HBO, 2001.
Recipe for a Perfect Christmas, Lifetime, 2005.

Television Scores; Pilots:
Once a Thief (movie; also known as *John Woo's "Once a Thief"* and *John Woo's "Violent Tradition"*), syndicated, 1996.

Television Scores; Episodic:
Ray Bradbury Theatre, 1990–92.
Kung Fu: The Legend Continues, Fox, 1992–96.
Free Willy (animated), ABC, 1994.
John Woo's "Once a Thief," syndicated, 1997.
Power Play, UPN, 1999.
New Tales from the Cryptkeeper, CBS, 1999.
Code Name: Eternity (also known as *Code: Eternity*), syndicated, 1999.
Corduroy, PBS, 2000.
King, 2003.
Franny's Feet, 2003.
Queer as Folk, Showtime, 2005.

Also composed music for *Freaky Friday,* CBS.

Television Background Music; Episodic:
Tales from the Cryptkeeper, ABC, 1993–94.

Television Themes; Episodic:
The Zack Files, ITV and Fox, 2000–2001.

Television Theme Music: Episodic:
Get Ed, ITV and Fox Family, 2005.

Radio Scores:
Vanishing Point and *Birdie French,* CBC, 1987–93.

OTHER SOURCES

Electronic:
Amin Bhatia Website, http://wwwbhatiamusic.com, July 20, 2007.

BLOOMFIELD, George 1930–

PERSONAL

Born 1930, in Montreal, Quebec, Canada; married Barbara Amiel, 1965 (divorced, 1971); married Louisa "Jane" Varalta.

Career: Director, producer, actor, and writer. Previously owned a theater company in Montreal, Quebec, Canada.

Awards, Honors: Gemini Award nomination, best direction in a dramatic or comedy series, Academy of Canadian Cinema and Television, 1987, for *The Campbells;* Gemini Award nomination, best direction in a dramatic or comedy series, 1993, for *Neon Rider;* Gemini Award nomination, best direction in a dramatic program or miniseries, 1993, for *Wojeck: Out of the Fire;* Gemini Award nomination, best direction in a dramatic or comedy series, 1994, for *North of 60;* Gemini Awards (with others), best direction in a dramatic or comedy series, 1995, best dramatic series, 1996, 1997, and Canada's Choice Awards (with others), Academy of Canadian Cinema and Television, 1996, 1997, all for *Due South;* Gemini Award nominations, best dramatic series (with others), 1998, and best direction in a dramatic series, 1998 (for episode "Dead Guy Running") and 1999, all for *Due South;* CBC Anik Award, best director.

CREDITS

Television Director; Series:
Second City TV (also known as *SCTV* and *Second City Revue*), syndicated, 1977–79.
Custard Pie, CBC, 1977.
SCTV Channel, Cinemax, 1983.
Fraggle Rock (also known as *Fraggle Rock with Jim Henson's Muppets* and *Jim Henson's "Fraggle Rock"*), HBO, 1983.
War of the Worlds (also known as *War of the Worlds: The Second Invasion*), syndicated, multiple episodes, 1988–89.
My Secret Identity, CTV, 1988.
E.N.G., Lifetime, multiple episodes, 1990.
Neon Rider, syndicated, multiple episodes, 1990–92.
Street Legal, CBC, multiple episodes, 1990–91.
Emily of New Moon, 1998.
The Associates, CTV, 2001.
Wild Card (also known as *Zoe Busiek: Wild Card*), Lifetime, 2003.
The Jane Show, Global, 2006.

Also director of *King of Kensington,* CBC.

Television Producer; Series:
Producer, *Peep Show,* 1975–76.
Creative producer, *Due South* (also known as *Direction: Sud*), CBS, 1995.
Creative producer, *Due South* (also known as *Un tandem de choc*), CTV, 1997.

Television Director; Movies:
Love on the Nose, 1974.
Nellie McClung, 1978.
Riel, CBC, 1979.
Wojeck: Out of the Fire, CBC, 1992.
The Awakening (also known as *Harlequin's "The Awakening"* and *La force d'aimer*), CBS, 1993.
TekWar: TekLords, syndicated, 1994.

Love and Murder (also known as *Criminal Instincts: Love and Murder* and *Crimes et passion*), Lifetime, 2000.

Deadly Appearances (also known as *Criminal Instincts: Deadly Appearances* and *e prix du silence*), Lifetime, 2000.

Television Director; Episodic:
"Soap Box Derby," *Sharon, Lois & Bram's Elephant Show* (also known as *The Elephant Show*), 1986.
"Sleepover," *Sharon, Lois & Bram's Elephant Show* (also known as *The Elephant Show*), 1986.
"First Day," *The Campbells,* syndicated, 1986.
Friday the 13th (also known as *Friday the 13th: The Series* and *Friday's Curse*), syndicated, 1987.
"High Society," *Road to Avonlea* (also known as *Avonlea* and *Tales from Avonlea*), Disney Channel, 1992.
"Old Friends, Old Wounds," *Road to Avonlea* (also known as *Avonlea* and *Tales from Avonlea*), Disney Channel, 1992.
"The Act of Hares," *North of 60,* CBC, 1993.
"Sisters of Mercy," *North of 60,* CBC, 1993.
"Ciao, Baby," *North of 60,* CBC, 1993.
"Where the Heart Is," *Lonesome Dove: The Series,* 1994.
"The Allys," *Hawkeye,* syndicated, 1995.
"The Awakening," *The Outer Limits* (also known as *The New Outer Limits*), Showtime and syndicated, 1995.
(And coproducer) "The Man Who Knew Too Little," *Due South* (also known as *Direction: Sud*), CBS, 1995.
(And coproducer) "An Invitation to Romance," *Due South* (also known as *Direction: Sud*), CBS, 1995.
"Quake!," *Kung Fu: The Legend Continues,* 1995.
"Tek Posse," *TekWar* (also known as *TekWar: The Series*), syndicated, 1995.
"A Terrible Beauty," *EZ Streets,* CBS, 1997.
"Escape," *La Femme Nikita* (also known as *Nikita*), USA Network, 1997.
"Choice," *La Femme Nikita* (also known as *Nikita*), USA Network, 1997.
"Innocent," *La Femme Nikita* (also known as *Nikita*), USA Network, 1997.
"Mountie on the Bounty: Part 1," *Due South* (also known as *Un tandem de choc*), CTV, 1998.
(And producer) "Family Matters," *Doc,* PAX, 2001.
"Murder Is Corny," *A Nero Wolfe Mystery* (also known as *Nero Wolfe*), Arts and Entertainment, 2002.
"Poison a la Carte," *A Nero Wolfe Mystery* (also known as *Nero Wolfe*), Arts and Entertainment, 2002.

Also directed episodes of *Adderly* and *Beggars and Choosers,* Showtime.

Television Producer; Episodic:
Executive producer, "The Victim," *Peep Show,* 1975.
Executive producer, "The Lie Chair," *Peep Show,* 1975.

Television Director; Other:
Henry V, 1966.
African Journey (special), 1989.
(And producer) *Doc* (pilot), PAX, 2001.

Television Appearances; Movies:
Sampson, *Escape from Iran: The Canadian Caper* (also known as *Desert Blades*), CBS, 1981.
Dr. Mueller, *The Park Is Mine,* HBO, 1986.

Television Appearances; Specials:
John Candy: The E! True Hollywood Story, E! Entertainment Television, 2001.

Television Appearances; Episodic:
"Now You See Him, Now You Don't," *Seeing Things,* CBC, 1984.
Lawyer, "Dust to Dust," *War of the Worlds* (also known as *War of the Worlds: The Second Invasion*), syndicated, 1989.
Video store customer, The Blue Line," *Due South* (also known as *Direction: Sud*), CBS, 1995.
Zoltan Motherwell, "Burning Down the House," *Due South* (also known as *Un tandem de choc*), CTV, 1997.
Lawyer, *Doc,* PAX, c. 2000.

Film Director:
Ground Handling of Aircraft, Part 2: Winter Operations (short documentary), National Film Board of Canada, 1958.
The Threshold: The Immigrant Meets the School (short documentary; also known as *Le portique: L'immigrant et l'ecole*), National Film Board of Canada, 1959.
Teamwork in Farm Research (short documentary; also known as *Travail d'equipe et recherches agricoles*), National Film Board of Canada, 1959.
The Mine Makers (short documentary), National Film Board of Canada, 1959.
The Scouler Case (short documentary), National Film Board of Canada, 1960.
Jenny, Cinerama, 1969.
To Kill a Clown, Twentieth Century–Fox, 1972.
(And editor) *Child Under a Leaf* (also known as *Love Child*), Cinema Financial, 1974.
Nothing Personal, Orion, 1980.
Double Negative (also known as *Deadly Companion*), Quadrant Films, 1980.
The Argon Quest, 1990.
African Journey 2, National Film Board of Canada, 1990.
Jacob Two Two Meets the Hooded Fang, Odeon Films, 1999.

According to some sources, also directed *Avonture van die Swart Hings Animation* (animated film).

Film Appearances:

Reverend Thomas Thanner, *Spasms* (also known as *Death Bite*), Producers Distributing, 1983.

Prego, *And Then You Die*, 1987.

RECORDINGS

Videos:

Himself, *Ride Forever*, Network Video, 2006.

WRITINGS

Films:

Ground Handling of Aircraft, Part 2: Winter Operations (short documentary), National Film Board of Canada, 1958.

The Scouler Case (short documentary), National Film Board of Canada, 1960.

Jenny, Cinerama, 1969.

To Kill a Clown, Twentieth Century–Fox, 1972.

Child Under a Leaf (also known as *Love Child*), Cinema Financial, 1974.

The Argon Quest (also based on story by Bloomfield), 1990.

BOLL, Uwe 1965–

PERSONAL

Born June 22, 1965, in Wermelskirchen, West Germany. *Education:* Studied film, marketing, and management at the University of Cologne and the University of Seigen; earned Ph.D. in literature.

Addresses: *Office*—Boll Kg, Fullsichel 7, 51399, Germany. *Publicist*—Wanstrom and Associates, 687 Denman St., Suite 43513, Vancouver V6G 3C7 Canada.

Career: Producer, director, and screenwriter. BOLL KG (a film production company), 1992—; TanusFilm (a production company), producer and director, 1994–2000; Began making Super 8 films as a child.

CREDITS

Film Work:

Hand camera operator and director, *German Fried Movie*, 1991.

Director and producer, *Barschel—Mord in Genf?*, Kinowelt Home Entertainment, 1993.

Director and producer, *Amoklauf*, Screen Power Home Entertainment, 1994.

Director and executive producer, *Das erste semester* (also known as *The First Semester*), United International Pictures, 1997.

Coproducer, *Fiasko* (also known as *Fiasco*), Starmedia Home Entertainment, 2000.

Coproducer, *L'amour, l'argent, l'amour* (also known as *L'Amour* and *Love, Money, Love*), EuroVideo, 2000.

Executive producer, *Angels Don't Sleep Here* (also known as *Backflash 2: Angels Don't Sleep Here*), Lions Gate Films, 2001.

Director and executive producer, *Blackwoods*, Boll Films, 2002.

Director and executive producer, *Heart of America* (also known as *Home Room*), MTI Home Video, 2003.

Director and producer, *House of the Dead* (also known as *House of the Dead: Le jeu ne fait que commencer*), Artisan Entertainment, 2003.

Director and executive producer, *Alone in the Dark*, Lions Gate Films, 2005.

Director and producer, *BloodRayne*, Romar Entertainment, 2005.

Director and executive producer, *In the Name of the King: A Dungeon Siege Tale* (also known as *Schwerter des konigs—Dungeon Siege*), 2007.

Director and executive producer, *Seed*, Freestyle Releasing, 2007.

Director, executive producer, and producer, *Postal*, Freestyle Releasing, 2007.

Director and executive producer, *BloodRayne II: Deliverance*, Visual Entertainment, 2007.

Film Appearances:

Danger seeker, *German Fried Movie*, 1991.

Himself, *Behind the House: Anatomy of the Zombie Movement* (documentary short), Artisan Entertainment, 2004.

Himself, *The Making Of: "House of the Dead"* (documentary), 2004.

Postal, 2007.

Television Work; Movies:

Director and producer, *Sanctimony*, Cinemax, 2000.

Television Appearances; Episodic:

Himself, *Tagesthemen*, 2004.

Himself, *HypaSpace* (also known as *HypaSpace Daily* and *HypaSpace Weekly*), Space Channel, 2006.

Himself, "Video Game Movies," *Space Top 10 Countdown*, Space Channel, 2006.

RECORDINGS

Music Videos:

Director, Nightwish's "Wish I Had an Angel," 2004.

WRITINGS

Screenplays:
German Fried Movie, 1991.
Barschel—Mord in Genf?, 1993.
Amoklauf, Screen Power Home Entertainment, 1994.
Das erste semester (also known as *The First Semester*), United International Pictures, 1997.
Blackwoods, Boll Films, 2002.
(Story only) *Heart of America* (also known as *Home Room*), MTI Home Video, 2003.
Seed, Freestyle Releasing, 2007.
Postal, Freestyle Releasing, 2007.

Television Movies:
Sanctimony, Cinemax, 2000.

Books:
Wrote *Wie man in Deutschland einen film drehen muss* (*How to Make a Move in Germany*); *Die gattung serie und ihre genres* (*Series and Their Genres*).

OTHER SOURCES

Periodicals:
Wired Magazine, December, 2006.

BOND, Timothy 1942–
    (Tim Bond)

PERSONAL

Born February 19, 1942, in Ottawa, Ontario, Canada; son of C. C. J. and Elizabeth (maiden name, Berton) Bond. *Education:* Carleton University, Ottawa, B.S., B.A., 1965. *Avocational Interests:* Flying, computing.

Addresses: *Agent*—Lee Dinstman, Agency for the Performing Arts, 405 South Beverly Dr., Beverly Hills, CA 90210.

Career: Director and writer. Stratford Festival, Stratford, Ontario, Canada, assistant director, 1966–68.

Member: Directors Guild of America, Writers Guild of America, Directors Guild of Canada (vice president, 1987), Alliance of Canadian Cinema, Television, and Radio Artists.

Awards, Honors: Gemini Award nomination (with others), best writing in a dramatic series, Academy of

Canadian Cinema and Television, 1989, for *Friday the 13th;* Gemini Award nomination, best direction in a dramatic or comedy series, 1992, for Top Cops.

CREDITS

Television Director; Movies:
Till Death Do Us Part (also known as *Madhouse*), 1982.
One Night Only, 1986.
Rapture, 1993.
TekWar: TekLab, syndicated, 1994.
Night of the Twisters, The Family Channel, 1996.
Running Wild, Showtime, 1997.
The Shadow Men, 1997.
Perfect Little Angels, Fox Family Channel, 1998.
Loving Evangeline (also known as *Harlequin's "Loving Evangeline"* and *En quete de verite*), 1998.
Diamond Girl (also known as *Harlequin's "Diamond Girl"* and *Un amour inattendu*), The Movie Channel, 1998.
Sweet Deception (also known as *Sweet Lies*), Fox Family Channel, 1998.
Eve's Christmas, Lifetime, 2004.
Truth, Lifetime, 2005.
Lesser Evil, Lifetime, 2006.
Gospel of Deceit, Lifetime, 2006.
Family in Hiding, Lifetime, 2006.
(As Tim Bond) *The Secrets of Comfort House,* Lifetime, 2006.

Television Director; Series:
The Campbells, CTV, c. 1986–87.
Hot Shots, 1986–87.

Television Director; Specials:
First Offender, HBO, 1987.
Goosebumps: The Haunted Mask, 1995.
Goosebumps: Night of the Living Dummy III, 1997.

Television Director; Episodic:
"Nina Who?," *Adderly,* CBS, 1986.
"Nemesis," *Adderly,* CBS, 1987.
"Boogie Board Blues," *My Pet Monster* (animated), 1987.
"Limo," *Night Heat,* 1987.
"Silk," *Night Heat,* 1988.
"The Way Home," *Hard Time on Planet Earth,* CBS, 1989.
"In the Driver's Seat," *Alfred Hitchcock Presents,* NBC, 1989.
"South by Southwest," *Alfred Hitchcock Presents,* NBC, 1989.
"The Vengeance Factor," *Star Trek: The Next Generation* (also known as *Star Trek: TNG*), syndicated, 1989.
"The Most Toys," *Star Trek: The Next Generation* (also known as *Star Trek: TNG*), syndicated, 1990.

Sweating Bullets, 1991.
Scene of the Crime, 1991.
"They Eat Horses, Don't They?" *Due South* (also known as *Direction: Sud*), CBS, 1994.
"What's Up Doc," *Side Effects,* CBC, 1994.
"Capital Offence," *Forever Knight,* syndicated, 1994.
"Eggheads," *Sliders,* Fox, 1995.
"Valerie 23," *The Outer Limits* (also known as *The New Outer Limits*), Showtime and syndicated, 1995.
"The Wedding of Alcmene," *Hercules: The Legendary Journeys,* syndicated, 1996.
"The Power," *Hercules: The Legendary Journeys,* syndicated, 1996.
The New Ghostwriter Mysteries, 1997.
"She's Come Undone," *Mutant X,* syndicated, 2004.

Also directed episodes of *Animorphs* (animated; also known as *AniTV*), Nickelodeon; *The Edison Twins,* CBC; *E.N.G.,* Lifetime; *Friday the 13th* (also known as *Friday's Curse* and *Friday the 13th: The Series*), syndicated; *Goosebumps* (also known as *Ultimate Goosebumps*); *Hitchhiker* (also known as *Deadly Nightmares* and *Le voyageur*), HBO; *My Secret Identity,* syndicated; *One Life to Live,* ABC; *Robocop* (also known as *RoboCop: The Series*), syndicated; *Top Cops; Touched by an Angel,* CBS; and *War of the Worlds* (also known as *War of the Worlds: The Second Invasion*), syndicated.

Film Director:
Deadly Harvest, New World, 1977.
The Lost World, Worldvision Home Video, 1992.
Return to the Lost World, 1992.
High Explosive (also known as *High Explosive*), Prophecy Entertainment, 2000.
She, Prophecy Entertainment, 2001.

Stage Director:
The Royal Hunt of the Sun, Winnipeg, Manitoba, Canada, 1978.
Eight to the Bar, 1979.
A History of American Film, Seattle, WA, 1980.
Arsenic and Old Lace, England, 1980.
The Man Who Came to Dinner, Toronto, Ontario, Canada, 1981.
The Dresser, Vancouver, British Columbia, Canada, 1981.

Director of more than 150 other stage plays.

WRITINGS

Television Movies:
She Cried Murder, 1974.
Till Death Do Us Part (also known as *Madhouse*), 1982.
The Quilt of Hathor, 1989.

Television Episodes:
Sweating Bullets, 1991.
Scene of the Crime, 1991.

Also writer for episodes of *Friday the 13th* (also known as *Friday's Curse* and *Friday the 13th: The Series*), syndicated; and *Hercules: The Legendary Journeys,* syndicated.

Television Scripts; Other:
Oakmount High, 1985.
Night Heat, 1987.
Over My Dead Body, 1991.

Screenplays:
Black Christmas, 1973.
Happy Birthday to Me, Columbia, 1981.

BONERZ, Peter 1938–

PERSONAL

Born August 6, 1938, in Portsmouth, NH; son of Christopher Andrew (a military intelligence officer) and Elfrieda Anne (maiden name, Kern) Bonerz; married Rosalind DiTrapani, December 13, 1963; children: Eric, Eli. *Education:* Marquette University, B.S., 1960.

Addresses: *Agent*—Creative Artists Agency, 2000 Avenue of the Stars, Los Angeles, CA 90212. *Manager*—George Shapiro, Shapiro/West and Associates, 141 El Camino Dr., Suite 205, Beverly Hills, CA 90212.

Career: Director and actor. The Committee (improvisational comedy troupe), San Francisco, CA, member of company, 1963–69; University of California, Los Angeles, instructor in acting and directing, 1991–94; University of Southern California, instructor, 1999. *Military service:* U.S. Army, 1961–63.

Awards, Honors: Directors Guild of America Award nomination (with others), outstanding directorial achievement in a comedy series, 1992, for "Uh Oh: Part 2," *Murphy Brown;* Emmy Award nomination, outstanding directing in a comedy series, 1993, for "You Say Potato, I Say Potato," *Murphy Brown;* Directors Guild of America Award nomination, outstanding directorial achievement in a comedy series, 1994, for "Angst for the Memory," *Murphy Brown;* some sources also cite Annual CableAce Award nomination, National Cable Television Association, 1996.

CREDITS

Television Director; Series:
ALF, NBC, multiple episodes, 1986–87.

Murphy Brown, CBS, multiple episodes, between 1991 and 1998.

Friends, NBC, multiple episodes, between 1994 and 1998.

Good Morning, Miami, NBC, multiple episodes, 2003–2004.

The Stones, CBS, 2004.

Television Director; Episodic:

The Bob Newhart Show, CBS, 1974.

When Things Were Rotten, 1975.

Good Heavens, 1976.

Szysznyk, 1977.

Apple Pie, ABC, 1978.

Archie Bunker's Place, CBS, 1979.

Park Place, CBS, 1981.

9 to 5, ABC, 1982.

Suzanne Pleshette Is Maggie Briggs, CBS, 1984.

It's Your Move, NBC, 1984.

"All Tied Up," *E/R,* CBS, 1985.

"A Change in Policy," *E/R,* CBS, 1985.

"The Honeybunnies," *George Burns Comedy Week,* CBS, 1985.

"Dating Henry," *You Again?,* NBC, 1986.

"A New Life," *You Again?,* NBC, 1986.

"All You Need Is Love," *You Again?,* NBC, 1986.

My Sister Sam, CBS, 1986.

The Thorns, ABC, 1988.

Doctor Doctor, 1989.

1st & Ten (also known as *1st and Ten: In Your Face!*), HBO, 1990.

Flying Blind, Fox, 1992.

"Prima Dava," *Love & War,* 1993.

"Oh Give Me a Home Where the Mathers Don't Roam," *Wings,* NBC, 1994.

"Sleepless in Nantucket," *Wings,* NBC, 1994.

"Sweeps Week," *NewsRadio* (also known as *The Station*), NBC, 1995.

"The Breakup," *NewsRadio* (also known as *The Station*), NBC, 1995.

"Star and Comet Collide! Giant Bugs Invade!," *The Naked Truth* (also known as *Wilde Again*), NBC, 1995.

Pearl, CBS, 1996.

Just Shoot Me!, NBC, 1997.

Three Sisters, NBC, 2001.

"The Easter Rebellion," *The Fighting Fitzgeralds,* NBC, 2001.

"Arianna," *My Big Fat Greek Life,* CBS, 2003.

"Val and Holly's Not Boyfriends," *What I Like About You,* The WB, 2004.

"Oh Baby," *Living with Fran,* The WB, 2005.

"Who's the Parent?," *Living with Fran,* The WB, 2005.

"Joey and the ESL," *Joey,* NBC, 2005.

"Joey and the Holding Hands," *Joey,* NBC, 2006.

"Joey and the Beard," *Joey,* NBC, 2006.

Also directed episodes of *Animaniacs* (also known as *Steven Spielberg Presents "Animaniacs"*), Fox; *Foley Square,* CBS; *Friends and Lovers; Getting Personal; Home Improvement,* ABC; *Hope & Gloria,* NBC; *The Hughleys,* ABC; *Likely Stories, Vol. 4; Mary Tyler Moore* (also known as *The Mary Tyler Moore Show*); *Minor Adjustments; Movie Stars,* The WB; *Mr. Rhodes,* NBC; *Room for Two,* ABC; *Soul Man,* ABC; *Together We Stand* (also known as *Nothing Is Easy*), CBS; *True Colors;* and *The Two of Us,* CBS.

Television Director; Pilots:

Sheila, CBS, 1977.

Father O Father, ABC, 1977.

A Dog's Life, NBC, 1979.

G.I.s, CBS, 1980.

Love, Natalie, NBC, 1980.

High Five, NBC, 1982.

In Security, CBS, 1982.

Back Together, CBS, 1984.

The Recovery Room, CBS, 1985.

Good Morning, Miss Bliss (also known as *What Now, Mrs. Davis*), NBC, 1987.

Julie Brown: The Show, CBS, 1989.

Drive, Fox, 2006.

Television Director; Other:

Sharing Richard (movie), CBS, 1988.

The Sweet Spot (miniseries), Comedy Central, 2002.

Television Appearances; Series:

Dr. Jerry Robinson, *The Bob Newhart Show,* CBS, 1972–76.

Franklin Hart, Jr., *9 to 5,* ABC, 1982–83.

George Bernstein–Flynn, *Three Sisters,* NBC, 2001–2002.

Television Appearances; Movies:

Carter Dowling, *How to Break Up a Happy Divorce,* NBC, 1976.

Andrew McLaren, *Mirror, Mirror,* NBC, 1979.

Phil Tanton, *Your Place ... or Mine,* CBS, 1983.

Pete Benfield, *Circle of Violence: A Family Drama* (also known as *Circle of Violence*), CBS, 1986.

Television Appearances; Miniseries:

Girard, *The Bastard* (also known as *The Kent Chronicles*), syndicated, 1978.

Television Appearances; Specials:

Stanley, "A Storm in Summer" (also known as "The Merchant of Scarsdale"), *Hallmark Hall of Fame* (also known as *Hallmark Television Playhouse*), NBC, 1970.

A World of Love, 1970.

Story Theatre, syndicated, 1971.

The Bob Newhart Show 19th Anniversary Special, CBS, 1991.

Voice, *Wisconsin: An American Portrait,* 2000.

"Bob Newhart: The Last Sane Man," *Biography,* Arts and Entertainment, 2001.

Himself, *Look Out Haskell, It's Real: The Making of "Medium Cool,"* 2001.

(Uncredited) Dr. Jerry Robinson (in archive footage), *On Stage at the Kennedy Center: The Mark Twain Prize,* PBS, 2002.

Intimate Portrait: Suzanne Pleshette, Lifetime, 2002.

TV Land Landmarks: Breaking the Mold, TV Land, 2004.

The 3rd Annual TV Land Awards (also known as *TV Land Awards: A Celebration of Classic TV*), TV Land, 2005.

Television Appearances; Pilots:

Chips, "The Pirates of Flounder Bay," *Summer Fun,* ABC, 1966.

Peter Stefan, *Elke,* CBS, 1971.

Tony Sheridan, *Dad's a Dog,* ABC, 1990.

George Bernstein–Flynn, *Three Sisters,* NBC, 2001.

Television Appearances; Episodic:

Boswell, "Morticia, the Writer," *The Addams Family,* ABC, 1965.

Proctor, "Oh, How We Danced," *Hey, Landlord,* 1967.

Larry Yorkin, "7 1/4: Part 2," *That Girl,* 1968.

Earl, "The Ransom," *Hawaii Five–0* (also known as *McGarrett*), 1970.

George Harvard, "Death Is a Seven Point Favorite," *McMillan & Wife,* 1971.

Doctor, "TV or Not TV," *Sanford and Son,* 1972.

"Mr. Right," *Good Heavens,* 1976.

Himself, *Stumpers!,* NBC, 1976.

Henry Stokes, "The Prison Game," *Visions,* 1977.

"The Borrowing," *George Burns Comedy Week,* CBS, 1985.

Calhoun Fletcher, "The Perfect Foil," *Murder, She Wrote,* CBS, 1986.

Voice of insurance agent, "Family Challenge," *Dinosaurs* (animated), ABC, 1991.

Jerry Robinson, "Better to Have Loved and Flossed," *Bob,* 1993.

(Uncredited) Theatre patron, "The One with the Screamer," *Friends,* NBC, 1997.

Peter, "Totally Tool Time," *Home Improvement,* ABC, 1997.

Dr. Robins, "The Cameo Episode," *George & Leo,* CBS, 1997.

Voice of Rabbi Katz, "Ron the Man," *Kim Possible* (animated; also known as *Disney's "Kim Possible"*), Disney Channel, 2003.

Himself, "Wacky Neighbors," *TV Land's Top Ten,* TV Land, 2005.

Also appeared in "U.S.A.," *Hollywood Television Theatre;* and as Charles Berkus in an episode of *Love & War.*

Film Appearances:

Perry, *Funnyman,* New Yorker, 1967.

Gus, *Medium Cool,* Paramount, 1969.

Himself, *A Session with the Committee,* 1969.

Mr. Bentley, *What Ever Happened to Aunt Alice?,* Cinerama, 1969.

Captain J. S. McWatt, *Catch–22,* Paramount, 1970.

Sergei, *Jennifer on My Mind,* United Artists, 1971.

Buck, *Fuzz,* United Artists, 1972.

Dr. Leonard Miller, *Serial,* Paramount, 1980.

Randall Kendall, *Nobody's Perfekt,* Columbia, 1981.

Ed Weinberger, *Man on the Moon* (also known as *Der Mondmann*), Universal, 1999.

Film Director:

Nobody's Perfekt, Columbia, 1981.

Police Academy 6: City under Siege, Warner Bros, 1989.

Stage Appearances:

(Off–Broadway debut) Member of ensemble, *The Premise,* The Premise, 1962.

(Broadway debut) Member of ensemble, *Story Theatre* (also known as *Paul Sills' "Story Theatre"*), Ambassador Theatre, 1970–71.

President Hale, *The White House Murder Case,* Circle in the Square Downtown, New York City, 1970.

Stage Director:

Oscar and Felix: A New Look at the Odd Couple, Geffen Playhouse, Westwood, CA, 2002.

WRITINGS

Screenplays:

(With John Korty) *Funnyman,* New Yorker, 1967.

BOTSFORD, Sara 1951–

PERSONAL

Born April 8, 1951, in Dobie, Ontario, Canada; married Alan Scarfe (an actor; divorced); children: two, including Jonathan Scarfe (an actor).

Addresses: *Agent*—Silver Massetti and Szatmary, 8730 West Sunset Blvd., Suite 440, West Hollywood, CA 90069.

Career: Actress, producer, director, and writer.

Awards, Honors: Genie Award nomination, best actress, Academy of Canadian Cinema and Television, 1983, for *By Design*; Gemini Award nomination, Academy of Canadian Cinema and Television, 1992, and Gemini Award, 1993, both best actress in a continuing leading dramatic role, for *E.N.G.*; Gemini Award nomination, best actress in a leading role in a dramatic program or miniseries, 1998, for *The Arrow*.

CREDITS

Television Appearances; Series:
Lilith McKechnie, *As the World Turns*, CBS, 1988, 1990.
Ann Hildebrandt, *E.N.G.*, Lifetime, 1990.
Mercedes DePedroso, *The Wright Verdicts*, CBS, 1995.
Norma St. Claire, *The Lot*, AMC, 1999.
Ellen Baines Heart, *Canooks*, 2007.

Television Appearances; Movies:
Maggie, *The Fighting Men* (also known as *Men of Steel*), CBC, 1977.
Tricia, *Crossbar*, CBC, 1979.
Janice, *Fatal Memories* (also known as *The Eileen Franklin Story*), NBC, 1992.
Eve, *My Breast*, CBS, 1994.
Heather Allen, *Dangerous Offender: The Marlene Moore Story*, CBC, 1996.
Dead Innocent (also known as *Eye*), HBO, 1996.
Bonnie, *The Fixer*, Showtime, 1998.
Mrs. Farber, *Our Guys: Outrage at Glen Ridge* (also known as *Outrage in Glen Ridge*), ABC, 1999.
Harriet Nelson, *Ricky Nelson: Original Teen Idol* (also known as *Ricky Nelson* and *The Ricky Nelson Story*), VH1, 1999.
Meredith Farley, *Burn: The Robert Wraight Story* (also known as *Terres brulantes: L'histoire de Robert Wraight*), CTV, 2003.

Television Appearances; Miniseries:
Kate O'Hara, *The Arrow* (also known as *Project Arrow*), CBC, 1997.
Mrs. Kathleen Sinclair, *Trudeau*, CBC, 2002.

Television Appearances; Episodic:
Lucy Rogers, *The Guiding Light*, CBS, three episodes, 1984.
Angelica, "The Lock Box," *The Equalizer*, CBS, 1985.
Eleanor Purvis, "A Matter of Honour," *Street Legal*, CBC, 1987.
Dakota Graham, "Family Passions," *Madison*, Global, 1994.
Rhonda, "My Momma's Back," *Pointman*, syndicated, 1995.
Mayor Anita Ross, "The Weaker Sex," *Sliders*, Fox, 1995.
"A Question of Truth," *New York News*, CBS, 1995.

Lee Colwell, "A Rock and a Hard Place," *Black Harbour*, CBC, 1997.
Lee Colwell, "You Can't Get There from Here," *Black Harbour*, CBC, 1997.
Diane (some sources cite Sarah) Posner, "Passion," *Law & Order*, NBC, 1997.
"A Lady in a Black Dress," *Beyond Belief: Fact or Fiction*, Fox, 1998.
Maria Schviller, "Self–Inflicted," *Total Recall 2070* (also known as *Total Recall: The Series*), Showtime, 1999.
Dr. Gail Cowlings, "The Shroud," *The Outer Limits* (also known as *The New Outer Limits*), Showtime and syndicated, 1999.
Attorney Post, "The Green Monster," *Ally McBeal*, Fox, 1999.
Jenny McGarry, "Five Votes Down," *The West Wing*, NBC, 1999.
Judge Evelyn LaVoy, "Media Relations," *Family Law*, CBS, 2000.
Laura Boulton, "The God Thing," *Judging Amy*, CBS, 2000.
Lucia Burns, "Don't Fence Me In," *The District*, CBS, 2001.
Lauren Ruder, "Believers," *Crossing Jordan*, NBC, 2001.
Helen Walsh, "Healthy McDowell Movement," *NYPD Blue*, ABC, 2002.
Elinor Galbraithe, "Live by the Sword," *Tom Stone* (also known as *Stone Undercover*), CBC, 2003.
Roberta Kanner, "Party Girl," *Without a Trace* (also known as *W.A.T.*), CBS, 2005.
Allen Barnes, "Loyal," *The L Word*, Showtime, 2005.
Allen Barnes, "Land Ahoy," *The L Word*, Showtime, 2005.
Susan Weinar, "The Running Man," *Numb3rs* (also known as *Num3ers*), CBS, 2006.
Guest star, "Moon Giver," *Three Minutes over Milford*, ABC Family Channel, 2006.
Dr. Helen Berkley, "Brothers in Arms," *Navy NCIS: Naval Criminal Investigative Service* (also known as *NCIS* and *NCIS: Naval Criminal Investigative Service*), CBS, 2007.

Television Appearances; Other:
Mrs. Jacobs, "The Hand Me Down Kid," *ABC Afterschool Special*, ABC, 1983.
Estelle Burroughs, *Sophie*, 2007.
Ellen Baines Heart, *Canooks* (pilot), 2007.

Television Work:
Associate producer, *E.N.G.* (series), Lifetime, 1990.
Producer and director, *Canooks* (pilot), 2007.
Producer and director, *Canooks* (series), 2007.

Film Appearances:
Angie Olaffsen, *By Design* (also known as *Sur mesure*), Atlantic Releasing, 1982.

Kelly Leonard, *Deadly Eyes* (also known as *Night Eyes* and *The Rats*), Warner Bros., 1982.

Gail Phillips, *Still of the Night*, Metro–Goldwyn–Mayer/ United Artists, 1982.

Ridley Taylor, *Murder by Phone* (also known as *Bells, The Calling*, and *Hell's Bells*), New World, 1982.

Maude Ryan, *The Gunrunner*, New World Home Video, 1984.

Barbara, *Legal Eagles*, Universal, 1986.

Lady Sarah Billings, *Jumpin' Jack Flash*, Twentieth Century–Fox, 1986.

Je t'aime woman, *Thick as Thieves* (also known as *Comme des voleurs*), 1991.

Obstruction of Justice, Oasis International, 1995.

Mrs. Barry and Frau Schiller, *Anne: Journey to Green Gables*, Sullivan Entertainment, 2004.

Christine Lord, *Tremors 4: The Legend Begins*, Universal Studios Home Video, 2004.

Mrs. Carmichael, *Eulogy*, Lions Gate Films, 2004.

Kathy Williams, *The Fog*, Columbia, 2005.

Stage Appearances:

Isabelle Bird, Joyce, and Nell, *Top Girls*, New York Shakespeare Festival, Estelle R. Newman Theatre, Public Theatre, New York City, 1983.

Charlotte, *The Real Thing*, Plymouth Theatre, New York City, c. 1984–85.

Kate Miller, *The Cover of Life*, American Place Theatre, New York City, 1994.

Also appeared as Tamara de Lempicka in an off– Broadway production of *Tamara*.

RECORDINGS

Videos:

You're on the Set of "Tremors 4: The Legend Begins, Universal Studios Home Video, 2004.

WRITINGS

Television Series:
Canooks, 2007.

Television Pilots:
Canooks, 2007.

BRADSHAW, John 1952–
(Jon Bradshaw)

PERSONAL

Born in 1952, in Stratford, Ontario, Canada.

Addresses: *Agent*—Great North Artists Management, Inc., 350 Duponte, Toronto M5R 1V9 Canada. *Manager*—Wisdom Literary, 287 South Robertson Blvd., Suite 258, Beverly Hills, CA 90211.

Career: Director, editor, producer, and screenwriter.

Awards, Honors: Independent Spirit Award nomination (with Alan Rudolph), best screenplay, Independent Features Project, 1989, for *The Moderns*; Video Premiere Award nomination, best director, DVD Exclusive Awards, 2001, for *Full Disclosure*.

CREDITS

Film Director:
Not Another Love Story, Canadian Filmmakers Distribution Centre, 1978.

That's My Baby (also known as *Je veux un bebe*), Gemini Film Productions, 1984.

The Big Slice, New City Releasing, 1991.

Specimen, Combustion Film Productions, 1996.

Lethal Tender (also known as *Deadly Currents*), Republic Pictures, 1997.

The Undertaker's Wedding (also known as *Ji epouse un croque–mort*), Astra Cinema, 1997.

Reaper (also known as *The Reaper*), World International Network, 1998.

Breakout (also known as *Breakout: Batteries Included* and *3 ninjas et l'invention du siecle*), 1998.

Triggerman, Trimuse Entertainment, 2001.

Full Disclosure, First Look Pictures Releasing, 2001.

Sleeping Dogs Lie (short), 2006.

Film First Assistant Director:
Fireballs, 1987.

Still Life (also known as *Art Killer Framed* and *Still Life: The Fine Art of Murder*), 1988.

Hostile Takeover (also known as *The Devastator* and *The Office Party*), MTI Home Video, 1988.

Red Blooded American Girl, Prism Pictures, 1990.

The Swordsman, 1993.

Red Hot, 1993.

April One, Astral Films, 1993.

Stalked (also known as *Traquee*), Republic Pictures, 1994.

Relative Fear (also known a *Le silence d'Adam* and *The Child*), Republic Pictures, 1994.

Death Wish V: The Face of Death (also known as *Death Wish 5: The Face of Death* and *Death Wish: The Face of Death*), Trimark Pictures, 1994.

The Paper Boy (also known as *The Paperboy*), Allegro Films, 1994.

No Exit (also known as *Fatal Combat*), No Exit Productions, 1995.

Meet Prince Charming, New City Releasing, 1999.

Film Assistant Director:
Soul Survivor, 1994.
Waiting for Michelangelo, 1995.

Film Second Assistant Director:
Caribe, Miramax, 1987.

Film Additional Unit Director:
Gladiator Cop (also known as *Gladiator Cop: The Swordsman II*), Monarch Home Video, 1994.

Film Editor:
Not Another Love Story (also known as *Je veux un bebe*), Canadian Filmmakers Distribution Centre, 1978.
That's My Baby, Gemini Film Productions, 1984.

Film Producer:
Not Another Love Story, Canadian Filmmakers Distribution Centre, 1978.

Film Coproducer:
Waiting for Michelangelo, 1995.

Film Associate Producer:
No Exit (also known as *Fatal Combat*), No Exit Productions, 1995.
Full Disclosure, First Look Pictures Releasing, 2001.

Television First Assistant Director; Movies:
Murder One, 1988.
(Second unit) *Liar's Edge,* 1992.
The Legend of the Ruby Silver, ABC, 1996.
Happy Face Murders, Showtime, 1999.
Zebra Lounge (also known as *Rendez–vous au Zebra Lounge*), HBO, 2001.
Hunger Point, Lifetime, 2003.
Martha, Inc.: The Story of Martha Stewart (also known as *Driven to Succeed* and *Martha Stewart— L'obcession du success*), NBC, 2003.
Crazy for Christmas, Lifetime, 2005.

Television Director; Movies:
The Battle of Vimy Ridge art 1: Setting the Stage, 1997.
The Battle of Vimy Ridge art 2: Keys to Victory, 1997.
The Battle of Vimy Ridge art 3: The Battle Looms, 1997.
20.13 ord im Blitzlicht (also known as *2013—Thou Shalt Not Kill*), 2000.
Killing Moon, 2000.
Between Truth and Lies, Lifetime, 2006.
Obituary, Lifetime, 2006.
They Come Back, Lifetime, 2007.

Television Work; Movies:
Footage provider, *A Family Divided,* NBC, 1995.

WRITINGS

Screenplays:
Not Another Love Story, Canadian Filmmakers Distribution Centre, 1978.
(Narration only; as Jon Bradshaw) *She Dances Alone,* 1981.
That's My Baby (also known as *Je veux un bebe*), 1984.
(As Jon Bradshaw; with Alan Rudolph) *The Moderns,* Alive Films, 1988.
The Big Slice, New City Releasing, 1991.
Specimen, Combustion Film Productions, 1996.
The Undertaker's Wedding (also known as *J'i epouse un croque–mort*), Astra Cinema, 1997.

Film Stories:
(As Jon Bradshaw) *80 Blocks from Tiffany,* 1979.

BROWN, George H.
    See WERTMULLER, Lina

BURROWS, James 1940–
    (Jim Burrows, Jimmy Burrows)

PERSONAL

Full name, James Edward Burrows; born December 30, 1940, in Los Angeles, CA; son of Abe (a writer and director) and Ruth (maiden name, Levinson) Burrows; married Linda Solomon, July 17, 1981 (divorced, 1993); married Debbie Easton, 1997; children: three, including Ellie. *Education:* Oberlin College, B.A., 1962; Yale University, M.F.A., 1965.

Addresses: *Agent*—Robert Broder, International Creative Management, 10250 Constellation Way, 9th Floor, Los Angeles, CA 90067.

Career: Director and producer. Worked as stage manager for his father, Abe Burrows; Arlington Park Theatre, Arlington Park, IL, stage director, 1970s; Charles Burrows Charles Productions, Los Angeles, cofounder, 1982; Three Sisters Entertainment, producer.

Awards, Honors: Emmy Awards, outstanding directing in a comedy series, 1980, 1981, Emmy Award nomination, outstanding directing in a comedy series, 1982, and Directors Guild of America Award nomination, outstanding directing in a comedy series, 1982, all for *Taxi;* Emmy Awards, outstanding directing in a comedy series, 1983, 1991, and outstanding comedy series (with others), 1983, 1984, 1989, 1991, Emmy Award nominations, outstanding directing in a comedy series, 1984, 1985, 1986, 1987, 1988, 1989, 1990, 1992, 1993, and outstanding comedy series (with others), 1985, 1986, 1987, 1988, 1990, 1992, 1993, Directors Guild of America Awards, outstanding directing in a comedy series, 1984, 1991, and Directors Guild of America Award nominations, outstanding directing in a comedy series, 1990, 1992, 1993, all for *Cheers;* Emmy Award nomination (with others), outstanding informational special, 1990, for *Cheers: Special 200th Episode Celebration;* Directors Guild of America Award (with others), outstanding directing in a comedy series, 1994, for *Frasier;* Emmy Award nomination, outstanding directing in a comedy series, 1995, and Directors Guild of America Award nomination, outstanding directing in a comedy series, 1996, both for *Friends;* Emmy Award nomination, outstanding directing in a comedy series, 1996, for *3rd Rock from the Sun;* Creative Achievement Award, American Comedy Awards, 1996; Emmy Award nomination, outstanding directing in a comedy series, and Directors Guild of America Award nomination, outstanding directing in a comedy series, both 1998, for *Dharma & Greg;* Emmy Award (with others), outstanding comedy series, 2000, Emmy Award nominations, outstanding directing for a comedy series, 1999, 2000, 2001, 2002, 2003, 2005, and outstanding comedy series (with others), 2001, 2002, 2003, 2004, 2005, Directors Guild of America Award (with others), outstanding directing in a comedy series, 2001, Directors Guild of America Award nominations, outstanding directing in a comedy series, 1999, 2000, 2002, 2003, 2004, 2006, and Golden Laurel Award nominations (with others), television producer of the year in episodic category, Producers Guild of America, 2003, 2004, all for *Will & Grace;* Special Lifetime Achievement Award, Banff Television Festival, 2003; Career Tribute Award, U.S. Comedy Festival, 2006; inducted into Academy of Television Arts and Sciences Hall of Fame, 2006.

CREDITS

Television Producer; Series:
(With others; and cocreator) *Cheers,* NBC, 1982–84.

Television Executive Producer; Series:
(With others) *Cheers,* NBC, 1984–93.
All Is Forgiven, NBC, 1986.
The Tortellis, NBC, 1987.
(With others) *Flesh 'n' Blood,* NBC, 1991.
The Secret Lives of Men, 1998.
Will & Grace, NBC, 1999–2006.
The Class, CBS, 2006–2007.

Television Director; Series:
The Bob Newhart Show, CBS, 1975–77.

Laverne & Shirley (also known as *Laverne & Shirley & Company* and *Laverne & Shirley & Friends*), ABC, 1976–77.
Taxi, ABC, 1978–82, then NBC, 1982–83.
Cheers, NBC, 1982–93.
Frasier, NBC, 1993–97.
Friends, NBC, between 1994 and 1998.
NewsRadio (also known as *The Station*), NBC, 1995–96.
Will & Grace, NBC, 1998–2006.
The Class, CBS, 2006–2007.

Television Director; Episodic:
The Mary Tyler Moore Show, CBS, 1970–77.
Friends and Lovers (also known as *Paul Sand in "Friends and Lovers"*), CBS, 1974–75.
The Tony Randall Show, ABC, 1976.
Busting Loose, CBS, 1977.
"John's Mother," *The Betty White Show,* CBS, 1977.
"The Job," *Rhoda,* CBS, 1977.
"One Is a Number," *Rhoda,* CBS, 1977.
Szysznyk, CBS, 1977.
"Christmas," *Lou Grant,* CBS, 1977.
"Ida Alone," *Rhoda,* CBS, 1978.
"All Work and No Play," *Rhoda,* CBS, 1978.
We've Got Each Other, CBS, 1978.
"Play Misty for John," *The Betty White Show,* CBS, 1978.
On Our Own, CBS, 1978.
Free Country, ABC, 1978.
Husbands, Wives and Lovers, CBS, 1978.
"I Do," *A New Kind of Family,* 1979.
"Punt, Pass, and Kick," *The Stockard Channing Show,* CBS, 1980.
Good Time Harry, NBC, 1980.
"All You Need Is Love," *Night Court,* NBC, 1984.
Premiere episode, *All Is Forgiven,* NBC, 1986.
Premiere episode, *The Hogan Family* (also known as *The Hogans, Valerie,* and *Valerie's Family*), NBC, 1986.
Premiere episode, *The Marshall Chronicles,* ABC, 1990.
Flying Blind, Fox, 1992.
Partners, Fox, 1995–96.
The Preston Episodes, 1995.
"Brains and Eggs," *3rd Rock from the Sun* (also known as *3rd Rock* and *Life as We Know It*), NBC, 1996.
"See Dick Run," *3rd Rock from the Sun* (also known as *3rd Rock* and *Life as We Know It*), NBC, 1996.
Chicago Sons, 1997–98.
George & Leo, CBS, 1997–98.
"The Audition," *Union Square,* NBC, 1997.
Conrad Bloom, 1998.
The Secret Lives of Men, 1998.
Ladies Man, CBS, 1999.
Cursed (also known as *The Weber Show*), NBC, 2000.
The Stones, CBS, 2004.
"Everything I Know About Men," *Courting Alex,* CBS, 2006.
"Substitute, *Teachers,* NBC, 2006.

Also directed episodes of *The Associates; Best of the West; Cafe Americain; Dharma & Greg,* ABC; *Fay,* NBC; *Jesse,* NBC; *Men Behaving Badly* (also known as *It's a Man World),* NBC; *Phyllis,* CBS; and *The Ted Knight Show,* CBS.

Television Director; Pilots:

Bumpers, NBC, 1977.
Calling Dr. Storm, M.D., NBC, 1977.
Roosevelt and Truman, CBS, 1977.
The Plant Family, CBS, 1978.
Your Place or Mine?, CBS, 1978.
Butterflies, NBC, 1979.
Best of the West, ABC, 1981.
Every Stray Dog and Kid, NBC, 1981.
Goodbye Doesn't Mean Forever, NBC, 1982.
At Your Service, NBC, 1984.
P.O.P., NBC, 1984.
"In the Lions Den," *CBS Summer Playhouse,* CBS, 1987.
The Tortellis, NBC, 1987.
Dear John, 1988.
Channel 99, NBC, 1988.
Down Home, NBC, 1990.
Wings, NBC, 1990.
The Boys Are Back (also known as *The Fanelli Boys),* NBC, 1990.
Roc, Fox, 1991.
Flesh 'n' Blood, NBC, 1991.
Pacific Station, NBC, 1991.
Frasier, NBC, 1993.
Friends, NBC, 1994.
NewsRadio (also known as *The Station),* NBC, 1995.
Partners, Fox, 1995.
Caroline in the City (also known as *Caroline),* NBC, 1995.
Hudson Street, ABC, 1995.
Pearl, 1996.
The Nerd, NBC, 1996.
Fired Up, 1997.
Veronica's Closet, NBC, 1997.
Will & Grace, NBC, 1998.
Stark Raving Mad, NBC, 1999.
Madigan Men, ABC, 2000.
Cursed (also known as *The Weber Show),* NBC, 2000.
Dexter Prep, ABC, 2002.
Good Morning, Miami, NBC, 2002.
Bram and Alice, CBS, 2002.
Two and a Half Men, CBS, 2003.
Beverly Hills S.U.V., NBC, 2004.
Four Kings, NBC, 2006.
The Class, CBS, 2006.
Back to You, Fox, 2007.
Traveling in Packs, ABC, 2007.
The Mastersons of Manhattan, NBC, 2007.
The Rich Inner Life of Penelope Cloud, CBS, 2007.
The Big Bang Theory, CBS, 2007.

Television Executive Producer; Pilots:

Tikiville, NBC, 2001.
Last Dance, NBC, 2001.

Television Director; Specials:

Big Shots in America, NBC, 1985.
Segment director, *Time Warner Presents the Earth Day Special,* ABC, 1990.
Segment director, "Cheers," "Disneyland's 35th Anniversary Celebration," *Disneyland* (also known as *Disney's Wonderful World, The Disney Sunday Movie, The Magical World of Disney, Walt Disney, Walt Disney Presents, Walt Disney's Wonderful World of Color,* and *The Wonderful World of Disney),* NBC, 1990.
(And executive producer) *Cheers: Special 200th Episode Celebration,* NBC, 1990.

Television Director; Movies:

(As Jim Burrows) *More than Friends* (also known as *Love Me and I'll Be Your Best Friend),* ABC, 1978.

Television Appearances; Specials:

Cheers: Special 200th Episode Celebration, NBC, 1990.
Intimate Portrait: Lea Thompson, Lifetime, 1998.
The "Frasier" Story, 1999.
Influences: From Yesterday to Today, CBS, 1999.
Ted Danson: One Lucky Guy, Arts and Entertainment, 2000.
Inside TV Land: The Pitch, TV Land, 2001.
Cheers, Arts and Entertainment, 2001.

Television Appearances; Episodic:

Agent, "The Lady in Red," *Rhoda,* CBS, 1974.
Maintenance man, "Halls of Hartley," *The Bob Newhart Show,* CBS, 1976.
Guest, *The Midnight Special,* 1981.
(Uncredited) Man who knocks, "One for the Road," *Cheers,* NBC, 1993.
(Uncredited) Film director, "The One with the Butt," *Friends,* NBC, 1994.
Inside the Actors Studio, Bravo, 2003.
(As Jimmy Burrows) "Valerie Bonds with the Cast," *The Comeback,* HBO, 2005.
(As Jimmy Burrows) "Valerie Shines under Stress," *The Comeback,* HBO, 2005.

Television Appearances; Pilots:

(As Jimmy Burrows) *The Comeback,* HBO, 2005.

Television Appearances; Awards Presentations:

The 43rd Annual Primetime Emmy Awards Presentation, Fox, 1991.
The 10th Annual American Comedy Awards, ABC, 1996.

Television Appearances; Miniseries:
TV Land Moguls, TV Land, 2004.
The 100 Most Memorable TV Moments, TV Land, 2004.

Stage Work:
Assistant stage manager, *Holly Golightly,* 1967.
Stage manager, *Forty Carats,* Morosco Theatre, New York City, 1968–70.
Director, *The Castro Complex,* Stairway Theatre, 1970.
Director, *Last of the Red Hot Lovers,* Arlington Park Theatre, Arlington Heights, IL, 1972–73.
Director, *Goodbye, Charlie,* Arlington Park Theatre, 1972–73.
Director, *Charley's Aunt,* Arlington Park Theatre, 1972–73.
Director, *The Man Who Came to Dinner,* Steppenwolf Theatre Company, Chicago, IL, then Barbican Theatre, London, both 1998.

Also directed off–Broadway dinner theatre productions.

Major Tours:
Stage manager for a touring production of *Cactus Flower,* U.S. cities.

Film Director:
Partners (also known as *Zwei irre typen auf heisser spur*), Paramount, 1982.

Film Appearances:
Broadway: Beyond the Golden Age (documentary; also known as *B.G.A. 2* and *Broadway: The Golden Age Two*), Second Act Productions, 2007.

WRITINGS

Television Series:
Cheers, NBC, 1982–93.

OTHER SOURCES

Books:
Newsmakers, Issue 3, Thomson Gale, 2005.

Periodicals:
Broadcasting and Cable, May 22, 1995, p. 30; January 24, 2005, p. 4A.
Entertainment Weekly, March 26, 2004, pp. 30–36.
Newsweek, September 11, 1995, p. 73.

C

CAHILL, Steve 1964–

PERSONAL

Original name, Stanley Fritz; born September 21, 1964. *Education:* New York University, M.F.A.; attended the U.S. Naval Academy, 1983–85.

Addresses: *Agent*—Silver, Massetti and Szatmary, 8730 West Sunset Blvd., Suite 440, West Hollywood, CA 90069.

Career: Actor.

CREDITS

Film Appearances:
Frank, *A Thousand Acres,* Buena Vista, 1997.
Lieutenant at Pentagon, *Peal Harbor* (also known as *Pearl Harbour*), Buena Vista, 2001.
Chris, *The Inner Circle,* PorchLight Entertainment, 2003.

Television Appearances; Series:
Bascombe Moody, *One Life to Live,* ABC, 1994.
Frank, *Frank Leaves for the Orient,* Comedy Central, 1999.
Assistant district attorney Don Harrison, *NYPD Blue,* ABC, 2001–2002.

Television Appearances; Miniseries:
Torb Macdonald, *J.F.K.: Reckless Youth,* ABC, 1993.
Hue, *Seduced by Madness: The Diane Borchadt Story* (also known as *Seduced by Madness*), NBC, 1996.

Television Appearances; Movies:
Andy Chase, *Color Me Perfect,* Lifetime, 1996.
Will Fontaine, *Close to Dangerous,* ABC, 1997.

Ed Hawkins, *Goldrush: A Real Life Alaskan Adventure* (also known as *Gold Rush!*), ABC, 1998.

Television Appearances; Episodic:
Beverly Hills 90210, Fox, 1994.
Todd, *Can't Hurry Love,* CBS, 1995.
Water guy, *Newsradio,* NBC, 1995.
The Single Guy, NBC, 1996.
Dave, *High Incident,* ABC, 1996.
Tom "T. J." Jansen, "Life's Too Short," *Party of Five,* Fox, 1997.
Dr. Brian Haywood, "The Murder of Mark Sloan," *Diagnosis Murder,* CBS, 1997.
Brent Morrison, "Out and In," *Union Square,* NBC, 1998.
Stan, "Estrogen," *Fantasy Island,* UPN, 1998.
Bryce Kilbourne, *DiResta,* UPN, 1998.
Attorney for the co–op, "Free Dental," *The Practice,* ABC, 1999.
Patrick Wells, "Drew's Reunion," *The Drew Carey Show,* ABC, 1999.
Family Law, CBS, 2000.
Michael, *3rd Rock from the Sun,* NBC, 2000.
Dr. Bertolf, "Ye Olde Freedom Inn," *Judging Amy,* CBS, 2003.

CAMPBELL, Graeme 1954–

PERSONAL

Born 1954, in Montreal, Quebec, Canada.

Career: Director, writer, and film editor.

Awards, Honors: CableACE Award nomination, best episode of an anthology, National Cable Television Association, 1991, for "The Earthmen," *The Ray Bradbury*

Theatre; Gemini Award, best director of a dramatic program or miniseries, Academy of Canadian Cinema and Television, 1992, for *Deadly Betrayal: The Bruce Curtis Story;* Gemini Award, best director of a children's or youth program or series, 2005, for "You Can't Always Get What You Want," *Instant Star.*

CREDITS

Television Director; Series:
Instant Star, CTV, multiple episodes, beginning 2005.

Television Director; Movies:
Deadly Betrayal: The Bruce Curtis Story (also known as *Journey into Darkness: The Bruce Curtis Story*), NBC, 1991.
The Disappearance of Vonnie, CBS, 1994.
The Man in the Attic, CBS and Showtime, 1995.
Deadlocked: Escape from Zone 14 (also known as *Deadlock 2*), Fox, 1995.
Talk to Me, ABC, 1996.
Unforgivable, CBS, 1996.
Volcano: Fire on the Mountain (also known as *Fire on the Mountain*), ABC, 1997.
Country Justice (also known as *Family Rescue*), CBS, 1997.
Dream House, UPN, 1998.
At the Mercy of a Stranger, CBS, 1999.
Out of Sync (also known as *Lip Service*), VH1, 2000.
Dangerous Child (also known as *Un fils en colere*), Lifetime, 2001.
Guilt by Association (also known as *Coupable par amour*), Court TV, 2002.
Going for Broke, Lifetime, 2003.

Television Director; Episodic:
"'Til Death Do Us Part," *The Hidden Room,* Lifetime, 1991.
"The Earthmen," *The Ray Bradbury Theatre* (also known as *Mystery Theatre, The Bradbury Trilogy, Le monde fantastique de Ray Bradbury,* and *Ray Bradbury presente*), HBO, 1992.
"Peter Peletire," *Top Cops,* 1992.
"Fair Trade," *North of 60,* CBC, 1992.
"Evelyn," *Road to Avonlea* (also known as *Avonlea* and *Tales from Avonlea*), Disney Channel, 1992.
"By the Book," *The Odyssey,* CBC, 1992.
"Smokescreen," *Ready or Not* (also known as *Les premieres fois*), Showtime, 1993.
"Double Talk," *Ready or Not* (also known as *Les premieres fois*), Showtime, 1993.
"Wild Life," *Ready or Not* (also known as *Les premieres fois*), Showtime, 1993.
"The Big Gulp," *Ready or Not* (also known as *Les premieres fois*), Showtime, 1993.
"Challenge," *Kung Fu: The Legend Continues,* 1993.

"Out of the Woods," *Kung Fu: The Legend Continues,* 1994.
"Enter the Tiger," *Kung Fu: The Legend Continues,* 1994.
"Living Hell," *The Outer Limits* (also known as *The New Outer Limits*), Showtime and syndicated, 1995.
"Sixteen Candles," *Twice in a Lifetime,* PAX, 1999.
"Ashes to Ashes," *Twice in a Lifetime,* PAX, 1999.
"Double Exposure," *Twice in a Lifetime,* PAX, 1999.
Dooley Gardens, 1999.
"Meaning of Death," *Mutant X,* syndicated, 2001.
"Crime of the New Century," *Mutant X,* syndicated, 2001.

Also directed episodes of *Degrassi: The Next Generation* (also known as *Degrassi—La nouvelle generation*), Noggin; *The Eleventh Hour,* CTV; *Naturally Sadie,* CTV; *Strange Days at Blake Holsey High* (also known as *Black Hole High*), Discovery Kids Channel; and *Street Justice,* syndicated.

Television Director; Other:
G–Saviour (live–action special; also known as *Gundam Savior*), 1999.
Everest (miniseries), 2007.

Film Director:
Into the Fire (also known as *Legend of Lone Wolf* and *The Legend of Wolf Lodge*), Moviestore Entertainment, 1988.
Still Life (also known as *Art Killer Framed* and *Still Life: The Fine Art of Murder*), Prism Entertainment, 1988.
Blood Relations, Miramax, 1988.
Murder One, Miramax, 1988.
Nico the Unicorn, Kingsborough Greenlight Pictures, 1998.

Film Editor:
Cimarrones, 1982.
Cowboys Claim, 1985.

WRITINGS

Screenplays:
Cowboys Claim, 1985.
Still Life (also known as *Art Killer Framed* and *Still Life: The Fine Art of Murder*), Prism Entertainment, 1988.

CAMPBELL, Ken Hudson 1963–
(Ken Campbell)

PERSONAL

Born April 6, 1963.

Addresses: *Agent*—TalentWorks, 3500 West Olive Ave., Suite 1400, Burbank, CA 91505; Danis Panaro Nist, 9201 West Olympic Blvd., Beverly Hills, CA 90212.

Career: Actor and comedian. Member of Second City, Chicago, IL. Founder of the improvisational comedy group Contents under Pressure. Appeared in advertisements and provided the voice of Bob the baby for various advertisements.

CREDITS

Film Appearances:
Santa, *Home Alone*, Twentieth Century–Fox, 1990.
Man in hallway, *Groundhog Day*, Columbia, 1993.
Seaman Buckman, *Down Periscope* (also known as *Abajo el periscopio, Cilgin denizalti, Giu le mani dal mio periscopio, Locos a bordo, Mission—Rohr frei!, Nagi peryskop, Nao mexas no meu periscopio, Periskope dol!, Perskooppi pystyyn, Titta, vi dyker!, Touche pas a mon periscope, Tuez a viz ala,* and *Y a–t–il un commandant pour sauver la Navy?*), Twentieth Century–Fox, 1996.
First wolf, *The Jungle Book: Mowgli's Story* (also known as *Das Dschungelbuch: Mowglis Abenteuer*), Buena Vista Home Video, 1998.
(As Ken Campbell) Max Lennert, *Armageddon* (also known as *Armageddon—Das jungste Gericht* and *Armageddon—giudizio finale*), Buena Vista, 1998.
Shangri–La, 1998.
(As Ken Campbell) Eliot Rosewater and Gilbert, *Breakfast of Champions*, Warner Bros., 1999.
(As Ken Campbell) Biker, *Coyote Ugly* (also known as *Coyote Bar, Coyote Girls, Show Bar, El Bar Coyote, Le ragazze del Coyote Ugly, Sakaltanya,* and *Wygrane marzenia*), Buena Vista, 2000.
(As Ken Campbell) Hal (some sources cite Al), *The Ladies Man* (also known as *The Ladies' Man*), Paramount, 2000.
(As Ken Campbell) Voice of baker, *Joseph: King of Dreams* (animated musical; also known as *Giuseppe il re dei sogni, Joosef—unten kuningas, Jose: El rey de los suenos, Josef—droemmarnas konung,* and *Joseph—Koning der Traeume*), DreamWorks Home Entertainment/Universal Home Video, 2000.
(As Ken Campbell) Voice of Po, *Titan A.E.* (animated; also known as *Planet Earth, Titan, Titan A.E.: After Earth, Titan: After Earth,* and *Titan—Depois da destruicao da terra*), Twentieth Century–Fox, 2000.
(As Ken Campbell) Animal control officer, *Dr. Dolittle 2* (also known as *Doctor Dolittle 2, DR2, DR.2, Docteur Dolittle 2, Elaeintohtori 2,* and *Il Dottor Dolittle 2*), Twentieth Century–Fox, 2001.
(As Ken Campbell) Police officer in gym, *Showtime* (also known as *Flics en direct, Showtime, policias en TV,* and *Showtime—Vegtelen & keptelen*), Warner Bros., 2002.

(As Ken Campbell) Tom, *Boat Trip*, Artisan Entertainment, 2002.
(As Ken Campbell) Chester, *Street of Pain* (short film), AtomFilms, 2003.
Sean, *A One Time Thing*, Trust Ranch Studios, 2004.
(As Ken Campbell) Writer, *Bewitched*, Columbia, 2005.

Television Appearances; Series:
Animal (Lust), *Herman's Head*, Fox, 1991–94.
Eddie, *Local Heroes*, Fox, 1996.
Voice of Barry, *God, the Devil and Bob* (animated; also known as *Dieu, le diable et Bob*), NBC, 2000.
Voice of Baby Bob, *Baby Bob* (also known as *Bob: O bebe falante*), CBS, 2002–2003.

Television Appearances; Miniseries:
Dr. Tom Manton, *Chiefs*, CBS, 1983.
Richard Henry Lee, *George Washington*, CBS, 1984.

Television Appearances; Movies:
Crash, ABC, 1978.
Member of the ensemble, *Life as We Know It!*, 1991.
(As Ken Campbell) Bruce, *Under Wraps*, Disney Channel, 1997.
Security guard, "Happy Birthday," *On the Edge*, Showtime, 2001.

Television Appearances; Specials:
Comedy Central Spotlight: Kelsey Grammer, Comedy Central, 1996.

Television Appearances; Episodic:
Voice of Crazy Lou, "Leader of the Pack," *Dinosaurs*, ABC, 1992.
Ken, "The Seven," *Seinfeld*, NBC, 1996.
Voice, "Exile in Guyville," *Duckman* (animated; also known as *Duckman: Private Dick/Family Man*), USA Network, 1996.
Roland (a cab driver), "A Year in the Life," *The Naked Truth* (also known as *Wilde Again*), NBC, 1997.
Gil, "Caroline and the Drycleaner," *Caroline in the City* (also known as *Caroline*), NBC, 1998.
Glenn (a bus driver), "The Blank Page," *Strangers with Candy*, Comedy Central, 2000.
(As Ken Campbell) Joe (a police officer), "The Free Lunch," *My Big Fat Greek Life* (also known as *My Big Fat Greek Wedding, Casamento grego—A serie,* and *Kreikkalainen naimakauppa*), CBS, 2003.
(As Ken Campbell) Roland Huff, "Blessed Are They," *The Practice*, ABC, 2003.
(As Ken Campbell) Roland Huff, "Cause of Action," *The Practice*, ABC, 2003.
(As Ken Campbell) Roland Huff, "The Heat of the Passion," *The Practice*, ABC, 2003.
(As Ken Campbell) Roland Huff, "The Lonely People," *The Practice*, ABC, 2003.

(As Ken Campbell) Spencer, "Bear Drop Soup," *The Loop,* Fox, 2006.

Appeared as Jerry Potsweiler, *Fantasy Island,* ABC.

Television Appearances; Pilots:
Detective Furie, *Cops and Robin,* NBC, 1978.
Animal (Lust), *Herman's Head,* Fox, 1991.

Appeared as Willy in *Manhattan Man,* Fox; also appeared in *Us?,* NBC; and *World on a String,* Fox.

Television Work; Series:
Creative consultant, *Local Heroes,* Fox, 1996.

Major Tours:
Appeared in tours with Second City.

RECORDINGS

Video Games:
Voice, *The X–Fools,* 1998.

CAMPBELL, Nicholas 1952–
    (Nick Campbell)

PERSONAL

Born March 24, 1952, in Toronto, Ontario, Canada; married Reimi Kobyashi (divorced); married Harmeet Alhuwalia (separated).

Career: Actor, director, and writer. Also worked as assistant director.

Awards, Honors: Genie Award nominations, best supporting actor, Academy of Canadian Cinema and Television, 1982, for *The Amateur,* and 1983, for *Killing 'em Softly;* Gemini Award nomination, best actor in a dramatic program or miniseries, Academy of Canadian Cinema and Television, 1988, for *Hoover vs. the Kennedys: The Second Civil War;* Gemini Award nomination, best actor in a dramatic program, 1997, for *Mother Trucker: The Diana Kilmury Story;* Gemini Award, best actor in a dramatic program or miniseries, 1998, for *Major Crime;* Gemini Award nominations, best actor in a continuing leading dramatic role, 2000, 2003, 2004, 2005, and Gemini Award, best actor in a continuing leading dramatic role, 2001, all for *Da Vinci's Inquest;* Directors Guild of Canada Award nomina-

tion (with others), outstanding achievement in a television drama series, 2003, for "For Just Bein' Indian," *Da Vinci's Inquest;* Genie Award nomination, best supporting actor, 2001, for *New Waterford Girl;* Gemini Award, best guest actor in a dramatic series, 2001, for "Steel Drums," *Blue Murder;* Gemini Award nomination, best actor in a dramatic program or miniseries, 2004, for *Human Cargo;* Gemini Award nomination, best actor in a continuing leading dramatic role, 2006, for *Da Vinci's City Hall.*

CREDITS

Film Appearances:
Marine, *The Omen* (also known as *Omen I, Omen I: The Antichrist,* and *Omen I: The Birthmark*), Twentieth Century–Fox, 1976.
Captain Glass, *A Bridge Too Far,* United Artists, 1977.
U.S.S. Wayne crew member, *The Spy Who Loved Me,* United Artists, 1977.
Billy "The Kid" Brocker, *Fast Company,* Topar Films, 1979.
Chris, *The Brood* (also known as *David Cronenberg's "The Brood"* and *La clinique de la terreur*), New World, 1979.
Jason Caball, *The Shape of Things to Come* (also known as *H. G. Wells' "The Shape of Things to Come"*), Film Ventures International, 1979.
Tony, *Yesterday* (also known as *Gabrielle, Scoring, This Time Forever,* and *The Victory*), Cinepix Film Properties, 1979.
Radio operator at Palmer Station, *Day of Resurrection* (also known as *The End, Virus,* and *Fukkatsu no hi*), 1980.
Bill Darcy, *Dirty Tricks,* Avco–Embassy, 1981.
Schraeger, *The Amateur,* Twentieth Century–Fox, 1981.
Roger Michaels, *Trapped* (also known as *Baker County, U.S.A., The Killer Instinct,* and *Le village de la mort*), Jensen Farley, 1982.
Clifford, *Killing 'em Softly* (also known as *Man in 5A*), 1982.
Danny, "For Life" (also known as "Por vida"), *Love,* Coup Films, 1982.
Frank Dodd, *The Dead Zone,* Paramount, 1983.
Henderson, *Terminal Choice* (also known as *Critical List, Death Bed, Death List,* and *Trauma*), Almi Pictures, 1985.
Sniffer, *Certain Fury,* New World, 1985.
Joey, *Knights of the City* (also known as *Cry of the City*), New World, 1986.
Corporal Brill, *Going Home* (also known as *Soldats en transit*), Opix Films, 1987.
Vincent, *Shades of Love: Champagne for Two,* 1987.
Cast member of zombie beach party III, *The Pink Chiquitas,* Shapiro Entertainment, 1987.
Albert Morse, *Rampage,* Miramax, 1988.
Hank, *Naked Lunch* (also known as *Le festin nu*), Twentieth Century–Fox, 1991.

Sean MacFern, *Shadows of the Past* (also known as *Mortelle amnesie*), Telefilm Canada, 1991.

Nick Papadopoulos, *The Big Slice,* New City Releasing, 1991.

Scott, *Shadow of the Wolf* (also known as *Agaguk*), Triumph Releasing, 1992.

Don, *Bordertown Cafe,* National Film Board of Canada, 1993.

Robert Neilson, *Jungleground,* Norstar Releasing, 1995.

Kyle's dad, *The Boys Club* (also known as *Secrets d'ados*), A–Pix Entertainment, 1997.

Frankie Gooland, *A Cool, Dry Place,* Twentieth Century–Fox, 1998.

East Side Showdown, National Film Board of Canada, 1998.

Francis Pottie, *New Waterford Girl* (also known as *La fille de New Waterford*), Alliance Atlantis Communications, 1999.

All the Fine Lines, 1999.

Jude's father, *Saint Jude,* Behaviour Distribution, 2000.

Bruce, *We All Fall Down,* Road Cone, 2000.

(As Nick Campbell) Donald, *Prozac Nation,* Miramax, 2000.

At Shepherd Park, 2001.

Simon, *Full Disclosure,* First Look Pictures Releasing, 2001.

(As Nick Campbell) Ollie, *New Year's Day,* Les Films du Losange, 2001.

Ross Fleming, *Turning Paige* (also known as *Pages de vie*), Film Option International, 2001.

Dad, *Siblings* (also known as *Secret de famille*), Monarch Home Video, 2004.

Sporty Lewis, *Cinderella Man,* Universal, 2005.

Al Johnson, *14 Days in Paradise,* 2007.

Film Director:

Stepping Razor: Red X, Northern Arts Entertainment, 1992.

Boozecan, Annex Entertainment, 1994.

Television Appearances; Series:

Nick Fox, *The Insiders,* ABC, 1985.

Tom Morgan, *Street Legal,* CBC, 1992–93.

Dominic Da Vinci, *Da Vinci's Inquest,* CBC, 1998–2005.

Mayor Dominic Da Vinci, *Da Vinci's City Hall,* CBC, 2005–2006.

Television Appearances; Miniseries:

Robert "Bobby" Kennedy, *Hoover vs. the Kennedys: The Second Civil War,* syndicated, 1987.

Lucas, *The Sleep Room* (also known as *Le pavillon de l'oubli*), Lifetime, 1998.

Congressman Joseph Kennedy, *Thanks of a Grateful Nation* (also known as *The Gulf War*), Showtime, 1998.

Jery Fisher, *Human Cargo,* CBC, 2004.

Host, *Trudeau II: Maverick in the Making,* CBC, 2005.

Prairie Giant: The Tommy Douglas Story, CBC, 2006.

Shorty McAdoo, *The Englishman's Boy,* CBC, 2007.

Television Appearances; Movies:

Turk, *Come Back, Little Sheba* (also known as *Laurence Olivier Presents: "Come Back, Little Sheba"*), NBC, 1977.

Mac, *Just Jessie,* 1981.

The July Group, CBC, 1981.

Larry, *Children of the Night,* CBS, 1985.

Dark Horse, 1985.

Ben Gardner, *In Defense of a Married Man,* ABC, 1990.

Bryon Hurd, *Split Images,* 1992.

Guy Simonds, *In Desperate Battle: Normandy 1944* (also known as *The Valour and the Horror, Part 3, La bataille de Normandie,* and *La bravoure et le mepris, partie 3*), CBC, 1992.

Man on highway, *The Diary of Evelyn Lau,* CBC, 1993.

Richard Noel, *Betrayal of Trust* (also known as *Under the Influence*), 1994.

Jack Tibbins, *Guitarman,* 1994.

Vic, *No Contest,* 1994.

Clayton Oliver, *Butterbox Babies* (also known as *Les nourrissons de la misere*), CBC, 1995.

Mark Forbes, *Dancing in the Dark,* Lifetime, 1995.

Malcolm Stone, *No Greater Love* (also known as *Danielle Steel's "No Greater Love"*), NBC, 1996.

Karl Weber, *We the Jury,* USA Network, 1996.

Jack Vlahovic, *Mother Trucker: The Diana Kilmury Story* (also known as *Teamster* and *La route de l'espoir*), TNT, 1996.

Billy Quinn, *Major Crime,* Lifetime, 1997.

Doggett, *Blood on Her Hands,* ABC, 1998.

Doug Hart (some sources cite Max Warner), *Hard to Forget* (also known as *Harlequin's "Hard to Forget"* and *Amoureux d'une ombre*), Showtime, 1998.

Rusty Zuvic, *Happy Face Murders,* Showtime, 1999.

100 Days in the Jungle, 2002.

John Reilly, *The Life,* CTV, 2004.

Host, *H2O* (also known as *H2O: The Last Prime Minister*), CBC, 2004.

Television Appearances; Episodic:

Roger, "Some Enchanted Evening," *Bless This House,* Thames, 1976.

Eddie Collins, "A Matter of Balance," *Space: 1999* (also known as *Spazio: 1999*), syndicated, 1976.

Roger Houghton, "The Hunt," *The Littlest Hobo,* syndicated, 1980.

Undercover cop, "Maintain the Right," *For the Record,* CBC, 1980.

Title role, "Shattered Vows," *The Hitchhiker* (also known as *Deadly Nightmares* and *Le voyageur*), HBO, 1983.

Title role, "When Morning Comes," *The Hitchhiker* (also known as *Deadly Nightmares* and *Le voyageur*), HBO, 1983.

Title role, "Split Decision," *The Hitchhiker* (also known as *Deadly Nightmares* and *Le voyageur*), HBO, 1983.

Toby Clark, "Death Strip," *T. J. Hooker,* ABC, 1984.

Jason "Doc" Gifford, "Inn at the End of the Road," *Airwolf* (also known as *Lobo del aire*), 1985.

Jason "Doc" Gifford, "Prisoner of Yesterday," *Airwolf* (also known as *Lobo del aire*), 1985.

Kyle Booker, "Obie's Law," *Night Heat,* 1985.

Michael "Mike" Devitt, "Back in Fashion," *Diamonds,* CBC, 1989.

Westic, "Power Play," *Counterstrike* (also known as *Force de frappe*), 1990.

Ron Smith, "Native Warriors," *Counterstrike* (also known as *Force de frappe*), 1991.

Tom Becker, "Range of Motion," *Beyond Reality,* USA Network, 1991.

Agent Ingram, "Moneymaker/Calling Cards," *Secret Service,* 1992.

Michael Brody, "The First Battle," *The Hidden Room,* 1993.

Graham Corrigan, "Eye Witness," *Kung Fu: The Legend Continues,* syndicated, 1995.

Kit O'Brady, "Double Eagle," *Highlander* (also known as *Highlander: The Series*), syndicated, 1995.

Nigel Ellis, "An Invitation to Romance," *Due South* (also known as *Direction: Sud*), CBS, 1995.

Colonel Stewart, "White Light," *F/X: The Series,* 1996.

Tom Wyler, "Turnaround," *Black Harbour,* CBC, 1997.

Simon, "The Two Headed Man," *Spoken Art,* Bravo!, 1997.

(As Nick Campbell) Robert Wallace, "The Other Woman," *The Hunger,* 1998.

Himself, "Pawn to King Four," *Made in Canada* (also known as *The Industry*), CBC, 1998.

Russell Beacham, "The Winding Cloth," *Psi Factor: Chronicles of the Paranormal,* syndicated, 1999.

Frank Daniels, "Better Luck Next Time," *The Outer Limits* (also known as *The New Outer Limits*), 1999.

Bryce, "Fatal Error," *Code Name: Eternity* (also known as *Code: Eternity*), Sci–Fi Channel, 2000.

Dominic Da Vinci, *Royal Canadian Air Farce* (also known as *Air Farce*), CBC, 2000.

"Father and Sons," *Prince Street,* NBC, 2000.

Eugene Sandler, "Steel Drums," *Blue Murder* (also known as *En quete de preuves*), Global, 2001.

Colonel Percy Brown, "Disguise for Murder," *A Nero Wolfe Mystery* (also known as *Nero Wolfe*), Arts and Entertainment, 2001.

Andy Krasicki, "Door to Death," *A Nero Wolfe Mystery* (also known as *Nero Wolfe*), Arts and Entertainment, 2001.

Grayson, "Mr. Monk and the Other Woman," *Monk,* USA Network, 2002.

Open Mike with Mike Bullard (also known as *The Mike Bullard Show* and *Open Mike*), Global, 2002.

Weasel the Fence, "Cash Call," *Tom Stone* (also known as *Stone Undercover*), CBC, 2004.

Gordon, "Bumpy Cover," *The Eleventh Hour,* CTV, 2005.

Also appeared in an episode of *Playmakers,* ESPN.

Television Appearances; Other:
James Wilson Morrice, *The Lust of His Eyes,* 1994.

Presenter, *21st Annual Gemini Awards* (special), Global, 2006.

Also appeared, according to some sources, in a special titled *The Science of Art,* 1998.

Television Director; Episodic:
"In the Bear Pit," *Da Vinci's Inquest,* CBC, 2002.

"For Just Bein' Indian," *Da Vinci's Inquest,* CBC, 2003.

"Seven Tentacles," *Da Vinci's Inquest,* CBC, 2004.

"Must Be a Night for Fires," *Da Vinci's Inquest,* CBC, 2005.

"Zero to Sixty Pretty Quick," *Da Vinci's City Hall,* CBC, 2005.

"Dante's Inferno," *Intelligence,* CBC, 2007.

Also directed episodes of *Diamonds,* CBC.

RECORDINGS

Videos:
The Making of "We All Fall Down," Critical Mass Releasing, 2002.

WRITINGS

Screenplays:
Stepping Razor: Red X, Northern Arts Entertainment, 1992.

Television Episodes:
Directed episodes of the series *Diamonds,* CBC.

CANONERO, Milena

PERSONAL

Born in Turin, Italy; married Marshall Bell (an actor). *Education:* Studied costume design and art history.

Addresses: *Agent*—International Creative Management, 10250 Constellation Way, Ninth Floor, Los Angeles, CA 90067.

Career: Costume designer, costume consultant, costume advisor, production designer, visual consultant, and producer. Also a fashion designer.

Member: Costume Designers Guild.

Awards, Honors: Academy Award, best costume design, and Film Award nomination, best costume design, British Academy of Film and Television Arts, both with Ulla–Britt Soederlund (name also spelled Ulla–Britt Soderlund), 1976, for *Barry Lyndon;* Academy Award, best costume design, and Film Award, best costume design, British Academy of Film and Television Arts, both 1982, for *Chariots of Fire;* Coty American Fashion Critics' Award, 1984, for a line of men's clothing she designed; Saturn Award nomination, best costumes, Academy of Science Fiction, Horror, and Fantasy Films, 1984, for *The Hunger;* Film Award, best costume design, British Academy of Film and Television Arts, 1986, for *The Cotton Club;* Academy Award nomination, best costume design, 1986, and Film Award nomination, best costume design, British Academy of Film and Television Arts, 1987, both for *Out of Africa;* Academy Award nomination, best costume design, 1989, for *Tucker: The Man and His Dream;* Academy Award nomination, best costume design, Film Award nomination, best costume design, British Academy of Film and Television Arts, and Saturn Award nomination, best costumes, all 1991, for *Dick Tracy;* Academy Award nomination, best costume design, Golden Satellite Award nomination, best costume design, International Press Academy, and Sierra Award nomination, best costume design, Las Vegas Film Critics Society, all 2000, for *Titus;* Career Achievement Award—Film, Costume Designers Guild, 2001; Academy Award nomination, best costume design, and Golden Satellite Award nomination, best costume design, both 2002, for *The Affair of the Necklace;* Costume Designers Guild Award, excellence in costume design for film—contemporary, 2005, for *The Life Aquatic with Steve Zissou;* Costume Designers Guild Award nomination, excellence in costume design for film—contemporary, 2005, for *Ocean's Twelve;* Sierra Award, best costume design, Phoenix Film Critics Society Award, best costume design, and Satellite Award nomination, best costume design, all 2006, Academy Award, best achievement in costume design, Film Award nomination, best costume design, British Academy of Film and Television Arts, and Costume Designers Guild Award nomination, excellence in costume design—period, all 2007, all for *Marie Antoinette.*

CREDITS

Film Costume Designer:
A Clockwork Orange (also known as *Stanley Kubrick's "Clockwork Orange"*), Warner Bros., 1971.

Barry Lyndon, Warner Bros., 1975.
The Disappearance, 1977.
Midnight Express, Columbia, 1978.
The Shining (also known as *Stanley Kubrick's "The Shining"*), Warner Bros., 1980.
Chariots of Fire (also known as *Ates arabalari, Carros de fuego, Carrozas de fuego, Carruagens de fogo, Die Stunde des Siegers, Les chariots de feu, Momenti di gloria, Momentos de gloria, Ohnive vozy, Rydwany ognia, Triumfens ogonblick, Tuezszekerek,* and *Tulivaunut*), Twentieth Century–Fox, 1981.
The Hunger (also known as *Aclik, Az ehseg, Begierde, Blodsghunger, El ansia, Fome de viver, Les predateurs, Miriam si sveglia a mezzanotte,* and *Verenjano*), Metro–Goldwyn–Mayer, 1983.
The Cotton Club (also known as *Gengszterek klubja*), Orion, 1984.
Give My Regards to Broad Street, Twentieth Century–Fox, 1984.
Out of Africa (also known as *Africa mia, Africa minha, Benim Afrikam, Jenseits von Afrika, La mia Africa, Memorias de Africa, Memories d'Africa, Minun Afrikkani, Mit Afrika, Mitt Afrika, Out of Africa—Souvenirs d'Afrique, Pera apo tin Afriki, Pozegnanie z Afryka, Souvenirs d'Afrique,* and *Tavol Afrikatol*), Universal, 1985.
Barfly, Cannon, 1987.
Haunted Summer, Cannon, 1988.
Tucker: The Man and His Dream (also known as *Tucker, Tucker—Ein Mann und sein Traum, Tucker, el hombre y su sueno, Tucker—en man och hans droem, Tucker: L'homme et son reve, Tucker—mies ja unelma, Tucker—O homem e o seu sonho, Tucker—Um homem e seu sonho,* and *Tucker, un uomo e il suo sogno*), Paramount, 1988.
Dick Tracy, Buena Vista, 1990.
Mio caro dottor Grasler (also known as *The Bachelor*), Greycat Films, 1991.
The Godfather: Part III (also known as *Mario Puzo's "The Godfather: Part III," The Death of Michael Corleone, Baba III, Boter 3, Der pate—Teil III, Der pate 3, El padri III, El padrino. Parte III, El padrino III, Gudfadern del III, Il padrino parte terza, Keresztapa 3., Kmotr 3, Kummisetae III, Le parrain 3, Le parrain III, Mario Puzo's "Der Pate—Teil III," O padrinho: Parte III, O poderoso chefao III,* and *Ojciec chrzestny III*), Paramount, 1990, included in the video compilation *The Godfather Trilogy: 1901–1980* (also known as *La trilogia de el padrino: 1901–80*), Paramount Home Video, 1992.
Fatale (also known as *Damage* and *Verhaengnis*), New Line Cinema, 1992.
Single White Female (also known as *Drusha Shutafa Ravaka, Enlig pige soger, Ensam ung kvinna soeker ..., Inserzione pericolosa, J. F. partagerait appartement, Jeune femme chercher colocataire, Jovem procura companheira, Mujer blanca soltera bus-*

ca ..., *Mujer soltera busca, Mulher solteira pro-cura ..., Nuori naimaton nainen, Sublokatorka,* and *Weiblich, ledig, jung sucht ...*), Columbia, 1992.

Death and the Maiden (also known as *La jeune fille et la mort*), Fine Line Features, 1994.

Love Affair (also known as *Perfect Love Affair, A sors utjai, Kutsuvat sitae rakkaudeksi, Love Affair—Segredos do coracao, Love affair—un grande amore, O amor da minha vida, Rendez–vous avec le destin, Segredos do coracao, Sipur Shel Ahava,* and *Un asunto de amor*), Warner Bros., 1994.

Only You (also known as *Him* and *Just in Time*), TriStar, 1994.

(With Elisabetta Beraldo) *Camilla,* Miramax, 1995.

Bulworth (also known as *Tribulations, Bulworth—Candidato em perigo, Bulworth—Il senatore, El senador Bulworth, Koko kansan Bulworth,* and *Politicamente incorreto*), Twentieth Century–Fox, 1998.

Titus (also known as *Titusz*), Fox Searchlight Pictures, 1999.

In the Boom Boom Room, 2000.

The Affair of the Necklace (also known as *A Kiralynoe nyakeke, Afera naszyjnikowa, Das Halsband der Koenigin, El misterio del collar, Farlig intrig, L'affaire du collier, L'intrigo della collana, La intriga del collar, O caso do colar,* and *O enigma do colar*), Warner Bros., 2001.

Solaris, Twentieth Century–Fox, 2002.

"Equilibrium," *Eros,* Warner Independent Pictures, 2004.

The Life Aquatic with Steve Zissou (also known as *Life Aquatic, The Life Aquatic, Untitled Wes Anderson Project, Acquatici lunatici, Die Tiefseetaucher, Edes vizi elet, La vida acuatica, con Steve Zissou, La vie aquatique, Le avventure acquatiche di Steve Zissou, Mereelu Steve Zissou seltis, Steve Zissou vedenalainen maailma, Vida acuatica,* and *Vida acuatica, con Steve Zissou*), Buena Vista, 2004.

Ocean's Twelve (also known as *Ocean's 12, Doze homens e outro segredo, La nueva gran estafa, Le retour de Danny Ocean, Oceani kaksteist,* and *Ocean's twelve: Dogrywka*), Warner Bros., 2004.

Belle toujours, New Yorker Films, 2006.

Marie Antoinette (also known as *Maria Antonieta, Maria Antonieta—La reina adolescente, Maria Antonietta,* and *Maria Antouaneta*), Columbia, 2006.

I vicere (also known as *The Viceroys*), Institut del Cinema Catala/Jean Vigo Italia/Televisio de Catalunya (TV3), 2007.

The Darjeeling Limited, Fox Searchlight Pictures, 2008.

Film Producer:

Associate producer, *Good Morning, Babylon* (also known as *Good morning Babilonia*), Vestron Pictures, 1987.

Associate producer, *Mamba* (also known as *Fair Game*), Management Corporation Entertainment Group, 1988.

(With others) *Naked Tango* (also known as *Kielletty tango, Nackter Tango, Nagie tango, Tango desnudo,* and *Tango nudo*), 1990, New Line Cinema, 1991.

Film Work; Other:

Visual consultant, *Barfly,* Cannon, 1987.

Costume advisor, *Mamba* (also known as *Fair Game*), Management Corporation Entertainment Group, 1988.

Costume design consultant, *Lost Angels* (also known as *The Road Home*), Orion, 1989.

Costume consultant, *Reversal of Fortune* (also known as *A szerencse forgando, Die Affaere der Sunny von B., El misterio von Bulow, Il mistero von Bulow, Le mystere von Bulow, Mysteriet von Buelow, O reverso da fortuna, Odmiana losu, Onnen kulissit, Reveses da fortuna,* and *To gyrisma tis tyhis*), Warner Bros., 1990.

Production designer, *Single White Female* (also known as *Drusha Shutafa Ravaka, Enlig pige soger, Ensam ung kvinna soeker ..., Inserzione pericolosa, J. F. partagerait appartement, Jeune femme chercher colocataire, Jovem procura companheira, Mujer blanca soltera busca ..., Mujer soltera busca, Mulher solteira procura ..., Nuori naimaton nainen, Sub-lokatorka,* and *Weiblich, ledig, jung sucht ...*), Columbia, 1992.

Television Costume Designer; Series:

Miami Vice (also known as *Gold Coast* and *Miami Unworthiness*), NBC, c. 1986–89.

Television Costume Designer; Specials:

Arabella (opera), 1994.

Television Appearances; Specials:

Herself, *Stanley Kubrick: A Life in Pictures* (documentary), Cinemax, 2001.

Television Appearances; Awards Presentations:

The 54th Annual Academy Awards, ABC, 1982.

The 79th Annual Academy Awards, ABC, 2007.

Stage Work:

Costume designer, *Arabella* (opera), Metropolitan Opera House, New York City, 1994.

Production designer and costume designer, *Amadeus,* Italian production, 1999–2000.

Designer for other operas, including *Die Fledermaus,* Metropolitan Opera House, and productions in Vienna, Austria and Italy.

RECORDINGS

Videos:
Herself, *The Making of "Titus"* (short), Twentieth Century–Fox Home Entertainment, 2000.
Herself, *Designing Affair: The Making of "Affair of the Necklace"* (short), Warner Home Video, 2001.
Herself, *The Making of "Marie Antoinette"* (short), Sony Pictures, 2007.

CARTER, Rick 1952–
(Richard Carter)

PERSONAL

Full name, Richard Carter; born 1952, in Los Angeles, CA.

Addresses: *Agent*—The Gersh Agency, 232 North Canon Dr., Beverly Hills, CA 90210.

Career: Production designer, cinematographer, and art director.

Member: Art Directors Guild.

Awards, Honors: Academy Award nomination (with Nancy Haigh), best art direction–set decoration, 1995, for *Forrest Gump*; Golden Satellite Award nomination, outstanding art direction, International Press Academy, and Excellence in Production Design Award nomination (with others), feature film, Art Directors Guild, both 1998, for *Amistad*; AFI Film Award nomination, AFI production designer of the year, AFI awards, and Excellence in Production Design Award nomination (with others), feature film—period or fantasy films, Art Directors Guild, both 2002, for *Artificial Intelligence: AI*.

CREDITS

Film Production Designer:
Magic Journeys (short), Walt Disney Attractions, shown as a part of an attraction at various Disney theme parks, beginning 1982.
Back to the Future, Part II (also known as *Paradox*), Universal, 1989.
Three Fugitives (also known as *Das Bankentrio, In fuga per tre, Kolme karkuria, Os tres fugitivos, Shlosha B'Menusa, Tre paa rommen, Tre paa rymmen, Tres fugitivos,* and *Trois fugitifs*), Buena Vista, 1989.
Back to the Future, Part III (also known as *Three*), Universal, 1990.

Death Becomes Her (also known as *A morte fica–vos tao bem, A morte lhe cai bem, Der Tod steht ihr gut, Doden kler henne, Doeden klaer henne, Ha–Muv'it Nae La, Kuolema pukee haentae, La mort vous va si bien, La morte ti fa bella, La muerte le sienta bien, La muerte os sienta tan bien, Smrt ji lepo pristoji,* and *Ze smiercia jej do twarzy*), Universal, 1992.
Jurassic Park (also known as *JP, Jurassic park—O parque dos dinossauros, Jurassic park: Parc jurassic, Jurassic Park: Parque jurasico, Jurski park, Le parc jurassic, O parque jurassico, Parc jurassic, Park Ha–Yura, Park jurajski,* and *Parque jurassico*), Universal, 1993.
Forrest Gump, Paramount, 1994.
Amistad (also known as *Amistad–Das Sklavenschiff*), DreamWorks, 1997.
The Lost World: Jurassic Park (also known as *Jurassic Park: The Lost World, Jurassic Park 2, The Lost World, The Lost World: Jurassic Park 2, Den tapte verden: Jurassic Park, El mundo perdido: Jurassic Park, Ha–Olum Ha–Avude, Il mondo perduto: Jurassic Park, Izgubljeni svet, Kadonnut maailma: Jurassic Park, Le monde perdu: Jurassic park, O mundo perdido: Jurassic Park, Vergessene Welt: Jurassic Park,* and *Zaginiony swiat: Jurassic park*), Universal, 1997.
Cast Away (also known as *Brodolom, Cast away—tuuliajolla, Cast away—Verschollen, Kaldale uhutud, Naufragiatul, Naufrago, O naufrago, Seul au monde,* and *Szamkivetett*), Twentieth Century–Fox, 2000.
What Lies Beneath (also known as *A verdade escondida, Apparences, Bag facaden—What lies beneath, Dolt under ytan, Le verita nascoste, Lo que la verdad esconde, Revelacao, Revelaciones, Salaisuus pinnan alla,* and *Schatten der Wahrheit*), Twentieth Century–Fox, 2000.
Artificial Intelligence: AI (also known as *A.I., A.I. Artificial Intelligence, A.I.: Artificial Intelligence, A.I. artificiell intelligens, A.I. inteligencia artifical, A.I.—Inteligencia Artifical, A.I. intelligence artificielle, A.I.: Intelligence artificielle, A.I. intelligenza artificiale, A.I.—Kuenstliche Intelligenz, A.I. Kunstig intelligens, A.I.—Mesterseges ertelem, A.I.: Tehniti noimosyni,* and *A.I.—Tekoaely*), Warner Bros., 2001.
The Polar Express (animated; also known as *Polar Express, Boreal Express, Der Polarexpress, El expreso polar, Le pole express, Napapiirin pikajuna, O expresso polar,* and *Polarexpressen*), Warner Bros., 2004, IMAX version released as *The Polar Express: An IMAX 3D Experience*.
Munich, Universal, 2005.
War of the Worlds (also known as *Out of the Night, Party in Fresno,* and *Uncle Sam*), Paramount, 2005.

Film Cinematographer:
(As Richard Carter) *Second–Hand Hearts,* Paramount, 1981.

(As Richard Carter) *The Adventures of Buckaroo Banzai: Across the 8th Dimension* (also known as *The Adventures of Buckaroo Banzai, Buckaroo Banzai, As aventuras de Buckaroo Banzai, Buckaroo Banzai—Die 8. Dimension, Hotet fraan aattonde dimensionen, Las aventuras de Buckaroo Banzai, Les aventures de Buckaroo Banzaie, Les aventures de Buckaroo Banzaie a travers la 8e dimension, Les aventures de Buckaroo Banzaie a travers la huitieme dimension, Oi peripeteies tou Buckaroo Banzai stin 8i diastasi, Przygody Buckaroo Banzai,* and *Superaessae—Buckaroo Banzai*), Twentieth Century–Fox, 1984.

The Slugger's Wife (also known as *Neil Simon's "The Slugger's Wife"*), Columbia, 1985.

The Goonies (also known as *Arkajalat, Die Goonies, I goonies, Les goonies, Los Goonies, Os goonies,* and *The goonies—doedskallegaenget*), Warner Bros., 1985.

(As Richard Carter) *Talking Walls* (also known as *Motel Vacancy*), New World Pictures, 1987.

(Uncredited) *Empire of the Sun* (also known as *A nap birodalma, Auringon valtakunta, Das Reich der Sonne, El imperio do sol, Empire du soleil, Imperio do sol, Imperium slonca, Imperyat Ha–Shemesh, L'empire du soleil, L'imperi del sol, L'impero del sole, O imperio do sol, Solens rige,* and *Solens rike*), Warner Bros., 1987.

Film Assistant Art Director:

(Uncredited) *Bound for Glory* (also known as *Afti i gi einai i diki mou gi, By nie pelzah, Dieses Land ist mein Land, En route pour la gloire, Esta terra e minha, Esta tierra es mi tierra, Questa terra e la mia terra, Taemae maa on minun,* and *Woody Guthrie—lyckans land*), United Artists, 1976.

The China Syndrome, Columbia, 1979.

Film Work; Other:

Set designer, *The China Syndrome,* Columbia, 1979.

Fourth dimensional consultant, *Contact,* Warner Bros., 1997.

Film Appearances:

Himself, *Looking Back at the Future* (documentary), Agenda Films, 2006.

Television Production Designer; Series:

Amazing Stories (also known as *Steven Spielberg's "Amazing Stories"*), NBC, c. 1985–87.

Television Appearances; Specials:

Himself, *Back to the Future Part II Featurette: A Behind the Scenes Look,* 1989.

Himself, *What Lies Beneath: Constructing the Perfect Thriller,* 2001.

Television Appearances; Episodic:

Himself, "What Lies Beneath," *HBO First Look,* HBO, 2000.

Himself, "War of the Worlds: The Final Invasion," *HBO First Look,* HBO, 2005.

RECORDINGS

Videos:

Himself, *The Making of "Jurassic Park,"* Universal Home Video, 1995.

Himself, *The Making of "Lost World,"* Universal Studios Home Video, 1997.

Himself, *The Making of "Amistad"* (short), DreamWorks Home Entertainment, 1999.

Himself, *Beyond Jurassic Park,* Universal Studios Home Video, 2001.

Himself, *Building the World of Gump: Production Design* (short), Paramount, 2001.

Himself, *AI: From Drawings to Sets* (short), DreamWorks Home Entertainment/Warner Bros., 2002.

Himself, *AI/FX* (short), DreamWorks Home Entertainment/Warner Bros., 2002.

Himself, *Creating AI* (short), DreamWorks Home Entertainment, 2002.

Himself, *"War of the Worlds": Production Diaries, East Coast—Beginning* (short), DreamWorks Home Entertainment, 2005.

Himself, *"War of the Worlds": Production Diaries, West Coast—War* (short), DreamWorks Home Entertainment, 2005.

Himself, *"War of the Worlds": Production Diaries, East Coast—Exile* (short), DreamWorks Home Entertainment, 2005.

Himself, *Munich: The Experience* (short), Universal Studios Home Video, 2006.

Himself, *Munich: The Mission—The Team* (short), Universal Studios Home Video, 2006.

Himself, *Munich: The On–Set Experience* (short), Universal Studios Home Video, 2006.

Himself, *Munich: Portrait of an Era* (short), Universal Studios Home Video, 2006.

CARTER, Thomas

PERSONAL

Born in Austin, TX. *Education:* Graduated from college; attended Southwest Texas State University.

Addresses: *Office*—Thomas Carter Company, 3000 West Olympic Blvd., Building 4, Suite 2224, Santa Monica, CA 90404. *Agent*—Creative Artists Agency, 2000 Avenue of the Stars, Los Angeles, CA 90067.

Career: Director, producer, actor, and writer. Thomas Carter Company, Santa Monica, CA, principal.

Member: Directors Guild of America, Writers Guild of America, West.

Awards, Honors: Emmy Award nomination, outstanding directing in a drama series, 1984, for "Midway to What?," an episode of *Hill Street Blues;* Directors Guild of America Award (with others), outstanding directorial achievement in dramatic shows—night, and Emmy Award nomination, outstanding directing in a drama series, both 1985, for "The Rise and Fall of Paul the Wall," an episode of *Hill Street Blues;* Emmy Award nomination, outstanding directing in a drama series, 1989, for "Conversations with the Assassin," an episode of *Midnight Caller;* Emmy awards, outstanding directing in a drama series, 1990, for "Promises to Keep," and 1991, for "In Confidence," both episodes of *Equal Justice;* Golden Satellite Award (with others), best miniseries or motion picture made for television, International Press Academy, 1997, and Emmy Award (with David Blocker), outstanding made for television movie, 1998, both for *Don King: Only in America;* Black Movie Award, outstanding achievement in directing, 2005, Black Reel Award, best director, 2006, and Image Award nomination, outstanding directing in a feature film/television movie, National Association for the Advancement of Colored People (NAACP), 2006, all for *Coach Carter.*

CREDITS

Television Work; Series:
Creator and executive producer, *Equal Justice,* ABC, 1990–91.
Executive producer, *Under One Roof,* CBS, 1995.
Producer, *UC: Undercover* (also known as *Undercover*), NBC, 2001–2002.
Executive producer, *Hack,* CBS, 2002–2004.

Television Director; Miniseries:
A Year in the Life (also known as *Ein Schicksalsjahr*), NBC, 1986.

Television Director; Movies:
Under the Influence (also known as *Aparencias*), CBS, 1986.
Bronx County, 1998.

Television Executive Producer; Movies:
Someone She Knows (also known as *Murder in the Neighborhood, Han tuntee murhaajan,* and *Sie kannte ihren Killer*), NBC, 1994.
The Uninvited (also known as *Victim of the Haunt, House of Terror, Hantee, La casa delle luci, La mal-*

dicion, Maldicao satanica, and *Stimmen aus dem Grab*), CBS, 1996.
Don King: Only in America (also known as *Don King: O dono dos ringues, Don King: O rei do boxe, Don King: Seulement en Amerique,* and *Don King—Una storia tutta americana*), HBO, 1997.
Five Desperate Hours (also known as *Amenazada, Epaetoivon tunnit, 5 horas de desespero,* and *Fuenf Stunden Todesangst*), NBC, 1997.
Ali: An American Hero (also known as *Ali vs. Clay, Ali: Amerykanski bokser,* and *Ali: En amerikansk hjaelte*), Fox, 2000.
Trapped in a Purple Haze (also known as *Un ragazzo contro* and *Wenn Mutterliebe zur Hoelle wird*), ABC, 2000.
Christmas Rush (also known as *Breakaway*), TBS, 2002.

Executive producer of other projects.

Television Work; Other; Movies:
Executive film consultant, *Heat Wave* (also known as *Emeutes en Californie, Heat Wave—onda di fuoco, Kuuma aalto,* and *Tensao brutal*), TNT, 1990.

Television Director; Episodic:
"Me?," *The White Shadow,* CBS, 1979.
Bret Maverick, episodes beginning c. 1981.
"Bypass," *St. Elsewhere,* NBC, 1982.
"Legionnaires," *St. Elsewhere,* NBC, 1982.
"Samuels and the Kid," *St. Elsewhere,* NBC, 1982.
"The Sell–Out," *Fame,* NBC, 1982.
"The Strike," *Fame,* NBC, 1982.
"Tomorrow's Farewell," *Fame,* NBC, 1982.
"You're Steele the One for Me," *Remington Steele,* NBC, 1982.
Hill Street Blues, NBC, episodes from 1982–84.
"Brother's Keeper," *Miami Vice* (also known as *Gold Coast* and *Miami Unworthiness*), NBC, 1984.
"Arthur, or the Gigolo" (also known as "Gigolo"), *Alfred Hitchcock Presents,* NBC, 1985.
"Final Escape," *Alfred Hitchcock Presents,* NBC, 1985.
"Dorothy and Ben," *Amazing Stories,* NBC, 1986.
"Miscalculation," *Amazing Stories,* NBC, 1986.
"One for the Road," *Amazing Stories,* NBC, 1986.
"Don't I Know You From Somewhere?," *A Year in the Life,* NBC, 1987.
"Conversations with the Assassin," *Midnight Caller,* NBC, 1988.
"The Price of Justice," *Equal Justice,* ABC, 1990.
"Promises to Keep," *Equal Justice,* ABC, 1990.
"End Game," *Equal Justice,* ABC, 1991.
"In Confidence," *Equal Justice,* ABC, 1991.
"Rooms," *Under One Roof,* CBS, 1995.
"Life on the Wire," *UC: Undercover* (also known as *Undercover*), NBC, 2001.
"Favors," *Hack,* CBS, 2002.

Director of "Play It Again, Milt," an unaired episode of *Bay City Blues,* NBC.

Television Work; Other; Episodic:
Supervising producer, "Conversations with the Assassin," *Midnight Caller,* NBC, 1988.

Television Director; Pilots:
St. Elsewhere, NBC, 1982.
Trauma Center, ABC, 1983.
Call to Glory, ABC, 1984.
Miami Vice (also known as *Gold Coast* and *Miami Unworthiness*), NBC, 1984.
"Cold Steel and Neon," *Heart of the City,* ABC, 1986.
Midnight Caller, NBC, 1988.
Equal Justice, ABC, 1990.
Divas, Fox, 1995.
Under One Roof, CBS, 1995.
Michael Hayes, CBS, 1997.
The Last Defense, CBS, 1998.
Hack, CBS, 2002.
Partners and Crime (also known as *Violent Crime*), CBS, 2003.
Hitched, Fox, 2005.
Company Town, CBS, 2006.

Television Executive Producer; Pilots:
Divas, Fox, 1995.
The Last Defense, CBS, 1998.
Hack, CBS, 2002.
Company Town, CBS, 2006.

Executive producer of *Wanted* and other projects.

Television Appearances; Series:
Ray Gun (a center kid), *Szysznyk,* CBS, 1977–78.
James Hayward, *The White Shadow,* CBS, 1978–81.

Television Appearances; Specials:
Story of a People: The Black Road to Hollywood, ABC, c. 1990.

Television Appearances; Awards Presentations:
The 43rd Annual Primetime Emmy Awards Presentation, 1991.

Television Appearances; Episodic:
Jerry, "Florida's Night Out," *Good Times,* CBS, 1976.
Second teenager, "To Kill a Tank," *The Blue Knight,* CBS, 1976.
Bobby, "One Strike and You're Out," *What's Happening!!,* ABC, 1977.
Patient, "The Winchester Tapes," *M*A*S*H* (also known as *MASH*), CBS, 1977.
Chris, "Physical," *Lou Grant,* CBS, 1978.

Donald Lilly, "Invasion of the Third World Body Snatchers," *Hill Street Blues,* NBC, 1982.
Himself, "Miami Vice," *The E! True Hollywood Story* (also known as *Miami Vice: The E! True Hollywood Story* and *THS*), E! Entertainment Television, 2001.
Himself, "African Americans in Television," *Inside TV Land* (also known as *Inside TV Land: African Americans in Television*), TV Land, 2002.

Film Director:
Swing Kids (also known as *Os ultimos rebeldes, Rebeldes del swing, Swing Kids—de sista rebellerna, Swing Kids—giovani ribelli,* and *Swing Kids—rytmin kapinalliset*), Buena Vista, 1993.
Metro (also known as *El negociador, Gliniarz z metropolii, Ket tusz koezoett, La flic de San Francisco, Metro—Verhandeln ist reine Nervensache, Tuhannen tilanteen mies,* and *Uno sbirro tuttofare*), Buena Vista, 1997.
Save the Last Dance (also known as *El ultimo baile, Espera al ultimo baile, Nee pour danser, No balanco do amor, Pasion y baile, Save the last dance—viimeinen tanssi,* and *Szivem erted rapes*), Paramount, 2001.
Coach Carter (also known as *All Day Long, Coach Carter—Treino para a vida,* and *Juego de honor*), Paramount, 2005.

Film Work; Executive Producer:
Coach Carter (also known as *All Day Long, Coach Carter—Treino para a vida,* and *Juego de honor*), Paramount, 2005.

Film Appearances:
Player, *The Monkey Hu$tle* (also known as *The Monkey Hustle* and *El barri es nostre*), American International Pictures, 1976.
Dean Hampton, *Almost Summer,* Universal, 1978.
Orderly John, *Whose Life Is It Anyway?,* Metro–Goldwyn–Mayer/United Artists, 1981.

RECORDINGS

Videos:
Himself, *The Making of "Save the Last Dance"* (short), Paramount, 2001.
Himself, *The White Shadow: Director's Debut* (short), Twentieth Century–Fox Home Entertainment, 2006.
Himself, *The White Shadow: A Series of Memories Preview* (short), Twentieth Century–Fox Home Entertainment, 2006.
Himself, *The White Shadow: The Shadow of Bruce Paltrow* (short), Twentieth Century–Fox Home Entertainment, 2006.

WRITINGS

Teleplays; Episodic:
(Stories) *Under One Roof,* CBS, episodes in 1995.

Teleplays; Pilots:
(Story) *Equal Justice*, ABC, 1990.
(And story) *Divas*, Fox, 1995.

Author of the pilot *Crazy Love*, NBC.

CATES, Gilbert 1934–
   (Gil Cates)

PERSONAL

Original name, Gilbert Katz; born June 6, 1934, in New York, NY; son of Nathan (a dress manufacturer) and Nina (maiden name, Peltzman) Katz; brother of Joseph Cates (a director and producer); uncle of Phoebe Cates (an actress); married Betty Jane Dubin, February 9, 1957 (divorced); married Judith Reichman (a gynecologist and writer), January 25, 1987; children: (first marriage) Melissa Beth, Jonathan Michael (a film editor), David Sawyer (a music editor), Gilbert Lewis, Jr. (an actor, director, producer, and writer); (second marriage) Ronit Reichman, Anat Reichman (stepchildren). *Education:* Syracuse University, B.A., 1955, M.A., 1965; trained at Neighborhood Playhouse School of the Theatre, New York City, 1953; studied with Robert Lewis, New York City, 1959. *Avocational Interests:* Fencing, photography.

Addresses: *Office*—Cates/Doty Productions, 10920 Wilshire Blvd., Suite 830, Los Angeles, CA 90024-6510. *Agent*—William Morris Agency, 1 William Morris Place, Beverly Hills, CA 90212.

Career: Producer and director. Syracuse University, Syracuse, NY, instructor in speech and drama, 1955; University of California, Los Angeles, dean of School of Theatre, Film, and Television, 1990–97, artistic director of Geffen Playhouse, Los Angeles, beginning 1994; Cates/Doty Productions, Beverly Hills, CA, producer and director. Childville, Inc., member of board of directors, 1966–73; Israeli Cancer Research Fund, member of board of directors, 1992–94. Previously worked as a page at National Broadcasting Company.

Member: Directors Guild of America (honorary life member; vice president of eastern region, 1965, and western region, beginning 1980; national president, 1983–87; national secretary–treasurer, 1997—), Academy of Motion Picture Arts and Sciences (member of board of governors of directors' branch, 2002–05; chair of board of directors), American Academy of Television Arts and Sciences, Actors' Equity Association (member of eastern regional board of directors, 1962–63),

League of New York Theaters, Tau Delta Phi, Friars Club (member of board of governors), Women in Film (member of board of directors, 1993–94; vice president, 2003).

Awards, Honors: Best short film award, International Film Importers and Distributors, 1962; San Francisco Film Festival citation, 1963, for *The Painting*; Image Award, National Association for the Advancement of Colored People, and TV Scout Award, excellence in television, 1972, both for *To All My Friends on Shore*; Chancellor's Medal, Syracuse University, 1974; Emmy Award nomination, outstanding directing in a limited series or special, 1985, for "Consenting Adult," *An ABC Theatre Presentation*; Robert B. Aldrich Achievement Award, Directors Guild of America, 1989; Emmy Award, outstanding variety, music, or comedy program, 1991, Emmy Award nominations, outstanding variety, music, or comedy special, 1990, annually, 1993–95, 1997–99, 2001, 2003, 2005–06, and Golden Laurel Award nomination, television producer of the year in variety television, Producers Guild of America, 2006, all for *The … Annual Academy Awards*; Emmy Award nomination, outstanding directing in a miniseries or special, 1990, for *Do You Know the Muffin Man?*; Emmy Award nomination, outstanding directing in a miniseries or special, 1991, for *Absolute Strangers*; Directors Guild of America Award nomination, outstanding direction in dramatic specials, 1991, for *Call Me Anna*; received star on Hollywood Walk of Fame, 1994; Jimmy Doolittle Award for Outstanding Contribution to Los Angeles Theatre, 1998; Lifetime Directors Achievement Award, Caucus of Producers, Writers, and Directors, 1998; L.A. Ovation Award, 1999; Arents Award, Syracuse University, 2003; President's Award, Directors Guild of America, 2005; Board of Governors Award, American Society of Cinematographers, 2005; Filmmaker Award, Cinema Audio Society, 2007; Citation Award, Edinburgh Film Festival.

CREDITS

Television Work; Movies:
Producer and director, *To All My Friends on Shore*, CBS, 1972.
Director, *The Affair* (also known as *Love Song*), ABC, 1973.
Director, *Johnny, We Hardly Knew Ye*, NBC, 1977.
Supervising producer and director, *Country Gold*, CBS, 1982.
Producer, *The Kid from Nowhere*, NBC, 1982.
Director, *Hobson's Choice*, CBS, 1983.
Producer and director, *Burning Rage* (also known as *Coalfire*), CBS, 1984.
Producer and director, *Child's Cry* (also known as *Child's Play* and *Who Hears the Child's Cry*), CBS, 1986.

Producer and director, *Fatal Judgment* (also known as *Fatal Dosage*), CBS, 1988.

Director, *My First Love* (also known as *One More Time* and *Second Chance*), ABC, 1989.

Director, *Do You Know the Muffin Man?*, CBS, 1989.

Producer and director, *Call Me Anna* (also known as *Call Me Anna: The Patty Duke Story* and *My Name Is Anna*), ABC, 1990.

Executive producer and director, *Absolute Strangers* (also known as *Matter of Privacy*), CBS, 1991.

Executive producer (with Donna Mills), *In My Daughter's Name* (also known as *Overruled*), CBS, 1992.

Executive producer and director, *Confessions: Two Faces of Evil,* 1994.

Television Work; Specials:
Producer and director, *After the Fall,* NBC, 1974.

Producer and director (with brother Joseph Cates), *Circus Lions, Tigers, and Melissa Too,* NBC, 1977.

Executive producer (with J. Cates), "Have I Got a Christmas for You," *Hallmark Hall of Fame,* NBC, 1977.

Executive producer (with J. Cates), "Fame," *Hallmark Hall of Fame,* NBC, 1978.

Executive producer (with J. Cates), *Country Night of Stars,* NBC, 1978.

Executive producer (with J. Cates), *Country Night of Stars II,* NBC, 1978.

Executive producer, *Stubby Pringles Christmas,* NBC, 1978.

Executive producer (with J. Cates), *Country Stars of the 70s,* NBC, 1979.

Executive producer (with J. Cates), *Skinflint,* NBC, 1979.

Executive producer (with J. Cates), *Elvis Remembered: Nashville to Hollywood,* NBC, 1980.

Executive producer (with J. Cates), *Fifty Years of Country Music,* NBC, 1981.

Director, *Johnny Cash Christmas, 1983,* CBS, 1983.

Director (with J. Cates), *Johnny Cash: Christmas on the Road,* CBS, 1984.

Director, *The 10th Anniversary Johnny Cash Christmas Special,* CBS, 1985.

Director, "Consenting Adult," *An ABC Theatre Presentation,* ABC, 1985.

Producer, *The ... Annual Academy Awards,* ABC, annually, 1989–95, 1997–99, 2001, 2003, 2005–2006.

Producer, *To Life, America Celebrates Israel's 50th,* CBS, 1998.

(Sometimes credited as Gil Cates) Executive producer, *An American Celebration at Ford's Theatre,* ABC, annually, 1999, 2001–2006.

Producer, *America Celebrates Ford's Theater,* ABC, 1999.

Executive producer, *Sunday at the Oscars,* ABC, 1999.

Executive producer, *Oscar Countdown,* ABC, 2001.

(As Gil Cates) Producer and director, "A Death in the Family," *Masterpiece Theatre,* PBS, 2002.

Executive producer, *Rockin' for the U.S.A.: A National Tribute to the U.S. Military,* CBS, 2002.

(As Gil Cates) Executive producer and director, *Collected Stories,* PBS, 2002.

(As Gil Cates) Executive producer, *Oscar Countdown,* ABC, 2003.

(As Gil Cates) Executive producer, *CBS at 75* (also known as *CBS at 75: A Primetime Celebration*), CBS, 2003.

Executive producer, *Oscar Countdown,* ABC, 2005, 2006.

Also worked as producer and director of specials featuring Ice Follies, the Worlds Fair, and Aquacade, all ABC, 1965.

Television Work; Series:
Producer (with Roger Peterson and Chester Feldman), *I've Got a Secret* (game show), CBS, between 1952 and 1967.

Producer and director, *Mother's Day* (game show), ABC, c. 1958–59.

Haggis Baggis (game show), NBC, 1958–59.

Producer and director, *Camouflage* (game show), ABC, 1961–62.

Creator, producer, and director, *Hootenanny,* ABC, 1962.

Executive producer and director, *International Showtime,* NBC, 1962–64.

Producer and director, *Faerie Tale Theatre* (also known as *Shelley Duvall's "Faerie Tale Theatre"*), Showtime, 1982.

Television Work; Miniseries:
Executive producer and director, *Innocent Victims,* ABC, 1996.

(As Gil Cates) Executive producer, *NetForce* (also known as *Tom Clancy's "NetForce"*), ABC, 1999.

Television Director; Episodic:
"Rapunzel," *Faerie Tale Theatre* (also known as *Shelley Duvall's "Faerie Tale Theatre"*), Showtime, 1983.

"Goldilocks and the Three Bears," *Faerie Tale Theatre* (also known as *Shelley Duvall's "Faerie Tale Theatre"*), Showtime, 1984.

(As Alan Smithee) "Paladin of the Lost Hour," *The Twilight Zone,* 1985.

Also directed episodes of *Picture This* and *Reach for the Stars,* both 1960s.

Television Work; Other:
Producer and director, *Electric Showcase,* ABC, 1965.

Producer, *Off Campus* (pilot), CBS, 1977.

Producer and director, *One More Time,* ABC, 1988.

Television Appearances; Specials:
Intimate Portrait: Pam Dawber, Lifetime, 2002.
(As Gil Cates) *The Awards Show Awards Show,* Trio, 2003.

Television Guest Appearances; Episodic:
Sunday Morning Shootout, AMC, 2007.

Film Work:
Producer and director, *The Painting* (short film), Union Films, 1962.
Producer and director, *Rings around the World,* Columbia, 1967.
Producer and director, *I Never Sang for My Father,* Columbia, 1970.
Director, *Summer Wishes, Winter Dreams,* Columbia, 1973.
Producer and director, *One Summer Love* (also known as *Dragonfly*), American International Pictures, 1976.
Director, *The Promise* (also known as *Face of a Stranger*), Universal, 1979.
Executive producer and director, *The Last Married Couple in America,* Universal, 1980.
Producer and director, *Oh, God! Book II* (also known as *Tracy and Friend*), Warner Bros., 1980.
Director, *Backfire,* Vidmark, 1989.

Film Appearances:
50 Years of Action!, 1986.
Himself, *Pesel Ha'Zahav,* 1999.
(As Gil Cates) Mr. Walsh, *$pent* (also known as *Spent*), Regent Entertainment, 2000.
Going through Splat: The Life and Work of Stewart Stern (documentary), Rosen/Ward, 2005.
(As Gil Cates) *Who Needs Sleep?,* 2006.

Stage Work:
Stage manager, *Shinbone Alley,* Broadway Theatre, New York City, 1957.
Associate producer (with Joseph Cates), *Spoon River Anthology* (later renamed *Spoon River*), Booth Theatre, New York City, 1963, then Royal Court Theatre, London, 1964.
Producer (with Jack Farren), *You Know I Can't Hear You When the Water's Running* (four one–acts), Ambassador Theatre, New York City, 1967–68, then Broadhurst Theatre, New York City, 1968–69.
Producer, *I Never Sang for My Father,* Longacre Theatre, New York City, 1968.
Producer, *The Chinese* and *Dr. Fish* (double–bill), Ethel Barrymore Theatre, New York City, 1970.
Producer (with Roy N. Nevans and Albert J. Schiff), *Solitaire/Double Solitaire* (double–bill), John Golden Theatre, New York City, 1971.
Director, *The Price,* Long Wharf Theatre, New Haven, CT, 1971.

Director, *Voices,* Ethel Barrymore Theatre, 1972.
Producer (with Matthew Alexander) and director, *Tricks of the Trade,* Brooks Atkinson Theatre, New York City, 1980.
Director, *Collected Stories,* 1999.
Director, *Under the Blue Sky,* Geffen Playhouse, Los Angeles, 2002.
Director, *Paint Your Wagon,* 2004.
Director, *Cat on a Hot Tin Roof,* 2005.
Director, *A Picasso,* Audrey Skirball Kenis Theatre, Los Angeles, 2007.

Also producing director of *Six Dance Lessons in Sex Weeks,* Geffen Playhouse, Los Angeles.

Major Tours:
Producer, *You Know I Can't Hear You When the Water's Running,* U.S. cities, 1967, and London, 1968.

WRITINGS

Television Movies:
Child's Cry (also known as *Child's Play* and *Who Hears the Child's Cry*), CBS, 1986.

OTHER SOURCES

Periodicals:
Hollywood Reporter, November 30, 1988, pp. 16 and 20.
Variety, November 26, 2001, p. A13.

CAULFIELD, Maxwell 1959–
    (Maxwell Caufield)

PERSONAL

Original name, Maxwell Maclaine; born November 23, 1959, in Glasgow, Scotland; son of Peter Nelby and Oriole Maclaine; married Juliet Mills (an actress), December 2, 1980; stepchildren: Sean Alquist, Mellisa (an actress).

Addresses: *Agent*—Cunningham, Escott, Dipene and Associates, 10635 Santa Monica Blvd., Suite 140, Los Angeles, CA 90025.

Career: Actor. Began career in show business as a nude dancer at Windmill Theatre, London, England.

Member: Screen Actors Guild, Actors' Equity Association (U.S. and England).

Awards, Honors: *Theatre World* Award, 1979, for *Class Enemy.*

CREDITS

Film Appearances:
Michael Carrington, *Grease 2,* Paramount, 1982.
Bill, *Electric Dreams,* Metro–Goldwyn–Mayer, 1984.
Roy Alston, *The Boys Next Door* (also known as *Big Shots*), New World, 1985.
Private Ray Ellis, *The Supernaturals,* Republic, 1987.
Eric Garrison, *Mind Games,* Metro–Goldwyn–Mayer, 1989.
George Abbott, *Project: Alien* (also known as *Fatal Sky* and *No Cause for Alarm*), ITC, 1990.
Joe Moore, *Exiled in America* (also known as *Exiled*), 1990.
Shane, *Sundown* (also known as *Sundown: The Vampire in Retreat*), Vestron, 1991.
Szalona ambicja (also known as *Crazy Ambition*), 1991.
Shaughnessy, *Dance with Death,* 1991.
Mickey, *Waxwork II: Lost in Time* (also known as *Lost in Time* and *Space Shift: Waxwork II*), 1992.
Garland, *Midnight Witness* (also known as *Maximum Force 2*), 1992.
David Cole, *Animal Instincts,* 1992.
William Robert Sloan, *No Escape, No Return,* 1993.
Victor Brandt, *In a Moment of Passion* (also known as *Europejska noc* and *In der Haut des Killers*), 1993.
Colonel Strong Vincent, *Gettysburg,* New Line Cinema, 1993.
Man in bathrobe, *Calendar Girl,* Sony Pictures Releasing, 1993.
Nick, *Alien Intruder,* 1993.
Adam Cestare, *Inevitable Grace,* Silverstar Productions, 1994.
Rex Manning, *Empire Records* (also known as *Empire* and *Rock and Fun*), Warner Bros., 1995.
Voice of Alistair Smythe, *Spider–Man: Sins of the Fathers* (animated), New World Entertainment, 1996.
Derek Leigh, *Prey of the Jaguar,* Jfw Productions, 1996.
Sweeney, *Oblivion 2: Backlash* (also known as *Backlash: Oblivion 2*), Full Moon, 1996.
Bob, *The Real Blonde,* Paramount, 1997.
British agent, *The Man Who Knew Too Little* (also known as *Agent Null Null Nix* and *Agent Null Null Nix—Bill Murray in hirnloser mission*), Warner Bros., 1997.
Jeff Thompson, *Divine Lovers,* 1997.
Smut, 1999.
Barry Gordon, *More to Love,* 1999.
Tom, *Dazzle,* 1999.
Daniel Summer, *The Perfect Tenant,* Trimark Pictures, 2000.

Agent Jim Carpenter, *Submerged* (also known as *Destination: Impact*), New City Releasing, 2000.
Mark Connor, *Overnight Sensation,* 2000.
Harlan Moss, *Facing the Enemy,* World International Network, 2001.
Keith, *The Hit,* Lietuvos Kinostudija, 2001.
Tom, *Dog Lover's Symphony,* Tehito Films/Tiger Ad Productions, 2006.
Narrator, *Hannari—Geisha Modern,* 2006.
Alex Mcdowell, *Dreamcity,* L&P Productions, 2007.

Film Work:
Associate producer, *Facing the Enemy,* World International Network, 2001.

Television Appearances; Series:
Miles Colby, a recurring role, *Dynasty,* ABC, 1985–86.
Miles Andrew Colby, *The Colbys* (also known as *Dynasty II: The Colbys*), 1985–87.
Voice of Alistair Smythe, *Spider–Man* (animated), 1995–97.
Pierce Riley, a recurring role, *All My Children* (also known as *AMC*), ABC, 1996–97.
Rafe Barrett, *Strip Mall,* Comedy Central, 2000–2001.
Jim Brodie, *Casualty,* BBC1, 2003–2004.

Television Appearances; Miniseries:
Alain Marais, *Till We Meet Again* (also known as *Judith Krantz's "Till We Meet Again"*), CBS, 1989.
Miles Colby, *Dynasty: The Reunion,* 1991.

Television Appearances; Movies:
Jeff, *The Parade* (also known as *Hit Parade*), CBS, 1984.
Phil Serulla, *Blue Bayou* (also known as *Orleans*), NBC, 1990.
Ian Levin, *The Rockford Files: Godfather Knows Best,* 1996.
Stuart, *Missing Pieces,* CBS, 2000.
Silas, *Dragon Storm,* Sci–Fi Channel, 2004.
Griffin, *Cry of the Winged Serpent,* Sci–Fi Channel, 2006.
Mayor Schmitz, *The Great San Francisco Earthquake,* Channel 4, 2006.

Television Appearances; Specials:
Captain Stanhope, *Journey's End,* 1983.
"Hayley Mills: Seeing Double," *Biography,* Arts and Entertainment, 1999.

Television Appearances; Pilots:
Jason Croft, *Beverly Hills, 90210,* Fox, 1990.

Television Appearances; Episodic:
Scotty Ferguson, "Starr Knight," *The Powers of Matthew Star,* 1983.

Alex Morrison, "Pitfalls," *Hotel* (also known as *Arthur Hailey's "Hotel"*), 1987.

Roger Travis, "J. B. As in Jailbird," *Murder, She Wrote,* CBS, 1988.

Jason Croft, "Class of Beverly Hills," *Beverly Hills, 90210,* Fox, 1990.

"Cellmates," *Monsters,* 1990.

Van Gelder, "Regal Connection," *Counterstrike* (also known as *Force de frappe*), 1990.

Derek Padley, "From the Horse's Mouth," *Murder, She Wrote,* CBS, 1991.

Andrew Strauss/David Lewis, "Return Engagement: Part 1," *Dr. Quinn, Medicine Woman,* CBS, 1994.

Himself, "Crossing the Line," *Sirens,* 1994.

David Lewis, "Ready or Not," *Dr. Quinn, Medicine Woman,* CBS, 1995.

"The Boy General," *The Lazarus Man,* 1996.

(As Maxwell Caufield) Tony Berelli, "The Maya Connection," *Mike Hammer, Private Eye,* 1998.

Brian, "Veronica's Bridal Shower," *Veronica's Closet,* NBC, 1998.

Armand, "True Course," *The Love Boat: The Next Wave,* 1998.

Rodney, "The Fran in the Mirror," *The Nanny,* CBS, 1999.

Helmut Volker, "Man in the Middle," *La Femme Nikita* (also known as *Nikita*), USA Network, 2000.

Helmut Volker, "Love, Honor and Cherish," *La Femme Nikita* (also known as *Nikita*), USA Network, 2000.

Stevens, "A Star Is Boned," *Son of the Beach,* FX Network, 2000.

Jim Brodie, "Casualty @ Holby City: Part Two," *Holby City* (also known as *Holby*), BBC, 2004.

The Paul O'Grady Show (also known as *The New Paul O'Grady Show*), ITV, 2004.

GMTV, ITV, 2004.

Stage Appearances:

(New York debut) Demetrius, *Hot Rock Hotel,* Truck and Warehouse Theatre, New York City, 1978.

Cuthbert and understudy for Derek, *Once a Catholic,* Helen Hayes Theatre, New York City, 1979.

Iron (Herron), *Class Enemy,* Players Theatre, New York City, 1979.

Ralph, *Hitting Town,* Zephyr Theatre, Los Angeles, 1980.

Frazer, *Crimes and Dreams,* Theatre Four, New York City, 1980.

Sloane, *Entertaining Mr. Sloane,* Westside Mainstage Theatre and Cherry Lane Theatre, New York City, 1981–82, later Mark Taper Forum, Los Angeles, 1987.

Peter, *Salonika,* New York Shakespeare Festival, Anspacher Theatre, Public Theatre, New York City, 1985.

Dennis, *Loot,* Mark Taper Forum, 1987.

Richard Loeb, *Never the Sinner,* Citadel Theatre, Edmonton, Alberta, Canada, 1991.

Gerald Croft, *An Inspector Calls,* Royale Theatre, New York City, 1995.

Chance Wayne, *Sweet Bird of Youth,* Williamstown Theatre Festival, Williamstown, MA, 1995.

John, *My Night with Reg,* Intar Hispanic American Theatre, New York City, 1997.

Duchotel, *He Hunts,* Geffen Playhouse, Westwood, CA, 2002.

George Love, *Tryst,* Promenade Theatre, New York City, 2006.

Harry Hawk, *Our Leading Lady,* Manhattan Theatre Club Stage II, New York City, 2007.

In the 1980s appeared as Horace, *The Inheritors,* Mirror Repertory Company, Real Theatre, Theatre at St. Peter's Church, New York City; as Captain Stanhope, *Journey's End,* Cast Theatre, Los Angeles; as Winston Smith, *1984,* Cast Theatre; and as Ben Gordon, *Paradise Lost,* Mirror Repertory Company, Real Theatre, Theatre at St. Peters Church.

Major Tours:

John Merrick, *The Elephant Man,* Florida cities, c. 1980.

Milo Tindle, *Sleuth,* U.S. cities, 1988.

RECORDINGS

Video Games:

Voice of James Bond, *007: Nightfire,* Electronic Arts, 2002.

Audio Books:

(With Marina Sirtis) *Griffin and Sabine: An Extraordinary Correspondence,* Publishing Mills, 1993.

Enduring Love, Publishing Mills, 1998.

OTHER SOURCES

Periodicals:

New York Times, September 4, 1981.

People Weekly, April 29, 1985, p. 128; February 13, 1995, p. 77.

Psychotronic Video, Issue 35, 2001, pp. 57–61.

CHAMBERLIN, Kevin 1963–

PERSONAL

Born November 25, 1963, in Baltimore, MD; raised in Moorestown, NJ. *Education:* Rutgers University, B.F.A., 1985.

Addresses: *Agent*—Gregg Klein, Abrams Artists Agency, 9200 Sunset Blvd., Suite 1130, Los Angeles, CA 90069.

Career: Actor. Drama Department (theatre company), member of company; also voice coach, pianist, and composer.

Awards, Honors: Antoinette Perry Award nomination, best featured actor, and Drama Desk Award nomination, best actor in a play, 2000, both for *Dirty Blonde;* Antoinette Perry Award nomination, best featured actor, and Drama Desk Award nomination, best actor in a play, 2001, both for *Seussical: The Musical.*

CREDITS

Television Appearances; Series:
Victor, *New York News,* CBS, 1995.
Fred Smedressman, *State of Mind,* Lifetime, 2007.

Television Appearances; Miniseries:
Daniel McCurtin, *LIBERTY! The American Revolution,* PBS, 1997.
Cat Man, *Kingpin,* NBC, 2003.

Television Appearances; Movies:
Cutler, *Letters from a Killer,* 1998.
Policeman, *Earthly Possessions,* HBO, 1999.
Moody, *The Valley of Light,* CBS, 2007.

Television Appearances; Pilots:
Lenny, *Inconceivable,* NBC, 2005.
Massage client, *Crumbs,* ABC, 2006.
Harvey, *Twenty Good Years,* NBC, 2006.
Fred Smedressman, *State of Mind,* Lifetime, 2007.

Television Appearances; Specials:
Referee, "Summer Stories: The Mall—Part 3," *ABC Afterschool Special,* ABC, 1992.

Television Appearances; Episodic:
Roger Berry, "Redemption," *Law & Order: Special Victims Unit* (also known as *Law & Order: SVU* and *Special Victims Unit*), NBC, 2001.
Mr. Bronkowsky, "Charity Cases," *Ed,* NBC, 2001.
Mr. Bronkowsky, "Ends and Means," *Ed,* NBC, 2002.
Gary Fisk, "Hang On to Me," *Without a Trace* (also known as *W.A.T.*), CBS, 2003.
Guy in waiting room, "Lilith Needs a Favor," *Frasier,* NBC, 2003.
Dr. Pendelton, "Mandi/Randi," *Nip/Tuck,* FX Network, 2003.
Wallace, "The Lemonade Stand," *According to Jim,* ABC, 2003.

Wayne, "Cross My Heart," *It's All Relative,* ABC, 2004.
Prosecutor Eams, "The People vs. Sergius Kovinsky," *The D.A.,* ABC, 2004.
Neville, "You Really Got Me," *Crossing Jordan,* NBC, 2005.
Dave, "Tony Whine–Man," *Listen Up,* CBS, 2005.
Carl, "Ubusy?," *Jake in Progress,* ABC, 2005.
Carl, "Boys' Night Out," *Jake in Progress,* ABC, 2005.
Carl, "Henry Porter and the Coitus Interruptus," *Jake in Progress,* ABC, 2005.
Momma, "Secrets," *Sex, Love & Secrets,* UPN, 2005.
Second patient (The Flash), "Super Men," *CSI: NY,* CBS, 2006.
Lionel, "Canadian," *So noTORious,* VH1, 2006.
Aron Malsky, "Godsend," *Heroes,* NBC, 2007.
Aron Malsky, "Distractions," *Heroes,* NBC, 2007.
Aron Malsky, "Run!," *Heroes,* NBC, 2007.

Appeared in an episode of *Late Show with David Letterman.*

Stage Appearances:
Preacher Mervin Oglethorpe, *Smoke on the Mountain,* McCarter Theatre, Princeton, NJ, 1988, then Lamb's Theatre, New York City, 1990.
Raymond, *Neddy,* American Place Theatre, New York City, 1990.
Member of ensemble, *My Favorite Year* (musical), Vivian Beaumont Theatre, Lincoln Center, New York City, 1992–93.
Feargus and other roles, *Abe Lincoln in Illinois,* Vivian Beaumont Theatre, Lincoln Center, 1993–94.
Stanley, *One Touch of Venus* (concert), City Center Theatre, New York City, 1996.
Dimas, *Triumph of Love* (musical), Royale Theatre, New York City, 1997–98.
Amos Hart, *Chicago* (musical), Shubert Theatre, New York City, 1998.
As Thousands Cheer, Drama Department, Greenwich House Theatre, New York City, 1998–99.
Charlie and other roles, *Dirty Blonde,* New York Theatre Workshop, Helen Hayes Theatre, New York City, 2000–2001.
Horton the Elephant, *Seussical: The Musical* (also known as *Seussical*), Richard Rodgers Theatre, New York City, 2000–2001.
Captain Mike, *Wonder of the World,* Manhattan Theatre Club Stage I, New York City, 2001–2002.
Buzz Richards, *Applause* (musical), Freud Playhouse, University of California, Los Angeles, 2005.
Gaetano Proclo, *The Ritz,* Roundabout Theatre Company, Studio 54, New York City, 2007.

Also appeared in *Juno,* Vineyard Theatre, New York City; *Wise Guys,* New York Theatre Workshop; and *Ziegfeld Follies of 1936,* City Center Theatre, New York City; appeared in regional productions at McCarter Theatre, Princeton, NJ; Paper Mill Playhouse, Millburn,

NJ; Repertory Theatre of St. Louis, St. Louis, MO; Williamstown Theatre Festival, Williamstown, MA; and Yale Repertory Theatre, New Haven, CT.

Film Appearances:
An actor, *Funny,* Original Cinema, 1988.
Charles Weiss, *Die Hard: With a Vengeance* (also known as *Die Hard 3*), Twentieth Century–Fox, 1995.
Carl Mickley, *In & Out,* Paramount, 1997.
Perry's "ex", *Trick,* Fine Line, 1999.
Wayne, *Herman U.S.A.* (also known as *Taking a Chance on Love*), Two Silks Releasing, 2001.
Frank the bouncer, *Road to Perdition,* DreamWorks, 2002.
Harold Speck, *Suspect Zero* (also known as *Suspect 0*), Paramount, 2004.
Mr. Scanlon, *Christmas with the Cranks,* Columbia, 2005.
Charlie Baker, *Loudmouth Soup,* Dendrobium Films, 2005.
Gus Boyle, *Bound by Lies* (also known as *The Long Dark Kiss*), Lightning Entertainment, 2005.
Marty, *Lucky Number Slevin* (also known as *Lucky # Slevin, Lucky Number S7evin,* and *The Wrong Man*), Metro–Goldwyn–Mayer, 2006.
Officer Jennings, *The Girl Next Door* (also known as *Jack Ketchum's "The Girl Next Door"*), Modern Girls Productions, 2007.

WRITINGS

Screenplays:
Loudmouth Soup, Dendrobium Films, 2005.

CHANG, Gary 1953–

PERSONAL

Full name, Gary Kington Chang; born February 22, 1953, in Minneapolis, MN; son of Melvin and Diana (maiden name, Lee) Chang; married Margaret Ann Craig, February 14, 1982. *Education:* Attended Tufts University, 1971; Carnegie–Mellon University, B.F.A., 1975; California Institute of Arts, M.F.A., 1977. *Avocational Interests:* Cooking, tennis.

Addresses: *Agent*—Soundtrack Music Associates, 2229 Cloverfield Blvd., Santa Monica, CA 90405.

Career: Composer, studio musician, synthesizer programmer, and producer. Pianist with a quartet in Pittsburgh, PA, c. 1970s; Fairlight Instruments, West Los Angeles, CA, product specialist, 1980–82; Gary Chang Co., Newhall, CA, composer and studio musician, 1982–85; Gary Chang Music Co., Inc., Newhall, principal and film music composer, 1985—. Rolandcorp USA, product consultant, 1985–89.

Member: American Federation of Musicians, Society of Composers and Lyricists.

Awards, Honors: National Endowment for the Arts grant, 1977; BMI Film Music Award, Broadcast Music, Inc. Film and Television Awards, 1993, for *Under Siege;* Golden Reel Award nomination (with others), best sound editing, direct to video category, Motion Picture Sound Editors, 2006, for *Left Behind: A World at War.*

CREDITS

Film Work:
Music performer, *Metalstorm: The Destruction of Jared–Syn,* Universal, 1983.
Song producer, "Dream Montage," and music performer, *The Breakfast Club,* Universal, 1985.
Music arranger, additional electronic music, *The Color of Money,* Buena Vista, 1986.
Music performer, *52 Pick–Up,* Cannon, 1986.
Music performer, *Firewalker,* Cannon, 1986.
Song producer, "Bring Me a Dream," *Death Warrant,* Metro–Goldwyn–Mayer, 1990.
Song producer, "Dangerous" and "Standing in the Shadows," *The Perfect Weapon,* Paramount, 1991.
Music producer, *The Island of Dr. Moreau,* New Line Cinema, 1996.

Television Appearances:
Himself, *Kat—jagten paa gyset,* 2001.

RECORDINGS

Albums; Soundtrack Recordings:
A Shock to the System, Windham Hill Jazz, 1990.
Under Siege, Varese Sarabande, 1993.
Island of Dr. Moreau, Milan, 1996.

WRITINGS

Television Music Composer; Movies:
A Killer Among Us, CBS, 1990.
Rising Son, TNT, 1990.
83 Hours 'til Dawn, CBS, 1990.
Donor, CBS, 1990.
Murder in New Hampshire: The Pamela Wojas Smart Story, CBS, 1991.

The Nightman (also known as *The Watchman*), NBC, 1992.

In the Line of Duty: Siege at Marion (also known as *Children of Fury*), NBC, 1992.

Shadow of a Stranger, 1992.

The Last Hit, 1993.

Double Deception, 1993.

(Including song "When the Rain Starts to Fall") *A Family Torn Apart* (also known as *Sudden Fury: A Family Torn Apart*), ABC, 1993.

Full Eclipse, 1993.

Deep Red, Sci–Fi Channel, 1994.

Against the Wall, HBO, 1994.

The Burning Season, HBO, 1994.

Nowhere to Hide, 1994.

Fatherland, 1994.

The Avenging Angel, 1995.

Original Sins (also known as *Acts of Contrition*), 1995.

Twisted Desire, 1996.

Twilight Man, 1996.

The Limbic Region, Showtime, 1996.

Murder Live!, NBC, 1997.

Under Pressure (also known as *Bad Day on the Block* and *The Fireman*), 1997.

A Soldier's Sweetheart, 1998.

Blackout Effect (also known as *747*), 1998.

Silencing Mary (also known as *Campus Justice*), NBC, 1998.

Mind Games (also known as *Trauma*), 1998.

A Bright Shining Lie, HBO, 1998.

At the Mercy of a Stranger, CBS, 1999.

Locked in Silence, Showtime, 1999.

Chameleon 2: Death Match, UPN, 1999.

The Crossing, Arts and Entertainment, 2000.

Runaway Virus, 2000.

A Vision of Murder: The Story of Donielle, CBS, 2000.

Range of Motion, Lifetime, 2000.

Path to War, HBO, 2002.

The Glow, Fox, 2002.

Sniper 2, 2002.

The Diary of Ellen Rimbauer, ABC, 2003.

Rush of Fear, Lifetime, 2003.

Word of Honor, TNT, 2003.

Television Music Composer; Miniseries:

Andersonville, TNT, 1996.

George Wallace, TNT, 1997.

Storm of the Century (also known as *Stephen King's "Storm of the Century"* and *La tempete du siecle*), ABC, 1999.

Rose Red (also known as *Stephen King's "Rose Red"*), ABC, 2002.

Kingdom Hospital (also known as *Stephen King's "Kingdom Hospital"*), ABC, 2004.

Television Music Composer; Episodic:

"Hunger Chic," *Trying Times,* PBS, 1989.

"The Boss," *Trying Times,* PBS, 1989.

"Death and Taxes," *Trying Times,* PBS, 1989.

Premiere episode, *The Marshall Chronicles,* ABC, 1990.

Main title theme music, "The Dead Letter," *Eerie, Indiana,* NBC, 1991.

Television Music Composer; Other:

"Harold Clurman: A Life of Theatre" (special), *American Masters,* PBS, 1989.

WIOU (pilot), CBS, 1990.

Film Music Composer:

Additional music, *The Breakfast Club,* Universal, 1985.

3:15 the Moment of Truth (also known as *Showdown at Lincoln High, 3:15,* and *3:15 a Time to Die*), Dakota Entertainment, 1986.

52 Pick–Up, Cannon, 1986.

Firewalker, Cannon, 1986.

Sticky Fingers, Spectrafilm, 1988.

The House of Usher (also known as *The Fall of the House of Usher*), 1988.

(With Michael Kamen) *Dead–Bang,* Warner Bros., 1989.

Additional music, *Next of Kin,* Warner Bros., 1989.

A Shock to the System, Corsair, 1990.

(And songwriter) *Death Warrant,* Metro–Goldwyn–Mayer/United Artists, 1990.

Miami Blues, Orion, 1990.

The Perfect Weapon, Paramount, 1991.

Under Siege (also known as *Piege en haute mer*), Warner Bros., 1993.

Sniper, TriStar, 1993.

F.T.W. (also known as *F.T.W.: Fuck the World* and *Last Ride*), 1994.

The Walking Dead, Savoy Pictures, 1995.

Im sog des boesen (also known as *Deadly Measures, Desperate Measures, In the Flesh, Nanny's Nightmare, Undercurrent,* and *Desperate–Verzweifelt*), 1995.

The Substitute, Orion, 1996.

The Island of Dr. Moreau, New Line Cinema, 1996.

Double Team (also known as *The Colony*), Columbia, 1997.

Kat, EuroVideo, 2001.

Sam's Lake, Knick Knack Productions/Maverick Films/Mirovision/One Eye Open/.40 Caliber, 2005.

Left Behind: World at War, Columbia, 2005.

English as a Second Language, 2005, Inferno Distribution, 2007.

CHUANG, Susan

PERSONAL

Career: Actress.

CREDITS

Film Appearances:
Ya–Li, *A State of Mind,* York Entertainment, 1998.
Pei Pei, *The Big Thing,* 2000.
Angela, *The Ride Home* (short), 2000.
Rebecca, *Alcatraz Avenue,* 2000.
Jodi Chang, *Tremors 3: Back to Perfection,* Universal Home Entertainment, 2001.
Hallmark mom, *Like Mike,* Twentieth Century–Fox, 2002.
Lotus, *S1m0ne,* New Line Cinema, 2002.
Iman Asswipe, *BraceFace Brandi* (short), 2002.
Kiko, *Melvin Goes to Dinner,* Arrival Pictures, 2003.
Tobin, *Miss Congeniality 2: Armed & Fabulous,* Warner Bros., 2005.
Ticket agent, *Smile,* B.D. Fox Marketing and Distribution, 2005.
Press conference reporter, *Bewitched,* Sony, 2005.
Reporter, *See Anthony Run* (short), 2005.
Suzy, *American Fusion,* 2005.

Television Appearances; Series:
Susan, *Dharma & Greg,* ABC, 1999–2002.
Frannie Ching, *Cold Case,* CBS, 2004–2007.

Television Appearances; Movies:
Female news anchor, *The Matthew Shepard Story* (also known as *L'affaire Matthew Shepard*), NBC, 2002.
Nina Wu, *Wendy Wu: Homecoming Warrior,* Disney Channel, 2006.

Television Appearances; Episodic:
Bank teller, "Serendipity," *Chicago Hope,* CBS, 1998.
Jane Chafin, " ... And a Nice Chianti," *7th Heaven* (also known as *Seventh Heaven*), The WB, 1998.
Nurse, "The Baby," *Party of Five,* Fox, 1998.
Reporter number two, "End of Games," *The Practice,* ABC, 1999.
Monique, "Which Prue Is It, Anyway?," *Charmed,* The WB, 1999.
Monique, "The Power of Two," *Charmed,* The WB, 1999.
Nurse, "Graduation Day: Part 2," *Buffy the Vampire Slayer* (also known as *BtVS, Buffy,* and *Buffy the Vampire Slayer: The Series*), The WB, 1999.
Roxanne's mom, "Corruption," *Oh Baby,* Lifetime, 1999.
Kim, "The Billboard," *Suddenly Susan,* NBC, 1999.
Woman, *Family Law,* CBS, 1999.
Nurse number two, "Rabbit Punch," *Battery Park,* NBC, 2000.
Interviewer, "A Midsummer Night's Nightmare," *Zoe, Duncan, Jack & Jane* (also known as *Zoe* and *Zoe ...*), The BW, 2000.
Miss Swift, "Stealing the Spotlight," *The Jersey,* Disney Channel, 2000.

The nurse, "The Enforcer," *Hang Time,* NBC, 2000.
Lily Chang, ""A Little Dad'll Do Ya," *NYPD Blue,* ABC, 2002.
Travel agent, "Palm Springs, California," *The Sweet Spot,* Comedy Central, 2002.
Michelle Wu, "The Cost of Freedom," *The Division* (also known as *The Heart of the City*), Lifetime, 2003.
"The One with Rachel's Dream," *Friends,* NBC, 2003.
"A Vote of Confidence," *Charlie Lawrence,* CBS, 2003.
Kathleen, "Mr. Monk Goes to the Theater," *Monk,* USA Network, 2003.
Pilates instructor, "Antonia Ramos," *Nip/Tuck,* FX Channel, 2003.
Attending physician, "Groundhog Summer," *Las Vegas,* NBC, 2003.
Bloodhound cop, "Coming of Rage," *CSI: Crime Scene Investigation* (also known as *CSI: Weekends, CSI: Las Vegas, C.S.I.,* and *Les Experts*), CBS, 2003.
Ying–Mei Kranski, "Dancing Beene," *Oliver Beene,* Fox, 2003.
Ying–Mei Kranski, "Babysitting," *Oliver Beene,* Fox, 2003.
Penny, *Significant Others,* Bravo, 2004.
Dr. Chase, "Control," *Huff,* Showtime, 2004.
Christine, "Valerie Stands Up for Aunt Sassy," *The Comeback,* HBO, 2005.
Captain Trish Wong, "Toy Soldiers," *E–Ring,* NBC, 2005.
Jing Chen, "Five Little Indians," *The Evidence,* 2006.
Bonnie, "Perseverance," *Help Me Help You,* ABC, 2006.
Herself, *Comedy Zen,* 2006.
Sun, "Single Dates," *The Winner,* Fox, 2007.

CHUCKLESTEIN, Shecky
   See OSWALT, Patton

CONNOLLY, John G.
   (John Connolly, John Gleeson Connolly)

PERSONAL

Career: Actor.

CREDITS

Film Appearances:
(As John Connolly) Baton inmate, *Poison,* Zeitgeist Films, 1991.
Charles, *A, B, C ... Manhattan* (also known as *Avenue A, B, C ... Manhattan*), 1997.
Dink, *Cost of Living,* 1997.
John Woods, *Whatever,* Sony Pictures Classics, 1998.

Serge, *My Sister's Wedding,* 2001.

Assistant director, *Ali,* Columbia, 2001.

(As John Connolly) Roger O'Malley, *Stolen Summer,* Miramax, 2002.

Man with flowers, *Flowers* (short), 2002.

Paul, *Last Day* (short), 2002.

(Uncredited) Norm the contractor, *The Company* (also known as *The Company—Das Ensemble*), Sony Pictures Classics, 2003.

Reporter, *Mr. 3000,* Buena Vista, 2004.

Lieutenant Alabama "Bama" Cobb, *xXx: State of the Union* (also known as *xXx 2: The Next Level, Cold Circle & Intersection,* and *xXx: The Next Level*), Sony, 2005.

Dean, *Homeland,* 2007.

Television Appearances; Miniseries:

(As John Connolly) DaCosta, *Internal Affairs,* CBS, 1988.

Television Appearances; Movies:

(As John Connolly) James Brady, *The Day Reagan Was Shot,* Showtime, 2001.

(As John Connolly) Mr. Oulendorf, *Sons of Mistletoe,* CBS, 2001.

(As John Connolly) Plumber, *The Pentagon Papers,* FX Channel, 2003.

(As John Connolly) District attorney, *The Wives He Forgot,* Lifetime, 2006.

Television Appearances; Pilots:

Lieutenant Arra, *New York Undercover* (also known as *Uptown Undercover*), Fox, 1994.

Television Appearances; Episodic:

Art, "High on the Hog," *New York Undercover* (also known as *Uptown Undercover*), Fox, 1995.

Happy hour guy, "Jim Carrey/Soundgarden," *Saturday Night Live* (also known as *SNL*), NBC, 1996.

Anderson, "Burden," *Law & Order,* NBC, 1998.

"Bay of Married Pigs," *Sex and the City,* HBO, 1998.

(As John Connolly) Harold Storum, *JAG,* 1999.

Satch, "Saturday Night," *Walker, Texas Ranger* (also known as *Ranger*), CBS, 2001.

Sergeant Mike McLaren, "Day 5: 9:00 a.m.–10:00 a.m.," *24,* Fox, 2006.

(As John Gleeson Connolly) Keller, "Games of Chance," *The Unit,* CBS, 2007.

WRITINGS

Screenplays:

(As John Connolly) *Eddie,* 1996.

CORMACK, Danielle

PERSONAL

Married Hayden Anderson; children: one.

Career: Actress and writer. Author of plays produced in New Zealand.

Awards, Honors: New Zealand Film and Television Awards, best actress, 1997, for *Topless Women Talk about Their Lives;* International Fantasy Film Award, best actress, Fantasporto, 2000, for *Siam Sunset.*

CREDITS

Film Appearances:

Molly, *The Last Tattoo,* Capella International, 1994.

Vera, *A Game with No Rules* (short), Der KurzFilmVerleih, 1994.

Liz, *Topless Women Talk about Their Lives,* Palace, 1997.

Chrissy Dunn and Carol Dunn, *Via Satellite,* 1998.

Grace, *Siam Sunset,* United International Pictures, 1999.

Bunnie, *Channelling Baby,* Oceania Parker, 1999.

Lucinda, *The Price of Milk,* Lot 47 Films, 2000.

Tony, *Without a Paddle,* Paramount, 2004.

Wife, *The Pool* (short), 2005.

Viola, *River Queen,* Twentieth Century–Fox, 2005.

Pregnant woman, *Perfect Creature,* Twentieth Century–Fox, 2006.

Television Appearances; Series:

Tania, *Gloss,* TV New Zealand, 1987.

Nurse Alison Rayner Warner, *Shortland Street,* 1992–95, 1997.

Ephiny, *Xena: Warrior Princess,* syndicated, 1995–2001.

Raina, *Cleopatra 2525,* syndicated, 2000.

Maddie, *Maddigan's Quest,* TV2 and BBC, 2006.

Television Appearances; Miniseries:

Herself, *Intrepid Journeys 2,* TV New Zealand, 2004.

Television Appearances; Movies:

Samsara, *Amazon High,* 1997.

Lynn Fabrizio, *Maiden Voyage* (also known as *Maiden Voyage: Ocean Hijack*), 2004.

Television Appearances; Episodic:

Meghan Kelly, "Sitting Ducks," *High Tide,* syndicated, 1994.

Jill McMillan, "Dead Heat," *High Tide,* syndicated, 1995.

Lady Marie DeValle, "Les Contemptibles," *Hercules: The Legendary Journeys,* syndicated, 1997.

Ephiny, "Prodigal Sister," *Hercules: The Legendary Journeys,* syndicated, 1997.

Ephiny, "Sky High," *Hercules: The Legendary Journeys,* syndicated, 1999.

Samsara, "Lifeblood," *Xena: Warrior Princess,* syndicated, 2000.

Catherine the Great, "A Horse of a Different Color," *Jack of All Trades,* 2000.

Dimity Rush, "Perfect Little Rosebud," *Rude Awakenings,* TV New Zealand, 2007.

Also appeared in *The Call Up; Marlin Bay; Overnight.*

Stage Appearances:
East, New Zealand and Swiss cities, 1994.

Also appeared in *Arcadia; The Learner's Stand; Return of the Summer Street Seven; Spare Prick.*

COSTO, Oscar L. 1953–
 (Oscar Costo, Oscar Luis Costo)

PERSONAL

Born July 11, 1953, in Havana, Cuba; married Vivian Wu (an actress), December 30, 1996.

Career: Producer and director. Mar de Oro Films, partner.

Awards, Honors: Video Premiere Award nomination, best live–action video premiere movie, DVD Exclusive Awards, 2001, for *Prancer Returns.*

CREDITS

Film Work:
Associate producer and production manager, *The Unholy,* Vestron Pictures, 1988.

Associate producer and production manager, *Midnight Crossing,* Vestron Pictures, 1988.

Producer and unit production manager, *Judgment* (also known as *Hitz*), Vidmark Entertainment, 1989.

Producer, *Excessive Force,* New Line Cinema, 2001.

(As Oscar Luis Costco) Coproducer, *Kinamand* (also known as *Chinaman*), Nordisk Film Biografdistribution, 2005.

Director and producer, *Shanghai Red,* 2006.

Television Work; Series:
(Uncredited) Co–executive producer and producer, *Sins of the City,* USA Network, 1998.

Television Work; Movies:
Coproducer, *Somebody Has to Shoot the Picture,* HBO, 1990.

Unit production manager, *Psycho IV: The Beginning,* NBC, 1991.

Producer, *Murder 101,* 1991.

Producer and unit production manager, *Red Wind,* 1991.

(Uncredited) Producer and unit production manager, *White Lie,* 1991.

Coproducer, *The Broken Cord,* ABC, 1992.

Producer and unit production manager, *Blindsided,* 1993.

Producer, second unit director, and unit production manager, *Vanishing Son,* 1994.

Producer, *Vanishing Son II,* syndicated, 1994.

Producer, *Vanishing Son III,* syndicated, 1994.

Producer, unit manager, and second unit director, *Vanishing Son IV,* syndicated, 1994.

Producer and unit production manager, *Dead Air,* Showtime, 1994.

Producer, *The Chippendales Murder,* USA Network, 2000.

Director, *My Funny Valentine,* 2000.

(As Oscar Luis Costco) Co–executive producer and producer, *Prancer Returns,* USA Network, 2001.

Producer, *Hitched,* USA Network, 2001.

Producer, *Saint Sinner* (also known as *Clive Barker's "Saint Sinner"*), Sci–Fi Channel, 2002.

(As Oscar Luis Costco) Producer, *Stealing Christmas,* USA Network, 2003.

Director, *Encrypt,* Sci–Fi Channel, 2003.

(As Oscar Luis Costco) Producer, unit production manager, and second unit director, *The Last Ride,* USA Network, 2004.

Television Director; Specials:
My Funny Valentine, 2000.

Television Producer; Episodic:
"Vapors," *SeaQuest DSV* (also known as *SeaQuest 2032*), NBC, 1994.

"When We Dead Awaken," *SeaQuest DSV* (also known as *SeaQuest 2032*), NBC, 1994.

"Dagger Redux," *SeaQuest DSV* (also known as *SeaQuest 2032*), NBC, 1995.

"Splashdown," *SeaQuest DSV* (also known as *SeaQuest 2032*), NBC, 1995.

Television Production Manager; Episodic:
"Dagger Redux," *SeaQuest DSV* (also known as *SeaQuest 2032*), NBC, 1995.

"Splashdown," *SeaQuest DSV* (also known as *SeaQuest 2032*), NBC, 1995.

Television Director; Episodic:
New York Undercover (also known as *Uptown Undercover*), Fox, 1994.
"Dream Weaver," *SeaQuest DSV* (also known as *SeaQuest 2032*), NBC, 1995.
"Dagger Redux," *SeaQuest DSV* (also known as *SeaQuest 2032*), NBC, 1995.
"Spindrift," *SeaQuest DSV* (also known as *SeaQuest 2032*), NBC, 1995.
"Resurrection," *SeaQuest DSV* (also known as *SeaQuest 2032*), NBC, 1995.
Swift Justice, 1996.
(As Oscar Costo) "The Good, the Bad and the Wealthy," *Sliders,* Fox, 1996.
"In Dino Veritas," *Sliders,* Fox, 1996.
The Burning Zone, UPN, 1996.
Dark Skies, NBC, 1996.
Viper, NBC, 1997.
413 Hope Street, 1997.
"Prison Story," *The Pretender,* NBC, 1997.
Soldier of Fortune, Inc. (also known as *S.O.F., Inc., S.O.F. Special Ops Force,* and *SOF, Inc.*), syndicated, 1997.
The Net, USA Network, 1998.
Three, 1998.
(As Oscar Costco) "The Pack," *Special Unit 2* (also known as *SU2*), UPN, 2001.
(As Oscar Costco) "The Waste," *Special Unit 2* (also known as *SU2*), UPN, 2001.
"The Skin," *Special Unit 2* (also known as *SU2*), UPN, 2001.
"The Eve," *Special Unit 2* (also known as *SU2*), UPN, 2001.
"The Love," *Special Unit 2* (also known as *SU2*), UPN, 2001.

WRITINGS

Screenplays:
Shanghai Red, 2006.

COX, Christina 1971–

PERSONAL

Born July 31, 1971, in Toronto, Ontario, Canada; father, an automotive executive. *Education:* Studied acting at Ryerson University Theatre School, Ryerson University.

Addresses: *Agent*—Metropolitan Talent Agency, 4500 Wilshire Blvd., Second Floor, Los Angeles, CA 90010; Paradigm, 360 North Crescent Dr., North Building, Beverly Hills, CA 90210. *Manager*—Brillstein–Grey Entertainment, 9150 Wilshire Blvd., Suite 350, Beverly Hills, CA 90212; Lauren Levitt and Associates, 1525 West Eighth Ave., Third Floor, Vancouver, British Columbia V6J 1T5, Canada.

Career: Actress.

Awards, Honors: Gemini Award nomination, best performance by an actress in a continuing leading dramatic role, Academy of Canadian Cinema and Television, 1998, for *F/X: The Series.*

CREDITS

Television Appearances; Series:
Angela "Angie" Ramirez, *F/X: The Series* (also known as *F/X, F/X: Efeitos mortais, F/X, effets speciaux,* and *F/X—murha tilauksesta*), CTV (Canada) and syndicated, 1996–98.
Jessica Capshaw, *The Crow: Stairway to Heaven* (also known as *The Crow, Witch Crow, El cuervo,* and *O corvo*), syndicated, 1998–99.
Vicki Nelson, *Blood Ties,* Lifetime, beginning 2007.

Television Appearances; Movies:
Detective Elizabeth "Beth" Jordan, *No One Could Protect Her,* ABC, 1996.
Natalie Grenier, *A Brother's Promise: The Dan Jansen Story,* CBS, 1996.
Officer Ida Cruz, *Mistrial,* HBO, 1996.
Volunteer, *Sins of Silence,* CBS, 1996.
Aurora, *Code Name Phoenix* (also known as *Code Name—Phoenix, Codigo: Phoenix,* and *Koodinimi Phoenix*), UPN, 2000.
Peta, *Jane Doe* (also known as *Runaway Jane*), USA Network, 2001.

Television Appearances; Episodic:
Jeanne d'Arc, "Dying to Know You," *Forever Knight,* CBS, 1992.
Jeanne d'Arc, "For I Have Sinned," *Forever Knight,* CBS, 1992.
Caroline Morgan, "Free Willie," *Due South* (also known as *Due South: The Series* and *Direction: Sud*), CTV (Canada) and CBS, 1994.
Jeanne d'Arc, "Faithful Followers," *Forever Knight,* syndicated, 1994.
Motorcycle police officer, "Close Call," *Forever Knight,* syndicated, 1994.
Caroline Morgan, "Vault," *Due South* (also known as *Due South: The Series* and *Direction: Sud*), CTV (Canada) and CBS, 1995.
Kyra, "Quake!," *Kung Fu: The Legend Continues,* syndicated, 1995.

Tessa Jones, "The Debt Collectors," *The Hardy Boys,* syndicated, 1995.

Lucy, "When She Was Good," *Lonesome Dove: The Outlaw Years,* syndicated, 1996.

Prostitute in limousine, "Petty Tyranny," *The Newsroom* (also known as *Tehdaeaempae uutiset*), CBC, 1996.

Jody Nolan, "Joshua," *First Wave,* Sci–Fi Channel, 1998.

T'akaya, "Spirits," *Stargate SG–1* (also known as *La porte des etoiles* and *Stargaate SG–1*), Sci–Fi Channel, Showtime, and syndicated, 1998.

Haley Simmons, "Second Chances," *Earth: Final Conflict* (also known as *EFC, Gene Roddenberry's "Battleground Earth," Gene Roddenberry's "Earth: Final Conflict," Invasion planete Terre,* and *Mission Erde: Sie sind unter uns*), syndicated, 1999.

Haley Simmons, "Thicker Than Blood," *Earth: Final Conflict* (also known as *EFC, Gene Roddenberry's "Battleground Earth," Gene Roddenberry's "Earth: Final Conflict," Invasion planete Terre,* and *Mission Erde: Sie sind unter uns*), syndicated, 1999.

Deb, "Skin Deep," *The Outer Limits* (also known as *The New Outer Limits*), Showtime, Sci–Fi Channel, and syndicated, 2000.

Haley Simmons, "Take No Prisoners," *Earth: Final Conflict* (also known as *EFC, Gene Roddenberry's "Battleground Earth," Gene Roddenberry's "Earth: Final Conflict," Invasion planete Terre,* and *Mission Erde: Sie sind unter uns*), syndicated, 2000.

Jessica "Jessie" Wilson, "GeoCore," *PSI Factor: Chronicles of the Paranormal* (also known as *PSI Factor*), CanWest Global Television and syndicated, 2000.

Sasha, "The Shift," *Code Name: Eternity* (also known as *Code: Eternity*), syndicated, 2000.

"Castle Keep," *Dark Realm* (also known as *Le monde des tenebres*), Sci–Fi Channel, 2000.

Lieutenant Kershaw, "Sentinel," *Stargate SG–1* (also known as *La porte des etoiles* and *Stargaate SG–1*), Sci–Fi Channel, Showtime, and syndicated, 2002.

Becky Dolan, "The Grift," *Mutant X,* syndicated, 2003.

Margo, "Damsels in De–Stress," *She Spies* (also known as *B.A.I.T., Ele spioneaza, Kemcsajok,* and *Superespias*), syndicated, 2003.

Sherry Stephens, "Sherry Darlin'," *Cold Case,* CBS, 2003.

Aleiss, "Exalted Reason, Resplendent Daughter," *Andromeda* (also known as *Gene Roddenberry's "Andromeda"*), syndicated, 2004.

Jenny Moylan, "Stalkerazzi," *CSI: Miami,* CBS, 2004.

Pamela, "Braveheart," *The Chris Isaak Show,* Showtime, 2004.

Annette Raines, "Love Hurts," *House M.D.* (also known as *House*), Fox, 2005.

CHP officer Morris, "Man Hunt," *Numb3rs* (also known as *Numbers* and *Num3ers*), CBS, 2005.

Linda Barstow, "Wings," *Eyes,* ABC, 2005.

Wendy, *This Is Wonderland* (also known as *Wonderland* and *La corte di Alice*), CBC, 2005.

Appeared in other programs, including *E.N.G.,* CTV (Canada) and Lifetime.

Television Appearances; Pilots:

Angela "Angie" Ramirez, *F/X: The Illusion* (also known as *F/X, F/X: The Series, F/X: Efeitos mortais, F/X, effets speciaux,* and *F/X—murha tilauksesta*), CTV (Canada) and syndicated, 1996.

Nora Delaney (some sources cite name as Nora Dechene), *Nikki & Nora,* UPN, 2004.

Alex Dion, *The Line,* TNT, 2005.

Appeared as Lynn in the unaired pilot of *Girlfriends,* The WB.

Film Appearances:

Tricia, *Common Ground,* 1990.

Deb, *Spike of Love,* 1995.

Kelly, *Street Law* (also known as *Law of the Jungle*), Triboro Entertainment Group, 1995.

Angel, *The Donor* (also known as *The Doner* and *The Giver*), Donor Productions, 1997.

Kim, *Better Than Chocolate* (also known as *Meilleur que le chocolat*), Trimark Pictures, 1999.

Cassandra Diaz, *Sometimes a Hero* (also known as *Cold Vengeance*), Amsell Entertainment, 2000.

Eve Logan, *The Chronicles of Riddick* (also known as *Pitch Black 2, Pitch Black 2: Chronicles of Riddick, Riddick, A batalha de Riddick, Kroniki Riddicka, La batalla de Riddick, Las cronicas de Riddick, Les chroniques de Riddick, Riddick—Chroniken eines Kriegers,* and *Riddickin aikakirja*), Universal, 2004, director's cut released as *The Chronicles of Riddick: The Director's Cut.*

Suzie Blaine, *Max Havoc: Ring of Fire* (also known as *O kyklos tis fotias*), 2006.

Margaret Whitehead, *Ascension Day* (also known as *3/5 of a Man*), Freedom Reign Productions/Oxbow Productions, 2007.

Film Stunt Performer:

Million Dollar Baby (also known as *Rope Burns, Golpes del destino, La fille a un million de dollars, Menina de ouro, Miljoni dollari tuedruk,* and *Za wszelka cene*), Warner Bros., 2004.

Stage Appearances:

Appeared in *Road* and *Twelfth Night* (also known as *Twelfth Night, or What You Will*).

OTHER SOURCES

Periodicals:

Advocate, August 31, 1999, pp. 58–59.

Cult Times, February, 2001, p. 11.

Electronic:

Christina Cox, http://www.christinacox.com, April 20, 2007.

D

DAKOTA, Alan
    See BALTES, Alan

DALE, Holly 1953–

PERSONAL

Born December 23, 1953, in Toronto, Ontario, Canada. *Education:* Sheridan College, degree in media arts, 1977.

Addresses: *Agent*—The Kaplan Stahler Gumer Braun Agency, 8383 Wilshire Blvd., Suite 923, Beverly Hills, CA 90211. *Manager*—Course Management, 15159 Greenleaf St., Sherman Oaks, CA 91403.

Career: Producer, director, and editor. Spectrum Films, Inc., Toronto, Ontario, cofounder (with Janis Cole) and partner; director of numerous commercials. Canadian Centre for Advanced Film Studies, resident, 1988; member of juries for film competitions; teacher of acting workshops and lectures at universities worldwide. Municipality of Metropolitan Toronto, member of arts advisory board, 1992. French Connection (massage parlor), assistant manager, c. 1973.

Awards, Honors: Genie Award (with Janis Cole), best theatrical documentary, Academy of Canadian Cinema and Television, 1982, Red Ribbon, American Film and Video Festival, 1983, both for *P4W: Prison for Women;* Genie Award nomination (with Cole), best theatrical documentary, Gold Plaque, Chicago International Film Festival, 1985, Red Ribbon, American Film and Video Festival, 1986, all for *Hookers on Davie;* named best lecture/performing artist, Canadian Organization of Campus Activities, 1986; Theatrical Achievement

Award (with Cole), producer of the year, Canadian Film and Television Association, 1988; Genie Award nomination (with Cole), best feature length documentary, Lillian Gish Award, Los Angeles Women in Film, Red Ribbon, American Film and Video Festival, 1989, all for *Calling the Shots;* Bessie Award, Marketing Awards of Excellence, 1993, for public service announcements for United Way; Toronto Arts Award for Excellence in Media Arts (with Cole), City of Toronto, 1994; Gemini Award nominations, best direction in a dramatic program or miniseries, Academy of Canadian Cinema and Television, 1998, for *Dangerous Offender;* Craft Award nominations, outstanding achievement in direction, Directors Guild of Canada, 2002, for *A Nero Wolfe Mystery;* Gemini Award nomination, best direction in a dramatic series, 2003, for *Bliss.*

CREDITS

Film Work:
(With Janis Cole) Producer, director, and editor, *Cream Soda* (short), Canadian Filmmakers Distribution Centre, 1976.

Editor, *Point of No Return,* International Film Distributors, 1976.

Assistant producer and casting director, *Starship Invasions* (also known as *Alien Encounter, Project Genocide,* and *War of the Aliens*), Warner Bros., 1977.

Producer, *Plague* (also known as *Induced Syndrome, —3: The Gemini Strain,* and *Mutation*), Group 1 International Distributing Organization, 1978.

(With Cole) Producer, director, and editor, *The Thin Line* (documentary; also known as *The Thin Blue Line*), National Film Board of Canada, 1977.

(With Cole) Producer, director, and editor, *Minimum Charge, No Cover* (documentary), 1978.

Casting director, *Firebird 2015 AD,* 1981.

(With Cole) Producer, director, and editor, *Hookers on Davie* (documentary), Pan–Canadian Film Distributors, 1984.

(With Cole) Producer, director, and editor, *Calling the Shots* (documentary), Pan–Canadian Film Distributors, 1988.
Director, *Dead Meat,* E.I. Video, 1989.
Associate producer, *Ethan Frome,* Miramax, 1993.
Director, *Blood & Donuts,* Live Entertainment, 1995.

Film Appearances:
Television interviewee, *Starship Invasions* (also known as *Alien Encounter, Project Genocide,* and *War of the Aliens*), Warner Bros., 1977.

Television Work; Movies:
Coproducer, codirector, and coeditor, *No Place like Home,* CHCH, 1991.
Director, *Dangerous Offender* (also known as *Dangerous Offender: The Marlene Moore Story*), CBC, 1996.
Director, *Wolfe Goes Out: A Nero Wolfe Mystery,* Arts and Entertainment, 2000.
Director, *Absolution,* Lifetime, 2006.
Director, *Wednesday's Child,* Lifetime, 2007.

Television Work; Specials:
(With Cole) Producer, director, and editor, *P4W: Prison for Women* (documentary), CBC, 1981.

Television Work; Pilots:
(With Cole) Producer, director, and editor, *Quiet on the Set: Filming Agnes of God,* HBO, c. 1985.
Director, *Tracker,* 2001.

Television Director; Episodic:
"Agnes Macphail," *Heritage Series,* CBC, 1991.
"Murphy," *Heritage Series,* CBC, 1993.
"In Sickness and in Health," *Side Effects,* CBC, 1994.
"Sharper Than a Serpent's Tooth," *Traders,* Lifetime and Global, 1996.
"The Accident," *Exhibit A* (also known as *Exhibit 2: Secrets of Forensic Science* and *Secrets of Forensic Science*), 1997.
"Bone of Contention," *Exhibit A* (also known as *Exhibit 2: Secrets of Forensic Science* and *Secrets of Forensic Science*), 1997.
The City (also known as *Deep in the City*), CTV, 1999.
Twice in a Lifetime, CTV and PAX, 1999.
Amazon (also known as *Peter Benchley's "Amazon"*), syndicated, 1999.
First Wave, Sci–Fi Channel, 1999–2000.
"Door to Death," *A Nero Wolfe Mystery* (also known as *Nero Wolfe*), 2001.
"Christmas Party," *A Nero Wolfe Mystery* (also known as *Nero Wolfe*), 2001.
"All Chocked Up," *Relic Hunter* (also known as *Relic Hunter—Die Schatzjagerin* and *Sydney Fox*), syndicated, 2001.
"Double Down," *Tracker,* syndicated, 2002.

"A Made Guy," *Tracker,* syndicated, 2002.
"Thieves' Honor," *Jeremiah,* Showtime, 2002.
"Valentine's Day in Jail," *Bliss* (also known as *Bliss II*), Oxygen, 2002.
"Leaper," *Bliss* (also known as *Bliss II*), Oxygen, 2002.
"Thieves' Honor," *Jeremiah,* Showtime, 2002.
"Above the Law," *Just Cause,* PAX, 2002.
"Buried Past," *Just Cause,* PAX, 2003.
"Lies, Speculation & Deception," *Just Cause,* PAX, 2003.
"Nina's Muse," *Bliss* (also known as *Bliss II*), Oxygen, 2003.
"Cat Got Your Tongue," *Bliss* (also known as *Bliss II*), Oxygen, 2003.
Sue Thomas: F.B.Eye, 2003–2005.
"Home," *Stargate: Atlantis* (also known as *La porte d'Atlantis* and *Stargate: Atlantis*), Sci–Fi Channel, 2004.
"Blindsided," *Doc,* PAX, 2004.
The Collector, CityTV, 2004–2006.
Wildfire, ABC Family, 2005.
"Last Night," *1–800–MISSING* (also known as *Missing*), Lifetime, 2005.
"Exposure," *1–800–MISSING* (also known as *Missing*), Lifetime, 2006.
"Double Take," *1–800–MISSING* (also known as *Missing*), Lifetime, 2006.
"So Shall Ye Reap," *1–800–MISSING* (also known as *Missing*), Lifetime, 2006.
"The Lies That Bind," *Kyle XY,* ABC Family, 2006.
"Blue–Eyed Blues," *Angela's Eyes,* Lifetime, 2006.
"The Good–Bye Room," *Cold Case,* CBS, 2007.
"Stone Cold," *Blood Ties,* Lifetime, 2007.
"What Lies Beneath," *Durham County,* 2007.
"The Lady of the Lake," *Durham County,* 2007.
"Divide and Conquer," *Durham County,* 2007.
"Guys and Dolls," *Durham County,* 2007.

Also directed "Wrapped," *Blood Ties,* Lifetime.

WRITINGS

Film Scripts:
Coauthor, *Calling the Shots* (documentary), Pan–Canadian Film Distributors, 1988.

Television Pilots:
(With Cole) *Quiet on the Set: Filming Agnes of God,* HBO, c. 1985.

Other:
Contributor, *Calling the Shots: Profiles of Women Filmmakers,* edited by Janis Cole, Quarry Press (Kingston, Ontario), 1993.

OTHER SOURCES

Books:
Women Filmmakers and Their Films, St. James Press, 1998.

Electronic:

Holly Dale Website, http://www.hollydaledirector.com, July 20, 2007.

DALLAS, Keith 1978(?)–
　　(Keith "Blackman" Dallas, Kieth Dallas)

PERSONAL

Born c. 1978, in Jamaica; raised in Vancouver, British Columbia, Canada.

Career: Actor. Also known as Kieth Dallas.

CREDITS

Film Appearances:

Bouncer at Silk's, *Romeo Must Die* (also known as *Romeo debe morir, Romeo deve morire, Romeo deve morrer, Romeo doit mourir, Romeon on kuoltava, Romeu tem que morrer,* and *Sa moara Romeo*), Warner Bros., 2000.

Detective, *Trixie,* Columbia/TriStar, 2000.

Henchman, *The Stickup,* Promark Entertainment Group, 2001.

Third heckler, *Say It Isn't So* (also known as *Diga que nao e verdade, Dime que no es cierto, Dime que no es verdad, Dimmi che non e vero, Ei voi olla totta, Ohne Worte, Skojar du, eller?,* and *Trop c'est trop*), Twentieth Century–Fox, 2001.

Lunchbox, *I Spy* (also known as *I–Spy*), Columbia/TriStar, 2002.

Young man, *Liberty Stands Still* (also known as *Liberty stands still—Im Visier des Moerders*), Lions Gate Films, 2002.

Cook, *The Hot Karl II,* Gastown Films, 2003.

Spend Mart clerk, *A Guy Thing* (also known as *Cosa de hombres, Cosas de tios, Cose da machi, Gelegenheit macht Liebe, Ivresse et consequences, Louco por elas, Miehen mieli,* and *Typiquement masculin*), Metro–Goldwyn–Mayer, 2003.

Orderly, *Riding the Bullet,* Innovation Film Group, 2004.

The bartender, *Fallen* (short film), A Muse Productions, 2005.

Cab driver, *The Sisterhood of the Traveling Pants* (also known as *The Sisterhood of the Travelling Pants, Eine fuer 4, 4 amiche e un paio di jeans, Neljae tyttoeae ja maagiset farkut, Quatre filles et un jean, Quatro amigas e um jeans viajante, Systrar I jeans,* and *Uno para todas*), Warner Bros., 2005.

Melvin the security guard, *Underclassman,* Miramax, 2005.

(As Keith "Blackman" Dallas) Big Leroy, *Snakes on a Plane* (also known as *Anaconda 3, Flight 121, Pacific Air Flight 121, Pacific Air 121, Snake Flight, SoaP, Venom, Des serpents dans l'avion, Maod lennukis, Serpentes a bordo, Serpents a bord, Serpientes a bordo, Terror a bordo,* and *Terror en el aire*), New Line Cinema, 2006.

Offensive lineman, *Final Destination 3* (also known as *Final Destination 3–D, Destination finale 3, Destino final 3, Final destination 3—viimeinen maeaeraenpaeae, Premonicao 3, Put bez povratka 3,* and *Vlepo to thanato sou 3*), New Line Cinema, 2006.

Officer Porter, *When a Man Falls in the Forest,* Redwood Palms Pictures, 2007.

Security guard, *Kickin It Old Skool,* Yari Film Group Releasing, 2007.

Keith Mendlesson, *Control Alt Delete,* Hard Drive Films, 2008.

Television Appearances; Series:

Sal Repisto, *Intelligence* (also known as *Hiszerzoek* and *Servicio de inteligencia*), CBC, beginning 2006.

Dave Graham, *Blood Ties,* Lifetime, beginning 2007.

Television Appearances; Movies:

First Demon fan, "H–E Double Hockey Sticks" (also known as "Demons et merveilles," "Entrando numa fria," and "Griffelkin—Ein Teufel auf Abwegen"), *The Wonderful World of Disney,* ABC, 1999.

Agent Orange, *Oh, Baby* (also known as *Bratty Babies, Menudos bebes, Paroles de bebes, Solos en casa,* and *Zwei Superbabies starten durch*), 2001.

Executive, *Till Dad Do Us Part,* Fox Family Channel, 2001.

Jamal, *Double Bill* (also known as *A Tale of Two Wives*), Oxygen, 2003.

Bouncer, *5ive Days to Midnight* (also known as *Five Days to Midnight*), Sci-Fi Channel, 2004.

Big man, *School of Life,* ABC Family Channel, 2005.

Bob, *Chasing Christmas,* ABC Family Channel, 2005.

Inmate, *A Little Thing Called Murder,* Lifetime, 2006.

Television Appearances; Episodic:

"Brothers," *Neon Rider,* syndicated, 1992.

First head, "The Football," *Seven Days* (also known as *7 Days* and *Seven Days: The Series*), UPN, 1999.

Archduke, "DefCon," *Level 9* (also known as *Nivel 9* and *Unite 9*), UPN, 2000.

O. G., "I and I Am a Camera," *Dark Angel* (also known as *James Cameron's "Dark Angel"*), Fox, 2001.

Arnold, "The Brink," *Seven Days* (also known as *7 Days* and *Seven Days: The Series*), UPN, 2001.

Security guard, "Instant Karma," *Strange Frequency,* VH1, 2001.

Freddie Mac, "City on Fire," *UC: Undercover* (also known as *Undercover*), NBC, 2001.

Kent, "The Ducks Are Too Depressing," *Da Vinci's Inquest*, CBC, 2003.

Man, "Memphis," *The Twilight Zone*, UPN, 2003.

Jerome, "The Prodigal Son," *Black Sash* (also known as *The Black Sash* and *The Bounty Hunter*), The WB, 2003.

Second guard, "The Prosecutor," *The Collector*, Space Television and City TV, 2004.

Bouncer, "No Life Like It," *Cold Squad*, CTV, 2004.

Shanks, "Woman Seeking Dead Husband: Smokers Okay, No Pets," *Psych*, USA Network, 2006.

Appeared in *Smallville* (also known as *Smallville: Beginnings* and *Smallville: Superman the Early Years*), The WB (later The CW). Appeared as Charles in "Disappearances," an unaired episode of *Still Life*, Fox.

Television Appearances; Pilots:

Impatient man, *Dead Like Me* (also known as *Dead Girl, Mitt liv som doed,* and *Tan muertos como yo*), Showtime, 2003.

RECORDINGS

Videos:

Himself, *Meet the Reptiles* (short), New Line Home Video, 2006.

Himself, *Pure Venom: The Making of "Snakes on a Plane"* (short), New Line Home Video, 2006.

Himself, *Snakes on a Set: Behind the Scenes* (short), New Line Home Video, 2006.

Video Games:

Voice of House, *Def Jam Fight for NY*, Electronic Arts, 2004.

DAVIES, Kimberley 1973–
(Kimberly Davies)

PERSONAL

Born February 20, 1973, in Ballarat, Victoria, Australia; married Jason Harvey (a doctor), 1997; children: Isabella, Joshua.

Addresses: *Agent*—Kazarian/Spencer & Associates, 11969 Ventura Blvd., Third Floor, Box 7409, Studio City, CA 91604. *Manager*—Evolution Entertainment, 901 North Highland Ave., Los Angeles, CA 90038.

Career: Actress. Appeared in advertisements and promotional trailers. Also known as Kimberly Davies.

CREDITS

Television Appearances; Series:

Annalise, *Neighbours* (also known as *Buren, Vecinos, Veiens,* and *Los voisins*), Ten Network (Australia), 1993–96.

Host, *Just Kidding!,* [Australia], c. 1995–96.

Laura Sinclair, *Pacific Palisades* (also known as *Brentwood* and *L.A. Affairs*), Fox, 1997.

Herself, *Celebrity Circus,* Nine Network (Australia), beginning 2005.

Herself, *I'm a Celebrity, Get Me Out of Here!,* Independent Television (England), beginning 2005.

Herself, *Dancing with the Stars,* Seven Network (Australia), beginning 2007.

Television Appearances; Movies:

Agent Lock, *Storm Catcher,* HBO, 1999.

Cheryl McManus, *Close Contact,* Seven Network (Australia), 1999.

Regina, *The Magicians* (also known as *Death by Magic*), UPN, 2000.

Isabelle, *The Shrink Is In,* Oxygen, 2001.

Luann, *South Pacific* (musical; also known as *Rodgers & Hammerstein's "South Pacific," Al sur del pacifico,* and *Ao sul do pacifico*), ABC, 2001.

Rhonda Newcombe, *Seconds to Spare,* USA Network, 2002.

Television Appearances; Specials:

The Bob Downe Special, 1996.

Television Appearances; Episodic:

Herself, "Keeping Up Appearances," *Frontline* (also known as *Behind the Frontline* and *Breaking News*), Australian Broadcasting Corporation, 1995.

Betty, "Directly from My Heart to You," *Twisted Tales* (also known as *Twisted*), Nine Network (Australia), 1996.

Trudy, "The Return," *Viper,* syndicated, 1998.

Amber Lamonte, "The Iceman Taketh," *Early Edition,* CBS, 1999.

Rhonna Sendahl, "Killer App," *Silk Stalkings,* USA Network, 1999.

Angela Prune, "Boy Next Door," *Ally McBeal,* Fox, 2000.

Inga, "Hello Charlie," *Spin City* (also known as *Spin*), ABC, 2000.

Jade (also known as Amber), "Occasionally Amber," *Early Edition,* CBS, 2000.

Jennifer Hutton, "Tsuris," *Profiler,* NBC, 2000.

Elaine Lowe, "A Sense of Community," *The Invisible Man* (also known as *I–Man, El hombre, Invisible Man—Der Unsichtbare,* and *Naekymaetoen mies*), Sci–Fi Channel, 2001.

Adrienne Turner, "The One Where the Stripper Cries," *Friends* (also known as *Across the Hall, Friends Like Us, Insomnia Cafe,* and *Six of One*), NBC, 2004.

Annalise, "Friends for Twenty Years," *Neighbours* (also known as *Buren, Vecinos, Veiens,* and *Los voisins*), Ten Network (Australia), 2005.

Herself, *This Morning* (also known as *This Morning with Richard and Judy*), Independent Television (England), 2005.

Herself, "Superchallenge: Heat 1 and Heat 2," *Temptation* (also known as *The New Sale of the Century*), 2006.

Television Appearances; Pilots:

Maya, "The Rats of Rumfordton," *It's True,* CBS, 1998.

Film Appearances:

Ariel, *True Love and Chaos,* Westside Films, 1997.

Bettina Barnes and Diane, *Psycho Beach Party* (also known as *Verano bizarro*), Strand Releasing/CinemaVault Releasing, 2000.

Hostess, *The Next Best Thing* (also known as *The Red Curtain, Algo casi perfecto, Det naest baesta, Det naestbedste, Ein Freund zum Verlieben, Ha–davar ha–tov ha–ba, Le bonheur … ou presque, Sai che c'e di nuovo?, Sobrou pra voce, Tatli suerpriz, Una pareja casi perfecta,* and *Un couple presque parfait*), Paramount, 2000.

Bartender, *Made* (also known as *Crime desorganizado, Karski kaksikko,* and *Le match*), Artisan Entertainment, 2001.

Mrs. Zilinski, *Feather Pimento* (short film), Cafeteria Inc., 2001.

Kelly, *The Month of August,* Angelic Entertainment, 2002.

Darbie, *Death to the Supermodels* (also known as *Operacion bikini*), Metro–Goldwyn–Mayer Home Entertainment, 2005.

RECORDINGS

Videos:

Herself, *Kimberley Davies: Your Body's Callin',* Delta Music, 2004.

Video Games:

Voice of Alura McCall, *007: Nightfire,* Electronic Arts, 2002.

OTHER SOURCES

Periodicals:

Filmink, October, 1998, p. 41.

Mayfair, Volume 31, issue 3, 1996, pp. 96–97.

Stuff, August, 2000, pp. 112–15.

DAVIS, Don S. 1942–
(Don Davis, Don Sinclair Davis)

PERSONAL

Full name, Don Sinclair Davis; born August 4, 1942, in Aurora, MO; son of M. T. Davis (a lumberyard owner); married (divorced); married Ruby Fleming, July, 2003. *Education:* Southwest Missouri State College, B.S., theatre and art; Southern Illinois University, M.A., 1970, Ph.D., 1982. *Avocational Interests:* Painting, woodcarving, drawing, golfing.

Addresses: *Agent*—GVA Talent Agency (Greater Vision Agency), 9229 Sunset Blvd., Suite 320, Hollywood, CA 90069.

Career: Actor. Worked as a stunt performer; worked as a college instructor, including work at the University of British Columbia; also an artist working with various media. Appeared at science fiction conventions. *Military service:* U.S. Army, began as second lieutenant, became captain, served c. 1960s.

Awards, Honors: Director's Award, best supporting actor, Fright–Fest, 2003, for *Savage Island;* Leo Award nomination, dramatic series: best supporting performance by a male, Motion Picture Arts & Sciences Foundation of British Columbia, 2004, for *Stargate SG–1.*

CREDITS

Television Appearances; Series:

Chief Sterling, *Broken Badges,* CBS, 1990–91.

Major Garland Briggs, *Twin Peaks* (also known as *Northwest Passage*), ABC, 1990–91.

Mr. Winslow, *Madison* (also known as *Working It out at Madison*), CanWest Global Television, 1994–96.

Major general (later lieutenant general) George S. Hammond, *Stargate SG–1* (also known as *La porte des etoiles* and *Stargaate SG–1*), Sci–Fi Channel, Showtime, and syndicated, 1997—.

Television Appearances; Miniseries:

Rodeo announcer, *The Luck of the Draw: The Gambler Returns* (also known as *Der Beste Spieler weit und breit—Sein hoechster Einsatz*), NBC, 1991.

General Harlan Ford, *Atomic Train* (also known as *Atomic Train—Zugfahrt ins Jenseits, Riesgo final,* and *Zugfahrt ins Jenseits*), NBC, 1999.

Television Appearances; Movies:

(As Don Davis) Capcom, "Hero in the Family" (also known as "Apina–faija," "Auf der Suche nach dem geheimnisvollen Kristall," "Familjens hjaelte," "Foervandlingen," and "Un eroe in famiglia"), *The Disney Sunday Movie* (also known as *Disneyland, Disneylandia, Disney's Wonderful World, The Magical World of Disney, Walt Disney, Walt Disney Presents, Walt Disney's Wonderful World of Color,* and *The Wonderful World of Disney*), ABC, 1986.

(As Don Davis) Customer, *That Secret Sunday,* CBS, 1986.

Mr. Haskell, *Spot Marks the X,* Disney Channel, 1986.

(As Don Davis) Surgeon, *I–Man,* ABC, 1986.

(As Don Davis) Coroner's assistant, *Deadly Deception,* CBS, 1987.

(As Don Davis) Jury foreperson, *Sworn to Silence,* ABC, 1987.

Gun salesperson, *Body of Evidence,* CBS, 1988.

(As Don Davis) Dr. Bennett, *The Lady Forgets,* CBS, 1989.

Earle Gardner, *Matinee* (also known as *Midnight Matinee*), c. 1989.

(As Don Davis) Dr. Bauman, *Hitler's Daughter,* USA Network, 1990.

(As Don Davis) *Memories of Murder* (also known as *Murhan kuvia, Omicidio nell'ombra,* and *Toedliche Erinnerung*), Lifetime, 1990.

Congressperson Howard K. Apples, *Blood River,* CBS, 1991.

Deputy Mack, *Captive,* ABC, 1991.

Jake Madison, *Omen IV: The Awakening* (also known as *A profecia maldita, La malediction IV—L'eveil, La profecia IV: el renacer, Omen IV—Das Erwachen, Omen IV: Ondskans haemnd, Omen IV: presagio infernale,* and *Omen IV: riivaajan paluu*), Fox, 1991.

Philip Baywood, *Posing: Inspired by Three Real Stories* (also known as *I Posed for Playboy*), CBS, 1991.

(As Don Davis) Third deputy, *Deadly Intentions ... Again?* (also known as *Attrazioni omicide, Intencao de matar, Intenciones asesinas, Intencoes assassinas, Jusqu'a ce que la crime nous separe, Koston aika, Med doedlig avsikt ...?,* and *Toedliche Absichten*), ABC, 1991.

Bertie, *Columbo: A Bird in the Hand ...,* ABC, 1992.

Bill Stevens, *Dead Ahead: The Exxon Valdez Disaster* (also known as *Disaster at Valdez*), HBO, 1992.

McCann, *Calendar Girl, Cop Killer? The Bambi Bembenek Story* (also known as *The Heart of the Lie, Au coeur du mensonge, Im Herzen der Luege,* and *Szczere klamstwo*), ABC, 1992.

Dave, *Miracle on Interstate 880* (also known as *Miracle on I–880*), NBC, 1993.

Judge Gray, *Final Appeal* (also known as *L'ultime proces*), NBC, 1993.

Man at book launch, *The Diary of Evelyn Lau,* CBC, 1993.

Mr. Harper, *Without a Kiss Goodbye* (also known as *Falsely Accused* and *The Laurie Samuels Story*), CBS, 1993.

Franklin Graves, *One More Mountain,* ABC, 1994.

Sherwin Francis, *Someone Else's Child* (also known as *Lost and Found*), ABC, 1994.

Whitney, *Avalanche* (also known as *Atrapados en la montana, Avalancha, Avalanche—Geisel im Schnee, Inferno bianco,* and *Lavinen*), Fox and CTV (Canada), 1994.

Detective Larson, *A Family Divided,* NBC, 1995.

Glen Holt, *A Dream Is a Wish Your Heart Makes: The Annette Funicello Story* (also known as *A Dream Is a Wish Your Heart Makes*), CBS, 1995.

Kevin Carroll, Sr., *Shadow of a Doubt,* NBC, 1995.

Mr. Smith, *The Ranger, the Cook and a Hole in the Sky* (also known as *Hole in the Sky*), ABC, 1995.

Sergeant Dills, *Black Fox,* CBS, 1995.

Sergeant Dills, *Black Fox: The Price of Peace,* CBS, 1995.

Sheriff, *Beauty's Revenge* (also known as *Midwest Obsession*), NBC, 1995.

(As Don Davis) Vice admiral Dunleavy, *She Stood Alone: The Tailhook Scandal* (also known as *Brutale Exzesse—Skandal in der Navy* and *Em nome de nacao*), ABC, 1995.

(As Don Davis) Agent Roy Church, *In Cold Blood,* CBS, 1996.

Byron Holcomb, *Brothers of the Frontier,* ABC, 1996.

Chief Payne, *The Limbic Region,* Showtime, 1996.

Colonel Zapf, *Prisoner of Zenda, Inc.* (also known as *Double Play*), Showtime, 1996.

Dewey, *The Angel of Pennsylvania Avenue* (also known as *L'ange de Noel*), Family Channel, 1996.

Dunbar, *Kidz in the Wood,* NBC, 1996.

Detective Church, *The Stepsister,* USA Network, 1997.

Hank, *Dad's Week Off* (also known as *National Lampoon's "Dad's Week Off"*), The Movie Channel, 1997.

Man, *Tricks,* Showtime, 1997.

(As Don Davis) Mayor Bob Hart, *Volcano: Fire on the Mountain* (also known as *Fire on the Mountain, Le reveil du volcan, Volcano, la montagne de feu, Vulcano: Fogo na montanha,* and *Vulkan—Berg in Flammen*), ABC, 1997.

Warden, *The Escape,* The Movie Channel, 1997.

Alexander Daniels, *Hostage Negotiator,* USA Network, 2001.

(As Don Davis) Voice of Wild Bill, *G.I. Joe: Spy Troops the Movie* (animated), 2003.

NRC Carl Mansfield, *Meltdown* (also known as *American Meltdown*), fX Channel, 2004.

Police chief, *Child of Mine* (also known as *Blick zurueck ins Verderben* and *Pesadelo*), 2005.

Neil Chapman, *Loch Ness,* Sci–Fi Channel, 2007.

Television Appearances; Specials:
(As Don Davis) *Miracles and Other Mysteries,* ABC, 1991.

Himself, *Stargate SG–1: The Lowdown,* Sci–Fi Channel, 2003.

Television Appearances; Awards Presentations:
First Annual Spaceys, Space, 2003.

Television Appearances; Episodic:

Benny, "Goodbye Delvecchio's, Hello World," *Joanie Loves Chachi*, ABC, 1982.

Agent Ruck, "Beans Finds His Dad but ...: Part 1," *The New Adventures of Beans Baxter*, Fox, 1987.

(As Don Davis) Cement truck driver, "Blow Out," *MacGyver*, ABC, 1987.

Principal Harris, "Blindsided," *21 Jump Street*, Fox, 1987.

Frank, "Chapel of Love," *21 Jump Street*, Fox, 1988.

Howard Usher, "The Bay Mystery," *The Beachcombers* (also known as *Beachcombers*), CBC, 1988.

Wyatt Porter, "The Endangered," *MacGyver*, ABC, 1988.

Dr. Morris, "Stairway to Heaven," *Wiseguy*, CBS, 1989.

Josiah Richmond, "Over the Line," *Bordertown* (also known as *Les deux font la loi*), Family Channel and CanWest Global Television, 1989.

Prison guard, "Flat Out," *Booker* (also known as *Booker, P.I.*), Fox, 1989.

"Burn Out," *Unsub*, NBC, 1989.

Judge Richard Bartke, "Bound for Glory," *L.A. Law*, NBC, 1990.

Judge, "Crazy," *Booker* (also known as *Booker, P.I.*), Fox, 1990.

Prison warden, "2245," *21 Jump Street*, Fox, 1990.

Lieutenant Donnelly, "Film at Eleven," *21 Jump Street*, syndicated, 1991.

Sheriff Dan Filcher, "Aliens Ate My Lunch," *Nightmare Cafe*, NBC, 1992.

Warden Vernon Howard, "Little Girl Lost," *Knots Landing*, CBS, 1992.

Palance, "The Return of Amanda," *Highlander* (also known as *Highlander: The Series*), syndicated, 1993.

Sergeant Pritchard, "Honor and Trust," *Street Justice*, syndicated, 1993.

Admiral Farallon, "Tango Blue," *M.A.N.T.I.S.*, Fox, 1994.

Birdwell, "Grand Delusion," *Birdland*, ABC, 1994.

Captain William Scully (Dana Scully's father), "Beyond the Sea," *The X-Files*, Fox, 1994.

Captain William Scully (Dana Scully's father), "One Breath," *The X-Files*, Fox, 1994.

(As Don Davis) Lloyd Hillegas, "Blood Ties," *Northern Exposure*, CBS, 1994.

Sergeant Thorne, "A Few Dead Men," *Cobra*, syndicated, 1994.

Chief O'Neill, *Traps*, CBS, 1994.

Detective Wilson, "The Living Hell," *The Outer Limits* (also known as *The New Outer Limits*), Showtime, Sci-Fi Channel, and syndicated, 1995.

General Callahan, "The Voice of Reason," *The Outer Limits* (also known as *The New Outer Limits*), Showtime, Sci-Fi Channel, and syndicated, 1995.

Former sheriff Crew, "Hero," *Profit* (also known as *Jim Profit—Ein Mann geht ueber Leichen*), Fox, 1996.

Harold Taggart, "The Inheritance," *Poltergeist: The Legacy*, Showtime and syndicated, 1996.

Lloyd, "Street Pirates," *Viper*, syndicated, 1996.

Mr. Washington, "Honey, It's No Fun Being an Illegal Alien," *Honey, I Shrunk the Kids: The TV Show* (also known as *Disney's "Honey, I Shrunk the Kids: The TV Show"* and *Honey, I Shrunk the Kids*), syndicated, 1998.

Wilton Fisker, "Crossroads," *The Sentinel*, UPN, 1998.

Del, "Farm Boys," *The Chris Isaak Show*, Showtime, 2002.

Dr. Tate, "Memphis," *The Twilight Zone*, UPN, 2003.

Avineri, "The Eschatology of Our Present," *Andromeda* (also known as *Gene Roddenberry's "Andromeda"*), syndicated, 2004.

General George S. Hammond, "Home," *Stargate: Atlantis* (also known as *Atlantis, Csillagkapu—Atlantisz, La porte d'Atlantis*, and *Stargaate: Atlaantis*), Sci-Fi Channel, 2004.

MTAC control officer, "Chained," *Navy NCIS: Naval Criminal Investigative Service* (also known as *Naval CIS, Navy CIS, Navy NCIS, NCIS*, and *NCIS: Naval Criminal Investigative Service*), CBS, 2004.

(In archive footage) Avineri, "The Heart of the Journey: Part 1," *Andromeda* (also known as *Gene Roddenberry's "Andromeda"*), syndicated, 2005.

Reverend Don Butler, "In God We Trust," *The West Wing* (also known as *West Wing* and *El ala oeste de la Casablanca*), NBC, 2005.

Senator Harlan Ellis (some sources cite name as Arlin Ellis), "Saved," *The Dead Zone* (also known as *Stephen King's "Dead Zone"*), USA Network, 2005.

Senator Harlan Ellis (some sources cite name as Arlin Ellis), "Vanguard," *The Dead Zone* (also known as *Stephen King's "Dead Zone"*), USA Network, 2005.

Senator Harlan Ellis (some sources cite name as Arlin Ellis), "Forbidden Fruit," *The Dead Zone* (also known as *Stephen King's "Dead Zone"*), USA Network, 2006.

Appeared in other programs, including *Two* (also known as *Gejagt—Das zweite Gesicht*), CTV (Canada) syndicated. Some sources cite appearances in other programs, including appearances as a one man band in "The Comic/The Golden Hour" and "Hit Man/The Swimmer," both 1979 episodes of *The Love Boat*, ABC; and an appearance in "The Man Who Knew Nothing at All," an episode of *Fly by Night*, CBS, 1991.

Television Appearances; Pilots:

One man band, *Don't Call Us*, CBS, 1976.

Top of the Hill, CBS, 1989.

Chief Sterling, *Broken Badges*, CBS, 1990.

Major Garland Briggs, *Twin Peaks* (also known as *Northwest Passage*), ABC, 1990.

"The Euphio Question/All the King's Horses," *Monkey House* (also known as *Kurt Vonnegut's "Monkey House"* and *Kurt Vonnegut's "Welcome to the Monkey House"*), Showtime, 1991.

Tiger Larkin, *The Marshal*, ABC, 1995.

(As Don Davis) Former sheriff Crew, *Profit* (also known as *Jim Profit—Ein Mann geht ueber Leichen*), Fox, 1996.

Major general George S. Hammond, *Stargate SG–1: Children of the Gods,* Showtime and syndicated, 1997.

Thornton, *Just Cause,* PAX TV, 2002.

Mr. McCallum, *Psych,* USA Network, 2006.

Television Appearances; Other:

Appeared as Norris (an American gambler) in "Steele of the Mounties," *Historica Minutes,* broadcast on Canadian networks and in Canadian schools.

Television Work; Series:

Double for Dana Elcar, *MacGyver,* ABC, c. 1985–92.

Film Appearances:

(As Don Davis) Railroad brakeman, *The Journey of Natty Gann,* Buena Vista, 1985.

(As Don Davis) Buddy, *Malone,* Orion, 1987.

Prison gate guard, *Stakeout,* Buena Vista, 1987.

Veterinarian, *Watchers,* Universal/Concorde Pictures, 1988.

(As Don Davis) Phil Clowson, *Beyond the Stars* (also known as *Personal Choice*), TMS Pictures (The Movie Store), c. 1988.

(As Don Davis) Commando, *Rescue Force* (also known as *Rescue Team*), 1989.

Dr. Fleischer, *Look Who's Talking* (also known as *Daddy's Home, Allo maman, ici bebe!, De quoi j'me mele, Hei, kuka puhuu, I kto to mowi, Kdopak to mluvi, Kuck' mal wer da spricht!, Mira quien habla, Nicsak, ki beszel, Olha quem esta falando, Olha quem fala, Schau mal, wer da spricht, Senti chi parla,* and *Titta han snackar!*), Columbia/TriStar, 1989.

Dr. Fleischer, *Look Who's Talking Too* (also known as *Allo maman, c'est encore moi, De quoi j'me mele encore, Glej kdo se oglasa 2, Hei, kuka puhuu myoes, I kto to mowi 2, Kuck' mal, wer da spricht— Teil 2, Mira quien habla tambien, Olha quem esta falando tambem, Olha quem fala ... tambem, Senti chi parla 2,* and *Titta hon snackar ocksaa!*), TriStar, 1990.

(As Don Sinclair Davis) Dr. Norman, *Waiting for the Light,* Mundial, 1990.

Sergeant, *Chaindance* (also known as *Common Bonds*), New City Releasing, 1990.

Dr. Fields, *Hook,* TriStar, 1991.

Doheny, *Mystery Date,* Orion, 1991.

Haig, *Cadence* (also known as *Count a Lonely Cadence* and *Stockade*), New Line Cinema, 1991.

Charlie Collins (Racine coach), *A League of Their Own* (also known as *Pretty League, Eine Klasse fuer sich, Ella dan el golpe, Ich wlasna liga, Liga de mulheres, Omaa luokkaansa, Ragazze vincenti, Tjejligan, Uma equipe muito especial, Un equipo muy especial,* and *Une equipe hors du commun*), Columbia, 1992.

Major Garland Briggs, *Twin Peaks: Fire Walk with Me* (also known as *Teresa Banks and the Last Seven Days of Laura Palmer* and *Twin Peaks*), New Line Cinema, 1992.

Police gun instructor, *Kuffs,* Universal, 1992.

Probation officer, *Hero* (also known as *Accidental Hero*), Columbia, 1992.

Reverend Willie Rose, *Needful Things,* Columbia, 1993.

Stuart, *Cliffhanger* (also known as *Cliffhanger—l'ultima sfida* and *Cliffhanger, traque au sommet*), TriStar, 1993.

Earl Pomerance, *Max* (also known as *Max—em busca da esperanca, Meu filho Max,* and *Wenn die Liebe den Tod besiegt*), Apple Pie Pictures, 1994.

Dr. Martin, *Hideaway,* TriStar, 1995.

Sergeant Grazer, *Alaska,* Columbia, 1996.

Stook, *The Fan,* Columbia/TriStar, 1996.

(Don Davis) Man in car, *Con Air* (also known as *A Fegyencjarat, Air bagnards, Con Air—A rota da fuga, Con Air: convictos en el aire, Con air—Lento vapauteen, Fortaleza voadora, Les ailes de l'enfer, Letalo prekletih, Lot skazancow,* and *Vanglaekspress*), Buena Vista, 1997.

Cardinal de la Jolla, *The 6th Day* (also known as *On the Sixth Day, The Sixth Day, A l'aube du 6e jour, A l'aube du 6eme jour, Den 6. dag, El sexto dia, El 6 dia, El 6. dia, I 6i mera, Il sesto giorno, Le sixieme jour, O sexto dia, O 6 dia, Siesty den, 6. paeivae, 6:e dagen,* and *Ziua a sasea*), Columbia, 2000.

Golf shirt man, *Suspicious River,* Beyond Films, 2000.

Mayflower best in show judge Everett Bainbridge, *Best in Show* (also known as *Dogumentary*), Warner Bros., 2000.

The Artist's Circle (short film), AtomFilms, 2000.

The chief, *Deadly Little Secrets,* 2001.

Keith Young, *Savage Island* (also known as *Deadman's Island*), Miridien Entertainment, 2003.

Bob Fleming, *Miracle* (also known as *El milagro* and *Milagro*), Buena Vista, 2004.

Voice of computer representation of George S. Hammond, *Stargate SG–3000,* Metro–Goldwyn–Mayer, 2004, also part of an attraction at Space Park Bremen in Germany.

(As Don Davis) Voice of Wild Bill, *G.I. Joe: Valor vs. Venom* (animated), Paramount Home Video, 2004.

Will, *Passing Darkness* (short film), Maderfilm Productions, 2005.

Joseph, *Beneath,* Paramount Classics, c. 2006.

Mr. Fernot, *The Still Life,* Polychrome Pictures, 2007.

Celebrity Art Show (documentary), Albion Entertainment, 2007.

Seed, Kinostar, 2007.

RECORDINGS

Videos:

(Uncredited) George S. Hammond, *The Secret Files of the SGC* (short), Metro–Goldwyn–Mayer/United Artists Home Entertainment, 2003.

DEAN, Ron

PERSONAL

Career: Actor.

CREDITS

Film Appearances:
A Labor of Love, 1975.
The Last Affair (also known as *Wife, Husband & Friends*), Cinematix Releasing, 1976.
Plesko, *Continental Divide,* Universal, 1981.
Detective with bullhorn, *Risky Business,* Warner Bros., 1983.
Kowalski, *The Big Score,* Vestron Video, 1983.
Guard, *Teachers,* Warner Home Video, 1984.
Vegetable House, 1985.
Mr. Clark, Andrew's father, *The Breakfast Club,* Universal, 1985.
Brennan, *Code of Silence,* Metro–Goldwyn–Mayer, 1985.
Pop, *Pink Nights,* 1985.
Ed Bedsole, *Nothing in Common,* TriStar, 1986.
Guy in crowd, *The Color of Money,* Buena Vista, 1986.
Mourner, *Light of Day,* TriStar, 1987.
Policeman number two, *Big Shots,* Warner Bros., 1987.
Detective Lukich, *Above the Law* (also known as *Nico* and *Nico: Above the Law*), Warner Bros., 1988.
Pat Flanagan, *Cocktail,* Buena Vista, 1988.
Lester, *Elvis Stories* (short), 1989.
Stan Lubinski, *Cold Justice,* Sony Pictures Entertainment, 1989.
Karl Richards, *The Package,* Metro–Goldwyn–Mayer/United Artists Home Entertainment, 1989.
Duke's father, *Shaking the Tree,* Castle Hill Productions, 1992.
Umpire Owens, *The Babe,* Universal, 1992.
Detective Kelly, *The Fugitive,* Warner Bros., 1993.
Coach Yonto, *Rudy,* TriStar, 1993.
Johnny Sulari, *The Client,* Warner Bros., 1994.
Sven Pettersson, *Anglagard—andra sommaren* (also known as *Angel Farm 2, Angel Farm, the Second Summer,* and *House of Angels: The Second Summer*), 1994.
Nick's boy, *Steal Big Steal Little,* Savoy Pictures, 1995.
Detective at McCann House, *Eye for an Eye,* Paramount, 1996.
Sergeant Nick Zingaro, *Chain Reaction,* Twentieth Century–Fox, 1996.
Dick, *35 Miles from Normal,* 1997.
Gus, *Night of the Lawyers,* 1997.
Old snack trucker, *Chicago Cab* (also known as *Hellcab*), Castle Hill Productions, 1998.
Willie the hot dog vendor, *Sailorman* (short), 2000.
Sam G, *Joey Petrone: TV Cop* (short), 2001.

Swimming Upstream, Newmark/Echelon Entertainment Group, 2002.
Lou, *Lana's Rain,* ISA Releasing, 2002.
Judge Ruben, *Wild Things 2,* Columbia, 2004.
Brooks, *The Wild Card,* Ardustry Home Entertainment, 2004.
Captain Larsen, *Voices from the Grave,* 2006.
Navy captain, *The Guardian,* Buena Vista, 2006.

Television Appearances; Series:
Sergeant Gino Gianelli, *Lady Blue,* ABC, 1985.
Chief Kramer, *Crime Story,* NBC, 1986–87.
Detective Kenny Branigan, *Angel Street,* CBS, 1992.
Detective Marion Zeke Crumb, *Early Edition,* CBS, 1996–2000.

Television Appearances; Movies:
Lathrop, *Heart of Steel,* ABC, 1983.
The Lost Honor of Kathryn Beck (also known as *Act of Passion*), CBS, 1984.
Ernie, *The Toughest Man in the World,* CBS, 1984.
Sergeant Gino Gianelli, *Lady Blue,* ABC, 1985.
The Birthday Boy, 1986.
Sullivan, *Dream Breakers* (also known as *In Evil's Grasp*), CBS, 1989.
Lieutenant Jerry Brunetto, *Legacy of Lies,* USA Network, 1992.

Television Appearances; Pilots:
Chief Kramer, *Crime Story,* NBC, 1986.
Jimmy, *Glory Days,* NBC, 1987.
Sergeant Hill, *Hammer, Slammer & Slade,* ABC, 1990.
Detective Kenny Branigan, *Angel Street* (movie), CBS, 1992.
Gwong, *Mystery Dance,* ABC, 1995.

Television Appearances; Episodic:
"The Two Hundred Underwacker Street Bridge," *The Duke,* NBC, 1979.
Detective number two, "The Chicago Connection," *T. J. Hooker,* ABC, 1985.
"Phantom Pain," *Wiseguy,* CBS, 1988.
Detective Tom Neally, "DEA," *DEA,* Fox, 1990.
Fire Chief Newton, "Great Balls of Fire," *Perfect Strangers,* ABC, 1991.
John Doe, "The Spy Who Came in from the Old," *Flying Blind,* Fox, 1992.
Frank, "You Can't Tell a Crook by His Cover," *Frasier,* NBC, 1994.
Mr. Mackey, "Double Abandando," *NYPD Blue,* ABC, 1994.
Red O'Connell, *The Good Life,* NBC, 1994.
Frank, "Retirement Is Murder," *Frasier,* NBC, 1995.
Tony "Red Sauce" Falcone, "The Maltese Falcone," *Pig Sty,* UPN, 1995.
Lou the lawyer, "Unwilling Witness," *Murder, She Wrote,* CBS, 1995.

Mr. Zafrani, "Jobs," *Life's Work,* ABC, 1996.

Mr. Zafrani, "Gobbledegook," *Life's Work,* ABC, 1996.

Frank, "Where Every Bloke Knows Your Name," *Frasier,* NBC, 1998.

"The Good Fight," *ER,* NBC, 1998.

Baseball scout, "Vigilance and Care," *Chicago Hope,* CBS, 1999.

"Liar's Club: Part 2," *Family Law,* CBS, 2001.

Mr. Howard Evans, "Joan Meets the Parents," *What About Joan,* ABC, 2001.

Police captain, "The Brothers," *Special Unit 2* (also known as *SU2*), UPN, 2001.

Police captain, "The Waste," *Special Unit 2* (also kwon as *SU2*), UPN, 2001.

Mr. Zafrani, "The House of Stewart," *Raising Dad,* The WB, 2002.

"Justice," *Karen Sisco,* ABC, 2003.

"Wedding Party," *The Handler,* CBS, 2004.

Tom Broderick, "Full Disclosure," *The West Wing,* NBC, 2004.

Willie, "Legacy," *Without a Trace* (also known as *W.A. T.*), CBS, 2004.

Joe Brockhurst, "The Brothers Grim," *NYPD Blue,* ABC, 2004.

Joe Brockhurst, "Peeler? I Hardley Knew Her," *NYPD Blue,* ABC, 2004.

Joe Brockhurst, "Traylor Trash," *NYPD Blue,* ABC, 2004.

Joe Brockhurst, "What's Your Poison?," *NYPD Blue,* ABC, 2004.

Woody, "Turn of the Screws," *CSI: Crime Scene Investigation* (also known as *C.S.I., CSI: Weekends, CSI: Las Vegas,* and *Les Experts*), CBS, 2004.

Slim Callahan, "Still Bill's Dad," *Still Standing,* CBS, 2004.

Peter Watson, "Dirty Bomb," *Numb3rs* (also known as *Num3ers*), CBS, 2005.

Karl, "Eat a Peach," *Six Feet Under,* 2005.

Troy Cage in 2005, "Colors," *Cold Case,* CBS, 2005.

Slim, "Still Deceitful," *Still Standing,* CBS, 2006.

DEMITA, John 1956(?)–
(John De Mita, John Demita, John Dimita)

PERSONAL

Born c. 1956; married Julia Fletcher, c. 1992; children: Conner, Holly.

Career: Actor. Taught theater arts at the College of the Canyons, Santa Clarita, CA; taught theater at El Camino College, Torrance, CA.

CREDITS

Film Appearances:

(As John Demita), Voice, "A" gai waak (also known as "A" ji hua, Jackie Chan's "Project A," Mark of the Dragon, Operazione pirati, Pirate Patrol, and Project A), Buena Vista Home Video, 1983.

(English version) Additional voices, *Tenku no shiro Rapyuta* (animated; also known as *Castle in the Sky* and *Laputa: The Flying Island*), Streamline Pictures, 1986.

Brad, *Spellbinder,* Metro–Goldwyn–Mayer, 1988.

(English version) Additional voices, *Majo no takkyubin* (animated; also known as *Kiki's Delivery Service*), Buena Vista Home Video, 1989.

Agent Spoon, *Steel and Lace,* Fries Entertainment, 1991.

Television news crew, *Universal Soldier,* Columbia TriStar, 1992.

Chipper, *The Opposite Sex and How to Live with Them,* Miramax, 1993.

(English version) Voice, *Zhong Nan Hai bao biao* (also known as *Chung Nam Hoi bo biu, The Defender,* and *The Bodyguard from Beijing*), Dimension Films, 1994.

Voice of Valkus, *Final Fantasy: Legend of the Crystals* (animated), Urban Vision Entertainment, 1994.

Voice of D–Boy, *Tekkaman Blade 2,* 1994.

Sir William of Dearborne, *Josh Kirby ... Time Warrior: Chapter 1, Planet of the Dino–Knights,* 1995.

Fazio, *Leprechaun 3,* Trimark Pictures, 1995.

William of Dearborn, *Josh Kirby ... Time Warrior: Chapter 2, the Human Pets,* 1995.

(English version) Voice of Kuriowa, *Psycho Driver* (animated), 1995.

(English version) Additional voices, *Biohunter* (animated), Urban Vision Entertainment, 1995.

Voice of Operative A, *Tenchi Muyo! In Love* (animated; also known as *Tenchi the Movie* and *Tenchi: The Movie*), Pioneer Entertainment, 1996.

(As John Dimita; English version) Voice of Tsui Chik and Black Mask, *Hak hap* (also known as *Black Mask* and *Hei xia*), Artisan Entertainment, 1996.

Huang Long, *Twilight of the Dark Master* (animated), Urban Vision Entertainment, 1997.

(English version) Voice of Kohroku, *Mononoke–hime* (animated; also known as *Princess Mononoke*), Dimension Films, 1997.

Joe Kuruma, *Hurricane Polymar* (animated), Urban Vision Entertainment, 1998.

(As John De Mita) Additional voices, *Gen 13* (animated), 1999.

Voice of Alan Elbourne and priest, *Banpaia hanta D* (animated; also known as *Vampire Hunter D* and *Vampire Hunter D: Bloodlust*), Manga Films, 2000.

(Uncredited) Voice of BCR soldier and space station technician, *Final Fantasy: The Spirits Within* (animated; also known as *Fainaru fantaji*), Columbia, 2001.

Chuck Farrell, *Megiddo: The Omega Code 2* (also known as *Megiddo*), Gener8Xion Entertainment, 2001.

Additional voice, *Lilo & Stitch* (animated), Buena Vista, 2002.

Additional voice, *Waking Up in Reno,* Miramax, 2002.

Voice of teacher, "Kid's Story," *The Animatrix* (animated), Warner Bros., 2003.

Voice of guard, *Thru the Moebius Strip* (animated), Fantastic Films International,. 2005.

Film Work:

Automated dialogue replacement (ADR), *Snow Falling on Cedars,* Universal, 1999.

(As John Demita) ADR, *Memento,* Newmarket Films, 2000.

ADR, *Undercover Brother,* Universal, 2002.

ADR, *Win a Date with Tad Hamilton!,* DreamWorks, 2004.

ADR, *Diary of a Mad Black Woman,* Lionsgate, 2005.

ADR, *The Return,* Rogue Pictures, 2006.

ADR, *Ask the Dust,* Paramount Vantage, 2006.

ADR, *Tyler Perry's "Daddy's Little Girls,"* Lionsgate, 2007.

ADR, *Pride,* Lionsgate, 2007.

ADR, *Dead Silence,* Universal, 2007.

Television Appearances; Series:

Arthur Newton, *Santa Barbara,* NBC, 1989.

Eric, *The Pursuit of Happiness,* NBC, 1995.

Additional voices, *Spawn* (also known as *Todd McFarlane's "Spawn"*), HBO, 1997.

Voice of Cleitus and Haphaestion, *Alexander Senki* (animated; also known as *Alexander* and *Reign: The Conqueror*), Fuji and Cartoon Network, 1997.

Count D, *Pet Shop of Horrors,* 2000.

Col. Clifford Blakely, *JAG,* CBS, 2001–2005.

Dosu Kinuta, *Naruto* (animated), Cartoon Network and YTV, 2002.

Television Appearances; Miniseries:

Dan Smith, *I Know My First Name Is Steven* (also known as *The Missing Years*), NBC, 1989.

Television Appearances; Movies:

Greg Anderson, *Brotherly Love,* CBS, 1985.

(As John De Mita) Scott McDonald, *Perry Mason: The Case of the Lethal Lesson,* NBC, 1989.

Vatican priest, *Child of Darkness, Child of Light,* USA Network, 1991.

Major Powers, *Without Warning,* CBS, 1994.

Peter Duchin, *Life of the Party: The Pamela Harriman Story* (also known as *Life of the Party: Pamela Harriman*), Lifetime, 1998.

Harry Y. Esterbrook, *Inherit the Wind,* Showtime, 1999.

Television Appearances; Specials:

Lieutenant Engleman, "The Mine," *Vietnam War Story,* HBO, 1987.

Announcer, *The 2001 Genesis Awards,* Animal Planet, 2001.

Television Appearances; Episodic:

Mr. Horn, "Teacher, Teacher," *The Facts of Life,* NBC, 1985.

George, "Kentucky Rye," *The Twilight Zone,* CBS, 1985.

Carl, "Coffee, Tea, or Steele," *Remington Steele,* NBC, 1985.

Young agent, "The Castro Connection," *Hunter,* NBC, 1986.

Tom, "Judy Miller, Come On Down," *Freddy's Nightmares* (also known as *Freddy's Nightmares: A Nightmare on Elm Street: The Series*), syndicated, 1988.

"In the Still of My Pants," *Hooperman,* ABC, 1989.

Lieutenant Henry Driscoll, "I Wish It Would Rain," *Tour of Duty,* CBS, 1989.

Eric Thomas, "A Merry Little Christmas," *Knots Landing,* CBS, 1990.

Hornsby, "The Suspect," *Matlock,* NBC, 1991.

Sam number two, "Stand Up for the Bastards," *The Jackie Thomas Show,* ABC, 1993.

Romulan, "Timescape," *Star Trek: The Next Generation* (also known as *Star Trek: TNG*), syndicated, 1993.

Jerry McVey, "Book of Renovation, Chapter 1," *L.A. Law,* NBC, 1993.

The Clinic, Comedy Central, 1995.

Cop, *John Grisham's "The Client,"* CBS, 1995.

Bob, "It's a Mad, Mad, Mad, Mad Eric," *Ned and Stacey,* Fox, 1997.

Quinn, "Peak Experience," *Silk Stalkings,* USA Network, 1997.

(As John Demita) Ursath, "Ransom," *Conan* (also known as *Conan the Adventurer*), syndicated, 1997.

Sales clerk, "Gifts," *Party of Five,* Fox, 1998.

Dr. Steven Jensen, "Slide by Wire," *Sliders,* Sci–Fi Channel, 1999.

Deputy Director John Keane, "Sleeping Dragons," *18 Wheels of Justice,* TNN, 2000.

Deputy Director John Keane, "Con Truck," *18 Wheels of Justice,* TNN, 2000.

Caller, "The Gay–Straight Alliance," *Once and Again,* ABC, 2002.

(Uncredited) Jason Garbett, "Mea Culpa," *CSI: Crime Scene Investigation* (also known as *C.S.I., CSI: Las Vegas, CSI: Weekends,* and *Les Experts*), CBS, 2004.

Also appeared as Lieutenant Engleman, "The Mine," *Vietnam War Story.*

RECORDINGS

Video Games:

Harry Reese, *Eraser—Turnabout,* 1996.

(English version) Voice of Luzzu, Barthello, Hypello, and Graav, *Fainaru fantaji X* (also known as *FFX, Final Fantasy X,* and *Final Fantasy X International*), Square Electronic Arts, 2001.

(Uncredited) Voice of Zhou Yu, *Shin sangoku muso 3* (also known as *Dynasty Warriors 4, Dynasty Warriors 4: Hyper,* and *Shin sangoku musou—Hyper*), KOEI Corp., 2003.

(English version) Voice of Barkeep, Hypello, and Barthello, *Final Fantasy X–2* (also known as *Fainaru fantajii X–2*), Square Enix Company, 2003.

(Uncredited) Voice of Zhou Yu, *Shin sangoku muso 3 mushoden* (also known as *Dynasty Warriors 4: Xtreme Legends*), KOEI Corp., 2003.

(English version; uncredited) Voice of Zhou Yu, *Shin sangoku muso 3: Empires* (also known as *Dynasty Warriors 4: Empires*), KOEI Corp., 2004.

(English version) Additional voices, *Fainaru fantaji XII* (also known as *Finally Fantasy XII*), Square Enix Company, 2006.

DESANDO, Anthony 1965–
(Anthony De Sando, Anthony de Sando, Anthony Joseph De Santis)

PERSONAL

Born December 4, 1965, in Jersey City, NJ.

Addresses: *Agent*—Domain, 9229 Sunset Blvd., Suite 415, Los Angeles, CA 90069. *Manager*—Allman/Rea Management, 141 Barrington, Suite E, Los Angeles, CA 90049.

Career: Actor.

CREDITS

Film Appearances:
Frankie Needles, *New Jack City,* Warner Bros., 1991.
Victor Lebrun, *Grand Isle,* 1991.
Vinnie Madano, *Out for Justice,* Warner Bros., 1991.
(As Anthony de Sando) *A Walk with Death,* 1993.
Hub Cap World, 1994.
Derrick, *Party Girl,* Overseas FilmGroup, 1994.
Nicky, *Federal Hill,* 1994.
Victor, *Two Bits* (also known as *A Day to Remember*), Miramax, 1995.
Pino, *Kiss Me, Guido,* Paramount, 1997.
Rilke, *Frogs for Snakes,* The Shooting Gallery International, 1998.
Kenny Paliski, *Just the Ticket,* United Artists, 1999.
A Day in Black and White (also known as *In Black and White*), 1999.
Sean Rickhart, *Cement,* Keystone Film Partners XIX, 1999.
Angel Gonzalez, *Double Parked,* Castle Hill, 1999.

Joey Zito, *The Whole Shebang,* 2 Match, 2000.
Mario, *Plan B,* Franchise Pictures, 2001.
Frank Mantovani, *Ciao America,* 2002.
(As Anthony de Sando) Frank the dog walker, *A Guide to Recognizing Your Saints,* First Look International, 2006.
Dennis Mangenelli, *Beer League* (also known as *Artie Lange's "Beer League"*), Freestyle Releasing, 2006.

Television Appearances; Series:
Alex DePalma, *L.A. Law,* NBC, 1992.
Detective Costa Papadakis, *Under Suspicion,* CBS, 1994–95.
Tony Amato, *New York News,* CBS, 1995.
Grant Noone, *One Life to Live,* ABC, 1996.
Brendan Filone, *The Sopranos,* HBO, 1999.
Vince Verbena, *Welcome to New York,* CBS, 2000.

Television Appearances; Miniseries:
Albert LaManna, *Vendetta: Secrets of a Mafia Bride* (also known as *Bride of Violence, Donna d nore,* and *A Family Matter*), syndicated, 1991.
Albert LaManna, *Vendetta II: The New Mafia* (also known as *Bride of Violence 2* and *Donna d nore 2*), HBO, 1993.

Television Appearances; Movies:
Bobby Malto, *The Return of Eliot Ness,* NBC, 1991.
Bobby, *Hysterical Blindness,* HBO, 2002.

Television Appearances; Pilots:
Carly, CBS, 1998.

Television Appearances; Episodic:
Harvey Doss, "Alice Doesn't Fit Here Anymore," *NYPD Blue,* ABC, 1997.
Siddhartha, "The Drought," *Sex and the City,* HBO, 1998.
Andy Stallworth, "Crackdown," *Martial Law,* CBS, 1998.
Brett Tunney, "Exposing Faith," *Third Watch,* NBC, 2001.
Father Paul, "Miracles & Wonders," *Crossing Jordan,* NBC, 2002.
Paul, "Til Death Do Us Part," *Crossing Jordan,* NBC, 2004.
(As Anthony Joseph de Santis) Anthony DeBellis, "Upstairs Downstairs," *Without a Trace* (also known as *W.A.T.*), CBS, 2004.
Detective Reed, "Man Hunt," *Numb3rs* (also known as *Num3ers*), CBS, 2005.
Himself, "Beer League Special," *Howard Stern on Demand* (also known as *Howard TV on Demand*), 2006.
(As Anthony De Sando) Joey Mazzaro, "A Grizzly Murder," *CSI: Miami,* CBS, 2007.

RECORDINGS

Video Games:
Voice of Reggie, *"The Sopranos": Road to Respect,* THQ, 2006.

WRITINGS

Film Additional Music:
Cement, 1999.

DeSCENNA, Linda 1949–
    (Linda De Scenna, Linda Descenna)

PERSONAL

Born November 14, 1949, in Warren, OH; daughter of Jack Loveless (an accountant) and Dorothy (a homemaker; maiden name, Sabey) DeScenna; married Ric McElvin (a lead man), December 8, 1984. *Education:* Graduated from Kent State University, 1971, with degrees in cinematography and painting.

Addresses: *Agent*—The Skouras Agency, 1149 Third St., 3rd Floor, Santa Monica, CA 90403.

Career: Set decorator and production designer. Previously worked as a studio secretary and cocktail waitress, Hollywood, CA.

Member: International Alliance of Theatrical Stage Employees and Moving Picture Operators of the U.S. and Canada (I.A.T.S.E.).

Awards, Honors: Academy Award nomination (with others), best art direction—set decoration, 1980, for *Star Trek: The Motion Picture;* Academy Award nomination (with Lawrence G. Paull and David L. Snyder), best art direction—set decoration, 1983, for *Blade Runner;* Academy Award nomination (with J. Michael Riva and Bo Welch), best art direction—set decoration, 1986, for *The Color Purple;* Academy Award nomination (with Ida Random), best art direction—set decoration, 1989, for *Rain Man;* Academy Award nomination (with Ferdinando Scarfiotti), best art direction—set decoration, 1993, for *Toys.*

CREDITS

Film Set Decorator:
Star Trek: The Motion Picture, Paramount, 1979.
Fatso, Twentieth Century–Fox, 1979.

It's My Turn (also known as *A Perfect Circle*), Columbia, 1980.
Blade Runner, Warner Bros., 1982.
Second Thoughts, Universal, 1982.
Brainstorm, United Artists, 1983.
Spacehunter: Adventures in the Forbidden Zone (also known as *Adventures in the Creep Zone* and *Road Gangs*), Columbia, 1983.
The Lonely Guy, Universal, 1984.
The Adventures of Buckaroo Banzai: Across the Eighth Dimension (also known as *The Adventures of Buckaroo Banzai*), Twentieth Century–Fox, 1984.
(As Linda De Scenna) *The Falcon and the Snowman,* Orion, 1985.
The Goonies, Warner Bros., 1985.
The Color Purple, Warner Bros., 1985.
Back to School, Orion, 1986.
Harry and the Hendersons (also known as *Bigfoot* and *Bigfoot and the Hendersons*), Universal, 1987.
Summer School, Paramount, 1987.
(As Linda De Scenna) *Someone to Watch Over Me,* Columbia, 1987.
Moving, Warner Bros., 1988.
Scrooged, Paramount, 1988.
Rain Man, Metro–Goldwyn–Mayer/United Artists, 1988.
(As Linda De Scenna) *Back to the Future Part II,* Universal, 1989.
Avalon, Tri–Star, 1990.
Defending Your Life, Warner Bros., 1991.
The Rocketeer, Buena Vista, 1991.
(As Linda De Scenna) *Honeymoon in Vegas,* Lobel Bergman Productions, 1992.
Toys, Fox–Baltimore Pictures, 1992.
Wolf, 1994.

Film Production Designer:
Jimmy Hollywood, 1994.
Bye Bye, Love, 1995.
Father of the Bride Part II, 1995.
A Family Thing, Metro–Goldwyn–Mayer/United Artists, 1996.
Liar Liar, Universal, 1997.
(As Linda Descenna) *Mouse Hunt,* DreamWorks, 1997.
Patch Adams, Universal, 1998.
Galaxy Quest, DreamWorks, 1999.
Dragonfly (also known as *Im zeichen der libelle*), Universal, 2001.
Bringing Down the House, Buena Vista, 2003.
Bruce Almighty, Universal, 2003.
The Pacifier (also known as *Gnome* and *Le pacifacteur*), Buena Vista, 2005.
Yours, Mine and Ours, Paramount, 2005.
Evan Almighty, Universal, 2007.

Film Appearances:
Shower guest, *Father of the Bride Part II,* 1995.

Television Set Decorator:
Worked on *Logan's Run; Fantastic Journey.*

DONATO, Marc 1989–
  (Mark Donato)

PERSONAL

Born March 2, 1989, in Toronto, Ontario, Canada; brother of Tanya Donato (an actress).

Addresses: *Agent*—(voice) Cunningham/Escott/Slevin and Doherty Talent Agency, 10635 Santa Monica Blvd., Suite 140, Los Angeles, CA 90025. *Manager*—Ted Schachter, Schachter Entertainment, 1157 South Beverly Dr., 2nd Floor, Los Angeles, CA 90035.

Career: Actor. Appeared in television commercials.

Awards, Honors: Young Artist Award (with others), best performance by a young ensemble in a television movie, pilot, or made–for–video movie, 1999, for *The Sweetest Gift;* Young Artist Award, best actor age ten or under in a television movie or pilot, and Daytime Emmy Award nomination, outstanding performer in a children's special, both 2000, for *Locked in Silence;* Young Artist Award nomination, best young actor in a voice–over role for television, film, or video, 2001, for "The Animal Shelf," *It's Itsy Bitsy Time;* Young Artist Award nomination, best supporting young actor in a television movie or special, 2002, for *Dangerous Child;* Young Artist Award nomination, best guest–starring young actor in a television drama series, 2002, for *Twice in a Lifetime;* Young Artist Award, best supporting young actor in a feature film, 2003, for *White Oleander;* Young Artist Award nomination, best guest–starring young actor in a television series, 2004, for *Doc;* Young Artist Award nomination, best leading young actor in an international feature film, 2005, for *The Blue Butterfly;* Young Artist Award nomination, best young actor in a voice–over role, 2006, for *Heisei tanuki gassen pompoko;* Young Artist Award nomination (with others), best young ensemble in a television series, 2006, for *Degrassi: The Next Generation.*

CREDITS

Television Appearances; Series:
Tucker James at age five, *Flash Forward,* ABC, 1996.
Voice of young Matthias, *Redwall* (animated; also known as *Brian Jacques' "Redwall"*), PBS, 1999.

Tyler, *Rescue Heroes* (also known as *Rescue Heroes: Global Response Team*), CBS, 1999.
Voice of young Martin, *Mattimeo: A Tale of Redwall* (animated; also known as *Brian Jacques' "Mattimeo: A Tale of Redwall"*), PBS, 2000.
Rich, *Clubhouse,* CBS, 2004–2005.
Derek Haig, a recurring role, *Degrassi: The Next Generation* (also known as *Degrassi—La nouvelle generation*), N Network, 2005–2007.

Television Appearances; Movies:
Ultimate Betrayal, CBS, 1994.
Ryan, *Fatal Vows: The Alexandra O'Hara Story,* CBS, 1994.
Beau, *The Morrison Murders: Based on a True Story,* USA network, 1996.
(As Mark Donato) Aaron Dubroski, *Double Jeopardy* (also known as *Victim of the Night*), 1996.
Paul, "Marie Taquet," *Rescuers: Stories of Courage— Two Couples,* Showtime, 1998.
Chip Martin, *The Sweetest Gift,* Showtime, 1998.
Mark, *Bone Daddy* (also known as *Palmer's Bones* and *L'affaire Palmer*), HBO, 1998.
Kevin, *The Time Shifters* (also known as *Thrill Seekers* and *The Timeshifters*), TBS, 1999.
Stephen Cline, *Locked in Silence,* Showtime, 1999.
Leo Cambridge, *Dangerous Child* (also known as *Un fils en colere*), Lifetime, 2001.
Voice of Wiggle, *Miss Spider's Sunny Patch Kids* (animated), Nickelodeon, 2003.

Television Appearances; Episodic:
David, "Ghost Ship," *Tales from the Cryptkeeper* (also known as *New Tales from the Cryptkeeper*), 1993.
Little boy, "A Cop, a Mountie, and a Baby," *Due South* (also known as *Direction: Sud*), CBS, 1994.
Martin Bindernagle, "Lucky Numbers," *Side Effects,* CBC, 1995.
Little boy, "An Eye for an Eye," *Due South* (also known as *Direction: Sud*), CBS, 1995.
Little kid, "Vault," *Due South* (also known as *Direction: Sud*), CBS, 1995.
Dewey Lester, "Mixed Up Masks," *Noddy,* PBS, 1998.
Voice, "The Animal Shelf," *It's Itsy Bitsy Time,* Fox Family Channel, 2000.
Mikey at age twelve, "Then Love Came Along," *Twice in a Lifetime,* PAX, 2001.
Joshua Valentine, "Crime of the New Century," *Mutant X,* syndicated, 2001.
Joseph Orien, "Burning at Crooked Lake," *Real Kids, Real Adventures,* Global, 2002.
Andrew Spinner, "Who Wants to Be a Millionaire," *Doc,* PAX, 2004.

Television Appearances; Other:
Jack at age three, *J.F.K.: Reckless Youth* (miniseries), ABC, 1993.

Thomas Logan, *Dear America: Standing in the Light* (special; also known as *Dear America 04, Standing in the Light,* and *Dear America: Standing in the Light—The Captive Story of Catharine Carey Logan, Delaware Valley, Pennsylvania, 1763*), HBO, 1999.

Film Appearances:

Conners child, *The Killing Machine* (also known as *The Killing Man*), 1994.

Nodding first grader, *Billy Madison,* Universal, 1995.

Mike Hillary at age eight, *Specimen,* Combustion Film Productions, 1996.

Mason Ansel, *The Sweet Hereafter* (also known as *De beaux lendemains*), Fine Line, 1997.

Zackary, *A Boy's Own Story,* 1997.

Robbie Mackessy, *A Map of the World* (also known as *Unschuldig verfolgt*), First Look Pictures Releasing, 1999.

Adam, *Pay It Forward,* Warner Bros., 2000.

Camera, 2000.

Davey Thomas, *White Oleander* (also known as *Weisser Oleander*), Warner Bros., 2002.

Pete Carlton, *The Blue Butterfly* (also known as *Mariposa azul* and *Le papillon bleu*), PorchLight Entertainment, 2004.

(English version) Voice of Sasuke, *Heisei tanuki gassen pompoko* (also known as *Pom polo* and *The Raccoon War*), Buena Vista Home Video, 2005.

OTHER SOURCES

Periodicals:

Kids Tribute, fall, 2001, p. 30.

DONOVAN, Elisa 1971–

PERSONAL

Original name, Lisa Donovan; born February 3, 1971, in Poughkeepsie, NY; daughter of Jack (a business executive) and Charlotte Donovan. *Education:* Attended New School for Social Research; trained for the stage at Michael Chekhov Studio, New York City. *Avocational Interests:* Horseback riding, painting.

Addresses: *Manager*—Seven Summits Pictures and Management, 8906 West Olympic Blvd., Ground Floor, Beverly Hills, CA 90211.

Career: Actress. Enviro–thon, spokesperson. Previously worked as a bartender and waitress.

CREDITS

Television Appearances; Series:

Amber Princess Mariens, *Clueless,* 1996–97, then UPN, 1997–99.

Morgan Cavanaugh, *Sabrina, the Teenage Witch* (also known as *Sabrina Goes to College* and *Sabrina*), The WB, 2000–2003.

Television Appearances; Movies:

Ivana, *Encino Woman* (also known as *California Woman*), ABC, 1996.

Lori Seefer, *The Best Actress,* E! Entertainment Television, 2000.

Eve Simon, *Eve's Christmas,* Lifetime, 2004.

June Baldwin, *Framed for Murder,* Lifetime, 2007.

Television Appearances; Specials:

E! Rack–n–Roll: Behind the Scenes, E! Entertainment Television, 1999.

Rocky Horror: 25th Anniversary Special, VH1, 2000.

Clueless: The E! True Hollywood Story, E! Entertainment Television, 2001.

Presenter, *The 35th Annual Victor Awards,* Fox Sports, 2001.

101 Biggest Celebrity Oops, E! Entertainment Television, 2004.

101 Most Unforgettable SNL Moments, E! Entertainment Television, 2004.

Television Appearances; Episodic:

Tanya, "Puppy Love," *Blossom,* NBC, 1994.

Tanya, "The Wedding," *Blossom,* NBC, 1994.

Holly, "Simon Gets Carl a Job, *Simon,* The WB, 1995.

Tina Douglas, "Ballad of D. B. Cooper," *Renegade,* 1995.

Ginger LaMonica, "Home Is Where the Tart Is," *Beverly Hills, 90210,* Fox, 1995.

Ginger LaMonica, "Buffalo Gals," *Beverly Hills, 90210,* Fox, 1995.

Ginger LaMonica, "Flying," *Beverly Hills, 90210,* Fox, 1996.

Ginger LaMonica, "Bleeding Hearts," *Beverly Hills, 90210,* Fox, 1996.

Amber, "Jack Gets Tough," *Just Shoot Me,* NBC, 1999.

Politically Incorrect (also known as *P.I.*), ABC, 1999, 2002.

The Late Late Show with Craig Kilborn (also known as *The Late Late Show*), CBS, 2000.

Annie, "A Key Exchange," *Jack & Jill,* The WB, 2000.

Annie, "Starstruck," *Jack & Jill,* The WB, 2000.

Late Night with Conan O'Brien, NBC, 2001.

Hollywood Squares (also known as *H2* and *H2: Hollywood Squares*), syndicated, 2001.

Shelby Crawford, "Sins of the Father," *Judging Amy,* CBS, 2004.

Shelby Crawford, "Roadhouse Blues," *Judging Amy,* CBS, 2004.

"Voting Electible Dysfunction," *Crossballs: The Debate Show* (also known as *Crossballs*), Comedy Central, 2004.

Rebecca Kemp, "Dead and Unburied," *Navy NCIS: Naval Criminal Investigative Service* (also known as *NCIS* and *NCIS: Naval Criminal Investigative Service*), CBS, 2006.

I Really Wanna Direct, E! Entertainment Television, 2007.

"Eating Disorders, Fame, and the Pressure to Be Thin in Hollywood," *The Dr. Keith Ablow Show,* 2007.

Appeared as Jennifer Xavier, *Oh Baby,* Lifetime; appeared in episodes of *Loving,* ABC; *Switched,* ABC Family Channel; and *The Test,* FX Network.

Television Appearances; Pilots:
Cheryl, *Justice League of America,* 1997.

Film Appearances:
Female lover, *Cafe Babel,* 1995.
Amber, *Clueless* (also known as *I Was a Teenage Teenager* and *No Worries*), Paramount, 1995.
Crazy actress, *Guns on the Clackamas,* PlympCorp Productions, 1995.
Cambi, *A Night at the Roxbury,* Paramount, 1998.
E. D., *15 Minutes,* 1999.
Salli McDonnell, *Loving Jezebel* (also known as *Chasing Beauties*), Shooting Gallery, 1999.
Nora, *Pop,* 1999.
Alexandra, *Rebound Guy* (short film), IFILM, 2001.
Mae, *Liars Club* (also known as *Save Me a Seat*), Odyssey Pictures/Stony Island Films, 2001.
Annabella Morris, *Wolves of Wall Street,* Blockbuster Video, 2002.
Herself, *Bandwagon,* 2004.
A Girls' Guide to Depravity (short film), 2004.
Susie, *TV: The Movie* (also known as *National Lampoon's "TV the Movie"*), Xenon Pictures, 2006.
Malika, *Kiss Me Again,* Monarch Home Video, 2006.
Martina, *The Bliss,* Society Entertainment/LP3 Pictures/La Vie en Rose, 2006.

Stage Appearances:
The Vagina Monologues, Canon Theatre, Beverly Hills, CA, 2001.

RECORDINGS

Videos:
"*Clueless*": *Fashion 101,* Paramount Home Video, 2005.
"*Clueless*": *Language Arts,* Paramount Home Video, 2005.

"*Clueless*": *We're History,* Paramount Home Video, 2005.

Appeared in the music videos "Here" by Lucious Jackson and "I Drive Myself Crazy" by 'N Sync.

WRITINGS

Contributor to books, including *Feeding the Fame,* 2006, and *Chicken Soup for the Teenage Soul.*

OTHER SOURCES

Periodicals:
People Weekly, December 2, 1996, p. 71.

DONOVAN, Jeffrey 1968–
(Jeff Donovan)

PERSONAL

Born in 1968, in Amesbury, MA. *Education:* Attended Bridgewater State College and University of Massachusetts at Amherst; New York University, M.F.A.

Addresses: *Agent*—Paradigm, 360 North Crescent Dr., North Bldg., Beverly Hills, CA 90210. *Publicist*—I/D Public Relations, 8409 Santa Monica Blvd., West Hollywood, CA 90069.

Career: Actor.

Awards, Honors: Method Fest Award, best supporting actor, 2003, for *Sam & Joe.*

CREDITS

Film Appearances:
Katz, *Inside Out,* 1994.
Pete Gulley, *Throwing Down,* 1995.
Henry Addison, *Sleepers,* Warner Bros., 1996.
Thomas Mason, *Catherine's Grove,* Catherine's Grove, Inc., 1997.
Julio, *Bait* (also known as *Piege*), Warner Bros., 2000.
Jeffrey Patterson, *Books of Shadows: Blair Witch 2* (also known as *Book of Shadows: Blair Witch Project 2, BW2,* and *BWP2*), Artisan Entertainment, 2000.
Robert Jennings, *Purpo$e* (also known as *Purpose*), Lakeshore Entertainment, 2001.

(As Jeff Donovan) Pascal, *Final Draft,* Shoreline Entertainment, 2003.

Eric, *Sam & Joe,* Z Films, 2003.

Vance, *Hitch,* Columbia, 2005.

Cal Percell, *Come Early Morning,* Bold Films/Roadside Attractions, 2006.

Clay Driscoll, *Believe in Me,* IFC Films, 2007.

Paul, *Expecting,* Ambush Entertainment, 2007.

Television Appearances; Series:
Dwayne "Popper" Collins, *Another World* (also known as *Another World: Bay City*), 1997.

Brad Ulrich, *The Beat,* UPN, 2000.

Detective Inspector Dave Creegan, *Touching Evil,* USA Network, 2004.

William Ivers, a recurring role, *Crossing Jordan,* NBC, 2007.

Television Appearances; Movies:
Randy Pitzer, *Critical Choices,* Showtime, 1996.

Bobby, *When Trumpets Fade* (also known as *Hamburger Hill 2*), HBO, 1998.

Television Appearances; Pilots:
Detective Inspector Dave Creegan, *Touching Evil,* USA Network, 2004.

Enemies, ABC, 2006.

Television Appearances; Miniseries:
Agent number one, *Witness to the Mob,* NBC, 1998.

Television Appearances; Episodic:
Edward "Eddie" Nicodos, "Jeopardy," *Law & Order,* NBC, 1995.

Newton/Miles Dell, "Thrill of the Kill," *Homicide: Life on the Street* (also known as *Homicide*), NBC, 1995.

Billy Webber, "The Wild and the Innocent," *Millennium,* Fox, 1997.

Kyle, "Dragon House: Parts 1 & 2," *The Pretender,* NBC, 1997.

Kyle, "Red Rock Jarod," *The Pretender,* NBC, 1998.

Kyle (in archive footage), "Amnesia," *The Pretender,* NBC, 1998.

Kyle, "Mr. Lee," *The Pretender,* NBC, 1999.

Tom, "These Shoes Were Made for Cheatin'," *Spin City,* ABC, 1999.

Tom, "The Mayor May Not," *Spin City,* ABC, 1999.

Daniel Germaine, "Lagrimas," *Witchblade,* TNT, 2002.

Todd Kendrick, "Nothing to Lose," *CSI: Miami,* CBS, 2005.

Dr. Julian Sloan, "Vigilante," *Threshold,* CBS, 2006.

(As Jeff Donovan) Second fan, "The Limo," *Yes, Dear,* CBS, 2006.

Steve Wagner, "Mr. Monk and the Astronaut," *Monk,* USA Network, 2006.

Michael, "Fight or Flight," *Burn Notice,* USA Network, 2007.

Appeared as Jacob Reese in an episode of *Law & Order,* NBC.

Stage Appearances:
Diomedes, *Troilus and Cressida,* Shakespeare in the Park, Delacorte Theatre, Public Theatre, New York City, 1995.

Skyscraper, Greenwich House Theatre, New York City, 1997.

Seth, *Freedomland,* Playwrights Horizons Theatre, New York City, 1998.

Teiresias, *Oedipus,* Classic Stage Company, New York City, 1998.

With Six You Get Musical Beds, 1999.

Gene, *Things You Shouldn't Say Past Midnight,* Promenade Theatre, New York City, 1999.

Clint, *The Glory of Living,* Manhattan Class Company Theatre, New York City, 2001.

Made Broadway debut in *An Inspector Calls;* appeared as Marco, *A View from the Bridge,* Roundabout Theatre Company, New York City production.

DREW, Rick

PERSONAL

Career: Writer and producer.

CREDITS

Television Work; Series:
Story editor, *Check It Out!,* USA Network, 1985.

Story editor, *MacGyver,* ABC, 1987–88.

Executive script consultant, *MacGyver,* ABC, 1988–89.

Executive story consultant, *MacGyver,* ABC, 1989–90.

Associate producer, *Lonesome Dove: The Outlaw Years,* syndicated, 1995.

Consulting producer, *PSI Factor: Chronicles of the Paranormal,* syndicated, 1996.

Producer, *The Immortal,* syndicated, 2000.

Executive consultant, *Code Name: Eternity,* Sci-Fi Channel, 2003–2004.

Television Director; Episodic:
"The Endangered," *PSI Factor: Chronicles of the Paranormal,* syndicated, 1998.

Film Work:
Production assistant, *Ruckus* (also known as *Big Ruckus in a Small Town, Ruckus in Madoc Country,* and *The Loner*), 1981.

WRITINGS

Screenplays:
Inhabited, PorchLight Entertainment, 2003.

Television Movies:
Life in a Day (also known as *Antidote*), UPN, 1999.
Combustion (also known as *Silent Killer*), Lifetime, 2004.
Meltdown (also known as *Meltdown: Days of Destruction*), Sci–Fi Channel, 2006.
Tell Me No Lies, Lifetime, 2007.

Television Episodes:
The Paul Anka Show, syndicated, 1983.
"Roots and Wings," *Danger Bay,* CBC, 1987.
"Deep Trouble," *Danger Bay,* CBC, 1987.
"The Birdman," *Danger Bay,* CBC, 1987.
MacGyver, ABC, 1988–90.
African Skies, Family Channel, 1991.
"Secrets," *Neon Rider,* syndicated, 1991.
"On the Line," *Neon Rider,* syndicated, 1992.
"Incident at Vernon River," *Road to Avonlea* (also known as *Avonlea* and *Tales from Avonlea*), Disney Channel and CBC, 1993.
"The Great Race," *Road to Avonlea* (also known as *Avonlea* and *Tales from Avonlea*), Disney Channel and CBC, 1994.
"Where the Heart Is," *Lonesome Dove: The Series,* syndicated, 1994.
"Last Stand," *Lonesome Dove: The Series,* syndicated, 1994.
"Blood Money," *Lonesome Dove: The Series,* syndicated, 1994.
"The More Things Change," *Road to Avonlea* (also known as *Avonlea* and *Tales from Avonlea*), Disney Channel and CBC, 1995.
"The Nature of the Beast," *Lonesome Dove: The Outlaw Years,* syndicated, 1995.
"Thicker Than Water," *Lonesome Dove: The Outlaw Years,* syndicated, 1995.
"The Hideout," *Lonesome Dove: The Outlaw Years,* syndicated, 1995.
PSI Factor: Chronicles of the Paranormal, syndicated, 1997–2000.
Police Academy: The Series, syndicated, 1997–98.
Welcome to Paradox, Sci–Fi Channel, 1998.
The Adventures of Shirley Holmes: Detective, Fox Family, 1998.
The Immortal, syndicated, 2000–2001.
"Serpent's Kiss," *BeastMaster,* syndicated, 2001.

Guinevere Jones, 2002.
Code Name: Eternity, Sci–Fi Channel, 2003–2004.
The Collector, City TV, 2004.
Young Blades, Independent Television, 2004–2005.
Zixx: Level Two, YTV, 2005.
"Heart of Fire," *Blood Ties,* Lifetime, 2007.

DRUMMOND, Alice 1929–

PERSONAL

Original name, Alice Ruyter; born May 21, 1929, in Pawtucket, RI; daughter of Arthur (an auto mechanic) and Sarah Irene (a secretary; maiden name, Alker) Ruyter; married Paul Drummond, March 3, 1951 (divorced 1975). *Education:* Brown University, B.A.

Addresses: *Agent*—Paradigm, 360 North Crescent Dr., North Building, Beverly Hills, CA 90210.

Career: Actress.

Member: Actors' Equity Association, Screen Actors Guild, American Federation of Television and Radio Artists.

Awards, Honors: Antoinette Perry Award nomination, best supporting or featured actress in a play (dramatic), 1970, for *The Chinese and Dr. Fish;* Drama Desk award nomination, outstanding featured actress in a play, 1976, for *A Memory of Two Mondays.*

CREDITS

Stage Appearances:
Bea, *A Toy for the Clowns* (produced with *Wretched for the Lionhearted*), East End Theatre, New York City, 1962.
Mrs. Barker, *The American Dream* (produced with *The Zoo Story*), Cherry Lane Theatre, New York City, 1962.
Mrs. Jones and midwife, *The Lunatic View,* Lucille Lortel Theatre, New York City, 1962.
Sweet of You to Say So [and] *Squirrel,* American National Theatre and Academy (ANTA) Matinee Series, Lucille Lortel Theatre, 1962.
Anne of Cleves, *Royal Gambit,* Equity Library Theatre, Master Theatre, New York City, 1963.
Helen, *A Doll's House,* Theatre Four, New York City, 1963.

Isabel Lawland, *The Blue Boy in Black,* Masque Theatre, New York City, 1963.

Townsperson and understudies for the roles of Mrs. Peterson and a townsperson, *The Ballad of the Sad Cafe,* Martin Beck Theatre, New York City, 1963–64.

Queen Boudicca, *The Giants' Dance,* Cherry Lane Theatre, 1964.

Eloisa Brace, *Malcolm,* Shubert Theatre, New York City, 1965–66.

Mrs. Lee, *The Chinese and Dr. Fish* (one–act), Ethel Barrymore Theatre, New York City, 1970.

Mrs. Carpenter, *The Carpenters,* American Place Theatre, New York City, 1970–71.

Ann Honeywell, *Chas. Abbott & Son,* Roundabout Theatre, New York City, 1971.

Flo and understudy for the role of a street lady, *Thieves,* Broadhurst Theatre, New York City, 1974, and Longacre Theatre, New York City, 1974–75.

Christine Schoenwalder and understudies for the roles of Flo Owens, Irma Kronkite, and Mrs. Helen Potts, *Summer Brave,* American National Theatre and Academy (ANTA) Playhouse, New York City, 1975.

Agnes, *A Memory of Two Mondays* (produced with *27 Wagons Full of Cotton*), Playhouse Theatre, New York City, 1976.

Miss Crews, *Boy Meets Girl,* Phoenix Theatre Company, New York City, 1976.

Mrs. Varney, *Secret Service,* Phoenix Theatre Company, New York City, 1976.

Dorothy Mumford, *Some of My Best Friends,* Longacre Theatre, 1977.

Killings on the Last Line, American Place Theatre, 1980.

Gay Wellington, *You Can't Take It with You,* Plymouth Theatre, New York City, 1983–84.

Nell, *Endgame,* Samuel Beckett Theater, New York City, 1984.

Sweet Bird of Youth, Theatre Royal Haymarket, London, 1985.

Ruth, *Marvin's Room,* Playwrights Horizons, New York City, 1991–92, then Minetta Lane Theatre, New York City, 1992.

Appeared in other productions, including appearances as Lucy and Martha, *Gallows Humor,* as Marion, *Go Show Me a Dragon,* and as Persephone, *Enter a Free Man,* all off–Broadway productions.

Film Appearances:

Woman in elevator, *Where's Poppa?* (also known as *Going Ape!*), United Artists, 1970.

Mrs. Dawson, *Man on a Swing,* Paramount, 1974.

Mrs. Ramsey, *Thieves,* Paramount, 1977.

Zharko's nurse, *King of the Gypsies,* Paramount, 1978.

Mrs. Novack, *Hide in Plain Sight,* United Artists, 1980.

Mrs. Deever, *Eyewitness* (also known as *The Janitor*), Twentieth Century–Fox, 1981.

Governor's secretary, *The Best Little Whorehouse in Texas* (musical; also known as *The Best Little Cathouse in Texas*), Universal, 1982.

Librarian, *Ghostbusters* (also known as *Ghost Busters, Ghostbusters: The Supernatural Spectacular, Eis cacafantasmas, Ghostbusters–Acchiappafantasmi, Ghostbusters—Die Geisterjaeger, Ghostbusters—Gli acchiappafantasmi, Ghostbusters—haamujengi, Krotitele duchu, Los cazafantasmas, Os caca–fantasmas, Pogromcy duchow, S.O.S. fantomes, Spoekligan,* and *Szellemirtok*), Columbia, 1984.

Maltha, *The Suicide Club* (also known as *Clube do suicidio, Il club dei suicidi, Klub samobojcow, Tod oder Joker,* and *Vaarallinen leikki*), Angelika Films, 1988.

Mrs. Dinges, *Funny Farm* (also known as *Aventuras y desaventuras de un yuppie en el campo, L'allegra fattoria, Livet paa landet, Maalla on mukavaa, Que bem que se esta no campo,* and *Uma fazenda do barulho*), Warner Bros., 1988.

Mrs. Powell, *Running on Empty* (also known as *A bout de course, Ahava B'Milkud, Die Flucht ins Ungewisse, Elaemaenae pakotie, Flykt utan maal, O peso de um passado, Un lugar en ninguna parte,* and *Vivere in fuga*), Warner Bros., 1988.

Woman at hearing, *The House on Carroll Street,* Orion, 1988.

Site committee member, *Animal Behavior,* Millimeter Films, 1989.

Carolyn, "Cat from Hell" segment, *Tales from the Darkside: The Movie* (also known as *Darkside, les contes de la nuit noire, El gato infernal, Geschichten aus der Schattenwelt, I delitti del gatto nero, Opowiesc o zmroku,* and *Pimeae puoli*), Paramount, 1990.

Lucy Fishman, *Awakenings* (also known as *Cas probuzeni, Despertares, Ebredesek, Heraeaemisiae, L'eveil, Oppvaakningen, Prebujenja, Przebudzenia, Risvegli, Tempo de despertar, Uppvaknanden, Xypnimata,* and *Zeit des Erwachens*), Columbia, 1990.

Martha, *Me & Veronica,* Arrow Releasing, 1992.

Mrs. Breen, *Money for Nothing* (also known as *The Joey Coyle Story, Banii n–aduc fericirea, Das Million–Ding, Der Preis fuer eine Million, Dinheiro a borla, Dinheiro, pra que dinheiro?, Milionario per caso, Nyhjaeae tyhjaestae,* and *Que no hacer con un millon de dolares!*), Buena Vista, 1993.

Dinner guest, *I.Q.* (also known as *A teoria do amor, Ahava ·tomeat, Ask ve zeka, El genio del amor, Formula para amar, Genio per amore, I.Q.—A szerelem relativ, I.Q.—Liebe ist relativ, I.Q. (Q.I.), L'amour en equation,* and *Rakkauden yhtaeloe*), Paramount, 1994.

Hattie, *Nobody's Fool* (also known as *Hvem er fuldkommen?, Kukaan ei ole taeydellinen, La vita a modo mio, Naiwniak, Ne imejte me za norca, Ni un pelo de tonto, Nobody's Fool—Auf Dauer unwiderstehlich, Nobody's Fool—Ein charmanter Dickkopf, O indomavel—Assim e minha vida, Senki bolondja, Un homme presque parfait, Vidas simples,* and *Yasamin icinden*), Paramount, 1994.

Mrs. Finkle, *Ace Ventura: Pet Detective* (also known as *Ace Ventura, Ace Ventura—Allati nyomozo, Ace Ventura: Detective Animal, Ace Ventura, detective chiens et chats, Ace Ventura—Detective pour chiens et chats, Ace Ventura—Ein tierischer Detektiv, Ace Ventura—L'acchiappanimali, Ace Ventura—Lemmikkidekkari, Ace Ventura mene l'enquete, Ace Ventura—Nori detektiv, Ace Ventura: Psi detektyw, Ace Ventura—Um detetive diferente, Ace Ventura, un detective diferente, Den galopperande detektiven,* and *Detective zoon*), Warner Bros., 1994.

Clara, *To Wong Foo, Thanks for Everything, Julie Newmar* (also known as *Extravagances, High Heels, To Wong Foo, A Wong Foo, gracias por todo, Julie Newmar, A Wong Foo, grazie di tutto! Julie Newmar, A Wong Foo, merci pour tout Julie Newmar, Hvala za vse, Os tres mosqueteiros do amor, Para Wong Foo, obrigada por tudo! Julie Newmar, Reinas o reyes, Reinas o reyes?,* and *Wong Foo, koesz mindent! Julie Newmar*), Universal, 1995.

Grandma Rose, *Jeffrey* (also known as *Jeffrey—De caso com a vida*), Orion, 1995.

Betsy (Amelia's neighbor), *Walking and Talking* (also known as *Confidencias, Mariage ou celibat, Parlando e sparlando, Propos et confidences,* and *Walking talking: nadie es perfecto*), Miramax, 1996.

Edith, *Just in Time* (short film), Flatland Pictures, 1996.

Aunt Susan, *In & Out* (also known as *A boldogito nem, Dentro e fora, In & Out—Rosa wie die Liebe, Je ali ni?, Le pot aux roses, Sera que ele e?,* and *Ute eller inte*), Paramount, 1997.

Carlotta Douglas, *Office Killer* (also known as *La asesina de la oficina, Mente paranoica,* and *Office Killer—L'impiegata modello*), Miramax, 1997.

Harriet, *'Til There Was You* (also known as *Ate tu apareceres ..., Ha–Dereh el Ha–Osher, Hasta que te encontre, Idoeszamitasom eloett, L'amour de ma vie, Si on s'aimait, Solo se ilm destino,* and *Zwei Singles in L.A.*), Paramount, 1997.

Mrs. Mann, *Commandments,* Universal/Gramercy Pictures, 1997.

Diner grandmother, *Advice from a Caterpillar* (also known as *Trzej mezczyzni i ona*), 1999.

Lady with cash, *Just the Ticket* (also known as *Gary & Linda, The Ticket Scalper, Ticket to Love, Biglietti ... d'amore, Bilhete caido do ceu, Billets pour deux, Como caido del cielo, Meu adoravel sonhador, Rakastunut huijari,* and *Un bilet in plus*), United Artists, 1999.

Postal clerk, *The Love Letter* (also known as *A carta anonima, Carta de amor, Der Liebesbrief, Destina-*

taire inconnu, Lettera d'amore, and *Rakkauskirje*), DreamWorks, 1999.

Stella, *I'll Take You There,* DEJ Productions, 1999.

Helen, *Joe Gould's Secret,* USA Films, 2000.

Aunt Millie Hodge, *The Rising Place,* Warner Bros., 2001.

Grandma Dottie, *Pieces of April,* United Artists, 2003.

Mrs. Brevoort, *House of D* (also known as *Delitos menores, El incomprendido,* and *Reflexos da amizade*), Lions Gate Films, 2004.

Miss Benvenuti, *The Honeymooners,* Paramount, 2005.

Elizabeth, *Chronic Town,* Grey Jumper Productions, 2008.

Television Appearances; Series:

Loretta Jardin, *Where the Heart Is,* CBS, 1971–73.

Frances Heine, *Park Place,* CBS, 1981.

Mary Callahan, *Lenny,* CBS, 1990–91.

Rosa Escobar, *Frannie's Turn,* CBS, 1992.

Television Appearances; Miniseries:

Mabel Baldwin, *The Best of Families,* PBS, 1977.

Alger Hiss's secretary, "Concealed Enemies," *American Playhouse,* PBS, 1984.

Television Appearances; Movies:

Helen, *Money, Power, Murder.* (also known as *Dinheiro, poder e assassinio, Moerderische News,* and *Vaarallisilla jaeljillae*), CBS, 1989.

Anna, *Daybreak* (also known as *Bloodstream*), HBO, 1993.

Old woman in jalopy, *Earthly Possessions,* HBO, 1999.

Appeared as Mrs. Milligan, *The Milligan Case.*

Television Appearances; Specials:

Mrs. Ewing, "Particular Men," *Playhouse New York,* PBS, 1972.

Mrs. Varney, "Secret Service," *Great Performances,* PBS, 1977.

Gay Wellington, "You Can't Take It with You," *Great Performances,* PBS, 1984.

Also appeared as Mommy, *The Sandbox,* PBS.

Television Appearances; Episodic:

Nurse Jackson, *Dark Shadows,* ABC, 1967 (multiple episodes).

Mavis Tuttle, "Harry and the Rock Star," *Night Court,* NBC, 1984.

"Nocturne," *The Equalizer,* CBS, 1986.

Alice Beeker, "Murder," *Night Court,* NBC, 1987.

Mrs. Rinde, "The Band Singer," *Kate & Allie,* CBS, 1988.

Juror, "Here's a Major Organ Interlude," *The Days and Nights of Molly Dodd,* Lifetime, 1989.

Nana Lil, "With This Ring," *Grace under Fire* (also known as *Grace under Pressure*), ABC, 1994.

Zelda, "Mayhem," *Law & Order* (also known as *Law & Order Prime*), NBC, 1994.

Mrs. Haggis, "Thin Line," *New York News,* CBS, 1995.

Mrs. Bagley, "Neighborhood Watch," *Cosby,* CBS, 1996.

Mrs. Spencer, "Suffragette City," *Spin City* (also known as *Spin*), ABC, 2000.

Mrs. Shroeder, "Memory Lane," *Ed* (also known as *Stuckeyville*), NBC, 2002.

Hannah Francis, "The Honeymoon Suite," *The Jury,* Fox, 2004.

Lydia Tuffalo, "Ass Fat Jungle," *Boston Legal* (also known as *Fleet Street, The Practice: Fleet Street,* and *The Untitled Practice*), ABC, 2005.

Appeared in other programs, including *As the World Turns,* CBS; *Guiding Light,* CBS; *Love of Life,* CBS; and *Search for Tomorrow,* CBS and NBC.

Television Appearances; Pilots:

Grace Barringer, *Sanctuary of Fear* (also known as *Father Brown, Detective, Girl in the Park, Sanctuary of Death, Il santuario della paura, Padre Brown, Detective,* and *Peter Brown laesst sich nicht bluffen*), NBC, 1979.

Mrs. Klein, *Nikki & Alexander,* NBC, 1989.

Mrs. Bingham, *Trinity,* NBC, 1998.

DUDGEON, Neil

PERSONAL

Born in Doncaster, South Yorkshire, England. *Education:* Trained for the stage at Royal Academy of Dramatic Arts, 1982–85.

Addresses: *Agent*—International Creative Management, 10250 Constellation Way, 9th Floor, Los Angeles, CA 90067; (voice work) Lip Service Casting Ltd., 4 Kingly Street, London W1B 5PE, England.

Career: Actor. Appeared in commercials.

CREDITS

Television Appearances; Miniseries:

"Moggy" Cattermole, *Piece of Cake,* PBS, 1988.

Tom Edmonds, *Nice Town,* BBC, 1992.

William Doria, *Resnick: Rough Treatment,* BBC, 1992.

Puppeteer's assistant, *The History of Tom Jones, a Foundling* (also known as *Henry Fielding's "Tom Jones"*), Arts and Entertainment, 1997.

Vince Yallop, *Four Fathers,* ITV, 1999.

Deputy Inspector Duncan Warren, *Messiah* (also known as *Messiah I: The First Killings*), BBC, 2001.

Deputy Inspector Duncan Warren, *Messiah 2: Vengeance Is Mine,* BBC, 2002.

Brian Richards, *The Planman,* ITV, 2003.

Deputy Inspector Duncan Warren, *Messiah: The Promise,* BBC, 2004.

Deputy Inspector Duncan Warren, *Messiah: The Harrowing,* BBC, 2005.

Television Appearances; Movies:

Vlasek, *Red King, White Knight,* HBO, 1989.

Crowson, *Night Voice,* BBC, 1990.

Eric Volkner, *Revolver,* NBC, 1992.

Lieutenant Gibbons, *Sharpe's Eagle,* PBS, 1993.

Sex crimes cop, *Fatherland,* HBO, 1994.

Dr. Neil McFarlane, *Breakout,* BBC, 1997.

Detective Constable Spence, *Our Boy,* BBC, 1997.

David, *The Gift,* BBC, 1998.

Dennis, *Dirty Tricks,* Carlton, 2000.

Matt Dempsey, *The Return,* ITV, 2003.

Lestrade, *Sherlock Holmes and the Case of the Silk Stocking,* BBC, 2004, PBS, 2005.

Coming down the Mountain, BBC1, 2007.

Television Appearances; Series:

Ken Andrews, *Common As Muck,* BBC, 1994.

George Moody, a recurring role, *The Mrs. Bradley Mysteries,* BBC America, 1998–2000.

Harry, *Sorted,* BBC, 2006.

Television Appearances; Specials:

Voice of the miller, "Leaving London," *The Canterbury Tales,* HBO, 1998.

Voice of the miller, "The Journey Back," *The Canterbury Tales,* HBO, 2000.

Narrator, *Humanzee: The Human Chimp,* Discovery Channel, 2003.

Joe Haines, *The Lavender List,* BBC4, 2006.

Doctor, *Imprints,* Channel 4, 2007.

Television Appearances; Episodic:

Brink, "Road," *Alive TV,* PBS, 1985.

Garry, *London's Burning,* ITV, 1988.

Jimmy, "Next Year in Jerusalem," *Saracen,* Central, 1989.

Deputy superintendent Graham Bentley, "Bin Diving," *Lovejoy,* Arts and Entertainment, 1991.

Mick, "Sins of Omission," *Casualty,* BBC1, 1991.

Deputy Superintendent Alan Hanson, "Lies and Damned Lies," *Between the Lines* (also known as *Inside the Line*), BBC, 1992.

Detective constable Costello, "Nothing to Hide," *A Touch of Frost,* ITV, 1994.

Deputy constable Marty Brazil, premiere episode, *Out of the Blue,* BBC, 1995.

David Michaels, "The Way through the Woods," *Inspector Morse,* PBS, 1997.

Daniel Bolt, "Garden of Death," *Midsomer Murders,* Arts and Entertainment, 2000.

Edward Buttimore, "Rage," *Murder in Mind,* BBC America, 2002.

Alan Richmond, *Rose and Maloney,* ITV, 2005.

Brian Peterson, *The Street,* ITV, 2006.

Roman Pretty, *Roman's Empire,* 2007.

Film Appearances:

Brink, *Road,* 1987.

(Uncredited) Policeman, *Prick Up Your Ears,* 1987.

Sergeant Rudkin, *Fools of Fortune,* New Line Cinema, 1990.

Priest, *Skallagrigg,* 1994.

Neil Payne *Different for Girls* (also known as *Crossing the Border*), First Look Pictures Releasing, 1996.

Detective constable Spence, *Our Boy,* 1997.

Holdsworth, *It Was an Accident,* Pathe, 2000.

Richard Jackson, *Breathtaking,* IAC Film, 2000.

Taxi driver, *Bridget Jones: The Edge of Reason* (also known as *Bridget Jones 2* and *Bridget Jones: L'age de raison*), 2004.

After 8, 2006.

Joshua, *Son of Rambow,* Paramount Vantage, 2007.

Stage Appearances:

Moggy Catermole, *Piece of Cake,* 1988.

Joe, *Crackwalker,* 1992.

Henry Bollingbroke, *Richard II,* Royal Exchange Theatre, Manchester, England, 1993.

John Worthing, *The Importance of Being Earnest,* Royal Exchange Theatre, 1993–94.

Larry, *Closer,* Royal National Theatre, Lyttelton Theatre, London, 1997.

Tinker, *Cleansed,* Royal Court Theatre, London, 2001.

Ian, *Blasted,* Jerwood Theatre Upstairs, Royal Court Theatre, London, 2001.

Sergeant, *Mountain Language,* Jerwood Theatre Downstairs, Royal Court Theatre, 2001.

Devlin, *Ashes to Ashes,* Jerwood Theatre Downstairs, Royal Court Theatre, 2001.

Radio Appearances:

In a Glass Darkly, 2003.

Christian, *The Pilgrim's Progress* (miniseries), 2004.

Artist, *Voices from Another Room,* BBC4, 2004.

E–F

ELSEN, John 1964–

PERSONAL

Born August 23, 1964.

Addresses: *Agent*—Cornerstone Talent Agency, 37 West 20th St., Suite 1108, New York, NY 10011.

Career: Actor.

CREDITS

Film Appearances:
Ali, Wendy's husband, *The Incredibly True Adventure of Two Girls in Love,* 1995.
Stone, *Turbulence,* Metro–Goldwyn–Mayer, 1997.
Joe/Banquo, *Macbeth in Manhattan,* The Asylum, 1999.
Deli guy, *The Out–of–Towners,* Paramount, 1999.
New York City cop, *The Thomas Crown Affair,* Metro–Goldwyn–Mayer, 1999.
Officer number one, *The Yards,* Miramax, 2000.
Uniform cop in Metronome, *Shaft* (also known as *Shaft—Noch Fragen?*), Paramount, 2000.
Chicago airport security, *Meet the Parents,* Universal, 2000.
Desk sergeant, *Woman Found Dead in Elevator,* 2000.
Interrogating detective, *Love the Hard Way* (also known as *Love the Hard Way—Atemios in New York*), Kino International, 2001.
Tony, *The Jimmy Show,* First Look International, 2001.
Cop, *Dummy,* Artisan Entertainment, 2002.
West of Here, 2002.
UPS delivery man, *Loverboy,* Screen Media Films, 2005.

Television Appearances; Series:
Officer Perry, a recurring role, *All My Children,* ABC, 2001–2002.

Television Appearances; Movies:
Heckler, *Mary and Rhoda,* ABC, 2000.

Television Appearances; Pilots:
Court officer Billy, *Queens Supreme,* CBS, 2003.

Television Appearances; Episodic:
Uniform cop, "Ice Follies," *NYPD Blue,* ABC, 1993.
Uniform cop, "Rockin' Robin," *NYPD Blue,* ABC, 1994.
Christian Brock, *Swift Justice,* UPN, 1996.
Cop, "Gentleman's Agreement," *Spin City,* ABC, 1998.
McNair, "In a Yellow Wood," *Trinity,* NBC, 1998.
Policeman number one, "A Single Life," *Law and Order: Special Victims Unit* (also known as *Law & Order: SVU* and *Special Victims Unit*), NBC, 1999.
Halberstam, "Patterns," *Third Watch,* NBC, 1999.
Pete, *Cosby,* CBS, 1999.
Weatherbee, "Sophomore Jinx," *Law and Order: Special Victims Unit* (also known as *Law & Order: SVU* and *Special Victims Unit*), NBC, 1999.
Hank, "Marathon," *Law and Order,* NBC, 1999.
Reporter, *Wonderland,* ABC, 2000.
Mark, *Hack,* CBS, 2000.
Man number one, "Valentine's Day," *Ed,* NBC, 2001.
"Let's Make a Night of It," *100 Centre Street,* Arts and Entertainment, 2001.
Security officer, "Save the Country," *The Education of Max Bickford,* CBS, 2002.
Officer Yorn, "Two Tonys," *The Sopranos,* HBO, 2004.

Stage Appearances:
The Way of the World, New York Shakespeare Festival, New York City, 1991.

Jason, *Sin,* McGinn–Cazale Theatre, New York City, 1995.

World of Mirth, Theatre Four, New York City, 2001.

EVE, Trevor 1951–

PERSONAL

Full name, Trevor John Eve; born July 1, 1951, in Birmingham, England; son of Stewart Frederick and Elsie (maiden name, Hamer) Eve; married Sharon Patricia Maughan (an actress), March 1, 1980; children: Alice Eve (an actress), James Jonathan (Jack), George Francis. *Education:* Studied acting at the Royal Academy of Dramatic Art; studied architecture at Kingston Polytechnic (now Kingston University). *Avocational Interests:* Golf, tennis.

Addresses: *Agent*—International Creative Management, Oxford House, 76 Oxford St., London W1N 0AX, England.

Career: Actor and producer. Appeared in advertisements. Projector Productions, producer. Royal Academy of Dramatic Art, associate. Child Hope International (a charity), patron.

Member: Chelsea Arts Club, Hurlingham Club, Queen's Club, Wentworth Club.

Awards, Honors: Laurence Olivier Theatre Award, best actor in a new play, Society of West End Theatre, 1982, for *Children of a Lesser God;* Laurence Olivier Theatre Award, best actor in a supporting role, 1997, for *Uncle Vanya.*

CREDITS

Film Appearances:
Man in shower, *Children,* 1976.

Jonathan Harker, *Dracula* (also known as *Dracula '79* and *Dracula—Eine Love Story*), Universal, 1979.

Matinee idol, *Scandal* (also known as *Escandalo, Scandal—il caso Profumo, Scandale, Skandaali,* and *Skandalen*), Miramax, 1989.

Alphonse Malard, *Mirage* (also known as *Miragem*), 1990.

Knight, *In the Name of the Father* (short film), American Film Institute, 1992.

Karl Stall, *Aspen Extreme* (also known as *Aspen—Dinheiro, seducao e perigo, Aspen extreme, Aspen—miljonaarien paratiisi, Aspen—Sci estremo, Fuera de pistas, Ski radical,* and *Zwei Asse im Schnee*), Buena Vista, 1993.

Jack Lane, *Don't Get Me Started,* 1994.

Jay, *Appetite,* New City Releasing, 1998.

Mike, *Next Birthday,* 1998.

Professor Morton Cropper, *Possession,* USA Films, 2002.

Velior, *Troy* (also known as *Untitled "The Iliad" Project, Troia, Troie, Troija, Troja, Trooja,* and *Troya*), Warner Bros., 2004.

Some source cite appearances in *The Knight's Tale* and *Psychotherapy.*

Television Appearances; Series:
London Belongs to Me, Thames Television, beginning 1977.

Eddie Shoestring, *Shoestring,* BBC, 1979–80, Entertainment Channel, 1982.

Dr. Jonathan MacKensie, *Shadow Chasers* (also known as *Shadowchasers*), ABC, 1985–86.

Ricky Fortune, *Dear John* (also known as *Dear John: USA, Divorciados, John Ha–Yakar, Mein Lieber John,* and *Querido John*), NBC, c. 1989.

Albert Tyburn, *Heat of the Sun,* Carlton Television, 1998, broadcast on *Mystery!* (also known as *Mystery!: Heat of the Sun*), PBS, 1999.

Detective superintendent Peter Boyd, *Waking the Dead,* BBC, 2001—.

Television Appearances; Miniseries:
Gordon Taylor, *A Brother's Tale,* Granada Television, 1983.

Tom Schwartz, *Lace,* ABC, 1984.

Jeremiah "Jem" Merlyn, *Jamaica Inn,* Harlech Television and syndicated, 1985.

Denys Finch Hatton, *Beryl Markham: A Shadow on the Sun* (also known as *Shadow on the Sun, Afrika, mein Leben, Etelaen auringon varjossa, Grosse Liebe Afrika,* and *Schatten auf der Sonne*), London Weekend Television and CBS, 1988.

Charles Stewart Parnell, *Parnell & the Englishwoman,* BBC, 1991, broadcast on *Masterpiece Theatre* (also known as *ExxonMobil Masterpiece Theatre* and *Mobil Masterpiece Theatre*), PBS, c. 1992.

Duncan Matlock, *The Politician's Wife* (also known as *The Politician's Wife: Stand by Him, The Politician's Wife: Echo Chamber, The Politician's Wife: Body Politic,* and *A mulher do politico*), Channel 4 (England), 1995, broadcast on *Masterpiece Theatre* (also known as *ExxonMobil Masterpiece Theatre* and *Mobil Masterpiece Theatre*), PBS, 1996, also broadcast on CBC.

Alex Kyle, *An Evil Streak* (also known as *Evilstreak*), London Weekend Television, 1999.

Mr. Murdstone, *David Copperfield,* BBC, 1999, broadcast on *Masterpiece Theatre* (also known as *ExxonMobil Masterpiece Theatre* and *Mobil Masterpiece Theatre*), PBS, 2000.

John Paxton, *Lawless,* Independent Television (England), 2004.

Patrick Stowe, *The Family Man* (also known as *Fadar vaar* and *Isa meidaen*), BBC, 2006.

Television Appearances; Movies:

The Portrait, 1975.

Hindle Wakes (also known as *Laurence Olivier Presents: "Hindle Wakes"*), Granada Television, 1976.

Louis de Franchi and Lucien de Franchi, *The Corsican Brothers* (also known as *Vendetta*), CBS, 1985.

Felix Cramer, *A Sense of Guilt,* BBC, 1990.

Paul LaFlore, *The President's Child,* CBS, 1992.

Alex Fisher, "Black Easter" (also known as "No Man's Land"), *Screen Two,* BBC, 1994.

Malcolm Iverson, *Murder in Mind* (also known as *Meurtre a l'esprit, Mielen varjot,* and *Toedliche Gedanken*), [Great Britain], 1994.

Mark, *For Love Alone: The Ivana Trump Story* (also known as *Ivana Trump's "For Love Alone"*), CBS, 1996.

Kanahan, *The Tribe,* BBC, 1998.

Neil Tannahill, *Doomwatch: Winter Angel* (also known as *Coaccion misteriosa* and *Katastrophe im schwarzen Loch*), Channel 5 (England), 1999.

Television Appearances; Specials:

Richard, *A Wreath of Roses,* Granada Television, 1988, broadcast on *Masterpiece Theatre* (also known as *ExxonMobil Masterpiece Theatre* and *Mobil Masterpiece Theatre*), PBS, 1989.

Torvald Helmer, *A Doll's House,* BBC, 1992.

Television Appearances; Awards Presentations:

Presenter, *The Laurence Olivier Awards 2003,* 2003.

Television Appearances; Episodic:

Julian Fontaine, "Tinker, Tailor, Liar, Thief," *Murder, She Wrote,* CBS, 1992.

Max Kendall, "The Last Time I Saw Paris," *Jack's Place,* ABC, 1992.

Himself, *Breakfast,* BBC, 2001.

Himself, *GMTV,* Independent Television (England), 2004.

Himself, *Top Gear* (also known as *Top Gear Xtra*), BBC, 2005, 2006.

Television Appearances; Pilots:

Dr. Jonathan MacKensie, *Shadow Chasers* (also known as *Shadowchasers*), ABC, 1985.

Tripper Day, *Life on the Flipside,* NBC, 1988.

Dave Stone, *The Stone Age,* BBC, 1989.

Frederick Paddington, *Up to No Good,* ABC, 1992.

In Security, NBC, 1992.

Detective chief inspector Peter Boyd, *Waking the Dead,* BBC, 2000.

Television Producer; Movies:

Alice through the Looking Glass (also known as *Alice i spegellandet, Alice im Spiegelland,* and *Alicja po drugiej stronie*), Channel 4 (England), 1998, HBO, 1999.

Cinderella (also known as *Cendrillon rhapsodie* and *Cenicienta*), Channel 4, 1999, Bravo, 2000.

Television Executive Producer; Specials:

Twelfth Night, or What You Will (also known as *Twelfth Night*), Channel 4 (England), 2003.

Stage Appearances:

Paul McCartney, *John, Paul, George, Ringo ... and Bert,* Lyric Theatre, London, 1974.

Riccardo, *Filumena,* Lyric Theatre, 1977.

James Leeds, *Children of a Lesser God,* Mermaid Theatre, then Albery Theatre, both London, 1981.

Leo Lehrer, *The Genius,* Royal Court Theatre, London, 1983.

Dexter, *High Society,* National Theatre, Victoria Palace Theatre, London, 1987.

Man Beast and Virtue, National Theatre, Cottesloe Theatre, London, 1989.

The Winter's Tale, Young Vic, London, 1991.

Inadmissible Evidence, Royal National Theatre, London, 1993.

Dr. Astrov, *Uncle Vanya,* Albery Theatre, 1996.

RECORDINGS

Audiobooks:

Daphne Du Maurier, *Jamaica Inn,* Listen for Leisure, 1981.

OTHER SOURCES

Periodicals:

Radio Times, January 13, 1990, pp. 4–5; March 18, 2006, pp. 10–12, 15.

EYRE, Peter 1942–

PERSONAL

Born March 11, 1942, in New York, NY; son of Edward Joseph (a banker) and Dorothy Pelline (maiden name, Acton) Eyre. *Education:* Attended Portsmouth Priory, Portsmouth, RI, and Downside Abbey, Stratton–on–the–Fosse, Somerset, England. *Politics:* Democrat. *Avocational Interests:* Music.

Addresses: *Office*—Original Productions, 308 West Verdugo Ave., Burbank, CA 91502. *Agent*—ICM, Ltd., Oxford House, 76 Oxford St., London W1D 1BS England.

Career: Actor and writer. Worked with Royal Shakespeare Company at Old Vic Theatre, London; worked with various regional theatres in the United Kingdom; Original Productions, Burbank, CA, managing director; also worked at Original Productions U.K. Entertainment.

Member: International PEN, Groucho Club.

Awards, Honors: Children's Award nomination (with Nic Ayling), best factual, British Academy of Film and Television Arts, 2002, for *Art Attack*.

CREDITS

Film Appearances:
Art director, *Having a Wild Weekend* (also known as *Catch Us If You Can*), Warner Bros., 1965.
Cinna, the poet, *Julius Caesar,* American International Pictures, 1970.
Priest, *The Pied Piper* (also known as *The Pied Piper of Hamelin*), Paramount, 1972.
Otto Mahler, *Mahler,* 1974.
George Tesman, *Hedda,* Brut Productions, 1975.
Edward, *La luna* (also known as *Luna*), Twentieth Century–Fox, 1979.
Casiodorus Rex, *Dragonslayer,* Paramount, 1981.
Walter, *Couples and Robbers,* 1981.
Reverend Borenius, *Maurice,* Cinecom, 1987.
Gott, *Just Ask for Diamond* (also known as *Diamond Edge*), Kings Road Entertainment, 1988.
Norton Shaw, *Mountains of the Moon,* TriStar Pictures, 1990.
Humphreys, *Let Him Have It* (also known as *L'age de vivre*), 1991.
Mr. Pope, *Orlando,* Sony Pictures Classics, 1992.
Lord Halifax, *The Remains of the Day,* Columbia Pictures, 1993.
Lord Apthorpe, *Princess Caraboo,* 1994.
Sabartes, *Surviving Picasso,* Warner Bros., 1996.
English tango fan, *The Tango Lesson* (also known as *La lecon de tango, La leccion de tango,* and *Tango–Feiber*), Sony Pictures Classics, 1997.
The Doge, *Dangerous Beauty* (also known as *The Honest Courtesan* and *A Destiny of Her Own*), Warner Bros., 1998.
Jarvis, *The Golden Bowl* (also known as *La coupe d'or*), Lions Gate Films, 2000.
Lord Hallsham, *From Hell,* Twentieth Century–Fox, 2001.
Monsieur Bassenge, *The Affair of the Necklace,* Warner Bros., 2001.

Bartholemew Gray, *Still Life* (short), 2005.
United States ambassador, *The Situation,* Shadow Distribution, 2006.

Television Appearances; Series:
Various roles, *The Last Machine,* BBC, 1995.
Forstater, *The Vanishing Man,* ITV, 1998.

Television Appearances; Miniseries:
Chubinov, *The Birds Fall Down,* BBC, 1978.
Main, *Spyship,* BBC, 1983.
Basil Plante, *The Two Mrs. Grenvilles,* NBC, 1987.
Roberts, *Scarlett,* CBS, 1994.
Vizir, *Joseph* (also known as *The Bible: Joseph, Die Bibel: Josef,* and *Joseph in Egypt*), TNT, 1995.
Chief physician, *Merlin,* NBC, 1998.
Arthur Quigley, *Cambridge Spies,* BBC, 2003.

Television Appearances; Movies:
A Misfortune, BBC, 1973.
Will Nugent, *Sharpe's Gold,* 1995.
Forstater, *The Vanishing Man,* 1996.
Simeon Landor, *Dalziel and Pascoe: An Advancement of Learning* (also known as *Dalziel and Pascoe*), BBC and Arts and Entertainment, 1996.
Frogface footman, *Alice in Wonderland* (also known as *Alice im Wunderland*), BBC, then ABC, 1999.
The priest, *Don Quixote,* TNT, 2000.
Butler Simpson, *Bertie and Elizabeth,* ITV1 and PBS, 2002.

Also appeared in *The Death of Socrates,* BBC.

Television Appearances; Specials:
Eric Colston, *Memento Mori,* BBC, then PBS, 1992.
Sigmund Freud, *The Question of God: Sigmund Freud & C. S. Lewis,* PBS, 2004.

Television Appearances; Episodic:
"The Return to Imray," *The Indian Tales of Rudyard Kipling,* BBC, 1964.
Knave of Hearts, "Alice in Wonderland," *The Wednesday Play,* BBC, 1966.
Kiril, Glagolyev's son, "Platonov," *Play of the Month,* BBC, 1971.
Trevor, "Thank You Very Much," *Play for Today,* BBC1, 1971.
West, "None of Your Business," *Callan,* ITV, 1972.
George Fitzwilliam, "The Secret of the Foxhunter," *The Rivals of Sherlock Holmes,* 1973.
Doran, "Doran's Box," *Play for Today,* BBC1, 1976.
Kurt, "Vienna, November 1908," *The Young Indiana Jones Chronicles,* 1993.
Various roles, *The Last Machine,* 1995.
Simeon Landor, "An Advancement of Learning," *Dalziel and Pascoe,* BBC, 1996.

Bishop of Norfolk, "Innocency of Life," *Kavanaugh QC,* ITV, 1998.

The registrar, "The One After Ross Says Rachel," *Friends,* NBC, 1998.

The registrar, "The One with Ross's Wedding: Part 2," *Friends,* NBC, 1998.

Michael Durban, "For Love nor Money," *Hetty Wainthropp Investigates,* BBC1, 1998.

Leonard Pike, "Strangler's Wood," *Midsomer Murders,* 1999.

Accusator Nigidius, "The Spoils," *Rome,* BBC, 2005.

Headley Madrigal, "A Picture of Innocence," *Midsomer Murders,* ITV and Arts and Entertainment, 2007.

Stage Appearances:

Thane, *Macbeth,* Old Vic Company, Dublin, Ireland, 1960.

Tom Perry, *The Tower,* Hampstead Theatre Club, London, 1964.

Alexeyev, *Oblomov,* Lyric Theatre, London, 1964, re–titled *Son of Oblomov,* Comedy Theatre, London, 1964.

Title role, *Benito Cereno,* Mermaid Theatre, London, 1967.

Prince Arthur, *Early Morning,* Royal Court Theatre, London, 1968.

Feste, *Twelfth Night,* Nottingham Playhouse, Nottingham, England, c. 1968–70.

Banquo, *Macbeth,* Nottingham Playhouse, c. 1968–70.

Konstantin, *The Seagull,* Nottingham Playhouse, c. 1968–70.

Dinsdale, *The Ruling Class,* Nottingham Playhouse, c. 1968–70.

Edgar, *King Lear,* Nottingham Playhouse, c. 1968–70.

Prince Myshkin, *The Idiot,* Nottingham Playhouse, c. 1968–70.

Title role, *The Silence of St. Just,* Gardener Centre, Brighton, England, 1971.

Guildenstern, *Rosencrantz and Guildenstern Are Dead,* Liverpool, England, 1972.

Konstantin, *The Seagull,* Chichester Festival, Chichester, England, 1973.

Major Tarver, *Dandy Dick,* Chichester Festival, 1973.

Ivan, *Notes from the Underground,* Open Space Theatre, London, 1973.

Oswald, *Ghosts,* Greenwich Theatre, London, 1974.

Konstantin, *The Seagull,* Greenwich Theatre, 1974.

Hamlet, Greenwich Theatre, 1974.

Axel, *Comrades,* Royal Shakespeare Company, 1974.

Peters, *The Beast,* Royal Shakespeare Company, 1974.

Christian Maske, *The Snob,* Open Space Theatre, 1974.

George Tesman, *Hedda Gabler,* Aldwych Theatre, London, 1975.

Toozenbach, *Three Sisters,* Cambridge Theatre, London, 1976.

The friend, *Stevie,* Vaudeville Theatre, London, 1977.

Philip, *News,* Soho Poly, 1977.

Raskolnikov, *Crime and Punishment,* Haymarket Theatre, Leicester, England, 1978.

Dolokbov, *War and Peace,* Haymarket Theatre, 1978.

Cain, *Abel and Cain,* Haymarket Theatre, 1978.

Jacques, *As You Like It,* Bristol Old Vic Theatre, Bristol, England, 1978.

The cardinal, *The Duchess of Malfi,* Birmingham Repertory Theatre, Birmingham, England, 1978.

Alceste, *The Misanthrope,* Birmingham Repertory, 1979.

Ferdinando, *Country Life,* Citizens Theatre, Glasgow, Scotland, 1979, then Lyric Theatre, 1980.

Polonius, *Hamlet,* Almeida Theatre, London, then Belasco Theatre, New York City, 1995.

Chere Maitre, Almeida Theatre, 1996, then New York, 1997, 1998, then London, 1999.

Duke of York, *Richard II,* Old Vic Theatre, London, 2005.

Also appeared as Edgar, *King Lear,* Old Vic Theatre, London; in *The Red Noses* and *The Desert Air,* both Royal Shakespeare Company.

Major Tours:

Thane, *Macbeth,* Russian and Polish cities, 1961.

George Tesman, *Hedda Gabler,* Royal Shakespeare Company, Canadian, American, and Australian cities, 1975.

Stage Director:

Stoop, Soho Poly, 1978.

Siblings, Lyric Hammersmith Theatre, London, 1989.

Bajazet, Almeida Theatre, New York City, 1990.

Ken in Smoking with Lulu, W Yorks Playhouse, 2000, then Soho Theatre, New York City, 2002.

Arthur in Camera Obscura, Almeida Theatre, 2002.

WRITINGS

Translator:

(With T. Alexander) Klus Mann, *Siblings: The Children's Story,* 1992.

Other:

Contributed to various periodicals, including *Vogue, Harpers, Vanity Fair,* and *Interview.*

FANNING, Tony
(Anthony Fanning)

PERSONAL

Full name, Anthony Fanning.

Career: Cinematographer, production designer, art director, and set designer.

Member: Art Directors Guild.

Awards, Honors: Excellence in Production Design Award nomination (with others), feature film, Art Directors Guild, 1998, *Amistad;* Emmy Award (with others), outstanding art direction for a single camera series, and Excellence in Production Design Award (with Jon Hutman), television series, Art Directors Guild, both 2000, for the pilot of *The West Wing;* Excellence in Production Design Award (with others), feature film—period or fantasy film, Art Directors Guild, 2005, *Lemony Snicket's A Series of Unfortunate Events.*

CREDITS

Film Cinematographer:

The Mighty Ducks (also known as *Champions, The Mighty Ducks Are the Champions, A hora dos campeoes, Jeu de puissance, Les petits champions, Los campeones, Maestarna, Mestarit, Mestarit—kiekkokaukalon kauhut, Mighty Ducks—Das Superteam, Somos los mejores,* and *Stoffa da campioni*), Buena Vista, 1992.

The Indian in the Cupboard, Columbia, 1995.

Amistad (also known as *Amistad—Das Sklavenschiff*), DreamWorks, 1997.

October Sky, MCA/Universal, 1999.

What Lies Beneath (also known as *A verdade escondida, Apparences, Bag facaden—What lies beneath, Dolt under ytan, Le verita nascoste, Lo que la verdad esconde, Revelacao, Revelaciones, Salaisuus pinnan alla,* and *Schatten der Wahrheit*), Twentieth Century–Fox, 2000.

What Women Want (also known as *Ce que femme veut, Ce que veulent les femmes, Ce–si doresc femeile?, Det kvinner vil ha, Do que as mulheres gostam, En que piensan las mujeres?, Lo que ellas quieren, Mi kell a noenek?, Mitae nainen haluaa, O que as mulheres querem, Vad kvinnor vill ha,* and *Was Frauen wollen*), Paramount, 2000.

Spider–Man (also known as *Spiderman* and *Spider–Man: The Motion Picture*), Columbia, 2002.

Intolerable Cruelty (also known as *Divorce Show, Intolerable, Achzareyoot Beelty Nisbelet, Crueldad intolerable, Dibosu shou, Ein (Un)moeglicher Haertefall, El amor cuesta caro, Intolerable cruaute, O amor custa caro, Okrucienstwo nie do przyjecia, Prima ti sposo, poi ti rovino, Sietaemaetoentae julmuutta,* and *Talumatu julmus*), Universal, 2003.

The Polar Express (animated; also known as *Polar Express, Boreal Express, Der Polarexpress, El expreso polar, Le pole express, Napapiirin pikajuna, O expresso polar,* and *Polarexpressen*), Warner Bros., 2004, IMAX version released as *The Polar Express: An IMAX 3D Experience.*

Ocean's Twelve (also known as *Ocean's 12, Doze homens e outro segredo, La nueva gran estafa, Le retour de Danny Ocean, Oceani kaksteist,* and *Ocean's twelve: Dogrywka*), Warner Bros., 2004.

Lemony Snicket's A Series of Unfortunate Events (also known as *Lemony Snicket, A Series of Unfortunate Events, Lemony Snicket: Ellendige avonturen, Lemony Snicket, una serie de eventos desafortunados, Lemony Snicket–Una serie di sfortunati eventi, Desventuras em serie, Lemony Snicket—Raetselhafte Ereignisse, Lemony Snicketi sari onnetuid lugusid, Lemony Snicketin surkeiden sattumuksien sarja, Lemony Snickets beraettelser om syskonen Baudelaires olycksaliga liv, Lemony Snickets beraettelser om syskonen Baudelairs olycksaliga liv, Lemony Snickets—En ulykke kommer sjaeldent alene, Les desastreuses aventures des orphelins Baudelaire, Les desastreuses aventures des orphelins Baudelaire d'apres Lemony Snicket, Syskonen Baudelairs olycksaliga liv, Un seguit de desgracies catastrofiques de Lemony Snicket, Una serie de catastroficas desdichas de Lemony Snicket, Una serie de eventos desafortunados,* and *Una serie de infortunados eventos. Lemony Snicket*), Paramount, 2004.

Munich, Universal, 2005.

Ocean's Thirteen (also known as *Ocean's 13, 13, I symmoria ton dekatrion, Oceanovih trinaset,* and *Trinadtsat druzey Oushena*), Warner Bros., 2007.

Film Production Designer:

Nancy Drew (also known as *Nancy Drew: The Mystery in Hollywood Hills*), Warner Bros., 2007.

Fire Bay, Dragon Fire Films, 2008.

Harold & Kumar 2 (also known as *Harold and Kumar Go to Amsterdam*), New Line Cinema, 2008.

Film Art Director:

(As Anthony Fanning) Assistant art director, *Forrest Gump,* Paramount, 1994.

Assistant art director, *Nell,* Twentieth Century–Fox, 1994.

Assistant art director, *Quiz Show* (also known as *Kviz, Kviz–show, Quiz Show—A verdade dos bastidores, Quiz Show—Der Skandal, Quiz Show: El dilema, Quiz Show—tupla ja kuitti,* and *Sike*), Buena Vista, 1994.

Supervising art director, *Jingle All the Way,* Twentieth Century–Fox, 1996.

Supervising art director, *War of the Worlds* (also known as *Out of the Night, Party in Fresno,* and *Uncle Sam*), Paramount, 2005.

Film Set Designer:

Wild Hearts Can't Be Broken, Buena Vista, 1991.

The Hudsucker Proxy (also known as *Hudsucker—Der grosse Sprung*), Warner Bros., 1994.

Television Cinematographer; Movies:
Keep the Change (also known as *Le mystere du ranch, Punto di svolta,* and *Ritorno a casa*), TNT, 1992.

Television Art Director; Pilots:
The West Wing (also known as *West Wing* and *El ala oeste de la Casablanca*), NBC, 1999.

Stage Set Designer:
Two Trains Running, Walter Kerr Theatre, New York City, 1992.
Art, South Coast Repertory Theatre, Costa Mesa, CA, 2000.
A Naked Girl on Appian Way, South Coast Repertory Theatre, Segerstrom Stage, 2005.

FARACY, Stephanie 1952–

PERSONAL

Born January 1, 1952, in Brooklyn, NY; *Education:* Wesleyan University, B.A., English and drama; attended Yale School of Drama.

Addresses: *Manager*—MBST Entertainment, 345 North Maple Dr., Suite 200, Beverly Hills, CA 90210.

Career: Actress.

CREDITS

Film Appearances:
Corinne, *Heaven Can Wait,* Paramount, 1978.
Babbette, *Scavenger Hunt,* Twentieth Century–Fox, 1979.
Angel Childress, *When You Comin Back, Red Ryder?,* Columbia, 1979.
Susie Davis, *Blind Date* (also known as *Blake Edwards' "Blind Date"*), TriStar, 1987.
Connie Ripley, *The Great Outdoors,* Universal, 1988.
Jenny Dennison, *Hocus Pocus,* Buena Vista, 1993.
Stephanie's mother, *Sideways,* Twentieth Century–Fox, 2004.
Letitia Vanglider, *Surviving Christmas,* DreamWorks, 2004.
Anna, *Flightplan,* Buena Vista, 2005.

Television Appearances; Series:
Gail Collins, *The Last Resort,* CBS, 1979–80.
Valerie Wood, *Goodnight, Beantown,* CBS, 1983–84.
Tracy Doyle, *Eye to Eye,* ABC, 1985.
Regina "Reggie" Hewitt, *His & Hers,* CBS, 1990.

Ellen Freeman, *True Colors,* Fox, 1990–92.
Mary Parker, *The Lot,* AMC, 1999.
Suzette Michaels, *Charlie Lawrence,* CBS, 2003.

Television Appearances; Miniseries:
Judy, *The Thorn Birds,* ABC, 1983.
Debbie Lee Claggett, *James A. Michener's "Space"* (also known as *Space*), CBS, 1985.
Katy, *American Geisha,* CBS, 1986.
Florence Schiffer, *Sidney Sheldon's "Windmills of the Gods"* (also known as *Windmills of the Gods*), CBS, 1988.
Candi Moretti, *Tales of the City* (also known as *Armistead Maupin's "Tales of the City"*), PBS, 1993.

Television Appearances; Movies:
Jennifer O'Connor, *Carpool,* CBS, 1983.
Kate Harris, *Classified Love,* CBS, 1986.
Beth Babyak, *Bridesmaids,* CBS, 1989.
Lynn, *The Only Way Out,* 1993.
Dr. Otis, *Run for the Dream: The Gail Devers Story,* Showtime, 1996.
Mrs. Marlowe, *Safety Patrol* (also known as *Disney's "Safety Patrol"* and *Safety Patrol!*), ABC, 1998.
Selma Drown, *The Rockford Files: If It Bleeds ... It Leads,* CBS, 1999.

Television Appearances; Pilots:
Typist, *Return of the Worlds Greatest Detective,* CBS, 1976.
Rozzie Webber, *Bumpers,* NBC, 1977.
Lieutenant Hope Phillips, *The Fighting Nightingales,* CBS, 1978.
Title role, *Stephanie,* CBS, 1981.
Judy Gillette, *Hotel,* ABC, 1983.
Goldie Hawkins, *Goldie and the Bears,* ABC, 1985.
Linda Monroe, *The Johnny Chronicles,* ABC, 2002.

Television Appearances; Episodic:
Debra Lee, "Excuse Me, May I Cut In?" *Laverne and Shirley* (also known as *Laverne & Shirley & Company* and *Laverne & Shirley & Friends*), ABC, 1976.
"It's the Willingness," *Visions,* PBS, 1980.
The Tonight Show Starring Johnny Carson, NBC, 1980.
Lisa, "Have I Got a Girl for You," *Trapper John, M.D.,* CBS, 1981.
"Little Miseries," *Insight,* syndicated, 1981.
"The Other Man—Mr. Roarke," *Fantasy Island,* ABC, 1983.
Private Sherry Stern, "Judy's Cousin," *Private Benjamin,* CBS, 1983.
Mama Malone, CBS, 1984.
"Honey Beats the Odds," *The Love Boat,* ABC, 1984.
Amy Sayler, "Novel Connection," *Magnum, P.I.,* CBS, 1986.
Amy Sayler, "Magnum on Ice: Part Two," *Murder, She Wrote,* CBS, 1986.

Janice Fletcher, "Class of '72," *Hotel*, ABC, 1987.

Susie, *The Pursuit of Happiness*, 1995.

Paula Houston, "Family Values," *Silk Stalkings*, USA Network, 1996.

Sally Redding, "The Quality of Mercy," *Touched by an Angel*, CBS, 1996.

Carol, "Single and Hating It," *Wings*, NBC, 1996.

Joan Sayers, "Hostile Convergence," *Dark Skies*, NBC, 1996.

Pamela, "Foreplay," *Pauly*, Fox, 1997.

Carole Fordham, "And That's the Way It Was?," *Murphy Brown*, CBS, 1997.

Lucy, "A Cross to Bear," *Boston Common*, NBC, 1997.

Voice, "Fallout," *Extreme Ghostbusters* (animated), syndicated, 1997.

Mimi, "Voyage of the Damned," *Frasier*, NBC, 1997.

Myra Dolan, "All in the Family," *Chicago Hope*, CBS, 1997.

Joyce Cullman, "Gigolo Jarod," *The Pretender*, NBC, 1998.

Faye, "Caroline and the Sandwich," *Caroline in the City* (also known as *Caroline*), NBC, 1998.

Lucille, "Sometimes You Feel Like a Nut," *Maggie Winters*, CBS, 1999.

Elizabeth Daryl, "Dog Gone," *Stark Raving Mad*, 2000.

Mrs. Adams, "Where's the Justice in That?," *Any Day Now*, 2000.

Mrs. Flynn, "The Invisible Mom," *Bette*, CBS, 2001.

Nancy Moore, "Best Man," *Providence*, NBC, 2001.

Eva, "Nice in White Satin," *Will & Grace*, NBC, 2003.

Mimi, "Boo!," *Frasier*, NBC, 2004.

Laura, "Key Ingredients," *Out of Practice*, CBS, 2005.

Stella, "Heavy Meddle," *Stacked*, Fox, 2005.

Mrs. Sullivan, "What I Am," *Grey's Anatomy*, ABC, 2006.

Stage Appearances:

The Dark at the Top of the Stairs, Ivanhoe Theatre, Chicago, IL, 1974.

Faye Streber, *Temporary Help*, Contemporary Theatre, Seattle, WA, 1999.

Also appeared in *Status Quo Vadis*, Chicago, IL; *Angel City* and *A History of the American Film*, both Mark Taper Forum, Los Angeles Music Center, Los Angeles.

FERRI, Claudia

PERSONAL

Born in Montreal, Quebec, Canada.

Addresses: *Contact*—MCM, 7012 St–Laurent, Suite 200, Montreal, Quebec H2S 3E2 Canada.

Career: Actress. Appeared in television commercials.

Awards, Honors: Jutra Award nomination, best supporting actress, Radio and Television Canada, Canadian Comedy Award nomination, film—pretty funny performance—female, 2004, both for *Mambo Italiano;* Montreal Award, outstanding performance—female, Alliance of Canadian Cinema, Television, and Radio Artists, 2005, for *Ciao Bella*.

CREDITS

Film Appearances:

Second reporter, *Sleeping with Strangers*, 1994.

John Oxenberger's girlfriend, *Hard Core Logo*, Miramax, 1996.

Maura Ramirez, *The Assignment* (also known as *Le Mandat*), Sony Pictures Entertainment, 1997.

Female officer, *Running Home*, 1999.

Ruth Levine, *Stardom* (also known as *15 Moments*), Lions Gate Films, 2000.

Audrey Wettering, *Artificial Lies* (also known as *Le Manipulateur*), 2000.

Ruth Levine, *Stardom* (also known as *15 Moments, Stardom,* and *Stardom—Le Culte de la celebrite*), 2000.

Mrs. Urbain, *Soother* (short), 2001.

Connie, *Killing Time* (short), 2001.

Lena Savage, *Dead Awake*, Nu Image, 2001.

Anna Barberini, *Mambo Italiano*, Samuel Goldwyn Films, 2003.

Agent Bolton, *Wargames: The Dead Code*, Metro–Goldwyn–Mayer, 2007.

Television Appearances; Series:

Triplex, 1994.

Christina Panzonni, *Omerta–Le Dernier des hommes d'honneur* (also known as *Omerta 3*), 1999.

Elena Batista, *Ciao Bella*, 2003.

Anna Bertoli, *Les aventures tumultueuses de Jack Carter*, 2003.

Dr. Audrey Habedian, *Naked Josh*, Oxygen, 2005–2006.

Roxy Calvert, *Durham County*, 2007.

Television Appearances; Miniseries:

Christina Favara, *Omerta II–La loi du silence*, 1997.

Fanny Labruzzo (older), *Bonanno: A Godfather's Story* (also known as *The Youngest Godfather*), Showtime, 1999.

Lucia Alarcon, *Race to Mars*, Discovery Channel Canada, 2007.

Television Appearances; Movies:

Girl outside salsa bar, *Born to Run*, Fox, 1993.

Giordano, *36 Hours to Die* (also known as *Sursis: 36 heures*), TNT, 1999.
Audrey Wettering, *Artificial Lies* (also known as *Le manipulateur*), Lifetime, 2000.
Leah, *Snow in August,* Showtime, 2001.
Nurse Donovan, *After Amy* (also known as *No Ordinary Baby*), 2001.
Norma Alvarado, *Saving Milly,* 2005.
Tina, *Hunt for Justice* (also known as *Jagd nach Gerechtigkeit*), MyNetwork, 2005.
Dr. Horowitz, *Tipping Point,* Lifetime, 2007.
Joan, *Too Young to Marry,* Lifetime, 2007.

Television Appearances; Episodic:
Danielle, "Cease Fire," *MacGyver,* 1989.
Devereaux's woman, "Freefall," *Highlander* (also known as *Highlander: The Series*), syndicated, 1992.
Kate Armstrong, "The Suction Method," *The Hunger,* Showtime, 2000.
Doctor, "Hard to Keep a Good Man Down," *Alienated,* The Space Channel, 2003.
Arlette Berlanger, *Nos etes,* 2006.

OTHER SOURCES

Electronic:
Claudia Ferri Website, http://www.claudiaferri.com, June 7, 2007.

FLIEGER, Jean
   See ST. JAMES, Jean

FLITTER, Josh 1994–

PERSONAL

Born August 25, 1994, in Ridgewood, NJ; son of Steve (a regional sales manager) and Carla (a former professional singer) Flitter. *Avocational Interests:* Playing baseball and hockey.

Addresses: *Manager*—MBST Entertainment, 345 North Maple Dr., Suite 200, Beverly Hills, CA 90210.

Career: Actor. Appeared in television commercials for Office Depot, Toyota Sienna, Southwest Airlines, DiGiorno pizza, SBC Communications, MasterCard, Chex cereal, and UPS delivery service.

Awards, Honors: Young Artist Award nomination, best performance in a feature film—supporting young actor, 2006, for *The Greatest Game Ever Played; Advertising Age* Award, best actor, for Office Depot commercial.

CREDITS

Film Appearances:
Young Bully, *Eternal Sunshine of the Spotless Mind,* Focus Features, 2004.
Jake, *Duane Hopwood,* IFC Films, 2005.
(Uncredited) Little Boy, *Hide and Seek,* Twentieth Century–Fox, 2005.
Eddie Lowery, *The Greatest Game Ever Played,* Buena Vista, 2005.
Stewart, *Big Momma's House 2,* Twentieth Century–Fox, 2006.
Voice of Budderball, *Air Buddies,* Buena Vista Home Entertainment, 2006.
Corky, *Nancy Drew,* Warner Bros., 2007.
Choir boy, *License to Wed,* Warner Bros., 2007.

Television Appearances; Pilots:
Henry Tammer, *Prodigy/Bully,* NBC, 2006.

Television Appearances; Episodic:
Cub scout number two, "Once Bitten," *Whoopi,* 2003.
Little Tommy, "Back in the Saddle," *Ed,* NBC, 2004.
Nathan, "Maybe–Sitting," *Phil of the Future,* 2005.
Himself, *Situation: Comedy,* Bravo, 2005.
Himself, "Cinderella: Part 2—The Premiere," *Super Short Show* (also known as *Mike's Super Short Show*), Disney Channel, 2005.
The Tonight Show with Jay Leno, NBC, 2005, 2007.
Jimmy Kimmel Live!, ABC, 2007.

Also appeared in *All My Children,* ABC; *One Life to Live,* ABC; *Blue's Clues,* Nickelodeon.

FLYNN, Colleen 1962–

PERSONAL

Born May 23, 1962, in NJ; married Stephen Hornyak (an actor), 1990.

Addresses: *Agent*—TalentWorks, 3500 West Olive Ave., Suite 1400, Burbank, CA 90069. *Manager*—Envision Entertainment, 9255 W. Sunset Blvd., Suite 500, Los Angeles, CA 90069.

Career: Actress.

Awards, Honors: Emmy Award nomination, outstanding guest actress in a drama series, 1995, for *ER.*

CREDITS

Film Appearances:
Ruthie, *Last Exit to Brooklyn* (also known as *Letzte ausfahrt Brooklyn*), 1989.
Adult Jessica *Late for Dinner,* SVS Video, 1991.
Sara Meinhold, *The Temp,* Paramount, 1993.
Coast Guard Captain, *Clear and Present Danger,* United International Pictures, 1994.
Woman on the bridge, *Pay It Forward,* 2000.

Television Appearances; Series:
Lisa Koufax, *Under Cover,* Fox, 1991.
Dr. Pam Blondel, *Flipper,* syndicated, 1995–96.
Paulette Charbonnet, *Orleans,* CBS, 1997.
Carolyn McGrail, *To Have and to Hold,* CBS, 1998.
Lolly Wetzel, a recurring character, *Judging Amy,* CBS, 2000–2004.

Television Appearances; Miniseries:
Maria Hawn, *Trial: The Price of Passion,* NBC, 1992.

Television Appearances; Movies:
Lisa Koufax, *Under Cover,* Fox, 1991.
Annie Britton, *Victim of Love: The Shannon Mohr Story,* NBC, 1993.
In the Best of Families: Marriage, Pride and Madness (also known as *Bitter Blood*), 1994.
Lianne Melrose, *Incident at Deception Ridge* (also known as *Terror at Deception Ridge*), USA Network, 1994.
Serving in Silence: The Margarethe Cammermeyer Story (also known as *Serving in Silence*), NBC, 1995.
Maggie Fergus, *Two Mothers for Zachary,* ABC, 1996.
Ruby Martin, *The Devil's Child,* ABC, 1997.

Television Appearances; Pilots:
Lisa, *Under Cover* (also known as *The Company*), 1991.
Sherman Oaks, Showtime, 1999.

Television Appearances; Episodic:
Dr. Colleen Flaherty Richards, "The Big Bang," *China Beach,* CBS, 1990.
Dr. Colleen Flaherty Richards, "Juice," *China Beach,* CBS, 1990.
Dr. Colleen Flaherty Richards, "Hello, Goodbye," *China Beach,* CBS, 1991.
Christine Riordan, "The Naked and the Wed," *Civil Wars,* ABC, 1992.
Lindsay Kerr, "David Is Authorized," *Class of '96,* 1993.
Lisbeth, *The Road Home,* CBS, 1994.

Janine Messersmith, "Sisters," *VR.5,* 1995.
Jodi O'Brian, "Love's Labor Lost," *ER,* NBC, 1995.
Michele Fazekas, "Detour," *The X–Files,* Fox, 1997.
Colleen Azar, "All Things," *The X–Files,* Fox, 2000.
Janice Bonner, "Prisoner of Love," *Philly,* ABC, 2001.
Rebecca Turner, "Samuel Rising," *Roswell* (also known as *Roswell High*), UPN, 2001.
Katherine Fielding, "As If By Fate," *Crossing Jordan,* NBC, 2002.
Katherine Kent, "Silent Partner," *Without a Trace* (also known as *W.A.T.*), CBS, 2002.
Strong Medicine, Lifetime, 2002.
Wendy Stuart, "Coming Home," *The Practice,* ABC, 2004.
Wendy Stuart, "Pre–Trial Blues," *The Practice,* ABC, 2004.
Wendy Stuart, "Mr. Shore Goes to Town," *The Practice,* ABC, 2004.
Lorna, "Passion of the Wick," *The Drew Carey Show,* ABC, 2004.
Chief of human resources, "Surprise," *Everwood* (also known as *Our New Life in Everwood*), The WB, 2005.
Jillian Thompson, "You Are Here," *The Closer,* TNT, 2005.
Lacy Jensen, "Voices," *Ghost Whisperer,* CBS, 2005.
Emily, "Superstar," *Cold Case,* CBS, 2005.
Julia's doctor, "Quentin Costa," *Nip/Tuck,* FX Channel, 2005.
Julia's doctor, "Cherry Peck," *Nip/Tuck,* FX Channel, 2005.
Julia's doctor, "Cindy Plumb," *Nip/Tuck,* FX Channel, 2006.
Julia's doctor, "Monica Wilder," *Nip/Tuck,* FX Channel, 2006.
Josh's mother, "The Shot," *Close to Home,* CBS, 2006.
Enid, "The Jerk," *House M.D.* (also known as *M.D.*), Fox, 2007.

FOH SHEN, Freda
(Freda Fo Shen)

PERSONAL

Addresses: *Agent*—Greene & Associates, 190 North Canon Dr., Suite 200, Beverly Hills, CA 90210.

Career: Actress.

CREDITS

Film Appearances:
Reporter, *Without a Trace,* (also known as *W.A.T.*), 1983.

Self–defense teacher, *Crossing Delancey,* Warner Bros., 1988.
Television newscaster, *The Dream Team,* 1989.
Nurse with addict, *Longtime Companion,* 1989.
Nurse, *Funny About Love,* 1990.
Ah Ling, *1000 Pieces of Gold,* 1990.
Berkeley registrar, *Basic Instinct* (also known as *Ice Cold Desire*), TriStar, 1992.
Maid, *Born Yesterday,* Buena Vista, 1993.
Polygraph technician, *The Glimmer Man,* Warner Bros., 1996.
Doctor Marsh, *Daddy Girl,* Live Entertainment, 1996.
Voice of Fa Li, *Mulan* (animated), Buena Vista, 1998.
(As Freda Fo Shen) Marge, *American Virgin* (also known as *Live Virgin*), Granite Releasing, 2000.
Voice of Chinese food lady, *Dude, Where's My Car?,* 2000.
Bon, *Planet of the Apes,* Twentieth Century–Fox, 2001.
Nurse, *Coastlines,* Curb Entertainment, 2002.
Melinda Barrows, *A Mighty Wind,* Warner Bros., 2003.
Doughnut woman, *The Ladykillers,* Buena Vista, 2004.
Voice of Fa Li, *Mulan II* (animated), Buena Vista Home Video, 2004.
Voice of Collen's mom, *Harlequin,* 2004.
May–Li Wong, *Red Doors,* Emerging Pictures, 2005.

Television Appearances; Series:
Doctor Noriko Weinstein, *Silk Stalkings,* USA Network and CBS, 1993.
Mrs. Lee, *Gideon's Crossing,* ABC, 2000–2001.
Dr. Chao, *Everwood* (also known as *Our New Life in Everwood*), The WB, 2005.
Dr. Perrin, *Close to Home,* CBS, 2006–2007.

Television Appearances; Movies:
Ticket agent, *Senior Trip!,* CBS, 1981.
Alice, *Those Secrets,* ABC, 1992.
Alien Nation: Millennium, Fox, 1996.
Janet Lee Cheung, *Cracker: White Ghost,* Arts and Entertainment, 1996.
Mrs. Yung, *Safety Patrol* (also known as *Disney's "Safety Patrol"* and *Safety Patrol!*), ABC, 1998.
Tida Woods, *The Tiger Woods Story,* Showtime, 1998.
Sharon Farr, *Invisible Child,* Lifetime, 1999.
Arlene, *Horse Sense,* Disney Channel, 1999.
Doctor Kwan, *Miracle in Lane 2,* Disney Channel, 2000.
Savanah Cummings, *NTSB: The Crash of Flight 323,* ABC, 2004.

Television Appearances; Specials:
Lynn Watson, "The Almost Royal Family," *ABC Afterschool Specials,* ABC, 1984.
Martin Luther King: The Dream and the Drum, PBS, 1986.

Television Appearances; Pilots:
Doctor Wallace, *L.A. Med,* ABC, 1997.

Television Appearances; Episodic:
"Mask of Deceit," *Khan!,* 1975.
Cliff's patient, "That's Not What I Said," *The Cosby Show,* NBC, 1987.
Mrs. Kishi, "Dawn and the Haunted House," *The Baby–Sitters Club,* 1990.
"The Talisman," *Renegade,* 1992.
Doctor Kaufman, *Doogie Howser, M.D.,* ABC, 1992.
Doctor Michelle Peck, "No Pain, No Gain," *Sisters,* NBC, 1994.
Miss Minor, "Homework," *Party of Five,* Fox, 1994.
Nurse, "Injustice for All," *Courthouse,* CBS, 1995.
Jean, "Fun City," *New York News,* CBS, 1995.
Miss Minor, "Spring Breaks: Part 2," *Party of Five,* Fox, 1996.
Nurse Whiteford, "Forever Jung," *Nowhere Man,* UPN, 1996.
Doctor Janet Yang, "Till Death Do Us Part," *Nash Bridges,* CBS, 1996.
Janet Lee Cheung, "White Ghost," *Cracker,* ABC, 1996.
Kikomo, "The World at Your Feet," *Arli$$,* HBO, 1997.
Lieutenant Commander Doctor Monica Chen, "Heroes," *JAG,* CBS, 1997.
Doctor Searles, "Growing Pains," *Chicago Hope,* CBS, 1997.
Nurse Eileen Martin, *Michael Hayes,* CBS, 1997.
Lt. Commander Chen, "Heroes," *JAG,* CBS, 1997.
Hearing specialist, "Split Second," *ER,* NBC, 1998.
Hearing specialist, "Vanishing Act," *ER,* NBC, 1998.
Nurse Laura Chase, "Denial," *L.A. Doctors* (also known as *L.A. Docs*), CBS, 1998.
Lady Alice Selleck, "Those Boots Were Made for Stalking," *To Have and To Hold,* CBS, 1998.
Ms. Gordan, "The Legacy," *7th Heaven* (also known as *7th Heaven: Beginnings* and *Seventh Heaven*), The WB, 1998.
Hearing specialist, "Getting to Know You," *ER,* NBC, 1999.
Ms. Gordan, "Sin," *7th Heaven* (also known as *7th Heaven: Beginnings* and *Seventh Heaven*), The WB, 1999.
Dr. Aldmen, "Team Play," *Chicago Hope,* CBS, 1999.
Ms. Gordan, "Words," *7th Heaven* (also known as *7th Heaven: Beginnings* and *Seventh Heaven*), The WB, 2000.
Mrs. Lee, "The Gift," *Gideon's Crossing,* ABC, 2000.
Mrs. Lee, "The Way," *Gideon's Crossing,* ABC, 2000.
Mrs. Lee, "The Routine Case," *Gideon's Crossing,* ABC, 2000.
Deputy District Attorney Judith Kemp, "Telling Lies: Part 1," *Family Law,* CBS, 2000.
Mrs. Simmons, "Do No Harm," *Strong Medicine,* Lifetime, 2000.
"Mothers and Daughters," *The Division* (also known as *Heart of the City*), Lifetime, 2001.
Dean Hackett, "Panacea," *Roswell* (also known as *Roswell High*), UPN, 2002.
Legal counsel Reed, "Life Sentence," *The Court,* ABC, 2002.
Curator, "Moo," *The Agency,* CBS, 2002.

Irene Taft, "Little Man," *Without a Trace* (also known as *W.A.T.*), 2002.
Doctor, "Day 2: 11:00 a.m.–12 p.m.," *24,* Fox, 2002.
Doctor, "Day 2: 1:00 p.m.–2 p.m.," *24,* Fox, 2002.
Marti Kino, "Handle with Care," *For the People* (also known as *Para la gente*), Lifetime, 2002.
Judge Amy Okubo, "Equal Justice," *The Practice,* ABC, 2003.
Judge Levinson, "A Mind Is a Terrible Thing to Lose," *Century City,* CBS, 2004.
Captain Lynda Chang, "Coming Home," *JAG,* CBS, 2004.
Miriam Chen–Pew, "An Innocent Man," *Jack & Bobby,* The WB, 2004.
Dr. Chang, "Guilty," *Desperate Housewives,* ABC, 2004.
Dr. Ann Kumi, "Smile," *Boston Legal,* ABC, 2006.

Also appeared as Miss Maekawa, "The PSA Story," *Buddies;* Lady Alice Selleck, "Who's Sorry Next," *To Have and To Hold,* CBS.

Stage Appearances:
Proscenium servant, sailor, townsperson, and Shogun's wife, *Pacific Overtures,* Winter Garden Theatre, New York City, 1976.
Royal dancer, royal wife, and understudy Tuptim, *The King and I,* Uris Theatre, New York City, 1977–78.
Understudy Madame Aung, *Plenty,* Joseph Papp Public Theatre, New York City, 1982.
Nancy Wing, *Yellow Fever,* 47th Street Theatre, New York City, 1983.
Lady Nijo and Mrs. Kidd, *Top Girls,* Estelle R. Newman Theatre, Public Theatre, New York City, 1983.
The Ups and Downs of Theophilus Maitland, Dallas Theatre Center, Dallas, TX, 1985.
Joanna Lu, television reporter, *Execution of Justice,* Virginia Theatre, New York City, 1986.
Gyoko, *Shogun, the Musical,* Marquis Theatre, New York City, 1990–91.
Hiro, East West Players, Silver Lake, CA, 1994.
Sweeney Todd, East West Players, 1994.
Phyllis, *Follies,* East West Players, David Henry Hwang Theatre, Los Angeles, 2000.

RECORDINGS

Video Games:
Voice of Admiral Alice Liu, *Star Trek: Bridge Commander,* Activision, 2002.

FRANZ, Elizabeth 1941–

PERSONAL

Original name, Elizabeth Frankovich; born June 18, 1941, in Akron, OH; daughter of Joseph (a factory worker) and Harriet Frankovich; married Edward "Ed" Binns (an actor), 1983 (died December 4, 1990). *Education:* Trained for the stage at the American Academy of Dramatic Arts.

Addresses: *Agent*—Mitchell K. Stubbs & Associates, 8675 West Washington Blvd., Suite 203, Culver City, CA 90232.

Career: Actress. Worked as a teacher of creative drama for teenagers, Westchester, NY, and as a secretary.

Member: Actors' Equity Association, American Federation of Television and Radio Artists, Screen Actors Guild.

Awards, Honors: Obie Award, performance, *Village Voice,* c. 1980, and Drama Desk Award nomination, outstanding actress in a play, 1982, both for *Sister Mary Ignatius Explains It All for You;* Antoinette Perry Award nomination, best featured actress in a play, 1983, for *Brighton Beach Memoirs;* Antoinette Perry Award, best performance by a featured actress in a play, Jeff Award, best actress in a supporting role—play, Joseph Jefferson Awards Committee, Drama Desk Award nomination, outstanding actress in a play, and Outer Critics Circle Award nomination, outstanding actress—play, all 1999, Elliot Norton Award, outstanding actress, large company, Boston Theater Critics Association, and Ovation Award, best featured actress in a play, LA Stage Alliance, both 2001, all for the stage production of *Death of a Salesman;* Emmy Award nomination, outstanding supporting actress in a miniseries or a movie, 2000, and Screen Actors Guild Award nomination, outstanding performance by a female actor in a television movie or miniseries, 2001, both for the television production of *Death of Salesman;* Antoinette Perry Award nomination, best featured actress in a play, and Drama Desk Award nomination, outstanding featured actress in a play, both 2002, for *Mornings at Seven.*

CREDITS

Stage Appearances:
In White America, Players Theatre, New York City, 1965.
Ruth Ann Chenier, *Death of the Well–Loved Boy,* St. Mark's Playhouse, New York City, 1967.
Ambassador, attendant, courtier, and soldier, *Rosencrantz and Guildenstern Are Dead,* Alvin Theatre, New York City, 1967–68.
Girl, *One Night Stands of a Noisy Passenger,* Actors Theatre, New York City, 1970.
Woman, *Atheist in a Foxhole,* Westside YWCA, Clark Center, New York City, 1974.
Marilyn, *Augusta,* Playwrights Horizons, then Theatre de Lys, both New York City, 1975.

Long Day's Journey into Night, Indiana Repertory Theatre, Indianapolis, IN, 1975.

Charlotta Ivanovna, *The Cherry Orchard,* New York Shakespeare Festival, Lincoln Center, Vivian Beaumont Theater, New York City, 1977.

The Seagull, Yale Repertory Theatre, New Haven, CT, 1979.

Sister Mary Ignatius, *Sister Mary Ignatius Explains It All for You,* off–Broadway production, beginning 1979, Playwrights Horizons, 1981, then Westside Arts Theatre, New York City, 1981–84.

Children of the Sun, Mirror Repertory Company, Theatre at St. Peter's Church, New York City, 1981.

Sally's Gone, She Left Her Name, Center Stage Theatre, Baltimore, MD, 1981.

Sarah Siddons, *The Actor's Nightmare,* Playwrights Horizons, 1981, then Westside Arts Theatre, New York City, 1981–84.

Kate Jerome, *Brighton Beach Memoirs,* Center Theatre Group, Ahmanson Theatre, Los Angeles, 1982, Alvin Theatre, 1983–85, and Neil Simon Theatre, New York City, 1985–86.

Miss Furnival, *Light Comedies,* Center Theatre Group, Ahmanson Theatre, 1984.

Lady, *The Time of Your Life,* Mirror Repertory Company, Theatre at St. Peter's Church, 1985.

Nora (Mrs. Lawrence Hiller), *The Octette Bridge Club,* Music Box Theatre, New York City, 1985.

The Madwoman of Chaillot, Mirror Repertory Company, Theatre at St. Peter's Church, c. 1985.

Yelena, *Children of the Sun,* Theatre at St. Peter's Church, 1985–86.

Kate Jerome, *Broadway Bound,* Broadhurst Theatre, New York City, 1986–88.

Ida, *The Cemetery Club,* Brooks Atkinson Theatre, New York City, 1990.

Dividing the Estate, Great Lakes Theater Festival, Cleveland, OH, 1990.

Mrs. Bridgenorth, *Getting Married,* Circle in the Square Theatre, New York City, 1991.

Abbess, *The Comedy of Errors,* New York Shakespeare Festival, Public Theater, Delacorte Theater, New York City, 1992.

Almira Gulch and the Wicked Witch of the West, *The Wizard of Oz* (musical), Paper Mill Playhouse, Millburn, NJ, 1992.

Mademoiselle Gabrielle, *The Madwoman of Chaillot,* Williamstown Theatre Festival, Main Stage, Williamstown, MA, 1993.

Eleanor of Aquitaine, *The Lion in Winter,* Cleveland Play House, Cleveland, OH, c. 1993.

Dolly Levi (title role), *The Matchmaker,* McCarter Theatre, Princeton, NJ, 1994.

Maria Vasilyevna Voinitskaya, *Uncle Vanya,* Circle in the Square Theatre, New York City, 1995.

Mother, *Minutes from the Blue Route,* Atlantic Theater Company, New York City, 1997.

Woman in Mind, Berkshire Theatre Festival, Main Stage, Stockbridge, MA, 1997.

Kate, *The Cripple of Inishmaan,* New York Shakespeare Festival, Joseph Papp Public Theater, Newman Theater, New York City, 1998.

Linda Loman, *Death of a Salesman,* Eugene O'Neill Theatre, New York City, 1999, Center Theatre Group, Ahmanson Theatre, Los Angeles, 2000, also produced in the Chicago and Boston areas.

Lola, *Model Apartment,* Long Wharf Theatre, New Haven, CT, 2001.

Aaronetta Gibbs, *Mornings at Seven,* Lyceum Theatre, New York City, 2002.

Cassandra and Lucy, *such small hands* (solo show), Syracuse Stage, Syracuse, NY, 2003.

Halie, *Buried Child,* National Theatre, Lyttelton Theatre, London, 2004.

Eleanor, *The Bird Sanctuary,* Pittsburgh Public Theater, O'Reilly Theater, Pittsburgh, PA, 2005.

Miss Haversham, *Great Expectations,* 2005.

Ellie, *Howard Katz,* Roundabout Theatre Company, Laura Pels Theatre, New York City, 2007.

Mary Ellis, *The Autumn Garden,* Williamstown Theatre Festival, Main Stage, 2007.

Appeared as Eliza Doolittle, *My Fair Lady* (musical), and as Alma, *Summer and Smoke,* both Dorset Playhouse, Dorset, VT; appeared as Amanda, *The Glass Menagerie;* appeared in *The Real Inspector Hound* and *Yesterday Is Over,* both New York City; appeared in other productions, including *Agnes of God, Hamlet,* and *A View from the Bridge.* Appeared in productions with the Repertory Theatre of St. Louis, St. Louis, MO, 1968; Trinity Square Players, Providence, RI, 1972–73; Arena Stage, Washington, DC, 1977–78; Mirror Theatre Company, New York City; and with the Akron Shakespeare Festival, Akron, OH.

Film Appearances:

Dear Dead Delilah, Avco–Embassy, 1972.

Doctor, *Pilgrim, Farewell,* Post Mills, 1980.

Grace Foster, *The Secret of My Success* (also known as *The Secret of My Succe$s*), Universal, 1987.

Pru Buckman, *Jacknife,* Cineplex Odeon Films, 1989.

Jane Dillon, *School Ties* (also known as *Codigo de honor, Der Aussenseiter, La difference, Scuola d'onore,* and *Zar Ba'Migrash*), Paramount, 1992.

Joanna, *Sabrina* (also known as *Sabrina (y sus amores)*), Paramount, 1995.

Aunt Lucille, *The Pallbearer* (also known as *Happy Blue, Amigo desconhecido, Der Zufallslover, El funebrero, Identitate furata, Le porteur, Mi desconocido amigo, Tre amici un matrimonio e un funerale,* and *Vaenner och flickvaenner*), Miramax, 1996.

Leda Rossington, *Thinner* (also known as *Stephen King's "Thinner," La peau sur les os, L'occhio del male, Maldicao, Sorvadj El, Stephen King's "Thinner"—Der Fluch,* and *Vainottu*), Paramount, 1996.

Miss Barzakian, *The Substance of Fire* (also known as *La esencia del fuego, L'essencia del foc, Plaagad av skuld, Revers de fortune,* and *Syyllisyyden taakka*), Miramax, 1996.

Mrs. Bundrass (a social worker), *Twisted,* Leisure Time Features, 1996.

(Uncredited) *Walking to the Waterline,* Goldheart Pictures, 1998.

Bea Greenberg, *A Fish in the Bathtub,* Curb Entertainment, 1999.

Bev Scheel, *Christmas with the Kranks* (also known as *John Grisham's "Skipping Christmas," Skipping the Holidays, Christmas geonneodwigi, Fuga del Natale, Julfritt, Um Natal muito, muito louco, Un Noel de folie!, Una Navidad de locos,* and *Verrueckte Weihnachten*), Columbia, 2004.

Doris Highsmith, *Loopy* (short film), 2004.

Sissel, *The Reader* (short film), Freshwater Films, 2005.

Some sources cite an appearance in *Story of a Bad Boy* (also known as *El despertar de la innocencia*), 1999.

Television Appearances; Series:
Alma Rudder, *Another World* (also known as *Another World: Bay City*), NBC, 1982–83.
Helen Wendall, *As the World Turns,* CBS, 1994–95.

Television Appearances; Miniseries:
Josephine McCormack, "The Three Sisters," *A Girl Thing,* Showtime, 2001.

Television Appearances; Movies:
Mother, *Love and Other Sorrows,* PBS, 1989.
Becky Brown, *Face of a Stranger* (also known as *Das Fremde Gesicht, Kohtalon sormi,* and *Vieraat kasvot*), CBS, 1991.
Maryanne's mother, *Shameful Secrets* (also known as *Going Underground*), ABC, 1993.
Mrs. Stromberg, *It's Nothing Personal* (also known as *Bounty Hunter* and *La vengeance au coeur*), NBC, 1993.
Dorothy, *An Unexpected Love* (also known as *This Much I Know, Un amor inesperado,* and *Un amour inattendu*), Lifetime, 2003.

Television Appearances; Specials:
Grace Stepney, "The House of Mirth," *Great Performances,* PBS, 1981.
Mrs. Rice, "The Rise and Rise of Daniel Rocket," *American Playhouse,* PBS, 1986.
"The Joy That Kills," *American Playhouse,* PBS, 1986.
Dottie McCann (title role), "Dottie," *American Playhouse,* PBS, 1987.
Augusta, *Saint Gaudens: Masque of the Golden Bowl,* PBS, 1988.
Cecile Nelson, "A Town's Revenge," *ABC Afterschool Specials,* ABC, 1989.
Alice Kelly, "Notes for My Daughter," *ABC Afterschool Specials,* ABC, 1995.

Broadway '99: Launching the Tony Awards, PBS, 1999.
Linda Loman, *Death of a Salesman,* Showtime, 2000.

Television Appearances; Awards Presentations:
The 50th Annual Tony Awards, PBS, 1999.
Seventh Annual Screen Actors Guild Awards (also known as *Screen Actors Guild Seventh Annual Awards*), TNT, 2001.

Television Appearances; Episodic:
Mrs. O'Rourke, "Original Sin," *Spenser: For Hire,* ABC, 1985.
"The Mother Instinct," *Monsters,* syndicated, 1989.
Marsha, "Hair," *Roseanne,* ABC, 1990.
Marsha, "I'm Hungry," *Roseanne,* ABC, 1990.
Gladys Lear (Norma's mother), "Life Upside–Down," *Sisters,* NBC, 1994.
Gladys Lear (Norma's mother), "Deceit," *Sisters,* NBC, 1995.
Vivian Galloway, "Convictions," *Judging Amy,* CBS, 2000.
Mia, "The Ins and Outs of Inns," *Gilmore Girls* (also known as *Gilmore Girls: Beginnings* and *The Gilmore Way*), The WB, 2001.
Vivian Galloway, "The Treachery of Compromise," *Judging Amy,* CBS, 2001.
Evelyn Shelby, "Look Again," *Cold Case,* CBS, 2003.
Alison Bishop, "Married with Children," *Law & Order* (also known as *Law & Order Prime*), NBC, 2004.
Jeannette Henley, "Scavenger," *Law & Order: Special Victims Unit* (also known as *Law & Order's Sex Crimes, Law & Order: SVU,* and *Special Victims Unit*), NBC, 2004.

Appeared as Emma, *Dear John* (also known as *Dear John: USA, Divorciados, John Ha–Yakar, Mein Lieber John,* and *Querido John*), NBC; and in *The Equalizer,* CBS.

Radio Work:
Worked as a production assistant on *Celebrity Corner.*

FYFE, Jim

PERSONAL

Married Leslie Klein (an actress); children: Hailey.

Career: Actor. Some sources cite work as a stand–up comedian.

CREDITS

Film Appearances:
Terry Dieter, *A Kiss before Dying* (also known as *Besame antes de morir, Der Kuss vor dem Tode, Een*

kus voor je sterft, En Kyss foere doeden, Pocalunek przed smiercia, Suudelma ennen kuolemaa, Um beijo antes de morrer, Um beijo ao morrer, Um beijo para a morte, Un bacio prima di morire, Un baiser avant de mourir, and *Un beso antes de morir*), Universal, 1991.

Nichols, *The Program* (also known as *The Challenge—Die Herausforderung, Lobos universitarios,* and *Ut a csucsra*), Buena Vista, 1993.

Stuart, *The Frighteners* (also known as *Robert Zemeckis Presents: "The Frighteners," Agarrame esos fantasmas, Chasseurs de fantomes, Fantomes contre fantomes, Kummituskopla, Os espiritos, Sevimli hayaletler, Sospesi nel tempo,* and *Toerjoen ki a frasz!*), Universal, 1996.

Roy, *The Real Blonde,* Paramount, 1997.

Anthony (bed and breakfast clerk), *Walking to the Waterline,* Goldheart Pictures, 1998.

Guy, *Kill the Man* (also known as *Como vencer na vida, En blek kopia, Kill the Man—Vom Kopiertrottel zum Millionaer,* and *Original i copia*), Summit Entertainment, 1999.

Second server, *Moonlight Mile* (also known as *Baby's in Black, Goodbye Hello, El compromiso, La vida continua, Moonlight mile—surun tie, Moonlight mile—Voglia di ricominciare,* and *Vida que segue*), Buena Vista, 2002.

Linda's lawyer, *Duane Hopwood,* IFC Films, 2005.

Night manager, *Full Grown Men,* Grottofilms, 2006.

Television Appearances; Series:

Various characters, *Encyclopedia,* HBO, beginning c. 1986.

Emile Berkoff, *Tanner '88* (also known as *Tanner: A Political Fable*), HBO, 1988.

William "Willie" Loomis and Benjamin "Ben" Loomis, *Dark Shadows* (also known as *Dark Shadows Revival*), NBC, 1991.

Jeb McCall, Quint, and Robogeek, *Ain't It Cool News,* beginning c. 2001.

Emile Berkoff, *Tanner on Tanner* (also known as *Tanner '04*), Sundance Channel, 2004.

Chairman, *Hey! Spring of Trivia,* Spike TV, beginning c. 2004.

Television Appearances; Movies:

Elliot Riley, *Alien Nation: Dark Horizon* (also known as *Alien Nation: Horizonte perdido* and *Muukalaiset—tuuma taivaanranta*), Fox, 1994.

"Star Struck" (also known as "Como conquistar uma estrela"), *CBS Sunday Afternoon Showcase,* CBS, 1994.

Roger Zalman, *Power 98,* HBO, 1996.

Cutler, *Phantom Force,* Sci–Fi Channel, 2004.

Television Appearances; Specials:

Host, *Buy Me That! A Kid's Survival Guide to TV Advertising,* HBO, 1989.

Host, *Earth to Kids: A Guide to Products for a Healthy Planet,* HBO, 1990.

Host, *Buy Me That Too! A Kid's Survival Guide to TV Advertising,* HBO, 1991.

Host, *Buy Me That 3! A Kid's Guide to Food Advertising,* HBO, 1992.

Tracey Takes on New York, HBO, 1993.

Host, *Going, Going, Almost Gone! Animals in Danger,* HBO, 1994.

Television Appearances; Episodic:

Cleary, "Life Choice," *Law & Order* (also known as *Law & Order Prime*), NBC, 1991.

Andre, "My Daughter's Keeper," *The Sinbad Show* (also known as *Sinbad* and *Ein Vater fuer zwei*), Fox, 1993.

Robert Picard, "Virus," *Law & Order* (also known as *Law & Order Prime*), NBC, 1993.

Agent Moore, "Fresh Prince: The Movie," *The Fresh Prince of Bel–Air,* NBC, 1994.

Scott Zachary, "No Kids Allowed," *Something Wilder,* CBS, 1994.

Lyle Friedman, "Grayson, Inc.," *Models, Inc.,* Fox, 1995.

Monty, "First Class," *The Wayans Bros.,* The WB, 1995.

Les Fenster, "Goode Feelings," *Goode Behavior,* UPN, 1996.

Dr. Harvey Snow, "All Hell Breaks Loose," *Pacific Palisades,* Fox, 1997.

First businessperson, "Food," *Tracey Takes On ...,* HBO, 1997.

Man, "Airport," *NewsRadio* (also known as *News Radio, The Station, Dias de radio,* and *Dies de radio*), NBC, 1997.

Dennis, "EMP," *Team Knight Rider* (also known as *El equipo fantastico, Nom de code: TKR, Oi ippotes tis asfaltou,* and *Ritariaessaet*), ABC, 1998.

Dennis, "Et Tu Dante," *Team Knight Rider* (also known as *El equipo fantastico, Nom de code: TKR, Oi ippotes tis asfaltou,* and *Ritariaessaet*), ABC, 1998.

Dennis, "Sky One," *Team Knight Rider* (also known as *El equipo fantastico, Nom de code: TKR, Oi ippotes tis asfaltou,* and *Ritariaessaet*), ABC, 1998.

Dr. Teodir Bleauteau, "Touched by an Amnesiac," *Buddy Faro,* CBS, 1998.

Mark Breslin, "Strangers on the Net," *Smart Guy,* The WB, 1998.

James "Jimmy the geek" Belmont, "Three of a Kind," *The X–Files,* Fox, 1999.

"Honey, It's a Billion Dollar Brain," *Honey, I Shrunk the Kids: The TV Show* (also known as *Disney's "Honey, I Shrunk the Kids: The TV Show"* and *Honey, I Shrunk the Kids*), syndicated, 1999.

Teacher, "Daddy's Girl," *Once and Again,* ABC, 2000.

"Honey, I'm Spooked," *Honey, I Shrunk the Kids: The TV Show* (also known as *Disney's "Honey, I Shrunk the Kids: The TV Show"* and *Honey, I Shrunk the Kids*), syndicated, 2000.

Kimmy the geek, "All about Yves," *The Lone Gunman* (also known as *Lone Gunmen, Au coeur du complot,* and *Die Einsamen Schutzen*), Fox, 2001.

Kimmy the geek, "Tango de los Pistoleros," *The Lone Gunman* (also known as *Lone Gunmen, Au coeur du complot,* and *Die Einsamen Schutzen*), Fox, 2001.

Mr. Lowell, "Life out of Balance," *Once and Again,* ABC, 2001.

Bill, "Tuxedo Hill," *Law & Order: Criminal Intent* (also known as *Law & Order: CI*), NBC, 2002.

Appeared in other programs, including an appearance as Larry in *Minor Adjustments,* NBC and UPN.

Television Appearances; Pilots:

William "Willie" Loomis and Benjamin "Ben" Loomis, *Dark Shadows* (also known as *Dark Shadows Revival*), NBC, 1990.

T.V. Guys, Fox, 1994.

Kimmy the geek, *The Lone Gunman* (also known as *Lone Gunmen, Au coeur du complot,* and *Die Einsamen Schutzen*), Fox, 2001.

Stage Appearances:

Carney and Hennessey, *Biloxi Blues,* Neil Simon Theatre, New York City, 1985–86.

Troy Le Flame, "Coup d'etat," and Chris, "Remedial English," *Young Playwrights Festival 1986,* Playwrights Horizons, New York City, 1986.

Dick, *Moonchildren,* McGinn–Cazale Theatre, New York City, 1987.

Moran, *Legs Diamond* (musical), Mark Hellinger Theatre, New York City, 1988–89.

Steven Flowers, *Privates on Parade,* Union Square Theatre, New York City, 1989.

Young Martello, *Artist Descending a Staircase,* Helen Hayes Theatre, New York City, 1989.

Corneilius Hackl, *The Matchmaker,* Union Square Theatre, New York City, 1991.

Archie, Gresham, unemployed police officer, fisherman, and Bumfork tramp, *On the Bum,* Playwrights Horizons, 1992.

A Normal Guy, Primary Stages, New York City, 1993.

The Fourth Wall, Pasadena Playhouse, Pasadena, CA, 1994.

Albert Amundson, *A Thousand Clowns,* Roundabout Theatre Company, Criterion Center Stage Right, New York City, 1996.

All in the Timing (one–act plays), Geffen Playhouse, Hartford, CT, 1998.

Multiple characters, *Merton of the Movies,* Geffen Playhouse, Los Angeles, 1999.

Also appeared in *Confessions of a Ladykiller, The Dysfunctional Show,* and *Romeo and Juliet,* all Los Angeles productions.

RECORDINGS

Videos:

Himself, *The Making of "The Frighteners,"* Universal Studios Home Video, 1998.

Video Games:

Voices of Earl Weatherby, Fitch, and Verne Wiggins, *Red Dead Revolver,* Rockstar Games, 2004.

Audiobooks:

S. E. Hinton, *The Outsiders,* Listening Library, 1988.

Suzie Kline, *Herbie Jones,* Listening Library, 1996.

WRITINGS

Teleplays; Episodic:

Exhale with Candice Bergen, Oxygen, episodes beginning c. 2000.

Ain't It Cool News, episodes beginning c. 2001.

Writings for the Stage:

A Normal Guy, Primary Stages, New York City, 1993.

G

GALINO, Valeria
     See **GOLINO, Valeria**

GARITO, Ken 1968–

PERSONAL

Born December 27, 1968, in Brooklyn, NY. *Education:* Brooklyn College, B.F.A.; studied acting at the Actor's Gym and with Susan Batson and Fred Kareman.

Addresses: *Agent*—Bauman, Rednaty and Shaul Agency, 5757 Wilshire Blvd., Suite 473, Los Angeles, CA 90036.

Career: Actor.

Member: Actor's Equity Association, American Federation of Television and Radio Artists, Screen Actors Guild.

Awards, Honors: Screen Actor's Guild Award (with others), outstanding performance by the cast of a motion picture, for *Crash.*

CREDITS

Film Appearances:
Don, *School Ties,* 1992.
Louie, *Clockers,* Universal, 1995.
Title role, *Charlie Hoboken,* Northern Arts Entertainment, 1998.
Brian, *Summer of Sam,* Buena Vista, 1999.
Mark, *The Curse,* 1999.

Fronterz, 2004.
Bruce, *Crash* (also known as *L.A. Crash*), Lions Gate Films, 2004.
Tommy Z, *Cloud 9,* Twentieth Century–Fox Home Entertainment, 2006.
Willy, *10th & Wolf,* THINKFilm, 2006.

Television Appearances; Series:
Arthur "Dizzy" Manselli, *The Heights,* Fox, 1992.

Television Appearances; Movies:
Cadet Lewis Ostheim, *Assault at West Point: The Court–Martial of Johnson Whittaker* (also known as *Assault at West Point*), Showtime, 1994.

Television Appearances; Pilots:
Billy, *Prince Street,* NBC, 1997.

Television Appearances; Episodic:
As the World Turns, 1997.
Montgomery, "DNR," *Law and Order,* NBC, 1999.
Uniform cop number one, *Law and Order: Special Victims Unit* (also known as *Law & Order: SVU* and *Special Victims Unit*), NBC, 1999.
Kevin Russo, "Teenage Wasteland," *Law & Order,* NBC, 2001.
Dan Corely, "The Good Doctor," *Law & Order: Criminal Intent* (also known as *Law & Order: CI*), NBC, 2001.
Zahn, "Recovery Time," *Strong Medicine,* Lifetime, 2002.
Lenny Gano, "A Little Dad'll Do Ya," *NYPD Blue,* ABC, 2002.
Johnny Malgrove, "Blood," *The Lyon's Den,* NBC, 2003.
Tucker, "Committed," *CSI: Crime Scene Investigation* (also known as *C.S.I., CSI: Las Vegas,* and *CSI: Weekends,* and *Les Experts*), CBS, 2005.
"Run, Piper, Run," *Charmed,* The WB, 2005.
Rob Giarusso, "And Here's Mike with the Weather," *Las Vegas,* NBC, 2006.

Dr. Rucker, "The Elephant in the Room," *Commander in Chief,* 2006.
Joseph Dellamonte, "Overkill," *The Closer,* 2006.

Stage Appearances:
Jake Singer, *Peacetime,* Workshop of the Players Art (WPA) Theatre, New York City, 1992.
Understudy Joey and Josh, *Conversations with My Father,* Royale Theatre, New York City, 1992–93.
Dash, *Watbanaland,* WPA Theatre, 1995.
Mr. Kodti, *On House,* WPA Theatre, 1997.
Nick Cristano, *Over the River and Through the Woods,* John Houseman Theatre, New York City, 1998–2000.

Also appeared in *Drink,* One Dream Theatre; as Johnny Nunzio, *Tony 'n Tina's Wedding,* Artificial Intelligence, New York City; Calvin, *Magic Hands Freddy,* Ensemble Studio Theatre.

OTHER SOURCES

Electronic:
Ken Garito Website, http://www.kengarito.com, July 13, 2007.

GASSNER, Dennis 1948–

PERSONAL

Born in 1948, in Canada. *Education:* Studied fine arts and architecture at University of Oregon; studied filmmaking and advertising design at Art Center College of Design, Pasadena, CA.

Addresses: *Agent*—The Gersh Agency, 232 North Canon Dr., Beverly Hills, CA 90210.

Career: Production designer. Designed dossier and helped create the advertising campaign for *Apocalypse Now,* 1978–79; became staff designer at Francis Ford Coppola's Zoetrope Studios, 1979. Previously worked as a record cover designer.

Awards, Honors: Academy Award nomination (with Nancy Haigh), best art direction, 1991, for *Barton Fink;* Academy Award (with Haigh), best art direction, 1991, for *Bugsy;* Los Angeles Film Critics Association Award, best production design, 1994, for *The Hudsucker Proxy;* Film Award, best production designer, British Academy of Film and Television Arts, and Golden Satellite Award, best art direction, International Press Academy, 1999,

both for *The Truman Show;* Film Award nomination, best production design, British Academy of Film and Television Arts, 2001, for *O Brother, Where Art Thou?;* Excellence in Production Design Award nomination (with Chris Gorak and Lance Hammer), feature film—period or fantasy films, Art Directors Guild, 2002, for *The Man Who Wasn't There;* Excellence in Production Design Award nomination (with others), feature film—period or fantasy films, 2002, Academy Award nomination (with Haigh), best art direction—set decoration, Film Award, best production design, British Academy of Film and Television Arts, Golden Satellite Award nomination (with Richard L. Johnson), best art direction, 2003, all for *Road to Perdition;* Film Award nomination, best production design, British Academy of Film and Television Arts, 2004, for *Big Fish;* Excellence in Production Design Award nomination (with others), feature film—contemporary, 2006, for *Jarhead.*

CREDITS

Film Production Designer:
Rumble Fish, Universal, 1983.
Wisdom, Twentieth Century–Fox, 1986.
The Hitcher, TriStar, 1986.
In the Mood (also known as *The Woo Woo Kid*), Lorimar, 1987.
Like Father, Like Son, TriStar, 1987.
Earth Girls Are Easy, Vestron, 1989.
Field of Dreams, Universal, 1989.
Miller's Crossing, Twentieth Century–Fox, 1990.
The Grifters, Miramax, 1990.
Barton Fink, Twentieth Century–Fox, 1991.
Bugsy, TriStar, 1991.
Hero (also known as *Accidental Hero*), Columbia, 1992.
The Hudsucker Proxy (also known as *Hudsucker—Der grosse sprung*), Warner Bros., 1994.
Waterworld, Universal, 1995.
The Truman Show, Paramount, 1998.
Himself, *The "Field of Dreams" Scrapbook* (documentary; also known as *The Making of the "Field of Dreams" Scrapbook*), Universal Studios Home Video, 1998.
O Brother, Where Art Thou? (also known as *O Brother*), Buena Vista, 2000.
The Man Who Wasn't There, USA Films, 2001.
Road to Perdition, DreamWorks, 2002.
Big Fish, Columbia, 2003.
The Ladykillers, Buena Vista, 2004.
Jarhead (also known as *Jarhead—Willkommen im dreck*), Universal, 2005.
Ask the Dust, Paramount Classics, 2006.
The Golden Compass (also known as *His Dark Materials: Northern Lights*), New Line Cinema, 2007.

Film Title Designer:
Sylvester, 1985.
The Hitcher, TriStar, 1986.

Under the Cherry Moon, Warner Bros., 1986.
Static, Siren Releasing, 1986.

Film Graphic Designer:
One from the Heart, Sony Pictures Releasing, 1982.
Hammett, Orion, 1982.
Rumble Fish, Universal, 1983.

Film Work; Other:
Production assistant, *Apocalypse Now,* United Artists, 1979.

Film Appearances:
Himself, *How's It' Going to End? The Making of "The Truman Show"* (documentary short), Paramount Pictures Home Entertainment, 2005.
Himself, *Faux Finishing: The Visual Effects of "The Truman Show"* (documentary short), Paramount Pictures Home Entertainment, 2005.

Television Work; Movies:
Set decorator, *Wet Gold,* 1984.

Television Appearances; Specials:
Himself, *The Making of "Road to Perdition,"* 2002.

Television Appearances; Episodic:
Himself, "Road to Perdition," *HBO First Look,* HBO, 2002.

OTHER SOURCES

Periodicals:
Theatre Crafts, November, 1991, p. 44.

GIL, Arturo 1960–

PERSONAL

Born March 13, 1960, in New Orleans, LA; raised in San Juan, Puerto Rico.

Addresses: *Agent*—Coralie Jr. Theatrical Agency, 4789 Vineland Ave., Suite 100, North Hollywood, CA 91602.

Career: Actor and stunt performer. Appeared in several advertisements. Worked as a disc jockey in New Orleans, a short wave radio engineer, and a computer operator; has a FCC (Federal Communications Commission) license.

Member: Screen Actors Guild, American Federation of Television and Radio Artists.

CREDITS

Film Appearances:
Mutant child, *Space Hunter: Adventures in the Forbidden Zone* (also known as *Adventures in the Creep Zone, Road Gangs, Avaruustaistelija, Cacadores no espaco, Cazador del espacio: Aventuras en la zona prohibida, Il cacciatore dello spazio, Kosmiczne lowy, Le guerrier de l'espace, Spacehunter—Jaeger im All,* and *Spacehunter—uppdrag I den foerbjudna zonen*), Columbia, 1983.
Human pyramid, *Grunt! The Wrestling Movie* (also known as *Grunt—Der Wrestling Film, Grunt—luunmurskaaja,* and *Naamioitu murskaaja*), New World Pictures, 1985.
Member of the Dinks, *Spaceballs* (also known as *Planet Moron, A mais louca odisseia no espaco, Avaruusboltsit, Balle spaziali, Bilele spatiale, Det vaaras foer rymden, Kosmiczne jaja, La folle histoire de l'espace, La loca historia de las galaxias, Mel Brooks "Spaceballs," Rumnodderne, S.O.S.—Tem um louco solto no escapo, Spaceballs—Mel Brooks' verrueckte Raumfahrt, Svermirske loptice,* and *Uergolyhok*), Metro–Goldwyn–Mayer, 1987.
Windy Winston, *The Garbage Pail Kids Movie* (also known as *Chlopaki z kubla na smieci, Die Schmuddelkinder, La pandilla basura,* and *Roskisriivioet*), Atlantic Releasing, 1987.
Giddy, *Snow White* (also known as *Cannon Movie Tales: Snow White, Snow White and the Seven Dwarfs, Snow White: A Cannon Movie Tale, Lumikki ja 7 kaeaepioetae, Schneewittchen,* and *Snoevit och de sju dvagarna*), c. 1987, Cannon Video, 1989.
Human xylophone, *The Dark Backward* (also known as *The Man with Three Arms*), Greycat Films/Strand Releasing, 1991.
Second station, *Bill and Ted's Bogus Journey* (also known as *Bill & Ted's Excellent Adventure II, Bill and Ted Go to Hell, Bill & Teds galna mardroemsresa, Bill & Ted's verrueckte Reise in die Zukunft, Bill e Ted—Dois loucos no tempo, Bill es Ted halali turaja, Bill og Ted drar til helvete, Bill si Ted ajung in iad, Bill y Ted 2, Billin ja Tedin maailma, El alucinante viaje de Bill y Ted, Les aventures de Bill et Ted, Les folles aventures de Bill et Ted,* and *Un mitico viaggio*), Orion, 1991.
Bulldog, *Mom and Dad Save the World* (also known as *Dick and Marge Save the World, Mom and Dad retten die Welt,* and *O salvador do mundo*), Warner Bros., 1992.
Clown, *Freaked* (also known as *Hideous Mutant Freekz*), Lauren Film, 1993.
First little person acrobat, *Silent Tongue* (also known as *Le gardien des espirits*), Trimark Pictures, 1993.

Rotoscope, *Last Action Hero* (also known as *Extremely Violent, Az utolso akciohoes, Den siste action-hjaelten, Der Letze Action Held, El ultimo gran heroe, El ultimo heroe en accion, L'ultim gran heroi, Last action hero—l'ultimo grande eroe, Le dernier des heros, O ultimo grande heroi,* and *Zadnja velika pustolovscina*), Columbia, 1993.

Drunk at pub, *Leprechaun 2* (also known as *Leprechaun II, One Wedding and Lots of Funerals, El duende 2,* and *Leprechaun II—Der Killerkobold kehrt zurueck*), Trimark Pictures, 1994.

Jester, *Mime's Eye* (short film), 1994.

Winston, *Ghoulies IV* (also known as *Skritci*), Cinetel Films, 1994.

The Bavarian baby, *The Fantasticks* (musical), United Artists, 1995.

Nick, *The Adventures of Mary–Kate and Ashley: The Case of the Christmas Caper* (also known as *Mary–Kate and Ashley's Christmas Caper*), 1995.

Arturo the jester, *Father Frost,* Plaza Entertainment, 1996.

Goateed man, *Slappy and the Stinkers* (also known as *Free Slappy, Stinkers, Sacre Slappy, Slappy e a turma, Slappy och busligan, Slappy und die Rasselbande,* and *Slappy—vallaton veijari*), TriStar, 1998.

Midget Paul, *Dirty Work* (also known as *Sale boulot*), Metro–Goldwyn–Mayer, 1998.

Plate spinner, *BASEketball* (also known as *Baseketball, BASEketball: Muchas pelotas en juego, Die Sportskanonen,* and *SEKOpallo*), MCA/Universal, 1998.

Voice, *Sinbad: Beyond the Veil of Mists* (animated), Phaedra Cinema, 2000.

Buddy Bear, *My First Day* (short film), My First Day Productions, 2001.

Fellinesque paparazzi, *Glam,* Storm Entertainment, 2001.

Rat guard, *Monkeybone* (live action and animated), Twentieth Century–Fox, 2001.

Sinister, *A Light in the Forest,* RGH/Lions Share Pictures, 2002.

Dancing Yosemite Sam, *Looney Tunes: Back in Action* (live action and animated; also known as *Looney Tunes: The Movie, Looney Tunes Back in Action: The Movie, The Untitled Looney Tunes Project, Les Looney Tunes passent a l'action, Looney Tunes: Behazra L'Action, Looney tunes: De nuevo en accion, Looney Tunes—De volta a acao, Looney Tunes: Les revoila!, Looney tunes: Taas kehissae,* and *Runi chunzu: Bakku in akushon*), Warner Bros., 2003.

Eenie Anna, *Wasabi Tuna,* Cafe Entertainment Studios, 2003, Indican Pictures, 2006.

Announcer angel, *Angels with Angles* (also known as *Everything's George*), InVision Entertainment, 2005.

Clerk (Mr. L), *Office Court* (short film), 2005.

The client, *Do Not Disturb* (also known as *A Bellman, a Hooker, and a Rabbi ...,* *Last Grave,* and *My Last Grave*), Jed I. Goodman Productions, 2007.

Oompa Loompa, *Epic Movie* (also known as *Big Movie, Bob Bailey, Fantastic Movie, Suur film, Una loca pelicula epica, Una pelicula epica,* and *Wielkie kino*), Twentieth Century–Fox, 2007.

Agent One–Fifth, *Agent One–Half* (also known as *Agent 1/2*), Willow Tree Productions, 2008.

Film Stunt Performer:

Leprechaun 2 (also known as *Leprechaun II, One Wedding and Lots of Funerals, El duende 2,* and *Leprechaun II—Der Killerkobold kehrt zurueck*), Trimark Pictures, 1994.

Leprechaun 3 (also known as *El duende 3*), Trimark Pictures, 1995.

Leprechaun 4: In Space (also known as *Leprechaun 4, Space Platoon, El duende 4,* and *Leprechaun: Destination cosmos*), Trimark Pictures, 1996.

Television Appearances; Series:

Happy, *Comic View's "Blackberry Inn"* (also known as *The Blackberry Inn*), Black Entertainment Television (BET), beginning c. 1995.

Various characters, *The Man Show,* Comedy Central, 1999–2003.

Cecil, *Passions* (also known as *Harmony's Passions* and *The Passions Storm*), NBC, 2002.

Dr. Damnnearkilter, *Cram,* Game Show Network (GSN), beginning c. 2003.

Machete, *Estudio 2,* KRCA (Los Angeles), beginning c. 2005.

Lil Lil Burrows, *Saul of the Mole Men* (also known as *Saul of the Mole People* and *S.T.R.A.T.A.*), Cartoon Network, beginning 2007.

Television Appearances; Movies:

Lefty, *The Munsters' Scary Little Christmas* (also known as *Munsterien joulu, Munsters froehliche Weihnachten,* and *O Natal de familia monstro*), 1996.

Wahoo, *Twice upon a Christmas* (also known as *Crazy Christmas, Rudolfa's Revenge, La fille du Pere Noel,* and *Natal em perigo*), PAX TV, 2001.

Appeared in other programs, including appearances as Geep, *Geep from out of Space;* as Horny, *Howie Mandel and the 7 Dwarves;* and as a Spanish leprechaun, *Pepe Plata's Leprechaun.*

Television Appearances; Specials:

Druid and elf, *A Spinal Tap Reunion: The 25th Anniversary London Sell–Out* (also known as *NBC Concerts Presents Spinal Tap* and *A Spinal Tap Reunion*), NBC, 1992.

Little person, *The AMC Project: The Talent Collector,* American Movie Classics, 2004.

Robot, *That's So Suite Life of Hannah Montana,* Disney Channel, 2006.

Television Appearances; Episodic:

Second little person, "Charity, Schmarity," *The Jackie Thomas Show,* ABC, 1992.

Spewey, "Spewey and Me," *Get a Life,* Fox, 1992.
Winston and Wind, "Aliens Ate My Lunch," *Nightmare Cafe,* NBC, 1992.
Paul Bunion, *The Edge,* Fox, 1992.
Beezle, "Honey, the Bunny Bit It," *Honey, I Shrunk the Kids: The TV Show* (also known as *Disney's "Honey, I Shrunk the Kids: The TV Show"* and *Honey, I Shrunk the Kids*), syndicated, 1998.
Dancing baby, "X–Happily Ever After," *Unhappily Ever After* (also known as *Unhappily ...*), The WB, 1998.
Lars, "Dr. Solomon's Traveling Alien Show," *3rd Rock from the Sun* (also known as *3rd Rock* and *Life as We Know It*), NBC, 1998.
Alonzo, "Quarantine," *The Parkers* (also known as *Die Parkers*), UPN, 1999.
Meowth, "Artie Comes to Town," *The Norm Show* (also known as *Norm*), ABC, 1999.
Water man, "Becker the Elder," *Becker,* CBS, 1999.
Male elf, "Sabrina's Perfect Christmas," *Sabrina, the Teenage Witch* (also known as *Sabrina* and *Sabrina Goes to College*), The WB, 2000.
Olaf, "Honey, I'm Spooked," *Honey, I Shrunk the Kids: The TV Show* (also known as *Disney's "Honey, I Shrunk the Kids: The TV Show"* and *Honey, I Shrunk the Kids*), syndicated, 2000.
White rabbit, "Syd in Wonderland," *Providence,* NBC, 2000.
"Mommy Dearest," *Strip Mall,* Comedy Central, 2000.
Cupid, "Fire and Brimstone," *Black Scorpion* (also known as *Roger Corman Presents "Black Scorpion"*), Sci–Fi Channel, 2001.
Douglas McGrath, "The Obstacle Course," *Ally McBeal,* Fox, 2001.
First Village person, "The Boys in the Band," *Just Shoot Me,* NBC, 2001.
Hillel, "Christmas? Christmas!," *Just Shoot Me,* NBC, 2001.
Stinky, "Happily Ever After," *Charmed,* The WB, 2002.
First Oompa Loompa, *Mind of Mencia,* Comedy Central, 2005.

Appeared as Elvis, *Ally McBeal,* Fox; as a tailor, *Candid Camera;* as a night person, *Days of Our Lives* (also known as *Cruise of Deception: Days of Our Lives, Days, DOOL, Des jours et des vies, Horton–sagaen, I gode og onde dager, Los dias de nuestras vidas, Meres agapis, Paeivien viemaeae, Vaara baesta aar, Zeit der Sehnsucht,* and *Zile din viata noastra*), NBC; as a prisoner, *General Hospital* (also known as *Hopital central* and *Hospital general*), ABC; as Mr. Schwartz, *Married ... with Children* (also known as *Not the Cosbys*), Fox; as a ring master, *The Mike O'Malley Show,* NBC; as a little person, *Rude Awakening,* Showtime; as Clarence, *Weekly World News,* USA Network; as an accomplice, *What Would You Do,* Nickelodeon; and as a singing mechanic, *The X Show,* fX Channel.

Television Appearances; Pilots:
Braggell, *Skwids: Troll Trouble* (also known as *Skwids*), Nickelodeon, 1996.

GKOLINO, Baleria
 See GOLINO, Valeria

GLOVER, Susan
 (Suzan Glover)

PERSONAL

Addresses: *Agent*—Reisler Talent Inc., 2022 de la Montagne, Suite 304, Montreal, Quebec H3G 1Z7, Canada.

Career: Actress.

CREDITS

Film Appearances:
Voice, *The Marvelous Land of Oz,* 1987.
Third reporter, *Criminal Law,* Hemdale Film Corp., 1988.
Without Work: Is Everyone Here Crazy, 1989.
Barmaid, *Malarek,* 1989.
Voice, *Nathael and the Seal Hunt* (also known as *Nathael et la chasse aux phoques*), 1990.
Voice, *The Phoenix,* 1990.
A Touch of Murder, 1990.
Voice, *Divine Fate* (also known as *Destin divin*), 1993.
(English version) Voice of Izabella, *Jungledret* (also known as *Amazon Jack, Go Hugo Go, Hugo the Movie Star, Jungle Jack,* and *Jungledyret Hugo*), 1993.
Nose number three, *Dr. Jekyll and Ms. Hyde,* Savoy Pictures, 1995.
Flower box woman, *Rainbow* (also known as *Les voyageurs de l'arc–en–ciel*), Vine International, 1995.
Narrator, *Mystery of the Maya,* 1995.
Rosa, *Dead Innocent* (also known as *Eye*), 1996.
Voice of Alfred, *La freccia azzurra* (also known as *Der blaue pfeil, La fleche bleue, How the Toys Saved Christmas,* and *The Blue Arrow*), 1996.
Presidential aide number two, *The Peacekeeper* (also known as *Hellbent* and *Red Zone*), Warner Bros., 1997.
Candy, *Suspicious Minds,* Trimark Pictures, 1997.
Dr. Peterson's receptionist, *For Hire,* Fries Film Group, 1997.
Judy Grant, *Random Encounter* (also known as *Rencontre fortuite*) Columbia TriStar Home Video, 1998.
Mrs. Schmidt, *Hysteria,* 1998.
Teri Kolchek, *Going to Kansas City,* 1998.
Voice of Tigress, *The Animal Train,* 1999.
Wife, *Two Thousand and None* (also known as *SOS la vie*), Pandora Film, 2000.

Claire Crosby, *Stardom* (also known as *15 Moments* and *Stardom—Le culte de la celebrite*), Lions Gate Films, 2000.

Phyllis Ryder, *Heart: The Marilyn Bell Story* (also known as *Marilyn Bell: Une histoire de coeur*), 2001.

Rod's wife, *Savage Messiah* (also known as *Moise: L'affaire Roch Theriault*), Christal Films, 2002.

Mrs. Hull, *The Struggle* (short), S. Solomon Pictures, 2002.

Alice, *Jack & Ella*, 2002.

Valda, *Jericho Mansions*, Equinox Films, 2003.

Television Appearances; Series:
Voice of General Jinjur, *The Wonderful Wizard of Oz* (animated), 1987.

Voices of Lucille Omitsu, Princess Violet Tokugawa, and Lucinda, *Samurai Pizza Cats* (animated; also known as *Kyatto ninden teyandee*), 1991.

Mrs. Tompkins, *The Little Lulu Show*, HBO, 1996.

Countess May Hem, *Night Hood*, 1996.

Voice, Princess Sissi, (animated), 1997.

Voice of Barb, *X–Chromosome* (animated), Oxygen, 1999.

Sarah, *Naked Josh* (also known as *Les lecons de Josh*), Oxygen and Showcase Television Canada, 2004–2006.

Also appeared as mom, *What's with Andy?*, Fox Family.

Television Appearances; Miniseries:
Doctor McMain, *Vendetta II: The New Mafia* (also known as *Bride of Violence 2* and *Donna d nore 2*), HBO, 1993.

Emmy Gorling, *Nuremberg*, TNT, 2000.

Television Appearances; Movies:
Additional voice, *David Copperfield* (also known as *Charles Dickens "David Copperfield"*), PBS, 1993.

Mrs. Hammersmith, *Satan's School for Girls*, ABC, 2000.

English actress, *The Audrey Hepburn Story*, ABC, 2000.

Amelie Martell, *Wall of Secrets* (also known as *Le mur des secrets*), Lifetime, 2003.

Helene Van Damme, *The Reagans*, Showtime, 2003.

Sales lady, *I Do (But I Don't)*, Lifetime, 2004.

Art collector, *False Pretenses*, Lifetime, 2004.

Tanya, *Living with the Enemy*, Lifetime, 2005.

Television Appearances; Specials:
Just for Laughs: Montreal Comedy Festival, 1999.
Gerda's mother, *Ten Days to Victory*, 2005.

Television Appearances; Episodic:
Olga, "The Tale of the 13th Floor," *Are You Afraid of the Dark?*, Nickelodeon, 1993.

Mrs. Basinger, "Crossing the Line," *Sirens*, 1994.

Parasol lady, "The Tale of Train Magic," *Are You Afraid of the Dark?*, Nickelodeon, 1995.

Voice of Paula, "Charley and Mimmo," *It's Itsy Bitsy Time* (animated), Fox, 1999.

Noelle Attoll, "Sock It to Me," *Radio Active*, 1999.

Noelle Attoll, "Dr. Tanya," *Radio Active*, 1999.

Noelle Attoll, "Morgan Unplugged," *Radio Active*, 1999.

Additional voice, "Miss Galaxy 5000," *Tripping the Rift*, Sci–Fi Channel, 2004.

Additional voice, "The Sidewalk Soiler," *Tripping the Rift*, Sci–Fi Channel, 2004.

Additional voice, "2001 Space Idiocies," *Tripping the Rift*, Sci–Fi Channel, 2004.

Television Work; Movies:
Stand–in for Linda Smith, *The Phone Call*, 1989.

Television Work; Specials:
Producer and director, *The Philosopher Stoned* (documentary), 2006.

RECORDINGS

Video Games:
Voice, *Jagged Alliance 2*, Ubi Soft Entertainment, 1999.

(As Suzan Glover) *Splinter Cell* (also known as *Tom Clancy's "Splinter Cell"*), Ubi Soft Entertainment, 2002.

Voice, *Prince of Persia: Warrior Within*, Masteronic Ltd., 2004.

Additional voices, *Splinter Cell: Chaos Theory*, 2005.

WRITINGS

Television Specials:
The Philosopher Stoned (documentary), 2006.

GOEN, Bob 1954–
(Robert Goen)

PERSONAL

Full name, Robert Kuehl Goen; born December 1, 1954, in Long Beach, CA; son of Robert and Mildred (maiden name, Kuehl) Goen; married Sabrina, 1988 (divorced, 1997); married Marianne Curan (a television personality), March 20, 2004; children: (first marriage) Maxwell. *Education:* San Diego State University, B.S., telecommunications and film, 1976; also attended Long Beach City College, Long Beach, CA.

Addresses: *Agent*—Rebel Entertainment Partners, Inc., 5700 Wilshire Blvd., Suite 456, Los Angeles, CA 90036.

Career: Reporter, host, and actor. KFOX (radio station), Long Beach, CA, news reader, 1977; KPRO–FM, Riverside, CA, disc jockey (some sources also cite producer and director), 1977–81; KESQ–TV, Palm Springs, CA, anchor, reporter, producer, writer, and editor, 1981–86. Worked as a bartender. Founder of the Bob Goen Lexus Celebrity Golf Classic (fund–raiser for the Make–A–Wish Foundation).

Awards, Honors: Two Daytime Emmy Award nominations, outstanding game show host, for *Wheel of Fortune;* inducted into the Long Beach City College Hall of Fame.

CREDITS

Television Appearances; Series:
Host, *Perfect Match,* syndicated, beginning 1986.
Host, *Home Shopping Game* (also known as *The Home Shopping Game Show*), CBS and syndicated, 1987.
Host, *Blackout,* CBS, 1988.
Host, *Great Weekend,* syndicated, 1988.
Host, *Wheel of Fortune,* CBS, 1989–91, NBC, 1991.
Host, *The Hollywood Game,* CBS, 1992.
Host, *Born Lucky,* Lifetime, beginning 1992.
Correspondent, *Entertainment Tonight* (also known as *E.T., ET Weekend, Entertainment This Week,* and *This Week in Entertainment*), syndicated, 1993–96.
Anchor and host, *Entertainment Tonight* (also known as *E.T., ET Weekend, Entertainment This Week,* and *This Week in Entertainment*), syndicated, 1996–2004.
Host, *ET in TV Land,* TV Land, beginning 2003.
Himself, *Poker Royale: The James Woods Gang vs. The Unabombers,* GSN (Game Show Network), 2005.
Host, *That's the Question,* GSN (Game Show Network), beginning 2006.

Television Appearances; Specials:
Host, *Lifetime Salutes Mom,* Lifetime, 1987.
Pledge host, *Star–athon '92: A Weekend with the Stars,* syndicated, 1992.
Host, *The Miss Universe Pageant,* CBS, 1994, 1995, 1996.
Host, *The Miss USA Pageant,* CBS, 1994, 1995, 1996.
Host, *The Miss Teen USA Pageant,* CBS, 1994, 1996.
Host, *The Orange Bowl Parade,* CBS, 1995.
Host, *Entertainment Tonight Presents: The Dukes of Hazzard—The Untold Story,* 1999.
Host, *Entertainment Tonight Presents: Indiana Jones—Behind the Adventure,* 2000.
Host, *Entertainment Tonight Presents: The Love Boat—Secrets from the Ship,* 2000.
Host, *Entertainment Tonight Presents: The Real Designing Women,* 2000.
The Making of "Jimmy Neutron," 2001.
Host, *Countdown to the Emmys 2003,* Fox, 2003.
Himself, *AKC/Eukanuba National Championship 2006 Live 2–Day Event,* The Discovery Channel and Animal Planet, 2006.
Big Break All–Star Challenge, 2006.

Television Appearances; Episodic:
(As Robert Goen) Reporter, "No More Mr. Nice Guy," *Freddy's Nightmares* (also known as *Freddy's Nightmares: A Nightmare on Elm Street: The Series, Freddy, le cauchemar de vos nuits, Freddyn painajaiset, Las pesadillas de Freddy,* and *Les cauchemars de Freddy*), syndicated, 1988.
Television announcer, "The End of the World," *Freddy's Nightmares* (also known as *Freddy's Nightmares: A Nightmare on Elm Street: The Series, Freddy, le cauchemar de vos nuits, Freddyn painajaiset, Las pesadillas de Freddy,* and *Les cauchemars de Freddy*), syndicated, 1988.
Bink Warmington, "Games People Play," *Perfect Strangers,* ABC, 1989.
Himself, "Vowel Play," *L.A. Law,* NBC, 1990.
Himself, "Suckup," *Space Ghost Coast to Coast* (live action and animated; also known as *SGC2C*), Cartoon Network, 1997.
Himself, "Thankless–Giving," *Hiller and Diller,* ABC, 1997.
Himself, "Veronica's Husband Won't Leave," *Veronica's Closet* (also known as *Veronica, El secreto de Veronica, Les dessous de Veronica, Los secretos de Veronica, Os segredos de Veronica,* and *Veronican salaisuudet*), NBC, 1997.
Himself, "Once a Secretary, Always a Secretary," *The Nanny,* CBS, 1998.
Himself, "The Other Cheek," *Chicago Hope,* CBS, 1998.
Himself, "Superstar," *Cosby,* CBS, 1999.
Himself, *Rock & Roll Jeopardy!,* VH1, 1999.
Himself, "Mary Hart: Heart's Ambition," *Biography* (also known as *A&E Biography: Mary Hart*), Arts and Entertainment, 2000.
Host, "In/Famous," *Robbery Homicide Division* (also known as *Metro* and *R.H.D./LA: Robbery Homicide Division/Los Angeles*), CBS, later USA Network, 2002.
Himself, *Good Day Live,* syndicated, 2002.
Himself, "The Last Action Queero," *I'm with Her* (also known as *Elaemaeae taehden kanssa*), ABC, 2003.
Himself, *The Wayne Brady Show,* syndicated, 2003.
Himself, "The Peck–Peck," *I'm with Her* (also known as *Elaemaeae taehden kanssa*), ABC, 2004.
Himself, *Larry King Live,* Cable News Network, 2004.
Voice of Bob Glimmer, "Blondes Have More Fun/Five Days of F.L.A.R.G.," *The Fairly OddParents* (animated; also known as *The Fairly GodParents, The*

Fairly Odd Parents, and *Oh My! GodParents*), Nickelodeon, 2005.

Appeared as himself in "Do Not Go Squealing into That Good Night," an unaired episode of *Style and Substance,* CBS.

Television Appearances; Pilots:
Himself, *I'm with Her* (also known as *Elaemaeae taehden kanssa*), ABC, 2003.

Appeared in other pilots.

Film Appearances:
Game show host, *Wicked Stepmother* (also known as *A madrasta, En haexa till styvmorsa, Ma belle–mere est une sorciere, Noita muuttaa taloon, Strega per un giorno,* and *Tanz der Hexen*), Metro–Goldwyn–Mayer, 1989.
Himself, *Homage,* Arrow Releasing, 1995.
Himself (host of *Entertainment Tonight*), *Junket Whore* (documentary), 1998.
Voice of newscaster, *Jimmy Neutron: Boy Genius* (animated), Paramount, 2001.

Radio Appearances:
Host of *The Keith and Bob Show,* broadcast by a Long Beach City College radio station. Appeared in other radio productions.

GOLINO, Valeria 1966–
(Valeria Galino, Baleria Gkolino)

PERSONAL

Born October 22, 1966, in Naples, Italy; father, a scholar and literary critic; mother, a painter.

Addresses: *Agent*—Creative Artists Agency, 9830 Wilshire Blvd., Beverly Hills, CA 90212. *Manager*—Alan Siegel Entertainment, 345 North Maple Dr., Suite 375, Beverly Hills, CA 90210.

Career: Actress. Also worked as a model. Also known as Baleria Gkolino.

Awards, Honors: Golden Lion Award, best actress, Venice International Film Festival, 1986, and Nastro d'Argento (Silver Ribbon), best actress, Italian National Syndicate of Film Journalists, 1987, both for *Storia d'amore;* Grolla d'oro (Golden Grolle), 1997, and

David di Donatello Award nomination, best actress in a leading role, 1998, both for *Le acrobate;* Nastro d'Argento (Silver Ribbon), best actress, 2002, David di Donatello Award nomination, best actress, 2003, and Mons International Festival of Love Films Award, best actress, 2003, all for *Respiro;* Nastro d'Argento nomination (Silver Ribbon nomination), best actress, 2004, for *Prendimi e portami via;* Nastro d'Argento nomination (Silver Ribbon nomination), best actress, 2006, for *Texas;* Innovator Award, CinemaItalianStyle, 2006; David di Donatello Award, Flaiano Film Festival Award, and Nastro d'Argento nomination (Silver Ribbon nomination), all best actress, 2006, Premio d'inverno, Festival delle cerase, 2007, and Grolla d'oro (Golden Grolle), all for *La guerra di Mario.*

CREDITS

Film Appearances:
Adalgisa De Andreiis, *Scherzo del destino in agguato dietro l'angolo come un briganti da strada* (also known as *A Joke of Destiny, A Joke of Destiny Lying in Wait around the Corner Like a Bandit, A Joke of Destiny Lying in Wait around the Corner Like a Robber, A Joke of Destiny Lying in Wait around the Corner Like a Street Bandit*), Samuel Goldwyn Company, 1983.
Girl in bikini, *Blind Date* (also known as *Deadly Seduction*), New Line Cinema, 1984.
(Uncredited) *Sotto ... sotto ... strapazzato da anomala passione* (also known as *Softly, Softly* and *Sotto ... sotto*), 1984.
Caterina, *Detective School Dropouts* (also known as *Dumb Dicks, Private Detectives,* and *Asilo di polizia*), 1985.
Mara, *Piccoli fuochi* (also known as *Little Fires* and *Little Flames*), 1985.
Bruna Assecondati, *Storia d'amore* (also known as *Love Story* and *A Tale of Love*), 1986.
Claudia Marchetti, *Dernier ete a Tanger* (also known as *Last Summer in Tangiers* and *L'ete dernier a Tanger*), 1987.
Francesca, *Figlio mio infinitamente caro* (also known as *My Dearest Son*), 1987.
Nora Treves, *Gli occhiali d'oro* (also known as *The Gold Rimmed Glasses* and *Les lunettes d'or*), European Classics, 1987.
Gina Piccolapupula, *Big Top Pee–wee* (also known as *Big Top Pee–Wee—la mia vita picchiatella, Manege frei fuer Pee Wee,* and *Wielki Pee–wee*), Paramount, 1988.
Sandra Parini, *Paura e amore* (also known as *Fear and Love, Love and Fear, Three Sisters, Fuerchten und Lieben,* and *Trois soeurs*), 1988.
Susanna, *Rain Man* (also known as *Cuando dos hermanos se encuentran, Encontro de irmaos, Esoeember, Ish Ha–Geshem, Kisni covek, Rainman, Rain man—l'uomo della pioggia, Sademies,* and *Yagmur adam*), Metro–Goldwyn–Mayer/United Artists, 1988.

Gemma Rosselli, *Acque di primavera* (also known as *Torrents of Spring* and *Les eaux printanieres*), Millimeter Films, 1989.

Jeanne de Luynes, *La putain du roi* (also known as *The King's Mistress, The King's Whore,* and *La donna del re*), Miramax, 1990.

Tracce di vita amorosa (also known as *Traces of an Amorous Life*), c. 1990.

Lia Spinelli, *Year of the Gun* (also known as *Brigadas vermelhas, Crimenes y secretos, El ano de las armas, L'anno del terrore, Vaekivallan vuosi,* and *Verliebt in die Gefahr*), Triumph Releasing, 1991.

Maria, *The Indian Runner* (also known as *Indian Runner*), Metro–Goldwyn–Mayer, 1991.

Ramada Thompson, *Hot Shots!* (also known as *Hot Shots: An Important Movie!, Ases pelos ares, Des pilotes en l'air, Hot Shots! Die Mutter aller Filme, Hot shots!—Hoejdarna, Hot shots!—kaikkien elokuvien aeiti, Hot shots: la madre de todos los desmadres, Napihnjenci,* and *Top gang, ases muito loucos*), Twentieth Century–Fox, 1991.

Anita, *Puerto escondido,* 1992.

Ramada Rodham Hayman, *Hot Shots! Part Deux* (also known as *Hot Shots 2, Hot Shots! 2, Hot Shots 2! The Exploitation, Ases pelos Ares 2, Des pilotes en l'air 2, Hot shot 2, Hot Shots! Der 2. Versuch, Hot Shots 2—kaikkien jatko–osien aeiti, Napihnjenci 2,* and *Top Gang 2, a missao*), Twentieth Century–Fox, 1993.

Giulietta Guicciardi von Gallenberg, *Immortal Beloved* (also known as *Amada immortal, Amata immortale, Amor immortal, Halhatatlan kedves, Ikuinen rakkaus, Ludwig van B., Ludwig van B.—Meine unsterbliche Geliebte, Nesmrtno ljubljena, Oluemsuez sevgi, Paixao imortal,* and *Sonate au clair de lune*), Columbia, 1994.

Marta, *Come due coccodrilli* (also known as *Like Two Crocodiles* and *Comme deux crocodiles*), 1994.

Sarah Novak and Beth Holly, *Clean Slate* (also known as *Blackout, Blackout—Ein Detektiv sucht sich selbst, Blackout—Und taeglich gruessen die Ganoven, Borron y cuenta nueva, E tudo o sono levou, Memoria curta, O cao zarolho,* and *Trou de memoire*), Metro–Goldwyn–Mayer, 1994.

Athena, "The Missing Ingredient" segment, *Four Rooms* (also known as *Four Rooms and a Hotel, Grand Hotel, Groom service, Araba's Hadarim, Cuatro habitaciones, Cztery pokoje, Doert oda, 4 quartos, Negy szoba, Neli tuba, Neljae huonetta, Silvester in fremden Betten,* and *Stiri sobe*), Miramax, 1995.

Delores, *Submission* (short film), 1995.

Terri, *Leaving Las Vegas* (also known as *Adieu Las Vegas, Adios a Las Vegas, Adjo Las Vegas, Despedida em Las Vegas, Elveda Las Vegas, Farvael Las Vegas, Las Vegas, vegallomas, Liebe bis in den Tod, Morrer em Las Vegas, Via da Las Vegas,* and *Zbogom Las Vegas*), United Artists, 1995.

Elizabeth Laughton, *An Occasional Hell,* Greenlight Productions, 1996.

Ida, *Escoriandoli,* 1996.

Secretary, *Danza della fata confetto,* 1996.

Taslima, *Escape from L.A.* (also known as *John Carpenter's "Escape from L.A.," Los Angeles 2013, Bekstvo iz Los Andjelesa, Escape de Los Angeles, Flucht aus L.A., Flykten fraan L.A., Fuga da Los Angeles, Fuga de Los Angeles, Ha–Briha M'Los Angeles, John Carpenter's "Flucht aus L.A.," Los Angeles'tan kacis, Menekueles Los Angelesboel, Pako L.A.:sta, Pobeg iz Los Angelesa, 2013: rescate en L.A.,* and *Ucieczka z Los Angeles*), Paramount, 1996.

I sfagi tou kokora (also known as *Slaughter of the Cock* and *La strage del gallo*), 1996.

Il fratello minore (short film), 1996, Istituto Luce, 2000.

Maria, *Le acrobate* (also known as *The Acrobat*), Mikado, 1997.

Sylvie Otti, *Side Streets,* Cargo Films, 1997.

Bravo Randy, c. 1997.

Silvia, *L'albero delle pere* (also known as *The Pear Tree* and *Shooting the Moon*), RaiTrade, 1998.

Actress, *Tipota,* 1999.

Anita, *Harem suare* (also known as *Le dernier harem*), Medusa Distribuzione, 1999.

Jamie, *Spanish Judges* (also known as *Ruthless Behavior*), Cargo Films, 1999.

Constanza Vero, *Ivansxtc* (also known as *Ivans XTC., Ivansxtc (To Live and Die in Hollywood),* and *Ivans xtc. (To Live and Die in Hollywood)*), Artistic License Films, 2000.

Lilly, "Goodnight Lilly, Goodnight Christine" segment, *Things You Can Tell Just by Looking at Her* (also known as *Azelet maga, Ce que je sais d'elle ... d'un simple regard, Coisas que eu poderia dizer so de olhar para ela, Coisas que voce pode dizer so de olhar para ela, Con solo mirarte, Con tan solo mirarla, Cosas que diria con solo mirarla, Coses que diries nomes de mirar–la, Gefuehle, die man sieht, Gefuehle, die man sieht ... Things you can tell, Julmia totuuksia, Le cose che so di lei, Regards de femmes,* and *Tout ce qu'on peut apprendre d'une femme au premier regard*), United Artists, 2000.

Nina, *Controvento* (also known as *Against the Wind*), Istituto Luce, 2000.

To tama (also known as *Evagora's Vow* and *Word of Honor*), 2000.

Italian actress (hotel guest), *Hotel,* Moonstone Entertainment, 2001, Innovation Film Group, 2003.

Anna, *L'inverno* (also known as *Winter*), Farfilms/Psycho Film/Rai Cinema, 2002.

Lupe Marin, *Frida* (also known as *Frida Kahlo*), Miramax, 2002.

Grazia, *Respiro* (also known as *Respiro: Grazia's Island*), Medusa Distribuzione, 2002, Sony Pictures Classics, 2003.

Luciana, *Prendimi e portami via* (also known as *Take Me Away*), 2003.

Camille Vrinks, *36 quai des orfevres* (also known as *36, Asuntos pendientes, Fiender emellan, 36—Toedliche Rivalen, Vallan piiri,* and *Vromikos kosmos*), Tartan USA, 2004.

Elisa, *Alive,* Media Blasters/TFM Distribution, 2004.

L'italienne (the Italian woman), *San–Antonio,* Pathe, 2004.

Carmen Holgado, *Ole!,* ARP Selection, 2005.

Guilia, *La guerra di Mario* (also known as *Mario's War, Shad–sky,* and *Solo un bambino*), Medusa Distribuzione, 2005.

Maria, *Texas,* Fandango/Medusa Film, 2005.

Rita, *A casa nostra* (also known as *Our Country*), 01 Distribuzione, 2006.

Valeria, *Solo cinque minuti* (short film), ANEC, 2006.

Agata, *Il sole nero* (also known as *Black Sun*), 2007.

Chiara, *La ragazza del lago* (also known as *Vieni a casa mia*), Indigo Film, 2007.

Natalia Petrovna, *Le reve de la nuit d'avant* (also known as *Actress*), Wild Bunch, 2007.

Parrucchiera, *Lascia perdere, Johnny,* Medusa Distribuzione, 2007.

Sandra, *Ma place au soleil* (also known as *My Place in the Son*), Studio Canal, 2007.

Eleni, *The Dust of Time,* c. 2008.

Caos calmo, Fandango, 2008.

Cash, TFM Distribution, 2008.

Some sources cite an appearance in the film *Il y des jours ... et des lunes* (also known as *There Were Days ... and Moons, Ci sono dei giorni ... e delle lune ..., So sind die Tage und der Mond,* and *Tem dias de lua cheia*), AFMD/Roissy Films, 1990.

Film Producer:

I sfagi tou kokora (also known as *Slaughter of the Cock* and *La strage del gallo*), 1996.

Television Appearances; Miniseries:

Nunzia, *La vita che verra* (also known as *La storia siamo noi* and *Ombre sull'ofanto*), [Italy], 1998.

(Sometimes credited as Valeria Galino) Calpurnia, *Julius Caesar* (also known as *Caesar* and *Giulio Cesare*), TNT, 2002.

Television Appearances; Movies:

Justine, *Alexandria Hotel,* 1998.

Television Appearances; Specials:

Hearts of Hot Shots Part Deux: A Filmmaker's Apology, 1993.

(In archive footage) Ramada, *Twentieth Century–Fox: The Blockbuster Years,* 2000.

Television Appearances; Awards Presentations:

Presenter, *The 1992 MTV Movie Awards,* MTV, 1992.

The 49th Annual Golden Globe Awards, 1992.

Presenter, *The 1993 MTV Movie Awards,* MTV, 1993.

The 52nd Annual Golden Globe Awards, TBS, 1995.

Television Appearances; Episodic:

Eugenie Kolchenko, "Red Wind," *Fallen Angels* (also known as *Perfect Crimes, Crime perfecte,* and *24 horas para a morte*), Showtime, c. 1995.

Herself, *On ne peut pas plaire a tout le monde* (also known as *ONPP, ONPP vu de la loge, ONPP vu de la plage, ONPP vu du bocal,* and *ONPP vu du desert*), 2003, 2005.

Herself, *On a tout essaye* (also known as *Les douze coups d'on a tout essaye, On a tout essaye et on a garde le meilleur, On a tout essaye, meme le prime,* and *On a tout essaye, meme sans le patron*), 2004.

Herself, *Tout le monde en parle,* 2004.

(Uncredited) Susanna, *80s,* Televisio de Catalunya (TV3, Spain), 2005.

Herself, *L'hebdo cinema,* 2007.

RECORDINGS

Videos:

Herself, *Hot Shots: The Making of an Important Movie* (short), Twentieth Century–Fox Home Entertainment, 1991.

Herself, *Beloved Beethoven,* Columbia/TriStar Home Video, 1999.

Herself, *Un'isola nell'isola: retroscena dal set di respiro* (short), Fandango, 2002.

Herself, *The Journey of Rain Man* (short), Metro–Goldwyn–Mayer Home Entertainment, 2004.

Qui veut la peau d'Olivier Marchal?, Gaumont Home Video, 2005.

Music Videos:

R.E.M., "Bittersweet Me," 1995.

GORDON, Matt

PERSONAL

Career: Actor.

Awards, Honors: Gemini Award nomination, best performance by an actor in a featured supporting role in a dramatic series, Academy of Canadian Cinema and Television, 2003, for *The Eleventh Hour.*

CREDITS

Television Appearances; Series:

Camera operator, *Foreign Objects,* CBC, c. 2001.

Murray Dann, *The Eleventh Hour,* CTV (Canada), c. 2003–2005.

Doc, *Rent–a–Goalie,* Showcase, 2006–2007.

Waldo Butters, *The Dresden Files,* Sci–Fi Channel, beginning 2007.

Television Appearances; Miniseries:

Would Be Kings, CTV (Canada), 2007.

Television Appearances; Movies:

Acting instructor, *Murder among Friends* (also known as *Isabella Rocks, Assassinato entre amigos,* and *Parceiros da lei*), 2001.

Tony (a photographer), *Say Nothing* (also known as *Le piege d'une liaison*), Cinemax, 2001.

Luis, *Trouser Accidents,* Bravo! (Canada), 2004.

Phil, *Evel Knievel* (also known as *Evel*), TNT, 2004.

Bill Vigars, *Terry,* CTV (Canada), 2005.

Carson Evans, *Mayday* (also known as *CBS Sunday Movie* and *Panik a fedelzeten*), CBS, 2005.

Petronivich, *A Stranger Here Myself,* Bravo! (Canada), 2005.

Albert, *Earthstorm* (also known as *Angelos tou fegariou*), Sci–Fi Channel, 2006.

Wayne, *Wedding Wars* (also known as *Wedding March*), Arts and Entertainment, 2006.

Television Appearances; Episodic:

Bettor, "Resurrection," *Earth: Final Conflict* (also known as *EFC, Gene Roddenberry's "Battleground Earth," Gene Roddenberry's "Earth: Final Conflict," Invasion planete Terre,* and *Mission Erde: Sie sind unter uns*), syndicated, 1997.

"Politics of Love," *Once a Thief* (also known as *John Woo's "Once a Thief," John Woo's "The Thief," John Woo's Violent Tradition, Kerran varas, aina varas?, Ladrao que rouba ladrao, Les repentis,* and *Matar a un ladron*), CTV (Canada) and syndicated, 1998.

Noah, "Flow," *Platinum,* UPN, 2003.

Ryan Thorpe, "The Checkered Flag," *Doc,* PAX TV, 2003.

Conservative patron, "Muffin Buffalo," *Wonderfalls* (also known as *Maid of the Mist* and *Touched by a Crazy Person*), Fox, 2004.

Darren, " … You Love Men," *Jeff Ltd.,* CTV (Canada), 2004.

Nolan Blackledge, "Dream Lover," *Mutant X,* syndicated, 2004.

Russell Berlin, "Homework," *Kevin Hill,* UPN, 2004.

Wayne, "The Game," *Tilt,* ESPN, 2005.

(Uncredited) Wayne, "Risk Tolerance," *Tilt,* ESPN, 2005.

Ed Baranyk, *This Is Wonderland* (also known as *Wonderland* and *La corte di Alice*), CBC, 2005.

Film Appearances:

Ken, *Pushing Tin* (also known as *A la limite, Alit under kontroll, Alto controle, Erotikes ataraksis, Falso tracciato, Fuera de control, Les aiguilleurs, Mi espacio,*

Riskirajoilla, Turbulenzen—und andere Katastrophen, and *Turnul de control*), Twentieth Century–Fox, 1999.

Mac McConnell, *Apartment Hunting,* Alliance Atlantis Communications, 2000.

TTC attendant, *Saint Monica* (also known as *Sainte Monica*), Allumination Filmworks/Seville Pictures, 2002.

Frank, *Shall We Dance* (also known as *Shall We Dance?, Shall We Dance? (Bailamos?), Shall We Dance? La nouvelle vie de Monsieur Clark, Bailamos?, Danca comigo?, Darf ich bitten?, Kas tantsime?, Saanko luvan?,* and *Si on dansait?*), Miramax, 2004.

Constable White, *Looking for Angelina,* The Galaxy Group, c. 2004, KOAN Inc., 2005.

Coach Henderson, *Full of It* (also known as *The Life and Lies of Sam Leonard, Nothing but the Truth,* and *The Whole Truth*), New Line Cinema, 2007.

Greg Fulton, *Your Beautiful Cul de Sac Home,* Pushmower Pictures, 2007.

GREENHUT, Robert 1942(?)–

PERSONAL

Some sources cite born March 18, 1942; born in New York, NY; children: Jennifer. *Education:* Studied music at the University of Miami.

Addresses: *Agent*—The Gersh Agency, 130 West 42nd St., New York, NY 10036.

Career: Producer, director, production manager, and production supervisor. Robert Greenhut Productions, New York City, founder and producer; Foundry Film Partners, founder (with Jon Ein).

Member: Directors Guild of America.

Awards, Honors: Directors Guild of America Award (with others), outstanding directorial achievement in motion pictures, 1978, for *Annie Hall;* Film Award (with Woody Allen), best film, British Academy of Film and Television Arts, 1986, for *The Purple Rose of Cairo;* Los Angeles Film Critics Association Award, best film, 1986, Academy Award nomination, best picture, 1987, and Film Award nomination, best film, British Academy of Film and Television Arts, 1987, all with others, for *Hannah and Her Sisters;* Film Award nomination (with Allen), best film, British Academy of Film and Television Arts, 1988, for *Radio Days;* Eastman Kodak Award, 1989, for lifetime achievement; Crystal Apple Award, mayor's office of New York City, 1989; Film Award nomination (with Allen), best film, British Academy of Film and Television Arts, 1991, for *Crimes and Misdemeanors;* Independent Spirit Award nomination, best feature, Independent Feature Project/West, 1995, for *Bullets over Broadway;* Golden Satellite Award nomination (with others), best motion picture—comedy or musical, International Press Academy, 1997, for *Everyone Says I Love You;* High Hopes Award (with others), Munich Film Festival, 1998, for *With Friends Like These ...*

CREDITS

Film Work:

Production assistant, *The Tiger Makes Out* (also known as *Der Tiger schlaegt zurueck* and *Um tigre de alcova*), Columbia, 1967.

Production manager: New York, *Husbands* (also known as *Aviomiehet, Ehemaenner, Maridos,* and *Mariti*), Columbia, 1970.

Production manager, *Where's Poppa?* (also known as *Donde esta papa?, Poikamiehen painajaiset, Senza un filo di classe, Var ar poppa? sa kaeringen,* and *Wo is' Papa?*), United Artists, 1970.

Unit production manager, *The Owl and the Pussycat,* Columbia, 1970.

First assistant director, *Panic in Needle Park,* Twentieth Century–Fox, 1971.

Production manager, assistant director, and producer, *Born to Win* (also known as *Addict* and *Born to Lose*), United Artists, 1971.

Assistant director, *Last of the Red Hot Lovers,* Paramount, 1972.

Production supervisor, *Tom Sawyer* (musical; also known as *A Musical Adaptation of Mark Twain's "Tom Sawyer"*), United Artists, 1973.

Associate producer, *Huckleberry Finn* (musical; also known as *Mark Twain's "Huckleberry Finn": A Musical Adaptation*), United Artists, 1974.

Associate producer, *Lenny,* United Artists, 1974.

Associate producer, *Dog Day Afternoon* (also known as *Ahar Ha–Tzohoraem Shel Poranoot, En satans eftermiddag, En skaev eftermiddag, Hikinen iltapaeivae, Hundstage, Kanikulai delutan, Laembe paerastlouna, Pieskie popoludnie, Quel pomeriggio di un giorno da cani, Tarde de perro, Tarde de perros, Um dia de cao,* and *Un apres–midi de chien*), Warner Bros., 1975.

Associate producer, *The Front* (also known as *Aldrig i livet, Der Strohmann, El testaferro, Il prestanome, La tapadera, Le prete–nom, Musta lista, O testa de ferro, Straamanden,* and *Testa–de–ferro por acaso*), Columbia, 1976.

Executive producer and production manager, *Annie Hall* (also known as *Anhedonia, It Had to Be Jew, A Roller Coaster Named Desire, Annie og jeg, Der Stadtneurotiker, Dos extranos amantes, Ha–Roman Sheli im Annie, Io & Annie, Mig og Annie, Nevrikos erastis, Noivo neurotico, noiva nervosa,* and *O nevrikos erastis*), United Artists, 1977.

Executive producer, *Interiors* (also known as *Innenleben, Interieurs, Interiores, Intimidade, Sisaekuvia,* and *Vivodasok*), United Artists, 1978.

Associate producer and production manager, *Hair* (musical; also known as *Hair—Birakin guenes iceri girsin, Hario, Pelo,* and *Vlasy*), United Artists, 1979.

Executive producer, *Manhattan,* United Artists, 1979.

Producer, *Stardust Memories,* United Artists, 1980.

Producer and first assistant director, *Arthur,* Warner Bros., 1981.

Producer, *A Midsummer Night's Sex Comedy* (also known as *Comedia sexual en una noche de verano, Comedie erotique d'une nuit d'ete, Eine Sommernachts–Sexkomoedie, En midsommarnatts sexkomedi, En midsommernats sexkomedi, Kesaeyoen seksikomedia, La comedia sexual de una noche de verano, Szentivaneji szexkomedia, Uma comedia sexual numa noite de verao,* and *Una commedia sexy in una notte di mezza estate*), Orion, 1982.

Executive producer, *The King of Comedy* (also known as *El rei de la comedia, El rey de la comedia, Konungur grinsins, Koomikkojen kuningas, Krol komedii, La valse des pantins, Melech Ha–Comedia, O rei da comedia,* and *Re per una notte*), Twentieth Century–Fox, 1983.

Producer, *Zelig,* Warner Bros., 1983.

Producer, *Broadway Danny Rose,* Orion, 1984.

Producer, *The Purple Rose of Cairo,* Orion, 1985.

Producer, *Hannah and Her Sisters,* Orion, 1986.

(With Mike Nichols) Producer, *Heartburn,* Paramount, 1986.

Producer, *Radio Days* (also known as *A era do radio, A radio aranykora, Dias da radio, Dias de radio,* and *Dies de radio*), Orion, 1987.

Producer, *September,* Orion, 1987.

Executive producer (with Laurence Mark) and unit production manager, *Working Girl* (also known as *Armas de mujer, Die Waffen der Frauen, Dolgozo lany, O femeie face cariera, Podnikava divka, Pracujaca dziewczyna, Quand les femmes s'en melent, Secretaria ejecutiva, Uma mulher de sucesso, Uma secretaria de futuro, Una donna in carriera, Working girl—med huvudet paa skaft!, Working girl—Quand les femmes s'en melent,* and *Working girl—tieni huipulle*), Twentieth Century–Fox, 1988.

Producer, *Another Woman,* Orion, 1988.

Producer (with James L. Brooks) and unit production manager, *Big* (also known as *Big—isoksi yhdessae, Duzy, Petit bonhomme, Quero ser grande, Quisiera ser grande,* and *Vreau sa fiu mare*), Twentieth Century–Fox, 1988.

Producer, *Crimes and Misdemeanors,* Orion, 1989.

Producer, "Oedipus Wrecks," *New York Stories,* Buena Vista, 1989.

Executive producer, *Postcards from the Edge* (also known as *Bons baisers d'Hollywood, Cartoline dall'inferno, Glooyot M'Ha–Haim, Gruesse aus*

Hollywood, Hilsen fra Hollywood, Lembrancas de Hollywood, Pocztowki znad krawedzi, Pohlednice z Hollywoodu, Postales desde el filo, Recuerdos de Hollywood, Terveisiae unelmien reunalta, and *Vykort fraan droemfabriken*), Columbia, 1990.

Producer, *Alice,* Paramount, 1990.

Producer, *Quick Change* (also known as *Con la poli en los talones, Ein Verrueckt genialer Coup, Hold–up a New York, Hurtige penge, Keikka putkessa, Kesef Kal, Latwy szmal, Monnaie courante, Nao tenho troco, No tengo cambio, Pare to harti kai treha, Scappiamo col malloppo, Snabba pengar, Um assalto genial,* and *Viszem a bankot*), Warner Bros., 1990.

Executive producer, *Regarding Henry,* Paramount, 1991.

Producer, *Husbands and Wives,* TriStar, 1992.

Producer, *A League of Their Own* (also known as *Pretty League, Eine Klasse fuer sich, Ella dan el golpe, Ich wlasna liga, Liga de mulheres, Omaa luokkaansa, Ragazze vincenti, Tjejligan, Uma equipe muito especial, Un equipo muy especial,* and *Une equipe hors du commun*), Columbia, 1992.

Producer, *Shadows and Fog* (also known as *Arnyekok es koed, Cienie i mgla, Neblina e sombras, Ombre e nebbia, Ombres et brouillard, Ombres i boira, Schatten und Nebel, Skuggor och dimma, Skygger og taage, Sombras e nevoeiro, Sombras y niebla, Sombras y nieblas,* and *Varjoja ja sumua*), Orion, 1992.

Producer, *Manhattan Murder Mystery,* TriStar, 1993.

Executive producer, *Wolf* (also known as *A farkas, Lobo, Loup, Volk, Wolf—Das Tier im Manne, Wolf—la belva e fuori,* and *Ze'ev*), Columbia, 1994.

Producer, *Bullets over Broadway,* Miramax, 1994.

Producer, *Renaissance Man* (also known as *Army Intelligence* and *By the Book*), Buena Vista, 1994.

Producer, *Mighty Aphrodite,* Miramax, 1995.

Executive producer and soundtrack executive producer, *The Preacher's Wife,* Buena Vista, 1996.

Producer, *Everyone Says I Love You* (musical; also known as *Woody Allen Fall Project 1995, Alla saeger I love you, Alle sagen—I love you, Alle siger I love you, Herkes seni seviyorum der, Kolam Omrim Ani Ohev Otach, Oloi lene s'agapo, Toda a gente diz quie te amo, Todos dicen I Love You, Todos dicen que te amo, Todos dicen te quiero, Todos dizem eu te amo, Tout le monde dit—I love you, Tutti dicono I love you,* and *Varazsige: I Love You*), Miramax, 1996.

Producer, *With Friends Like These …,* Winner Communications/Mom's Roof, Inc., 1998.

Executive producer, *Jump,* Arrow Releasing, 1999.

Executive producer, *Siegfried & Roy: The Magic Box* (documentary; also known as *The Magic Box*), IMAX Corporation, 1999.

Producer and unit production manager, *The White River Kid* (also known as *White River*), New City Releasing, 1999.

Co–executive producer, *Company Man,* Paramount, 2000.

Consultant, *Black Knight* (also known as *Chevalier noir, El caballero negro, Enas ippotis mavra halia, Le chevalier black, Locuras en la edad media, Loucuras na idade media,* and *Ritter Jamal—Eine schwarze Komoedie*), Twentieth Century–Fox, 2001.

Production executive and preproduction consultant, *Seabiscuit,* Universal, 2003.

Producer, *Stateside* (also known as *Sinners*), Samuel Goldwyn Films, 2004.

Consulting producer, *The Marconi Bros.,* Blueprint Film Group/Old World Films, 2006.

Producer, *Final Me Guilty* (also known as *Find Me Guilty: The Jackie Dee Story, Beni suclu bulun, Declaradme culpable, Final me guilty—uskomaton oikeudenkaeynti, Jugez–moi coupable,* and *Prova a incastrarmi*), Yari Film Group Releasing, 2006.

Unit production manager: additional photography, *The Departed* (also known as *Infernal Affairs, A tegla, Agents troubles, Departed—Unter Feinden, Dvostruka igra, Ha–Shtoolim, Infiltracja, Infiltrados, Kahe tule vahel, Koestebek, Les infiltres, Los infiltrados, O pliroforiodotis, Os infiltrados, The Departed—Entre inimigos,* and *The Departed—Il bene e il male*), Warner Bros., 2006.

Special teams coach, *Garfield: A Tail of Two Kitties* (live action and animated; also known as *Garfield 2, Garfield—Pacha royal, Gustaf 2,* and *Karvinen 2*), Twentieth Century–Fox, 2006.

Executive producer and unit production manager, *August Rush,* Warner Bros., 2007.

Some sources cite Greenhut as the director and producer of *The Wedding Contract,* Premiere Marketing & Distribution.

Film Appearances:

(Uncredited) Director of Irish play, *Stateside* (also known as *Sinners*), Samuel Goldwyn Films, 2004.

Television Work; Movies:

Associate producer, *The Silence,* NBC, 1975.

Associate producer and production manager, *Panic in Echo Park,* NBC, 1977.

Producer, *Don't Drink the Water,* ABC, 1994.

GRESHAM, Gloria 1946(?)–

PERSONAL

Born c. 1946, in Indianapolis, IN; daughter of Gloria Mae Gresham; father, a television engineer; married

"Doc" Erickson (a producer). *Education:* Graduated from Indiana University, 1967.

Addresses: *Office*—Costume Designers Guild, 13949 Ventura Blvd., Suite 309, Sherman Oaks, CA 91423–3570.

Career: Costume designer.

Member: Costume Designers Guild.

Awards, Honors: Academy Award nomination, best achievement in costume design, 1991, for *Avalon;* Saturn Award nomination, best costumes, Academy of Science Fiction, Fantasy and Horror Films, 1994, for *Last Action Hero.*

CREDITS

Film Costume Designer:
Just Tell Me What You Want, Warner Bros., 1980.
Urban Cowboy, Paramount, 1980.
Zorro, the Gay Blade, Twentieth Century–Fox, 1981.
Author! Author!, Twentieth Century–Fox, 1982.
Diner, Metro–Goldwyn–Mayer/United Artists, 1982.
The Escape Artist, Orion/Warner Bros., 1982.
Without a Trace, Twentieth Century–Fox, 1983.
Body Double, Columbia, 1984.
(With Francine Jamison and Jim Tyson) *Fletch,* Universal, 1984.
(With Kendall Errair and Barton K. James) *Footloose,* Paramount, 1984.
(With Bernie Pollack) *The Natural,* Tri–Star, 1984.
8 Million Ways to Die, Tri–Star, 1986.
Tin Men, Buena Vista, 1987.
Outrageous Fortune, Buena Vista, 1987.
Midnight Run, Universal, 1988.
Twins, Universal, 1988.
Lucky Stiff (also known as *That Shamrock Touch*), 1988.
Ghostbusters II (also known as *Ghostbusters 2*), Columbia, 1989.
The War of the Roses, Twentieth Century–Fox, 1989.
When Harry Met Sally (also known as *When Harry Met Sally*), Columbia, 1989.
Avalon, Tri–Star, 1990.
Kindergarten Cop, Universal, 1990.
Misery, Columbia, 1990.
V.I. Warshawski (also known as *V.I. Warshawski, Detective in High Heels*), Buena Vista, 1991.
Beethoven (also known as *Beethoven: Story of a Dog*), Universal, 1992.
A Few Good Men, 1992.
Last Action Hero, 1993.
Disclosure, 1994.
North, 1994.

Boys on the Side (also known as *Avec ou sans hommes*), 1995.
The American President, 1995.
Sleepers, Warner Bros., 1996.
Ghosts of Mississippi (also known as *Ghosts from the Past*), Sony Pictures Entertainment, 1996.
Sphere, Warner Bros., 1998.
Six Days Seven Nights (also known as *6 Days 7 Nights*), Buena Vista, 1998.
Liberty Heights, Warner Bros., 1999.
Rules of Engagement (also known as *Les regles d'engagement, Rules–sekunden der entscheidung,* and *Rules of Engagement—Die regeln des krieges*), Paramount, 2000.
The Kid (also known as *Disney's "The Kid"*), Buena Vista, 2000.
Bandits, Metro–Goldwyn–Mayer, 2001.
The Hunted, Paramount, 2003.
Envy, DreamWorks, 2004.
The Last Shot, Buena Vista, 2004.
Annapolis, Buena Vista, 2006.

Film Work; Other:
Costume coordinator, *The Wiz,* 1978.
Costume designer assistant, *The Brink Job,* 1978.

Film Appearances:
Herself, *How Harry Met Sally,* 2000.

Television Costume Assistant; Movies:
Johnny, We Hardly Knew Ye, NBC, 1977.

Television Costume Designer; Specials:
Leslie's Folly, Showtime, 1994.
I Am Your Child, ABC, 1997.

Stage Costume Designer:
A Black Quartet, Tambellinis Gate Theatre, then Frances Adler Theatre, both New York City, 1969.
The Way It Is!!!, New Lincoln Theatre, 1969.
Show Me Where the Good Times Are, Edison Theatre, New York City, 1970.
Forty Carats, tour of U.S. cities, 1974.
Rockabye Hamlet, Minskoff Theatre, New York City, 1976.

Stage Work; Other:
Assistant to Mr. Aulisi, *Weekend with Feathers,* Shubert Theatre, New Haven, CT, then on tour of U.S. cities, 1976.

SIDELIGHTS

Gloria Gresham's favorite films are *Avalon* and *Diner.*

OTHER SOURCES

Periodicals:
People Weekly, spring, 1990, p. 122.

GRIFFIN, Tim
(Tim Griffen, Timothy Collins Griffin)

PERSONAL

Addresses: *Agent*—Pakula, King and Associates, 9229 West Sunset Blvd., Suite 315, Los Angeles, CA 90069.

Career: Actor.

CREDITS

Film Appearances:
Orientation advisor, *Higher Learning,* Columbia, 1995.
Wright Herman, *Lover Girl* (also known as *Lover Girls*), Bedford Entertainment/Xanadeux, 1997.
The older Nick Wilson, *Wind River,* Lions Gate Films, 1998.
Timmy, *Boys and Girls,* Dimension Films, 2000.
Officer Griffin, *Cherish,* Fine Line, 2002.
John Nevins, *The Bourne Supremacy* (also known as *Die Bourne verschwoerung*), Universal, 2004.
Tony, *Kids in America,* Launchpad Releasing/Slowhand Cinema Releasing, 2005.
Police captain and detective, *Danika,* Universal, 2006.

Television Appearances; Series:
Ronny O'Malley, a recurring role, *Grey's Anatomy,* ABC, between 2005 and 2007.

Television Appearances; Movies:
For the Very First Time (also known as *Til I Kissed Ya*), NBC, 1991.
Dwight, *Evolver,* Sci–Fi Channel, 1995.

Television Appearances; Episodic:
John Conlan, "Murder Most Ancient," *In the Heat of the Night,* NBC, 1989.
Gil Reynolds, "Brotherly Love," *Hunter,* NBC, 1990.

Gene, "Her Father's Daughter," *Who's the Boss?,* ABC, 1990.
Tommy, "F.N.G.," *China Beach,* ABC, 1990.
Dirk, "Jerry's Journey," *Parker Lewis Can't Lose* (also known as *Parker Lewis*), Fox, 1992.
Messenger, *A League of Their Own,* CBS, 1993.
Jason, "The Rave," *Saved by the Bell: The College Years,* NBC, 1994.
Devin, "Live for Today," *Dead at 21,* MTV, 1994.
Rod, "Bikini Camp Slasher," *Weird Science,* USA Network, 1995.
Second fraternity guy, "Lowenstein's Lament," *Cybill,* CBS, 1996.
Jacob, "Electric Twister Acid Test," *Sliders,* Fox, 1996.
Nicky Mink, "Rumpelstiltskin," *Pacific Blue,* USA Network, 1997.
Bart Valen, "Full Contact," *Walker, Texas Ranger,* CBS, 1997.
Bart Valen, "Rookie," *Walker, Texas Ranger,* CBS, 1997.
Travis, *Port Charles,* ABC, 1997.
Richie Grayson, "Love and War," *Party of Five,* Fox, 1998.
Richie Grayson, "Gifts," *Party of Five,* Fox, 1998.
Tom Boxdollar, "HAARP Attack," *Seven Days* (also known as *Seven Days: The Series*), UPN, 1999.
The rabbit, "Animal Pragmatism," *Charmed,* The WB, 2000.
Bill Deverell, "Angel's Flight," *Family Law,* CBS, 2001.
(As Tim Griffen) "The Mission," *JAG,* CBS, 2002.
"Baggage," *7th Heaven* (also known as *Seventh Heaven* and *7th Heaven: Beginnings*), The WB, 2003.
John Rose, "Remember," *The Guardian,* CBS, 2004.
Detective Chris Leinberger, "Mousetrap," *Medical Investigation,* NBC, 2005.
Baron, "Day 4: 8:00 p.m.–9:00 p.m.," *24,* Fox, 2005.
Roy Barnes, "Fatal Retraction," *The Closer,* TNT, 2005.
Marine Sergeant Malcolm Porter, "Light Sleeper," *Navy NCIS: Naval Criminal Investigative Service* (also known as *NCIS* and *NCIS: Naval Criminal Investigative Service*), CBS, 2006.
Captain John Evans, "The Gallant Hero & the Tragic Victor," *ER,* NBC, 2006.
Captain John Evans, "21 Guns," *ER,* NBC, 2006.
Morgan Eliot, "Manhunt," *The Unit,* CBS, 2006.

Also appeared as a ruffian in an episode of *Empty Nest,* NBC.

Television Appearances; Other:
(As Timothy Collins Griffin) Matthew Robinson, "Taking a Stand," *ABC Afterschool Special,* ABC, 1989.
Mark Tomlinson, *Against the Grain* (pilot), NBC, 1993.

H

HARMON, Angie 1972–
(Angie Harmon–Sehorn, Angie Sehorn)

PERSONAL

Original name, Angela Michelle Harmon; born August 10, 1972, in Dallas, TX; daughter of Lawrence Paul Harmon (a model and hospital information network executive) and Daphne Demar Caravageli (a model); married Jason Sehorn (a professional football player), June 9, 2001; children: Finley Faith, Avery Grace. *Education:* Graduated from Highland Park High School, Dallas, TX, 1990. *Religion:* Christian.

Addresses: *Agent*—United Talent Agency, 9560 Wilshire Blvd., Suite 500, Beverly Hills, CA 90212. *Manager*—John Carrabino Management, 100 North Crescent Dr., Suite 323, Beverly Hills, CA 90210.

Career: Actress. Began working as a model as a child; worked as a runway model as an adult; appeared in television commercials, including Neutrogena skin products and Purina Dog Chow; appeared in print ads for Neutrogena skin products.

Awards, Honors: Screen Actors Guild Award nominations (with others), outstanding performance by an ensemble in a drama series, 1999, 2000, 2001, 2002, all for *Law and Order.*

CREDITS

Film Appearances:
Pam, *Lawn Dogs,* Strand Releasing, 1997.
Voice of Barbara Gordon, *Batman Beyond: Return of the Joker* (animated; also known as *Return of the Joker* and *Batman of the Future: Return of the Joker*), Warner Bros., 2000.

Herself, *The Acting Class,* 2000.
Page Hensen, *Good Advice,* Family Room Entertainment, 2001.
Ronica Miles, *Agent Cody Banks* (also known as *L'agent Cody Banks*), Metro–Goldwyn–Mayer, 2003.
Anna, *The Deal,* Front Street Productions, 2005.
Veronica Cleeman, *Fun with Dick and Jane* (also known as *Alternative Career* and *Fun with Dick & Jane*), Sony, 2005.
Kate Crawford, *End Game,* Metro–Goldwyn–Mayer, 2006.
Rose, *Seraphim Falls,* Samuel Goldwyn Films, 2006.
Eve Goode, *The Good Mother* (also known as *Glass House: The Good Mother* and *The Glass House 2*), Screen Gems, 2006.

Television Appearances; Series:
Ryan McBride, *Baywatch Nights* (also known as *Detectives on the Beach*), syndicated, 1995–97.
Amanda Reardon, *C-16: FBI* (also known as *C–16*), ABC, 1997–98.
Assistant district attorney Abbie Carmichael, *Law and Order,* NBC, 1998–2001.
Assistant district attorney Abbie Carmichael, *Law and Order: Special Victims Unit* (also known as *SVU* and *Special Victims Unit*), NBC, 1999–2000.
Dr. Nora Campbell, *Inconceivable,* NBC, 2005.
Lindsay Boxer, *Women's Murder Club,* ABC, 2007.

Television Appearances; Movies:
Susan Wilson, *Video Voyeur: The Susan Wilson Story,* Lifetime, 2002.

Television Appearances; Pilots:
Bethany Steele, *Secrets of a Small Town,* ABC, 2006.
Lindsay Boxer, *Women's Murder Club,* ABC, 2007.

Television Appearances; Specials:
The 18th Annual American Fashion Awards, E! Entertainment Television, 1999.

The 5th Annual Screen Actors Guild Awards, TNT, 1999.
Presenter, *The 52nd Annual Primetime Emmy Awards,* ABC, 2000.
VH1/Vogue Fashion Awards, VH1, 2000, 2001.
VH1 Divas Live: The One and Only Aretha Franklin (also known as *VH1 Divas Live: The One and Only Aretha Franklin—A Benefit Concert for VH1 Save the Music Foundation*), VH1, 2001.
Intimate Portrait: Vera Wang, Lifetime, 2002.
(As Angie Harmon Sehorn) Host, *Together: Stop Violence Against Women,* Lifetime, 2003.
Politics: A Pop Culture History, VH1, 2004.
CMT: The Greatest—Sexiest Southern Women, Country Music Television, 2006.
Presenter, *8th Annual A Home for the Holidays with Rod Stewart,* 2006.

Television Appearances; Episodic:
Debbie Prentice, "Offshore Thunder," *Renegade,* 1995.
Ryan McBride, "Sail Away," *Baywatch,* syndicated, 1996.
Tonight Show with Jay Leno, NBC, 1999, 2000, 2005.
Larry King Live, CNN, 2000.
Voice of Commissioner Barbara Gordon, "King's Ransom," *Batman Beyond* (animated; also known as *Batman of the Future*), The WB, 2000.
The Rosie O'Donnell Show, syndicated, 2000, 2002.
Entertainment Tonight (also known as *E.T.*), syndicated, 2003, 2007.
The Oprah Winfrey Show (also known as *Oprah*), syndicated, 2004.
The O'Reilly Factor, Fox News, 2004.
The View, ABC, 2004.
Kathy Griffin: My Life on the D–List, Bravo, 2006.

OTHER SOURCES

Periodicals:
Glamour, April, 2000, p. 288.
People Weekly, October 12, 1998, p. 91.
Redbook, February, 2004, p. 106.
Texas Monthly, September, 2000, p. 144.
TV Guide, April 1, 2000, p. 46.

HARRIS, John
  See YOUNG, Burt

HARRIS, Lynn

PERSONAL

Addresses: *Office*—Warner Bros. Pictures, Inc., 4000 Warner Blvd., Burbank, CA 91522.

Career: Producer and script supervisor. Warner Bros., Burbank, CA, executive vice president of production.

CREDITS

Film Script Supervisor:
(Second unit) *The Drifter,* Concorde Pictures, 1988.
Monday Morning (also known as *Class of Fear*), 1990.
Dollman, Paramount Home Video, 1991.
Arcade, Full Moon Entertainment, 1993.
Kalifornia, Gramercy Pictures, 1993.
Dead Connection (also known as *Final Combination* and *Lights Out*), 1994.
A Passion to Kill (also known as *Rules of Obsession*), A–Pix Entertainment, 1994.

Film Co–Executive Producer:
Se7en, New Line Cinema, 1995.
Boogie Nights, New Line Cinema, 1997.

Film Executive Producer:
Bed of Roses, New Line Cinema, 1996.
Blade, New Line Cinema, 1998.
Body Shots, New Line Cinema, 1999.
And (uncredited) production executive, *Magnolia* (also known as *mag–no'li–a*), New Line Cinema, 1999.
Town & Country (also known as *Town and Country*), New Line Cinema, 2001.
Life as a House, New Line Cinema, 2001.
Blade II, New Line Cinema, 2002.
About a Boy (also known as *About a Boy oder: der tag det toten ente* and *Pour un garcon*), Universal, 2002.
S1m0ne, New Line Cinema, 2002.
Highwaymen (also known as *Pourchasse*), New Line Cinema, 2003.

Film Studio Executive:
Town & Country, New Line Cinema, 2001.
Life As a House, New Line Cinema, 2001.
S1m0ne, New Line Cinema, 2002.
Blade II, New Line Cinema, 2002.
Highwaymen (also known as *Pourchasse*), New Line Cinema, 2003.
The Notebook, New Line Cinema, 2004.
We Are Marshall, Warner Bros., 2006.
Zodiac, Paramount, 2007.

Film Producer:
The Notebook, New Line Cinema, 2004.
Blade: Trinity, New Line Cinema, 2004.

Television Script Supervisor; Series:
Malibu Shores, NBC, 1996.

7th Heaven (also known as *Seventh Heaven*), The WB, 1996–99.

Television Work; Miniseries:
Production coordinator, *Passion and Paradise* (also known as *Murder in Paradise*), 1989.
Script supervisor, *Gone in the Night,* 1996.

Television Script Supervisor; Movies:
Fatal Charm, Showtime, 1990.
Invasion of Privacy, USA, 1992.
In the Shadows, Someone's Watching, NBC, 1993.
Natural Selection (also known as *Dark Reflection*), Fox, 1994.
Roseanne and Tom: Behind the Scenes, NBC, 1994.
Witch Hunt, HBO, 1994.
Moment of Truth: Eye of the Stalker (also known as *Eye of the Stalker*), NBC, 1995.
A Friend's Betrayal (also known as *Stolen Youth*), NBC, 1996.
A Nightmare Come True (also known as *A Dream of Murder*), CBS, 1997.

Television Work; Movies:
Assistant to producers, *Manhunt: Search for the Night Stalker,* 1989.

Television Work; Specials:
A Laugh, a Tear, syndicated, 1990.

Television Director; Episodic:
"Stand Up," *7th Heaven* (also known as *Seventh Heaven*), The WB, 2003.

HARRIS, Wood 1969–
(Sherwin David Harris)

PERSONAL

Full name, Sherwin David Harris; born October 17, 1969, in Chicago, IL; son of John and Mattie Harris. *Education:* Attended New York University graduate acting program.

Career: Actor. Appeared in Rockport shoe advertisement, 2007.

Awards, Honors: Image Award nomination, outstanding supporting actor in a motion picture, National Association for the Advancement of Colored People, Blockbuster Entertainment Award nomination, favorite supporting actor—drama, 2001, both for *Remember the Titans.*

CREDITS

Film Appearances:
(As Sherwin David Harris) Motaw, *Above the Rim,* Asso Film, 1994.
Cafe 24 busboy, *As Good As It Gets,* TriStar, 1997.
Al Swayze, *Celebrity,* Miramax, 1998.
Officer Henderson, *The Siege,* Twentieth Century–Fox, 1998.
Chicky, *Committed* (also known as *Non Stop Girl*), Miramax, 2000.
Julius Campbell, *Remember the Titans,* Buena Vista, 2000.
Clayton, *The Gold Cup,* 2000.
Will, *Train Ride,* 2000.
Are You Cinderella?, 2000.
Ace, *Paid in Full,* Dimension Films, 2002.
Tony, *MVP,* 2003.
Brax, *Dirty,* Silver Nitrate Releasing, 2005.
Dion Element, *Southland Tales,* Samuel Goldwyn Films, 2006.
Dr. Sidney Zachary, *Ways of the Flesh* (also known as *The Heart Specialist*), 2006.
Gabriel Marx, *Jazz in the Diamond District,* 2007.
Dayvon, *4 Life,* 2007.

Television Appearances; Series:
Avon Barksdale, *The Wire,* HBO, 2002–2004.

Television Appearances; Movies:
Ellis Alves, *Spenser: Small Vices* (also known as *Robert B. Parker "Small Vices"*), 1999.
Jimi Hendrix, *Hendrix* (also known as *A Room Full of Mirrors: The Jimi Hendrix Story*), Showtime, 2000.
Billy Dixon, *Rhapsody,* 2000.

Television Appearances; Specials:
The 2000 Blockbuster Entertainment Awards, Fox, 2000.
The 32nd NAACP Image Awards, Fox, 2001.
My Coolest Years, VH1, 2004.
BET Hip–Hop Awards, Black Entertainment Television, 2006.

Television Appearances; Episodic:
Hector, "Moby Greg," *NYPD Blue,* ABC, 1996.
Tony, "The Rules," *Cosby,* CBS, 1997.
Officer Gordon Wood, "Plan B," *Oz,* 1997.
Shadow, "Going Native," *New York Undercover* (also known as *Uptown Undercover*), Fox, 1998.
Himself, *Russell Simmons Presents Def Poetry* (also known as *Def Poetry* and *Def Poetry Jam*), HBO, 2002.
Marvin Gardens/Dwayne Grant, "Another Life," *The Twilight Zone,* UPN, 2003.
The Wendy Williams Experience, 2006.

Murphy, "The Art of Reckoning," *Numb3rs* (also known as *Num3ers*), CBS, 2007.

Stage Appearances:

Troilus and Cressida, Delacorte Theatre, New York City, 1995.

Sid, *Waiting for Lefty,* Blue Light Theatre Company, Classic Stage Company Theatre, New York City, 1997.

Also appeared as Private First Class Melvyn Peterson, *A Soldier's Play.*

RECORDINGS

Music Videos:

"Through the Wire," *Kanye West: College Dropout—Video Anthology,* Universal Music and Video Distribution, 2005.

Martin Luther's "Daily Bread," 2005.

Also appeared in Common's "Testify."

HAWTHORNE, Elizabeth

PERSONAL

Married Raymond Hawthorne (an actor); children: Sophia (an actress), Emmeline (an actress).

Career: Actress. Theatre Corporate, member of company, 1974–84; Mercury Theatre, member of company, 1984–92.

Awards, Honors: Film Award, best supporting actress, New Zealand Film and Television Awards, 2000, for *Savage Honeymoon;* Theatre Actress of the Year Award.

CREDITS

Film Appearances:

Suzanne Maxwell, *Hot Target,* Crown International Pictures, 1985.

Bernice, *Jack Be Nimble,* 1993, then Cinevista, 1994.

Mrs. Benton, *Alex* (also known as *Alex: The Spirit of a Champion*), Isambard Productions/New Zealand Film Corporation/New Zealand On Air/Total Film and Television, 1993.

Henrietta Simpson, *The Last Tattoo,* Capella International, 1994.

Anne, *The Beach* (short), Der KurzFilmVerleih, 1995.

Magda Rhys–Jones, *The Frighteners* (also known as *Robert Zemeckis Presents "The Frighteners"*), Universal, 1996.

The Bar, 1997.

Maisy Savage, *Savage Honeymoon,* Rocket Pictures, 2000.

Charlotte Morrison, *Jubilee,* South Pacific Pictures, 2000.

Detective Shoorwell, *Exposure* (also known as *Exposure—Gefahrliche enthullung, Naked Terror,* and *Der tod steht modell*), 2000.

Pat Kelly, *No One Can Hear You,* Mainline Releasing, 2001.

Mrs. MacReady, *The Chronicles of Narnia: The Lion, the Witch, and the Wardrobe* (also known as *The Chronicles of Narnia*), Buena Vista, 2005.

Doctor–LA, *Jinx Sister,* 2007.

30 Days of Nights, Columbia, 2007.

Also appeared in *Memory and Desire.*

Television Appearances; Series:

Dr. Julia Thornton, *Shortland Street,* TV New Zealand, 1995–96.

Various roles, *Hercules: The Legendary Journeys,* syndicated, 1995–99.

Voice of Hera, *Cleopatra 2525,* syndicated, 2000–2001.

Liz Brasch, *Spin Doctors,* 2001.

Television Appearances; Miniseries:

Patricia McCardle, *The Tommyknockers* (also known as *Stephen King's "The Tommyknockers"*), ABC, 1993.

Caroline, *Greenstone,* Odyssey, 1999.

Television Appearances; Movies:

Hanlon: In Defence of Minnie Dean, 1985.

First party guest, *Adrift,* CBS, 1993.

Queen Omphale, *Hercules and the Lost Kingdom* (also known as *Hercules: The Legendary Journey—Hercules and the Lost Kingdom*), syndicated, 1994.

Susan Ellis, *Lawless,* 1999.

Judge Harriet Caldwell, *Raising Waylon,* CBS, 2004.

Joan Rivers, *Not Only But Always,* CBC and Channel 4, 2004.

Eleanor Harrison, *The Man Who Lost His Head,* ITV, 2007.

Also appeared in *Plainclothes.*

Television Appearances; Specials:

Various historical figures, *This Is It,* TV3, 1999.

Television Appearances; Episodic:

Voice of Hera, "The Treasure of Zeus: Part 3: What a Crockery," *Young Hercules,* 1998.

Voice of Hera, "Down and Out in Academy Hills," *Young Hercules,* 1998.
Voice of Hera, "Herc's Nemesis," *Young Hercules,* 1998.
Voice of Hera, "Valley of the Shadow," *Young Hercules,* 1999.

RECORDINGS

Video Games:
Voice of Mrs. MacCready, *The Chronicles of Narnia: The Lion, the Witch and the Wardrobe,* Buena Vista Games, 2005.

HENDERSON, Meredith 1983–

PERSONAL

Full name, Meredith Janet Anne Henderson; born November 24, 1983, in Ontario, Canada; daughter of Mark Henderson (a musician with the group Tangleroot) and Laura Parsons (Tangleroot's manager); sister of Beth (an actress and musician with Tangleroot), Noah (an actor and musician with Tangleroot), and Rebecca "Beki" Henderson (an actress and musician with Tangleroot). *Avocational Interests:* Reading.

Career: Actress.

Awards, Honors: Gemini Award nomination, best performance in a children's or youth program or series, Academy of Canadian Cinema and Television, 1998, Gemini Award, best performance in a children's or youth program or series, 1999, both for *The Adventures of Shirley Holmes.*

CREDITS

Film Appearances:
Jaynie Nightingale, *Kayla* (also known as *Kayla—Mein freund aus der wildnis*), 1999.
Woman's voice, *Beachbound* (short), 2004.
Sara Wexler, *Heartstopper,* Anchor Bay Entertainment, 2006.
Nellie Russell, *The Assassination of Jesse James by the Coward Robert Ford* (also known as *The Assassination of Jesse James*), Warner Bros., 2007.

Film Work:
Executive producer and producer, *Shut Up and Deal,* 2007.

Television Appearances; Series:
Shirley Holmes, *The Adventures of Shirley Holmes,* YTV and Fox Family, 1996–2000.
Phoebe Sutton, *Big Sound,* Global, 2000.
Cleo Bellows, *MythQuest,* CBC and PBS, 2001.
Callie Leeson, *Queer as Folk* (also known as *Q.A.F.* and *Queer as Folk*), Showtime, 2004–2005.
Hilary Dunbar, *The Best Years,* 2007.

Television Appearances; Miniseries:
Young Maddie, *Beach Girls,* Lifetime, 2005.
Marlene, *Everest,* 2007.

Television Appearances; Movies:
Aurora, *The Song Spinner,* Showtime, 1995.
Anna Schiller, *A Wind at My Back Christmas,* 2001.
Tara Norris, *Stranger at the Door* (also known as *Un etranger parmi nous*), Lifetime, 2004.

Television Appearances; Specials:
Eileen Shania Twain, *Shania: A Life in Eight Albums* (also known as *Shania—Une vie en huit albums*), CBC, 2005.

Television Appearances; Episodic:
Cara Renfield, "Vampire Breath," *Goosebumps* (also known as *Ultimate Goosebumps*), Fox, 1996.
"Good Harvest," *The Fearing Mind,* Fox Family, 2000.
Geena, "Blackboard Jungle," *Just Cause,* PAX, 2003.
Sara Denton, "White Whale," *1–800–Missing* (also known as *Missing*), Lifetime, 2003.
Button's girlfriend, "Pizza Boys Are Missing," *Puppets Who Kill,* Comedy Central, 2004.
Two of four wives, "Strange Bedfellows," *The Eleventh Hour,* CTV, 2004.
Nikki Slovak/Caryn Harris, "Rules of Engagement," *The Dresden Files,* Sci–Fi Channel, 2007.

Also appeared as student, "Eliza," *Strange World,* ABC.

HENRY, John
See RICHARDSON, Jay

HEYMAN, David 1961–

PERSONAL

Full name, David Jonathan Heyman; born July 26, 1961, in London, England; son of John (a producer) and Norma (a producer) Heyman.

Addresses: *Office*—Heyday Films, 4000 Warner Blvd., Burbank, CA 91522; 5 Denmark St., London WC2H8LP United Kingdom.

Career: Producer and actor. Warner Bros., creative executive, beginning 1986; United Artist, vice president, c. late 1980s.

Member: Academy of Motion Pictures Arts and Sciences, British Academy of Film and Television Arts.

Awards, Honors: Children's Award nomination (with Chris Columbus and Steve Kloves), best feature film, British Academy of Film and Television Arts, Alexander Korda Award nomination (with Columbus), best British film, British Academy of Film and Television Arts, both 2002, for *Harry Potter and the Sorcerer's Stone;* Children's Award nomination (with Columbus and Kloves), best feature film, British Academy of Film and Television Arts, 2003, for *Harry Potter and the Chamber of Secrets;* ShoWest Award, producer of the year, National Association of Theater Owners, 2003; Children's Award (with Columbus, Mark Radcliffe, and Alfonso Cuaron), best feature film, British Academy of Film and Television Arts, 2004, Alexander Korda Award nomination (with Columbus, Radcliffe, and Cuaron), best British film, British Academy of Film and Television Arts, 2005, both for *Harry Potter and the Prisoner of Azkaban.*

CREDITS

Film Producer:
Juice (also known as *Angel Town 2*), Paramount, 1992.
The Stoned Age (also known as *Tack's Chicks*), 1994.
Ravenous, Twentieth Century–Fox, 1996.
Harry Potter and the Sorcerer's Stone (also known as *Harry Potter and the Philosopher's Stone*), Warner Bros., 2001.
Harry Potter and the Chamber of Secrets (also known as *Harry Potter und die kammer des schreckens*), Warner Bros., 2002.
Harry Potter and the Prisoner of Azkaban, Warner Bros., 2004.
Harry Potter and the Goblet of Fire, Warner Bros., 2005.
Harry Potter and the Order of the Phoenix, Warner Bros., 2007.
I Am Legend, Warner Bros., 2007.

Film Executive Producer:
The Daytrippers (also known as *En route vers Manhattan*), Columbia TriStar, 1996.
Taking Lives, 2004.

Film Work; Other:
Worked as a production runner for *Ragtime* and *A Passage to India.*

Film Appearances:
Eldad, *Bloomfield* (also known as *The Hero*), AVCO Embassy Pictures, 1971.
Pinot Noir, *Cookin'* (short), 1997.
Mr. Janus, *Ravenous,* Twentieth Century–Fox, 1999.
Nathalie's pimp, *The Lost Son,* 1999.
Himself, *Build a Scene* (documentary short), 2003.
Himself, *Creating the Vision* (documentary short), 2004.
Himself, *Conjuring a Scene* (documentary short), 2004.
Himself, *Preparing for the Yule Ball* (documentary short), 2006.
Himself, *The Maze: The Third Task* (documentary short), 2006.
Himself, *In Too Deep: The Second Task* (documentary short), 2006.
Himself, *He Who Must Not Be Named* (documentary short), 2006.
Himself, *Harry vs. the Horntail: The First Task* (documentary short), 2006.

Television Producer; Series:
Threshold, CBS, 2005.

Television Producer; Movies:
Blind Justice (also known as *Canaan's Way*), HBO, 1994.

Television Executive Producer; Pilots:
Crime Prevention Unit, ABC, 2007.

Television Appearances; Specials:
J. K. Rowling and the Story of Harry Potter, Arts and Entertainment, 2002.
Best Ever Family Films, 2005.
Inside "Harry Potter and the Goblet of Fire," 2005.
"Harry Potter": Behind the Magic, Granada, 2005.
The 100 Greatest Family Films, Channel 4, 2005.

HIGGINS, Jonathan
(Johnathan Higgins)

PERSONAL

Career: Actor.

CREDITS

Television Appearances; Series:
Chad Daniels, *Odyssey 5,* Showtime, 2002–2003.
Colm Dresden, *The Dresden Files,* Sci–Fi Channel, beginning 2007.

Television Appearances; Miniseries:

George Littell, *Thanks of a Grateful Nation* (also known as *The Gulf War*), Showtime, 1997.

Joe Kennedy, *Bonanno: A Godfather's Story* (also known as *The Family, Family: The Life and Times of Joseph Bonanno, The Youngest Godfather,* and *Nejmladsi kmotr*), Showtime, 1999.

Sergeant Hodges, *Widows* (also known as *Aenkornas haemnd, As viuvas,* and *Braquage au feminin*), ABC, 2002.

Culver, *Covert One: The Hades Factor* (also known as *Eletveszely, El factor Hades, El primer encubrimiento de Robert Ludlum—El factor Hades, Laboratorio mortale, Mystiki omada 1—To agima tou Adi, O factor Hades,* and *Operaatio Haades*), CBS, 2006.

Television Appearances; Movies:

Doug Schmidt, *Execution of Justice* (also known as *Um crime politico*), Showtime, 1999.

Father Bell, *Blessed Stranger: After Flight 111* (also known as *A tragedia do voo 111* and *Le drame du vol 111*), CTV (Canada), 2000.

Jonathan Matthews, *The Bookfair Murders* (also known as *Intriga em Frankfurt* and *Mord paa bogmessen*), CTV (Canada), 2000.

Darryl F. Zanuck, *Bojangles,* Showtime, 2001.

Pat McKinley, *Final Jeopardy* (also known as *Tentative de meurtre* and *Vida em risco*), ABC, 2001.

William Hockman, *Life in the Balance* (also known as *Crime em evidencia, L'innocence en sursis, Med livet som indsats,* and *Pendiente de un hilo*), Lifetime, 2001.

Franklin Roosevelt, *The Man Who Saved Christmas* (also known as *O homem que salvou o natal*), CBS, 2002.

Medic, *Lathe of Heaven* (also known as *O flagelo dos ceus*), Arts and Entertainment, 2002.

Peter Edelman, *RFK* (also known as *Little Brother* and *RFK—vaativa vastuu*), fX Channel, 2002.

Army officer at Rand, *The Pentagon Papers* (also known as *Les hommes du Pentagone, Los archivos del Pentagono, Segredos do Pentagono,* and *Traicion en Pentagono*), fX Channel, 2003.

Greg McLainey, *The Crooked E: The Unshredded Truth about Enron* (also known as *A verdadeira historia de uma fraude* and *Lo scandalo Enron*), CBS, 2003.

Harry Brewer, *A Woman Hunted* (also known as *Outrage* and *Une femme aux abois*), Lifetime, 2003.

Jerry Dennings, *Crimes of Passion* (also known as *Coupable de seduction*), Lifetime, 2005.

John Cuti, *Martha behind Bars* (also known as *Martha Stewart: Behind Bars*), CBS, 2005.

Frank, *Housesitter* (also known as *The Housesitter* and *La maison du secret*), 2007.

Victor, *Framed for Murder* (also known as *Amistades enganosas*), Lifetime, 2007.

Television Appearances; Episodic:

Herbie, "Trial Marriage," *Once a Thief* (also known as *John Woo's "Once a Thief," John Woo's "The Thief,"*
John Woo's Violent Tradition, Kerran varas, aina varas?, Ladrao que rouba ladrao, Les repentis, and *Matar a un ladron*), CTV (Canada) and syndicated, 1997.

Professor Joseph Gates, "Trade Off," *Soldier of Fortune, Inc.* (also known as *SOF, Inc., S.O.F., Inc.,* and *S.O.F. Special Ops Force*), syndicated, 1998.

Thomas Ryan, "The Christmas Angel," *Little Men,* PAX TV, 1998.

Mr. Dundonald, "The Afterlife," *Traders* (also known as *Haute finance*), CanWest Global Television and Lifetime, c. 1998.

Jeff, "Between Heaven and Hell," *Earth: Final Conflict* (also known as *EFC, Gene Roddenberry's "Battleground Earth," Gene Roddenberry's "Earth: Final Conflict," Invasion planete Terre,* and *Mission Erde: Sie sind unter uns*), syndicated, 1999.

Booth Danforth, *Leap Years,* Showtime, 2001 (multiple episodes).

"Revenge," *Largo Winch* (also known as *Largo Winch—Gefaehrliches Erbe* and *Largon kosto*), 2001.

Jasper, "Carnivores," *The Shield* (also known as *The Barn* and *Rampart*), fX Channel, 2002.

Jasper, "The Quick Fix," *The Shield* (also known as *The Barn* and *Rampart*), fX Channel, 2003.

"The Candidate," *Doc,* PAX TV, 2003.

Norman Culver, "Sniper Shot, Intern Hot," *Wild Card* (also known as *Zoe Busiek: Wild Card*), Lifetime, 2004.

Ellis Wood, "We Are Coming Home," *Missing* (also known as *1–800–Missing*), Lifetime, 2005.

Detective Harley Krost, "Off the Meter," *The Unit,* CBS, 2006.

Television Appearances; Pilots:

President, *An American in Canada* (also known as *Frostbite*), CBC, 2002.

Film Appearances:

Findlay, *Short for Nothing,* [Canada], 1998.

(As Johnathan Higgins) Officer Michaell, *The Boondock Saints* (also known as *Mission des dieux*), Lions Gate Films, 1999.

Detective Rakowski, *Bruiser* (also known as *Devil's Mask*), Lions Gate Films, 2000.

David Brewster, *The House on Turk Street* (also known as *No Good Deed*), Remstar Distribution, 2002, MAC Releasing, 2003.

(As Johnathan Higgins) Phillip, *Beyond Borders* (also known as *Amar peligrosamente, Amor sem fronteiras, Amore senza confini–Beyond borders, Au–dela des frontieres, Jenseits aller Grenzen, Mas alla de las fronteras, Pera apo ta synora,* and *Yli rajojen*), Paramount, 2003.

Colin Naylor, *A Different Loyalty,* Lions Gate Films, 2004.

Boston announcer, *Saint Ralph,* Odeon Films, 2004, Samuel Goldwyn Films, 2005.

Embry Wallis, *The Greatest Game Ever Played* (also known as *Das groesste Spiel seines Lebens, El juego que hizo historia, El piu bel gioco della mia vita,* and *Juego de honor*), Buena Vista, 2005.

Vord, *Guy X,* 2005.

HINES, Cheryl 1965–

PERSONAL

Full name, Cheryl Ruth Hines; born September 21, 1965, in Miami Beach, FL; daughter of Rosemary Harbolt (an administrative assistant); married Paul Young (a manager), December 30, 2002; children: Catherine Rose. *Education:* University of Central Florida, B.A., communications and theater performance; also attended West Virginia University and Florida State University; studied improvisation and acting at The Groundlings Theater.

Addresses: *Agent*—Endeavor, 9601 Wilshire Blvd., 3rd Floor, Beverly Hills, CA 90210. *Manager*—Principato/Young Management, 9465 Wilshire Blvd., Suite 880, Beverly Hills, CA 90212.

Career: Actress. The Groundlings, Los Angeles, CA, member. Also worked as a hotel bartender.

Awards, Honors: Emmy Award nominations, outstanding supporting actress in a comedy series, 2003, 2006, Gracie Allen Award, outstanding supporting actress in a comedy series, American Women in Radio and Television, 2005, Screen Actors Guild Award nomination (with others), outstanding performance by an ensemble in a comedy series, 2006, all for *Curb Your Enthusiasm.*

CREDITS

Film Appearances:
Sheila, *Cheap Curry and Calculus,* 1996.
Catering manager, *Along Came Polly,* Universal, 2004.
Roxanne, *Cake,* Lions Gate Films, 2005.
Sally Crowder, *Our Very Own,* Miramax, 2005.
Sally, *Herbie Fully Loaded,* Buena Vista, 2005.
Bickford Shmeckler's Cool Ideas, Screen Media Films, 2006.
Jamie Munro, *RV* (also known as *RV: Runaway Vacation* and *Die chaoscamper RV*), Columbia, 2006.
Casey Nudelman, *Keeping Up with the Steins,* Miramax, 2006.
Herself, *Barry Sonnenfeld: The Kosher Cowboy* (documentary short), Sony Pictures Home Entertainment, 2006.

Herself, *Robin Williams: A Family Affair* (documentary short), Sony Pictures Home Entertainment, 2006.
Herself, *History of "Curb Your Enthusiasm": So Far* (short), Home Box Office Home Video, 2006.
Herself, *History of "Curb Your Enthusiasm": Even Further* (short), Home Box Office Home Video, 2006.
Herself, *RV Nation: The Culture of Road Warriors* (documentary short), Sony Pictures Home Entertainment, 2006.
Becky, *Waitress,* Fox Searchlight Pictures, 2007.
Lainie Schwartzman, *The Grand* (documentary), 2007.

Television Appearances; Series:
Cheryl David, *Curb Your Enthusiasm,* HBO, 2000—.
Voice of Kate, *Father of the Pride* (animated), NBC, 2004–2005.

Television Appearances; Movies:
Rose Goodman, *Double Bill* (also known as *A Tale of Two Wives*), Oxygen, 2003.

Television Appearances; Specials:
Cheryl David, *Larry David: Curb Your Enthusiasm,* HBO, 1999.
I Love the '80s, VH1, 2002.
The Award Show Awards Show, TRIO, 2003.
Presenter, *The 31st Annual American Music Awards,* ABC, 2003.
The Three Stooges 75th Anniversary Special, NBC, 2003.
"Sex and the City": A Farewell, HBO, 2004.
Presenter, *The 30th Annual People's Choice Awards,* CBS, 2004.
Presenter, *The 2004 Radio Music Awards,* NBC, 2004.
The 31st Annual People's Choice Awards, CBS, 2005.
AFI's 100 Years, 100 "Movie Quotes": The Greatest Lines from American Film, CBS, 2005.
Celebrity Autobiography: In Their Own Words, Bravo, 2005.
The WIN Awards 2006, PAX, 2006.
The 58th Annual Primetime Emmy Awards, NBC, 2006.
Comic Relief 2006, TBS and HBO, 2006.
Reel Comedy: RV, Comedy Central, 2006.

Television Appearances; Episodic:
Nurse, *Unsolved Mysteries,* NBC, 1997.
Debbie, "Poetry in Notion," *Suddenly Susan,* NBC, 1998.
Helen, "Six Degrees of Marlon," *The Wayons Bros.,* The WB, 1998.
The Test, FX Channel, 2001.
Spencer's mother, "Annoying Kid," *Everybody Loves Raymond* (also known as *Raymond*), CBS, 2002.
Trailer park lady, "Terrorist Training: Part 1," *Reno 911!,* Comedy Central, 2003.
Hollywood Squares (also known as *H2* and *H2: Hollywood Squares*), syndicated, 2003.

Dr. Linda, "Did Wanda Say a Four Letter Word?," *Wanda at Large,* Fox, 2003.

Ask Rita, syndicated, 2003.

Good Day Live, syndicated, 2004.

Ellen: The Ellen DeGeneres Show, syndicated, 2004, 2006, 2007.

Jimmy Kimmel Live, ABC, 2004, 2006.

"Tournament 4, Game 4," *Celebrity Blackjack,* Gams Show Network, 2004.

"Tournament 4, Game 2," *Celebrity Poker Showdown,* Bravo, 2004.

"Tournament 6, Game 4," *Celebrity Poker Showdown,* Bravo, 2005.

"Tournament 6 Championship," *Celebrity Poker Showdown,* Bravo, 2005.

Weekends at the DL, Comedy Central, 2005.

The Late Late Show with Craig Ferguson, CBS, 2005, 2006.

Last Call with Carson Daly, NBC, 2005, 2006, 2007.

Best Week Ever, VH1, 2006.

Paige Cox, "My New God," *Scrubs,* NBC, 2006.

Live with Regis and Kelly, syndicated, 2006.

The Megan Mullally Show, syndicated, 2006.

"Cheryl Hines," *Talkshow with Spike Feresten,* 2006.

Entertainment Tonight (also known as *E.T.*) syndicated, 2007.

Late Night with Conan O'Brien (also known as *Conan O'Brien*), NBC, 2007.

Television Work; Series:

Executive producer, *Campus Ladies,* Oxygen, 2005–2007.

Television Work; Episodic:

Director, "No Means No," *Campus Ladies,* Oxygen, 2006.

Stage Appearances:

Merry Samson, *Beverly Winwood Presents the Actors Showcase,* Groundlings Theatre, Los Angeles, CA, 2002.

**HIRSH, David Julian
(David Hirsh)**

PERSONAL

Born in Montreal, Quebec, Canada. *Education:* Studied criminology at the University of Toronto; studied acting at the Lee Strasberg Theater Institute and the Actor's Studio.

Addresses: *Agent*—Agency for the Performing Arts, 405 S. Beverly Dr., Beverly Hills, CA 90212. *Manager*—Gilbertson, Kincaid, and Associates, 501 Santa Monica Blvd., Suite 301, Santa Monica, CA 90401.

Career: Actor. Also worked as a personal bartender to Calvin and Kelly Klein.

Awards, Honors: Gemini Award (with Steve Markle), best performing arts program or series or arts documentary program or series, Academy of Canadian Cinema and Television, 2005, for *Camp Hollywood.*

CREDITS

Film Appearances:

Lloyd, *Blue Hill Avenue,* Artisan Entertainment, 2001.

Jeremy, *OHM,* 2001.

(As David Hirsh) Freddie Cannon, *Confessions of a Dangerous Mind* (also known as *Confessions d'un homme dangereaux*), Miramax, 2002.

(As David Hirsh) Barton, *Noel,* Red Rose Productions, 2004.

Himself, *The Dinner,* 2007.

Television Appearances; Series:

Josh Adler, *Leap Years,* Showtime, 2001.

Josh Gould, *Naked Josh* (also known as *Les lecons de Josh*), Showcase Television Canada and Oxygen, 2004–2006.

Max, *Love Bites,* 2006.

Television Appearances; Movies:

(As David Hirsh) Blair, *Crime in Connecticut: The Return of Alex Kelly,* CBS, 1999.

Benjamin Pierce, *Coast to Coast,* Showtime, 2003.

Jon Peter, *Sombre Zombie,* 2005.

Tom, *The Roommate,* 2007.

Jake, *St. Urbain's Horseman,* CBC, 2007.

Television Appearances; Specials:

Himself, *Camp Hollywood,* 2004.

Television Appearances; Episodic:

(As David Hirsh) Kronen, "New Regime," *La Femme Nikita* (also known as *Nikita*), USA Network, 1998.

Zeke, "Matchmaker, Matchmaker," *Twice in a Lifetime,* CTV and PAX, 2000.

Danny Valance, "Legacy," *Largo Winch* (also known as *Largo Winch—Gefahrliches Erbe*), Mystery Channel, 2001.

Open Mike with Mike Bullard (also known as *Open Mike* and *The Mike Bullard Show*), Global, 2002.

Jason, "Bet Your Life," *Just Cause,* PAX, 2002.

Thomas Berke, "The Outsider," *The Dead Zone* (also known as *Stephen King's "The Dead Zone"*), USA Network, 2003.

Zack Shannon, "Summer in the City," *CSI: NY* (also known as *CSI: New York*), CBS, 2005.

Zack Shannon, "Grand Murder at Central Station," *CSI: NY* (also known as *CSI: New York*), CBS, 2005.
Zack Shannon, "Zoo York," *CSI: NY* (also known as *CSI: New York*), CBS, 2005.

Television Work; Specials:
Producer, *Camp Hollywood,* 2004.

Stage Appearances:
Appeared in *One Hundred Gates,* Off–Broadway production.

WRITINGS

Television Specials:
Camp Hollywood, 2004.

HOLDEN, Gina 1975–

PERSONAL

Born March 17, 1975, in Smithers, British Columbia, Canada. *Education:* Graduated from college with honors; studied dance.

Addresses: *Agent*—Kirk Talent Agencies, Inc., 134 Abbott St., Suite 402, Vancouver, British Columbia V6E 1T7, Canada.

Career: Actress. Worked as a model and appeared in advertisements. Worked as a volunteer for various causes.

CREDITS

Television Appearances; Series:
Rachel Scofield, *Reunion,* Fox, 2005.
Claire, *Da Vinci's City Hall,* CBC, 2005–2006.
Coreen Fennel, *Blood Ties,* Lifetime, beginning 2007.
Dale Arden, *Flash Gordon,* Sci–Fi Channel, beginning 2007.

Television Appearances; Miniseries:
Louise, *Roughing It* (also known as *Mark Twain's "Roughing It"*), The Hallmark Channel, 2002.

Television Appearances; Movies:
Nervous student, *Perfect Romance* (also known as *Keyword: Love, Perfect Match, Le parfait amour,* and *Romance perfecto*), Lifetime, 2004.

Diana Coles, *Murder on Spec* (also known as *Trophy Wife* and *Heritage criminel*), Lifetime, 2006.

Television Appearances; Specials:
Carrie Dreyer, *Death's Design: Making "Final Destination 3,"* 2006.

Television Appearances; Episodic:
Angela Wilkins, "Die Like an Egyptian," *Killer Instinct* (also known as *Deviant Behavior, The Gate,* and *Pahuuden jaeljillae*), Fox, 2005.
Aubry and Chrystal Henderson, "The Last Goodbye," *The Dead Zone* (also known as *Stephen King's "Dead Zone"*), USA Network, 2005.
Haley Collins, "Wendigo," *Supernatural,* The WB, 2005.
Twink, "Lynch Pin," *The L Word* (also known as *Earthlings*), Showtime, 2005.
Bethany Cadman, "Speak Now or Forever Hold Your Piece," *Psych,* USA Network, 2006.

Television Appearances; Pilots:
New girl at *Milk, The L Word* (also known as *Earthlings*), Showtime, 2004.

Film Appearances:
LV receptionist, *Fantastic Four* (also known as *Fantastic 4, Fantastik doertlue, Les quatre fantastiques, Los cuatro fantasticos,* and *Quarteto fantastico*), Twentieth Century–Fox, 2005.
Sam, *"LTD.,"* Answer Produktions, 2005.
Amanda, *The Butterfly Effect 2* (also known as *El efecto mariposa 2* and *L'effet papillon 2*), New Line Cinema, 2006.
Carrie Dreyer, *Final Destination 3* (also known as *Final Destination 3–D, Destination finale 3, Destino final 3, Final destination 3—viimeinen maeaeraenpaeae, Premonicao 3, Put bez povratka 3,* and *Vlepo to thanato sou 3*), New Line Cinema, 2006.
Pretty young assistant, *Man about Town,* Lions Gate Films, 2006.
Carrie Adams, *Alien vs. Predator: AVP2* (also known as *Alien vs. Predator 2*), Twentieth Century–Fox, 2007.
Fourth protester, *Battle in Seattle,* Remstar Distribution, 2007.
Hope Eastbrook, *The Christmas Cottage,* Lionsgate, 2007.
Young assistant, *Code Name: The Cleaner,* New Line Cinema, 2007.

RECORDINGS

Videos:
Herself, *Dead Teenager Movie* (short), New Line Home Video, 2006.
Herself, *Kill Shot: The Making of "Final Destination 3,"* New Line Home Video, 2006.

HOLDEN, Laurie 1972(?)–

PERSONAL

Born December 17, 1972 (some sources say 1973), in Los Angeles, CA; daughter of Larry Holden (an actor) and Adrienne Ellis (an actress); stepdaughter of Michael Anderson (a director). *Education:* University of California at Los Angeles, B.A., theatre arts, 1993; also studied economics at McGill University, Montreal, Canada; studied acting at The Webber Douglas Academy of Art and The Larry Moss Acting Studio. *Avocational Interests:* Working with children's charities.

Addresses: *Agent*—Innovative Artists, 1505 10th St., Santa Monica, CA 90401. *Publicist*—Perception Public Relations, 3940 Laurel Canyon Blvd., Suite 169, Studio City, CA 91604.

Career: Actress. Won Look of the Year modeling pageant, Toronto, Ontario, Canada.

Awards, Honors: Natalie Wood Acting Award, University of California at Los Angeles, 1993; Gemini Award nomination, best performance by an actress in a guest role in a dramatic series, Academy of Canadian Cinema and Television, 1996, for *Due South.*

CREDITS

Film Appearances:
Karen, *Separate Vacations,* Alliance, 1986.
Matt's girl, *Physical Evidence,* Columbia, 1989.
Vicki, *Expect No Mercy,* Imperial Entertainment, 1995.
Detective Ally Marsey, *Past Perfect,* Nu Image, 1996.
Adele Stanton, *The Majestic,* Warner Bros., 2001.
Billy, *Meet Market,* Cut Entertainment Group, 2004.
Marge Maggs, *Bailey's Billion$,* Echo Bridge Entertainment, 2005.
Debbie McIlvane, *Fantastic Four,* Twentieth Century–Fox, 2005.
Cybil Bennett, *Silent Hill,* TriStar, 2006.
Herself, *Path of Darkness: Making "Silent Hill"* (documentary), Sony Pictures Home Entertainment, 2006.
Amanda Dumfries, *The Mist,* Weinstein Company, 2007.

Television Appearances; Series:
Scales of Justice, 1990.
Claire, *Family Passions* (also known as *Macht der leidenschaft*), CTV, 1994.
Darlene Kubolek, *Destiny Ridge,* CanWest Global, 1994–96.

Marita Covarrubias, a recurring character, *The X–Files,* Fox, 1996–2000.
Mary Travis, *The Magnificent Seven,* CBS, 1998–2002.

Television Appearances; Miniseries:
Marie Wilder, *The Martian Chronicles,* 1980.
Princess Deshkova, *Young Catherine,* TNT, 1991.

Television Appearances; Movies:
Rachel, *TekWar: TekLab* (also known as *TekLab*), syndicated, 1994.
Mabel Dunham, *The Pathfinder,* Showtime, 1996.
Beth Polasky, *The Alibi,* ABC, 1997.
Scarlett, *Echo* (also known as *Dead Echo*), ABC, 1997.
Bonnie Lorrine, "Fool's Gold," *Dead Man's Gun,* Showtime, 1997.
Scales of Justice, 1998.
Amy Ryan, *The Man Who Used to Be Me* (also known as *Race Through Time* and *Rencontre avec le passe*), Fox, 2000.

Television Appearances; Specials:
Inside the X–Files, Fox, 1998.

Television Appearances; Episodic:
Erin, "Gemini and Counting," *Captain Power and the Soldiers of the Future,* 1988.
Joyce Morrison and Judith Carswell, "The Hardboiled Mystery," *Father Dowling Mysteries* (also known as *Father Dowling Investigates*), 1991.
Suki, "Larceny, Inc./Reach Out and Rob Someone/Jet Threat," *The Secret Service,* 1993.
Jill Kennedy, "Letting Go," *Due South,* CTV and CBS, 1995.
Debra Campbell, "Homeland," *Highlander* (also known as *Highlander: The Series*), syndicated, 1995.
Sherri Sampson, "What You Don't Know Can Kill You," *Murder, She Wrote,* CBS, 1996.
Cora Jennings/Sarah Browning, "Thirteenth Generation," *Poltergeist: The Legacy,* 1996.
Madeline Reynolds, "Many Happy Returns," *Two,* 1996.
Susan McLaren, "Breaking Point," *The Outer Limits* (also known as *The New Outer Limits*), Showtime and syndicated, 2000.
Herself, "The Majestic," *HBO First Look,* HBO, 2001.
Piper Moran, "Shabbas Bloody Shabbas," *Big Sound,* Global, 2001.

Stage Appearances:
Appeared in *Cat on a Hot Tin Roof.*

RECORDINGS

Video Games:
Voice of Marita Covarrubias, *The X Files: Resist or Serve,* Vivendi Universal Games, 2004.

OTHER SOURCES

Periodicals:
People Weekly, May 18, 1998, p. 191.
TV Guide, February 13, 1999, p. 5.

HOLMES, David 1969–

PERSONAL

Born February 14, 1969, in Belfast, Northern Ireland.

Addresses: *Agent*—First Artists Management, 16000 Ventura Blvd., Suite 605, Encino, CA 91436.

Career: Composer and music supervisor. Previously worked as a club DJ, song producer, magazine writer, concert promoter, chef, and hairdresser; Mogwai (a cafe), owner and operator.

Awards, Honors: Online Film Critics Society Award nomination, best original score, BMI Film Music Award, 2002, both for *Ocean's Eleven;* British Independent Film Award nomination, best technical achievement, 2003, for *Buffalo Soldiers;* BMI Film Music Award, 2005, for *Ocean's Twelve.*

CREDITS

Film Work:
Arranger of "Something More," *Three Chords and a Wardrobe* (short), AtomFilms, 1998.
Song performer of "Minus 61 in Detroit," *One Day in September* (documentary), Sony Pictures Classics, 1999.
Music supervisor, *Buffalo Soldiers* (also known as *Army Go Home!* and *Buffalo Soldiers—Army Go Home!*), Miramax, 2001.
Performer of "Gone (The Kruder & Dorfmeister Session)," *Zoolander,* Paramount, 2001.
Performer of "Rodney Yates," "Gritty Shaker," and "69 Police," *Ocean's Eleven* (also known as *11* and *O11*), Warner Bros., 2001.
Music composition supporter, *"Ocean's Elevens": The Look of the Con* (short), Warner Bros., 2002.
Performer of "No Man's Land," *Code 46,* United Artists, 2003.
Music supervisor, *Ocean's Twelve,* Warner Bros., 2004.
Producer, *The 18th Electricity Plan* (short), 2006.

RECORDINGS

Albums:
This Film's Crap, Let's Slash the Seats, 1995.
Let's Get Killed, 1997.
Essential Mix, 1998.
Stop Arresting Artists, 1998.
Bow Down to the Exit Sign, 1999.
Holmes on the Decks, 2000.
Come Get It I Got It, 2001.
David Holmes Presents The Free Association, 2003.

Music Videos:
Directed "69 Police."

WRITINGS

Film Scores:
Resurrection Man, Gramercy Pictures, 1997.
Three Chords and a Wardrobe (short), AtomFilms, 1998.
Resurrection Man, PolyGram, 1998.
Out of Sight, Universal, 1998.
Buffalo Soldiers (also known as *Army Go Home!* and *Buffalo Soldiers—Army Go Home!*), Miramax, 2001.
Ocean's Eleven (also known as *11* and *O11*), Warner Bros., 2001.
Analyze That, Warner Bros., 2002.
Code 46, United Artists, 2003.
Stander, Newmarket Films, 2003.
Ocean's Twelve, Warner Bros., 2004.
The War Within, Magnolia Pictures, 2005.
Ocean's Thirteen (also known as *13*), Warner Bros., 2007.

Film Songs:
"Minus 61 in Detroit," *One Day in September,* Sony Pictures Classics, 1999.
"Rodney Yates," "Gritty Shaker," and "69 Police," *Ocean's Eleven* (also known as *11* and *O11*), Warner Bros., 2001.
"No Man's Land," *Code 46,* United Artists, 2003.

Television Scores; Movies:
Supply & Demand (also known as *Lynda La Plante's "Supply & Demand, Raw Recruit"*), 1997.

HOOPER, Nicholas
(Nick Hooper)

PERSONAL

Addresses: *Agent*—Cool Music, 1A Fisher's Land, Chiswick, London W4 1RX United Kingdom.

Career: Composer.

Awards, Honors: Television Award nomination, best original television music, British Academy of Film and Television Arts, 2002, for *The Way We Live Now;* Television Award nomination, best original television music, British Academy of Film and Television Arts, 2004, for *State of Play;* Television Award, best original television music, British Academy of Film and Television Arts, 2004, for *The Young Visiters;* Television Award nomination, best original television music, British Academy of Film and Television Arts, 2006, for *The Girl in the Cafe;* Television Award, best original television music, British Academy of Film and Television Arts, 2007, for *"Prime Suspect": The Final Act.*

CREDITS

Television Appearances; Episodic:
Shoplifter, "The Feral Element," *Legacy of the Silver Shadow,* 2002.

WRITINGS

Film Scores:
Land of the Tiger (documentary), 1985.
The Weaver's Wife (short), 1991.
Good Looks (short), 1992.
Punch (short), 1996.
The Tichborn Claimant, Redbus Film Distribution, 1998.
The Heart of Me, THINKFilm, 2002.
Harry Potter and the Order of the Phoenix, Warner Bros., 2007.

Television Scores; Series:
Wild and Dangerous, Animal Planet, 2000.
Messiah, BBC, 2000–2004.
The Future Is Wild, 2002.

Television Scores; Miniseries:
The Way We Live Now, BBC and PBS, 2001.
State of Play, BBC1 and BBC America, 2003.
Messiah: The Promise, BBC, 2004.

Television Scores; Movies:
The Time Traveller, 1993.
The Secret, BBC, 2002.
Loving You (also known as *The Rainbow Room*), ITV, 2003.
The Young Visiters, BBC, 2003.
(As Nick Hooper) *Bloodlines,* 2005.
(As Nick Hooper) *The Cost of Living,* 2005.
The Girl in the Cafe, HBO, 2005.
(As Nick Hooper) *My Family and Other Animals,* PBS, 2005.
(As Nick Hooper) *The Best Man,* BBC America, 2006.

The Chatterley Affair, 2006.
"Prime Suspect": The Final Act (also known as *"Prime Suspect" 7: The Final*), 2006.

Television Incidental Music; Specials:
Wildfilm, PBS, 1995.

Television Scores; Specials:
Tigers of Kanha, NBC, 1999.
In Search of Maneaters: Tigers of the Sundarbans, Animal Planet, 1999.
Inside the Animal Mind, PBS, 2000.
Elephant Island, Discovery Channel, 2000.
Elephants of Sand River, Discovery Channel, 2000.

Television Scores; Episodic:
(As Nick Hooper) "India: Land of the Tiger," *Nature,* PBS, 1982.
Nature, BBC, 1996–2005.
"Lonely," *Blue Murder,* Global, 2004.

HORSDAL, Chelah 1973–

PERSONAL

Full name, Chelah Phoebe Horsdal; born June 19, 1973, in Vancouver Island, British Columbia, Canada; daughter of Valdy (a folk singer; full name, Paul Valdemar Horsdal) and Kathleen Mary (an artist, teacher, and hospice counselor; maiden name, Fraser) Horsdal. *Education:* Studied acting.

Career: Actress. Worked as a model and appeared in advertisements.

Awards, Honors: Leo Award nomination, best performance by a female in a short drama, Motion Picture Arts & Sciences Foundation of British Columbia, 2006, for *Dark Room.*

CREDITS

Film Appearances:
Young mother, *Paycheck,* Paramount, 2003.
Botox's friend, *Connie and Carla,* Universal, 2004.
Jan, *The Truth about Miranda,* Wheelbarrow Films, 2004.
Sharon, *Pursued,* First Independent Pictures, 2004.
Alice, *Dark Room* (short film), 12th Sign Creations/Room 7 Productions, 2005.
Prostitute, *Seeking Fear,* Purewebb Films, 2005.

Third assistant district attorney, *The Exorcism of Emily Rose,* Screen Gems, 2005.

Blind secretary, *Hollow Man II* (also known as *El hombre sin sombra 2*), Destination Films, 2006.

Minivan mother, *X–Men: The Last Stand* (also known as *X–Men: Final Decision, X–Men 3, X3, X–me-hed—viimane vastuhakk, X–men—Conflitto finale, X–Men—Der letzte Widerstand, X–men—I teliki anametrisi, X–men—L'affrontement final, X–men—L'engagement ultime, X–men—La batalla final, X–Men—O confronto final, X–men—Ostatni bastion, X–men—posledniyat sblasak, X–men—uppgo-erelsen, X–men—viimeinen kohtaaminen, X–Men 3—Hamiflat Ha'acharon, X–men 3—La batalla final,* and *X–men 3—La decision final*), Twentieth Century–Fox, 2006.

Security guard, *The Pink Panther* (also known as *The Birth of the Pink Panther, The Mask of the Pink Panther, A pantera cor de rosa, Der rosarote Panther, La pantera rosa, La panthere rose, O roz panthiras, Rosa Pantern,* and *Vaaleanpunainen pantteri*), Metro–Goldwyn–Mayer, 2006.

Cheryll Witherspoon, *Burning Mussolini,* Burning Mussolini Productions, 2007.

Darcy Benson, *Alien vs. Predator: AVP2* (also known as *Alien vs. Predator 2*), Twentieth Century–Fox, 2007.

Joanne, *Ashes Fall* (short film), Blindpictures, 2007.

Miranda, *Addicted,* Yari Film Group Releasing, 2007.

Susan, *Elegy* (also known as *Elegy: Dying Animal*), Metro–Goldwyn–Mayer, 2007.

Woman in elevator, *Vice,* Romar Entertainment, 2007.

Janice, *Passengers,* Columbia, 2008.

Television Appearances; Series:

Lieutenant Womack, *Stargate SG–1* (also known as *La porte des etoiles* and *Stargaate SG–1*), Sci–Fi Channel, Showtime, and syndicated, beginning 2004.

Television Appearances; Miniseries:

Officer of the Royal Canadian Mounted Police (RCMP, the Mounties), *Human Cargo* (also known as *Third World*), CBC, 2004.

Lori Corbett, *Fallen,* ABC Family Channel, 2006.

Television Appearances; Movies:

Second female police officer, *The Life,* CTV (Canada), 2004.

Stefani the rental car woman, *5ive Days to Midnight* (also known as *Five Days to Midnight*), Sci–Fi Channel, 2004.

Mother, *Marker,* [Canada], 2005.

Cynthia Lewis, *A Decent Proposal,* [Canada], 2006.

Molly's mother, *Nightmare,* 2007.

Television Appearances; Specials:

Cindy, "Crossroads: A Story of Forgiveness" (also known as "Road to Forgiveness" and "Road to Redemption"), *Hallmark Hall of Fame,* CBS, 2007.

Television Appearances; Episodic:

Call girl, "Lifestyles of the Rich and Infamous," *The Hat Squad,* CBS, 1993.

Female paramedic, "Amazing Grace," *Mysterious Ways* (also known as *One Clear Moment, Anexegeta phainomena, Les chemins de l'etrange, Mysterious ways—les chemins de l'etrange, Rajatapaus,* and *Senderos misteriosos*), NBC and PAX TV, 2000.

Second reporter, "Listen," *Mysterious Ways* (also known as *One Clear Moment, Anexegeta phainomena, Les chemins de l'etrange, Mysterious ways—les chemins de l'etrange, Rajatapaus,* and *Senderos misteriosos*), NBC and PAX TV, 2002.

Admissions officer, "Haunted," *Tru Calling* (also known as *Heroine, Tru,* and *True Calling*), Fox, 2003.

Misabo Ahm, "Pieces of Eight," *Andromeda* (also known as *Gene Roddenberry's "Andromeda"*), syndicated, 2003.

Third police constable, "Thanks for the Toaster Oven," *Da Vinci's Inquest,* CBC, 2003.

Doctor Walker, "Voices over Water," *Cold Squad,* CTV (Canada), 2004.

First police constable, "Okay It's Official," *Da Vinci's Inquest,* CBC, 2004.

Janet Miller, "Collision," *The Dead Zone* (also known as *Stephen King's "Dead Zone"*), USA Network, 2004.

Cute librarian, "Hookman," *Supernatural,* The WB, 2005.

Dr. McCann, "Lexmas," *Smallville* (also known as *Smallville Beginnings* and *Smallville: Superman the Early Years*), The WB, 2005.

Frances Elwood, "H. P. Lovecraft's 'Dreams in the Witch–House,'" *Masters of Horror,* Showtime, 2005.

Heather Woodland, "Extreme Aggressor," *Criminal Minds,* CBS, 2005.

Jane Kelsey, "1988," *Reunion,* Fox, 2005.

Jeanine (Carrie's mother), "Wake–Up Call," *The 4400,* USA Network and SKY, 2005.

Mrs. Annie Tropek, "The Power of Love," *Renegadepress.com,* TVOntario (TVO) and Aboriginal Peoples Television Network, 2005.

Gail Esterbrook, "A Shock to the System," *Saved,* TNT, 2006.

Gail Esterbrook, "Tango," *Saved,* TNT, 2006.

Ivy Beckman, "Five Little Indians," *The Evidence,* ABC, 2006.

Janet, "The Burden of Truth," *Whistler,* CTV (Canada) and The N (Noggin), 2006.

Janet, "Meltdown," *Whistler,* CTV (Canada) and The N (Noggin), 2006.

Janet, "Will the Real Beck …?," *Whistler,* CTV (Canada) and The N (Noggin), 2006.

Mother, "Goodnight, Moon," *Three Moons over Milford,* ABC Family Channel, 2006.

Pretty redhead, "For What It's Worth," *Men in Trees* (also known as *A ferfi fan terem*), ABC, 2006.

Psychic, "Labia Majora," *The L Word* (also known as *Earthlings*), Showtime, 2006.

Psychic, "Lobsters," *The L Word* (also known as *Earthlings*), Showtime, 2006.

Weather girl, "Dead Flowers," *Godiva's,* Bravo, 2006.

Beth, "Game, Set ... Muuurder?," *Psych,* USA Network, 2007.

Didi Cassidy, "Crossroads: Parts 1 & 2," *Battlestar Galactica* (also known as *Galactica, Galactica—Estrella de combate,* and *Taisteluplaneetta Galactica*), Sci–Fi Channel, 2007.

Lauren Brooks, "Love, Money, and a Six Olive Martini," *Exes and Ohs* (also known as *Exes & Oh's*), Logo, 2007.

Lauren Brooks, "Pole Dancing and Other Forms of Therapy," *Exes and Ohs* (also known as *Exes & Oh's*), Logo, 2007.

Appeared as Tammi in "Not Fade Away," an unaired episode of *Still Life,* Fox.

Television Appearances; Pilots:
Juliet, *The Virgin of Akron, Ohio,* Lifetime, c. 2007.

HUDLIN, Reginald 1961–
(Reggie Hudlin)

PERSONAL

Full name, Reginald Alan Hudlin; born December 15, 1961, in Centerville, MO (some sources cite Centerville, IL); son of Warrington W., Sr., (a teacher and insurance executive) and Helen (a teacher; maiden name, Cason) Hudlin; brother of Warrington Hudlin (a producer, director, and actor); married Chrisette Suter, November 30, 2002. *Education:* Harvard University, B.A. (cum laude), 1983.

Addresses: *Office*—BET Networks, One BET Plaza, 1235 W Street NE, Washington, D.C. 20018. *Agent*—Paradigm, 360 North Crescent Dr., North Bldg., Beverly Hills, CA 90210. *Manager*—3 Arts Entertainment, 9460 Wilshire Blvd., 7th Floor, Beverly Hills, CA 90212.

Career: Director, writer, producer, and actor. Illinois State Arts Council, artist–in–residence, 1984–85; University of Wisconsin, Milwaukee, visiting film lecturer, 1985–86; Olgivy and Mather Advertising Agency, New York City, copywriter, 1986; Hudlin Bros. Inc., New York City, founder (with brother Warrington Hudlin) and president, 1986–?; Hudlin Bros. Records, founder (with Warrington Hudlin), 1996–?; Black Entertainment Television (BET), president and chief programming executive, 2005—; with Warrington Hudlin has produced music videos for such groups as Heavy D and the Boyz.

Awards, Honors: Student Academy Award—New England region, best film, 1983, for *House Party* (short); Best Film Award, Black Cinema Society, 1984; named National Endowment for the Arts fellow, 1985; Lillian Award, Delta Sigma Theta Sorority, 1990; Filmmakers Trophy—dramatic, Cinematography Award—dramatic, and Grand Jury Prize nomination—dramatic, all Sundance Film Festival, Critics Award nomination, Deauville Film Festival, all 1990, and Independent Spirit Award nominations, best director and best first feature (with Warrington Hudlin), 1991, all for *House Party* (feature–length); recipient of Key to City of Newark, NJ, 1990; named to Black Filmmakers Hall of Fame, 1990; Clarence Muse Award, Black Filmmakers Hall of Fame, 1991; Starlight Award, Black American Cinema Society, 1993; CableACE Award (with others), best dramatic or theatrical special, 1995, for *Cosmic Slop;* Black Cinema Award, Deep Ellum Film Festival, 2001; received grants from the Black Filmmakers Foundation.

CREDITS

Film Director:
House Party! (short), 1983.
The Kold Waves (short), 1984.
Reggie's World of Soul (short), 1985.
House Party, New Line Cinema, 1990.
Boomerang, Paramount, 1992.
The Great White Hype, Twentieth Century–Fox, 1996.
The Ladies Man (also known as *The Ladies' Man*), Paramount, 2000.
Servicing Sara (also known as *Mann umstandehalber abzugeben! Oder: Scheiden ist suB* and *Scheiden ist suB*), Paramount, 2001.

Other Film Work:
(As Reggie Hudlin) Sound, "Dr. Dobermind," *Fright Show* (also known as *Cinemagic*), 1985.
Executive producer (with Warrington Hudlin), *Bebe's Kids* (animated; also known as *Robin Harris' "Bebe's Kids"*), Paramount, 1992.
Producer, *Ride,* Miramax/Dimension Films, 1998.
Director, *Robin Harris: Live from the Comedy Act Theater,* Visual Arts Entertainment, 2006.

Film Appearances:
(As Reggie Hudlin) Dog 4, *She's Gotta Have It,* Island Pictures, 1986.
Burglar number one, *House Party,* New Line Cinema, 1990.
Street hustler, *Boomerang,* Paramount, 1992.
Reporter 31, *Posse,* Gramercy Pictures, 1993.
Voice of Rodney Roach, *Joe's Apartment,* Warner Bros., 1996.
Aloysius, *The Ladies Man* (also known as *The Ladies' Man*), Paramount, 2000.

Himself, *We Don't Die, We Multiply: The Robin Harris Story* (documentary), 2006.

Television Work; Series:
Producer, *The Bernie Mac Show,* Fox, 2003–2006.
Executive producer, *The Boondocks* (animated), Cartoon Network, 2005–2007.

Television Work; Movies:
Worked as executive producer and director, *Bat Out of Hell,* HBO.

Television Work; Specials:
Director, *Cosmic Slop,* HBO, 1994.
Executive producer and director, *The Last Days of Russell,* 1995.
Executive producer and director, *Richard Pryor: The Funniest Man Dead or Alive,* Black Entertainment Television, 2005.
Network executive producer, *Bring That Year Back 2006: Laugh Now, Cry Later,* Black Entertainment Television, 2006.

Television Work; Pilots:
Director, *Everybody Hates Chris,* UPN, 2005.
Executive producer and director, *Wifey,* Black Entertainment Television, 2007.

Television Director; Episodic:
"When Worlds Colitis," *City of Angels,* CBS, 2000.
The Bernie Mac Show, Fox, 2001.
Everybody Hates Chris, UPN, 2005.

Television Appearances; Specials:
Canned Ham: The Ladies Man, Comedy Central, 2000.
Acapulco Black Film Festival, HBO, 2000.
America Beyond the Color Line with Henry Louis Gates Jr. (also known as *American Beyond the Color Line*), 2002.
(As Reggie Hudlin) *Heroes of Black Comedy,* 2002.
It's Black Entertainment, Showtime, 2002.
Intimate Portrait: Tisha Campbell–Martin, Lifetime, 2002.
Made You Look: Top 25 Moments of BET History, Black Entertainment Television, 2005.
Parliament Funkadelic: One Nation Under Groove, PBS, 2005.
Bring Back That Year 2006: Laugh Now, Cry Later, Black Entertainment Television, 2006.

Television Appearances; Episodic:
Dialogue with Black Filmmakers, 1992.
Tavis Smiley, PBS, 2004.
Dennis Miller, CNBC, 2005.
Showbiz Tonight, CNN, 2005.

WRITINGS

Screenplays:
House Party! (short), 1983.
The Kold Waves (short), 1984.
Reggie's World of Soul (short), 1985.
House Party, New Line Cinema, 1990.
Bebe's Kids (animated; also known as *Robin Harris' "Bebe's Kids"*), Paramount, 1992.
Robin Harris: Live from the Comedy Act Theater, Visual Arts Entertainment, 2006.

Film Songs:
"I Ain't Havin It," "Straight Jackin " and "Freedom Song," *Bebe's Kids* (animated; also known as *Robin Harris' Bebe's Kids*), Paramount, 1992.

Television Specials:
The Last Days of Russell, 1995.

Television Episodes:
The Boondooks (animated), Cartoon Network, 2005–2007.

Comic Books/Graphic Novels:
(With Aaron McGruder and Kyle Baker) *Birth of a Nation,* Crown, 2004.
Black Panther, Marvel Comics, 2004–2005.

OTHER SOURCES

Books:
Contemporary Black Biography, Vol. 9, Gale Research, 1995.

Periodicals:
Entertainment Weekly, July 23, 2004, p. 81.
Essence, November, 2005, p. 86.
Film Comment, May/June, 1990, pp. 65–69.
Newsweek, December 26, 2001, p. 21.
New York Times, July 26, 1992, pp. H9, H12–13.

J–K

JAMES, Peter Francis 1956–

PERSONAL

Born September 16, 1956, in Chicago, IL.

Addresses: *Agent*—Abrams Artists Agency, 9200 Sunset Blvd., Suite 1130, Los Angeles, CA 90069.

Career: Actor.

Awards, Honors: Black Reel Award nomination, network or cable—best supporting actor, 2003, for *The Rosa Parks Story;* Drama Desk Award (with others), outstanding ensemble performance, 2006, for *Stuff Happens;* Obie Award, performance, *Village Voice,* 2006, Lucille Lortel Award, outstanding lead actor, League of Off–Broadway Theatres and Producers, 2007, both for *Stuff Happens;* Obie Award for *The Maids.*

CREDITS

Film Appearances:
Various roles, *Coriolanus,* 1979.
Lawrence, *Montana* (also known as *Nothing Personal*), Columbia TriStar, 1998.
Man at party, *Joe Gould's Secret,* USA Films, 2000.
Marc Forrest, *The Pack,* 2007.

Television Appearances; Series:
Blake Stevens, *As the World Turns,* 1989–1990.
Judge Kevin Beck, *Law & Order: Special Victims Unit* (also known as *Law & Order: SVU* and *Special Victims Unit*), NBC, 2000.
Joe Morgan, *The Guiding Light* (also known as *Guiding Light*), CBS, 2000.

Television Appearances; Miniseries:
Isaac Coles, *The Wedding* (also known as *Oprah Winfrey Presents "The Wedding"*), 1998.

Television Appearances; Movies:
Edmund Tyrone, *Long Day's Journey Into Night,* 1982.
Janitor, *The Cabinet of Dr. Ramirez,* PBS, 1991.
Dr. Broyard, *Ruby Bridges,* ABC, 1998.
Martin Holly, *Double Platinum,* ABC, 1999.
Alfred Livingston, *Love Song,* MTV, 2000.
Raymond Parks, *The Rosa Parks Story,* CBS, 2002.

Television Appearances; Specials:
Horatio, *Hamlet,* PBS, 1990.
Announcer, *Master of the Martial Arts Presented by Wesley Snipes,* TNT, 1998.

Television Appearances; Episodic:
Thurgood Marshall, "Simple Justice," *The American Experience,* PBS, 1993.
Mr. Connel, "Quid Pro Quo," *New York Undercover* (also known as *Uptown Undercover*), CBS, 1998.
Voice, *Courage the Cowardly Dog* (animated), Cartoon Network, 1999.
Dr. Piskell, "Men," *Third Watch,* NBC, 2000.
Jahfree Neema, "A Failure to Communicate," *Oz,* HBO, 2003.
Jahfree Neema, "4giveness," *Oz,* HBO, 2003.
Jahfree Neema, "A Day in the Death," *Oz,* HBO, 2003.
Jahfree Neema, "Exeunt Omnes," *Oz,* HBO, 2003.

Stage Appearances:
Octavious Caesar, *Julius Caesar,* Anspacher Theatre, Public Theatre, New York City, 1979.
Various roles and understudy lieutenant, *Coriolanus,* Delacorte Theatre, New York City, 1979.
Understudy various roles, *The American Clock,* Biltmore Theatre, New York City, 1980.
Edmund Tyrone, *Long Day's Journey Into Night,* Anspacher Theatre, Public Theatre, 1981.

Halberdier/Lovell, *King Richard III,* Delacorte Theatre, 1983.

Henry, *The Skin of Our Teeth,* Classic Stage Company Theatre (CSC), New York City, 1986.

Benvolio, *Romeo and Juliet,* Anspacher Theatre, Public Theatre, 1988.

Landolfo, *Enrico V,* Union Square Theatre, New York City, 1988–89.

Pisanio, *Cymbeline,* Estelle R. Newman Theatre, Public Theatre, New York City, 1989.

Horatio, *Hamlet,* Anspacher Theatre, Public Theatre, 1990.

Clitandre, *The Learned Ladies,* CSC Theatre, 1991.

Mr. Lewis, "Secrets," and Dr. Green, "I'm Not Stupid," *Young Playwrights Festival 1991,* Playwrights Horizons Theatre, New York City, 1991.

Provost, *Measure for Measure,* Delacorte Theatre, 1993.

Claire, *The Maids,* CSC Theatre, 1993.

Jupiter, *Amphitryon,* CSC Theatre, 1995.

Aenas, *Troilus and Cressida,* Delacorte Theatre, 1995.

Man and Baron Docteur, *Venus,* Martinson Hall, Public Theatre, New York City, 1996.

Ventidius, *Antony and Cleopatra,* Anspacher Theatre, Public Theatre, 1997.

Captain Byers, *Judgment at Nuremberg,* Longacre Theatre, New York City, 2001.

Pisanio, *Cymbeline,* Lucille Lortel Theatre, New York City, 2002.

Robert Alexander Trigor, *Drowning Crow,* Manhattan Theatre Club, New York City, 2004.

Don Pedro, *Much Ado About Nothing,* Delacorte Theatre, 2004.

Bill Ray, *On Golden Pond,* Cort Theatre, New York City, 2005.

Colin Powell, *Stuff Happens,* Public Theatre, New York City, 2006.

Also appeared in *Gem of the Ocean* and *Midsummer,* both Los Angeles.

Stage Director:
The Misanthrope, Classic Stage Company Theatre (CSC), New York City, 1995.

_____

JENKINS, Paul

PERSONAL

Born in Philadelphia, PA.

Career: Actor.

CREDITS

Film Appearances:
Tony, *The Organization,* Metro–Goldwyn–Mayer, 1971.

James Brower, *One Is the Lonely Number* (also known as *Two Is a Happy Number*), Metro–Goldwyn–Mayer, 1972.

Policeman, *Chinatown,* Paramount, 1974.

Television stage manager, *Network,* Metro–Goldwyn–Mayer, 1976.

Dr. Royston, *I Never Promised You a Rose Garden,* New World Pictures, 1977.

Sean Daniels, *Night Games* (also known as *Jeux erotiques de nuit* and *Love Games*), AVCO Embassy Pictures, 1980.

Hawker, *Hard to Hold,* Universal, 1984.

Playtronics lobby guard, *Sneakers,* Universal, 1992.

Bukowski, *Great Poets Die ...,* (short), 1997.

Television Appearances; Series:
Professor Parks, *The Waltons,* CBS, 1974–76.

Ed, *Dynasty,* ABC, 1981.

Television Appearances; Miniseries:
Dance emcee, *The Last Convertible,* NBC, 1979.

Television Appearances; Movies:
Deputy, *Outrage!,* ABC, 1973.

Paul Martinson, *Fear on Trial,* CBS, 1975.

Terry, *The November Plan,* 1976.

Lieutenant Kevin O'Malley, *Law & Order,* NBC, 1976.

District attorney Edison, *Mrs. R's Daughter,* NBC, 1979.

Bob Paikowski, *I Take These Men* (also known as *Surprise, Surprise!*), CBS, 1983.

Steelworker, *Heart of a Champion: The Ray Mancini Story,* CBS, 1985.

Lawrence Newman, *Winchell,* HBO, 1998.

Nan's father, *Minotaur,* Sci–Fi Channel, 2006.

Television Appearances; Pilots:
Al Stabile, *The Marcus–Nelson Murders* (movie; also known as *Kojak: "The Marcus–Nelson Murders"*), CBS, 1973.

Teddy Durham, *The Imposter* (movie), NBC, 1975.

Montvallier, *Panache,* ABC, 1976.

Television Appearances; Episodic:
Sergeant Baker, "The Moose," *M*A*S*H,* CBS, 1972.

"Lost Sunday," *Mannix,* CBS, 1972.

Jake, *The Young and the Restless* (also known as *Y&R*), CBS, 1973.

Clive, "All the Dead Were Strangers," *Mannix,* CBS, 1973.

Joe Wilson, "Something in the Woodwork," *Night Gallery* (also known as *Rod Serling's "Night Gallery"*), NBC, 1973.

Glenn, "Heartbreak Keith," *The Partridge Family,* ABC, 1973.

Charlie Durand, "The Twenty–Four Karat Plague," *The Streets of San Francisco,* ABC, 1973.

Charlie Durand, "The Twenty–Five Caliber Plague," *The Streets of San Francisco,* ABC, 1974.

Timmy Oakes, "The Only Way Out," *Kojak,* CBS, 1974.

Towers, "Death Watch," *The Rookies,* ABC, 1974.

Chet, "The Prisoner," *Cannon,* CBS, 1974.

Stan Gorrick, "Profit and Loss: Profit," *The Rockford Files* (also known as *Jim Rockford, Private Investigator*), NBC, 1974.

Simon Lloyd, "The Farnsworth Stratagem," *The Rockford Files* (also known as *Jim Rockford, Private Investigator*), NBC, 1975.

Martin Spetler, "The Games Children Play," *Cannon,* CBS, 1975.

"Day of Execution," *The Manhunter,* CBS, 1975.

Dan Purcell, "The Plastic Connection," *Caribe,* ABC, 1975.

Tom Jenkins, "Fool's Dare," *Isis* (also known as *The Secret of Isis*), CBS, 1975.

Ludford, "Mister Five and Dime," *Harry O,* ABC, 1976.

"A Slight Case of Murder," *The Blue Knight,* CBS, 1976.

"Odyssey of Death: Parts 1 & 2," *Police Story,* NBC, 1976.

Barney, "Monster Manor," *Police Story,* NBC, 1976.

Gareth Hudson, "The Trouble with Warren," *The Rockford Files* (also known as *Jim Rockford, Private Investigator*), NBC, 1976.

Bill Goodson, "I Love You, Rosey Malone," *Starsky and Hutch,* ABC, 1977.

Jack Efros, "Scandal," *Lou Grant,* CBS, 1978.

Boyle, "Off the Record," *Mrs. Columbo* (also known as *Kate Columbo, Kate Loves a Mystery,* and *Kate the Detective*), NBC, 1979.

Kirby, "Blackout," *Lou Grant,* CBS, 1980.

Kenny the bartender, "The Shadow of Death," *Quincy M.E.* (also known as *Quincy*), NBC, 1982.

Roger Johnson, "The New Man," *Tales from the Darkside,* syndicated, 1984.

Lawson, "Think Blue," *Hunter,* NBC, 1985.

Anthony Martin, *Lime Street,* ABC, 1985.

Older bearded trucker, "Dead Run," *The Twilight Zone,* CBS, 1986.

Duncan Parker, "The Last Laugh," *Falcon Crest,* CBS, 1989.

Detective, "Twice Victim," *Knots Landing,* CBS, 1989.

District attorney, "Devil on My Shoulder," *Knots Landing,* CBS, 1990.

Gavin Malloy, "Flashpoint," *Walker, Texas Ranger* (also known as *Walker*), CBS, 1996.

Reporter, *Michael Hayes,* CBS, 1997.

Detective Kate, "The Inmates," *Ally McBeal,* Fox, 1998.

Desk cop, *Vengeance Unlimited,* ABC, 1998.

Father Carroll, "Rings of Saturn," *Party of Five,* Fox, 1999.

Martin Sheffield, "Access," *The West Wing,* NBC, 2004.

Father Pat McGuire, "Yo, Adrian," *Cold Case,* CBS, 2005.

Also appeared in "B. J. and the Seven Lady Truckers," *B. J. and the Bear,* NBC.

JO-JO 1990–
(JoJo, Joanna Levesque, Jojo Levesque)

PERSONAL

Full name, Joanna Noelle Levesque; born December 20, 1990, in Brattleboro, VT; daughter of Joel Levesque and Diana Blagden (a cleaning lady, a church soloist, and theater performer).

Addresses: *Agent*—International Creative Management, 10250 Constellation Way, 9th Floor, Los Angeles, CA 90067.

Career: Actress and singer.

Awards, Honors: Teen Choice Award nomination, movies—choice breakout (female), 2006, for *Aquamarine.*

CREDITS

Film Appearances:

(As JoJo) Young Elizabeth, *Developing Sheldon,* 2002.

Herself, *Robin Williams: A Family Affair* (documentary short), Sony Pictures Home Entertainment, 2006.

Herself, *JoJo: The Pop Princess* (documentary short), Sony Pictures Home Entertainment, 2006.

Herself, *Barry Sonnenfeld: The Kosher Cowboy* (documentary short), Sony Pictures Home Entertainment, 2006.

Hailey, *Aquamarine,* Twentieth Century–Fox, 2006.

Cassie Munro, *RV* (also known as *RV: Runaway Vacation* and *Die chaoscamper RV*), Columbia, 2006.

Television Appearances; Specials:

(As JoJo) *The Teen Choice Awards 2004,* Fox, 2004.

(As JoJo) *MTV Video Music Awards 2004,* MTV, 2004.

Performer, *Jingle Ball Rock,* Fox, 2004.

The 2004 Radio Music Awards, NBC, 2004.

(As JoJo) Co–host, *Hope Rocks: The Concert with a Cause,* 2005.

(As Joanna Levesque) *The 2005 Teen Choice Awards,* Fox, 2005.

(As Joanna Levesque) *American Top 40 Live,* Fox, 2005.

(As JoJo) *The JammX Kids All Star Dance Special,* 2006.

(As Joanna Levesque) *The Second JammX Kids All Star Dance Special,* 2006.

(As JoJo) *A Capitol Fourth,* 2006.

(As JoJo) Presenter, *The 2006 American Music Awards,* 2006.

(As Joanna Levesque) Music performer, *The 2006 Miss Teen USA Pageant,* NBC, 2006.

(As Jojo Levesque) *Reel Comedy: RV,* 2006.

Television Appearances; Episodic:

(As JoJo) Herself, "Oatmeal," *Kids Say the Darndest Things,* CBS, 1998.

(As JoJo) Contestant, *Destination Stardom* (also known as *From Hawaii ... Destination Stardom*), 1999, 2000.

(As JoJo) Michelle, "Bernie Mac Dance Party," *The Bernie Mac Show,* Fox, 2002.

(As JoJo) Young Linda Rondstadt, "Tidings of Comfort and Joy," *American Dreams* (also known as *Our Generation*), NBC, 2004.

(As JoJo) *On–Air with Ryan Seacrest,* syndicated, 2004.

(As JoJo) *G–giga.de* (also known as *Giga Green* and *NBC Giga*), 2004.

(As JoJo) *Total Request Live* (also known as *TRL* and *Total Request Live with Carson Daly*), MTV, 2004, 2006.

(As JoJo) *The Tony Danza Show,* syndicated, 2004.

(As JoJo) Performer, *America's Most Talented Kid* (also known as *America's Most Talented Kid*), NBC, 2004.

(As JoJo) *This Morning* (also known as *This Morning with Richard and Judy*), ITV, 2004.

(As Joanna Levesque) *Punk'd,* MTV, 2004.

(As JoJo) *Top of the Pops Saturday,* BBC, 2004.

(As JoJo) *Best Hit USA,* 2004.

(As JoJo) *Live with Regis and Kelly,* syndicated, 2004, 2006.

(As JoJo) Musical guest, *The VIP,* 2005.

(As JoJo) Herself, "Swine Song," *Skunked TV,* 2005.

(As JoJo) "Secrets of Music Superstars," *The Tyra Banks Show,* UPN, 2006.

(As JoJo) *The Tonight Show with Jay Leno* (also known as *Jay Leno*), NBC, 2006.

(As JoJo) *Ellen: The Ellen DeGenres Show,* syndicated, 2006.

(As JoJo) *The Megan Mullally Show,* syndicated, 2006.

(As JoJo) *The View,* ABC, 2006.

RECORDINGS

Albums:

Jojo, Universal, 2004.

The High Road, Blackground/Universal, 2006.

JONES, Eddie 1955–

PERSONAL

Born 1955, in Washington, PA; married Anita Khanzadian (a director). *Education:* Studied acting.

Addresses: *Agent*—Martin Gage, The Gage Group, 14724 Ventura Blvd., Suite 505, Sherman Oaks, CA 91403.

Career: Actor. Worked at a service station in Los Angeles.

CREDITS

Film Appearances:

Blackie, *Bloodbrothers* (also known as *A Father's Love*), Warner Bros., 1978.

Lieutenant Olson, *On the Yard,* Midwest, 1978.

Officer Curdy, *The First Deadly Sin,* Filmways Pictures, 1980.

Ned Chippy, *Prince of the City,* Warner Bros., 1981.

Watchman, *Q* (also known as *Q: The Winged Serpent, Serpent,* and *The Winged Serpent*), United Film Distribution, 1982.

Jack Peurifoy, *When the Mountains Tremble* (documentary), New Yorker Films, 1983.

Third police officer, *Trading Places,* Paramount, 1983.

Chief O'Brien, *C.H.U.D.,* New World Pictures, 1984.

Cassidy, *Invasion U.S.A.,* Cannon, 1985.

Charlie McWilliams, *The New Kids* (also known as *Striking Back*), Columbia, 1985.

William McKenna, *Year of the Dragon,* Metro–Goldwyn–Mayer, 1985.

Police patient, *The Believers,* Orion, 1987.

Tom Kelly, *Apprentice to Murder,* New World Pictures, 1988.

Sean Katz, *American Blue Note* (also known as *Fakebook*), Panorama Entertainment, 1989.

Benny, *Cadillac Man,* Orion, 1990.

Mintz, *The Grifters,* Miramax, 1990.

Mr. Hagen, *Stanley & Iris,* Metro–Goldwyn–Mayer, 1990.

Malcolm, *The Rocketeer,* Buena Vista, 1991.

Buddy Wallace, *Sneakers,* Universal, 1992.

Dave Hooch, *A League of Their Own,* Columbia, 1992.

Johnny the landlord, *Conversations,* 1994.

Earl, *Dancer, Texas Pop. 81,* TriStar, 1998.

Father Reilly, *Tru Friends,* 1998.

Emmett McFadden, *Return to Me* (also known as *Distance Calls, Dos vidas contigo, Droit au coeur, Feitico do coracao, Hechizo del corazon, Palaa luokseni, Regressa para mim, Reviens–moi,* and *Zurueck zu dir*), Metro–Goldwyn–Mayer, 2000.

Moonglow bartender, *The Singing Detective* (musical), Paramount Classics, 2003.

Samuel Riddle, *Seabiscuit,* Universal, 2003.

Salchak, *The Terminal,* DreamWorks, 2004.

Marty Goldberg, *Fighting Tommy Riley,* Freestyle Releasing, 2005.

Sheriff Bo Stevens, *Disconnect,* Dreamscape Cinema, 2005.

Harold, *Angst,* Dreamscape Cinema, 2006.

Television Appearances; Series:
Dr. Matt Steele, *Young Dr. Malone,* NBC, 1961.
Sam Evans and Bailiff Henry Evans, *Dark Shadows* (also known as *Dark Shadows Revival* and *La malediction de Collinwood),* NBC, 1991.
Jonathan Kent, *Lois & Clark: The New Adventures of Superman* (also known as *Lois & Clark* and *The New Adventures of Superman),* ABC, 1993–97.
Charles "the Official" Borden, *The Invisible Man* (also known as *I–Man, El hombre, Invisible Man—Der Unsichtbare,* and *Naekymaetoen mies),* Sci–Fi Channel, 2000–2002.

Provided the voice of Sam for the English version of *The Big O* (anime; also known as *Big O* and *The Big O II),* Cartoon Network, originally broadcast on Sun TV.

Television Appearances; Miniseries:
Sweeney, *Doubletake,* CBS, 1985.
Barney Koster, *I'll Take Manhattan,* CBS, 1987.
Jim Fitzgerald, *The Kennedys of Massachusetts,* ABC, 1990.

Television Appearances; Movies:
Captain, *Case Closed* (also known as *Death by Diamonds),* CBS, 1988.
Detective Mike Devlin, *She Was Marked for Murder,* NBC, 1988.
Edward "Matty" Mattingly, *Kojak: Flowers for Matty* (also known as *Flowers for Matty),* ABC, 1990.
Detective Harry Boland, *Us,* CBS, 1991.
C. D. Holloway, *The Positively True Adventures of the Alleged Texas Cheerleader–Murdering Mom,* HBO, 1993.
Commissioner Fisette, *The Return of Ironside,* NBC, 1993.
Detective Ayers, *Final Appeal* (also known as *L'ultime proces),* NBC, 1993.
Victim of Love: The Shannon Mohr Story (also known as *Crimes of Passion: Victim of Love),* NBC, 1993.
Lieutenant Byrnes (some sources cite Lieutenant Jones), *Ed McBain's "87th Precinct: Lightning"* (also known as *Ed McBain's "87th Precinct"),* NBC, 1995.
Mac Brophy, *Body Language,* 1995.
Wilson Hartwick, *Letter to My Killer,* USA Network, 1995.
Secretary of War Edwin McMasters Stanton, *The Day Lincoln Was Shot,* TNT, 1998.
Judge Prestwich, *Stranger in My House* (also known as *Total Stranger),* Lifetime, 1999.

Television Appearances; Episodic:
Michael O'Rourke, "Original Sin," *Spenser: For Hire,* ABC, 1985.
Howard Winslow, "Joyride," *The Equalizer,* CBS, 1986.
J. D. Hayes, "Company Man," *Spenser: For Hire,* ABC, 1988.

Lieutenant Brannigan, "Heart of Justice," *The Equalizer,* CBS, 1989.
Lieutenant Brannigan, "Past Imperfect," *The Equalizer,* CBS, 1989.
Lieutenant Brannigan, "Silent Fury," *The Equalizer,* CBS, 1989.
Lieutenant Brannigan, "The Visitation," *The Equalizer,* CBS, 1989.
Benjamin Taylor, "Man behind the Badge," *The Young Riders,* ABC, 1990.
Dr. Frank, "The Chickens Come Home to Roost," *Grand,* NBC, 1990.
Dr. Frank, "An Obtuse Triangle," *Grand,* NBC, 1990.
Dr. Frank, "One Way Out," *Grand,* NBC, 1990.
Gus Zaret, "The Inquisition," *WIOU,* CBS, 1990.
Chief Colin Young, "The Assassination: Parts 1 & 2," *Matlock,* NBC, 1992.
Dr. Kluger, "The Magnificent Six," *Cheers,* NBC, 1992.
Ed Stewart, "Blindside," *Bodies of Evidence,* CBS, 1993.
Himself, "Maxwell Said Knock You Out," *In the House,* UPN, 1996.
Noah, "Last Call," *Touched by an Angel,* CBS, 1997.
Mr. Merrin, "Naming Names," *Party of Five,* Fox, 1998.
"Temptation and Responsibility," *Hyperion Bay,* The WB, 1998.
"Truth or Consequences," *Hyperion Bay,* The WB, 1999.
"Young and on Fire," *Hyperion Bay,* The WB, 1999.
Himself, "Living Design/Eco: Environmental Consciousness," *It's Christopher Lowell* (also known as *The Christopher Lowell Show),* The Discovery Channel, 2002.
Judge Wells, "The Long Goodbye," *Judging Amy,* CBS, 2003.
Judge Wells, "Dancing in the Dark," *Judging Amy,* CBS, 2004.
Judge Wells, "Disposable," *Judging Amy,* CBS, 2004.
Himself, "Action Heroes," *My First Time,* TV Land, 2005.
Pete O'Malley, "It Happened One Night," *Crossing Jordan* (also known as *Untitled Tim Kring Project),* NBC, 2005.

Appeared in other programs, including an appearance as Arnie Kellogg, *EZ Streets,* CBS; and as Marvin Klein, *Michael Hayes,* CBS. Appeared in "The Least Wonderful Time of the Year," an unaired episode of *To Have & to Hold,* CBS.

Television Appearances; Pilots:
Victor Muldoon, "Trick or Treat (Pilot)," *Tales from the Darkside,* syndicated, 1983.
Gus Zaret, *WIOU,* CBS, 1990.
Sam Evans, *Dark Shadows* (also known as *Dark Shadows Revival* and *La malediction de Collinwood),* NBC, 1991.
Jonathan Kent, *Lois & Clark: The New Adventures of Superman* (also known as *Lois & Clark* and *The New Adventures of Superman),* ABC, 1993.

Charles "the Official" Borden, *The Invisible Man* (also known as *I–Man, El hombre, Invisible Man—Der Unsichtbare,* and *Naekymaetoen mies*), Sci–Fi Channel, 2000.

Older man, *Ghost Whisperer,* CBS, 2005.

Stage Appearances:

That Championship Season, Booth Theatre, New York City, 1974.

Ellis, *Curse of the Starving Class,* New York Shakespeare Festival, Public Theater, Estelle R. Newman Theater, New York City, 1978.

Mike, *The Ruffian on the Stair,* South Street Theatre, New York City, 1978.

Sheriff George McKinstry, *Devour the Snow,* John Golden Theatre, New York City, 1979.

Ellis, *Curse of the Starving Class,* Studio Arena Theatre, Buffalo, NY, 1980.

An Act of Kindness, Harold Clurman Theatre, New York City, 1980.

Hal, *Big Apple Messenger,* Workshop of the Players Art Theatre, New York City, 1981.

Jass, New Dramatists Theatre, New York City, 1981.

Dr. Joe Quigly, *The Freak,* Douglas Fairbanks Theatre, New York City, 1982.

Tarsh, *Maiden Stakes,* St. Clement's Theatre, New York City, 1982.

Whitaker Chambers, *Knights Errant,* INTAR Theatre, New York City, 1982.

A Touch of the Poet, Whole Theatre Company, Montclair, NJ, 1982.

Edwin, "Slacks," *Triple Feature,* Stage 73, Manhattan Theatre Club, New York City, 1983.

Ed Burke, *Burkie,* Hudson Guild Theatre, New York City, 1984.

Weston, *Curse of the Starving Class,* INTAR Theatre, 1985, then Promenade Theatre, New York City, 1985–86.

Dee, "Pilgrim," *Sorrows and Sons,* Vineyard Theatre, New York City, 1986.

Alan, *The Downside,* Long Wharf Theatre, New Haven, CT, 1987.

Leonard Christofferson, "The Tablecloth of Turin," *Bigfoot Stole My Wife,* Manhattan Punch Line, New York City, 1987.

Gordon Tate, *April Snow,* Manhattan Theatre Club Stage II, New York City, 1988.

Dad, *The Dreamer Examines His Pillow,* McCadden Place Theatre, Hollywood, CA, beginning 2007.

Also appeared in other productions, including *The Skirmishers,* Interact Theatre Company, actor. Apprentice for summer stock productions.

OTHER SOURCES

Periodicals:
TV Zone, March, 2001, pp. 46–49.

JORDAN, Claudia 1973–

PERSONAL

Born April 12, 1973, in Providence, RI. *Education:* Studied broadcasting and journalism at Baldwin Wallace College. *Avocational Interests:* Cooking.

Addresses: *Agent*—Identity Talent Agency, 9107 Wilshire Blvd., Suite 450, Beverly Hills, CA 90210.

Career: Actress and model. Appeared in television commercials, including Coors Light beer, Sears department stores, Pepsi products, and Visa. Previously worked at *Providence American* newspaper and WHDH–TV, Boston, MA. Miss Rhode Island Teen USA, 1990; Miss Rhode Island USA, 1997.

CREDITS

Film Appearances:
Trippin', October Films, 1999.

Pretty woman at party, *Retiring Tatiana,* Tapeworm Video Distributors, 2000.

Simone lookalike, *S1m0ne,* New Line Cinema, 2002.

Nora's Hair Salon, DEJ Productions, 2004.

Television Appearances; Series:
Guest correspondent, *The Best Damn Sports Show Period,* Fox Sports, 2001.

Model, *The Price Is Right,* CBS, 2001–2003.

Entertainment reporter, *54321,* 2003.

Cohost, *Modern Girl's Guide to Life,* 2003.

Correspondent, *Livin' Large,* 2004–2005.

Model number nine, *Deal or No Deal,* NBC, 2005—.

Television Appearances; Movies:
Sexy lady, *Little Richard,* NBC, 2000.

Television Appearances; Specials:
(Uncredited) Model, *The Price Is Right 30th Anniversary Special,* CBS, 2002.

(Uncredited) Model, *The Price Is Right Primetime Specials,* CBS, 2002.

(Uncredited) Model, *The Price Is Right Million Dollar Spectacular,* CBS, 2003.

Presenter, *The 9th Annual Soul Train Lady of Soul Awards,* The WB, 2003.

Judge, *Miss Universe 2006 Pageant,* NBC, 2006.

Television Appearances; Episodic:
Vanessa, "Movin' On Up," *City Guys,* NBC, 1999.

Natasha, "Lovers and Other Strangers," *Jack & Jill,* The WB, 2000.

(Uncredited) Model, *The New Price Is Right,* CBS, 2001, 2003.

Herself, *The Bold and the Beautiful* (also known as *Belleza y poder*), CBS, 2002.

Dog Eat Dog (game show), 2002.

Herself, "Goodbye, Mr. Chips," *One on One,* UPN, 2005.

Ms. Bonita, "They Work Hard for His Honey," *That's So Raven* (also known as *That's So Raven!*), Disney Channel, 2005.

The Big Idea with Donny Deutsch, CNBC, 2006, 2007.

Guest correspondent, *Ballers,* 2007.

RECORDINGS

Video Games:

Model, *Deal or No Deal* (also known as *Imagination DVD TV Games: "Deal or No Deal"*), Imagination Games, 2006.

Videos:

Girl, "Quit Playing Games with My Heart," *Backstreet Boys: All Access Video,* 1998.

OTHER SOURCES

Electronic:

Claudia Jordan Website, http://www.claudiajordan.net, July 20, 2007.

KAY, Stephen T.
(Stephen Kay, Stephen Thomas Kay)

PERSONAL

Addresses: *Agent*—International Creative Management, 10250 Constellation Way, 9th Floor, Los Angeles, CA 90067. *Manager*—Principal Entertainment, 1964 Westwood Blvd., Suite 400, Los Angeles, CA 90025.

Career: Actor, director, and writer. Appeared in television commercial for AT&T telecommunications.

CREDITS

Film Director:

(As Stephen Kay) *Two Over Easy* (short), 30–Minute Movie, 1994.

The Last Time I Committed Suicide, New City Releasing, 1997.

(As Stephen Kay) *Get Carter,* 2000.

(As Stephen Kay) *Boogeyman* (also known as *Boogeyman—Der schwarze mann*), Screen Gems, 2005.

Film Appearances:

Soldier numbert wo, *The Zero Boys,* Lightening Video, 1986.

Movie director, *Lethal Weapon 3,* Warner Bros., 1992.

Devon, *Angel 4: Undercover* (also known as *Angel 4: Assault with a Deadly Weapon*), LIVE Video, 1993.

Singer, *October 22,* Millennium Films, 1998.

Bald dude, Gilbert's pal, *The Mod Squad,* Metro–Goldwyn–Mayer, 1999.

(Uncredited) Man at party, *Get Carter,* Warner Bros., 2000.

(As Stephen Thomas Kay) Tony Pindella, *Angel Eyes* (also known as *Ojos de angel*), Warner Bros., 2001.

Television Work; Miniseries:

Executive producer, and director, *Fallen,* ABC Family, 2006.

Television Director; Movies:

Wasted, MTV, 2002.

(As Stephen Kay) *The Dead Will Tell,* CBS, 2004.

The Commuters, 2005.

The Hunt for the BTK Killer, CBS, 2005.

Television Director; Episodic:

(As Stephen Kay) "All In," *The Shield,* FX Channel, 2004.

"Ain't That a Shame," *The Shield,* FX Channel, 2005.

(As Stephen Kay) "Family," *Saved,* TNT, 2006.

(As Stephen Kay) "Who Do You Trust?," *Saved,* TNT, 2006.

(As Stephen Kay) "Code Zero," *Saved,* TNT, 2006.

(As Stephen Kay) "It's Different for Girls," *Friday Night Lights,* NBC, 2006.

(As Stephen Kay) "Blinders," *Friday Night Lights,* NBC, 2007.

Television Appearances; Series:

Reginald Jennings, a recurring character, *General Hospital,* ABC, 1992—.

Peter Rucker, *Deadly Games,* 1995–97.

Television Appearances; Movies:

Counselor, *Wasted,* MTV, 2002.

Television Appearances; Episodic:

(As Stephen Kay) Editor, "Going Limp," *thirtysomething,* ABC, 1990.

(As Stephen Kay) Ralph, "Permanent Wave—June 2, 1983," *Quantum Leap,* ABC, 1991.

Vincent Polaski, "Dead to Rights," *Murder, She Wrote,* CBS, 1993.

Ray Gasner, *Moon Over Miami,* ABC, 1993.

Salesman, "Jack the Ripper," *Unhappily Ever After* (also known as *Unhappily ...*), The WB, 1995.

Darren Crosley, "Something Foul in Flappieville," *Murder, She Wrote,* CBS, 1996.

Dr. Lachman, "Love, Death & Soda," *The Home Court,* NBC, 1996.

Hawkins, "Fight or Flight," *Party of Five,* Fox, 1997.

"Vanessa Marcil," *Intimate Portrait,* Lifetime, 2003.

WRITINGS

Screenplays (as Stephen Kay):
Two Over Easy (short), 30–Minute Movie, 1994.
The Last Time I Committed Suicide, New City Releasing, 1997.
The Mod Squad, Metro–Goldwyn–Mayer, 1999.

KELLY, Brendan 1964–

PERSONAL

Full name, Brendan Joseph Kelly; born September 28, 1964, in Dublin, Ireland; married Sandra Saraya Salvador; children: four.

Addresses: *Manager*—Allman/Rea Management, 141 Barrington, Suite E, Los Angeles, CA 90049.

Career: Actor.

Awards, Honors: Audience Award, best short, Williamsburg Brooklyn Film Festival, 1999, for *Franky Goes to Hollywood.*

CREDITS

Film Appearances:
Nino Scrocco, *Sweet Lies,* 1988.
Hank Hansen, *Loser* (also known as *"Loser": The Movie*), Animas Pictures, 1991.
Guard Cone, *Malcolm X* (also known as *X*), Warner Bros., 1992.
Ray, *Fly by Night,* 1993.
Big Chief, *Clockers,* MCA/Universal, 1995.
Norman, Terell's chauffeur, *Devil in a Blue Dress,* TriStar, 1995.
Private Cox, *The Rock,* Buena Vista, 1996.

Teddy, *The Devil's Own,* Columbia, 1997.
Conrad, *Con Air,* Buena Vista, 1997.
Sergei, *The Lizzie McGuire Movie,* Buena Vista, 2003.
Mad Dog, *Cellular* (also known as *Final Call—Wenn er auflegt, muss sie sterben*), New Line Cinema, 2004.
Mr. George, *Victim,* 2007.

Film Work:
Director and producer, *Franky Goes to Hollywood* (short), Warner Home Video, 1999.

Television Appearances; Series:
Mike Savage, *Acapulco H.E.A.T.,* syndicated, 1993–94.

Television Appearances; Movies:
Lovey Norris, *Jesse Stone: Death in Paradise,* CBS, 2006.

Television Appearances; Pilots:
Mike Mooney, *Hollywood Confidential* (movie), UPN, 1997.
Drug enforcement agent Joe Vacco, *Wanted,* TNT, 2005.

Television Appearances; Episodic:
Lex Monroe, "Tarzan and the Deadly Cargo," *Tarzan,* syndicated, 1993.
Lex Monroe, "Tarzan and the Jewel of Justice," *Tarzan,* syndicated, 1994.
Charlie, "Diefenbaker's Day off," *Due South* (also known as *Direction: Sud*), CTV and CBS, 1994.
Harry Donovan, "Knock You Out," *New York Undercover* (also known as *Uptown Undercover*), Fox, 1995.
Ollie Stenzel, "No Good Deed," *Big Apple,* CBS, 2001.
Wolfgang Cutler, "Impotence," *Oz,* HBO, 2002.
Wolfgang Cutler, "See No Evil, Hear No Evil, Smell No Evil," *Oz,* HBO, 2002.
Wolfgang Cutler, "Sonata da Oz," *Oz,* HBO, 2002.
Wolfgang Cutler, "A Failure to Communicate," *Oz,* HBO, 2002.
Gavin Loughery, "The Vision Thing," *NYPD Blue,* ABC, 2004.
Gerry McCourt, "Death Goes On," *Crossing Jordan,* NBC, 2005.

KELLY, Joanne 1980–

PERSONAL

Born 1980, in Newfoundland, Canada. *Education:* Acadia University, B.A., drama and English, 2000; studied voice, acting, movement, and dance; attended workshops.

Addresses: *Agent*—Fountainhead Talent, Inc., 131 Davenport Rd., Toronto, Ontario M5R 1H8, Canada. *Manager*—Burstein Company, 15304 Sunset Blvd., Suite 208, Pacific Palisades, CA 90272.

Career: Actress.

Member: Alliance of Canadian Cinema, Television and Radio Artists.

Awards, Honors: Gemini Award nomination, best performance by an actress in a leading role in a dramatic program or miniseries, Academy of Canadian Cinema and Television, 2006, for *Playing House;* won a provincial gold medal in badminton and a provincial silver medal in volleyball.

CREDITS

Film Appearances:
Madonna Brassaurd, *The Bay of Love and Sorrows* (also known as *La baie de l'amour et des regrets*), Odeon Films, 2002.
Slug (short film), 2002.
Sophie Nichols, *Crime Spree* (also known as *Wanted*), DEJ Productions/Alliance Atlantis Communications, 2003.
Sasha, *Going the Distance* (also known as *National Lampoon's "Going the Distance"*), Seville Pictures, 2004.
Julia, *Remembering Phil,* Prevalent Films, 2007.

Television Appearances; Series:
Liberty "Libby" Kaufman, *Jeremiah* (also known as *Jeremiah—Krieger des Donners*), Showtime and The Movie Network (Canada), beginning 2003.
Sarah, *Slings and Arrows,* The Movie Network (Canada), beginning 2005.
Sara Collins, *Vanished* (also known as *Kadotettu*), Fox, 2006–2007.

Appeared in *The Newsroom,* CBC.

Television Appearances; Miniseries:
Appeared as Nadia in *The Treasure of Ugarit.*

Television Appearances; Movies:
Loreena, *Mafia Doctor* (also known as *El doctor de la familia* and *O doutor da Mafia*), CBS, 2003.
Jenna Breeden, *Whiskey Echo* (also known as *Whiskey echo*), CBC, 2005.
Joanna Parks, *Solar Strike* (also known as *Solar Attack*), Sci–Fi Channel, 2005.
Simone, *Selling Innocence,* CTV (Canada), 2005.

Frannie Mackenzie, *Playing House* (also known as *Un mere a l'epreuve*), CTV (Canada) and Lifetime, 2006.
Kelly, *I Am an Apartment Building,* Bravo!FACT, 2006.
Laurie Dwyer, *Heyday!,* CBC, 2006.

Television Appearances; Specials:
Appeared as Strato and young Cato, *Julius Caesar,* Bravo! (Canada).

Television Appearances; Episodic:
Kim, "The Future Revealed," *Mutant X,* syndicated, 2002.
Mata Hari, "Secrets and Lies," *Mentors,* Family Channel (Canada), 2002.
Zareth, "Remember When," *Tracker,* syndicated, 2002.
Zareth, "To Catch a Dessarian," *Tracker,* City TV and syndicated, 2002.
Trudy Jennings, "Sisters," *Snakes & Ladders,* CBC, 2004.
Bianca, "Bad Blood," *The Dresden Files,* Sci–Fi Channel, 2007.
Bianca, "Storm Front," *The Dresden Files,* Sci–Fi Channel, 2007.

Appeared in other programs, including *Largo Winch* (also known as *Largo Winch—Gefaehrliches Erbe* and *Largon kosto*).

Television Appearances; Pilots:
Jesse Peretz, *The Catch,* ABC, 2005.
Sara Collins, *Vanished* (also known as *Kadotettu*), Fox, 2006.

Stage Appearances:
Carol, *Oleanna,* Castaway Horse, Theatre Passe Muraille Backspace, Toronto, Ontario, Canada, 2004.

Appeared as Mariana, *Measure for Measure,* as Starveling and an understudy for Hermia, *A Midsummer Night's Dream,* and as a servant and a soldier, *Romeo and Juliet,* all Shakespeare by the Sea; as Strato and young Cato, *Julius Caesar;* as a witch, *Macbeth,* Hurly-Burly Theatre Company, New York City; as a servant and soldier, *Romeo and Juliet,* Minack Theatre, Cornwall, England; as Rachel, *Seven Stories,* Same Plan Co–op; and as Hagholzer, *The Visit.* Appeared as Portia, *Julius Caesar,* and as Mrs. Morgan Organ and Lilly Smalls, *Under Milk Wood,* both Acadia University Theatre Company.

Major Tours:
Appeared as Hagholzer, *The Visit,* English cities.

Stage Producer:
Oleanna, Castaway Horse, Theatre Passe Muraille Backspace, Toronto, Ontario, Canada, 2004.

KLEIN, Linda

PERSONAL

Career: Actress and producer. Registered nurse; medical producer and technical medical consultant for dozens of films, including *Bulworth, I Am Sam,* and *Ocean's Eleven,* and television programs, including series in which she appears as a nurse.

CREDITS

Television Appearances; Series:
Nurse Linda, *Nip/Tuck,* FX Network, 2003–2006.
Nurse Linda, a recurring role, *Grey's Anatomy,* ABC, 2005–2006.

Television Appearances; Pilots:
Operating room technician, *Chicago Hope,* CBS, 1994.
Nurse Linda, *Nip/Tuck,* FX Network, 2003.
Nurse, *Friday Night Lights,* NBC, 2006.

Television Appearances; Movies:
Nightingales, NBC, 1988.

Television Appearances; Episodic:
Nurse Klein, "Educating Janine," *Doogie Howser, M.D.,* ABC, 1992.
Nurse Klein, "Club Medicine," *Doogie Howser, M.D.,* ABC, 1992.
Nurse Klein, "There's a Riot Going On," *Doogie Howser, M.D.,* ABC, 1992.
Medical attendant, "True Confessions," *NYPD Blue,* ABC, 1993.
Emergency medical service paramedic, "Up on the Roof," *NYPD Blue,* ABC, 1994.
Second nurse, "Wild Irish Woes," *Brooklyn South,* CBS, 1997.
Third nurse, "The Heavens Can Wait," *Chicago Hope,* CBS, 1999.
Operating room nurse, "The Golden Hour," *Chicago Hope,* CBS, 1999.
Delivery room doctor, "The Trip," *Six Feet Under,* HBO, 2001.
Female corps member, "Adrift: Part 2," *JAG,* CBS, 2001.
Surgical nurse, "5:00 a.m.–6:00 a.m.," *24,* Fox, 2001.
Third nurse, "Chapter Eighteen," *Boston Public,* Fox, 2001.
Nurse, "Chapter Forty–Four," *Boston Public,* Fox, 2002.
Surgical nurse, "Time of Death," *MDs,* ABC, 2002.
Nurse, "Mr. Monk Takes Manhattan," *Monk,* USA Network, 2004.

Nurse, "What to Do While You're Waiting," *Friday Night Lights,* NBC, 2007.

Appeared as Nurse Duffy, *City of Angels,* CBS.

Television Work; Series:
Associate producer, *Chicago Hope,* CBS, c. 1999–2000.
Producer, *Grey's Anatomy,* ABC, 2007.

Film Appearances:
Nurse, *Hard to Kill* (also known as *Seven Year Storm*), 1990.
Third doctor, *Very Bad Things,* Polygram Films, 1998.
Chicago Hope paramedic, *Frankie and Johnny Are Married,* IFC Films, 2004.

WRITINGS

Television Episodes:
Writer for episodes of the series *Chicago Hope,* CBS.

KLOVES, Steve 1960–
(Steven Kloves)

PERSONAL

Born March 18, 1960, in Austin, TX; father, an aerospace engineer; mother, a teacher and former newspaper columnist; married Kathy Kloves (a writer and producer); children: Callie Blake, Christopher James. *Education:* Attended the University of California, Los Angeles.

Addresses: *Agent*—Creative Artists Agency, 2000 Avenue of the Stars, Los Angeles, CA 90067.

Career: Screenwriter and director. Previously worked delivering scripts for an agency.

Awards, Honors: Screen Award nomination, best screenplay written directly for the screen, Writers Guild of America, 1990, for *The Fabulous Baker Boys;* Sierra Award, best screenplay—adapted, Las Vegas Film Critics Society, Boston Society of Film Critics Award, best screenplay, 2000, Academy Award nomination, best writing—screenplay based on material previously produced or published, Screen Award nomination, best screenplay based on material previously produced or published, Writers Guild of America, Scripter Award (with Michael Chabon), University of Southern California, Online Film Critics Award nomination, best screenplay, ALFS Award nomination, screenwriter of the year, London Critics Circle Film Awards, Golden Globe Award nomination, best screenplay—motion picture, Chicago Film Critics Association Award nomination, best screenplay, Broadcast Film Critics Association Award, best screenplay—adapted, Film Award nomination, best screenplay—adapted, British Academy of Film and Television Arts, 2001, all for *Wonder Boys*; Children's Award nomination (with David Heyman and Chris Columbus), best feature film, British Academy of Film and Television Arts, 2002, for *Harry Potter and the Sorcerer's Stone*; Children's Award nomination (with Heyman and Columbus), best feature film, British Academy of Film and Television Arts, 2003, for *Harry Potter and the Chamber of Secrets*; Saturn Award nomination, best writer, Academy of Science Fiction, Fantasy and Horror Films, 2005, for *Harry Potter and the Prisoner of Azkaban*; Saturn Award nomination, best writing, Academy of Science Fiction, Fantasy and Horror Films, 2006, for *Harry Potter and the Goblet of Fire*.

CREDITS

Film Director:
(As Steven Kloves) *The Fabulous Baker Boys,* 1989.
Flesh and Bone, 1993.

Film Appearances:
Himself, *Conversation with J. K. Rowling and Steve Kloves* (documentary short), 2003.
Himself, *Creating the Vision* (documentary short), 2004.

WRITINGS

Screenplays:
(As Steven Kloves) *Racing with the Moon,* Paramount, 1984.
(As Steven Kloves) *The Fabulous Baker Boys,* Twentieth Century–Fox, 1989.
Flesh and Bone, Paramount, 1993.
Wonderboys (also known as *Die Wonder Boys* and *Wonderboys–lauter wunderknaben*), Paramount, 2000.
Harry Potter and the Sorcerer's Stone (also known as *Harry Potter and the Philosopher's Stone*), Warner Bros., 2001.
Harry Potter and the Chamber of Secrets (also known as *Harry Potter und die kammer des schreckens*), Warner Bros., 2002.
Harry Potter and the Prisoner of Azkaban, Warner Bros., 2004.
Harry Potter and the Goblet of Fire, Warner Bros., 2005.

KOENIG, Andrew 1968–
(Josh A. Koenig, Joshua Koenig)

PERSONAL

Full name, Joshua Andrew Koenig; born August 17, 1968, in Los Angeles, CA; son of Walter Koenig (an actor).

Career: Film editor, producer, director, writer, and actor. Happy Trailers HD, film editor for short trailers. Charles Whittman Reilly and Friends (improvisational group), performer in the Los Angeles area, including appearances at Second City Los Angeles and 10 West.

CREDITS

Television Appearances; Series:
(Sometimes credited as Josh A. Koenig or Joshua Koenig) Richard "Boner" Stabone, *Growing Pains,* ABC, 1985–89.
G.I. Joe (animated), syndicated, 1990.

Television Appearances; Episodic:
"Champagne High," *21 Jump Street,* Fox, 1988.
Jon, "You Can Count on Me," *My Two Dads,* NBC, 1989.
Tumak, "Sanctuary," *Star Trek: Seep Space Nine* (also known as *Deep Space Nine, DS9,* and *Star Trek: DS9*), syndicated, 1993.

Television Appearances; Other:
Second guy in locker room, *The Great O'Grady* (special), Showtime, 1993.
Scott, *The Theory of Everything* (movie), Trinity Broadcasting Network, 2006.

Television Work:
Film editor and director, *Good Boy* (movie), AMC, 2003.
Film editor, *White Space* (special), 2005.

Film Work:
Executive producer, director, and film editor, *Woman in a Green Dress* (short film), Monkey Go Lucky Entertainment Circle, 2004.
Director, *Instinct vs. Reason,* 2004.
Film editor, *Gonzo Utopia* (short documentary), Happy Trailers HD, 2006.
Film editor, *Jukebox: From Edison to Ipod* (short documentary), Happy Trailers HD, 2007.

Film Appearances:
The Joker, *Batman: Dead End* (short film), TheForce.Net, 2003.

RECORDINGS

Videos:
Fangoria's Weekend of Horrors, Media Home Entertainment, 1986.

WRITINGS

Films:
Woman in a Green Dress (short film), Monkey Go Lucky Entertainment Circle, 2004.

Television Movies:
Good Boy, AMC, 2003.

KORKES, Jon
(John Korkes)

PERSONAL

Career: Actor.

CREDITS

Film Appearances:
First burglar, *The Out of Towners,* Paramount, 1970.
Snowden, *Catch–22,* Paramount, 1970.
Kenny Newquist, *Little Murders,* Twentieth Century–Fox, 1971.
First Hawk, *Un Homme est mort* (also known as *The Outside Man, Funerale a Los Angeles,* and *A Man Is Dead*), United Artists, 1972.
Dental corpsman, *Cinderella Liberty,* Twentieth Century–Fox, 1973.
David, *The Day of the Dolphin,* AVCO Embassy Pictures, 1973.
Rudy Keppler of the *Chicago Examiner, The Front Page,* 1974.
Jeffrey, *Two–Minute Warning,* Universal, 1976.
Frank, *Between the Lines,* Midwest Films, 1977.
Dr. Paul Hendricks, *Jaws of Satan* (also known as *King Cobra*), Metro–Goldwyn–Mayer, 1981.
Sam, *Worth Winning,* Twentieth Century–Fox, 1989.
Tim Calhoun, *Syngenor,* Southgate Entertainment, 1990.
Fuzby Robinson, *Too Much Sun,* New Line Cinema, 1991.
Chemistry lab professor, *Getting Away with Murder,* Savoy Pictures, 1996.
Counselor, *Riding in Cars with Boys,* Columbia, 2001.

Film Work:
Director, *Who Was That Man* (short), 1998.

Television Appearances; Series:
Officer Tom Robinson, *Oz,* HBO, 2001–2003.

Television Appearances; Miniseries:
The Blue Knight, NBC, 1973.
Thad Crawford, *The Word,* CBS, 1978.

Television Appearances; Movies:
The Carpenters, 1974.
Randolph, *The Storyteller,* NBC, 1977.
Justice Department man, *Terrorist on Trial: The United States vs. Salim Ajami* (also known as *Hostile Witness* and *In the Hands of the Enemy*), CBS, 1988.
(As John Korkes) Jack Hudson, *Highway Heartbreaker,* CBS, 1992.

Television Appearances; Pilots:
Husband, *What's Alan Watching?,* CBS, 1989.

Television Appearances; Episodic:
Victor Koch, "The Different Ones," *Night Gallery* (also known as *Rod Serling's "Night Gallery"*), NBC, 1971.
Mr. Bradford, "Archie and the F.B.I.," *All in the Family,* CBS, 1972.
Officer Cosgrove, "The Ticket," *Maude,* CBS, 1972.
Beck Wilson, "Angels in the Snow," *Mary Tyler Moore* (also known as *The Mary Tyler Moore Show*), CBS, 1973.
Satch, "The Torch Man," *The Rookies,* ABC, 1975.
Terry Nash, "The Set–Up: Parts 1 & 2," *Starsky and Hutch,* ABC, 1977.
"Pistol Packing Enos," *Enos,* CBS, 1981.
Winston guy, "I See England, I See France, I See Maddie's Netherworld," *Moonlighting,* ABC, 1989.
Boomer Mason, "Heartbeat," *Homicide: Life on the Street* (also known as *Homicide*), NBC, 1995.
Stu, "My Name Is Asher Kingsley," *The Larry Sanders Show,* HBO, 1996.
Attorney for Burt Malone, "Narcosis," *Law & Order,* NBC, 2000.
Carl McFarland, *The Beat,* UPN, 2000.
Wally Sullivan, "A Ministering Angel," *Big Apple,* CBS, 2001.
Attorney Terence Moore, "Sacrifice," *Law & Order: Special Victims Unit* (also known as *Law & Order: SVU* and *Special Victims Unit*), NBC, 2001.
Ralph Bannerman, "Blink," *Law & Order: Criminal Intent* (also known as *Law & Order: CI*), NBC, 2003.
The Jury, Fox, 2004.

Stage Appearances:
Kenny Newquist, *Little Murders,* Circle in the Square Downtown, New York City, 1969.
(As John Korkes) Waldo, *The Carpenters,* American Place Theatre, New York City, 1970–71.
Private Sheldon Grossbart, "Defender of the Faith," and Doctor, "Epstein," *Unlikely Heroes: 3 Philip Roth Stories,* Plymouth Theatre, New York City, 1971.

L

LAMIA, Jenna

PERSONAL

Education: Attended Amherst College, New York University, and the Sorbonne.

Addresses: *Agent*—Endeavor, 9601 Wilshire Blvd., 3rd Floor, Beverly Hills, CA 90210. *Manager*—Crysis Management, 3800 Barham Blvd., Suite 409, Los Angeles, CA 90068.

Career: Actress. Appeared in television commercials, including Budweiser beer and Visa Checkcard.

Awards, Honors: AudioFile Award, performance, for *The Girl with the Peal Earring;* AudioFile Award, performance, for *The Secret Life of Bees.*

CREDITS

Film Appearances:
Girl teen, *Hi–Life,* Lions Gate Films, 1998.
Paddy, *Corkscrew Hill* (animated short), Busch Gardens, 2001.
Sparkle, *Nowhere to Go But Up* (also known as *Happy End* and *I Want to Be Famous*), 2003.
Rain Forsyth, *Drowning,* 2004.
Shelby, *Something's Wrong in Kansas,* 2007.
Voice of Lake, *The Story of a Mother,* 2007.

Television Appearances; Series:
Carrie Schillnger, *Oz,* HBO, 2000–2002.

Television Appearances; Episodic:
Poppy Downes, "Old Habits—New Beginnings," *Strangers with Candy,* Comedy Central, 1999.

Ali, *The Guiding Light* (also known as *Guiding Light*), CBS, 1999.
Ali, "Damaged Goods," *Brutally Normal,* 2000.
Siobhan Miller, "Taken," *Law & Order: Special Victims Unit* (also known as *Law & Order: SVU* and *Special Victims Unit*), NBC, 2000.
Alice Blossom, "Hawks and Handsaws," *Without a Trace* (also known as *W.A.T.*), CBS, 2004.
Gina Bell, "Old Yeller," *NYPD Blue,* ABC, 2004.
Christine Britton, "Last Rites," *The Jury,* Fox, 2004.

Stage Appearances:
(Broadway debut) Mildred, *Ah, Wilderness,* Lincoln Center, 1998.
Glory of Living, New York City, 2001.
Daughter, *Bedbound,* New York City, 2003.
Tina, *Intrigue with Faye,* New York City, 2003.

Also appeared in *Much Ado About Nothing; Twelfth Night; Sara Say Goodbye; No Mercy; Afternoon of the Elves;* as Constance Congdon, *Tales of the Lost Formicans;* Witch, *Macbeth;* Howard Korder, *Boy's Life.*

RECORDINGS

Video Games:
Voice of female hostage and Melinda Kline, *S.W.A.T. 4,* Vivendi Universal Games, 2005.
Voice of female hostage 1, Rita Winston, and Female 911 officer, *SWAT 4: The Stetchkov Syndicate,* Irrational Games, 2006.
Voice of Qara, Dory the beggar girl, and Laleen spirit, *Neverwinter Nights,* 2006.

Taped Readings:
Hey Nostradomus! by Douglas Coupland, 2003.

Also read Cynthia Leitich Smith's *Rain Is Not My Indian Name;* Tracy Chevalier's *The Girl with the Pearl Earring;* Sue Monk Kidd's *The Secret Life of Bees.*

LASSEZ, Sarah

PERSONAL

Born in Sherbrooke, Quebec, Canada; daughter of Jean–Louis (a computer scientists) and Catherine (a computer scientist) Lassez. *Education:* New York University, B.F.A.

Addresses: *Agent*—(literary) Dan Strone, Trident Media Group, 41 Madison Ave., 36th Floor, New York, NY 10010. *Manager*—Beth Holden–Garland, Untitled Entertainment, 331 North Maple Dr., 3rd Floor, Beverly Hills, CA 90210.

Career: Actress.

Awards, Honors: Feature Film Award, best supporting actress in a dramatic feature, New York International Independent Film and Video Festival, 1998, for *The Blackout;* Silver Lake Award, best performance, Los Angeles Silver Lake Film Festival, 2006, for *Mad Cowgirl.*

CREDITS

Film Appearances:
Jane, *The Still Point,* Colosimo Film Productions, 1985.
Angela Estelle Morales, *Roosters,* IRS Releasing, 1993.
The Foot Shooting Party (short film), Buena Vista, 1994.
Melody, *Loving Deadly,* Barron Productions, 1994.
Laura, *Malicious,* Republic Pictures Home Video, 1995.
Polly (Egg), *Nowhere,* Fine Line, 1997.
Second Annie, *The Blackout,* Trimark Pictures, 1997.
Julie, *Alexandria Hotel,* 1998.
Kate Williams, *The Clown at Midnight,* Fried Film Group/Hallmark Entertainment, 1998.
Heather, *Sleeping Beauties,* 1999.
Previous, *The Gold Cup,* Full Circle Studios, 2000.
Frances at age twenty–five, *The Sleepy Time Gal,* Antarctic Pictures, 2001.
Samantha, *The Tag* (short film), 2001.
Abby Berkhoff, *In Pursuit,* 2001.
Rosebud, *Chatroom* (short film), Made in Italy Productions, 2003.
Coranette, *Rien, voila l'ordre,* Wallworks, 2003.
Karina, *Until the Night,* Pathfinder Pictures, 2004.
Sophi, *Brothel,* Mount Parnassus Pictures, 2006.
Therese, *Mad Cowgirl,* Cinema Epoch, 2006.
Anna Dichter, *Fade,* Klondike 5 Productions, 2006.

Television Appearances; Movies:
Angie, *Midnight Runaround,* syndicated, 1994.
Francesca, *The Shaggy Dog,* ABC, 1994.
Ashley, *The Ultimate Lie,* NBC, 1996.

Connie Binoculars, *The Outfitters,* Sundance Channel, 1999.

Television Appearances; Episodic:
Cynda, "Something Out of Nothing," *Party of Five,* Fox, 1994.

Television Appearances; Other:
Gilda Steinberg, "Educating Mom," *ABC Afterschool Special,* ABC, 1996.
Heather Norland, *Hollywood Confidential* (pilot), UPN, 1997.

WRITINGS

Books:
(With Gian Sardar) *Psychic Junkie: A Memoir,* Simon Spotlight Entertainment, 2006.

OTHER SOURCES

Books:
Lassez, Sarah, and Gian Sardar, *Psychic Junkie: A Memoir,* Simon Spotlight Entertainment, 2006.

Periodicals:
Detour, November, 1997, p. 1.
Interview, October, 1993, p. 1.
MovieMaker, October, 1997, p. 1.
People, July 24, 2006.

Electronic:
Sarah Lassez Official Site, http://www.sarahlassez.com, May 19, 2007.

LAWRENCE, Mark Christopher 1964–

PERSONAL

Born May 22, 1964, in Los Angeles, CA. *Education:* Attended University of Southern California; trained at Los Angeles Theatre Center.

Addresses: *Agent*—House of Representatives, 400 South Beverly Dr., Suite 101, Beverly Hills, CA 90212; (commercials) Cunningham/Escott/Slevin & Doherty Talent Agency, 10635 Santa Monica Blvd., Suite 140, Los Angeles, CA 90025.

Career: Actor, singer, voice performer, and comedian. Performed with San Francisco Mime Troupe; stand–up comedian; appeared in commercials for NyQuil sleep aid, 2001, American Dairy Association and Oreo cookies, 2002, and Best Buy electronics stores, 2003.

Member: American Federation of Television and Radio Artists (past president of local branch), Screen Actors Guild (past vice president of local branch), Actors' Equity Association.

Awards, Honors: DramaLogue Award for *Minamanta;* Image Award, National Association for the Advancement of Colored People, for *Glass House.*

CREDITS

Film Appearances:
Construction worker, *Caddyshack II,* Warner Bros., 1988.
Attila, *Listen to Me,* Columbia, 1989.
Burly attendant, *Terminator 2: Judgment Day* (also known as *T2, T2: Extreme Edition, T2: Ultimate Edition, T2—Terminator 2: Judgment Day, El exterminator 2,* and *Le terminator 2—Le jugement dernier*), TriStar, 1991.
Cop, *Child's Play 3* (also known as *Child's Play 3: Look Who's Stalking*), Universal, 1991.
Tone Def, *Fear of a Black Hat,* Samuel Goldwyn Company, 1994.
Rono, *Crimson Tide,* Buena Vista, 1995.
Prison guard, *Tales from the Hood,* Savoy Pictures, 1995.
Rollo, *That Darn Cat,* Buena Vista, 1997.
Third "brotha", *Sprung,* Trimark Pictures, 1997.
Lil' Ass Gee, *Caught in the Spray* (short film), 1998.
Wig shop owner, *Senseless,* Miramax/Dimension Films, 1998.
Manager of the Angels, *Molly,* Metro–Goldwyn–Mayer, 1999.
E. J., *Retiring Tatiana,* Tapeworm Video Distributors, 2000.
Go with the Fro (short film), 2001.
Friend at Leo's party, *Planet of the Apes,* Twentieth Century–Fox, 2001.
Fourth lying man, *Two Can Play That Game,* Columbia TriStar/Screen Gems, 2001.
Simms, *K–PAX* (also known as *K–PAX—Alles ist moeglich*), MCA/Universal, 2001.
Danny G., *Lost Treasure,* Blockbuster Video, 2003.
Christopher Mello, *Garfield* (also known as *Garfield: The Movie*), Twentieth Century–Fox, 2004.
Wes Trogden, *Christmas with the Kranks,* Columbia, 2004.
Wesley, *Fair Game,* Urbanworks, 2005.
Construction worker, *The Island,* DreamWorks, 2005.
Wayne, *The Pursuit of Happyness,* Columbia, 2006.

Also appeared (according to some sources) in the films *Ghost Dad* and *Police Academy VI.*

Film Work; Voice for Automated Dialogue Replacement (ADR):
The Wood, Paramount, 1999.
Hearts in Atlantis, Warner Bros., 2001.

Television Appearances; Miniseries:
Fats Domino, *Shake, Rattle, and Roll: An American Love Story,* CBS, 1999.

Television Appearances; Series:
Fletcher Williams, *The George Wendt Show,* CBS, 1995.
Hank, *Kelly Kelly,* The WB, 1998.
Bill, *The Mullets,* UPN, 2003.

Television Appearances; Movies:
Jack Spays, *12:01,* Fox, 1993.
Pagoda disc jockey, *The Rockford Files: Murder and Misdemeanors,* CBS, 1997.
Pop, *Tiger Cruise,* Disney Channel, 2004.
Calvin's dad, *Life Is Ruff,* Disney Channel, 2005.
Duty sergeant, *Ordinary Miracles,* Hallmark Channel, 2005.

Television Appearances; Episodic:
Mark, "A Home, a Loan," *Roc* (also known as *Roc Live*), Fox, 1991.
Black gentleman, "Driving My Mama Back Home," *Designing Women,* CBS, 1992.
Mr. Powell, "Hasta la Vista," *Evening Shade,* CBS, 1992.
Skycap, "The Airport," *Seinfeld,* NBC, 1992.
Security guard, "Hollywood Swinging: Part 2," *Martin,* Fox, 1993.
Trekker, "Where Have You Gone, Joe DiMaggio?," *Murphy Brown,* CBS, 1994.
Boss, "The Race," *Seinfeld,* NBC, 1994.
Chris, "Deandra and Them," *The Show,* Fox, 1996.
Bartender, "Gobble, Gobble, Dick, Dick," *3rd Rock from the Sun* (also known as *Life as We Know It* and *3rd Rock*), NBC, 1996.
Big Dave, "A Boy and His Doll," *Coach,* ABC, 1997.
Mr. Kirkpatrick, "Child's Play," *Sister, Sister,* The WB, 1997.
Quires, "A Few So–so Men," *Malcolm & Eddie,* UPN, 1998.
Hank, "The Perfect Game," *Touched by an Angel,* CBS, 2000.
First sheriff, "Traffic Jam," *Malcolm in the Middle,* Fox, 2000.
Tony, "The Daddies Group," *Yes, Dear,* CBS, 2001.
Matt, *Emeril,* NBC, 2001.
Arnold, "Do the Hustle," *Dharma & Greg,* ABC, 2001.
"Second Chance," *Crossing Jordan,* NBC, 2004.

Deana, "Pressure Drop," *Grounded for Life,* The WB, 2004.
Bar bouncer, "Girls' Night Out," *Reba,* The WB, 2004.
John, "Waiting for Oprah," *Hot Properties,* ABC, 2005.
Jack Knox, "Stole P's HD Cart," *My Name Is Earl,* NBC, 2006.

Appeared as Tom, *Hearts Afire,* CBS; as Clyde, *High Incident,* ABC; and as Russell, *Men Behaving Badly,* NBC; also appeared in episodes of *American Dreams,* NBC; *Hill Street Blues; In Living Color,* Fox; *Method and Red,* Fox; and *Weeds,* Showtime.

Television Appearances; Pilots:
Chris, *The Show,* Fox, 1996.

Stage Appearances:
Appeared as Alexis, *Anthony and Cleopatra,* Del and Alice's father, *Minamanta,* Basilio, *Life Is a Dream,* and as Duncan and Richard, *The Black Horror Show,* all Los Angeles Theatre Center, Los Angeles; Fezziwig, *A Christmas Carol,* interviewer, *Love, Janis,* man standing still, *Nuevo California,* and as Gratiano, *The Merchant of Venice,* all San Diego Repertory Theatre, San Diego, CA; Matthew, *Cotton Patch Gospel,* Lambs Players Theatre, San Diego, CA; Quince and Engeus, *A Midsummer Night's Dream,* La Jolla Playhouse, La Jolla, CA; Bunthorne, *Patience,* Bing Theatre, Los Angeles; multiple roles, *Ripped Van Winkle,* San Francisco Mime Group, San Francisco, CA; Kenneth, *South of Where We Live,* Thomas J. Ford Theatre; Habu Stop, *Tracers,* Gap Theatre; Larry, *What a Good Black Man Needs,* Dee Abdullah Theatre; also appeared in *Glass House.*

RECORDINGS

Videos:
Performer and editor, *SHOUT! An Evening of Gospel Comedy,* Prater Dudz Entertainment, 2006.

WRITINGS

Video Scripts:
Performer and editor, *SHOUT! An Evening of Gospel Comedy,* Prater Dudz Entertainment, 2006.

OTHER SOURCES

Electronic:
Mark Christopher Lawrence Official Site, http://www.markchristopherlawrence.com, May 13, 2007.

LEMELIN, Stephanie 1979–

PERSONAL

Full name, Stephanie Nicole Lemelin; born June 29, 1979, in Quebec, Canada (some sources say Sewell, NJ); daughter of Rejean (a professional goalie and goalie coach) and Rona Lemelin. *Education:* University of Pennsylvania, undergraduate degree, Communications and English, 2001. *Avocational Interests:* Krav Maga.

Addresses: *Agent*—Paradigm, 360 North Crescent Dr., North Bldg., Beverly Hills, CA 90210. *Manager*—Nine Yards/Roklin Management, 8530 Wilshire Blvd., 5th Floor, Beverly Hills, CA 90211.

Career: Actress.

CREDITS

Film Appearances:
Marianne, *Late Summer* (short), 2001.
(Uncredited) Woman number two, *The 40 Year Old Virgin* (also known as *The 40 Year–Old Virgin* and *The 40–Year–Old Virgin*), Universal, 2005.
Laurie, *The Thirst,* MTI Home Video, 2006.
Jenny Purdy, *Raising Flagg,* Cinema Libre Studio, 2006.
Kat, *Limbo Lounge,* 2007.

Also appeared in *Me, Myself, and Irene.*

Film Work:
Associate producer, *The Thirst,* 2006.

Television Appearances; Series:
Thorne, *Cavemen,* ABC, 2007.

Television Appearances; Movies:
Gabrielle Watson, *Anonymous Rex,* Sci–Fi Channel, 2004.

Television Appearances; Pilots:
Titletown, Fox, 2003.
Missy, *Dirtbags,* Fox, 2005.
Caroline, *Worst Week of My Life,* Fox, 2006.
Ally Sullivan, "Killer," *CSI: Crime Scene Investigation* (also known as *CSI: Las Vegas, CSI: Weekends, C.S.I.,* and *Les Experts*), CBS, 2006.
Thorne, *Cavemen,* ABC, 2007.

Television Appearances; Episodic:
Tara, "The Day After," *Undeclared,* Fox, 2002.
Stephanie, "Love Freakin' Story," *The Mullets,* UPN, 2003.
Michelle, "Chris' College Friend," *Run of the House,* 2003.
Christie, "Malcolm Visits College," *Malcolm in the Middle,* Fox, 2004.
Danielle, "The Lady Doth Protest Too Much," *Out of Practice,* CBS, 2006.

LENNON, Thomas 1970–
    (Tom Lennon)

PERSONAL

Born August 9, 1970, in Chicago, IL; married Jenny Robertson (an actress). *Education:* Graduated from New York University.

Addresses: *Agent*—Creative Artists Agency, 2000 Avenue of the Stars, Los Angeles, CA 90067. *Manager*—Principato/Young Management, 9465 Wilshire Blvd., Suite 880, Beverly Hills, CA 90212.

Career: Actor, writer, producer, and director. Appeared in television commercials, including Starburst candy, Sprint communications, and Snickers candy; The State (comedy troupe), cofounder.

CREDITS

Film Appearances:
(As Tom Lennon) Geoff, *Aisle Six,* 1991.
(As Tom Lennon) Moonie, *A Friend of Dorothy* (short), 1994.
Voice of documentaries, *Drop Dead Gorgeous* (also known as *Gnadenlos schon*), New Line Cinema, 1999.
Census taker, *Row Your Boat,* Gullane Pictures, 2000.
Doctor, *Memento,* Newmarket Films, 2000.
Eric Montclare, *Out Cold,* Buena Vista, 2001.
The priest, *Boat Trip,* Artisan Entertainment, 2002.
Pete Morse, *A Guy Thing,* Metro–Goldwyn–Mayer, 2003.
Thayer, *How to Lose a Guy in 10 Days* (also known as *Wie werde ich ihn los in 10 tagen*), Paramount, 2003.
Roger Walker, *Le Divorce,* Twentieth Century–Fox, 2003.
Himself, *Bachelor Party Confidential* (documentary short), Metro–Goldwyn–Mayer Home Entertainment, 2003.

Himself, *Inside "A Guy Thing"* (documentary short), Metro–Goldwyn–Mayer Home Entertainment, 2003.
(As Tom Lennon) Marshall, *Heights,* Sony Pictures Classics, 2004.
D.U.G., *The Godfather of Green Bay,* Blue Moon Pictures, 2005.
Voice of Eddie the computer, *The Hitchhiker's Guide to the Galaxy,* Buena Vista, 2005.
Larry Murphy, *Herbie Fully Loaded,* Buena Vista, 2005.
Videographer, *Conversations with Other Women,* Fabrication Films, 2005.
Campus rent–a–cop, *Bickford Shmeckler's Cool Ideas,* Screen Media Films, 2006.
Richie's friend, *The Ten,* THINKFilm, 2007.
Lieutenant Jim Dangle, *Reno 911!: Miami* (also known as *"Reno 911!: Miami": The Movie*), Twentieth Century–Fox, 2007.
Schroeder Duncan, *Eden Court,* 2007.
Karl Wolfschtagg, *Balls of Fury,* Rogue Pictures, 2007.
Himself, *Living with Lew,* 2007.

Film Work:
Co–editor, *Aisle Six,* 1991.
Executive producer, *Reno 911!: Miami* (also known as *"Reno 911!: Miami": The Movie*), Twentieth Century–Fox, 2007.
Producer, *Balls of Fury,* Rogue Pictures, 2007.

Also made *The Waiters* (short).

Television Appearances; Series:
Various characters, *You Wrote It, You Watch It,* MTV, 1992.
Various characters, *The State,* MTV, 1994–95.
Meredith Laupin, *Viva Variety,* Comedy Central, 1997.
Chester E. Donge, *MDs,* 2002.
Lieutenant Jim Dangle, *Reno 911!,* Comedy Central, 2003–2007.

Television Appearances; Specials:
Various characters, *The State's 43rd Annual All–Star Halloween Special,* CBS, 1995.
Mr. Laupin, *The Viva in Vegas Special,* Comedy Central, 1998.
(As Tom Lennon) Host, *Reel Comedy: "Taxi,"* Comedy Central, 2004.
Comedy Central's Bar Mitzvah Bash!, Comedy Central, 2004.
Spike TV's Video Games Awards 2006, Spike TV, 2006.
Reel Comedy: "Reno 911!: Miami," Comedy Central, 2007.

Television Appearances; Episodic:
Voice, *Disney's "Hercules"* (animated), 1998.
Randall, "The One in Vegas: Parts 1 & 2," *Friends,* NBC, 1999.

Ernie, "Finders Keepers," *Jesse,* NBC, 1999.

Painter number one, *Everything's Relative,* NBC, 1999.

Ernie, "Small Time Felon: The Jesse Warner Story: Part 2," *Jesse,* NBC, 2000.

Voice of landlord, "Tarzan and the Mysterious Visitor," *The Legend of Tarzan* (animated; also known as *Disney's "The Legend of Tarzan"*), UPN and syndicated, 2001.

Voice, "Kimitation Nation," *Kim Possible* (animated; also known as *Disney's "Kim Possible"*), Disney Channel, 2002.

Animal trainer Tom Reynolds, *The Late Late Show with Craig Kilborn* (also known as *The Late Late Show*), CBS, 2004.

Voice of Vic, "Skin of Eeeeeeeevil!!!," *Brandy & Mr. Whiskers* (animated), Disney Channel, 2004.

(As Tom Lennon) *The Late Late Show with Craig Ferguson,* CBS, 2005, 2006.

Voice of Vic, "Any Club that Would Have Me as a Member ...," *Brandy & Mr. Whiskers* (animated), Disney Channel, 2006.

(Uncredited) Kevin Federline, *The Late Late Show with Craig Ferguson,* CBS, 2006.

Gary, "You're Getting Sleepy," *Stacked,* Fox, 2006.

Talkshow with Spike Feresten, 2006.

Lieutenant Jim Dangle, *Last Call with Carson Daly,* NBC, 2007.

"Reno 911!: Miami," *Making a Scene,* 2007.

Television Work; Series:

Creator, *The State,* MTV, 1993.

Creator, *Viva Variety,* Comedy Central, 1997.

Executive producer and (uncredited) creator, *Reno 911!,* Comedy Central, 2003–2007.

Television Work; Specials:

Creator, *The State's 43rd Annual All–Star Halloween Special,* CBS, 1995.

Television Work; Episodic:

Director, *Reno 911!,* Comedy Central, 2005.

WRITINGS

Screenplays:

Taxi (also known as *New York Taxi* and *Taxi 2004*), Twentieth Century–Fox, 2004.

The Pacifier (also known as *Gnome* and *Le pacifacteur*), Buena Vista, 2005.

Herbie Fully Loaded, Buena Vista, 2005.

Let's Go to Prison, Universal, 2006.

Night at the Museum, Twentieth Century–Fox, 2006.

Reno 911!: Miami (also known as *"Reno 911!: Miami": The Movie*), Twentieth Century–Fox, 2007.

Balls of Fury, Rogue Pictures, 2007.

Television Specials:

The State's 43rd Annual All–Star Halloween Special, CBS, 1995.

Television Episodes:

You Wrote It, You Watch It, MTV, 1992.

The State, MTV, 1993.

Viva Variety, Comedy Central, 1997.

"Bogie Nights," *Strangers with Candy,* Comedy Central, 1999.

(Uncredited) *Reno 911!,* Comedy Central, 2003–2007.

LENNON, Thomas F. 1951–
(Thomas Lennon, Thomas Furneaux Lennon, Tom Lennon)

PERSONAL

Born November 3, 1951, in Washington, DC. *Education:* Yale University, graduate (magna cum laude), 1973.

Career: Documentary filmmaker, producer, and writer. Association of Independent Video/Filmmakers, New York City, 1975–78; ABC News, New York City, associate producer and writer, 1979–83, then producer–director and writer, 1983–87; Lennon Documentary Group, founder and president, 1987—; Columbia School of Journalism, guest lecturer, 1990. The Fourth World Movement, New York City, volunteer, 1990.

Member: Writers Guild of America, Directors Guild of America.

Awards, Honors: Emmy Award (with others), outstanding individual achievement in writing, 1984, for "To Save Our Schools, to Save Our Children"; Emmy Award nomination (with others), outstanding individual achievement in writing, 1985, for "Growing Old in America"; Christopher Award, c. 1986, for *At a Loss for Words ... Illiterate in America;* National Black Producers Award, c. 1988, for *Racism 101;* Blue Ribbon, American Film and Video Association, c. 1989, for "Demon Rum"; Television Award (with Shelby Steele), Writers Guild of America, Best Current Events Documentary, San Francisco Film Festival, 1991, both for "Seven Days in Bensonhurst"; Television Award (with others), documentary—current events, Writers Guild of America, 1994, for "The Choice of '92"; Television Award nomination (with Mark Zwonitzer), documentary—other than current events, Writers Guild of America, 1996, for "The Battle of the Bulge: World War II's Deadliest Battle"; Grand Jury Prize nomination—

documentary, Sundance Film Festival, Emmy Award (with Michael Epstein), outstanding informational special, Academy Award nomination (with Epstein), best documentary feature, 1996, Film Award nomination, best documentary—other than current events, Writers Guild of America, and George Foster Peabody Broadcasting Award, University of Georgia, 1997, all for "The Battle Over Citizen Kane"; Television Award nomination (with Thomas N. Brown), documentary—other than current events, Writers Guild of America, 1999, for *The Irish in America: Long Journey Home*; Emmy Award nominations, outstanding directing for non–fiction programming (with Ed Bell) and outstanding non–fiction special–traditional (with others), 2003, for *Unchained Memories: Readings from the Slave Narratives*; Television Award nomination (with others), documentary—other than current events, Writers Guild of America, 2004, for *Becoming American: The Chinese Experience*; Pare Lorentz Award nomination (with Ruby Yang), International Documentary Association, 2006, Academy Award (with Yang), best documentary—short subjects, 2007, both for *The Blood of Yingzhou District*.

CREDITS

Film Producer:
Racism 101, 1988.
The Blood of Yingzhou District (documentary short; also known as *Yingzhou de haizi*), 2006.

Television Work; Specials:
Producer and director, *At a Loss for Words ... Illiterate in America*, PBS, 1986.
Senior producer, *On Values: Talking with Peggy Noonan*, PBS, 1995.
Producer and director, *The Irish in America: Long Journey Home*, PBS, 1998.
Producer and director, *Unchained Memories: Readings from the Slave Narratives* (documentary), 2003.
Producer, *Julia's Story*, 2005.

Television Work; Episodic:
Director, "To Save Our Schools, to Save Our Children," *ABC News Closeup*, ABC, 1984.
Producer and director, "Growing Old in America," *ABC News Closeup*, ABC, 1985.
"The Favored Few," *20/20*, ABC, 1986.
"Shoplifters," *20/20*, ABC, 1988.
Producer, "Demon Run," *The American Experience*, PBS, 1989.
Producer and director, "Coming from Japan" (also known as "The Giant from Japan"), *Frontline*, PBS, 1992.
Producer, "The Choice '92," *Frontline*, PBS, 1992.

Producer, "Tabloid Truth: The Michael Jackson Scandal," *Frontline*, PBS, 1994.
Director, "The Battle of the Bulge: World War II's Deadliest Battle," *The American Experience*, PBS, 1994.
Director and producer, "The Battle over Citizen Kane," *The American Experience*, PBS, 1996.
Senior Producer, "The Pilgrimage of Jesse Jackson," *Frontline*, PBS, 1996.
Producer and director, "Jefferson's Blood," *Frontline*, PBS, 2000.
Producer, "The Hurricane of '38," *The American Experience*, PBS, 2001.
Director and series producer, "No Turning Back," *Becoming American: The Chinese Experience*, PBS, 2003.
Series producer, "Gold Mountain Dreams," *Becoming American: The Chinese Experience*, PBS, 2003.
Producer, "Between Two Worlds," *Becoming American: The Chinese Experience*, PBS, 2003.
Series producer, "Becoming American: Personal Journeys," *Becoming American: The Chinese Experience*, PBS, 2003.
Director, "One Nation Under Law," *The Supreme Court*, PBS, 2007.
Director, "A New Kind of Justice," *The Supreme Court*, PBS, 2007.
Director, "The Rehnquist Revolution," *The Supreme Court*, PBS, 2007.
Director, "A Nation of Liberties," *The Supreme Court*, PBS, 2007.

WRITINGS

Documentary Scripts:
Racism 101, 1988.

Television Specials:
(With Mark Zwonitzer) *Battle of the Bulge*, 1995.
The Irish in America: Long Journey Home, PBS, 1998.

Television Episodes:
(With others) "To Save Our Schools, to Save Our Children," *ABC News Closeup*, ABC, 1984.
"Growing Old in America," *ABC News Closeup*, ABC, 1985.
"The Favored Few," *20/20*, ABC, 1986.
"Shoplifters," *20/20*, ABC, 1988.
(With Shelby Steele) "Seven Days in Bensonhurst," *Frontline*, PBS, 1990.
"Coming from Japan" (also known as "The Giant from Japan"), *Frontline*, PBS, 1992.
"The Choice '92," *Frontline*, PBS, 1992.
(With Richard Ben Cramer) "Tabloid Truth: The Michael Jackson Scandal," *Frontline*, PBS, 1994.

"The Battle of the Bulge: World War II's Deadliest Battle," *The American Experience,* PBS, 1994.

"The Battle over Citizen Kane," *The American Experience,* PBS, 1996.

"Jefferson's Blood," *Frontline,* PBS, 2000.

"The Hurricane of '38," *The American Experience,* PBS, 2001.

"No Turning Back," *Becoming American: The Chinese Experience,* PBS, 2003.

"Gold Mountain Dreams," *Becoming American: The Chinese Experience,* PBS, 2003.

"Between Two Worlds," *Becoming American: The Chinese Experience,* PBS, 2003.

LEVESQUE, Joanna
See JO-JO

LEVESQUE, Jojo
See JO-JO

LIGON, Tom 1945–
(Thomas Lignon)

PERSONAL

Full name, Thomas Bryant Ligon; born September 10, 1945, in New Orleans, LA; married K. C. (an actress), December 31, 1976. *Education:* Studied English at Yale University.

Career: Actor.

CREDITS

Film Appearances:

Teenager, *Nothing But a Man,* Cinema V, 1964.

Horton Fenty, *Paint Your Wagon,* Paramount, 1969.

Chester Jump, *Jump* (also known as *Fury on Wheels*), Cannon, 1971.

Lamar, *The Last American Hero* (also known as *Hard Driver*), Twentieth Century–Fox, 1973.

Sanders, *Joyride,* American International Pictures, 1977.

Cameo, *Young Doctors in Love,* Twentieth Century–Fox, 1982.

Mr. Ingalis, *Cutting Class,* Republic Pictures Home Video, 1989.

Oliver, *I Believe in America,* 2006.

Chief Joseph Spataford, *Serial,* 2007.

Television Appearances; Series:

T. D. Drinkard, *A World Apart,* ABC, 1970–71.

Lucas Lorenzo Prentiss, *The Young and the Restless* (also known as *Y&R*), CBS, 1978–82.

Coach Billy Bristow, *Loving,* ABC, 1983–84.

Addison, *Santa Barbara,* NBC, 1987.

Bailey Thompson, *Another World* (also known as *Another World: Bay City*), NBC, 1995.

#01Y208, *Oz,* HBO, 2001–2003.

Television Appearances; Movies:

Childs, *The Execution of Private Slovik,* NBC, 1974.

Lester Carter, *Judge Horton and the Scottsboro Boys,* NBC, 1976.

Alan Campbell, *F. Scott Fitzgerald in Hollywood,* ABC, 1976.

Phillip Russo, *The Demon Murder Case* (also known as *The Rhode Island Murders*), NBC, 1983.

Television Appearances; Specials:

Voice, *School: The Story of American Public Education,* PBS, 2001.

Television Appearances; Episodic:

"The Legacy," *Southern Baptist Hour,* 1964.

Clifford, "The Honeymooners: Operation Protest," *The Jackie Gleason Show,* CBS, 1970.

David, "The Loser," *Medical Center,* CBS, 1971.

"The Black Box Murders," *Wide World Mystery,* 1975.

Young man, "The Set–Up: Parts 1 & 2," *Starsky and Hutch,* ABC, 1977.

"Silky Chamberlin," *Police Woman,* NBC, 1977.

Miller, "The Blue Angels," *Charlie's Angels,* ABC, 1977.

Wills, "The Ten–Second Client," *Rosetti and Ryan,* NBC, 1977.

Phelps, "Lyman P. Dokker, Fed," *Baretta,* ABC, 1977.

"Operation Stand–Down," *Baa Baa Black Sheep* (also known as *Black Sheep Squadron*), NBC, 1978.

"The Ten Percent Solution," *Dallas,* CBS, 1987.

T. Justin Moore, "Simple Justice," *The American Experience,* PBS, 1993.

Scott Hampton, "Switch," *Law & Order,* NBC, 1995.

Gillespie, "True North," *Law & Order,* NBC, 1998.

Malcolm Sanford, "Panic," *Law & Order,* NBC, 2000.

Bluebell Agency Executive, "Care," *Law & Order: Special Victims Unit* (also known as *Law & Order: SVU* and *Special Victims Unit*), NBC, 2001.

Phil Brucker, "B*tch," *Law & Order,* NBC, 2003.

Stage Appearances:

Steve Kozlek, *Have I Got a Girl for You,* Music Box Theatre, New York City, 1963.

Orson, *Your Own Thing,* Orpheum Theatre, New York City, 1968–70.

Skipper Allen, *Love Is a Time of Day,* Music Box Theatre, 1969.

Jeff Dolan, *Angela,* Music Box Theatre, 1969.

Eugene Winter, *Geniuses,* New York City, 1982–83.

Roger Freed, *A Backer's Audition,* American Jewish Theatre, New York City, 1992.

Orgon and Visitor, *Tartuffe: Born Again* (also known as *Tartuffe*), Circle in the Square Theatre, New York City, 1996.

Clay, *BAFO (Best and Final Offer),* New York City, 1998.

H. C. Curry, *The Rainmaker,* Center Stage, Baltimore, MD, 2003.

The Audience, Connelly Theatre, New York City, 2005.

All the Way Home, Transport Group, Connelly Theatre, 2006.

Tiger, *Bengal Tiger at the Baghdad Zoo,* Lark Theatre, New York City, 2007.

Also appeared as Kilroy, *Camino Real;* in *Our Town,* New York City; *Den of Thieves,* New York City; *The Golf Ball,* New York City; *Another Paradise,* New York City; *Quills; Picasso at Lapin Agile; Anything Goes; Lawyers; Dracula; 1776; Evelyn and the Polka King.*

LIPTON, Peggy 1947(?)–

PERSONAL

Born August 30, 1947 (some sources cite 1948), in New York, NY; daughter of Harold (a corporate lawyer) and Rita (an artist) Lipton; married Quincy Jones (a producer, composer, actor, music conductor and arranger, and executive), September 14, 1974 (divorced, c. 1987); children: Kidada (an actress), Rashida. *Avocational Interests:* New Age spiritualism, hatha–yoga.

Addresses: *Agent*—Progressive Artists Agency, 400 S. Beverly Dr., Suite 216, Beverly Hills, CA 90212. *Manager*—THJ Management, 405 E. 54th St., Suite 3H, New York, NY 10022.

Career: Actress. Worked previously as a model, singer, and songwriter.

Awards, Honors: Golden Globe Award, best actress in a television drama, 1971, and Golden Globe Award nominations, best actress —drama, 1970, 1972, and 1973, Emmy Award nominations, outstanding continued performance by an actress in a leading role, 1969,

1970, 1970 and 1972, all for *The Mod Squad;* Soap Opera Digest Award nomination, outstanding supporting actress, 1991, for *Twin Peaks.*

CREDITS

Film Appearances:

Mosby's Marauders (also known as *Willie and the Yank*), 1966.

Laurie Kramer, *Blue,* 1968.

A Boy … a Girl (also known as *The Sun's Up*), 1969.

I'm Gonna Git You Sucka, 1988.

Television correspondent, *War Party,* 1988.

Mom, *The Purple People Eater,* Concorde, 1988.

Kathleen Crowe, *Kinjite: Forbidden Subjects,* Cannon, 1989.

Rita, *True Identity,* 1991.

Norma Jennings, *Twin Peaks: Fire Walk with Me* (also known as *Twin Peaks*), 1992.

Ellen March, *The Postman,* Warner Bros., 1997.

Roxanne Rochet, *The Intern,* Moonstone Entertainment, 2000.

Laurabel Pierce, *Skipped Parts,* Trimark Pictures, 2000.

Janice, *Jackpot,* Sony Pictures Classics, 2001.

Television Appearances; Series:

Joanna, *The John Forsythe Show,* NBC, 1965–66.

Julie Barnes, *The Mod Squad,* ABC, 1968–73.

Norma Jennings, *Twin Peaks,* ABC, 1990.

Hadley Larson, *Angel Falls,* CBS, 1993.

Television Appearances; Miniseries:

Olivia Owens, *Secrets* (also known as *Judith Krantz's "Secrets"*), 1992.

Gloria Steinem, *The 70s,* NBC, 2000.

Television Appearances; Movies:

Julie Barnes, *The Return of the Mod Squad,* ABC, 1979.

Assistant district attorney, *Addicted to His Love,* (also known as *Sisterhood*), ABC, 1988.

Jane Sims, *Fatal Charm,* 1992.

Helen Stroud, *The Spider and the Fly,* Lifetime, 1994.

Nancy Weston, *Deadly Vows,* Fox, 1994.

Carol Mills, *Justice for Annie: A Moment of Truth Movie,* NBC, 1996.

Television Appearances; Specials:

Twin Peaks and Cop Rock: Behind the Scenes, ABC, 1990.

Presenter, *The Screen Actors Guild Awards,* 1997.

An All Star Party for Aaron Spelling, ABC, 1998.

The Mod Squad: The E! True Hollywood Story, E! Entertainment Television, 2000.

Quincy Jones: In the Pocket, PBS, 2001.
ABC's 50th Anniversary Celebration, ABC, 2003.

Television Appearances; Episodic:
Secretary, "Your Witch Is Showing," *Bewitched,* 1965.
Selma, "And Then I Wrote ...," *Mr. Novak,* 1965.
Mary Winters, "Night Fever," *The Alfred Hitchcock Hour,* 1965.
"The Wolves up Front, the Jackals Behind," *The Virginian,* 1966.
Bride, "Wall of Crystal," *The Invaders,* 1967.
Oralee Prentiss, "Willie and the Yank: The Deserter," *Disneyland* (also known as *Disney's Wonderful World, The Disney Sunday Movie* and *The Wonderful World of Disney*), 1967.
Oralee Prentiss, "Willie and the Yank: The Mosby Raiders," *Disneyland* (also known as *Disney's Wonderful World, The Disney Sunday Movie* and *The Wonderful World of Disney*), 1967.
"A Song Called Revenge," *Bob Hope Presents the Chrysler Theatre* (also known as *The Chrysler Theater* and *Universal Star Time*), 1967.
Girl in museum, "Flight Plan," *The F.B.I.,* 1967.
Jenny Grimmer, "Elizabeth's Odyssey," *The Road West,* 1967.
The Hollywood Palace, ABC, 1969.
This Is Tom Jones, ABC, 1969.
The David Frost Show, syndicated, 1970.
"Working Girl," *The Hitchhiker,* 1989.
"The Cast of Twin Peaks," *The Phil Donahue Show,* syndicated, 1990.
Later with Bob Costas, NBC, 1990.
Miss Jenkins, the schoolteacher, "Miss Jenkins," *Wings,* NBC, 1994.
Kelly McQueen Foster, "What Makes Sammy Run," *Popular,* The WB, 2000.
Kelly McQueen Foster, "Two Weddings and a Funeral," *Popular,* The WB, 2000.
Kelly McQueen Foster, "Timber," *Popular,* The WB, 2000.
Kelly McQueen Foster, "Baby, Don't Do It," *Popular,* The WB, 2000.
Politically Incorrect, ABC, 2000.
"Quincy Jones: In the Pocket," *American Masters,* PBS, 2001.
Olivia Reed, "The Frame," *Alias,* ABC, 2004.
Olivia Reed, "Hourglass," *Alias,* ABC, 2004.
Marsha, "The Turkey Triangle," *Cuts,* 2005.
Dateline NBC, NBC, 2005.

Stage Appearances:
The Guys, Flea Theatre, New York City, 2002.

RECORDINGS

Videos:
Mother, *Black or White,* 1991.

Mother, *Dangerous: The Short Films* (also known as *Michael Jackson–Dangerous: The Short Films*), 1993.
Mother, *Michael Jackson: Video Greatest Hits–HIStory,* 1995.
Reflections on the Phenomenon of 'Twin Peaks', 2002.
The mother, *Michael Jackson: Number Ones,* 2003.

Albums:
Singer on the album *Peggy Lipton.*

WRITINGS

Songs:
Wrote the song "L.A. Is My Lady," recorded by Frank Sinatra.

OTHER SOURCES

Periodicals:
People Weekly, September 8, 1986; April 4, 1988; May 12, 1997, pp. 180.

LIPTON, Robert 1943–

PERSONAL

Born November 20, 1943, in New York, NY; brother of Peggy Lipton (an actress); married Maria Masters, 1983 (divorced, 1988).

Career: Actor.

CREDITS

Film Appearances:
Dick Marsh, *Maryjane,* American International Pictures, 1968.
Antonio, *Blue,* Paramount, 1968.
First aide, *Bullitt,* Warner Bros./Seven Arts, 1968.
Charlie Newcombe, *Tell Them Willie Boy Is Here,* Universal, 1969.
Jess Clayton, *Diamante Lobo* (also known as *A Bullet from God, God's Gun,* and *Pistola di Dio*), Irwin Yablans, 1976.
Jon David, *Chatterbox,* American International Pictures, 1977.
Dave Roberts, *F.I.S.T.,* United Artists, 1978.

Tom, *Death Spa* (also known as *Witch Bitch*), MPI Home Video, 1988.

Major Derek Johnson, *Lethal Woman* (also known as *The Most Dangerous Woman Alive*), VidAmerica, 1989.

Chopper pilot, *Die Hard 2* (also known as *Die Hard 2: Die Harder*), Twentieth Century–Fox, 1990.

Max, *A Woman, Her Man, and her Futon*, First Look International, 1992.

Dr. Rivera, *Morella* (also known as *The Cloning of Morella*), Taurus Entertainment Company, 1997.

Television Appearances; Series:

Tom Steinberg, *The Survivors* (also known as *Harold Robbins' "The Survivors"*), 1969.

Dr. Jeff Ward, *As the World Turns*, CBS, 1978–84.

Andre, *One Life to Live*, ABC, 1985.

Television Appearances; Miniseries:

Mike Loomis, *Vanished*, NBC, 1971.

Television Appearances; Movies:

Philip, *Silent Night, Lonely Night*, NBC, 1969.

Luke, *Marriage: Year One*, NBC, 1971.

Dex, *See the Man Run* (also known as *The Second Face*), ABC, 1971.

Ralph, *Awake and Sing!*, 1972.

Alex Gordon, *Dr. Max*, CBS, 1974.

First doctor, *Kate's Secret*, NBC, 1986.

(Uncredited) *Desperado: The Outlaw Wars*, NBC, 1989.

Richard Josephson, *The Secretary*, CBS, 1995.

Television Appearances; Pilots:

Ray, *Home*, ABC, 1987.

Television Appearances; Episodic:

Radio man, "The Creature," *Voyage to the Bottom of the Sea*, ABC, 1965.

Helmsman, "The Enemies," *Voyage to the Bottom of the Sea*, ABC, 1965.

George, "And Then I Wrote ...," *Mr. Novak*, NBC, 1965.

Jerry Brewster, "Twenty Six Ways to Spell Heartbreak: A, B, C, D ...," *Ben Casey*, ABC, 1966.

Jerry Brewster, "Pull the Wool Over Your Eyes, Here Comes the Cold Wind of Truth," *Ben Casey*, ABC, 1966.

Scott, "Homecoming," *Marcus Welby, M.D.* (also known as *Robert Young, Family Doctor*), ABC, 1969.

Adam Randall, "The Sins of the Father," *The Virginian* (also known as *The Men from Shiloh*), NBC, 1970.

Bryan Marsh, "Brink of Doom," *Medical Center*, CBS, 1970.

Bobbie Sudberry, "The Other Kind of Spy," *The Name of the Game*, NBC, 1970.

Billy Wizard, "Why I Blew Up Dakota," *The Name of the Game*, NBC, 1970.

"Quadrangle for Death," *Dan August*, ABC, 1970.

Jimmy Chard, "One Hour to Kill," *Ironside* (also known as *The Raymond Burr Show*), NBC, 1970.

Ross Sutton, "Cynthia," *Marcus Welby, M.D.* (also known as *Robert Young, Family Doctor*), ABC, 1971.

Alfred Cummings, "Love, Peace, Brotherhood and Murder," *Ironside* (also known as *The Raymond Burr Show*), NBC, 1971.

"The People versus Nelson," *The D.A.*, 1971.

Public defender, "Justice Is a Sometime Thing," *The Bold Ones: The Lawyers* (also known as *The Lawyers*), NBC, 1971.

Jason, "Crime Club," *The Mod Squad*, ABC, 1972.

"The Covenant," *Marcus Welby, M.D.* (also known as *Robert Young, Family Doctor*), ABC, 1975.

"Squeeze Play," *Matt Helm*, ABC, 1975.

Stallman, "Two Frogs on a Mongoose," *Police Story*, NBC, 1976.

Quiney, "Terror on Ward One," *Charlie's Angels*, ABC, 1977.

"Everybody Pays the Fare," *Baretta*, ABC, 1977.

Burton Levine, "A Second Self," *Street Hawk*, ABC, 1985.

Darrell Prescott, "The Wrong Way Home," *Scarecrow and Mrs. King*, CBS, 1985.

Martin Grattop, "Murder in the Afternoon," *Murder, She Wrote*, CBS, 1985.

Dan Rivers, "Children's Children," *Highway to Heaven*, NBC, 1986.

Richard Abbott, "Obituary for a Dead Anchor," *Murder, She Wrote*, CBS, 1986.

"Somebody to Love," *Houston Knights*, CBS, 1987.

Colin Hale, "Class Act," *Murder, She Wrote*, CBS, 1989.

"Hello and Goodbye," *L.A. Law*, NBC, 1993.

"Postmortem Madness," *Melrose Place*, Fox, 1995.

Richard Mason, "Patriot," *Walker, Texas Ranger* (also known as *Walker*), CBS, 1996.

Head surgeon, "One Son," *The X–Files*, Fox, 1999.

Richard Mason, "Countdown," *Walker, Texas Ranger* (also known as *Walker*), CBS, 1999.

Jenkins, "Zero Tolerance," *Judging Amy*, CBS, 2000.

Judge Dubin, "Valor," *JAG*, CBS, 2001.

Special agent Charles Renford, "Inter Arma Silent Legs," *The Practice*, ABC, 2001.

Techno president, "Wasteland," *The District*, 2002.

Harold Aspis, *Fastlane*, Fox, 2002.

"Hawks and Handsaws," *Without a Trace* (also known as *W.A.T.*), CBS, 2004.

Stage Appearances:
Pitching to the Star, 2002.

LLOYD, Norman 1914–

PERSONAL

Born November 8, 1914, in Jersey City, NJ; married Peggy Craven (some sources cite Peggy Hirsdansky), June 29, 1936; children: Susanna Baird, Michael Lloyd. *Education:* Attended New York University, c. 1930–32.

Addresses: *Agent*—The Blake Agency, 1327 Ocean Ave., Suite J, Santa Monica, CA 90401.

Career: Actor, producer, and director. Eva LeGallienne's Civic Repertory Theatre, New York City, member of company, 1932–33; Mercury Theatre, New York City, founder (with Orson Welles and John Houseman) and member of company.

Member: Actors' Equity Association, Screen Actors Guild, Screen Directors Guild of America, Academy of Motion Pictures Arts and Sciences.

Awards, Honors: Emmy Award nomination (with others), outstanding dramatic series, 1970, for *The Name of the Game;* Emmy Award nomination, outstanding special—comedy or drama, 1974, for *Steambath.*

CREDITS

Stage Appearances:
(Stage debut) *Liliom,* Civic Repertory Theatre, New York City, 1932.
Club, *Alice in Wonderland,* Civic Repertory Theatre, 1932.
Faneres, *A Secret Life,* Apprentice Theatre, New School for Social Research, New York City, 1933.
Naked, Apprentice Theatre, 1934.
Fear, Apprentice Theatre, 1934.
The Armored Train, Apprentice Theatre, 1934.
The Call of Life, Apprentice Theatre, 1934.
Title role, *Dr. Knock,* Apprentice Theatre, 1934, then Peabody Playhouse, Boston, MA, 1935.
(Broadway debut) Japhet, *Noah,* Longacre Theatre, 1935.
Kleist, *Gallery Gods,* Peabody Playhouse, 1935.
Salesman and Judge Brandeis, *Triple–A Plowed Under,* Living Newspaper Unit, Federal Theatre, Biltmore Theatre, New York City, 1936.
Clown, *Injunction Granted,* Living Newspaper Unit, Federal Theatre, Biltmore Theatre, 1936.
Consumer, *Power,* Living Newspaper Unit, Federal Theatre, Ritz Theatre, New York City, 1937.

Cinna, *Julius Caesar,* Mercury Theatre, New York City, 1937.
Roger/Hodge, *The Shoemaker's Holiday,* Mercury Theatre, 1938.
Johnny Appleseed, *Everywhere I Roam,* National Theatre, New York City, 1938.
Quack, the medicine man, *Medicine Show,* New Yorker Theatre, New York City, 1940.
One of the Four, *Liberty Jones,* Shubert Theatre, New York City, 1941.
Dawson, *Village Green,* Henry Miller's Theatre, New York City, 1941.
Sandy, *Ask My Friend Sandy,* Biltmore Theatre, 1943.
Mosca, *Volpone,* Las Palmas Theatre, Los Angeles, 1945.
Fool, *King Lear,* National Theatre, 1950.
The Devil, *Don Juan in Hell,* La Jolla Playhouse, La Jolla, CA, 1953.
Mr. Dockwiler, *Madame, Will You Walk,* Phoenix Theatre, New York City, 1953.
Lucio, *Measure for Measure,* American Shakespeare Festival, Stratford, CT, 1956, then Phoenix Theatre, 1957.
Sir Andrew Undershaft, *Major Barbara,* Mark Taper Forum, Los Angeles Music Center, Los Angeles, 1971.
The Will and Bart Show, Williamstown Theatre, Williamstown, MA, 1992.

Also appeared at Deertrees Theatre, Harrison, ME, 1937.

Stage Director:
The Road to Rome, La Jolla Playhouse, La Jolla, CA, 1948.
The Cocktail Party, La Jolla Playhouse, 1951.
(With Hume Cronyn) *Madam, Will You Walk,* Phoenix Theatre, New York City, 1953.
The Golden Apple, Phoenix Theatre, then Alvin Theatre, New York City, both 1954.
The Taming of the Shrew, American Shakespeare Festival, Stratford, CT, 1956, then Phoenix Theatre, 1957.

Also directed *The Lady's Not for Burning.*

Film Appearances:
(Film debut) Frye, *Saboteur,* Universal, 1942.
Organist, *Who Done It?,* 1942.
The Southerner, United Artists, 1945.
Archimbeau (some sources cite Archibald), *A Walk in the Sun* (also known as *Salerno Beach*), Twentieth Century–Fox, 1945.
Dewitt Pyncheon, *A Letter for Evie,* Metro–Goldwyn–Mayer, 1945.
Jasper Goodwin, *The Unseen,* Paramount, 1945.

Peter Moran, *Within These Walls,* Twentieth Century–Fox, 1945.

Mr. Garnes (some sources cite Garmes), *Spellbound* (also known as *Alfred Hitchcock's "Spellbound"*), United Artists, 1945.

Adam Leckie, *The Green Years,* Metro–Goldwyn–Mayer, 1946.

Sammy, *Young Widow,* United Artists, 1946.

Dr. Troyanski, *The Beginning or the End,* Metro–Goldwyn–Mayer, 1947.

Dr. Sturdevant, *No Minor Vices,* Metro–Goldwyn–Mayer, 1948.

Tallien, *The Black Book* (also known as *Reign of Terror*), Eagle–Lion, 1949.

Sleeper, *Scene of the Crime,* Metro–Goldwyn–Mayer, 1949.

Jim Murphy, *Calamity Jane and Sam Bass,* Universal, 1949.

Patout, *Buccaneer's Girl,* Universal, 1950.

Troubador, *The Flame and the Arrow,* Warner Bros., 1950.

Al Molin, *He Ran All the Way,* Universal, 1951.

Anton, *The Light Touch,* Metro–Goldwyn–Mayer, 1951.

Sutro, *M,* 1951.

Bodalink, *Limelight,* United Artists, 1952.

Baracca, *Flame of Stamboul,* Columbia, 1957.

Dr. Steven Lipscomb, *Audrey Rose,* United Artists, 1977.

Carl Billings, *FM* (also known as *Citizen's Band*), Universal, 1978.

Monsignore, *Jaws of Satan* (also known as *King Cobra*), United Artists, 1980.

Carruthers, *The Nude Bomb* (also known as *Maxwell Smart and the Nude Bomb* and *The Return of Maxwell Smart*), Universal, 1980.

Mr. Nolan, *Dead Poets Society,* 1989.

Father Vasco, *Journey of Honor* (also known as *Shogun Warrior* and *Shogun Mayeda*), 1992.

Mr. Letterblair, *The Age of Innocence,* 1993.

President of Wassamotta U., *The Adventures of Rocky and Bullwinkle,* Universal, 2000.

Charlie: The Life and Art of Charles Chaplin, Warner Home Video, 2003.

Kenneth, *Photosynthesis,* Filmmakers Alliance, 2005.

The professor, *In Her Shoes,* Twentieth Century–Fox, 2005.

Broadway: Beyond the Golden Age (also known as *B.G.A. 2* and *Broadway: The Golden Age Two*), Second Act, 2007.

Television Appearances; Series:

Dr. Daniel Auschlander, *St. Elsewhere,* NBC, 1982–88.

Therapist, *Home Fires,* 1992.

Dr. Isaac Mentnor, *Seven Days* (also known as *Seven Days: The Series*), UPN, 1998–2000.

Television Appearances; Movies:

(Television debut) *Streets of New York,* NBC, 1939.

Amys Penrose, *The Dark Secret of Harvest Home,* NBC, 1978.

Roland Fielding, *Beggarman, Thief,* NBC, 1979.

Father Manfred, *Amityville: The Evil Escapes* (also known as *The Amityville Horror: The Evil Escapes, Part 4* and *Amityville IV: The Evil Escapes*), NBC, 1989.

Aaron, *The Omen,* 1995.

Secretary Swenson, *Fail Safe,* CBS, 2000.

Madison Bowers, *The Song of the Lark,* 2001.

District attorney Asher Silverman, "We the People," *The Practice,* 2003.

Television Appearances; Specials:

Une legende une vie: Citizen Welles, 1974.

The American Film Institute Salute to Alfred Hitchcock, 1979.

NBC's Sixtieth Anniversary Celebration, NBC, 1986.

Surviving a Heart Attack, Lifetime, 1988.

Jean Renoir: Part One–From La Belle Epoque to World War II, 1993.

Jean Renoir: Part Two–Hollywood and Beyond, 1994.

Alfred Hitchcock, Arts and Entertainment, 1994.

Television's Christmas Classics, CBS, 1994.

Aaron, *The Omen,* Fox, 1995.

The Battle over Citizen Kane, PBS, 1996.

Hitchcock: Shadow of a Genius (also known as *Dial H for Hitchcock* and *Dial H Hitchcock: The Genius behind the Showman*), Turner Classics, 1999.

Hitchcock, Selznick, and the End of Hollywood, PBS, 1999.

Reputations: Alfred Hitchcock, 1999.

Chaplin Today: Monsieur Verdoux, 2003.

The John Garfield Story, TCM, 2003.

Television Appearances; Episodic:

Francis Oberon, "We Must Kill Toni," *The United States Steel Hour* (also known as *The U.S. Steel Hour*), 1956.

"The Plunge," *Kraft Television Theatre* (also known as *Kraft Mystery Theatre* and *Kraft Theatre*), 1956.

Duke of Buckingham, "Trial of Colonel Blood," *On Trial* (also known as *The Joseph Cotten Show* and *The Joseph Cotten Show: On Trial*), 1957.

Johnny, "The Earring," *General Electric Theater* (also known as *G. E. Theater*), 1957.

Lieutenant, "Nightmare in 4–D," *Alfred Hitchcock Presents,* CBS, 1957.

Charles, "Design for Loving," *Alfred Hitchcock Presents,* CBS, 1958.

Harold Stern, "Delusion," *Alcoa Presents,* 1959.

"Slezak and Son," *New Comedy Showcase,* 1960.

The little man, "The Little Man Who Was There," *Alfred Hitchcock Presents,* CBS, 1960.

Leo Thorby, "Maria," *Alfred Hitchcock Presents,* CBS, 1961.

"A Talk with Hitchcock," *Telescope,* 1964.

Norman, "Nightbirds," *The Most Deadly Game,* 1970.

Dickon, "Scarecrow," *Hollywood Television Theatre,* PBS, 1971.

"Operation: Mr. Felix," *O'Hara, U.S. Treasury,* 1972.

Henry Mallory, "A Feast of Blood," *Night Gallery,* 1972.

Lewis, "The Gondola," *Hollywood Television Theatre,* PBS, 1973.

Harry Fine, "Night of the Piraeus," *Kojak,* 1975.

Cornelius Sumner, *Quincy M.E.* (also known as *Quincy*), 1982.

The Match Game/Hollywood Squares Hour, 1984.

Professor, "Laura's Struggle," *The Paper Chase* (also known as *The Paper Chase: The Fourth Year, The Paper Chase: The Graduation Year, The Paper Chase: The Second Year* and *The Paper Chase: The Third Year*), 1985.

Merlin, "The Last Defender of Camelot," *The Twilight Zone,* 1986.

Lloyd Marcus, "If the Frame Fits," *Murder, She Wrote,* CBS, 1986.

General Leand Masters, "Day One," *Wiseguy,* 1989.

General Leand Masters, "Day Four," *Wiseguy,* 1989.

General Leand Masters, "Day Seven," *Wiseguy,* 1989.

General Leand Masters, "Day Nine," *Wiseguy,* 1989.

Philip Arkham, "The Committee," *Murder, She Wrote,* CBS, 1991.

Gordon Wimsatt, "Oceans White with Phone," *Civil Wars,* ABC, 1992.

Professor Richard Galen, "The Chase," *Star Trek: The Next Generation,* 1993.

Edward St. Cloud, "Murder in White," *Murder, She Wrote,* CBS, 1993.

"George" Lyle Bartlett, "Bye George," *Wings,* NBC, 1996.

"The Battle Over Citizen Kane," *The American Experience,* 1996.

"Vincent Price: The Versatile Villain," *Biography,* 1997.

Rabbi and District attorney Asher Silverman, "Part V," *The Practice,* ABC, 1997.

Rabbi and District attorney Asher Silverman, "Part VI," *The Practice,* ABC, 1997.

Rabbi and District attorney Asher Silverman, "Line of Duty," *The Practice,* ABC, 1998.

"Hitchcock, Selznick and the End of Hollywood," *American Masters,* 1998.

Television Appearances; Miniseries:
Family Portraits: Alfred Hitchcock, 1995.

Television Appearances; Pilots:
Dr. Isaac Mentnor, *Seven Days,* UPN, 1998.

Television Director; Series:
Revue, CBS, 1950–52.

The Adventures of Kit Carson (also known as *Kit Carson*), 1951.

Alfred Hitchcock Presents, 1958–1962.

Insight, 1960.

The Alfred Hitchcock Hour, 1963–64.

Hollywood Television Theatre, PBS, 1972–73.

Television Producer; Series:
The Alfred Hitchcock Hour, 1962.

The Name of the Game, NBC, 1969–70.

Hollywood Television Theatre, PBS, 1972–73, then executive producer, 1974.

Tales of the Unexpected (also known as *Roald Dahl's "Tales of the Unexpected"*), syndicated, 1979–80.

Television Executive Producer; Series:
Hollywood Television Theatre, PBS, 1974.

Six Characters in Search of an Author (also known as *Hollywood Television Theatre: Six Characters in Search of an Author*), 1976.

Television Director; Episodic:
"Mr. Lincoln," *Omnibus,* NBC, 1952.

The Jail, ABC, 1961.

The Jar, CBS, 1964.

Journey to the Unknown (also known as *Out of the Unknown*), 1968.

"Youth from Vienna," *Tales of the Unexpected* (also known as *Roald Dahl's Tales of the Unexpected*), syndicated, 1979.

Television Producer; Episodic:
Journey to the Unknown (also known as *Out of the Unknown*), 1968.

Television Director; Movies:
The Smugglers, NBC, 1966.

Companions in Nightmare, NBC, 1967.

Columbo: Lady in Waiting, NBC, 1971.

Television Producer; Movies:
The Smugglers, NBC, 1966.

Companions in Nightmare, NBC, 1967.

What's a Nice Girl Like You ...?, 1971.

The Bravos, ABC, 1972.

Awake and Sing!, 1972.

Shadow of a Gunman, 1972.

The Gondola, 1973.

Carola, 1973.

Steambath, 1973.

The Man of Destiny, 1973.

The Carpenters, 1974.

The Stye of the Blind Pigs, 1974.

Double Solitaire, 1974.

The Chinese Prime Minister, 1974.
Nourish the Beast, 1974.
For the Use of the Hall, 1975.
Knuckle, 1975.
The Ashes of Mrs. Reasoner, 1976.
The Last of Mrs. Lincoln, 1976.
The Fatal Weakness, 1976.
The Hemingway Play, 1977.
And the Soul Shall Dance, 1978.
Actor (also known as *Actor, the Paul Muni Story),* 1978.
Tales of the Unexpected, 1979.

Television Work; Specials:
Executive producer, *Another Part of the Forest,* 1972.

RECORDINGS

Videos:
Saboteur: A Closer Look, Universal Studios Home Video, 2000.
Dead Poets: A Look Back, Buena Vista, 2006.

WRITINGS

Books:
Stages (autobiography), 1993.

OTHER SOURCES

Periodicals:
Classic Images, April, 2000, pp. 73–77.
Starlog, December, 1998.

LOMBARDOZZI, Domenick 1976–
    (Dom Lombardozzi, Dominick Lombardozzi)

PERSONAL

Original name, Domenico Lombardozzi; born March 25, 1976, in the Bronx, New York.

Addresses: *Agent*—The Gersh Agency, 232 North Canon Dr., Beverly Hills, CA 90210. *Manager*—Leverage Management, 3030 Pennsylvania Ave., Santa Monica, CA 90404.

Career: Actor.

CREDITS

Film Appearances:
(As Dominick Lombardozzi) Nicky Zero, *A Bronx Tale,* Savoy Pictures, 1993.
Joey Chips, *Kiss Me, Guido,* Paramount, 1997.
Key, *54* (also known as *Fifty–Four),* Miramax, 1998.
Policeman One, *Side Streets,* Cargo Films, 1998.
Cyrill, *Just One Time,* Cowboy Booking International, 1999.
Tow truck driver, *For Love of the Game,* MCA/Universal, 1999.
Frankie, *The Young Girl and the Monsoon,* Artistic License, 1999.
Todd, *The Yards,* Miramax, 2000.
Schmitty, *Jungle Juice,* Bayshore Entertainment, 2001.
(Uncredited) Counterman, *Kate & Leopold,* Miramax, 2001.
Eddie Iovine, *Love in the Time of Money,* Blow Up Pictures, 2002.
Wyatt, *Phone Booth,* Twentieth Century–Fox, 2002.
G. Q., *S.W.A.T.,* Columbia, 2003.
Artie Bottolota, Jr., *Carlito's Way: Rise to Power,* Universal, 2005.
Jerry McQueen, *Find Me Guilty* (also known as *Find Me Guilty: The Jackie Dee Story),* Yari Film Group, 2006.
Leo Sullivan, *Freedomland,* Sony, 2006.
Switek, *Miami Vice,* Universal, 2006.

Television Appearances; Series:
Detective Thomas "Herc" Hauk, *The Wire,* HBO, 2002–2007.

Television Appearances; Movies:
Moose Skowron, *61** (also known as *61),* HBO, 2001.
Cueball, *The Man,* 2007.

Television Appearances; Specials:
Himself, *"The Wire": It's All Connected,* HBO, 2006.

Television Appearances; Pilots:
Cueball, *The Man,* CBS, 2007.

Television Appearances; Episodic:
Jason Vitone, "Ambitious," *Law & Order,* NBC, 1999.
"The Beat Goes On," *The Beat,* UPN, 2000.
Ralph Galino, "A Cock and Balls Story," *Oz,* HBO, 2000.
Ralph Galino, "Obituaries," *Oz,* HBO, 2000.
Max Legazi, "Johnny Got His Gold," *NYPD Blue,* ABC, 2001.
Detective Barry Newcastle, "Childhood Memories," *Third Watch,* NBC, 2001.

Marcus Peluso, "Too Jung to Die," *The Jury,* Fox, 2001.
Joe Petro, "Blue Wall," *Law & Order: Trial by Jury,* NBC, 2005.
Dom, "Dominated," *Entourage,* HBO, 2006.
Dom, "Guys and Dolls," *Entourage,* HBO, 2006.

LURIE, John 1952–

PERSONAL

Born December 14, 1952, in Worcester, MA (some sources say Minneapolis, MN).

Career: Actor and composer. The Lounge Lizards (an experimental music group), member and leader; John Lurie National Orchestra, founder.

Awards, Honors: ASCAP Award, top box office film, American Society of Composers, Authors and Publishers, 1996, Grammy Award nomination, best instrumental composition written for a motion picture or for television, 1997, for *Get Shorty.*

CREDITS

Film Appearances:
Rome '78, 1978.
Sax player, *Permanent Vacation,* 1980.
The Lizard, *The Offenders,* B Movies, 1980.
Underground U.S.A., New Cinema, 1980.
Men in Orbit, 1981.
The saxophonist, *Subway Riders,* Hep Pictures, 1981.
Himself, *New York Beat Movie* (also known as *Downtown 81* and *Glenn O'Brien's "New York Beat Movie"*), 1981.
Slater, *Paris, Texas,* Twentieth Century–Fox, 1984.
Willie, *Stranger Than Paradise,* Samuel Goldwyn Company, 1984.
Neighbor saxophonist, *Desperately Seeking Susan,* Orion, 1985.
Jack, *Down by Law* (also known as *Down by Law—Alles im griff*), Island Pictures, 1986.
The Kitchen Presents "Two Moon July" (documentary; also known as *Two Moon July*), 1986.
Cusatelli, *Il piccolo diavolo* (also known as *The Little Devil*), 1988.
James, *The Last Temptation of Christ,* Universal, 1988.
Himself, *Location Production Footage: "The Last Temptation of Christ"* (documentary short), Universal, 1988.
Sparky, *Wild at Heart* (also known as *David Lynch's "Wild at Heart"*), Samuel Goldwyn Company, 1990.
Himself, *John Lurie and the Lounge Lizards Live in Berlin* (documentary), Telecom Japan, 1992.

Saxophone player, *Blue in the Face* (also known as *Brooklyn Boogie*), Miramax, 1995.
Coker, *Just Your Luck* (also known as *Whiskey Down*), PolyGram Video, 1996.
Distinguished man, *New Rose Hotel,* Avalanche Home Entertainment, 1998.
Downtown 81, Zeitgeist Films, 2000.
Frank, *Sleepwalk,* 2001.
Himself, *5 Sides of a Coin* (documentary), Seventh Art Releasing, 2003.
Face Addict, Funny Balloons, 2005.
TV Party (documentary), BrinkDVD, 2005.

Film Work:
Director, *Men in Orbit,* 1978.
Saxophonist, *Permanent Vacation,* 1980.
Saxophonist, *Subway Riders,* 1981.
Assistance, *Heaven,* Island Pictures, 1987.
Guitar and harmonica, *Mystery Train,* Orion, 1989.
Musician, *Animal Factory,* New City Releasing, 2000.

Television Appearances; Series:
Guest host VJ, *VH1 New Visions,* VH1, 1986.
Fishing with John, IFC and Bravo, 1991.
#97P528 Greg Penders, *Oz,* HBO, 2001–2003.
Narrator, *Animal Cops: Detroit,* Animal Planet, 2002.
Narrator, *Animal Cops—Houston,* Animal Planet, 2003–2004.

Television Appearances; Movies:
(Archive footage) Willie, *Wanderlust,* 2005.

Television Appearances; Specials:
Host, *Are You Comfortable?,* 2003.

Television Appearances; Episodic:
Himself, "Hooky/Mermaid Man and Barnacleboy II," *SpongeBob Square Pants* (animated; also known as *SpongeBob*), Nickelodeon, 2000.
Jack, *Cinema mil,* 2005.

Television Executive Producer; Movies:
Are You Comfortable?, 2003.

Television Director; Episodic:
Fishing with John, 1991.

WRITINGS

Film Scores:
Stranger Than Paradise Part One: The New World, 1982.
Variety, Horizon Films, 1983.
Stranger Than Paradise, Samuel Goldwyn Company, 1984.

City Limits, 1985.
Down by Law (also known as *Down by Law—Alles im griff*), New Yorker Films, 1987.
Mystery Train, Orion, 1989.
Keep It for Yourself (short), 1991.
Blue in the Face (also known as *Brooklyn Boogie*), Miramax, 1995.
Get Shorty, Metro–Goldwyn–Mayer/United Artists, 1995.
Manny & Lo, Sony Pictures Classics, 1996.
Na krasnom modrom Dunaji (also known as *On the Beautiful Blue Danube*), 1997.
Excess Baggage, Columbia, 1997.
Lulu on the Bridge, Trimark Pictures, 1998.
Clay Pigeons (also known as *Clay Pigeons—Lebende Ziele* and *Lebende Ziele*), Gramercy Pictures, 1998.
Animal Factory, New City Releasing, 2000.
Face Addict, Funny Balloons, 2005.

Film Additional Music:

The Loveless (also known as *Breakdown*), 1982.
Slam Dance, Island Pictures, 1987.

Television Scores; Movies:

Police Story: Monster Manor, ABC, 1988.

Television Main Title Theme; Specials:

Late Night with Conan O'Brien: 10th Anniversary Special, NBC, 2003.

Television Scores; Episodic:

"Massai: Jambo!," *Arsenal Atlas,* 1987.
"Mauritius—Zanzibar—Dar es salam," *Arsenal Atlas,* 1987.
Fishing with John, IFC and Bravo, 1991.

Television Music; Episodic:

Composed music for *Late Night with Conan O'Brien* (also known as *Conan O'Brien*), NBC.

Stage Music:

The Hairy Ape, Selwyn Theatre, New York City, 1997.

M

MANTELL, Michael
    (Michael Mantel, Michael A. Mantel, Michael Albert Mantel)

PERSONAL

Career: Actor.

Awards, Honors: Florida Film Critics Award (with others), best ensemble cast, 2004, for *A Mighty Wind;* Copper Wing Award (with others), best ensemble, Phoenix Film Festival, 2006, for *Self Medicated.*

CREDITS

Film Appearances:
(As Michael Albert Mantel) Mr. Love, *The Brother from Another Planet,* Cinecom International, 1984.
(As Michael A. Mantel) Doolin, *Matewan,* Cinecom International, 1987.
Abe Attell, *Eight Men Out,* Orion, 1988.
Businessman, *The Appointments of Dennis Jennings,* 1988.
Dr. Popovich, *Reversal of Fortune,* Warner Bros., 1990.
Coral Bay owner (some sources cite Coral Ray owner), *Little Man Tate,* Orion, 1991.
Deputy Warren, *Out of the Rain* (also known as *End of Innocence*), Artisan Entertainment, 1991.
Zimmer, *City of Hope,* 1991.
Dr. Kline, *Passion Fish,* Miramax, 1992.
Aaron Holder, *The Night We Never Met,* Miramax, 1993.
Harold, *Dead Funny,* A–Pix Entertainment, 1994.
Pennebaker, *Quiz Show,* Buena Vista, 1994.
Sam, *Bed of Roses,* New Line Cinema, 1996.
Soldier, *Alien Force,* 1996.
Angry customer, *The Velocity of Gary,* Columbia TriStar Home Video, 1998.

Taylor Woods (some sources cite Taylor Cook), *Deterrence,* Paramount, 1999.
Dr. Jeff Bleckner, *Gun Shy,* Buena Vista, 2000.
Kleiman, *Lost Souls,* New Line Cinema, 2000.
Harold Fishbein, *Allerd Fishbein's in Love,* 2000.
Dell, *Rangers,* 2000.
Dr. Frazier at cryogenic institute, *Artificial Intelligence: AI* (also known as *A.I.: Artificial Intelligence*), Warner Bros., 2001.
Stewart, *Secretary,* Lions Gate Films, 2002.
Deputy mayor, *A Mighty Wind,* Warner Bros., 2003.
Dr. Reinholtz, *Self Medicated,* 2005.
Glen, *The World's Fastest Indian,* Magnolia Pictures, 2005.
Dr. Meisenbach, *Thank Your for Smoking,* Fox Searchlight, 2006.
Dr. Stan, *Ocean's' Thirteen* (also known as *13*), Warner Bros., 2007.

Television Appearances; Series:
Louis Begg, *Love and Marriage,* Fox, 1996.
David Rayburn, *State of Grace,* 2001.

Television Appearances; Movies:
Dr. Friedman, *Against Her Will: An Incident in Baltimore,* CBS, 1992.
Lester Correl, *Power 98,* HBO, 1996.
Dennis Smith, *Voice from the Grave: From the Files of "Unsolved Mysteries"* (also known as *Crimes of Passion: Voice from the Grave, From the Files of "Unsolved Mysteries:" Voice from the Grave,* and *Unsolved Mysteries: Voice from the Grave*), NBC, 1996.
Dr. Reuben Avery, *Sins of the Mind,* USA Network, 1997.
Larry, *Alien Nation: The Udara Legacy,* Fox, 1997.
Stephen Royer, *Blackout Effect* (also known as *747*), NBC, 1998.
Art Rupe, *Little Richard,* NBC, 2000.
David Lehmann, *Chain of Command,* HBO, 2000.

Gerry, *A Private Affair,* Black Entertainment Television, 2000.

Sidney Schlenker, *When Billie Beat Bobby* (also known as *Bille contre Bobby: La bataille des sexes*), ABC, 2001.

Television Appearances; Pilots:

Joseph Shapiro, *Ally McBeal,* Fox, 1997.

Dr. Boaz, *Strange World,* ABC, 1999.

Television Appearances; Specials:

"Taking a Stand," *ABC Afterschool Special,* ABC, 1989.

Interviewee, *Workplace Violence: Danger on the Job,* Arts and Entertainment, 2001.

Television Appearances; Episodic:

William Wright, "Company Man," *Spenser: For Hire,* 1988.

Cutler, "Die Laughing," *B. L. Stryker,* ABC, 1989.

Jimmy Newton, "The Witness," *Matlock,* NBC, 1990.

Edward Kay, "Mushrooms," *Law & Order,* NBC, 1991.

Morris Hoffman, "Breeder," *Law & Order,* NBC, 1994.

Steve White, "Rockin' Robin," *NYPD Blue,* ABC, 1994.

Mr. Burtis, "Couch Potatoes," *Roseanne,* ABC, 1995.

Howard Sewell, "The Farthest Man from Home," *Space: Above and Beyond,* Fox, 1995.

Howard Sewell, "Hostile Visit," *Space: Above and Beyond,* Fox, 1995.

Howard Sewell, "Choice or Chance," *Space: Above and Beyond,* Fox, 1995.

Dr. Underman, "Injustice for All," *Courthouse,* CBS, 1995.

Mr. Rosenthal, "Benefactors," *Party of Five,* Fox, 1996.

Howard Sewell, "The Angriest Angel," *Space: Above and Beyond,* Fox, 1996.

Rabbi Bennett, *High Incident,* ABC, 1996.

Mr. Hendricks, "Saturn," *The Secret World of Alex Mack* (also known as *Alex Mack*), 1996.

Henry Garner, "An American Dream," *Cracker* (also known as *Cracker: Mind Over Murder* and *Fitz*), ABC, 1997.

Cedric Davison, "Return of Crumb," *Early Edition,* CBS, 1998.

Prosecutor, "These Boots Were Made for Stalking," *To Have & to Hold,* CBS, 1998.

Prosecutor, "Driveway to Heaven," *To Have & to Hold,* 1998.

Gas man, "Is There a Woogy in the House?," *Charmed,* The WB, 1999.

Dr. James Riley, "Alpha," *The X–Files,* Fox, 1999.

Oliver Simon, "City Of ...," *Angel* (also known as *Angel: The Series*), The WB, 1999.

Clifford Bell, "Love and Money," *Family Law,* CBS, 1999.

Mr. Spencer, "Abby Road," *ER,* NBC, 2000.

Charles Lassiter, "Human Touch," *Judging Amy,* CBS, 2000.

Oliver Simon, "Eternity," *Angel* (also known as *Angel: The Series*), The WB, 2000.

Ray Garth, "Narcosis," *Law & Order,* NBC, 2000.

James Dupree, "The Ultimate Question," *Hollywood Off–Ramp,* E! Entertainment Television, 2000.

Donnie, "The Lost," *Third Watch,* NBC, 2000.

"Miracle at the Cucina," *That's Life,* CBS, 2001.

Doctor, "Everyone Deserves to Be Loved," *Any Day Now,* Lifetime, 2001.

Jamie Hotchkiss, "Bad Moon Rising," *The West Wing,* NBC, 2001.

Howard Gordon, "Gordo's Bar Mitzvah," *Lizzie McGuire,* Disney Channel, 2002.

Howard Gordon, "Mom's Best Friend," *Lizzie McGuire,* Disney Channel, 2002.

"The Prisoner," *The Agency,* CBS, 2002.

Steve Hillenburg, "Day 2: 9:00 p.m.–10:00 p.m.," *24,* Fox, 2003.

Fred Larson, "A Tale of Poes and Fire," *Gilmore Girls* (also known as *Gilmore Girls: Beginnings*), The WB, 2003.

Dr. Stevens, "Forever," *CSI: Crime Scene Investigation* (also known as *C.S.I., CSI: Las Vegas, CSI Weekends,* and *Les experts*), CBS, 2003.

Bernard Freedman, "Things She Said," *The Lyon's Den,* NBC, 2003.

Field, "Blind Eye," *The District,* CBS, 2003.

Car salesman, "The Letter," *Miracles,* ABC, 2003.

Shelly Lukens, "Full Disclosure," *The West Wing,* NBC, 2004.

Alan Lowell, "On the Fence," *NYPD Blue,* ABC, 2004.

Doctor, "The Dare," *Six Feet Under,* HBO, 2004.

Roger Shyler, "Necessary Risks," *Crossing Jordan,* NBC, 2004.

Nyles, "The Other Side of the Tracks," *Medium,* NBC, 2005.

"The Limit," *Just Legal,* The WB, 2005.

Ken Westin, "Honor," *Cold Case,* CBS, 2005.

Larry Carlyle, "The Man on Death Row," *Bones,* Fox, 2005.

(As Michael Mantel) Mercer, "The Safe Harbor," *The O.C.,* Fox, 2006.

Norman Elby, "LAPD Blue," *Shark,* CBS, 2006.

James Corwin, "The Thing with Feathers," *Without a Trace* (also known as *W.A.T.*), CBS, 2006.

Jesse Abrams, "Road Rage," *Close to Home,* CBS, 2007.

Appeared as Jimmy Demonico, *Law & Order: Special Victims Unit* (also known as *Law & Order: SVU* and *Special Victims Unit*), NBC; and in episodes of *American Dreams,* NBC; *100 Centre Street,* Arts and Entertainment; and *Strong Medicine,* Lifetime.

Television Appearances; Other:

Theo Bloom, *Wild Things: Diamonds in the Rough,* 2005.

Stage Appearances:

Rabbi, *The Tenth Man,* Vivian Beaumont Theatre, Lincoln Center, New York City, 1989–90.

Harry Scupp and Mr. Blum, *Bad Habits,* Manhattan Theatre Club Stage I, New York City, 1990.

MARCH, Stephanie 1974–

PERSONAL

Full name, Stephanie Caroline March; born July 23, 1974, in Dallas, TX; son of John Abe March IV and Laura Len Irwin; married Bobby Flay (a chef), February 20, 2005. *Education:* Northwestern University, B.S., theatre and Hispanic studies, 1996. *Avocational Interests:* Reading, traveling, swimming, yoga, and dance.

Addresses: *Agent*—The Gersh Agency, 232 North Canon Dr., Beverly Hills, CA 90210. *Publicist*—I/D Public Relations, 8409 Santa Monica Blvd., West Hollywood, CA 90069.

Career: Actress.

CREDITS

Film Appearances:
Coasting, 2000.
Kim, *Focus Room* (short), Hellespont Films, 2003.
Nikki, *Head of State,* DreamWorks, 2003.
Julie, *Mr. & Mrs. Smith,* Twentieth Century–Fox, 2005.
Kay, *East Broadway* (also known as *Falling for Grace*), 2006.
Cathy, *Flannel Pajamas,* Gigantic Pictures, 2006.
Julia, *The Treatment,* New Yorker Films, 2006.
Stephanie, *Copy That* (short), 2006.
Herself, *Stephanie March: "Conviction"* (short), Universal, 2006.

Television Appearances; Series:
Assistant district attorney Alexandra Cabot, *Law & Order: Special Victims Unit* (also known as *Law & Order: SVU* and *Special Victims Unit*), NBC, 2000–2005.
Host, *What America Eats with PARADE,* 2004.
Alexandra Cabot, *Conviction,* NBC, 2006.

Television Appearances; Movies:
Miss Forsythe, *Death of a Salesman,* Showtime, 2000.
Cissy Hathaway, *Jesse Stone: Night Passage,* CBS, 2006.

Television Appearances; Specials:
Celebrity Weddings: In Style (also known as *In Style: Celebrity Weddings*), ABC, 2006.

Television Appearances; Episodic:
Arlene, "A Bris Is Just a Bris," *Early Edition,* CBS, 1997.
Herself, *Boy Meets Grill with Bobby Flay,* 2002.
Herself, "Head of State," *HBO First Look,* HBO, 2003.
The Caroline Rhea Show, syndicated, 2003.
Extra TV, syndicated, 2003, 2004.
Gretchen Thomas, "Blind Date," *30 Rock,* NBC, 2006.

Stage Appearances:
(Broadway debut) Miss Forsythe, *Death of a Salesman,* Chicago, IL, 1998, then Eugene O'Neill Theater, New York City, 1999.
Lady Caroline, *Enchanted April,* Hartford Stage Company, Hartford, CT, 2000.
Linda MacArthur, *Talk Radio!,* Long Acre Theatre, New York City, 2007.

Made professional debut as Helena, *A Midsummer Night's Dream,* Chicago, IL.

MARGOLIN, Arnold

PERSONAL

Brother of Stuart Margolin (an actor).

Career: Writer, producer, director, and actor.

Awards, Honors: Emmy Award (with Charles Fox), outstanding achievement in music, lyrics, and special material, 1970, for theme music, *Love, American Style;* Emmy Award nominations (with others), outstanding comedy series, 1970, 1971, both for *Love, American Style.*

CREDITS

Film Appearances:
Dr. Whitehat, *Young Doctors in Love,* Twentieth Century–Fox, 1982.
Mr. Vanderway, *Exit to Eden,* Savoy Pictures, 1994.
Max, *Bull Run,* FireRock Entertainment, 2006.

Television Producer; Series:
The McLean Stevenson Show, NBC, 1976.
Supervising producer, *Private Benjamin,* CBS, 1981.
(And supervising producer) *Growing Pains,* ABC, 1985–86.
One Big Family, syndicated, 1986.
(And creator) *A Family for Joe,* NBC, 1990.
(And creator) *Promised Land* (also known as *Land of the Brave*), CBS, 1998–99.

Also executive producer of *Love, American Style,* ABC; and story editor, *My Mother the Car,* NBC.

Television Producer; Pilots:
(And director) *Two Boys,* NBC, 1970.
Going Places, NBC, 1973.
That's My Mama, ABC, 1974.
The Orphan and the Dude, ABC, 1975.
Harry and Maggie, CBS, 1975.
(And director) *Walkin' Walter,* ABC, 1977.
The Dooley Brothers, CBS, 1979.
Creator and executive producer, *A Family for Joe,* NBC, 1990.

Television Producer; Movies:
Between Love and Honor, CBS, 1995.

Television Director; Episodic:
"Love and the Spaced–Out Chick," *Love, American Style,* ABC, 1972.

Also directed episodes of *Private Benjamin,* CBS.

Television Appearances; Movies:
Dorian Dupree, *He's Not Your Son,* CBS, 1984.

Television Appearances; Episodic:
Arnold, "Sizzling Sidney," *Hey, Landlord,* 1966.
Beatnik, "Czech Your Wife, Sir?," *Hey, Landlord,* 1967.
"Love and the Sack," *Love, American Style,* ABC, 1971.
"Love and the Hip Arrangement," *Love, American Style,* ABC, 1972.
Reverend Tebbits, "Finale," *Promised Land* (also known as *Home of the Brave*), CBS, 1999.

WRITINGS

Screenplays:
Star Spangled Girl, Paramount, 1971.
Snowball Express, Buena Vista, 1972.
Russian Roulette, Avco Embassy, 1975.
The Adventures of Mary–Kate & Ashley: The Case of the Sea World Adventure (also based on story by Margolin), Dualstar Productions, 1995.
The Adventures of Mary–Kate & Ashley: The Case of the Mystery Cruise (also based on story by Margolin), Dualstar Productions, 1995.
Bull Run, FireRock Entertainment, 2006.

Television Movies:
A Good Sport, CBS, 1984.
He's Not Your Son, CBS, 1984.
Between Love and Honor, CBS, 1995.

Television Pilots:
Two Boys, 1970.
The Orphan and the Dude, ABC, 1975.
Harry and Maggie, CBS, 1975.
The Dooley Brothers, CBS, 1979.
A Family for Joe, NBC, 1990.

Television Episodes:
"Take a Tramp to Lunch This Week," *The Smothers Brothers Show,* CBS, 1965.
"It Don't Mean a Dang if It Ain't Got That Twang," *The Smothers Brothers Show,* CBS, 1965.
"Mr. Big Curtsies Out," *Mr. Terrific,* CBS, 1967.
"His Two Right Arms," *Mary Tyler Moore* (also known as *The Mary Tyler Moore Show*), CBS, 1972.
"Weekend Fantasy," *Growing Pains,* ABC, 1985.
"The Love Song of M. Aaron Seaver," *Growing Pains,* ABC, 1986.
One Big Family, syndicated, 1986.
"Vengeance Is Mine," *War of the Worlds* (also known as *War of the Worlds: The Second Invasion*), syndicated, 1989.
"Rain Dance," *The Wild Thornberrys* (animated), Nickelodeon, 1999.

Also writer for episodes of *The Andy Griffith Show* (also known as *Andy of Mayberry*), CBS; *Love, American Style,* ABC; *My Mother the Car; O.K. Crackerby!; Private Benjamin,* CBS; *Promised Land* (also known as *Home of the Brave*), CBS; *Touched by an Angel,* CBS; and *Wind at My Back,* CBC.

Television Specials:
The Adventures of Mary–Kate and Ashley: Mystery on the High Seas (also based on story by Margolin), ABC, 1995.

Television Music; Series:
Composer and lyricist, theme song, *Love, American Style,* ABC, 1969.

MARTIN, Ivan
(Yvan Martin)

PERSONAL

Career: Actor.

CREDITS

Film Appearances:
Wits End, *Bad Liver & a Broken Heart* (short), 1996.
Love, etc., Phaedra Cinema, 1996.

Indie veejay, *Coming Soon,* Unapix Entertainment Productions, 1999.

Ray, *Sleepwalk,* 2001.

(As Yvan Martin) Igor, *I Am Josh Polonski's Brother,* 2001.

Guilty of Love (short), 2001.

Galaxie executive, *Hollywood Ending,* DreamWorks, 2002.

Jim, *High Times Potluck,* Ardustry Home Entertainment, 2002.

Serge, *People I Know* (also known as *Im inneren kreis* and *Der innere kreis*), Miramax, 2002.

Lorenzo, *The Lucky Ones,* Universal, 2003.

Nick, *Prey for Rock & Roll,* Mac Releasing, 2003.

Ricky, *Rhythm of the Saints,* 2003.

Neville, *The Deep and Dreamless Sleep* (also known as *Project 350*), 2004.

Christopher Ambrose, *Homecoming,* 2005.

Sean, *Funny Valentine,* Xenon Pictures, 2005.

Frank Halsey, *Long Distance,* Image Entertainment, 2005.

Bartender, *Winter Passing,* Focus Features, 2005.

Rocco, *One Last Thing …,* Magnolia Pictures, 2005.

Juego (short), 2006.

Pablito, *Un Franco, 14 Pesetas,* 2006.

Charlie, *9A,* 2006.

Morris Anson, *Neal Cassady,* 2007.

Television Appearances; Miniseries:
Nicky's friend, *Witness to the Mob,* NBC, 1998.

Television Appearances; Episodic:
Ivan Fonseca, "Neighbors," *Ed,* NBC, 2002.

Jerome, "Hooked," *Law & Order: Special Victims Unit* (also known as *Law & Order: SVU* and *Special Victims Unit*), NBC, 2005.

Kenny Giacolone, "The Fleshy Part of the Thigh," *The Sopranos,* HBO, 2006.

MATENOPOULOS, Debbie 1974–

PERSONAL

Original name, Thespina "Despina" Matenopoulos; born December 13, 1974, in Richmond, VA; father a woodworker; mother a beauty salon operator; married Jay Faires (a music producer), July 5, 2003. *Education:* Attended Virginia Commonwealth University, 1992–94; New York University, B.A., 1997.

Addresses: *Manager*—Steven Greener, Handprint Entertainment, 1100 Glendon Ave., Suite 1000, Los Angeles, CA 90024. *Publicist*—Howard Bragman, Fifteen Minutes Public Relations, 8436 West Third St., Suite 650, Los Angeles, CA 90048.

Career: Actress, broadcast correspondent, and producer.

Awards, Honors: Daytime Emmy Award nomination (with others), outstanding talk show host, 1999, for *The View.*

CREDITS

Television Appearances; Series:
Cohost, *The View,* ABC, 1997–99.

Cohost, *The Screening Room,* TV Guide Channel, 1999.

Celebrity Deathmatch (also known as *MTV's "Celebrity Deathmatch"*), MTV, 2000–2002.

Cohost, *Good Day Live,* Fox, 2004–2005.

Television Appearances; Specials:
The 2001 TV Guide Awards, Fox, 2001.

Test the Nation, Fox, 2003.

"Celebrity Weddings," *VH1: All Access,* VH1, 2004.

100 Greatest Kid Stars, VH1, 2005.

I Love the Holidays, VH1, 2005.

20 Greatest Celebreality Moments, VH1, 2006.

Host, *Fashion Police Golden Globes 2006,* 2006.

Correspondent, *Live from the Red Carpet: The 2006 Emmy Awards,* 2006.

Host, *E!'s Live Countdown to the Academy Awards,* E! Entertainment Television, 2006.

Host, *E!'s Live Countdown to the Emmys,* E! Entertainment Television, 2006.

Host, *E!'s Live Countdown to the Academy Awards,* E! Entertainment Television, 2007.

Host, *E!'s Live Countdown to the Golden Globes,* E! Entertainment Television, 2007.

Host, *E!'s Live Countdown to the Grammys,* E! Entertainment Television, 2007.

Cohost, *Live from the Red Carpet: The 2007 Academy Awards,* 2007.

Correspondent, *Live from the Red Carpet: The 2007 Golden Globe Awards,* 2007.

Television Appearances; Miniseries:
The 100 Scariest Movie Moments, Bravo, 2004.

I Love the '90s: Part Deux, VH1, 2005.

I Love the 80's 3-D, VH1, 2005.

I Love Toys, VH1, 2006.

I Love the '70s: Volume 2, VH1, 2006.

Television Appearances; Episodic:
Herself, "The Six Southern Gentlemen of Tennessee," *Sports Night,* ABC, 1998.

Woman at party, *General Hospital,* ABC, 1998.
(Uncredited) *Saturday Night Live* (also known as *SNL*), NBC, 1999.
The Howard Stern Radio Show, syndicated, 1999.
Howard Stern, E! Entertainment Television, 1999.
The Roseanne Show, syndicated, 2000.
The Test, FX Network, 2001.
Judge, *He's a Lady,* TBS, 2004.
Jimmy Kimmel Live, ABC, 2005.
Joanna, "The Big Dollars & Sense Episode," *Half & Half,* UPN, 2005.
Celebrity cohost, *Queer Edge with Jack E. Jett & Sandra Bernhard,* 2005.
The Big Idea with Donny Deutsch, CNBC, 2005.
Host, *The Daily 10,* 2006.
Host, "Miami," *Instant Beauty Pageant,* 2006.
The View, ABC, 2006.

Appeared in an episode of *American Dreams,* NBC.

Film Appearances:
Lisa Swayzak, *Endsville,* Stick Figure Productions, 2000.
Angryman, Blue Mutt Productions, 2001.
Herself, *Knocked Up,* Universal, 2007.

Film Work:
Executive producer, *Angryman,* Blue Mutt Productions, 2001.

RECORDINGS

Videos:
Voice, *Celebrity Deathmatch* (video game; also known as *MTV's "Celebrity Deathmatch"*), Gotham Games/ Take2 Interactive, 2003.
Herself, *The Great 80's TV Flashback,* Universal Studios Home Video, 2006.

OTHER SOURCES

Periodicals:
People Weekly, March 30, 1998, p. 16.

McFARLAND, Rebecca

PERSONAL

Addresses: *Agent*—Don Buchwald and Associates, 6500 Wilshire Blvd., Suite 3300, Los Angeles, CA 90048.

Career: Actress.

CREDITS

Television Appearances; Series:
Christine, *The Army Show,* The WB, 1998.
Val Gibson, *Working,* NBC, 1998–99.

Television Appearances; Pilots:
Fargo, Trio, 2003.
Adeline, *Hollis & Rae,* ABC, 2006.

Television Appearances; Movies:
Jan Kyles, *A Place Called Home,* Hallmark Channel, 2004.

Television Appearances; Episodic:
"Stodermayer," *The Big Easy,* USA Network, 1996.
Janie, "Murder Can Be Contagious," *Diagnosis Murder,* CBS, 1996.
Anna, "The Little Kicks," *Seinfeld,* NBC, 1996.
Allie McNeil, "Soft Targets," *Pacific Blue,* USA Network, 1997.
Amber, "Guilt by Association," *Silk Stalkings,* USA Network, 1997.
Francey, "Handicaps," *Party of Five,* Fox, 1997.
Jane Oliver, "Citizen Canine," *Total Security,* ABC, 1997.
Penelope, "A Girl's Gotta Live in the Real World," *Jenny,* NBC, 1997.
Talli, "Random Thoughts," *Star Trek: Voyager* (also known as *Voyager*), UPN, 1997.
Barbara Ann, "Grace Under–funded," *Grace Under Fire,* ABC, 1998.
Loretta, "What Are Friends For?," *Union Square,* NBC, 1998.
Debbie Lefcowitz, "Wandalust," *Maximum Bob,* ABC, 1998.
Nancy, "While You Weren't Sleeping," *The Norm Show* (also known as *Norm*), ABC, 1999.
Rachel Borden, "Blown Away," *Philly,* ABC, 2001.
Donna Finer, "Johnny Got His Gold," *NYPD Blue,* ABC, 2001.
Melissa, "Taking Sides," *Once and Again,* ABC, 2002.
Jennifer Prince, "Low Blow," *NYPD Blue,* ABC, 2002.
Jason Kent's attorney, "Play with Fire," *CSI: Crime Scene Investigation* (also known as *C.S.I., CSI: Las Vegas, CSI Weekends,* and *Les experts*), CBS, 2003.
Dr. Ellie Bergen, "Graboid Rights," *Tremors,* Sci–Fi Channel, 2003.
Lynn, "Chris–Crossed," *Charmed,* The WB, 2003.
Leanne, "Alan Harper, Frontier Chiropractor," *Two and a Half Men,* CBS, 2003.
"Sweet Child of Mine," *Century City,* CBS, 2004.
Leanne, "An Old Flame with a New Wick," *Two and a Half Men,* CBS, 2004.

Detective Rachel Rapp, "Doppelgaenger," *Navy NCIS: Naval Criminal Investigative Service* (also known as *NCIS* and *NCIS: Naval Criminal Investigative Service*), CBS, 2005.

Leanne, "Something Salted and Twisted," *Two and a Half Men,* CBS, 2005.

Marla, "Ascendant," *Night Stalker,* ABC, 2006.

Susanne Derr, "It's Different for Girls," *Friday Night Lights,* NBC, 2006.

Leanne, "My Damn Stalker," *Two and a Half Men,* CBS, 2007.

Vanessa Leary, "Art," *Eyes,* ABC, 2007.

Susan Rodriguez, "Storm Front," *The Dresden Files,* Sci–Fi Channel, 2007.

Film Appearances:

Second theatre girl, *Scream 2,* Dimension Films, 1997.

Molly Fitzsimmons, *Art House,* Asylum, 1998.

Polly, *Elvis Tooka Bullet,* Dream Entertainment, 2001.

Caren, *LA Blues,* LA Blues, 2007.

McMANUS, Jim

PERSONAL

Raised in the United Kingdom.

Addresses: *Agent*—Arlene Thornton & Associates, 12711 Ventura Blvd., Suite 490, Studio City, CA 91604.

Career: Actor.

CREDITS

Television Appearances; Series:

Bernard, *Casting Off,* Thames Television, 1988.

Stanley Chambers, *Trouble in Mind,* London Weekend Television, beginning 1991.

Television Appearances; Miniseries:

Cab driver, *Young Charlie Chaplin* (also known as *Charlie Chaplin, Charlie the Kid, Chaplins barndom,* and *O jovem Charlie Chaplin*), Thames Television, 1988, broadcast on *WonderWorks* (also known as *WonderWorks: Young Charlie Chaplin*), PBS, 1989.

Tricky Reeves, *Tipping the Velvet* (also known as *Besant el vellut*), BBC and BBC America, 2002.

Television Appearances; Movies:

Driver, *Running Late* (also known as *Hetki lyoe*), [Great Britain], 1992.

Smithers, *Sharpe's Siege* (also known as *Die Scharfschutzen—Todfeinde*), Independent Television (England), 1996.

Pawnbroker, *Hornblower: Loyalty* (also known as *Horatio Hornblower 3, Hornblower and the Hotspur,* and *Hornblowerin seikkailut: Lojaalisuus*), Independent Television and Arts and Entertainment, 2003.

Television Appearances; Episodic:

Sam, "Seven for a Secret—Never to Be Told," *Dixon of Dock Green,* BBC, 1975.

Ollie Parsons, "Visiting Fireman," *The Sweeney,* Independent Television (England), 1976.

Sam, "Domino," *Dixon of Dock Green,* BBC, 1976.

Ophthalmologist, "The Invisible Enemy: Part 1," *Doctor Who,* BBC, 1977.

Truck driver's friend, "Heroes," *The Professionals,* Independent Television, 1978.

Accrington Stanley, "The Anastasia Syndrome," *Juliet Bravo,* BBC, 1980.

Alex, "It Never Rains ...," *Only Fools and Horses,* BBC, 1982.

George, "Looking for Mickey," *Minder,* Independent Television, 1982.

Wassermann, "Evacuation," *The Bill,* Independent Television, 1988.

Mr. Blake, "What Kind of Man?," *The Bill,* Independent Television, 1990.

Sir Cedric Sackbutt, "Cedric Sackbutt's Search for a Song," *T–Bag and the Pearls of Wisdom,* Independent Television, 1990.

Station master Dutton, "Friends Like These," *Press Gang,* Independent Television, 1990.

Reginald, *The House of Eliott,* BBC and Arts and Entertainment, 1992.

Brian, "A Fridge Too Far," *Minder,* Independent Television, 1994.

First police officer, "Masterchef," *Chef!,* BBC, 1994.

"Hospital Entrepreneurs," *Jack and Jeremy's Real Lives,* Channel 4 (England), 1996.

Police officer, *Underworld,* Channel 4, 1997.

Bill Watson, "Hard Cash," *The Bill,* Independent Television, 1998.

Brian Merry, "How I Won the War," *Goodnight Sweetheart,* BBC, 1999.

Mr. Green, "Bad for Your Health: Parts 1 & 2," *The Bill,* Independent Television, 2000.

Jack Hampton, "Golden Years," *Doctors* (also known as *Laegerne*), BBC, 2002.

Clive Formby, "Down to Earth," *Heartbeat* (also known as *Classic Heartbeat*), Independent Television, 2004.

Clive Formby, "Money, Money, Money," *Heartbeat* (also known as *Classic Heartbeat*), Independent Television, 2004.

Himself, *Best Week Ever,* VH1, 2004.

Film Appearances:

(Uncredited) Man at water station, *The Day the Earth Caught Fire* (also known as *The Day the Sky Caught Fire*), Universal, 1961.

Barman, *Sweeney 2* (also known as *Sweeney Two*), EMI, 1978.

Himself, *Players* (also known as *Smash, Gracze, Kaksinpeli, L'ultimo gioco, Pasiones en juego,* and *Spiel mit der Liebe*), Paramount, 1979.

Police officer, *Murder by Decree* (also known as *Sherlock Holmes and Saucy Jack* and *Sherlock Holmes: Murder by Decree*), Avco–Embassy, 1979.

Bike salesperson, *Silver Dream Racer,* J. Arthur Rank, 1980, Almi Pictures, 1983.

Hammett, *Just Ask for Diamond* (also known as *Diamond's Edge*), Twentieth Century–Fox, 1988.

Detective, *Buddy's Song,* Trimark Pictures, 1990.

Mr. Critchley, *Dangerous Lady,* Warner Sisters Productions, 1995.

Chef, *Lawless Heart* (also known as *Coracao sem lei*), Optimum Releasing, 2002, First Look Pictures Releasing, 2003.

Machine (short film), London Film School, 2003.

Aberforth Dumbledore, *Harry Potter and the Order of the Phoenix* (also known as *Tip Top, Hari Poter i Red Feniksa, Harry Potter e a Ordem da Fenix, Harry Potter e l'ordine della Fenice, Harry Potter en de orde van de feniks, Harry Potter es a Foenix Rendje, Harry Potter et l'ordre du phenix, Harry Potter i l'orde del Fenix, Harry Potter ja feeniksin kilta, Harry Potter och fenixordern, Harry Potter og foniksordenen, Harry Potter und der Orden des Phoenix,* and *Harry Potter y la orden del Fenix*), Warner Bros., 2007.

McNAIRY, Scoot

PERSONAL

Addresses: *Agent*—The Group Management, 7507 Sunset Blvd., Suite 204, Los Angeles, CA 90046. *Manager*—4Dog Management, 7505 Sunset Blvd., Suite 204, Los Angeles, CA 90046.

Career: Actor. Appeared in television commercials, including Axe Click fragrance, 2006.

CREDITS

Film Appearances:
Russell, *Wrong Numbers,* 2001.
Untitled, *Plugged In* (short), 2002.
Ryan, *Sexless,* 2003.
Jack, *Wonderland,* Lions Gate Films, 2003.
Friend number one, *Silenced* (short), 2003.
Stoner, *D.E.B.S.,* Samuel Goldwyn Films, 2004.
Dale, *White Men in Seminole Flats* (short), 2004.

(Uncredited) DJ at club, *Sleepover,* Metro–Goldwyn–Mayer, 2004.
Augie, *Herbie Fully Loaded,* Buena Vista, 2005.
Charles, *Marcus,* Warner Home Video, 2006.
Army–Jacket, *Art School Confidential,* Sony Pictures Classics, 2006.
Beatnik number one, *Bobby,* Weinstein Company, 2006.
Harold Grey, *The Shadow Effect* (short), 2006.
Dan, *Mr. Fix It,* First Look International, 2006.
Wilson, *In Search of a Midnight Kiss,* 2007.
Frank Jeffries, *Twisted,* 2007.
Peter, *Wednesday Again,* 2007.
Ferret, *The Listening Party,* 2007.

Film Work:
Producer, *In Search of a Midnight Kiss,* 2007.

Television Appearances; Movies:
Jake, *More, Patience,* 2006.

Television Appearances; Pilots:
More, Patience, Fox, 2006.

Television Appearances; Episodic:
Henry, "My Best Friend is a Big Fat Slut," *Good Girls Don't,* Oxygen, 2004.
Trevor, "All Alone," *Six Feet Under,* HBO, 2005.
T. J., "Meth Murders," *Close to Home,* CBS, 2005.
Dean Thomas Stilton, "The Hot One," *Jake in Progress,* ABC, 2006.
Dean Thomas Stilton, "Eyebrow Girl vs. Smirkface," *Jake in Progress,* ABC, 2006.
Fast food worker, "Something Blue," *How I Met Your Mother,* CBS, 2007.

RECORDINGS

Music Videos:
Appeared in Death Cab for Cutie's "A Movie Script Ending" and Regina Spektor's "Fidelity."

MEISLE, Kathryn

PERSONAL

Married Marcus Giamatti (an actor and musician; divorced).

Addresses: *Agent*—Gersh Agency, 232 North Canon Dr., Beverly Hills, CA 90210. *Manager*—James Suskin, James Suskin Management, 253 West 72nd St., Suite 1014, New York, NY 10023.

Career: Actress.

Awards, Honors: Drama Desk Award nomination, outstanding featured actress in a play, 1993, for *As You Like It;* Antoinette Perry Award nomination, best actress in a featured role, and Joe A. Callaway Award, best performance in a classic drama, Actors' Equity Association, both 2003, for *Tartuffe.*

CREDITS

Stage Appearances:
Salome, *Dandy Dick,* Roundabout Theatre Company, Union Square Theatre, New York City, 1988.

Desdemona, *Othello,* New York Shakespeare Festival, Delacorte Theatre, Public Theatre, New York City, 1991.

As You Like It, New York Shakespeare Festival, Public Theatre, 1993.

Frances Parnell, *Racing Demon,* Vivian Beaumont Theatre, Lincoln Center, New York City, 1995.

Hortensia, *The Rehearsal,* Roundabout Theatre Company, Criterion Center Stage Right Theatre, New York City, 1996–97.

Grace Harkaway, *London Assurance,* Roundabout Theatre Company, Criterion Center Stage Right Theatre, 1997.

Elvira, *Blithe Spirit,* New Jersey Shakespeare Festival, Community Theatre, Morristown, NJ, 1997.

Mabel, *The Most Fabulous Story Ever Told,* New York Theatre Workshop, Minetta Lane Theatre, New York City, 1998–99.

Helena, *A Midsummer Night's Dream,* Center Theatre Group, Ahmanson Theatre, Los Angeles, 1999.

Measure for Measure, Center Theatre Group, Ahmanson Theatre, 1999.

Flinty McGee and Florence DeRoot, *Old Money,* Mitzi E. Newhouse Theatre, New York City, 2000–2001.

Nathalie Derrien, *What You Get and What You Expect* (also known as *Ce qui arrive et ce qu'on attend*), New York Theatre Workshop, 2000.

The Game of Love and Chance, Theatre Ten Ten, New York City, 2000.

Olivia, *Twelfth Night,* New York Shakespeare Festival, Delacorte Theatre, Public Theatre, 2002.

Elmira, *Tartuffe,* Roundabout Theatre Company, American Airlines Theatre, New York City, 2002–2003.

Nancy Robin, *Living Out,* Second Stage Theatre, New York City, 2003.

Marie–Louise Durham, *The Constant Wife,* Roundabout Theatre Company, American Airlines Theatre, 2005.

Deborah, *A Touch of the Poet,* Roundabout Theatre Company, Studio 54 Theatre, New York City, 2005–2006.

Appeared in *A Month in the Country* and *Philadelphia, Here I Come,* both Guthrie Theatre, Minneapolis, MN; *School for Scandal,* Shakespeare Theatre, Washington, DC; *She Stoops to Conquer,* Long Wharf Theatre, New Haven, CT; *Twelfth Night,* Arena Stage, Baltimore, MD; and *Wonderful Tennessee,* McCarter Theatre, Princeton, NJ; also appeared in *Misalliance.*

Film Appearances:
Marcie Elliott, *Basket Case 2,* Shapiro/Glickenhaus Entertainment, 1990.

Susan, *Chicken Delight,* 1991.

Mrs. Carpenter, *That Night* (also known as *One Hot Summer*), Warner Bros., 1992.

Mary Wright, *Rosewood,* Warner Bros., 1997.

Cecilia Kelly, *You've Got Mail,* Warner Bros., 1998.

Mildred, *Down* (also known as *The Elevator* and *The Shaft*), First Floor Features, 2001.

Television Appearances; Episodic:
Juliet Crawford, *Loving,* ABC, 1983.

Catherine Moody, "By Hooker, by Crook," *Law & Order,* NBC, 1990.

The Cosby Mysteries, NBC, 1994.

Mrs. Rockwell, "To Your Health," *Oz,* HBO, 1997.

Susan Young, "Under the Influence," *Law & Order,* NBC, 1998.

Helen, "Once for the Books," *Cosby,* CBS, 1999.

Gina Silver, "Disrobed," *Law & Order: Special Victims Unit* (also known as *Law & Order: SVU* and *Special Victims Unit*), NBC, 2000.

Mrs. Rockwell, "Even the Score," *Oz,* HBO, 2001.

Ms. Guhler (some sources cite Susan Schooler), "The Cook of the Money Pot," *Judging Amy,* CBS, 2002.

Katherine Manning, "Hawks and Handsaws," *Without a Trace* (also known as *W.A.T.*), CBS, 2004.

Saundra Castle, "The Vote," *The Guardian,* CBS, 2004.

Janet Welker, "My Dinner with Andy," *NYPD Blue,* ABC, 2004.

Janet Welker, "I Like Ike," *NYPD Blue,* ABC, 2004.

Mrs. Seaborne, "Shootout," *CSI: Miami,* CBS, 2005.

Alice Webb, "Three Parties," *Brothers & Sisters,* ABC, 2007.

Television Appearances; Other:
Cindy London, *One Life to Live* (series), 1988.

The Cosby Mysteries (movie; also known as *Guy Hanks I*), NBC, 1994.

Dolly Madison, *Sally Hemings: An American Scandal* (miniseries), CBS, 2000.

MONET, Daniella 1989–
(Daniella Zuvic)

PERSONAL

Full name, Daniella Monet Zuvic; born March 1, 1989.

Addresses: *Agent*—The Gersh Agency, 232 North Cannon Dr., Beverly Hills, CA 90210. *Manager*—LA Entertainment, 1317 N. San Fernando Blvd., Suite 155, Burbank, CA 91504.

Career: Actress.

CREDITS

Film Appearances:
Young Angie, *Follow Your Heart,* DMG Entertainment, 1998.
Sarah, *Simon Says,* 2006.
Gabby Kramer, *Taking 5,* Lions Gate Films, 2007.
Inga, *Nancy Drew,* Warner Bros., 2007.

Television Appearances; Series:
Megan Kleinman, *Listen Up,* CBS, 2004–2005.

Television Appearances; Episodic:
(As Daniella Zuvic) Corey at age eight, "Avenging Angel," *Pacific Blue,* USA Network, 1997.
(As Daniella Zuvic) Joyce Fitzsimmons, "Heartache," *American Dreams* (also kwon as *Our Generation*), NBC, 2003.
(As Daniella Zuvic) Joyce Fitzsimmons, "Where the Boys Are," *American Dreams* (also known as *Our Generation*), NBC, 2003.
(As Daniella Zuvic) Joyce Fitzsimmons, "Secrets and Lies," *American Dreams* (also known as *Our Generation*), NBC, 2003.
Bethany, "Still Negotiating," *Still Standing,* CBS, 2003.
Missy Kleinfeld, "No Right Way," *8 Simple Rules ... for Dating My Teenage Daughter,* ABC, 2003.
Missy Kleinfeld, "Get Real," *8 Simple Rules ... for Dating My Teenage Daughter,* ABC, 2004.
Missy Kleinfeld, "Opposites Attract: Part 1," *8 Simple Rules ... for Dating My Teenage Daughter,* ABC, 2004.
Missy Kleinfeld, "Finale Part Un," *8 Simple Rules ... for Dating My Teenage Daughter,* ABC, 2004.
Karen, "Go Bernie, It's Your Birthday," *The Bernie Mac Show,* Fox, 2004.
Rebecca, "Surprise," *Zoey 101,* Nickelodeon, 2006.
Rebecca, "Chase's Girlfriend," *Zoey 101,* Nickelodeon, 2006.
Rebecca, "Zoey's Balloon," *Zoey 101,* Nickelodeon, 2006.

MORGAN, Jaye P. 1931–

PERSONAL

Original name, Mary Margaret Morgan; born December 3, 1931, in Mancos, CO; sister of Bob Morgan, Charlie Morgan, Dick Morgan, and Duke Morgan (all singers).

Career: Actress. Began performing at the age of three with the family vaudeville act, The Morgan Family; sang with Hank Penny, c. late 1940s, and the Frank De Vol Orchestra, 1950–53; toured the United States with her nightclub act, 1955.

Awards, Honors: Voted best female singer of 1954, *Down Beat* magazine; *Cash Box* magazine award, best female vocalist, 1955; named best new female vocalist, *Record Whirl* magazine.

CREDITS

Film Appearances:
(With The Morgan Family) *Stars Over Broadway,* Warner Bros., 1935.
Singer, *Frank DeVol and His Orchestra* (short), Universal, 1953.
Magda, *The All–American Boy,* Warner Bros., 1973.
Stop–It nurse, *Loose Shoes* (also known as *Coming Attractions* and *Quackers*), National American Films, 1980.
Herself, *The Gong Show Movie,* Universal, 1980.
Kate Parker, *Night Patrol,* New World Pictures, 1984.
Celebrity number two, *Home Alone 2: Lost in New York* (also known as *Home Alone II*), Twentieth Century–Fox, 1992.
Herself, *Confessions of a Dangerous Mind* (also known as *Confessions d'un homme dangereux*), Miramax, 2002.

Television Appearances; Series:
Stop the Music, ABC, 1949.
The Robert Q. Lewis Show, 1954–55.
Coke Time (also known as *Coke Time with Eddie Fisher*), NBC, 1955.
The Perry Como Show (also known as *Perry Como's Kraft Music Hall* and *The Chesterfield Supper Club*), 1955.
The Jaye P. Morgan Show, NBC, 1956.
The Gong Show, NBC, 1976.
Performer, *The Chuck Barris Rah–Rah Show,* NBC, 1978.
The $1.98 Beauty Show, syndicated, 1978.

Television Appearances; Pilots:
Plush Horse singer, *Adventures of Nick Carter,* NBC, 1972.

Television Appearances; Specials:
Sonja Henie's Holiday on Ice, NBC, 1956.
Honeymoon Game, 1971.
Burt and the Girls, NBC, 1973.
The Don Rickles Show, CBS, 1975.
Host, *The All–American College Comedy Show,* CBS, 1979.

Anything for a Laugh—Twenty Years of the Best of the Chuck Barris Show, ABC, 1985.
TV's Most Censored Moments, TRIO and USA Network, 2002.

Television Appearances; Episodic:

Singer, *The Colgate Comedy Hour* (also known as *Colgate Summer Comedy Hour, Colgate Variety Hour,* and *Michael Todd Revue*), NBC, 1955.

Singer, "Ice Capades," *The Steve Allen Show* (also known as *The Steve Allen Plymouth Show*), NBC, 1956.

The Dinah Shore Chevy Show (also known as *The Dinah Shore Show*), NBC, 1956.

The Julius LaRosa Show, 1957.

Singer, *Toast of the Town* (also known as *The Ed Sullivan Show*), CBS, 1958, 1959.

"On Stage with Music," *The Bell Telephone Hour,* NBC, 1959.

"Fun Fair," *Startime* (also known as *Ford Startime* and *Lincoln–Mercury Startime*), NBC, 1960.

"John Wayne Show," *The Jack Benny Program* (also known as *The Jack Benny Show*), CBS, 1960.

Sally Dwight, "Money and the Minister," *General Electric Theater* (also known as *G. E. Theater*), CBS, 1961.

Patti Maxwell, "Patti's Tune," *Hennesey,* CBS, 1962.

Ruth Evans, "Sunday Father," *The Eleventh Hour,* NBC, 1964.

Nightclub singer, "Second Chorus," *My Three Sons,* ABC, 1964.

Maggie Feeney, "Cap'n Ahab," *Vacation Playhouse,* CBS, 1965.

Claudia Farrell, "A Falling Star," *My Three Sons,* CBS, 1966.

Ginny McCabe, "The Girl from Missouri," *The Outsider,* NBC, 1969.

The Real Tom Kennedy Show, 1970.

The Tonight Show Starring Johnny Carson, NBC, 1970–73.

Panelist, *Mantrap,* syndicated, 1971.

"Love and the Mistress," *Love, American Style,* ABC, 1971.

The Virginia Graham Show, 1972.

Match Game 73, CBS, 1973.

Herself, "The Songwriter," *The Odd Couple,* ABC, 1973.

Judy Farrell, "The Noise of a Quiet Weekend," *Lucas Tanner,* NBC, 1975.

Rhyme and Reason, ABC, 1976.

Break the Bank, 1976, 1977.

The Cross–Wits, syndicated, 1977.

The Merv Griffin Show, syndicated, 1977.

The Muppet Show, syndicated, 1977.

Olivia, "Gopher's Greatest Hits/The Vacation/One Rose a Day," *The Love Boat,* ABC, 1979.

Canada After Dark, CBC, 1979.

Celebrity Cooks, CBC, 1979.

Helen Brackett, "Double Play," *Simon & Simon,* CBS, 1984.

Cora Matthews/Cora Rush, "Son of the Groom," *Too Close for Comfort* (also known as *The Ted Knight Show*), syndicated, 1984.

The Howard Stern Show, syndicated, 1992.

"The Gong Show," *E! True Hollywood Story,* E! Entertainment Television, 2003.

Hollywood Squares (also known as *H2* and *H2: Hollywood Squares*), syndicated, 2003.

Television Theme Song Performer: Series:

Fay, NBC, 1975.

Stage Appearances:

Annie Get Your Gun, Pittsburgh Civic Light Orchestra, Pittsburgh, PA, and Melody Top Theatre, Chicago, IL, 1960.

Guys and Dolls, 1961.

Also appeared in *The Tender Trap; The Unsinkable Molly Brown; The Pajama Game,* St. Louis Municipal Opera, St. Louis, MS; *Funny Girl; Nunsense; Miss Margarida's Way; The Fabulous Palm Springs Follies;* as Miss Mona, *The Best Little Whorehouse in Texas.*

Major Tours:

Sugar Babies, U.S. cities, 1981–82.

RECORDINGS

Albums:

Jaye P. Morgan and Orchestra, Royale, 1954, 1955, 1956.

Jaye P. Morgan Sings, Allegro, 1956.

Jaye P. Morgan Sings with Frank DeVol's Orchestra, Allegro Royale, 1956.

Jaye P. Morgan, RCA Victor, 1956.

The House of Jaye P. Morgan, Concord, 1957.

Jaye P. Morgan—Just You, Just Me, RCA Victor, 1958.

Jaye P. Morgan, Rondolette, 1958.

Jaye P. Morgan Slow & Easy, Metro–Goldwyn–Mayer, 1959.

Jaye P. Morgan Up North, Metro–Goldwyn–Mayer, 1960.

Jaye P. Morgan Down South, Metro–Goldwyn–Mayer, 1960.

Jaye P. Morgan That Country Sound, Metro–Goldwyn–Mayer, 1961.

Jaye P. Morgan Life Is Just a Bowl of Cherries, Tops Mayfair, 1962.

Montgomery Ward 90th Anniversary Presents Jaye P. Morgan, R.R.I. Records, 1962.

Jaye P. Morgan, Candor Records, 1976.

Jaye P. Morgan Lately!, Dejavu Record Company, 2005.

Singles:

"That's All I Want From You," 1954.

"Are You Lonesome Tonight?," 1959.

"A Song For You," 1971.

OTHER SOURCES

Electronic:
Jaye P. Morgan Website, http://www.jayepmorgan.com, July 20, 2007.

MORGAN, Jeffrey Dean 1966–
(Jeffrey D. Morgan)

PERSONAL

Born April 22, 1966, in Seattle, WA; son of Richard Dean and Sandy Thomas; divorced. *Avocational Interests:* Rooting for the Seattle Seahawks.

Addresses: *Agent*—William Morris Agency, One William Morris Place, Beverly Hills, CA 90212. *Publicist*—Nancy Iannios Public Relations, 8271 Melrose Ave., Suite 102, Los Angeles, CA 90046.

Career: Actor. Founder of a graphic art company in Seattle, WA. Affiliated with charities. Also known as Jeffrey D. Morgan.

Awards, Honors: Tater Tot awards, E! Entertainment Television, c. 2006, best guest star, for *Grey's Anatomy* and *Supernatural,* and biggest tearjerker, for *Grey's Anatomy.*

CREDITS

Television Appearances; Series:
Nature photographer Jack Hawkins, *Extreme* (also known as *Extreme—Das Leben am Abgrund*), ABC, 1995.
Dr. Edward Marcase, *The Burning Zone* (also known as *Burning Zone—Expedition Killervirus, Burning Zone: Menace imminente, Vaaravyoehyke,* and *Zona peligrosa*), UPN, 1996–97.
Judah Baldwin, *Weeds* (also known as *Nancy uel a fueben* and *Weeds—Kleine Deals unter Nachbarn*), Showtime, beginning 2005.
John Winchester, *Supernatural* (also known as *Sobrenatural*), The WB, 2005–2006, The CW, 2006–2007.
Denny Duquette, a recurring character, *Grey's Anatomy* (also known as *Complications, Procedure, Surgeons, Under the Knife,* and *Grey's Anatomy—Die jungen Aerzte*), ABC, 2006–2007.

Television Appearances; Miniseries:
Musician in cafe, *Naomi & Wynonna: Love Can Build a Bridge* (also known as *Love Can Build a Bridge*), NBC, 1995.

Television Appearances; Movies:
Jesse, *In the Blink of an Eye,* ABC, 1996.
Todd Hunter, *Legal Deceit,* Cinemax, 1997.

Television Appearances; Specials:
Bobby Debeneke, *Black Sheep,* Fox, 1994.
It's Hot in Here: UPN Fall Preview, UPN, 1996.
Host and narrator, *Grey's Anatomy: Every Moment Counts,* ABC, 2007.

Television Appearances; Episodic:
Weapons officer, "Shadow," *JAG,* NBC, 1995.
Sid, "El Sid," *Sliders,* Fox, 1996.
Jake Horbart, "Child of Hope," *Walker, Texas Ranger,* CBS, 2000.
Larkin (a fire fighter), "Child of Hope," *ER* (also known as *Emergency Room*), NBC, 2001.
Daniel Glenn, "The Test," *The Practice,* ABC, 2002.
Father William Natali, "Forgive Me, Father," *The Division* (also known as *Heart of the City*), Lifetime, 2002.
Sam Ryan, "Provider," *Angel* (also known as *Angel: The Series, Angel—Jaeger der Finsternis,* and *Skoteinos angelos*), The WB, 2002.
Wally (CIA technician), "Defending His Honor," *JAG,* NBC, 2002.
Wally (CIA technician), "Enemy Below," *JAG,* NBC, 2002.
Bill Nowlin, "All for Our Country," *CSI: Crime Scene Investigation* (also known as *C.S.I., CSI: Las Vegas, CSI: Weekends,* and *Les experts*), CBS, 2003.
Xindi (Reptilian), "Carpenter Street," *Enterprise* (also known as *Star Trek: Enterprise, Star Trek: Series V,* and *Star Trek: Untitled Fifth Series*), UPN, 2003.
Geoffrey Pine, "Two Pair," *Tru Calling* (also known as *Heroine, Tru,* and *True Calling*), Fox, 2004.
Mike, "Give Daddy Some Sugar," *The Handler* (also known as *Joe Renato, Street Boss, FBI: Operations secretes,* and *Peitetehtaevissae*), CBS, 2004.
Steven Leight, "Mr. Monk Takes Manhattan," *Monk,* USA Network, 2004.
Joe Zukowski, "The Accomplice," *The O.C.* (also known as *California Teens, Newport Beach, O.C., O.C., California, Orange County, A Narancsvidek, O.C.—Um estranho no paraiso,* and *Zycie na fali*), Fox, 2005.
Himself, "Should I Spy on My Kids?," *Rachael Ray* (also known as *RR*), syndicated, 2007.

Appeared as Mike in "The Big Fall," an unaired episode of *The Handler* (also known as *Joe Renato, Street Boss, FBI: Operations secretes,* and *Peitetehtaevissae*), CBS.

Television Appearances; Pilots:
Shay Astor, *Mystery Dance,* ABC, 1995.
Dr. Edward Marcase, *The Burning Zone* (also known as *Burning Zone—Expedition Killervirus, Burning*

Zone: Menace imminente, Vaaravyoehyke, and *Zona peligrosa*), UPN, 1996.

John Winchester, *Supernatural* (also known as *Sobrenatural*), The WB, 2005.

Some sources cite an affiliation with *Correspondents,* ABC.

Film Appearances:

Sharkey, *Uncaged* (also known as *Angel in Red* and *Vice Zone*), Concorde–New Horizons, 1991.

Jack Bennett, *Dillinger and Capone,* Concorde–New Horizons, 1995.

Ramone, *Undercover Heat* (also known as *Undercover*), A–pix Entertainment, 1995.

Todd Hunter, *Legal Deceit* (also known as *The Promised Land*), 1997.

Billy, *Road Kill,* Trident Releasing, 1999.

Daniel, *Something More* (short musical), 2003.

Tom Newman, *Six: The Mark Unleashed* (also known as *Six—La hermandad*), American World Pictures/ ChristianCinema.com, 2004.

Detective Cole Davies, *Chasing Ghosts,* American World Pictures, 2005.

The sheriff, *Dead & Breakfast,* Anchor Bay Entertainment, 2005.

Dale, *Jam,* Thanksgiving Films, 2006.

Brad, *Kabluey,* Whitewater Films, 2007.

Bruce, *The Adventures of Beatle Boyin,* 2007.

Patrick, *The Accidental Husband,* Yari Film Group Releasing, 2007.

Rick, *Live!,* Atlas Entertainment/Mosaic Media Group, 2007.

William, *P.S., I Love You,* Warner Bros., 2007.

American Girl (also known as *Kit Kittredge: An American Girl Mystery*), New Line Cinema/ Picturehouse Entertainment, 2008.

Days of Wrath, Foxy Films/Independent/Mandalay Alliance Entertainment, 2008.

Stage Appearances:

Appeared in stage productions, including the musicals *Grease* and *West Side Story.*

RECORDINGS

Videos:

Himself, *The Making of "Six"* (short), Signal Hill Pictures, 2004.

OTHER SOURCES

Periodicals:

TV Guide, February 6, 2006, p. 6.

MORRISON, Jennifer 1979–
(Jenny Morrison)

PERSONAL

Full name, Jennifer Marie Morrison; born April 12, 1979, in Chicago, IL; daughter of David (a teacher and high school band director) and Judy Morrison (a teacher); engaged to Jesse Spencer (an actor), December 23, 2006. *Education:* Loyola University, B.A., theater and English minor, 2000; studied acting at Steppenwolf Theatre Company.

Addresses: *Agent*—Abrams Artists Agency, 9200 Sunset Blvd., Suite 1130, Los Angeles, CA 90069. *Manager*— John Carrabino Management, 100 North Crescent Dr., Suite 323, Beverly Hills, CA 90210.

Career: Actress. Worked as a child model, appearing in print ads for JC Penney and Montgomery Ward department stores, as well as television commercials, including Rice Krispies cereal and Mondos.

CREDITS

Film Appearances:

(Film debut; As Jenny Morrison) Meaghan Eastman, *Intersection,* Paramount, 1994.

Denice, *Miracle on 34th Street,* Twentieth Century–Fox, 1994.

(As Jenny Morrison) Samantha Kozac, *Stir of Echoes,* Artisan Entertainment, 1999.

Amy Mayfield, *Urban Legends: Final Cut* (also known as *Legendes urbaines 2, Legenddes urbaines: La suite,* and *Leyendas urbanas: corte final*), Columbia, 2000.

Joyce, *The Zeroes,* 2001.

Sonya Mallow, *Design,* 2002.

Alicia, *Nantucket,* 2002.

Annie, *Girl Fever* (also known as *100 Women*), Bleiberg Entertainment, 2002.

Jamie, *Grind,* Warner Bros., 2003.

Chris, *Mall Cop,* 2004.

Missy Vanglider, *Surviving Christmas,* DreamWorks, 2004.

Sarah, *Lift* (short), 2004.

Jade, *Mr. & Mrs. Smith,* Twentieth Century–Fox, 2005.

Gabrielle Winters, *Flourish,* Cinequest Distribution, 2006.

Big Stan, Metro–Goldwyn–Mayer, 2007.

Film Work:

Producer, *Flourish,* 2006.

Television Appearances; Series:
Dr. Allison Cameron, *House M.D.,* Fox, 2004—.

Television Appearances; Movies:
Callie, *Big Shot: Confessions of a Campus Bookie,* FX Channel, 2002.
Lily Bowser, *The Sure Hand of God* (also known as *Sinners Need Company*), Lifetime, 2004.
Princess Diana, *The Murder of Princess Diana,* Lifetime, 2007.

Television Appearances; Specials:
The 2005 Billboard Music Awards, Fox, 2005.
The 58th Annual Primetime Emmy Awards, NBC, 2006.
House Unplugged, 2006.

Television Appearances; Pilots:
Megan, *The Random Years,* 2002.

Television Appearances; Episodic:
Gwen, "Let Sleeping Dogs Fry," *The Chronicle* (also known as *News from the Edge*), Sci–Fi Channel, 2001.
Melissa Dunnigan, "Most Likely to Succeed," *Touched by an Angel,* CBS, 2001.
Melanie Shea Thompson, "The Lost Weekend," *Dawson's Creek,* The WB, 2001.
Melanie Shea Thompson, "Sleeping Arrangements," *Dawson's Creek,* The WB, 2002.
Mandy Singer, "In Too Deep," *Any Day Now,* Lifetime, 2002.
Megan, *The Random Years,* UPN, 2002.
Herself, "The Video Shoot," *Newlyweds: Nick & Jessica,* MTV, 2003.
Herself, "Ashlee Moves Onward and Upward," *The Ashlee Simpson Show,* MTV, 2004.
Herself, "Ashlee Verses Her Label," *The Ashlee Simpson Show,* MTV, 2004.
Herself, "Valentine's Bummer," *The Ashlee Simpson Show,* MTV, 2004.

RECORDINGS

Video Games:
Intelligence officer Kirce James, *Command & Conquer 3: Tiberium Wars,* Electronic Arts, 2007.

Music Videos:
Appeared in Nick Lachey's "Shut Up."

OTHER SOURCES

Electronic:
Jennifer Morrison Website, http://www.jennifer morrison.net, July 20, 2007.

MYRIN, Arden 1973–

PERSONAL

Born December 10, 1973, in Little Compton, RI; father an accountant; mother a real estate agent. *Education:* Colorado College, graduated; trained with Groundlings, Los Angeles.

Addresses: *Agent*—Innovative Artists Talent and Literary Agency, 1505 10th St., Santa Monica, CA 90401. *Manager*—Steve Caserta, Sanders Armstrong Caserta Management, 2120 Colorado Blvd., Suite 120, Santa Monica, CA 90404.

Career: Actress and comedian. Improv Olympics, member of company in Chicago, IL, and Los Angeles; appeared in commercials for KFC restaurants, 2005, and other products.

CREDITS

Film Appearances:
Mary, *Deconstructing Harry,* Fine Line, 1997.
Student, *In & Out,* Paramount, 1997.
Wendy, *I Think I Do,* Strand Releasing, 1998.
Stewardess with luggage, *The Imposters,* Twentieth Century–Fox, 1998.
Stacey, *30 Days,* Arrow Releasing, 2000.
Darcy's assistant, *What Women Want,* Paramount, 2000.
Lorraine, *Bubble Boy,* Buena Vista, 2001.
Lucy, *Highway,* New Line Cinema, 2002.
Hippie girl, *Auto Focus,* Sony Pictures Classics, 2002.
Larry's coworker, *Farm Sluts* (short film), Mad–Hoc Media, 2003.
Julie, *Soul Mates* (short film), 2003.
Sarah, *Dry Cycle* (also known as *Spin, Shoot & Run*), Newmark Films, 2003.
Emily, *Kinsey,* Fox Searchlight, 2004.
Bunny LeVine, *Whistlin' Dixie* (short film), Faeries Revenge Productions/Siren Films, 2004.
Daisy, *Christmas with the Kranks,* Columbia, 2004.
Patty, *Heart of the Beholder,* Beholder Productions, 2005.
Foreperson, *I'm Not Gay* (short film), Big Film Shorts, 2005.
Sara, *Evan Almighty,* Universal, 2007.

Television Appearances; Series:
Abby Cosgrove, *Working,* NBC, 1997–99.
Caramel, *On the Spot,* The WB, 2003.
Member of ensemble, *Mad TV,* Fox, 2005–2007.
Guest host, *That's So Hollywood,* 2007.

Television Appearances; Episodic:

Amy, "She Loves Me Yeah, Yeah, Yeah," *Just Shoot Me!,* NBC, 1999.

Cheryl, "The Ex Factor," *Nikki,* The WB, 2000.

Brenda, "The One with the Stain," *Friends,* NBC, 2001.

Girl, "Eight Simple Rules for Dating a Celebrity," *I'm With Her,* ABC, 2004.

Miss Nude Reno 1, "Dangle's Wife Visits," *Reno 911!,* Comedy Central, 2004.

(Uncredited) Wendy, "Dinner Date with Death," *Kitchen Confidential,* Fox, 2005.

Claude, "Bridesmaids Revisited," *Gilmore Girls* (also known as *Gilmore Girls: Beginnings*), The WB, 2006.

Marcy, "The Breakup," *Modern Men,* The WB, 2006.

Late Night with Conan O'Brien, 2006.

Television Appearances; Other:

Daphne, *The Royale* (movie), AMC, 1996.

Sherman's March (pilot), NBC, 2000.

What's Up, Peter Fuddy?, 2001.

VH1 Big in 06 Awards (special), VH1, 2006.

Stage Appearances:

Catherine, *Boston Marriage,* Martinson Hall, Public Theatre, New York City, 2002.

N–O

NELSON, Judd 1959–

PERSONAL

Full name, Judd Asher Nelson; born November 28, 1959, in Portland, ME; son of Leonard (an attorney) and Merle (an attorney and politician) Nelson. *Education:* Haverford College, degree in philosophy; studied acting at the Stella Adler Conservatory. *Avocational Interests:* Golf, reading, writing, motorbiking.

Addresses: *Office*—Lighthouse Entertainment, 409 North Camden Dr., Suite 202, Beverly Hills, CA 90210. *Agent*—Aaron R. Kogan, Metropolitan Talent Agency, 4500 Wilshire Blvd., Second Floor, Los Angeles, CA 90010.

Career: Actor. Affiliated with Lighthouse Entertainment, Beverly Hills, CA.

Awards, Honors: Golden Globe Award nomination, best performance by an actor in a miniseries or motion picture made for television, 1988, for *Billionaire Boys Club;* Silver Bucket of Excellence Award (with others), MTV Movie awards, 2005.

CREDITS

Film Appearances:
Eddie Keaton, *Making the Grade* (also known as *The Last American Preppy*), Metro–Goldwyn–Mayer/United Artists/Cannon, 1984.
Alec Newbary, *St. Elmo's Fire,* Columbia, 1985.
John Bender, *The Breakfast Club,* Universal, 1985.
Phil Hicks, *Fandango,* Warner Bros., 1985.
Billy Turner, *Blue City,* Paramount, 1986.

Voices of Hot Rod and Rodimus Prime, *The Transformers: The Movie* (animated; also known as *Matrix Forever, The Transformers, Transformers the Movie: Apocalypse! Matrix Forever, Transformers the Movie: Mokushiroku matrix yo eien ni,* and *Transformers: Matrix yo eien ni*), De Laurentiis Entertainment Group, 1986.
Robin "Stormy" Weathers, *From the Hip,* De Laurentiis Entertainment Group, 1987.
(Uncredited) Motorcycle police officer, *Never on Tuesday,* Palisades Entertainment, 1988.
Arthur "Buck" Taylor, *Relentless,* New Line Cinema, 1989.
Himself, *Far Out Man* (also known as *Soul Man II*), 1990.
Marty Malt, *The Dark Backward* (also known as *The Man with Three Arms*), Strand Releasing, 1991.
Officer Nick Peretti, *New Jack City,* Warner Bros., 1991.
Andrew Blumenthal, *Primary Motive,* Blossom Pictures, 1992.
David Mirkin, *Entangled* (also known as *Fatal Attack* and *Les veufs*), 1993.
Jimmy, *Every Breath,* 1993.
Harry Mirapolsky, *Flinch,* 1994.
Jimmie Wing, *Airheads,* Twentieth Century–Fox, 1994.
Phil Gallo, *Caroline at Midnight* (also known as *Someone's Watching*), 1994.
Prisoner, *Hail Caesar,* 1994.
Hit man, *For a Few Lousy Dollars,* Front Row Communications/Malofilm Distribution/Showcase Entertainment, 1996.
Nathaniel Burke, *Steel,* Warner Bros., 1997.
Ken Knowles, *Light It Up,* Twentieth Century–Fox, 1999.
Harold Peters, *Falcon Down,* New City Releasing, 2000.
Max, *The Cure for Boredom* (also known as *Sex & Bullets*), Showcase Entertainment, 2000.
Rufus the buck–toothed sluggard, *Endsville,* Stick Figure Productions, 2000.

Quitz, *Dark Asylum* (also known as *Return to Death Row*), Lions Gate Films, 2001.

Sheriff, *Jay and Silent Bob Strike Back* (also known as *VA5* and *View Askew 5*), Miramax/Dimension Films, 2001.

Jack Jones, *Deceived,* Third Millennium, 2002.

Brian Nathanson, *White Rush,* Canon Films, 2003.

Father Brian, *The Lost Angel,* Franchise Pictures, 2003.

Himself, *Oh, What a Lovely Tea Party* (documentary), View Askew Productions, 2004.

Ziad, *The Freediver,* 2004, 111 Pictures, 2006.

Shep, *Lethal Eviction,* The Asylum Home Entertainment, 2005.

Kevin, *Little Hercules in 3–D,* Little Hercules, 2006.

TV: The Movie (also known as *National Lampoon's "TV the Movie"*), Xenon Pictures, 2006.

Ella's father, *The Caretaker,* Turkey Ranch Productions, 2007.

Jonathan Usher, *Nevermore,* Dayton Street Productions, 2007.

Reporter, *A Single Woman,* Heroica Films, 2007.

Steven P. D. Landry, *Netherbeast Incorporated,* 2007.

Film Work:

Associate producer, *White Rush,* Canon Films, 2003.

Television Appearances; Series:

Jack Richmond, *Suddenly Susan,* NBC, 1996–99.

Television Appearances; Miniseries:

Joseph "Joe" Hunt, *Billionaire Boys Club,* NBC, 1987.

Television Appearances; Movies:

Lieutenant Pete Dunham, *Out of the Ashes* (also known as *Hiroshima: Out of the Ashes*), NBC, 1990.

Gideon, *Conflict of Interest,* 1993.

Dr. Jennings, *Blindfold: Acts of Obsession* (also known as *Blindfold*), USA Network, 1994.

Paul Kinsey, *Circumstances Unknown,* USA Network, 1995.

Matt Curran, *Blackwater Trail,* 1996.

Alan Freed, *Mr. Rock 'n' Roll: The Alan Freed Story* (also known as *The Big Beat Heat* and *Mr. Rock and Roll*), NBC, 1999.

Jack Hulka, "The New Adventures of Spin and Marty: Suspect Behavior," *The Wonderful World of Disney,* ABC, 2000.

Phillip Warren, *The Spiral Staircase* (also known as *Le secret du manoir*), Fox Family Channel, 2000.

Stanley Caldwell, *Cabin by the Lake,* USA Network, 2000.

Aaron Roberts, *The Lost Voyage,* 2001.

Alex, *Cybermutt* (also known as *Rex: Le cyber chien*), Animal Planet, 2002.

Darryl Bedford, *Santa, Jr.,* The Hallmark Channel, 2002.

George, *Three Wise Guys,* USA Network, 2005.

Eric Bryce, *The Black Hole,* Sci–Fi Channel, 2006.

Television Appearances; Specials:

Shattered If Your Kid's on Drugs (also known as *Shattered* and *Shattered If Your Kid Are on Drugs*), 1986.

Vietnam soldier, *Funny, You Don't Look 200* (also known as *Funny, You Don't Look 200: A Constitutional Vaudeville*), ABC, 1987.

Voice, *Dear America: Letters Home from Vietnam* (also known as *Dear America*), HBO, 1987.

Unauthorized Biography: Jane Fonda, syndicated, 1988.

Host, *Harley–Davidson: The American Motorcycle,* TBS, 1993.

Host, *Unmasked: Exposing the Secrets of Deception,* NBC, 1998.

Himself, *Outer Limits Farewell Tribute,* Showtime and syndicated, 2000.

(In archive footage) Himself, *Survivor: The Australian Outback—The Reunion,* CBS, 2001.

Himself, *Playboy: Inside the Playboy Mansion,* Arts and Entertainment, 2002.

(In archive footage) Himself, *Mouthing Off: 51 Greatest Smartasses,* Comedy Central, 2004.

Television Appearances; Awards Presentations:

The ALMA Awards, ABC, 1998.

Presenter, *The Thirteenth Annual Genesis Awards* (also known as *The 13th Annual Genesis Awards*), Animal Planet, 1999.

Host, *The 2001 Genesis Awards,* Animal Planet, 2001.

Television Appearances; Episodic:

Police officer, "Camille," *Moonlighting,* ABC, 1986.

Himself, *The Howard Stern Show,* syndicated, 1991.

Gaston, "What's Cookin'?," *Tales from the Crypt* (also known as *HBO's "Tales from the Crypt"*), HBO, 1992.

Guest host, *Later* (also known as *Later with Bob Costas, Later with Cynthia Garrett,* and *Later with Greg Kinnear*), NBC, 1994.

Himself, *The Rosie O'Donnell Show,* syndicated, 1997, 1998, 1999.

Himself, *Hollywood Squares* (also known as *H2* and *H2: Hollywood Squares*), syndicated, 1998.

Sin City Spectacular (also known as *Penn & Teller's "Sin City Spectacular"*), FX Channel, 1998.

Himself, *Late Night with Conan O'Brien,* NBC, 1999.

"The Brat Pack," *The E! True Hollywood Story* (also known as *The Brat Pack: The E! True Hollywood Story* and *THS*), E! Entertainment Television, 1999.

Harry Longworth, "Something about Harry," *The Outer Limits* (also known as *The New Outer Limits*), Showtime, Sci-Fi Channel, and syndicated, 2000.

(In archive footage) Himself, "Survivor: Back from the Outback," *Survivor,* CBS, 2001.

Mick Sheridan, "Time of Your Death," *CSI: Crime Scene Investigation* (also known as *C.S.I., CSI: Las Vegas, CSI Weekends,* and *Les experts*), CBS, 2006.

Ollie, "Fleeting Cheating Meeting," *Las Vegas* (also known as *Casino Eye*), NBC, 2007.

Sander Gillis, "The Ride–In," *CSI: New York,* CBS, 2007.

Television Appearances; Pilots:

Martin Potter, "More Than a Feeling," *Strange Frequency,* VH1, 2001.

Michael McNamara, *Sideliners,* c. 2006.

Stage Appearances:

Henry Hitchcock, *Sleeping Dogs,* Mark Taper Forum, Los Angeles, 1986.

Sling and bartender, *Planet Fires,* Mark Taper Forum, 1986.

Orphans, Burt Reynolds Dinner Theatre, Jupiter, FL, 1986.

Paulie, *Temple,* American Jewish Theatre, New York City, 1988.

Jonathan, *Carnal Knowledge,* Martin R. Kaufman Theatre, New York City, 1990.

Appeared as Roy, *Domino Courts;* as Wolfgang Amadeus Mozart, *Mozart and Salieri;* and as Don Juan, *The Stone Guest.* Appeared in *The Seagull,* Los Angeles Theater Company; and in *Wrestlers;* appeared in productions with the Shoestring Theatre Company (some sources cite name as the Shoestring Shakespeare Company), 1976–78.

RECORDINGS

Videos:

Himself, *Road to "New Jack City"* (short), New Wave Entertainment, 2005.

Music Videos:

John Parr, "St. Elmo's Fire (Man in Motion)," 1985.

Simple Minds, "Don't You (Forget about Me)," 1985.

WRITINGS

Screenplays:

Every Breath, 1993.

OTHER SOURCES

Periodicals:

Entertainment Weekly, September 20, 1996, p. 64.

People Weekly, April 19, 1999, p. 121; October 18, 1999, p. 151.

NIGAM, Anjul 1965–

PERSONAL

Born December 15, 1965, in Kanpur, India; immigrated to the United States, c. 1967; son of Lakshmi Narayan and Sushila Devi Nigam; married Anjalika Mathur (an actress and producer), November 24, 2001; children: Nikaash Mathur Nigam. *Education:* New York University, Tisch School of the Arts, B.F.A., 1988. *Politics:* Democratic. *Religion:* Hinduism. *Avocational Interests:* Writing, stand–up comedy, juggling, soccer, tennis.

Addresses: *Agent*—House of Representatives, 400 South Beverly Dr., Suite 101, Beverly Hills, CA 90212. *Manager*—DiSante Frank & Co., 10061 Riverside Dr., Suite 377, Toluca Lake, CA 91602.

Career: Actor. Appeared in advertisements. New York University, worked in scene study construction, 1986–89, and as a drama coach, 1987–89; Children's Entertainment Company, Los Angeles, performer, beginning 1990.

Member: Screen Actors Guild, Actors Equity Association, American Federation of Television and Radio Artists.

Awards, Honors: Named Cheshire Community Theatre scholar, 1984; and Kiwanis scholar, 1984–88.

CREDITS

Film Appearances:

Singh, *House Party 2* (also known as *Kid'n Play—Det vilda partyt, Micsoda buli 2., Os estudantes devem estar loucos,* and *Sekopaeiden kotibileet*), New Line Cinema, 1991.

The courier, *The Fifteen Minute Hamlet* (short film), 1995.

Karna, *Two Rivers,* Two Rivers Productions, 1999.

Tow truck driver, *King of the Korner* (also known as *King of LA*), Vine International Pictures, 2000.

Jarred, *Speaking of Sex,* Lionsgate, 2001.

Salman, *The First $20 Million Is Always the Hardest,* Twentieth Century–Fox, 2002.

Rajeev, *Winter Break* (also known as *Snow Job*), 2003.

Candor City Hospital (short film), HelloBox Films, 2003.

Todd, *Death and Taxis,* Clearwater Pictures/Magnum Independent Pictures, 2004.

Boyfriend, *Looking for Comedy in the Muslim World,* Warner Independent Pictures, 2005.

Singh, *Taken,* Twentieth Century–Fox, 2008.

Film Work:
Member of automated dialogue replacement group, *The Bourne Supremacy* (also known as *A Bourne-csapda, A supremacia Bourne, Bournuv mytus, Die Bourne Verschwoerung, El mito de Bourne, La mort dans la peau, La supremacia de Bourne, Medusan isku,* and *Sti skia ton kataskopon*), Universal, 2004.

Television Appearances; Series:
Mamoj Nakshi, *MDs* (also known as *Meds* and *The Oath*), ABC, 2002.

(Often uncredited) Dr. Raj Prahbu, *Grey's Anatomy* (also known as *Complications, Procedure, Surgeons, Under the Knife,* and *Grey's Anatomy—Die jungen Aerzte*), ABC, beginning 2005.

Television Appearances; Miniseries:
Uday Shankar, *NetForce* (also known as *Tom Clancy's "NetForce"*), ABC, 1999.

Television Appearances; Movies:
Rahman, *Silver Strand,* Showtime, 1995.

Dr. Sanjay, *The Lake* (also known as *Das Grauen am See, Hvad soen gemte, Il mistero del lago, Noiduttu jaervi, O lago, O lago sangrento, Rivages mortels,* and *Sjoen*), NBC, 1998.

Television Appearances; Specials:
Hakim, "Back When We Were Grownups," *Hallmark Hall of Fame,* CBS, 2004.

Television Appearances; Episodic:
Sesame Street (also known as *Canadian Sesame Street, The New Sesame Street, Open Sesame, Sesame Park,* and *Les amis de Sesame*), PBS, 1987, 1988.

Raj, "Fortunate Son," *Growing Pains,* ABC, 1989.

Second substitute, "Mike, the Teacher," *Growing Pains,* ABC, 1990.

Anjul, "Tower of Power," *Parker Lewis Can't Lose* (also known as *Parker Lewis*), Fox, 1991.

Sanjay Khandwhalla, "The Young & the Rest of Us," *Murphy Brown,* CBS, 1993.

Lip (the driver), "Don't Go to Springfield," *Sisters,* NBC, 1996.

Alex Ghandar, "Fortune's Fools," *ER* (also known as *Emergency Room*), NBC, 1997.

Kumar, "The Truth Is Out There," *NYPD Blue,* ABC, 1997.

Voice, "Seeds of Destruction," *Extreme Ghostbusters* (animated; also known as *El regreso de los cazafantasmas* and *Tosi viilee haamujengi*), syndicated, 1997.

Vijay, "Danger Zone," *Nash Bridges* (also known as *Bridges*), CBS, 1998.

Mall worker, "Denial," *Get Real* (also known as *Asuntos de familia, Helt aerligt!, Irti arjesta, La famille Green, Realitatile vietii,* and *Sechs unter einem Dach*), Fox, 1999.

Raji, "Gobble, Gobble," *Providence,* NBC, 2001.

Television commercial director, "Setting Precedents," *Arli$$* (also known as *Arliss*), HBO, 2001.

Rajeeb Khandewahl, "Blood Lust," *CSI: Crime Scene Investigation* (also known as *C.S.I., CSI: Las Vegas, CSI: Weekends,* and *Les experts*), CBS, 2002.

Professor Bahlah, *Days of Our Lives* (also known as *Cruise of Deception: Days of Our Lives, Days, DOOL, Des jours et des vies, Horton–sagaen, I gode og onde dager, Los dias de nuestras vidas, Meres agapis, Paeivien viemaeae, Vaara baesta aar, Zeit der Sehnsucht,* and *Zile din viata noastra*), NBC, 2003.

Dr. Alhabah, "Lipstick on Your Panties," *Huff* (also known as *!Huff* and *Huff—terapian tarpeessa*), Showtime, 2004.

Dr. Renfro, "Vector," *Numb3rs* (also known as *Numbers* and *Num3ers*), CBS, 2005.

Doctor, "Light Sleeper," *Medium,* NBC, 2005.

Harish Lev, "Tanglewood," *CSI: NY,* CBS, 2005.

Alex Neuville, "Dr. Feelbad," *Shark,* CBS, 2006.

Appeared in other programs, including *Blossom,* NBC; *Life Goes On* (also known as *Glenbrook*), ABC; and *Wake, Rattle & Roll* (also known as *Jump, Rattle & Roll* and *Despierta peque y al loro*), syndicated. Appeared as Fareed in "Family Values," an unaired episode of *Skin,* Fox. Provided a voice characterization for "The Perfect Shot," an unaired episode of *Mowgli: The New Adventures of the Jungle Book* (animated; also known as *Viidakkopoika Mowgli*), Fox.

Stage Appearances:
Minnesota Moon, 1986.
The Park, 1987.
Norm and Ahmed, 1990.

O'BYRNE, Brian F. 1967–
   (Brian O'Byrne)

PERSONAL

Given name is pronounced Bree–un; born May 16, 1967, in County Cavan, Ireland. *Education:* Trained at Samuel Beckett Centre for Drama and Theatre, Trinity College, Dublin.

Addresses: *Agent*—Jason Gutman, Gersh Agency, 232 North Canon Dr., Beverly Hills, CA 90210.

Career: Actor.

Awards, Honors: Antoinette Perry Award nomination, best feature actor in a play, and *Theatre World* Special Award (with others), best ensemble performance, both 1998, for *The Beauty Queen of Leenane;* Antoinette Perry Award nomination, best actor in a play, 1999, and *Irish Times* Award, best actor, both for *The Lonesome West;* Antoinette Perry Award, best featured actor in a play, Lucille Lortel Award, outstanding lead actor, League of Off–Broadway Theatres and Producers, New York Drama Critics Circle Award, outstanding performance, Obie Award, outstanding performance, *Village Voice,* and Drama Desk Award nomination, all 2004, for *Frozen;* Obie Award, outstanding performance, 2004, Lucille Lortel Award nomination, outstanding lead actor, 2005, Drama Desk Award, best actor, 2005, and Outer Critics Circle Award, outstanding actor in a play, 2005, all for *Doubt;* Drama Desk Award nomination, best actor in a play, 2006, for *Shining City;* Antoinette Perry Award nomination, best actor in a play, and Drama Desk Award nomination, both 2007, for "Voyage," *The Coast of Utopia.*

CREDITS

Film Appearances:
Sonny, *Avenue X* (short film), 1994.
Graham Crouch, *Electricity* (short film), Dun Laoghaire Institute of Art, Design, and Technology, 1997.
Jessop, *The Last Bus Home,* Goutte d'Or Distribution, 1997.
Timmy, *The Fifth Province,* Ocean Films/Strawberry Vale Films, 1997.
George, *An Everlasting Piece,* Columbia/DreamWorks, 2000.
(As Brian O'Byrne) Gestapo interrogator, *The Grey Zone,* Lions Gate Films, 2001.
Gerry, *Disco Pigs,* Renaissance Films, 2001.
Darill Miller, *Bandits,* Metro–Goldwyn–Mayer, 2001.
Richie Markey, *The Mapmaker,* Grand Pictures/Oil Factory, 2001.
Mick, *Intermission,* IFC Films, 2004.
Mick, *Easy,* Magic Lamp Releasing, 2004.
(As Brian O'Byrne)) Father Horvak, *Million Dollar Baby,* Warner Bros., 2004.
The man, *In an Instant,* Eye Wonder Films/LPK Productions, 2005.
Lewes, *The New World,* New Line Cinema, 2005.
Dr. Sweet, *Bug,* Lions Gate Films, 2006.
Sean, *No Reservations,* Warner Bros., 2007.
Bobby, *Before the Devil Knows You're Dead,* Capitol Films, 2007.

Stage Appearances:
Philly Cullen, *The Playboy of the Western World,* Irish Repertory Theatre, New York City, 1990.
James Hennessy, *Seconds Out,* New York Shakespeare Festival, LuEsther Hall, Public Theatre, New York City, 1993.
Tom Valiunus, *The Sisters Rosensweig,* Ethel Barrymore Theatre, New York City, 1993–94.
Merryweather, *Hapgood,* Mitzi E. Newhouse Theatre, New York City, 1994–95.
Pato Dooley, *The Beauty Queen of Leenane,* Atlantic Theatre Company, Walter Kerr Theatre, New York City, 1998–99.
Valene Connor, *The Lonesome West,* Lyceum Theatre, New York City, 1999.
Vic, *Smelling a Rat,* Samuel Beckett Theatre, New York City, 2002.
Dad, *bedbound,* Irish Repertory Theatre, 2003.
Ralph, *Frozen,* Manhattan Class Company, Circle in the Square, New York City, 2004.
Father Flynn, *Doubt,* Manhattan Theatre Club, Walter Kerr Theatre, 2005–2006.
Ian, *Shining City,* Biltmore Theatre, New York City, 2006.
Alexander Herzen, *The Coast of Utopia* (contains "Voyage," "Shipwreck," and "Salvage"), Vivian Beaumont Theatre, Lincoln Center, New York City, 2006–2007.

Appeared in Irish productions of *The Leenane Trilogy* (contains *The Beauty Queen of Leenane, Lonesome in the West,* and *Skull in Connemara*) Druid Royal Court Theatre, Galway, Ireland; appeared in *Angel,* Pedal/Crank Theatre; *The Country Boy,* Buffalo, NY; *The Drum,* Co–Motion Theatre, Dublin, Ireland, and Irish Repertory Theatre, New York City; *Good Evening Mr. Collins,* Abbey Theatre, Dublin, Ireland; *Grandchild of Kings,* Irish Repertory Theatre; *Hackney Office,* Druid Royal Court Theatre; *Marking,* Pure Orange Theatre; *Moll,* Irish Repertory Theatre; *Philadelphia Here I Come,* Irish Repertory Theatre; *Sharon's Grave,* Gate Theatre, Dublin, Ireland; *A Thousand Hours of Love,* Theatre for a New City; and *The Woman Who Walked into Doors,* Helix Theatre, Dublin, Ireland; also appeared in *The Madame MacAdam Traveling Theatre.*

Television Appearances; Miniseries:
Luke, *Amongst Women,* BBC2, 1998.
Title role, *Alexander Hamilton,* PBS, 2007.

Television Appearances; Movies:
Larry, *The Blackwater Lightship,* CBS, 2004.

Television Appearances; Specials:
Happy Birthday Oscar Wilde, BBC, 2004.

Television Appearances; Episodic:

"An Act of Violence," *Joe Forrester,* 1976.

(As Brian O'Byrne) Father Rooney, "One of a Kind," *Valerie* (also known as *The Hogan Family, The Hogans,* and *Valerie's Family*), NBC, 1986.

Padraic Connelly, Number 01C972, "Orpheus Descending," *Oz,* HBO, 2001.

Padraic Connelly, Number 01C972, "Even the Score," *Oz,* HBO, 2001.

Padraic Connelly, Number 01C972, "Famous Last Words," *Oz,* HBO, 2001.

Liam Connors, "Ghost," *Law & Order: Special Victims Unit* (also known as *Law & Order: SVU* and *Special Victims Unit*), NBC, 2005.

Television Appearances; Awards Presentations:

The 58th Annual Tony Awards (also known as *The 2004 Tony Awards*), CBS, 2004.

The 59th Annual Tony Awards, CBS, 2005.

O'DONNELL, David

PERSONAL

Married Jennifer Aspen (an actress), September 2, 2006. *Education:* Studied at the Beverly Hills Playhouse.

Career: Actor.

CREDITS

Film Appearances:

Hand–holding man, *The Trigger Effect* (also known as *Der grosse Stromausfall—Eine Stadt im Ausnahmezustand, Efect de recul, Efeito domino, Efeitos na escuridao, Effetto Blackout, El efecto domino, Elektrosokk, Kaikki yhteydet poikki, Nuits mortelles,* and *Reactions en chaine*), Gramercy Pictures, 1996.

Young airman, *Air Force One* (also known as *AFO, Air Force One: Avion presidentiel, Air Force One, el avion del presidente, Avion presidencial, Az elnoek kueloengepe, Forca aerea 1, Forca aerea um, Presidendi lennuk,* and *Ugrabitev*), Columbia, 1997.

Mole boy, *Eating L.A.* (also known as *Eating LA*), All Channel Films Distribution, 1999.

Lieutenant Bruce Wilhemy, *Thirteen Days* (also known as *13 Days, Kolmetoista paeivaeae, 13 dager, Trece dias, Tredici giorni, Treize jours, Tretten dage, Tretton dagar, Treze dias,* and *Treze dias que abalaram o mundo*), New Line Cinema, 2000.

Billy Elliot, *Red Zone,* Red Zone, 2001.

First assistant director, *L.A. Twister,* Indican Pictures, 2004.

Gui, *The End of Suffering* (short film; also known as *Something True*), 2005.

Handsome man, *Guy in Row Five,* Odessa/Paper Moon Films, 2005.

Jake, *Dirty Love,* Palisades Pictures/First Look International, 2005.

Paulo, *The Rain Makers,* Image Entertainment, 2005.

Desmond, *Dear Me,* Shutter Star Pictures, 2007.

Television Appearances; Series:

Alex, *Undressed* (also known as *MTV's "Undressed"*), MTV, 1999.

Television Appearances; Miniseries:

Michael Giancamo, *Bella Mafia,* CBS, 1997.

Television Appearances; Movies:

Nick, *Made Men* (also known as *Fausse donne* and *Los duros*), HBO, 1999.

George, *The Big Time* (also known as *Livs levande*), TNT, 2002.

Stephen Fox, *Silent Warnings* (also known as *Dark Harvest, Warnings, Vaaran merkit, Warnings—Die Zeichen sind da, Warnings—presagi di morte,* and *Warnings—sentiras el miedo*), Sci–Fi Channel, 2003.

C. J., *Magma: Volcanic Disaster,* Sci–Fi Channel, 2006.

Television Appearances; Episodic:

Carey, "Ted and Carey's Bogus Adventure," *NYPD Blue,* ABC, 1996.

Young man, "Family Secrets," *7th Heaven* (also known as *Seventh Heaven* and *7th Heaven: Beginnings*), The WB, 1996.

Cooper Riggs, "Vanished," *JAG,* CBS, 1997.

Ramage, "A River of Candy Corn Runs through It," *Sabrina, the Teenage Witch* (also known as *Sabrina* and *Sabrina Goes to College*), ABC, 1997.

Ramage, "Sabrina, the Teenage Boy," *Sabrina, the Teenage Witch* (also known as *Sabrina* and *Sabrina Goes to College*), ABC, 1997.

Kent Damarr, "When Cheerleaders Attack," *Melrose Place,* Fox, 1998.

Tony, "'80s Night," *Beverly Hills 90210,* Fox, 1999.

Johnny MacClay, "What's Family Got to Do with It?," *That's Life,* CBS, 2002.

Jeb, "Sub Rosa," *Navy NCIS: Naval Criminal Investigative Service* (also known as *Naval CIS, Navy CIS, Navy NCIS, NCIS,* and *NCIS: Naval Criminal Investigative Service*), CBS, 2003.

Renalto, "Recipe for Disaster," *One on One,* UPN, 2006.

Appeared in other programs, including *Arli$$* (also known as *Arliss*), HBO; and *Fantasy Island,* ABC.

Television Appearances; Pilots:
Chuck, *Unhappily Ever After* (also known as *Unhappily ...*), The WB, 1995.

RECORDINGS

Video Games:
Provided the voice of Maddog in *The Best of 911 Paramedic.*

O'HURLEY, Shannon

PERSONAL

Original name, Shannon Hurley; born in HI. *Education:* Attended American Conservatory Theatre, San Francisco, CA, Boston Conservatory of Music, Boston, MA, and London Academy of Music and Dramatic Arts, London.

Addresses: *Agent*—Pakula, King and Associates, 9229 West Sunset Blvd., Suite 315, Los Angeles, CA 90069.

Career: Actress. Circle X Theatre Company, Los Angeles, member of company, 1997–2002.

CREDITS

Film Appearances:
Song performer, *At Play in the Fields of the Lord,* Universal, 1991.
Susan Schiffer, *Copycat,* Warner Bros., 1995.
Didi Jeffries, *Pain Angel* (short film), 1999.
District attorney Joyce Rafferty, *Legally Blonde,* Metro–Goldwyn–Mayer, 2001.
Pre–crime public service announcer, *Minority Report,* Twentieth Century–Fox, 2002.
Scream Queen, Tatiana Bliss Picture, 2003.
All–American mom, *Bad News Bears,* Paramount, 2005.
Danika, Universal, 2006.

Television Appearances; Movies:
Blair, *The Barefoot Executive,* ABC, 1995.

Television Appearances; Episodic:
Programmer, "The Thaw," *Star Trek: Voyager* (also known as *Voyager*), UPN, 1996.
Shannon, "High Rollers," *Renegade,* USA Network and syndicated, 1996.

Tibby Hendricks, "Athletes ARE Role Models," *Arli$$,* HBO, 1996.
Reporter, "A Little Faith," *Party of Five,* Fox, 1997.
"Wild Fire," *The Burning Zone,* UPN, 1997.
"The Court–Martial of Sandra Gilbert," *JAG,* CBS, 1997.
"It's the Real Thing, Baby," *Pensacola: Wings of Gold,* syndicated, 1997.
Grechen Schoobauer, "You Gotta Love This Game," *Arli$$,* HBO, 1999.
Nancy Fine, "Witch Hunt," *Judging Amy,* CBS, 1999.
Yvonne, "Blind Eye," *Profiler,* NBC, 1999.
Billy's mother, "The Bearer of Bad Tidings," *Becker,* CBS, 2000.
Anne Voss, "Brand X," *The X–Files,* Fox, 2000.
Susan Gallipagamus, "Chapter Thirteen," *Boston Public,* Fox, 2001.
Donna Alcott, "The Grass Is Always Pinker," *All About Us,* NBC, 2001.
Donna Alcott, "No Questions Asked," *All About Us,* NBC, 2001.
Donna Alcott, "Behind the Music," *All About Us,* NBC, 2001.
"Children Are the Most Important Thing," *Any Day Now,* Lifetime, 2001.
Betty O'Keefe, "Truth Hurts," *Any Day Now,* Lifetime, 2002.
Angela Provazolli, "Trial by Magic," *Charmed,* The WB, 2002.
Annie Randall, "Sparkle," *The Guardian,* CBS, 2004.
Mrs. Truesdale, "Running to Stand Still," *Desperate Housewives,* ABC, 2004.
Ria Prince, "The Real World Rittenhouse," *Strong Medicine,* Lifetime, 2004.
Ria Prince, "Family Practice," *Strong Medicine,* Lifetime, 2005.
Rachel Tinsley, "La Bomba," *NYPD Blue,* ABC, 2005.
Mrs. Truesdale, "My Heart Belongs to Daddy," *Desperate Housewives,* ABC, 2005.
Susan Wertz, "2162 Votes," *The West Wing,* NBC, 2005.
Phyllis Deaver, "Smile," *Boston Legal,* ABC, 2006.
Estelle Pope, "No Good Deed," *The Closer,* TNT, 2006.

Some sources cite appearance as Anette Landon in an episode of *Family Law,* CBS.

Stage Appearances:
Appeared in *And What Give Up Show Biz,* Mason Street Theatre, San Francisco, CA; as Chris, *Dancing at Lughnasa,* Berkeley Repertory Company, Berkeley, CA, and Arizona Theatre Company, Tucson, AZ; as Vixen, *The Eight: Reindeer Monologues,* Circle X Theatre Company, Los Angeles; in *Inflagrante Gothicto;* in *Irving Berlin in Review,* Lorraine Hansberry Theatre, San Francisco, CA; as Marsha, *The Loman Family Picnic,* Marin Theatre Company, Marin, CA; as Helena, *A Midsummer Night's Dream;* as Caitlin, *Over the River and into the Woods,* El Portal Center, Los Angeles; as

Corey, *Show and Tell*, Circle X Theatre Company; and in the title role, *The Unsinkable Molly Brown*, Peninsula Civic Light Opera, San Mateo, CA.

OSWALT, Patton 1969–
(Shecky Chucklestein, Patton P. Oswalt)

PERSONAL

Born January 27, 1969, in Portsmouth, VA; married Michelle McNamara (a writer), September 24, 2005. *Education:* College of William and Mary, graduated, 1991.

Addresses: *Agent*—Gregory McKnight, Creative Artists Agency, 2000 Avenue of the Stars, Los Angeles, CA 90067. *Manager*—Dave Roth, Generate Management, 1545 26th St., Suite 200, Santa Monica, CA 90404.

Career: Actor, voice performer, comedian, writer, and producer. Standup comedian at comedy clubs around the United States, 1996—; organizer and touring member of Comedians of Comedy, 2004; appeared in commercials for Nike shoes, 1999, Sierra Mist soft drinks, 2004, and other products.

CREDITS

Television Appearances; Series:
HBO Comedy Showcase, HBO, 1995.
Make Me Laugh, 1997.
HBO Comedy Half–Hour, HBO, 1997.
Spence Olchin, *The King of Queens*, CBS, 1998–2007.
Late Night with Conan O'Brien, NBC, multiple episodes, beginning 2000.
Tough Crowd with Colin Quinn, Comedy Central, 2002.
Voice of Professor Dementor, a recurring role, *Kim Possible* (animated; also known as *Disney's "Kim Possible"*), Disney Channel, between 2003 and 2007.

Television Appearances; Miniseries:
I Love the '80s, VH1, 2002.
On the Road, History Channel, 2003.
The Comedians of Comedy, Comedy Central, 2005.

Television Appearances; Specials:
Pulp Comics, Comedy Central, 1994.
Comics Come Home 3, Comedy Central, 1997.
"Patton Oswalt," *Comedy Central Presents*, Comedy Central, 1999.

The Comedy Central Presents the New York Friars Club Roast of Jerry Stiller, Comedy Central, 1999.
NFL All–Star Comedy Blitz, CBS, 1999.
VH1 Big in '03, VH1, 2003.
Patton Oswalt: No Reason to Complain, Comedy Central, 2004.
Host, *Reel Comedy: Starsky & Hutch*, Comedy Central, 2004.
Host, *Reel Comedy: Dodgeball, a True Underdog Story*, Comedy Central, 2004.
Mouthing Off: 51 Greatest Smartasses, Comedy Central, 2004.
Best Summer Ever, VH1, 2004.
Ultimate Super Heroes, Ultimate Super Villains, Ultimate Super Vixens, Bravo, 2004.
VH1 Big in '04, VH1, 2004.
VH1 Big in 05 Awards, VH1, 2005.
Host, *Reel Comedy: Wedding Crashers*, Comedy Central, 2005.
Last Laugh '05 (also known as *Comedy Central's "Last Laugh '05"*), Comedy Central, 2005.
Host, *Reel Comedy: Night at the Museum*, Comedy Central, 2006.
Voice of Mr. Groin, *The Amazing Screw–on Head*, Sci–Fi Channel, 2006.
Comedy Central Roast of William Shatner, Comedy Central, 2006.
Last Laugh '06 (also known as *Comedy Central's "Last Laugh '06"*), Comedy Central, 2006.

Television Appearances; Pilots:
Spence Olchin, *The King of Queens*, CBS, 1998.
Host, *Happy Game Fun Bomb*, Comedy Central, 2005.
Himself, *Root of All Evil*, Comedy Central, 2007.

Television Appearances; Episodic:
Clerk, "The Couch," *Seinfeld*, NBC, 1994.
Crippled person in wheelchair, *Mad TV*, Fox, 1995.
Full Frontal Comedy, Showtime, 1995.
Voice, *Dr. Katz: Professional Therapist* (animated), Comedy Central, 1995.
Guy, "The Trainer," *NewsRadio* (also known as *The Station*), NBC, 1996.
Famous Mortimer, "Operation Hell on Earth," *Mr. Show with Bob and David* (also known as *Mr. Show*), HBO, 1996.
(As Patton P. Oswalt) Seymour, "Bad Influence," *The Weird Al Show*, CBS, 1997.
Man in restaurant, "Patriotism, Pepper, and Professionalism," *Mr. Show with Bob and David* (also known as *Mr. Show*), HBO, 1998.
The List, VH1, 1999.
Happy Hour, USA Network, 1999.
Voice of Eldon Michaels, "Sentries of the Lost Cosmos," *Batman Beyond* (animated; also known as *Batman of the Future*), The WB, 2000.
Voice of Helmet, "Renaissance," *Home Movies*, 2002.

Voice of Specs/Spectral, "Trouble Squared," *Static Shock* (animated), The WB, 2002.

Voice of Boomer, *Crank Yankers,* Comedy Central, 2002, 2003.

(As Shecky Chucklestein) Voice of DP/Skeeter, "Frat Aliens," *Aqua Teen Hunger Force* (animated; also known as *ATHF*), Cartoon Network, 2003.

Voice of DP/Skeeter, "The Last One," *Aqua Teen Hunger Force* (animated; also known as *ATHF*), Cartoon Network, 2003.

Pyramid (game show), syndicated, 2003.

Jimmy Kimmel Live, ABC, 2003, 2004, 2005, 2007.

Voice of comic book writer, "The Big Superhero Wish!," *The Fairly OddParents* (animated), Nickelodeon, 2004.

Voice of Zynx, "Pioneer Island," *Tom Goes to the Mayor* (animated), Cartoon Network, 2004.

Kenny Rogers assassin, "Security for Kenny Rogers," *Reno 911!,* Comedy Central, 2004.

Dungeon master, "Junior Gets Married," *Reno 911!,* Comedy Central, 2004.

Dungeon master, "Not Without My Mustache," *Reno 911!,* Comedy Central, 2004.

Dungeon master, "Dangle's Wife Visits," *Reno 911!,* Comedy Central, 2004.

"Sex and the City, NASCAR, and More," *Best Week Ever,* VH1, 2004.

Shorties Watchin' Shorties, Comedy Central, 2004.

Carter Bogie, "Kids Putt–Putt/Double Dutch," *Cheap Seats: Without Ron Parker* (also known as *Cheap Seats*), ESPN, 2005.

Dennis Miller, CNBC, 2005.

"Perfect 10's the Women," *TV Land's Top Ten,* TV Land, 2005.

"Character You Love to Hate," *TV Land's Top Ten,* TV Land, 2005.

Himself, "A Look Behind the Scenes," *Tom Goes to the Mayor* (animated), Cartoon Network, 2005.

Too Late with Adam Carolla, Comedy Central, 2005.

Last Call with Carson Daly, NBC, multiple appearances, 2005, 2006.

Voice of Cosmo Krank (Toymaker), "Cash for Toys," *The Batman* (animated), The WB, 2006.

Guest host, *Live at Gotham,* Comedy Central, 2006.

(As Shecky Chucklestein) Voice of Jesus Ezekian Jesus, "Ezekial," *Aqua Teen Hunger Force* (animated; also known as *ATHF*), Cartoon Network, 2006.

Boozehammer of Galen, "Spanish Mike Returns," *Reno 911!,* Comedy Central, 2006.

Boozehammer of Galen, "Son of a Chechekevitch," *Reno 911!,* Comedy Central, 2006.

The Henry Rollins Show, 2006.

Boozehammer of Galen, "Ex–Wife and Her New Husband," *Reno 911!,* Comedy Central, 2007.

Multiple roles, "Let's Go," *Human Giant,* 2007.

Film critic, "The Illusionators," *Human Giant,* 2007.

Appeared as Bob, *American Dad,* Fox; and as restaurant manager, *Campus Ladies,* Oxygen Media.

Television Appearances; Other:
Sleep, 1996.
Robbery, 1996.
Lottery, 1996.
Leslie, *Super Nerds,* 2000.

Television Work; Miniseries:
Creator and executive producer, *The Comedians of Comedy,* Comedy Central, 2005.

Film Appearances:
Mind Control (short film), Comedy Central, 1995.
Quarrantine (short film), Comedy Central, 1996.
Stingray radio operator, *Down Periscope,* Twentieth Century–Fox, 1996.
Vermin (short film), Comedy Central, 1998.
First "auteur," *Desperate but Not Serious* (also known as *Reckless + Wild*), New City Releasing, 1999 (later broadcast on television by HBO, 2001.
Delmer Darion, *Magnolia* (also known as *mag–no'li–a*), New Line Cinema, 1999.
Blue–collar guy, *Man on the Moon* (also known as *Der Mondmann*), Universal, 1999.
Monkey photographer, *Zoolander,* Paramount, 2001.
Disc jockey, *The Vinyl Battle* (short film), Open Road, 2002.
Dozer, *Run Ronnie Run,* New Line Cinema, 2002.
Shelly, *ZigZag,* Silver Nitrate Films, 2002.
Larry, *Calendar Girls,* Buena Vista, 2003.
Disc jockey at disco, *Starsky & Hutch,* Warner Bros., 2004.
Felix, *See This Movie,* Slamdance on the Road, 2004.
Clerk at impound office, *Taxi* (also known as *New York Taxi* and *Taxi 2004*), Twentieth Century–Fox, 2004.
Hedges, *Blade: Trinity,* New Line Cinema, 2004.
Buddha, *Outpost,* Blue Cactus Pictures/Bubble Quandary, 2004.
Cake pervert, *Cake Boy,* Image Entertainment, 2004.
Himself, *The Comedians of Comedy* (documentary), Vitagraph Films, 2005.
Realtor, *Clark and Michael* (short film), Innertube, 2006.
Techie guy, *Failure to Launch,* Paramount, 2006.
Fred, *Sex and Death 101,* Avenue Pictures/S & D Productions/Sandbar Pictures, 2007.
Jeff Spoder, *Reno 911! Miami* (also known as *Reno 911! Miami: The Movie*), Twentieth Century–Fox, 2007.
Roger, *Greetings from Earth* (short film), 2007.
Voice of Remy, *Ratatouille* (animated), Buena Vista, 2007.
The Hammer, *Balls of Fury,* Rogue Pictures, 2007.
Milo, *All Roads Lead Home,* Waldo West Productions, 2007.
Himself, *Heckler* (documentary), Jizzy Entertainment, 2007.
Himself, *The Sophisticated Misfit* (documentary), Smee Entertainment, 2007.

Film Work:
Executive producer, *The Comedians of Comedy* (documentary), Vitagraph Films, 2005.

RECORDINGS

Videos:
Voice of radio caller in Heartland Values with Nurse Bob, *Grand Theft Auto: Liberty City Stories* (video game), Rockstar Games, 2005.
Voices of New World Order caller and reporter, *Grand Theft Auto: Vice City Stories* (video game), Take Two Interactive Software, 2006.
Producer and performer, *The Comedians of Comedy: Live at the El Rey*, Lord Loudoun, 2006.

Appeared as Carl the Corndog in "Another Perfect Day" by American Hi–Fi.

Albums:
Feelin' Kinda Patton (comedy album), United Musicians Collective, 2004, unedited version released as *222*, 2004.
Werewolves and Lollipops, Sub Pop Records, 2007.

WRITINGS

Television Specials:
"Patton Oswalt," *Comedy Central Presents*, Comedy Central, 1999.
Patton Oswalt: No Reason to Complain, Comedy Central, 2004.
MTV Special: "Dodgeball—A True Underdog Story," MTV, 2004.

Television Miniseries:
The Comedians of Comedy, Comedy Central, 2005.

Television Scripts; Other:
Sleep, 1996.
Robbery, 1996.
Lottery, 1996.

Film Scripts:
Mind Control (short film), Comedy Central, 1995.
Quarrantine (short film), Comedy Central, 1996.
Vermin (short film), Comedy Central, 1998.
The Comedians of Comedy (documentary), Vitagraph Films, 2005.

P

PALFFY, David 1969–
(David Pallfy)

PERSONAL

Born March 5, 1969, in Canada; married Erica Durance (an actress), January 8, 2005.

Career: Actor.

Awards, Honors: AMPIA Award, best actor, Annual Alberta Film & Television Awards, Alberta Motion Picture Industry Association, 1986, for *Storm.*

CREDITS

Film Appearances:

Lowell, *Storm* (also known as *Turbulences, Haudattu saalis,* and *Junge Scharfschuetzen*), Cannon, c. 1986.

Mass grave soldier, *Full Metal Jacket* (also known as *Stanley Kubrick's "Full Metal Jacket"*), Warner Bros., 1987.

Brent, *Little Girls Don't Kill,* 1989.

Gawky soldier, *The Fourth War,* Cannon, 1990.

David, *Affair Play,* Concorde Film, 1995.

Art, *Urban Safari,* Warwick Pictures, 1996.

Falco, *L.A.P.D.: To Protect and to Serve* (also known as *LAPD, LAPD Conspiracy, LAPD: Policia de Los Angeles,* and *Policia de Los Angeles—Corrupcion total*), Fries Film Group, 2001.

First pimp, *Replicant* (also known as *The Replicant, A replica, Asesino perfecto, Le clone, Replicant—tappajan kopio, Replicante,* and *Replikans*), Artisan Entertainment, 2001.

Sleazy man, *Ballistic: Ecks vs. Sever* (also known as *Ballistic, Ecks vs. Sever,* and *X vs. Sever*), Warner Bros., 2002.

Castillo, *House of the Dead* (also known as *House of the dead: Le jeu ne fait que commencer*), Artisan Entertainment, 2003.

Vince, *Firefight,* Concorde–New Horizons, 2003.

Prison guard, *Edison* (also known as *Edison Force*), Millennium Films, 2005.

Film Work:

Some sources state that Palffy was a stunt double on the film *The Chronicles of Riddick* (also known as *Pitch Black 2, Pitch Black 2: Chronicles of Riddick, Riddick, A batalha de Riddick, Kroniki Riddicka, La batalla de Riddick, Las cronicas de Riddick, Les chroniques de Riddick, Riddick—Chroniken eines Kriegers,* and *Riddickin aikakirja*), Universal, 2004, director's cut released as *The Chronicles of Riddick: The Director's Cut.*

Television Appearances; Series:

John Marr, *Eyes of a Cowboy,* beginning 1998.

Bailey Gallanson, *Cold Squad,* CTV (Canada), 1999–2000.

Anubis, *Stargate SG–1* (also known as *La porte des etoiles* and *Stargaate SG–1*), Sci–Fi Channel, Showtime, and syndicated, 2002–2004.

Voice of Leon Papas for English version, *Master Keaton* (anime), beginning 2003, series originally broadcast in Japan by NTV, beginning 1998.

Television Appearances; Miniseries:

Jim, *De Zomer van '45* (also known as *Kesae–45*), NCRV Television (the Netherlands), 1991.

Television Appearances; Movies:

Gustavo Vasquez, *My Mother, the Spy* (also known as *Droles d'espionnes!, Minha mae e uma espia,* and *Spionin auf Urlaub*), Lifetime, 2000.

Agent Wesson, *Oh, Baby* (also known as *Bratty Babies, Menudos bebes, Paroles de bebes, Solos en casa,* and *Zwei Superbabies starten durch*), 2001.

Joseph "Gunboat" Curtis, "Ladies and the Champ," *The Wonderful World of Disney,* ABC, 2001.

Prosecutor, *He Sees You When You're Sleeping* (also known as *Mary Higgins Clark and Carol Higgins Clark's "He Sees You When You're Sleeping," Ce soir je veillerai sur toi,* and *Un angel para ellas*), PAX TV, 2002.

Nazir, *Premonition* (also known as *The Psychic*), 2003.

Telly Savalas, *Behind the Camera: The Unauthorized Story of "Charlie's Angels,"* NBC, 2004.

Bruno Slinger, *Third Man Out,* Here! TV, 2005.

Mark Fairfield, *Criminal Intent* (also known as *Amour et premeditation*), Lifetime, 2005.

Phleg, *Bloodsuckers* (also known as *Vampire Wars: Battle for the Universe*), Sci–Fi Channel, 2005.

Marcel, *Caved In* (also known as *Caved In: Prehistoric Terror*), Sci–Fi Channel, 2006.

Television Appearances; Specials:

Himself, *Storm: In the Making,* [Canada], c. 1986.

Male agitator, *The Sports Pages* (also known as *Caderno de esportes*), Showtime, 2001.

Television Appearances; Episodic:

Fred Marr, "The Sweetest Sting," *Friday the 13th* (also known as *Friday's Curse, Friday the 13th: The Series, The 13th Hour, Aaveita ja kummituksia, Erben des Fluchs, Kauhun kammio, L'entrepot du diable, Misterio para tres, Pentek 13, Perjantain kirous,* and *Vendredi 13*), syndicated, 1989.

(As David Pallfy) "Clay Pigeon," *Neon Rider,* syndicated, 1990.

"Hand to Hand," *Bordertown* (also known as *Les deux font la loi*), Family Channel and CanWest Global Television, 1990.

Pietr, "Sanctuary," *Street Justice,* syndicated, 1991.

Jim Davies, "Witness," *The Commish,* ABC, 1992.

Krueger, "Catcher," *Street Justice,* syndicated, 1992.

Detective Michael Ritter, "Hello ... Again," *Street Justice,* syndicated, 1993.

Jack Graham, *Coverstory,* NCRV Television (the Netherlands), 1993.

Porter, "MIG–89," *Viper,* syndicated, 1996.

Beck, "Secret," *The Sentinel,* UPN, 1997.

Dark man, "Max," *The X–Files,* Fox, 1997.

Dark man, "Tempus Fugit," *The X–Files,* Fox, 1997.

Captain, "It Came from out of the Sky," *Night Man* (also known as *NightMan*), syndicated, 1998.

Dr. LaBlanc, "The Winning of Morticia Addams," *The New Addams Family,* Fox Family Channel, 1998.

Dr. Sorensen, "The Time Is Now," *Millennium,* Fox, 1998.

Jules Vandeveer, "Old Acquaintance," *Viper,* syndicated, 1998.

Father Peter, "Never Say Die," *The Crow: Stairway to Heaven,* syndicated, 1999.

Kramer, "Blank Slate," *The Outer Limits* (also known as *The New Outer Limits*), Showtime, Sci-Fi Channel, and syndicated, 1999.

Mel, "Last Man Standing," *The Net,* USA Network, 1999.

Sokar, "The Devil You Know," *Stargate SG–1* (also known as *La porte des etoiles* and *Stargaate SG–1*), Sci–Fi Channel, Showtime, and syndicated, 1999.

Sokar, "Jolinar's Memories," *Stargate SG–1* (also known as *La porte des etoiles* and *Stargaate SG–1*), Sci–Fi Channel, Showtime, and syndicated, 1999.

(Uncredited) Sokar, "Serpent's Song," *Stargate SG–1* (also known as *La porte des etoiles* and *Stargaate SG–1*), Sci–Fi Channel, Showtime, and syndicated, 1999.

Rourk, "Freezone," *Freedom,* UPN, 2000.

"Unearthed," *First Wave,* Sci–Fi Channel, 2000.

Mariano Cuchillo, "Tango des los Pisoleros," *The Lone Gunmen,* Fox, 2001.

Ursari, "The Devil Take the Hindmost," *Andromeda* (also known as *Gene Roddenberry's "Andromeda"*), syndicated, 2001.

"The Pyramid of Doom," *Los Luchadores,* Fox, 2001.

Cory, "Deux Ex Machina," *Jeremiah,* Showtime, 2003.

Academician Ler–Near, "Machinery of the Mind," *Andromeda* (also known as *Gene Roddenberry's "Andromeda"*), syndicated, 2004.

(Uncredited) Himself, "Erica Durance Leaves Upset," *Howard Stern on Demand* (also known as *Howard TV on Demand*), In Demand, 2006.

(In archive footage) Himself, "Best of 10/09–10/12," *Howard Stern on Demand* (also known as *Howard TV on Demand*), In Demand, 2006.

Fritz, "Death Goes On," *Blade: The Series* (also known as *Blade—Die Jagt geht weiter*), Spike, 2006.

Appeared as a police officer (some sources cite Ricky) in *The Hat Squad,* CBS.

Television Appearances; Pilots:

Fritz, *Blade: The Series* (also known as *Blade—Die Jagt geht weiter*), Spike, 2006.

RECORDINGS

Video Games:

Voice of Caleb, *Need for Speed: Underground 2,* Electronic Arts, 2004.

PALILLO, Ron 1949(?)–
(Ronald G. Paolillo)

PERSONAL

According to some sources, surname is sometimes spelled "Pallilo"; born April 2, 1949 (some sources cite

1954), in Cheshire (some sources cite nearby New Haven), CT; son of Gabriel and Carmel Paolillo. *Education:* University of Connecticut at Storrs, B.A., 1972; also attended Fairfield University, Fairfield, CT.

Career: Actor and voice performer. Touring performer in Shakespearean plays; corporate speaker. Also taught at University of Connecticut, c. 1999; artist, with drawings exhibited in New York, Hawaii, and California; also illustrator of children's books, including (as Ronald G. Paolillo) *The Red Wings of Christmas* by Wesley Eure, Pelican Publishing, 1992, and *A Gift for the Contessa* by Michael Mele, Pelican Publishing, 1997.

CREDITS

Television Appearances; Series:
Arnold Horshack, *Welcome Back, Kotter,* ABC, 1975–79.
Voice of Sergeant Squealy, *Laverne and Shirley in the Army* (animated; also known as *Laverne & Shirley*), ABC, 1981.
Voice of Sergeant Squealy, *Mork & Mindy/Laverne & Shirley/Fonz Hour* (animated; also known as *Laverne and Shirley with the Fonz*), ABC, 1982.
Voice of Rubik, *Rubik, the Amazing Cube* (animated), ABC, 1983.
Voice, *The Adventures of Don Coyote and Sancho Panda* (animated), syndicated, 1990.
Gary Warren, *One Life to Live,* ABC, 1994.

Television Appearances; Miniseries:
Hever, "Tower of Babel," *Greatest Heroes of the Bible,* NBC, 1978.
I Love the '70s, VH1, 2003.
The 100 Greatest TV Quotes & Catchphrases, TV Land, 2006.

Television Appearances; Specials:
Welcome Back Kotter: The E! True Hollywood Story, E! Entertainment Television, 2000.
Celebrity Boxing 2, Fox, 2002.
ABC's 50th Anniversary Celebration, ABC, 2003.

Television Appearances; Pilots:
Spike Mitchell, *The Invisible Woman,* NBC, 1983.

Television Appearances; Episodic:
The Captain and Tennille, ABC, 1976.
Match Game 73 (also known as *Match Game* and *Match Game 77*), CBS, 1977.
Al Breyer, "The Gopher's Opportunity/Home Sweet Home/Switch," *The Love Boat,* ABC, 1979.

"Food/Fuel: Fueling Machines," *3–2–1 Contact,* PBS, 1980.
Casper Martin, "Lose One, Win One/For the Record/Mind My Wife," *The Love Boat,* ABC, 1981.
Mutner, "The Wild One," *Alice,* CBS, 1981.
Zack, "Mexican Slayride: Part 1," *The A–Team,* NBC, 1983.
Nick, "Journey to a Spacecraft," *CHiPs* (also known as *CHiPs Patrol*), NBC, 1983.
Charlie Arbis, "The Beverly Hills Social Club," *Matt Houston,* ABC, 1983.
Attorney Norman Lester, "Hooray for Homicide," *Murder, She Wrote,* CBS, 1984.
Kussman, "Elusive Butterfly," *Trapper John, M.D.,* CBS, 1986.
Jason Weinstein, "Rites of Passage," *Cagney & Lacey,* CBS, 1986.
Voice of ordinary guy, "Planet of the Capes," *Darkwing Duck* (animated), ABC and Disney Channel, 1991.
"Horschak's Law," *Ellen* (also known as *These Friends of Mine*), ABC, 1996.
"When the Vow Breaks: Parts 1 & 2," *Ellen* (also known as *These Friends of Mine*), ABC, 1996.
Arnold Dingfelder Horshak, "The Welcome Back Show," *Mr. Rhodes,* NBC, 1997.
Voice, "Westward, No!," *Duckman: Private Dick/Family Man* (animated), 1997.
The Rosie O'Donnell Show, syndicated, 1997.
"Kid Stars," *VH–1: Where Are They Now?,* VH1, 2000.
"Lovable Losers: Geeks & Nerds," *TV Land's Top Ten,* TV Land, 2005.
"Small Screen, Big Stars," *TV Land's Top Ten,* TV Land, 2005.
"Character You Love to Hate," *TV Land's Top Ten,* TV Land, 2005.
"Greatest TV Romances," *TV Land's Top Ten,* TV Land, 2005.

Television Work; Series:
Additional voices, *Potsworth & Co.* (animated), syndicated, 1990.

Film Appearances:
Frankey, *Skatetown, U.S.A.,* Columbia, 1979.
Trinculo, *The Tempest,* Bard Productions, 1983.
Surf II (also known as *Surf II: The End of the Trilogy*), International Film Marketing, 1984.
Pappion, *Doin' Time,* Warner Bros., 1985.
Allen Hawes, *Jason Lives: Friday the 13th Part VI* (also known as *Friday the 13th Part VI: Jason Lives*), Paramount, 1986.
Ronnie, *Committed,* Highlight Video, 1988.
Matt, *Hellgate,* New World Video, 1989.
Torchy, *Snake Eater* (also known as *Soldier*), Moviestore Entertainment, 1989.
Torchy, *Snake Eater II: The Drug Buster,* Starlight, 1990.
Tony, *Wind,* Columbia TriStar, 1992.

Himself, *Dickie Roberts: Former Child Star* (also known as *Dickie Roberts: (Former) Child Star*), Paramount, 2003.

Dougie Styles, *Trees 2: The Root of All Evil,* Pioneer Motion Pictures, 2004.

Professor Walker, *The Guardians,* RuffHouse Productions, 2006.

Stage Appearances:

A Closer Walk with Patsy Cline (musical), West Palm Beach, FL, 1999–2000.

Inherit the Wind, Ivoryton Playhouse, Ivoryton, CT, 2004.

Appeared in New York City productions of *Hot l Baltimore* and *Summer Brave.*

Major Tours:

Appeared in a touring production of *A Midsummer Night's Dream.*

Stage Director:

A Closer Walk with Patsy Cline (musical), West Palm Beach, FL, 1999–2000.

PARDO, Don 1918–

PERSONAL

Full name, Dominick George Pardo; born February 22, 1918, in Westfield, MA; children: Jimmy Pardo (a comedian).

Career: Actor and television announcer. National Broadcasting Company, New York City, staff announcer for network radio programs, including *The Magnificent Montague,* 1950–51, and for numerous television programs, including *The Price Is Right,* 1956–63, *Jeopardy!,* 1964–75, and *Saturday Night Live,* 1975—. WGRF–FM Radio, Buffalo, NY, opening announcer for *College of 97 Rock Knowledge;* WNBC–TV, New York City, news announcer; voice for commercials, including Frosted Cheerios breakfast cereal, 1995.

CREDITS

Film Appearances:

Announcer, *The Sex O'clock News,* 1984.

Guess That Tune host, *Radio Days,* Orion, 1987.

Jay, *Stay Tuned,* Warner Bros., 1992.

(Uncredited) Announcer, *Honeymoon in Vegas,* Columbia, 1992.

Himself, *The Godson,* Sterling Home Entertainment, 1998.

Television Appearances; Series:

Announcer, *Remember This Date,* 1950.

Announcer, *Winner Take All,* 1952.

Announcer, *Three Steps to Heaven,* 1953.

Announcer, *Judge for Yourself* (also known as *The Fred Allen Show*), 1953.

Announcer, *Choose Up Sides* (game show), 1953.

Announcer, *Droodles* (game show), 1954.

Announcer, *The Price is Right,* 1956–63.

Announcer, *Charge Account* (also known as *The Jan Murray Show*), 1960.

Announcer, *Concentration* (game show), 1962–63.

Announcer, *Jeopardy,* 1964–75.

Announcer, *Eye Guess* (game show), 1966–69.

Announcer, *Three on a Match* (game show), 1971–74.

Announcer, *Winning Streak* (game show), 1974–75.

Announcer, New York segments, *Wheel of Fortune,* 1975, 1988.

Announcer, *Saturday Night Live* (also known as *SNL*), NBC, 1975—.

Television Appearances; Episodic:

Announcer, *The Colgate Comedy Hour,* three episodes, 1951–53.

Announcer, *Jackpot,* 1975.

Late Night with David Letterman, NBC, 1988.

"Where No White Man Has Ever Gone Before," *History Bites,* History Television, 2001.

Himself, "Medium Rare," *Oz,* HBO, 2001.

Himself, "Conversions," *Oz,* HBO, 2001.

Television Appearances; Other:

Announcer, *Max Liebman Presents: Promenade,* 1955.

Announcer, *Those Wonderful TV Game Shows,* 1984.

Announcer, *Totally Minnie* (also known as *Disney's "Totally Minnie"*), 1987.

Announcer for "Histeria Night Live" segments, *Histeria!* (series), The WB, 1998.

Announcer, *Saturday Night Live: 25th Anniversary,* NBC, 1999.

Announcer, *Saturday Night Live Weekend Update Halftime Special,* NBC, 2003.

Announcer, *Live from New York: The First 5 Years of Saturday Night Live,* NBC, 2005.

RECORDINGS

Albums:

(Contributor) Frank Zappa, *Zappa in New York,* re-release version, 1993.

Videos:

Game show announcer, "I Lost on Jeopardy," *The Compleat Al* (comedy compilation), Fox Video, 1985.

Dr. Demento 20th Anniversary Collection, Rhino Home Video, 1991.

Announcer, *Saturday Night Live Christmas* (compilation of previously broadcast comedy segments), Trimark Video, 1999.

Pardo's appearance as a game show announcer for the "Weird Al" Yankovic comedy sketch titled "I Lost on Jeopardy" has been included in several of Yankovic's subsequent video compilations. His work as an announcer for the television series *Saturday Night Live* has been included in archive footage for several video compilations featuring cast members such as Jon Lovitz, Robin Williams, Dan Aykroyd, Mike Myers, Chris Rock, and Molly Shannon.

PARDUCCI, Paul

PERSONAL

Career: Actor, producer, director, and writer.

Member: Mensa.

CREDITS

Film Appearances:

Jack Cheese, *Silent but Deadly,* Troma Entertainment, 1987.

Sancho, *Hot Splash,* 1988.

Pizza assistant, *Punch the Clock,* 1990.

Eddie, *Thrill Kill Video Club,* Surf Reality Productions, 1991.

Paul, *Cracking Up,* 1994, Phaedra Cinema, 1998.

Leon, *Hard Time,* Mystique Films, 1996.

Bear/Petrovich, *A Gun, a Car, a Blonde,* Showcase Entertainment, 1997.

Police officer, *Good Burger,* Paramount, 1997.

Man in shower, *Switchback,* Paramount, 1997.

Rocco, *The Unknown Cyclist,* Trident Releasing, 1998.

Ronnie, *Hitman's Run,* Lions Gate Films, 1999.

Louis Schrankhart, *The Interview* (short film), Pardco Pictures, 2000.

Title role, *Uncle Joe's Garage* (short film), 2001.

Interviewer, *Evp,* 2003.

Film Producer and Director:

The Interview (short film), Pardco Pictures, 2000.

Uncle Joe's Garage (short film), 2001.

Evp, 2003.

Television Appearances; Series:

Title role, *Nightmare Boss,* 2006.

Television Appearances; Specials:

The pancreas supervisor, *Inside Eddie Johnson,* Nickelodeon, 1996.

Title role, *The Uncle Paul Show,* Cartoon Network, 1996.

Television Appearances; Episodic:

Himself, *Night after Night,* 1992.

"Comedy Bootcamp," *Short Attention Span Theatre,* Comedy Central, 1993.

Bud, "The Jack Buckner Society," *Madman of the People,* NBC, 1994.

Dave, "Sweet Denial," *Platypus Man,* UPN, 1995.

Officer Bryant, *The Young and the Restless* (also known as *Y&R*), CBS, 1995.

Big Tony, "Ring of Fire," *The John Larroquette Show* (also known as *Larroquette*), NBC, 1996.

Captain Perry, "Black Ops," *JAG,* NBC, 1996.

Joey, "Autumn 'Foilage,'" *Boston Common,* NBC, 1996.

Prison guard, "How to Turn a Minus into a Plus," *Arli$$,* HBO, 1996.

Gorko, "The Pleasure Planet Principle, or G Marks the Spot," *Homeboys in Outer Space,* UPN, 1996.

First "repo" man, "Nobody's Perfect," *Murphy Brown,* CBS, 1996.

Dante, "The Gym," *Mad About You,* NBC, 1996.

Centurion, "I, Chettus," *Weird Science,* USA Network, 1997.

Lou, "Family Un–Ties," *Home Improvement,* ABC, 1997.

Doug, "Bully for Dave," *The Naked Truth* (also known as *Wilde Again*), NBC, 1997.

Deke Williams, "Elliott the Geek," *Just Shoot Me!,* NBC, 1998.

The guard, "The April Fools," *Kenan & Kel,* Nickelodeon, 1999.

Mike Delaney, "Physician Heal Thyself," *Becker,* CBS, 1999.

Construction worker, "Four Colds and a Funeral," *Stark Raving Mad,* NBC, 1999.

(Uncredited) First policeman, "The Remains of the Date," *Girlfriends,* UPN, 2000.

Policeman, *The Amanda Show,* Nickelodeon, 2000.

Murphy, "Sick Popples/When Cheerleaders Attack," *The Amanda Show,* Nickelodeon, 2000.

The Amanda Show, Nickelodeon, 2001.

Dave Tiarrez, "Nariz a Nariz," *NYPD Blue,* ABC, 2001.

Coach, "Hall of Fame," *The Bernie Mac Show,* Fox, 2002.

Alan, "He Shoots, They Snore," *Will & Grace,* NBC, 2002.

Earl, "Out Damned Spot," *Dr. Vegas,* CBS, 2004.

Barney in 1983, "It's Raining Men," *Cold Case,* CBS, 2005.

Cyrus, "Goodbye for Now," *Desperate Housewives,* ABC, 2005.

Captain Kyle Henning, "A Boy in a Bush," *Bones,* Fox, 2005.

Coach Remmers, "The Dance Contest," *Drake & Josh,* Nickelodeon, 2006.

Television Appearances; Other:
Voice of Bill the Bear, *The Zoonatiks in Home Sweet Home* (animated), 1997.

Television Work:
Creator, *The Uncle Paul Show* (special), Cartoon Network, 1996.

Creator, producer, and director, *Nightmare Boss* (series), 2006.

RECORDINGS

Video Games:
Voice of Gordy, *Jak and Daxter: The Precursor Legacy* (also known as *Jak and Daxter*), Sony Computer Entertainment, 2001.

WRITINGS

Films:
The Interview (short film), Pardco Pictures, 2000.
Uncle Joe's Garage (short film), 2001.
Evp, 2003.

Television:
The Zoonatiks in Home Sweet Home (animated), 1997.
Nightmare Boss (series), 2006.

PARIKH, Devika
(Davika Parikh)

PERSONAL

Education: Syracuse University, graduated; trained for the stage at Beverly Hills Playhouse, Beverly Hills, CA.

Addresses: *Agent*—Henderson/Hogan/McCabe, 247 South Beverly Dr., Beverly Hills, CA 90212.

Career: Actress, comedian, and voice performer. Foxy, Fine & Funny (comedy troupe), member of company; improvisational comic (with others) at such clubs as Comedy Store, Underground Improv, and Upfront Comedy Theatre; appeared in commercials for Checkers and Rally's restaurants, Kraft foods, Sears department stores, and other products.

CREDITS

Television Appearances; Series:
Bonnie, a recurring role, *The West Wing,* NBC, 1999–2003.

Television Appearances; Movies:
Hostess, *Nothing but the Truth,* CBS, 1995.
Rhonda Reese, *Judgment Day,* HBO, 1999.
Cheryl Reed, *Dancing in September,* HBO, 2000.
Silvia Penniman, *Little Richard,* NBC, 2000.
Brenda Brass, *Something to Sing About,* syndicated, 2000.
Vikki, *Book of Love: The Definitive Reason Why Men Are Dogs,* Black Entertainment Television, 2005.

Television Appearances; Episodic:
Shanice, *Rhythm & Blues,* NBC, 1992.
First King Beef girl, "Boyz 'R Us," *Martin,* Fox, 1992.
First King Beef girl, "Baby It's Cole'd in Here," *Martin,* Fox, 1992.
Gayle, "Will Goes a Courtin'," *The Fresh Prince of Bel–Air,* NBC, 1993.
Second woman, "Strictly Business," *The Sinbad Show* (also known as *Sinbad*), Fox, 1993.
Monique "Slumber Party," *Sister, Sister,* ABC, 1994.
Girl, "Women Rises in World, Falls on Face!," *The Naked Truth* (also known as *Wilde Again*), ABC, 1996.
Tina, "Mother of Invention," *In the House,* UPN, 1996.
Natalie Baxter, "An Officer and a Homegirl," *The Wayans Bros.,* The WB, 1996.
Second nurse, "All in the Family," *Chicago Hope,* CBS, 1997.
Barbara, "Shades of Gray," *The Jamie Foxx Show,* The WB, 2000.
Master of ceremonies, "Frasier's Edge," *Frasier,* NBC, 2001.
"La Nina Perdida," *Resurrection Blvd.,* Showtime, 2002.
Maureen Kingsley, "12:00 a.m.–1:00 a.m.," *24,* Fox, 2001.
(As Davika Parikh) Maureen Kingsley, "4:00 a.m.–5:00 a.m.," *24,* Fox, 2001.
Maureen Kingsley, "8:00 a.m.–9:00 a.m.," *24,* Fox, 2002.
Maureen Kingsley, "12:00 p.m.–1:00 p.m.," *24,* Fox, 2002.
Mary, "Single Mama, Drama," *Girlfriends,* UPN, 2003.
Bella, "Can Two Wrongs Make a Right?," *The Parkers,* UPN, 2004.
DeeDee, "Who Brought the Jive Turkey?," *One on One,* UPN, 2004.

Reporter, "True Colors," *That's So Raven!,* Disney Channel, 2005.

Yolanda Jenkins, "Food for Thought," *That's So Raven!,* Disney Channel, 2005.

Delilah, "Janie, Shut Up!," *Eve,* UPN, 2005.

Olivia Hopkins, "Secrets and Lies," *Criminal Minds,* CBS, 2006.

Also appeared in at least one episode of *In Living Color,* Fox; and in *Kenan & Kel,* Nickelodeon.

Television Appearances; Other:
Bonnie, *The West Wing* (pilot), NBC, 1999.

Melanie, "Out–of–Body Experience" (special), *Black Filmmaker Showcase,* Showtime, 2004.

Appeared in a pilot titled *Cold Shoulder,* NBC.

Film Appearances:
Barbara, *How to Be a Player* (also known as *Def Jam's "How to Be a Player"*), Gramercy, 1997.

N'Dea Strawberry, *Strawberry's Letter,* OnyxQuest Entertainment, 2001.

Caught, 2002.

Marsha Mello, *Mello's Kaleidoscope* (short film), Mo Mello Productions, 2002.

Jail intake reporter, *S.W.A.T.,* Columbia, 2003.

Fatima, *Air Marshal,* Lions Gate Films Home Entertainment, 2003.

Woman on bus, *Our Father* (short film), 2004.

Voice of news reporter, *Madagascar* (animated), DreamWorks, 2005.

Herself, *Angels Can't Help but Laugh* (documentary), Nina Holiday Entertainment, 2007.

Some sources cite role of Wanda in the film *Hair Show,* UrbanWorks Entertainment, 2004; role of Gina, *Menage,* University of Southern California; and appearances in *CB4,* MCA/Universal, 1993, and *Where the F#"? Is Lochman,* American Film Institute.

Film Work:
Additional voices, *The Jungle Book2* (animated), Buena Vista, 2003.

Some sources cite voice work in the films *Something New,* Focus Features, 2006; and *I Think I Love my Wife,* Fox Searchlight, 2007.

Stage Appearances:
Appeared as Keisha and Margaret, *Culture Shock,* Theatre of the Arts; gravedigger, *Hamlet,* Knightsbridge Theatre, Los Angeles; Celia, *Hatful of Rain,* Off Ramp Theatre, St. Louis, MO; Edwina Beard, *South of Where*

We Live, Ebony Showcase Theatre, Los Angeles; Joanne, *Vanities,* Complex Theatre; and Dr. Cohen, *The Visit,* Hudson Avenue Theatre, Los Angeles.

Major Tours:
Appeared in multiple roles in a West Coast tour of *1001 Black Inventions.*

PARK, Linda 1978–

PERSONAL

Born July 9, 1978, in South Korea; immigrated to the United States; daughter of Kellie Park. *Education:* Boston University, B.F.A., acting, 2000; studied at the London Academy of Music and Dramatic Art and the Royal Academy of Dramatic Art; studied voice and dance. *Avocational Interests:* Ballroom dancing.

Addresses: *Agent*—SDB Partners, 1801 Avenue of the Starts, Suite 902, Los Angeles, CA 90067. *Manager*—Seven Summit Pictures & Management, 8906 West Olympic Blvd., Ground Floor, Beverly Hills, CA 90211.

Career: Actress. Underground Asylum (theatre company), cofounder; American Fight Directors, certified actor combatant; San Jose Stage Company, worked as an intern. Appeared at science fiction conventions. Affiliated with charities.

CREDITS

Television Appearances; Series:
Ensign Hoshi Sato, *Enterprise* (also known as *Star Trek: Enterprise, Star Trek: Series V,* and *Star Trek: Untitled Fifth Series*), UPN, 2001–2005.

Sally Lance, *Raines,* NBC, 2007.

Television Appearances; Episodic:
Anna Lin, "Fag," *Popular* (also known as *Suositut*), The WB, 2001.

Herself, *Jeopardy!,* syndicated, 2003.

Television Appearances; Pilots:
Ensign Hoshi Sato, "Broken Bow: Parts 1 & 2," *Enterprise* (also known as *Star Trek: Enterprise, Star Trek: Series V,* and *Star Trek: Untitled Fifth Series*), UPN, 2001.

Sally Lance, *Raines,* NBC, 2007.

Stage Appearances:
Meet Me in St. Louis (musical), c. 1985.

Fuchsia, Underground Asylum, Hollywood, CA, 2003.

Vanessa, *Roger & Vanessa*, Latchmere Theatre, London, 2004.
Clytemnestra, *Agamemnon*, Vortex Theatre Company, St. Veronica's Church, New York City, 2005.

Appeared as Maggie (Maggie the Cat), *Cat on a Hot Tin Roof*; as Ophelia, *Hamlet*; and as Helen, *The Trojan Women*. Appeared in other musicals; appeared in other productions, including *The Phantom Tollbooth* (musical), *Cyrano de Bergerac, Lysistrata, Mad Forest,* and *Richard III.*

Stage Producer:
(With others) *Roger & Vanessa,* Latchmere Theatre, London, 2004.

Film Appearances:
Hannah, *Jurassic Park III* (also known as *The Extinction: Jurassic Park 3, JP3, Jurassic Park 3, Jurassic Park 3: Breakout, Jurassic Park 3: The Extinction, Return to the Island: Jurassic Park 3, Jurassic Park III: Parque jurasico III, Jurski park 3, Le parc jurassique III,* and *Parc jurassic III*), Universal, 2001.
Party goer, *Taken,* Superstitious Entertainment, 2002.
Min, *Geldersma* (short film), Quality Time Productions/Luminous Pictures, 2004.
Renee Hansen, *Spectres* (also known as *Soul Survivor*), Xenon Pictures, 2004.
Kate, *Honor,* Hologram Entertainment/Arc2 Intertainment/TVX, 2006.
Shen, *My Prince, My Angel* (short film), My Prince, My Angel, 2006.

Film Executive Producer and Producer:
My Prince, My Angel (short film), My Prince, My Angel, 2006.

WRITINGS

Writings for the Stage:
Created material with the Underground Asylum (theatre company).

OTHER SOURCES

Periodicals:
Dreamwatch, April, 2004.
DW, November, 2002.
San Jose Mercury News, February 5, 2003.
Starlog, March, 2005.
Star Trek Monthly, November, 2002.
TV Zone, November, 2001, pp. 30–32; December, 2001.

TV Zone Special, September, 2002, pp. 34–37.
Yolk, Volume 8, 2001.

PARKER, Anthony Ray

PERSONAL

Addresses: *Manager*—Roland Gotingco, Meissner Management, 122 Riley St., Paddington, New South Wales 2021, Australia.

Career: Actor.

CREDITS

Television Appearances; Series:
Garage Sale, 1998.
Chip Dexter, *Shortland Street,* TV New Zealand, 1998.
Host, *Guess Who's Coming to Dinner?,* 1998–2001.
Member of North Team, *Celebrity Treasure Island,* 2001.
Host, *Second Honeymoon,* 2001.
Beefy con, *Prison Break: Proof of Innocence,* 2006.

Television Appearances; Movies:
Minotaur, *Hercules in the Maze of the Minotaur,* syndicated, 1994.
Security guard, *Every Woman's Dream,* CBS, 1996.
Fire captain, *Superfire* (also known as *Firefighter—Inferno in Oregon* and *Superfire—Inferno in Oregon*), ABC, 2002.
Umpire, *Eddie's Million Dollar Cook–off,* Disney Channel, 2003.

Television Appearances; Episodic:
Richard, *McKenna,* ABC, 1994.
Iphicles, "The Gauntlet," *Hercules: The Legendary Journeys,* syndicated, 1995.
Minotaur, "The Sword of Veracity," *Hercules: The Legendary Journeys,* syndicated, 1996.
Valerus, "Once a Hero," *Hercules: The Legendary Journeys,* syndicated, 1996.
Second Kimo bodyguard, "The Romanoff Affair," *One West Waikiki,* syndicated, 1996.
Bacchus, "Girls Just Wanna Have Fun," *Xena: Warrior Princess* (also known as *Xena*), syndicated, 1996.
Pinullus, "A Comedy of Eros," *Xena: Warrior Princess* (also known as *Xena*), syndicated, 1997.
Title role, "The Deliverer," *Xena: Warrior Princess* (also known as *Xena*), syndicated, 1997.

Mephistopheles, "The Haunting of Amphipolis," *Xena: Warrior Princess* (also known as *Xena*), syndicated, 2000.
Voice of Thornox, "Disappearing Act," *Power Rangers: Dino Thunder* (animated), Fox, 2004.

Television Appearances; Specials:
Happy Birthday 2 You, TV2, 2000.

Film Appearances:
Deputy, *The Frighteners* (also known as *Robert Zemeckis Presents: "The Frighteners"*), Universal, 1996.
Webster, *Nightmare Man,* Isambard Productions/WingNut Films, 1999.
Dozer, *The Matrix,* Warner Bros., 1999.
Morgan, *The Marine,* Twentieth Century–Fox, 2006.
First officer, *Two–Eleven* (short film), Velvet Revolution Pictures, 2007.
Slim, *Urban Assault,* Renegade Worldwide, 2007.

RECORDINGS

Videos:
Voice of Dozer, *The Matrix: Path of Neo* (video game), Atari/Shiny Entertainment/Warner Bros. Interactive Entertainment, 2005.
Declassified: The Making of "The Marine," WWE Films, 2006.

PARKER, Monica

PERSONAL

Addresses: *Agent*—Mitchell K. Stubbs & Associates, 8675 W. Washington Blvd., Suite 203, Culver City, CA 90232.

Career: Actress, writer, and producer.

CREDITS

Film Appearances:
Fat girl, *The Merry Wives of Windsor,* 1972.
Keep It in the Family, 1973.
My Pleasure Is My Business, Brian, 1975.
Running, Universal, 1979.
Gloria Washburn, *Improper Channels,* Crown International Pictures, 1979.
Corinne, *The Woman in Red,* 1984.

Police Academy 2: Their First Assignment, Warner Bros., 1985.
Terminal Choice, Almi Pictures, 1985.
Sally, *He's My Girl,* Scotti Brothers Pictures, 1987.
Jessica, *Switching Channels,* TriStar, 1988.
All's Fair, Moviestore Entertainment, 1989.
Mrs. Tindermarsh, *The Road to Wellville,* Sony, 1994.
Janice Moran, *A Perfect Murder,* Warner Bros., 1998.
Nailed, Curb Entertainment, 2001.
Population 436, Sony Pictures Entertainment, 2006.
Hannah, *Nancy Drew,* Warner Bros., 2007.

Television Appearances; Movies:
Jane, *Stand By Your Man,* CBS, 1981.
Dolores, *Scorned and Swindled,* CBS, 1984.
Dorothy, *Through the Eyes of a Killer,* CBS, 1992.
Greta, *Miracle on Interstate 880* (also known as *Miracle on I–880*), NBC, 1993.
Haru's secretary, *Long Shadows,* PBS, 1994.
Marie, *The Other Woman,* CBS, 1995.
Coroner, *If Looks Could Kill* (also known as *If Looks Could Kill: From the Files of "America's Most Wanted"* and *If Looks Could Kill: The John Hawkins Story*), Fox, 1996.
Goldie, *Radiant City,* ABC, 1996.
Nadine, *At the End of the Day: The Sue Rodriguez Story* (also known as *Le combat de Sue Rodriguez*), Lifetime, 1998.
May Bolton, *The Color of Love: Jacey's Story,* CBS, 2000.
Irma Van Wyck, *Recipe for a Perfect Christmas,* Lifetime, 2005.
Louise, *Post Mortem,* 2007.

Television Appearances; Specials:
Voice, *What Have We Learned, Charlie Brown?* (animated), CBS, 1983.

Television Appearances; Pilots:
Betty, *One Night Band,* CBS, 1983.

Television Appearances; Episodic:
Ladonna, "Deep Throat," *The X–Files,* Fox, 1993.
Madame Tarot, "Day of the Dead," *Lonesome Dove: The Outlaw Years,* syndicated, 1995.
Hannah Parkins, "Evidence of Malice," *Murder, She Wrote,* CBS, 1996.
Allergic woman, "Ground Zero," *ER,* NBC, 1997.
Nurse Stryker, "Rescue Me," *Diagnosis Murder,* CBS, 1999.
Alana, "No Fare," *Martial Law,* CBS, 2000.
Mrs. Vanjec, "Bye Bye Binnie," *Just Shoot Me!,* NBC, 2001.

Television Work; Movies:
Coproducer, *A Kiss So Deadly,* NBC, 1996.
Executive producer, *Hunger Point,* Lifetime, 2003.

Executive producer, *Home By Christmas,* Lifetime, 2006.

Executive producer, *The Party Never Stops: Diary of a Binge Drinker,* Lifetime, 2007.

WRITINGS

Television Movie Stories:
A Kiss So Deadly, NBC, 1996.
Home By Christmas, Lifetime, 2006.

Television Episodes:
An Evening at Improv, PBS, 1981.
Who's the Boss?, ABC, 1984.

PARMET, Phil 1942–

PERSONAL

Full name, Philip Alan Parmet; born March 7, 1942, in Princeton, NJ; married, wife's name Lisa (a costume designer). *Education:* Attended Fairleigh Dickinson University and University of Pennsylvania.

Addresses: *Agent*—Jasan Pagni, Paradigm, 360 North Crescent Dr., North Bldg., Beverly Hills, CA 90210.

Career: Cinematographer and video game director. Also photography director for music videos by Bruce Springsteen, Led Zeppelin, Meatloaf, the Temptations, and other recording artists; worked as documentary filmmaker, photographer, and camera operator; still photographer, with solo and group shows in New York City, Los Angeles, and European cities.

Member: International Cinematographers Guild.

CREDITS

Film Cinematographer:
(With others) *Elephant with Seven Feet* (documentary), 1966.
(Uncredited) *The Song Remains the Same* (documentary; also known as *Led Zeppelin: The Song Remains the Same*), Warner Bros., 1976.
(Contributor) *Harlan County U.S.A.* (documentary), Cinema 5 Distributing, 1976.
Baby Snakes (documentary with animation), Intercontinental Absurdities, 1979.

He Makes Me Feel Like Dancin' (documentary), Edgar J. Scherick Associates, 1984.
Directed by William Wyler, 1986.
Fatal Mission (also known as *Enemy*), Anchor Bay Entertainment, 1990.
Street Hunter, 21st Century Film, 1990.
American Dream (documentary), Cabin Creek Films, 1990.
In the Soup (also known as *In the Soup–alles kino* and *In the Soup—un mare di guai*), Triton Pictures, 1992.
Distant Justice, Columbia TriStar, 1992.
Distant Cousins (also known as *Desperate Motive*), New Line Cinema, 1993.
Two Small Bodies (also known as *Two Small Bodies— Zwei Koerper*), Castle Hill, 1994.
Nina Takes a Lover, Triumph Releasing, 1994.
Cyborg 3: The Recycler (also known as *Cyborg 3* and *Cyborg 3: The Creation*), Prism Leisure/Warner Vision Entertainment, 1994.
The Fifteen Minute Hamlet (short film), cin–cine, 1995.
"The Wrong Man" segment, *Four Rooms,* Miramax, 1995.
Under the Hula Moon, Trident Releasing, 1995.
Big Ell's, 1995.
364 Girls a Year (also known as *The Last Bachelor*), Lost Studios, 1996.
Flipping, Dove International, 1997.
The Lovemaster, Rocket Pictures Home Video, 1997.
Girly Magazine Party, 1997.
Voices Unheard, 1998.
Devil Doll/Ring Pull (short film), Fuel/Ministry of Information, 1999.
Love and Action in Chicago, New Films International, 1999.
Next Stop, Eternity (short film), Seventh Art Releasing, 2000.
The Cutting Room (short film), 2001.
13 Moons, Lot 47 Films, 2002.
American Gun, Miramax, 2002.
Heavy Put–Away (short film), Fox Searchlight, 2004.
Dallas 362, 2003, ThinkFilm, 2005.
The Devil's Rejects (also known as *TDR—The Devil's Rejects*), Lions Gate Films, 2005.
Symbiopsychotaxiplasm: Take 2 ½ (documentary), Criterion Collection, 2006.
Lonesome Jim, IFC Films, 2006.
The Dog Problem, ThinkFilm, 2006.
Halloween: The Shape of Horror (short film), Compass International Pictures, 2006.
"Werewolf Women of the SS" segment, *Grindhouse* (also known as *Quentin Tarantino's "Death Proof"* and *Robert Rodriguez's "Planet Terror"*), Weinstein Co., 2007.
Blue State, Eagle Vision/Paquin Films, 2007.
Halloween, Metro–Goldwyn–Mayer, 2007.

Film Work; Other:

Coproducer and codirector, *Driving to Ground Zero*, 2001.

Film Appearances:

Baby Snakes (documentary with animation), Intercontinental Absurdities, 1979.
Symbiopsychotaxiplasm: Take 2 ½ (documentary), Criterion Collection, 2006.

Television Cinematographer; Movies:

The Last Days of Frankie the Fly (also known as *Frankie the Fly*), HBO, 1997.
Mind Games, ABC, 1998.
Black and White, HBO, 1999.
Animal Factory, Cinemax, 2000.
Run for the Money (also known as *Hard Cash*), USA Network, 2002.
Bastards of the Party, HBO, 2006.

Television Cinematographer; Specials:

"No Maps on My Taps," *American Masters*, PBS, 1979.
(Contributor) *L.A. Homefront/The Fires Within*, Showtime, 1994.
(Contributor) "John Brown's Holy War," *The American Experience*, PBS, 2000.

Television Cinematographer; Other:

Women: Stories of Passion (series), Showtime, 1996.
Orleans (miniseries), CBS, 1997.

RECORDINGS

Video Director:

Loadstar: The Legend of Tully Bodine (video game), 1994.
Ripper (video game), Take2 Interactive, 1996.

Video Appearances:

30 Days in Hell (also known as *30 Days in Hell: The Making of "The Devil's Rejects"*), Lions Gate Films Home Entertainment, 2005.

OTHER SOURCES

Periodicals:

International Photographer, February, 1997, pp. 27–31.

Electronic:

Phil Parmet Official Site, http://www.byeye.com, May 19, 2007.

PAU, Peter 1952–
(Tak–Hai Pau)

PERSONAL

Cantonese spelling of name is Baau Tak Hei; Mandarin spelling of name is Bao De Xi; born 1952, in Hong Kong (now China); son of Fong Pao (an actor and director) and Su Liu (an actress). *Education:* School of the San Francisco Art Institute, B.F.A., 1983.

Addresses: *Agent*—David Gersh, Gersh Agency, 232 North Canon Dr., Beverly Hills, CA 90210.

Career: Cinematographer, director, producer, and actor. Also photographer, including commercial work. Formerly worked as a bank clerk in Hong Kong.

Member: Hong Kong Society of Cinematographers.

Awards, Honors: Hong Kong Film Award nomination, best cinematography, 1988, for *Wai si–lei chuen kei;* Hong Kong Film Award nomination (with Hang–Sang Poon), best cinematography, 1989, for *He Bo;* Hong Kong Film Award, best cinematography, 1990, for *Bu tuo wa de ren;* Hong Kong Film Award nomination (with Wing–Hung Wong), best cinematography, 1990, for *Dip hyut shueng hung;* Hong Kong Film Award nomination (with Sun Yip Li), best cinematography, 1991, for *Qin yong;* Hong Kong Film Award nominations (with others), best cinematography, 1992, for *Hoyat gwan tsoi* and for *Wei si li zhi ba wang xie jia;* Hong Kong Film Award, best cinematography, 1992, for *Gau yat san diu hap lui;* Hong Kong Film Award, best cinematography, 1994, for *Bai fa mo nu zhuan;* Hong Kong Film Award nomination, best cinematography, 1995, for *Hua qi Shao Lin;* Hong Kong Film Award nominations, best cinematography, 1996, and Video Premiere Award, best cinematography, DVD Exclusive Awards, 2001, both for *Ye ban ge sheng;* Hong Kong Film Award nominations, best cinematography, 1999, for *Ngon na ma dak lin na,* and 2000, for *Ban zhi yan;* Boston Society of Film Critics Award, Los Angeles Film Critics Association Award, New York Film Critics Circle Award, nomination for Golden Frog, Camerimage Awards, and nomination for Golden Horse Award, Golden Horse Film Festival, all 2000, Academy Award, Film Award nomination, British Academy of Film and Television Arts, American Society of Cinematographers Award nomination, British Society of Cinematographers Award nomination, Chicago Film Critics Association Award, Dallas–Fort Worth Film Critics Association Award, Florida Film Critics Circle Award, Hong Kong Film Award, Golden Satellite Award nomination,

International Press Academy, and Online Film Critics Society Award, all 2001, all best cinematography, for *Crouching Tiger, Hidden Dragon;* Hong Kong Film Award nomination, best cinematography, 2002, for *Bak ging lok yue liu;* Asia–Pacific Film Festival Award, 2002, and Hong Kong Film Award nomination, 2003, both best cinematography, for *The Touch;* Hawaii International Film Festival Award, excellence in cinematography, 2002; Hong Kong Film Award and Golden Horse Award, both best cinematography, 2006, for *Ru guo—Ai;* Hong Kong Film Award nomination, best cinematography, 2006, for *Wu ji.*

CREDITS

Film Cinematographer:
(And director) *The Temptation of Dance,* 1984.
Tian mi shi liu sui (also known as *Sweet Sixteen*), 1986.
Wai si–lei chuen kei (also known as *Legend of Wisely, Legend of Wu, Legend of the Golden Pearl, Die 7. Macht, Wisely Legend,* and *Wei si li chan ji*), Rin–Film–Verleih, 1987.
He bo, 1988.
Gong xi duo qing (also known as *The Greatest Lover*), 1988.
Bu tuo wa de ren (also known as *A Fishy Story* and *Bat tuet mat dik yan*), 1989.
Ji dong ji xia (also known as *The Iceman Cometh* and *Time Warriors*), 1989.
Du shen (also known as *God of Gamblers* and *Dao san*), 1989, subtitled version, Rim, 1996.
Dip hyut shueng hung (also known as *Just Heroes, The Killer,* and *Die xue shuang xiong*), subtitled version, Circle Films, 1990.
Xiao ao jiang hu (also known as *Swordsman*), Golden Princess/Long Shong Pictures/Newport Films, 1990.
Qin yong (also known as *A Terracotta Warrior* and *Gu jin da zhan qin yon qing*), Art & Talent Group, 1990.
Jing gu jyun ga (also known as *Tricky Brains, The Ultimate Trickster,* and *Zheng gu zhuan jia*), Win's Movie Productions, 1991.
Wei si li zhi ba wang xie jia (also known as *Bury Me High* and *Wai si–lei ji ba wong se gaap*), New Dawn Pictures, 1991.
Hoyat gwan tsoi loi (also known as *Till We Meet Again, When My Dear Come Again, Au revoir mon amour,* and *He ri jun zai lai*), 1991.
Bo Hao (also known as *To Be Number One* and *Bai Hao*), Golden Harvest/Johnny Mak Productions, 1991.
Gau yat san diu hap lui (also known as *Saviour of the Soul, Terrible Angel,* and *Jiu yi shen diao xia lu*), Team Work Production House, 1991.
Haomen yeyan (also known as *The Banquet*), 1991.
Du xia II zhi Shang Hai tan du sheng (also known as *God of Gamblers III: Back to Shanghai*), 1991.

Sam sei goon (also known as *Interrogate to Death, Justice, My Foot!,* and *Shen si guan*), Cosmopolitan Film Productions, 1992.
Leung goh nuijen, yat goh leng, yat goh m leng (short film; also known as *Too Happy for Words*), Jackie & Willie Productions, 1992.
Chikio gouyeung (also known as *Naked Killer* and *Chi luo gao yang*), 1992, subtitled version, Rim, 1995.
Se diu ying hung ji dung sing sai jau (also known as *The Eagle Shooting Heroes, Dong cheng xi jiu,* and *She diao ying xiong zhi dong chen xi jiu*), Het Tone Production, 1993.
Bai fa mo nu zhuan (also known as *The Bride with White Hair, Baak faat moh lui chuen,* and *Jiang–hu: Between Love and Glory*), subtitled version, Century Pacific, 1994.
Huang Fei–hung zhi wu: long cheng jian ba (also known as *Once Upon a Time in China V* and *Wong Fei–Hung V*), 1994.
Hua qi Shao Lin (also known as *American Shaolin, National Treasure, Treasure Hunt,* and *Fa kei siu lam*), 1994, subtitled version, Rim, 1996.
Jin yu man tang (also known as *The Chinese Feast* and *Gam yuk moon tong*), Mandarin Films, 1995.
Ye ban ge cheng (also known as *The Phantom Lover* and *Ye boon goh sing*), Mandarin Films/Sil–Metropole Organization, 1995.
Xiu Xiu han ta de nan ren (also known as *Sau sau woh sze dik laam yan*), 1995.
Hua yue jia qi (also known as *Love in the Time of Twilight*), 1995.
Double Team (also known as *The Colony*), Columbia/Trimark Pictures, 1997.
(And coproducer) *Warriors of Virtue,* Metro–Goldwyn–Mayer, 1997.
Ngon na ma dak lin na (also known as *Anna Magdalena*), 1998.
Bride of Chucky, MCA/Universal, 1998.
Ban zhi yan (also known as *Metade Fumaca*), Art Port/GAGA Communications/Media Asia Distribution, 1999.
Crouching Tiger, Hidden Dragon (also known as *Ngo foo chong lung* and *Wo hu cang long*), subtitled version, Sony Pictures Entertainment, 2000.
Dracula 2000 (also known as *Dracula 2001* and *Wes Craven Presents "Dracula 2000"*), Miramax/Dimension Films, 2000.
Bak Ging lok yue liu (also known as *Beijing Rocks* and *Bei Jing le yu lu*), 2001.
(And director) *The Touch* (also known as *Tian mai chuan qi*), Miramax, 2002.
Ru guo—Ai (also known as *Perhaps Love*), Shaw Organisation, 2005.
Wu ji (also known as *The Promise* and *Mo gik*), subtitled version, Warner Independent Pictures, 2006.
Shoot 'em Up, New Line Cinema, 2007.

Film Director:
Wu du qing chou (also known as *Misty*), 1992.

Film Appearances:
(Uncredited) Szeto, *Fei zhou he shang* (also known as *Crazy Safari, The Gods Must Be Crazy III, Vampires Must Be Crazy,* and *Fei jau woh seung*), 1991.
Chef from North West Restaurant, *Jin yu man tang* (also known as *The Chinese Feast* and *Gam yuk moon tong*), Mandarin Films, 1995.

OTHER SOURCES

Periodicals:
Current Biography, February, 2002, pp. 63–66.

PEARSON, Andrea C. 1977–
        (Andrea Pearson, Andrea Persun)

PERSONAL

Full name, Andrea Carina Pearson; born September 29, 1977, in Washington, D.C. *Education:* Graduated from the International Community School of Abidjan, 1998; studied theatre in college.

Career: Actress. Appeared in advertisements.

CREDITS

Television Appearances; Series:
(As Andrea Pearson) Priscilla Carter, a recurring role, *7th Heaven* (also known as *Seventh Heaven* and *7th Heaven: Beginnings*), The WB, 2000–2001.
Gia Campbell, *General Hospital* (also known as *Hopital central* and *Hospital general*), ABC, 2002–2003.
Gia Campbell, *Port Charles* (also known as *Port Charles: Desire, Port Charles: Fate, Port Charles: The Gift, Port Charles: Miracles Happen, Port Charles: Naked Eyes, Port Charles: Secrets, Port Charles: Superstitions, Port Charles: Surrender, Port Charles: Tainted Love, Port Charles: Tempted, Port Charles: Time in a Bottle,* and *Port Charles: Torn*), ABC, 2002–2003.

Television Appearances; Episodic:
Herself, "Wise Queen," *The Charlie Horse Music Pizza,* PBS, 1998.
(As Andrea Pearson) Jackie, "Pier Pressure," *City Guys,* NBC, 2000.
Nora, "High Anxiety," *Dawson's Creek,* The WB, 2001.

Nora, "Hotel New Hampshire," *Dawson's Creek,* The WB, 2001.
(Uncredited) Nora, "Use Your Disillusion," *Dawson's Creek,* The WB, 2001.
(As Andrea Pearson) Second female student, "Eric Visits," *Undeclared,* Fox, 2001.
Herself, *Soap Talk,* SOAPnet, 2003, 2004.
First customer, "Why Can't We Be Friends," *Cuts,* UPN, 2005.
(As Andrea Pearson) Lily, "The Disconnect," *The O.C.* (also known as *California Teens, Newport Beach, O.C., O.C., California, Orange County, A Narancs-videk, O.C.—Um estranho no paraiso,* and *Zycie na fali*), Fox, 2005.
(As Andrea Pearson) Lily, "The Pot Stirrer," *The O.C.* (also known as *California Teens, Newport Beach, O.C., O.C., California, Orange County, A Narancs-videk, O.C.–Um estranho no paraiso,* and *Zycie na fali*), Fox, 2006.

Television Appearances; Pilots:
April, *Ruling Class,* Fox, 2001.
Denise, *Las Vegas* (also known as *Casino Eye*), NBC, 2006.

Film Appearances:
Jewel, *American Gun* (also known as *Amerikka aseiden armolla* and *Xafnikos thanatos*), Buena Vista Home Video, 2002.

RECORDINGS

Video Games:
(As Andrea Persun) Voice, *Freedom Fighters,* EA Games, 2003.
(As Andrea Persun) Voices, *SOCOM U.S. Navy SEALs: Fireteam Bravo 2,* Sony Computer Entertainment America, 2006.

OTHER SOURCES

Periodicals:
Soap Opera Digest & Weekly, June, 2003.

PELLINGTON, Mark 1962–

PERSONAL

Born March 17, 1962, in Baltimore, MD; son of Bill Pellington (a professional football player); married Jennifer Barrett (a costume designer; died July 30, 2004); children: one. *Education:* University of Virginia, B.A.

Addresses: *Agent*—United Talent Agency, 9560 Wilshire Blvd., Suite 500, Beverly Hills, CA 90212. *Manager*—Tom Lassally, 3 Arts Entertainment, 9460 Wilshire Blvd., 7th Floor, Beverly Hills, CA 90212.

Career: Director, producer, actor, and writer. Music Television Network, worked as member of on–air promotions team; director of music videos and commercials; also worked as graphic designer, including material for the television series *Homicide: Life on the Street.*

Awards, Honors: Emmy Award nomination, outstanding individual achievement in graphic design and title sequences, 1993, for *Homicide: Life on the Street;* MTV Video Music Award, best direction, 1993, for "Jeremy"; nomination for Grand Jury Prize, dramatic category, Sundance Film Festival, 1997, for *Going All the Way;* nomination for Grand Prix, Paris Film Festival, 1999, for *Arlington Road.*

CREDITS

Film Work:
Director, *Going All the Way,* Gramercy, 1997.
Director, *Arlington Road,* Screen Gems, 1999.
Executive producer, *No Maps for These Territories,* 2000.
Director, *The Mothman Prophecies,* Sony Pictures Entertainment, 2002.
Executive producer, *OT: Our Town* (documentary), Film Movement, 2003.
Executive producer, *Time Well Spent* (short film), 2004.
Executive producer, *The Man from Earth* (also known as *Jerome Bixby's "The Man from Earth"*), Falling Sky Entertainment, 2007.

Film Appearances:
Bill Dooler, *Jerry Maguire,* TriStar, 1996.
Freddy, *Almost Famous,* DreamWorks, 2000.
Bartender and voice of Indrid Cold, *The Mothman Prophecies,* Sony Pictures Entertainment, 2002.

Television Director; Episodic:
"Blood Ties: Part 2," *Homicide: Life on the Street* (also known as *Homicide*), NBC, 1997.
Cold Case, CBS, multiple episodes, between 2003 and 2007.

Television Director; Specials:
Punch and Judy Get Divorced, PBS, 1992.
Rock the Vote, Fox, 1992.
Television: The Drug of the Nation, PBS, 1993.
Father's Daze, PBS, 1994.

Television Director; Other:
Words in Your Face, 1991.
United States of Poetry (miniseries), PBS, 1995.
Destination Anywhere (movie), VH1, 1997.

Television Appearances; Specials:
Lesley Ann Warren: A Cinderella Story (also known as *Celebrity: Lesley Ann Warren*), Arts and Entertainment, 2000.

Television Appearances; Episodic:
Sonic Cinema, Sundance Channel.

RECORDINGS

Videos:
Director, *U2: Achtung Baby* (also known as *U2: Achtung Baby, the Videos, the Cameos, and a Whole Lot of Interference from ZOO–V*), PolyGram Video/Uni Distribution, 1992.
Director, *Pearl Jam: Single Video Theory,* Epic/Sony Music Entertainment, 1998.
Himself, *Hidden Vulnerability: A Look into the Making of "Arlington Road,"* Columbia TriStar Home Video, 1999.
Producer, director, and himself, *Day by Day: A Director's Journey Part I* (also known as *Day by Day: A Director's Journey—The Road In*), 2003.
Producer, director, and himself, *Day by Day: A Director's Journey Part II* (also known as *Day by Day: A Director's Journey—The Road Home*), 2003.
Director, "Beautiful Girl," *I'm Only Looking: The Best of INXS,* Rhino Home Video, 2004.
Director, "Everybody's Changing," *Strangers,* Interscope Records, 2005.
Director, *U2 3D,* 3uality Digital Entertainment, 2007.

Director of numerous music videos, including "Jeremy" by Pearl Jam, 1992; "One" by U2, 1992; "Beautiful Girl" by INXS, 1993; "Rooster" by Alice in Chains, 1993; "Hobo Humpin' Slobo Babe" by Whale, 1994; "Ladykillers" by Lush, 1996; "We're in This Together" by Nine Inch Nails, 1999; "Do You Realize" by Flaming Lips, 2002; "Halflight" by Tomanadandy, 2002; "Lonesome Day" by Bruce Springsteen, 2002; "Gravedigger" by Dave Matthews, 2003; "Best of You" by Foo Fighters, 2005; "Everybody's Changing" by Keane, 2005; "Falling by the Wayside" by People in Planes, 2005; "Black Lodge" by Anthrax; and "Butterfly" by Screaming Tree.

WRITINGS

Television Movies:
Destination Anywhere, VH1, 1997.

PERSUN, Andrea
  See PEARSON, Andrea C.

PFLIEGER, Jean
  See ST. JAMES, Jean

PHILLIPS, Joseph C. 1962–
  (Joseph Phillips)

PERSONAL

Full name, Joseph Connor Phillips; born January 17, 1962, in Denver, CO; son of Dr. Clarence Phillips (a pediatrician); married Nicole, 1994; children: Connor, Ellis, Samuel. *Education:* New York University, B.F.A., acting, 1983; studied communications at the University of the Pacific; studied acting with Michael Howard, Chicago City Limits, and Nora Dunfree; also graduated from culinary school.

Addresses: *Agent*—Don Buchwald & Associates, 6500 Wilshire Blvd., Suite 2200, Los Angeles, CA 90048.

Career: Actor. Also worked as a writer, columnist, television and radio commentator, acting workshop teacher, and public speaker. Sickle Cell Disease Association of America, ambassador; George W. Bush Presidential campaign, 2004, co–chair of the African American steering committee; Republican National Committee's African American Advisory Board, member; California African American Museum, member of state board of directors; Claremont Institute fellow, 2005.

Member: Screen Actors Guild, American Federation of Television and Radio Artists, Actors Equity Association, Academy of Television Arts and Sciences, Alpha Phi Alpha.

Awards, Honors: Image Award nominations, outstanding actor in a daytime drama series, National Association for the Advancement of Colored People (NAACP), 1997, 1998, 1999, for *General Hospital.*

CREDITS

Film Appearances:
Waymon Tinsdale III, *Strictly Business,* Warner Bros., 1991.
A Fare to Remember, 1998.

Michael, *Let's Talk About Sex,* Fine Line Features, 1998.
Robert Mitchellson, *Getting Played,* New Line Home Video, 2005.

Television Appearances; Series:
Lieutenant Martin Kendall, *The Cosby Show,* NBC, 1985–92.
Justus Ward, *General Hospital,* ABC, 1994–98.
J. T. Morse, *Vanished,* Fox, 2006.

Television Appearances; Movies:
Luke Jordan, *Midnight Blue,* Black Entertainment Television, 2000.
Detective McKinley, *Perfect Murder, Perfect Town: JonBenet and the City of Boulder,* CBS, 2000.

Television Appearances; Specials:
George Murchison, *A Raisin in the Sun,* PBS, 1989.
Night of 100 Stars III, NBC, 1990.
Sex, Shock & Censorship in the 90's, Showtime, 1993.
Justus Ward, *General Hospital: Twist of Fate,* ABC, 1996.
Himself and Lieutenant Martin Kendall, *The Cosby Show: A Look Back,* NBC, 2002.

Television Appearances; Pilots:
J. T. Morse, *Vanished,* Fox, 2006.

Television Appearances; Episodic:
Daryl, "Cliff in Love," *The Cosby Show,* 1985.
Billy Harris, *Hothouse,* ABC, 1988.
Matt Johnson, "Poison," *A Man Called Hawk,* ABC, 1989.
Lieutenant Martin Kendall, "Forever Hold Your Peace," *A Different World,* NBC, 1989.
James, *The Larry Sanders Show,* HBO, 1992.
Louis White, *Crime & Punishment,* NBC, 1993.
Kent, *Me and the Boys,* ABC, 1994.
Derrick, "The Ex–files," *Martin,* Fox, 1995.
Jeremy Mills IV, "Not So Silent Partner," *Living Single* (also known as *My Girls*), Fox, 1996.
Dexter, *High Incident,* ABC, 1996.
James, "The Book," *The Larry Sanders Show,* HBO, 1997.
Mark Sanborn, "Family Is Family," *Any Day Now,* Lifetime, 1999.
(As Joseph Phillips) Martin, "To Halve or Halve Not," *City of Angels,* CBS, 2000.
Harrison's doctor, "Ur–ine Trouble," *Popular,* The WB, 2000.
Reverend Reggie Wright, "Mama, I Want to Sing," *The Parkers,* UPN, 2001.
Bill, "Separation Anxiety," *The King of Queens,* CBS, 2001.
Lowry's attorney, "Look Closer," *Judging Amy,* CBS, 2001.

Geiger, "Kayus Ex Machina," *V.I.P.* (also known as *V.I.P.—Die Bodyguards*), syndicated, 2001.

"The Cosby Kids," *E! True Hollywood Story,* E! Entertainment Television, 2001.

Mayor Morgan Douglas, "Blindsided," *The District,* CBS, 2003.

Mayor Morgan Douglas, "Where There's Smoke," *The District,* CBS, 2003.

Mayor Morgan Douglas, "Criminally Insane," *The District,* CBS, 2003.

Mayor Morgan Douglas, "Rage," *The District,* CBS, 2003.

E! 101 Most Awesome Moments in Entertainment, E! Entertainment Television, 2004.

Langley, "Blood Is Thicker," *Las Vegas,* NBC, 2004.

Graham Krell, "Compulsion," *CSI: Crime Scene Investigation* (also known as *CSI: Weekends, CSI: Las Vegas, C.S.I.,* and *Les Experts*), CBS, 2005.

Coach Braxton, "Friends with Benefits," *Jack & Bobby,* The WB, 2005.

"Centennial," *Las Vegas,* NBC, 2005.

Marcus Johnson, "Transitions," *Without a Trace* (also known as *W.A.T.*), CBS, 2005.

Marcus Johnson, "Second Sight," *Without a Trace* (also known as *W.A.T.*), CBS, 2005.

Marcus Johnson, "End Game," *Without a Trace* (also known as *W.A.T.*), CBS, 2005.

Marcus Johnson, "The Thing with Feathers," *Without a Trace* (also known as *W.A.T.*), CBS, 2006.

Stage Appearances:

George Murchison, *A Raisin in the Sun,* Union Square Theatre, New York City, 1986.

Second citizen, senator, soldier, and Cominius, Roman general, *Coriolanus,* Joseph Papp Public Theatre, New York City, 1988–89.

Also appeared in *Six Degrees of Separation,* Broadway production; as title role, *Dreaming Emmett.*

WRITINGS

Stage Plays:

Professor Lombooza Lomboo, 4305 Theatre, Los Angeles, 2000.

Nonfiction:

He Talk Like a White Boy, Running Press Book, 2006.

Contributed to *Entertainment Weekly* and numerous other periodicals; author of a weekly syndicated columnists.

OTHER SOURCES

Electronic:

Joseph C. Phillips Website, http://www.josephcphillips.com, July 6, 2007.

PIERCE–ROBERTS, Tony 1944(?)–
(Tony Pearce Roberts)

PERSONAL

Full name, Anthony Pierce–Roberts; born December 24, 1944 (some sources cite 1945), in Birkenhead, Cheshire, England; grew up in Rhodesia (now Zimbabwe).

Addresses: *Agent*—Skouras Agency, 1149 Third St., 3rd Floor, Santa Monica, CA 90403.

Career: Cinematographer. Former member of Central African Film Unit; British Broadcasting Corp., camera assistant, 1967–71, director of photography, 1972–80; photography director for commercials and documentary films; also photographer and camera operator, sometimes credited as Tony Pearce Roberts.

Member: British Society of Cinematographers.

Awards, Honors: Television Award nomination, best camera operator, British Academy of Film and Television Arts, 1980, for *Tinker, Tailor, Soldier, Spy;* Television Award nomination (with John Else), best camera operator, British Academy of Film and Television Arts, 1981, for "Caught on a Train," *BBC2 Playhouse;* Television Award nomination, best camera operator, British Academy of Film and Television Arts, 1983, for *A Voyage round My Father* and *P'tang, Yang, Kipperbang;* Best Cinematography Award, British Society of Cinematographers, and New York Film Critics Award, best cinematographer, both 1986, Academy Award nomination, best cinematography, Film Award nomination, best cinematography, British Academy of Film and Television Arts, American Society of Cinematographers Award nomination, outstanding achievement in cinematography in theatrical releases, and *Evening Standard* British Film Award, best technical or artistic achievement, all 1987, all for *A Room with a View;* Best Cinematography Award, British Society of Cinematographers, 1992, Academy Award nomination and Film Award nomination, British Academy of Film and Television Arts, both best cinematography, American Society of Cinematographers Award nomination, outstanding achievement in cinematography in theatrical releases, and Golden Frog nomination, Camerimage, all 1993, all for *Howards End;* Film Award nomination, best cinematography, British Academy of Film and Television Arts, 1994, for *The Remains of the Day.*

CREDITS

Film Cinematographer:

Arabian Time–Machine (documentary), 1979.

Moonlighting (also known as *Schwarzarbeit*), Universal, 1982.
A Private Function, Island Alive, 1984.
Frog Dance: Solos and Indulgences '80–'84 (documentary), 1984.
A Room with a View, Cinecom, 1986.
A Tiger's Tale, Atlantic Releasing, 1988.
Out Cold (also known as *Stiffs* and *Where's Ernie?*), Hemdale, 1989.
Slaves of New York, TriStar, 1989.
Mr. & Mrs. Bridge, Miramax, 1990.
White Fang, Buena Vista, 1991.
Howards End, Sony Pictures Classics, 1992.
The Dark Half, Orion, 1993.
Splitting Heirs, Universal, 1993.
The Remains of the Day, Columbia, 1993.
The Client, Warner Bros., 1994.
Disclosure, Warner Bros., 1994.
Haunted, October Films, 1995.
Surviving Picasso, Warner Bros., 1996.
Jungle 2 Jungle (also known as *Un Indien a New York*), Buena Vista, 1997.
Paulie (also known as *A Parrot's Tale*), DreamWorks, 1998.
Something to Believe In, Warner Bros., 1998.
Asterix et Obelix contre Cesar (also known as *Asterix and Obelix Take On Caesar, Asterix & Obelix vs. Caesar, Asterix e Obelix contro Cesare, Asterix & Obelix gegen Caesar,* and *Asterix—Sig ueber Casar*), Miramax, 1999.
Blackadder Back & Forth (short film; also known as *Time for Blackadder*), VCI Distribution, 1999.
(Contributor) *The Bone Collector,* Universal, 1999.
The Trench (also known as *La tranchee*), Somme Productions, 2000.
Kiss Kiss (Bang Bang), Offline Releasing, 2000.
The Golden Bowl (also known as *La coupe d'or*), Lions Gate Films, 2001.
The Glow (short film), Glory Film, 2001.
The Importance of Being Earnest, Miramax, 2002.
Underworld, Screen Gems, 2003.
De–Lovely (also known as *Just One of Those Things*), Metro–Goldwyn–Mayer, 2004.
Separate Lies (also known as *A Way Through the Weeds*), Fox Searchlight, 2005.
Doom (also known as *Doom—Der Film*), Universal, 2005.
Lights2: Return of the Shadow (short film), Glory Film, 2005.
Home of the Brave, Metro–Goldwyn–Mayer, 2006.
J'aurais voulu etre un danseur (also known as *Gone for a Dance*), Artemis Productions, 2007.

Television Photography Director; Miniseries:
Days of Hope, BBC, 1975.
"Double Echo" segment, *The Mind Beyond,* BBC, 1976.
"Brensham People" segment, *Going, Going, Gone,* 1976.
Tinker, Tailor, Soldier, Spy, PBS, 1979.

Nobody's Hero, 1982.
The Bourne Identity, ABC, 1988.
Dinotopia, ABC, 2002.

Television Photography Director; Movies:
The Fight Against Slavery, BBC, 1974.
The Good Soldier, 1980.
A Voyage round My Father, 1982.
P'tang, Yang, Kipperbang (also known as *First Love: P'tang, Yang, Kipperbang* and *Kipperbang*), Channel 4, 1982.
The Cold Room (also known as *The Prisoner*), HBO, 1984.
No Place Like Home, CBS, 1989.

Television Photography Director; Specials:
"Hard Labour," *Play for Today,* BBC1, 1973.
Orders from Above, 1975.
"A Story to Frighten the Children," *Play for Today,* BBC1, 1976.
"Early Struggles," *Play for Today,* BBC1, 1976.
Who Was Jesus?, 1976.
"Dinner at the Sporting Club," *Play for Today,* BBC1, 1978.
"Caught on a Train," *BBC2 Playhouse,* BBC2, 1980.

Television Photography Director; Episodic:
"Someone from the Welfare," *Tuesday Documentary,* BBC, 1973.
"Satan Superstar," *Everyman,* BBC, 1977.
"A Little Outing," *Premiere,* BBC, 1977.
"The School Teacher," *Americans,* 1977.
"The General," *Americans,* 1977.
"Listen to Me," *Shoestring,* 1979.

PITTS, Greg 1970–

PERSONAL

Born January 21, 1970, in Sarasota, FL. *Education:* University of South Florida, theatre degree, 1992; trained with the Groundlings Theatre Company, c. 1994–97. *Avocational Interests:* Water sports.

Addresses: *Agent*—Innovative Artists, 1505 10th St., Santa Monica, CA 90401. *Manager*—Flutie Entertainment, 6500 Wilshire Blvd., Suite 2240, Los Angeles, CA 90048.

Career: Actor. Appeared in advertisements. Worked as a postproduction coordinator in the animation industry and held a variety of jobs.

CREDITS

Film Appearances:

Drew, *Office Space* (also known as *Alles routine, Como enlouquecer seu chefe, Cubiculos de la oficina, Enredos de oficina, Hivatali patkanyok, Impiegati ... male!, Konotorrotter, Konttorirotat, La folie du travail, O insustentavel peso do trabalho, Risutora man, Trabajo basura,* and *34 heures c'est deja trop*), Twentieth Century–Fox, 1999.

Vincent Van Gogh, *Studio Notes* (short film), 1999.

Alex at the age of twenty, *Panic* (also known as *Panic—Der Tod hat Tradition, Panico, Panik, Panikos,* and *Volte–face*), Artisan Entertainment, 2000.

Fiji Mermaid waiter, *Coyote Ugly* (also known as *Coyote Bar, Coyote Girls, Show Bar, El Bar Coyote, Le ragazze del Coyote Ugly, Sakaltanya,* and *Wygrane marzenia*), Buena Vista, 2000.

Quentin (video store clerk), *Beethoven's 3rd* (also known as *Beethoven 3, Beethoven III, Beethovens trea, Beethoven—To taxidi, Beethoven: Urlaub mit Hindernissen, Beethovenin kolmas, Beethoven 3: De excursion con la familia,* and *Beethoven 3—Uma familia em apuros*), Universal Studios Home Video, 2000.

Deputy Trousdale, *Speaking of Sex*, Lionsgate, 2001.

Keith, *Rebound Guy*, IFILM, 2001.

Video man, *I Shaved My Legs for This*, 2001.

Tee, *The Third Wheel* (also known as *Duetto a tre, Hilfe, ich habe ein Date!, Kolmas pyoerae, Una noche perfecta,* and *Une soiree parfaite*), Miramax, 2002.

Camera operator, *Idiocracy* (also known as *3001, Untitled Mike Judge Comedy, Idiokracja, Idioluutio,* and *La idiocracia*), Twentieth Century–Fox, 2006.

Jason, *Bachelor Party 2*, Twentieth Century–Fox Home Entertainment/Blue Star Pictures, 2007.

Bickford Shmeckler's Cool Ideas, Screen Media Films, 2007.

Television Appearances; Series:

Chud (some sources cite Chio) McGraf, *Sister, Sister,* ABC, c. 1994–95, The WB, 1995–99.

Billy McCarthy (some sources cite Billy Cavanaugh), *Damon*, Fox, 1998.

Charles "Charlie" Gamble, *Normal, Ohio* (also known as *Butch, Don't Ask, Goodman, The John Goodman Project,* and *Untitled John Goodman Project*), Fox, 2000.

Jerry O'Malley, *Grey's Anatomy* (also known as *Complications, Procedure, Surgeons, Under the Knife,* and *Grey's Anatomy—Die jungen Aerzte*), ABC, beginning 2005.

Tommy "Whitey" White, *Sons & Daughters*, ABC, 2006.

Television Appearances; Movies:

Duffy, *Witness Protection* (also known as *Mafian taehtaeimessae, Protecao a testemunha, Proteccao de uma testemunha, Protejan al testigo, Skyddat vittne, Temoin a charge,* and *Testigo protegido*), HBO, 1999.

Officer Jones, *Unconditional Love* (also known as *Who Shot Victor Fox, Amor a toda prova, Amor incondicional, Amours suspectes, Insieme per caso, Un amour absolu, Vallaton rakkaus, Vem skoet Victor Fox?,* and *Wer totete Victor Fox?*), Starz!, 2002.

Television Appearances; Episodic:

Chuck, "On a Clear Day You Can Hear Forever," *Suddenly Susan*, NBC, 1999.

McNeely, "What Bravery Is," *Chicken Soup for the Soul,* PAX TV, 1999.

Mark, "Party All the Time," *Eve* (also known as *The Opposite Sex*), UPN, 2004.

Valet, "Unbearable," *CSI: Criminal Scene Investigation* (also known as *C.S.I, CSI: Las Vegas, CSI: Weekends,* and *Les experts*), CBS, 2005.

Television Appearances; Pilots:

Billy McCarthy (some sources cite Billy Cavanaugh), *Damon*, Fox, 1998.

Brad, *Kilroy*, HBO, 1999.

Generation Gap, The WB, 2002.

Appeared as Luke MacGregor, *The MacGregors* (also known as *Untitled Marsh McCall Project*), NBC.

Stage Appearances:

Smooth Down There (sketch comedy show), the Groundlings, 1997.

Appeared in *A Boy's Life, The Good Woman of Setzuan, An Indian Straw Hat, Scooter Thomas Makes It to the Top of the World,* and *The Skin of Our Teeth,* all University of South Florida.

Major Tours:

Performed in a touring improvisational team and in stunt show with a Wild West theme.

WRITINGS

Writings for the Stage:

Smooth Down There (sketch comedy show), the Groundlings, 1997.

With others, contributed material for a touring improvisational team.

OTHER SOURCES

Electronic:

Greg Pitts, http://www.gregpitts.com, May 11, 2007.

POPE, Dick 1947–
(Richard Pope)

PERSONAL

Born 1947, in Bromley, Kent, England.

Addresses: *Agent*—International Creative Management, 10250 Constellation Way, 9th Floor, Los Angeles, CA 90067.

Career: Cinematographer. British Broadcasting Corporation, camera operator for documentary films shot in Africa; photography director for commercials and music videos; also works as camera operator, sometimes credited as Richard Pope.

Member: British Society of Cinematographers.

Awards, Honors: Television Award nomination, best camera operator, British Academy of Film and Television Arts, 1988, for *Porterhouse Blue;* Catalonian International Film Festival Award, best cinematography, 1990, for *The Reflecting Skin;* nomination for Camerimage Golden Frog, International Film Festival of the Art of Cinematography, 1995, for *Nothing Personal;* Camerimage Golden Frog, 1996, for *Secrets & Lies;* Camerimage Special Award (with Mike Leigh), best duo—director and cinematographer, 1999; Golden Frog, 2004, for *Vera Drake;* San Diego Film Critics Society Award, best cinematography, 2006, Camerimage Silver Frog, 2006, Academy Award nomination, best cinematography, 2007, and American Society of Cinematographers Award nomination, outstanding cinematography in a theatrical release, 2007, all for *The Illusionist.*

CREDITS

Film Cinematographer:

Women in Rock (documentary; also known as *Girls Bite Back*), Stein Film, 1980.

Punk and Its Aftershocks (documentary; also known as *British Rock* and *British Rock—Ready for the 80s*), Stein Film, 1980.

Urgh! A Music War, Filmways, 1981.

Alan Bush: A Life (documentary), Black Sun Productions, 1983.

Coming Up Roses (also known as *Rhosyn a Rhith*), Mainline Releasing, 1986, subtitled version, Skouras, 1987.

The Girl in the Picture, Samuel Goldwyn Company, 1986.

The Fruit Machine (also known as *Wonderland*), Vestron, 1988.

Life Is Sweet, Forum Distribution, 1990.

The Reflecting Skin (also known as *L'enfant miroir*), Virgin Vision, 1990.

Naked (also known as *Mike Leigh's "Naked"*), Fine Line, 1993.

The Air Up There, Buena Vista, 1994.

An Awfully Big Adventure, Fine Line, 1995.

Nothing Personal, 1995, Trimark Pictures, 1997.

Secrets & Lies (also known as *Secrets et mensonges*), October Films, 1996.

Career Girls, October Films, 1997.

Swept from the Sea (also known as *Amy Foster* and *Balaye par la mer*), TriStar, 1998.

(Contributor) *Phantoms* (also known as *Dean Koontz's "Phantoms"*), Dimension Films, 1998.

Topsy–Turvy, October Films/USA Films, 1999.

The Debt Collector, Madman Entertainment, 2000.

The Way of the Gun, Artisan Entertainment, 2000.

Thirteen Conversations About One Thing (also known as *13 Conversations*), Cony Pictures Classics, 2002.

All or Nothing, Metro–Goldwyn–Mayer, 2002.

Nicholas Nickleby, United Artists, 2002.

Vera Drake, Fine Line, 2004.

The Illusionist, Yari Film Group/Freestyle Releasing, 2006.

Man of the Year, Universal, 2006.

Honeydripper, Emerging Pictures, 2007.

Television Photography Director; Miniseries:

"Protest and Reform" segment, *The Christians,* 1977.

The Do Gooders, 1979.

Diary of a Maasai Village, BBC, 1984.

Porterhouse Blue, Channel 4, 1987.

The Blackheath Poisonings, PBS, 1992.

Television Photography Director; Movies:

Fool's Gold: The Story of the Brink's–Mat Robbery, Arts and Entertainment, 1992.

A Sense of History, 1992.

Pleasure (also known as *Alan Bleasdale Presents "Pleasure"*), Channel 4, 1994.

Life's a Bitch, 1995.

Deadly Voyage, HBO, 1996.

Television Photography Director; Specials:

Credo: Jean's Way, 1978.

Islam, 1979.

"Dark City" (also known as "Strong City"), *Screen One,* BBC, 1990.

The Great Kandinsky, PBS, 1995.

Television Photography Director; Series:

World in Action, Granada, between 1970 and 1979.

Forever Green, ITV, 1989.

Television Photography Director; Episodic:
"The Knockers' Tale," *Our Lives,* Channel 4, 1983.

RECORDINGS

Videos:
Himself, *Creating a Classic: The Making of "Nicholas Nickleby,"* MGM Home Entertainment, 2003.

POWELL, Sandy 1960–

PERSONAL

Born April 7, 1960, in London, England. *Education:* Studied theater design at London's Central School of Art.

Addresses: *Agent*—International Creative Management, 10250 Constellation Way, 9th Floor, Los Angeles, CA 90067. *Contact*—c/o Drury House 34–43 Russell St., London WC2B 5HA England.

Career: Costume designer. Began career designing for fringe theater and dance productions.

Awards, Honors: *Evening Standard* British Film Award, best technical and artistic achievement, 1992, for *Edward II, The Miracle,* and *The Pope Must Die;* Academy Award nomination, best costume design, *Evening Standard* British Film Award, best technical and artistic achievement, Film Award nomination, best costume design, British Academy of Film and Television Awards, 1994, all for *Orlando;* Film Award nomination, best costume design, British Academy of Film and Television Arts, Saturn Award, best costumes, Academy of Science Fiction, Fantasy, and Horror Films, 1995, both for *Interview with the Vampire: The Vampire Chronicles;* Academy Award nomination, best costume design, Golden Satellite Award nomination, outstanding costume design, International Press Academy, Film Award nomination, best costume design, British Academy of Film and Television Arts, 1998, all for *The Wings of the Dove;* Academy Award, best costume design, Film Award nomination, best costume design, British Academy of Film and Television Arts, 1999, both for *Shakespeare in Love;* Film Award, best costume design, British Academy of Film and Television Arts, Academy Award nomination, best costume design, 1999, both for *Velvet Goldmine;* Film Award nomination, best costume design, British Academy of Film and Television Arts, 2000, for *The End of the Affair;* Genie Award nomination, best achievement in costume design, Academy of Canadian Cinema and Television,

2000, for *Felicia's Journey;* Academy Award nomination, best costume design, Golden Satellite Award nomination, best costume design, Online Film Critics Society Award nomination, best costume design, Film Award nomination, best costume design, British Academy of Film and Television Arts, 2003, all for *Gangs of New York;* Phoenix Film Critics Society Award nomination, best costume design, Online Film Critics Society Award, best costume design, 2003, for *Far from Heaven;* Academy Award, best achievement in costume design, Golden Satellite Award nomination, best costume design, Sierra Award, best costume design, Las Vegas Film Critics Society, Costume Designers Guild Award nomination, excellence in costume design for film—period/fantasy, Film Award nomination, best costume design, British Academy of Film and Television Arts, 2005, all for *The Aviator;* British Independent Film Award nomination, best technical achievement, Film Award nomination, best costume design, British Academy of Film and Television Arts, 2005, Academy Award nomination, best achievement in costume design, 2006, all for *Mrs. Henderson Presents.*

CREDITS

Film Costume Designer:
Caravaggio, Cinevista, 1986.
("Louise") *Aria,* Miramax, 1987.
The Last of England, International Film Circuit, 1988.
Stormy Monday, Atlantic Releasing Corp., 1988.
For Queen and Country, Atlantic Releasing Corp., 1988.
Killing Dad or How to Love Your Mother, Palace Pictures, 1989.
Venus Peter, Starlight, 1989.
Shadow of China (also known as *China Shadow*), New Line Cinema, 1990.
The Miracle, Miramax, 1991.
The Pope Must Die, Miramax, 1991.
Edward II, Fine Line Features, 1991.
Orlando, Sony Pictures Classics, 1992.
The Crying Game, Miramax, 1992.
Being Human, Warner Bros., 1993.
Wittgenstein, Zeitgeist Films, 1993.
Interview with the Vampire: The Vampire Chronicles (also known as *Interview with the Vampire*), Warner Bros., 1994.
Rob Roy, United Artists, 1995.
Michael Collins, Warner Bros., 1996.
The Butcher Boy, Geffen Pictures, 1997.
The Wings of the Dove, Miramax, 1997.
Velvet Goldmine, Miramax, 1998.
Hilary and Jackie, October Films, 1998.
Shakespeare in Love, Miramax, 1998.
Felicia's Journey (also known as *Le voyage de Felicia*), Artisan Entertainment, 1999.
Miss Julie, Metro–Goldwyn–Mayer, 1999.
The End of the Affair, Columbia, 1999.

Far from Heaven (also known as *Loin du paradis*), Focus Features, 2002.
Gangs from New York, Miramax, 2002.
Sylvia, Focus Features, 2003.
The Aviator, Miramax, 2004.
Mrs. Henderson Presents, Weinstein Company, 2005.
The Departed, Warner Bros., 2006.
The Other Boleyn Girl, Columbia, 2007.

Film Work; Other:
Assistant storeman, *Anna and the King,* Twentieth Century–Fox, 1999.

Film Appearances:
Seamstress, *Edward II,* Fine Line Features, 1991.
Herself, *Making of "Mrs. Henderson Presents"* (documentary short), 2006.

Television Costume Designer; Episodic:
"Didn't You Kill My Brother?," *The Comic Strip Presents ...,* 1988.

Television Appearances; Specials:
Shakespeare in Love and Film, 1999.
The 71st Annual Academy Awards, ABC, 1999.
A Life Without Limits: The Making of "The Aviator," FX Channel, 2004.
The 77th Annual Academy Awards, ABC, 2005.

Television Appearances; Episodic:
Appeared as herself, "Far from Heaven," *Anatomy of a Scene,* Sundance Channel.

PRATT, Victoria 1970–
(Vicky Pratt)

PERSONAL

Full name, Victoria Ainsle Pratt; born December 18, 1970, in Chesley, Ontario, Canada; married T. J. Scott (a director), December 28, 2000. *Education:* York University, degree (summa cum laude), kinesiology; studied acting at Actors Network, Toronto, Ontario. *Avocational Interests:* Kickboxing, Shotokan karate.

Addresses: *Agent*—Don Buchwald and Associates, 6500 Wilshire Blvd., Suite 2200, Los Angeles, CA 90048. *Manager*—Gilbertson, Kincaid and Associates, 501 Santa Monica Blvd., Suite 301, Santa Monica, CA 90401.

Career: Actress. York University, Downsview, Ontario, Canada, worked at Human Performance Laboratory.

Awards, Honors: Medal, Canadian Track and Field Championships, 1990; Saturn Award nomination, best supporting actress in a television series, Academy of Science Fiction, Horror, and Fantasy Films, 2004, for *Mutant X.*

CREDITS

Film Appearances:
(As Vicky Pratt) Ding, *Legacy,* Quantum Entertainment, 1998.
(Uncredited) Fitness instructor, *Whatever It Takes,* 1999.
Charlie, *Blacktop* (also known as *La route de la peur*), 2000.
(As Vicky Pratt) Jennifer, *The Mallory Effect,* Indican Pictures, 2002.
Herself, *Ham & Cheese,* IndustryWorks, 2004.
(Uncredited) Herself, *Double Dare* (documentary), Balcony Releasing, 2004.
Kelli, *Comedy Hell,* 2005.
Herself, *Reinventing the House: Making a Bloody Sequel* (documentary short), 2006.
Sara, *What Love Is,* Big Sky Motion Pictures, 2007.
Carrie Rieger, *Brotherhood of Blood,* 2007.

Television Appearances; Series:
Cohost, *Go for It!,* 1996.
(As Vicky Pratt) Jackie Janczyk, *Once a Thief* (also known as *John Woo's "Once a Thief"*), Fox, 1998.
(As Vicky Pratt) Wilkes, *Forbidden Island,* 1999.
Rose "Sarge," *Cleopatra 2525,* syndicated, 2000–2001.
Shalimar Fox, *Mutant X,* 2001–2004.
Naomi Leeds, *Dirty Sexy Money,* ABC, 2007.
Andrea Battle, *Day Break,* ABC, 2006–2007.

Also appeared as cohost, *Personal Edge.*

Television Appearances; Movies:
Charlie, *Blacktop,* HBO, 2000.
Callie, *Hush,* Lifetime, 2005.
Corporal Tara Jeffries, *Murder at the Presidio,* USA Network, 2005.
Simms, *Mayday,* CBS, 2005.
Henson, *House of the Dead 2* (also known as *House of the Dead 2: All Guts, No Glory* and *House of the Dead II: Dead Aim*), Sci–Fi Channel, 2005.
Nicole, *Kraken: Tentacles of the Deep,* Sci–Fi Channel, 2006.
Laney Hennessy, *Her Fatal Flaw,* Lifetime, 2006.
Jamie, *Wednesday's Child,* Lifetime, 2007.

Television Appearances; Pilots:
Andrea Battle, *Day Break,* ABC, 2006.
Naomi Leeds, *Dirty Sexy Money,* ABC, 2007.

Television Appearances; Specials:
2nd Annual Spaceys, Space, 2004.

Also appeared in *Go for It,* Discovery Channel.

Television Appearances; Episodic:
(As Vicky Pratt) Cyane, "Adventures in the Sin Trade:
   Parts 1 & 2," *Xena: Warrior Princess,* syndicated,
   1998.
(As Vicky Pratt) Claire Wilson/Gia, "Tomorrow," *First
   Wave,* Sci–Fi Channel, 2000.
The Test, FX Channel, 2001.
Pyramid, syndicated, 2004.

Also appeared in *Galleger; Off the Record.*

RECORDINGS

Videos:

Appeared in *Musclemag's Fitness Video;* (with Rob
Fletcher) in *Karatics: The Ultimate Workout.*

WRITINGS

Contributor to *Serious Strength Training,* a book by
Tudor O. Bompa. Author of a monthly column in
Oxygen.

OTHER SOURCES

Periodicals:
Toronto Star, January 23, 2000.

Electronic:
Victoria Pratt Website, http://www.victoriaprattonline.
   com, July 20, 2007.

PRINZI, Frank
   (William Snyder)

PERSONAL

Education: New York University, graduate film program.

Addresses: *Agent*—The Gersh Agency, 232 North
Canon Dr., Beverly Hills, CA 90210.

Career: Cinematographer, director, and camera
operator.

Member: American Society of Cinematographers.

Awards, Honors: Emmy Award, outstanding individual
achievement in cinematography for a series, 1992,
Emmy Award nomination, outstanding individual
achievement in cinematography for a series, 1993,
American Society of Cinematographers Award nomination, outstanding achievement in cinematography in a
regular series, 1993, all for *Northern Exposure.*

CREDITS

Film Cinematographer:
Sleepwalk, First Run Features, 1986.
Chief Zabu, 1986.
The Critical Years (short), 1987.
Seven Women—Seven Sins, ASA Communications,
   1987.
A Better Tomorrow II (also known as *Yinghung bunsik
   II* and *The Color of a Hero II*), 1987.
The Suicide Club, Angelika Films, 1988.
The Prince of Pennsylvania, New Line Cinema, 1988.
Night of the Living Dead, Columbia, 1990.
(Seattle) *The Silent Alarm,* 1993.
Living in Oblivion, Sony, 1995.
Sex & the Other Man, 1995.
The Grave, New City Releasing, 1996.
She's the One, Twentieth Century–Fox, 1996.
The Real Blonde, Paramount, 1997.
No Looking Back, PolyGram, 1998.
200 Cigarettes, Paramount, 1999.
The Best Man, Universal, 1999.
Chinese Coffee, Fox Searchlight, 2000.
Sidewalks of New York, Paramount, 2001.
Five Minutes, Mr. Welles (short), 2005.
Trumbo (documentary), 2007.

Film Work; Other:
Gaffer and key grip, *Stranger Than Paradise,* Samuel
   Goldwyn Company, 1984.
Assistant camera, *The Brother from Another Planet,* Ci-
   necom Pictures, 1984.
Assistant camera, *Day of the Dead* (also known as
   George A. Romero's "Day of the Dead"), United
   Film Distribution Company, 1985.
Additional camera operator, *Krush Groove,* Warner
   Bros., 1985.
First assistant camera, *She's Gotta Have It,* Island
   Pictures, 1986.
Second camera operator, *School Daze,* Columbia,
   1988.
Additional camera operator, *Do the Right Thing,*
   Universal, 1989.

Additional photography, *Resident Alien,* Greycat Films, 1990.

Additional photography, *Paris Is Burning,* Prestige Films, 1990.

Additional camera operator, *Jungle Fever,* Universal, 1991.

Second unit photographer, *The Ice Storm,* Fox Searchlight, 1997.

Coproducer, *Sidewalks of New York,* Paramount, 2001.

Television Cinematographer; Miniseries:
Witness to the Mob, NBC, 1998.

Television Cinematographer; Movies:
Tad, Family Channel, 1995.
Stolen Women: Captured Hearts, CBS, 1997.
Firehouse, 1997.
The David Cassidy Story, NBC, 2000.

Television Cinematographer; Specials:
The Fig Tree (also known as *Wonderworks: "The Fig Tree"*), PBS, 1987.
Dottie, PBS, 1987.
Blue Window, PBS, 1987.
Journey Into Genius (also known as *Eugene O'Neill: "Journey Into Genius"*), PBS, 1988.
Steven Wright in "The Appointments of Dennis Jennings," HBO, 1989.
Ask Me Again, PBS, 1989.

Television Producer; Specials:
Dottie, PBS, 1987.

Television Cinematographer; Pilots:
Mystery Dance, ABC, 1995.

Television Cinematographer; Episodic:
True Blue, NBC, 1989.
(As William Snyder) *"Sleep Well, Professor Oliver," Gideon Oliver* (also known as *By the Rivers of Babylon*), ABC, 1989.
Northern Exposure, CBS, 1991–93.
Deadline, NBC, 2000.
Law & Order: Criminal Intent (also known as *Law & Order: CI*), NBC, 2004–2006.

Television Director; Episodic:
"Sleeping with the Enemy," Northern Exposure, CBS, 1993.
Law & Order: Criminal Intent (also known as *Law & Order: CI*), NBC, 2002–2007.

Television Appearances; Episodic:
Two Drink Minimum, Comedy Central, 1993.

Himself, *"Sidewalks of New York," Anatomy of a Scene,* Sundance, 2001.

PROTAT, Francois

PERSONAL

Career: Cinematographer.

Awards, Honors: Genie Award nomination, best achievement in cinematography, Academy of Canadian Cinema and Television, 1981, for *Fantastica;* Genie Award nomination, best achievement in cinematography, 1985, for *Le crime d'Ovide Plouffe;* Genie Award, best achievement in cinematography, 1986, for *Joshua Then and Now;* Best Artistic Contribution (with Jacques Loiseleux), Montreal World Film Festival, Genie Award nomination, best achievement in cinematography, 1994, both for *Kabloonak.*

CREDITS

Film Cinematographer:
A Time to Consider (documentary), 1972.
La faim des caves (documentary), 1973.
(Second unit) *Bingo* (also known as *Bingo! En pleine gueule*), Ambassador Film Distributors, 1974.
Rene Simard au Japon (documentary), Les Distributions Cine–Capitale, 1974.
Les Ordres (also known as *Orderers* and *Orders*), New Yorker Films, 1974.
Le tribunal de la famille (documentary; also known as *The Family Court*), 1974.
Nursing en obstetrique, 1974.
Le maitre (documentary), 1974.
L'orientation (documentary), 1974.
Processus administratif (documentary), 1974.
The French World Comes to Quebec (also known as *Le monde s'en vient a Quebec*), National Film Board of Canada, 1975.
Rappelle–toi (documentary), 1975.
Les chevaux ont–lis des ailes? (documentary), 1975.
La tete de Normande St–Onge (also known as *Normande* and *The Head of Normande St. Onge*), Fred Baker Films, 1975.
Jos Carbone, 1976.
Chanson pour Julie, Cinepix Film Properties, 1976.
(Second unit) *Parlez–nous d'amour,* 1976.
Pygmalion, 1976.
L'ange et la femme (also known as *The Angel and the Woman*), 1977.
Panique, Les Films Mutuels, 1977.
Tomorrow Never Comes, Cinepix Film Properties, 1978.

La jument vapeur (also known as *Dirty Dishes*), Quartet Films, 1978.

Jacob Two–Two Meets the Hooded Fang, Cinema Shares International, 1978.

Eclair au chocolat (also known as *Chocolate Eclair*), Les Films Mutuels, 1979.

Au revoir a lundi (also known as *Bye, See You Monday* and *See You Monday*), United Artists, 1979.

L'arrache–coeur (also known as *Heart Break*), J.–A. Lapointe Films, 1979.

Fantastica, Les film Mutuels, 1980.

Les plouffe (also known as *The Plouffe Family*), Cine 360, 1981.

The Kinky Coaches and the Pom Pom Pussycats (also known as *Crunch* and *Heartbreak High*), Summa Vista, 1981.

Tulips, AVCO Embassy Pictures, 1981.

Scandale, Ambassador Film Distributors, 1982.

The Hot Touch (also known as *Coup de maitre* and *Peter Dion*), Twentieth Century–Fox, 1982.

Killing 'em Softly (also known as *Man in 5A*), Prism Pictures, 1982.

Running Brave, Buena Vista, 1983.

Le crime d'Ovide Plouffe (also known as *Murder in the Family* and *The Crime of Ovide Plouffe*), 1984.

La guerre des tuques (also known as *The Dog Who Stopped the War* and *The Great Snowball War*), Cinema Plus Distribution, 1984.

The Surrogate (also known as *Blind Rage*), Cinema International Canada, 1984.

Joshua Now and Then, Twentieth Century–Fox, 1985.

Separate Vacations, Alliance, 1986.

Flag, 1987.

(Second unit) *Wild Thing,* Atlantic Releasing, 1987.

Switching Channels, 1988.

The Kiss, TriStar, 1988.

Winter People, Columbia, 1989.

Speed Zone! (also known as *Cannonball Fever*), Orion, 1989.

Weekend at Bernie's (also known as *Hot and Cold*), Twentieth Century–Fox, 1989.

Beautiful Dreamers, Hemdale Film Corp., 1990.

Clearcut, Northern Arts Entertainment, 1991.

Les amoureuses, Cine 360 Inc., 1993.

Brainscan, Triumph, 1994.

Kabloonak (also known as *Nanook*), Raven Releasing, 1995.

Johnny Mnemonic (also known as *Fugitivo del futuro* and *Johnny Mnemonique*), Columbia TriStar, 1995.

Senior Trip (also known as *La folle excursino de National Lampoon* and *National Lampoon's "Senior Trip"*), New Line Cinema, 1995.

La–haut, un roi au–dessus des nuages (also known as *Above the Clouds* and *La–haut*), Vision Distribution, 2003.

Film Work; Other:
Special effects, *Kamouaska,* France Film, 1973.

Camera operator, *Il etait une fois dans l'est* (also known as *Once Upon a Time in the East*), Cine–Art, 1974.

Camera, *The Hot Touch* (also known as *Coup de maitre* and *Peter Dion*), Twentieth Century–Fox, 1982.

Executive in charge of production, *Le crime d'Ovide Plouffe* (also known as *Murder in the Family* and *The Crime of Ovide Plouffe*), 1984.

Camera operator, *Beautiful Dreamers,* Hemdale Film Corp., 1990.

Television Cinematographer; Series:
Chris Cross, Showtime, 1993.
The Hunger, Showtime, 1998–2000.
Tag, 1999.

Television Cinematographer; Movies:
Til Death Do Us Part (also known as *Madhouse*), 1982.
Between Friends (also known as *Nobody Makes Us Cry*), HBO, 1983.
In Defense of a Married Man, ABC, 1990.
The Return of Eliot Ness, NBC, 1991.
Mark Twain and Me, Disney Channel, 1991.
A Little Piece of Heaven, NBC, 1991.
Last Wish, ABC, 1992.
The Diamond Fleece (also known as *The Great Diamond Robbery*), USA Network, 1992.
A Town Torn Apart (also known as *Doc: The Dennis Littky Story*), NBC, 1992.
Ghost Mom (also known as *Bury Me In Niagara*), Fox, 1993.
A Vow to Kill, USA Network, 1995.
The Song Spinner, Showtime, 1995.
Tails You Live, Heads You're Dead, USA Network, 1995.
Family of Corps (also known as *Une famille de flics*), CBS, 1995.
The Haunting of Lisa (also known as *Les premonitions de Lisa*), Lifetime, 1996.
Hostile Advances: The Kerry Ellison Story, Lifetime, 1996.
Whiskers (also known as *Moustaches*), Showtime, 1997.
Valentine's Day (also known as *Protector*), HBO, 1998.
Crime in Connecticut: The Story of Alex Kelly (also known as *Le retour d'Alex Kelly*), CBS, 1999.
Time at the Top (also known as *L'ascenseur du temps*), Showtime, 1999.
Louise, 2005.

Television Work; Episodic:
Assistant camera, "Premiers contacts" and "Experiences d'une famille," *Le combat des sourds,* 1974.

Cinematographer, "Shattered Vows," *The Hitchhiker,* 1983.

Cinematographer, "Cats Out of the Bag," *Lassie,* YTV and Animal Planet, 1996.

Cinematographer, "Mayor for a Day," *Lassie,* YTV and Animal Planet, 1998.

PROULX, Brooklynn 1999–
(Brooklyn Proulx)

PERSONAL

Full name, Brooklyn Marie Proulx; born April 27, 1999, in Cranbrook, British Columbia, Canada. *Avocational Interests:* Ice skating.

Addresses: *Manager*—1 Management, 9000 Sunset Blvd., Suite 1550, Los Angeles, CA 90069.

Career: Actress. Also appeared in television commercials.

CREDITS

Film Appearances:
(As Brooklyn Proulx) Jenny at age four, *Brokeback Mountain,* Focus Features, 2005.
Sophie, *Six Figures,* 2005.
Mary James, *The Assassination of Jesse James by the Coward Robert Ford* (also known as *The Assassination of Jesse James*), Warner Bros., 2007.

Television Appearances; Movies:
Paris Jackson, *Man in the Mirror: The Michael Jackson Story,* VH1, 2004.
Emma Weihenmayer at age six, *Touch the Top of the World,* Arts and Entertainment, 2006.
Amanda, *Don't Cry Now,* Lifetime, 2007.
Hayley Newtone, *The Newtones,* 2007.
Taryn, *Christmas Miracle,* Lifetime, 2007.

Television Appearances; Pilots:
Maddie Drew, "Bring It On, Earl," *Saving Grace,* TNT, 2007.

PURPURO, Sandra

PERSONAL

Addresses: *Agent*—Metropolitan Talent Agency, 4500 Wilshire Blvd., 2nd Floor, Los Angeles, CA 90010.

Career: Actress.

CREDITS

Film Appearances:
Cricket, *Toad Warrior* (also known as *Hell Comes to Frogtown III*), 1996.

A, *Swimsuit: The Movie,* Pathfinder Pictures, 1997.
Sunsplit, 1997.
Irate woman, *My F–ing Job,* 1997.
Qayla, *Atlantis Falling,* 2000.
Cricket, *Max Hell Comes to Frogtown* (also known as *Max Hell Frog Warrior*), Light Source Entertainment, 2002.
Rosie, *The Job,* Lions Gate Films Home Entertainment, 2003.
Sam, *Man vs. Monday* (short), 2006.
Kristin Elias, *On the Brink* (short), 2006.
Mistress, *The Lucky Girl,* 2006.

Also appeared in *Wired for Jane.*

Television Appearances; Series:
Liz Labella, *DiResta,* UPN, 1998.
Thea Harris, *The Beat,* UPN, 2000.
Katherine McClain, *Oz,* HBO, 2001–2002.

Television Appearances; Movies:
Kate Atkins, *Living Straight,* 2003.
District attorney Sarah Lovell, *Wild Things: Diamonds in the Rough,* 2005.

Television Appearances; Pilots:
Marsha Simon, *Adam,* ABC, 1996.
Born in the USA, Fox, 2007.

Television Appearances; Episodic:
Spike, *Misery Loves Company,* Fox, 1995.
Angie, "Lucky Puck," *Maybe This Time,* ABC, 1996.
Marie Louise Farego, "Caroline and the Movie," *Caroline in the City* (also known as *Caroline*), NBC, 1996.
Celia, "A Fight to Remember," *Life with Roger,* The WB, 1997.
Theresa, "Taillight's Last Gleaming," *NYPD Blue,* ABC, 1997.
Mariella, *413 Hope Street,* Fox, 1997.
Pam, "Opposites Distract," *Party of Five,* Fox, 1998.
Grace, "Best Laid Plans," *Wasteland,* ABC, 1999.
Angela Zarelli, "Little Abner," *NYPD Blue,* ABC, 2000.
Angela Zarelli, "Roll Out the Barrel," *NYPD Blue,* ABC, 2000.
Mrs. Perrault, "Survival of the Fittest," *ER,* NBC, 2001.
Barbara Romano, "The Foot," *Six Feet Under,* HBO, 2001.
Maria Sandoval, "The Quest: Parts 1 & 2," *The Huntress,* USA Network, 2001.
Mrs. Hampton, "The Test," *The Practice,* ABC, 2002.
Gina Palestina, "Momento," *That's Life,* CBS, 2002.
Tereza Varela, "Dragonchasers," *The Shield,* FX Channel, 2002.
Tereza Varela, "Carnivores," *The Shield,* FX Channel, 2002.

Hairdresser, *Without a Trace* (also known as *W.A.T.*), CBS, 2002.

Birthing class mom, *The Young and the Restless* (also known as *Y&R*), CBS, 2002.

Shelley Stark, "Last Laugh," *CSI: Crime Scene Investigation* (also known as *C.S.I., CSI: Las Vegas, CSI: Weekends,* and *Les Experts*), CBS, 2003.

Gloria Flores, "Bruno Comes Back," *The Handler,* CBS, 2003.

Lisa Perez, "Gun of a Son," *10–8: Officers on Duty* (also known as *10–8* and *10–8: Police Patrol*), ABC, 2003.

Strong Medicine, Lifetime, 2003.

Wanda Does It, Comedy Central, 2004.

(Uncredited) Television correspondent, "Mexico," *Threat Matrix,* ABC, 2004.

Brenda, *The Young and the Restless* (also known as *Y&R*), CBS, 2004.

Sophia, "Shall We Fight," *Quintuplets,* Fox, 2004.

Annie Jansen, "Up on the Roof," *Blind Justice,* ABC, 2005.

Mona, "Weekend in Bangkok with Two Olympic Gymnasts," *Two and a Half Men,* CBS, 2005.

Antonia Difara, "Frank's Best," *Cold Case,* CBS, 2005.

Prostitute, "We're Gonna Be All Right," *Desperate Housewives,* ABC, 2006.

Miss Zeiger, "Bomb Shelter," *Malcolm in the Middle,* Fox, 2006.

Dr. Barbara Young, "The Man in the Cell," *Bones,* Fox, 2007.

Marina, "Needle in the Haystack," *House M.D.* (also known as *House*), Fox, 2007.

Also appeared as Wendy, "What the Past Will Bring," *Bull,* TNT.

Stage Appearances:

Louise Blaine, *Prom Queens Unchained,* Top of the Gate, New York City, 1991.

Roustabout, *Carnival,* York Theatre at St. Peter's, New York City, 1993.

Cha–Cha Degregorio and understudy Betty Rizzo, *Grease,* Eugene O'Neill Theatre, New York City, 1994–98.

Q–R

QUINN, Iris

PERSONAL

Born in Amherst, Nova Scotia, Canada; married Fred Henderson (an actor); children: Joey Quinn. *Education:* Mount Allison University, creative writing and English literature degree, 1972.

Addresses: *Agent*—Pacific Artists Management, 685–1285 West Broadway, Vancouver, British Columbia V6H 3X8 Canada.

Career: Actress. Performed at The Charlottetown Festival, 1972; University of British Columbia, faculty guest artist.

CREDITS

Film Appearances:
Woman on porch, *Dangerous Intentions,* New Films International, 1995.
Jonas' wife, *Hideaway,* TriStar, 1995.
Farley's sister, *Listen,* Devin Entertainment, 1996.
Kansas City hostess, *Duets,* Buena Vista, 2000.
Sarah, *The Telescope* (short), 2002.
Kyle's mother, *The Perfect Score* (also known as *Voll gepunktet*), Paramount, 2004.
Mrs. Strutmyer, *Slither,* Universal, 2006.
Mrs. Mathers, *Of Golf and God,* 2006.

Television Appearances; Series:
Voice of Tandy, *The Cramp Twins* (animated), Cartoon Network, 2001.
Marguerite, *Master Keaton,* 2003.

Television Appearances; Miniseries:
Mark's mom, *Out of Order,* 2003.

Television Appearances; Movies:
Mrs. Schmidt, *Whose Child Is This? The War for Baby Jessica,* ABC, 1993.
Woman on porch, *Dangerous Intentions,* CBS, 1995.
Trudy, *Ronnie & Julie* (also known as *Ronnie et Julie*), Showtime, 1997.
April, *Tricks,* Showtime, 1997.
Claire, *Cuori in campo* (also known as *Greener Fields* and *World Cup '98*), Cinemax, 1998.
Nurse number two, *Sweetwater* (also known as *Sweetwater: A True Rock Story*), VH1, 1999.
Ginger, *I Was a Teenage Faust,* Showtime, 2002.
Camazotz Lady, *A Wrinkle in Time* (also known as *Un raccourci dans le temps*), ABC, 2003.
Catherine, *I'll Be Seeing You* (also known as *Mary Higgins Clark's "I'll Be Seeing You"* and *Un jour tu verras*), PAX, 2004.
Carol Kennedy, *12 Hours to Live,* Lifetime, 2006.
Evelyn, *What Comes Around,* Lifetime, 2006.

Television Appearances; Pilots:
Mrs. Sloan, *Breaking News,* Bravo, 2002.

Television Appearances; Episodic:
Dr. James, *The Heights,* Fox, 1992.
Lillian Daniels, "Miracle Man," *The X–Files,* Fox, 1994.
Dr. Burns, "When the Bough Breaks," *Madison,* Global, 1995.
Vira, "Ancient History," *Action Man,* syndicated, 1995.
Eleanor Huntoon, "Medicine Man," *Dead Man's Gun,* Showtime, 1997.
Julie Chaney, "Finkelman's Folly," *The Sentinel,* UPN, 1998.
Joanne Patterson, "Cul–De–Sac," *First Wave,* Sci–Fi Channel, 1998.
Emily Ogilvie, "The Womanizer," *Dead Man's Gun,* Showtime, 1999.

Liz, "Pretty Fly for a Dead Guy," *Cold Squad,* CTV, 1999.

"Among My Souvenirs," *Hollywood Off–Ramp,* E! Entertainment Television, 2000.

Rachel, "Twin," *So Weird,* Disney Channel, 2000.

Paloma, "Crazy," *Mysterious Ways,* NBC, 2000.

Mrs. Anders, "Studio D," *The Immortal,* syndicated, 2000.

Elizabeth Miller, "Doe Re: Me," *John Doe,* Fox, 2002.

Roxanne Lytusiak, "Live by the Sword," *Tom Stone* (also known as *Stone Undercover*), CBC, 2003.

Dr. Aveeno, "Alien Man," *Alienated,* The Space Channel, 2004.

Diane Bradford, "The Best Laid Plans," *Life As We Know It,* ABC, 2004.

Diane Bradford, "Secrets & Lies," *Life As We Know It,* ABC, 2004.

Mrs. Walters, "The Filth: Part 1," *Cold Squad,* CTV, 2005.

Mrs. Walters, "And the Fury: Part 2," *Cold Squad,* CTV, 2005.

Marjorie, "New York Fiction: Part 2," *Men in Trees,* ABC, 2006.

RECORDINGS

Video Games:

Underwater elder, *Frogger Beyond,* 2002.

Voice of Helena Chang, *Dreamfall: The Longest Journey* (also known as *Den Lengste reisen: Drommefall*), Aspyr Media, 2006.

OTHER SOURCES

Electronic:

Iris Quinn Website, http://irisquinn.com, July 6, 2007.

RAIDER, Brad 1975–

PERSONAL

Born April 28, 1975, in Philadelphia, PA.

Addresses: *Agent*—James/Levy Management, 3500 West Olive Ave., Suite 1470, Burbank, CA 91505; Metropolitan Talent Agency, 4500 Wilshire Blvd., 2nd Floor, Los Angeles, CA 90010. *Manager*—Robert Stein Management, 345 North Maple Dr., Suite 217, Beverly Hills, CA 90210.

Career: Actor.

CREDITS

Film Appearances:

Footballer, *Second Skin,* 1998.

Eric, *Greener Mountains,* 2004.

Rob Shorwell, *Americanizing Shelley,* Rocky Mountain Pictures, 2007.

Television Appearances; Series:

Max Perch, *The Trouble with Normal,* ABC, 2000.

Television Appearances; Movies:

Jay Garvey, *Spring Break Lawyer,* MTV, 2001.

Educating Lewis, 2004.

Television Appearances; Specials:

Rick, *Everything But the Girl,* NBC, 2001.

Television Appearances; Pilots:

Gregg Glass, *That Was Then,* 2002.

Marcus, *More, Patience,* Fox, 2006.

Television Appearances; Episodic:

Hey guy, "Suffragette City," *Spin City,* ABC, 2000.

Theo Williams, "Hearts and Minds," *The Education of Max Bickford,* CBS, 2001.

Theo Williams, "In the Details," *The Education of Max Bickford,* CBS, 2001.

Gregg Glass, "Mayor May Not," *That Was Then,* ABC, 2002.

Mark, "Kiss and Don't Tell," *Rock Me Baby,* UPN, 2004.

Todd, "The Guide to Being in the Mood," *The Bad Girl's Guide,* UPN, 2005.

Todd, "The Guide to Doing It Now," *The Bad Girl's Guide,* UPN, 2005.

Miles, "The Homewrecker," *Modern Men,* The WB, 2006.

Justin, "The Lying Game," *CSI: NY,* CBS, 2007.

Also appeared as Gregg Glass, "Under Noah's Certain Terms," *That Was Then,* ABC; Chip, "Nipple Effect," *Coupling* (also known as *Coupling U.S.*), NBC; Michael number two, "Miss Communication," *Miss Match,* NBC.

RAMIREZ, Sara 1975–

PERSONAL

Born August 31, 1975, in Mazatlan, Sinaloa, Mexico; immigrated to the United States; father, an oceanographer and in technology; mother's name, Luisa Varges (a singer, actress and principal). *Education:* San Diego School of Creative and Performing Arts, graduated; the Juilliard School, New York City, graduated from the drama division.

Addresses: *Agent*—Cornerstone Talent Agency, 37 West 20th St., Suite 1108, New York, NY 10011. *Publicist*—Nancy Seltzer and Associates, 6220 Del Valle Dr., Los Angeles, CA 90048.

Career: Actress.

Member: Screen Actors Guild, Actors' Equity Association.

Awards, Honors: Outer Critics Circle Award nomination, outstanding actress in a musical, 1999, for *The Gershwins' "Fascinating Rhythm"*; Antoinette Perry Award, best performance by a featured actress in a musical, Outer Critics Circle Award, outstanding featured actress in a musical, Broadway.com Audience awards, favorite featured actress and favorite breakthrough performance, and Broadway.com Audience Award nomination, favorite diva performance, all 2005, for *Monty Python's "Spamalot"*; Special Civil Rights Award (with Chris Sieber), Gay Pride awards, 2005; Screen Actors Guild Award (with others), outstanding performance by an ensemble in a drama series, and ALMA Award nomination, outstanding actress—television series, miniseries, or television movie, American Latin Media Arts awards, both 2007, for *Grey's Anatomy*.

CREDITS

Television Appearances; Series:
Dr. Calliope "Callie" Torres, *Grey's Anatomy* (also known as *Complications, Procedure, Surgeons, Under the Knife,* and *Grey's Anatomy—Die jungen Aerzte*), ABC, 2006—.

Television Appearances; Awards Presentations:
Dr. Calliope "Callie" Torres, *Grey's Anatomy: Complications of the Heart,* ABC, 2006.
Dr. Calliope "Callie" Torres, *Grey's Anatomy: Straight to the Heart,* ABC, 2006.
Dr. Calliope "Callie" Torres, *Grey's Anatomy: Under Pressure,* ABC, 2006.
Dr. Calliope "Callie" Torres, *Grey's Anatomy: Every Moment Counts,* ABC, 2007.
Herself, *Anatomia Unplugged,* Cuatro, 2007.

Television Appearances; Awards Presentations:
The 55th Annual Tony Awards, CBS, 2001.
The 59th Annual Tony Awards, CBS, 2005.

Presenter, *The 60th Annual Tony Awards,* CBS, 2006.
Presenter, *2006 ALMA Awards,* ABC, 2006.
2007 ALMA Awards, 2007.

Television Appearances; Episodic:
Carol, "About Last Night," *Spin City* (also known as *Spin*), ABC, 2000.
Gwen Girard, "The Tys That Bind," *Third Watch,* NBC, 2000.
Linda, "The Crier," *Welcome to New York* (also known as *Gaffigan*), CBS, 2000.
Mrs. Barrera, "Baby Killer," *Law & Order: Special Victims Unit* (also known as *Law & Order's Sex Crimes, Law & Order: SVU,* and *Special Victims Unit*), NBC, 2000.
Lisa Perez, "Chameleon," *Law & Order: Special Victims Unit* (also known as *Law & Order's Sex Crimes, Law & Order: SVU,* and *Special Victims Unit*), NBC, 2002.
Hannah, *As the World Turns,* CBS, 2003.
Irma, "Who's Your Daddy?," *NYPD Blue,* ABC, 2004.
Herself, "On Location: Oprah on the Set of Grey's Anatomy," *The Oprah Winfrey Show* (also known as *Oprah*), syndicated, 2006.
Guest cohost, *The View,* ABC, 2006.
Musical guest, *The Late Late Show with Craig Ferguson* (also known as *The Late Late Show*), CBS, 2006.
Herself, *Entertainment Tonight* (also known as *Entertainment This Week, E.T., ET Weekend,* and *This Week in Entertainment*), syndicated, multiple episodes in 2006, 2007.
Herself, *eTalk Daily* (also known as *eTalk* and *e–Talk Daily*), CTV (Canada), 2006, 2007.
Dr. Calliope "Callie" Torres, "The Other Side of This Life: Parts 1 & 2," *Grey's Anatomy* (also known as *Complications, Procedure, Surgeons, Under the Knife,* and *Grey's Anatomy—Die jungen Aerzte*), ABC, 2007, broadcast as the pilot for *Private Practice* (also known as *Untitled Grey's Anatomy Spin–Off*), ABC.
Herself, *Corazon de ...,* Television Espanola (TVE, Spain), 2007.
Herself, *The View,* ABC, 2007.

Appeared in other programs, including *Talk to Me.*

Television Appearances; Pilots:
Vena, *Star Patrol,* Fox, 2000.
Gabriella Martinez, *Baseball Wives,* HBO, 2002.
Naked Hotel (also known as *ABC/Armyan Bernstein Luxury Hotel Drama, Hotel Project,* and *Untitled John Corbett/ABC Project*), ABC, 2003.
Dr. Calliope "Callie" Torres, "The Other Side of This Life: Parts 1 & 2," *Private Practice* (also known as *Untitled Grey's Anatomy Spin–Off*), ABC, 2007, broadcast as an episode of *Grey's Anatomy* (also known as *Complications, Procedure, Surgeons, Under the Knife,* and *Grey's Anatomy—Die jungen Aerzte*), ABC.

Stage Appearances:

Hair (musical), Starlight Theatre, Balboa Park, San Diego, CA, 1994.

Wahzinak and member of the ensemble, *The Capeman* (musical), Marquis Theatre, New York City, 1998.

Josie, *Barrio Babies* (musical), Denver Center Theatre Company, Denver, CO, 1999.

The Gershwins' "Fascinating Rhythm" (revue), Longacre Theatre, New York City, 1999.

Felicia, *A Class Act* (musical), Ambassador Theatre, New York City, 2001.

Member of the ensemble, *Dreamgirls* (musical benefit), Ford Center for the Performing Arts, New York City, 2001.

Petra, *A Little Night Music* (musical), Ravinia Festival, Ravinia Festival Pavilion, Ravinia, IL, 2002.

The Vagina Monologues, Westside Theatre, New York City, c. 2002.

Marquise de Merteuil, *The Game* (musical), Barrington Stage Company, Pittsfield, MA, 2003.

"Sara Ramirez with Hollis Resnik at the Ravinia," *Martinis and the Martin* (concert), Ravinia Festival, 2003.

Bravo! Bernstein (Musical Theatre Works [MTW] twentieth anniversary gala concert), Hudson Theatre, New York City, 2003.

Cabaret & Main (cabaret revue), Williamstown Theatre Festival, Main Stage, Williamstown, MA, 2004.

The Lady of the Lake, *Monty Python's "Spamalot"* (musical; also known as *Spamalot*), Shubert Theatre (now LaSalle Bank Theatre), Chicago, IL, 2004–2005, then Shubert Theatre, New York City, 2005.

Appeared as Alicia, *Piano,* IACD/American Repertory Theatre, Cambridge, MA. Performed in concerts, galas, and benefit productions, including *The Barrington Stage Company Gala.* Appeared in workshops, including *Carnival,* Radio City Musical Hall, New York City; and *The Wild Party,* Manhattan Theatre Center, New York City; appeared in the workshops *The Laura Nyro Project* and *Lennon.*

Film Appearances:

Rose (Zabar's cashier), *You've Got Mail* (also known as *You Have Got Mail, You've Got M@il, A Szerelem halojab@an, C'e posta per te, Du har m@il, e–m@il fuer Dich, Masz wiadomosc, Mens@gem pra voce, Mesaj pentru tine, Sinulle on posti@, Tienes un e–mail, Tiens un e–mail, Voce tem uma mensagem, Vous avez un message,* and *Vous avec un mess@age*), Warner Bros., 1998.

Female ensemble member, *Chicago* (musical; also known as *Chicago: The Musical*), Miramax, 2002.

Police officer at carjacking, *Spider–Man* (also known as *Spiderman, Spider–Man: The Motion Picture, El hombre arana, Homem–Aranha, Omul paianjen, Pokember, Spider–Man—Haemaehaekkimies,* and *Spindelmannen*), Columbia, 2002.

Belkis, *Washington Heights,* 2002, Mac Releasing, 2003.

Voice of Peggy Fears, *When Ocean Meets Sky* (documentary), 2003.

Lisa, *Going Under,* 2004, Argot Pictures, 2006.

RECORDINGS

Albums; with Others:

Chicago (soundtrack), Sony, 2003.

Monty Python's "Spamalot" (original Broadway cast recording), Decca Broadway, 2005.

Appeared in a cast recording of *The Capeman.*

Video Games:

Voice of Lammy, *UnJammer Lammy,* Sony Computer Entertainment America, 1999.

Voice of Lammy, *PaRappa the Rapper 2,* 2001.

OTHER SOURCES

Electronic:

Sara Ramirez.com. The Official Website, http://www.sararamirez.com, May 21, 2007.

RASH, Jim

PERSONAL

Born in Charlotte, NC.

Addresses: *Agent*—Creative Artists Agency, 2000 Avenue of the Stars, Los Angeles, CA 90067. *Manager*—Principato/Young Management, 9465 Wilshire Blvd., Suite 880, Beverly Hills, CA 90212; Jeff Morrone Management, 9350 Wilshire Blvd., Suite 224, Beverly Hills, CA 90212.

Career: Actor. The Groundlings, company member, 2004; appeared in television commercial for Cheez–It Twisterz snacks, 2005.

CREDITS

Film Appearances:

Accountant, *Auto Motives* (short), 2000.

Amateur porn guy, *One Hour Photo,* Fox Searchlight Pictures, 2002.

Jane's assistant, *Hiding in Walls* (short), 2002.

Head teacher's assistant Phillip, *Slackers* (also known as *Les complices*), Screen Gems, 2002.

Technician, *Minority Report,* Twentieth Century–Fox, 2002.

Studio executive number two, *S1m0ne,* New Line Cinema, 2002.

Caller, *Wrong Hollywood Number* (short), 2003.

George, *George & Gracie* (short), 2003.

Mr. Grayson/Stitches, *Sky High,* Buena Vista, 2005.

Katherine's secretary, *Partner(s),* 2005.

(Scenes deleted) Beauregard St. Pompadeux, *Cook–Off!,* 2006.

Slapsy Doodle, *MaxiDoodles: Behind the Makeup* (short), Six Foot Seven Films, 2006.

Goose, *Balls of Fury,* Rogue Pictures, 2007.

Television Appearances; Series:
Cotton, *Thanks,* CBS, 1999.
Mitchell Tuit, *Katie Joplin,* The WB, 1999.
Clerk/Fenton, *That '70s Show,* Fox, 2002–2006.
Various roles, *Reno 911!,* Comedy Central, 2003–2004.
Jonathan, *Help Me Help You,* 2006.

Television Appearances; Movies:
Hackett, 2007.

Television Appearances; Specials:
Himself, *Sketch Pad 2,* 2003.

Television Appearances; Pilots:
Loomis (movie), CBS, 2001.
Vice Principal Eugene Wolgenmoth, *Hackett,* Fox, 2007.

Television Appearances; Episodic:
Production assistant, "Local Hero," *Cybill,* CBS, 1995.
Pollster, "Movies," *Tracey Takes On ...,* HBO, 1997.
Carl, "Good Val Hunting," *Working,* NBC, 1998.
Eddie Blatt, "Becker the Elder," *Becker,* CBS, 1999.
Bart, "Big Sissies," *Clueless,* 1999.
Census guy, "Scary Hughley," *The Hughleys,* UPN, 2000.
Bull, TNT, 2000.
Quimby, "Vanished: Part 1," *The Practice,* ABC, 2001.
Jeff, *The Fighting Fitzgeralds,* NBC, 2001.
Salesman, "The Receipt," *According to Jim,* ABC, 2002.
Rob McLyle, "Claude the Liar," *Less than Perfect,* ABC, 2002.
Dougy, *Baby Bob,* CBS, 2002.
Todd Benton, "Random Acts of Violence," *CSI: Crime Scene Investigation* (also known as *CSI: Las Vegas, CSI: Weekends, C.S.I.,* and *Les Experts*), CBS, 2003.
Court therapist, "All the Rage," *The Guardian,* CBS, 2003.
Stalker, "Check/Mate," *Coupling,* NBC, 2003.

Dr. Joel Sanderson, "Left for Dead," *Navy NCIS: Naval Criminal Investigative Service* (also known as *NCIS* and *NCIS: Naval Criminal Investigative Service*), CBS, 2004.
Lewis, "Philip in a China Shop," *It's All Relative,* ABC, 2004.
Nervous male passenger, "The Last One: Part 2," *Friends,* NBC, 2004.
Voice of gatekeeper, Jefferson, and announcer, "Test of Time/A Kick in the Asgard," *Grim & Evil* (animated; also known as *The Grim Adventures of Billy & Mandy*), Cartoon Network, 2004.
Freddie Blake, "Rivals and Departures," *Jake in Progress,* ABC, 2005.
Brent, "Love Is in the Airplane," *Will & Grace,* NBC, 2005.
Hodge, "Halfway Impotent," *Halfway Home,* Comedy Central, 2007.

Also appeared as Harris Van Doren, "Jake or Fake?," *The Naked Truth* (also known as *Wilde Again*), NBC; Harris Van Doren, "Bob & Carol & Ted & Alice, Except with Different Names," *The Naked Truth* (also known as *Wilde Again*), NBC.

Television Work; Pilots:
Co–executive producer, *Adopted,* 2005.

Television Director; Episodic:
Lovespring International, Lifetime, 2005.

Stage Appearances:
Willard Carrington, *Beverly Winwood Presents the Actors Showcase,* Groundlings Theatre, Los Angeles, 2002.

Also appeared in *Reunion; Holed Up; Pirates of Penzance; Harvey; Flowers for Algernon.*

WRITINGS

Television Pilots:
Adopted, 2005.

RATNER, Bill

PERSONAL

Married Aleka Corwin (an art director); children: two.

Addresses: *Agent*—Cunningham, Escott, Slevin & Doherty, 10635 Santa Monica Blvd., suite 130, Los Angeles, CA 90025.

Career: Actor and voice artist. Provides voice–overs for local television newscasts including WCVB in Boston, MA, and WESH in Daytona Beach and Orlando, FL; provided voice work for numerous commercials, including McDonalds, Apple Computer, Microsoft, Honda automobiles, Hilton Hotels, and Procter & Gamble products.

CREDITS

Film Appearances:
Special effects voices, *Explorers*, Paramount, 1985.
Voice of Flint, *G.I. Joe: The Movie* (animated; also known as *Action Force: The Movie*), Celebrity Home Entertainment, 1987.
Character voice, *Lobster Man from Mars*, Electric Pictures, 1989.
Voice of announcer, *Fat Albert*, Twentieth Century–Fox, 2004.
Voice of Humpty Dumpty, *Geppetto's Secret* (animated), 2005.

Television Appearances; Series:
Voice, *Meatballs and Spaghetti*, CBS, 1982.
Voice of Flint and Cobra Trooper, *G.I. Joe* (animated; also known as *Action Force* and *Chijo saikyo no Expert Team G.I. Joe*), syndicated, 1985.
Announcer, *Missing/Reward*, syndicated, 1989.
Announcer, *Haywire*, Fox, 1990.
Announcer, *Stuntmasters*, syndicated, 1991.
Narrator, *Secret Passages*, 2002.
Narrator, *Impact: Stories of Survival*, 2004, Discovery Health Channel.

Television Appearances; Specials:
George, *The Christmas Tree Train*, 1983.
George, *Which Witch Is Which?*, 1984.
Voice of Flint, *G.I. Joe: The Revenge of Cobra* (animated), 1984.
George, *The Turkey Caper*, 1985.
Voice of Flint, *G.I. Joe: Arise, Serpentor, Arise!* (animated; also known as *Action Force: Arise, Serpentor, Arise!*), 1986.
Announcer, *Miracle and Other Mysteries*, ABC, 1991.
Announcer, *The Last Days of World War II* (also known as *The Last Days of WWII*), 1995.
Announcer, *The 1996 Clio Awards*, Fox, 1996.
Announcer, *Comedy Club Superstars*, ABC, 1996.
Narrator, *The Berlin Airlift: First Battle of the Cold War* (documentary), History Channel, 1998.
Narrator, *Masters of Fantasy: Vincent Price*, Sci–Fi Channel, 1998.
Narrator, *Evel Knievel: The E! True Hollywood Story*, E! Entertainment Television, 1998.
Narrator, *The Missouri: A Journey with Stephen Ambrose* (documentary), History Channel, 1999.

Narrator, *The Greatest Supermodels*, The Learning Channel, 1999.
Narrator, *The Greatest Relief Organization: The Red Cross*, The Learning Channel, 1999.
Narrator, *Air Force One: A History*, History Channel, 1999.
Narrator, *Mt. Everest: The Fatal Climb* (documentary), Discovery Channel, 1999.
Narrator, *The Greatest Boxer: Muhammad Ali*, The Learning Channel, 2000.
Narrator, *Greatest Space Explorer: Hubble Telescope*, The Learning Channel, 2000.
Narrator, *Sarge!*, History Channel, 2001.
Newsreel voice, *Goin' to Chicago*, PBS, 2001.
Narrator, *The Greatest Monument: Mt. Rushmore*, The Learning Channel, 2002.
Narrator, *Search for the Mothman*, 2002.
Narrator, *THS Investigates: Love Behind Bars*, E! Entertainment Television, 2005.

Television Appearances; Pilots:
Voice of interceptor, *Interceptor*, syndicated, 1989.

Television Appearances; Episodic:
Voice of Flint and Dashiell R. Faireborn, *Transformers* (animated; also known as *Super God Robot Force, Tatakae! Cho robot seimeitai Transformer, The Transformers, Transformer 2010*, and *Transformers: Generation 1*), syndicated, 1986.
Voice of Stu Simmons, *AAAHH!!! Real Monsters* (animated), Nickelodeon, 1994.
Narrator, "Air Force One: A History," *Modern Marvels*, History Channel, 1997.
Narrator, "The Magnum," *Modern Marvels*, History Channel, 2002.
Narrator, "Car Tech of the Future," *Modern Marvels*, History Channel, 2005.
Voice of Flint, "North by North Quahog," *Family Guy* (animated; also known as *Padre de familia*), Fox, 2005.
Voice of narrator, "Gwen 10," *Ben 10* (animated), Cartoon Network, 2006.
Voice, "A Day at the Circus," *Robot Chicken* (animated), Cartoon Network, 2006.

RECORDINGS

Video Games:
Voice of narrator, *King's Quest VI: Heir Today, Gone Tomorrow*, 1992.
Voice, *Forgotten Realms: Baldur's Gate—Dark Alliance II*, 2004.

WRITINGS

Television Specials:
Narrator, *Mt. Everest: The Fatal Climb* (documentary), Discovery Channel, 1999.

OTHER SOURCES

Electronic:
Bill Ratner Website, http://www.billratner.com, July 6, 2007.

REEVES, Perrey
(Perry Reeves)

PERSONAL

Born in New York, NY. *Avocational Interests:* Meditation and yoga.

Career: Actress. Built a yoga retreat in Costa Rica; works with the International Fund for Animal Welfare.

Awards, Honors: Screen Actors Guild Award nomination (with others), outstanding performance by an ensemble in a comedy series, 2007, for *Entourage.*

CREDITS

Film Appearances:
Kristen De Silva, *Child's Play 3* (also known as *Child's Play 3: Look Who's Stalking* and *Child's Play III*), Universal, 1991.
Amy, *Kicking and Screaming,* Trimark Pictures, 1995.
Holly, *Smoke Signals* (also known as *Le secret des cendres*), Miramax, 1998.
Amanda, *The Suburbans,* TriStar, 1999.
Marissa Jones, *Old School,* DreamWorks, 2003.
Jessie, associate number four, *Mr. & Mrs. Smith,* Twentieth Century–Fox, 2005.
Michelle, *Undiscovered,* Lions Gate Films, 2005.
Marni, *American Dreamz,* Universal, 2006.
Adrienne Stafford, *Boy of Pigs,* 2007.
Sergeant Berger, *Vicious Circle,* 2007.

Television Appearances; Series:
Daphne, *The Lyon's Den,* NBC, 2003.
Mrs. Ari, *Entourage,* HBO, 2004—.

Television Appearances; Movies:
Lauren, *The Preppie Murder,* ABC, 1989.
Suzanne Dwyer, *The Return of Ironside,* NBC, 1993.
Zoe Moon, *Escape to Witch Mountain,* ABC, 1995.
Maizie, *An Element of Truth,* CBS, 1995.

Television Appearances; Pilots:
Laura, *Mothers, Daughters and Lovers* (movie; also known as *American River*), NBC, 1989.
Hannah Mathewson, *Plymouth* (movie), ABC, 1991.

Television Appearances; Episodic:
(As Perry Reeves) Tracy Hill, "Just Say No! High," *21 Jump Street,* Fox, 1990.
Pepper, "Child's Play," *The Flash,* CBS, 1990.
"Truth and Consequences," *Doogie Howser, M.D.,* ABC, 1991.
"If This Is Adulthood, I'd Rather be In Philadelphia," *Doogie Howser, M.D.,* ABC, 1991.
Perrette Davis, "The Lemon Tomato Juice Hour," *Homefront,* ABC, 1992.
Perrette Davis, "Can't Say No," *Homefront,* ABC, 1992.
Perrette Davis, "Appleknocker to Wed Tomatohawker," *Homefront,* 1992.
"The Last Motel," *Red Shoe Diaries* (also known as *Zalman King's "The Red Shoe Diaries"*), Showtime, 1994.
Kristen Kilar, "3," *The X–Files,* Fox, 1994.
Susan Constable, "The Murder Channel," *Murder, She Wrote,* CBS, 1994.
Taryn, *Sliders,* 1996.
Brooke, "A Cute Triangle," *Off Centre,* The WB, 2001.
Linda's neighbor, "Recipe for Murder," *CSI: Crime Scene Investigation* (also known as *CSI: Las Vegas, CSI: Weekends, C.S.I.* and *Les Experts*), CBS, 2003.
Julia, "Hurricane Anthony," *CSI: Miami,* CBS, 2003.
Karen Herzfeld, "Too Close to Call," *Medium,* NBC, 2005.

Also appeared in (as Perry Reeves) "The Car," *Too Something* (also known as *New York Daze*), Fox.

REEVES, Saskia 1962–

PERSONAL

Born in 1962, in London, England. *Education:* Studied acting with London Guildhall School of Speech and Drama.

Career: Actress. Also did voice work for television commercials and read books for vocalpoint.net.

CREDITS

Film Appearances:
Sarah Gilmartin, *December Bride,* M.D. Wax Courier, 1990.
Antonia McGill, *Antonia and Jane,* Miramax, 1991.

Natalie, *Close My Eyes,* Castle Hill, 1991.
Helen, *In the Border Country,* 1991.
Isobel Heatherington, *The Bridge,* 1992.
Louise Duffield, *Traps,* Filmopolis Pictures, 1994.
Lynda, *I.D.* (also known as *Undercover*), Sales Company, 1995.
Miriam, *Butterfly Kiss* (also known as *Killer on the Road*), Cinepix Film Properties, 1995.
Jean, *Different for Girls* (also known as *Crossing the Border*), First Look Pictures Releasing, 1996.
Joy, *L.A. Without a Map* (also known as *I Love L.A.* and *Los Angeles Without a Map*), United Media, 1998.
Maria Ann McCardle, *Heart,* Feature Film Company, 1999.
Ticks, 1999.
Bubbles (short), 2001.
Rosa, *The Tesseract,* First Look International, 2003.
Mum, *The Knickerman* (short), 2004.
Mother, *Fast Learners* (short), 2006.

Television Appearances; Series:
Chloe Marsh, *Plotlands,* BBC, 1997.

Television Appearances; Miniseries:
Edwina, *A Woman of Substance,* 1983.
Lady Jessica Atreides, *Dune* (also known as *Frank Herbert's "Dune," Frank Herbert's "Dune—Der Wusternplanet,"* and *Der Wustenplanet*), Sci-Fi Channel, 2000.
Julie Hopcroft, *Suspicion,* ITV, 2003.
Cassie Mahy, *Island at War,* ITV and PBS, 2004.
Eileen Judd, *The Commander: Virus,* ITV, 2005.

Television Appearances; Series:
Sheila Rabey, *Afterlife,* BBC America and ITV, 2006.

Television Appearances; Movies:
Greta Samsa, *Metamorphosis,* 1987.
Rosie, *Children Crossing,* BBC, 1990.
Lady Marsham, *Citizen Locke,* 1994.
Selina Roberts, *Cruel Train,* BBC, 1995.
Mrs. Cratchit, *A Christmas Carol,* TNT, 1999.
Meryl Rogers, *A Line in the Sand,* Anglia, 2004.
Louise Doyle, *The Strange Case of Sherlock Holmes & Arthur Conan Doyle,* BBC, 2005.
Lady Mountbatten, *The Last Days of the Raj,* Channel 4, 2007.

Television Appearances; Specials:
Phillipa Monaghan, "In My Defence," *Two Monologues: In My Defence/A Chip in the Sugar,* PBS, 1992.
Narrator, *A Very British Psycho* (documentary), 1997.

Television Appearances; Episodic:
Pretty Girl, "Daddy's Girls," *Lytton's Diary,* 1985.

Dr. Laurie Poole, "Breaking Glass," *Waking the Dead,* BBC, 2003.
Mary Alton, "If TV Goes Down the Tube," *If,* BBC, 2005.
Sheila Rabey, "Daniel One & Two," *Afterlife,* ITV and BBC America, 2005.
Eileen Edwards, "Natural Causes," *The Inspector Lynley Mysteries,* BBC1 and PBS, 2006.
Sally Bernard, *Spooks* (also known as *MI–5*), BBC1 and Arts and Entertainment, 2006.

Stage Appearances:
Beatrice, *Much Ado About Nothing,* Majestic Theatre, Brooklyn Academy of Music, New York City, then Playhouse Theatre, London, both 1998.
Carol, *Orpheus Descending,* Donmar Warehouse Theatre, London, 2000.

OTHER SOURCES

Periodicals:
Empire, issue 32, 1992, pp. 44–45.

REKERT, Winston 1949–
    (Winston A. Rekert)

PERSONAL

Born July 10, 1949, in Vancouver, British Columbia, Canada; father, a logger.

Addresses: *Agent*—Silver, Massetti and Szatmary Ltd., 8730 Sunset Blvd., Suite 440, Los Angeles, CA 90069.

Career: Actor. Virtue/Rekert Productions, cofounder, partner, and producer, c. 1990–94. Also worked as a logger.

Awards, Honors: Genie Award nomination, best performance by an actor in a leading role, Academy of Canadian Cinema and Television, 1981, for *Suzanne;* Genie Award nomination, best performance by an actor in a leading role, 1982, for *Heartaches;* Genie Award nomination, best performance by an actor in a leading role, 1985, and best actor, Critic's Choice Awards, Festival of Festivals, both for *Walls;* Genie Award nomination, best performance by an actor in a leading role, 1987, for *The Blue Man;* Gemini Award, best performance by a lead actor in a continuing dramatic role, Academy of Canadian Cinema and Television, 1987, Gemini Award nomination, best performance by a lead actor in a continuing dramatic role, 1988, both for *Adderly;* Sir Peter Ustinov Award, Banff Television Festival, 1993; Gemini Award nomination (with others), best dramatic series, 1993, 1995, Gemini Award nomination, best performance by an actor in a continuing leading dramatic role, 1994, all for *Neon Rider;* Gemini Award nomination, best performance by an actor in a guest role in a dramatic series, 2001, for *Cold Squad;* Gemini Award, best performance by an actor in a guest role in a dramatic series, 2003, for *Blue Murder.*

CREDITS

Film Appearances:
Prairie Landscapes, 1977.
Nicky Callaghan, *Suzanne,* Twentieth Century–Fox, 1980.
Marcello DiStassi, *Heartaches,* 1981, then Motion Picture Marketing, 1982.
Antonio Montoya, *Your Ticket Is No Longer Valid* (also known as *Finishing Touch, A Slow Descent into Hell,* and *L'ultime passion*), Ambassador Film Distributors, 1981.
John, "The Black Cat in the Black Mouse Socks," *Love,* Coup Films, 1982.
Sean Phelan, *Dead Wrong* (also known as *The Columbia Connection, Entrapment,* and *Death Fighter*), Sounder Productions, 1983.
Danny Baker, *Walls* (also known as *Lock Up*), Jerico Films, 1984.
Detective Langevin, *Agnes of God,* Columbia, 1985.
Tom McTeague, *Toby McTeague* (also known as *Toby*), Filmline International, 1986.
Dorian Kruger, *High Stakes,* 1986.
Orrin Mercer, *Harlequin's "Loving Evangeline"* (also known as *En quete de verite*), 1998.
Carl, *The Last Stop* (also known as *Dernier arret*), Sterling Home Entertainment, 2000.
Eliah Savage, *Savage Island* (also known as *Deadman's Island*), Ardustry Home Entertainment, 2003.
Homeless man, *Breakdown* (short), Quat Media, 2006.
Dr. Larry, *Trapped Ashes,* 2006.
Larry, *Honeymoon with Mom,* Regent Worldwide Sales, 2006.

Television Appearances; Series:
Voice of Mungo Baobab, *Droids* (animated; also known as *Droids: The Adventures of R2D2 and C3PO* and *Star Wars: Droids*), ABC, 1985.
V. H. Adderly, *Adderly,* CBC and Disney Channel, 1986–87.
Michael Terry, *Neon Rider,* syndicated, 1990–94.

Television Appearances; Miniseries:
Max, *Brothers by Choice,* CBC, 1986.
Chet, *Glory! Glory!,* HBO, 1989.

The stranger, *Roughing It* (also known as *Mark Twain's "Roughing It"*), Hallmark Channel, 2002.

Television Appearances; Movies:
Who'll Save Our Children?, 1978.
Paul Sharpe, *The Blue Man* (also known as *Eternal Evil*), 1985.
Brian, *The World's Oldest Living Bridesmaid,* CBS, 1990.
Paul Gatlin, *Voices from Within* (also known as *Silhouette*), NBC, 1994.
Rick Dion, *Falling from the Sky: Flight 174* (also known as *Freefall: Flight 174*), ABC, 1995.
Captive Heart: The James Mink Story, CBS, 1996.
Bill DeCreeft, *To Brave Alaska,* ABC, 1996.
Chet, *Moonlight Becomes You,* Family Channel, 1998.
Jack, *A Cooler Climate,* Showtime, 1999.
Reed Halverson, *Murder at the Cannes Film Festival,* E! Entertainment Television, 2000.
Ty Corbett, *Cabin Pressure* (also known as *Hijack'd*), PAX, 2001.
Mason, *Wicked Minds* (also known as *Espirits tordus*), 2002.
Peter Lang, *Before I Say Goodbye* (also known as *Mary Higgins Clark's "Before I Say Goodbye"* and *Mary Higgins Clark: "Avant de te dire adieu"*), PAX, 2003.
Fred, *A Date with Darkness: The Trial and Capture of Andrew Luster,* Lifetime, 2003.
Joe Cunningham, *Undercover Christmas* (also known as *L'amour en cadeau* and *Undercover Lover*), CBS, 2003.
William, *Eve's Christmas,* Lifetime, 2004.
Wayne Newton, *Behind the Camera: The Unauthorized Story of "Diff'rent Strokes,"* NBC, 2006.
Frank Dolan, *The Secret of Hidden Lake,* Lifetime, 2006.

Television Appearances; Specials:
Voice of Mungo Baobab, *The Great Heap,* ABC, 1986.

Television Appearances; Episodic:
James, "Photo Finish," *The Littlest Hobo,* CTV and syndicated, 1981.
Kurt Malcolm, "Showdown," *Night Heat,* 1986.
"The Otters Return," *Danger Bay,* CBC and Disney Channel, 1987.
Tony Azzarella, "State of Mind," *Street Legal,* CBC, 1988.
Tony Azzarella, "A Powerful Prison Story," *Street Legal,* CBC, 1988.
Sheriff Clint Maitland, "Rebellion," *Lonesome Dove: The Series,* syndicated, 1995.
(As Winston A. Rekert) Frank Orsini, "Strange Bedfellows," *Due South* (also known as *Un tandem de choc*), CBS, 1997.

Cordesh, "The Tok'ra: Parts 1 & 2," *Stargate SG–1* (also known as *La porte des etoiles*), Showtime and syndicated, 1998.

Himself, *Terminal City,* CBC, 1998.

Reed Callum, "Valentine," *Psi Factor: Chronicles of the Paranormal,* syndicated, 1999.

General Beckett, "The Return of Maggie Beckett," *Sliders,* Sci–Fi Channel, 1999.

Agent Armstrong, "Like Father, Like Monk," *Secret Agent Man,* UPN, 2000.

"Among My Souvenirs," *Hollywood Off–Ramp,* E! Entertainment Television, 2000.

General Robert Ruxton, "Attention Deficit," *Higher Ground,* 2000.

Horace Burke, "Skywatchers," *First Wave,* 2000.

Detective Pet Chorney, "Loyalties," *Cold Squad,* CTV, 2000.

Sergeant Pete Chorney, "Loose Ends: Parts 1 & 2," *Cold Squad,* CTV, 2001.

Reverend James Cole, "A Man of God," *Mysterious Ways,* PAX, 2002.

Zeus, "The Shards of Rimini," *Andromeda* (also known as *Gene Roddenberry's "Andromeda"*), syndicated, 2002.

"America's Most Wanted," *Blue Murder* (also known as *En quete de preuves*), Global, 2003.

Otis Hardwicke, "The Old Man," *The Collector,* City TV, 2004.

Young Blades, Independent Television, 2004.

Wade Carson—the celebrity, "Rubbing Shoulders," *Godiva's,* Bravo, 2006.

Priest, "Lay Down Your Burdens: Part 2," *Battlestar Galactica,* Sci–Fi Channel, 2006.

Priest, "Exodus: Part 2," *Battlestar Galactica,* Sci–Fi Channel, 2006.

Priest, "Collaborators," *Battlestar Galactica,* Sci–Fi Channel, 2006.

The L Word, Showtime, 2006.

Jonah Greeley, "Roadkill," *Supernatural,* The CW, 2007.

Also appeared as Sam Norris, "Bloodhounds Can't Fly," *The Great Detective.*

Television Work; Series:

Cocreator and executive producer, *Neon Rider,* syndicated, 1990.

Television Director; Episodic:

"The Good, the Bad and Eleanor," *Neon Rider,* syndicated, 1992.

"Brothers," *Neon Rider,* syndicated, 1992.

"Moving On: Parts 1 & 2," *Neon Rider,* syndicated, 1994.

WRITINGS

Television Episodes; Stories:

"The Good, the Bad and Eleanor," *Neon Rider,* syndicated, 1992.

RHIMES, Shonda 1970–
(Shonda Lynn Rhimes)

PERSONAL

Full name, Shonda Lynn Rhimes; born January 13, 1970, in University Park, IL; father, a university administrator; mother, a university professor; children: Harper. *Education:* Dartmouth College, B.A., English literature and creative writing, 1991; University of Southern California School of Cinema and Television, M.F.A., 1994.

Addresses: *Office*—Shondaland, 4151 Prospect Ave., Los Feliz Tower, 4th Floor, Los Angeles, CA 90027; c/o ABC TV, 500 S. Buena Vista St., Burbank, CA 91521. *Agent*—International Creative Management, 10250 Constellation Way, Los Angeles, CA 90067.

Career: Producer, writer, and director. Shondaland (production company), Los Angeles, CA, principal. Black Underground Theatre and Arts Association, director. Previously worked in advertising and at a mental health facility.

Awards, Honors: Gary Rosenberg Writing Fellowship, University of Southern California; Black Reel Award nomination, best screenplay—original or adapted, 2005, for *The Princess Diaries 2: Royal Engagement;* Emmy Award nominations, outstanding drama series (with others) and outstanding writing for a drama series, Television Producer of the Year Award in Episodic—Drama, nomination (with others), Producers Guild of America Golden Laurel Awards, Television Award (with others), new series, Writers Guild of America, Television Award nomination (with others), dramatic series, Writers Guild of America, 2006, Television Producer of the Year Award in Episodic—Drama (with others), Producers Guild of America Golden Laurel Awards, Image Award, outstanding writing in a dramatic series, National Association for the Advancement of Colored People, 2007, all for *Grey's Anatomy.*

CREDITS

Television Work; Series:

Creator, executive producer, and (as Shonda Lynn Rhimes) show runner, *Grey's Anatomy,* ABC, 2005—.

Creator and executive producer, *Private Practice,* ABC, 2007—.

Television Work; Pilots:

Executive producer and show runner, *Private Practice,* ABC, 2007.

Television Work; Specials:
Research director, *Hank Aaron: Chasing the Dream* (documentary), TBS, 1995.

Television Appearances; Episodic:
Tavis Smiley, PBS, 2005.
ABC News Nightline, ABC, 2006.
"On Location: Oprah on the set of 'Grey's Anatomy,'" *The Oprah Winfrey Show,* syndicated, 2006.
Entertainment Weekly (also known as *E.T.*), syndicated, 2007.

Film Work:
Director, *Blossoms and Veils* (short), 1998.

WRITINGS

Television Movies:
Introducing Dorothy Dandridge (also known as *Face of an Angel*), 1999.

Television Pilots:
Private Practice, ABC, 2007.

Television Episodes:
Grey's Anatomy, ABC, 2005—.
Private Practice, ABC, 2007—.

Screenplays:
Blossoms and Veils (short), 1998.
(Uncredited rewrite) *Frida,* Miramax, 2002.
Crossroads, Paramount, 2002.
The Princess Diaries 2: Royal Engagement, Buena Vista, 2004.

OTHER SOURCES

Periodicals:
Ebony, October, 2005.
Written By, September, 2005.

RICHARDSON, Jay
(John Henry)

PERSONAL

Career: Actor. Appeared in commercial for Injury HelpLine (law firm), 2007.

CREDITS

Film Appearances:
Ron, *The Newlydeads,* City Lights, 1987.
Samanski, *Evil Spawn* (also known as *Alien Within, Alive by Night, Deadly Sting,* and *Metamorphosis*), Camp Video, 1987.
First phantom, *Terror Night* (also known as *Bloody Movie*), 1987, Retromedia Entertainment, 2004.
Aaron Pendleton, *Beverly Hills Vamp,* Vidmark Entertainment, 1988.
Bill Weston, *Death Row Diner,* Camp Motion Pictures, 1988.
Jack Chandler, *Hollywood Chainsaw Hookers* (also known as *Hollywood Hookers*), Camp Motion Pictures, 1988.
Prison sergeant major, *Alienator,* Image Entertainment, 1989.
Boris, *L.A. Heat,* PM Video, 1989.
Edison, *Slash Dance,* Simitar Video, 1989.
Abbott, *Brothers in Arms,* Republic, 1989.
Mueller, *Time Burst: The Final Alliance,* AIP Home Video, 1989.
Johnny Ventura, *Terminal Force,* Prism Pictures, 1989.
Kilrenney, *Marked for Murder,* Highlight Video, 1989.
Jay, *The Channeler,* Magnum Video, 1990.
Mr. Adams, *Witchcraft II: The Temptress,* Academy Entertainment, 1990.
Commissioner, *Vice Academy Part 2,* 1990.
Omar, *Wizards of the Demon Sword,* Troma Entertainment, 1991.
Wheelchair Willie, *Street Soldiers,* Curb/Esquire Films, 1991.
Commissioner, *Vice Academy Part 3,* Rick Sloane Productions, 1991.
Cybernator, Vista Home Video, 1991.
Richard Trent, *Bad Girls from Mars,* 1991, Vidmark Entertainment, 1994.
Lieutenant Wanamaker, *Inner Sanctum,* New Line Cinema, 1991.
Terry Munroe, *Haunting Fear,* Concorde–New Horizons/Troma Entertainment, 1991.
Detective McKenzie, *Mind, Body & Soul,* AIP Home Video, 1992.
Mr. Kurtz, *Munchie,* New Horizons Home Video, 1992.
San Jose ticket agent, *Honeymoon in Vegas,* Columbia, 1992.
Matthew Cameron, *Original Intent,* Skouras, 1992.
Dr. Scott Callister, *Sins of Desire,* Cinetel Films, 1993.
Philip Grimes, *Divorce Law* (also known as *California Brief Affairs* and *Illegal Affairs*), Vista Street Entertainment, 1993.
Munchie Strikes Back, Concorde–New Horizons, 1994.
The commissioner, *Vice Academy 4* (also known as *Vice Academy Part 4*), Rick Sloane Productions, 1994.

(Uncredited) Mike's father, *Hollywood Hills 90028,* Peacock Films, 1994.

Mike, *Teenage Exorcist,* Action International Pictures, 1994.

Jake Michaels, *Starstruck,* 1995.

Bartell, *Hard Bounty,* C/FP Video, 1995.

Chief Tanner, *Dead Giveaway,* Abril Video, 1995.

Public relations guy, *Destination Vegas,* New Concorde, 1995.

Michael, *Killing for Love,* Vital Exchanges, 1995.

Charles Walters, *Smooth Operator* (also known as *Forbidden Games 2*), 1995.

Mr. Snazowski, *You Snooze You Lose,* I.Q. Entertainment, 1995.

Bob Gordon, *Attack of the 60 Foot Centerfolds,* New Horizons Home Video, 1995.

Richard Jordan, *Victim of Desire* (also known as *Implicated*), Concorde–New Horizons, 1995.

Marty Walters, *My Uncle the Alien,* PM Entertainment, 1996.

Dr. Condon, *Sorceress II: The Temptress* (also known as *Legion of Evil: Sorceress II* and *Sorceress 2*), New Horizons Home Video, 1996.

Commissioner, *Vice Academy 5,* Cinequanon Pictures International, 1996.

Hawkins, *Demolition High,* Astra Cinema/New City Releasing, 1996.

Tommy Stompanato, *Fugitive Rage* (also known as *Caged Fear*), A–Pix Entertainment/Royal Oaks Entertainment, 1996.

Ronnie, *Gator King,* 1997.

Commissioner, *Vice Academy Part 6,* A Plus Entertainment, 1999.

(As John Henry) Lieutenant Cannon, *Reasonable Doubt* (also known as *The Baptist* and *Crime Scene*), American World Pictures, 2001.

Mr. Slider, *Thy Neighbor's Wife* (also known as *Poison*), New City Releasing, 2001.

Thornton, *Passion Crimes* (also known as *Every Woman Has a Secret*), After Dark Pictures/New City Releasing, 2001.

Ted Nightingale, *13 Erotic Ghosts,* Retromedia Entertainment, 2002.

Mayor Carl Baxter, *Deadly Stingers,* Twentieth Century–Fox, 2003.

Cruise ship captain, *Lost Treasure,* Blockbuster Video, 2003.

H. G., *Treasure Hunt,* New Concorde, 2003.

Hugh Janus, *Final Examination,* Artisan Entertainment, 2003.

Captain Sam, *Bikini Airways,* Retromedia Entertainment, 20023.

Dean Grundy, *The Bikini Escort Company* (also known as *The Erotic Escort Company*), American Independent Productions/Krazy Karwash Kompany, 2004.

Dr. Matthews, *Teenage Cavegirl,* Retromedia Entertainment, 2004.

Dr. R. J. Reynolds, *Genie in a String Bikini* (also known as *The Erotic Dreams of Jeannie*), Retromedia Entertainment, 2004.

Richard Daninsky, *Tomb of the Werewolf,* Alliance Atlantis Video, 2004.

Narrator, *Bikini a Go Go* (also known as *Curse of the Erotic Tiki*), American Independent Productions/ Retromedia Entertainment, 2004.

Warden Kendrick, *Bikini Chain Gang,* Image Entertainment, 2005.

Danny, *Sunland Heat* (also known as *Dragoness*), Artist View Entertainment, 2005.

Dr. Richards, *The Witches of Breastwick,* All Channel Films Distribution, 2005.

Warden Kendrick, *Bikini Round–up,* Image Entertainment, 2005.

Film Work:

Associate producer, *Teenage Exorcist,* Action International Pictures, 1994.

Television Appearances; Movies:

Officer Minion, *Out of Time,* NBC, 1988.

Tom Peck, *Mob Boss,* syndicated, 1990.

Mr. Jennings, *Dreamrider,* Showtime, 1993.

Professor Lamar, *Witch Academy* (also known as *Little Devils*), USA Network, 1995.

John, *The Wasp Woman* (also known as *Forbidden Beauty* and *Roger Corman Presents "The Wasp Woman"*), Showtime, 1995.

Professor Steadman, *Visions,* syndicated, 1996.

Captain Hightower, *Maximum Revenge* (also known as *Maximum Security*), HBO, 1997.

Derek, *Little Cobras: Operation Dalmatian* (also known as *Dalmatian Fever*), HBO, 1997.

General Gardner, *Storm Trooper,* Showtime, 1998.

Detective Beddinger, *Monkey Business,* Showtime, 2000.

Foster, *The Curse of the Komodo,* Sci–Fi Channel, 2004.

Dr. Trent, *A.I. Assault* (also known as *Shockwave*), Sci–Fi Channel, 2006.

Television Appearances; Episodic:

Gordon Williams, "Highest Bidder," *Hot Line,* 1994.

Simon, "Freudian Slip," *Love Street,* Showtime, 1995.

Jerry, "Finders Keepers," *Erotic Confessions,* HBO, 1996.

Television Appearances; Other:

Armand Kabakian, *Irresistible Impulse,* 1996.

Sam, *General Hospital* (series), ABC, 1998.

The Day the Music Died (special), VH1, 1999.
Detective Trout, *Haunting Desires,* 2004.
Detective Blake, *Lust Connection,* 2005.
Dr. William Richardson, *Komodo vs. Cobra* (also known as *Komodo vs. King Cobra* and *KVC: Komodo vs. Cobra*), 2005.

RECORDINGS

Video Game:
Voice of Jay Jacobson, *Voyeur,* Philips Interactive Media of America, 1993.

ROBERTS, Emma 1991–

PERSONAL

Full name, Emma Rose Roberts; born February 10, 1991, in Rhinebeck, NY; daughter of Eric Roberts (an actor) and Kelly Cunningham (a producer); niece of Julia Roberts (an actress).

Addresses: *Manager*—Sweeney Management, 8755 Lookout Mountain Ave., Los Angeles, CA 90046.

Career: Actress.

Awards, Honors: Young Artist Award nomination, best performance in a television series (comedy or drama)—leading young actress, Teen Choice Award nomination, choice television breakout performance—female, 2005, Young Artist Award nomination (with others), outstanding young performers in a television series, 2005, 2006, Blimp Award nomination, favorite television actress, Kids' Choice Awards, 2007, all for *Unfabulous;* ShoWest Award, female star of tomorrow, ShoWest Convention, 2007.

CREDITS

Film Appearances:
Delilah, *BigLove* (short), Apollo Cinema, 2001.
Young Kristina Jung, *Blow,* New Line Cinema, 2001.
Sister, *Grand Champion,* American Family Movies, 2002.
Amelia, *Spymate,* Miramax, 2006.
Claire, *Aquamarine,* Twentieth Century–Fox, 2006.
Title role, *Nancy Drew,* Warner Bros., 2007.

Television Appearances; Series:
Addie Singer, *Unfabulous,* Nickelodeon, 2004–2007.

Television Appearances; Specials:
The Teen Choice Awards 2005, Fox, 2005.
Nickelodeon Kids' Choice Awards '06, Nickelodeon, 2006.
Nickelodeon Kids' Choice Awards '07 (also known as *Nickelodeon's 20th Annual Kids' Choice Awards*), Nickelodeon, 2007.
Presenter, *The 42nd Annual Academy of Country Music Awards,* CBS, 2007.

Television Appearances; Episodic:
Addie, "Honor Council," *Drake & Josh,* Nickelodeon, 2004.
Late Show with David Letterman (also known as *The Late Show*), CBS, 2004.
Ellen: The Ellen DeGeneres Show, syndicated, 2005.
Live with Regis and Kelly, syndicated, 2005, 2007.
Entertainment Tonight (also known as *E.T.*), syndicated, 2007.

RECORDINGS

Albums:
Unfabulous and More: Emma Roberts, Columbia, 2005.

OTHER SOURCES

Periodicals:
USA Today, January 6, 2005.

Electronic:
Emma Roberts Website, http://www.EmmaRoberts.net, July 25, 2007.

ROBERTS, Jeremy 1954–
  (Jerry Roberts)

PERSONAL

Born 1954, in Birmingham, AL; married Cerlette Lamme (a professional ice skater), October 10, 1995; children: one daughter.

Addresses: *Agent*—The Gage Group, 14724 Ventura Blvd., Suite 505, Sherman Oaks, CA 91403.

Career: Actor. American Conservatory Theater, former member of touring company. Appeared in advertisements. Held various jobs, including working as a truck driver, waiter, bartender, and in a restaurant. *Military service:* U.S. Marine Corps; served in Vietnam.

CREDITS

Film Appearances:

First SWAT police officer, *Christmas Vacation* (also known as *National Lampoon's "Christmas Vacation," National Lampoon's "Winter Holiday," Ett paeron till farsa firar jul, Fars fede juleferie, Hilfe, es weihnachtet sehr, Hjelp, vi maa paa juleferie, Joulupuu on kaervennetty, Karacsonyi vakacio, Le sapin a les boules, Que parodia de Natal, Schoene Bescherung, Socorro! Ya es Navidad, S.O.S.! Ya es Navidad, Un natale esplosivo,* and *Witaj swiety Mikolaju*), Warner Bros., 1989.

Gus, *The Marrying Man* (also known as *Too Hot to Handle*), Buena Vista, 1991.

Lieutenant Dimitri Valtane, *Star Trek VI: The Undiscovered Country,* Paramount, 1991.

Truck driver, *Late for Dinner,* Sony Pictures Releasing, 1991.

Paul, *Jack and His Friends,* Arrow Releasing, 1992.

Second biker, *Sister Act,* Buena Vista, 1992.

Sonny, *Diggstown* (also known as *Midnight Sting*), Metro–Goldwyn–Mayer, 1992.

Spenser, *The People under the Stairs* (also known as *Wes Craven's "The People under the Stairs," As criaturas atras das paredes, Das Haus der Vergessenen, De mensen onder de trap, El sotano del miedo, Kellarivaekeae, La casa nera, La gente detras de las paredes, Le sous–sol de la peur, Ondskans hus,* and *Os prisioneiros da cave*), Universal, 1992.

Bobby the bouncer, *The Mask,* New Line Cinema, 1994.

Brad Skoog, *Stuart Saves His Family* (also known as *Como salvar sua familia, Rescate familiar, Sekopaeiden seurakunta, Stuart sauve sa famille,* and *Stuart Stupid—Eine Familie zum Kotzen*), Paramount, 1995.

Guard, *Money Train,* Columbia, 1995.

Lone Justice 2, Triboro Entertainment Group, 1995.

Charlie, *Quiet Days in Hollywood* (also known as *The Way We Are*), Overseas FilmGroup, 1997.

Detective Jerry Moore, *No Strings Attached* (also known as *The Last Obsession*), Redwood Communications, 1997.

Patrick, *Running Time,* 1997.

Hook, *Jungle Boy,* Jungle Boy Film Productions, 1998.

Tom Jones, *The Thirteenth Floor* (also known as *The 13th Floor, Abwaerts in die Zukunft, El piso 13, Etajul 13, Il tredicesimo piano, Le treizieme etage, Nivel 13, Nivell 13, O 13 andar, Passe virtuel, 13: e vaaningen, 13F,* and *13. kerros*), Columbia, 1999.

Bobby Victory, *The Mexican* (also known as *Mexican, A mexicana, A mexikoi, La mexicana, Le mexicain, Meksikaneren,* and *Mexican—Eine heisse Liebe*), DreamWorks, 2001.

Russell, *Windfall,* FWP Productions, 2001.

Second goon, *Wheelmen,* Stretch Pix, 2002.

Crazy Dave, *Herbie Fully Loaded* (also known as *Herbie, Herbie the Love Bug, Herbie fulltankad, Herbie fully loaded—Ein toller kaefer startet durch, Herbie—Il super maggiolino, Katsaridaki gia panta, La coccinelle revient, La coccinelle—Tout equipee,* and *Riemukupla—Tankki taeynnae*), Buena Vista, 2005.

Television Appearances; Miniseries:

Ed McCall, *False Arrest,* ABC, 1991.

Detective Jim Beck, *Knots Landing: Back to the Cul–de–Sac,* CBS, 1997.

Television Appearances; Movies:

Slick, *Peter Gunn,* ABC, 1989.

Garnsey, *Don't Touch My Daughter* (also known as *Nightmare*), NBC, 1991.

Scarface, *Black Out* (also known as *A.K.A.* and *Midnight Heat*), HBO, 1996.

Tanner, *Phoenix,* Sci–Fi Channel, 1997.

Heavy man, *Dangerous Waters* (also known as *Imminent Danger*), Fox, 1999.

Television Appearances; Specials:

"Black Pudding," *The Edge,* HBO, 1989.

Television Appearances; Episodic:

Doctor, "Just Desserts," *Three Up, Two Down,* BBC, 1985.

"Smoke Gets in Your Eyes," *Jake and the Fatman,* CBS, 1987.

Officer, "Full Marital Jacket," *L.A. Law,* NBC, 1988.

Carl Grant, "The Secret," *Paradise* (also known as *Guns of Paradise*), CBS, 1989.

Kidnapper, "Deadline," *Freddy's Nightmares* (also known as *Freddy's Nightmares: A Nightmare on Elm Street: The Series, Freddy, le cauchemar de vos nuits, Freddyn painajaiset, Las pesadillas de Freddy,* and *Les cauchemars de Freddy*), syndicated, 1989.

Man, "Losing Control," *Hard Time on Planet Earth,* CBS, 1989.

Sergeant Stokley, "Test of Wills," *Murder, She Wrote,* CBS, 1989.

"The Cleveland Indian," *Hardball,* NBC, 1989.

"Swallowed Alive," *21 Jump Street,* Fox, 1989.

Doug, "Friends or Lovers?," *Wings,* NBC, 1990.

Hugh Leyton, "The Informer: Parts 1 & 2," *Matlock,* NBC, 1990.

Police officer, "Whose Mid–Life Crisis Is It Anyway," *Doogie Howser, M.D.,* ABC, 1990.

"Goodbye: Parts 1 & 2," *Jake and the Fatman,* CBS, 1990.

Nichols, "Room Service," *Hunter,* NBC, 1991.

Chauffeur, "The Limo," *Seinfeld,* NBC, 1992.

Keefer, "Baths and Showers," *Knots Landing,* CBS, 1992.

Agent Kreton, "The President's Coming," *Bakersfield P.D.,* Fox, 1993.

Bill Swill, "Mail Order Brides," *The Adventures of Brisco County, Jr.* (also known as *Brisco County Jr.*), Fox, 1993.

Bill Swill, "No Man's Land," *The Adventures of Brisco County, Jr.* (also known as *Brisco County Jr.*), Fox, 1993.

Jake, "Billy," *Renegade,* USA Network and syndicated, 1993.

Jay, "Crime and Punishment," *Roseanne,* ABC, 1993.

John Dunhill, "Turpitude," *Picket Fences,* CBS, 1993.

Hugh Bell Borgers, *Ned Blessing: The Story of My Life and Times,* CBS, 1993.

"The Entertainer," *Space Rangers,* CBS, 1993.

"War and Peace," *Roseanne,* ABC, 1993.

Officer Friendly, "Sex Ed," *Weird Science,* USA Network, 1994.

"Rabbit Redux," *Renegade,* USA Network and syndicated, 1994.

Kenny, "An Uncle in the Business," *Renegade,* USA Network and syndicated, 1995.

(As Jerry Roberts) Meso'Clan, "Hippocratic Oath," *Star Trek: Deep Space Nine* (also known as *Deep Space Nine, DS9,* and *Star Trek: DS9*), syndicated, 1995.

Derkus "Derk" Petronicus, "Mercenary," *Hercules: The Legendary Journeys* (also known as *Hercules*), syndicated, 1996.

Inspector Michaels, "The ABC's of Murder," *Diagnosis Murder,* CBS, 1996.

Lieutenant Dimitri Valtane, "Flashback," *Star Trek: Voyager* (also known as *Voyager*), UPN, 1996.

Thersites, "A Fist Full of Dinars," *Xena: Warrior Princess* (also known as *Xena*), syndicated, 1996.

Hank Race (some sources cite Hank Davis), *Moloney,* CBS, c. 1996.

Efram Bartlett, "Keys," *The Pretender,* NBC, 1997.

Fenton Boggs, "Born under a Bad Sign," *Renegade,* USA Network and syndicated, 1997.

Harland Groves, "Cop in a Box," *Pacific Blue,* USA Network, 1997.

Harrison Peak, "Peak Experience," *Silk Stalkings,* USA Network, 1997.

Richard Alan Hance, "The Thin White Line," *Millennium,* Fox, 1997.

Tim Summers, "Episode 126," *Prisoner* (also known as *Caged Women, Prisoner: Cell Block H, Women behind Bars, Women in Prison, Kvinnofaengelset,* and *Kvinnofangelset*), Ten Network (Australia), 1997.

Tim Summers, "Episode 133," *Prisoner* (also known as *Caged Women, Prisoner: Cell Block H, Women behind Bars, Women in Prison, Kvinnofaengelset,* and *Kvinnofangelset*), Ten Network, 1997.

Whistler, "It's the Real Thing, Baby," *Pensacola: Wings of Gold,* syndicated, 1997.

Clyde, *Sunset Beach,* NBC, 1997 (multiple episodes).

"Fools Russian," *Brooklyn South,* CBS, 1997.

Beck, "California Reich," *Sliders,* Sci–Fi Channel, 1998.

Flint, "One Day out West," *The Magnificent Seven,* CBS, 1998.

Kakistos, "Faith, Hope & Trick," *Buffy the Vampire Slayer* (also known as *BtVS, Buffy,* and *Buffy the Vampire Slayer: The Series*), The WB, 1998.

Limousine driver, *Three,* The WB, 1998.

Aiden, "Paradise Found," *Xena: Warrior Princess* (also known as *Xena*), syndicated, 1999.

Benjamin Hanley, "To Serve and Protect," *Profiler,* NBC, 1999.

George Vincent, "Agua Mala," *The X–Files,* Fox, 1999.

Michael Mills, "Call of the Wild," *L.A. Heat,* TNT, 1999.

Nate Krill, "Captive Hearts," *Martial Law,* CBS, 1999.

Xersos, "Be Deviled," *Hercules: The Legendary Journeys* (also known as *Hercules*), syndicated, 1999.

Bartlett, "Ghosts from the Past," *The Pretender,* NBC, 2000.

Cal, "The Invitation," *Touched by an Angel,* CBS, 2000.

(Uncredited) Gibbs, "Ex Libris," *Charmed,* The WB, 2000.

Odell, "Three Lucky Ladies on the Line," *Any Day Now,* Lifetime, 2000.

Alan Neel, "An Early Frost," *The Practice,* ABC, 2001.

Alan Neel, "Payback," *The Practice,* ABC, 2001.

Alan Neel, "The Thin Line," *The Practice,* ABC, 2001.

Huiclov De Fehrn, "Flash to Bang," *The Invisible Man* (also known as *I–Man, El hombre, Invisible Man—Der Unsichtbare,* and *Naekymaetoen mies*), Sci–Fi Channel, 2001.

Huiclov De Fehrn, "Money for Nothing: Part 1," *The Invisible Man* (also known as *I–Man, El hombre, Invisible Man—Der Unsichtbare,* and *Naekymaetoen mies*), Sci–Fi Channel, 2001.

Larry, "Laughlin It Up," *Dead Last,* The WB and YTV (Canada), 2001.

Lieutenant Earl J. Rubidoux, "Live: From Death Row," *Seven Days* (also known as *7 Days* and *Seven Days: The Series*), UPN, 2001.

Officer Peters, "The West Texas Round–Up and Other Assorted Misdemeanors," *Going to California,* Showtime, 2002.

Earl Ambrose, "Daddy's Girl," *Dragnet* (also known as *L.A. Dragnet*), ABC, 2003.

Georgie, "Future Malcolm," *Malcolm in the Middle* (also known as *Fighting in Underpants*), Fox, 2003.

Mr. Arnz, "Crash and Burn," *CSI: Crime Scene Investigation* (also known as *C.S.I.*, *CSI: Las Vegas*, *CSI Weekends*, and *Les experts*), CBS, 2003.

Sam Carver, "Dead Woman Walking," *CSI: Miami*, CBS, 2003.

"Power Play," *For the People* (also known as *Para la gente*), Lifetime, 2003.

Dewey, "Mr. Monk Takes His Medicine," *Monk*, USA Network, 2004.

Mark Watt, "Marlon's Brando," *Blind Justice*, ABC, 2005.

"Luck Be a Lady," *Crossing Jordan* (also known as *Untitled Tim Kring Project*), NBC, 2005.

Mel Stoltz, "Spit & Eggs," *Veronica Mars*, The CW, 2006.

Twenty Good Years (also known as *20 Good Years*), NBC, 2006.

Mel Stoltz, "Postgame Mortem," *Veronica Mars*, The CW, 2007.

Appeared as Russell Washington, *Days of Our Lives* (also known as *Cruise of Deception: Days of Our Lives*, *Days*, *DOOL*, *Des jours et des vies*, *Horton–sagaen*, *I gode og onde dager*, *Los dias de nuestras vidas*, *Meres agapis*, *Paeivien viemaeae*, *Vaara baesta aar*, *Zeit der Sehnsucht*, and *Zile din viata noastra*), NBC; as Quinn, *Raven*, CBS; and as Duke, *The Unit*, CBS. Appeared in *Eighteen Wheels of Justice* (also known as *18 Wheels of Justice*, *Highway to Hell—18 Raeder aus Stahl*, *La loi du fugitif*, and *Oikeutta tien paeaell*), The National Network; and *Jack and Jill*, The WB. Appeared as Gary Slaton in "The Kids Are All Right?," an unaired episode of *To Have & to Hold*, CBS.

Television Appearances; Pilots:

Second police officer, *Doogie Howser, M.D.*, ABC, 1989.

Huiclov De Fehrn, *The Invisible Man* (also known as *I–Man*, *El hombre*, *Invisible Man—Der Unsichtbare*, and *Naekymaetoen mies*), Sci–Fi Channel, 2000.

"The Good Guy" (also known as "Junkyard Dog"), *The Law and Mr. Lee* (also known as *The Henry Lee Project* and *The Law and Henry Lee*), CBS, c. 2003.

Major Tours:

Appeared in tours with the American Conservatory Theater.

RECORDINGS

Video Games:

Voice of Lieutenant Colonel John "Gash" Dekker, *Wing Commander IV: The Price of Freedom*, Electronic Arts, 1995.

Voice of Colonel John "Gash" Dekker, *Wing Commander: Prophecy* (also known as *Wing Commander V*), 1997.

Voice of Kakistos, *Buffy the Vampire Slayer: Chaos Bleeds*, Fox Interactive/Vivendi Universal Games, 2003.

OTHER SOURCES

Periodicals:
Cult Times, September, 1997, p. 11; July, 1999, p. 11.

Electronic:
JeremyRoberts.com, http://www.jeremyroberts.com, March 27, 2007.

ROBERTS, Tony Pearce
   See PIERCE–ROBERTS, Tony

ROBIE, Wendy 1953–
   (Wendie Robie)

PERSONAL

Born October 6, 1953, in Cincinnati, OH; children: Samantha. *Education:* Earned degree in English literature.

Career: Actress. Will & Company, associate art director. Also worked as an English teacher.

Awards, Honors: *After Dark* Award, outstanding body of work, 2005, for appearances with Next Theatre Company, Chicago, IL.

CREDITS

Film Appearances:
Woman and mom, *The People Under the Stairs* (also known as *Wes Craven's "The People Under the Stairs"*), Universal, 1991.

(Scenes deleted) Nadine Hurley, *Twin Peaks: Fire Walk with Me,* New Line Cinema, 1992.

Zealot at police station, *Vampire in Brooklyn* (also known as *Wes Craven's "Vampire in Brooklyn"*), Paramount, 1995.

Melanie Sardes, *The Glimmer Man,* Warner Bros., 1996.

Principal Joyce Saunders, *Devil in the Flesh* (also known as *Dearly Devoted*), Alliance Video, 1998.

Bernice, *The Dentist 2* (also known as *The Dentist 2: Brace Yourself*), Trimark Pictures, 1998.

Prince, *Romeo and Juliet,* 2000.

Dr. Thalama, *The Attic Expeditions* (also known as *Horror in the Attic*), DEJ Productions, 2001.

Ms. Tebbit, *Fairies* (short), 2003.

Television Appearances; Series:

Nadine Hurley, *Twin Peaks,* 1990–91.

Television Appearances; Movies:

Vonda White, *Prophet of Evil: The Ervil LeBaron Story,* CBS, 1993.

Dr. Horton, *A Place for Annie,* ABC, 1994.

Mary Burnett, *Lost Voyage,* 2001.

Television Appearances; Episodic:

June Reed, "Sandcastles," *Baywatch,* syndicated, 1991.

Mrs. Takin, "Trilogy: Part 2 (For Your Love)—June 14, 1966," *Quantum Leap,* NBC, 1992.

"The DaDa Effect," *Ultraman: The Ultimate Hero* (also known as *Ultraman Powered*), 1994.

Nurse, "Mind Games," *Viper,* NBC, 1994.

Ulani, "Destiny," *Star Trek: Deep Space Nine* (also known as *DS9, Deep Space Nine,* and *Star Trek: DS9*), syndicated, 1995.

Mrs. Cathcart, "Private School," *Sister, Sister,* The WB, 1995.

Kate Balfour, "Hostile Convergence," *Dark Skies,* NBC, 1996.

Harriet Davidson, "The Art of War," *C–16: FBI,* ABC, 1998.

(As Wendie Robie) Elaine, "Dog Day After New Year," *Party of Five,* Fox, 2000.

Trish, "The Toolshed Behind the Church," *Any Day Now,* Lifetime, 2000.

Nun, "Penance," *The Magnificent Seven,* CBS, 2000.

Stage Appearances:

Suzie, *Omnium Gatherum,* Next Theatre Company, Chicago, IL, 2004.

A Delicate Balance, 2004.

Lilith, *The Love Song of J. Robert Oppenheimer,* Next Theatre Company, 2005.

Woman, *The Long Christmas Ride Home,* Next Theatre Company, 2005.

Hecuba, 2006.

Radio Appearances:

Narrator, *In the Family,* 2005.

RECORDINGS

Video Games:

Insane patient, *Zork: Nemesis,* 1996.

ROBINSON, Zuleikha 1977–

PERSONAL

Born June 29, 1977, in London, England. *Education:* Graduated from the American Academy of Dramatic Arts.

Addresses: *Agent*—Finch and Partners, 4–8 Heddon St., London W1B 4BS United Kingdom; The Gersh Agency, 232 North Canon Dr., Beverly Hills, CA 90210. *Manager*—Artistry Entertainment, 525 Westbourne Dr., Los Angeles, CA 90048.

Career: Actress.

CREDITS

Film Appearances:

Lester Moore's assistant, *Timecode,* Screen Gems, 2000.

Suzie, *Slash,* First Look International, 2002.

Jazira, *Hidalgo* (also known as *Dash*), Buena Vista, 2004.

Jessica, *The Merchant of Venice* (also known as *Il mercante di Venezia* and *William Shakespeare's "The Merchant of Venice"*), Sony Pictures Classics, 2004.

Moushumi Mazumdar, *The Namesake,* Fox Searchlight, 2006.

Television Appearances; Series:

Yves Adele Harlow, *The Lone Gunmen,* Fox, 2001.

Eva Marquez, *New Amsterdam,* Fox, 2007.

Gaia, *Rome,* HBO, 2007.

Television Appearances; Pilots:

Eva Marquez, *New Amsterdam,* Fox, 2007.

Television Appearances; Episodic:

Yves Adele Harlow/Lois Runtz, "Jump the Shark," *The X–Files,* Fox, 2002.

RODGERS, R. E.
(Rick Rodgers, R E Rogers)

PERSONAL

Career: Actor. Appeared in public service announcements for Office of National Drug Policy, 2003.

CREDITS

Film Appearances:

(As Rick Rodgers) Nick, *School Ties,* Paramount, 1992.

Officer Sanchez, *Ed's Next Move,* Orion Classics, 1996.

Uniform cop, *The Thomas Crown Affair,* Metro–Goldwyn–Mayer, 1999.

David Paxton, *Little Man* (short), The Cinema Guild, 1999.

Delongpre, *Bad Boys II* (also known as *Good Cops: Bad Boys II*), Sony Pictures Entertainment, 2003.

Oldfield, *Live Free or Die,* THINKFilm, 2006.

Film Work:

Directed *JEER4; The Last Guy To Let You Down* (short).

Television Appearances; Series:

Scarface, *The Guiding Light* (also known as *Guiding Light*), 2001.

#9ZR492, *Oz,* HBO, 1998–2002.

Niko, *Jonny Zero,* Fox, 2005.

Television Appearances; Miniseries:

(As R E Rogers) Detective Ron Gosage, *Perfect Murder, Perfect Town: JonBenet and the City of Boulder,* 2000.

Television Appearances; Pilots:

Niko, *Jonny Zero,* Fox, 2005.

Television Appearances; Episodic:

Officer Oliver, "Navy Blues," *Law & Order,* NBC, 1997.

Darryl Kern, "Manhunt," *Law & Order: Special Victims Unit* (also known as *Law & Order: SVU* and *Special Victims Unit*), NBC, 2001.

Officer Zimny, "Last Rites," *The Jury,* NBC, 2004.

Officer Tommy Callahan, "Goliath," *Law & Order: Special Victims Unit* (also known as *Law & Order: SVU* and *Special Victims Unit*), NBC, 2005.

Mitchell Mackenzie, "Traffic," *Numb3rs* (also known as *Num3ers*), CBS, 2006.

Stage Appearances:

Edward, *Dedication or the Stuff of Dreams,* 59E59 Theatre, New York City, 2005.

Also appeared as junior, *Stonewall Jackson's House,* American Place Theatre, New York City.

ROSE, Gabrielle 1954–
(Gay Rose)

PERSONAL

Born 1954, in Canada; married Hrothgar Mathews (an actor).

Career: Actress. Also voice performer for commercials.

Awards, Honors: Genie Award nominations, best leading actress, Academy of Canadian Cinema and Television, 1988, for *Family Viewing,* and 1990, for *Speaking Parts;* National Board of Review Award (with others), best ensemble, and Genie Award nomination, best leading actress, both 1997, for *The Sweet Hereafter;* Gemini Award nomination, best guest actress in a dramatic series, Academy of Canadian Cinema and Television, 1998, for "Rita Brice," *Cold Squad;* Gemini Award nomination, best supporting actress in a dramatic program or miniseries, 1998, for *The Sleep Room;* two Gemini Award nominations, both best leading actress in a dramatic program or miniseries, 1999, for *Milgaard* and *Win, Again!;* Gemini Award nomination, best guest actress in a dramatic series, 2002, for "Dead Dog Rain: Part 1," *Tom Stone.*

CREDITS

Film Appearances:

Exercise matron, *The Journey of Natty Gann,* Buena Vista, 1985.

Dorothy Finnehard (some sources cite Dorothy Rinehart), *The Stepfather* (also known as *Stepfather I*), New Century Vista, 1987.

Sandra, *Family Viewing,* Cinephile, 1988.

Clara, *Speaking Parts,* Zeitgeist Films, 1990.

Connie, *Lighthouse* (also known as *Stranded*), Erin Features, 1991.

Mimi, *The Adjuster* (also known as *L'expert en sinistres*), Orion, 1992.

Lillian Severn, *The Portrait,* 1992.

Bobbie, *Kanada,* 1993.

Alex, *Valentine's Day,* 1994.

Off Key (short film), 1994.

Claire, *Sleeping with Strangers,* 1994.

Judge Marshall, *Timecop,* Universal, 1994.

Dolores Driscoll, *The Sweet Hereafter* (also known as *De beaux lendemains*), Fine Line, 1997.

Sister, *Altarpiece* (short film), Smash Arts, 1998.

Dr. D'Ambrosia, *Shrink* (short film), Hoodoo Films, 1998.

Helen's mother Joyce, *A Feeling Called Glory* (short film), 1999.

Georgia, *Double Jeopardy* (also known as *Doppelmord* and *Double condemnation*), Paramount, 1999.

Ruth Seraph, *The Five Senses,* Fine Line, 2000.

Covetousness, *Lift* (short film), 2000.

Nurse, *Legs Apart* (short film), Toronto International Film Festival, 2000.

Ellen Kanachowski, *The Rhino Brothers,* Rhino Brothers, 2001.

The Waiting Room, Inter–Muses Productions, 2001.

Mother, *Speak* (short film), Spacecake Productions, 2001.

Mrs. Fitz, *Go–Go Boy (Prelude)* (short film), 2000, 2002.

Beth Thompson, *Beauty Shot* (short film), Red Hall Productions, 2002.

Candace, *Casanova at Fifty* (short film), Canadian Broadcasting Corp., 2003.

Ida, *The Delicate Art of Parking,* Horizon Entertainment, 2003.

Wendy, *Eighteen,* TLA Releasing, 2005.

Publishing executive, *Where the Truth Lies,* ThinkFilm, 2005.

Cyd, *Missing in America,* First Look International, 2005.

Dr. Mercedes Kent, *Sisters,* Voltage Pictures, 2006.

Mrs. Wheeler, *Catch and Release,* Columbia, 2007.

Delinda, *In the Name of The King: A Dungeon Siege Tale,* Freestyle Releasing, 2007.

Helen, *Jeannie Learns to Cook* (short film), 2007.

Mrs. Locke, *Beneath,* Paramount, 2007.

Television Appearances; Series:

Jason's mother, *Northwood,* CBC, 1991.

Moorehead, a recurring role, *Dark Angel* (also known as *James Cameron's "Dark Angel"*), Fox, 2002.

Toni Mastroianni–Tan, a recurring role, *Robson Arms,* CTV, between 2005 and 2007.

Television Appearances; Miniseries:

June (some sources cite Jane) Graham, *Love and Hate: The Story of Colin and Joanne Thatcher* (also known as *Love and Hate: A Marriage Made in Hell*), NBC, 1989.

Nurse Stephens, *The Sleep Room* (also known as *Le pavillon de l'oubli*), Lifetime, 1998.

Dr. Harriet Penzler, *Taken* (also known as *Steven Spielberg Presents "Taken"*), Sci–Fi Channel, 2002.

Cappie, *The Atwood Stories,* 2003.

Television Appearances; Movies:

Assistant, *Secrets of a Married Man,* NBC, 1984.

Victim's friend, *Blackout,* HBO, 1985.

Julie Trenton, *Love, Mary,* CBS, 1985.

Sister Anne Elizabeth, *Devlin,* Showtime, 1992.

Anne, *Dieppe,* CBC, 1993.

Dodie, *Other Women's Children,* Lifetime, 1993.

Jackie Miller, *Whose Child Is This? The War for Baby Jessica,* ABC, 1993.

Sarah Berger, *While Justice Sleeps,* NBC, 1994.

Jeannie Locke, *My Mother's Ghost,* Fox Family Channel, 1996.

Joan, *Home Song* (also known as *LaVyrle Spencer's "Home Song"*), CBS, 1996.

Win, Again!, CBC, 1999.

Joyce Milgaard, *Milgaard* (also known as *Hard Time: The David Milgaard Story* and *Erreur judiciaire: l'histoire de David Milgaard*), Lifetime, 1999.

Mary Maculwain, *Trapped,* USA Network, 2001.

Dell Carter, *Hush,* Lifetime, 2005.

Rose, *Augusta, Gone,* Lifetime, 2006.

Kay, *Cleaverville,* Lifetime, 2007.

Television Appearances; Episodic:

(As Gay Rose) Brenda, "Things that Go Bump in the Night," *Rising Damp,* YTV, 1975.

Jayne Reynolds, "Fever of the Blood," *Street Legal,* CBC, 1987.

Mrs. Carol Rudkin, "John Doe," *Neon Rider,* syndicated, 1990.

Jesse's mother, "Straight Home," *Neon Rider,* syndicated, 1992.

Mrs. Frank, "Catcher," *Street Justice,* syndicated, 1992.

Dr. McNeely, "The Puck Stops Here," *The Commish,* ABC, 1992.

Linda Stone, "Hero," *The Commish,* ABC, 1993.

Anita Budahas, "Deep Throat," *The X–Files,* Fox, 1993.

Dr. Zenzola, "The Host," *The X–Files,* Fox, 1994.

Mrs. Winslow, "Family Passions," *Madison,* Global, 1994.

Mrs. Winslow, "Family Affairs," *Madison,* Global, 1995.

Christina Fox–Arturo, "Eggheads," *Sliders,* Fox, 1995.

Hester Tarbell, "Day of the Dead," *Lonesome Dove: The Outlaw Years,* syndicated, 1995.

Esther, "Town Without Pity," *Poltergeist: The Legacy,* Showtime, 1996.

Emily Watson, "Breaking Ground," *The Sentinel,* UPN, 1997.

Aging stripper, "Somehow, Satan Got Behind Me," *Millennium,* Fox, 1998.

Beverly Abbot, "Tess," *Cold Squad,* CTV, 1998.

Welcome Lady, "Saturn Dreaming of Mercury," *Millennium,* Fox, 1999.

Andrea Taffley, *Beggars and Choosers,* Showtime, 1999.

Mrs. Craven, "Intentions," *Mysterious Ways,* PAX, 2000.

Arleen Arkin, "Metamorphosis," *Smallville* (also known as *Smallville Beginnings* and *Smallville: Superman the Early Years*), The WB, 2001.

"The Last to Know," *Just Cause,* PAX, 2002.

Lenore MacDonald, "Dead Dog Rain: Parts 1 & 2," *Tom Stone* (also known as *Stone Undercover*), CBC, 2002.

Kathryn Wentworth, "A Town Without Pity," *Peacemakers,* USA Network, 2003.

Esther Stokes, "Cock of the Walk," *Cold Squad,* CTV, 2004.

Mother, "Rubadub Sub," *Young Blades,* Independent Television, 2005.

Mrs. Stampwell, "Coming Home," *The Dead Zone* (also known as *Stephen King's "Dead Zone"*), 2005.

Gayle, "Womyn's Weekend," *Alice, I Think,* CTV, 2006.

Mrs. King, "The Woman King," *Battlestar Galactica,* Sci–Fi Channel, 2007.

Appeared in *Dead Zone,* USA Network; as Mrs. Wilkins, *Killer Instinct,* Fox; as Carol, *The L Word,* Showtime.

Television Appearances; Other:

(As Gay Rose) Jan, *Machinegunner,* 1976.

(As Gay Rose) *She Loves Me* (special), BBC, 1978.

The Private Capital, 1989.

Colleen McIntyre, *Three Moons over Milford* (pilot), ABC Family Channel, 2006.

ROSE, Nectar

PERSONAL

Addresses: *Agent*—Joel King, Pakula/King and Associates, 9229 West Sunset Blvd., Suite 315, Los Angeles, CA 90069. *Manager*—David Sweeney, Sweeney Management, 8755 Lookout Mountain Ave., Los Angeles, CA 90046.

Career: Actress.

CREDITS

Film Appearances:

(Uncredited) Stripper, *Independence Day* (also known as *ID4*), Twentieth Century–Fox, 1996.

(Uncredited) Marilyn Monroe, *L.A. Confidential,* Warner Bros., 1997.

Nervous cheerleader, *Bring It On,* Universal, 2000.

Butter, *Stealing Roy* (short film), IFILM, 2001.

Freshman girl with David, *Legally Blonde,* Metro–Goldwyn–Mayer, 2001.

Sara Fratelli, *Not Another Teen Movie* (also known as *Sex Academy*), Columbia, 2001.

Jamie, *Extreme Dating,* Franchise Pictures, 2004.

Blonde in office, *50 First Dates,* Columbia, 2004.

Delia Rodgers, *The Hazing* (also known as *Dead Scared*), Lightning Entertainment, 2004.

Flirty girl, *Able Edwards,* Graphic Films, 2004.

Aubrey, *Pan Dulce,* 3rd Grade Teacher Productions, 2004.

(Uncredited) Stewardess, *A Lot Like Love,* Buena Vista, 2005.

Cyndi, *Tweek City,* Madacy Entertainment, 2005.

Paradise, *Bad News Bears,* Paramount, 2005.

Lenore, *Serenity,* Universal, 2005.

Shelly, *Bull Run,* FireRock Entertainment, 2006.

Eva, *Roman,* Echo Bridge Home Entertainment, 2006.

Karina, *The Iron Man,* Karim Movies, 2006.

Jackie, *Kush,* Auteur Entertainment, 2006.

Hooker, *The Brothers Solomon,* Screen Gems, 2007.

Television Appearances; Series:

Daphne Wallace, *Spyder Games,* MTV, 2001.

Television Appearances; Movies:

Diana, *The List,* ABC Family Channel, 2006.

Television Appearances; Episodic:

Danielle, "Trust Me or Don't Trust Me," *Off Centre,* The WB, 2001.

Kimberly, "I Can't Get No Satisfaction," *That '70s Show,* Fox, 2004.

Dottie, "The Sea Is a Harsh Mistress," *Two and a Half Men,* CBS, 2006.

RECORDINGS

Videos:

Interviews with Roman People, Echo Bridge Home Entertainment, 2007.

ROSEWOOD, Olivia

PERSONAL

Addresses: *Agent*—Julia Buchwald, Don Buchwald and Associates, 6500 Wilshire Blvd., Suite 2200, Los Angeles, CA 90048.

Career: Actress, producer, director, and writer.

CREDITS

Film Appearances:
Toy piano fan, *Colin Fitz* (also known as *Colin Fitz Lives!*), Baby Shark/River One Films, 1997.
Stacy/Fawn, *Where's Marlowe?*, Paramount, 1999.
Self Storage, Zero Pictures, 1999.
Beth from Denver, *Almost Famous,* DreamWorks, 2000.
Margaret, *Dirt* (also known as *Dumber than Dirt*), MAC Releasing, 2001.
Dana, *Orange County,* Paramount, 2002.
Tami, *A Midsummer Night's Rave,* Velocity Home Entertainment, 2002.
Bob and Rob's assistant, *Hiding in Walls,* Out of Pocket Films, 2002.
Mary, *The Pick Up* (short film), CineMagic Productions, 2003.
Fight Ballet (short film), 2005.
Granola girl, *Break a Leg,* MTI Home Video, 2006.

Film Work:
Director, *The Pick Up* (short film), CineMagic Productions, 2003.
Executive producer and director, *Fight Ballet* (short film), 2005.

Television Appearances; Movies:
Alicia, *In Quiet Night* (also known as *You Belong to Me Forever*), Lifetime, 1998.

Television Appearances; Specials:
"G Force," *Date Squad,* Cinemax, 2001.

Television Appearances; Episodic:
"Teacher's Pet," *Silk Stalkings,* USA Network, 1998.
Caroline Bell, "O Captain, My Captain," *L.A. Doctors* (also known as *L.A. Docs*), CBS, 1999.
Alison Carpenter, "Play with Fire," *CSI: Crime Scene Investigation* (also known as *C.S.I., CSI: Las Vegas, CSI Weekends,* and *Les experts*), CBS, 2003.

WRITINGS

Film Scripts:
The Pick Up (short film), CineMagic Productions, 2003.

RYDER, Lisa 1970–

PERSONAL

Born October 26, 1970, in Edmonton, Alberta, Canada. *Education:* University of Toronto, degree, theatre; studied ballet at Edmonton School of Ballet, jazz dance at Metro Movement, Toronto, Ontario, and improvisation at Second City. *Avocational Interests:* Bicycling, fitness workouts.

Addresses: *Agent*—Lucas Talent, Sun Tower 100 West Pender St., 7th Floor, Vancouver V6B 1R8 Canada.

Career: Actress. Bald Ego Productions (theatre company), cofounder and co–artistic director; Equity Showcase Theatre, member of board of directors. Appeared on posters for KISS–FM (Toronto, Ontario, Canada), 1997.

Awards, Honors: Gemini Award nomination, best performance by an actress in a feature supporting role in a dramatis series, Academy of Canadian Cinema and Television, 2001, for *Andromeda.*

CREDITS

Film Appearances:
Kim, *City of Dark,* 1997.
Halley, *Strands* (short), 1997.
Joey, *Stolen Heart* (also known as *North of Fargo*), Norstar Entertainment, 1998.
Kay–Em 14, *Jason X* (also known as *Friday the 13th Part 10*), New Line Cinema, 2001.
Herself and Kay–Em 14, *By Any Means Necessary: The Making of "Jason X"* (documentary), New Line Home Video, 2002.
Estelle Freisen, *Lemon* (short), 2004.

Also appeared in *Das Hammr.*

Television Appearances; Series:
Detective Tracy Vetter, *Forever Knight,* syndicated, 1995, USA Network and syndicated, 1995–96.
Beka Valentine, *Andromeda* (also known as *Gene Roddenberry's "Andromeda"*), NBC, 2000–2005.

Television Appearances; Movies:
Sam, *Blackheart,* 1999.
Shelby, *Secret Lives,* Lifetime, 2005.

Television Appearances; Episodic:
Alana, "Magic Trick," *Kung Fu: The Legend Continues,* 1994.
Angela Mosler, "Beyond the Law," *Forever Knight,* syndicated, 1994.
Kris, "The Walking Shoe Incident," *The Newsroom,* CBC, 1996.
Mary Callwood, "Devolution," *Psi Factor: Chronicles of the Paranormal,* syndicated, 1997.

Kate Boone, "Decision," *Earth: Final Conflict* (also known as *EFC, Gene Roddenberry's "Earth: Final Conflict," Invasion planete Terre,* and *Mission Erde: Sie sind unter uns*), syndicated, 1997.

Kate Boone, "Truth," *Earth: Final Conflict* (also known as *EFC, Gene Roddenberry's "Earth: Final Conflict," Invasion planete Terre,* and *Mission Erde: Sie sind unter uns*), syndicated, 1997.

Janie Bain, "The Case of the Real Fake," *The Adventures of Shirley Holmes,* YTV, 1998.

Dr. Grace, "Brightness Falls," *Total Recall 2070* (also known as *Total Recall: The Series*), 1999.

Jane Easterbrook, "The Spanish Prisoner," *Wind at My Back,* CBC, 2001.

Jane Easterbrook, "Secrets and Lies," *Wind at My Back,* CBC, 2001.

Also appeared as Kris, "Deeper, Deeper," *The Newsroom,* CBC; Kris, "The Kevorkian Joke," *The Newsroom,* CBC; Kris, "Petty Tyranny," *The Newsroom,* CBC; Lady Macbeth, *Virtual Classroom: Shakespeare;* in *Movie Television,* CTV.

Stage Appearances:
Sexy woman, *Cafe Naked,* Bald Ego Productions, University of Toronto, Toronto, Ontario, Canada, 1993.

Vic, *Panting of the Victors,* Bald Ego Productions, 1994.

Joyce, *Possible Worlds,* Bald Ego Productions, 1997.

Maria, *The Paradise,* Bald Ego Productions, 1997.

Maureen, *Put Me Away* (solo show), Bald Ego Productions, 1998.

Also appeared as Mirror, *And He Lost His Head,* Bald Ego Productions, University of Toronto, Toronto, Ontario, Canada; Lucille Dupuis, *Baggage;* Geraldine, *The City Wears a Slouch Hat,* Bald Ego Productions; Priscilla Lamprey, *Crater;* Trotsky, *Exilum;* the prophet, *Gulf;* as Marilyn Monroe, *Insignificance;* Kate, *Insomnia;* Ricky, *Kyotopolis;* Macduff, *Macbeth;* Eurydice, *Orpheus;* Sammi, *Proposals;* Sieglinde, *Slay Me;* "Ph. D.," *Threepenny Epic Cabaret,* Bald Ego Productions; Phoefe, *Trembling Tongues,* Toronto Fringe Festival, Toronto, Ontario, Canada; Recklesshead, *Wisdom;* second woman, *The Witnesses;* in *Sleepers Awake!,* Theatre Centre East; *Touch.*

Stage Choreographer:
Cafe Naked, Bald Ego Productions, University of Toronto, Toronto, Ontario, Canada, 1993.

Panting of the Victors, Bald Ego Production, 1994.

Put Me Away (solo show), Bald Ego Productions, 1998.

WRITINGS

Stage:
Coauthor, *Cafe Naked,* Bald Ego Productions, University of Toronto, Toronto, Ontario, Canada, 1993.

Coauthor, *Panting of the Victors,* Bald Ego Productions, 1994.

Coauthor, *The Paradise,* Bald Ego Productions, 1997.

Coauthor, *Put Me Away* (solo show), Bald Ego Productions, 1998.

Also author of *Baggage.*

S

ST. JAMES, Jean
(Jean Flieger, Jean Pflieger)

PERSONAL

Children: Martin Starr (an actor).

Career: Actress.

CREDITS

Film Appearances:

Female customer, *Wishmaster* (also known as *Wes Craven's "Wishmaster"*), Live Entertainment/Live Film & Mediaworks, 1997.

Waitress in San Diego, *The Big Empty,* Asylum, 1997.

Dede, *Broken and Bleeding,* Nostromo Entertainment, 1998.

Hospital nurse, *Motel Blue,* MTI Home Video, 1999.

Susan Harold, *Demon Under Glass,* BCI Eclipse, 2002.

Isabel, *Seventy–Seven Below* (short film), 2004.

Waitress, *D.E.B.S.,* Samuel Goldwyn Films, 2005.

Mom, *Art School Confidential,* Sony Pictures Classics, 2006.

Julie Sparks, *George Bush Goes to Heaven,* Hermosa Beach Filmworks, 2006.

Cassandra, *The Professor's Daughter* (short film), University of Southern California, 2007.

Repo, Revel Entertainment, 2007.

Jenny, *One Long Night,* American World Pictures, 2007.

Aunt Rebecca, *Privileged,* Glass House Productions, 2007.

Film Appearances as Jean Pflieger:

Job interviewer, *Cocktail,* Buena Vista, 1988.

Lori, *Nightmare at Noon* (also known as *Death Street*), Omega Entertainment, 1988.

Second secretary, *Warm Summer Rain,* 1989.

Psychiatric patient, *Death Becomes Her,* Universal, 1992.

(Credited as Jean Flieger) Linda, *Last Dance,* Rocky Point Productions, 1992.

Ms. Buchanan, *Class of 1999 II: The Substitute,* Vidmark Entertainment, 1994.

Jeweler, *Ice,* PM Entertainment Group, 1994.

Selby's neighbor, *Serial Killer,* Starlight, 1995.

Me and the King, Comment Films, 1995.

Mother, *Lion Strike* (also known as *Ring of Fire 3: Lion Strike*), PM Entertainment Group, 1995.

Client's wife, *Safe,* Sony Pictures Classics, 1995.

Ms. McCoy, *Eight Days a Week,* 1997, Legacy Releasing, 1999.

Television Appearances; Movies:

(As Jean Pflieger) Hotel manager, *Ray Alexander: A Taste for Justice,* NBC, 1994.

Sheila, *Babylon 5: The River of Souls* (also known as *The River of Souls*), TNT, 1998.

(Uncredited) Sally, *Mystery Woman,* Hallmark Channel, 2003.

Helga Hauptfuhrer, *Mini's First Time,* HBO, 2006.

Television Appearances; Episodic:

Melissa's mother, "Don't Be a Stranger," *Against the Grain,* NBC, 1993.

Mom, "Paul Is Dead," *Mad About You,* NBC, 1994.

Mrs. Wurtz, "Backstage Pass," *Saved by the Bell: The New Class,* NBC, 1996.

Waitress, "Big Angry Virgin from Outer Space," *3rd Rock from the Sun* (also known as *Life as We Know It* and *3rd Rock*), NBC, 1996.

Mrs. Rudisill, *Moloney,* CBS, 1996.

Mother, "The Touching Game," *Mad About You,* NBC, 1997.

"The Apparition," *Beyond Belief: Fact or Fiction* (also known as *Beyond Belief*), Fox, 1997.

Foreperson of Malzone jury, "The Blessing," *The Practice,* ABC, 1997.

Dance instructor, "A Swing and a Mrs.," *Melrose Place,* Fox, 1998.

Helen Rickman, "Once in a Blue Moon," *The Pretender,* NBC, 1998.

Mrs. Parrish, "Last Tango in Hartford," *Judging Amy,* CBS, 1999.

Taffy Hubbard, "Scorpio Rising," *Martial Law,* CBS, 2000.

Hilda, "The One with Rachel's Assistant," *Friends,* NBC, 2000.

Irate mother, "Kill Me Now," *Gilmore Girls* (also known as *Gilmore Girls: Beginnings*), The WB, 2000.

Second mom, "Presenting Lorelai Gilmore," *Gilmore Girls* (also known as *Gilmore Girls: Beginnings*), The WB, 2001.

Airport ticket agent, *Passions* (also known as *Harmony's Passions* and *Passions Storm*), NBC, 2001.

Natalie Clarkson, "Awakenings," *The Practice,* ABC, 2001.

Saleslady, "It's a Wonderful Life," *Three Sisters,* NBC, 2001.

Nurse, "Diagnosis Val," *V.I.P.* (also known as *V.I.P.—Die Bodyguards*), syndicated, 2002.

Laughing Beverly Hills shopper, "Nick Takes Over the Rodeo," *The Nick Cannon Show,* Nickelodeon, 2002.

April, "Brave New World," *The Division* (also known as *Heart of the City*), Lifetime, 2002.

Female lawyer, "Soul Survivor," *Charmed,* The WB, 2003.

Cancer patient, "Endorsement," *Skin,* Fox, 2003.

Mrs. Harris, "Forbidden Fruit," *Run of the House,* The WB, 2003.

Cecile, "Sex Kills," *House, M.D.* (also known as *House*), Fox, 2006.

Claire Henderson, "Psychodrama," *Criminal Minds,* CBS, 2006.

Betty, "Giving Up the Ghost," *Ghost Whisperer,* CBS, 2006.

Middle–aged woman, "I'd Rather Be in Philadelphia," *Gilmore Girls* (also known as *Gilmore Girls: Beginnings*), CW Network, 2007.

Appeared as saleslady, *Dark Angel,* Fox; and as an older woman, *Weeds,* Showtime.

Television Appearances as Jean Pflieger; Episodic:

Personal secretary, "The 21–Inch Sun," *Amazing Stories* (also known as *Steven Spielberg's "Amazing Stories"*), NBC, 1987.

Wedding guest, "Something Borrowed, Someone Blue," *Murder, She Wrote,* CBS, 1989.

"A Death in the Family," *Hardball,* NBC, 1990.

Mary Connors, "The Reporter," *Hunter,* NBC, 1991.

Jury foreperson, "Truth and Consequences," *Gabriel's Fire,* ABC, 1991.

Customer, "Frank & Son," *Step by Step,* ABC, 1991.

"Salmonella Is Coming to Town," *Anything but Love,* ABC, 1991.

"Marty Walks," *Anything but Love,* ABC, 1992.

Beth, "Burned," *Melrose Place,* Fox, 1992.

Beverly, *New York Daze,* Fox, 1995.

Television Appearances; Other:

Mrs. Williams, *General Hospital* (series), ABC, 1993.

Maria Covington, *Felicity* (pilot), The WB, 1998.

SANDE, Theo Van de
  See van de SANDE, Theo

SAROSSY, Paul 1963–

PERSONAL

Born April 24, 1963, in Barrie, Ontario, Canada; married Geraldine O'Rawe (an actress); children: one. *Education:* York University, B.F.A., film, 1986.

Addresses: *Agent*—KM Reps, Inc., 29 Fraser Ave., Suite 4, Toronto, Ontario M6K 1Y7 Canada; Skouras Agency, 1149 Third St., 3rd Floor, Santa Monica, CA 90403.

Career: Cinematographer.

Member: Canadian Society of Cinematographers, British Society of Cinematographers.

Awards, Honors: Genie Award, best achievement in cinematography, Academy of Canadian Cinema and Television, 1994, for *Exotica;* American Society of Cinematographers Award nomination, outstanding achievement in cinematography in miniseries, 1996, for *Picture Windows;* Genie Award, best achievement in cinematography, 1997, Golden Slate Award, Csapnivalo Awards, 2000, both for *The Sweet Hereafter;* Best Director of Photography, Valladolid International Film Festival, 1997, for *Affliction* and *The Sweet Hereafter;* Independent Spirit Award nomination, best cinematography, Independent Features Project, 1999, for *Affliction;* Canadian Society of Cinematographers Award, best cinematography in a television drama, 1999, for *Rocky Marciano;* Best Director of Photography, Valladolid International Film Festival, 1999, Genie Award, best achievement in cinematography, Canadian Society of Cinematographers Award nomination, best cinematography in a theatrical feature, 2000, all for *Felicia's*

Journey; Jury Prize, Raindance Film Festival, British feature, "New Blood" Award, Cognac festival du Film Policier, Maverick Spirit Award, Cinequest San Jose Film Festival, Douglas Hickox Award nomination, British Independent Films, 2002, all for *Mr. In–Between;* Genie Award nomination, best achievement in cinematography, 2003, for *Perfect Pie;* Kodak New Century Award, Canadian Society of Cinematographers, 2004; Genie Award, best achievement in cinematography, Canadian Society of Cinematographers Award, best cinematography in a theatrical feature, 2005, both for *Head in the Clouds;* Gemini Award nomination, best photography in a comedy, variety or performing arts program or series, Academy of Canadian Cinema and Television, 2006, for *Black Widow;* Canadian Society of Cinematographers Award, best cinematography in a theatrical feature, 2007, for *The Wicker Man.*

CREDITS

Film Cinematographer:
Speaking Parts, Manuel Salvador, 1989.
White Room, 1990.
Terminal City Ricochet, Festival Films, 1990.
Revenge of the Radioactive Reporter, Astral Films, 1990.
Montreal vu par ... (also known as *Montreal Sextet* and *Six variations sur un theme*), 1991.
Masala, Strand Releasing, 1991.
The Adjuster (also known as *L'expert en sinistres*), Orion Classics, 1991.
Giant Steps, 1992.
Ordinary Magic, 1993.
Love & Human Remains (also known as *Armour et restes humains*), Sony Pictures Classics, 1993.
Satie and Suzanne, Rhombus International, 1994.
Exotica, Miramax, 1994.
(Stories from) The Land of Cain (short), 1995.
Blood & Donuts, Live Entertainment, 1995.
Mariette in Ecstasy, 1996.
Lulu, Alliance, 1996.
Picture Perfect, Twentieth Century–Fox, 1997.
The Sweet Hereafter (also known as *De beaux lendemains*), Fine Line Features, 1997.
Affliction, Lions Gate Films, 1997.
Jerry and Tom, Lions Gate Films, 1998.
Pete's Meteor, First Look Ventures, 1998.
Felicia's Journey (also known as *Le voyage de Felicia*), Artisan Entertainment, 1999.
The Line (short), 2000.
(Second unit) *X–Men* (also known as *X–Men 1.5*), Twentieth Century–Fox, 2000.
Lakeboat, Cowboy Book International, 2000.
Duets, Buena Vista, 2000.
On the Nose, Capitol Films, 2001.
Ararat, Miramax, 2002.
Paid in Full, Dimension Films, 2002.

Perfect Pie (also known as *La voie du destin*), Odeon Films, 2002.
The Snow Walker, First Look International, 2003.
Head in the Clouds (also known as *Juegos de mujer*), Sony Pictures Classics, 2004.
Where the Truth Lies, THINKFilm, 2005.
The River King, Myriad Pictures, 2005.
Black Widow, Rhombus International, 2005.
Ripley Under Ground, Fox Searchlight, 2005.
The Wicker Man, Warner Bros., 2006.
One Way, 2006.
Blaze, 2006.
Charlie Bartlett, Metro–Goldwyn–Mayer, 2007.
The Secret (also known as *Si j'etais toi*), 2007.
All Hat, Odeon Films, 2007.

Film Work:
Additional photographer, *Twist* (documentary), Triton Pictures, 1992.
Associate producer, *Lakeboat,* 2000.
Director, *Mr. In–Between* (also known as *The Killing Kind*), Verve Pictures, 2001.

Film Appearances:
Himself, *The Making of "Ararat"* (documentary short), Miramax, 2003.

Television Cinematographer; Movies:
Grand Larceny, CBC, 1991.
The Facts Behind the Helsinki Roccomatios, 1994.
Mistrial, HBO, 1996.
A Portrait of Arshile, 1996.
Rocky Marciano, Showtime, 1999.
Jerry & Torn, Showtime, 1999.
Rated X, Showtime, 2000.
Krapp's Last Tape, Channel 4, 2000.
No Night is Too Long, BBC, 2002.
The Man Who Saved Christmas, CBS, 2002.
Soldier's Girl, Showtime, 2003.
Martha, Inc.: The Story of Martha Stewart (also known as *Driven to Succeed*), NBC, 2003.
The Incredible Mrs. Ritchie (also known as *L'incroyable Mme Richie*), Showtime, 2003.
The Survivors Club, CBS, 2004.
Eight Days to Live, CTV, 2006.

Television Cinematographer; Pilots:
Dark Eyes, ABC, 1995.

Television Cinematographer; Specials:
Krapp's Last Tape, PBS, 2001.

Television Cinematographer; Episodic:
"Soir Blue," *Picture Windows* (also known as *Picture Windows: Language of the Heart*), Showtime, 1994.

SAVIDES, Harris 1957–

PERSONAL

Born September 28, 1957, in New York, NY. *Education:* School of Visual Arts, degree in film and still photography.

Addresses: *Agent*—The Skouras Agency, 1149 Third St., 3rd Floor, Santa Monica, CA 90403.

Career: Cinematographer. Began career as fashion photographer; also worked as a cinematographer on television commercials.

Member: American Society of Cinematographers.

Awards, Honors: MTV Video Music Award, best music video cinematography, 1993, for Madonna's "Rain"; MTV Video Music Award, best music video cinematography, 1994, for REM's "Love Hurts"; MTV Video Music Award, 1998, for Fiona Apple's "Criminal"; Music Video Production Association Award nomination, 2001, for Macy Gray's "I Try"; New York Film Critics Circle Award, best cinematographer, 2003, for both *Elephant* and *Gerry;* Independent Spirit Award nomination, best cinematography, Independent Features Project, 2003, for *Gerry;* Independent Spirit Award nomination, best cinematography, 2004, for *Elephant;* MTV Video Music Award nomination, 2005, for Coldplay's "Speed of Sound"; Independent Spirit Award nomination, best cinematography, 2006, for *Last Days.*

CREDITS

Film Cinematographer:
Heaven's Prisoners, New Line Cinema, 1996.
The Game, PolyGram, 1997.
Illuminata, Artisan Entertainment, 1998.
The Yards, Miramax, 2000.
Finding Forrester, Columbia, 2000.
The Follow (short; also known as *The Hire: The Follow*), BMW Films, 2001.
Gerry, Miramax, 2002.
Elephant, HBO Films, 2003.
Birth, Fine Line Features, 2004.
Last Days, 2005.
Zodiac, Paramount, 2007.
Margot at the Wedding, Paramount, 2007.
American Gangster, Universal, 2007.

Film Work; Other:
Additional photographer, *Se7en,* New Line Cinema, 1995.

Additional cinematographer, *Chop Suey* (documentary), Zeitgeist Films, 2001.

Film Appearances:
911 operator, *Se7en,* New Line Cinema, 1995.
Ankles, *The Game,* PolyGram, 1997.
Himself, *The Work of Director Jonathan Glazer* (documentary), Palm Pictures, 2005.

Television Cinematographer; Movies:
Lake Consequence, Showtime, 1993.

Television Cinematographer; Specials:
The Investigator, Showtime, 1994.
Robbie Robertson: Going Home, Disney Channel, 1995.

RECORDINGS

Music Videos (as Cinematographer):
Tom Waits' "Goin' Out West," 1992.
REM's "Love Hurts," 1993.
Madonna's "Rain," 1994.
Nine Inch Nail's "Closer," 1994.
Madonna's "Bedtime Story," 1995.
Michael Jackson's "Scream," 1995.
The Rolling Stones' "Like a Rolling Stone," 1995.
Fiona Apple's "Criminal," 1997.
"Scream," *Michael Jackson: HIStory on Film—Volume II,* Sony Music, 1997.
Sonic Youth's "Little Trouble Girl," 1999.
Macy Gray, "I Try," 1999.
"Rain," *Madonna; The Video Collection 93:99,* Warner Reprise Video, 1999.
Radiohead's "I Might Be Wrong," 2001.
"Like a Rolling Stone," *The Work of Director Michel Gondry,* Palm Pictures, 2003.
Coldplay's "Speed of Sound," 2004.
"Criminal," "Scream," "Bedtime Story," "Closer," and "Rain," *The Work of Director Mark Romanek,* Palm Pictures, 2005.

Exercise Videos (as cinematographer):
Cindy Crawford: The Next Challenge Workout, 1993.

SAVINI, Tom 1946–

PERSONAL

Born November 3, 1946, in Pittsburgh, PA; married Nancy Hare, 1984; children: Lia (an actress). *Education:* Attended Carnegie–Mellon University.

Career: Actor, special effects makeup artist, special effects supervisor, director, stunt performer, and stunt coordinator. Tom Savini Ltd. (special effects company), principal; Terrormania (haunted house attraction), Pittsburgh, PA, owner; Douglas School of Business, Monessen, PA, teacher of makeup special effects classes. Worked as a teenager in a traveling group that presented horror and magic shows at movie theatres; other work as a teenager included volunteer monster creator and makeup designer for a local television program called *Chiller Theatre*, Pittsburgh, PA; Optic Nerve Studios, Inc., special effects creator, 1994. *Military service:* Served as combat photographer in Vietnam.

Awards, Honors: Saturn Award nomination, best makeup, Academy of Science Fiction, Fantasy, and Horror Films, 1980, for *Dawn of the Dead;* Saturn Award, best makeup, 1986, for *Day of the Dead;* Lifetime Achievement Award, New York City Horror Film Festival, 2003.

CREDITS

Film Appearances:

Arthur, *Martin*, Libra Films International, 1979.

Blades, *Dawn of the Dead* (also known as *Dawn of the Living Dead, George A. Romero's "Dawn of the Dead," Zombie: Dawn of the Dead, Zombies, Zombies: Dawn of the Dear,* and *Zombi*), United Film Distribution, 1979.

Nicky, *Effects* (also known as *Death's Director* and *The Manipulator*), International Harmony, 1980.

Disco boy, *Maniac,* Analysis Film Releasing, 1980.

Morgan, *Knightriders* (also known as *George A. Romero's "Knightriders"*), United Film Distribution, 1981.

Second garbage man, *Creepshow* (also known as *Cuentos de ultratumba*), Warner Bros., 1982.

Himself, *Il mondo dell'orrore di Dario Argento* (documentary; also known as *Dario Argento's World of Horror*), Vidmark Entertainment, 1985.

Himself, *Document of the Dead,* 1985.

Spirit of Jack the Ripper, *The Ripper,* Liberty Home Video, 1986.

The creep, *Creepshow 2,* New World, 1987.

Himself, *Drive-in Madness!* (documentary; also known as *Screen Scaries*), Imagine Video, 1987.

(Uncredited) The monomaniac, "The Black Cat" segment, *Due occhi diabolici,* Taurus Entertainment, 1991.

Himself, *Dario Argento: Master of Horror* (documentary), Vidmark Entertainment, 1991.

News photographer, *Innocent Blood* (also known as *A French Vampire in America*), Warner Bros., 1992.

Lieutenant Ron Vargo, *Heartstopper* (also known as *Dark Craving*), 1993, Tempo Video, 1996.

Roland, *The Demolitionist,* Simitar Video, 1995.

Sex Machine, *From Dusk to Dawn,* Dimension Films, 1996.

Himself, *Halloween ... The Happy Haunting of America!* (documentary), Chuck Williams Productions/Whiz Bang Entertainment, 1997.

Deputy Hughs, *Children of the Living Dead,* Spartan Home Entertainment, 2001.

Eddie Rao, *Eyes Are Upon You* (also known as *Demon Lust*), 2001.

Uncle Joe, *The Monster Man,* 2001.

Rouge, *Web of Darkness,* Renegade Films/Savage Armadillo Productions, 2001.

Salt Lake City detective, *Ted Bundy* (also known as *Bundy*), First Look International, 2002.

Stranger, *Blood Bath,* 2002.

Jesus Christ, *Zombiegeddon,* Nickel Duck Productions/Wild Range Productions, 2003.

Kane, *Vicious,* MTI Home Video, 2003.

County sheriff, *Dawn of the Dead,* Universal, 2004.

The higher power, *The Absence of Light,* New Illusions Pictures, 2004.

Victor Tonelli, *Unearthed,* Pheromone Films, 2004.

Himself, *UnConventional* (documentary), Revolution Earth Productions, 2004.

Man, "The Psychic" segment, *Death 4 Told,* Asylum, 2005.

Stephen, *Forest of the Damned* (also known as *Demonic, Johannes Roberts' "Demonic,"* and *Johannes Roberts' "Forest of the Damned"*), American World Pictures, 2005.

Machete zombie, *Land of the Dead* (also known as *George A. Romero's "Land of the Dead," Land of the Dead—Le territoire des morts,* and *Le terre des morts*), Universal, 2005.

Cabby, *A Dream of Color in Black and White,* Lions Gate Films, 2005.

Fate, 2005.

Sheriff, *Beyond the Wall of Sleep,* Lions Gate Films Home Entertainment, 2006.

Prester John, *Sea of Dust,* 309 Productions, 2006.

Himself, *American Scary* (documentary), Z–Team Productions, 2006.

Deputy Tolo, "Planet Terror" segment, *Grindhouse* (also known as *Quentin Tarantino's "Death Proof"* and *Robert Rodriguez's "Planet Terror"*), Dimension Films, 2007.

Killer, *Horrorween,* Adirondack International Pictures, 2007.

Matthew, *Small Time Crime,* 72nd Street Productions, 2007.

Going to Pieces: The Rise and Fall of the Slasher Film (documentary), ThinkFilm, 2007.

Film Work; Makeup Artist or Special Effects Makeup Artist:

Deathdream (also known as *Dead of Night, The Night Andy Came Home, Night Walk, The Veteran, Whispers,* and *Soif de sang*), MPI Home Video, 1972.

Deranged (also known as *Deranged: Confessions of a Necrophile*), American International Pictures, 1974.

Dawn of the Dead (also known as *Dawn of the Living Dead, George A. Romero's "Dawn of the Dead," Zombie: Dawn of the Dead, Zombies, Zombies: Dawn of the Dead,* and *Zombi*), United Film Distribution, 1979.

Martin, Libra, 1979.

Effects (also known as *Death's Director* and *The Manipulator*), International Harmony, 1980.

Eyes of a Stranger, Warner Bros., 1980.

Friday the 13th, Paramount, 1980.

(And horror sequence designer) *The Burning,* Filmways, 1981.

(And stunt coordinator) *Maniac,* Analysis Film Distribution, 1981.

The Prowler (also known as *The Graduation* and *Rosemary's Killer*), Sandhurst, 1981.

Nightmares in a Damaged Brain (also known as *Blood Splash, Nightmare,* and *Schizo*), 21st Century Film, 1981.

Xiao sheng pa pa (also known as *Till Death Do We Scare* and *Siu sang ong ong*), 1982.

(With others) *Alone in the Dark,* New Line Cinema, 1982.

Creepshow (also known as *Cuentos de ultratumba*), Warner Bros., 1982.

Midnight (also known as *Backwoods Massacre*), Independent International Pictures, 1983.

(And special effects supervisor) *Friday the 13th—The Final Chapter* (also known as *Friday the 13th: Last Chapter* and *Friday the 13th: Part 4*), Paramount, 1984.

Day of the Dead (also known as *George A. Romero's "Day of the Dead"*), United Film, 1985.

Maria's Lovers, Cannon, 1985.

The Texas Chainsaw Massacre, Part 2 (also known as *The Texas Chainsaw Massacre 2*), Cannon, 1986.

Invasion U.S.A., Cannon, 1986.

Monkey Shines (also known as *Ella* and *Monkey Shines: An Experiment in Fear*), Orion, 1988.

Red Scorpion (also known as *Red Exterminator*), Shapiro–Glickenhaus Home Video, 1989.

(And supervisor) *Due occhi diabolici,* Taurus Entertainment, 1991.

Bloodsucking Pharaohs in Pittsburgh (also known as *Picking Up the Pieces*), Paramount Home Entertainment, 1991.

Trauma (also known as *Dario Argento's "Trauma"*), Republic, 1993.

Heartstopper (also known as *Dark Craving*), 1993, Tempo Video, 1996.

Killing Zoe, October Films, 1994.

Backstreet Justice (also known as *Dead Wrong*), Prism Pictures, 1994.

Special effects supervisor, *Cutting Moments* (short film), 1997.

Special makeup effects supervisor, *Cold Hearts,* 1999, Synapse Films, 2002.

Special effects supervisor, *Web of Darkness,* Renegade Films/Savage Armadillo Productions, 2001.

Ted Bundy (also known as *Bundy*), First Look International, 2002.

Film Work; Other:

Director, *Night of the Living Dead,* Columbia, 1990.

Stunt coordinator, *Children of the Living Dead,* Spartan Home Entertainment, 2001.

Television Appearances; Specials:

A Night of Movie Magic, The Discovery Channel, 1995.

The American Nightmare, Independent Film Channel, 2000.

Dario Argento: En Eye for Horror, 2000.

Hollywood Goes to Hell, 2000.

Bogeyman II: Masters of Horror, Sci–Fi Channel, 2004.

Dream of the Dead: George Romero, 2005.

Television Appearances; Miniseries:

A–Z of Horror (also known as *Clive Barker's "A–Z of Horror"*), 1997.

The 100 Scariest Movie Moments, Bravo, 2004.

Television Appearances; Episodic:

"Horror Makeup: Fright Factories," *Movie Magic,* 1995.

Peter Reynolds, "Lost Boy," *Sheena,* 2000.

Voice, "Worst Episode Ever," *The Simpsons* (animated), Fox, 2001.

"Frightvition 2002," *The Midnight Movie,* 2002.

Appeared in "Halloween Candy," *Tales from the Darkside,* syndicated.

Television Appearances; Other:

Motorcyclist, *The Boy Who Loved Trolls,* 1984.

Chemical/weapons engineer, *Mr. Stitch,* Sci–Fi Channel, 1996.

Television Makeup Effects Specialist:

The Assassination File (also known as *Out in the Cold*), 1996.

(And designer) *Mr. Stitch,* Sci–Fi Channel, 1996.

Television Director; Episodic:

Directed an episode of *Tales from the Dark Side,* syndicated.

RECORDINGS

Videos:

Scream Greats, Vol. 1: Tom Savini, Master of Horror Effects (also known as *Scream Greats, Vol. 1*), Paramount Home Video, 1986.

Il mondo di Dario Argento 2: Il museo degli orrori di Dario Argento, 1997.

The Dead Walk: Remaking a Classic, Columbia TriStar Home Video, 1999.

Two Masters' Eyes, 2003.

Savini's EFX, 2003.

The Many Days of "Day of the Dead," 2003.

Behind the House: Anatomy of the Zombie Movement, Artisan Entertainment, 2004.

Creature Feature: 50 Years of the Gill–Man, Cinematic Heroes/Gill Film, 2004.

Tom Savini: The Early Years, Blue Underground, 2004.

Interviewee and director, *Chill Factor: House Call* (also known as *Tom Savini's "Chill Factor"*), 2004.

The Dead Will Walk, Anchor Bay Entertainment, 2004.

(In archive footage) *Nightmares in Foam Rubber,* 2004.

After Effects: Memories of Pittsburgh Filmmaking, Synapse Films, 2005.

The Shark Is Still Working, Finatic Productions, 2006.

The Witch's Dungeon: 40 Years of Chills, Colorbox Studios, 2006.

Texas Frightmare Weekend 2006, Triple C Productions, 2006.

Flesh Wounds: Seven Stories of the Saw, Dark Sky Films, 2006.

It Runs in the Family: The Making of a Sequel, Metro–Goldwyn–Mayer, 2006.

Appeared as teacher and created special makeup effects for the music video "Twisted Sister: Come Out and Play," Atlantic Video, 1986; appeared in and created makeup for "Be Chrool to Your Scuel" by Twisted Sister.

WRITINGS

Nonfiction:

Grande Illusions, Imagine, 1983, reprinted as *Bizarro!,* Harmony Books, 1986, then as *Grande Illusions: A Learn–by Example Guide to the Art and Technique of Special Make–up Effects from the Films of Tom Savini,* 1993.

Grande Illusions, Book II, Michelucci, 1988.

Contributor to periodicals.

OTHER SOURCES

Books:

International Dictionary of Films and Filmmakers, Volume 4: Writers and Production Artists, 4th edition, St. James Press, 2000.

Periodicals:

Aspire!, January, 2000, pp. 4–6.

Dark Side, December, 2002, pp. 26–32.

Fangoria, March, 1996, pp. 64–68.

Electronic:

Tom Savini Official Site, http://www.savini.com, April 13, 2007.

SCHOOLER, Heidi

PERSONAL

Education: Studied at the Actors Studio; studied acting, comedy, improvisation, voice, and voice–over work with various instructors.

Addresses: *Agent*—Coast to Coast Talent Group, 3350 Barham Blvd., Los Angeles, CA 90068; The Michael Abrams Group, 2934 Beverly Glen Circle, Suite 453, Bel Air, CA 90077; The Osbrink Agency, 4343 Lankershim Blvd., Suite 100, Universal City, CA 91602.

Career: Actress. Provided voice work for advertisements. Provided the voice of Lois Lane for the project *Superman 2.*

Member: Actors' Equity Association, American Federation of Television and Radio Artists, Screen Actors Guild.

Awards, Honors: Schooler's performance as Mary Magdalene in *He Was Here* was named a star turn by *LA Weekly.*

CREDITS

Film Appearances:

(Uncredited) New Haven reporter, *The Doors* (also known as *The Doors: la leyenda, Ha–Dlatot, Les Doors,* and *O mito de uma geracao*), TriStar, 1991.

Courtesan, *Dracula* (also known as *Bram Stoker's "Dracula," Bram Stokers "Dracula," Bram Stokerin Dracula, Dracula d'apres Bram Stoker, Dracula d'apres l'oeuvre de Bram Stoker, Dracula de Bram Stoker, Dracula, de Bram Stoker, Drakoulas,* and *Drakula*), Columbia, 1992.

Liz, *Bimbo Penitentiary* (also known as *Cuffdunk and Roundtree*), 1992.

Katrina, *The Wedding Project,* 1999.

Meg, *Cut* (short film), 2003.

Hedy Lamarr, *Calling Hedy Lamarr,* Lone Star Productions/Mischief Films, 2004.

Laughing housewife, *Natural Born Salesman* (short film), American Film Institute, 2005.

Lilli, *Inland Empire,* 518 Media/Absurda, 2006.

Psychiatric ward woman, *Beautiful Dreamer,* Image-
works Entertainment International, 2006.
Sarah, *The Shabbos Bigfoot* (short film), Studio 203,
2006.
A Mock Time: A Star Trek Wedding, c. 2007.
Girrl, W.O.W. Filmz, c. 2008.

Appeared as Larissa, *8 o'clock Madness* (short film); as
Frankie, *In the Claire de Lune* (short film); as Candy,
Special Delivery; and in *Protestskaya.*

Film Line Producer:
Assistant line producer, *Hash Brown's,* DreamReel
Productions, 1999.
Random Shooting in L.A., Collaboration Filmworks,
2002.

Television Appearances; Series:
Herself, *Your Reality Checked* (also known as *Reality
Check*), Fine Living Network, beginning c. 2003.

Television Appearances; Movies:
Karen, *Strange Voices,* NBC, 1987.

Television Appearances; Episodic:
Sara at the Maple Clinic, *General Hospital,* ABC, 1987
(multiple episodes).
Young girl, "The Wedding," *Heartbeat* (also known as
Herzschlag des Lebens—Goettinnen in Weiss and
Sydaemen asialla), ABC, 1988.
Courtesan in "The Cask of Amontillado" segment,
"Edgar Allan Poe: Terror of the Soul," *American
Masters,* PBS, 1995.
(Uncredited) Female detective, "Doctor's Orders," *Me-
dium,* NBC, 2006.

Television Appearances; Other:
Appeared in *Snow White,* Nickelodeon; and in *Pizza
Man.*

Stage Appearances:
The Yiddish Trojan Women, West Coast Jewish Theatre,
Studio City, CA, 1996.
Myra, "The Long Goodbye," *Signposts: An Evening of
Rarely Performed One-Acts,* Rose Alley Theater,
Venice, CA, 2002.
Danielle, *Me Too,* Stella Adler Theatre, Los Angeles,
2006.
Getting Sara Married, Westside Jewish Community
Center, Los Angeles, 2006.
Got Nerve (solo show), c. 2007.

Appeared as Miss Metcalf, *Dark of the Moon,* and as a
wife, *La ronde,* both Actors Studio, Los Angeles; as Lisa,
Do Over, and as Moth, *Dreamers,* both West Coast

Ensemble; as Cordelia, *King Lear,* and as Natasha, *Three
Sisters* (musical), both Bare Bones Theatre; as Hermia,
A Midsummer Night's Dream, and as Juliet, *Romeo and
Juliet,* both Syracuse Classics Workshop; as Diane, *Big
Time,* Beverly Hills Playhouse, Beverly Hills, CA; as
Jane Lane, *Demolition Downtown,* NoHo Theatre and
Arts Festival, North Hollywood, CA; as Mary
Magdalene, *He Was Here,* Rose Alley Theater; as Mag,
Lovers, Saw Mill Theatre, NY; as Annie Sullivan, *The
Miracle Worker,* Veterans Theatre, Los Angeles; as
Anya, *Reach for the Stars* (rock musical), SIR Studio
Theatre; and as Kathy, *Vanities,* American Musical and
Dramatic Academy, New York City.

Major Tours:
Karen, *Stand through the Eyes of a Child,* U.S. cities,
2007.

WRITINGS

Writings for the Stage:
Got Nerve (solo show), c. 2007.

OTHER SOURCES

Electronic:
Heidi Schooler, http://heidischooler.nowcasting.com,
May 11, 2007.

SCHREIBER, Nancy

PERSONAL

Born in Detroit, MI. *Education:* Studied psychology and
art history at the University of Michigan.

Addresses: *Agent*—Montana Artists Agency, 7715
Sunset Blvd., 3rd Floor, Los Angeles, CA 90046.

Career: Cinematographer and camera operator. Began
film career as a production assistant, best boy electric,
and gaffer on films and television commercials; served
as a cinematographer on over one hundred music
videos for artists such as Aretha Franklin, Billy Joel,
Sting, and Billy Idol. American Film Institute, adjunct
professor, 1993–94.

Member: American Society of Cinematographers.

Awards, Honors: Independent Spirit Award nomination,
best cinematography, Independent Features Project,
1994, for *Chain of Desire;* Golden Frog nomination,

Camerimage, 1994, for *Dead Beat;* Emmy Award nomination, outstanding individual achievement—informational programming, 1996, for *The Celluloid Closet;* Vision Award, Women in Film Crystal Awards, 1997; Cinematography Award—dramatic, Sundance Film Festival, 2004, for *November.*

CREDITS

Film Cinematographer:
Different Drummer–Elvin Jones, 1979.
Possum Living, 1980.
The Last to Know, New Day Films, 1981.
Ladykiller, 1986.
Promises to Keep, 1988.
Interior Decorator from Hell, 1988.
Painting the Town: The Illusionistric Murals of Richard Haas, 1989.
Trapped Alive, 1990.
Fat Monroe (short), 1990.
Through the Wire (documentary), Original Cinema, 1990.
Kiss Me a Killer, Califilm, 1991.
Thank You and Good Night, 1991.
Visions of Light (documentary; also known as *Visions of Light: The Art of Cinematography*), Kino International, 1992.
Chain of Desire, Prism Pictures, 1992.
Liberators: Fighting on Two Fronts in World War II (documentary), 1992.
Trapped Alive, AIP Home Video, 1993.
The Obit Writer (short), 1993.
The Soft Kill, 1994.
Dead Beat (also known as *The Phone Perfector*), Live Entertainment, 1994.
Girl in the Cadillac, Columbia TriStar Home Video, 1995.
The Celluloid Closet (also known as *Celluloid Closet* and *Gefangen in der traumfabik*), Sony Pictures Classics, 1995.
Just in Time (short), 1996.
"M" Word, 1996.
Scorpion Spring, New Line Home Video, 1996.
Cater–Waiter (short), 1996.
The Curse of the Inferno (also known as *The Stick Up*), 1997.
Nevada, Storm Entertainment, 1997.
The Silver Screen: Color Me Lavender, Planet Pictures, 1997.
Butter (also known as *Never 2 Big*), Live Entertainment, 1998.
Standoff, Trimark Pictures, 1998.
Your Friends & Neighbors, Gramercy, 1998.
The Source (documentary), 1999.
Breathe In, Breathe Out (documentary), 2000.
Shadow Magic (also known as *Xi yang jing*), 2000.

Book of Shadows: Blair Witch 2 (also known as *BW2, BWP2,* and *Book of Shadows: Blair Witch Project 2*), Artisan Entertainment, 2000.
Stranger Inside, 2001.
Buying the Cow, Destination Films, 2002.
Rules of Love, 2002.
Robert Capra: In Love and War (documentary), 2003.
The Failures, Yankke Films, 2003.
Red Roses and Petrol, World Wide Motion Pictures Corp., 2003.
Piggy Banks, American World Pictures, 2004.
November, IFC Films, 2004.
The Nearly Unadventurous Life of Zoe Cadwaulder (short), 2004.
Imaginary Witness: Hollywood and the Holocaust (documentary), 2004.
Loverboy, Screen Media Films, 2005.
American Gun, IFC Films, 2005.
The Nines, Newmarket Films, 2007.
Flakes, 2007.
Letting Go of God, 2007.

Film Work; Other:
Production assistant and best boy electric, *The Werewolf of Washington,* 1973.
Gaffer, *The Other Half of the Sky: A China Memoir,* 1975.
Director, *Possum Living,* 1980.
Additional photography, *Seeing Red,* 1983.
Additional camera operator, *High Wire* (documentary short), New Films International, 1984.
Additional photographer, *Diego Rivera: I Paint What I See* (documentary), New Deal Films, 1992.
Camera operator, *Chains of Desire,* 1992.
Camera operator, *The Soft Kill,* 1994.
Additional photographer, *The Winner,* Norstar Entertainment, 1996.
Additional camera operator, *Walter Rosenblum: In Search of Pitt Street* (documentary), 1999.
Additional cinematographer, *Amy's Orgasm* (also known as *Amy's O* and *Why Love Doesn't Work*), Magic Lamp Releasing, 2001.
Additional photographer, *Ghost World,* United Artists, 2001.
Additional cinematography, *Shut Up & Sing,* Weinstein Company, 2006.
Additional camera operator, *Third Ward TX* (documentary), 2007.

Film Appearances:
Cinematographer Style, 2006.

Television Cinematographer; Miniseries:
The Hamptons, ABC, 2002.

Television Cinematographer; Movies:
Lush Life, Showtime, 1993.
Thicker Than Blood, TNT, 1998.

Lessons Learned, 2000.
"Fat Monroe," *The Wilgus Stories,* 2000.
Stranger Inside, HBO, 2001.
"Reaching Normal," *On the Edge,* Showtime, 2001.
Path to War, HBO, 2002.

Television Work; Movies:
Gaffer, *Six American Families,* 1976.
Gaffer, *Scenes from a Lifetime: Moving Up,* 1978.
Camera operator, additional photography, and lighting, *Forgotten Silver,* 1995.
Additional camera operator, *Mrs. Harris,* HBO, 2005.

Television Cinematographer; Specials:
Kids on Kids on Kids, HBO, 1987.
The Creative Spirit, PBS, 1992.
(Interviews) *In a New Light,* ABC, 1992.
Missing Parents, Showtime, 1994.
Smart Sex, MTV, 1994.
A Personal Journey with Martin Scorsese Through American Movies, 1995.
The Good, the Bad and the Beautiful, TBS, 1996.
The Making of "Alien: Resurrection" (documentary short), Sci–Fi Channel, 1997.
My America ... Or Honk if You Love Buddha (documentary), PBS, 1997.
HBO Real Sex 20: Ladies Night, HBO, 1998.
Warner Bros. 75th Anniversary: No Guts, No Glory, TNT, 1998.
Influenza 1918, PBS, 1998.
Forever Hollywood, 1999.
100 Years of Women, Lifetime, 1999.
(Host shoot) *Shooting War* (also known as *Shooting War: World War II Cameraman*), ABC, 2000.
The Hamptons, ABC, 2002.
Precinct Hollywood, AMC, 2005.
Imaginary Witness: Hollywood and the Holocaust, AMC, 2005.

Television Work; Specials:
Gaffer, *Six American Families,* 1976.
Gaffer, *Scenes from a Lifetime: Moving Up,* 1978.
Additional stills animation, *Spirit to Spirit: Nikki Giovanni,* PBS, 1987.
Photography, *Greatest Sports Upsets,* HBO, 1987.
Photography, *The Wild West,* syndicated, 1993.
Camera operator, *Reba!,* NBC, 1994.
Additional photography, *The Story of Mothers & Daughters,* ABC, 1997.
Additional camera, *Where It's At: The Rolling Stone State of the Union,* ABC, 1998.
Camera, *Warner Bros. 75th Anniversary: No Guts, No Glory,* TNT, 1998.
Additional photography, *Reno Finds Her Mom,* HBO, 1998.
Additional photography, *Paradise Lost 2: Revelations,* HBO, 2000.
Camera, *Size Matters: A Real Sex Xtra,* HBO, 2001.

Camera, *Real Sex 26: Lessons in Love and Lust,* HBO, 2001.
Production staff, "How Oscar Changed Me," *The 75th Annual Academy Awards,* ABC, 2003.
Additional camera, *Peter Jennings Reporting: I Have a Dream,* ABC, 2003.
Lighting designer, *Pretty Things,* HBO, 2004.

Television Cinematographer; Episodic:
"Dawn and the Haunted House," *The Baby–Sitters Club,* HBO, 1990.
"Visions of Love," *Hot Line,* 1994.
"Influenza 1918," *The American Experience,* PBS, 1998.
The Hollywood Fashion Machine, AMC, 1999.
"The Crash of 1929," *The American Experience,* PBS, 2004.
Cathouse: The Series, HBO, 2004.
"Valerie Triumphs at the Upfronts," *The Comeback,* HBO, 2005.
"Valerie Bonds with the Cast," *The Comeback,* HBO, 2005.
The Ghost Whisperer, CBS, 2006.
Heartland, TNT, 2006.
"The Cradle Will Rock," *Ghost Whisperer,* 2007.

Television Work; Episodic:
Camera operator, "Film in the Television Age," *American Cinema,* PBS, 1995.
Camera operator, "Climbing the Mountain: Part 1," *Dr. 90210,* E! Entertainment Television, 2004.

RECORDINGS

Videos:
Camera operator, *Van Morrison: The Concert,* Polydor Music Video, 1990.
Cinematographer: host sequence, *Playboy: The Story of X* (documentary), Playboy Home Video, 1998.

SCOVELL, Nell

PERSONAL

Married Colin Summers (a camera operator).

Addresses: *Agent*—Greg Hodes, Endeavor, 9601 Wilshire Blvd., 3rd Floor, Beverly Hills, CA 90210.

Career: Writer, producer, and director. Worked as staff writer for the magazine *Spy.*

CREDITS

Television Work; Series:
Story editor, *Newhart,* CBS, 1982.
Coproducer, *Coach,* ABC, 1991–92.
Producer, *Coach,* ABC, 1992–93.
Supervising producer, *Murphy Brown,* CBS, 1993–94.
Creator, *Sabrina, the Teenage Witch* (also known as *Sabrina* and *Sabrina Goes to College*), ABC, 1996.
Co–executive producer, *Charmed,* The WB, 2001–2002.
Coproducer, *Presidio Med,* CBS, 2003.
Producer, *Navy NCIS: Naval Criminal Investigative Service* (also known as *NCIS* and *NCIS: Naval Criminal Investigative Service*), CBS, 2006–2007.

Also executive producer of the series *Sabrina, the Teenage Witch* (also known as *Sabrina* and *Sabrina Goes to College*), ABC.

Television Work; Other:
Contributing producer, *The Coach Retrospective: Mary Hart Goes One on One with "Coach"* (special), ABC, 1994.
Creator, *Sabrina Goes to Rome* (movie), ABC, 1998.
Executive producer and director, *Hayley Wagner, Star* (movie), Showtime, 1999.
Executive producer, *Criminology 101* (pilot; also known as *Not a Clue*), CBS, 2003.

WRITINGS

Television Series:
The Smothers Brothers Comedy Hour, CBS, 1988–89.
Sibs, ABC, 1991–92.
Coach (also based on story by Scovell), ABC, multiple episodes, 1991–93.
Sabrina, the Teenage Witch (also known as *Sabrina* and *Sabrina Goes to College*), ABC, 1996–97, and The WB, 2001.
Charmed, The WB, multiple episodes, 2001–2002.

Also writer for *Late Night with David Letterman,* NBC.

Television Pilots:
The TV Wheel, HBO, 1995.
Sabrina, the Teenage Witch (also known as *Sabrina* and *Sabrina Goes to College*), ABC, 1996.
Criminology 101 (also known as *Not a Clue*), CBS, 2003.

Television Movies:
Hayley Wagner, Star, HBO, 1999.
Hello Sister, Goodbye Life, ABC Family Channel, 2006.

Television Specials:
Contributing writer, *The Coach Retrospective: Mary Hart Goes One on One with "Coach"* (special), ABC, 1994.

Television Episodes:
"Get Dick," *Newhart,* CBS, 1989.
"Good Neighbor Sam," *Newhart,* CBS, 1990.
"Father Goose," *Newhart,* CBS, 1990.
"One Fish, Two Fish, Blowfish, Blue Fish," *The Simpsons* (animated), Fox, 1991.
"Ticket to Writhe," *Murphy Brown,* CBS, 1993.
"Bah Humboldt," *Murphy Brown,* CBS, 1993.
"The Fifth Anchor," *Murphy Brown,* CBS, 1994.
"The Tip of the Silverburg," *Murphy Brown,* CBS, 1994.
"A Little Deb Will Do You," *The Critic,* ABC, 1994.
"Urges," *Space Ghost Coast to Coast* (also known as *SGC2C*), Cartoon Network, 1995.
"Runaway Sydney," *Providence,* NBC, 1999.
"You Bet Your Life," *Providence,* NBC, 1999.
"And Baby Makes Death," *The War Next Door,* USA Network, 2000.
"Secrets," *Presidio Med,* CBS, 2002.
"Mr. Monk and the Election," *Monk,* USA Network, 2005.
"Mr. Monk Goes to the Office," *Monk,* USA Network, 2005.
"Dead and Unburied," *Navy NCIS: Naval Criminal Investigative Service* (also known as *NCIS* and *NCIS: Naval Criminal Investigative Service*), CBS, 2006.
"Driven," *Navy NCIS: Naval Criminal Investigative Service* (also known as *NCIS* and *NCIS: Naval Criminal Investigative Service*), CBS, 2006.
"Dead Man Walking," *Navy NCIS: Naval Criminal Investigative Service* (also known as *NCIS* and *NCIS: Naval Criminal Investigative Service*), CBS, 2007.

Screenplays:
Honey, We Shrunk Ourselves, 1997.

Other:
Short stories anthologized in *More Mirth of a Nation.* Contributor to periodicals, including *New York Times Magazine, Rolling Stone, Self, Tatler, Vanity Fair,* and *Vogue.*

SEATLE, Dixie

PERSONAL

Career: Actress.

Awards, Honors: Genie Award nomination, best supporting actress, Academy of Canadian Cinema and Television, 1982, for *Ticket to Heaven;* Gemini Award, 1987, and Gemini Award nomination, 1989, both best actress in a continuing dramatic role, Academy of Canadian Cinema and Television, for *Adderly;* Gemini Award, best featured supporting actress in a dramatic series, 2002, for *Paradise Falls.*

CREDITS

Television Appearances; Series:
Sheila, *A Gift to Last,* CBC, 1978.
Mona Ellerby, *Adderly,* CBS, 1986–87.
Bea Sutton, *Paradise Falls,* Showtime, 2001–2004.

Television Appearances; Miniseries:
Sarah Osborn, *Salem Witch Trials,* CBS, 2002.
Signy Bok, *Lives of the Saints,* CTV, 2004.

Television Appearances; Movies:
Amazing Grace, *The Glitter Dome,* HBO, 1984.
Camilla Bowles, *The Women of Windsor,* 1992.
Officer Terri Orloff, *Stranger in Town,* Showtime, 1998.
Gertie Moser, *The Lady in Question,* Arts and Entertainment, 1999.
Pat Swendon, *Range of Motion,* Lifetime, 2000.
Joanna Bull, *Gilda Radner: It's Always Something,* ABC, 2002.
Sherrill Delaney, *The Pact,* Lifetime, 2002.
Eleanor Hess, *The Piano Man's Daughter* (also known as *La fille de l'homme au piano*), CBC, 2003.

Television Appearances; Episodic:
Mrs. Donnen, "Napoleon," *The Littlest Hobo,* syndicated, 1982.
Marlowe—Private Eye, 1986.
Kate Chaffee, "Neighbors," *Night Heat,* 1986.
Danny's mom, "Race against Time," *Katts and Dog* (also known as *Rin Tin Tin: K–9 Cop*), The Family Channel, 1988.
Teri Novak, "So Shall Ye Reap," *War of the Worlds* (also known as *War of the Worlds: The Second Invasion*), syndicated, 1989.
Betty Schultz, "A Tangled Web," *E.N.G.,* Lifetime, 1990.
Sara, "Love and Duty," *E.N.G.,* Lifetime, 1992.
Jane, "Point Blank," *Neon Rider,* syndicated, 1992.
Elizabeth Wade, "The Color of Mad," *Beyond Reality,* Fox, 1992.
Barbara Norton, "Spin Doctor," *Forever Knight,* CBS, 1992.
Francine Decker, "Black and White in Color," *Street Legal,* CBC, 1993.
Sharon, "Flying Fists of Fury II," *Kung Fu: The Legend Continues,* syndicated, 1995.

Aunt Benna, "How I Got My Shrunken Head: Parts 1 & 2," *Goosebumps* (also known as *Ultimate Goosebumps*), 1998.
Beth Botrelle, "The Ladies Man," *Due South* (also known as *Un tandem de choc*), CTV, 1998.
Laura Young, "Body and Soul," *Psi Factor: Chronicles of the Paranormal,* syndicated, 1999.
Lily Ledoux, "The Ballad of Steeley Joe," *The Secret Adventures of Jules Verne,* Sci–Fi Channel, 2000.
"Encumbered," *The Associates,* CTV, 2001.
Dr. Roe, "Sacred Ground," *Screech Owls,* YTV, 2002.
Mrs. Judy Goldstein, "Reversal of Fortune," *Street Time,* Showtime, 2002.
Mrs. Judy Goldstein, "On Goldie Pond," *Street Time,* Showtime, 2003.

Appeared as Lorene in an episode of *Doc,* PAX.

Television Appearances; Other:
I Love a Man in Uniform, 1983.

Stage Appearances:
Better Living, CentreStage, Toronto, Ontario, Canada, 1986.
The Stillborn Lover, Stratford Festival Theatre, Stratford, Ontario, Canada, 1995.
Equus, Stratford Festival Theatre, 1997.
Marmee, *Little Women,* Stratford Festival Theatre, 1997.
The "other woman," *Death of a Salesman,* Stratford Festival Theatre, 1997.
The Real Thing (staged reading), 2000.
Melissa Good, *Patience,* Great Canadian Theatre Company, 2001.

Appeared in *Ashes,* Manitoba Theatre Centre, Winnipeg, Manitoba, Canada; *Crossing Over,* Factory Theatre, Toronto, Ontario, Canada; *The Merry Wives of Windsor* and *Othello,* both Stratford Festival Theatre, Stratford, Ontario, Canada; *The Philadelphia Story,* Grand Theatre, London, Ontario, Canada; *Taking Over,* Factory Theatre; *Thirteen Hands,* Canadian Stage, Toronto; and *Twelfth Night,* Young People's Theatre, Toronto.

Film Appearances:
Sarah, *Ticket to Heaven,* United Artists, 1981.
Betty Anne, *Hank Williams: The Show He Never Gave,* Simcom Limited, 1982.
"The Black Cat in the Black Mouse Socks," in *Love,* Coup Films, 1982.
Mrs. Collins, *Joe's So Mean to Josephine,* Alliance, 1996.
Jacob's mom, *Jacob Two Two Meets the Hooded Fang,* Odeon Films, 1999.

Radio Appearances:
Reader, "Alias Grace," *The Book Reading,* ABC (Australia), 1998, then CBC, 1999.

Poetry reader for the series *Between the Covers,* CBC.

RECORDINGS

Videos:
Narrator, *Abortion: Stories from North and South* (also known as *La avortement—histoire secrete*), Cinema Guild/National Film Board of Canada, 1984.

SEHORN, Angie
   See HARMON, Angie

SHARP, Keesha 1973–

PERSONAL

Full name, Keesha Ulrika Sharp; born 1973, in Brooklyn, NY. *Education:* Boston Conservatory, B.F.A. *Avocational Interests:* Boxing, kick–boxing, writing, music.

Addresses: *Agent*—Craig Gartner, Endeavor, 9601 Wilshire Blvd., 3rd Floor, Beverly Hills, CA 90210. *Publicist*—Klear Public Relations, 827 North Hollywood Way, Suite 506, Burbank, CA 91505.

Career: Actress and singer. Also occasional stunt performer.

CREDITS

Film Appearances:
Party girl, *Pootie Tang,* Paramount, 2001.
Debbie, *American Adobo,* Outrider Pictures, 2002.
First sister, *Malibu's Most Wanted,* Warner Bros., 2003.
Chanel, *Leprechaun: Back 2 tha Hood,* Lions Gate Films, 2003.
Edna, *Never Die Alone,* Fox Searchlight, 2004.
Angela, *Bull Run,* FireRock Entertainment, 2006.

Television Appearances; Series:
Monica Charles Brooks, *Girlfriends,* UPN, 2002–2006, CW Network, 2006–2007.
Sheila Ridenhour, a recurring role, *Everybody Hates Chris,* UPN, 2005–2006.

Television Appearances; Episodic:
Lauren, "The Crier," *Welcome to New York,* CBS, 2000.
Grace, "Walking Wounded," *Third Watch,* NBC, 2001.
Charlene, "Pique," *Law & Order: Special Victims Unit* (also known as *Law & Order: SVU* and *Special Victims Unit*), NBC, 2001.
Linda Berry, "Church," *The Tracy Morgan Show,* NBC, 2004.
Linda Berry, "Weird Science," *The Tracy Morgan Show,* NBC, 2004.
Lexi, "Still Flirting," *Still Standing,* CBS, 2004.

Stage Appearances:
Living in the Wind, American Place Theatre, New York City, 2000.
Eat the Runt, American Place Theatre, 2001.

Appeared in productions of *Jitney* and *Seven Guitars.*

Major Tours:
Toured U.S. cities in the musical *Carousel.*

SHEA, Dan 1954–

PERSONAL

Full name, Daniel Joseph Shea; born December 23, 1954, in Hespeler (now Cambridge), Ontario, Canada; married, wife's name Chris (divorced); children: Joey (an actress), Stephanie. *Education:* University of Waterloo, B.S. (with honors).

Addresses: *Office*—c/o *Stargate SG–1* Productions, Bridge Studios, 240 Boundary Rd., Burnaby, British Columbia, Canada V5M 3Z3.

Career: Actor and stunt coordinator. Appeared in commercials; also worked as stunt performer, stunt double, and hockey consultant.

CREDITS

Television Appearances; Series:
Sergeant Siler, a recurring role, *Stargate SG–1* (also known as *La porte des etoiles*), Showtime, 1998–2002, then Sci–Fi Channel, 2002—.

Television Appearances; Movies:
Comic, *Blackout,* HBO, 1985.
Policeman, *Through the Eyes of a Killer* (also known as *The Master Builder*), CBS, 1992.

Pilot, *Arctic Blue,* HBO, 1993.

Tall musher, *Call of the Wild,* CBS, 1993.

Toronto Maple Leaf goon, *Net Worth,* CBC, 1995.

Other inspector, *The Inspectors,* Showtime, 1998.

Joe, *Heaven's Fire* (also known as *L'enfer en plein ciel* and *Inferno der Flammen*), Fox Family Channel, 1999.

Baggage handler, *Romantic Comedy 101,* E! Entertainment Television, 2001.

Television Appearances; Episodic:

Biker, "Renegade," *MacGyver,* ABC, 1989.

Van driver, "Deep Cover," *MacGyver,* ABC, 1990.

Guy in first group, "His Master's Voice," *Wiseguy,* CBS, 1990.

"Nowhere Fast," *Neon Rider,* syndicated, 1991.

Sentry, "Vengeance Is Mine," *Hawkeye,* syndicated, 1995.

Soldier, "The Bounty," *Hawkeye,* syndicated, 1995.

Stewart Billings, "Victoria's Secret," *Two,* syndicated, 1996.

(Uncredited) Deputy, "Christmas Carol, *The X–Files,* Fox, 1997.

Fight announcer, "Sweet Science," *The Sentinel,* UPN, 1998.

Deputy, "Bad Boys," *Dead Man's Gun,* Showtime, 1999.

Cop, "Down to Earth," *The Outer Limits* (also known as *The New Outer Limits*), Showtime and syndicated, 2000.

Old man/cop, "Alienshop," *The Outer Limits* (also known as *The New Outer Limits*), Showtime and syndicated, 2001.

Bartender, "The First Freshman," *Seven Days* (also known as *Seven Days: The Series*), UPN, 2001.

Sergeant Siler, "Rising: Part 1," *Stargate: Atlantis* (also known as *La porte d'Atlantis*), Sci–Fi Channel, 2004.

Policeman, "Bloody Mary," *Supernatural,* The WB, 2005.

Sergeant Siler, "The Return: Part 1," *Stargate: Atlantis* (also known as *La porte d'Atlantis*), Sci–Fi Channel, 2006.

Television Appearances; Specials:

Himself, *Sci Fi Inside: Sci Fi Friday,* Sci–Fi Channel, 2005.

Television Stunt Coordinator; Series:

Stargate SG–1 (also known as *La porte des etoiles*), Showtime, 1997–2002, then Sci–Fi Channel, 2002—.

Television Stunt Coordinator; Movies:

Net Worth, CBC, 1995.

H–E Double Hockey Sticks, ABC, 1999.

Snow Queen, 2002.

Television Stunt Coordinator; Episodic:

"9 Lives," *Psych,* NBC, 2006.

Film Appearances:

Weston, *Underclassman,* Miramax, 2005.

Fisherman, *The Fog,* Columbia, 2005.

Third cleaner, *Connor's War,* Sony Pictures Home Entertainment, 2006.

Film Stunt Coordinator:

Slap Shot 2: Breaking the Ice, Universal Home Entertainment, 2002.

OTHER SOURCES

Periodicals:

TV Zone, September, 2001, pp. 68–69.

TV Zone Special, July, 2002, pp. 28–29.

SHEN, Freda Fo
See FOH SHEN, Freda

SHORT, John

PERSONAL

Career: Actor, producer, and writer. Barn (theatre), cofounder, 1994, and teacher; stage actor at Actors Theatre of Louisville, Louisville, KY, Syracuse Stage, Syracuse, NY, and John F. Kennedy Center for the Performing Arts. Loyola Marymount University, acting teacher; teacher at Camp Bravo summer workshop. Also works as a photographer.

Awards, Honors: Drama Desk Award nomination, outstanding featured actor in a musical, 1985, for *Big River.*

CREDITS

Film Appearances:

Curtis, *Maximum Overdrive,* De Laurentiis Entertainment Group, 1986.

Assistant director, *A Fine Mess* (also known as *Blake Edwards' "A Fine Mess"*), Columbia, 1986.

Cub reporter Pesky Miller, *Brenda Starr,* Columbia TriStar, 1989.

Resident, *Gross Anatomy* (also known as *A Cut Above*), Buena Vista, 1990.

First John, *Peephole,* 1992.

Corny "Buster" Robins, *Diggstown* (also known as *Midnight Sting*), Metro–Goldwyn–Mayer, 1992.

INCO White, *Apollo 13* (also released as *Apollo 13: The IMAX Experience*), MCA/Universal, 1995.

Harley's associate, *The Associate,* Buena Vista, 1996.

Agent Dewey, *Ransom,* Buena Vista, 1996.

Mr. Howard, *Shiloh 2: Shiloh Season,* Warner Bros., 1999.

Acting coach, *Welcome to Hollywood,* Phaedra Cinema, 2000.

Tiny "Who" man, *How the Grinch Stole Christmas* (also known as *Dr. Seuss' "How the Grinch Stole Christmas," The Grinch,* and *Der Grinch*), Universal, 2000.

Alden, *The Pickets* (short film), Cinevative Productions, 2002.

Ned Becker, *Christmas with the Kranks,* Columbia, 2004.

Film Work:

Executive producer, *The Pickets* (short film), Cinevative Productions, 2002.

Television Appearances; Movies:

Tour guide, *The Other Lover,* CBS, 1985.

Uma, *Angel in Green,* CBS, 1987.

Television Appearances; Series:

Father Charles "Chuck" Cavanaugh, Jr., *The Cavanaughs,* CBS, 1986.

Television Appearances; Episodic:

Reimer, "Love Thy Neighbor," *Trapper John, M.D.,* CBS, 1985.

"Out with the New, Inn with the Old," *Newhart,* CBS, 1985.

Dr. Brandon Falsey, "The Last One," *St. Elsewhere,* NBC, 2988.

"Stand by Your Man," *21 Jump Street,* Fox, 1989.

Pee Wee Reese, "Boys of Summer," *Brooklyn Bridge,* CBS, 1991.

Steve Bannister, "Buzzy Money," *Coach,* ABC, 1993.

Technician, "Recovery," *JAG,* NBC, 1996.

Warren Snail, "Part I," *The Practice,* ABC, 1997.

"Good Fellows," *Providence,* NBC, 1999.

Warren Hungerford, "Vigilante," *The District,* CBS, 2001.

Commercial director, "Precautions," *Strong Medicine,* Lifetime, 2002.

Dr. Phillip "Phil" Spivey, "The Price," *Angel* (also known as *Angel: The Series*), The WB, 2002.

Drake, "Regeneration," *Enterprise* (also known as *Star Trek: Enterprise*), UPN, 2003.

Riley Sheets, "The Hubbert Peak," *The West Wing,* NBC, 2004.

Dr. Raymond Young, "'Til We Meat Again," *Boston Legal,* ABC, 2005.

Dr. Schlansky, "Wake Up," *ER,* NBC, 2005.

Coach Braddock, "The Shot," *Close to Home,* CBS, 2006.

Appeared in an episode of *Ally McBeal,* Fox; and as Crawford Dunn, *The Marshal,* ABC.

Stage Appearances:

Tom Sawyer, *Big River* (musical), Eugene O'Neill Theatre, New York City, 1985–87.

RECORDINGS

Video Games:

Voice of Ensign Foster, *Silent Steel,* Tsunami Entertainment, 1995.

WRITINGS

Film Scripts:

The Pickets (short film), Cinevative Productions, 2002.

SIE, James 1962–

PERSONAL

Born December 18, 1962, in Summit, NJ; half–brother of Allison Sie (an actress and producer).

Addresses: *Agent*—Terry Rhodes, International Creative Management, 10250 Constellation Way, 9th Floor, Los Angeles, CA 90067; (voice work) Danis, Panaro & Nist, 9201 West Olympic Blvd., Beverly Hills, CA 90212.

Career: Actor and voice artist.

Member: Screen Actors Guild, American Federation of Television and Radio Artists, Actors' Equity Association.

CREDITS

Television Appearances; Animated Series:

Voices of Chow and other characters, *Jackie Chan Adventures,* The WB, 2000–2005.

Voice of Mr. Chang, *The Infinite Darcy,* 2004.

Voice of Sam Chang, *Game Over,* UPN, 2004.

Voices of cabbage merchant and others, *Avatar: The Last Airbender,* Nickelodeon, 2005–2006.

Television Appearances; Episodic:

"Chinatown," *The Untouchables,* syndicated, 1993.

Man in line, "Ringing Up Baby," *Dharma & Greg,* ABC, 1998.

Deliverer, "The Getaway," *It's Like, You Know ...,* ABC, 1999.

Waiter, "The Thanks You Get," *For Your Love,* The WB, 1999.

Deliverer, "Home for the Holidays," *Providence,* NBC, 1999.

Lana Dagchen, "Playing God," *Family Law,* CBS, 2000.

Fifth student, "A Walk in the Woods," *ER,* NBC, 2001.

Shoe salesman, "PreWitched," *Charmed,* The WB, 2001.

Voice of Confucius, "Confucius Say Way Too Much," *Time Squad* (animated), Cartoon Network, 2001.

Restaurant critic, "Crouching Tiger, Hidden Val," *V.I.P.* (also known as *V.I.P.—Die Bodyguards*), syndicated, 2001.

Chemistry teacher, "Short Story," *Even Stevens,* Disney Channel, 2002.

Multiple voices, "Returning Japanese," *King of the Hill* (animated), Fox, 2002.

Voice of Nozawa, "The Fat and the Furious," *King of the Hill* (animated), Fox, 2002.

Multiple voices, "Night and Deity," *King of the Hill* (animated), Fox, 2003.

Walter Hagan, "The Friendly Skies," *Without a Trace* (also known as *W.A.T.*), CBS, 2003.

Voice of General Kwan, "Initiation," *Justice League* (animated; also known as *JL* and *Justice League Unlimited*), Cartoon Network, 2004.

Voice of wind dragon, "Ultimatum," *Justice League* (animated; also known as *JL* and *Justice League Unlimited*), Cartoon Network, 2004.

Voice of Kwan, "Parental Bonding," *Danny Phantom* (animated), Nickelodeon, 2004.

Voice of Nguc, "Orange You Sad I Did Say Banana?," *King of the Hill* (animated), Fox, 2005.

Voices of elderly monk, Yoo Yee, and ninja, "Crouching Jimmy, Hidden Sheen," *The Adventures of Jimmy Neutron: Boy Genius* (animated), Nickelodeon, 2005.

Voice of Louie Hong Fa, "Block–Long Hong Kong Terror," *What's New, Scooby–Doo?* (animated), The WB, 2005.

Voices of Kal Yee, Mr. Kellington, and ninja, "Out of the Past," *The Life and Times of Juniper Lee* (animated), 2005.

FBI technician, "Sacrifice," *Numb3rs* (also known as *Num3ers*), CBS, 2005.

Voice of Kwan, "Beauty Marked," *Danny Phantom* (animated), Nickelodeon, 2006.

Voice of Kwan, "Reality Trip," *Danny Phantom* (animated), Nickelodeon, 2006.

Voice of Cory, "Boyz on da Run: Parts 1–3," *Shorty McShorts' Shorts* (animated), Disney Channel, 2006.

Voice of Master Pho, "Master Pho," *The Replacements* (animated), 2006.

Voice of Chen Lin, "X Is for Xanadu," *W.I.T.C.H.* (animated), ABC Family Channel, 2006.

Narrator and voice of Monkey Butt, "Dugly Uckling's Treasure Quest," *Random! Cartoons* (animated), 2007.

Appeared in "Montana Sassy/Justice," an episode of *Nip/Tuck,* FX Network; also appeared in episodes of *America's Most Wanted,* Fox; *Early Edition,* CBS; and *Port Charles,* ABC.

Television Appearances; Other:

FBI technician, *Numb3rs* (pilot; also known as *Num3ers*), CBS, 2005.

Voice of Kwan, *Danny Phantom: Reign Storm* (special), Nickelodeon, 2005.

Television Work; Movies:

Additional voices, *The Batman vs. Dracula: The Animated Movie* (animated), Cartoon Network, 2005.

Additional voices, *Hellboy Animated: Sword of Storms* (animated), Cartoon Network, 2006.

Film Appearances:

Ken Lim, *Chain Reaction,* Twentieth Century–Fox, 1996.

Luke, *Strawberry Fields* (also known as *What Happened to Her?* and *the Strawberry Fields*), Phaedra Cinema, 1997.

Vincent Ling, *U.S. Marshals,* Warner Bros., 1998.

Sergeant James, *Bats,* Columbia, 1999.

Steven, *Ghost World,* United Artists, 2001.

Voices of freaky male and elk dad, *Ice Age: The Meltdown* (animated; also known as *Ice Age 2*), Twentieth Century–Fox, 2006.

Appeared in the film *Beautiful,* Destination Films.

Stage Appearances:

Talking with My Hands (solo show), East West Players, Mark Taper Forum, Los Angeles Music Center, Los Angeles, 1999.

Also appeared as Hymen, *As You Like It,* Bailiwick Repertory Theatre, Chicago, IL; as Fred, then as Dick Wilkins, *A Christmas Carol,* Goodman Theatre, Chicago; Commediant, *Don Quichotte,* Lyric Opera; Dale, *FOB,* Angel Island Theatre, Chicago; Lucky, *Immortal-*

ity, Indecent Exposure Company; Victor, *Lizard Music,* Lifeline Theatre, Chicago; John Lee, *Porcelain,* Eclipse Theatre, Chicago; Milton, *The Promise,* Lifeline Theatre; Michael Ito, *Santa Anita '42,* Illinois Theatre Center, Chicago; Paulie, *Straight as a Line,* Primary Stages and Playwrights Horizon Theatre, both New York City; Ariel, *The Tempest,* Oak Park Shakespeare Festival, Oak Park, IL; son, *Wonderland* (workshop production), Mark Taper Forum, Los Angeles Music Center, Los Angeles; and Mrs. Which, *A Wrinkle in Time,* Lincoln Center Institute, New York City.

RECORDINGS

Video Games:

Voices of Bruce Lee and young Bruce Lee, *Bruce Lee: Quest of the Dragon,* Universal Interactive Studios, 2002.

Voice, *Command & Conquer: Generals,* Electronic Arts/ Westwood Studios, 2003.

(English version) Voice, *Tenchu san* (also known as *Tenchu: Wrath of Heaven*), Activision, 2003.

Voice, *Command & Conquer: Generals Zero Hour,* EA Games, 2003.

Voices of Diem, Vietnamese soldiers, prisoners, and civilians, *ShellShock: Nam '67,* Eidos Interactive, 2004.

Additional voices, *Shark Tale,* DreamWorks, 2004.

Voice, *Red Ninja: End of Honor,* Vivendi Universal Games, 2005.

Voices of monk, cop, and civilian, *Narc,* Midway Games, 2005.

Voice of Sunfire, *X–Men Legends II: Rise of Apocalypse,* Activision, 2005.

Voice of Fin Fang Foom, *Marvel: Ultimate Alliance,* Activision, 2006.

Additional voices, *SOCOM U.S. Navy SEALs: Fireteam Bravo 2,* Sony Computer Entertainment America, 2006.

Voice of Dennis, *Lost Planet: Extreme Condition,* Capcom Entertainment, 2006.

WRITINGS

Stage Shows:

Talking With My Hands (solo show), East West Players, Mark Taper Forum, Los Angeles Music Center, Los Angeles, 1999.

SKOTCHDOPLE, James W.
(James Skotchdople, Jim Skotchdople)

PERSONAL

Career: Producer and assistant director.

CREDITS

Film Second Assistant Director:

Turk 182!, Twentieth Century–Fox, 1985.

A Chorus Line, Columbia, 1985.

The Money Pit, Universal, 1986.

Brighton Beach Memoirs (also known as *Neil Simon's "Brighton Beach Memoirs"*), Universal, 1986.

(As James Skotchodople) *Mannequin,* Twentieth Century–Fox, 1987.

Ishtar, Columbia, 1987.

The Untouchables, Paramount, 1987.

(As Jim Skotchdople; New York) *The Believers,* Orion, 1987.

Biloxi Blues (also known as *Neil Simon's "Biloxi Blues"*), Universal, 1988.

Moon Over Parador, Universal, 1988.

Scrooged, Paramount, 1988.

Dead Bang (also known as *Dead–Bang*), Warner Bros., 1989.

Revenge, Columbia, 1990.

Sand (also known as *Sandstorm*), Showcase Entertainment, 2000.

Film First Assistant Director:

Days of Thunder, Paramount, 1990.

What About Bob?, Buena Vista, 1991.

The Last Boy Scout, Geffen Pictures, 1991.

HouseSitter, Universal, 1992.

Sleepless in Seattle, TriStar, 1993.

True Romance (also known as *Breakaway*), Warner Bros., 1993.

Mixed Nuts (also known as *Lifesavers*), TriStar, 1994.

Crimson Tide, Buena Vista, 1995.

The Fan, Sony Pictures Entertainment, 1996.

Green Day: Bullet in a Bible (documentary), Warner Bros., 2005.

Film Associate Producer:

Naked Tango (also known as *Tango desnudo*), New Line Cinema, 1991.

Sleepless in Seattle, TriStar, 1993.

Crimson Tide, Buena Vista, 1995.

Film Coproducer:

True Romance (also kwon as *Breakaway*), Warner Bros., 1993.

Film Producer:

Company Man, Paramount, 2000.

Sand (also known as *Sandstorm*), Showcase Entertainment, 2000.

Film Executive Producer:

Mixed Nuts (also known as *Lifesavers*), TriStar, 1994.

The Fan, TriStar, 1996.

Enemy of the State, Buena Vista, 1998.
Spy Game, Universal, 2001.
Man on Fire, Twentieth Century–Fox, 2004.
Bewitched, Columbia, 2005.

Film Work; Other:
(As Jim Skotchdopole) Production assistant, *Eddie and the Cruisers,* Embassy Pictures, 1983.
Production assistant, *Firstborn* (also known as *First Born* and *Moving In*), Paramount, 1984.
Unit production manager: Morocco, *Spy Game,* Universal, 2001.
Line producer: California, "Deathproof," *Grindhouse* (also known as *Quentin Tarantino's "Death Proof"*), Weinstein Company, 2007.

Film Appearances:
Himself, *Vengeance Is Mine: Reinventing "Man on Fire"* (documentary), Twentieth Century–Fox Home Entertainment, 2005.

Television Work; Movies:
Production assistant, *A Doctor's Story,* NBC, 1984.

Television Appearances; Specials:
Himself, *The Making of "Man on Fire,"* 2004.

Television Appearances; Episodic:
Himself, "Man on Fire," *HBO First Look,* HBO, 2004.

SKY, Jennifer 1977–

PERSONAL

Original name, Jennifer Danielle Wacha; born October 13, 1977, in Palm Beach, FL; married Alex Band (a musician), July 25, 2004. *Avocational Interests:* Running, skiing, outdoor activities.

Addresses: *Agent*—Innovative Artists, 1505 Tenth St., Santa Monica, CA 90401. *Manager*—The Collective, 9100 Wilshire Blvd., Suite 700 West, Beverly Hills, CA 90212.

Career: Actress. Worked as a model, beginning c. 1990; appeared in television commercials.

CREDITS

Film Appearances:
Sorority girl, *Shallow Hal* (also known as *Schwer verliebt*), Twentieth Century–Fox, 2001.

Tina, *Shop Club,* 2002.
Charlie, *My Little Eye,* Focus Features, 2002.
Hot girl, *Fish Without a Bicycle,* Romar Entertainment, 2003.
Janet, *Never Die Alone,* Fox Searchlight Pictures, 2004.
Courtney, *Meet Market,* Cut Entertainment Group, 2004.
Lola the secretary, *The Helix Loaded,* Romar Entertainment, 2005.

Television Appearances; Series:
Lisa Foxworth, *Emerald Cove,* Disney Channel, 1994.
Sarah Webber, *General Hospital,* ABC, 1997–98.
Amarice, *Xena: Warrior Princess,* syndicated, 1999.
Cleopatra "Cleo," *Cleopatra 2525,* syndicated, 2000–2001.

Television Appearances; Movies:
Judy Adams, *Our Son, the Matchmaker,* CBS, 1996.
Jane, *Trigger Happy,* Independent Film Channel, 2001.
Vanessa, *Columbo: Columbo Likes the Nightlife,* 2003.

Television Appearances; Pilots:
Cassidy Shaw, *Fastlane,* Fox, 2002.

Television Appearances; Episodic:
Girl in store, "Sympathy for the Deep," *SeaQuest DSV* (also known as *SeaQuest 2032*), NBC, 1994.
April, "Jet Ski Race," *Out of the Blue,* ABC, 1995.
Heidi, "The Pack," *Buffy the Vampire Slayer* (also known as *BtVS, Buffy,* and *Buffy the Vampire Slayer: The Series*), The WB, 1997.
Bree Hopkins, "Rumpelstiltskin," *Pacific Blue,* USA Network, 1997.
Callie, "Blind Eye for Hire," *Sins of the City,* USA Network, 1998.
Vanessa Griggs/Laura, "Possession," *Boomtown,* NBC, 2002.
Zephyr's assistant Matilda, "Abra Cadaver," *CSI: Crime Scene Investigation* (also known as *CSI: Las Vegas, CSI: Weekends, C.S.I.,* and *Les Experts*), CBS, 2002.
Cassidy Shaw, "Slippery Slope," *Fastlane,* Fox, 2003.
Mabel Stillman, "The Power of Three Blondes," *Charmed,* The WB, 2003.
Melissa, "The Magic Bullet," *Dragnet* (also known as *L.A. Dragnet*), ABC, 2003.
Cookie Devine/Sara Piper, "Innocent," *CSI: Miami,* CBS, 2004.
Sara Piper, "Game Over," *CSI: Miami,* CBS, 2005.

Stage Appearances:
Appeared as Julie, *Romeo and Juliet,* Martin County Theatre, FL; Frenchie, *Grease.*

SLOANE, Lindsay 1977–

PERSONAL

Full name, Lindsay Sloane Leikin; born August 8, 1977, in Queens (some sources say Long Island), NY; married Dar Rollins (an agent), 2004. *Religion:* Jewish.

Addresses: *Agent*—Endeavor, 9601 Wilshire Blvd., 3rd Floor, Beverly Hills, CA 90210. *Manager*—Thruline Entertainment, 9250 Wilshire Blvd., Suite 100, Beverly Hills, CA 90212.

Career: Actress. Appeared in print ads for Freshlook ColorBlends contact lenses; appeared in short film, *Fluffers*, www.atomfilms.com.

Awards, Honors: Young Artist Award nomination, best performance in a television comedy—supporting young actress, 1997, for *Mr. Rhodes*.

CREDITS

Film Appearances:
(Uncredited) Girl student, *The Faculty*, Dimension Films, 1998.
Dalia, *Win a Date*, 1998.
Daphne, *Seven Girlfriends*, 1999.
Big Red, *Bring It On*, Universal, 2000.
Melissa Peyser, *The In–Laws* (also known as *Ein ungleiches Paar* and *Wild Wedding–ein ungleiches Paar*), Warner Bros., 2003.
Minnie, *Exposed*, Mainline Releasing, 2003.
Rebecca, *Dog Gone Love*, MTI Home Video, 2004.
Laurel Simon, *The TV Set*, THINKFilm, 2006.
Chloe, *Over My Dead Body* (also known as *How I Met My Boyfriend's Dead Fiance*), Universal, 2007.
Marcy, *The Accidental Husband*, Yari Film Group Releasing, 2007.

Television Appearances; Series:
Alice Pedermeir, *The Wonder Years*, 1991–93.
Zoey Miller, *Mr. Rhodes*, NBC, 1996.
Valerie Birkhead, *Sabrina, the Teenage Witch* (also known as *Sabrina*), ABC, 1997–99.
Marcy Sternfeld/Kim Peterson, *Grosse Pointe*, The WB, 2000–2001.
Karly Stone, *The Stones*, CBS, 2004.

Television Appearances; Movies:
Fin, *Sabrina, Down Under*, ABC, 1999.
Wendy, *Student Affairs*, 1999.
She Said/He Said, 2006.

Television Appearances; Specials:
Voice of big sister, *Why, Charlie Brown, Why?* (animated), CBS, 1990.
Tina, "Between Mother and Daughter," *CBS Schoolbreak Special*, CBS, 1995.
Stars team member, *Basebrawl: MTV Rock N' Jock*, MTV, 2001.

Television Appearances; Pilots:
Sasha Hoffman, *Help Me Help You*, ABC, 2006.

Television Appearances; Episodic:
Ruthie, "Halloween," *My So–Called Life*, ABC, 1994.
Rebecca Gold, "Intolerance," *Promised Land* (also known as *Home of the Brave*), CBS, 1997.
Debbie Rainer, "Close Quarters," *Working*, NBC, 1997.
Jennifer, "Haus Arrest," *Dharma and Greg*, ABC, 1997.
Voice of Jackie, "Earth Mover," *Batman Beyond* (animated), The WB, 1999.
Patty, "Eric Gets Suspended," *That 70s Show*, Fox, 1999.
Patty, "Kitty and Eric's Night Out," *That 70s Show*, Fox, 2000.
Stacy, Zoey's friend, "Six Meetings before Lunch," *The West Wing*, NBC, 2000.
Summer Raynes, "Boys in the Band," *M.Y.O.B.*, NBC, 2000.
Officer Gloria, "Blood, Sweat & Fitz," *The Fighting Fitzgeralds*, NBC, 2001.
Lara, "Instant Karma," *Strange Frequency 2*, VH1, 2001.
Lisa B., "Blowing Free: Parts 1 & 2," *Going to California*, Showtime, 2001.
Lisa B., "The Big Padoodle," *Going to California*, Showtime, 2001.
Chelsea, "Jewel Heist," *Greg the Bunny*, Fox, 2002.
Nicole, "I Wanna Be Sedated," *Entourage*, HBO, 2006.
The Late Late Show with Craig Ferguson, CBS, 2006.
Sasha Hoffman, "The Mattress," *Help Me Help You*, ABC, 2006.
Sasha Hoffman, "Perverse Psychology," *Help Me Help You*, ABC, 2006.

Also appeared in "The Popcorn Machine," *Too Something* (also known as *New York Daze*), Fox; as Daphne, "Matchmaker, Matchmaker," *Miss Match*, NBC.

Stage Appearances:
Appeared in *The Emperor's New Clothes; Say Yo Ho Ho; Rumors;* and *Cabaret*.

SMITH, Iain 1949–

PERSONAL

Full name, Iain Alistair Robertson Smith; born January 8, 1949, in Glasgow, Scotland; son of Nathaniel Lawrence Albert and Anne Cameron (maiden name,

Urquhart) Smith; married Isabel Buchanan, July 1, 1975; children: three. *Education:* Graduated from London Film School, 1971. *Avocational Interests:* Reading, theater, cinema, Scottish painting, walking, philosophy, and travel.

Addresses: *Office*—U.K. Film Council, 10 Little Poland St., London W1W 7JG United Kingdom. *Manager*—Sandra Marsh Management, 9150 Wilshire Blvd., Suite 220, Beverly Hills, CA 90212.

Career: Producer. Cofounder of a production company, which produced television commercials, documentaries, children's feature films, and low budget dramas in the 1970s and 1980s; Applecross Productions, founder, 1987. UK Film Council, board member; Creative Scotland, board member; Film Skills Strategy Committee, chairperson; British Film Advisory Group, deputy chairman; Children's Film and Television Foundation, director; Production Guild of Great Britain, vice president; British Film Commission, deputy chairman; previously served on the boards of the Scottish Film Council, Scottish Film Production Fund, and Scottish Film Training Trust; National Film and Television School, former governor.

Member: Scottish Film Training Trust (founding member), British Screen Advocacy Council and Skillset, British Academy of Film and Television Arts, British Film Institute.

Awards, Honors: Outstanding Achievement Award, British Academy of Film and Television Arts Awards—Scotland, 2005, for outstanding achievement in film.

CREDITS

Film Associate Producer:
Local Hero, Warner Bros., 1983.
The Killing Fields, Warner Bros., 1984.
The Mission, Warner Bros., 1986.

Film Producer:
The Frog Prince (also known as *French Lesson*), Warner Bros., 1984.
Killing Dad or How to Love Your Mother, Palace Pictures, 1989.
Seven Years in Tibet, Sony, 1997.
Alexander (also known as *Alexandre*), Warner Bros., 2004.
Children of Men, Universal, 2006.
The Fountain, Warner Bros., 2006.

Also worked as producer, *My Childhood,* BFI.

Film Coproducer:
Hearts of Fire, Lorimar Home Video, 1987.
City of Joy (also known as *La cite de la joie*), TriStar, 1992.
Mary Reilly, TriStar, 1996.
The Fifth Element (also known as *le cinquieme element*), Columbia, 1997.

Film Executive Producer:
1492: Conquest of Paradise (also known as *1492, 1492: Christophe Colomb, 1492: La conquete du paradis,* and *1492: La conquista del paraiso*), Paramount, 1992.
Entrapment (also known as *Verlockende Falle*), Twentieth Century–Fox, 1999.
Spy Game, Universal, 2001.
Cold Mountain, Miramax, 2003.

Film Work; Other:
Unit production manager, *La mort en direct* (also known as *Death Watch—Der gerkaufte tod, Death in Full View, Deathwatch,* and *Der gekaufte tod*), Embassy Home Entertainment, 1980.
Location manager, *Chariots of Fire,* Twentieth Century–Fox, 1981.
Line producer: London, *Planet of the Apes,* Twentieth Century–Fox, 2001.

Film Appearances:
Ambassador Cathcart, *Spy Game,* 2001.
Himself, *Resurrecting "Alexander"* (documentary short), Warner Home Video, 2005.

Television Work; Miniseries:
Unit manager, *Prime Suspect 7: The Final Act,* PBS, 2006–2007.

Television Appearances; Episodic:
Himself, "The Mission," *Omnibus,* BBC, 1986.

SMITH, J. W.

PERSONAL

Career: Actor.

CREDITS

Film Appearances:
A. C. Turnbull, *The Warriors,* Paramount, 1979.
Will, *Deal of the Century,* Warner Bros., 1983.

Black kidnapper, *D.C. Cab* (also known as *Street Fleet* and *Mr. T and Company*), 1983.

Police officer, *Girls Just Want to Have Fun,* New World, 1985.

Mercenary, *Let's Get Harry* (also known as *The Rescue*), TriStar, 1986.

Man at auto wrecking yard, *Crossroads,* Columbia, 1986.

First dealer, *Outrageous Fortune,* Buena Vista, 1987.

Salim, *Red Heat,* Columbia TriStar, 1988.

Pimp, *K–9,* 1989.

Larry, *Johnny Handsome,* Columbia TriStar, 1989.

Willie, *False Identity,* 1990.

Sergeant Walter Hodo, *Downtown,* 1990.

Sporty Black, *Bloodfist III: Forced to Fight* (also known as *Forced to Fight*), New Horizon, 1991.

Video dealer, *Deep Cover,* United International Pictures, 1992.

Detective Clich, *Don't be a Menace to South Central While Drinking Your Juice in the Hood* (also known as *Don't be a Menace*), Miramax, 1996.

Calvin, *Hoodlum,* United Artists, 1997.

Postman, *Why Do Fools Fall in Love,* Warner Bros., 1998.

Red, *Spanish Judges* (also known as *Ruthless Behaviour*), 1999.

Mess guard, *Undisputed* (also known as *Undisputed— Sieg ohne ruhm*), Miramax, 2002.

Souled Out, Anthem Pictures, 2005.

Television Appearances; Miniseries:

Nathaniel Carter, *The Atlanta Child Murders,* CBS, 1985.

Vincent, *House of Frankenstein,* NBC, 1997.

Television Appearances; Movies:

Synanon man, *Attack on Fear,* CBS, 1984.

The Children of Times Square (also known as *Street Wise*), ABC, 1986.

L.A. Takedown (also known as *L.A. Crimewave* and *Made in L.A.*), NBC, 1989.

Vincent, *House of Frankenstein 1997,* 1997.

Television Appearances; Specials:

Voice of doorman and factory worker, *Happy Prince: An Animated Special From "The Happily Ever After: Fairy Tales for Children"* (animated), 1999.

Television Appearances; Pilots:

The Last Days of Russell, ABC, 1995.

Television Appearances; Episodic:

Citizen, "Domestic Beef," *Hill Street Blues,* 1982.

Citizen, "Officer of the Year," *Hill Street Blues,* 1982.

"The Arrival," *Falcon Crest,* 1982.

Roller, "Death by Kiki," *Hill Street Blues,* 1983.

Cabbie, "Yesterday It Rained," *Knots Landing,* 1984.

Roach, "Once a Hero," *Airwolf* (also known as *Lobo del aire*), 1984.

Arthur Baker, "Suitcase," *Hill Street Blues,* 1986.

Referee, "One of the Boys," *Valerie* (also known as *The Hogan Family, The Hogans,* and *Valerie's Family*), 1986.

Walt Buckner, "Fifty Ways to Floss Your Lover," *L.A. Law,* NBC, 1987.

Rik, "Rakers," *Max Headroom* (also known as *Max Headroom: 20 Minutes Into the Future*), 1987.

Rik, "Body Banks," *Max Headroom* (also known as *Max Headroom: 20 Minutes Into the Future*), 1987.

Rik, "Security Systems," *Max Headroom* (also known as *Max Headroom: 20 Minutes Into the Future*), 1987.

"The Mafia Priest Mystery: Part 1" (also known as "The Renegade Priest Mystery")," *Father Dowling Mysteries,* 1989.

Charley Ledbetter, "The Man Who Was Death," *Tales From the Crypt* (also known as *HBO's "Tales From the Crypt"*), HBO, 1989.

Jake, "Stake–Out," *Family Matters,* ABC, 1989.

Eddie, "Pool Hall Blues—September 4, 1954," *Quantum Leap,* NBC, 1989.

Larry Sheflo, "Hello, Goodbye," *Life Goes On,* ABC, 1991.

Peanuts, "Hard Bargains," *Reasonable Doubts,* NBC, 1991.

Peanuts, "Making Dirt Stick," *Reasonable Doubts,* NBC, 1991.

Jack Knife, "Roc Works for Joey," *Roc,* Fox, 1992.

Walt, "Wedding Bells & Box Boys," *Sister, Sister,* The WB, 1994.

Sheriff, "The Closer I Get to You," *Martin,* Fox, 1994.

Man with bandaged head, *Sister, Sister,* The WB, 1994–95.

Shelton, "The Shawn–Shank Redemption," *The Wayans Bros.,* The WB, 1995.

Steve, "X–Cops," *The X–Files,* Fox, 2000.

(Uncredited) "South Side Story," *The Hughleys,* UPN, 2001.

Stuart, "The Princeless Bride," *Touched by an Angel,* CBS, 2002.

Construction Worker number two, "Inky Dinky Don't," *Listen Up,* CBS, 2005.

Prefect of Wanganui, "The Prefect of Wanganui," *Reno 911!,* Comedy Central, 2005.

Stage Appearances:

Jim, *We Interrupt This Program ...,* Ambassador Theatre, New York City, 1975.

Gunn, *So Nice, They Named It Twice,* Joseph Papp Public Theater, New York City, 1976.

SMITH, Marcy
See WALKER, Marcy

SNYDER, William
See PRINZI, Frank

SOSNOVSKA, Olga 1972–

PERSONAL

Born May 21, 1972, in Warsaw, Poland; immigrated to England, c. 1983; married Sendhil Ramamurthy, 1999. *Education:* Studied acting at the Webber Douglas Academy, London.

Addresses: *Agent*—Cornerstone Talent Agency, 37th West 20th St., Suite 1108, New York, NY 10011. *Manager*—Andy Freedman Personal Management, 20 Ironsides St. Suite 18, Marina Del Rey, CA 90292.

Career: Actress. Appeared in television commercials for DeBeers Diamonds, 2004, and Thomasville Furniture Store, 2005.

CREDITS

Film Appearances:
Preserve, 1999.
Simone, *House of D,* Lions Gate Films, 2004.
Debbie, *Ocean's Thirteen* (also known as *13*), Warner Bros., 2007.

Television Appearances; Series:
Lena Kundera, *All My Children,* ABC, 2002–2004.
Fiona Carter, *Spooks* (also known as *MI–5*), BBC, 2004–2005.

Television Appearances; Miniseries:
Keda, *Gormenghast,* BBC2 and BBC America, 2000.
Atalanta, *Jason and the Argonauts,* NBC, 2000.
Andrea Patton, *Take Me,* ITV, 2001.
Linda, *The Lost Empire* (also known as *Monkey King—Ein Krieger zwischen den welten*), NBC, 2001.

Television Appearances; Movies:
Appeared in *The Queen and Her Lover,* BBC.

Television Appearances; Specials:
The 30th Annual Daytime Emmy Awards, ABC, 2003.

Television Appearances; Episodic:
Tanya, "Sons: Part 2," *The Vice,* ITV, 1999.

Marie–Helene, *Monarch of the Glen,* BBC Scotland and BBC America, 2001.
Jean Marie Lofficier, "Probability," *Law & Order: Criminal Intent* (also known as *Law & Order: CI*), NBC, 2003.
Velida Prinskka, "House Calls," *Law & Order,* NBC, 2003.
The View, ABC, 2003.
SoapTalk, Soap Net, 2003.
Natalya Chernus, "Honor Among Thieves," *Criminal Minds,* CBS, 2007.

Stage Appearances:
Lucille Cadeau, *House,* City Center Theatre, New York City, 2002.
Lucille Cadeau, *Garden,* City Center Theatre, 2002.

Also appeared as Rosaline, *Much Ado About Nothing,* Cliveden Open Air Theatre, Cliveden, England; Jemima, *A Busy Day,* Bristol Old Vic and West End Theatre, London.

SPANO, Vincent 1962–

PERSONAL

Born October 18, 1962, in Brooklyn, NY; married Crista.

Addresses: *Agent*—Innovative Artists, 1505 10th St., Santa Monica, CA 90401. *Manager*—Next Stop Management, 2923 Pearl St., Santa Monica, CA 90405.

Career: Actor.

CREDITS

Stage Appearances:
(Stage debut) *The Shadow Box,* Morosco Theatre, New York City, 1977.
Tig, *Balm in Gilead,* Minetta Lane Theatre, New York City, 1984.

Film Appearances:
(Debut) Mark, *Over the Edge,* Warner Brothers, 1979.
Foster, *The Double McGuffin,* Mulberry Square, 1979.
Gas thief, *A Stranger Is Watching,* 1982.
Steve, *Rumble Fish,* Universal, 1983.
Sheik Capadilupo, *Baby, It's You,* Paramount, 1983.
Raj, *The Black Stallion Returns,* Metro–Goldwyn–Mayer/United Artists, 1983.
Johnny, *Alphabet City,* Atlantic, 1984.

Boris Lafkin, *Creator* (also known as *The Big Picture*), Universal, 1985.

Al Griselli, *Maria's Lovers,* Cannon, 1985.

Nicola Bonnano, *Good Morning Babylon* (also known as *Good Morning Babilonia*), Vestron, 1987.

Billy Moran, *And God Created Woman,* Vestron, 1987.

Peter, *Qualcuno in ascolto* (also known as *High Frequency*), 1988.

Carlo Goldoni, *Rouge Venise* (also known as *Venezia rosso sangue* and *Venetian Red*), 1989.

Mitchell Bryce, *Heart of the Deal,* 1990.

Anthony Rossano, *Oscar,* 1991.

Nick Rinaldi, *City of Hope,* 1991.

Antonio Balbi, *Alive* (also known as *Alive: The Miracle of the Andes*), 1993.

Matthew Berman, *Indian Summer* (also known as *L'ete indien*), 1993.

Franco Distassi, *The Ascent,* 1994.

Russell Clifton, *The Tie That Binds,* 1995.

Frank Cavatelli, *The Unknown Cyclist,* Trident Releasing, 1997.

Mark Demetrius, *No Strings Attached* (also known as *The Last Obsession*), Redwood Communications, 1997.

Al Stanco, *A Brooklyn State of Mind,* Miramax, 1997.

Zophael "Jones", *The Prophecy III: The Ascent* (also known as *God's Army III*), Dimension Films, 2000.

Ed Simms, *Texas Rangers,* Miramax, 2001.

Detective Steve Banks, *Silence* (also known as *The Only Witness*), Marvista Entertainment, 2003.

Miles, *A Modern Twain Story: The Prince and the Pauper,* 2007.

Devin Bayliss, *Nevermore,* 2007.

Film Work:

Director and cinematographer, *High Expectations* (short), 2002.

Director, *Betrunner* (short), 2004.

Television Appearances; Series:

Jackie Peterson, *Search for Tomorrow,* NBC, 1979.

Detective Alex Gage, *Prince Street,* NBC, 1997.

Television Appearances; Miniseries:

Scott Nash, *Medusa's Child,* ABC, 1997.

Television Appearances; Movies:

Dick, *Senior Trip!,* CBS, 1981.

Angel Perez, *The Gentleman Bandit* (also known as *The Bandit Priest*), CBS, 1981.

Mark Ciuni, *Blood Ties* (also known as *Il cugino americano*), Showtime, 1986.

Ted Harduval, *Afterburn,* HBO, 1992.

Jack, *Downdraft,* Showtime, 1996.

Balthazar, *The Christmas Path,* Fox, 1999.

Brett Becher, *The Deadly Look of Love* (also known as *Mine Forever* and *True Romance*), Lifetime, 2000.

Steven Binder, *Goosed,* The Movie Channel, 2000.

Jack, *Jenifer* (also known as *The Jenfier Estess Story*), CBS, 2001.

Jack Carver, *The Rats,* Fox, 2002.

Detective Steve Banks, *The Only Witness,* Lifetime, 2002.

Ryan Cawdor, *Deathlands: Homeward Bound,* Sci–Fi Channel, 2003.

Mark Decker, *Landslide,* Hallmark Channel, 2004.

Tony Di Cenzo, *The Engagement Ring,* TNT, 2005.

Robert Genaro, *Her Fatal Flaw,* Lifetime, 2006.

Troy Whitlock, *Pandemic,* Hallmark Channel, 2007.

Television Appearances; Specials:

Intimate Portrait: Rosanna Arquette, Lifetime, 2003.

Television Appearances; Episodic:

Officer Fine, "Two for the Show," *Tales from the Crypt* (also known as *HBO's "Tales from the Crypt"*), HBO, 1993.

Dan Ralston, "The Big One," *North Shore,* Fox, 2004.

Dan Ralston, "The Cook, the Waitress, the GM, and His Lover," *North Shore,* 2004.

FBI Agent Dean Porter, "Infiltrated," *Law & Order: Special Victims Unit* (also known as *Law & Order: SVU* and *Special Victims Unit*), 2006.

FBI Agent Dean Porter, "Florida," *Law & Order: Special Victims Unit* (also known as *Law & Order: SVU* and *Special Victims Unit*), 2007.

FBI Agent Dean Porter, "Screwed," *Law & Order: Special Victims Unit* (also known as *Law & Order: SVU* and *Special Victims Unit*), 2007.

Television Work; Movies:

Director, *Storm,* Fox, 1999.

Television Work; Specials:

Director, *In the Groove,* HBO, 1994.

Television Work; Episodic:

Director, "Two for the Show," *Tales from the Crypt* (also known as *HBO's "Tales from the Crypt"*), HBO, 1989.

SPHEERIS, Penelope 1945–
   (P. Spheeris)

PERSONAL

Born December 2, 1945, in New Orleans, LA; father, a circus carnival owner and side–show "strong man"; mother, a ticket taker for a traveling circus side show;

children: Anna Schoeller. *Education:* University of California, Los Angeles, B.A. and M.F.A., film; also studied at American Film Institute, Los Angeles.

Addresses: *Agent*—Gersh Agency, Inc., 232 North Canon Dr., Beverly Hills, CA 90210–5302.

Career: Director, producer, and writer. Rock 'n' Reel (music video production company), founder, 1974, and producer of music videos; Spheeris Films, filmmaker; appeared in print ads for the Directors Guild of America, 2001. Worked as a waitress for twelve years.

Member: Directors Guild of America, Writers Guild of America.

Awards, Honors: Freedom of Expression Award and Grand Jury Prize nomination, both Sundance Film Festival, and Jury Award, best documentary, Chicago Underground Film Festival, 1998, all for *The Decline of Western Civilization Part III;* Most Popular Documentary Award, Melbourne International Film Festival, 2001, for *We Sold Our Souls for Rock 'n Roll;* Spirit of Silver Lake Award, Los Angeles Silver Lake Film Festival, 2001; Pioneer Filmmaker Award, Deep Ellum Film Festival, 2001; Lifetime Achievement Award, Temecula Valley International Film Festival, 2003; Maverick Award, LA Femme Film Festival, 2005.

CREDITS

Film Work:
Editor, *Uncle Tom's Fairy Tales,* 1968.
Director, *I Don't Know,* 1971.
Producer, *Real Life,* Paramount, 1979.
Director, producer, additional photography, and (as P. Spheeris) additional cinematographer, *The Decline of Western Civilization* (documentary), Spheeris Films, 1981.
Director, *Suburbia* (also known as *Rebel Streets* and *The Wild Side*), New World, 1984.
Director, *The Boys Next Door* (also known as *Big Shots*), New World, 1985.
Director, *Hollywood Vice Squad* (also known as *The Boulevard*), Cinema Group, 1986.
Director, *Dudes,* Cineworld, 1986.
Director, *The Decline of Western Civilization II: The Metal Years* (documentary), New Line Cinema, 1986.
Director, *As Nasty As We Want to Be,* 1990.
Director, *Thunder and Mud,* 1990.
Director, *Wayne's World,* Paramount, 1992.
Director and producer, *The Beverly Hillbillies,* Twentieth Century–Fox, 1993.
Director, *The Little Rascals,* Universal, 1994.
Director, *Black Sheep,* Paramount, 1996.

Director, *Senseless,* Miramax/Dimension Films, 1998.
Director and camera operator, *The Decline of Western Civilization Part III* (documentary), Spheeris Films, 1998.
Director, *The Thing in Bob's Garage,* Act III Productions, 1998.
Director, *No Use Walking When You Can Stroll,* 1998.
Director, *Hollywierd,* 1999.
Director and cinematographer, *We Sold Our Souls for Rock 'n' Roll* (documentary), Divine Pictures, 2001.
Director, *Posers,* Miramax, 2001.
Director, *Closers,* Dimension Films, 2001.
Director and producer, *The Kid & I,* Slowhand Cinema Releasing, 2005.

Also made *Lifers Group: World Tour* (documentary short).

Film Appearances:
Naked Angels, 1969.
Star the witch, *The Ski Bum* (also known as *Point Zero*), 1971.
Margo, *The Second Coming of Suzanne* (also known as *Suzanne*), 1974.
Calling the Shots, 1988.
Nicky's mom, *Wedding Band,* 1990.
(Uncredited) Cameo, *Wayne's World,* Paramount, 1992.
Penelope Spheeris, *The Kid & I,* Slowhand Cinema Releasing, 2005.

Television Work; Movies:
Director, *The Crooked E: The Unshredded Truth About Enron,* CBS, 2003.

Television Work; Specials:
(With others) Director, *Decade,* MTV, 1989.
Segment director, "New Chicks," in "Prison Stories: Women on the Inside," *HBO Showcase,* HBO, 1991.
Director, *Visitors from the Unknown,* CBS, 1991.
Director, *UFO Abductions,* 1991.
Segment director, *The 75th Annual Academy Awards,* ABC, 2002.
Segment director, *Oscar Countdown 2003,* 2003.
Cinematographer, *Mississippi Rising,* 2005.

Television Work; Pilots:
Cocreator, executive producer, and director, *Danger Theatre,* Fox, 1993.
Director, *Dear Doughboy,* The WB, 2000.

Television Work; Episodic:
Producer: film segments, *Saturday Night Live* (also known as *SNL*), NBC, 1975–76.
Story editor, "One for the Road," *Roseanne,* ABC, 1990.
Director, "Prom Night," *Cracking Up,* 2004.

Television Appearances; Specials:
Decade, MTV, 1989.
VH1 Presents the '70s, VH1, 1996.
Canned Ham: Senseless, Comedy Central, 1998.
Intimate Portrait: Lea Thompson, Lifetime, 1998.
100 Greatest Artists of Hard Rock, VH1, 2000.
Ernest Goes to Hollywood: Jim Varney, the E! True Hollywood Story, E! Entertainment Television, 2001.
VH1 Presents the '80s, VH1, 2001.
The Beverly Hillbillies: The E! True Hollywood Story, E! Entertainment Television, 2001.
Herself, *Hollywood High,* AMC, 2003.
When Metal Ruled the World, VH1, 2004.
Z Channel: A Magnificent Obsession, Independent Film Channel, 2004.
The Story of Bohemian Rhapsody, BBC, 2004.
Heavy: The Story of Metal, VH1, 2005–2006.

Television Appearances; Episodic:
Independent View, PBS, 2002.
"Penelope Spheeris/John Doe," *The Henry Rollins Show,* Independent Film Channel, 2006.

WRITINGS

Film Scripts:
The Decline of Western Civilization (documentary), Spheeris Films, 1981.
Suburbia (also known as *Rebel Streets* and *The Wild Side*), New World, 1984.
(With Bert Dragin) *Summer Camp Nightmare* (also known as *The Butterfly Revolution*), Concorde, 1987.
(And story) *The Little Rascals,* Universal, 1994.

Television Pilot Stories:
Danger Theatre, Fox, 1993.

Television Episodes:
"Fender Bender," *Roseanne,* ABC, 1990.

OTHER SOURCES

Books:
Authors and Artists for Young Adults, Vol. 46, Gale Group, 2002.
International Dictionary of Films and Filmmakers, Volume 2: *Directors,* St. James Press, 1996.
Newsmakers 1989, Issue 4, Gale, 1989.
Women Filmmakers and Their Films, St. James Press, 1998.

Periodicals:
People Weekly, July 4, 1988, pp. 52–54.

SPOKE, Suanne

PERSONAL

Born in Meadville, PA.

Career: Actress.

CREDITS

Film Appearances:
Mrs. Travis, *An American Summer,* 1991.
Lecture woman number two, *Krippendorf's Tribe,* Buena Vista, 1998.
Bruno's woman, *P.U.N.K.S.* (also known as *Rebels*), 1999.
Mrs. Lippman, *More Dogs Than Bones,* 2000.
Autograph seeker, *There's Something About Meryl* (short), 2004.
Businesswoman, *War of the Worlds,* Paramount, 2005.
Drunk woman, *Peace* (short), 2005.
Lady One, *Crazylove,* PorchLight Entertainment, 2005.

Television Appearances; Miniseries:
Dorinda Morgan, *The Beach Boys: An American Family,* ABC, 2000.

Television Appearances; Movies:
Tourist wife, *Supreme Sanction,* HBO, 1999.
Ann B. Davis/Alice, *Growing Up Brady,* NBC, 2000.

Television Appearances; Episodic:
Girl in lobby, "Ladies of the Evening," *The Golden Girls,* CBS, 1986.
Officer Goodman, "The Lung Goodbye," *L.A. Law,* NBC, 1987.
Cop number two, "Izzy Ackerman or Is He Not," *L.A. Law,* NBC, 1989.
Customer, "The Jacket," *Seinfeld,* NBC, 1991.
"Brush with the Elbow of Greatness," *The Larry Sanders Show,* HBO, 1992.
Madame Sonia, *Step by Step,* ABC, 1992.
Miss Heitzman, "Reach for the Stars," *Getting By,* ABC, 1993.
Doctor Jerri McCorkle, *Lois and Clark: The New Adventures of Superman,* ABC, 1993.
Madame Sonia, "The Psychic," *Step by Step,* ABC, 1993.
Madame Sonia, "Feeling Forty," *Step by Step,* ABC, 1994.
Doctor, "The Labors of Love," *Beverly Hills, 90210,* Fox, 1994.
Jana, "One Flew Over the Courthouse," *Courthouse,* CBS, 1995.

Caterer, "The Wedding," *Party of Five,* Fox, 1995.
Rebecca, "Sexual Chemistry," *Hot Line,* 1996.
Big–haired woman, *Lois and Clark: The New Adventures of Superman,* ABC, 1996.
Woman, "Adventures of Rebound Girl," *Townies,* ABC, 1996.
Female police officer, "Little Red Corvette," *The Jamie Foxx Show,* The WB, 1997.
Penelope, "The Apartment," *Life with Roger,* The WB, 1997.
Obstetrician receptionist, "Random Acts," *ER,* NBC, 1997.
Manager, *Hangin' with Mr. Cooper,* ABC, 1997.
"Dying to Live," *Profiler,* NBC, 1997.
Prudish woman, "The Old West," *Unhappily Ever After* (also known as *Unhappily ... ,* The WB, 1997.
Bibi, "The Great Dickdater," *3rd Rock from the Sun* (also known as *3rd Rock* and *Life As We Know It*), NBC, 1998.
Mrs. Sardell, "Father's Keeper," *Clueless,* UPN, 1998.
Big Mark's mom, *Two of a Kind,* ABC, 1998.
Assistant director Bobbie Lopez, *Vengeance Unlimited,* ABC, 1998.
Maggie, "Went to a Garden Party," *Style and Substance,* 1998.
Mrs. Sardell, "Popularity," *Clueless,* UPN, 1999.
Woman customer, "Monday," *The X–Files,* Fox, 1999.
Receptionist, "Norm and the Prototype," *The Norm Show* (also known as *Norm*), ABC, 1999.
Eileen, *Passions,* 2000.
Patrice Patterson, "Zero Tolerance," *Judging Amy,* CBS, 2000.
Patrice Patterson, "You're Not the Boss of Me," *Judging Amy,* CBS, 2000.
Wanda, "Boxing Dharma," *Dharma and Greg,* 2000.
Iris, "Holy Craps," *That '70s Show,* Fox, 2001.
"There But for Fortune," *The Division* (also known as *Heart of the City*), Lifetime, 2001.
Irene, "Is She Really Going Out with Walt?," *Grounded for Life,* 2002.
Sophie Taylor/Marj Fennell, "Bad to Worse," *The Practice,* ABC, 2002.
Darlene Stimson, "Let's Make a Deal," *Dragnet* (also known as *L.A. Dragnet*), ABC, 2003.
Katey Mills in 2003, "Hitchhiker," *Cold Case,* CBS, 2003.
"As I Was Going to St. Ives," *The Division* (also known as *Heart of the City*), Lifetime, 2004.
Loreen, "Driving Miss Gilmore," *Gilmore Girls,* The WB, 2006.

Stage Appearances:
Appeared in *David's Mother,* Los Angeles.

STAFFORD, Michelle 1965–

PERSONAL

Born September 14, 1965, in Chicago, IL; father a lawyer; mother a film studio executive. Religion: Scientologist. *Religion:* Scientologist. *Avocational Interests:* Travel.

Addresses: *Agent*—Glick Agency, 1250 Sixth St., Suite 100, Santa Monica, CA 90401.

Career: Actress. Second Avenue Productions (theatre company), cofounder. Model for runway fashion shows in Europe, Japan, and the United States, and for print advertisements; appeared in commercials for Herbal Essences shampoo, 2001, Toyota Camry, 2006, and American Airlines. Also worked in sales. Philanthropist; volunteer with Citizens Commission on Human Rights and Hollywood Education and Literacy Project.

Awards, Honors: *Soap Opera Digest* Awards, outstanding female newcomer, 1996, outstanding villainess, 1997, outstanding lead actress, 2003, and *Soap Opera Digest* Award nominations, outstanding female scene stealer, 2001, and outstanding lead actress, 2005, Daytime Emmy Awards, outstanding supporting actress in a drama series, 1997, and outstanding lead actress in a drama series, 2004, Daytime Emmy Award nominations, outstanding lead actress in a drama series, 2003, 2005, Special Fan Award nomination, irresistible combination (with Peter Bergman), Daytime Emmy Awards, 2005, all for *The Young and the Restless;* award from National Foundation for Women Legislators.

CREDITS

Television Appearances; Series:
Frankie, *Tribes,* Fox, 1990.
Phyllis Summers Newman, *The Young and the Restless* (also known as *Y&R*), CBS, 1994–97, 2000—.
Joanna Hadley, *Pacific Palisades,* Fox, 1997.
Sheila Carter, a recurring role, *The Young and the Restless* (also known as *Y&R*), CBS, 2006, 2007.

Television Appearances; Movies:
Hotel guest, *Another Midnight Run,* syndicated, 1994.
Dawna, *Like Mother, Like Daughter,* Lifetime, 2007.

Television Appearances; Specials:
CBS Soap Break, CBS, 1995.
The All–American Thanksgiving Parade, CBS, 1996.
Host, *The All–American Thanksgiving Parade,* CBS, 2000, 2001.
CMT: 20 Sexiest Women, 2004.
CMT: 20 Sexiest Men, 2004.
CMT: The Greatest—20 Sexiest Women, 2006.
CMT: The Greatest—20 Sexiest Men, 2006.

Television Appearances; Episodic:
Laura Jessup, "The Posse," *Renegade,* USA Network and syndicated, 1994.

Amber, *The Watcher,* UPN, 1995.

Vanessa Evans, "Wrath of Con," *Players,* NBC, 1998.

April, "Two Guys, a Girl, and a Softball Team," *Two Guy, a Girl, and a Pizza Place* (also known as *Two Guys and a Girl*), ABC, 1998.

Trish, "Gangland: Parts 1 & 2," *Diagnosis Murder,* CBS, 1999.

Suzanne Moore, "Contemptuous Minds," *JAG,* CBS, 1999.

Nancy Biggs, "Val Point Blank," *V.I.P.* (also known as *V.I.P.—Die Bodyguards*), syndicated, 2000.

Herself, *Sex Wars,* 2000.

Herself, *Who Knows You Best?,* 2000.

Heather Murphy, "The First Temptation of Daphne," *Frasier,* NBC, 2001.

Linda Barnes, "The Bottle Show," *Judging Amy,* CBS, 2002.

Guest cohost, *Good Day Live,* syndicated, 2004.

Sydney, "Between First and Home," *Clubhouse,* CBS, 2004.

Soap Talk, Soap Network, 2004, 2006.

Mandi, "Desperate Housewitches," *Charmed,* The WB, 2005.

Wheel of Fortune, syndicated, 2006.

Herself, "Tyra's Soap Opera Spectacular," *The Tyra Banks Show,* CW Network, 2007.

Appeared as Babs, *Models Inc.,* Fox; also appeared in an episode of *Strong Medicine,* Lifetime.

Television Appearances; Awards Presentations:

Presenter, *The 28th Annual Daytime Emmy Awards,* NBC, 2001.

Presenter, *The 30th Annual Daytime Emmy Awards,* ABC, 2003.

18th Annual Soap Opera Digest Awards, Soap Network, 2003.

Presenter, *The 39th Annual Academy of Country Music Awards,* CBS, 2004.

The 31st Annual Daytime Emmy Awards, NBC, 2004.

The 32nd Annual Daytime Emmy Awards, CBS, 2005.

The 33rd Annual Daytime Emmy Awards, ABC, 2006.

Film Appearances:

Madam, *Body of Influence* (also known as *Indecent Advances*), 1993.

Bidder Suzanne Monroe, *Double Jeopardy* (also known as *Doppelmord* and *Double condamnation*), Paramount, 1999.

Suzanne, *Attraction,* 2000.

Rachel, *Lost,* 2002.

Rene, *Cottonmouth* (also known as *Lethal Force* and *Silent Justice*), 2002.

Taffeta Munro, *Vampires Anonymous,* 2003.

Ex-wife Jessica, *Totally Baked: A Pot-u-Mentary,* 2007.

OTHER SOURCES

Periodicals:
Soap Opera Digest, August, 2000.
Soap Opera Weekly, March 5, 2002.
TV Guide, July 15, 2000, p. 44; August 16, 2003, p. 46.

STANTON, Gabrielle G.
(Gabrielle Stanton)

PERSONAL

Married Harry Werksman (an actor).

Addresses: *Agent*—The Kaplan Stahler Gumer Braun Agency, 8383 Wilshire Blvd., Suite 923, Beverly Hills, CA 90211.

Career: Producer, writer, and story editor.

Awards, Honors: Emmy Award nomination (with others), outstanding dramatic series, 2006, Writers Guild of America Television Award (with others), new series, 2006, Writers Guild of America Television Award nomination (with others), dramatic series, 2006, 2007, all for *Grey's Anatomy.*

CREDITS

Television Work; Series:

Story editor and executive story editor, *Farscape,* Sci–Fi Channel, 1999.

Coproducer, *The Invisible Man* (also known as *I–Man*), Sci–Fi Channel, 2000.

Producer, *The Invisible Man* (also known as *I–Man*), Sci–Fi Channel, 2001.

Coproducer, *Veritas: The Quest,* ABC, 2003.

(As Gabrielle Stanton) Producer, *Grey's Anatomy,* ABC, 2005.

(As Gabrielle Stanton) Supervising producer, *Grey's Anatomy,* ABC, 2005–2006.

(As Gabrielle Stanton) Supervising producer, *Ugly Betty,* ABC, 2007.

Television Work; Pilots:

Co–executive producer, *Moonlight,* CBS, 2007.

Film Work:

Assistant (for Mr. Zaloom), *Encino Man* (also known as *California Man*), Buena Vista, 1992.

Film Appearances:

(As Gabrielle Stanton) Gabrielle, *Free Enterprise,* Regent Entertainment, 1998.

(As Gabrielle Stanton) Herself, *Where No Fan Has Gone Before: The Making of "Free Enterprise"* (documentary), Pioneer Entertainment, 1999.

WRITINGS

Television Movies:

(As Gabrielle Stanton) *Deathlands* (also known as *Deathlands: Homeward Bound*), Sci–Fi Channel, 2003.

Television Episodes:

(Story only) "The Reckoning," *Star Trek: Deep Space Nine* (also known as *DS9, Deep Space Nine,* and *Star Trek: DS9*), syndicated, 1998.

V.I.P. (also known as *V.I.P.—Die Bodyguards*), syndicated, 1998.

"Bliss," *Earth: Final Conflict* (also known as *EFC, Gene Roddenberry's "Earth: Final Conflict," Invasion planete Terre,* and *Mission Erde: Sie dind unter uns*), syndicated, 1999.

"Highjacked," *Earth: Final Conflict* (also known as *EFC, Gene Roddenberry's "Earth: Final Conflict," Invasion planete Terre,* and *Mission Erde: Sie dind unter uns*), syndicated, 1999.

"Message in a Bottle," *Earth: Final Conflict* (also known as *EFC, Gene Roddenberry's "Earth: Final Conflict," Invasion planete Terre,* and *Mission Erde: Sie dind unter uns*), syndicated, 1999.

"Home on the Remains," *Farscape,* Sci–Fi Channel, 2000.

(Story only) "My Three Crichtons," *Farscape,* Sci–Fi Channel, 2000.

"The Ugly Truth," *Farscape,* Sci–Fi Channel, 2000.

"Going Postal," *The Invisible Man* (also known as *I–Man*), Sci–Fi Channel, 2001.

"Den of Thieves," *The Invisible Man* (also known as *I–Man*), Sci–Fi Channel, 2001.

"A Sense of Community," *The Invisible Man* (also known as *I–Man*), Sci–Fi Channel, 2001.

"Exposed," *The Invisible Man* (also known as *I–Man*), Sci–Fi Channel, 2001.

"Who's Zoomin' Who?," *Grey's Anatomy,* ABC, 2005.

"Much Too Much," *Grey's Anatomy,* ABC, 2005.

(As Gabrielle Stanton) "Staring at the Sun," *Grey's Anatomy,* ABC, 2005.

(As Gabrielle Stanton) "Band–Aid Covers the Bullet Hole," *Grey's Anatomy,* ABC, 2006.

(As Gabrielle Stanton) "Petra–Gate," *Ugly Betty,* ABC, 2007.

Also appeared in "Sangraal," *Veritas: The Quest.*

STANZLER, Wendey

PERSONAL

Addresses: *Agent*—Amy L. Retzinger, Gersh Agency, 232 North Canon Dr., Beverly Hills, CA 90210. *Manager*—Rabiner/Damato Entertainment, 617 North Beverly Dr., Beverly Hills, CA 90210.

Career: Film editor and director.

Awards, Honors: Eddie Award (with Jennifer Beman), best edited documentary, American Cinema Editors, 1990, for *Roger & Me;* Eddie Award nomination, best edited half–hour series for television, 2001, for "Running with Scissors," *Sex and the City;* Eddie Award, best edited half–hour series for television, and Emmy Award nomination, outstanding single–camera picture editing for a comedy series, both 2003, for "Luck Be an Old Lady," *Sex and the City;* Eddie Award nomination (with Michael Berenbaum), best edited half–hour series for television, 2004, for "The Catch," *Sex and the City;* Emmy Award nomination, outstanding single–camera picture editing for a comedy series, 2004, and Eddie Award (with Berenbaum), best edited half–hour series for television, 2005, both for "An American Girl in Paris," *Sex and the City.*

CREDITS

Film Editor:

(And producer) *Roger & Me* (documentary; also known as *A Humorous Look at How General Motors Destroyed Flint, Michigan*), Warner Bros., 1989.

The Last Party (documentary), Live Entertainment/Triton Pictures, 1993.

The Making of " … And God Spoke" (also known as *… And God Spoke*), Live Entertainment, 1994.

The Pesky Suitor (short film), Genre Films, 1995.

Canadian Bacon, Gramercy, 1995.

I'm Not Rappaport, Gramercy, 1996.

Nick and Jane, Avalanche Releasing, 1997.

Gray Matters, Yari Film Group Releasing, 2007.

Film Work; Other:

Sound editor, *Stryker's War* (also known as *Thou Shalt Not Kill … Except*), Film World Distributors, 1985.

Television Director; Episodic:

"The Ick Factor," *Sex and the City,* HBO, 2004.

"Who's Zoomin' Who?," *Grey's Anatomy,* ABC, 2005.

"Deny, Deny, Deny," *Grey's Anatomy,* ABC, 2005.

"Much Too Much," *Grey's Anatomy*, ABC, 2005.

"What Have I Done to Deserve This?," *Grey's Anatomy*, ABC, 2006.

"The Window," *Love Monkey*, CBS, 2006.

"Hey 19," *Six Degrees*, ABC, 2006.

"A New Light," *Six Degrees*, ABC, 2006.

"I Know Things Now," *Desperate Housewives*, ABC, 2006.

"A Weekend in the Country," *Desperate Housewives*, ABC, 2006.

"Children and Art," *Desperate Housewives*, ABC, 2006.

"Gossip," *Desperate Housewives*, ABC, 2007.

"History Lessons," *Men in Trees*, ABC, 2007.

"I'm Coming Out," *Ugly Betty*, ABC, 2007.

"Mr. Monk Goes to the Hospital," *Monk*, USA Network, 2007.

Also director for *Head Cases*, Fox.

Television Editor; Series:
Senior editor, *TV Nation*, NBC, 1994.
Sex and the City, HBO, multiple episodes, 1999–2001.
Ed, NBC, 2000.

Also film editor for the series *City Arts* and *Now and Again*, CBS.

Television Editor; Other:
Secrets of the CIA, 1988.

STENSTROM, David
    (David Stentstrom)

PERSONAL

Career: Actor.

CREDITS

Film Appearances:
Pool player number two, *Critters*, New Line Cinema, 1986.
Lieutenant Durschlag, *Project X*, Twentieth Century–Fox, 1987.
Wally Fenster, *Acts of Betrayal*, New City Releasing, 1997.
Voice of Demonite, *Power Rangers Lightspeed Rescue—Titanium Ranger: Curse of the Cobra*, 2000.

Television Appearances; Series:
Neil Johnson, *General Hospital*, ABC, 1986.

Hal, *Masked Rider* (also known as *Saban's "Masked Rider"*), Fox and syndicated, 1995–96.

Voice of King Mondo, *Power Rangers Zeo* (also known as *ZeoRangers*), Fox, 1996.

Television Appearances; Movies:
Ellis, *What Price Victory*, ABC, 1988.
Clerk, *Fatal Judgment*, CBS, 1988.
(As David Stentstrom) Fred Clawson, *The Revenge of Al Capone* (also known as *Capone*), NBC, 1989.

Television Appearances; Episodic:
Treehouse builder number two, "Hurry–Up," *Out of Control*, Nickelodeon, 1984.
Waldo, *Out of Control*, Nickelodeon, 1984.
Photographer, "Something Borrowed, Someone Blue," *Murder, She Wrote*, CBS, 1989.
Husband, "The Fixer–Upper," *Murder, She Wrote*, CBS, 1990.
Budding comic, "Where Have You Gone, Billy Boy?," *Murder, She Wrote*, CBS, 1991.
Studio guard, "Postcards from the Faultline," *Gabriel's Fire*, ABC, 1991.
Blatchley, "Graduation Day," *Reasonable Doubts*, NBC, 1991.
National labor relations board representative, "All These Things Will I Give Thee," *Homefront*, ABC, 1992.
Todd, "Dangerous Reunions," *Doogie Howser, M.D.*, ABC, 1992.
Customer, "Teach Your Children Well," *Sisters*, NBC, 1992.
Craps player, "Love and Hate in Cabot Cove," *Murder, She Wrote*, CBS, 1993.
Alcoholics Anonymous man, *Models Inc.*, Fox, 1994.
Santa, *Beverly Hills 90210*, Fox, 1994.
Hal Stewart, *Masked Rider*, Fox and syndicated, 1995.
Security guard, "Up on the Roof," *Full House*, ABC, 1995.
Dr. Baker, *Sparks*, UPN, 1996.
(Uncredited) Voice of King Mondo, "Countdown to Destruction: Part 1," *Power Rangers in Space*, Fox, 1998.
Voice of Demonite, "Ryan's Destiny," *Power Rangers Lightspeed Rescue* (also known as *Operation Lightspeed*), Fox, 2000.
Voice of Demonite Clone, "Curse of the Cobra," *Power Rangers Lightspeed Rescue* (also known as *Operation Lightspeed*), Fox, 2000.
Bill Davies, "Roast Chicken," *The King of Queens*, CBS, 2000.
Cop, "The Thanksgiving Story: Parts 1 & 2," *Providence*, NBC, 2000.
(Uncredited) Voice of narrator, "Force from the Future: Part 1," *Power Rangers Time Force*, Fox, 2001.
Voice of Fearog, "Ransik Lives," *Power Rangers Time Force*, Fox, 2001.

Bitter man, "The Kids Are Alright," *Grounded for Life*, Fox, 2002.

STEWART, Marlene 1949–

PERSONAL

Full name, Marlene Jean Stewart; born August 25, 1949, in Boston, MA; daughter of William Edward and Germaine (maiden name, Cormier) Stewart. *Education:* University of California, Berkeley, B.A., European history, 1972, and M.A.; Fashion Institute of Technology, New York City, A.A., 1975; Fashion Institute of Design and Merchandising, Los Angeles, A.A., 1976.

Addresses: *Home*—1416 N. Havenhurst Dr. #1C, Los Angeles, CA 90046.

Career: Fashion and costume designer. Covers, Inc., owner and designer, 1978–84. Costume designer for music videos, including Madonna's "Material Girl" and "Dress You Up"; for concert tours, including Madonna's Virgin Tour, 1985, and World Tour, 1987; and for commercials for firms such as Levi Strauss and Chrysler. Wardrobe consultant for various performers, including Duran Duran, Eurythmics, Pointer Sisters, Madonna, Janet Jackson, Grace Jones, and Isabella Rosellini. Museum of Contemporary Art, member.

Member: Costume Designers Guild, National Academy of Video Arts and Sciences, American Film Institute, National Organization of Female Executives.

Awards, Honors: Named best costume designer, American Video Awards, 1985; Women in Film Award, American Film Institute, 1987.

CREDITS

Film Costume Designer:
Body Rock, New World, 1984.
Back to the Beach (also known as *Malibu Beach Girls*), Paramount, 1987.
Siesta, Lorimar, 1987.
The Women's Club, 1987.
Gingerale Afternoon, 1989.
Pet Sematary (also known as *Stephen King's "Pet Sematary"*), Paramount, 1989.
Wild Orchid, Vision, 1990.
Side Out, TriStar, 1990.
The Doors, TriStar, 1991.

JFK (also known as *JFK—Affaire non classee*), Warner Bros., 1991.
Terminator 2: Judgment Day (also known as *T2, El exterminator 2, Terminator 2—Le jugement dernier,* and *T2—Terminator 2: Judgment Day*), TriStar, 1991.
Pet Sematary II, Paramount, 1992.
Point of No Return (also known as *The Assassin* and *The Assassin–(Point of No Return)*), Warner Bros., 1993.
Dangerous Game (also known as *Snake Eyes*), Metro–Goldwyn–Mayer, 1993.
Falling Down (also known as *Chute libre*), Warner Bros., 1993.
True Lies, Twentieth Century–Fox, 1994.
The River Wild, Universal, 1994.
I'll Do Anything, Columbia, 1994.
To Wong Foo, Thanks for Everything, Julie Newmar, Universal, 1995.
The Phantom, Paramount, 1996.
Space Jam, Warner Bros., 1996.
The Saint, Paramount, 1997.
The X–Files (also known as *Aux frontieres du reel*), Twentieth Century–Fox, 1998.
Enemy of the State, Buena Vista, 1998.
Gone in Sixty Seconds, Buena Vista, 2000.
The Adventures of Rocky and Bullwinkle (also known as *Die abenteuer von Rocky und Bullwinkle*), Universal, 2000.
Coyote Ugly, Buena Vista, 2000.
Ali, Columbia, 2001.
Tears of the Sun, Columbia, 2003.
21 Grams, Focus Features, 2003.
Hitch, 2005.
The Holiday, Universal, 2006.
Stop Loss, Paramount, 2007.

Film Visual Consultant:
Blueberry Hill, 1988.

Film Costume Consultant:
(To Mr. Stone) *Alexander* (also known as *Alexander Revisited: The Final Cut* and *Alexandre*), Warner Bros., 2004.

Film Appearances:
Herself, *"Hitch": Style,* 2005.

Television Costume Designer; Series:
2000 Malibu Road, CBS, 1992.

Television Costume Designer: Movies:
Pair of Aces, CBS, 1990.

Television Costume Designer; Pilots:
Gang of Four, ABC, 1989.

Television Costume Designer; Episodic:
"Elysian Fields," *CBS Summer Playhouse,* CBS, 1989.
"Collection Completed," *Tales from the Crypt* (also known as *HBO's "Tales from the Crypt"*), HBO, 1989.

OTHER SOURCES

Periodicals:
Premiere, April, 1991, p. 50.

STOLLERY, Brian

PERSONAL

Career: Actor and stand–up comedian. As a comedian, served as the opening act for "Weird Al" Yankovic on two tours.

CREDITS

Film Appearances:
The captain, *Legends of the Fall,* Columbia TriStar, 1994.
Grad student, *Last of the Dogmen,* Savoy Pictures, 1995.
Birks clerk, *Waydowntown,* Lot 47 Films, 2000.
Father, *Rat Race* (also known as *Course folle*), Paramount, 2001.
Dr. Bruce Kearn, *Cover Story* (also known as *Ambition fatale*), Skouras Films, 2002.
Global safety salesman, *A Problem with Fear* (also known as *Parano*), Christal Films, 2003.

Television Appearances; Series:
Tom Weatherby, *Jake and the Kid,* Global, 1995.
Wally, *Tom Stone* (also known as *Stone Undercover*), CBC, 2002–2004.

Television Appearances; Miniseries:
Beamis, *Roughing It* (also known as *Mark Twain's "Roughing It"*), Hallmark Channel, 2002.
Bob Williams, *Karroll's Christmas,* Arts and Entertainment, 2004.
Samuel Fenwick, *Everest,* 2007.

Television Appearances; Movies:
Clinical clerk number two, *Prescription for Movie,* 1987.
Dr. Pitts, *Out of Nowhere,* ABC, 1997.
David Winston, *A Father's Choice,* CBS, 2000.
Hotel clerk, *High Noon,* TBS, 2000.

Abraham Best, *Children of Fortune,* CBS, 2000.
Case officer, *The Death and Life of Nancy Eaton,* Oxygen, 2003.
Rupert, *Burn: The Robert Wraight Story* (also known as *Terres brulantes: L'histoire de Robert Wraight*), CTV, 2003.
Male suit number one, *Picking Up & Dropping Off,* ABC Family, 2003.
Glenn Feather, *Call Me: The Rise and Fall of Heidi Fleiss,* USA Network, 2004.
Accident victim, *Lies My Mother Told Me,* Lifetime, 2005.
Bishop Whipple, *Bury My Heart at Wounded Knee,* HBO, 2007.
Drosselmeyers assistant, *The Secret of the Nutcracker,* 2007.

Television Appearances; Episodic:
"Buffalo Bill's Wild West Show," *Lonesome Dove: The Series,* syndicated, 1995.
Ed, "Hunting in the Dark," *North of 60,* CBC, 1997.
"Honey, You're So Transparent," *Honey, I Shrunk the Kids: The TV Show,* syndicated, 1998.
Ross Moreau, "Truant," *Caitlin's Way* (also known as *Caitlin, Montana*), Nickelodeon and YTV, 2002.

Also appeared in "The Rifle Company," *The Campbells,* syndicated.

STONE, Danton

PERSONAL

Born in Queens, NY.

Career: Actor.

Awards, Honors: Drama Desk Award (with others), outstanding ensemble acting, 1985, for *Balm in Gilead.*

CREDITS

Film Appearances:
Fighting student, *The Chosen,* Analysis Film Releasing Corp., 1981.
Farouk, *Joy of Sex* (also known as *National Lampoon's "The Joy of Sex"*), Paramount, 1984.
Joe, *Maria's Lovers,* Cannon, 1984.
Aldo, *Band of the Hand,* TriStar, 1986.
Hired killer, *Eight Men Out,* Orion, 1988.
Dr. Wolfe, *Checking Out,* Warner Bros., 1989.
Saabs, *Crazy People,* Paramount, 1990.

Tony Bella, *Once Around,* Universal, 1991.
Eric, *He Said, She Said,* Paramount, 1991.
Gruber, *McHale's Navy,* MCA/Universal, 1997.
Bob Berns, *Series 7: The Contenders,* USA Films, 2001.
Charles Peak, *Approaching Heaven,* 2004.
Len, *Focus Group* (short), 2004.
Bruce Wallace, *Palindromes,* Wellspring Media, 2004.

Television Appearances; Series:
Rodney Wilhoit, *Tom,* CBS, 1994.
Brownie, *The Tom Show,* The WB, 1997.

Television Appearances; Miniseries:
Detective Sal Marchetti, *Internal Affairs,* CBS, 1988.

Television Appearances; Movies:
Weston "Wes" Hurley, *Fifth of July,* Showtime and PBS, 1989.
Longo, *Tongs,* ABC, 1989.
Peter Sissman, *Darrow,* PBS, 1991.
Benny Lazarra, *With Murder in Mind* (also known as *With Savage Intent*), CBS, 1992.
Barry, *Rock the Boat* (also known as *Atlantis Conspiracy*), 2000.

Television Appearances; Specials:
J. T., "The Gift of Amazing Grace," *ABC Afterschool Specials,* ABC, 1986.

Television Appearances; Episodic:
Brad Steadman, "Accounts Receivable," *thirtysomething,* ABC, 1988.
Luigi, "Tongs," *Gideon Oliver* (also known as *By the Rivers of Babylon*), ABC, 1989.
Jerry Bowman, "Trouble with the Rubbles," *Roseanne,* ABC, 1991.
Jerry Bowman, "Tolerate Thy Neighbor," *Roseanne,* ABC, 1991.
Jerry Bowman, "Trick Me Up, Trick Me Down," *Roseanne,* ABC, 1991.
Jerry Bowman, "The Commercial Show," *Roseanne,* ABC, 1991.
Father Carmine, *The Heights,* Fox, 1992.
Dave Speckler, "Guys and Balls," *The Jackie Thomas Show,* ABC, 1993.
Pete Bennett, "A Picture's Worth ... $9.95," *Grace Under Fire,* ABC, 1993.
Neil Chase, "Dancing in the Dark," *My So–Called Life,* ABC, 1994.
Neil Chase, "Resolutions," *My So–Called Life,* ABC, 1995.
Neil Chase, "Weekend," *My So–Called Life,* ABC, 1995.
Jack Wilderman, "Angel," *Law & Order,* NBC, 1995.
"Neighborhood Watch," *Cosby,* CBS, 1996.
District attorney Pat Fortunato, "Losing Your Appeal," *Oz,* HBO, 1998.

District attorney Pat Fortunato, "Strange Bedfellows," *Oz,* HBO, 1998.
"Breaking In, Breaking Out, Breaking Up, Breaking Down," *Trinity,* NBC, 1999.
Mr. Sontag, "Commendatori," *The Sopranos,* HBO, 2000.
District attorney Pat Fortunato, "The Bill of Wrongs," *Oz,* HBO, 2000.
Mr. Nerolik, "Thieves Like Us," *Once and Again,* ABC, 2001.
"Closure," *Ed,* NBC, 2001.
Building superintendent, "Surveillance," *Law & Order: Special Victims Unit* (also known as *Law & Order: SVU* and *Special Victims Unit*), NBC, 2002.
Rick Morrissey, "Yesterday," *Law & Order: Criminal Intent* (also known as *Law & Order: CI*), NBC, 2002.
Patrick, "Unoriginal Sin," *Sex and the City,* HBO, 2002.
Officer Morgenstern, "Three Boys and a Gun," *The Jury,* Fox, 2004.
Officer Morgenstern, "The Boxer," *The Jury,* Fox, 2004.
Gerald Hanes, "No Good Deed," *Jonny Zero,* Fox, 2005.
Ed, "Homeless Hal," *Hope & Faith,* NBC, 2006.

Stage Appearances:
Israel James, *Mrs. Murray's Farm,* Circle Theatre, New York City, 1976.
Alfred Hugenberg/Bob, *Lulu,* Circle Theatre, 1978.
Weston Hurley, *Fifth of July,* Circle Theatre, 1978.
Say Goodnight Gracie, Playwrights Horizon Theatre, New York City, 1978.
Jack Gerabauldi, *In the Recovery Lounge,* Circle Theatre, 1979.
Weston Hurley, *Fifth of July,* New Apollo Theatre, New York City, 1980–82.
Don Tabaha, *Angels Fall,* Circle Theatre, 1983.
Joe, *Balm in Gilead,* Circle Repertory Theatre, New York City, 1984.
Eddie Pataco, *Dysan,* Circle Repertory Theatre, 1985.
Paul Forrest, *In This Fallen City,* Circle Repertory Theatre, 1986.
Chuck Galluccio, *Fortune's Fools,* Cherry Lane Theatre, New York City, 1995.
Mere Mortals and Others, Primary Stages Theatre, New York City, 1997.
Martini, *One Flew Over the Cuckoo's Nest,* Steppenwolf Theatre, Chicago, IL, 2000, then London and Royal Theatre, New York City, 2001.

SUTTON, Michael 1970–

PERSONAL

Born June 18, 1970, in Los Angeles, CA; father, a publicist. *Education:* California State University at Northridge, B.A., film production.

Career: Actor. Appeared in television commercials, including Miller Beer, Coca–Cola, and Tribe perfume. brandSUTTON (a public relations and marketing firm), founder and principal; Xenii (private membership community), co–founding partner and marketing president; Standing O Pictures (film production company), president. The Lodge Steakhouse, Beverly Hills, owner; Memphis (restaurant), Hollywood, CA, owner.

Awards, Honors: Young Artist Award nomination, best performance by a youth actor in a daytime series, 1995, Daytime Emmy Award nomination, outstanding supporting actor in a drama series, 1996, both for *General Hospital.*

CREDITS

Film Appearances:
Steve, *Inventing the Abbotts,* Twentieth Century–Fox, 1997.
James, *Error in Judgment,* 1998.
Zed, *Dark Nova,* 1999.
Jimmy Scrico, *Wanted,* York Entertainment, 1999.
American Intellectuals, Oak Island Films, 1999.
Ben, *My Daughter's Tears* (also known as *Against All Evidence* and *Meine tochter ist keine morderin*), 2002.
Kevin Ivine, *Hyper Sonic,* 2002.
Porn star, *Love Hollywood Style,* 2006.

Film Work:
Worked as a executive producer, *The Freshest Kids* (documentary).

Television Appearances; Series:
Michael "Stone" Cates, *General Hospital,* ABC, 1993–95.

Television Appearances; Movies:
Radu, *Dark Prince: The True Story of Dracula* (also known as *Dark Prince: Legend of Dracula* and *Dracula: The Dark Prince*), USA Network, 2000.

Television Appearances; Specials:
In a New Light: Sex Unplugged, ABC, 1995.
Hot Summer Soaps, ABC, 1995.
Soaps' Most Unforgettable Love Stories, ABC, 1998.

Television Appearances; Episodic:
Man in box, *Touched by an Angel,* CBS, 1994.

Himself, "Positive: A Journey into AIDS," *ABC Afterschool Specials,* ABC, 1995.

SUTTON, Ted

PERSONAL

Career: Actor.

CREDITS

Film Appearances:
Cop, *Her Alibi,* Warner Bros., 1989.
On the Block, Vidmark Entertainment, 1990.
District attorney, *Maxim Xul,* Magnum Video, 1991.
Flag officer, *G.I. Jane,* Buena Vista, 1997.
Pentagon employee, *Species II,* Metro–Goldwyn–Mayer, 1998.
Dr. Fred Lang, *Revolution #9,* Exile Pictures, 2002.
Sergeant First Class Cunningham, *Signs* (also known as *M. Night Shyamalan's "Signs"*), Buena Vista, 2002.
Chuck Farley, *Marci X,* Paramount, 2003.
Judge Baddin, *Fat Cats,* 2005.
Mr. Croshere, *Fortunes,* MTI Home Video, 2005.

Some sources cite appearance as anchor in the film *Elliot Fauman, Ph.D.,* Taurus Entertainment, 1990.

Television Appearances; Movies:
Trooper Black, *In the Blink of an Eye,* ABC, 1996.

Television Appearances; Episodic:
Robert, "Countdown," *Law & Order: Special Victims Unit* (also known as *Law & Order: SVU* and *Special Victims Unit*), NBC, 2001.
General Blaye, "Day 2: 1:00 a.m.–2:00 a.m.," *24.,* Fox, 2003.
Male driver, "Wild and the Innocent," *10–8: Officers on Duty* (also known as *10–8* and *10–8: Police Patrol*), ABC, 2004.
General Matthew Smithfield, "Coming Home," *JAG,* CBS, 2004.
Herb, "Mindhunters," *Cold Case,* CBS, 2004.
Recruitment officer, "Malice in Wonderland," *Charmed,* The WB, 2005.

Appeared as Al Pavlik in an episode of *Ed,* NBC.

T

PERSONAL

Born April 25, 1941, in Lyon, France; son of Rene (a writer and publicist) and Genevieve (maiden name, Dumond) Tavernier; married, wife's name Colo (a screenwriter; also known as Claudine O'Hagan), February 16 1965 (divorced, 1980); children: Nils (an actor), Tiffany (a writer). *Education:* Attended Sorbonne, University of Paris; also studied law.

Addresses: *Office*—Little Bear, 7–9 rue Arthur Groussier, 75010 Paris, France. *Agent*—Sam Cohn, International Creative Management, 10250 Constellation Way, 9th Floor, Los Angeles, CA 90067.

Career: Director, producer, and writer. Assistant to film director Jean–Pierre Melville, 1961; press agent for film producer Georges de Beauregard; freelance press agent, 1965–1972; Lumiere Institute, president; Little Bear, Paris, principal and producer.

Member: French Directors Guild (past president), Society of Dramatic Authors and Composers (vice president).

Awards, Honors: Prix Louis Delluc and Nugo Award, Chicago Film Festival, both 1973, OCIC Award, Silver Berlin Bear, and nomination for Golden Berlin Bear, all Berlin International Film Festival, 1974, for *L'Horloger de Saint–Paul;* Cesar Awards (with Jean Aurenche), best director and best screenplay, and Cesar Award nomination, best film, all Academie des Arts et Techniques du Cinema, and Critics Award, best film, French Syndicate of Cinema Critics, all 1976, for *Que la fete commence ...;* Cesar Award (with Aurenche), best screenplay, and

Cesar Award nominations, best director and best film, all 1977, for *Le Juge et l'assassin;* nomination for Golden Berlin Bear, Prix Unifrance, and Golden Asteroide, all 1980, and Cesar Award nomination (with David Rayfiel), best original script, 1981, all for *La Mort en direct;* nomination for Golden Palm, Cannes Film Festival, 1980, for *Une semaine de vacances;* Academy Award nomination, best foreign film, 1981, Cesar Award nominations, best director, best film, and best screenplay (with Aurenche), 1982, and Critics Award, best film, French Syndicate of Cinema Critics, 1982, all for *Coup de torchon;* Cannes Film Festival Award, best director, and nomination for Golden Palm, both 1984, Boston Society of Film Critics Award, best director, Film Award (with Alain Sarde), best foreign language film, British Academy of Film and Television Arts, Cesar Award (with Colo Tavernier), best screenplay adaptation, Cesar Award nominations, best director and best film, New York Film Critics Circle Award, best foreign film, and National Board of Review Award, best foreign film, all 1985, and Mainichi Film Concours Award, best foreign language film, 1986, all for *Un Dimanche a la campagne;* Silver Ribbon, best director of a foreign film, Italian National Syndicate of Film Journalists, 1987, and Bodil Award, best European Film, Bodil Festival, 1988, all for *'Round Midnight;* Special Prize of the Jury, European Film Awards, and Tokyo International Film Festival Award, best artistic contribution, both 1989, Film Award, best film not in the English language, British Academy of Film and Television Arts, and Cesar Award nominations, best director, best film, and best screenplay (with Jean Cosmos), all 1990, for *La Vie et rien d'autre;* Golden Palm nomination, Cannes Film Festival, 1990, for *Daddy Nostalgie;* special mention, Bergamo Film Meeting, 1992, for *La Guerre sans nom;* Cesar Award nominations, best director, best film, and best screenplay (with Michel Alexandre), all 1992, for *L.627;* Golden Berlin Bear and nomination for Golden Kikito, best Latin film, Gramado Film Festival, both 1995, for *L'Appat;* FIPRESCI Award, Solidarity Award, and nomination for Golden Seashell, all San Sebastian International Film Festival, 1996, Cesar Award, best director, and Cesar Award nominations, best film and best original screenplay (with Cosmos), Best European Film Award and People's Choice Award, both Denver International Film Festival, and Critics Award, best film, French Syndicate of Cinema Critics, all 1997, all for *Capitaine Conan;* Crystal Iris Award, Brussels International Film Festival, 1998; FIPRESCI Award, honorable mention for speciality of the topic, Prize of the Ecumenical Jury, and nomination for Golden Berlin Bear, all Berlin International Film Festival, Audience Award, San Sebastian International Film Festival, and Ecumenical Film Award, Norwegian International Film Festival, all 1999, and Fotogramas de Plata Award and Sant Jordi Award, both best foreign film, 2000, all for *Ca commence aujourd'hui;* Lifetime Achievement Award, Istanbul International Film Festival, 2001; nomination for Golden Berlin Bear, and Jury Awards, best director, best film, and best screenplay (with Cosmos), Fort Lauderdale International Film Festival, all 2002, for *Laissez–passer;* Audience Award, San Sebastian International Film Festival, 2005, for *Holy Lola.*

CREDITS

Film Director:

"Baiser de Judas" in *Les Baisers* (also known as *I Baci* and *Una Voglia matta di donna*), Rome–Paris Films/ Flora Films, 1963.

"Une Chance explosive" in *La Chance et l'amour* (also known as *Chance at Love* and *L'Amore e la chance*), Rome–Paris Films/ROTOR Film, 1964.

Assistant director, *Maciste, gladiatore di Sparta* (also known as *The Terror of Rome against the Son of Hercules* and *Maciste, gladiateur de Sparte*), 1964.

Assistant director, *Una Questione d'onore* (also known as *A Question of Honour*), 1965.

L'Horloger de Saint–Paul (also known as *The Clockmaker, The Clockmaker of St. Paul,* and *The Watchmaker of St. Paul*), Lira Films, 1972.

Que la fete commence ... (also known as *Let Joy Reign Supreme*), Fildebroc, 1975.

Le Juge et l'assassin (also known as *The Judge and the Assassin*), Lira Films, 1976.

Des Enfants gates (also known as *Spoiled Children*), Gaumont/Sara/Films 66/Little Bear, 1977.

(And coproducer) *La Mort en direct* (also known as *Deathwatch, Death Watch–Der Gekaufte Tod, Death in Full View, Der Gekaufte Tod,* and *The Continuous Katherine Mortenhoe*), Selta/Sara/Little Bear/FR–3/Gaumont, 1979.

(And producer) *Une Semaine de vacances* (also known as *A Week's Brief Vacation, A Week's Holiday,* and *A Week's Vacation,*), Sara Films/Little Bear Productions, 1980.

Coup de torchon (also known as *Clean Slate* and *Clean Up*), Films de la Tour/Little Bear Productions, 1981.

Philippe Soupault (also known as *Philippe Soupault et le surrealisme*), 1982.

(And producer, both with Robert Parrish) *Mississippi Blues* (also known as *October Country* and *Pays d'octobre*), Corinth Films, 1983.

Cine citron, 1983.

La 8eme generation, 1983.

(And producer) *Un Dimanche a la campagne* (also known as *A Sunday in the Country*), Metro–Goldwyn–Mayer, 1984.

'Round Midnight (also known as *Autour de minuit*), Warner Bros., 1986.

La Passion Beatrice (also known as *Beatrice, The Passion of Beatrice,* and *Quarto comandamento*), Samuel Goldwyn Company, 1987.

La Vie et rien d'autre (also known as *Life and Nothing But*), Orion, 1989.

Daddy Nostalgie (also known as *Daddy Nostalgia* and *These Foolish Things*), Avenue Entertainment, 1990.

50 Ans de cinema Americaine, 1991.

La Guerre sans nom (also known as *The Undeclared War*), 1991.

"Pour Aung San Suu Kyi, Myanmar" segment, *Contre l'oubli* (also known as *Against Oblivion, Lest We Forget,* and *Ecrire contre l'oubli*), 1992.

L.627, Kino International, 1992.

La Fille de d'Artagnan (also known as *D'Artagnan's Daughter, The Daughter of D'Artagnan,* and *Revenge of the Musketeers*), Miramax, 1994.

L'Appat (also known as *The Bait, Fresh Bait,* and *Live Bait*), 1995.

(And producer) *Capitaine Conan* (also known as *Captain Conan*), Bac Films, 1996.

De l'autre cote du periph (also known as *The Other Side of the Tracks*), 1998.

Ca commence aujourd'hui (also known as *It All Starts Today*), Independent Artists, 1999.

Spotlights on a Massacre: 10 Films Against 100 Million Antipersonnel Land Mines, 1999.

Histoires de vies brisees: les "double peine" de Lyon (documentary), Pierre Grise Distribution, 2001.

Laissez–passer (also known as *Safe Conduct* and *Salvocunducto*), subtitled version, Empire Pictures, 2002.

Holy Lola, TFM Distribution, 2004.

Film Producer:

La Question (also known as *The Question*), 1976.

Rue du pied de Grue, 1979.

La Trace (also known as *The Trace*), 1983.

Veillees d'armes (also known as *The Troubles We've Seen: A History of Journalism in Wartime, The Troubles weve seen—Die Geschichte der Kriegsberichterstattung,* and *Veillees d'armes: Histoire du journalisme en temps de guerre*), 1994.

Co–executive producer, *Fred,* 1997.

Coproducer, *Pas d'histoires!* (animated; also known as *Don't Make Trouble!*), Gebeka Films, 2001.

Film Appearances:

(Uncredited) *La Boulangere de Monceau* (also known as *The Baker of Monceau, The Baker's Girl of Monceau,* and *The Girl at the Monceau Bakery*), 1963.

Hotel Terminus: Klaus Barbie, His Life and Times, Samuel Goldwyn Company, 1988.

Infant of Paradise: Alexadre Trauner and the Development of Film Production Design, 1993.

Francois Truffaut: Portraits voles (also known as *Francois Truffaut: Stolen Portraits*), 1993.

Les Demoiselles ont eu 25 ans (also known as *The Young Girls Turn 25*), 1993.

L'Univers de Jacques Demy (also known as *The Universe of Jacques Demy* and *The World of Jacques Demy*), 1995.

Narrator, *Lumiere: The First Picture Show* (documentary), Kino Video, 1996.

Narrator, *The Lumiere Brothers' First Films,* 1996.

In the Shadow of Hollywood (documentary; also known as *A l'ombre d'Hollywood*), National Film Board of Canada, 2000.

Himself, *Claude Sautet ou La magie invisible* (documentary; also known as *Claude Sautet or the Invisible Magic* and *Claude Sautet oder die unsichtbare magie*), Les Grands Films Classiques, 2003.

Himself, *L'homme au cigare* (documentary), Rattlesnake Pictures, 2003.

Himself, *Cineastes an accio* (documentary; also known as *Cineastas en accion*), Kilimanjaro Productions, 2005.

Television Appearances; Specials:

Lyon, le regard interieur (also known as *Lyon, Inside Out*), 1988.

Un Film sur Bertrand Tavernier, 1996.

Cannes ... les 400 coups, 1997.

Blue Note: A Story of Modern Jazz, Bravo, 1997.

Clint Eastwood: Out of the Shadows, PBS, 2000.

Television Appearances; Episodic:

American Cinema, PBS, 1995.

Interviewee, "Michael Powell," *Artworks Scotland,* 2005.

Magacine, 2005.

Himself, *L'hebdo cinema,* 2006.

Television Appearances; Other:

Dialogue pour un portrait: Philippe Noiret, 1981.

Le petit Mitchell illustre, 1981.

Gilles Grangier, 50 ans de cinema, 1990.

Jean Renoir: Part One—From La Belle Epoque to World War II, 1993.

Jean Renoir: Part Two—Hollywood and Beyond, 1993.

The Making of an Englishman, 1995.

Philippe le bienheureux, 1996.

Quand le chat sourit, 1997.

Positif, une revue, 2003.

Jacques Deray: Le cinema ... ma vie, 2005.

Member of audience, *Premio Donostia a Willem Dafoe,* 2005.

(In archive footage) *Ceremonia de clausura,* 2005.

Television Director:

Lyon, le regard interieur (special; also known as *Lyon, Inside Out*), 1988.

La Lettre (movie), 1997.

Les enfants de Thies, 2001.

RECORDINGS

Videos:

Compositeurs/realisateurs, dialogue impossible?, 2002.

WRITINGS

Screenplays:

"Baiser de Judas" in *Les Baisers* (also known as *I Baci* and *Una Voglia matta di donna*), Rome–Paris Films/Flora Films, 1963.

"Une Chance explosive" in *La Chance et l'amour* (also known as *Chance at Love* and *L'Amore e la chance*), Rome–Paris Films/ROTOR Film, 1964.

Entre las redes (also known as *Mexican Slayride, Coplan ouvre le feu a Mexico, Coplan III,* and *Moresque: obiettivo allucinante*), 1966.

Capitaine Singrid (also known as *Captain Singrid, Capitao Singrid,* and *I mercenari muoiono all'alba*), 1967.

(With Jean Aurenche and Pierre Bost) *L'Horloger de Saint–Paul* (also known as *The Clockmaker, The Clockmaker of St. Paul,* and *The Watchmaker of St. Paul;* based on novel *L'Horloger d'Everton* by Georges Simenon), Lira Films, 1972, Joseph Green Pictures, 1976.

(With Aurenche) *Que la fete commence ...* (also known as *Let Joy Reign Supreme*), Fildebroc, 1975, Specialty Films, 1977.

(With Aurenche) *Le Juge et l'assassin,* Lira Films, 1976, released as *The Judge and the Assassin,* Libra Films, 1982.

(With Charlotte Dubreuil and Christine Pascal) *Des Enfants gates* (also known as *Spoiled Children*), Gaumont/Sara/Films 66/Little Bear, 1977, Corinth, 1981.

(With David Rayfiel) *La Mort en direct* (also known as *The Continuous Katherine Mortenhoe, Death in Full View, Deathwatch, Death Watch–Der Gekaufte Tod,* and *Der Gekaufte Tod;* based on story "The Unsleeping Eye" by David Compton), Selta/Sara/Little Bear/FR–3/Gaumont, 1979, Quartet Films, 1982.

(With Colo Tavernier and Marie–Francoise Hans) *Une Semaine de vacances* (also known as *A Week's Brief Vacation, A Week's Holiday,* and *A Week's Vacation*), Sara Films/Little Bear Productions, 1980, Biograph International, 1982.

(With Aurenche) *Coup de torchon* (also known as *Clean Slate* and *Clean Up;* based on novel *Pop. 1280* by Jim Thompson), Films de la Tour/Little Bear Productions, 1981, Biograph International/Quartet Films/Frank Moreno Co., 1982.

La Trace (also known as *The Trace*), 1983.
Mississippi Blues (also known as *October Country* and *Pays d'octobre*), Odessa/Little Bear Productions, 1983.
La 8eme generation, 1983.
(With Colo Tavernier) *Un Dimanche a la campagne* (also known as *A Sunday in the Country;* based on novel *Monsieur Ladmiral va bientot mourir* by Bost), Metro–Goldwyn–Mayer, 1984.
(With Rayfiel) *'Round Midnight* (also known as *Autour de minuit*), Warner Bros., 1986.
(With Laurent Heynemann and Phillippe Boucher) *Les Mois d'avril sont meurtriers* (also known as *April Is a Deadly Month),* Sara Films/CDF, 1986.
(With Cosmos) *La Vie et rien d'autre* (also known as *Life and Nothing But*), Orion, 1989.
(Dialogue) *Daddy Nostalgie* (also known as *Daddy Nostalgia* and *These Foolish Things*), Avenue Entertainment, 1990.
Der Gruene Berg, 1990.
La Guerre sans nom (also known as *The Undeclared War*), 1991, published (with Patrick Rotman) as *La Guerre sans nom: Les appeles d'Algerie, 1954–1962,* Editions du Seuil, 1992.
(With Michel Alexandre) *L.627,* Kino International, 1992.
La Fille de d'Artagnan (also known as *D'Artagnan's Daughter, The Daughter of D'Artagnan,* and *Revenge of the Musketeers*), Miramax, 1994.
(With C. Tavernier O'Hagan) *L'Appat* (also known as *The Bait, Live Bait,* and *Fresh Bait*), 1995.
(With Cosmos) *Capitaine Conan* (also known as *Captain Conan*), Bac Films, 1996.
(With Dominique Sampiero and daughter Tiffany Tavernier) *Ca commence aujourd'hui* (also known as *It All Starts Today*), Independent Artists, 1999.
Il avait dans le coeur des jardins introuvables, 2000.
(With Jose Giovanni) *Mon pere, il m'a sauve la vie* (also known as *My Father Saved my Life*), Bac Films, 2001.
(With Cosmos) *Laissez–passer* (also known as *Safe Conduct* and *Salvocunducto*), subtitled version, Empire Pictures, 2002.
Holy Lola, TFM Distribution, 2004.

Television Specials:
Lyon, le regard interieur (also known as *Lyon, Inside Out*), 1988.

Other:
(With Jean–Pierre Coursodon) *Trente ans de cinema Americaine* (nonfiction book; title means *Thirty Years of American Cinema*), Editions C.I.B., 1970.
(Compiler) *Amis americains: Retretiens avec les grands auteurs d'Hollywood,* Institut Lumiere, 1993.
50 Years of American Cinema (book), 1995.

Also contributed to periodicals, including *Cahiers du cinema* and *Positif.*

OTHER SOURCES

Books:
Zants, Emily, *Bertrand Tavernier: Fractured Narrative and Bourgeois Values,* Scarecrow Press, 1999.

Periodicals:
Cineaste, summer, 1998, p. 20.
Film Comment, November, 1998, p. 71.
Sight and Sound, July, 1999, pp. 12–15.

THOMAS, Bruce

PERSONAL

Addresses: *Agent*—Pakula/King and Associates, 9229 West Sunset Blvd., Suite 315, Los Angeles, CA 90069.

Career: Actor. Appeared in commercials as Batman for OnStar vehicle communications system, 2000–01.

CREDITS

Television Appearances; Series:
Trevor McEvoy, *The Bold and the Beautiful* (also known as *Belleza y poder*), CBS, 1999–2000.
Stephen Trager, a recurring role, *Kyle XY,* ABC Family Channel, 2006–2007.

Television Appearances; Movies:
Jim, *Just Desserts,* Hallmark Channel, 2004.
Mitch, *Life on Liberty Street,* Hallmark Channel, 2004.
Ted Howell, *A Boyfriend for Christmas,* Hallmark Channel, 2004.

Television Appearances; Episodic:
Trevor Winslow, "Exposure," *Models Inc.,* Fox, 1995.
Mike Lyons, "She Ain't Friendly, She's My Mother," *Ellen* (also known as *These Friends of Mine*), ABC, 1995.
David, "Happy Endings," *The John Larroquette Show* (also known as *Larroquette*), NBC, 1996.
Hank Bradley, "Leap of Faith," *Beverly Hills, 90210,* Fox, 1996.
Tom, "House of Blues," *Wings,* NBC, 1997.
Carl Schmidt, "Budget Cuts," *Beverly Hills, 90210,* 1998.
Carl Schmidt, "Dealer's Choice," *Beverly Hills, 90210,* 1998.
Carl Schmidt, "Don't Ask, Don't Tell," *Beverly Hills, 90210,* 1998.
Beau Tucker, "All Good Dogs Go to Heaven," *Providence,* NBC, 1999.

Dr. Joshua Locke, *Port Charles,* ABC, 2000.

Gene Trent (some sources cite Gene Traynor), "Dance of Danger," *Diagnosis Murder,* CBS, 2001.

(Uncredited) Batman, premiere episode, *Birds of Prey* (also known as *BOP*), The WB, 2002.

Reptilian soldier, "The Council," *Enterprise* (also known as *Star Trek: Enterprise*), UPN, 2004.

Reptilian soldier, "Countdown," *Enterprise* (also known as *Star Trek: Enterprise*), UPN, 2004.

Xindi–reptilian soldier, "Zero Hour," *Enterprise* (also known as *Star Trek: Enterprise*), UPN, 2004.

Dr. Wolfe, "War Crimes," *E–Ring,* NBC, 2006.

Megan's dad, "Mrs. Botwin's Neighborhood," *Weeds,* Showtime, 2006.

Appeared as Rocky Brush in an episode of *Nash Bridges,* CBS.

Television Appearances; Other:

(In archive footage) *Heroes of Comedy: Women on Top* (miniseries), Comedy Central, 2003.

Stephen Trager, *Kyle XY* (pilot), ABC Family Channel, 2006.

Film Appearances:

One of the Mini–Ash, *Army of Darkness* (also known as *Army of Darkness: Evil Dead 3, Army of Darkness: The Medieval Dead, Army of Darkness: The Ultimate Experience in Medieval Horror, Bruce Campbell vs. Army of Darkness,* and *Evil Dead 3*), Universal, 1993.

Bruce, *Secrets of a Chambermaid,* Mystique Films, 1998.

Floyd, *Thirteen Days,* New Line Cinema, 2000.

UPS guy, *Legally Blonde,* Metro–Goldwyn–Mayer, 2001.

UPS guy, *Legally Blonde 2: Red, White & Blonde,* Metro–Goldwyn–Mayer, 2003.

Peter, *Closing Escrow,* Awkward Silence Productions/16x9 Productions/HD Vision Studios, 2006.

Emotional man, *Escape* (short film), Radar Multimedia, 2006.

Jim Stanton, *Babysitter Wanted,* Imagination Worldwide, 2007.

THOMAS, Sharon 1946–

PERSONAL

Born in 1946; married Roger Tanaka, 1964 (divorced, 1966); married Christopher Cain (a director, writer, and producer), 1969; children: Dean (an actor), Krisinda (an actress), Roger.

Career: Actress.

CREDITS

Film Appearances:

Jenny Allen, *Grand Jury,* 1976.

Tina, *Sixth and Main,* National Cinema Network, 1977.

Fred, *Cuba Crossing* (also known as *Assignment: Kill Castro, Key West Crossing, Kill Castro, Solo fur zwei Superkiller, Sweet Dirty Tony, Sweet Violent Tony, The Mercenaries,* and *Todeskommando Schweinbucht*), Aurora, 1980.

Casino waitress, *The Stone Boy,* Twentieth Century–Fox, 1984.

Waitress, *Star Trek III: The Search for Spock,* Paramount, 1984.

Mrs. Unger, *The Flamingo Kid,* Twentieth Century–Fox, 1984.

Doctor, *That Was Then … This Is Now,* Paramount, 1985.

Kimberly, *The Principal,* TriStar, 1987.

Susan McSween, *Young Guns,* Twentieth Century–Fox, 1988.

Monique James, *Pure Country,* Warner Bros., 1992.

Cameo, *Eating Las Vegas* (short), 1997.

Television reporter, *Calendar Girls,* Buena Vista, 2003.

Voice of Dolly, *Firedog,* 2005.

Television Appearances; Series:

Mabel, *General Hospital,* ABC, 1982.

Paula, *Herndon,* 1983.

Television Appearances; Movies:

Angela, *Portrait of a Showgirl,* CBS, 1982.

Amy Donaldson, *Wheels of Terror,* USA Network, 1990.

Television Appearances; Specials:

Herself, *Who's Your Momma?,* 2004.

Television Appearances; Episodic:

Barbara, "A Ransom in Diamonds," *Barnaby Jones,* 1978.

Maisie, "The Green, Green Glow of Home," *Lois & Clark: The New Adventures of Superman* (also known as *Lois & Clark* and *The New Adventures of Superman*), ABC, 1993.

Pretentious lady, "Season's Greedings," *Lois & Clark: The New Adventures of Superman* (also known as *Lois & Clark* and *The New Adventures of Superman*), ABC, 1994.

Nun, "Just Say Noah," *Lois & Clark: The New Adventures of Superman* (also known as *Lois & Clark* and *The New Adventures of Superman*), ABC, 1995.

Sales lady, "Murder.com," *The Division* (also known as *Heart of the City*), Lifetime, 2003.

Celebrities Uncensored, E! Entertainment Television, 2003.

THRONE, Zachary 1967–
(Zach Throne)

PERSONAL

Born April 3, 1967 (some sources say July 9), in Hollywood, CA; married Samantha Throne.

Addresses: *Agent*—Artists Group, Ltd., 2049 Century Park East, Suite 4060, Los Angeles, CA 90067.

Career: Actor. Appeared in television commercials, including Bayer Nutritional Science. Also worked as a musician, appearing with Tribute to David Bowie, Mother Pearl, and Cody Carpenter.

CREDITS

Film Appearances:
Simon, *Suspicious Agenda,* Warner Music Vision, 1994.
Artie Samson, *Deceptions II: Edge of Deception* (also known as *Edge of Deception*), Warner Bros., 1995.
Dean Carter, *Soulmates,* Curb Entertainment, 1997.
Martin, *64 Disks* (short), 2002.

Television Appearances; Series:
Lenny Wieckowski, *The Heights,* Fox, 1992.
Howard, *Beverly Hills, 90210,* Fox, 1993–94.

Television Appearances; Movies:
Clay, *When You Remember Me,* ABC, 1990.
Jim Steinman, *Meat Loaf: To Hell and Back,* 2000.

Television Appearances; Episodic:
Larry Vogel, "Brightman SATyicon," *The Marshall Chronicles,* ABC, 1990.
Officer Stillman, "Marital Blitz," *Cop Rock,* ABC, 1990.
Officer Stillman, "No Noose Is Good Noose," *Cop Rock,* ABC, 1990.
Officer Stillman, "Bang the Potts Slowly," *Cop Rock,* ABC, 1990.
Voice of Mark Winkle, "The Unforgiven," *California Dreams* (also known as *Dreams*), NBC, 1994.
Danny, "Much Ado," *Party of Five,* Fox, 1994.
Danny, "Kiss Me Kate," *Party of Five,* Fox, 1994.
Danny, "Who Cares?," *Party of Five,* Fox, 1995.
Neil, "D&B, Inc.," *The Huntress,* USA Network, 2001.
Dr. Scott, "A Little Help from My Friends," *ER,* NBC, 2003.

Balloon vendor, "Homebodies," *CSI: Crime Scene Investigation* (also known as *C.S.I., CSI: Las Vegas, CSI: Weekends,* and *Les Experts*), CBS, 2003.
Nathan Singer, "Bleak House," *The Handler,* CBS, 2004.
Various voices, "Avatar Day," *Avatar: The Last Airbender* (animated), Nickelodeon, 2006.
Various voices, "Zuko Alone," *Avatar: The Last Airbender* (animated), Nickelodeon, 2006.

Television Work; Series:
Singing voice for actor Aaron Jackson, *California Dreams,* NBC, 1994–97.

RECORDINGS

Video Games:
Various voices, *Flushed Away,* D3P Publisher, 2006.

TIRELLI, Jaime
(Jaime Roman Tirelli, Jamie Tirelli)

PERSONAL

Married Millie; children: Gina, Ariana. *Education:* Graduated from American Academy of Dramatic Arts, 1975.

Career: Actor.

CREDITS

Film Appearances:
Street gang, *Marathon Man,* Paramount, 1976.
Jose, *Fort Apache the Bronx,* Twentieth Century–Fox, 1981.
WPCP announcer, *Soup for One,* Warner Bros., 1982.
Second taxi driver, *Author! Author!,* Twentieth Century–Fox, 1982.
Hector, *The Brother from Another Planet,* Cinecom Pictures, 1984.
Willie, *Sudden Death,* Marvin Films, 1985.
Spanish voice, *Big,* Twentieth Century–Fox, 1988.
Officer Rivera, *Rooftoops,* New Visions Pictures, 1989.
Maitre d', *Penn & Teller Get Killed* (also known as *Dead Funny*), Warner Bros., 1989.
Luis, *The Chair* (also known as *Hot Seat*), Imperial Entertainment, 1989.
Alvarez, *State of Grace,* Orion, 1990.
Fuentes, *City of Hope,* Samuel Goldwyn Company, 1991.

Oliver, *The House of the Spirits* (also known as *Andernes hus, A Casa dos Espiritos,* and *Das Geisterhaus*), Miramax, 1993.

Valentin, *Carlito's Way,* Universal, 1993.

Monitor, *The Cowboy Way,* Universal, 1994.

Popi, *Lotto Land,* Cinepix Film Properties, 1995.

Liquor store owner, *The Preacher's Wife,* Buena Vista, 1996.

Joe, *A Simple Wish* (also known as *The Fairy Godmother*), Universal, 1997.

Hector, *Girlfight,* Screen Gems, 2000.

Hector, *The Blue Diner* (also known as *La fonda azul*), First Look International, 2001.

Prison Song, New Line Cinema, 2001.

Marty, *Pinero,* Miramax, 2001.

Guillermo, *Washington Heights,* Mac Releasing, 2002.

Ralph, *All Night Bodega,* Xenon Pictures, 2002.

Don Armando, *Dirt,* Mac Releasing, 2003.

(As Jaime Roman Tirelli) Hispanic man, *Kinsey,* 2004.

Leticia's father, *Carlito's Way: Rise to Power,* Universal, 2005.

Popo, *I Believe in America,* 2006.

Beneficio, *Kill the Poor,* IFC Films, 2006.

T. C.'s dad, *The Groomsmen,* Bauer Martinez Studios, 2006.

Father, *Bella,* Inferno Distribution, 2006.

Yellow, Sony Pictures Entertainment, 2006.

Jose, *Santa Mesa,* 2007.

Simon, *Definitely, Maybe,* Universal, 2007.

Pawn shop owner, *The Brave One,* Warner Bros., 2007.

Father Gorbia, *The Ministers,* 2007.

Television Appearances; Series:

Orlando Lopez, *Ball Four,* CBS, 1976.

Television Appearances; Movies:

In the Line of Duty: The F.B.I. Murders, NBC, 1988.

The Old Man and the Sea (also known as *Ernest Hemingway's "The Old Man and the Sea"*), NBC, 1990.

Castillo, *It's Always Something,* ABC, 1990.

Lieutenant Aquila, *In the Line of Duty: Street War* (also known as *Urban Crossfire*), NBC, 1992.

Mike, *Strapped,* HBO, 1993.

Tropicana club owner, *Undefeated,* HBO, 2003.

Television Appearances; Pilots:

Pete Vasquez, *Mobile Medics,* CBS, 1977.

Student, *A Doctor's Story* (movie), NBC, 1984.

(As Jamie Tirelli) Principal, *The Prosecutors* (movie), NBC, 1996.

Television Appearances; Specials:

Panamanian, *Ask Me Again,* PBS, 1989.

Television Appearances; Episodic:

Detective Phil Grover, "Foxy Lady," *Starsky and Hutch,* ABC, 1978.

Gino, "Pot of Gold," *Wonder Woman* (also known as *The New Adventures of Wonder Woman* and *The New Wonder Woman*), CBS, 1978.

Ramon Scavosa, "The Lock Box," *The Equalizer,* CBS, 1985.

Gomez, "Free Verse," *Miami Vice,* NBC, 1986.

One Life to Live, ABC, 1987.

Manny, "Louis in Love," *Kate & Allie,* CBS, 1987.

Crime scene investigator Rivera, "Life Choice," *Law & Order,* NBC, 1991.

Chick Sullivan, "Benevolence," *Law & Order,* NBC, 1993.

Santana, "Mayhem," *Law & Order,* NBC, 1994.

New York Undercover, Fox, 1994.

Art Hutado, "Curt Russell," *NYPD Blue,* ABC, 1995.

New York News, CBS, 1995.

Ferdinand Ricardo, "The Truth and Nothing But ...," *Oz,* HBO, 1999.

Ferdinand Ricardo, "Napoleon's Boney Parts," *Oz,* HBO, 1999.

Ferdinand Ricardo, "Legs," *Oz,* HBO, 1999.

D'Arrigo, "A Teacher's Life," *Cosby,* CBS, 1999.

Sergeant Palatio, "Black, White and Blue," *Law & Order,* NBC, 2000.

Juan Gomez, "Lost Causes," *100 Centre Street,* Arts and Entertainment, 2001.

Jimmy Ramirez, "Legion," *Law & Order: Criminal Intent* (also known as *Law & Order: CI*), NBC, 2003.

Jimmy Ramirez, "Saving Face," *Law & Order: Criminal Intent* (also known as *Law & Order: CI*), NBC, 2005.

Dario Rodriguez, "The Line," *Law & Order: Trial by Jury,* NBC, 2005.

Espinoza, "Sorry, Wrong Number," *Kidnapped,* NBC, 2006.

"Acknowledgment," *Kidnapped,* NBC, 2007.

Also appeared as Elena, "The American Dream," *Leg Work.*

Stage Appearances:

Page, "Rubbers," and baseball player, "Yank 3, Detroit 0 Top of the Seventh," *Rubbers/Yank 3 Detroit 0 Top of the Seventh,* American Place Theatre, New York City, 1975.

Mr. Solares, *In the Summer House,* Vivian Beaumont Theatre, New York City, 1993.

Alacran, *Blade to the Heat,* Anspacher Theatre, Public Theatre, New York City, 1994.

Father Amador, *Chronicle of a Death Foretold,* Plymouth Theatre, New York City, 1995.

TORRES, Gina 1969–

PERSONAL

Born April 25, 1969, in New York, NY; married Laurence Fishburne (an actor and producer), September

20, 2002. *Education:* Attended High School of Music and Art (now La Guardia High School of Music and Art), New York City; also studied opera and jazz.

Addresses: *Agent*—Domain, 9229 Sunset Blvd., Suite 415, Los Angeles, CA 90069. *Manager*—Framework Entertainment, 9057 Nemo St., Suite C, West Hollywood, CA 90069.

Career: Actress. Former singer in a gospel choir. Also worked as a waitress and receptionist.

Awards, Honors: ALMA Award, outstanding lead actress in a syndicated drama series, America Latino Media Arts Awards, 2001, for *Cleopatra 2525;* Golden Satellite Award nomination, best performance by an actress in a supporting role in a series—drama, International Press Academy, 2004, for *Angel.*

CREDITS

Film Appearances:
Francine, *Bed of Roses,* New Line Cinema, 1996.
Maitre d', *The Substance of Fire,* Miramax, 1996.
Cas, *The Matrix Reloaded,* Warner Bros., 2003.
Cas, *The Matrix Revolutions,* Warner Bros., 2003.
Herself, *Here's How It Was: The Making of "Firefly"* (documentary short), Twentieth Century–Fox Home Entertainment, 2003.
Marcella, *Hair Show,* Innovation Film Group, 2004.
Herself, *"Angel": Season 4 Overview* (documentary; also known as *"Prophecies": Season 4 Overview*), Fox Box, 2004.
Herself, *Fatal Beauty and the Beast* (documentary short), Fox Box, 2004.
Stacey, *Fair Game,* Urbanworks, 2005.
Zoe, *Serenity,* Universal, 2005.
Herself, *Re–Lighting the Firefly* (documentary short), 2005.
Lilac, *Jam,* Starz! Encore Entertainment, 2006.
Aicha, *Five Fingers,* Lions Gate Films, 2006.
Herself, *A Filmmaker's Journey* (documentary short), 2006.
Brenda Cooper, *I Think I Love My Wife,* Fox Searchlight Pictures, 2007.
Carla Silva, *South of Pico,* 2007.

Television Appearances; Series:
Magdalena and other characters, *One Life to Live,* ABC, 1995–96.
Nebula, *Hercules: The Legendary Journeys,* syndicated, 1997–99.
Helen "Hel," *Cleopatra 2525,* syndicated, 2000–2001.
Anna Espinosa, a recurring character, *Alias,* ABC, 2001–2006.

Zoe Washburn, *Firefly* (also known as *Firefly: The Series*), Fox, 2002–2003.
Jasmine, *Angel* (also known as *Angel: The Series*), The WB, 2003.
Julia Milliken, *24,* Fox, 2004.
Voice of Vixen, *Justice League* (animated; also known as *JL*), Cartoon Network, 2004–2006.
Cheryl Carrera, *Standoff,* Fox, 2006.

Television Appearances; Movies:
Unnatural Pursuits, 1994.
LaMayne, *Dark Angel,* Fox, 1996.
Vicki Lee, *The Law and Mr. Lee,* 2003.

Television Appearances; Pilots:
Dr. Amy Ellis, *M.A.N.T.I.S.,* 1994.
Third opera patron, *Encore! Encore!,* NBC, 1998.
Cheryl Carrera, *Standoff,* Fox, 2006.

Television Appearances; Specials:
Presenter, *The 2001 ALMA Awards,* ABC, 2001.
Sci Fi Inside: "Serenity," Sci–Fi Channel, 2005.

Television Appearances; Episodic:
Laura Elkin, "Skin Deep," *Law & Order,* NBC, 1992.
Charlene, "Purple Heart," *Law & Order,* NBC, 1995.
Dominican woman, "E.R.," *NYPD Blue,* ABC, 1995.
House of Buggin', Fox, 1995.
Cleopatra, "King of Assassins," *Xena: Warrior Princess* (also known as *Xena*), syndicated, 1997.
Michelle Brubaker, "FTX: Field Training Exercise," *Profiler,* NBC, 1997.
Jeannette, *The Gregory Hines Show,* 1997.
Beth Hymson, casting director, "Yes, Virginia, There Is a Hercules," *Hercules: The Legendary Journeys,* syndicated, 1998.
Jenna Vogler, "Open Heart," *La Femme Nikita* (also known as *Nikita*), USA Network, 1998.
Stacy Trenton, "It's Not Karma, It's Life," *Any Day Now,* 2001.
Stacy Trenton, "Boy Will Be Boys," *Any Day Now,* 2002.
Dacia Banga, "Absolute Bastard," *The Agency,* 2003.
Sadie Harper, "Big Coal," *The Guardian,* CBS, 2003.
Sadie, "Shame," *The Guardian,* CBS, 2003.
Warden Hutton, "XX," *CSI: Crime Scene Investigation* (also known as *CSI: Las Vegas, CSI: Weekends, C.S.I.,* and *Les Experts*), CBS, 2004.
The Film Programme (also known as *Film 2005*), BBC, 2005.
Sadie, "Kavanaugh," *The Shield,* FX Channel, 2006.
Sadie, "Smoked," *The Shield,* FX Channel, 2006.
Sadie, "Of Mice and Lem," *The Shield,* FX Channel, 2006.
Tyra Hughes, "More Than This," *Without a Trace* (also known as *W.A.T.*), CBS, 2006.
Tavis Smiley, PBS, 2007.

Also appeared in *Sesame Street,* PBS.

Stage Appearances:

(Professional debut) *Dreamgirls* (musical), Downtown Cabaret, Bridgeport, CT, 1981.

Antigone, Off–Broadway production, 1987.

A Raisin in the Sun, Off–Broadway production, 1987.

A Soldier's Tale, 1987–88.

Sheila's Day, 1990.

Heliotrope Bouquet, 1990.

Pericles, 1991.

Blood Wedding, Off–Broadway production, 1992.

Marci Williams, *Face Value,* Cort Theatre, New York City, 1993.

(Broadway debut) Terri Clark, *The Best Little Whorehouse Goes Public,* Lunt–Fontanne Theatre, New York City, 1994.

Ma Rainey's Black Bottom, Off–Broadway production, 1994.

Alcmena, *Amphitryon,* Classic Stage Company, New York City, 1995.

The Wiz, 1998.

Dreamgirls, 1998.

Also appeared in *Jelly Belly,* Off–Broadway production; *Red Lights and Blues.*

RECORDINGS

Video Games:

Voice of Niobe, *The Matrix Online* (also known as *MxO*), Warner Bros. Interactive Entertainment, 2005.

OTHER SOURCES

Books:

Contemporary Black Biography, Vol. 52, Thomson Gale, 2006.

Electronic:

Gina Torres Website, http://www.gina-torres.com, July 25, 2007.

U–V

UZZAMAN, Badi 1939–
(Badi Uzzamann)

PERSONAL

Born 1939, in Phulpur, India.

Career: Actor.

CREDITS

Film Appearances:
Dealer, *My Beautiful Laundrette,* Orion Classics, 1985.
Mortician's assistant, *Cry Freedom,* Universal, 1987.
Ghost, *Sammy and Rosie Get Laid* (also known as *Sammy and Rosie*), Cinecom, 1987.
Shopkeeper, *Bellman and True,* Island, 1987.
Mr. Patel, *Personal Services,* 1987.
Family father, *Karachi,* 1989.
Indian body, *Lebewohl, Fremde,* 1991.
Ibrahim, *K2* (also known as *K2: The Ultimate High*), Miramax, 1991.
Dadaji's retainer, *Immaculate Conception,* Barcino Barcino Films, 1992.
Uncle, *Bhaji on the Beach,* 1993.
Wasim, *Son of the Pink Panther* (also known as *Blake Edwards "Son of the Pink Panther"* and *Il Figlio della pantera rosa*), Metro–Goldwyn–Mayer, 1993.
Anwar, *The Buddha of Suburbia,* 1993.
Old Ram, *Brothers in Trouble,* Alta Films, 1995.
Ranjan, *Bideshi,* 1995.
Man in mosque, *My Son the Fanatic,* Miramax, 1997.
Shopkeeper, *Babymother,* 1998.
Indian shopkeeper, *Mad Cows,* Entertainment Film, 1999.
(As Badi Uzzaman) Dr. Chandra, *You're Dead,* 1999.
Shopkeeper, *Kevin and Perry Go Large,* Icon Film, 2000.

Dr. Mackay, *The Fourth Angel* (also known as *Vengeance secrete*), Artisan Entertainment, 2001.
Passenger, *All or Nothing,* Metro–Goldwyn–Mayer, 2002.
Vikram, *Cross My Heart,* 2003.
Singh, *The Baby Juice Express,* Universal Home Video, 2004.
Hassan, *Yasmin,* 2004.
Kung fu waiter, *In Your Dreams,* Shoreline Entertainment, 2006.
Chemist, *Eastern Promises,* Focus Features, 2007.

Television Appearances; Series:
Rashid, *Tandoori Nights,* 1985.
Uncle Ram, *Specials,* BBC, 1991.

Television Appearances; Miniseries:
Ali, *The Singing Detective,* BBC and PBS, 1986.
Older Indian (in segment "Over and Out," *GBH,* Channel 4, 1991.
Morgue attendant, *Chimera* (also known as *Monkey Boy*), 1991.
Puran Kapoor, *Firm Friends,* 1992.
Anwar, *The Buddha of Suburbia,* BBC, 1993.
Mr. Ahmed, *Prime Suspect 5: Errors of Judgment,* 1996.
Flapper, *Gulliver's Travels,* NBC, 1996.
Shahid, *Holding On,* BBC and BBC America, 1997.
Uncle Mo, "Serving the Community," *Hetty Wainthropp Investigates III,* PBS, 2000.
Elderly Asian man, *Life Isn't All Ha Ha Hee Hee,* BBC, 2005.

Television Appearances; Movies:
Clinic registrar, *Frankenstein's Baby,* BBC, 1990.
Arshak, *Lie Down with Lions* (also known as *Red Eagle*), Lifetime, 1994.
Ajit Rao, *Milner,* 1994.
Mohanial, *Two Oranges and a Mango,* 1994.
Cracker: To Be a Somebody, Arts and Entertainment, 1995.

Shopkeeper, *Babymother,* Channel 4, 1998.
Abby, *Planespotting,* ITV, 2005.

Television Appearances; Specials:
Cab driver, *Mother Love,* PBS, 1990.

Television Appearances; Pilots:
Amar, "Outpost," *CBS Summer Playhouse,* CBS, 1989.

Television Appearances; Episodic:
Mr. Ahmed, "Home Beat," *The Bill,* ITV1, 1985.
Surinder's father, "Grand Expectations," *Boon,* ITV, 1986.
Mohun–Lal, "The Bombay Ducks," *Call Me Mister,* BBC, 1986.
Kartar Singh, "The Sign of Four," *The Return of Sherlock Holmes, Series II,* PBS, 1988.
Bharat Patel, "Victim of Circumstance," *Casualty,* BBC1, 1989.
Mr. Gopal, "Enemies," *The Bill,* ITV1, 1990.
Chip Van Owner, "Fat Chance," *Inspector Morse,* ITV and PBS, 1991.
Jasbeer, "Words of Advice," *Between the Lines* (also known as *Inside the Line*), 1992.
Mr. Patel, *Coronation Street* (also known as *Corrie*), 1993.
Shahid Ali, "To Be a Somebody," *Cracker,* ITV and Arts and Entertainment, 1994.
Mr. Jamal, *Crown Prosecutor,* 1995.
Old Indian Man, "Unknown Soldiers," *A Touch of Frost,* ITV, 1996.
Sharma, "Not Cricket," *Backup,* BBC, 1997.
Mr. Gupta, "Next of Kin," *Casualty,* BBC1, 1998.
Ramesh, "Ghost Squad: Part 1," *In Deep,* BBC, 2001.
Gupta, "Bridging the Gap," *Auf Wiedersehen, Pet,* BBC, 2002.
Grandad Usmani, *Clocking Off,* BBC, 2003.
Ranjith Mehta, "Perks of the Job," *Casualty,* BBC1, 2003.
Mr. Sardar, *Mile High,* Sky, 2004.
Hotel desk man, *The Grid,* BBC and TNT, 2004.
Suzie's father, "They Keep Killing Suzie," *Torchwood,* BBC, 2006.

VANDERVOORT, Laura 1984–

PERSONAL

Born September 22, 1984, in Toronto, Ontario, Canada. *Education:* Studied psychology and English at York University. *Avocational Interests:* Second degree black-belt in karate.

Career: Actress. Appeared in television commercials, including Philadelphia Cream Cheese and Smarties candy.

Awards, Honors: Young Artist Award nomination, best performance in a television movie (comedy)—leading young actress, 2001, for *Mom's Got a Date with a Vampire.*

CREDITS

Film Appearances:
Carolyn, *Troubled Waters,* 2006.
Kelly, *The Lookout,* Miramax, 2007.

Television Appearances; Series:
Sadie Harrison, *Instant Star,* N, 2004–2007.

Television Appearances; Movies:
Lauren, *Alley Cats Strike,* Disney Channel, 2000.
Chelsea Hansen, *Mom's Got a Date with a Vampire,* Disney Channel, 2000.
(Uncredited) Young girl, *Prom Queen: The Marc Hall Story* (also known as *Prom Queen*), CTV, 2004.
Carolyn, *Troubled Waters,* Lifetime, 2006.

Television Appearances; Specials:
E! Entertainer of the Year 2003, E! Entertainment Television, 2003.

Television Appearances; Pilots:
Ashley, *Falcon Beach,* Global and ABC Family, 2005.

Television Appearances; Episodic:
Nadine, "The Haunted House Game," *Goosebumps* (also known as *Ultimate Goosebumps*), Fox, 1997.
Sheena, "Deep Trouble: Parts 1 & 2," *Goosebumps* (also known as *Ultimate Goosebumps*), Fox, 1998.
Ashley Fox, "The Tale of the Laser Maze," *Are You Afraid of the Dark?,* Nickelodeon, 2000.
Misty Reynolds, "Even Steven," *Twice in a Lifetime,* PAX and CTV, 2000.
Tina, "Russian Roulette," *Mutant X,* syndicated, 2001.
The girl, *The Gavin Crawford Show,* Comedy Network, 2002.
Annis Bennington, "The Family Tree," *Doc,* PAX, 2004.
Gabbie, "Bad Girls," *Sue Thomas: F.B.Eye,* PAX, 2005.
Natalie, "Bad Blood," *The Dresden Files,* Sci–Fi Channel, 2007.
Miss Tangiers, "Big Shots," *CSI: Crime Scene Investigation* (also known as *C.S.I., CSI: Las Vegas, CSI: Weekends,* and *Les Experts*), CBS, 2007.

van de SANDE, Theo 1947–
(Theo Van De Sande, Theo Van de Sande, vdSande)

PERSONAL

Born May 10, 1947, in Tilburg, The Netherlands; immigrated to the United States, 1987. *Education:* Graduated from Dutch Film Academy, 1970.

Addresses: *Agent*—Paradigm, 360 North Crescent Dr., North Bldg., Beverly Hills, CA 90210.

Career: Cinematographer.

Awards, Honors: Golden Calf, best cinematography, 1982, 1987; Dutch Film Critics Award, 1982, for *Het meisje met het rode haar;* Dutch Film Critics Award, 1984, for *De illusionist;* Madrid Film Festival Award, best cinematography, 1987, for *De Wisselwachter.*

CREDITS

Film Cinematographer:
Drop–out (also known as *De meester kan me nog meer vertellen*), 1969.
Eigen Haard is goud waard, 1973.
Vaarwel (also known as *Farewell* and *The Romantic Agony*), 1973.
Naakt over de schutting (also known as *Naked Over the Fence*), City Film, 1973.
Dakota, 1974.
Straf (short), 1974.
Zwaarmoedige verhalen voor bij de centrale verwarming (also known as *Melancholy Tales* and *Zwaarmoedige verhalen*), 1975.
Soleil des hyenes (also known as *Sun of the Hyenas* and *The Hyena's Sun*), 1976.
Alle dagen feest (also known as *Every Day a Party*), 1976.
Het Debuut (also known as *The Debut*), 1977.
De plaats van de vreemdeling (documentary; also known as *The Alien's Place*), Icarus Films, 1977.
Dokter Vlimmen (also known as *Doctor Vlimmen*), Concorde, 1977.
Kasper in de onderwereld (also known as *De goden moeten hun getal hebben* and *Kasper in the Underworld*), 1979.
The Factory (documentary), 1979.
Mijn vriend (also known as *The Judge's Friend* and *Het verborgen Leven van Jules Depraeter*), Tuschinski 1979.
Verdronken Land (also known as *Drown Country*), 1980.

De witte (also known as *Filasse, Whitey,* and *De witte van Sichem*), Tuschinski, 1980.
Charlotte (also known as *Charlotte S.*), 1981.
Het meisje met het rode haar (also kwon as *The Girl with the Red Hair*), United Artists Classics, 1981.
Van de koele meren des doods (also known as *Hedwig: The Quiet Lakes*), 1982.
Golven (also known as *Waves*), 1982.
The Future of '36 (documentary; also known as *De toekomst van '36*), 1983.
Giovanni, 1983.
De Anna, 1983.
Schatjes! (also known as *Army Brats* and *Darlings!*), 1984.
De Schorpioen (also known as *The Scorpion*), 19894.
De illusionist (also known as *The Illusionist*), Castle Hill Productions, 1984.
We komen als vrienden (documentary; also known as *We Are Coming as Friends*), 1985.
De IJssalon (also known as *Private Releasing* and *The Ice–Cream Parlour*), Tuschinski Film Distribution, 1985.
Stranger at Home, Stichting Fugitive Cinema, 1985.
Het bittere kruid (also known as *Bitter Sweet*), Concorde Film, 1985.
De Aanslag (also known as *The Assault*), Cannon, 1986.
Mama is boos! (also known as *Hitting the Fan!*), 1986.
De Wisselwachter (also known as *The Pointsman*), Vestron Pictures, 1986.
Zoeken naar Eileen (also known as *Looking for Eileen*), 1987.
Der Madonna—Mann, Impuls, 1987.
(As Theo Van de Sande) *Crossing Delancy,* Warner Bros., 1988.
(As Theo Van de Sande) *Miracle Mile,* Twentieth Century–Fox, 1988.
Rooftops, New Visions Pictures, 1989.
The First Power (also known as *Pentagram, Possessed, Possessed by Evil,* and *Transit*), Orion, 1990.
Let the Good Times Roll (documentary), 1991.
Once Around, Universal, 1991.
Body Parts, Paramount, 1991.
Eyes of an Angel (also known as *The Tender*), Ascot Video, 1991.
(As Theo Van de Sande) *Wayne's World,* Paramount, 1992.
Big Girls Don't Cry … They Get Even (also known as *Stepkids*), New Line Cinema, 1992.
It Was a Wonderful Life (documentary), New Video Group, 1993.
Les hirondelles ne meurent pas a Jerusalem (also known as *Swallows Never Die in Jerusalem*), 1994.
Exit to Eden, Savoy Pictures, 1994.
Wet (short; also known as *Feucht*), 1995.
Bushwacked (also known as *Tenderfoots* and *The Tenderfoot*), Twentieth Century–Fox, 1995.
"Wet," Tales of Erotica (also known as *Erotic Tales*), Trimark Pictures, 1996.
Volcano, Twentieth Century–Fox, 1997.
Colors Straight Up (documentary), 1997.

(As Theo Van De Sande) *Blade,* New Line Cinema, 1998.

Cruel Intentions, Columbia, 1999.

Big Daddy, Columbia, 1999.

Little Nicky, New Line Cinema, 2000.

Double Take, Buena Vista, 2001.

(As Theo Van De Sande) *High Crimes,* Twentieth Century–Fox, 2002.

DysFunktional Family, Miramax, 2003.

Out of Time, Metro–Goldwyn–Mayer, 2003.

Little Black Book, Columbia, 2004.

Cowboy del Amor (documentary), Emerging Pictures, 2005.

Beauty Shop, Metro–Goldwyn–Mayer, 2005.

Your, Mine and Ours, Paramount, 2005.

(Los Angeles) *The Marine* (also known as *Marine*), Twentieth Century–Fox, 2006.

Steal a Pencil for Me, 2007.

Film Work; Other:

Assistant camera, *Wat zien ik* (also known as *Any Special Way, Business Is Business,* and *Diary of a Hooker*), 1971.

Assistant camera, *Joao en het mes* (also known as *A Face E o Rio* and *Joao*), City Film, 1972.

(As vdSande) Assistance, *Volgend jaar in Holysloot,* 1983.

Second unit director, *Double Take,* Buena Vista, 2001.

Coproducer, *Cowboy del Amor* (documentary), Emerging Pictures, 2005.

Producer, *Steal a Pencil for Me,* 2007.

Television Cinematographer; Series:

Q & Q, kunst—en vliegwerk, 1976.

Pim, 1983.

October Road, ABC, 2007.

The Riches, FX Channel, 2007.

Television Cinematographer; Movies:

De elektriseemachine van Wimshurst, 1978.

Tuesdays with Morrie (also known as *Oprah Winfrey Presents: "Tuesdays with Morrie"*), ABC, 1999.

Television Cinematographer; Specials:

Let the Good Times Roll, PBS, 1993.

Television Cinematographer; Pilots:

The Practice, ABC, 1997.

The Richies, 2007.

Television Cinematographer; Episodic:

"Een mislukte foto," *Q & Q* (also known as *Q en Q, een mislukte foto*), 1974.

"De ring in het bos," *Q & Q* (also known as *Q en Q, een mislukte foto*), 1974.

"De vrolijke zeug," *Q & Q* (also known as *Q en Q, een mislukte foto*), 1974.

"De familie Bennebroeck," *Q & Q* (also known as *Q en Q, een mislukte foto*), 1974.

"Reading the Pleasure," *Women: Stories for Passion,* Showtime, 1997.

"For the Sake of Science," *Women: Stories for Passion,* Showtime, 1997.

VAN OOSTRUM, Kees 1963–
(Kees VanOostrum, Kees van Oostrum, Kees Van Osstrom, Kees Von Oostrum)

PERSONAL

Born July 5, 1963, in Amsterdam, Netherlands. *Education:* Graduated from the American Film Institute.

Addresses: *Agent*—Endeavor, 9601 Wilshire Blvd., 3rd Floor, Beverly Hills, CA 90210.

Career: Cinematographer.

Member: Academy of Motion Pictures Arts and Sciences (cinematographers branch).

Awards, Honors: Emmy Award nomination, outstanding individual achievement in cinematography for a miniseries or a special, 1992, for *Miss Rose White;* American Society of Cinematographers Award nomination, outstanding achievement in cinematography in miniseries, 1993, for *The Burden of Proof;* Emmy Award nomination, outstanding individual achievement in cinematography for a miniseries or a special, American Society of Cinematographers Award, outstanding achievement in cinematography in miniseries, 1994, both for *Return to Lonesome Dove;* American Society of Cinematographers Award nomination, outstanding achievement in cinematography in miniseries, 1998, for *Medusa's Child;* American Society of Cinematographers Award nomination, outstanding achievement in cinematography in movies of the week/miniseries/pilot for basic or pay television, 2005, for *Spartacus.*

CREDITS

Film Cinematographer:

Nights at O'Rear's, 1980.

Certain Fury, New World Pictures, 1985.

Gettysburg, New Line Cinema, 1993.

Separate Lives, 1995.

Thinner (also known as *Stephen King's "Thinner"*), Artisan Entertainment, 1996.
Drive Me Crazy, Twentieth Century–Fox, 1999.
The Last Man Club, 2002.
Gods and Generals, Warner Bros., 2003.
Fields of Freedom, 2006.
We Fight to Be Free (short), Greystone Communications, 2006.
The Last Word, THINKFilms, 2007.

Film Director:
Het Bittere kruid (also known as *Bitter Sweet*), Concorde Films, 1985.
Dial 9 for Love (also known as *Men Are Dogs*), Amberlon Pictures, 2001.
We Fight to Be Free, 2006.

Film Work; Other:
Lighting, *Vliegen zonder Vieugels,* 1977.
Special effects director and special cinematographer, *Treasure: In Search of the Golden Horse,* Intravision, 1984.

Film Appearances:
Cinematographer Style, 2006.

Television Cinematographer; Miniseries:
Guts and Glory: The Rise and Fall of Oliver North, CBS, 1989.
Son of the Morning Star, ABC, 1991.
An Inconvenient Woman, ABC, 1991.
The Burden of Proof (also known as *Scott Turow's "The Burden of Proof"*), ABC, 1992.
Return to Lonesome Dove, CBS, 1993.
(As Kees Van Oostrom) *Degree of Guilt,* NBC, 1995.
Medusa's Child, ABC, 1997.
Spartacus, USA Network, 2004.

Television Camera Operator; Miniseries:
Return to Lonesome Dove, CBS, 1993.
(As Kees Van Oostrom) *Degree of Guilt,* NBC, 1995.

Television Cinematographer; Movies:
Kwiek graal, 1982.
Is da graal, he, 1982.
Her Life as a Man, NBC, 1984.
Crime of Innocence, NBC, 1985.
Something in Common, CBS, 1986.
A Time to Triumph, CBS, 1986.
A Case of Deadly Force, CBS, 1986.
Roses Are for the Rich, 1987.
(As Kees Van Oostrom) *Mistress,* CBS, 1987.
(As Kees VanOostrum) *The Karen Carpenter Story,* CBS, 1989.
Day One, CBS, 1989.
The Incident, CBS, 1990.

A Son's Promise, ABC, 1990.
Ivory Hunters (also known as *The Last Elephant*), TBS, 1990.
(As Kees Van Oostrum) *Long Road Home,* NBC, 1991.
Never Forget, TNT, 1991.
The Story Lady, NBC, 1991.
Miss Rose White, NBC, 1992.
In My Daughter's Name (also kwon as *Overruled*), CBS, 1992.
Somebody's Daughter, ABC, 1992.
Heartbeat (also known as *Danielle Steel's "Heartbeat"*), NBC, 1993.
There Was a Little Boy, CBS, 1993.
Torch Song (also known as *Judith Krantz's "Torch Song"*), ABC, 1993.
Men Don't Tell, CBS, 1993.
(As Kees van Oostrom) *Once in a Lifetime* (also known as *Danielle Steel's "Once in a Lifetime"*), NBC, 1994.
The Enemy Within, HBO, 1994.
Children of the Dark, CBS, 1994.
Jack Reed: A Search for Justice, NBC, 1994.
"Hart to Hart": Old Friends Never Die, NBC, 1994.
Journey, CBS, 1995.
From the Mixed–Up Files of Mrs. Basil E. Frankweiler, ABC, 1995.
Down Came a Blackbird (also known as *Ramirez*), Showtime, 1995.
Degree of Guilt, 1995.
The Christmas Tree, ABC, 1996.
Old Man (also known as *William Faulkner's "Old Man"*), CBS, 1997.
Before He Wakes, CBS, 1998.
You Know My Name (also known as *Bill Tilghman*), TNT, 1999.
Cupid & Cate, CBS, 2000.
A House Divided, Showtime, 2000.
Revenge of the Middle–Aged Woman, CBS, 2004.
The Madam's Family: The Truth About the Canal Street Brothel, CBS, 2004.
Snow Wonder, CBS, 2005.
The Water Is Wide, CBS, 2006.
(As Kees Von Oostrum) *A Perfect Day,* TNT, 2006.

Television Camera Operator; Movies:
A House Divided, Showtime, 2000.

Television Cinematographer; Pilots:
The Gifted One (movie), 1989.
Homeward Bound, ABC, 2002.

Television Cinematographer; Specials:
The Hand–Me–Down Kid, ABC, 1983.
(As Kees Von Oostrum) *Missing Persons—Four True Stories,* HBO, 1984.
Alfred G. Graebner Memorial High School Handbook of Rules and Regulations, CBS, 1984.

Television Director; Specials:
(As Kees Von Oostrum) *Missing Persons—Four True Stories,* HBO, 1984.

Television Work; Episodic:
Cinematographer, *Sable,* ABC, 1987.
Director, "Dead Heat," *The Hitchhiker* (also kwon as *Deadly Nightmares* and *Le voyageur*), HBO, 1987.
Cinematographer, *Second Noah,* ABC, 1996.
Cinematographer, *Profiler,* NBC, 1997–98.
Director, "Lethal Obsession," *Profiles,* NBC, 1998.

VDSANDE
    See van de SANDE, Theo

VELEZ, Lauren 1964–

PERSONAL

Born November 2, 1964, in Brooklyn, NY; daughter of Jose (a police officer) and Coco Velez; twin sister of Lorraine Velez (some sources say Maria Dolores; an actress); married Mark Gordon (a bartender and personal trainer), 1993. *Education:* Studied dance at the Alvin Alley American Dance Theatre; attended Kingsborough Community College for one semester.

Addresses: *Manager*—James/Levey Management, 3500 West Olive Ave., Suite 1470, Burbank, CA 91505.

Career: Actress. Also worked as a restaurant hostess and telephone operator.

Awards, Honors: Independent Spirit Award nomination, best female lead, 1995, Independent Features Project, for *I Like It Like That;* NCLR Bravo Award nomination, outstanding actress in a feature film, National Council of La Raza, 1996, for *City Hall;* NCLR Bravo Award, outstanding actress in a drama series, 1996, Image Award nominations, outstanding lead actress in a drama series, National Association for the Advancement of Colored People (NAACP), 1997, 1998, ALMA Award nomination, outstanding actress in a drama series, American Latin Media Arts Awards, 1998, all for *New York Undercover;* ALMA Award nomination, outstanding actress in a feature film, 1999, for *I Think I Do;* ALMA Award nominations, outstanding actress in a drama series, 1999, 2000, 2002, ALMA Award, outstanding actress in a television series, 2001, all for *Oz;* ALMA Award nomination, outstanding actress in a made–for–television movie or miniseries, 1999, for

Thicker Than Blood; Festival Prize, best supporting actress, Long Island International Film Expo, 2006, for *Serial;* Vision Award, best actress–drama, National Association of Multi–ethnicity in Communications, 2007, for *Dexter.*

CREDITS

Film Appearances:
(Film debut) Lisette Linares, *I Like It Like That,* Columbia, 1994.
Elaine Santos, *City Hall,* Columbia, 1996.
Carol, *I Think I Do,* Strand Releasing, 1997.
Nueba Yol III (bajo la nueva ley), kit parker films, 1997.
Buscando un sueno (also known as *In Search of a Dream*), Nova Creative Releasing, 1997.
Vicky, *The La Mastas,* 1998.
Rosa Sanchez, *Prince of Central Park,* Keystone Entertainment, 2000.
Prison counselor, *Prison Song,* New Line Cinema, 2001.
Maria Vasquez, *Barely Buzzed* (short), 2005.
Roseanne Crystal, *Serial,* 2007.

Television Appearances; Series:
Detective Nina Moreno, *New York Undercover,* 1995–98.
Dr. Gloria Nathan, *Oz,* HBO, 1997–2003.
Lieutenant Maria Laguerta, *Dexter,* Showtime, 2006—.

Television Appearances; Movies:
Camilla Lopez, *Thicker Than Blood,* TNT, 1998.
Agent Susan Mestre, *Love and Treason,* CBS, 2001.

Television Appearances; Specials:
The 1996 NCLR Bravo Awards, Fox, 1996.
Presenter, *The 12th Annual Hispanic Heritage Awards,* NBC, 1998.
Presenter, *Hispanic Heritage Awards,* NBC, 2000.
Presenter, *The 5th Annual ALMA Awards,* ABC, 2000.
Intimate Portrait: Rita Moreno, Lifetime, 2001.

Television Appearances; Episodic:
Claudine Palmeri, "The Hit Parade," *The Cosby Mysteries,* NBC, 1995.
Detective Arias, "Azrael's Breed," *Strange World,* ABC, 1999.
Ms. Torres, "Marathon," *Law & Order,* NBC, 1999.
Emily Sadler, "Clean Sweep," *Profiler,* NBC, 2000.
Emily Sadler, "Spin Doctor," *The Pretender,* NBC, 2000.
Stalker, *Resurrection Blvd.,* Showtime, 2000.
Detective Denise Beltran, "Redemption," *Dragnet* (also known as *L.A. Dragnet*), ABC, 2003.
Detective Denise Beltran, "For Whom the Whistle Blows," *Dragnet* (also known as *L.A. Dragnet*), ABC, 2003.

Attorney Shamal, "Home," *Law & Order: Special Victims Unit* (also known as *Law & Order: SVU* and *Special Victims Unit*), NBC, 2004.

Attorney Shamal, "Obscene," *Law & Order: Special Victims Unit* (also known as *Law & Order: SVU* and *Special Victims Unit*), NBC, 2004.

Dr. Vanessa Burke, "First Response," *Strong Medicine,* Lifetime, 2005.

Faye Templeton, "The Last Temptation," *Wanted,* TNT, 2005.

Elena Cabrera, "Knowing Her," *Medium,* NBC, 2006.

Claudia Gomez, "Undercurrents," *Numb3rs* (also known as *Num3ers*), CBS, 2006.

Claudia Gomez, "Hardball," *Numb3rs* (also known as *Num3ers*), CBS, 2006.

Claudia Gomez, "Contenders," *Numb3rs* (also known as *Num3ers*), CBS, 2006.

Stage Appearances:

Witch, *Into the Woods,* Martin Beck Theatre, New York City, 1987–89.

Mayne, *Intimate Apparel,* Roundabout Theatre Company, New York City, 2004.

Major Tours:

Appeared in *Dreamgirls,* U.S. cities.

VERA, Julia
(Julie Vera)

PERSONAL

Career: Actress.

CREDITS

Film Appearances:

Mrs. Galvin, *Lady Avenger,* Southgate Video, 1988.

Anna, *Homeboys,* 1992.

(As Julie Vera) Madre, *Gas, Food Lodging,* IRS Media, 1992.

Additional bus passenger number seven, *Speed,* Twentieth Century–Fox, 1994.

Mexican nun, *The Net,* Columbia, 1995.

Tear it Down, 1997.

Mama, *Across the Line,* 2000.

Hopi woman, *Role of a Lifetime,* PorchLight Entertainment, 2001.

Clara Blanca, *Blow,* New Line Cinema, 2001.

Vicki, *The Glass House,* Columbia, 2001.

Dona Gorgonia, *Real Women Have Curves,* HBO Independent Pictures, 2002.

Ramona Ramirez, *Pumpkin,* United Artists, 2002.

Dora, *White Like the Moon* (short), 2002.

Rita, *El Viaje: The Journey* (short), 2004.

Woman in community center, *Latin Dragon,* Screen Media Ventures, 2004.

Herself, *The X–Files: The Making of "The Truth"* (documentary), Twentieth Century–Fox Home Entertainment, 2004.

Oleta Diaz, *All Souls Day: Dia de los muertos* (also known as *Dia de los muertos*), IDT Entertainment, 2005.

Dona Carmen, *Day Shift* (short), Fox Searchlight, 2005.

Maria, *The Divorce Ceremony,* 2006.

Landlady, *Coda* (short), 2006.

Arcelia, *The Virgin of Juarez,* First Look International, 2006.

Rosario, *One Night With You,* 2006.

Montana, *Man in the Chair,* 2007.

Abuelita, *Gordon Glass,* 2007.

Television Appearances; Series:

Marta Morez, *General Hospital,* ABC, 1994.

Television Appearances; Miniseries:

Esperanza, *The Invaders,* The WB, 1995.

Delia's mother, *Kingpin,* NBC, 2003.

Television Appearances; Movies:

Teresa, *Safe House,* Showtime, 1998.

Emma Vega, *A Memory in My Heart,* CBS, 1999.

Hopi woman, *Role of a Lifetime,* NBC, 2000.

Television Appearances; Pilots:

Hispanic woman, *Sporting Chance,* CBS, 1990.

Yolanda, "Pilot: Parts 1 & 2," *Malibu Shores,* NBC, 1996.

Rosa, *Pasadena,* Fox, 2001.

Television Appearances; Specials:

Norma Martinez, *The Selena Murder Trial: The E! True Hollywood Story,* E! Entertainment Television, 1996.

Television Appearances; Episodic:

Margarite Sanchez, *L.A. Law,* NBC, 1990.

Rosa, *Simon,* The WB, 1995.

Housekeeper, "Angels We Have Heard on High," *Beverly Hills, 90210,* Fox, 1995.

Mrs. Lopez, "See Me," *Dangerous Minds,* ABC, 1996.

Yolanda, *Malibu Shores,* NBC, 1996.

Reyes y Rey, Telemundo, 1998.

Cuban lady, "Politics," *Tracey Takes On ...,* HBO, 1997.

Woman, "Fear of Flying," *L.A. Doctors* (also known as *L.A. Docs*), CBS, 1998.

Sister Rafaela, "Fever," *Air America,* syndicated, 1998.

Mrs. Lana Chee, "Dreamland," *The X–Files,* Fox, 1998.

Mrs. Lana Chee, "Dreamland II," *The X–Files,* Fox, 1998.

Maria, "Thanksgiving Until It Hurts," *Dharma & Greg,* ABC, 1999.

Mrs. Guitierez, "Mother's Day," *The Division* (also known as *Heart of the City*), Lifetime, 2001.

Wife, *Philly,* ABC, 2001.

"It's Val's Wonderful Life," *V.I.P.* (also known as *V.I.P.—Die Bodyguards*), syndicated, 2001.

Anna Rodriguez, Tony's sister, "Johnny got His Gold," *NYPD Blue,* ABC, 2001.

Indian woman, "The Truth," *The X–Files,* Fox, 2002.

Inez, "Strap On," *Fastlane,* Fox, 2003.

Cleaning woman, "Perfect Circles," *Six Feet Under,* HBO, 2003.

Maria Sanchez 2003, "Gleen," *Cold Case,* CBS, 2003.

Reina, "Freefall," *ER,* NBC, 2003.

Marisol Fuentes, "From the Grave," *CSI: Miami,* CBS, 2005.

Concepion, "Swish Out of Water," *Will & Grace,* NBC, 2005.

Abuela, *The Shield,* FX Channel, 2005.

Lupa Trejo, "Machismo," *Criminal Minds,* CBS, 2006.

VICTOR, Mark

PERSONAL

Addresses: *Office*—Mark Victor Productions, 2932 Wilshire Blvd., Suite 202, Santa Monica, CA 90403.

Career: Producer and writer. Mark Victor Productions, Los Angeles, CA, principal. Also worked as a lawyer in AZ.

CREDITS

Film Producer:
(With Michael Grais) *Poltergeist II: The Other Side* (also known as *Poltergeist 2* and *Poltergeist II*), Metro–Goldwyn–Mayer, 1986.

(With Michael Grais) *Marked for Death,* Twentieth Century–Fox, 1990.

Sleepwalkers (also known as *Sleepstalkers* and *Stephen King's "Sleepwalkers"*), Columbia, 1992.

(With Michael Grais) *Cool World* (animated), Paramount, 1992.

Adopt a Sailor, 2007.

Falling, 2007.

Film Executive Producer:
Great Balls of Fire!, Orion, 1989.

Christina's House, Metro–Goldwyn–Mayer, 1999.

Television Work; Movies:
Producer, *UFO Abductions,* 1991.

Executive producer, *Who Killed Atlanta's Children?* (also *Echo of Murder*), 2000.

Television Executive Producer; Specials:
Visitors from the Unknown, CBS, 1991.

Secrets of the Unknown, CBS, 1991.

Visitors from the Unknown, CBS, 1992.

WRITINGS

Screenplays:
(With Michael Grais) *Death Hunt,* Twentieth Century–Fox, 1981.

(With Michael Grais and Steven Spielberg) *Poltergeist,* Metro–Goldwyn–Mayer/United Artists, 1982.

(With Michael Grais) *Poltergeist II: The Other Side* (also known as *Poltergeist 2* and *Poltergeist II*), Metro–Goldwyn–Mayer, 1986.

(With Michael Grais) *Marked for Death,* Twentieth Century–Fox, 1990.

(With Michael Grais) *Cool World* (animated), Paramount, 1992.

Television Specials:
Visitors from the Unknown, CBS, 1991.

Secrets of the Unknown, CBS, 1991.

Visitors from the Unknown, CBS, 1992.

Television Episodes:
The Immortal, syndicated, 2000.

With Michael Grais, also wrote episodes of *Kojak,* CBS; *Baretta; Starsky and Hutch.*

---

von BRANDENSTEIN, Patrizia
(Patrizia Von Brandenstein)

PERSONAL

Born in AZ; father, an army warrant officer; married second husband, Stuart Wurtzel (a production designer); children: (second marriage) Kimberly. *Education:* Attended University of Alaska, Anchorage, and Catholic University of America; studied at Comedie Francaise, Paris, Lester Polakov's Studio, and HB Studio and Actors Studio, New York City.

Addresses: *Agent*—Mirisch Agency, 1875 Century Park East, Suite 2050, Los Angeles, CA 90067.

Career: Production designer, art director, and costume designer. La Mama Experimental Theatre Club, New York City, worked as seamstress, prop maker, and scene painter in the 1960s; American Conservatory Theatre, San Francisco, CA, various positions, 1966–74; Playhouse in the Park, Cincinnati, OH, costume designer, 1970–71.

Member: Local 800, New York Local 829.

Awards, Honors: Academy Award nomination (with others), best art direction—set decoration, 1982, for *Ragtime;* Academy Award (with Karel Cerny), best art direction—set decoration, 1985, and Film Award nomination, best production design for a film, 1986, British Academy of Film and Television Arts, both for *Amadeus;* Academy Award nomination (with William A. Elliott and Hal Gausman), best art direction—set decoration, 1988, for *The Untouchables;* Below–The–Line Award, Gotham Awards, 1993.

CREDITS

Film Production Designer:
Hester Street, 1975.
Girlfriends, Warner Bros., 1978.
Heartland, Levitt–Pickman, 1979.
Breaking Away, Twentieth Century–Fox, 1979.
Tell Me a Riddle, Filmways, 1980.
(With Tony Reading) *Ragtime,* Paramount, 1981.
(As Patrizia Von Brandenstein) *Silkwood,* Twentieth Century–Fox, 1983.
Touched, Lorimar Productions/Wildwood Partners, 1983.
Beat Street, Orion, 1984.
Amadeus (also known as *Peter Shaffer's "Amadeus"*), Orion, 1984.
A Chorus Line, Columbia, 1985.
The Money Pit, Universal, 1986.
No Mercy, TriStar, 1986.
The Untouchables, Paramount, 1987.
Betrayed, Metro–Goldwyn–Mayer/United Artists, 1988.
(As Patrizia Von Brandenstein) *Working Girl,* Twentieth Century–Fox, 1988.
The Lemon Sisters, Miramax, 1990.
(As Patrizia Von Brandenstein; with Doug Kraner) *State of Grace,* Orion, 1990.
Postcards from the Edge, Columbia, 1990.
Billy Bathgate, Buena Vista, 1991.
(As Patrizia Von Brandenstein) *Sneakers,* Universal, 1992.
Leap of Faith, Paramount, 1992.
Six Degrees of Separation, Metro–Goldwyn–Mayer, 1993.
The Quick and the Dead, TriStar, 1995.
(As Patrizia Von Brandenstein) *Just Cause,* Warner Bros., 1995.
The People vs. Larry Flynt (also known as *Larry Flynt*), Columbia, 1996.
Mercury Rising, Universal, 1998.

A Simple Plan (also known as *Ein einfacher plan* and *Un plan simple*), Paramount, 1998.
Man on the Moon (also known as *Der Mondmann*), Universal, 1999.
Shaft (also known as *Shaft—Noch fragen?*), Paramount, 2000.
The Emperor's Club, MCA/Universal, 2002.
(As Patrizia Von Brandenstein) *It Runs in the Family* (also known as *Family Business*), Metro–Goldwyn–Mayer, 2003.
The Ice Harvest, Focus Features, 2005.
All the King's Men (also known as *Das spiel der macht*), Sony, 2006.
Goya's Ghosts (also known as *Los fantasmas de Goya*), Samuel Goldwyn Company, 2006.
The Tourist, Twentieth Century–Fox, 2007.

Film Costume Designer:
(As Patrizia Von Brandenstein; with Jennifer Nichols) *Saturday Night Fever,* Paramount, 1977.
Between the Lines, Midwest, 1977.
A Little Sex, Universal, 1982.

Film Art Director:
Girlfriends, 1978.
(As Patrizia Von Brandenstein) *Breaking Away,* 1979.
Ragtime, 1981.

Film Work; Other:
Set designer, *The Candidate,* Warner Bros., 1972.
Researcher, *King of the Gypsies,* 1978.
Visual consultant, *The Untouchables,* Paramount, 1987.

Film Appearances:
Herself, *The Making of "Amadeus"* (documentary), Warner Home Video, 2002.
Herself, *Remembering "Ragtime"* (documentary short), Paramount Pictures, 2004.

Television Production Designer; Movies:
The Gardener's Son, 1977.
The Summer of My German Soldier, NBC, 1978.
My Old Man, CBS, 1979.
Witness Protection, HBO, 1999.
South Pacific (also known as *Rodgers & Hammerstein's "South Pacific"*), ABC, 2001.
(As Patrizia Von Bradenstein) *Plainsong,* 2004.

Television Art Director; Movies:
The Last Tenant, ABC, 1978.
Hardhat and Legs, CBS, 1980.
Barn Burning (also known as *The American Short Story Collection: "Barn Burning"*), 1980.

Television Work; Specials:
Visual consultant, *A Tale of Cinderella,* PBS, 1998.

Television Appearances; Specials:
The 57th Annual Academy Awards, ABC, 1985.

Stage Costume Designer:
Don't Shoot Mable It's Your Husband, Bouwerie Lane
    Theatre, New York City, 1968.
Rosmersholm, Stage Two, Roundabout Theatre, New
    York City, 1974.
Double Feature, Theatre at St. Peters Church, New York
    City, 1981.
Hizzoner!, Longacre Theatre, New York City, 1989.

Major Tours (As Costume Designer):
Dylan, U.S. cities, 1970.

OTHER SOURCES

Books:
International Dictionary of Films and Filmmakers,
    Volume 4: *Writers and Production Artists,* St. James
    Press, 1996.
Women Filmmakers and Their Films, St. James Press,
    1998.

Periodicals:
American Film, August, 1990, pp. 32–37, 46–47.

VON OOSTRUM, Kees
    See VAN OOSTRUM, Kees

W

WAISBREN, Ben
(Benjamin Waisbren)

PERSONAL

Career: Producer. Continental Entertainment Group, president.

CREDITS

Film Executive Producer:
Duane Hopwood, IFC Films, 2005.
(As Benjamin Waisbren) *V for Vendetta* (also known as *V wie Vendetta*), Warner Bros., 2005.
(As Benjamin Waisbren) *Poseidon,* Warner Bros., 2006.
(As Benjamin Waisbren) *The Good German,* Warner Bros., 2006.
(As Benjamin Waisbren) *Blood Diamond,* Warner Bros., 2006.
(As Benjamin Waisbren) *300,* Warner Bros., 2006.
Gardener of Eden, 2007.
First Born, First Look International, 2007.
Next, Paramount, 2007.
(As Benjamin Waisbren) *Nancy Drew,* Warner Bros., 2007.
Cassandra's Dream, Weinstein Company, 2007.
The Assassination of Jesse James by the Coward Robert Ford (also known as *The Assassination of Jesse James*), Warner Bros., 2007.

WAITES, Thomas G.
(T. G. Waites, Thomas Waites, Tom Waites)

PERSONAL

Born in Philadelphia, PA.

Career: Actor. Actors Studio, member; owns and operates an acting studio, New York, NY.

CREDITS

Film Appearances:
Chilly, *On the Yard,* Midwest Films, 1978.
(Uncredited) Fox, *The Warriors,* Paramount, 1979.
(As Thomas Waites) Jeff McCullaugh, *... And Justice for All,* Columbia, 1979.
(As Thomas Waites) Windows, *The Thing* (also known as *John Carpenter's "The Thing"*), Universal, 1982.
Broud, *The Clan of the Cave Bear,* Warner Bros., 1986.
Al Capone, *The Verne Miller Story* (also known as *Gangland* and *Verne Miller*), 1987.
Smittie, *Light of Day,* TriStar, 1987.
Officer Kelly, *Shakedown* (also known as *Blue Jean Cop*), Universal, 1988.
Frankie's man, *State of Grace,* Orion, 1990.
(As T. G. Waites) Gill, *McBain,* MCA/Universal, 1991.
Barricade captain, *Money Train,* Columbia, 1995.
Warden Andrews, *Timelock,* MTI Home Video, 1996.
Mulroney, *An American Affair,* 1997.
Sergeant, *Most Wanted,* New Line Cinema, 1997.
John Willio, *Rites of Passage,* World International Network, 1999.
(As Thomas Waites) Grip, *American Virgin* (also known as *Live Virgin*), Granite Releasing, 2000.
(As Thomas Waites) Carpet guy, *Nailed,* Curb Entertainment, 2001.

Television Appearances; Series:
Otis Price, *All My Children,* ABC, 1987.
Harry Stanton, *Oz,* HBO, 2001–2003.

Television Appearances; Movies:
The Other Side of Victory, 1976.
Howard, *The Face of Rage,* ABC, 1983.
Tink, *Flowers for Matty,* ABC, 1990.

Supply sergeant, *A Thousand Men and a Baby* (also known as *Narrow Escape*), CBS, 1997.

Television Appearances; Specials:
Paul, *O'Malley,* NBC, 1980.

Television Appearances; Episodic:
Thompson, "Bushido," *Miami Vice,* NBC, 1985.
Alan, "Abrams for the Defense," *Crime Story,* NBC, 1986.
Jim Kaufman, "Nightscape," *The Equalizer,* CBS, 1986.
Shep Morrow, "The Child Broker," *The Equalizer,* CBS, 1988.
Duke, *Another World* (also known as *Another World: Bay City*), NBC, 1989.
Craig Herman, "We Was Robbed," *NYPD Blue,* ABC, 1996.
Randy, airplane mechanic, "Slither," *Sliders,* Fox, 1997.
Crisis Center, NBC, 1997.
William Weaver, Sr., "Weaver of Hate," *NYPD Blue,* ABC, 1998.
White person, *Four Corners,* CBS, 1998.
George Speaker, "Big Brother's Secret," *Mike Hammer, Private Eye,* syndicated, 1998.
Second cop, "Becoming: Part 2," *Buffy the Vampire Slayer* (also known as *BtVS, Buffy,* and *Buffy the Vampire Slayer: The Series*), The WB, 1998.
Captain Lewis Webber, "Standoff," *Law & Order,* NBC, 2000.
Mo Turnman, bookie, "Jones," *Law & Order: Criminal Intent* (also known as *Law & Order: CI*), NBC, 2001.
Lance Brody, "A Murder Among Us," *Law & Order: Criminal Intent* (also known as *Law & Order: CI*), NBC, 2003.
Michael Gruzielanek, "The Boxer," *The Jury,* Fox, 2004.

Stage Appearances:
(As Thomas Waites) Bobby, *American Buffalo,* Circle in the Square Theatre, New York City, 1981–82.
(As Thomas Waites) *Pastorale,* McGinn–Cazale Theatre, New York City, 1982.
Alternate Dean Rebel, *Teaneck Tanzi: The Venus Flytrap,* Nederlander Theatre, New York City, 1983.
Ralph Berger, *Awake and Sing!,* Circle in the Square Theatre, 1984.
Robert, *Search and Destroy,* Circle in the Square Theatre, 1992.

Stage Work:
Director, *Six Goumbas and a Wannabe,* Players Theatre, New York City, 2001.
Director, *Golden Ladder,* Players Theatre, 2002.

RECORDINGS

Video Games:
(As Tom Waites) Fox, *The Warriors,* Rockstar Games, 2005.

WALKER, Marcy 1961–
(Marcy Smith)

PERSONAL

Born November 26, 1961, in Paducah, KY; father, an aeronautical field service engineer; married Stephen Ferris (an actor; divorced); married Billy Warlock (an actor), November 2, 1985 (divorced, 1987); married Stephan Collins (a cameraman), 1990 (divorced, 1991); married Robert Drew Primrose (an operator and audio technician), 1997 (divorced, February, 1999); married Doug Smith, December 11, 1999; children: (third marriage) Taylor. *Religion:* Christian.

Addresses: *Agent*—David Shapira and Associates, 193 North Robertson Blvd., Beverly Hills, CA 90211.

Career: Actress. Worked as children's ministry director at a church outside of Charlotte, NC, 2006—.

Awards, Honors: Daytime Emmy Award nominations, outstanding actress in a supporting role in a daytime drama series, 1983, 1984, *Soap Opera Digest* Award, outstanding supporting actress, 1997, Daytime Emmy Award nomination, outstanding lead actress in a drama series, 2001, all for *All My Children; Soap Opera Digest* Award nominations, outstanding young leading actress on a daytime serial, 1986, and favorite daytime super couple on a daytime serial (with A Martinez), 1986, 1988, 1989, *Soap Opera Digest* Awards, outstanding heroine—daytime, 1989, outstanding lead actress—daytime, 1990, outstanding super couple—daytime (with A Martinez), 1990, and best death scene—daytime, 1992, Daytime Emmy Award nominations, outstanding lead actress in a drama series, 1987, 1988, and Daytime Emmy Award, outstanding lead actress in a drama series, 1989, all for *Santa Barbara.*

CREDITS

Film Appearances:
Franny, *Hot Resort,* Cannon, 1985.
Rachel Parsons, *Talking About Sex,* 1994.

Television Appearances; Series:
Liza Colby Chandler, *All My Children,* ABC, 1981–84, 1995–2005.
Eden Capwell, *Santa Barbara,* NBC, 1984–91.
Christy Cooper, *Palace Guard,* CBS, 1991.
Tangie Hill, *The Guiding Light* (also known as *Guiding Light*), CBS, 1993–95.

Television Appearances; Movies:
Emmeline, *Life on the Mississippi,* PBS, 1980.
Caitlin Jones, *The Return of Desperado,* NBC, 1988.
Marie Ramsey, *Perry Mason: The Case of the Desperate Deception,* NBC, 1990.
Cindy, *Babies,* NBC, 1990.
Kate, *Midnight's Child,* Lifetime, 1992.
Ann Demski, *Overexposed,* ABC, 1992.
Rebecca/Christine, *Terror in the Shadows,* NBC, 1995.
Lieutenant Kathy Leone, *Sudden Terror: The Hijacking of School Bus #17,* ABC, 1996.

Television Appearances; Specials:
Presenter, *The 13th Annual Daytime Emmy Awards,* NBC, 1986.
The 14th Annual Daytime Emmy Awards, ABC, 1987.
The 15th Annual Daytime Emmy Awards, CBS, 1988.
Host, *Soap Opera Digest Awards,* NBC, 1988, 1989.
The 16th Annual Daytime Emmy Awards, NBC, 1989.
Soap Opera Awards, NBC, 1990.
Presenter, *The 18th Annual Daytime Emmy Awards,* CBS, 1991.
Presenter, *The 21st Annual Daytime Emmy Awards,* ABC, 1994.
Presenter, *The 24th Annual Daytime Emmy Awards,* ABC, 1997.
Presenter, *Soap Opera Update Awards,* Lifetime, 1997.
The 26th Annual Daytime Emmy Awards, CBS, 1999.
The 27th Annual Daytime Emmy Awards, ABC, 2000.
The 28th Annual Daytime Emmy Awards, NBC, 2001.

Television Appearances; Pilots:
Melanie Roston, *Bar Girls,* CBS, 1990.

Television Appearances; Episodic:
"Soap Stars and Their Real Life Families Week II," *Family Feud* (also known as *Family Fortune* and *The Best of Family Feud*), 1983.
"All My Children," *Biography,* Arts and Entertainment, 2003.

RECORDINGS

Videos:
Liza Colby Chandler, *Daytime's Greatest Weddings,* Buena Vista Home Video, 2004.

WEBSTER, Paul

PERSONAL

Addresses: *Office*—Kudos Film and Television, 12–14 Amwell St., London EC1R 1UQ, England.

Career: Producer and studio executive. Miramax, head of production; Film Four, chief executive; Kudos Film and Television, London, head of film group; also worked as production coordinator.

Awards, Honors: Independent Spirit Award nomination (with director James Gray), best first feature, Independent Features Project West, 1996, for *Little Odessa;* nomination for Alexander Korda Award for Best British Film (with others), British Academy of Film and Television Arts, 2006, for *Pride & Prejudice.*

CREDITS

Film Executive Producer:
Bob Roberts, Paramount, 1992.
Co–executive producer, *Posse,* Gramercy, 1993.
Co–executive producer, *Little Voice,* Miramax, 1998.
My Life So Far, Miramax, 1999.
Jump Tomorrow (also known as *Life: A User's Manual*), IFC Films, 2001.
My Brother Tom, Film Four, 2001.
Late Night Shopping, Film Four, 2001.
Buffalo Soldiers (also known as *Army Go Home!* and *Buffalo Soldiers—Army Go Home!*), 2001, Miramax, 2003.
The Warrior, 2001, Miramax, 2005.
Dog Eat Dog, Film Four, 2001.
Charlotte Gray (also known as *Die Liebe der Charlotte Gray*), Warner Bros., 2001.
The Emperor's New Clothes (also known as *I vestiti nuovi dell'imperatore*), Paramount, 2002.
Crush (also known as *Drei Freundinnen und ein Liebhaber* and *Heiraten fuer fortgeschrittene*), Sony Pictures Classics, 2002.
Lucky Break (also known as *Rein oder raus*), Paramount, 2002.
Birthday Girl, Miramax, 2002.
Miranda, First Look Pictures, 2002.
Once Upon a Time in the Midlands, Sony Pictures Classics, 2003.
The Principles of Lust, Film Four, 2003.
The Actors, Miramax, 2003.
To Kill a King, Film Four, 2003.
It's All About Love, Strand Releasing, 2004.
Diarios de motocicleta (also known as *The Motorcycle Diaries, Carnets de voyage, Die Reise des jungen Che,* and *Voyage a motocyclette*), Focus Features, 2005.

Film Producer:
Dream Demon, Palace Pictures, 1988.
The Tall Guy, Miramax, 1990.
Rubin and Ed, IRS Media, 1991.
Drop Dead Fred (also known as *My Special Friend*), New Line Cinema, 1991.
Romeo Is Bleeding, Gramercy, 1994.

Little Odessa, Fine Line, 1995.
The Pallbearer, Miramax, 1996.
Gridlock'd, Gramercy, 1997.
The Yards, Miramax, 2000.
Pride & Prejudice (also known as *Orgueil et prejuges*), Focus Features, 2005.
Atonement, Focus Features, 2007.

Film Associate Producer:

Wings of Death (short film), Palace Pictures, 1985.

RECORDINGS

Videos:

The Politics of Dating, Universal Studios, 2006.
The Bennets, Universal Studios, 2006.

WEINER, Zane 1953–

PERSONAL

Born July 11, 1953, in Holyoke, MA; son of Mathew (a retailer) and Helen Marie (a nurse; maiden name, Bernstein) Weiner. *Education:* University of New Hampshire, B.A., theatre, 1975. *Politics:* Democrat. *Religion:* Jewish. *Avocational Interests:* Fishing.

Career: Stage manager, production manager, producer, production executive, and writer.

Member: Actors' Equity Association.

Awards, Honors: Directors Guild of America Award (with others), outstanding directorial achievement in motion pictures, 2004, for *The Lord of the Rings: The Return of the King.*

CREDITS

Film Work:

Musical production coordinator, *The Cotton Club,* Orion Pictures, 1984.
Production assistant, *Blue Desert* (also known as *Silent Victim*), 1991.
Location manager: Mexico, *Ruby Cairo* (also known as *Deception* and *The Missing Link: Ruby Cairo*), 1993.
Location manager, *Wilder Napalm,* TriStar, 1993.
Location manager, *Deception,* Miramax, 1993.
Location manager, *China Moon,* Orion, 1994.

Unit production manager, *Rapa Nui,* Warner Bros., 1994.
Production supervisor, *The Fan,* Sony Pictures Entertainment, 1996.
Unit production manager, *Mighty Joe Young* (also known as *Mighty Joe*), Buena Vista, 1998.
Production supervisor: additional photography, *Senseless,* 1998.
Unit production manager, *October Sky,* Universal, 1999.
Unit production manager, *Wonder Boys* (also known as *Die Wonder Boys* and *Wonderboys—Lauter wunderknaben*), Paramount, 2000.
Coproducer and unit production manager, *The Crew,* Buena Vista, 2000.
Unit production manager and unit publicist, *The Lord of the Rings: The Fellowship of the Ring* (also known as *The Fellowship of the Ring* and *The Lord of the Rings: The Fellowship of the Ring: The Motion Picture*), New Line Cinema, 2001.
Unit production manager, *8 Mile,* Universal, 2002.
Unit production manager, *The Lord of the Rings: The Two Towers* (also known as *Der Herr der Ringe: Die zwei turme* and *The Two Towers*), New Line Cinema, 2002.
Coproducer and unit production manager, *The Long and Short of It* (short), 2003.
Unit production manager, *The Lord of the Rings: The Return of the King* (also known as *Der Herr der Ringe: Die Ruckkehr des konigs* and *The Return of the King*), New Line Cinema, 2003.
Unit production manager, *The Big Bounce,* Warner Bros., 2004.
Production executive, *Looking for Comedy in the Muslim World,* Warner Independent, 2005.
Production executive, *For Your Consideration,* Warner Independent Pictures, 2006.
Production executive, *Beowulf,* Warner Bros., 2007.

Also worked as music production coordinator, *Bright Angel;* music production coordinator, *Barton Fink.*

Stage Work:

Production stage manager, *Tuscaloosa's Calling Me But I'm Not Going,* Top of the Gate, New York City, 1975–76.
Production stage manager, *Ashes,* Joseph Papp Public Theatre, Anspacher Theatre, New York City, 1977.
Production stage manager, *Curse of the Starving Class,* Joseph Papp Public Theatre, Newman Theatre, New York City, 1978.
Production stage manager, *Julius Caesar,* Joseph Papp Public Theatre, Anspacher Theatre, 1979.
Stage manager, *Bosoms and Neglect,* Longacre Theatre, New York City, 1979.
Production stage manager, *Othello,* Delacorte Theatre, New York City, 1979.

Production stage manager, *Salt Lake City Skyline,* Joseph Papp Public Theater, Anspacher Theatre, 1980.

Stage manager, *Happy New Year,* Morosco Theatre, New York City, 1980.

Production stage manager, *Pirates of Penzance,* New York Shakespeare Festival, Delacorte Theatre, then Uris Theatre, New York City, 1980–81.

Stage manager, *Dreamgirls,* Imperial Theatre, New York City, 1981–85.

Stage manager, *The Life and Adventures of Nicholas Nickleby,* Broadhurst Theatre, New York City, 1986.

Stage manager, *Chess,* Imperial Theatre, 1988.

Production stage manager, *Only Kidding!,* Westside Theatre Upstairs, New York City, 1989.

Also worked as a stage manager, *Coriolanus,* New York Shakespeare Festival; stage manager, *A Chorus Line,* Shubert Theatre, New York City; *Ballroom,* Majestic Theatre, New York City.

Major Tours:

Worked as stage manager, *A Chorus Line,* international cities.

WRITINGS

Plays:

Wrote *Firetown; Lottery; Bad Luck Charlie;* and *The American Spirit.*

WERTMULLER, Lina 1926–

(George Brown, George H. Brown, Lina Wertmueller, Nathan Wich)

PERSONAL

Full name, Arcangela Felice Assunta Wertmueller von Elgg Espanol von Brauchich; born August 14, 1926, in Rome, Italy; daughter of Federico (a lawyer) and Maria Santa Maria Wertmueller; married Enrico Job (a sculptor, set designer, production designer, art director, and costume designer), 1968. *Education:* Academy of Theatre, Rome, graduated, 1951.

Career: Director and writer. Member of Maria Signorelli's puppet troupe, Italy, 1951–52; actress, stage manager, set designer, publicist, and writer for theatre, radio, and television, and producer and director of avante–garde plays, Italy, 1952–62; Liberty Films, cofounder; also worked as assistant director. Formerly worked as a schoolteacher. Venice Film Festival, member of jury, 1988.

Awards, Honors: Silver Sail, best direction of a feature film, Locarno International Film Festival, 1963, for *I Basilischi;* nomination for Golden Palm, Cannes Film Festival, 1972, for *Mimi metallurgico ferito nell'onore;* nomination for Golden Palm, 1973, for *Film d'amore e d'anarchia;* Academy Award nominations, best original screenplay written and best director, and Directors Guild of America Award nomination, outstanding direction, all 1977, for *Pasqualino settebellezze;* nomination for Golden Berlin Bear, Berlin International Film Festival, 1978, for *The End of the World in Our Usual Bed in a Night Full of Rain;* Crystal Award, Women in Film, 1985; nomination for Golden Prize, Moscow International Film Festival, 1985, for *Scherzo del destino in agguato dietro l'angolo come un brigante di strada;* Golden Berlin Bear nomination and Interfilm Award/Otto Dibelius Film Award, *Berliner Morgenpost* reader jury, Berlin International Film Festival, both 1986, for *Un complicato intrigo di donne, vicoli e delitti;* First Friendship Award, National Organization of Italian–American Women, 1987; named special commissioner, Centro Sperimentale di Cinematografia, 1988.

CREDITS

Film Director:

I Basilischi (also known as *The Basilisks* and *The Lizards*), Connoisseur, 1963.

Questa volta parliamo di uomini (also known as *Let's Talk About Men, Now Let's Talk About Men,* and *This Time Let's Talk About Men*), Archimede, 1965.

(As George Brown; musical numbers only) *Rita la zanzara* (also known as *Rita the Mosquito*), Mondial, 1966.

Non stuzzicate la zanzara (also known as *Don't Sting the Mosquito* and *Don't Tease the Mosquito*), Mondial, 1967.

Mimi metallurgico ferito nell'onore (also known as *The Seduction of Mimi, Mimi the Metalworker,* and *Wounded in Honor*), New Line Cinema, 1972.

Film d'amore e d'anarchia (also known as *Film of Love and Anarchy, Film of Love and Anarchy, This Morning at 10 in the Via dei Fiori at the Well–known House of Tolerance, Love and Anarchy, Film d'amore e d'anarchia, ovvero stamattina alle 10 in via dei Fiori nella nota casa di tolleranza,* and *D'Amore e d'anarchia*), Peppercorn–Wormser, 1973.

Tutto a posto e niente in ordine (also known as *All in Place and Nothing in Order, All Screwed Up, Everything Ready, Nothing Works,* and *Everything's in Order but Nothing Works*), New Line Cinema, 1974.

Travolti da un insolito destino nell'azzurro mare d'agosto (also known as *Swept Away* and *Swept Away ... by an Unusual Destiny in the Blue Sea of August*), Almi Cinema V, 1975.

(And coproducer) *Pasqualino settebellezze* (also known as *Pasqualino: Seven Beauties* and *Seven Beauties*), Almi Cinema V, 1976.

The End of the World in Our Usual Bed in a Night Full of Rain (also known as *A Night Full of Rain* and *La Fine del mondo nel nostro solito letto in una notte piena di pioggia*), Warner Bros., 1978.

Fatto di sangue fra due uomini per causa di una vedova si sospettano (also known as *Blood Feud* and *Revenge*), Associated Film Distribution, 1979.

E una domenica sera di novembre, 1981.

Scherzo del destino in agguato dietro l'angolo come un brigante di strada (also known as *A Joke of Destiny* and *A Joke of Destiny, Lying in Wait Around the Corner like a Bandit*), Samuel Goldwyn Company, 1983.

Sotto ... sotto ... strapazzato da anomala passione (also known as *Softly, Softly* and *Sotto ... sotto*), Columbia/Triumph, 1984.

Un complicato intrigo di donne, vicoli e delitti (also known as *Camorra, Camorra (A Story of Streets, Women, and Crime)*, *Camorra: The Naples Connection*, and *A Complex Plot About Women, Alleys and Crimes*), Cannon, 1986.

Notte d'estate, con profilo greco, occhi a mandorla e odore di basilico (also known as *Summer Night, with Greek Profile, Almond Eyes and Scent of Basil*), New Line Cinema, 1986.

Imago urbis, 1987.

"Bari" segment, *12 registi per 12 citta*, 1989.

In una notte di chiaro di luna (also known as *As Long as It's Love, Clair, Crystal or Ash, Fire or Wind, as Long as It's Love*, and *On a Moonlit Night*), 1989.

Io speriamo che me la cavo (also known as *Ciao, Professore!* and *Let's Hope I Make It*), Miramax, 1993.

Ninfa plebea (also known as *The Nymph*), 1996.

Metalmeccanico e parrucchiera in un turbine di sesso e di politica (also known as *The Blue Collar Worker and the Hairdresser in a Whirl of Sex and Politics* and *The Worker and the Hairdresser*), Medusa, 1996.

Ferdinando e Carolina, Medusa, 1999.

An Interesting State, 1999.

Peperoni ripieni e pesci in faccia (also known as *Too Much Romance ... It's Time for Stuffed Peppers*), Sharada Distribuzione, 2004.

Documentary Film Appearances:

Lina Wertmuller, 1977.

Zwischen Kino und Konzert—Der Komponist Nino Rota, 1993.

Un Amico magico: il maestro Nino Rota, 1999.

(Uncredited; in archive footage) *Luchino Visconti*, 1999.

Isa 9000 (short film), 2001.

Fellini, 2001.

Marcello, una vita dolce, Cinemien, 2007.

Television Director:

Il Giornalino di Gian Burasca (series; also known as *Gian Burrasca's Diary*), 1965.

(As Nathan Wich) *Il Mio corpo per un poker* (movie; also known as *The Belle Starr Story*), 1967.

Il Decimo clandestino (also known as *The Tenth One in Hiding* and *To Save Nine*), 1989.

Sabato, domenica e lunedi (movie; also known as *Saturday, Sunday and Monday*), 1990.

Francesca e Nunziata (also known as *Francesca and Nunziata*), 2001.

Television Appearances; Specials:

(In archive footage) *The Magic of Fellini*, 2002.

Stage Director:

Shimmy lagano tarantelle e vino, 1978.

Love and Magic in Mama's Kitchen, Spoleto, Italy, then LaMama Experimental Theatre Club, New York City, 1980.

L'Esibizionista, Teatro Nazionale, Rome, 1995.

WRITINGS

Screenplays:

I Basilischi (also known as *The Basilisks* and *The Lizards;* also based on story by Wertmueller), Connoisseur, 1963.

Questa volta parliamo di uomini (also known as *Let's Talk About Men, Now Let's Talk About Men*, and *This Time Let's Talk About Men*; also based on story by Wertmueller), Archimede, 1965.

Rita la zanzara (also known as *Rita the Mosquito*), Mondial, 1966.

Non stuzzicate la zanzara (also known as *Don't Sting the Mosquito* and *Don't Tease the Mosquito*), Mondial, 1967.

(With others) *Les Chemins de Kathmandu*, 1969.

(With Ottavio Jemma, Marcello Costa, and Pasquale Festa Campanile) *Quando le donne avevano la coda* (also known as *When Women Had Tails*), Film Ventures, 1970.

(With Sauro Scavolini, Gianfranco Calligarich, and Sergio Sollima) *Citta violenta* (also known as *The Family, Violent City*, and *La cite de la violence*), Universal, 1970.

Mimi metallurgico ferito nell'onore (also known as *The Seduction of Mimi, Mimi the Metalworker*, and *Wounded in Honor;* also based on story by Wertmueller), New Line Cinema, 1972.

Cari genitori (also known as *Dear Parents*), 1973.

(With Suso Cecchi d'Amico, Kenneth Ross, and Franco Zeffirelli) *Brother Sun, Sister Moon* (also known as *Fratello sole, sorella luna*), Paramount, 1973.

Film d'amore e d'anarchia (also known as *Film of Love and Anarchy, Film of Love and Anarchy, This Morning at 10 in the Via dei Fiori at the Well–known House of Tolerance, Love and Anarchy, Film d'amore e d'anarchia, ovvero stamattina alle 10 in via dei Fiori nella nota casa di tolleranza,* and *D'Amore e d'anarchia*), Peppercorn–Wormser, 1973.

Tutto a posto e niente in ordine (also known as *All in Place and Nothing in Order, All Screwed Up, Everything Ready, Nothing Works,* and *Everything's in Order but Nothing Works*), New Line Cinema, 1974.

Travolti da un insolito destino nell'azzurro mare d'agosto (also known as *Swept Away* and *Swept Away ... by an Unusual Destiny in the Blue Sea of August;* also based on story by Wertmueller), Almi Cinema V, 1975.

Pasqualino settebellezze (also known as *Pasqualino: Seven Beauties* and *Seven Beauties*), Almi Cinema V, 1976.

The End of the World in Our Usual Bed in a Night Full of Rain (also known as *A Night Full of Rain* and *La Fine del mondo nel nostro solito letto in una notte piena di pioggia*), Warner Bros., 1978.

Fatto di sangue fra due uomini per causa di una vedova—si sospettano (also known as *Blood Feud* and *Revenge*), Associated Film Distribution, 1979.

Scherzo del destino in agguato dietro l'angolo come un brigante di strada (also known as *A Joke of Destiny* and *A Joke of Destiny, Lying in Wait Around the Corner like a Bandit;* also based on story by Wertmueller), Samuel Goldwyn Company, 1983.

Sotto ... sotto ... strapazzato da anomala passione (also known as *Softly, Softly* and *Sotto ... sotto;* also based on story by Wertmueller), Columbia/Triumph, 1984.

Un complicato intrigo di donne, vicoli e delitti (also known as *Camorra, Camorra (A Story of Streets, Women, and Crime), Camorra: The Naples Connection,* and *A Complex Plot About Women, Alleys and Crimes;* also based on story by Wertmueller), Cannon, 1986.

(And composer of musical score, with Lello Greco) *Notte d'estate, con profilo greco, occhi a mandorla e odore di basilico* (also known as *Summer Night, with Greek Profile, Almond Eyes and Scent of Basil*), New Line Cinema, 1986.

In una notte di chiaro di luna (also known as *As Long as It's Love, Clair, Crystal or Ash, Fire or Wind, as Long as It's Love,* and *On a Moonlit Night*), 1989.

Io speriamo che me la cavo (also known as *Ciao, Professore!* and *Me Let's Hope I Make It*), Miramax, 1993.

Ninfa plebea (also known as *The Nymph*), 1996.

Metalmeccanico e parrucchiera in un turbine di sesso e di politica (also known as *The Blue Collar Worker and the Hairdresser in a Whirl of Sex and Politics* and *The Worker and the Hairdresser*), Medusa, 1996.

Ferdinando e Carolina, Medusa, 1999.

Peperoni ripieni e pesci in faccia (also known as *Too Much Romance ... It's Time for Stuffed Peppers*), Sharada Distribuzione, 2004.

Television Movies:

(As Nathan Wich) *Il Mio corpo per un poker* (also known as *The Belle Starr Story*), 1967.

Il Decimo clandestino (also known as *The Tenth One in Hiding* and *To Save Nine*), 1989.

Sabato, domenica e lunedi (also known as *Saturday, Sunday and Monday*), 1990.

Francesca e Nunziata (also known as *Francesca and Nunziata*), 2001.

Stage Plays:

Two and Two Are No Longer Four, 1968.

Shimmy lagano tarantelle e vino, 1978.

Love and Magic in Mama's Kitchen, Spoleto, Italy, then LaMama Experimental Theatre Club, New York City, 1980.

L'Esibizionista, Teatro Nazionale, Rome, 1995.

Other:

The Screenplays of Lina Wertmueller (contains *The Seduction of Mimi, Love and Anarchy, Swept Away by an Unusual Destiny in the Blue Sea of August,* and *Seven Beauties*), translated from Italian by Steven Wagner, New York Times Book Co., 1977.

The Head of Alvise (originally published in Italian as *La testa di Alvise*), translated by Nora Hoppe, William Morrow, 1982.

ADAPTATIONS

The 1972 film *Quando le donne persero la coda* (also known as *When Women Lost Their Tails* and *Toll trieben es die alten Germanen*) was based on an idea by Wertmueller. The film *Which Way Is Up?*, released by Universal in 1977, was adapted by Carl Gottlieb and Cecil Brown from Wertmueller's screenplay *Mimi metallurgico ferito nell'onore.* The film *Swept Away,* released by Columbia TriStar in 2002, was based on her 1975 screenplay *Travolti da un insolito destino nell/azzurro mare d'agosto.* The 1971 television miniseries *Nessuno deve sapere* was based on an idea by Wertmueller.

OTHER SOURCES

Books:

International Dictionary of Films and Filmmakers, 2nd edition, St. James Press, 1991.

Periodicals:

Savvy, January, 1985, p. 86.

WEST, Joel 1975–

PERSONAL

Born April 6, 1975, in Indianola, IA; son of Rob West and Jan Gipple (a veterinary technician); married Anna Bocci (an actress), August 2002; children: one. *Education:* Attended Buena Vista College. *Avocational Interests:* Photography, carpentry, landscaping, and writing.

Addresses: *Manager*—Seven Summits Pictures and Management, 8906 West Olympic Blvd., Ground Floor, Beverly Hills, CA 90211.

Career: Actor. Previously worked as a model for Calvin Klein, Versace, Armani, and Hugo Boss, among others; appeared in a television commercial for Bacardi; was an actor and producer for a small theater company in Los Angeles, CA. Also worked for a construction company and as a set designer and constructor.

CREDITS

Film Appearances:
Christopher, *The Smokers,* Metro–Goldwyn–Mayer Home Entertainment, 2000.
Kyle, *The Giving Tree* (also known as *Brutal Truth, Shaded Places,* and *The Brutal Truth*), Eternity Pictures, 2000.
Jeremy, *Krocodylus* (also known as *Blood Surf* and *Crocodile*), Trimark Pictures, 2000.
Joel, *The Elite,* PM Entertainment Group, 2001.
Blood Surf, 2001.
Zero, *Scorcher,* Buena Vista Home Video, 2002.
Niles Spencer, *Global Effect,* 2002.
Zednik, *Con Express,* 2002.
Slickster filmmaker, *All Features Great and Small* (short), 2005.
Starting Out in the Evening, 2007.

Also appeared in *The Journeyman* (short).

Film Work:
Worked as producer, *The Journeyman* (short).

Television Appearances; Series:
Shupe, *Oz,* HBO, 2000–2003.
Officer Aaron Jessop, *CSI: Miami,* CBS, 2003–2006.

Television Appearances; Specials:
Extreme Makeover: Wedding Edition, ABC, 2005.

Television Appearances; Episodic:
Model Homes, HGTV, 1998.
Rocco, "Kiss and Tell," *Felicity,* The WB, 2002.
(Uncredited) Malek, "Long Live the Queen," *Charmed,* The WB, 2002.
Selwin Burnet, *10–8,* ABC, 2003.
Staff Sergeant Finch, "The 7–10 Split," *American Dreams* (also known as *Our Generation*), NBC, 2004.
Chris, "Be Careful What You Wish For," *The Division* (also known as *Heart of the City*), Lifetime, 2004.
Raakin, "Borderland," *Enterprise* (also known as *Star Trek: Enterprise*), UPN, 2004.

Stage Appearances:
Fabian, *An Appalachian Twelfth Night,* The Globe Playhouse, West Hollywood, CA, 2002.

WRITINGS

Screenplays:
Wrote *The Journeyman* (short).

OTHER SOURCES

Electronic:
Joel West Website, http://www.joelwestcollection.com, July 7, 2007.

WHITE, Vanna 1957–

PERSONAL

Original name, Vanna Marie Rosich; born February 18, 1957, in North Myrtle Beach, SC; daughter of Miguel Angel and Joan Marie Rosich; stepdaughter of Herbert Stackley White, Jr. (a cafe owner); married George Santopietro (an actor and restaurateur), December 31, 1990 (divorced, May 15, 2002); children: Nicholas, Giovanna, one stepson. *Education:* Attended Atlanta School of Fashion Design.

Career: Actress and game show personality. Began career as a model, c. 1978; appeared in television commercials, Stove Top Stuffing, 1986, Choice Hotels, 1991, and Cybersonic2 power flosser, 2003; spokesperson for SpringAir mattresses, 1986—.

Awards, Honors: Star on Hollywood Walk of Fame, 2006.

CREDITS

Television Appearances; Series:
Letter turner, *Wheel of Fortune,* NBC, CBS, and syndicated, 1982—.
Voice of Lauri Sanders, *Captain Planet and the Planeteers* (animated; also known as *The New Adventures of Captain Planet*), 1990.

Television Appearances; Movies:
High school cheerleader, *Midnight Offerings,* 1981.
Venus, *Goddess of Love,* NBC, 1988.
Herself, *Meet the Munceys,* 1988.

Television Appearances; Specials:
The Jay Leno Show, NBC, 1986.
Herself, *The Flintstones' 25th Anniversary Celebration,* 1986.
Presenter, *The 13th Annual Daytime Emmy Awards,* NBC, 1986.
Game Show Biz, 1987.
Bob Hope With His Beautiful Easter Bunnies and Other Friends, 1987.
Special guest, *Totally Minnie* (also known as *Disney's "Totally Minnie"*), 1987.
Host, *The 1989 Clio Awards: The Best TV Commercials in the World,* syndicated, 1989.
MDA Jerry Lewis Telethon, 1990.
Happy Birthday, Bugs: 50 Looney Years, 1990.
Presenter, *The 18th Annual Daytime Emmy Awards,* CBS, 1991.
American Bandstand 40th Anniversary Special, ABC, 1992.
Herself, "Words Up!," *CBS Schoolbreak Special,* 1992.
Jim Thorpe Pro Sports Awards Presented by Footlocker, ABC, 1993.
The 22nd Annual Daytime Emmy Awards, NBC, 1995.
Merv Griffin's Fourth Annual New Year's Eve Live TV Special, syndicated, 1995.
A Salute to the American Red Cross, TNN, 1995.
Merv Griffin: Master of the Game, Arts and Entertainment, 1998.
Vanna White: Game Show Goddess, Arts and Entertainment, 1998.
The Great American History Quiz: Pursuit of Happiness, History Channel, 2000.
Presenter, *The 30th Annual Daytime Emmy Awards,* ABC, 2003.
The 32nd Annual Daytime Emmy Awards, CBS, 2005.

Television Appearances; Pilots:
Herself, *Contact: Talking to the Dead,* ABC, 2002.

Television Appearances; Episodic:
The New Price is Right, CBS, 1980.
Herself, "The Big Apple: Part 1," *Gimme a Break!,* 1984.
"Ted Knight," *This Is Your Life,* 1984.

Herself, "Wheel of Fortune," *The A–Team,* NBC, 1986.
Herself, "The Day Garry Moved In," *It's Garry Shandling's Show,* Fox and Showtime, 1986.
Herself, "The Wheel of Misfortune," *227,* 1986.
Herself, "Walking Point," *Simon & Simon,* CBS, 1987.
Herself, *Santa Barbara,* NBC, 1988.
Roxanne, "Cyrano de Mario," *The Super Mario Bros. Super Show!,* syndicated, 1989.
Herself, "Vowel Play," *L.A. Law,* NBC, 1990.
The Howard Stern Show, 1990.
Herself, "God Rest Ye Murray Gentleman," *L.A. Law,* NBC, 1990.
Coco/Helen Granowinner, "The Proposition," *Married ... with Children,* Fox, 1993.
Mrs. Moffatt, "The Test," *Full House,* ABC, 1994.
"Donna Mills," *Intimate Portrait,* Lifetime, 1998.
Herself, "Chelsea Gets an Opinion," *Style and Substance,* CBS, 1998.
"Vanna White," *Intimate Portrait,* Lifetime, 1999.
The Rosie O'Donnell Show, syndicated, 1999.
Howard Stern, 1999.
Herself, "A&E Biography: Nina van Horn," *Just Shoot Me,* NBC, 2000.
Herself, "Inner Tube," *The King of Queens,* CBS, 2001.
The Wayne Brady Show, syndicated, 2003.
Herself, "Charity Season," *Open Access,* The Tennis Channel, 2006.

Film Appearances:
Mickey, *Gypsy Angels,* 1980 (some sources cite 1994).
Reston girl, *Looker,* Warner Bros., 1981.
Doris, *Graduation Day,* RCA/Columbia, 1981.
Herself, *Double Dragon* (also known as *Double Dragon: The Movie*), Gramercy Pictures, 1993.
Herself, *Naked Gun 33 1/3: The Final Insult,* Paramount, 1994.
Herself, *Dirt Nap* (also known as *Two Tickets to Paradise*), 2006.

RECORDINGS

Videos:
Wrestlemania III, 1987.
Wrestlemania IV, 1988.

Also appeared in the Muppets music video *She Drives Me Crazy.*

Video Games:
Herself/hostess, *Wheel of Fortune,* 1998.

WRITINGS

Books:
(With Patricia Romanowski) *Vanna Speaks,* Warner Books (New York City), 1987.

Vanna's Afghans A to Z: 52 Crochet Favorites, Oxmoor House (Birmingham, AL), 1994.

Vanna's Afghans All Through the House, Oxmoor House (Birmingham, AL), 1997.

Vanna's Favorite Gift Afghans, Oxmoor House (Birmingham, AL), 1998.

Vanna's Favorite Crochet Gifts, Oxmoor House (Birmingham, AL), 2001.

OTHER SOURCES

Books:

Notable Hispanic American Women, Book 2, Gale, 1998.

WICH, Nathan
    See WERTMULLER, Lina

WILDING, Mark

PERSONAL

Addresses: *Agent*—Endeavor, 9601 Wilshire Blvd., 3rd Floor, Beverly Hills, CA 90210.

Career: Producer, writer, story editor, and actor.

Awards, Honors: Emmy Award nomination (with others) outstanding drama series, 2006, Writers Guild of America Television Award (with others), new series, 2006, Writers Guild of America Television Award nomination (with others), dramatic series, 2007, both for *Grey's Anatomy.*

CREDITS

Television Work; Series:

Coproducer, *Ellen* (also known as *These Friends of Mine*), ABC, 1994.

Executive story editor, *Caroline in the City* (also known as *Caroline*), 1995.

Producer, *The Tony Danza Show,* NBC, 1997.

Producer, *Working,* NBC, 1997–99.

Coproducer, *Charmed,* The WB, 2002–2003.

Supervising producer, *Charmed,* The WB, 2002–2005.

Coproducer, *Jake 2.0,* 2004.

Co-executive producer, *Grey's Anatomy,* ABC, 2005–2007.

Television Appearances; Episodic:

Boy, "Taste of Evil," *Out of the Unknown,* 1971.

Film Appearances:

Wuthering Heights, American International Pictures, 1970.

WRITINGS

Television Episodic:

"The Class Reunion," *Ellen* (also known as *These Friends of Mine*), 1994.

"The Go–Between," *Ellen* (also known as *These Friends of Mine*), 1994.

"Witches in Tights," *Charmed,* The WB, 2002.

"Dead Man Walking," *Jake 2.0,* 2004.

"Cheaper by the Coven," *Charmed,* The WB, 2004.

"Ordinary Witches," *Charmed,* The WB, 2005.

"Freaky Phoebe," *Charmed,* The WB, 2005.

"Owner of a Lonely Heart," *Grey's Anatomy,* ABC, 2005.

"17 Seconds," *Grey's Anatomy,* ABC, 2006.

"Where the Boys Are," *Grey's Anatomy,* ABC, 2006.

"Desire," *Grey's Anatomy,* ABC, 2007.

Also wrote episodes of *The Naked Truth* (also known as *Wilde Again*); *Jesse,* NBC; *Becker,* CBS; *Dave's World,* CBS; *Caroline in the City* (also known as *Caroline*), NBC; *Working,* NBC.

WILLIAMS, Scott
    See WINTERS, Scott William

WINCER, Simon 1943–

PERSONAL

Born 1943, in Sydney, New South Wales, Australia.

Addresses: *Agent*—Creative Artists Agency, 2000 Avenue of the Stars, Los Angeles, CA 90067.

Career: Director and producer.

Awards, Honors: Prize of the International Critics' Jury, Catalonian International Film Festival, and Australian Film Institute Award nomination, best director, both 1980, for *Harlequin;* Australian Film Institute Award nomination, best director, 1983, for *Phar Lap;* Emmy Award, outstanding director of a miniseries or special, 1989, and Directors Guild of America Award nomination, outstanding director of a dramatic special, 1990, both for *Lonesome Dove;* Bronze Wrangler Awards (with others), outstanding television feature film, Western Heritage Awards, 2002, for *Crossfire Trail,* and 2004, for *Monte Walsh.*

CREDITS

Film Director:

Harlequin (also known as *Dark Forces* and *The Minister's Magician*), New Image, 1980.

Snapshot (also known as *Day after Halloween, Day before Halloween, The Night after Halloween,* and *One More Minute*), Group 1, 1981.

Phar Lap (also known as *Phar Lap—Heart of a Nation*), Twentieth Century–Fox, 1984.

D.A.R.Y.L., Paramount, 1985.

(And producer, with Ian Jones) *The Lighthorsemen,* Cinecom, 1987.

Quigley Down Under (also known as *Quigley*), Metro–Goldwyn–Mayer, 1990.

Harley Davidson and the Marlboro Man, Metro–Goldwyn–Mayer, 1991.

The Adventures of Young Indiana Jones: Daredevils of the Desert, 1992.

Free Willy (also known as *Sauvez Willy*), Warner Bros., 1993.

(And producer) *Lightning Jack,* Savoy Pictures, 1994.

Operation Dumbo Drop (also known as *Dumbo Drop*), Buena Vista, 1995.

The Phantom, Paramount, 1996.

The Adventures of Young Indiana Jones: The Trenches of Hell, 1999.

The Adventures of Young Indiana Jones: Adventures in the Secret Service, 1999.

The Adventures of Young Indiana Jones: Oganga, the Giver and Taker of Life, 1999.

Crocodile Dundee in Los Angeles, Paramount, 2001.

The Young Black Stallion, Buena Vista, 2003.

NASCAR 3D: The IMAX Experience (also known as *NASCAR: The IMAX Experience*), Warner Bros., 2004.

Film Executive Producer:

The Man from Snowy River, Twentieth Century–Fox, 1982.

One Night Stand, 1983.

Television Director; Series:

(And producer) *Homicide,* Seven Network, 1964.

The Haunting of Hewie Dowker, 1976.

Prisoner: Cell Block H (also known as *Caged Women* and *Prisoner*), Ten Network, multiple episodes, 1980.

The Young Indiana Jones Chronicles, multiple episodes, 1992–93.

(And coproducer) *Ponderosa,* PAX, 2001.

Television Director; Movies:

The Girl Who Spelled Freedom (also known as *The Story of Linn Yann*), ABC, 1986.

The Last Frontier, CBS, 1986.

Bluegrass, CBS, 1988.

Flash, CBS, 1997.

The Echo of Thunder, CBS, 1998.

Escape: Human Cargo (also known as *Escape*), Showtime, 1998.

Murder She Purred: A Mrs. Murphy Mystery (also known as *Murder She Purred*), ABC, 1998.

(And co–executive producer) *Crossfire Trail* (also known as *Louis L'Amour's "Crossfire Trail"*), TNT, 2001.

Monte Walsh, TNT, 2003.

Television Director; Miniseries:

Against the Wind, syndicated, 1978.

Lonesome Dove, CBS, 1989.

P. T. Barnum, Arts and Entertainment, 1999.

Into the West, TNT, 2005.

Comanche Moon, CBS, 2007.

Television Director; Episodic:

Matlock Police, Ten Network, 1971.

The Box, Ten Network, 1974.

Cash and Company, Seven Network, 1975.

The Sullivans, Nine Network, 1976.

Young Ramsay, Seven Network, 1977.

Chopper Squad, Ten Network, 1978.

Also directed episodes of *Ryan* and *Tandarra,* Seven Network.

Television Appearances; Specials:

Lonesome Dove: The Making of an Epic, 1991.

The 100 Greatest Family Films, Channel 4, 2005.

RECORDINGS

Videos:

The Making of "The Echo of Thunder," 1998.

The Style & Sound of Speed, Warner Home Video, 2006.

Pushing the Limit: The Making of "Grand Prix," Warner Home Video, 2006.

WRITINGS

Television Episodes:
Chopper Squad, Ten Network, 1978.

OTHER SOURCES

Periodicals:
DGA, January, 2003, pp. 92–95.

WINTERS, Scott William 1965–
   (Scott Williams, Scott Winters)

PERSONAL

Born August 5, 1965, in New York, NY; father, an investment banker; brother of Dean Winters (an actor) and Bradford Winters (a writer); married Jennifer Logan, March 29, 2003; children: one.

Addresses: *Agent*—Domain, 9229 Sunset Blvd., Suite 415, Los Angeles, CA 90069. *Manager*—Anthem Entertainment, 6100 Wilshire Blvd., Suite 1170, Los Angeles, CA 90069.

Career: Actor. Also worked as a bartender.

CREDITS

Film Appearances:
Blow dried jerk, *The People vs. Larry Flynt* (also known as *Larry Flynt*), Columbia, 1996.
Clark, *Good Will Hunting,* Miramax, 1997.
(Uncredited) Clark/himself, *Jay and Silent Bob Strike Back,* Dimension Films, 2001.
Detective, *Mystic River,* Warner Bros., 2003.

Television Appearances; Series:
Cyril O'Reily, *Oz,* HBO, 1998–2003.
Senior Deputy Matt Jablonski, *10–8: Officers on Duty* (also known as *10–8* and *10–8: Police Patrol*), ABC, 2003–2004.
Detective Stan Hatcher, *NYPD Blue,* ABC, 2004.

Television Appearances; Pilots:
Jeff Kendall, *The Prosecutors* (movie), NBC, 1996.
Gary Domino, *13 Graves,* Fox, 2006.

Television Appearances; Specials:
The 6th Annual Sears Soul Train Christmas Starfest, UPN, 2003.

Television Appearances; Episodic:
(As Scott Winters) Eddie Dugan, "Partners and Other Strangers," *Homicide: Life on the Street* (also known as *Homicide*), NBC, 1997.
(As Scott Winters) Eddie Dugan, "Strangers and Other Partners," *Homicide: Life on the Street* (also known as *Homicide*), NBC, 1997.
Ellis, "Baptism of Fire," *Promised Land* (also known as *Home of the Brave*), CBS, 1998.
Ray, "Countdown," *The Pretender,* NBC, 1999.
Jack McNamara, "The Ring," *Angel* (also known as *"Angel": The Series*), The WB, 2000.
Damon Lawrence, "They Say It's Your Birthday," *The Beat,* UPN, 2000.
Ghost Goucher, "Asslane," *Fastlane,* Fox, 2003.
Ranger Randy Turman, "The Mountain," *The Dead Zone* (also known as *Stephen King's "The Dead Zone"*), USA Network, 2003.
John McCarthy, "Last Rites," *The Jury,* Fox, 2004.
Fred Kinnan, "Speed Kills," *CSI: Miami,* CBS, 2004.
Marvin, "Shark," *North Shore,* Fox, 2005.
Roger, "Under the Weather," *Crossing Jordan,* NBC, 2005.
Glen Nash, "Soft Target," *Numb3rs* (also known as *Num3ers*), CBS, 2005.
Frank Zane, "Juads," *Wanted,* TNT, 2005.
Wildfire, ABC Family, 2005.
Don Fitzgibbons, "Up in Smoke," *CSI: Crime Scene Investigation* (also known as *C.S.I., CSI: Las Vegas,* and *CSI: Weekends,* and *Les Experts*), CBS, 2006.
Detective McNamara, "Popping Cherry," *Dexter,* Showtime, 2006.
Detective McNamara, "Let's Give the Boy a Hand," *Dexter,* Showtime, 2006.
Detective Bates, "Burglary," *Eyes,* ABC, 2007.
Agent Samuels, "Day 6: 7:00 a.m.–8 a.m.," *24,* Fox, 2007.
Agent Samuels, "Day 6: 8:00 a.m.–9 a.m.," *24,* Fox, 2007.
Agent Samuels, "Day 6: 10:00 a.m.–11 a.m.," *24,* Fox, 2007.
Agent Samuels, "Day 6: 11:00 a.m.–12 p.m.," *24,* Fox, 2007.
Pogue, "Betrayal," *Lincoln Heights,* ABC Family, 2007.
Lieutenant Pogue, "Missing," *Lincoln Heights,* ABC Family, 2007.

WISHNOFF, Steven 1959–
   (Steve Wishnoff, Steven E. Wishnoff)

PERSONAL

Born August 10, 1959. *Avocational Interests:* Collector of 1960s and 1970s television trivia.

Career: Actor, talent coordinator, researcher, director, and producer. Volunteered at New York City schools' music and drama programs.

CREDITS

Television Work; Series:
Talent coordinator, *But Can They Sing?,* VH1, 2005.
Talent coordinator, *Celebrity Duets,* Fox, 2006.

Television Work; Specials:
Online producer, *TV Land Awards: A Celebration of Classic TV* (also known as *1st Annual TV Land Awards*), TV Land, 2003.
Online producer, *The Nick at Nite Holiday Special,* Nickelodeon, 2003.
Director and executive producer, *"Arrested Development": Making of a Future Classic,* TV Land, 2004.
Online producer, *The Second Annual TV Land Awards: A Celebration of Classic TV,* TV Land, 2004.
Talent supervisor, *The 2005 World Music Awards,* ABC, 2005.
Researcher, *"Knots Landing" Reunion: Together Again,* CBS, 2005.

Television Appearances; Series:
Tony Masters, *Oz,* HBO, 1999–2003.

Television Appearances; Episodic:
Also appeared as pregnant schoolgirl, "Yo' Fool Dump My Baby's Father," Richard Simmons, "Big Body Bigots," and as Ethel Mertz, "I Love Lucy But I Hate You," all *The Richard Bey Show* (also known as *9 Broadcast Plaza* and *People Are Talking*).

Film Appearances:
(Uncredited) Lucy Tania, *Stonewall,* Strand Releasing, 1995.
The fortune teller, *My Divorce,* 1997.
(As Steven E. Wishnoff) Prison drag queen, *Marci X,* Paramount, 2003.

Stage Appearances:
Appeared as Albin/Zaza, *La Cage Aux Folles;* Amos Hart, *Chicago;* Vivian McVanish, *Howard Crabtree's Whoop–Dee–Doo,* New York City.

WRITINGS

Television Specials:
"Arrested Development": Making of a Future Classic, TV Land, 2004.

WITTLIFF, William D. 1940–
(Bill Witliff, Bill Wittliff)

PERSONAL

Full name, William Dale Wittliff; born 1940, in Taft, TX; married Sally; children: Reid, Allison. *Education:* Graduated from the University of Texas, 1963.

Addresses: *Office*—Encino Press, 510 Baylor St., Austin, TX 78703. *Agent*—William Morris Agency, One William Morris Pl., Beverly Hills, CA 90212.

Career: Screenwriter, producer, and author. Encino Press, Austin, TX, founder, 1964.

Member: Academy of Motion Picture Arts and Sciences, Texas Philosophical Society, Texas Institute of Letters (president, 1974–78, member of executive council, 1979–90, fellow, 1993). Sundance Institute (former member of the board of trustees).

Awards, Honors: Christopher Award, 1985, for *Country;* seven Emmy Awards, National Critics Award, best miniseries and best television program, D. W. Griffith Award, best television miniseries, National Board of Review, International Monitor Award, best achievement in entertainment programming, Golden Globe Award, George Foster Peabody Broadcasting Award, best television miniseries, University of Georgia, 1989, Bronze Wrangler Award (with others), television feature film, Western Heritage Awards, Television Award, adapted long form, Writers Guild of America, 1990, all for *Lonesome Dove;* Western Heritage Award, outstanding fictional television drama, National Cowboy Hall of Fame, 1993, for *Ned Blessing: The Story of My Life and Times;* three Golden Globe Award nominations, including best motion picture, three Academy Award nominations, 1994, Bronze Wrangler Award (with others), theatrical motion picture, Western Heritage Awards, 1995, all for *Legends of the Fall.*

CREDITS

Film Work:
Producer and second unit director, *Raggedy Man,* Universal, 1981.
Coproducer, *Barbarosa,* Universal, 1982.
Producer, *Country,* Buena Vista, 1984.
(As Bill Wittliff) Producer and director, *Red Headed Stranger,* Alive Films, 1986.

(As Bill Wittliff) Executive producer, *The Cowboy Way,* Universal, 1994.

Producer, *Legends of the Fall,* 1994.

(As Bill Wittliff) Executive producer, *Lone Justice 2,* Triboro Entertainment Group, 1995.

Film Appearances:

Man in bar, *Resurrection,* 1980.

Television Work; Series:

Executive producer, *Ned Blessing: The Story of My Life and Times,* CBS, 1993.

Television Work; Miniseries:

Executive producer, *Lonesome Dove,* CBS, 1989.

Television Work; Pilots:

Executive producer, *Ned Blessing: The True Story of My Life* (movie; also known as *Lone Justice* and *Ned Blessing*), 1992.

Television Work; Episodic:

Producer, "Return to Plum Creek," *Ned Blessing: The Story of My Life and Times,* CBS, 1993.

Television Appearances; Episodic:

(As Bill Wittliff) Voice of Sheriff Nemeyer, "A Ghost Story," *Ned Blessing: The Story of My Life and Times,* CBS, 1993.

WRITINGS

Screenplays:

The Black Stallion, United Artists, 1979.

Honeysuckle Rose (also known as *On the Road Again*), Warner Bros., 1980.

Raggedy Man, Universal, 1981.

Barbarosa, Universal, 1982.

Country, Buena Vista, 1984.

(As Bill Wittliff) *Red Headed Stranger,* Alive Films, 1986.

(As Bill Wittliff) *The Cowboy Way,* Universal, 1994.

(As Bill Wittliff) *Legends of the Fall,* 1994.

Lone Justice 2, Triboro Entertainment Group, 1995.

(As Bill Wittliff) *The Perfect Scream* (also known as *Der Sturm*), Warner Bros., 2000.

Zapata: El Sueno del Heroe, 2004.

Television Miniseries:

(As Bill Wittliff) *Lonesome Dove,* CBS, 1989.

Television Movies:

Thaddeus Rose and Eddie, CBS, 1978.

Ned Blessing: The True Story of My Life (also known as *Lone Justice* and *Ned Blessing*), 1992.

Television Episodes:

"The Smink Brothers," *Ned Blessing: The Story of My Life and Times,* CBS, 1993.

Nonfiction:

(Editor; with Sheila Ohlendorf) *The Horseman of the Americas: An Exhibition from the Hall of the Horseman of the Americas,* University of Texas Humanities Research Center, 1968.

Novels:

(With Sara Clark) *Raggedy Man,* Pinnacle, 1979.

WOLSKY, Albert 1930–

PERSONAL

Born November 24, 1930, in Paris, France. *Education:* City College of the City University of New York, graduated.

Addresses: *Contact*—c/o Friedman and LaRosa, Inc., 747 Third Ave., New York, NY 10017–2803.

Career: Costume designer. California Institute of the Arts, Valencia, CA, guest artist and lecturer. Worked as a travel agent prior to 1960.

Member: International Alliance of Theatrical and Stage Employees, Academy of Motion Picture Arts and Sciences (member of board of governors).

Awards, Honors: Emmy Award nomination, best costume design for a drama special, 1977, for "Beauty and the Beast," *Hallmark Hall of Fame;* Academy Award, best costume design, 1980, and Film Award nomination, best costume design for a film, British Academy of Film and Television Arts, 1981, both for *All That Jazz;* Academy Award nomination, best costume design, 1983, for *Sophie's Choice;* Academy Award nomination, best costume design, 1986, for *The Journey of Natty Gann;* Academy Award, best costume design, 1992, for *Bugsy;* Academy Award nomination, best costume design, Saturn Award nomination, best costumes, Academy of Science Fiction, Fantasy and Horror Films, 1993, both for *Toys;* Lifetime Achievement Award, Costume Designers Guild, 1999; Saturn Award nomination, best costume design, Academy of Science Fiction, Horror, and Fantasy Films, 2000, for

Galaxy Quest; Golden Satellite Award nomination, best costume design, International Press Academy, Costume Design Guild Award nomination, excellence in costume design for film—period/fantasy, 2003, both for *Road to Perdition;* Hollywood Film Award, costume designer of the year, 2004.

CREDITS

Film Costume Designer:
The Heart Is a Lonely Hunter, Warner Bros./Seven Arts, 1968.
Popi, United Artists, 1969.
Lovers and Other Strangers, Cinerama, 1970.
Loving, Columbia, 1970.
Where's Poppa? (also known as *Going Ape*), United Artists, 1970.
Little Murders, Twentieth Century–Fox, 1971.
Born to Win (also known as *Addict* and *Born to Lose*), United Artists, 1971.
Lady Liberty (also known as *La mortadella* and *The Sausage*), United Artists, 1972.
The Last of the Red Hot Lovers, Paramount, 1972.
The Trial of the Catonsville Nine, Melville, 1972.
Up the Sandbox, National General, 1972.
Lenny, United Artists, 1974.
Harry and Tonto, Twentieth Century–Fox, 1974.
The Gambler, Paramount, 1974.
Next Stop, Greenwich Village, Twentieth Century–Fox, 1976.
Thieves, Paramount, 1977.
The Turning Point, Twentieth Century–Fox, 1977.
Fingers, Brut Productions, 1977.
An Unmarried Woman, Twentieth Century–Fox, 1978.
Grease, Paramount, 1978.
Moment by Moment, Universal, 1978.
Meteor, American International Pictures, 1979.
Manhattan, United Artists, 1979.
All That Jazz, Twentieth Century–Fox, 1979.
Willie and Phil, Twentieth Century–Fox, 1980.
The Jazz Singer, AFD, 1980.
(Costumes for Ms. Van Devere) *The Changeling* (also known as *L'enfant du diable*), 1980.
(Barbra Streisand's costumes) *All Night Long,* Universal, 1981.
Paternity, Paramount, 1981.
Tempest, Columbia, 1982.
Still of the Night, Metro–Goldwyn–Mayer/United Artists, 1982.
Sophie's Choice, Universal/AFD, 1982.
To Be or Not to Be, Twentieth Century–Fox, 1983.
Star 80, Warner Bros., 1983.
Moscow on the Hudson, Columbia, 1984.
The Falcon and the Snowman, Orion, 1985.
The Journey of Natty Gann, Buena Vista, 1985.
Crimes of the Heart, DD Entertainment, 1986.
Down and Out in Beverly Hills, Buena Vista, 1986.
Legal Eagles, Universal, 1986.

Nadine, TriStar, 1987.
Moon over Parador, Universal, 1988.
Chances Are, TriStar, 1989.
Cookie, Warner Bros., 1989.
Enemies, a Love Story, Twentieth Century–Fox, 1989.
She–Devil, Orion, 1989.
Funny about Love, Paramount, 1990.
Bugsy, TriStar, 1991.
Scenes from a Mall, Buena Vista, 1991.
Toys, Twentieth Century–Fox, 1992.
The Pickle (also known as *The Adventures of the Flying Pickle*), Columbia, 1993.
The Pelican Brief, Warner Bros., 1993.
Fatal Instinct, Metro–Goldwyn–Mayer, 1993.
Junior, Universal, 1994.
The Grass Harp, Fine Line Features, 1995.
Up Close and Personal, Buena Vista, 1996.
Striptease, Columbia, 1996.
Red Corner, Metro–Goldwyn–Mayer, 1997.
The Jackal (also known as *Le chacal* and *Der schakal*), Universal, 1997.
You've Got Mail, Warner Bros., 1998.
Runaway Bride, Paramount, 1999.
Galaxy Quest, DreamWorks Distribution, 1999.
Lucky Numbers (also known as *Le bon numero*), Paramount, 2000.
Road to Perdition, DreamWorks, 2002.
Maid in Manhattan (also known as *Made in New York*), Columbia, 2002.
The Manchurian Candidate, Paramount, 2004.
Jarhead (also known as *Jarhead—willkommen im dreck*), Universal, 2005.
Ask the Dust, Paramount Classics, 2006.
Across the Universe, Columbia, 2007.
Charlie Wilson's War, Universal, 2007.

Television Costume Designer; Movies:
A Hatful of Rain, 1968.

Television Costume Designer; Specials:
"Beauty and the Beast," *Hallmark Hall of Fame,* 1976.

Television Appearances; Specials:
The Hollywood Fashion Machine, 1995.
The Making of "Road to Perdition," 2002.

Television Appearances; Episodic:
"Road to Perdition," *HBO First Look,* HBO, 2002.

Stage Costume Designer:
Generation, Broadway production, 1964.
Your Own Thing, Orpheum Theatre, New York City, 1968–69.
Little Murders, Circle in the Square, New York City, 1969.
The White House Murder Case, Circle in the Square, 1970.

The Trial of the Catonsville Nine, Theatre at Good Shepherd–Faith Church, then Lyceum Theatre, New York City, 1971.

The Sunshine Boys, Broadhurst Theatre, New York City, 1972–73.

The Jockey Club Stakes, Cort Theatre, New York City, 1973.

All Over Town, Booth Theatre, New York City, 1974–75.

Hamlet, New York Shakespeare Festival, Delacorte Theatre, New York City, 1975.

27 Wagons Full of Cotton and *A Memory of Two Mondays* (double–bill), The Playhouse, New York City, 1976.

Sly Fox, Broadhurst Theatre, 1976–77.

Wine Untouched, Harold Clurman Theatre, New York City, 1979.

Tricks of the Trade, Brooks Atkinson Theatre, New York City, 1980.

Wally's Cafe, Brooks Atkinson Theatre, 1981.

One More Song/One More Dance, Joyce Theatre, New York City, 1983.

Ann Reinking ... Music Moves Me, Joyce Theatre, 1984–85.

Oliver Oliver, City Center Theatre, New York City, 1985.

Sly Fox, Ethel Barrymore Theatre, New York City, 2004.

Stage Work; Other:
Assistant to Miss Roth, *A Case of Libel,* Longacre Theatre, New York City, 1963–64.

Supervisor of men's costumes, *The Chinese Prime Minister,* Royale Theatre, New York City, 1964.

Assistant to Miss Zipprodt, *Fiddler on the Roof,* Imperial Theatre, New York City, 1964–67, then Majestic Theatre, 1967–70, Broadway Theatre, 1970–72.

Assistant to Ann Roth, *The Odd Couple,* Plymouth Theatre, New York City, 1965–66, then Eugene O'Neill Theatre, New York City, 1966–67.

Assistant to Mr. Wittop, *I Do! I Do!,* 46th Street Theatre, New York City, 1966–68.

Assistant to Theoni Aldredge, *Illya Darling,* Mark Hellinger Theatre, New York City, 1967–68.

Began career as assistant for Helene Pons during the original Broadway production of *Camelot.*

Major Tours (As Costume Designer):
Generation, U.S. cities, 1966–67.
Your Own Thing, U.S. cities, 1968–70.
The Sunshine Boys, U.S. cities, 1973–75.
All Over Town, U.S. cities, 1975.

WOLVETT, Jaimz
    See WOOLVETT, Jaimz

WOOD, Frank 1959–

PERSONAL

Born 1959, in Lincoln, MA; son of Robert Wood (a government official). *Education:* New York University, M.F.A., acting.

Addresses: *Agent*—The Jim Flynn Agency, 307 West 38th St., Suite 801, New York, NY 10018.

Career: Actor. Began professional career with People's Light and Theatre Company, Philadelphia, PA, 1987; worked with the Fifty Second Project; appeared in productions at Soho Repertory Theatre, Adobe Theatre, and Dallas Theatre Center.

Member: American Federation of Television and Radio Artists, Actors Equity Association, Screen Actors Guild.

Awards, Honors: Drama–Logue Award (with others), best ensemble, 1995, for *Kofman's Entrevista 187;* Antoinette Perry Award, best actor—featured role—play, 1999, for *Side Man.*

CREDITS

Film Appearances:
Doctor, *Down to You,* Miramax, 2000.
Oliver, *Small Time Crooks,* DreamWorks, 2000.
Frank Pollock, *Pollock,* Sony Pictures Classics, 2000.
McGeorge Bundy, *Thirteen Days,* New Line Cinema, 2000.
Hotel manger, *The Royal Tenenbaums,* Buena Vista, 2001.
Pediatrician, *In America,* Twentieth Century–Fox, 2002.
Michael Wormly, *People I Know* (also known as *Im inneren kreis* and *Der innere kreis*), Miramax, 2002.
Alex Montgomery, *The Undeserved,* 2004.
Berenson, *King of the Corner,* Ardustry Home Entertainment, 2004.
Assaulted commuter, *Keane,* Magnolia Pictures, 2004.
Lawrence, *The Favor,* Dark Knight Productions, 2006.
Bruce, *Flakes,* 2007.
Howard, *Dan in Real Life,* Buena Vista, 2007.

Television Appearances; Specials:
Performer, *The 53rd Annual Tony Awards,* CBS, 1999.

Television Appearances; Pilots:
Crazed man, *Medium,* NBC, 2005.

Television Appearances; Episodic:
Dr. Rutland, "Scrambled," *Law & Order,* NBC, 1998.
"Losing Streak," *Ed,* NBC, 2001.
Dean Ross, "Second Opinion," *The Sopranos,* HBO, 2001.
Fire chief, "Honor," *Third Watch,* NBC, 2001.
George Weems, "Chinoiserie," *Law & Order: Criminal Intent* (also known as *Law & Order: CI*), NBC, 2002.
Flight of the Conchords, HBO, 2007.

Also appeared in "This Land Is Your Land," *Line of Fire,* ABC.

Stage Appearances:
(Broadway debut) Gene, *Side Man,* Classic Stage Company Theatre. (CSC), New York City, 1998, then John Golden Theatre, New York City, 1998–99.
Christopher, *The Wax,* Playwrights Horizons Theatre, New York City, 2000–2001.
Jody, *Hollywood Arms,* Goodman Theater, Chicago, IL, 2002, then Cort Theatre, New York City, 2002–2003.
Vershinin, *Three Sisters,* American Repertory Theatre, Loeb Drama Center, Cambridge, MA, 2005–2006.
Adult men, *Spring Awakening,* Atlantic Theatre, New York City, 2006.
The Rainmaker, 2006.
Family and understudy journalist, *Spalding Gray: Stories Left to Tell,* Minetta Lane Theatre, New York City, 2007—.

Also appeared in *Kofman's Entrevista 187,* Padua Hills Playwrights Festival, Los Angeles; *Three Sisters; Tomorrowland; King of Rats; Dark Ride.*

WOOD, Martin

PERSONAL

Addresses: *Agent*—Agency for the Performing Arts, 405 South Beverly Dr., Beverly Hills, CA 90212.

Career: Producer, director, and writer.

Awards, Honors: Audience Award, best feature film, Toronto Sprockets International Film Festival for Children, 2001, for *The Impossible Elephant;* Directors Guild of Canada Team Award nomination, outstanding achievement in a television movie/miniseries/children's, 2002, Gemini Award nomination, best direction in a children's or youth program or series, Academy of

Canadian Cinema and Television, 2004, both for *The Impossible Elephant;* Leo Award nomination (with others), best dramatic series, Motion Picture Arts and Sciences Foundation of British Columbia, 2005, for *Stargate: Atlantis.*

CREDITS

Film Work:
Daily second assistant director, *The Road to Saddle River,* 1994.
Production manager and associate producer, *40,000 Years of Dreaming* (documentary), 1997.
Director, *Teenage Space Vampires* (also known as *Darkness Comes*), Full Moon Entertainment, 1998.
Director, *The Impossible Elephant* (also known as *The Incredible Elephant*), Peace Arch Entertainment Group, 2001.

Television Work; Series:
Creative consultant, *Stargate SG–1* (also known as *La Porte des etoiles*), Showtime then Sci–Fi Channel, 1998–2006.
Director, *Stargate SG–1* (also known as *La Porte des etoiles*), Showtime then Sci–Fi Channel, 1998–2006.
Coproducer, *Stargate SG–1* (also known as *La Porte des etoiles*), Sci–Fi Channel, 2003–2006.
Coproducer, *Stargate: Atlantis* (also known as *La porte d'Atlantis*), Sci–Fi Channel, 2004–2005.
Director, *Stargate: Atlantis* (also known as *La porte d'Atlantis*), Sci–Fi Channel, 2004–2007.
Supervising producer, *Stargate: Atlantis* (also known as *La porte d'Atlantis*), Sci–Fi Channel, 2005–2007.
Executive producer and producer, *Sanctuary,* 2007.

Television Work; Movies:
Second assistant director, *Home Movie,* 1992.
Director, *The Great Run of China,* 1995.
Director and producer, *Listen Up!,* 1997.
Director, *Vicki Gabereau: The Mouth That Roared,* 1999.
Director, *SIDS: Uncovering the Mystery,* 2000.
Director, *Sanctuary,* 2007.
Director, *Stargate: Continuum,* Sci–Fi Channel, 2008.

Television Work; Pilots:
First assistant director, *Them,* UPN, 1996.
Director, *Stargate Atlantis: Rising,* Sci–Fi Channel, 2004.

Television Work; Specials:
Director and associate producer, *SIDS: A Special Report,* 1995.
Director, *Pierre Burton: Canada's Arrogant Icon,* 1999.

Producer, *From Stargate to Atlantis: Sci Fi Lowdown,* 2004.

Television Work; Episodic:
Director, "Grand Plans," *Jake and the Kid,* Global, 1995.
Director, "No Time to Wave: The Life and Times of Ben Wicks," *Life and Times,* CBC, 1997.
First unit director and second unit director, "The Enemy Within," *Stargate SG–1* (also known as *La Porte des etoiles*), Showtime, 1997.
Second unit director, "The Broca Divide," *Stargate SG–1* (also known as *La Porte des etoiles*), Showtime, 1997.
Second unit director, "The First Commandment," *Stargate SG–1* (also known as *La Porte des etoiles*), Showtime, 1997.
Second unit director, "Emancipation," *Stargate SG–1* (also known as *La Porte des etoiles*), Showtime, 1997.
Director, "Air–Tight Alibi," *Silk Stalkings,* USA Network, 1997.
Director, "Ramone P.I.," *Silk Stalkings,* USA Network, 1998.
Director, "Cook's Tour," *Silk Stalkings,* USA Network, 1999.
Director, "The Three Phases of Claire," *The Invisible Man* (also known as *I–Man*), Sci–Fi Channel, 2001.
Director, "Trapped by Time," *Earth: Final Conflict* (also known as *EFC, Gene Roddenberry's "Earth: Final Conflict,"* *Invasion planete Terre,* and *Mission Erde: Sie sind unter uns*), syndicated, 2001.
Director, "Blood Ties," *Earth: Final Conflict* (also known as *EFC, Gene Roddenberry's "Earth: Final Conflict,"* *Invasion planete Terre,* and *Mission Erde: Sie sind unter uns*), syndicated, 2001.
Director, "Honor and Duty," *Earth: Final Conflict* (also known as *EFC, Gene Roddenberry's "Earth: Final Conflict,"* *Invasion planete Terre,* and *Mission Erde: Sie sind unter uns*), syndicated, 2001.
Director, "Subversion," *Earth: Final Conflict* (also known as *EFC, Gene Roddenberry's "Earth: Final Conflict,"* *Invasion planete Terre,* and *Mission Erde: Sie sind unter uns*), syndicated, 2001.
Director, "Over the Net," *Just Deal,* NBC, 2002.
Director, "Journeys End in Lovers Meeting," *Jeremiah,* Showtime, 2002.
Director, "Letters from the Other Side: Parts 1 & 2," *Jeremiah,* Showtime, 2002.
Director, "Rites of Passage," *Jeremiah,* Showtime, 2002.
Director, "Voices in the Dark," *Jeremiah,* Showtime, 2002.
Director, "Running on Empty," *Jeremiah,* Showtime, 2002.
Director, "The Dissonant Interval: Parts 1 & 2," *Andromeda* (also known as *Gene Roddenberry's "Andromeda"*), Sci–Fi Channel, 2004.
Director, "Totaled Recall," *Andromeda* (also known as *Gene Roddenberry's "Andromeda"*), Sci–Fi Channel, 2005.

Director, "One More Day's Light," *Andromeda* (also known as *Gene Roddenberry's "Andromeda"*), Sci–Fi Channel, 2005.
Director, "Chaos and the Stillness of It," *Andromeda* (also known as *Gene Roddenberry's "Andromeda"*), Sci–Fi Channel, 2005.
Director, *Sanctuary,* 2007.

Also worked as a first assistant director and second assistant director on episodes of *The Commish,* ABC.

Television Appearances; Specials:
Preview to Atlantis, 2004.
From Stargate to Atlantis: A Sci Fi Lowdown, Sci–Fi Channel, 2004.
Sci Fi Lowdown: Beyond the Stargate—Secrets Revealed, Sci–Fi Channel, 2005.
Sci Fi: Sci Fi Friday, Sci–Fi Channel, 2005.

Television Appearances; Episodic:
Wormhold X–Treme Director, "200," *Stargate SG–1* (also known as *La porte des etoiles*), Sci–Fi Channel, 2006.

WRITINGS

Screenplays:
Teenage Space Vampires (also known as *Darkness Comes*), Full Moon Entertainment, 1998.
1800 Seconds: Chasing Canada's Snowbirds (documentary), CBC International Sales, 2002.

Television Movies:
The Great Run of China, 1995.
Listen Up!, 1997.
SIDS: Uncovering the Mystery, 2000.

Television Episodic:
"No Time to Wave: The Life and Times of Ben Wicks," *Life and Times,* CBC, 1997.
Sanctuary, 2007.

WOOLVETT, Gordon Michael 1970–
(Gordon Woolvett, Gordon M. Woolvett)

PERSONAL

Born in 1970, in Hamilton, Ontario, Canada; brother of Jaimz Woolvett (an actor); married Michele Morand, January 15, 2000; children: Rogan. *Education:* Attended Theatre Aquarius. *Avocational Interests:* Writing, especially science fiction.

Addresses: *Agent*—Silver, Massetti and Szatmary/West Ltd., 8730 Sunset Blvd., Suite 440, Los Angeles, CA 90069. *Contact*—c/o Tribune Entertainment Co., 5800 Sunset Blvd., Los Angeles, CA 90028.

Career: Actor. Appeared as P.J. (program jockey) for YTV, in the early to mid 1990s; appeared in television commercials.

Awards, Honors: Gemini Award nomination, best performance by an actor in a supporting role, Academy of Canadian Cinema and Television, 1990, for *Princes in Exile;* Gemini Hottest Star Award, 2002.

CREDITS

Film Appearances:
Teddy Shapiro, *Joshua Then and Now,* Twentieth Century–Fox, 1985.
Teddy, *Going to War,* 1985.
The Journey Home, National Film Board of Canada, 1989.
Louis, *Princes in Exile,* 1990, then Fries Entertainment, 1991.
Jimmy, *Bordertown Cafe,* National Film Board of Canada, 1993.
(Uncredited) Male candy striper, *Canadian Bacon,* 1995.
Ricky, *Rude,* A–Pix Entertainment, 1995, then Alliance Entertainment, 1996.
Chip, *The Legend of Gator Face,* 1996.
Larry Eggers, *Shadow Builder* (also known as *Bram Stoker's "Shadowbuilder"*), Sterling Home Entertainment, 1997.
Spit, *Clutch,* Cineplex Odeon, 1998.
David "Dave" Collins, *Bride of Chucky* (also known as *Child's Play 4* and *Chucky*), Universal, 1998.
(As Gordon M. Woolvett) *Ice,* ABC/Trimark Pictures, 1999.
Walter, *The Highwayman,* Lions Gate Films, 1999.
Spike, *Everything's Gone Green,* First Independent Pictures, 2006.

Also appeared as Robby, *Manic;* in *Vietnaming.*

Film Work:
Producer and director, *Fracture* (short), 2006.

Television Appearances; Series:
Greg, *Airwaves,* CBC, 1986.
Brad, *Learning the Ropes,* syndicated, 1988–89.
Host, *Video & Arcade Top Ten,* YTV, 1991.
Host, *Nickelodeon Wildside Show,* Nickelodeon, 1993.
Herbert Pencroft, *Mysterious Island,* Family Channel, 1995.

(As Gordon Michael Woolvett) Reb, *Deepwater Black* (also known as *Mission Genesis*), Sci–Fi Channel, 1997.
Seamus Harper, *Andromeda* (also known as *Gene Roddenberry's "Andromeda"*), syndicated, 2000–2004, then Sci–Fi Channel, 2004–2005.
Voice of Thunderer/Peter Littlecloud, *The Seventh Portal,* 2000.

Television Appearances; Miniseries:
Soletski, *Family Pictures,* ABC, 1993.
Sergeant Sam Barlow, *Shattered City: The Halifax Explosion,* CBC, 2003.

Television Appearances; Movies:
Bobby, *Act of Vengeance,* HBO, 1986.
9B, CBC, 1986.
Rodney, *The World's Oldest Living Bridesmaid,* CBS, 1990.
Manic, 1993.
River's boyfriend, *X–Rated* (also known as *X–Rated: Liberty Street*), CBC, 1993.
Chip, *The Legend of Gator Face,* Showtime, 1996.
Paul, *Gone in a Heartbeat,* CBS, 1996.
Soldier, *Elvis Meets Nixon,* Showtime, 1997.
Little Jay, *Promise the Moon,* CBC, 1997.
Huddy, *Peacekeepers,* CBC, 1997.
Clyde, *My Date with the President's Daughter,* ABC, 1998.
Karen Young's victim, *Mind Games* (also known as *Trauma*), Showtime, 1998.
(As Gordon M. Woolvett) Soldier, *Ice* (also known as *Eis—wenn die welt erfriert*), ABC, 1998.
Frank McThomas, *Ultimate Deception,* USA Network, 1999.
Army ranger sergeant, *Ice,* ABC, 2000.
Clayton, *Secrets of an Undercover Wife,* Lifetime, 2007.

Also appeared as Paul, *Taken Away,* CBC; Chris Stokes, *Side Effects,* CBC; in *A Question of Justice,* CBS.

Television Appearances; Specials:
The 17th Annual Gemini Awards, 2002.

Television Appearances; Episodic:
Mitch, "Pariah," *Captain Power and the Soldiers of the Future,* 1987.
Second boy, "The Inheritance," *Friday the 13th* (also known as *Friday's Curse* and *Friday the 13th: The Series*), syndicated, 1987.
"It Only Hurts for a Little While," *My Secret Identity,* 1988.
"Decoy Ducks," *Katts and Dog* (also known as *Rin Tin Tin: K–9 Cop*), CTV and Family Channel, 1992.
Rat, "But When She Was Bad ... She Was Horrid: Parts 1 & 2," *Road to Avonlea,* CBC and Disney Channel, 1992.

John Cody, "Ike's New Buddy," *Maniac Mansion,* 1992.
Peter, "Allison's Restaurant," *The Mighty Jungle,* Family Channel, 1994.
Sean, "The Gang of Three," *Kung Fu: The Legend Continues,* syndicated, 1994.
Kyle the grocery boy, "Can't Run, Can't Hide," *Forever Knight,* syndicated, 1994.
Chris Stokes, "House of Caduceus," *Side Effects,* 1994.
Herbert Pencroft, "Genesis," *Mysterious Island,* 1995.
Herbert Pencroft, "Down Under," *Mysterious Island,* 1995.
Jules, "Bad Influence," *F/X: The Series,* syndicated, 1996.
Judge, "The Young and the Relentless," *Sliders,* Fox, 1996.
Gary, "The Haunting," *Psi Factor: Chronicles of the Paranormal,* syndicated, 1998.
Gary, "The Labyrinth," *Psi Factor: Chronicles of the Paranormal,* syndicated, 1998.
Marine corporal Gordon, "Cold Fusion," *Twilight Zone,* UPN, 2003.
Steve Jeffries, "Gifted," *Blood Ties,* Lifetime, 2007.

Also appeared in *E.N.G.,* CTV.

Television Director; Episodic:
"Reel Time," *The Heartbreak Cafe,* 2006.

WRITINGS

Television Episodes:
"Vault of the Heavens," *Andromeda* (also known as *Gene Roddenberry's "Andromeda"*), syndicated, 2003.
"Totaled Recall," *Andromeda* (also known as *Gene Roddenberry's "Andromeda"*), Sci–Fi Channel, 2003.
"Abridging the Devil's Divide," *Andromeda* (also known as *Gene Roddenberry's "Andromeda"*), syndicated, 2004.

OTHER SOURCES

Electronic:
Gordon Michael Woolvett Website, http://www. gmwoolvett.com, July 20, 2007.

WOOLVETT, Jaimz 1967–
(Jaimz Wolvett, Jaimz Woolvet, Jeimz Woolvet, Jaimz Woolvet.com)

PERSONAL

Original name, James Woolvett; born April 14, 1967, in Toronto, Ontario, Canada; brother of Gordon Woolvett (an actor).

Career: Actor.

Awards, Honors: Young Artist Award nomination, best young actor starring in an off–primetime or cable series, 1992, for *Dog House;* Gemini Award nomination, best performance by an actor in a featured supporting role in a dramatic program or miniseries, Academy of Canadian Cinema and Television, 1999, for *Milgaard.*

CREDITS

Film Appearances:
The Schofield Kid, *Unforgiven,* Warner Bros., 1992.
Ed, *The Dark,* Imperial Entertainment, 1994.
Lieutenant Dugan, *Dead Presidents,* Buena Vista, 1995.
Deputy Earl, *Rosewood,* Warner Bros., 1997.
Ward Minogue, *The Assistant,* Lions Gate Films, 1997.
Dominic Grace, *Sanctuary,* New City Releasing, 1997.
Larry, *Boogie Boy,* Sterling Home Entertainment, 1997.
Donald, *Reluctant Angel,* Blackwatch Releasing, 1998.
Vince, *Y2K* (also known as *Terminal Countdown*), PM Entertainment Group, 1999.
Ben, *Tail Lights Fade* (also known as *Le rallye*), Trimark Pictures, 1999.
Red Tenney, *Rites of Passage,* Davis Entertainment Classics/World International Network, 1999.
Leo, *The Guilty* (also known as *Coupable ou non–coupable*), Dogwood Pictures/J & M Entertainment/ Muse Entertainment, 1999.
(As Jaimz Woolvett.com) Mouse, *Beautiful Joe,* 2000.
Buddy Conner, *The Stepdaughter,* Trimark Pictures, 2000.
Going Back, GFT Entertainment, 2001.
Leo, *Global Heresy,* GFT Entertainment, 2001.
Power Play, First Look International, 2002.
Leo, *Global Heresy* (also known as *Au coeur du rock* and *Rock My World*), Screen Media Films, 2002.
Fingers, *A.K.A. Birdseye* (also known as *Birdseye*), 2002.
Nathan, *The Lazarus Child,* Warner Bros., 2004.

Television Appearances; Series:
Richie Underwood, *Dog House,* YTV, 1990.
Matt Scott, *White Fang* (also known as *Croc blanc*), 1993.

Television Appearances; Miniseries:
George Caron, *Hiroshima,* 1995.
Duke of Burgundy, *Joan of Arc* (also known as *Jeanne d'Arc*), CBS, 1999.

Television Appearances; Movies:
9B, CBC, 1986.
Scott Franz, *Deadly Betrayal: The Bruce Curtis Story* (movie; also known as *Journey into Darkness: The Bruce Curtis Story*), NBC, 1991.

(As Jaimz Woolvet) *Brothers' Destiny* (also known as *Long Road Home* and *The Road Home*), 1995.

Ensign Jasper Weston, *The Pathfinder*, 1996.

David E. Herold, *The Day Lincoln Was Shot*, TNT, 1998.

Ron Wilson, *Milgaard* (also known as *Hard Time: The David Milgaard Story* and *Erreur judiciate: l'histoire de David Milgaard*), 1999.

Tex, *Going Back* (also known as *Freres de guerre* and *Under Heavy Fire*), HBO, 2001.

Wagon train scout, *Love Comes Softly*, Hallmark Channel, 2003.

Jerry Collins, *Red Water*, TBS, 2003.

Gary Hinman, *Helter Skelter*, CBS, 2004.

Tex, *The Veteran*, 2006.

Television Appearances; Specials:

Jason, "Maggie's Secret," *CBS Schoolbreak Special*, CBS, 1990.

Television Appearances; Episodic:

Sean, "Forests of the Night," *E.N.G.*, CTV and Lifetime, 1989.

"Out of Control," *My Secret Identity*, syndicated, 1989.

Larry, "Terminal Rock," *War of the Worlds*, syndicated, 1989.

Chris Gray, "Home," *Street Legal*, CBC, 1989.

Steve Forret, "Running Man," *Neon Rider*, syndicated, 1990.

Tom, "The Prom," *C.B.C.'s Magic Hour*, CBC, 1990.

Captain Middleton, "Duty Bound," *Lonesome Dove: The Series*, 1994.

Booth Elliot, "Enter Prince Charming," *Road to Avonlea*, CBC and Disney Channel, 1994.

Booth Elliot, "The Minister's Wife," *Road to Avonlea*, CBC and Disney Channel, 1994.

Tommy Ness, "The Gang of Three," *Kung Fu: The Legend Continues*, syndicated, 1994.

Eric, "Escape," *La Femme Nikita* (also known as *Nikita*), USA Network, 1997.

Corporal Daryl Wetzel, "Father's Day," *JAG*, CBS, 1998.

Dean, "The Hunt," *Da Vinci's Inquest*, CBC, 1999.

Dean, "The Capture," *Da Vinci's Inquest*, CBC, 1999.

James Pearl, "The People vs. Eric Draven," *The Crow: Stairway to Heaven*, syndicated, 1999.

(Uncredited) James Pearl, "Birds of a Feather," *The Crow: Stairway to Heaven*, syndicated, 1999.

Steven Dalkowski, "Past Perfect," *The Fugitive*, CBS, 2001.

Midshipman Spencer, "Mutiny," *JAG*, CBS, 2001.

Himself, "The Western," *Film Genre* (also known as *Hollywood History*), 2002.

(As Jaimz Wolvett) Emergency medical technician number two, "Wing and a Prayer," *MDs*, ABC, 2002.

Tull, "Nymphs Just Wanna Have Fun," *Charmed*, The WB, 2003.

RECORDINGS

Video Games:

(As Jeimz Woolvet) Voice of Blackheart, *Marvel Super Heroes*, 1995.

(As Jaimz Woolvet) Voice of Blackheart and Mephisto, *Marvel Super Heroes vs. Street Fighter*, 1997.

WRITINGS

Television Episodes:

Wrote episodes of *White Fang* (also known as *Croc blanc*).

OTHER SOURCES

Electronic:

Jaimz Woolvett Website, http://www.jaimzwoolvett.com, July 20, 2007.

WORTHINGTON, Sam 1976–

PERSONAL

Full name, Samuel Worthington; born August 2, 1976, in Perth, Australia. *Education:* Graduated from the National Institute of Dramatic Art, Australia.

Addresses: *Agent*—Creative Artists Agency, 2000 Avenue of the Stars, Los Angeles, CA 90067. *Manager*—Industry Entertainment, 955 South Carrillo Dr., 3rd Floor, Los Angeles, CA 90048; Shanahan Management, Berman House, 91 Campbell St., Sydney 2010 Australia.

Career: Actor.

Awards, Honors: Australian Film Institute Award nomination, best performance by an actor in a leading role, 2000, for *Bootmen*; Film Critics Circle of Australia Award nomination, best supporting actor—male, 2002, for *Dirty Deeds*; Film Critics Circle of Australia Award nomination, best actor—male, Australian Film Institute Award, best actor in a leading role, 2004, both for *Somersault*.

CREDITS

Film Appearances:

Mitchell, *Bootmen*, Fox Searchlight Pictures, 2000.

Our hero, *Matter of Life* (short), Tropfest, 2001.

Corporal B. J. "Depot" Guidry, *Hart's War,* Metro–Goldwyn–Mayer, 2002.

Darcy, *Dirty Deeds* (also known as *Sacre boulot*), DEJ Productions, 2002.

Barry "Wattsy" Wirth, *Getting' Square,* Universal, 2003.

Ronnie, *Thunderstruck,* Icon Film Distribution, 2004.

Joe, *Somersault,* Magnolia Pictures, 2004.

Miles, *Blue Poles* (short), 2004.

Private first class Lucas, *The Great Raid,* Miramax, 2005.

Able, *Fink!,* 2005.

Macbeth, *Macbeth,* Truly Indie, 2006.

Himself, *The Faking Game* (short), 2006.

Neil, *Rogue,* Dimension Extreme, 2007.

Film Work:

Director and cinematographer, *Enzo* (short), Hypnotic, 2004.

Television Appearances; Series:

Howard Light, *Love My Way,* 2004–2005.

Dr. Sam Dash, *The Surgeon,* Ten Network, 2005.

Television Appearances; Specials:

Presenter, *The 2003 Australian Film Institute Awards,* ABC [Australia], 2003.

The Price of Freedom: Making "The Great Raid," FX Channel, 2005.

Narrator, *Battle of Long Tan,* 2006.

Television Appearances; Episodic:

Dunsmore, "Boomerang: Part 1," *JAG,* CBS, 2000.

Phillip Champion, "Able to Leap Tall Buildings," *Water Rats,* Nine Network, 2000.

Shane Donovan, "Bloodlines," *Blue Heelers,* Seven Network, 2000.

Rove Live, Ten Network, 2006.

Gus Rogers, "Delivery Man," *Two Twisted,* Nine Network, 2006.

Stage Appearances:

Made professional debut in *Judas Kiss,* Belvoir Street Theatre, Sydney, Australia.

WRITINGS

Screenplays:

Enzo (short), Hypnotic, 2004.

Film Scores:

Enzo (short), Hypnotic, 2004.

Y–Z

YIASOUMI, George

PERSONAL

Career: Actor.

CREDITS

Film Appearances:
Stage manager, *The Gold Diggers,* British Film Institute, 1983.
Primate sequences, *Greystoke: The Legend of Tarzan, Lord of the Apes,* Warner Bros., 1984.
Andre Breton, *Zina,* Virgin Films, 1985.
Japanese man, *Time After Time,* 1986.
Lady Kong, *King Kong Lives* (also known as *King Kong 2*), De Laurentiis Entertainment Group, 1986.
First valet, *Orlando,* Sony Pictures Classics, 1992.
Paris vampire, *Interview with the Vampire: The Vampire Chronicles* (also known as *Interview with the Vampire*), Warner Bros., 1994.
Photographer, *The Tango Lesson* (also known as *La lecon de tango, La leccion de tango,* and *Tango–Fieber*), Sony Pictures Classics, 1997.
A to Z, 1997.
Wrigley, the chauffeur, *The Borrowers,* PolyGram, 1997.
King Philip II of Spain, *Elizabeth* (also known as *Elizabeth: The Virgin Queen*), Gramercy Pictures, 1998.
Reporter, *The Man Who Cried* (also known as *The man who cried—Les larmes d'un homme*), Universal Focus, 2000.
Dauphin, *Quills* (also known as *Quills—Macht der besesenheit*), Fox Searchlight Pictures, 2000.
The strongman, *Sylvester* (short), Hired Gun, 2001.
Chef, *Swept Away* (also known as *Travolti dal destino*), Screen Gems, 2002.
Pog, *The Early Days* (short), 2003.

Barman, *Gladiatress,* Icon Film Distribution, 2004.
Kitchen boss, *Yes,* Sony Pictures Classics, 2004.

Television Appearances; Series:
Various roles, *Glam Metal Detectives,* BBC, 1995.

Television Appearances; Miniseries:
Bookman, *Gormenghast,* BBC2 and BBC America, 2000.
Ticket collector, *Dinotopia,* ABC, 2002.

Television Appearances; Movies:
Aristotle, *"Young Indiana Jones": Travels with Father,* Family Channel, 1996.
Alptraum im Airport (also known as *Midnight Flight*), 1998.
Felix, *Pompeii: The Last Day* (also known as *Pompeya—El ultimo dia*), BBC, 2003.

Television Appearances; Specials:
Teodoro Majocchi, *A Royal Scandal,* PBS, 1996.

Television Appearances; Pilots:
Appeared as cleric, *Baddiel's Syndrome.*

Television Appearances; Episodic:
Cato, "Up the Down Escalator," *Rockliffe's Babies,* BBC, 1987.
Writer, "Detectives on the Edge of a Nervous Breakdown," *The Comic Strip Presents ...,* BBC2, 1993.
Darren, "Space Virgins From Planet Sex," *The Comic Strip Presents ...,* BBC2, 1993.
Harry, "Gregory: Diary of a Nutcase," *The Comic Strip Presents ...,* BBC2, 1993.
Maltese Joe, "Yesterday's Hero," *The Bill,* ITV1, 1999.
Cart driver, "Four Men in a Plane," *The Comic Strip Presents ...,* Channel 4, 1999.
Larry, "Bed," *Sam's Game,* 2001.

Smiler Braithwaite, "A Very Ormston Christmas," *Born and Bred*, BBC and PBS, 2003.

Cruise manager, "Death on the Nile," *Poirot* (also known as *Agatha Christie's "Poirot"*), ITV and PBS, 2004.

Television Work; Series:
Script consultant, *Get Real*, Fox, 1998.

WRITINGS

Television Episodes:
Glam Metal Detectives (also kwon as *GMD*), BBC, 1995.

YOUNG, Burt 1940–
(John Harris)

PERSONAL

Original name, Jerry De Louise; born April 30, 1940, in New York, NY; son of Michael and Josephine De Louise; married, wife's name Gloria, May 20, 1961 (died, 1974); children: Richard (deceased), Anne Susan Morea (an actress). *Education:* Trained for the stage at Actors Studio, New York City. *Religion:* Roman Catholic.

Addresses: *Agent*—Christopher Barrett, Metropolitan Talent Agency, 4500 Wilshire Blvd., 2nd Floor, Los Angeles, CA 90010.

Career: Actor and writer. Artist, with work exhibited at Galerie 1225 Art et Vin, Montreal, Quebec, Canada, 2005, and Jade Nectar Gallery, New York City, 2006. White Crown Carpet Cleaners, president, 1964–67; Aurura Carpet Installation Company, president, 1966–69; Burt's Blues Tapes–Records, owner and operator, 1978; restaurant owner in Bronx, NY; also worked as boxer, baker, and truck driver. *Military service:* U.S. Marine Corps, 1957–59.

Member: Academy of Motion Picture Arts and Sciences, Writers Guild of America.

Awards, Honors: Academy Award nomination, best supporting actor, 1977, for *Rocky*.

CREDITS

Film Appearances:
(As John Harris) Gimpy, *Carnival of Blood* (also known as *Death Rides a Carousel*), 1970.

Willie Quarequlo, *The Gang That Couldn't Shoot Straight* (also known as *The Gang That Couldn't Shoot*), Metro–Goldwyn–Mayer, 1971.

First hood, *Born to Win* (also known as *Addict* and *Born to Lose*), 1971.

Lapides, *Across 110th Street*, 1972.

Master at arms, *Cinderella Liberty*, Twentieth Century–Fox, 1973.

Curly, *Chinatown*, Paramount, 1974.

Carmine, *The Gambler*, Paramount, 1974.

Mac, *The Killer Elite*, United Artists, 1975.

Sergeant Bernasconi, *Murph the Surf* (also known as *Live a Little, Steal a Lot* and *You Can't Steal Love*), American International Pictures, 1975.

Warden Durgom, *Harry and Walter Go to New York*, Columbia, 1976.

Paulie, *Rocky*, Metro–Goldwyn–Mayer/United Artists, 1976.

Sergeant Dominic Scuzzi, *The Choirboys* (also known as *Aenglarna*), Universal, 1977.

Augie Garvas, *Twilight's Last Gleaming* (also known as *Nuclear Countdown* and *Das Ultimatum*), Allied Artists, 1977.

Pig Pen/Love Machine, *Convoy*, United Artists, 1978.

Joe Shannon (title role), *Uncle Joe Shannon*, United Artists, 1978.

Paulie, *Rocky II*, United Artists, 1979.

Sergeant Royko, *Blood Beach*, 1981.

Eddie Cisco, *… All the Marbles* (also known as *The California Dolls*), Metro–Goldwyn–Mayer, 1981.

Paulie, *Rocky III*, Metro–Goldwyn–Mayer/United Artists, 1982.

Jerry Feldman, *Lookin' to Get Out*, Paramount, 1982.

Anthony Montelli, *Amityville II: The Possession*, Orion, 1982.

Phil, *Over the Brooklyn Bridge* (also known as *Across the Brooklyn Bridge* and *My Darling Shiksa*), Metro–Goldwyn–Mayer, 1984.

Joe, *Once upon a Time in America* (also known as *C'era una volta in America*), Warner Bros., 1984.

Bedbug Eddie, *The Pope of Greenwich Village*, (also known as *Village Dreams*), Metro–Goldwyn–Mayer, 1984.

Paulie, *Rocky IV*, Metro–Goldwyn–Mayer, 1985.

Lou the chauffeur, *Back to School*, Orion, 1986.

Harry, *Medium Rare*, 1987.

Andrews, *Blood Red*, Hemdale Releasing, 1988.

Clive, *Beverly Hills Brats*, Taurus Entertainment, 1989.

Big Joe, *Last Exit to Brooklyn* (also known as *Letzte Ausfahrt Brooklyn*), Cinecom International, 1989.

Rocco, *Wait Until Spring, Bandini* (also known as *Bandini, John Fante's "Wait Until Spring, Bandini," Aspetta primavera Bandini*, and *Le Ragioni del cuore*), Orion, 1989.

General Noriega, *Going Overboard* (also known as *Babes Ahoy*), 1989.

Paulie, *Rocky V*, Metro–Goldwyn–Mayer, 1990.

Luca Garibaldi, *Backstreet Dreams* (also known as *Backstreet Strays*), 1990.

Warden Boyle, *Club Fed*, 1990.

Georgie, *Betsy's Wedding,* Buena Vista, 1990.

Coach Mack, *Diving In,* Skouras, 1991.

Art Falco, *Bright Angel,* Hemdale Releasing, 1991.

George Maniago, *Americano rosso* (also known as *Red American*), 1991.

Sal DiMarco, *Excessive Force,* 1992.

Cattive ragazze, 1992.

Mancini, *Alibi perfetto* (also known as *Circle of Fear*), 1992.

Werner, *Berlin '39,* 1994.

Reno, *Tashunga* (also known as *North Star, Duello tra I ghiacci,* and *Grand nord*), Warner Bros., 1995.

Roy, *Red Blooded American Girl II* (also known as *Hit & Run, Hot Blooded,* and *Red Blooded 2*), 1995.

Opposite Corners, 1995.

Lorenzo, *She's So Lovely* (also known as *Call It Love*), Miramax, 1997.

Alberto Strachitella, *The Undertaker's Wedding* (also known as *J'ai epouse un croque–mort*), Astra Cinema, 1997.

Jack, *Kicked in the Head,* October Films, 1997.

J. C., *The Deli,* Golden Monkey Pictures, 1997.

Himself, *The Mouse,* Strand Releasing, 1997.

Heaven Before I Die, 1997.

One Deadly Road, 1998.

Joe McCollough, *The Florentine,* Bcb Productions, 1999.

Vito Graziosi, *Mickey Blue Eyes,* Warner Bros., 1999.

Joe, *Terra bruciata,* 1999.

Sydney Delacroix, *Loser Love,* Trident Releasing, 1999.

Bobby, *Blue Moon,* Curb Entertainment, 2000.

Don Ettore Visone, *L'uomo della fortuna,* Lion Pictures, 2000.

Dominic Piazza, *Very Mean Men,* Miracle Entertainment, 2000.

John Stoller, *The Day the Ponies Come Back,* 2000.

Frankie Chips, *Table One,* 2000.

Never Look Back, Giants Entertainment, 2000.

Himself, *Fight the Good Fight,* 2000.

The Boys Behind the Desk, 2000.

Sal Palermo, *Plan B,* Franchise Pictures, 2001.

Pasquale "Pop" Cugini, *Cugini,* Shooters Post and Transfer, 2001.

Hank Bartlowski, *The Boys of Sunset Ridge,* PorchLight Entertainment, 2001.

And She Was, Cinemavault Releasing International, 2002.

Uncle Louie, *Checkout,* Dream Entertainment, 2002.

Gino, *The Adventures of Pluto Nash* (also known as *Pluto Nash*), Columbia/Warner Bros., 2002.

2 Birds with 1 Stallone (documentary; also known as *Fight the Good Fight, Lou Loves People,* and *2 Birds with 1 Stallone: The Life Story of Lou Benedetti*), Lil Mama Pictures, 2002.

Santo Sposato, *Kiss the Bride,* 2002, Metro–Goldwyn–Mayer, 2004.

Mike Ameche, *Crooked Lines,* Cinemavault Releasing International, 2003.

Vincent Bublioni, *Shut Up and Kiss Me!,* American World Pictures, 2004.

Jack Stockman, *The Wager,* Icelandic Film/Prophecy Pictures, 2004.

Gus, *Downtown: A Street Tale,* Slowhand Cinema Releasing, 2004.

Sherman, *Land of Plenty,* IFC Films, 2005.

Voice of Bruno, *Firedog* (animated), Firedog LLC, 2005.

Murray, *Transamerica,* IFC Films, 2005.

Leo Singer, *Nicky's Game* (short film), SpaceTime Films/LaSalleHolland, 2005.

Artie Bottolota, Sr., *Carlito's Way: Rise to Power,* Universal, 2005.

(In archive footage) *Hubert Selby Jr.: It'll Be Better Tomorrow* (documentary), Eclectic DVD Distribution/Music Video Distributors, 2005.

Himself, *RevoLOUtion: The Transformation of Lou Benedetti,* Louniversal Releasing, 2006.

Paulie, *Rocky Balboa,* Metro–Goldwyn–Mayer, 2006.

Santino, *Oliviero Rising,* Astra Film, 2007.

Pops, *Blue Lake Massacre,* Red Rock, 2007.

J. T. Bates, *Hack!,* Smithfield Street Productions, 2007.

Mueller, *The Hideout,* Duea Film/Motion Pictures Midwest, 2007.

Murray, *Go Go Tales,* Bellatrix Media/Go Go Tales, 2007.

Television Appearances; Movies:

Ernie, *The Connection,* ABC, 1973.

Ace Tully, *The Great Niagara,* ABC, 1974.

Gustavino, *Hustling,* ABC, 1975.

Ralph Rodino, *Woman of the Year,* CBS, 1976.

Rocco Agnelli, *Daddy, I Don't Like It Like This,* CBS, 1977.

Lieutenant Palumbo, *Murder Can Hurt You,* ABC, 1980.

Fidel Fargo, *A Summer to Remember,* CBS, 1985.

Due vite un destino (also known as *The Final Contract*), 1992.

Detective Zimmer, *Double Deception,* NBC, 1993.

Mo Weinberg, *Columbo: Undercover,* ABC, 1994.

Mr. Ippolito, *Before Women Had Wings* (also known as *Oprah Winfrey Presents: "Before Women Had Wings"*), ABC, 1997.

Chief Frank Shea, *Firehouse,* 1997.

Gallagher, *Cuori in campo* (also known as *Greener Fields* and *World Cup '98*), Cinemax, 1998.

Television Appearances; Miniseries:

Vincente Dominici, *Vendetta: Secrets of a Mafia Bride* (also known as *Bride of Violence, A Family Matter,* and *Donna d'onore*), syndicated, 1991.

Vincente Dominici, *Vendetta II: The New Mafia* (also known as *Bride of Violence 2* and *Donna d'onore 2*), HBO, 1993.

Milai, *The Maharaja's Daughter* (also known as *Die Tochter des Maharadschas*), 1994.

Lou Benedetti, *Crocodile Shoes,* 1994.

Virginio Ballazzo, *The Last Don* (also known as *Mario Puzo's "The Last Don"*), CBS, 1997.

Oland, *Pensando all'Africa* (also known as *Thinking About Africa, Sotto il cielo dell'Africa,* and *Unter der sonne Afrikas*), 1998.

Television Appearances; Series:
You and Me Kid, 1983.
Nick Chase, *Roomies,* NBC, 1987.
Frank, *Alternate Realities,* 2002.

Television Appearances; Specials:
Split Personality, HBO, 1992.
Narrator, *City Dump: The Story of the 1951 CCNY Basketball Scandal,* HBO, 1998.
The Making of a Mobster: "Mickey Blue Eyes," 1999.
James Caan: Making a Scene, Arts and Entertainment, 2001.
"Sylvester Stallone," *Biography,* Arts and Entertainment, 2005.

Television Appearances; Episodic:
Lieutenant Willis, "L.I.P. (Local Indigenous Personnel)," *M*A*S*H*,* CBS, 1973.
Willy, "Keep Your Eye on the Sparrow," *Baretta,* 1975.
Johnny Checco, "Soldier in the Jungle," *Baretta,* 1976.
Solomon, "The Big Hand's in Trouble," *Baretta,* 1976.
Stuart Gaily, "The Family Hour," *The Rockford Files* (also known as *Jim Rockford, Private Investigator*), 1976.
Lupo Ramirez, "Give a Little, Take a Little," *Miami Vice,* NBC, 1984.
Louie Ganucci, "The Confirmation Day" (also known as "The Family"), *The Equalizer,* 1985.
Salesman, "Road Hog," *Alfred Hitchcock Presents,* 1986.
Gambler, "Split Personality," *Tales from the Crypt* (also known as *HBO's "Tales from the Crypt"*), HBO, 1992.
Mr. Riveto, "The Postman Always Moves Twice," *Bless This House,* CBS, 1995.
Jack "Soldier" Belmont, "Lucky," *Walker, Texas Ranger,* CBS, 1996.
Captain Parker, "Tempests," *The Outer Limits* (also known as *The New Outer Limits*), Showtime, then syndicated, 1997.
Lewis Darnell, "Mad Dog," *Law & Order,* NBC, 1997.
Jack "Soldier" Belmont, "Small Blessings," *Walker, Texas Ranger,* CBS, 1997.
The Howard Stern Radio Show, 2000.
Bobby "Bacala" Baccalieri, Sr., "Another Toothpick," *The Sopranos,* HBO, 2001.
Dino Mantoni, "Bruno Comes Back," *The Handler,* CBS, 2003.
Himself, "Winners & Losers & Whiners & Boozers: Part 2," *I'm With Her,* ABC, 2004.
(Uncredited) Himself, "Survival of the Fittest," *The Contender,* NBC, 2005.
(Uncredited) Himself, "Rivals," *The Contender,* NBC, 2005.

(Uncredited) Himself, "Injury Takes Its Toll," *The Contender,* NBC, 2005.
(Uncredited) Himself, "Heavy Hands," *The Contender,* NBC, 2005.

Television Appearances; Other:
Alec Rosen, *Serpico: The Deadly Game* (pilot), NBC, 1976.
Gioci de specchi, 2000.

Stage Appearances:
Smitty in "Escape from Deep Hammock During the Hurricane of '52," Dr. Pinkney in "The Organ Recital at the New Grand," and Bobby Terry in "The Men's Room," *The Men's Room,* Actors Repertory Theatre, New York City, 1982.
Jackie, *Cuba and His Teddy Bear,* New York Shakespeare Festival, Susan Stein Shiva Theatre, Public Theatre, then Longacre Theatre, both New York City, 1986.
S.O.S. (solo show), Actors Playhouse, New York City, 1988.
Eddie Carbone, *A View from the Bridge,* Los Angeles, 1995.

Appeared in *Rats,* Group Theatre.

WRITINGS

Screenplays:
Uncle Joe Shannon, United Artists, 1978.

Television Movies:
Daddy, I Don't Like It Like This, CBS, 1977.

Stage Shows:
S.O.S. (solo show), Actors Playhouse, New York City, 1988.

Also author of the script *A Letter to Alicia and the New York City Government, from a Man with a Bullet in His Head.*

OTHER SOURCES

Periodicals:
Bright Lights Film Journal, August, 2006.
People Weekly, August 11, 1986, p. 77.

Electronic:
Burt Young Official Site, http://burtyoungartandfilm.com, April 21, 2007.

ZAYAS, David

PERSONAL

Married Liza Colon (an actress). *Education:* Studied acting at Ernie Martin's studio.

Addresses: *Agent*—TalentWorks, 3500 West Olive Ave., Suite 1400, Burbank, CA 91505.

Career: Actor. LAByrinth Theatre Company, member, New York, NY, 1992—; appeared in television commercials, including Pepcid and Tums antacid tablets, and Pepsi products. Former New York Police Department policeman.

CREDITS

Film Appearances:
Jorge, *Lena's Dream,* 1997.
Lieutenant Ballard, *Bleach* (short), 1998.
Omar, *O.K. Garage* (also known as *All Revved Up*), New City Releasing, 1998.
Cop number one, *Scar City* (also known as *S.C.A.R.* and *Scarred City*), 1998.
Construction foreman, *Return to Paradise* (also known as *All for One*), MCA/Universal, 1998.
Osborne, *Rounders,* Miramax, 1998.
Hector, *Above Freezing,* 3DD Entertainment, 1998.
Policeman, *Stepmom,* Columbia, 1998.
Kingdom Come, 1999.
Cop in elevator, *Bringing Out the Dead,* Paramount, 1999.
Billy the cop, *Sam the Man,* 2000.
Officer Jerry Rifkin, *The Yards,* Miramax, 2000.
Alfred D'Angelo, *A Gentleman's Game,* First Look International, 2001.
David, *Washington Heights,* 2002.
Cynthia's dad, *Anne B. Real,* Screen Media Films, 2003.
La arana, *La arana* (short), 2003.
Paulie, *Mimmo & Paulie* (short), 2004.
Popo, *Brooklyn Bound,* Image Entertainment, 2004.
Guard, *Jailbait,* Kindred Media Group, 2004.
Detective Benson, *Bristol Boys,* Fabrication Films, 2005.
Charlie Russell, *The Interpreter* (also known as *L'interprete*), Universal, 2005.
Nestor, *Sangre/Blood* (short), 2005.
Antonio de la Maza, *La fiesta del chivo* (also known as *The Feast of the Goat*), 2005.
Robert Torres, *16 Blocks,* Warner Bros., 2006.
Eduardo, *The Savages,* Fox Searchlight, 2007.
Detective Dalberto, *Michael Clayton,* Warner Bros., 2007.
Hector, *Burning Mussolini,* 2007.

Television Appearances; Series:
Rei Morales, *The Beat,* UPN, 2000.
Enrique Morales, *Oz,* HBO, 2000–2003.
Angel Batista, *Dexter,* Showtime, 2006.
Javier, *Burn Notice,* 2007.

Television Appearances; Miniseries:
Super, *Angels in America,* HBO, 2003.
Lou Napoli, *The Path to 9/11,* ABC, 2006.

Television Appearances; Movies:
Code Team Blue Head, *Wit,* HBO, 2001.
Paulie, *Undefeated,* HBO, 2003.
Angel's father, *Angel* (also known as *Angel Rodriguez*), HBO, 2005.

Television Appearances; Pilots:
Hernan, *Conviction,* NBC, 2006.

Television Appearances; Episodic:
McGinty, "Savages," *Law & Order,* NBC, 1995.
Raoul Cervantes, "Causa Mortis," *Law & Order,* NBC, 1996.
Martinez, "The Enforcers," *New York Undercover* (also known as *Uptown Undercover*), Fox, 1996.
"Somebody's Lyin," *Feds,* CBS, 1997.
Carlos, "Flight," *Law & Order,* NBC, 1998.
Uniform cop number one, " ... To Forgive, Divine," *Trinity,* NBC, 1998.
Motoman, "Welcome to Camelot," *Third Watch,* NBC, 1999.
"These Shoots Are Made for Joaquin," *NYPD Blue,* ABC, 2000.
All My Children, ABC, 2000.
Detective Milton, "Protection," *Law & Order: Special Victims Unit* (also known as *Law & Order: SVU* and *Special Victims Unit*), NBC, 2002.
Jorge Gonzales, "Manhunt," *UC: Undercover,* NBC, 2002.
Prison guard, *The Guiding Light* (also known as *Guiding Light*), CBS, 2002.
John Mireles, "Smoke," *Law & Order,* NBC, 2003.
Fire marshal, "On Fire," *Law & Order: Criminal Intent* (also known as *Law & Order: CI*), NBC, 2006.
Carlos Costavo, "Brutus," *Numb3rs* (also known as *Num3ers*), CBS, 2006.
Quite Frankly with Stephen A. Smith, ESPN, 2006.
Gabriel Molina, "Crash and Burn," *Without a Trace* (also known as *W.A.T.*), CBS, 2007.
Alvarez, "Strange Bedfellows," *Shark,* CBS, 2007.
Ballistics Brian, "Grave Doubts," *The Closer,* TNT, 2007.

Stage Appearances:

Valdez, *Jesus Hopped the A Train,* Classic Stage Company Theatre, New York City, 2000.

Edwin, *Our Lady of 121st Street,* Union Square Theatre, New York City, 2003.

Cheche, *Anna in the Tropics,* New York City, 2003–2004.

Also appeared in *Divine Horseman, Francisco and Benny,* and *In Arabia, We'd All Be Kings,* all LAByrinth theatre company, New York City.

ZIMMER, Constance 1970–

PERSONAL

Born October 11, 1970, in Seattle, WA. *Education:* Attended the American Academy of Dramatic Arts. *Avocational Interests:* Gardening, photography, charity work, hiking, and book clubs.

Addresses: *Agent*—Innovative Artists, 1505 Tenth St., Santa Monica, CA 90401. *Manager*—Sweeney Management, 8755 Lookout Mountain Ave., Los Angeles, CA 90046.

Career: Actress. Appeared in television commercials for Triscuit Crackers, 1998, Chrysler automobiles, 2000, Budweiser beer, 2001, Rite Aid drugstores, and Duracell batteries. Petro Zillia, Los Angeles, partner; produced handmade jewelry, candles, greeting cards, and other items. Attends numerous celebrity benefits for charity; AIDS activism.

Awards, Honors: Drama–logue Award, best actress, for *Catholic School Girls.*

CREDITS

Film Appearances:

Zestfully clean woman, *Senseless,* Miramax, 1998.

Vicky Portenza, *Warm Blooded Killers,* 1999.

Kyle, *Farewell, My Love,* Win Entertainment, 1999.

Echo, *Spin Cycle,* 2000.

Assistant Kelly, *Home Room,* Innovation Film Group, 2002.

Corley James, *Just Pray* (short), 2005.

Angel, *Damaged Goods* (short), 2006.

Nicole, *The Hammer,* Hammer the Movie, 2007.

Chaos Theory, Warner Independent Pictures, 2007.

The director, *AmericanEast,* Distant Horizons, 2007.

Television Appearances; Series:

Beth, *The Fighting Fitzgeralds,* NBC, 2001.

Penelope "Penny" Barnes Barrington, *Good Morning Miami,* NBC, 2002–2004.

Sister Lilly Watters, *Joan of Arcadia,* CBS, 2004–2005.

Dana Gordon, *Entourage,* HBO, 2005–2006.

Brianna, *In Justice,* ABC, 2006.

Claire Simms, *Boston Legal,* ABC, 2006–2007.

Television Appearances; Miniseries:

I Love the '80s, VH1, 2002.

Television Appearances; Movies:

Girl in line, *The Day My Parents Ran Away* (also known as *Missing Parents*), Fox, 1993.

Female patient, *Quicksilver Highway,* Fox, 1997.

Cassie Tilman/Cassie Thomas, *Mystery Woman,* Hallmark Channel, 2003.

52 Fights, 2006.

Television Appearances; Specials:

Intimate Portrait: Suzanne Pleshette, Lifetime, 2002.

Television Appearances; Pilots:

Helmet Heads, The WB, 1999.

Naomi, *Out of Practice,* CBS, 2005.

Emily, *52 Flights,* ABC, 2006.

Television Appearances; Episodic:

Young woman patient, "The Quality of Mercy," *Babylon 5* (also known as *B5*), 1994.

Riot girl, "Just Coffee?," *Ellen* (also known as *These Friends of Mine*), ABC, 1997.

Lisa Byrd, "An Education in Murder," *Diagnosis Murder,* CBS, 1997.

LaVerne, "Tiffany, the Home Wrecker," *Unhappily Ever After* (also known as *Unhappily ...* , 1997.

Waitress number two, "The Wizard," *Seinfeld,* NBC, 1998.

Millie, "Reunion," *Beverly Hills, 90210,* Fox, 1998.

Vanessa, "Brother Can You Spare a Dime?," *The Wayans Bros.,* The WB, 1998.

Vanessa, "Six Degrees of Marlon," *The Wayans Bros.,* The WB, 1998.

Girl, "The Last Stand," *Felicity,* The WB, 1998.

Sunless, "The Rope," *Hyperion Bay,* The WB, 1998.

Jenny, "Fixer Upper," *The King of Queens,* CBS, 1998.

"The Takeover," *Hyperion Bay,* The WB, 1999.

Dana, "A Goy and His Dog," *Chicago Hope,* CBS, 1999.

Phoebe, "First Person Shooter," *The X–Files,* Fox, 2000.

Sandi, "Star 80 Proof," *Rude Awakening,* 2000.

Kristen, "Owl Show Ya," *The Trouble with Normal,* ABC, 2000.

Mary, "The Find," *Beyond Belief: Fact or Fiction?* (also known as *Beyond Belief*), 2000.

"The Thanksgiving: Parts 1 & 2," *Providence*, NBC, 2000.

Jessica Kagen, "Mr. Cherry Must Be Stopped," *Gideon's Crossing*, ABC, 2001.

Tori Spangler, "Subject: The Stone Room," *FreakyLinks*, Fox, 2001.

Pamela Tommasino, "Blown Away," *Philly*, ABC, 2001.

Siobhan! Ross, "The Yoko Factor," *My Guide to Becoming a Rock Star*, The WB, 2002.

Siobhan! Ross, "The Session," *My Guide to Becoming a Rock Star*, The WB, 2002.

Zoe Prentiss, "Dress for Success," *NYPD Blue*, ABC, 2004.

Greta, "Henry Porter and the Coitus Interruptus," *Jake in Progress*, ABC, 2005.

Guest, "Leachman Passes a Milestone/Golf/Stuff Styles & Jules Verne Gets the Star Treatment," *In the Mix* (also known as *In the Cutz*), Urban America, 2006.

The Megan Mullally Show, syndicated, 2006.

"Constance Marie," *My Celebrity Home*, E! Entertainment Television and Style Network, 2006.

Naomi, "The Lady Doth Protest Too Much," *Out of Practice*, CBS, 2006.

Kelly, "Oleander," *Notes from the Underbelly*, ABC, 2007.

Also appeared as Kaleigh, "A Girl's Gotta Come Through in a Clutch," *Jenny*, NBC; Siobhan! Ross, "The Deal," *My Guide to Becoming a Rock Star*, The WB.

Stage Appearances:

Appeared in *Catholic School Girls; Mousy Brown*.

OTHER SOURCES

Electronic:

Constance Zimmer Website, http://www.constancezimmer.com, July 25, 2007.

ZIMMERMAN, Joey 1986–
(J. Paul Zimmerman, Joseph Zimmerman)

PERSONAL

Full name, Joseph Paul Zimmerman; born June 10, 1986, in Albuquerque, NM; son of Kat Zimmerman. *Avocational Interests:* Baseball, fencing, hockey, writing, collecting cards, comics, and action figures.

Addresses: *Agent*—Innovative Artists Talent Agency, 1999 Avenue of the Stars, Los Angeles, CA 90067–6022.

Career: Actor. Appeared in television commercials, including GE Healthcare and McDonald's.

Awards, Honors: Young Artist Award nomination (with others), outstanding youth ensemble in a television series, 1994, for *The Mommies;* Young Artist Award nomination, best performance by a youth actor in a drama series, 1995, for *Earth 2;* Young Artist Award nomination, best performance by a guest–starring young performer in a television comedy series, 2000, for *Cupid;* Young Artist Award, best performance in a television comedy series—guest starring young performer, 2001, for *Becker;* Young Artist Award nomination, best performance in a television movie or special—supporting young actor, 2002, for *Halloweentown II: Kalabar's Revenge.*

CREDITS

Film Appearances:

Ben, *Mother's Boys*, Dimension Films, 1993.

Pir, *Beastmaster III: The Eye of Braxus* (also known as *Beastmaster III*), Animal Makers, 1995.

Adam Berkow, Jr., *Very Bad Things*, PolyGram Filmed Entertainment, 1998.

Timmy Taylor, *Treehouse Hostage*, Trimark Pictures, 1999.

Jimmy, *Whore*, 2000.

Film Work:

Executive producer, director, and editor, *Dogg's Hamlet, Cahoot's Macbeth*, 2005.

Television Appearances; Series:

Ulysses, *Earth 2*, NBC, 1994–95.

Eric Kipper, *Bailey Kipper's P.O.V.* (also known as *Bailey Kipper's Point of View*), CBS, 1996.

Television Appearances; Movies:

Gary Travis, *Jack Reed: Badge of Honor*, NBC, 1993.

Murder Between Friends, NBC, 1994.

Nicholas McConnell, *Killing Mr. Griffin* (also known as *Killing Griffin*), NBC, 1997.

John Keenan, *A Thousand Men and a Baby* (also known as *Narrow Escape*), CBS, 1997.

Dylan Piper, *Halloweentown*, Disney Channel, 1998.

(As Joseph Zimmerman) Dylan Piper Cromwell, *Halloweentown II: Kalabar's Revenge* (also known as *Halloweentown II*), 2001.

Dylan Piper Cromwell, *Halloweentown High*, 2004.

(As J. Paul Zimmerman) Dylan Piper, *Return to Halloweentown* (also known as *Halloweentown IV*), Disney Channel, 2006.

Television Appearances; Pilots:

Ulysses "Uly" Adair, *Earth 2*, NBC, 1994.

Television Appearances; Specials:
"Crosstown," *CBS Schoolbreak Special,* CBS, 1996.

Television Appearances; Episodic:
Kevin, *The Mommies,* NBC, 1993.
Dracula, "Halloween," *Frasier,* NBC, 1997.
Dennis, *Nothing Sacred,* 1997.
Chuckie, "Caroline and the Guys in the Bathroom," *Caroline in the City* (also known as *Caroline*), NBC, 1998.
"The Children's Hour," *Cupid,* ABC, 1999.
Matthew Anderson, "Happy Birthday," *Felicity,* The WB, 1999.
Young Hyde, "Reefer Madness," *That '70s Show,* Fox, 2000.
Jeff Andrews, "What Indifference a Day Makes," *Becker,* CBS, 2000.
Steven Jamison, "Summary Judgments," *The Practice,* ABC, 2000.
Steven Jamison, "Germ Warfare," *The Practice,* ABC, 2000.
Luke, "Talk to Me," *7th Heaven* (also known as *Seventh Heaven*), The WB, 2000.
Luke, "Gossip," *7th Heaven* (also known as *Seventh Heaven*), The WB, 2000.
Hyde at age thirteen, "Class Picture," *That '70s Show,* Fox, 2002.
Soda kid, "Lizzie's Eleven," *Lizzie McGuire,* Disney Channel, 2003.
Collins, "Only Connect," *The Jake Effect,* Bravo, 2006.

Also appeared as Young Pauly, *Pauly,* Fox.

Stage Appearances:
Appeared as young MacDuff, *Macbeth,* a Vortex production; in *The Legacy.*

WRITINGS

Screenplays:
Dogg's Hamlet, Cahoot's Macbeth, 2005.

ZITO, Chuck 1953–
(Charles Zito)

PERSONAL

Original name, Charles Zito, Jr.; born March 1, 1953, in the Bronx, NY; son of Charles and Gloria (maiden name, Frangione) Zito; married Kathy (divorced); children: Lisa. *Avocational Interests:* Karate (black belt).

Career: Actor and stunt performer. *Chuck Zito's View,* Sirius channel Howard 101, radio show host. Member of the Hell's Angels for twenty–five years as well as other motorcycle clubs; former Golden Gloves boxer; previously worked as a bodyguard through his Charlie's Angels Bodyguards Service, clients including Liza Minelli, Jean–Claude Van Damme, Mickey Rourke, Joan Rivers, Pamela Anderson, and Sylvester Stallone; worked at Scores Gentleman's Club, 2005–06; also worked as a manual laborer.

CREDITS

Film Appearances:
Mafia head, *Nyu Yoku no koppu* (also known as *New York Cop*), Overseas Film Group, 1993.
Prisoner, *Nowhere to Run,* Columbia, 1993.
Club bouncer, *Carlito's Way,* 1993.
Big cop, *Love Is a Gun,* 1994.
Tough guy, *Jimmy Hollywood,* Paramount, 1994.
Toots, *Viper* (also known as *Bad Blood*), Third Coast Entertainment, 1994.
Bartender, *Sensation,* 1995.
Jerry, *Squanderers* (also known as *Money to Burn*), New Line Home Video, 1996.
Frankie, *The Juror,* Columbia, 1996.
Tony, *Heaven's Prisoners,* New Line Cinema, 1996.
Zito, *The Funeral,* Echo Bridge Home Entertainment, 1996.
Dick, *Red Line,* Triboro Entertainment Group, 1996.
Guard number three, *Scar City* (also known as *S.C.A.R.* and *Scarred City*), 1998.
Guard at abandoned track, *No Code of Conduct,* Dimension Films, 1998.
Chuck, *Black and White,* Screen Gems, 1999.
Biker, *Me and Will,* Bedford Entertainment, 1999.
Tony Clifton biker, *Man on the Moon* (also known as *Der Mondmann*), Universal, 1999.
The cook, *Table One,* New Line Cinema, 2000.
Chuck, *This Thing of Ours,* Gabriel Film Group, 2003.
Anthony, *Brooklyn Bound,* Image Entertainment, 2004.
Vinnie, *Coalition,* Image Entertainment, 2004.
Rubenstein, *Tinsel Town,* 2005.
Captain Sallie, *Remedy,* Starline Pictures, 2005.
Freddy Knuckles, *Search for Bobby D,* Monarch Home Video, 2005.
Tony Esposito, *The Signs of the Cross,* 2005.
Buck, *Carlito's Way: Rise to Power,* Universal, 2005.
George Winfield, *Ghosts of Goldfield,* 2007.
Jailer number one, *Man in the Chair,* 2007.

Film Stunts:
Hudson Hawk, TriStar, 1991.
29th Street, Twentieth Century–Fox, 1991.
The Last Boy Scout, Geffen Pictures, 1991.
Neon City, Vidmark Entertainment, 1992.
Best of the Best 2, Twentieth Century–Fox, 1993.
The Chase, Twentieth Century–Fox, 1994.

True Lies, Twentieth Century–Fox, 1994.
North, Columbia, 1994.
Viper (also known as *Bad Blood*), 1994.
Kiss of Death, Twentieth Century–Fox, 1995.
Mallrats, Gramercy Pictures, 1995.
The Rock, Buena Vista, 1996.
Eraser, Warner Bros., 1996.
Maximum Risk (also known as *Bloodstone* and *The Exchange*), Columbia, 1996.
My Fellow Americans, Warner Bros., 1996.
Amistad, 1997.
A Perfect Murder, Warner Bros., 1998.
The Siege, Twentieth Century–Fox, 1998.
Enemy of the State, Buena Vista, 1998.
Point Blank, Sterling Home Entertainment, 1998.
Aa Ab laut chalen (also known as *Lets Go Back*), 1999.
Requiem for a Dream (also known as *Delusion Over Addiction*), Artisan Entertainment, 2000.
Gone in Sixty Seconds, Buena Vista, 2000.
15 Minutes (also known as *15 Minuten ruhm*), New Line Cinema, 2001.
City by the Sea (also known as *The Suspect*), Warner Bros., 2002.
New York Minute, Warner Bros., 2004.
The Forgotten (also known as *Stranger*), Columbia, 2004.

Film Work; Other:
(As Charles Zito) Set security, *The Indian Runner* (also known as *Indian Runner*), 1991.
Stunt coordinator, *Santa with Muscles,* Legacy Releasing Corp., 1996.

Television Appearances; Series:
Chucky "The Enforcer" Pancamo, *Oz,* HBO, 1998–2003.
WCW Nitro, 1999.

Television Appearances; Movies:
Jake, *Love, Cheat & Steal,* Showtime, 1993.
Harley biker, *Gia,* HBO, 1998.

Television Appearances; Specials:
Mickey Rourke: The E! True Hollywood Story, E! Entertainment Television, 1999.
Host, *Street Justice,* 2001.
UFC 44: Undisputed, 2003.
UFC 46: Supernatural, 2004.
UFC 47: It's On!, 2004.

Television Appearances; Episodic:
(Uncredited) "Hubris," *New York Undercover* (also known as *Uptown Undercover*), 1997.
Howard Stern, E! Entertainment Television, 1998, 2000.
The Howard Stern Radio Show, syndicated, 1999.
Mikey, "Val Point Blank," *V.I.P.* (also known as *V.I.P.—Die Bodyguards*), syndicated, 2000.
"Chuck Zito," *Howard Stern on Demand* (also known as *Howard TV on Demand*), 2006.
Rudy, *The Young and the Restless* (also known as *Y&R*), CBS, 2006.

Television Work; Series:
Stunts, *Oz,* HBO, 1997.

WRITINGS

Autobiographies:
(With Joe Layden) *Chuck Zito: Street Justice,* 2002.

OTHER SOURCES

Electronic:
Chuck Zito Website, http://www.chuckzito.com, July 20, 2007.

ZUVIC, Daniella
   See MONET, Daniella

Cumulative Index

To provide continuity with *Who's Who in the Theatre*, this index interfiles references to *Who's Who in the Theatre*, 1st–17th Editions, and *Who Was Who in the Theatre* (Gale, 1978) with references to *Contemporary Theatre, Film and Television*, Volumes 1–79.

References in the index are identified as follows:

CTFT and volume number—*Contemporary Theatre, Film and Television*, Volumes 1–79
WWT and edition number—*Who's Who in the Theatre*, 1st–17th Editions
WWasWT—*Who Was Who in the Theatre*

Aames, Willie 1960– CTFT–39
   Earlier sketches in CTFT–7, 18
Aaron, Caroline 1952– CTFT–71
   Earlier sketches in CTFT–22, 32
Aaron, Paul CTFT–15
Aarons, Alexander A. ?–1943 .... WWasWT
Aarons, Alfred E. ?–1936 .... WWasWT
Abady, Caroline Sidney
   See .... Aaron, Caroline
Abady, Josephine R. 1949–....................... CTFT–4
Abarbanell, Lina 1880–1963 .... WWasWT
Abba, Marta 1907–1988....................... WWasWT
Abbas, Hector 1884–1942.................... WWasWT
Abbati, Stefano CTFT–32
Abbensetts, Michael 1938– CTFT–13
   Earlier sketches in CTFT–6; WWT–17
Abbot, Rick
   See.. Sharkey, Jack
Abbott, Bruce 1954– CTFT–64
   Earlier sketch in CTFT–29
Abbott, Bud 1895(?)–1974...................... CTFT–16
Abbott, Chris CTFT–56
Abbott, George 1887–1995 .... CTFT–5
   Obituary in CTFT–14
   Earlier sketch in WWT–17
Abbott, John 1905– .... WWasWT
Abdul, Paula 1962(?)– CTFT–46
Abdul–Jabbar, Kareem 1947– CTFT–38
   Earlier sketch in CTFT–13
Abeille, Jean CTFT–34
Abel, Lionel 1910–.................................... CTFT–1
Abel, Walter 1898–1987 .... CTFT–5
   Earlier sketch in WWT–17
Abeles, Edward S. 1869–1919.............. WWasWT
Abeles, Sara
   See .... Gilbert, Sara
Abell, Tim 1968–.................................... CTFT–53
Abercrombie, Ian...................................... CTFT–38
Abercrombie, Lascelles 1881–1938....... WWasWT
Abernathy, Donzaleigh CTFT–41
Abingdon, W. L. 1859–1918 .... WWasWT
Abingdon, William 1888–1959 .... WWasWT
Ableman, Paul 1927–.............................. CTFT–11
Aborn, Milton 1864–?............................ WWasWT
Abraham, F. Murray 1939(?)– CTFT–72
   Earlier sketches in CTFT–1, 4, 22, 32
Abraham, Marc.. CTFT–41
Abraham, Paul ?–1960 .... WWasWT
Abrahams, A. E. 1873–1966.................. WWasWT

Abrahams, Doris Cole 1925– CTFT–5
   Earlier sketch in WWT–17
Abrahams, Doug CTFT–54
Abrahams, Jim 1944–.............................. CTFT–25
   Earlier sketches in CTFT–4, 15
Abrahams, Jon 1977–.............................. CTFT–72
   Earlier sketch in CTFT–34
Abrahamsen, Daniel Charles
   1952–... CTFT–1
Abrams, Celia
   See .... Raimi, Sam
Abrams, Gerald W. 1939–........................ CTFT–47
Abrams, Jeffrey 1966– CTFT–46
   Earlier sketch in CTFT–23
Abrams, Peter CTFT–43
Abravanel, Maurice 1903–1993 .... CTFT–1
   Obituary in CTFT–12
Abuba, Ernest 1947– CTFT–1
Acevedo, Kirk 1972–.............................. CTFT–64
   Earlier sketch in CTFT–29
Achard, Marcel 1900–1974 .... WWasWT
Acheson, James CTFT–71
   Earlier sketches in CTFT–12, 20, 32
Acheson, Mark CTFT–39
Achilles, Peter
   See .... Jarrico, Paul
Achurch, Janet 1864–1916 .... WWasWT
Acker, Amy 1976–.................................. CTFT–49
Ackerman, Andy 1957(?)– CTFT–40
Ackerman, Bettye 1928– CTFT–1
Ackerman, Chantal
   See................................... Akerman, Chantal
Ackerman, Harry S. 1912–1991 .... CTFT–3
   Obituary in CTFT–10
Ackerman, Leslie 1956– CTFT–33
   Earlier sketch in CTFT–7
Ackerman, Robert Allan 1945– CTFT–79
   Earlier sketches in CTFT–9, 35
Ackerman, Thomas E.............................. CTFT–65
Ackland, Joss 1928–.............................. CTFT–76
   Earlier sketches in CTFT–5, 34; WWT–17
Ackland, Rodney 1908– WWT–17
   Earlier sketch in WWasWT
Ackles, Jensen 1978– CTFT–68
Ackles, Kenneth V. 1916–1986 .... CTFT–4
Acklom, Rauff de Ryther Duan
   See .... Manners, David
Ackroyd, David 1940– CTFT–64
   Earlier sketches in CTFT–1, 12, 20, 29

Aco, Lucas
   See .... Lucas, Jonathan
Acovone, Jay 1955– CTFT–43
   Earlier sketch in CTFT–21
Acton–Bond, Acton .... WWasWT
Actor, Allen
   See .... Byron, Jeffrey
Adair, Jean ?–1953..................................... WWasWT
Adam, Ken 1921– CTFT–37
   Earlier sketches in CTFT–1, 12
Adam, Ronald 1896–1979 .... WWT–16
Ada–May
   See .... May, Ada
Adams, Amy.. CTFT–67
Adams, Brandon Quintin 1979–.............. CTFT–44
Adams, Brooke 1949– CTFT–53
   Earlier sketches in CTFT–2, 18
Adams, Casey
   See.. Showalter, Max
Adams, Dick 1889–................................ WWasWT
Adams, Don 1926– CTFT–33
   Earlier sketch in CTFT–3
Adams, Edie 1929(?)– CTFT–18
   Earlier sketches in CTFT–3; WWT–17
Adams, Enid–Raye 1973–........................ CTFT–76
Adams, Ida ?–1960 .... WWasWT
Adams, Jane 1965– CTFT–59
   Earlier sketch in CTFT–27
Adams, Jason 1963–................................ CTFT–63
Adams, Joey Lauren 1971(?)–................ CTFT–69
   Earlier sketches in CTFT–21, 31
Adams, Julie 1926– CTFT–43
   Earlier sketch in CTFT–1
Adams, Marla CTFT–42
Adams, Mason 1919–2005...................... CTFT–29
   Obituary in CTFT–64
   Earlier sketches in CTFT–1, 4, 18
Adams, Maud 1945–.............................. CTFT–33
   Earlier sketch in CTFT–6
Adams, Maude 1872–1953 .... WWasWT
Adams, Miriam 1907–........................... WWasWT
Adams, Molly CTFT–2
Adams, Polly CTFT–33
   Earlier sketch in CTFT–7
Adams, Robert .... WWasWT
Adams, Tony 1953–................................ CTFT–53
   Earlier sketches in CTFT–2, 10
Adams, W. Bridges
   See................................... Bridges–Adams, W.

Adams, Wayne 1930– CTFT–1
Adato, Perry Miller CTFT–11
Aday, Marvin Lee
    See .... Meat Loaf
Adcock, Danny 1948– CTFT–66
    Earlier sketch in CTFT–30
Addams, Dawn 1930–1985...................... CTFT–2
    Earlier sketch in WWT–17
Addie, Robert 1960– CTFT–28
Addinsell, Richard Stewart
    1904–1977 .... WWT–16
Addison, Anita W. CTFT–56
Addison, Carlotta 1849–1914............... WWasWT
Addison, John 1920–1998 .... CTFT–9
    Obituary in CTFT–24
Addison, Nancy 1948–............................ CTFT–31
Addison, Walter....................................... CTFT–68
Addy, Mark 1964(?)– CTFT–66
    Earlier sketch in CTFT–30
Addy, Wesley 1913–1996 .... CTFT–8
    Obituary in CTFT–16
    Earlier sketch in WWT–17
Ade, George 1866–1944 .... WWasWT
Adelman, Barry CTFT–46
Adelman, Sybil 1942– CTFT–3
Adelson, Gary 1954– CTFT–37
    Earlier sketch in CTFT–12
Aderer, Adolphe 1855–? .... WWasWT
Adjani, Isabelle 1955–............................ CTFT–28
    Earlier sketches in CTFT–3, 9, 16
Adler, Brian CTFT–40
Adler, Charles 1957–.............................. CTFT–79
    Earlier sketch in CTFT–36
Adler, Gilbert... CTFT–42
Adler, Jacob 1855–1962 .... WWasWT
Adler, Jerry 1929–.................................. CTFT–75
    Earlier sketches in CTFT–3, 33; WWT–17
Adler, Larry 1914– CTFT–4
Adler, Luther 1903–1984........................ CTFT–2
    Earlier sketch in WWT–17
Adler, Matt 1966–................................... CTFT–41
Adler, Ria Pavia
    See .... Pavia, Ria
Adler, Richard 1921–.............................. CTFT–14
    Earlier sketches in CTFT–4; WWT–17
Adler, Stella 1902– CTFT–3
    Earlier sketch in WWT–17
Adlon, Pamela Segall 1968– CTFT–73
Adlon, Percy 1935–................................ CTFT–33
    Earlier sketch in CTFT–8
Adonis, Frank CTFT–38
Adrian, Max 1903–................................ WWasWT
Adrienne, Jean 1905–............................ WWasWT
Adye, Oscar .... WWasWT
Affabee, Eric
    See .... Stine, R. L.
Affleck, Ben 1972–................................. CTFT–69
    Earlier sketches in CTFT–20, 31
Affleck, Casey 1975–.............................. CTFT–55
    Earlier sketch in CTFT–26
Agar, Dan 1881–1947 .... WWasWT
Agar, John 1921–2002............................ CTFT–43
    Earlier sketch in CTFT–8
Agate, May 1892– .... WWasWT
Agena, Keiko 1973–................................ CTFT–73
Ager, Nikita CTFT–73
Aghayan, Ray 1934– CTFT–53
    Earlier sketch in CTFT–11
Aguilar, George CTFT–42
Agut, Alicia CTFT–34
Agutter, Jenny 1952– CTFT–64
    Earlier sketches in CTFT–2, 18, 29
Ahern, Lloyd II 1942– CTFT–65

Aherne, Brian 1902–1986 .... WWasWT
Ahl, Kennet
    See .... Follows, Megan
Ahlander, Thecla Ottilia 1855–? .... WWasWT
Ahlers, Anny 1906–1933 .... WWasWT
Aidem, Betsy 1957– CTFT–72
    Earlier sketches in CTFT–3, 33
Aidman, Betty Linton CTFT–1
Aidman, Charles 1925–1993 .... CTFT–1
    Obituary in CTFT–12
Aiello, Danny 1933–............................... CTFT–70
    Earlier sketches in CTFT–5, 12, 21, 31
Aiello, Rick 1958–.................................. CTFT–71
Aiken, Liam 1990–.................................. CTFT–66
    Earlier sketch in CTFT–30
Aiken, Phil
    See.. Akin, Philip
Ailey, Alvin 1931–1989 .... CTFT–11
    Earlier sketch in CTFT–1
Aimee, Anouk 1932(?)– CTFT–64
    Earlier sketches in CTFT–2, 9, 18, 29
Ainley, Henry 1879–1967 .... WWasWT
Aitken, Maria 1945–............................... CTFT–13
    Earlier sketches in CTFT–4; WWT–17
Akalaitis, JoAnne 1937–.......................... CTFT–20
    Earlier sketches in CTFT–5, 12; WWT–17
Akayama, Dennis CTFT–49
Akbar, Tami
    See .... Roman, Tami
Aked, Muriel 1887–1955....................... WWasWT
Akerlind, Christopher CTFT–52
Akerman, Chantal 1950–......................... CTFT–46
    Earlier sketch in CTFT–23
Akerman, Jeremy 1942– CTFT–75
Akerman, Malin 1978–............................ CTFT–78
Akers, Karen 1945–................................ CTFT–39
    Earlier sketch in CTFT–4
Akin, Philip CTFT–41
Akins, Claude 1926–1994 .... CTFT–7
    Obituary in CTFT–12
    Earlier sketch in CTFT–2
Alaimo, Marc 1942–............................... CTFT–39
Alan, Devon 1991–................................. CTFT–68
Alan, Jane 1960–.................................... CTFT–74
Alan, Lori CTFT–49
Alanis
    See.................................... Morissette, Alanis
Alaskey, Joe CTFT–36
Alazraqui, Carlos 1963(?)– CTFT–40
Alba, Jessica 1981– CTFT–55
    Earlier sketch in CTFT–26
Albanese, Antonio 1964–........................ CTFT–34
Albanesi, Meggie (Margherita)
    1899–1923 .... WWasWT
Albee, Edward 1928–............................. CTFT–49
    Earlier sketches in CTFT–4, 14; WWT–17
Alberghetti, Anna Maria 1936– CTFT–20
Albert, Allan 1945–............................... WWT–17
Albert, Ben 1876–? .... WWasWT
Albert, Eddie 1908(?)– CTFT–40
    Earlier sketches in CTFT–2, 8, 18; WWT–17
Albert, Edward 1951–2006..................... CTFT–66
    Obituary in CTFT–73
    Earlier sketches in CTFT–1, 7, 18, 30
Albert, William 1863–? .... WWasWT
Albert–Lambert, Raphael 1865–? .... WWasWT
Albertson, Jack ?–1981 .... WWT–17
Albery, Bronson 1881–1971 .... WWasWT
Albery, Donald 1914–1988 .... CTFT–7
    Earlier sketch in WWT–17
Albery, Ian Bronson 1936–..................... WWT–17
Albright, Hardie 1903–......................... WWasWT
Alcala, Felix Enriquez............................. CTFT–56

Alcivar, Bob.. CTFT–12
Alcott, John 1931–1986 .... CTFT–28
    Earlier sketch in CTFT–23
Alda, Alan 1936–.................................... CTFT–66
    Earlier sketches in CTFT–1, 3, 10, 17, 30;
    WWT–17
Alda, Robert 1914–1986 .... CTFT–3
    Earlier sketch in WWT–17
Alda, Rutanya 1942(?)– CTFT–64
    Earlier sketches in CTFT–4, 18, 20
Alden, Hortense 1903–......................... WWasWT
Alden, Norman 1924–............................ CTFT–53
Alder, Eugene
    See .... Hackman, Gene
Alderson, Clifton 1864–1930................ WWasWT
Alderton, John 1940– CTFT–33
    Earlier sketches CTFT–5; in WWT–17
Aldin, Arthur 1872–? .... WWasWT
Aldon, Pamela Segall 1968– CTFT–73
    Earlier sketch in CTFT–38
Aldredge, Denny
    See .... Aldredge, Theoni V.
Aldredge, Theoni V. 1932–...................... CTFT–38
    Earlier sketches in CTFT–1, 11, 4; WWT–17
Aldredge, Tom 1928–.............................. CTFT–79
    Earlier sketches in CTFT–1, 9, 36
Aldrich, Charles T. 1872–?.................... WWasWT
Aldrich, Janet 1956–................................ CTFT–7
Aldrich, Rhonda CTFT–78
Aldrich, Richard 1902–1986 .... CTFT–3
    Earlier sketch in WWasWT
Aldrich, Robert 1918–1983 .... CTFT–2
Aldrich, Sarah 1975–.............................. CTFT–67
    Earlier sketch in CTFT–30
Aldridge, Michael 1920–1994 .... CTFT–3
    Obituary in CTFT–12
    Earlier sketch in WWT–17
Aldridge, Theoni V.
    See .... Aldredge, Theoni V.
Alea, Tomas Gutierrez 1928–1996 .... CTFT–25
Aleandri, Emelise.................................... CTFT–44
    Earlier sketch in CTFT–2
Aleandro, Norma 1936–.......................... CTFT–35
    Earlier sketch in CTFT–9
Alekan, Henri 1909–.............................. CTFT–13
Aleksander, Grant 1959–........................ CTFT–62
Aletter, Frank 1926–................................ CTFT–1
Alexander, Barbara Lee
    See .... Niven, Barbara
Alexander, Bill 1948– CTFT–11
    Earlier sketch in WWT–17
Alexander, Brett CTFT–48
Alexander, C. K. 1923–......................... WWT–17
Alexander, Denise 1939–........................ CTFT–31
Alexander, Erika 1969–.......................... CTFT–58
    Earlier sketches in CTFT–17, 27
Alexander, Flex....................................... CTFT–43
Alexander, George 1858–1918............. WWasWT
Alexander, Jace 1964–............................ CTFT–79
    Earlier sketch in CTFT–36
Alexander, Jane 1939–........................... CTFT–64
    Earlier sketches in CTFT–1, 4, 18, 29;
    WWT–17
Alexander, Janet ?–1961 .... WWasWT
Alexander, Jason 1959–.......................... CTFT–52
    Earlier sketches in CTFT–1, 8, 15, 25
Alexander, John CTFT–42
Alexander, John 1897– WWT–16
Alexander, Katherine 1901–................. WWasWT
Alexander, Kathleen................................ WWT–13
Alexander, Khandi 1957–........................ CTFT–46
    Earlier sketch in CTFT–23
Alexander, Lawrence 1939– CTFT–12

Alexander, Michael
    See .... Ballhaus, Michael
Alexander, Muriel 1898– .... WWasWT
Alexander, Robert A. 1929– CTFT–2
Alexander, Scott.................................. CTFT–29
Alexander, Terence 1923– CTFT–6
    Earlier sketch in WWT–17
Alexander, Terry CTFT–32
Alexandre, Rene 1885–1946 .... WWasWT
Alexi–Malle, Adam 1964– CTFT–64
    Earlier sketch in CTFT–29
Alfonso, Kristian 1964– CTFT–38
Ali, Tatyana 1979– CTFT–38
Alice, Mary 1941– CTFT–74
    Earlier sketches in CTFT–6, 33
Alison, Dorothy 1925– CTFT–1
Allam, Roger 1953– CTFT–72
    Earlier sketch in CTFT–32
Allan, Elizabeth 1910–1990 .... WWT–14
Allan, Jed 1937– CTFT–57
Allan, John B.
    See .... Westlake, Donald E.
Allan, Maud...................................... WWasWT
Allandale, Fred 1872–? .... WWasWT
Allen, A. Hylton 1879–? .... WWasWT
Allen, Adrienne WWT–14
Allen, Billie CTFT–1
Allen, Bob "Tex"
    See .... Allen, Robert
Allen, Byron 1961– CTFT–11
Allen, Chad 1974– CTFT–57
    Earlier sketches in CTFT–17, 27
Allen, Charles Leslie 1830–1917 .... WWasWT
Allen, Chesney 1896– .... WWasWT
Allen, Corey 1934– CTFT–8
Allen, Debbie 1950– CTFT–46
    Earlier sketches in CTFT–6, 13, 23
Allen, Dede 1924(?)– CTFT–53
    Earlier sketch in CTFT–9
Allen, Elizabeth 1934– CTFT–8
    Earlier sketch in WWT–17
Allen, Elizabeth Anne 1979– CTFT–73
Allen, Frank 1851–? .... WWasWT
Allen, Fred 1894–1956 .... CTFT–21
Allen, H. Marsh WWT–6
Allen, Irwin 1916–1991 .... CTFT–12
Allen, Jack 1907– WWT–17
Allen, Jay Presson 1922– CTFT–7
    Earlier sketch in CTFT–1
Allen, Jayne Meadows
    See .... Meadows, Jayne
Allen, Jed
    See.................................... Allan, Jed
Allen, Jeff
    See.................................... Allin, Jeff
Allen, Jo Harvey 1943(?)– CTFT–32
Allen, Joan 1956– CTFT–64
    Earlier sketches in CTFT–7, 19, 29
Allen, John Piers 1912– WWT–17
Allen, Jonelle 1944– CTFT–39
    Earlier sketch in CTFT–7
Allen, Karen 1951– CTFT–44
    Earlier sketches in CTFT–1, 4, 15
Allen, Kelcey 1875–1951 .... WWasWT
Allen, Krista 1971(?)– CTFT–79
    Earlier sketch in CTFT–36
Allen, Laura 1974– CTFT–68
Allen, Mel 1913– CTFT–15
Allen, Nancy 1950– CTFT–64
    Earlier sketches in CTFT–2, 5, 18, 29
Allen, Parry
    See .... Shen, Parry

Allen, Patrick 1927– CTFT–24
    Earlier sketch in WWT–17
Allen, Penelope CTFT–64
    Earlier sketches in CTFT–4, 20, 29
Allen, Peter 1944–1992 .... CTFT–9
    Obituary in CTFT–11
Allen, Phillip R. 1939– CTFT–22
    Earlier sketch in CTFT–11
Allen, Phylicia
    See .... Rashad, Phylicia
Allen, Rae 1926– CTFT–44
    Earlier sketch in WWT–17
Allen, Ralph G. 1934– CTFT–11
    Earlier sketch in WWT–17
Allen, Robert 1906–1998 .... CTFT–4
    Obituary in CTFT–32
Allen, Roland
    See .... Ayckbourn, Alan
Allen, Ron CTFT–43
Allen, Rosalind CTFT–60
Allen, Sage CTFT–34
Allen, Sheila 1932– CTFT–44
    Earlier sketch in WWT–17
Allen, Steve 1921– CTFT–25
    Earlier sketches in CTFT–4, 15
Allen, Tim 1953– CTFT–72
    Earlier sketches in CTFT–12, 21, 32
Allen, Todd CTFT–63
Allen, Vera 1897– CTFT–1
    Earlier sketch in WWasWT
Allen, Viola 1869–1948 .... WWasWT
Allen, Woody 1935– CTFT–51
    Earlier sketches in CTFT–1, 8, 15, 25;
    WWT–17
Allenby, Frank 1898–1953..................... WWasWT
Allenby, Peggy 1905–1967 .... WWasWT
Allen–Moritt, Krista
    See .... Allen, Krista
Allensworth, Carl 1908– CTFT–6
Allers, Franz 1906–1995 .... CTFT–1
    Obituary in CTFT–14
Alley, Kirstie 1955– CTFT–57
    Earlier sketches in CTFT–10, 17, 27
    Brief Entry in CTFT–5
Alleyne, John CTFT–15
Allgood, Sara 1883–1950 .... WWasWT
Allik, Vera Viiu CTFT–6
Allin, Jeff CTFT–57
Allinson, Michael WWT–1
Allison, Nancy 1954– CTFT–4
Allister, Claud 1891–1967 .... WWasWT
Allmon, Clinton 1941– CTFT–1
Allodi, James CTFT–68
Allport, Christopher CTFT–36
Allwine, Wayne CTFT–42
Allyson, June 1917–2006 .... CTFT–46
    Obituary in CTFT–72
Allman, Betsy CTFT–48
Almberg, John 1940– CTFT–2
Almendros, Nestor 1930–1992 .... CTFT–5
    Obituary in CTFT–10
Almodovar, Pedro 1951– CTFT–10
Almquist, Gregg 1948– CTFT–42
    Earlier sketches in CTFT–4, 20
Alonso, Johnny CTFT–62
Alonso, Laz CTFT–74
Alonso, Maria Conchita 1957– CTFT–48
    Earlier sketches in CTFT–7, 14, 24
Alonzo, John A. 1934– CTFT–10
Alpar, Gitta 1900– .... WWasWT
Alper, Jonathan 1950– CTFT–5
    Earlier sketch in WWT–17
Alswang, Ralph 1916–1979 .... WWT–17

Alt, Carol 1960– CTFT–38
    Earlier sketch in CTFT–14
Alt, James
    See.................................... Fitzpatrick, Jim
Alt, Natalie .... WWasWT
Alter, Lori Anne CTFT–78
Altman, Bruce CTFT–70
    Earlier sketches in CTFT–20, 31
Altman, Jeff 1951– CTFT–38
    Earlier sketch in CTFT–14
Altman, Robert 1925– CTFT–46
    Earlier sketches in CTFT–2, 7, 14, 23
Altman, Ruth .... WWasWT
Alton, John 1901–1996 .... CTFT–26
Alvarado, Angela CTFT–67
    Earlier sketch in CTFT–30
Alvarado, Trini 1967– CTFT–53
    Earlier sketches in CTFT–7, 18
Alvarez, George................................ CTFT–60
Alvin, John 1917– CTFT–9
Alzado, Lyle 1949– CTFT–8
Amalric, Mathieu 1965– CTFT–32
Amandes, Tom 1959– CTFT–63
Amanpour, Christiane 1958– CTFT–74
Amante, James
    See .... Band, Charles
Amante, Robert
    See .... Band, Charles
Amato, Mark 1965– CTFT–54
Ambient, Mark 1860–1937................... WWasWT
Ambrose, David 1943– CTFT–33
    Earlier sketches in CTFT–1, 5
Ambrose, Lauren 1978– CTFT–60
Ambrose, Tangie............................... CTFT–68
Ambrosone, John CTFT–53
Ambuehl, Cindy 1965– CTFT–59
Ameche, Don 1908–1993 .... CTFT–7
    Obituary in CTFT–12
    Earlier sketches in CTFT–2; WWT–17
Amelio, Gianni 1945– CTFT–15
Amenabar, Alejandro 1972– CTFT–38
Amendola, Tony CTFT–38
Ames, Florenz 1884–? .... WWasWT
Ames, Gerald 1881–1933 .... WWasWT
Ames, Leon 1901– .... WWasWT
Ames, Preston 1905–1983 .... CTFT–10
Ames, Robert 1893–1931 .... WWasWT
Ames, Rosemary 1906– .... WWasWT
Ames, Winthrop 1871–1937 .... WWasWT
Ami, Namon
    See.. Bercovici, Luca
Amic, Henri 1853–? .... WWasWT
Amick, Madchen 1970– CTFT–48
    Earlier sketches in CTFT–14, 24
Amiel, Denys 1884–? .... WWasWT
Amiel, Jon 1948– CTFT–43
    Earlier sketches in CTFT–12, 21
Amis, Suzy 1962(?)– CTFT–23
    Earlier sketch in CTFT–13
Amkraut, Alynne 1953– CTFT–11
Amos, John 1939(?)– CTFT–37
    Earlier sketches in CTFT–4, 13
Amos, Keith 1962–1998........................ CTFT–30
Amram, David 1930– CTFT–43
    Earlier sketch in CTFT–1
Amritraj, Ashok CTFT–76
Amsterdam, Morey 1914(?)–1996............. CTFT–9
    Obituary in CTFT–16
Ana–Alicia 1956(?)– CTFT–18
    Earlier sketch in CTFT–8
Anapau, Kristina 1979– CTFT–60
Anchia, Juan Ruiz 1949– CTFT–60
    Earlier sketch in CTFT–28

Ancier, Garth 1958(?)– CTFT–14
Anders, Allison 1954– CTFT–39
  Earlier sketch in CTFT–16
Anders, Glenn 1890– .... WWasWT
Anderson, Andy 1947– CTFT–69
Anderson, Anthony 1970– CTFT–68
  Earlier sketch in CTFT–30
Anderson, Audrey Marie CTFT–76
Anderson, Bob 1922– CTFT–46
Anderson, Brad 1964– CTFT–68
  Earlier sketch in CTFT–30
Anderson, Brent CTFT–57
Anderson, Chow
  See .... Chow Yun–Fat
Anderson, Craig CTFT–1
Anderson, D. C. CTFT–60
Anderson, Daphne 1922– WWT–17
Anderson, Daryl 1951– CTFT–69
Anderson, Dion CTFT–46
Anderson, Donna 1925– CTFT–11
Anderson, Eddie "Rochester"
  1905–1977 .... CTFT–22
Anderson, Erich CTFT–43
Anderson, Gillian 1968– CTFT–46
  Earlier sketches in CTFT–14, 23
Anderson, Gillian Bunshaft
  1943– CTFT–13
Anderson, Harry 1952– CTFT–47
  Earlier sketches in CTFT–6, 13, 23
Anderson, Haskell V. III 1942(?)– CTFT–74
  Earlier sketches in CTFT–4, 33
Anderson, J. Grant 1897– WWT–17
Anderson, Jamie CTFT–56
Anderson, Jo 1958– CTFT–52
Anderson, John 1922– CTFT–9
Anderson, John (Hargis) 1896–1943 ...... WWasWT
Anderson, John Murray 1886–1954 .... WWasWT
Anderson, Judith 1898–1992 .... CTFT–4
  Obituary in CTFT–10
  Earlier sketch in WWT–17
Anderson, Kevin 1960– CTFT–70
  Earlier sketches in CTFT–12, 21, 31
Anderson, Laurie 1947– CTFT–30
  Earlier sketches in CTFT–8, 18
Anderson, Lawrence 1893–1939 .... WWasWT
Anderson, Lindsay 1923–1994 .... CTFT–13
  Earlier sketches in CTFT–2, 6
Anderson, Loni 1945(?)– CTFT–64
  Earlier sketches in CTFT–2, 9, 18, 29
Anderson, Louie 1953– CTFT–43
  Earlier sketches in CTFT–12, 21
Anderson, Marina
  See .... D'Este, Coco
Anderson, Mary 1859–1940 .... WWasWT
Anderson, Maxwell 1888–1959 .... WWasWT
Anderson, Melissa Sue 1962– CTFT–36
  Earlier sketch in CTFT–10
  Brief Entry in CTFT–2
Anderson, Melody CTFT–4
Anderson, Michael 1920– CTFT–27
  Earlier sketch in CTFT–8
Anderson, Michael J. 1953– CTFT–58
Anderson, Michael, Jr. 1943– CTFT–33
  Earlier sketch in CTFT–6
Anderson, Mitchell 1961– CTFT–53
Anderson, Nathan 1969– CTFT–77
Anderson, Neil CTFT–60
Anderson, Pamela 1967– CTFT–41
  Earlier sketch in CTFT–20
Anderson, Paul S. W. 1965(?)– CTFT–63
Anderson, Paul Thomas 1970– CTFT–43
  Earlier sketch in CTFT–21
Anderson, Peter 1942– CTFT–11

Anderson, Richard 1926– CTFT–39
  Earlier sketch in CTFT–1, 17
Anderson, Richard Dean 1950– CTFT–53
  Earlier sketches in CTFT–8, 15, 25
Anderson, Robert Woodruff
  1917– WWT–17
Anderson, Rona 1928– WWT–17
Anderson, Sam CTFT–43
  Earlier sketch in CTFT–21
Anderson, Sarah Pia 1952– CTFT–37
  Earlier sketch in CTFT–12
Anderson, Stanley CTFT–38
Anderson, Steven CTFT–38
Anderson, Tami
  See .... Roman, Tami
Anderson, Wes 1969– CTFT–69
  Earlier sketch in CTFT–30
Anderson, William
  See .... West, Adam
Andersson, Bibi 1935– CTFT–33
  Earlier sketch in CTFT–7
Andersson, Harriet 1932– CTFT–44
  Earlier sketch in CTFT–8
Andoh, Adjoa CTFT–38
Andreeff, Starr 1965(?)– CTFT–31
Andreeva–Babakhan, Anna Misaakovna
  1923– .... WWasWT
Andrei, Damir CTFT–78
Andress, Ursula 1936– CTFT–39
  Earlier sketches in CTFT–3, 18
Andreva, Stella
  See .... Browne, Stella
Andrew, Leo 1957– CTFT–8
Andrews, Ann 1895– .... WWasWT
Andrews, Anthony 1948– CTFT–39
  Earlier sketches in CTFT–7, 18
Andrews, Dana 1909–1992 .... CTFT–4
  Obituary in CTFT–11
  Earlier sketch in WWT–17
Andrews, David 1952– CTFT–36
  Earlier sketch in CTFT–10
Andrews, Dick
  See .... Dick, Andy
Andrews, Eamonn 1922–1987 .... CTFT–2
Andrews, George Lee 1942– CTFT–1
Andrews, Giuseppe 1979– CTFT–51
Andrews, Harry 1911–1989 .... CTFT–7
  Earlier sketches in CTFT–2; WWT–17
Andrews, Jay
  See .... Wynorski, Jim
Andrews, Julie 1935– CTFT–38
  Earlier sketches in CTFT–1, 7, 14; WWasWT
Andrews, Maidie .... WWasWT
Andrews, Nancy 1924–1989 .... CTFT–8
  Earlier sketch in WWT–17
Andrews, Naveen 1969– CTFT–64
  Earlier sketches in CTFT–19, 29
Andrews, Peter
  See .... Soderbergh, Steven
Andrews, Real 1963– CTFT–23
Andrews, Robert 1895– .... WWasWT
Andrews, Tige CTFT–3
Andrews, Tod 1920– .... WWasWT
Andriole, David CTFT–71
Andros, Douglas 1931– CTFT–1
Angarano, Michael 1987– CTFT–78
Angel, Heather 1909–1986 .... CTFT–4
  Earlier sketch in WWasWT
Angel, Jack 1931(?)– CTFT–39
Angel, Vanessa 1963– CTFT–39
Angela, June 1959– CTFT–55
  Earlier sketch in CTFT–11

Angelopoulos, Theo 1936(?)– CTFT–22
  Earlier sketch in CTFT–11
Angelou, Maya 1928– CTFT–39
  Earlier sketches in CTFT–10, 17
Angelus, Muriel 1909– .... WWasWT
Angers, Avril 1922– CTFT–14
  Earlier sketch in WWT–17
Angie
  See .... Featherstone, Angela
Anglade, Jean–Hugues 1955– CTFT–68
  Earlier sketch in CTFT–30
Angle, Kurt 1968– CTFT–43
Anglim, Philip 1953– CTFT–41
  Earlier sketches in CTFT–20; WWT–17,
  CTFT–4
Anglin, Margaret 1876–1958 .... WWasWT
Anhalt, Edward 1914– CTFT–10
Anholt, Christien 1971– CTFT–40
Aniston, Jennifer 1969– CTFT–53
  Earlier sketches in CTFT–15, 25
Aniston, John 1937– CTFT–58
  Earlier sketches in CTFT–17, 27
Anka, Paul 1941– CTFT–60
Annabella 1912– .... WWasWT
Annakin, Ken 1914– CTFT–11
Annals, Michael 1938– WWT–17
Annaud, Jean–Jacques 1943– CTFT–37
  Earlier sketches in CTFT–3, 13
Annis, Francesca 1944(?)– CTFT–51
  Earlier sketches in CTFT–8, 15, 25
Ann-Margret 1941– CTFT–60
  Earlier sketches in CTFT–3, 9, 16, 28
Annunzio, Gabriele d' 1863–1938 .... WWasWT
Anouilh, Jean 1910–1987 .... CTFT–5
  Earlier sketch in WWT–17
Anouk
  See .... Aimee, Anouk
Ansara, Michael 1927(?)– CTFT–33
  Earlier sketch in CTFT–3
Ansell, John 1874–1948 .... WWasWT
Anselmo, Tony CTFT–37
Ansen, David 1945– CTFT–10
Ansley, Zachary CTFT–34
Anson, A. E. 1879–1936 .... WWasWT
Anson, George William 1847–1920 ...... WWasWT
Anspach, Susan 1939(?)– CTFT–53
  Earlier sketches in CTFT–3, 18
Anspacher, Louis K. 1878–1947 .... WWasWT
Anspaugh, David 1946– CTFT–39
  Earlier sketches in CTFT–8, 15
Anstey, Edgar 1907–1987 .... CTFT–4
  Obituary in CTFT–5
Anstey, F. 1856–1934 .... WWasWT
Anstruther, Harold .... WWasWT
Ant, Adam 1954– CTFT–38
  Earlier sketch in CTFT–14
Anthony, Joseph 1912– WWT–17
Anthony, Lysette 1963– CTFT–36
  Earlier sketch in CTFT–10
Anthony, Marc 1968– CTFT–66
  Earlier sketch in CTFT–30
Anthony, Michael 1920– CTFT–5
Antille, Lisa CTFT–3
Antin, Steve 1956– CTFT–36
Antoine, Andre 1857–1943 .... WWasWT
Anton, George CTFT–75
  Earlier sketch in CTFT–34
Anton, Susan 1950(?)– CTFT–29
  Earlier sketches in CTFT–3, 18
  Brief Entry in CTFT–2
Antona–Traversi, Camillo
  1857–1926 .... WWasWT

Antona–Traversi, Giannino
1860–1934........................... WWasWT
Antonio, Lou 1934– CTFT–43
Earlier sketch in CTFT–8
Antonioni, Michelangelo 1912(?)–........... CTFT–38
Earlier sketches in CTFT–6, 13
Antony, Hilda 1886–?.......................... WWasWT
Antoon, A. J. 1944–1992 .... CTFT–5
Obituary in CTFT–10
Earlier sketch in WWT–17
Antrobus, John 1933–........................... WWT–17
Anwar, Gabrielle 1970– CTFT–45
Earlier sketches in CTFT–13, 23
Aoki, Brenda Jean 1953–........................ CTFT–20
Apatow, Judd 1967–.............................. CTFT–72
Earlier sketch in CTFT–32
Apicella, John.................................... CTFT–38
Appel, Peter 1959–............................... CTFT–73
Earlier sketch in CTFT–32
Appel, Richard 1964– CTFT–25
Apple, Gary 1955–.................................. CTFT–3
Applebaum, Gertrude H. CTFT–1
Appleby, Dorothy 1908–1990 .... WWasWT
Appleby, Shiri 1978–.............................. CTFT–60
Applegate, Christina 1971– CTFT–45
Earlier sketches in CTFT–10, 17
Aprea, John 1941– CTFT–38
Apsion, Annabelle 1963–........................ CTFT–77
Earlier sketch in CTFT–34
Apted, Michael 1941–............................ CTFT–70
Earlier sketches in CTFT–1, 5, 12, 21, 31
Aquino, Amy CTFT–43
Arad, Avi 1948–.................................... CTFT–46
Araki, Gregg 1959–............................... CTFT–25
Arana, Tomas 1959–.............................. CTFT–72
Earlier sketch in CTFT–32
Aranha, Ray 1939–................................ CTFT–34
Earlier sketch in CTFT–3
Arau, Alfonso 1932– CTFT–50
Arbeit, Herman O. 1925– CTFT–18
Earlier sketch in CTFT–2
Arbenina, Stella 1887– .... WWasWT
Arbuckle, Maclyn 1866–1931 .... WWasWT
Arbus, Allan 1918– CTFT–6
Earlier sketch in CTFT–1
Arcand, Denys 1941–............................. CTFT–36
Earlier sketch in CTFT–10
Arcand, Nathaniel 1971– CTFT–63
Arce, Maria 1979–................................. CTFT–78
Arcenas, Loy 1953(?)–........................... CTFT–43
Earlier sketch in CTFT–9
Archer, Anne 1947– CTFT–47
Earlier sketches in CTFT–6, 13, 23
Archer, Beverly 1948–............................ CTFT–46
Archer, Joe .... WWasWT
Archer, John 1915–.............................. WWasWT
Archer, John 1953–................................. CTFT–2
Archer, Lee
See.. Ellison, Harlan
Archer, William 1856–1924.................. WWasWT
Archibald, Douglas 1919–....................... CTFT–11
Arcieri, Leila 1973–................................ CTFT–78
Ardant, Fanny 1949–............................. CTFT–47
Earlier sketch in CTFT–23
Arden, Edwin Hunter Pendleton
1864–1918.................................. WWasWT
Arden, Eve 1912–1990............................ CTFT–3
Earlier sketch in WWT–17
Arden, John 1930–............................... WWT–17
Ardolino, Emile 1943–1993 .... CTFT–10
Obituary in CTFT–12
Ardrey, Robert 1908–........................... WWasWT
Arell, Sherry H. 1950– CTFT–3

Arenal, Julie................................. CTFT–43
Earlier sketch in CTFT–2
Arenberg, Lee 1962–............................. CTFT–42
Aresco, Joey CTFT–60
Argarno, Michael
See .... Angarano, Michael
Argent, Edward 1931–........................... WWT–17
Argentina .... WWasWT
Argento, Asia 1975–.............................. CTFT–68
Argento, Dario 1940–............................ CTFT–33
Earlier sketch in CTFT–8
Argenziano, Carmen 1943–..................... CTFT–51
Earlier sketches in CTFT–8, 15, 25
Argo, Victor 1934–................................ CTFT–34
Argyle, Pearl 1910– .... WWasWT
Arias, Silvana 1977–.............................. CTFT–75
Arias, Yancey 1971–.............................. CTFT–74
Ariola, Julie CTFT–56
Aris, Ben 1937–.................................... CTFT–19
Earlier sketch in CTFT–3
Arkell, Elizabeth .... WWasWT
Arkell, Reginald 1882–1959 .... WWasWT
Arkin, Adam 1957–............................... CTFT–48
Earlier sketches in CTFT–7, 14, 24
Arkin, Alan 1934–................................. CTFT–39
Earlier sketches in CTFT–2, 11, 18; WWT–17
Arkin, Anthony 1967–........................... CTFT–48
Arkoff, Lou CTFT–37
Arkoff, Samuel Z. 1918– CTFT–3
Arkush, Allan 1948–.............................. CTFT–43
Earlier sketches in CTFT–13, 22
Arledge, Roone 1931–............................ CTFT–43
Earlier sketch in CTFT–4
Arlen, Harold 1905–1986 .... WWT–17
Arlen, Michael 1895–1956 .... WWasWT
Arlen, Stephen 1913–.......................... WWasWT
Arling, Joyce 1911–............................. WWasWT
Arlington, Billy 1873–? .... WWasWT
Arliss, George 1868–1946 .... WWasWT
Armen, Rebecca 1957–............................ CTFT–2
Armenante, Jillian 1968–........................ CTFT–44
Armendariz, Pedro, Jr. 1940– CTFT–42
Armin, Robert 1952–............................. CTFT–44
Armitage, Frank
See....................................... Carpenter, John
Armitage, Richard ?–1986 .... CTFT–4
Armstrong, Alun 1946– CTFT–45
Armstrong, Anthony 1897–................... WWasWT
Armstrong, Barney 1870–?................... WWasWT
Armstrong, Bess 1953–.......................... CTFT–77
Earlier sketches in CTFT–6, 35
Armstrong, Curtis 1953–........................ CTFT–51
Earlier sketches in CTFT–8, 15, 25
Armstrong, Gillian 1950–....................... CTFT–18
Earlier sketch in CTFT–7
Armstrong, Jack 1964– CTFT–52
Armstrong, Paul 1869–1915 .... WWasWT
Armstrong, R. G. 1917–.......................... CTFT–44
Earlier sketch in CTFT–8
Armstrong, Robert 1896– .... WWasWT
Armstrong, Samaire 1980– CTFT–66
Armstrong, Su CTFT–60
Earlier sketch in CTFT–28
Armstrong, Vaughn CTFT–40
Armstrong, Vic 1946–............................ CTFT–60
Earlier sketch in CTFT–28
Armstrong, Will Steven 1930–1969 .... WWasWT
Armstrong, William CTFT–77
Earlier sketch in CTFT–34
Armstrong, William 1882–1952............. WWasWT
Arnatt, John 1917–.............................. WWT–17
Arnaud, Yvonne 1892–1958 .... WWasWT

Arnaz, Desi 1917–1986 .... CTFT–4
Earlier sketch in CTFT–3
Arnaz, Desi, Jr. 1953– CTFT–1
Arnaz, Lucie 1951–................................ CTFT–43
Earlier sketches in CTFT–1; WWT–17
Arndt, Denis 1939–............................... CTFT–52
Arness, James 1923– CTFT–18
Earlier sketch in CTFT–3
Arnett, Peter 1934–............................... CTFT–48
Earlier sketch in CTFT–11
Arnett, Will 1970–................................ CTFT–71
Arnette, Jeanetta 1954– CTFT–77
Earlier sketch in CTFT–34
Arney, Randall CTFT–76
Earlier sketch in CTFT–32
Arngrim, Stefan 1955–........................... CTFT–65
Arnold, Bill
See .... Arnold, William
Arnold, Bonnie CTFT–29
Arnold, Danny 1925–1995....................... CTFT–3
Obituary in CTFT–15
Arnold, David 1962–.............................. CTFT–64
Earlier sketch in CTFT–28
Arnold, Edward 1890–1956.................. WWasWT
Arnold, Franz 1878–1960.................... WWasWT
Arnold, Jeanne 1931–............................. CTFT–8
Arnold, Phyl ?–1941 .... WWasWT
Arnold, Roseanne
See.. Roseanne
Arnold, Tichina 1971–........................... CTFT–66
Earlier sketch in CTFT–17
Arnold, Tom ?–1969 .... WWasWT
Arnold, Tom 1947– CTFT–4
Earlier sketch in WWT–17
Arnold, Tom 1959– CTFT–71
Earlier sketches in CTFT–13, 22, 32
Arnold, Victor 1936–............................. CTFT–38
Arnold, William CTFT–64
Earlier sketch in CTFT–29
Arnott, James Fullarton 1914–1982 .... CTFT–4
Earlier sketch in WWT–17
Arnott, Mark 1950–.............................. CTFT–44
Earlier sketch in CTFT–5
Arnott, Peter 1936– CTFT–3
Aronofsky, Darren 1969–........................ CTFT–59
Earlier sketch in CTFT–27
Aronson, Boris 1900–1980..................... WWT–17
Aronstein, Martin 1936–.......................... CTFT–4
Earlier sketch in WWT–17
Arquette, Alexis 1969–.......................... CTFT–48
Earlier sketch in CTFT–23
Arquette, Courteney Cox
See............................ Cox, Courteney
Arquette, David 1971–........................... CTFT–49
Earlier sketch in CTFT–23
Arquette, Lewis 1935–........................... CTFT–28
Arquette, Patricia 1968–........................ CTFT–71
Earlier sketches in CTFT–13, 22, 32
Arquette, Richmond 1963–..................... CTFT–46
Arquette, Rosanna 1959– CTFT–57
Earlier sketches in CTFT–2, 6, 14, 27
Arrabal, Fernando 1932–....................... WWT–17
Arrambide, Mario 1953–.......................... CTFT–3
Arrley, Richmond
See....................................... Noonan, Tom
Arrowsmith, William 1924– CTFT–1
Arroyave, Karina 1969–.......................... CTFT–44
Arroyo, Danny CTFT–70
Arsenio
See .... Hall, Arsenio
Arthur, Beatrice 1923–........................... CTFT–72
Earlier sketches in CTFT–4, 20, 32; WWT–17

Cumulative Index

Arthur, Carol
  See.. DeLuise, Carol
Arthur, Daphne 1925–............................ WWasWT
Arthur, Jean 1905(?)–1991 .... CTFT–10
  Earlier sketch in WWasWT
Arthur, Julia 1869–1950........................ WWasWT
Arthur, Karen 1941– CTFT–36
  Earlier sketch in CTFT–10
Arthur, Paul 1859–1928.......................... WWasWT
Arthur, Robert ?–1929 .... WWasWT
Arthur, Robert 1909–1986 .... CTFT–4
Arthur, Syd
  See.. Kapelos, John
Arthur–Jones, Winifred WWT–6
Arthurs, George 1875–1944 .... WWasWT
Artus, Louis 1870–? .... WWasWT
Arundale, Grace (Kelly) .... WWasWT
Arundale, Sybil 1882–1965 .... WWasWT
Arundell, Dennis 1898–1936 .... WWasWT
Asade, Jim 1936– CTFT–2
Asano, Tadanobu 1973–......................... CTFT–77
  Earlier sketch in CTFT–34
Asara, Mike
  See....................................... Ansara, Michael
Ash, Gordon ?–1929 .... WWasWT
Ash, Leslie 1960– CTFT–77
  Earlier sketch in CTFT–34
Ash, Maie 1888–? .... WWasWT
Ash, William 1977–............................... CTFT–77
  Earlier sketch in CTFT–34
Ashanti 1980– CTFT–67
Ashbrook, Dana 1967– CTFT–72
Ashbrook, Daphne 1966– CTFT–44
Ashby, Hal 1936–1988............................. CTFT–6
Ashby, Harvey CTFT–22
  Earlier sketch in CTFT–4
Ashby, Linden 1960–.............................. CTFT–64
  Earlier sketches in CTFT–19, 29
Ashcroft, Peggy 1907–1991..................... CTFT–4
  Obituary in CTFT–10
  Earlier sketch in WWT–17
Ashe, Eve Brent
  See... Brent, Eve
Asher, Jane 1946–................................... CTFT–8
  Earlier sketches in CTFT–2; WWT–17
Asher, William 1919–............................... CTFT–9
Asherson, Renee 1920–.......................... CTFT–44
  Earlier sketch in WWT–17
Ashfield, Kate CTFT–71
  Earlier sketch in CTFT–32
Ashford, Rob 1959– CTFT–72
  Earlier sketch in CTFT–32
Ashford, Matthew 1960–......................... CTFT–52
Ashley, Alyssa
  See... Indigo
Ashley, Christopher 1964–..................... CTFT–50
Ashley, Elizabeth 1939– CTFT–78
  Earlier sketches in CTFT–1, 8, 35; WWT–17
Ashley, Heather
  See... Chase, Heather
Ashley, Iris 1909– .... WWasWT
Ashley, Katie
  See... Lynn, Sherry
Ashman, Howard 1950–1991 .... CTFT–12
  Obituary in CTFT–9
  Earlier sketch in CTFT–1
Ashmore, Aaron 1979– CTFT–66
Ashmore, Basil 1951– WWT–17
Ashmore, Peter 1916– .... WWasWT
Ashmore, Shawn 1979– CTFT–62
Ashton, Ellis 1919–................................. CTFT–4
  Earlier sketch in WWT–17
Ashton, Frederick 1906–......................... WWasWT

Ashton, John 1948–................................. CTFT–58
  Earlier sketches in CTFT–6, 27
Ashton–Griffiths, Roger 1957–................. CTFT–64
  Earlier sketch in CTFT–29
Ashwell, Lena 1872–1957 .... WWasWT
Askew, Desmond 1972–.......................... CTFT–64
  Earlier sketch in CTFT–29
Askew, Luke 1937– CTFT–55
  Earlier sketch in CTFT–26
Askey, Arthur Bowden 1900–................. WWT–17
Askin, Leon 1907– CTFT–33
  Earlier sketch in CTFT–2
Askin, Peter 1946– CTFT–5
Asner, Edward 1929–............................... CTFT–38
  Earlier sketches in CTFT–1, 6, 13
Asner, Jules 1968–.................................. CTFT–66
Aspen, Jennifer 1973– CTFT–53
Asquith, Anthony 1902–1968 .... WWasWT
Asquith, Ward CTFT–3
Assante, Armand 1949– CTFT–70
  Earlier sketches in CTFT–4, 11, 20, 31
Asseyev, Tamara CTFT–19
  Earlier sketch in CTFT–3
Astaire, Adele 1898–1981 .... WWasWT
Astaire, Fred 1899–1987 .... CTFT–3
  Obituary in CTFT–5
  Earlier sketch in WWasWT
Astin, John 1930–.................................... CTFT–43
  Earlier sketches in CTFT–6, 22
Astin, MacKenzie 1973– CTFT–72
  Earlier sketch in CTFT–22
Astin, Patty Duke
  See... Duke, Patty
Astin, Sean 1971– CTFT–72
  Earlier sketches in CTFT–13, 22, 32
Astley, John.. WWasWT
Astredo, Humbert Allen............................ CTFT–1
Atal, Henri
  See.. Attal, Henri
Atherton, Ted... CTFT–77
Atherton, William 1947–......................... CTFT–72
  Earlier sketches in CTFT–4, 21, 32; WWT–17
Athis, Alfred 1873–? .... WWasWT
Atienza, Edward 1924– WWT–17
Atkin, Harvy 1942– CTFT–52
Atkin, Nancy 1904– .... WWasWT
Atkins, Christopher 1961–...................... CTFT–72
  Earlier sketches in CTFT–5, 33
  Brief Entry in CTFT–2
Atkins, Eileen 1934–............................... CTFT–72
  Earlier sketches in CTFT–4, 11, 22, 32;
  WWT–17
Atkins, Essence 1972– CTFT–75
Atkins, Robert 1886–1972 .... WWasWT
Atkins, Tom 1935– CTFT–49
Atkinson, Barbara 1926–......................... CTFT–3
  Earlier sketch in WWT–17
Atkinson, David..................................... CTFT–69
Atkinson, Don 1940–............................... CTFT–7
Atkinson, Harry 1866–? .... WWasWT
Atkinson, (Justin) Brooks 1894–1984...... WWT–17
Atkinson, Rosalind 1900–1977.............. WWT–16
Atkinson, Rowan 1955– CTFT–57
  Earlier sketches in CTFT–10, 17, 27
Atlas (William Hedley Roberts)
  1864–? .... WWasWT
Atlee, Howard 1926–............................... CTFT–1
Atom, Jackie
  See .... Peacock, Trevor
Attal, Henri.. CTFT–39
Attanasio, Paul 1959– CTFT–62
  Earlier sketch in CTFT–28

Attenborough, Richard 1923– CTFT–51
  Earlier sketches in CTFT–1, 8, 15, 25;
  WWT–17
Atteridge, Harold R. 1886–1938........... WWasWT
Atterton, Edward...................................... CTFT–40
Attias, Daniel... CTFT–40
Attles, Joseph 1903–............................... CTFT–1
Atwater, Edith 1911–1986.................... WWasWT
Atwill, Lionel 1885–1946 .... WWasWT
Atwood, Colleen 1950–............................ CTFT–62
  Earlier sketch in CTFT–28
Auberjonois, Rene 1940–......................... CTFT–41
  Earlier sketches in CTFT–2, 8, 15; WWT–17
Aubrey, James 1947–.............................. CTFT–3
  Earlier sketch in WWT–17
Aubrey, Madge 1902–1970 .... WWasWT
Auden, W. H. 1907–1973 .... WWasWT
Audley, Maxine 1923– CTFT–6
  Earlier sketch in WWT–17
Audran, Stephane 1932–......................... CTFT–39
  Earlier sketches in CTFT–8, 15
Augarde, Adrienne ?–1913 .... WWasWT
Augarde, Amy 1868–1959...................... WWasWT
August, Bille 1948–................................. CTFT–38
  Earlier sketch in CTFT–14
August, John 1971–................................. CTFT–43
August, Pernilla 1958– CTFT–46
  Earlier sketch in CTFT–23
Augustus, Sherman CTFT–65
  Earlier sketch in CTFT–29
Aukin, David 1942–................................. CTFT–43
  Earlier sketch in WWT–17
Auletta, Robert 1940– CTFT–1
Aulisi, Joseph G....................................... CTFT–39
  Earlier sketches in CTFT–8, 15; WWT–17
Ault, Marie 1870–1951 .... WWasWT
Aumont, Jean–Pierre 1913(?)– CTFT–22
  Earlier sketches in CTFT–4; WWT–17
Aurness, James
  See... Arness, James
Auster, Paul 1947– CTFT–23
Austin, Alana 1982–................................ CTFT–57
Austin, Charles 1878–1944 .... WWasWT
Austin, Denise 1957–.............................. CTFT–36
Austin, Lyn 1922– CTFT–1
Austin, Ray 1932– CTFT–55
  Earlier sketch in CTFT–11
Austin, Robert... CTFT–38
Austin, Steve 1964–............................... CTFT–44
Austrian, Marjorie 1934–......................... CTFT–4
Auteuil, Daniel 1950–............................. CTFT–33
  Earlier sketch in CTFT–8
Autry, Alan 1952– CTFT–26
Autry, Gene 1907–1998 .... CTFT–21
  Obituary in CTFT–24
Avalon, Frankie 1940– CTFT–41
  Earlier sketches in CTFT–3, 19
Avalos, Luis 1946– CTFT–78
  Earlier sketches in CTFT–5, 35
Avari, Erick CTFT–38
Avary, Roger 1965– CTFT–66
  Earlier sketch in CTFT–30
Avedis, Howard CTFT–1
Averback, Hy 1920–1997....................... CTFT–6
  Obituary in CTFT–19
Avery, James 1948–............................... CTFT–40
Avery, Margaret CTFT–38
  Earlier sketches in CTFT–8, 15
Avery, Tex 1909–1980 .... CTFT–13
Avian, Bob 1937–.................................... CTFT–38
  Earlier sketch in CTFT–13
Avildsen, John G. 1935– CTFT–10
Aviles, Rick 1954–1995........................... CTFT–27

Avital, Mili 1972– CTFT–70
    Earlier sketches in CTFT–20, 31
Avnet, Jon 1949– CTFT–65
    Earlier sketches in CTFT–2, 11, 19, 29
Avni, Ran 1941– CTFT–1
Avril, Suzanne .... WWasWT
Axelrod, George 1922– CTFT–22
    Earlier sketch in CTFT–4
Axelrod, Jack 1930– CTFT–79
Axelrod, Robert 1949– CTFT–42
Axton, David
    See .... Koontz, Dean R.
Axton, Hoyt 1938– CTFT–18
    Earlier sketch in CTFT–3
Axworthy, Geoffrey 1923– WWT–17
Ayanna, Charlotte 1976– CTFT–60
Ayckbourn, Alan 1939– CTFT–21
    Earlier sketches in CTFT–4, 12; WWT–17
Aycox, Nicki Lynn 1975– CTFT–63
Ayer, Debbon CTFT–68
Ayer, Nat. D. ?–1952 .... WWasWT
Ayers, David H. 1924– CTFT–1
Ayers, Sam CTFT–71
Ayers–Allen, Phylicia
    See .... Rashad, Phylicia
Aykroyd, Dan 1952– CTFT–47
    Earlier sketches in CTFT–6, 13, 23
Aylesworth, Reiko 1972– CTFT–52
Ayliff, Henry Kiell ?–1949 .... WWasWT
Aylmer, Felix 1889–1964 .... WWasWT
Aylward, John 1947– CTFT–38
Aynesworth, Allan 1865–1959 .... WWasWT
Ayr, Michael 1953– CTFT–9
Ayre, Kristian 1977– CTFT–78
Ayres, Lew 1908–1996 .... CTFT–15
    Obituary in CTFT–16
    Earlier sketch in CTFT–3
Ayrton, Norman 1924– WWT–17
Ayrton, Randle 1869–1940 .... WWasWT
Azaria, Hank 1964– CTFT–72
    Earlier sketches in CTFT–20, 32
Azenberg, Emanuel 1934– CTFT–5
    Earlier sketch in WWT–17
Azizi, Anthony 1969(?)– CTFT–74
Aznavour, Charles 1924– CTFT–29
    Earlier sketches in CTFT–2, 19
Azzara, Candy 1945– CTFT–44
    Earlier sketch in CTFT–1
Azzopardi, Mario 1950– CTFT–79
    Earlier sketch in CTFT–36

B

Baaf, Mohsen Makhmal
    See .... Makhmalbaf, Mohsen
Babatunde, Obba 1951– CTFT–69
    Earlier sketches in CTFT–21, 31
Babcock, Barbara 1937– CTFT–39
    Earlier sketches in CTFT–6, 18
Babcock, Debra Lee 1956– CTFT–5
Babcock, Todd 1969– CTFT–56
Babe, Thomas 1941– CTFT–5
    Earlier sketch in WWT–17
Babenco, Hector 1946(?)– CTFT–38
    Earlier sketch in CTFT–6
Bacall, Lauren 1924– CTFT–57
    Earlier sketches in CTFT–1, 7, 14, 27
Bacall, Michael CTFT–56
Bacarella, Mike CTFT–38

Baccarin, Morena 1979– CTFT–79
Baccus, Stephen 1969– CTFT–1
Bach, Barbara CTFT–2
Bach, Catherine 1954– CTFT–41
    Earlier sketches in CTFT–5, 18
    Brief Entry in CTFT–2
Bach, Reginald 1886–1941 .... WWasWT
Bach, Sebastian 1968– CTFT–40
Bacharach, Burt 1928(?)– CTFT–64
    Earlier sketches in CTFT–3, 19, 29
Bachchan, Amitabh 1942– CTFT–58
    Earlier sketch in CTFT–27
Bachman, Richard
    See .... King, Stephen
Bachmann, Conrad CTFT–58
Bacic, Steve 1965– CTFT–65
Backus, Jim 1913–1989 .... CTFT–6
Backus, Richard 1945– CTFT–20
    Earlier sketches in CTFT–4; WWT–17
Baclanova, Olga 1899– .... WWasWT
Bacon, Frank 1864–1922 .... WWasWT
Bacon, Jane 1895– .... WWasWT
Bacon, Kevin 1958– CTFT–69
    Earlier sketches in CTFT–5, 12, 21, 31
    Brief Entry in CTFT–2
Bacon, Mai 1898– .... WWasWT
Bacon, Michael CTFT–69
Badalamenti, Angelo 1937– CTFT–79
    Earlier sketches in CTFT–10, 36
Badale, Andy
    See .... Badalamenti, Angelo
Badalucco, Michael 1954– CTFT–61
    Earlier sketch in CTFT–28
Baddeley, Angela 1904–1976 .... WWT–16
Baddeley, Hermione 1906–1986 .... CTFT–4
    Earlier sketch in WWT–17
Bade, Tom 1946– CTFT–1
Badel, Alan 1923– WWT–17
Badel, Sarah 1943– CTFT–33
    Earlier sketches in CTFT–5; WWT–17
Badelt, Klaus CTFT–56
Bader, Diedrich 1968(?)– CTFT–61
    Earlier sketches in CTFT–17, 28
Badgley, Penn 1986– CTFT–73
Badham, John 1939– CTFT–39
    Earlier sketches in CTFT–1, 8, 15
Badie, Mina CTFT–74
Badiyi, Reza 1930(?)– CTFT–37
    Earlier sketch in CTFT–11
Badland, Annette CTFT–57
    Earlier sketch in CTFT–27
Baena, Chris
    See .... Minear, Tim
Baer, Hanania 1943– CTFT–41
    Earlier sketches in CTFT–19
Baer, Marian 1924– CTFT–1
Baer, Max, Jr. 1937– CTFT–6
Baffa, Christopher CTFT–65
    Earlier sketch in CTFT–29
Bagby, Larry 1974– CTFT–65
Bagdelamenti, Angelo
    See .... Badalamenti, Angelo
Bagden, Ronald 1953– CTFT–1
Bagley, Ben 1933– WWT–17
Bagley, Lorri 1973– CTFT–72
Bagley, Tim CTFT–38
Bagneris, Vernel 1949– CTFT–56
    Earlier sketch in CTFT–9
Bagnold, Enid 1889–1981 .... WWT–17
Bahnks, Jonathan
    See .... Banks, Jonathan
Bahns, Maxine 1971– CTFT–47
    Earlier sketch in CTFT–23

Bai, Ling
    See .... Ling, Bai
Bailey, Bill 1964– CTFT–72
    Earlier sketch in CTFT–32
Bailey, Eion 1976– CTFT–58
Bailey, Frederick 1946– CTFT–1
Bailey, G. W. 1945– CTFT–62
    Earlier sketches in CTFT–17, 28
Bailey, Gordon 1875–? .... WWasWT
Bailey, H. C. 1878–1961 .... WWasWT
Bailey, John 1942– CTFT–37
    Earlier sketches in CTFT–5, 13
Bailey, Pearl 1918–1990 .... CTFT–9
    Earlier sketches in CTFT–4; WWT–17
Bailey, Robin 1919–1999 .... CTFT–11
    Obituary in CTFT–24
    Earlier sketch in WWT–17
Bailey, Steven W. 1971– CTFT–79
Bailey–Smith, Michael
    See .... Smith, Michael Bailey
Bailon, Adrienne 1983– CTFT–76
Bain, Barbara 1931– CTFT–70
    Earlier sketches in CTFT–3, 19, 31
Bain, Conrad 1923– CTFT–20
    Earlier sketches in CTFT–4; WWT–17
Baines, Florence 1877–1918 .... WWasWT
Bainter, Fay 1891–1968 .... WWasWT
Baio, Scott 1961(?)– CTFT–65
    Earlier sketches in CTFT–5, 19, 29
    Brief entry in CTFT–2
Baird, Bil 1904–1987 .... CTFT–5
    Earlier sketch in WWT–17
Baird, Dorothea 1875–1933 .... WWasWT
Baird, Ethel .... WWasWT
Baird, Mary E. 1947– CTFT–1
Bairstow, Scott 1970– CTFT–65
    Earlier sketches in CTFT–20, 29
Baitz, Jon Robin 1961– CTFT–51
    Earlier sketch in CTFT–12
Bakalyan, Richard 1931– CTFT–56
Bakay, Nick 1964– CTFT–58
    Earlier sketches in CTFT–17, 27
Baker, Becky Ann 1953– CTFT–58
    Earlier sketch in CTFT–27
Baker, Benny 1907– .... WWasWT
Baker, Blanche 1956– CTFT–1
Baker, Carroll 1931– CTFT–34
    Earlier sketches in CTFT–1, 8
Baker, Davis Aaron 1963– CTFT–40
Baker, Dee Bradley CTFT–40
Baker, Diane 1938– CTFT–72
    Earlier sketches in CTFT–22, 32
Baker, Dylan 1959– CTFT–62
    Earlier sketch in CTFT–28
Baker, Elizabeth ?–1962 .... WWasWT
Baker, George 1885–? .... WWasWT
Baker, George 1931– CTFT–43
    Earlier sketches in CTFT–3; WWT–17
Baker, George Pierce 1866–1935 .... WWasWT
Baker, Ian 1947– CTFT–66
Baker, Iris 1901– .... WWasWT
Baker, Joe Don 1936– CTFT–75
    Earlier sketches in CTFT–6, 33
Baker, Josephine 1906–1975 .... WWT–16
Baker, Kathy 1950– CTFT–44
    Earlier sketches in CTFT–8, 15
Baker, Kenny 1934– CTFT–49
    Earlier sketch in CTFT–8
Baker, Lee ?–1948 .... WWasWT
Baker, Mark 1946– WWT–17
Baker, Mark
    See .... Linn–Baker, Mark

Baker, Norma Jean
See........................... Monroe, Marilyn
Baker, Paul 1911–............................. CTFT–1
Baker, Raymond 1948– CTFT–45
Earlier sketches in CTFT–1, 6
Baker, Rick 1950– CTFT–49
Earlier sketches in CTFT–6, 15, 24
Baker, Rod 1945–............................... CTFT–4
Baker, Roy Ward 1916–..................... CTFT–11
Baker, Scott
See........................... Thompson Baker, Scott
Baker, Simon 1969– CTFT–54
Baker, Tyler
See................................. Christopher, Tyler
Baker, Word 1923–1995...................... CTFT–1
Obituary in CTFT–15
Bakke, Brenda 1963(?)–...................... CTFT–51
Bakke, Tami
See........................... Clatterbuck, Tamara
Bakshi, Ralph 1938– CTFT–15
Earlier sketch in CTFT–6
Bakula, Scott 1954(?)–....................... CTFT–57
Earlier sketches in CTFT–7, 14, 27
Balaban, Bob 1945–........................... CTFT–72
Earlier sketches in CTFT–1, 6, 33
Balanchine, George 1904–1980 .... WWT–17
Balasky, Belinda 1947– CTFT–66
Balcer, Rene 1954–........................... CTFT–13
Balch, Marston 1901– CTFT–2
Balderston, John L. 1889–1954 .... WWasWT
Balding, Rebecca 1955–..................... CTFT–46
Baldridge, Mike CTFT–69
Baldwin, Adam 1962–......................... CTFT–57
Earlier sketches in CTFT–7, 14, 27
Baldwin, Alec 1958–........................... CTFT–70
Earlier sketches in CTFT–5, 12, 21, 31
Baldwin, Daniel 1960–....................... CTFT–23
Earlier sketch in CTFT–13
Baldwin, James 1924–1987................... CTFT–3
Baldwin, Judith 1946–....................... CTFT–58
Baldwin, Peter 1929–......................... CTFT–36
Earlier sketch in CTFT–11
Baldwin, Stephen 1966–..................... CTFT–46
Earlier sketches in CTFT–13, 23
Baldwin, William....................... CTFT–10
Bale, Christian 1974–......................... CTFT–65
Earlier sketches in CTFT–19, 29
Balfour, Eric 1977–........................... CTFT–40
Balfour, Katharine 1920–1990.............. CTFT–4
Balibar, Jeanne 1968–....................... CTFT–38
Balin, Ina 1937–1990......................... CTFT–9
Balk, Fairuza 1974– CTFT–72
Earlier sketches in CTFT–11, 22, 32
Ball, Lucille 1911–1989 .... CTFT–8
Earlier sketch in CTFT–3
Ball, Samuel 1974– CTFT–73
Ball, Sonja CTFT–48
Ball, William 1931–1991 .... CTFT–5
Obituary in CTFT–10
Earlier sketch in WWT–17
Ballantine, Carl 1922–....................... CTFT–63
Ballantyne, Paul 1909– CTFT–3
Earlier sketch in WWT–17
Ballard, Alimi CTFT–74
Ballard, Carroll 1937–......................... CTFT–8
Ballard, Kaye 1926–........................... CTFT–65
Earlier sketches in CTFT–1, 3, 19, 29
Ballard, Lucien 1908–1988 .... CTFT–7
Ballerini, Edoardo............................. CTFT–71
Earlier sketch in CTFT–32
Ballet, Arthur H. 1924–...................... WWT–17
Ballhaus, Michael 1935–...................... CTFT–62
Earlier sketches in CTFT–10, 17, 28

Balodis, Janis 1950– CTFT–11
Balsam, Martin 1919–1996 .... CTFT–7
Obituary in CTFT–16
Earlier sketches in CTFT–2; WWT–17
Balsam, Talia 1960–........................... CTFT–72
Earlier sketches in CTFT–7, 33
Baltes, Alan 1962–............................. CTFT–79
Baltz, Kirk....................................... CTFT–52
Bamber, Jamie 1973–......................... CTFT–65
Bamford, Maria 1970– CTFT–68
Bamman, Gerry 1941–......................... CTFT–65
Earlier sketches in CTFT–3, 18, 29
Bana, Eric 1968–............................... CTFT–75
Earlier sketch in CTFT–34
Banbury, Frith 1912–......................... CTFT–4
Earlier sketch in WWT–17
Bancroft, Anne 1931– CTFT–30
Earlier sketches in CTFT–1, 7, 18; WWT–17
Bancroft, Bob CTFT–71
Bancroft, Cameron 1967–................... CTFT–42
Bancroft, George Pleydell 1868–1956 .... WWasWT
Bancroft, Lady 1839–1921 .... WWasWT
Bancroft, Squire 1841–1926 .... WWasWT
Band, Charles 1951–........................... CTFT–49
Band, Richard 1958(?)–....................... CTFT–47
Banderas, Antonio 1960–..................... CTFT–72
Earlier sketches in CTFT–13, 22, 32
Banerjee, Victor 1946–....................... CTFT–79
Earlier sketches in CTFT–3, 9
Banes, Lisa 1955– CTFT–43
Earlier sketch in CTFT–21
Bangs, John Kendrick 1862–1922.......... WWasWT
Bankhead, Tallulah 1903–1968 .... WWasWT
Banks, Boyd 1964– CTFT–68
Banks, Dennis J. 1937–....................... CTFT–39
Earlier sketch in CTFT–16
Banks, Elizabeth 1974–....................... CTFT–77
Banks, Ernie Lee CTFT–40
Banks, Jonathan 1947–....................... CTFT–72
Earlier sketches in CTFT–7, 33
Banks, Leslie J. 1890–1952................... WWasWT
Banks, Linden................................... CTFT–55
Banks, Tyra 1973–............................. CTFT–48
Bannen, Ian 1928–............................. CTFT–5
Earlier sketch in WWT–17
Banner, Bob 1921–............................. CTFT–3
Bannerman, Celia 1946–...................... CTFT–5
Earlier sketch in WWT–17
Bannerman, Kay 1919–1991 .... CTFT–4
Obituary in CTFT–10
Earlier sketch in WWT–17
Bannerman, Margaret 1896– .... WWasWT
Bannister, Harry 1893–1961 .... WWasWT
Bannon, Jack 1940–........................... CTFT–33
Earlier sketch in CTFT–6
Bantry, Bryan 1956–........................... CTFT–1
Banyaer, Michael 1970–....................... CTFT–48
Bara, Theda 1890(?)–1955.................... CTFT–20
Baraka, Amiri 1934–........................... CTFT–7
Earlier sketch in WWT–17
Baranski, Christine 1952–.................... CTFT–64
Earlier sketches in CTFT–4, 11, 20, 29; WWT–17
Barbara, Joe..................................... CTFT–17
Barbeau, Adrienne 1945–.................... CTFT–64
Earlier sketches in CTFT–4, 20, 29
Barbee, Richard 1887– .... WWasWT
Barber, Frances 1958(?)–..................... CTFT–35
Earlier sketch in CTFT–9
Barber, Gary CTFT–79
Earlier sketch in CTFT–36
Barber, Gillian 1957–......................... CTFT–54

Barber, Glynis 1955–......................... CTFT–58
Earlier sketch in CTFT–27
Barber, John..................................... CTFT–1
Barbera, Joseph 1911–2006.................. CTFT–42
Obituary in CTFT–74
Earlier sketches in CTFT–1, 8, 18
Barberie, Jillian 1966–....................... CTFT–74
Barbor, H. R. 1893–1933 .... WWasWT
Barbour, Elly 1945–........................... CTFT–19
Earlier sketch in CTFT–2
Barbour, James 1966–......................... CTFT–62
Barbour, Joyce 1901– .... WWasWT
Barbour, Thomas 1921– CTFT–2
Barcelo, Randy 1946–......................... CTFT–4
Barclay, Paris 1956–........................... CTFT–59
Earlier sketch in CTFT–27
Barcroft, Roy 1902–1969..................... CTFT–21
Bard, Wilkie 1874–? .... WWasWT
Bardem, Javier 1969–......................... CTFT–75
Earlier sketch in CTFT–34
Bardon, Henry 1923–......................... WWT–17
Bardon, John 1921– CTFT–38
Bardot, Brigitte 1934– CTFT–3
Bareikis, Arija 1966–......................... CTFT–48
Barge, Gillian 1940– WWT–17
Barger, Greg
See................................. Berger, Gregg
Baring, Maurice 1874–1945 .... WWasWT
Barish, Keith CTFT–10
Barker, Bob 1923–............................. CTFT–70
Earlier sketches in CTFT–2, 19, 31
Barker, Clive 1931–........................... WWT–17
Barker, Clive 1952–........................... CTFT–43
Earlier sketches in CTFT–13, 22
Barker, Felix..................................... WWT–17
Barker, H. Granville–
See................... Granville–Barker, Harley
Barker, Helen Granville–
See................... Granville–Barker, Helen
Barker, Howard 1946– CTFT–14
Earlier sketch in WWT–17
Barker, Ronnie 1929–......................... CTFT–57
Earlier sketches in CTFT–7, 27; WWT–17
Barker, Sean
See................................. Hayter, David
Barkin, Ellen 1955(?)–....................... CTFT–72
Earlier sketches in CTFT–6, 13, 22, 32
Barkley, Deanne 1931–....................... CTFT–10
Barkworth, Peter 1929–...................... WWT–17
Barlog, Boleslaw 1906–....................... WWasWT
Barlow, Billie 1862–1937 .... WWasWT
Barlow, H. J. 1892–1970 .... WWasWT
Barnabe, Bruno 1905– WWT–17
Barnard, Ivor 1887–1953..................... WWasWT
Barner, Barry K. 1906–1965 .... WWasWT
Barnes, Art
See............................... Mumy, Bill
Barnes, Artie
See............................... Ferrer, Miguel
Barnes, Binnie 1905– .... WWasWT
Barnes, Christopher Daniel
1972–... CTFT–50
Barnes, Clive 1927– CTFT–3
Earlier sketch in WWT–17
Barnes, Fran 1931– CTFT–1
Barnes, Fred 1884–? .... WWasWT
Barnes, Howard 1904–1968 .... WWasWT
Barnes, J. H. 1850–1925 .... WWasWT
Barnes, Joanna 1934–......................... CTFT–6
Barnes, Kenneth (Ralph) 1878–1957 ..... WWasWT
Barnes, Peter 1931– CTFT–38
Earlier sketches in CTFT–5, 14; WWT–17

Barnes, Priscilla 1952(?)– CTFT–78
  Earlier sketches in CTFT–9, 35
Barnes, Susan CTFT–51
Barnes, Wade 1917– CTFT–4
Barnes, Winifred 1894–1935 .... WWasWT
Barnett, Ken
  See .... Francis, Freddie
Barnette, Alan.................................... CTFT–54
Barney, Jay 1913–1985............................ CTFT–1
Baron, Alec CTFT–5
Baron, David
  See .... Pinter, Harold
Baron, Evalyn 1948– CTFT–19
  Earlier sketch in CTFT–2
Baron, Joanne CTFT–63
Barondes, Elizabeth CTFT–58
Barone, Anita 1964– CTFT–63
Baronova, Irina 1919– .... WWasWT
Barr, Julia 1949– CTFT–62
Barr, Kathleen CTFT–40
Barr, Nathan CTFT–62
Barr, Patrick 1908–1985 .... WWT–17
Barr, Richard 1917–1989......................... CTFT–7
  Earlier sketch in WWT–17
Barr, Roseanne
  See .... Roseanne
Barranger, Millie S. 1937– WWT–17
Barratt, Augustus.............................. WWasWT
Barratt, Watson 1884–1962 .... WWasWT
Barrault, Jean–Louis 1910– .... WWasWT
Barre, Gabriel 1957– CTFT–4
Barrera, David CTFT–44
Barrett, Brendon Ryan 1986– CTFT–66
Barrett, Brent 1957– CTFT–58
Barrett, Edith 1906– .... WWasWT
Barrett, George 1869–1935 .... WWasWT
Barrett, Jacinda 1972– CTFT–73
Barrett, Leslie 1919– CTFT–4
  Earlier sketch in WWT–17
Barrett, Lester .... WWasWT
Barrett, Majel 1939– CTFT–39
Barrett, Oscar 1875–1941 .... WWasWT
Barrett, Rona 1936– CTFT–4
Barrett, Wilson 1900– .... WWasWT
Barretta, Bill CTFT–50
Barrett–Roddenberry, Majel
  See................................... Barrett, Majel
Barrie, Amanda 1939– WWT–17
Barrie, Barbara 1931– CTFT–64
  Earlier sketches in CTFT–3, 19, 29; WWT–17
Barrie, Chris 1960– CTFT–69
Barrie, Frank 1939– WWT–17
Barrie, James Matthew 1860–1937........ WWasWT
Barrington, Rutland 1853–1922.............. WWasWT
Barris, Chuck 1929– CTFT–6
Barron, Dana 1968– CTFT–52
Barron, David.................................... CTFT–79
Barron, Marcus 1925–1944 .... WWasWT
Barron, Muriel 1906– .... WWasWT
Barrow, Bernard 1927–1993.................... CTFT–11
  Obituary in CTFT–12
Barrowman, John 1968– CTFT–43
Barrs, Norman 1917– CTFT–1
Barry, B. Constance 1913– CTFT–1
Barry, B. H. 1940– CTFT–5
  Earlier sketch in CTFT–1
Barry, Christine 1911– .... WWasWT
Barry, Gene 1919(?)– CTFT–53
  Earlier sketches in CTFT–2, 5, 12, 18
Barry, Jack 1918–1984 .... CTFT–2
Barry, Joan 1901–1989 .... WWasWT
Barry, John 1933– CTFT–43
  Earlier sketches in CTFT–4, 11, 22

Barry, Lynda 1956– CTFT–14
Barry, Michael 1910–1988 .... CTFT–7
  Earlier sketch in WWT–17
Barry, Miranda Robbins 1951– CTFT–11
Barry, Paul 1931– CTFT–5
  Earlier sketch in CTFT–1
Barry, Philip 1896–1949 .... WWasWT
Barry, Raymond J. 1939– CTFT–79
  Earlier sketches in CTFT–1, 9, 35
Barry, Shiel 1882–1937 .... WWasWT
Barry, Thom CTFT–54
Barrymore, Diana 1921–1960 .... WWasWT
Barrymore, Drew 1975– CTFT–70
  Earlier sketches in CTFT–5, 12, 21, 31
  Brief Entry in CTFT–2
Barrymore, Ethel 1879–1959 .... WWasWT
Barrymore, Jaid 1946– CTFT–75
  Earlier sketch in CTFT–33
Barrymore, John 1882–1942 .... WWasWT
Barrymore, Lionel 1878–1954 .... WWasWT
Bart, Lionel 1930–1999 .... CTFT–3
  Obituary in CTFT–32
  Earlier sketch in WWT–17
Bart, Peter 1932– CTFT–2
Bart, Roger 1962– CTFT–58
  Earlier sketch in CTFT–27
Bartel, Paul 1938– CTFT–6
Bartenieff, George 1935– CTFT–1
Bartet, Jeanne Julia 1854– .... WWasWT
Barth, Cecil ?–1949 .... WWasWT
Barth, Eddie 1931– CTFT–49
Bartholomae, Phillip H. ?–1947............ WWasWT
Bartilson, Lynsey 1983– CTFT–46
Bartkowiak, Andrzej 1950– CTFT–62
  Earlier sketches in CTFT–16, 28
Bartlett, Basil 1905– .... WWasWT
Bartlett, Bonnie 1929– CTFT–74
  Earlier sketches in CTFT–6, 33
Bartlett, Cal CTFT–59
Bartlett, Clifford 1903–1936 .... WWasWT
Bartlett, D'Jamin 1948– CTFT–5
  Earlier sketch in WWT–17
Bartlett, Elise .... WWasWT
Bartlett, Erinn 1973– CTFT–73
Bartlett, Hall 1925(?)–1993 .... CTFT–1
  Obituary in CTFT–12
Bartlett, Michael 1901– .... WWasWT
Bartlett, Robin 1951– CTFT–41
Bartley, John S. CTFT–56
Bartok, Jayce 1972– CTFT–58
Barton, Dora ?–1966 .... WWasWT
Barton, Dorie CTFT–54
Barton, James 1890–1962...................... WWasWT
Barton, John 1928– CTFT–6
  Earlier sketch in WWT–17
Barton, Margaret 1926– .... WWasWT
Barton, Mary ?–1970 .... WWasWT
Barton, Mischa 1986– CTFT–58
  Earlier sketch in CTFT–27
Barton, Peter 1956– CTFT–48
  Earlier sketch in CTFT–9
Bartusiak, Skye McCole 1992– CTFT–51
Barty, Billy 1924(?)– CTFT–33
  Earlier sketch in CTFT–6
Barty, Jack 1888–1942.......................... WWasWT
Baruch, Steven CTFT–49
Baruchel, Jay CTFT–66
  Earlier sketch in CTFT–30
Baruck, Siri 1978– CTFT–65
Baryshnikov, Mikhail 1948– CTFT–48
  Earlier sketches in CTFT–3, 13
Basaraba, Gary 1959– CTFT–56
Basche, David Alan 1970– CTFT–68

Basco, Dante 1975– CTFT–72
  Earlier sketch in CTFT–32
Base, Guilio 1964– CTFT–34
Basehart, Richard 1914–1984 .... CTFT–2
  Earlier sketch in WWT–17
Basinger, Kim 1953– CTFT–44
  Earlier sketches in CTFT–6, 13, 22
  Brief Entry in CTFT–2
Baskcomb, A. W. 1880–1939 .... WWasWT
Baskcomb, Lawrence 1883–1962 .... WWasWT
Baskette, Lena
  See .... Basquette, Lina
Baskin, Elya 1951– CTFT–43
Basquette, Lina 1907–1994 .... CTFT–14
Bass, Alfie 1921–1987 .... CTFT–5
  Earlier sketch in WWT–17
Bass, George Houston 1938– CTFT–1
Bass, James Lance 1979– CTFT–63
Bass, Kingsley B., Jr.
  See .... Bullins, Ed
Bass, Ron 1942– CTFT–48
  Earlier sketches in CTFT–14, 24
Bassett, Alfred Leon 1870–? .... WWasWT
Bassett, Angela 1958– CTFT–46
  Earlier sketches in CTFT–13, 23
Bassett, Linda 1950– CTFT–79
  Earlier sketches in CTFT–8, 35
Bassett, William 1935– CTFT–38
Bassey, Jennifer................................. CTFT–27
Bataille, Henry 1872–1940...................... WWasWT
Bate, Anthony................................... WWT–17
Bateman, James
  See .... Gibson, Henry
Bateman, Jason 1969– CTFT–41
  Earlier sketches in CTFT–5, 19
  Brief Entry in CTFT–2
Bateman, Justine 1966– CTFT–64
  Earlier sketches in CTFT–2, 5, 18, 29
Bateman, Leah 1892– .... WWasWT
Bateman, Michael John 1947– CTFT–79
  Earlier sketch in CTFT–36
Bateman, Miss 1842–1917 .... WWasWT
Bateman, Virginia Frances
  See .... Compton, Mrs. Edward
Bateman, Zitlah 1900–1970 .... WWasWT
Bates, Alan 1934– CTFT–30
  Earlier sketches in CTFT–2, 7, 18; WWT–17
Bates, Bianche 1873–1941 .... WWasWT
Bates, Jeanne 1918– CTFT–27
Bates, Kathy 1948– CTFT–60
  Earlier sketches in CTFT–1, 10, 17, 28
Bates, Michael 1920– WWT–16
Bates, Ralph 1940–1991 .... CTFT–9
  Obituary in CTFT–16
Bates, Sally 1907– .... WWasWT
Bates, Thorpe 1883–1958...................... WWasWT
Bates, Tyler CTFT–79
Bateson, Timothy 1926– WWT–17
Bath, Hubert 1883– .... WWasWT
Batinkoff, Randall 1968– CTFT–66
  Earlier sketch in CTFT–30
Batley, Dorothy 1902– .... WWasWT
Batt, Bryan 1963– CTFT–58
Batten, Paul CTFT–57
Battle, Hinton 1956– CTFT–47
  Earlier sketches in CTFT–11, 23
Battles, John 1921– .... WWasWT
Batty, Archibald 1884–1961 .... WWasWT
Baty, Gaston 1885–1952 .... WWasWT
Bauchau, Patrick 1938– CTFT–39
Bauche, Vanessa 1973– CTFT–38
Bauer, Christopher.............................. CTFT–52
Bauer, Jamie Lyn 1949(?)– CTFT–17

Bauer, Kristin 1973– CTFT–76
   Earlier sketch in CTFT–34
Bauer, Steven 1956– CTFT–43
   Earlier sketches in CTFT–8, 15
Bauersmith, Paula 1909–1987 .... CTFT–5
   Earlier sketch in WWT–17
Baughan, Edward Algernon
   1865–1938 .... WWasWT
Baughman, Renee CTFT–2
Baum, Carol CTFT–64
   Earlier sketch in CTFT–29
Baumann, K. T. CTFT–1
Baumgarten, Craig 1949– CTFT–39
   Earlier sketches in CTFT–1, 16
Bausch, Pina 1940– CTFT–11
Bava, Mario 1914– CTFT–8
Bawn, Harry 1872–? .... WWasWT
Bax, Clifford 1886–1962 .... WWasWT
Bax, Kylie 1975– CTFT–68
Baxendale, Helen 1969(?)– CTFT–75
   Earlier sketch in CTFT–32
Baxley, Barbara 1927–1990 .... CTFT–2
   Earlier sketch in WWT–17
Baxley, Craig R. CTFT–68
Baxter, Alan 1908– .... WWasWT
Baxter, Anne 1923–1985 .... CTFT–3
   Earlier sketch in WWT–17
Baxter, Barry 1894–1922 .... WWasWT
Baxter, Beryl 1926– .... WWasWT
Baxter, Beverly 1891– .... WWasWT
Baxter, Cash 1937– CTFT–5
Baxter, Jane 1909– WWT–17
Baxter, Jennifer CTFT–67
Baxter, Keith 1935(?)– CTFT–37
   Earlier sketches in CTFT–4, 13; WWT–17
Baxter, Meredith 1947– CTFT–60
   Earlier sketches in CTFT–9, 16, 28
Baxter, Stanley 1926– WWT–17
Baxter, Trevor 1932– WWT–17
Baxter–Birney, Meredith
   See .... Baxter, Meredith
Bay, Frances 1918– CTFT–37
Bay, Howard 1912–1986 .... CTFT–4
   Earlier sketch in WWT–17
Bay, Michael 1965– CTFT–47
   Earlier sketch in CTFT–23
Baye, Nathalie 1948– CTFT–39
   Earlier sketches in CTFT–8, 15
Bayes, Nora 1880–1928 .... WWasWT
Bayler, Terence 1930– CTFT–19
   Earlier sketch in CTFT–3
Bayley, Caroline 1890– .... WWasWT
Bayley, Dame Iris
   See .... Murdoch, Dame (Jean) Iris
Bayley, Hilda ?–1971 .... WWasWT
Baylis, Lilian 1874–1937 .... WWasWT
Bayliss, Peter WWT–17
Bayly, Caroline .... WWasWT
Baynton, Henry 1892–1951 .... WWasWT
Beach, Adam 1972– CTFT–72
   Earlier sketch in CTFT–32
Beach, Ann 1938– WWT–17
Beach, Gary 1947– CTFT–1
Beach, Michael 1963(?)– CTFT–70
   Earlier sketches in CTFT–21, 31
Beacham, Stephanie 1947– CTFT–37
   Earlier sketches in CTFT–4, 13; WWT–17
Beachwood, Kermit
   See.. Miller, Matt K.
Beahan, Kate CTFT–68
Beaird, Betty 1939– CTFT–11
Beal, Jeff 1963– CTFT–58

Beal, John 1909–1997 .... CTFT–11
   Obituary in CTFT–17
   Earlier sketch in WWT–17
Beal, John 1947– CTFT–48
Bealby, George 1877–1931 .... WWasWT
Beale, Simon Russell 1961– CTFT–51
   Earlier sketch in CTFT–25
Beals, Jennifer 1963– CTFT–48
   Earlier sketches in CTFT–5, 14, 24
   Brief Entry in CTFT–2
Bean, Henry 1945– CTFT–53
   Earlier sketch in CTFT–16
Bean, Normal
   See .... Burroughs, Edgar Rice
Bean, Orson 1928– CTFT–60
   Earlier sketches in CTFT–3, 16, 28; WWT–17
Bean, Sean 1959(?)– CTFT–37
   Earlier sketch in CTFT–13
Beard, Jane CTFT–51
Beard, Winston
   See .... Goldman, James
Beardsley, Alice 1925– CTFT–1
Bearse, Amanda 1958– CTFT–30
   Earlier sketches in CTFT–8, 18
Beart, Emmanuelle 1965– CTFT–32
   Earlier sketch in CTFT–22
Beasley, Allyce 1954– CTFT–74
   Earlier sketches in CTFT–7, 33
Beasley, John 1943– CTFT–53
Beasley, William S. CTFT–44
   Earlier sketch in CTFT–22
Beat Takeshi
   See .... Kitano, Takeshi
Beaton, Cecil 1904–1980 .... WWT–16
Beatty, Harcourt .... WWasWT
Beatty, John Lee 1948– CTFT–38
   Earlier sketches in CTFT–2, 6, 13; WWT–17
Beatty, Lou, Jr. CTFT–75
   Earlier sketch in CTFT–34
Beatty, May ?–1945 .... WWasWT
Beatty, Nancy CTFT–68
Beatty, Ned 1937– CTFT–47
   Earlier sketches in CTFT–6, 13, 23
Beatty, Robert 1909– WWT–17
Beatty, Roberta 1891– .... WWasWT
Beatty, Warren 1937– CTFT–75
   Earlier sketches in CTFT–3, 11, 22, 32
Beauchamp, John ?–1921 .... WWasWT
Beaudoin, Michelle 1975– CTFT–60
   Earlier sketches in CTFT–17, 28
Beaufort, John 1912– WWT–17
Beaumont, Cyril William 1891– .... WWasWT
Beaumont, Diana 1909–1964 .... WWasWT
Beaumont, Gabrielle 1942– CTFT–23
   Earlier sketches in CTFT–1, 12
Beaumont, Hugh 1908–1982 .... WWasWT
Beaumont, John 1902– .... WWasWT
Beaumont, Kathryn 1938– CTFT–69
Beaumont, Muriel 1881–1957 .... WWasWT
Beaumont, Ralph 1926– CTFT–10
Beaumont, Roma 1914– .... WWasWT
Beauvais, Garcelle 1966– CTFT–44
Beaven, Jenny 1950– CTFT–47
   Earlier sketch in CTFT–23
Beaver, Jim 1950– CTFT–47
   Earlier sketches in CTFT–11, 23
Beaver, Terry CTFT–68
Bebel, Jean Paul Belmondo
   See .... Belmondo, Jean–Paul
Bebonis, Marcia
   See .... DeBonis, Marcia
Becher, John C. 1915–1986 .... WWT–17
Beck, Christophe CTFT–41

Beck, Frances Patricia 1937– CTFT–11
Beck, John 1943(?)– CTFT–36
   Earlier sketch in CTFT–9
Beck, Julian 1925–1985 .... CTFT–4
   Earlier sketch in WWT–17
Beck, Kimberly 1956– CTFT–9
Beck, Michael CTFT–3
Beck, Noelle 1968– CTFT–73
Beckel, Graham 1949– CTFT–79
   Earlier sketches in CTFT–9, 35
Becker, Gerry... CTFT–70
   Earlier sketch in CTFT–31
Becker, Harold 1950– CTFT–37
   Earlier sketch in CTFT–13
Becker, Josh 1958– CTFT–36
Becker, Tony 1963– CTFT–40
Beckerman, Bernard 1921– WWT–17
Beckett, Samuel 1906–1989 .... CTFT–4
   Obituary in CTFT–9
   Earlier sketch in WWT–17
Beckhard, Arthur J. .... WWasWT
Beckinsale, Kate 1973– CTFT–72
   Earlier sketch in CTFT–32
Beckley, Barbara.................................... CTFT–53
Beckley, Beatrice Mary 1885–? .... WWasWT
Beckman, Henry 1921(?)– CTFT–39
Beckman, John c. 1898–1989 .... CTFT–8
Beckwith, Reginald 1908–1965 .... WWasWT
Bed, Helen
   See .... Winn, Amanda
Bedard, Irene 1967– CTFT–60
   Earlier sketches in CTFT–16, 28
Bedelia, Bonnie 1952(?)– CTFT–60
   Earlier sketches in CTFT–3, 10, 17, 28
Bedells, Phyllis 1893–1985 .... WWasWT
Bedford, Brian 1935– CTFT–29
   Earlier sketches in CTFT–2, 11, 18; WWT–17
Bedford Lloyd, John............................... CTFT–62
Bedi, Kabir 1946– CTFT–53
Bee, Gillian Ferra
   See.................................... Ferrabee, Gillian
Beecher, Janet 1884–1955 .... WWasWT
Beechwood, Kermit
   See .... Miller, Matt K.
Beecroft, David 1960– CTFT–48
Beehan, Kate
   See .... Beahan, Kate
Beer, J. Weak
   See .... Weber, Jake
Beerbohm, Clarence Evelyn
   ?–1917 .... WWasWT
Beerbohm, Max 1872–1956 .... WWasWT
Beere, Bernard (Mrs.) 1856–? .... WWasWT
Beers, Francine CTFT–1
Beery, Noah, Jr. 1913(?)–1994 .... CTFT–3
   Obituary in CTFT–15
Beet, Alice ?–1931................................ WWasWT
Beggs, Richard 1942– CTFT–47
   Earlier sketches in CTFT–12, 23
Beghe, Jason 1960– CTFT–51
   Earlier sketch in CTFT–25
Begley, Ed 1901–1970 .... WWasWT
Begley, Ed, Jr. 1949– CTFT–72
   Earlier sketches in CTFT–4, 11, 22, 32
Begtrup, Mageina Tovah
   See .... Tovah, Mageina
Behan, Brendan 1923–1964 .... WWasWT
Behar, Joy 1943– CTFT–41
Behnken, Lucas 1979– CTFT–75
Behr, Ira Steven 1953– CTFT–39
Behr, Jason 1973–.................................. CTFT–67
   Earlier sketch in CTFT–30

Behrman, Samuel Nathaniel
    1893–1973 .... WWasWT
Beim, Norman 1923– CTFT–1
Beimler, Hans CTFT–49
Beiser, Brendan 1970– CTFT–78
Bejart, Maurice 1927– CTFT–11
Bel Geddes, Barbara 1922– CTFT–3
    Earlier sketch in WWT–17
Belack, Doris CTFT–44
Belafonte, Harry 1927– CTFT–35
    Earlier sketches in CTFT–1, 5
Belafonte, Shari 1954– CTFT–35
    Earlier sketch in CTFT–6
Belardinelli, Charles CTFT–61
    Earlier sketch in CTFT–28
Belasco, David 1853–1931 .... WWasWT
Belcher, Patricia CTFT–78
Beldon, Eileen 1901– WWT–17
Beldone, Phil "Cheech"
    See .... Ellison, Harlan
Belfrage, Bruce 1901– .... WWasWT
Belgrader, Andrei 1946– CTFT–19
    Earlier sketch in CTFT–2
Belkin, Jeanna 1924– CTFT–1
Belknap, Allen R. 1941– CTFT–18
    Earlier sketch in CTFT–2
Bell, Ann 1939(?)– CTFT–48
    Earlier sketches in CTFT–23; WWT–17
Bell, Barry 1951– CTFT–52
Bell, Catherine 1968– CTFT–61
    Earlier sketches in CTFT–17, 28
Bell, David 1954– CTFT–62
Bell, Digby Valentine ?–1917 .... WWasWT
Bell, Drake 1986– CTFT–74
Bell, E. E. 1955– CTFT–79
Bell, Enid 1888– .... WWasWT
Bell, Felicia M. CTFT–60
Bell, James (Harliee) 1891– .... WWasWT
Bell, John 1940– WWT–17
Bell, Kristen 1980– CTFT–65
Bell, Lake 1979– CTFT–72
Bell, Lynne 1944– CTFT–1
Bell, Marshall 1944– CTFT–57
    Earlier sketch in CTFT–27
Bell, Mary Hayley 1914– .... WWasWT
Bell, Michael CTFT–40
Bell, Nicholas
    Earlier sketch in CTFT–32
Bell, Stanley 1881–1952 .... WWasWT
Bell, Tobin 1942– CTFT–76
    Earlier sketch in CTFT–34
Bell, Tom 1932(?)– CTFT–35
    Earlier sketch in CTFT–9
Bell, Vanessa
    See .... Calloway, Vanessa Bell
Bella, Joseph F. 1940– CTFT–1
Bellamy, Bill 1965– CTFT–48
    Earlier sketch in CTFT–23
Bellamy, Earl 1917– CTFT–28
Bellamy, Franklyn 1886– .... WWasWT
Bellamy, Ned CTFT–42
Bellamy, Ralph 1904–1991 .... CTFT–6
    Obituary in CTFT–10
    Earlier sketches in CTFT–1; WWasWT
Bellardinelli, Charles
    See .... Belardinelli, Charles
Bellaver, Harry 1905–1993 .... CTFT–1
    Obituary in CTFT–12
Belle, Camilla 1986– CTFT–52
Belleville, Frederic de 1857– .... WWasWT
Bellew, Kyrie 1887– .... WWasWT
Bellis, Richard 1946– CTFT–56
Bellisario, Donald P. 1935– CTFT–10

Bellman, Gina 1966– CTFT–76
    Earlier sketch in CTFT–34
Bello, Maria 1967– CTFT–32
    Earlier sketch in CTFT–22
Bellocchio, Marco 1939– CTFT–29
Bellon, Roger CTFT–45
Bellonini, Edna 1903– .... WWasWT
Bellows, Gil 1967– CTFT–71
    Earlier sketches in CTFT–20, 32
Bellucci, Monica 1969(?)– CTFT–69
Bellwood, Pamela 1951– CTFT–21
Belmondo, Jean–Paul 1933– CTFT–31
    Earlier sketches in CTFT–7, 18
Belmore, Bertha 1882–1953 .... WWasWT
Belson, Jerry CTFT–7
Beltrami, Marco CTFT–70
    Earlier sketches in CTFT–21, 31
Beltran, Robert 1953– CTFT–61
    Earlier sketches in CTFT–16, 28
Belushi, Jim 1954– CTFT–47
    Earlier sketches in CTFT–3, 13, 23
    Brief Entry in CTFT–2
Belushi, John 1949–1982 .... CTFT–16
Belzer, Richard 1944– CTFT–71
    Earlier sketches in CTFT–12, 20, 32
Bemis, Cliff 1948– CTFT–79
Ben–Ami, Jacob 1890– .... WWasWT
Benard, Maurice 1963– CTFT–60
Ben–Ari, Neal 1952– CTFT–9
Benaventa, Jacinto 1866–1954 .... WWasWT
Benben, Brian 1956– CTFT–48
    Earlier sketches in CTFT–14, 24
Benchley, Peter 1940– CTFT–5
Benchley, Robert C. 1889– .... WWasWT
Bendall, Ernest Alfred 1846–1924 .... WWasWT
Bender, Candace Camille
    See .... Kita, Candace
Bender, Jack CTFT–79
    Earlier sketch in CTFT–36
Bender, Lawrence 1958– CTFT–31
    Earlier sketch in CTFT–21
Bendix, Simone 1967– CTFT–62
    Earlier sketch in CTFT–28
Bendix, William 1906–1994 .... CTFT–28
Benedetti, Caprice CTFT–61
Benedetti, Robert L. 1939– CTFT–36
    Earlier sketch in CTFT–11
Benedict, Amy 1964– CTFT–69
Benedict, Dirk 1945– CTFT–56
    Earlier sketches in CTFT–1, 23
Benedict, Jay 1951– CTFT–46
Benedict, Paul 1938– CTFT–70
    Earlier sketches in CTFT–3, 19, 31
Benedict, Robert Patrick CTFT–58
Benedict, Stewart Hurd 1924– CTFT–21
Benedicto, Lourdes 1974(?)– CTFT–74
Benedictus, David 1938– WWT–17
Benelli, Sem 1877–1949 .... WWasWT
Benett, Fran
    See .... Bennett, Fran
Benford, Starla CTFT–52
Benigni, Roberto 1952– CTFT–43
    Earlier sketch in CTFT–21
Bening, Annette 1958– CTFT–62
    Earlier sketches in CTFT–9, 16, 28
Benini, Ferruccio 1854–1925 .... WWasWT
Benison, Peter 1950– CTFT–37
Benjamin, Allan 1949– CTFT–3
Benjamin, Christopher 1934– CTFT–38
Benjamin, Louis 1922– WWT–17
Benjamin, Morris Edgar 1881–? .... WWasWT
Benjamin, P. J. 1951– CTFT–1
Benjamin, Paul CTFT–71

Benjamin, Richard 1938– CTFT–74
    Earlier sketches in CTFT–1, 5, 33
Bennes, John CTFT–52
Bennett, Alan 1934– CTFT–49
    Earlier sketches in CTFT–8, 15; WWT–17
Bennett, Arnold 1867–1931 .... WWasWT
Bennett, Charles 1899– .... WWasWT
Bennett, Daryl CTFT–49
Bennett, Elizabeth Ann CTFT–76
Bennett, Faith .... WWasWT
Bennett, Fran 1937– CTFT–62
    Earlier sketch in CTFT–1
Bennett, Harve 1930– CTFT–18
    Earlier sketch in CTFT–8
Bennett, Hywel 1944– CTFT–35
    Earlier sketches in CTFT–9; WWT–17
Bennett, Jeff 1962– CTFT–79
    Earlier sketch in CTFT–36
Bennett, Jill 1931– WWT–17
Bennett, Jill 1975– CTFT–78
Bennett, Jimmy 1996– CTFT–64
Bennett, Joan 1910–1990 .... CTFT–4
    Obituary in CTFT–9
    Earlier sketch in WWT–17
Bennett, Jonathan 1981– CTFT–71
Bennett, Lelia .... WWasWT
Bennett, Marcia CTFT–45
Bennett, Mark CTFT–63
Bennett, Matthew 1968– CTFT–62
Bennett, Meg 1948– CTFT–7
Bennett, Michael 1943–1987 .... CTFT–5
    Earlier sketch in WWT–17
Bennett, Nigel 1949– CTFT–37
Bennett, Peter 1917–1990(?) CTFT–9
    Earlier sketch in WWT–17
Bennett, Richard 1873–1944 .... WWasWT
Bennett, Richard Rodney 1936– CTFT–37
    Earlier sketch in CTFT–12
Bennett, Ruth CTFT–7
Bennett, Tony 1926– CTFT–6
Bennett, Vivienne 1905–1978 .... WWT–16
Bennett, Wilda 1894–1967 .... WWasWT
Bennett, Zachary 1980– CTFT–65
    Earier sketch in CTFT–29
Bennett–Gordon, Eve
    See .... Gordon, Eve
Benny, Jack 1894–1974 .... CTFT–20
Benrimo, J. Harry 1874–1942 .... WWasWT
Benrubi, Abraham 1969– CTFT–58
    Earlier sketch in CTFT–27
Benskin, Tyrone 1958– CTFT–39
Benskin, Tyrone DeCosta
    See .... Benskin, Tyrone
Benson, Amber 1977– CTFT–76
    Earlier sketch in CTFT–34
Benson, Frank R. 1858–1939 .... WWasWT
Benson, George 1911–1983 .... CTFT–3
    Earlier sketch in WWT–17
Benson, Jodi 1961– CTFT–70
    Earlier sketches in CTFT–21, 31
Benson, Lady ?–1946 .... WWasWT
Benson, Robby 1956– CTFT–67
    Earlier sketches in CTFT–8, 18, 30
Benson, Ruth 1873–1948 .... WWasWT
Benson–Landes, Wendy 1975(?)– CTFT–61
Bent, Buena ?–1957 .... WWasWT
Benthaak, Tushka
    See .... Bergen, Tushka
Benthall, Michael 1919–1956 .... WWasWT
Bentham, Frederick 1911– WWT–17
Bentivoglio, Fabrizio 1957– CTFT–34
Bentley, Eric 1916– WWT–17
Bentley, Irene ?–1940 .... WWasWT

Bentley, Robert CTFT–49
Bentley, Wes 1978– CTFT–67
   Earlier sketch in CTFT–30
Bentley, Will 1873–? .... WWasWT
Benton, Barbi 1950– CTFT–9
Benton, Robert 1932– CTFT–48
   Earlier sketches in CTFT–3, 14
Ben–Victor, Paul 1965– CTFT–64
   Earlier sketch in CTFT–29
Benz, Julie 1972(?)– CTFT–38
Benzali, Daniel 1950(?)– CTFT–62
   Earlier sketches in CTFT–16, 28
Bercovici, Luca 1957– CTFT–64
Berendt, Rachel ?–1957 .... WWasWT
Berenger, Tom 1950(?)– CTFT–61
   Earlier sketches in CTFT–3, 9, 16, 28
Berenson, Marisa 1947– CTFT–74
   Earlier sketches in CTFT–7, 33
Berenson, Stephen 1953– CTFT–3
Beresford, Bruce 1940– CTFT–37
   Earlier sketches in CTFT–6, 13
Beresford, Harry 1867–1944 .... WWasWT
Berfield, Justin 1986– CTFT–74
Berg, Barry 1942– CTFT–1
Berg, Gertrude 1899–1941 .... WWasWT
Berg, Greg
   See .... Berger, Gregg
Berg, Jeff 1947– CTFT–10
Berg, Peter 1964– CTFT–45
   Earlier sketch in CTFT–14
Bergen, Bob 1964– CTFT–37
Bergen, Candice 1946– CTFT–62
   Earlier sketches in CTFT–3, 10, 17, 28
Bergen, Nella 1873–1919 .... WWasWT
Bergen, Polly 1930– CTFT–38
   Earlier sketches in CTFT–6, 14
Bergen, Tushka 1969– CTFT–71
Berger, Anna CTFT–74
   Earlier sketches in CTFT–7, 33
Berger, Gregg CTFT–70
   Earlier sketches in CTFT–4, 21, 31
Berger, Henning 1872– .... WWasWT
Berger, Keith 1952– CTFT–18
   Earlier sketch in CTFT–2
Berger, Robert 1914– CTFT–1
Berger, Senta 1947– CTFT–1
Berger, Sidney L. 1936– CTFT–1
Berger, Stephen 1954– CTFT–1
Bergerat, Emile 1845–? .... WWasWT
Bergere, Jenica 1974– CTFT–44
Bergere, Lee CTFT–8
Bergere, Valerie 1872–1938 .... WWasWT
Bergeron, Philippe 1959– CTFT–46
   Earlier sketch in CTFT–23
Bergese, Micha 1945– CTFT–4
Berghof, Herbert 1909–1990 .... CTFT–4
   Earlier sketch in WWT–17
Bergin, Patrick 1951– CTFT–71
   Earlier sketches in CTFT–13, 22, 32
Bergman, Alan 1925– CTFT–53
   Earlier sketch in CTFT–10
Bergman, Andrew 1945– CTFT–67
   Earlier sketch in CTFT–11
Bergman, Daniel 1962– CTFT–21
Bergman, Ingmar 1918– CTFT–30
   Earlier sketches in CTFT–3, 19
Bergman, Ingrid 1915–1982 .... CTFT–1
   Earlier sketch in WWT–17
Bergman, J. Peter 1946– CTFT–1
Bergman, Marilyn 1929– CTFT–53
   Earlier sketch in CTFT–10
Bergman, Sandahl CTFT–7
Bergner, Elisabeth 1900–1986 .... WWT–17

Bergstrom, Hilda .... WWasWT
Beringer, Esme 1875–1936 .... WWasWT
Beringer, Mrs. Oscar 1856–1936 .... WWasWT
Beringer, Vera 1879–1964 .... WWasWT
Beristain, Gabriel CTFT–64
Berk, Michael CTFT–40
Berk, Tony ?–1988 .... CTFT–2
Berkeley, Ballard 1904–1988 .... WWasWT
Berkeley, Busby 1859–1976 .... WWT–16
Berkeley, Reginald Cheyne
   1890–1935 .... WWasWT
Berkeley, Wilma .... WWasWT
Berkeley, Xander 1955(?)– CTFT–67
   Earlier sketch in CTFT–30
Berkley, Elizabeth 1972(?)– CTFT–62
   Earlier sketches in CTFT–16, 28
Berkoff, Steven 1937– CTFT–79
   Earlier sketches in CTFT–10, 36; WWT–17
Berkson, Susan CTFT–3
Berle, Milton 1908– CTFT–31
   Earlier sketches in CTFT–3, 19; WWT–17
Berlin, Irving 1888–1989 .... CTFT–8
   Earlier sketch in WWT–17
Berlind, Roger 1930– CTFT–38
   Earlier sketches in CTFT–1, 12
Berliner, Ron 1958– CTFT–3
Berling, Charles 1958– CTFT–38
Berlinger, Joe 1963(?)– CTFT–38
Berlinger, Milton
   See .... Berle, Milton
Berlinger, Robert 1958– CTFT–62
Berlinger, Warren 1937– CTFT–5
   Earlier sketch in WWT–17
Berlyn, Alfred 1860–1936 .... WWasWT
Berman, Bruce 1952– CTFT–64
   Earlier sketch in CTFT–29
Berman, Danielle CTFT–29
Berman, Ed 1941– CTFT–5
   Earlier sketch in WWT–17
Berman, Len CTFT–40
Berman, Pandro S. 1905–1996 .... CTFT–21
Berman, Rick 1945– CTFT–46
   Earlier sketch in CTFT–23
Berman, Shelley 1926– CTFT–6
Bermange, Barry 1933– CTFT–11
Bermel, Albert 1927– CTFT–1
Bern, Art
   See .... Brauner, Artur
Bernadotte, Sirio
   See .... Argento, Dario
Bernard, Barney 1877–1924 .... WWasWT
Bernard, Carlos 1962– CTFT–69
Bernard, Crystal 1959– CTFT–62
   Earlier sketches in CTFT–16, 28
Bernard, Jason 1938–1996 .... CTFT–15
   Obituary in CTFT–16
   Earlier sketch in CTFT–8
Bernard, Jean Jacques 1888– .... WWasWT
Bernard, Kenneth 1930– CTFT–1
Bernard, Sam 1863–1927 .... WWasWT
Bernard, Tristan 1866–1947 .... WWasWT
Bernardi, Barry CTFT–36
Bernd, Art
   See .... Brauner, Artur
Bernede, Arthur .... WWasWT
Bernette, Sheila WWT–17
Bernhard, Harvey 1924– CTFT–23
   Earlier sketch in CTFT–4
Bernhard, Sandra 1955– CTFT–60
   Earlier sketches in CTFT–10, 17, 28
   Brief Entry in CTFT–6
Bernhardt, Kevin 1961– CTFT–62

Bernhardt, Melvin CTFT–2
   Earlier sketch in WWT–17
Bernhardt, Sarah 1845–1923 .... WWasWT
Bernheim, Shirl 1921(?)– CTFT–32
Bernsen, Collin CTFT–69
Bernsen, Corbin 1954– CTFT–43
   Earlier sketches in CTFT–7, 14
Bernstein, Adam 1960– CTFT–74
Bernstein, Aline 1882–1955 .... WWasWT
Bernstein, Armyan CTFT–62
   Earlier sketch in CTFT–28
Bernstein, Charles 1943– CTFT–43
   Earlier sketches in CTFT–11, 22
Bernstein, Elmer 1922– CTFT–32
   Earlier sketches in CTFT–4, 11, 22
Bernstein, Henry 1875–1953 .... WWasWT
Bernstein, Jay 1937– CTFT–5
Bernstein, Leonard 1918–1990 .... CTFT–11
   Earlier sketches in CTFT–3; WWT–17
Bernstein, Walter 1919– CTFT–33
   Earlier sketches in CTFT–1, 6
Beroza, Janet CTFT–2
Berr, Georges 1867–1942 .... WWasWT
Berr De Turique, Julien 1863–1923 .... WWasWT
Berri, Claude 1934– CTFT–55
   Earlier sketches in CTFT–8, 15, 26
Berridge, Elizabeth 1962– CTFT–37
   Earlier sketches in CTFT–5, 13
Berry, Adam CTFT–70
Berry, David 1943– CTFT–30
   Earlier sketches in CTFT–2, 18
Berry, Eric 1913– WWT–17
Berry, Halle 1968– CTFT–43
   Earlier sketches in CTFT–11, 22
Berry, James 1883–? .... WWasWT
Berry, John 1917– CTFT–11
Berry, Josh CTFT–76
Berry, Ken 1933– CTFT–8
Berry, Raymond
   See .... Barry, Raymond J.
Berry, Tom CTFT–75
Berry, Vincent 1987– CTFT–46
Berry, William Henry 1870–1951 .... WWasWT
Berryman, Michael 1948– CTFT–63
Berstein, Sheryl CTFT–40
Bertinelli, Valerie 1960– CTFT–37
   Earlier sketches in CTFT–3, 13
Bertolazzi, Carlo 1870–? .... WWasWT
Bertolucci, Bernardo 1940(?)– CTFT–47
   Earlier sketches in CTFT–4, 12, 23
Bertorelli, Toni CTFT–38
Bertram, Arthur 1860–1955 .... WWasWT
Bertram, Eugene 1872–1941 .... WWasWT
Bertram, Laura 1978– CTFT–61
Bertrand, Sandra 1943– CTFT–1
Beruh, Joseph 1924–1989 .... CTFT–8
   Earlier sketch in WWT–17
Besch, Bibi 1940–1996 .... CTFT–6
   Obituary in CTFT–16
   Earlier sketch in CTFT–1
Besier, Rudolf 1878–1942 .... WWasWT
Bessell, Ted 1942–1996 .... CTFT–9
   Obituary in CTFT–16
Bessette, Denise 1954– CTFT–30
   Earlier sketches in CTFT–2, 19
Besso, Claudia CTFT–79
Besson, Luc 1959– CTFT–37
Best, Ahmed 1974– CTFT–67
   Earlier sketch in CTFT–30
Best, Edna 1900–1974 .... WWasWT
Best, James 1926– CTFT–43
   Earlier sketch in CTFT–21
Best, Wayne CTFT–62

Betancourt, Anne.. CTFT–58
Bethencourt, Francis 1926–.................... WWT–17
Bethune, Ivy 1918–................................. CTFT–62
Bethune, Zina 1950(?)–............................. CTFT–9
Bettany, Paul 1971–................................ CTFT–74
Bettelheim, Edwin 1865–1938.............. WWasWT
Bettger, Lyle 1915–................................... CTFT–1
Betti, Laura 1934–.................................. CTFT–34
    Earlier sketch in CTFT–8
Bettis, Angela CTFT–71
    Earlier sketch in CTFT–32
Bettis, John 1946–................................... CTFT–23
    Earlier sketch in CTFT–12
Bettis, Valerie ?–1982 .... WWT–17
Betts, Daniel CTFT–62
    Earlier sketch in CTFT–28
Betts, Edward William 1881–?.............. WWasWT
Betts, Ernest WWT–11
Betts, Jack CTFT–46
Bevan, Faith 1896–................................. WWasWT
Bevan, Isla 1910–.................................... WWasWT
Bevan, Tim 1958–.................................... CTFT–74
Beveridge, J. D. 1844–1926 .... WWasWT
Beveridge, Ryan....................................... CTFT–79
Beverley, Trazana 1945–......................... CTFT–15
    Earlier sketch in CTFT–8
Bewes, Rodney 1937–............................. WWT–17
Bey, John Toles
    See.. Toles–Bey, John
Beyer, Elsie WWT–13
Beymer, Richard 1939(?)–....................... CTFT–41
    Earlier sketch in CTFT–9
Beyonce
    See .... Knowles, Beyonce
Bhatia, Amin CTFT–79
Bialik, Mayim 1975–............................... CTFT–48
    Earlier sketch in CTFT–13
Bibb, Leslie 1973(?)– CTFT–58
Bibby, Charles 1878–1917.................... WWasWT
Bibby, Jackie 1951(?)– CTFT–42
Bibi
    See .... Andersson, Bibi
Bicat, Tony 1945– WWT–17
Bick, Stewart CTFT–42
Bickford, Charles A. 1891–1933............ WWasWT
Bickford, David 1953–.............................. CTFT–4
Biddle, Adrian CTFT–62
    Earlier sketch in CTFT–28
Biddle, Ryan
    See .... Bittle, Ryan James
Biehn, Michael 1956–.............................. CTFT–53
    Earlier sketches in CTFT–8, 15, 25
Biel, Jessica 1982– CTFT–55
    Earlier sketch in CTFT–26
Bierko, Craig 1965(?)– CTFT–43
    Earlier sketch in CTFT–21
Bigelow, Kathryn CTFT–10
Biggar, Trisha CTFT–40
Biggs, Casey 1955– CTFT–39
Biggs, Jason 1978–.................................. CTFT–67
    Earlier sketch in CTFT–30
Biggs, Richard 1961– CTFT–48
    Earlier sketch in CTFT–23
Biggs–Dawson, Roxann
    See .... Dawson, Roxann
Bikel, Theodore 1924–............................. CTFT–33
    Earlier sketches in CTFT–5; WWT–17
Bilbrooke, Lydia 1888–1990.................. WWasWT
Bilderback, Nicole 1975–......................... CTFT–53
Bilhaud, Paul 1854–1933 .... WWasWT
Bill, Tony 1940–... CTFT–6
Biller, Kenneth CTFT–54
Billig, Robert 1947– CTFT–1

Billing, H. Chiswell 1881–1934 .... WWasWT
Billing, Roy CTFT–71
    Earlier sketch in CTFT–32
Billings, Earl 1945–................................. CTFT–50
Billings, Josh 1947–.................................. CTFT–5
Billingslea, Beau 1953–........................... CTFT–74
Billingsley, Barbara 1922–....................... CTFT–21
Billingsley, John 1960–............................ CTFT–41
    Earlier sketch in CTFT–34
Billingsley, Peter 1971–........................... CTFT–39
    Earlier sketches in CTFT–7, 18
Billington, Adeline 1825–? .... WWasWT
Billington, Ken 1946–.............................. CTFT–44
    Earlier sketches in CTFT–1, 4, 21
Billington, Kevin 1934–.......................... WWT–17
Billington, Michael 1939–...................... WWT–17
Billington, Stephen 1969– CTFT–38
Billy O
    See .... O'Sullivan, Billy
Bilowit, Ira J. 1925– CTFT–1
Bilson, Bruce 1928–................................. CTFT–55
Bilson, Danny.. CTFT–75
Bilson, Rachel 1981– CTFT–74
    Earlier sketch in CTFT–11
Biname, Charles 1949–............................ CTFT–48
    Earlier sketch in CTFT–15
Binder, Steve... CTFT–1
Bingham, Amelia 1869–1927 .... WWasWT
Bingham, Jeffrey 1946– CTFT–6
Bingham, Sallie 1937–.............................. CTFT–1
Bingham, Traci 1968–............................. CTFT–39
Binner, Margery 1908– .... WWasWT
Binney, Constance 1900– .... WWasWT
Binoche, Juliette 1964– CTFT–70
    Earlier sketches in CTFT–12, 20, 31
Binus, Judith 1944–.................................. CTFT–2
Binyon, Laurence 1869–1943................ WWasWT
Birch, Frank 1889–1956 .... WWasWT
Birch, Patricia 1934(?)–........................... CTFT–37
    Earlier sketches in CTFT–10; WWT–17
Birch, Thora 1982–.................................. CTFT–64
    Earlier sketch in CTFT–29
Bird, Brad CTFT–27
Bird, Cordwainer
    See .... Ellison, Harlan
Bird, David 1907–................................... WWT–17
Bird, John 1936–..................................... WWT–17
Bird, Richard 1894–1986 .... WWasWT
Birk, Raye 1944–..................................... CTFT–51
Birkell, Lauren CTFT–74
Birkelund, Olivia 1963–.......................... CTFT–53
Birkenhead, Susan CTFT–42
Birkett, Bernadette 1948–....................... CTFT–55
    Earlier sketch in CTFT–20
Birkett, Jeremiah CTFT–49
Birkett, Viva 1887–1934 .... WWasWT
Birmingham, George A. 1865–1950 ...... WWasWT
Birmingham, Gil CTFT–69
Birnbaum, Roger 1950(?)–....................... CTFT–36
    Earlier sketch in CTFT–11
Birney, David 1939–................................ CTFT–62
    Earlier sketches in CTFT–1, 5; WWT–17
Birney, Reed 1954–................................... CTFT–1
Biroc, Joseph 1903(?)–1996..................... CTFT–17
    Obituary in CTFT–16
    Earlier sketch in CTFT–10
Bishop, Alfred 1848–1928 .... WWasWT
Bishop, Andre 1948–............................... CTFT–49
    Earlier sketches in CTFT–1, 9
Bishop, Carole
    See .... Bishop, Kelly
Bishop, Conrad J. 1941– CTFT–1
Bishop, George Walter 1886–1965........ WWasWT

Bishop, Joey 1918– CTFT–7
Bishop, John
    See .... Willis, Ted
Bishop, John CTFT–69
Bishop, Kate 1847–1923 .... WWasWT
Bishop, Kelly 1944– CTFT–33
    Earlier sketches in CTFT–5; WWT–17
Bishop, Tony
    See .... Day, Mark
Bishop, Will 1867–1944 .... WWasWT
Bisno, Leslie 1953–................................... CTFT–6
Bisoglio, Val 1926–................................... CTFT–8
Bissell, James D. 1951–........................... CTFT–36
    Earlier sketch in CTFT–11
Bisset, Jacqueline 1944–.......................... CTFT–72
    Earlier sketches in CTFT–2, 6, 13, 22, 32
Bisset, Josie 1970–.................................. CTFT–23
Bisson, Yannick 1969– CTFT–51
Bisutti, Danielle CTFT–72
Bitterman, Adam CTFT–78
Bittle, Ryan James 1977–......................... CTFT–67
    Earlier sketch in CTFT–30
Bivens, Diane E. CTFT–1
Bivens, J. B. CTFT–39
Bivens, John Paul, Jr.
    See .... Bivens, J. B.
Bixby, Bill 1934–1993 .... CTFT–9
    Obituary in CTFT–12
    Earlier sketch in CTFT–3
Bjoernstrand, Gunnar 1909–1986 .... CTFT–22
Bjornson, Maria CTFT–12
Black, Alex 1989–................................... CTFT–69
Black, Alfred 1913–................................ WWasWT
Black, Claudia 1972(?)–........................... CTFT–62
    Earlier sketch in CTFT–28
Black, David 1931–................................. WWT–17
Black, Don 1936(?)–................................ CTFT–63
Black, Dorothy 1899– .... WWasWT
Black, Dorothy 1913–1985 .... CTFT–2
    Earlier sketch in WWT–17
Black, George 1890–1945 .... WWasWT
Black, George 1911–1970 .... WWasWT
Black, Jack 1969–................................... CTFT–72
    Earlier sketch in CTFT–32
Black, James CTFT–59
    Earlier sketches in CTFT–17, 27
Black, Karen 1942(?)–.............................. CTFT–70
    Earlier sketches in CTFT–4, 20, 31
Black, Lewis 1948– CTFT–64
Black, Lucas 1982– CTFT–47
    Earlier sketch in CTFT–23
Black, Malcolm 1928– CTFT–1
Black, Marina CTFT–71
Black, Mary CTFT–77
Black, Meghan CTFT–69
Black, Michael Ian 1971– CTFT–66
Black, Noel 1937– CTFT–18
    Earlier sketch in CTFT–2
Black, Shane 1961–................................. CTFT–36
    Earlier sketch in CTFT–11
Black, William
    See.. Suplee, Ethan
Blackburn, Richard.................................. CTFT–49
Blackler, Betty 1929–............................. WWasWT
Blackman, Eugene Joseph
    1922–... CTFT–1
Blackman, Fred J. 1879–1951 .... WWasWT
Blackman, Honor 1926– CTFT–70
    Earlier sketches in CTFT–4, 20, 31; WWT–17
Blackman, Robert CTFT–49
Blackmer, Sidney 1895–......................... WWasWT
Blackmore, Peter 1909– .... WWasWT
Blackwood, Christian 1942–.................... CTFT–11

Blacque, Taurean 1941(?) CTFT–57
    Earlier sketch in CTFT–8
Blade, Jake
    See .... Shaw, Scott
Blades, Ruben 1948– CTFT–70
    Earlier sketches in CTFT–5, 12, 21, 31
Blaine, Vivian 1921(?)–1995 .... CTFT–5
    Obituary in CTFT–15
    Earlier sketch in WWT–17
Blair, Isla 1944– CTFT–38
    Earlier sketch in WWT–17
Blair, Joyce 1932– WWT–17
Blair, Kevin
    See .... Spirtas, Kevin
Blair, Linda 1959– CTFT–70
    Earlier sketches in CTFT–3, 19, 31
Blair, Lionel 1931– WWT–17
Blair, Pamela 1949– CTFT–19
    Earlier sketch in CTFT–2
Blair, Selma 1972– CTFT–55
    Earlier sketch in CTFT–26
Blaisdell, Nesbitt 1928– CTFT–67
    Earlier sketches in CTFT–3, 19, 30
Blake, Andre B. CTFT–76
    Earlier sketch in CTFT–34
Blake, Betty 1920– CTFT–1
Blake, Charles H. 1916– CTFT–1
Blake, Ellen CTFT–65
Blake, Geoffrey 1962– CTFT–63
    Earlier sketch in CTFT–28
Blake, Harry 1866–? .... WWasWT
Blake, Josh 1975– CTFT–8
Blake, Noah 1964(?)– CTFT–62
Blake, Robert 1933(?)– CTFT–9
    Earlier sketch in CTFT–3
Blake, Yvonne 1938– CTFT–53
    Earlier sketch in CTFT–25
Blakeley, James 1873–1915 .... WWasWT
Blakelock, Denys 1901–1970 .... WWasWT
Blakely, Colin 1930–1987 .... CTFT–4
    Earlier sketch in WWT–17
Blakely, Susan 1948(?)– CTFT–77
    Earlier sketches in CTFT–6, 34
Blakemore, Michael 1928– CTFT–38
    Earlier sketches in CTFT–6, 13; WWT–17
Blakemore, Sean CTFT–69
Blakeslee, Susan CTFT–69
Blakley, Ronee 1946– CTFT–7
Blakiston, Clarence 1864–1943 .... WWasWT
Blalock, Jolene 1975– CTFT–46
Blanc, JB 1969– CTFT–70
Blanc, Jennifer 1974– CTFT–42
Blanc, Mel 1908–1989 .... CTFT–8
Blanchard, Rachel 1976– CTFT–47
    Earlier sketch in CTFT–23
Blanchard, Terence 1962– CTFT–65
    Earlier sketch in CTFT–29
Blanche, Ada 1862–1953 .... WWasWT
Blanche, Marie 1893– .... WWasWT
Blanche, Robert CTFT–68
Blanchett, Cate 1969– CTFT–69
    Earlier sketches in CTFT–21, 31
Bland, Alan 1897–1946 .... WWasWT
Bland, Joyce 1906–1963 .... WWasWT
Blaney, Charles E. ?–1944 .... WWasWT
Blaney, Norah .... WWasWT
Blank, Kenny 1977– CTFT–76
Blank, Les 1935– CTFT–14
Blankfield, Mark 1950– CTFT–44
Blasi, Rosa 1972– CTFT–73
Blatty, William Peter 1928– CTFT–21
    Earlier sketch in CTFT–4
Blaustein, Addie 1960– CTFT–52

Blavet, Emile 1838–? .... WWasWT
Blaxill, Peter 1931– CTFT–1
Blayney, May 1875–1953 .... WWasWT
Bleasdale, Alan 1946– CTFT–36
    Earlier sketch in CTFT–10
Bleckner, Jeff 1943– CTFT–69
    Earlier sketches in CTFT–4, 21, 31; WWT–17
Bledel, Alexis 1981– CTFT–73
Bledsoe, Tempestt 1973– CTFT–36
    Earlier sketch in CTFT–11
Bleeth, Yasmine 1972(?)– CTFT–60
    Earlier sketches in CTFT–16, 28
Bleibtreu, Moritz 1971– CTFT–67
    Earlier sketch in CTFT–30
Blendell, Troy CTFT–75
Blessed, Brian 1937– CTFT–53
    Earlier sketches in CTFT–8, 15, 25
Blethyn, Brenda 1946– CTFT–67
    Earlier sketches in CTFT–20, 30
Bleu, Corbin 1989– CTFT–78
Bley, Maurice G. 1910– CTFT–4
Blick, Newton 1899–1965 .... WWasWT
Blicker, Jason CTFT–46
Blier, Bernard 1916–1989 .... CTFT–8
Blier, Bertrand 1939– CTFT–30
    Earlier sketch in CTFT–8
Blinn, Holbrook 1872–1928 .... WWasWT
Blinn, William 1937– CTFT–53
    Earlier sketch in CTFT–10
Bliss, Boti 1975– CTFT–70
Bliss, Helena 1917– WWT–17
Bliss, Thomas A. CTFT–41
Blitzer, Wolf 1948– CTFT–40
Bloch, Robert 1917–1994 .... CTFT–2
    Obituary in CTFT–13
Bloch, Scotty 192(?)– CTFT–36
    Earlier sketches in CTFT–1, 11
Block, Larry 1942– CTFT–53
    Earlier sketches in CTFT–2, 8, 15, 25
Blocker, Dirk 1957– CTFT–58
Blomfield, Derek 1920–1964 .... WWasWT
Blommaert, Susan 1948– CTFT–62
    Earlier sketch in CTFT–28
Blomquist, Alan C. 1953– CTFT–56
    Earlier sketch in CTFT–26
Blondell, Joan 1909–1979 .... WWT–16
Bloodworth–Thomason, Linda
    1947(?)– CTFT–10
Bloom, Brian 1970– CTFT–43
    Earlier sketch in CTFT–21
Bloom, Claire 1931– CTFT–73
    Earlier sketches in CTFT–4, 11, 22, 32;
    WWT–17
Bloom, David 1964(?)– CTFT–40
Bloom, John
    See .... Briggs, Joe Bob
Bloom, John 1935– CTFT–48
    Earlier sketch in CTFT–11
Bloom, Lindsay 1955– CTFT–3
Bloom, Michael 1950– CTFT–4
Bloom, Orlando 1977– CTFT–43
Bloom, Verna CTFT–7
Bloomfield, George 1930– CTFT–79
    Earlier sketch in CTFT–36
Bloomfield, John CTFT–40
Bloomgarden, Kermit 1904–1976 .... WWT–16
Blore, Eric 1887–1959 .... WWasWT
Blossom, Henry Martyn, Jr.
    1866–1919 .... WWasWT
Blossom, Roberts 1924– CTFT–41
Blount, Helon 1929– CTFT–4
    Earlier sketch in WWT–17

Blount, Lisa 1957– CTFT–67
    Earlier sketches in CTFT–7, 18, 30
Blow, Sydney 1878–1961 .... WWasWT
Blu, Susan CTFT–47
Blucas, Marc 1972– CTFT–42
Bludworth, Bill
    See .... Morgan, Glen
    See .... Wong, James
Blue, Callum 1977– CTFT–68
Blue, Zachary
    See .... Stine, R.L.
Bluhm, Brady 1983– CTFT–70
Blum, Mark 1950– CTFT–53
    Earlier sketches in CTFT–8, 15, 25
Blum, Steven CTFT–48
Blumas, Trevor 1984– CTFT–67
Blumenfeld, Robert 1943– CTFT–3
Blumenkrantz, Jeff 1965– CTFT–74
    Earlier sketches in CTFT–8, 33
Blundell, Graeme 1945– WWT–17
Blunt, Emily 1983– CTFT–74
Bluteau, Lothaire 1957– CTFT–73
    Earlier sketches in CTFT–20, 32
Bluth, Don CTFT–25
    Earlier sketches in CTFT–6, 15
Bluthal, John 1929– CTFT–41
    Earlier sketch in CTFT–20
Blutig, Eduard
    See .... Gorey, Edward
Blyden, Larry 1925–1975 .... WWT–16
Blyth–Pratt, Charles Edward
    1869–? .... WWasWT
Blyth–Pratt, Violet .... WWasWT
Blythe, Benedick CTFT–67
Blythe, Bobby 1894– .... WWasWT
Blythe, Coralie 1880–1928 .... WWasWT
Blythe, John 1921– WWT–17
Blythe, Violet .... WWasWT
Boam, Jeffrey 1949– CTFT–10
Boardman, Chris 1954– CTFT–59
    Earlier sketch in CTFT–27
Boatman, Michael 1964– CTFT–62
    Earlier sketches in CTFT–16, 28
Bobadilla, Pepita .... WWasWT
Bobbie, Walter 1945– CTFT–20
Bobby, Anne 1967– CTFT–43
    Earlier sketch in CTFT–21
Bobby Z
    See .... Zajonc, Robert "Bobby Z"
Bobs, The Two .... WWasWT
Bocarde, Kevin CTFT–58
Bochco, Steven 1943– CTFT–47
    Earlier sketches in CTFT–6, 13, 23
Bocher, Christian 1962– CTFT–55
Bochner, Hart 1956(?)– CTFT–67
    Earlier sketches in CTFT–2, 18, 30
Bochner, Lloyd 1924–2005 .... CTFT–30
    Earlier sketches in CTFT–7, 18
    Obituary in CTFT–68
Bock, Jerry 1928– WWT–17
Bockstael, Robert CTFT–59
    Earlier sketch in CTFT–17
Bocquet, Gavin CTFT–48
    Earlier sketch in CTFT–23
Bode, Milton 1860–1938 .... WWasWT
Bode, Ralf D. CTFT–11
Boden, Richard 1953– CTFT–64
Bodie, Dr. Walford 1870–? .... WWasWT
Bodom, Borgchild WWT–7
Bodrov, Sergei 1948– CTFT–31
    Earlier sketch in CTFT–20
Boehmer, J. Paul 1965– CTFT–68
    Earlier sketch in CTFT–30

Cumulative Index

Boen, Earl 1941(?)– CTFT–42
   Earlier sketch in CTFT–20
Boers, Frank Jr.
   See .... Bonner, Frank
Boetticher, Budd 1916– CTFT–12
Bofshever, Michael 1950– CTFT–6
Boganny, Joe 1874–? .... WWasWT
Bogard, Travis 1918– CTFT–3
Bogarde, Dirk 1921(?)– CTFT–9
   Earlier sketch in WWasWT
Bogardus, Stephen 1954– CTFT–43
   Earlier sketch in CTFT–22
Bogart, Humphrey 1899–1957 .... WWasWT
Bogart, Paul 1919– CTFT–12
   Earlier sketch in CTFT–1
Bogdanov, Michael 1938– CTFT–10
   Earlier sketch in WWT–17
Bogdanovich, Peter 1939– CTFT–46
   Earlier sketches in CTFT–1, 4, 12, 23
Boggetti, Victor 1895– .... WWasWT
Bogin, Abba 1925– CTFT–1
Bogle, Warren
   See .... Bergman, Andrew
Bogosian, Eric 1953– CTFT–50
   Earlier sketches in CTFT–7, 14, 24
Bogush, Elizabeth 1977– CTFT–73
Bohannon, Judy CTFT–2
Bohay, Heidi CTFT–3
Bohen, Ian 1976– CTFT–60
Bohnen, Roman ?–1949 .... WWasWT
Bohrer, Corinne 1958– CTFT–64
Bohringer, Richard 1941– CTFT–29
Bohringer, Romane 1973– CTFT–30
Bohrman, David 1954– CTFT–13
Boht, Jean 1936– CTFT–8
Bokino, Carlo
   See .... Band, Charles
Bolam, James 1938– CTFT–70
   Earlier sketches in CTFT–5, 20, 31; WWT–17
Boland, Jennifer
Boland, Joanne 1975– CTFT–67
Boland, Mary 1885–1965 .... WWasWT
Bolasni, Saul CTFT–1
Bole, Cliff CTFT–39
Bolender, Bill CTFT–43
Boles, John 1900–1969 .... WWasWT
Boleslawski, Richard 1889–1937 .... WWasWT
Bolger, John 1954– CTFT–62
   Earlier sketches in CTFT–17, 28
Bolger, Ray 1904–1987 .... CTFT–3
   Earlier sketch in WWT–17
Boll, Uwe 1965– CTFT–79
Bollea, Terry
   See .... Hogan, Hulk
Bolm, Adolph 1887–1951 .... WWasWT
Bologna, Gabriel CTFT–78
Bologna, Joseph 1934(?)– CTFT–77
   Earlier sketches in CTFT–3, 9, 35
Bolotin, Craig CTFT–28
Bolt, David CTFT–54
Bolt, Jeremy CTFT–63
Bolt, Jonathan 1935– CTFT–3
Bolt, Robert 1924–1995 .... CTFT–12
   Obituary in CTFT–18
   Earlier sketches in CTFT–4; WWT–17
Bolton, Guy Reginald 1884–1979 .... WWT–16
Bonaduce, Danny 1959– CTFT–39
   Earlier sketch in CTFT–15
Bond, Acton ?–1941 .... WWasWT
Bond, C. G. 1945– WWT–17
Bond, Derek 1920– CTFT–1
Bond, Edward 1934– CTFT–16
   Earlier sketches in CTFT–4; WWT–17

Bond, Frederic 1861–1914 .... WWasWT
Bond, Gary 1940–1995 .... CTFT–3
   Obituary in CTFT–15
   Earlier sketch in WWT–17
Bond, Jessie 1853–1942 .... WWasWT
Bond, Lilian 1910– .... WWasWT
Bond, Samantha 1962– CTFT–62
   Earlier sketch in CTFT–28
Bond, Sheila 1928– CTFT–1
   Earlier sketch in WWasWT
Bond, Sudie 1928–1984 .... CTFT–1
   Earlier sketch in WWT–17
Bond, Timothy 1942– CTFT–79
   Earlier sketch in CTFT–36
Bondi, Beulah 1892–1981 .... WWasWT
Bondor, Rebecca CTFT–1
Bonerz, Peter 1938– CTFT–79
   Earlier sketches in CTFT–1, 11, 36
Bones, Ken CTFT–72
   Earlier sketch in CTFT–32
Bonet, Lisa 1967– CTFT–48
   Earlier sketch in CTFT–10
   Brief Entry in CTFT–4
Bonfils, Helen 1889–1972 .... WWasWT
Bonham Carter, Helena 1966– CTFT–47
   Earlier sketches in CTFT–7, 14, 23
Bonifant, J. Evan 1985– CTFT–76
   Earlier sketches in CTFT–22, 32
Bonilla, Michelle CTFT–56
Bon Jovi, Jon 1962– CTFT–70
   Earlier sketches in CTFT–21, 31
Bonnaire, Henri 1869–? .... WWasWT
Bonner, Frank 1942– CTFT–62
   Earlier sketch in CTFT–7
Bonneville, Hugh 1963– CTFT–56
   Earlier sketch in CTFT–26
Bonniere, Rene CTFT–36
Bonnot, Francoise CTFT–29
Bono 1960– CTFT–40
Bono, Sonny 1935–1998 .... CTFT–7
   Obituary in CTFT–22
Bonsall, Brian 1981– CTFT–14
Bonus, Ben ?–1984 .... WWT–17
Boockvor, Steve 1945– CTFT–1
Booke, Sorrell 1930–1994 .... CTFT–4
   Obituary in CTFT–13
   Earlier sketch in WWT–17
Bookstaver, Sandy 1973– CTFT–65
BoomK.A.T.
   See .... Manning, Taryn
Boone, Debby 1956– CTFT–1
Boone, Mark, Jr. 1955– CTFT–38
Boone, Pat 1934– CTFT–47
Boor, Frank ?–1938 .... WWasWT
Boorem, Mika 1987– CTFT–64
Boorman, John 1933– CTFT–48
   Earlier sketches in CTFT–6, 15
Boorstin, Jon CTFT–10
Boosler, Elayne 1952(?)– CTFT–11
Boot, Gladys ?–1964 .... WWasWT
Booth, James 1933– WWT–17
Booth, Judas
   See .... Lynch, David
Booth, Kristin 1974– CTFT–54
Booth, Lindy 1979– CTFT–44
Booth, Shirley 1898–1992 .... CTFT–4
   Obituary in CTFT–11
   Earlier sketch in WWT–17
Booth, Webster 1902– .... WWasWT
Boothby, Victoria CTFT–1
Boothe, Clare 1903–1987 .... WWasWT
Boothe, Power 1945– CTFT–1

Boothe, Powers 1949(?)– CTFT–69
   Earlier sketches in CTFT–4, 18, 30
Borden, Bill CTFT–60
   Earlier sketch in CTFT–28
Borden, Lizzie 1955– CTFT–12
Borden, Steve 1959– CTFT–69
   Earlier sketch in CTFT–30
Bordoni, Irene ?–1953 .... WWasWT
Boreanaz, David 1971– CTFT–58
   Earlier sketch in CTFT–27
Borell, Louis 1906– .... WWasWT
Borgnine, Ernest 1917(?)– CTFT–70
   Earlier sketches in CTFT–2, 7, 19, 31
Boris, Robert M. 1945– CTFT–5
Borlenghi, Matt 1967– CTFT–59
Borlin, Jean .... WWasWT
Borman, Kay
   See .... K Callan
Borman, M.
   See .... Skerritt, Tom
Born, Rosco 1950– CTFT–38
Borowitz, Katherine CTFT–34
Borrego, Jesse 1962– CTFT–75
   Earlier sketches in CTFT–5, 33
Borris, Clay 1950– CTFT–36
Borstein, Alex 1971– CTFT–70
Bosco, Philip 1930– CTFT–70
   Earlier sketches in CTFT–1, 4, 11, 21, 31;
   WWT–17
Bosley, Tom 1927– CTFT–44
   Earlier sketches in CTFT–4, 14; WWT–17
Bosse–Vingard, Harriet Sofie
   1878–? .... WWasWT
Bosson, Barbara 1939(?)– CTFT–40
   Earlier sketches in CTFT–7, 18
Bostock, Thomas H. 1899– .... WWasWT
Bostwick, Barry 1945(?)– CTFT–47
   Earlier sketches in CTFT–2, 5, 12, 23
Boswell, Charles CTFT–60
Bosworth, Kate 1983– CTFT–69
Botsford, Sara 1951– CTFT–79
Bott, Alan 1894– .... WWasWT
Bottin, Rob 1959(?)– CTFT–41
   Earlier sketch in CTFT–9
Botto, Juan Diego 1975– CTFT–34
Bottomley, Gordon 1874–1948 .... WWasWT
Bottoms, Joseph 1954– CTFT–41
   Earlier sketches in CTFT–4, 20
Bottoms, Sam 1955– CTFT–41
   Earlier sketches in CTFT–4, 20
Bottoms, Timothy 1951– CTFT–70
   Earlier sketches in CTFT–3, 20, 31
Boucher, Victor 1879–1942 .... WWasWT
Bouchier, Chili 1909– CTFT–6
   Earlier sketch in WWT–17
Boucicault, Aubrey 1869–1913 .... WWasWT
Boucicault, Dion G. 1859–1929 .... WWasWT
Boucicault, Mrs. Dion 1833–1916 .... WWasWT
Boucicault, Nina 1867–1950 .... WWasWT
Boughton, Rutland 1878–1960 .... WWasWT
Bould, Beckett 1880–? .... WWasWT
Boule, Kathryn 1949– CTFT–1
Boulter, Rosalyn 1916– .... WWasWT
Boulting, Sydney Arthur Rembrandt
   See .... Cotes, Peter
Boulton, Guy Pelham 1890– .... WWasWT
Bouquet, Michel 1926– CTFT–30
Bouquett, Tamara Tunie
   See .... Tunie, Tamara
Bourchier, Arthur 1863–1927 .... WWasWT
Bourgeois, John CTFT–44
Bourne, Adeline .... WWasWT

Bourne, Douglas
  See.. Doug, Doug E.
Bourne, J. R. 1970– CTFT–78
Bourne, Mel 1923– CTFT–48
  Earlier sketch in CTFT–10
Bourneuf, Philip 1912–1979 .... WWT–16
Boutsikaris, Dennis 1952– CTFT–62
  Earlier sketches in CTFT–16, 28
Bouwmeester, Louis 1842–? .... WWasWT
Bova, Joseph 1924– CTFT–4
  Earlier sketch in WWT–17
Bovasso, Julie 1930–1991 .... CTFT–7
  Obituary in CTFT–10
  Earlier sketch in WWT–17
Bovill, C. H. 1878–1918 .... WWasWT
Bovy, Berthe 1887– .... WWasWT
Bow, Clara 1905–1965 .... CTFT–20
Bowab, John 1933– CTFT–48
  Earlier sketch in CTFT–11
Bowden, Charles WWT–17
Bowe, David CTFT–77
  Earlier sketch in CTFT–34
Bowen, John CTFT–48
Bowen, John 1924– WWT–17
Bowen, John Pearson 1953– CTFT–13
Bowen, Julie 1970– CTFT–77
  Earlier sketch in CTFT–34
Bowen, Michael CTFT–62
  Earlier sketch in CTFT–28
Bowen, Roger 1932–1996 .... CTFT–7
  Obituary in CTFT–16
Bower, Marian ?–1945 .... WWasWT
Bower, Tom CTFT–77
  Earlier sketch in CTFT–34
Bowers, Faubion 1917– CTFT–2
Bowers, Lally 1917–1984 .... WWT–17
Bowers, Richard 1964– CTFT–41
Bowers, Robert Hood 1877–1941 .... WWasWT
Bowes, Alice ?–1969 .... WWasWT
Bowes, Janet Elizabeth 1944– CTFT–1
Bowie, David 1947– CTFT–69
  Earlier sketches in CTFT–3, 18, 30
Bowles, Anthony 1931– WWT–17
Bowles, Paul 1910– CTFT–1
Bowles, Peter 1936– CTFT–37
  Earlier sketches in CTFT–6, 13; WWT–17
Bowman, Chuck CTFT–52
Bowman, Nellie 1878–? .... WWasWT
Bowman, Rob 1960– CTFT–51
  Earlier sketches in CTFT–15, 25
Box, Edgar
  See.. Vidal, Gore
Box, John 1920– CTFT–10
Boxer, (Cyril) John 1909– WWT–17
Boxleitner, Bruce 1950– CTFT–45
  Earlier sketches in CTFT–3, 14
Boyar, Lombardo 1973– CTFT–77
  Earlier sketch in CTFT–34
Boyce, Rodger CTFT–65
Boyce, Todd 1961– CTFT–43
Boycea, Roger
  See .... Boyce, Rodger
Boyd, Billy 1968– CTFT–43
Boyd, Frank M. 1863–? .... WWasWT
Boyd, Guy CTFT–50
Boyd, Lynda CTFT–57
Boyd, Russell 1944– CTFT–40
Boyer, Charles 1899– .... WWasWT
Boyett, Robert L. 1942(?)– CTFT–13
Boyle, Billy 1945– WWT–17
Boyle, Danny 1956– CTFT–69
  Earlier sketch in CTFT–30

Boyle, Katie 1926– CTFT–11
  Earlier sketch in CTFT–1
Boyer, Katy CTFT–68
Boyle, Lara Flynn 1970– CTFT–58
  Earlier sketches in CTFT–10, 17, 27
Boyle, Lisa 1968– CTFT–38
Boyle, Peter 1935–2006 .... CTFT–64
  Obituary in CTFT–74
  Earlier sketches in CTFT–3, 9, 16, 29
Boyle, William 1853–1923 .... WWasWT
Boyne, Clifton 1874–1945 .... WWasWT
Boyne, Leonard 1853–1920 .... WWasWT
Bozman, Ron CTFT–78
Braban, Harvey 1883–? .... WWasWT
Bracco, Elizabeth CTFT–46
Bracco, Lorraine 1955(?)– CTFT–10
Bracco, Roberto 1863–1943 .... WWasWT
Brach, Gerard 1927– CTFT–6
Bracken, Eddie 1920– CTFT–41
  Earlier sketches in CTFT–3, 19; WWT–17
Bradbury, James H. 1857–1940 .... WWasWT
Bradbury, Malcolm 1932– CTFT–10
Bradbury, Ray 1920– CTFT–62
  Earlier sketches in CTFT–10, 17, 28
Braddock, Micky
  See .... Dolenz, Micky
Braden, Bernard 1916– .... WWasWT
Braden, William 1939– CTFT–18
  Earlier sketch in CTFT–2
Bradfield, W. Louis 1866–1919 .... WWasWT
Bradford, Jesse 1979– CTFT–69
  Earlier sketch in CTFT–30
Bradford, Richard 1937– CTFT–36
Bradley, Bart
  See.. Braverman, Bart
Bradley, Buddy 1908– .... WWasWT
Bradley, David 1942– CTFT–76
Bradley, Ed 1941–2006 .... CTFT–46
  Obituary in CTFT–74
  Earlier sketch in CTFT–23
Bradley, Elizabeth 1922–2000 .... CTFT–38
Bradley, Lillian Trimble 1875–1939 .... WWasWT
Bradshaw, John 1952– CTFT–79
  Earlier sketch in CTFT–36
Bradshaw, Terry 1948– CTFT–78
Brady, Leo 1917– CTFT–1
Brady, Orla 1961– CTFT–62
  Earlier sketch in CTFT–28
Brady, Scott 1924–1985 .... CTFT–2
Brady, Terence 1939– WWT–17
Brady, Veronica 1890–1964 .... WWasWT
Brady, Wayne 1972– CTFT–54
Brady, William A. 1863–1950 .... WWasWT
Brady, William A. 1900–1935 .... WWasWT
Brae, June 1918– .... WWasWT
Braeden, Eric 1941– CTFT–18
  Earlier sketch in CTFT–8
Braff, Zach 1975– CTFT–66
Braga, Brannon 1964– CTFT–49
Braga, Sonia 1950(?)– CTFT–38
  Earlier sketches in CTFT–7, 14
Bragaglia, Marinella .... WWasWT
Bragg, Bernard CTFT–3
Bragg, Melvyn 1939– CTFT–36
  Earlier sketch in CTFT–11
Braham, Horace 1893–1955 .... WWasWT
Braham, Leonora 1853–1931 .... WWasWT
Braham, Lionel .... WWasWT
Braham, Philip 1881–1934 .... WWasWT
Brahms, Caryl WWT–17
Braidwood, Tom 1948– CTFT–47
  Earlier sketch in CTFT–23
Braine, John 1922–1986 .... CTFT–4

Braithwaite, Lilian 1873–1948 .... WWasWT
Brakhage, Stan 1933– CTFT–42
  Earlier sketch in CTFT–20
Brambell, Wilfrid 1912–1985 .... WWT–17
Brammell, Abby 1979– CTFT–75
Bramon, Risa
  See .... Garcia, Risa Bramon
Branagh, Kenneth 1960– CTFT–39
  Earlier sketch in CTFT–9
Brancato, Chris CTFT–60
Brancato, John CTFT–61
Brancato, Lillo 1976– CTFT–50
  Earlier sketch in CTFT–43
Branch, Eileen 1911– .... WWasWT
Branch, William B. 1927– CTFT–13
Brand, Joshua 1952(?)– CTFT–11
Brand, Oscar 1920– CTFT–1
Brand, Steven 1967– CTFT–68
Brandauer, Klaus Maria 1944– CTFT–33
  Earlier sketches in CTFT–6, 33
Brandes, Marthe (Brunschwig)
  1862–1930 .... WWasWT
Brandis, Jonathan 1976– CTFT–40
Brandman, Michael CTFT–65
Brandman, Steven J. CTFT–65
Brando, Marlon 1924– CTFT–28
  Earlier sketches in CTFT–3, 10, 17
Brandon, Dorothy 1899?–1977 .... WWasWT
Brandon, Johnny CTFT–1
Brandon, Michael 1945– CTFT–64
  Earlier sketches in CTFT–7, 18, 29
Brandon–Thomas, Amy Marguerite
  1890– .... WWasWT
Brandon–Thomas, Jevan 1898– .... WWasWT
Brandt, Ivan 1903– .... WWasWT
Brandt, Yanna Kroyt 1933– CTFT–3
Brantley, Betsy 1955– CTFT–40
Brandy
  See .... Norwood, Brandy
Brandy, J. C. 1975– CTFT–69
Brannagh, Brigid 1972– CTFT–49
Brannon, Ash CTFT–28
Braoude, Patrick CTFT–34
Braschi, Nicoletta 1960– CTFT–27
Brass, Steffani 1992– CTFT–73
Brasseur, Albert Jules 1862–? .... WWasWT
Bratt, Benjamin 1963– CTFT–64
  Earlier sketches in CTFT–16, 29
Braugher, Andre 1962– CTFT–48
  Earlier sketches in CTFT–13, 23
Braughton, Fred
  See .... Murphy, Eddie
Braun, Steve 1976– CTFT–68
Brauner, Artur 1918– CTFT–31
  Earlier sketch in CTFT–21
Braverman, Bart 1946– CTFT–38
Braxton, Toni 1968(?)– CTFT–26
Bray, Thom 1954– CTFT–56
Bray, Yvonne de 1889– .... WWasWT
Brayton, Lily 1876–1953 .... WWasWT
Brazeau, Jay 1945– CTFT–72
  Earlier sketch in CTFT–32
Brazil, Scott CTFT–43
Brazzi, Rossano 1916–1994 .... CTFT–10
  Obituary in CTFT–15
Bread, Kim
  See.. Cleese, John
Brecher, Egon 1885–1946 .... WWasWT
Breck, Peter 1929– CTFT–60
Breckenridge, Alex 1982– CTFT–69
Breckenridge, Laura CTFT–68
Breckman, Andy 1955– CTFT–76

Brecusse, Leslie
　See .... Bricusse, Leslie
Breen, Helen 1902– .... WWasWT
Breen, Patrick 1960– CTFT–64
　Earlier sketch in CTFT–29
Breen, Robert 1914–1990 .... CTFT–2
Breese, Edmund 1871–1936 .... WWasWT
Bregman, Martin 1931– CTFT–41
　Earlier sketches in CTFT–1, 5, 19
Bregman, Tracey E. 1963– CTFT–58
Breker, Eric CTFT–71
Bremner, Ewen CTFT–69
　Earlier sketch in CTFT–30
Brendon, Nicholas 1971– CTFT–68
Brennan, Eileen 1938– CTFT–52
　Earlier sketches in CTFT–1, 8, 15, 25
Brenneman, Amy 1964– CTFT–53
　Earlier sketches in CTFT–15, 25
Brenner, Albert 1926– CTFT–11
Brenner, David 1945– CTFT–53
　Earlier sketches in CTFT–2, 18
Brenner, Dori CTFT–9
Brenner, Lisa 1974– CTFT–68
Brenner, Randy 1955– CTFT–3
Brent, Eve 1930– CTFT–63
　Earlier sketch in CTFT–28
Brent, Romney 1902–1976 .... WWasWT
Brenton, Howard 1942– CTFT–6
　Earlier sketch in WWT–17
Brereton, Austin 1862–1923 .... WWasWT
Breslin, Abigail 1966– CTFT–75
Breslin, Spencer 1992– CTFT–62
Bressack, Celia 1956– CTFT–3
Bresson, Robert 1907– CTFT–8
Brest, Martin 1951– CTFT–7
Brett, Jeremy 1935(?)–1995 .... CTFT–8
　Obituary in CTFT–15
　Earlier sketches in CTFT–3; WWT–17
Brett, Stanley 1879–1923 .... WWasWT
Breuer, Jim 1967– CTFT–75
Breuer, Lee 1937– CTFT–5
　Earlier sketch in WWT–17
Breuer, Marita CTFT–34
Breuler, Robert CTFT–32
Brewster, Jordana 1980– CTFT–56
　Earlier sketch in CTFT–26
Brewster, Paget 1969– CTFT–64
　Earlier sketch in CTFT–29
Brewster, Towsend Tyler 1924– CTFT–1
Brialy, Jean–Claude 1933– CTFT–39
　Earlier sketch in CTFT–16
Brian, Donald 1877–1948 .... WWasWT
Brice, Fanny 1891–1951 .... WWasWT
Brickman, Marshall 1941– CTFT–6
Bricusse, Leslie 1931– CTFT–53
　Earlier sketches in CTFT–9; WWT–17
Bridge, Andrew 1952– CTFT–39
　Earlier sketch in CTFT–14
Bridge, Peter 1925– WWT–17
Bridges, Beau 1941– CTFT–60
　Earlier sketches in CTFT–3, 10, 17, 28
Bridges, Brooke Marie 1991– CTFT–73
Bridges, James 1936–1993 .... CTFT–4
　Obituary in CTFT–12
Bridges, Jeff 1949– CTFT–60
　Earlier sketches in CTFT–3, 10, 17, 28
Bridges, Jimmy 1960– CTFT–71
Bridges, Jordan 1973– CTFT–69
　Earlier sketch in CTFT–30
Bridges, Lloyd 1913–1998 .... CTFT–11
　Obituary in CTFT–21
　Earlier sketch in CTFT–3
Bridges, Penny Bae 1990– CTFT–73

Bridges, Robert 1937– CTFT–3
Bridges, Sean CTFT–68
Bridges, Todd 1965– CTFT–70
　Earlier sketches in CTFT–20, 31
Bridges–Adams, W. 1889–1965 .... WWasWT
Bridgewater, Leslie 1893– .... WWasWT
Bridgewater, Stephen 1953– CTFT–67
　Earlier sketch in CTFT–30
Bridie, James 1888–1951 .... WWasWT
Brien, Alan 1925– WWT–17
Briercliffe, Nellie ?–1966 .... WWasWT
Brierley, David 1936– WWT–17
Briers, Richard 1934– CTFT–36
　Earlier sketches in CTFT–9; WWT–17
Brieux, Eugene 1858–1932 .... WWasWT
Briggs, Hedley 1907–1968 .... WWasWT
Briggs, Joe Bob 1953– CTFT–57
　Earlier sketches in CTFT–15, 25
Brighouse, Harold 1882–1958 .... WWasWT
Bright, Kellie 1976– CTFT–77
　Earlier sketch in CTFT–34
Bright, Richard 1937– CTFT–31
　Earlier sketches in CTFT–4, 20
Brightman, Sarah 1961– CTFT–38
　Earliers sketch in CTFT–13
Brightman, Stanley 1888–1961 .... WWasWT
Brighton, Pam 1946– WWT–17
Brightslymoore, Sir Willups
　See .... Cross, David
Briley, John 1925– CTFT–20
　Earlier sketch in CTFT–10
Brill, Charlie CTFT–46
Brill, Fran 1946– CTFT–51
　Earlier sketches in CTFT–1, 8, 15, 25
Brill, Mitzi McCall
　See .... McCall, Mitzi
Brill, Robert CTFT–40
Brill, Steven CTFT–64
　Earlier sketch in CTFT–28
Brillstein, Bernie CTFT–72
　Earlier sketches in CTFT–6, 33
Brimble, Nick CTFT–34
Brimley, Wilford 1934– CTFT–37
　Earlier sketches in CTFT–6, 13
Brinckerhoff, Burt 1936– CTFT–57
　Earlier sketches in CTFT–11, 22
Brinkley, Ritch CTFT–46
Brion, John 1963(?)– CTFT–64
　Earlier sketch in CTFT–29
Brisbane, Katharine 1932– CTFT–4
　Earlier sketch in WWT–17
Brisbin, David CTFT–77
　Earlier sketch in CTFT–34
Briscoe, Brent 1961– CTFT–58
Brisson, Carl 1895–1965 .... WWasWT
Brisson, Frederick 1913–1984 .... WWT–17
Bristow, Charles 1928– WWT–17
Brittany, Morgan 1951– CTFT–78
　Earlier sketches in CTFT–7, 35
Britton, Christopher CTFT–54
Britton, Connie 1968– CTFT–64
　Earlier sketches in CTFT–16, 29
Britton, Tony 1924– CTFT–14
　Earlier sketch in WWT–17
Broad, Jay 1930– CTFT–18
　Earlier sketch in CTFT–2
Broad, William
　See .... Idol, Billy
Broadbent, Jim 1949– CTFT–55
　Earlier sketch in CTFT–26
Broadhurst, George H. 1866–1952 .... WWasWT
Broadhurst, Kent 1940– CTFT–30
　Earlier sketches in CTFT–2, 19

Broberg, Jan
　See .... Felt, Jan Broberg
Broccoli, Albert R. 1909–1996 .... CTFT–6
　Obituary in CTFT–16
Broccoli, Barbara 1960– CTFT–63
　Earlier sketch in CTFT–28
Brockett, Oscar G. 1923– WWT–17
Brocklebank, Daniel 1979– CTFT–69
　Earlier sketch in CTFT–30
Brocksmith, Roy 1945– CTFT–41
　Earlier sketches in CTFT–2, 18
Brockway, Amie 1938– CTFT–2
Broderick, Beth 1959– CTFT–37
　Earlier sketch in CTFT–13
Broderick, Helen 1891–1959 .... WWasWT
Broderick, Matthew 1962– CTFT–42
　Earlier sketches in CTFT–4, 11, 20
Brodkin, Herbert 1912–1990(?) CTFT–10
Brody, Adam 1979(?)– CTFT–60
Brody, Adrien 1973– CTFT–55
　Earlier sketch in CTFT–26
Brodziak, Kenn 1913– WWT–17
Brogden, Gwendoline 1891– .... WWasWT
Brogger, Ivar 1947– CTFT–6
　Earlier sketches in CTFT–1, 6
Brogi, Giulio 1935– CTFT–34
Brokaw, Cary 1951– CTFT–72
　Earlier sketches in CTFT–11, 22, 32
Brokaw, Tom 1940– CTFT–41
　Earlier sketch in CTFT–6
Brolin, James 1940(?)– CTFT–41
　Earlier sketches in CTFT–7, 14
Brolin, Josh 1968– CTFT–72
　Earlier sketches in CTFT–22, 32
Brolly, Shane CTFT–71
Bromberg, J. 1904–1951 .... WWasWT
Bromka, Elaine 1950– CTFT–1
Bromley–Davenport, Arthur
　1867–1946 .... WWasWT
Bron, Eleanor 1940– CTFT–34
　Earlier sketch in WWT–17
Bronson, Charles 1921(?)– CTFT–23
　Earlier sketches in CTFT–3, 12
Bronwyn–Moore, Lisa
　See .... Moore, Lisa Bronwyn
Brook, Clive 1887–1974 .... WWasWT
Brook, Faith 1922– CTFT–41
　Earlier sketches in CTFT–4, 20; WWT–17
Brook, Jayne 1962– CTFT–46
Brook, Lesley 1917– .... WWasWT
Brook, Peter 1925– CTFT–10
　Earlier sketch in WWT–17
Brook, Sara WWT–17
Brooke, Cynthia 1875–1949 .... WWasWT
Brooke, Mrs. E. H. ?–1915 .... WWasWT
Brooke, Emily ?–1953 .... WWasWT
Brooke, Harold 1910– WWT–17
Brooke, Paul CTFT–34
　Earlier sketch in WWT–17
Brooke, Sarah .... WWasWT
Brookes, Jacqueline 1930– CTFT–7
　Earlier sketch in WWT–17
Brookfield, Charles Hallam Elton
　1857–1913 .... WWasWT
Brook–Jones, Elwyn 1911–1962 .... WWasWT
Brooks, Albert 1947– CTFT–45
　Earlier sketches in CTFT–6, 14
Brooks, Angelle 1967– CTFT–60
Brooks, Avery 1948– CTFT–64
　Earlier sketches in CTFT–9, 16, 29
Brooks, Charles David III
　1939– CTFT–3

Brooks, David 1920–1999 .... CTFT–1
    Obituary in CTFT–32
Brooks, David Allen 1947– CTFT–49
Brooks, Garth 1962– CTFT–41
Brooks, James L. 1940– CTFT–62
    Earlier sketches in CTFT–3, 10, 17, 28
Brooks, Jason 1966– CTFT–74
Brooks, Jeff 1950– CTFT–1
Brooks, Joel CTFT–70
    Earlier sketches in CTFT–4, 20, 31
Brooks, Louis 1906–1985 .... CTFT–27
Brooks, Mel 1926– CTFT–50
    Earlier sketches in CTFT–1, 6, 13, 24
Brooks, Norman G. 1926– CTFT–4
Brooks, Randy CTFT–57
Brooks, Richard 1912–1992 .... CTFT–10
Brooks, Richard 1962(?)– CTFT–64
    Earlier sketches in CTFT–17, 28
Brooks, Virginia Fox
    See .... Vernon, Virginia
Broones, Martin 1892– .... WWasWT
Brophy, Brian CTFT–54
Brosnan, Pierce 1953– CTFT–50
    Earlier sketches in CTFT–6, 13, 24
Brosten, Harve 1943– CTFT–2
Brothers, Joyce 1929(?)– CTFT–65
    Earlier sketches in CTFT–17, 29
Brotherson, Eric 1911–1989 .... CTFT–9
    Earlier sketch in WWT–17
Brouett, Albert .... WWasWT
Brough, Colin 1945– CTFT–1
Brough, Fanny Whiteside
    1854–1914 .... WWasWT
Brough, Mary 1863–1934 .... WWasWT
Brough, Mrs. Robert ?–1932 .... WWasWT
Broughton, Bruce 1945– CTFT–35
    Earlier sketch in CTFT–7
Broughton, Jessie 1885–? .... WWasWT
Broughton, Phyllis 1862?–1926 .... WWasWT
Broun, Heywood 1888–1939 .... WWasWT
Broun, Heywood Hale 1918– CTFT–1
Browder, Ben 1962– CTFT–63
    Earlier sketch in CTFT–28
Brower, Jordan 1981– CTFT–69
    Earlier sketch in CTFT–30
Brown, Amelda CTFT–38
Brown, Arvin 1940– CTFT–53
    Earlier sketches in CTFT–2, 8, 15, 25;
    WWT–17
Brown, Barry M. 1942– CTFT–8
    Earlier sketch in CTFT–1
Brown, Billy Aaron 1981– CTFT–74
Brown, Blair 1946(?)– CTFT–38
    Earlier sketches in CTFT–6, 14
Brown, Brennan CTFT–51
Brown, Bryan 1947(?)– CTFT–57
    Earlier sketches in CTFT–7, 14, 26
Brown, Chelsea 1947(?)– CTFT–20
Brown, Clancy 1959– CTFT–65
    Earlier sketches in CTFT–16, 29
Brown, David 1916– CTFT–70
    Earlier sketches in CTFT–3, 19, 31
Brown, Don CTFT–40
Brown, Dwier 1959– CTFT–54
Brown, Ernie
    See .... Lively, Ernie
Brown, Garrett
    See .... Brown, Garrett M.
Brown, Georg Stanford 1943– CTFT–72
    Earlier sketches in CTFT–7, 33
Brown, George H.
    See .... Wertmuller, Lina

Brown, Georgia 1933–1992 .... CTFT–9
    Obituary in CTFT–16
    Earlier sketch in WWT–17
Brown, Graham 1924– CTFT–9
Brown, Harry Joe 1892(?)–1972 .... CTFT–26
Brown, Ivor 1891–1974 .... WWasWT
Brown, Jim 1936(?)– CTFT–78
    Earlier sketches in CTFT–9, 35
Brown, Joe E. 1892–1973 .... WWasWT
Brown, John Mason 1900–1969 .... WWasWT
Brown, John Russell 1923– WWT–17
Brown, Julie 1958– CTFT–36
    Earlier sketch in CTFT–9
Brown, Kathryne Dora CTFT–52
Brown, Kenneth H. 1936– CTFT–4
    Earlier sketch in CTFT–2
Brown, Kermit 1939(?)– CTFT–9
    Earlier sketch in CTFT–1
Brown, Kimberlin 1961– CTFT–58
Brown, Kimberly J. 1984– CTFT–49
Brown, Lew 1899–1958 .... WWasWT
Brown, Lionel 1888–1964 .... WWasWT
Brown, Louise .... WWasWT
Brown, Olivia 1960(?)– CTFT–46
Brown, Orlando 1987– CTFT–73
Brown, Pamela 1917–1975 .... WWasWT
Brown, Pat Crawford 1929– CTFT–58
Brown, Peter 1935– CTFT–53
Brown, R. Nelson CTFT–67
Brown, Ralph 1957– CTFT–40
Brown, Robert Curtis
    See .... Curtis–Brown, Robert
Brown, Robert N. CTFT–11
Brown, Roberta CTFT–41
Brown, Roger Aaron CTFT–36
Brown, Ruth 1928–2006 .... CTFT–48
    Obituary in CTFT–75
    Earlier sketch in CTFT–11
Brown, Sam O.
    See .... Edwards, Blake
Brown, Sarah 1975– CTFT–60
Brown, Sharon 1962– CTFT–57
Brown, Susan 1932– CTFT–58
Brown, Tyne Daly
    See .... Daly, Tyne
Brown, W. Earl 1963– CTFT–43
Brown, William F. 1928– CTFT–1
Brown, Wren T. 1964– CTFT–74
Brown, Yvette Nicole 1971– CTFT–78
Brown, Zack 1949– CTFT–37
    Earlier sketches in CTFT–1, 11
Browne, Coral 1913–1991 .... CTFT–4
    Obituary in CTFT–10
    Earlier sketch in WWT–17
Browne, E. Martin 1900–1980 .... WWT–17
Browne, Irene 1896–1965 .... WWasWT
Browne, Kale 1950– CTFT–65
    Earlier sketches in CTFT–17, 29
Browne, Laidman 1896–1961 .... WWasWT
Browne, Louise .... WWasWT
Browne, Marjorie 1913– .... WWasWT
Browne, Maurice 1881–1955 .... WWasWT
Browne, Pattie 1869–1934 .... WWasWT
Browne, Roscoe Lee 1925– CTFT–73
    Earlier sketches in CTFT–4, 11, 22, 32;
    WWT–17
Browne, Stella 1906– .... WWasWT
Browne, W. Graham 1870–1937 .... WWasWT
Browne, Wynyard (Barry)
    1911–1964 .... WWasWT
Browning, Alistair CTFT–74
Browning, Emily 1988– CTFT–63
Browning, Ryan 1974– CTFT–52

Browning, Susan 1941– CTFT–20
    Earlier sketches in CTFT–4; WWT–17
Brownlow, Kevin 1938– CTFT–5
Brown–Potter, Mrs.
    See .... Potter, Cora Urquhart
Broyles, William, Jr. 1944– CTFT–66
Brubaker, James D. 1937– CTFT–58
    Earlier sketch in CTFT–27
Bruce, Alison 1962– CTFT–76
Bruce, Brenda 1922(?)–1996 .... CTFT–9
    Obituary in CTFT–16
    Earlier sketch in WWT–17
Bruce, Carol 1919– CTFT–48
    Earlier sketches in CTFT–15; WWT–17
Bruce, Christopher 1945– CTFT–28
    Earlier sketch in CTFT–15
Bruce, Edgar K. 1893– .... WWasWT
Bruce, Nigel 1895–1953 .... WWasWT
Bruce, Shelley 1965– CTFT–1
Bruce, Susan 1957– CTFT–3
Bruce, Tonie Edgar 1892–1966 .... WWasWT
Bruce–Potter, Hilda 1888– .... WWasWT
Bruckheimer, Jerry 1945– CTFT–72
    Earlier sketches in CTFT–1, 6, 33
Bruckner, Agnes 1985– CTFT–59
Bruckner, Amy 1991– CTFT–75
Bruford, Rose Elizabeth 1904– WWT–17
Brugge, Pieter Jan CTFT–29
Bruhanski, Alex CTFT–54
Brule, Andre .... WWasWT
Brule, Robin CTFT–66
Brune, Adrienne 1892– .... WWasWT
Brune, Clarence M. 1870–? .... WWasWT
Brune, Gabrielle 1912– .... WWasWT
Brune, Minnie Tittell 1883–? .... WWasWT
Bruning, Francesca 1907– .... WWasWT
Bruno, Albert 1873–1927 .... WWasWT
Bruno, Dylan 1972– CTFT–43
Bruno, John CTFT–65
    Earlier sketch in CTFT–29
Bruns, George 1914(?)–1983 .... CTFT–22
Bruns, Philip 1931– CTFT–60
Brunton, Dorothy 1893– .... WWasWT
Bruskotter, Eric CTFT–41
Brustein, Robert 1927– WWT–17
Bruton, Margo CTFT–6
Bryan, Dora 1924– CTFT–5
    Earlier sketch in WWT–17
Bryan, Hal 1891–1948 .... WWasWT
Bryan, Herbert George ?–1948 .... WWasWT
Bryan, Kenneth 1953–1986 .... CTFT–2
Bryan, Peggy 1916– .... WWasWT
Bryan, Robert 1934– CTFT–8
    Earlier sketch in WWT–17
Bryan, Zachary Ty 1981– CTFT–58
    Earlier sketch in CTFT–27
Bryant, Charles 1879–1948 .... WWasWT
Bryant, Clara 1985– CTFT–69
Bryant, J. V. 1889–1924 .... WWasWT
Bryant, Michael 1928– CTFT–37
    Earlier sketches in CTFT–13; WWT–17
Bryant, Peter CTFT–49
Bryantsev, Alexandr Alexandrovich
    1883–1961 .... WWasWT
Bryce, Ian 1956– CTFT–57
    Earlier sketch in CTFT–26
Bryce, Scott CTFT–58
Bryceland, Yvonne 1925–1992 .... CTFT–7
    Obituary in CTFT–10
    Earlier sketch in WWT–17
Bryden, Bill 1942– CTFT–28
    Earlier sketches in CTFT–6, 15; WWT–17
Bryden, Ronald 1927– WWT–17

Brydone, Alfred 1863–1920 .... WWasWT
Bryer, Vera 1905– .... WWasWT
Bryggman, Larry 1938– CTFT–50
Earlier sketches in CTFT–9, 16
Bryniarski, Andrew CTFT–40
Bryning, John 1913– .... WWasWT
Brynner, Yul 1920–1985 .... CTFT–3
Earlier sketch in WWT–17
Brynolfsson, Reine 1953– CTFT–47
Earlier sketch in CTFT–23
Bubrosa, Marje
See .... Barbour, James
Buchanan, Ian 1957(?)– CTFT–57
Earlier sketch in CTFT–26
Buchanan, Jack 1891–1957 .... WWasWT
Buchanan, Maud .... WWasWT
Buchanan, Thompson 1877–1937 .... WWasWT
Buchholz, Bob CTFT–74
Buchholz, Horst 1933– CTFT–1
Buchinsky, Charles
See .... Bronson, Charles
Buck, Chris CTFT–29
Buck, David 1936–1989 .... CTFT–8
Earlier sketch in WWT–17
Buck, Detlev 1962– CTFT–32
Buckham, Bernard 1882–1963 .... WWasWT
Bucklaw, Alfred .... WWasWT
Buckler, Hugh C. 1870–1936 .... WWasWT
Buckley, A. J. 1978– CTFT–76
Buckley, Betty 1947– CTFT–37
Earlier sketches in CTFT–1, 4, 13
Buckley, May 1875–? .... WWasWT
Buckman, Phil 1969– CTFT–65
Earlier sketch in CTFT–29
Buckmaster, John 1915– .... WWasWT
Buckner, Robert 1906– CTFT–23
Bucksey, Colin CTFT–62
Buckstone, J. C. 1858–1924 .... WWasWT
Buckstone, Rowland 1860–1922 .... WWasWT
Buckton, Florence 1893– .... WWasWT
Budig, Rebecca 1973– CTFT–62
Budries, David 1953– CTFT–11
Earlier sketch in CTFT–1
Buell, Bill 1952– CTFT–53
Earlier sketches in CTFT–1, 25
Bufanda, Brad 1983– CTFT–74
Bufman, Zev 1930– CTFT–4
Earlier sketch in WWT–17
Buhagiar, Valerie 1964– CTFT–56
Bui, Tony 1973(?)– CTFT–30
Buist, Walter Scott 1860–? .... WWasWT
Bujold, Genevieve 1942– CTFT–44
Earlier sketches in CTFT–3, 11, 22
Bukowski, Bobby 1953– CTFT–58
Bulen, Steve CTFT–52
Bulgakov, Leo 1889–1948 .... WWasWT
Bull, Peter 1912–1984 .... CTFT–1
Earlier sketch in WWasWT
Bullard, Thomas 1944– CTFT–9
Earlier sketch in CTFT–1
Bullins, Ed 1935– CTFT–7
Earlier sketch in WWT–17
Bulloch, Jeremy 1945– CTFT–47
Earlier sketch in CTFT–23
Bullock, Christopher 1934– WWT–17
Bullock, Donna 1955– CTFT–66
Earlier sketches in CTFT–3, 19, 30
Bullock, Eldon 1952– CTFT–4
Bullock, John Malcolm 1867–1938 .... WWasWT
Bullock, S. Scott CTFT–38
Bullock, Sandra 1964– CTFT–71
Earlier sketches in CTFT–13, 22, 32
Buloff, Joseph 1899–1985 .... WWT–17

Bumpass, Rodger CTFT–41
Bumstead, Henry 1915– CTFT–36
Earlier sketch in CTFT–10
Bunce, Alan 1903–1965 .... WWasWT
Bunch, Velton Ray CTFT–39
Bundy, William 1924– WWT–17
Bunker, Edward 1933– CTFT–31
Bunnage, Avis WWT–17
Bunston, Herbert 1870–1935 .... WWasWT
Bunuel, Luis 1900–1983 .... CTFT–29
Buono, Cara 1974– CTFT–66
Earlier sketch in CTFT–30
Buono, Victor 1938–1981 .... CTFT–2
Burbidge, Douglas 1895–1959 .... WWasWT
Burbridge, Edward CTFT–4
Earlier sketch in WWT–17
Burch, Shelly 1959(?)– CTFT–19
Earlier sketch in CTFT–2
Burchill, William ?–1930 .... WWasWT
Burden, Hugh 1913–1985 .... WWT–17
Burden, Suzanne 1958– CTFT–38
Burdis, Ray 1958– CTFT–69
Earlier sketch in CTFT–30
Burditt, Jack CTFT–66
Burditt, Joyce CTFT–69
Burdon, Albert 1900– .... WWasWT
Bure, Candace Cameron 1976– CTFT–57
Earlier sketch in CTFT–26
Burfield, Joan
See .... Fontaine, Joan
Burge, Gregg 1957(?)–1998 .... CTFT–23
Burge, Stuart 1918– CTFT–8
Earlier sketch in WWT–17
Brugess, Don CTFT–46
Burgess, Muriel 1926– CTFT–4
Burghardt, Arthur 1947– CTFT–52
Burghoff, Gary 1943– CTFT–62
Earlier sketch in CTFT–8
Burgi, Richard 1958– CTFT–44
Burgin, Polly
See .... Bergen, Polly
Burgis, Kathleen 1907– .... WWasWT
Burgon, Geoffrey 1941– CTFT–37
Earlier sketch in CTFT–12
Burk, Robert
See .... Burke, Robert John
Burke, Alfred 1918– CTFT–32
Earlier sketch in WWT–17
Burke, Billie 1885–1970 .... WWasWT
Burke, Billy CTFT–54
Burke, Chris 1965– CTFT–8
Burke, David 1934– WWT–17
Burke, David CTFT–61
Burke, Delta 1956– CTFT–39
Earlier sketches in CTFT–7, 15
Burke, Joe Michael 1973– CTFT–69
Burke, Kathy 1964– CTFT–47
Earlier sketch in CTFT–23
Burke, Marie 1894– .... WWasWT
Burke, Marylouise CTFT–50
Burke, Michael Reilly CTFT–63
Burke, Patricia 1917– WWT–17
Burke, Robert Easton
See .... Easton, Robert
Burke, Robert John 1955– CTFT–69
Earlier sketch in CTFT–30
Burke, Tom 1890–1969 .... WWasWT
Burkholder, Scott CTFT–50
Burkley, Dennis 1945– CTFT–40
Burks, Robert 1910–68 .... CTFT–27
Burks, Willis II 1935– CTFT–68
Earlier sketch in CTFT–30

Burley, Dennis
See .... Burkley, Dennis
Burley, Mark A. 1951– CTFT–37
Earlier sketch in CTFT–13
Burlingame, Lloyd WWT–17
Burmester, Leo 1944– CTFT–70
Earlier sketches in CTFT–20, 31
Burnaby, G. Davy 1881–1949 .... WWasWT
Burnand, Francis Cowley 1836–1917 ..... WWasWT
Burne, Arthur 1873–1945 .... WWasWT
Burne, Nancy 1912–1954 .... WWasWT
Burnett, Carol 1933– CTFT–54
Earlier sketches in CTFT–1, 8, 16, 26;
WWT–17
Burnett, Charles 1944– CTFT–40
Burnett, Frances Hodgson
1849–1924 .... WWasWT
Burnett, John F. CTFT–11
Burnett, Mark 1960(?)– CTFT–50
Burnham, Barbara 1900– .... WWasWT
Burns, Brooke 1977(?)– CTFT–54
Burns, Catherine Lloyd 1961– CTFT–56
Burns, David 1902–1971 .... WWasWT
Burns, Edward 1968– CTFT–43
Earlier sketch in CTFT–22
Burns, Eileen CTFT–6
Burns, Francis
See .... Gelbart, Larry
Burns, George 1896–1996 .... CTFT–17
Obituary in CTFT–16
Earlier sketches in CTFT–3, 9
Burns, Heather 1974– CTFT–73
Burns, Jere 1954– CTFT–37
Earlier sketch in CTFT–13
Burns, Kathleen Kinmont
See .... Kinmont, Kathleen
Burns, Kelly
See .... O'Byrne, Kehli
Burns, Ken 1953– CTFT–44
Earlier sketches in CTFT–11, 22
Burns, Kevin 1955– CTFT–46
Burns, Martha CTFT–50
Burns, Ralph 1922– CTFT–24
Earlier sketch in CTFT–12
Burns, Regan 1968– CTFT–68
Burns, Ric 1955(?)– CTFT–28
Burns, Tex
See .... L'Amour, Louis
Burns–Bisogno, Louisa 1936– CTFT–1
Burnside, R. H. 1870–1952 .... WWasWT
Burr, Anne 1920– .... WWasWT
Burr, Jeff 1963(?)– CTFT–54
Burr, Raymond 1917–1993 .... CTFT–9
Obituary in CTFT–12
Earlier sketch in CTFT–3
Burr, Robert WWT–17
Burrell, Daisy 1893– .... WWasWT
Burrell, John 1910– .... WWasWT
Burrell, Pamela 1945– CTFT–4
Burrell, Sheila 1922– CTFT–41
Earlier sketches in CTFT–20; WWT–17
Burress, Hedy 1973– CTFT–48
Earlier sketch in CTFT–23
Burrill, Ena 1908– .... WWasWT
Burroughs, Edgar Rice 1875–1950 .... CTFT–27
Burroughs, Jackie 1939(?)– CTFT–65
Earlier sketch in CTFT–29
Burroughs, Robert C. 1923– CTFT–3
Burroughs, William S. 1914–1997 .... CTFT–17
Obituary in CTFT–18
Earlier sketch in CTFT–10
Burrows, Abe 1910–1984 .... CTFT–2
Earlier sketch in WWT–17

Burrows, Darren E. 1966– CTFT–34
Burrows, James 1940– CTFT–79
   Earlier sketches in CTFT–10, 36
Burrows, Saffron 1973– CTFT–58
   Earlier sketch in CTFT–27
Burson, Greg CTFT–50
Burstyn, Ellen 1932– CTFT–72
   Earlier sketches in CTFT–1, 6, 13, 22, 32
Burt, Laura 1872–1952 .... WWasWT
Burton, Corey 1955– CTFT–41
Burton, Donald 1934– CTFT–11
Burton, Frederick 1871–1975 .... WWasWT
Burton, Hilarie 1982– CTFT–66
Burton, Kate 1957– CTFT–66
   Earlier sketches in CTFT–2, 18, 30
Burton, Langhorne 1880–1949 .... WWasWT
Burton, LeVar 1957– CTFT–65
   Earlier sketches in CTFT–7, 18, 29
Burton, Margaret 1924–1984 .... WWT–17
Burton, Percy 1878–1948 .... WWasWT
Burton, Richard 1925–1984 .... CTFT–2
   Earlier sketch in WWT–17
Burton, Richard P. 1878–? .... WWasWT
Burton, Steve 1970– CTFT–67
   Earlier sketch in CTFT–30
Burton, Tim 1958(?)– CTFT–54
   Earlier sketches in CTFT–9, 16, 26
Burton, Tony CTFT–46
Burton, Warren 1944– CTFT–58
Burton–Hill, Clemency CTFT–69
Burtt, Ben 1948– CTFT–10
Burum, Stephen H. 1939– CTFT–48
   Earlier sketches in CTFT–12, 23
Burwell, Carter 1955– CTFT–62
   Earlier sketch in CTFT–28
Bury, John 1925– WWT–17
Busa, George
   See .... Buza, George
Buscemi, Steve 1957– CTFT–45
   Earlier sketches in CTFT–15, 25
Busch, Adam 1978– CTFT–69
Busch, Charles 1954– CTFT–36
   Earlier sketch in CTFT–10
   Brief sketch in CTFT–6
Busey, Gary 1944– CTFT–38
   Earlier sketches in CTFT–1, 6, 14
Busey, Jake 1971(?)– CTFT–48
   Earlier sketch in CTFT–23
Busfield, Timothy 1957– CTFT–53
   Earlier sketches in CTFT–8, 15, 25
Bush, Barbara
   See .... Tyson, Barbara
Bush, Grand L. 1955– CTFT–51
Bush, Norman 1933– CTFT–4
Bush, Rebecca 1968– CTFT–75
Bush, Sophia 1982– CTFT–69
Bushell, Anthony 1904– .... WWasWT
Buskirk, June Van
   See .... Van Buskirk, June
Busley, Jessie 1869–1950 .... WWasWT
Busse, Margaret .... WWasWT
Bussell, Darcey 1969– CTFT–48
   Earlier sketch in CTFT–13
Bussert, Meg 1949– CTFT–1
Bussieres, Pascale 1968(?)– CTFT–34
Butala, Jenna
   See .... Elfman, Jenna
Butcher, Ernest 1885–1965 .... WWasWT
Butcher, Kasan 1973– CTFT–74
Butkus, Dick 1942– CTFT–47
   Earlier sketch in CTFT–7
Butler, Bill 1931– CTFT–43
   Earlier sketches in CTFT–11, 22

Butler, Brett 1958– CTFT–41
   Earlier sketch in CTFT–20
Butler, Dan 1954– CTFT–58
   Earlier sketches in CTFT–17, 27
Butler, Dean 1956– CTFT–56
Butler, Gerard 1969– CTFT–54
Butler, Paul CTFT–69
   Earlier sketch in CTFT–30
Butler, Richard William 1844–1928 ...... WWasWT
Butler, Robert 1927– CTFT–56
   Earlier sketches in CTFT–1, 12, 23
Butler, Tom CTFT–50
Butler, Yancy 1970– CTFT–68
   Earlier sketches in CTFT–20, 30
Butleroff, Helen 1950– CTFT–3
Butlin, Jan 1940– WWT–17
Butt, Alfred Bart 1878–1962 .... WWasWT
Butterworth, Charles 1896–1946 .... WWasWT
Butterworth, Clara .... WWasWT
Butti, Enrico Annibale 1868–1912 .... WWasWT
Button, Jeanne 1930– WWT–17
Buttons, Red 1919–2006 .... CTFT–37
   Obituary in CTFT–73
   Earlier sketches in CTFT–6, 13
Buttram, Pat 1916–1994 .... CTFT–9
   Obituary in CTFT–12
Butz, Norbert Leo 1969(?)– CTFT–50
Buxton, Sarah 1965– CTFT–60
Buy, Margherita CTFT–32
Buza, George CTFT–74
Buzas, Jason 1952– CTFT–19
   Earlier sketch in CTFT–2
Buzo, Alexander 1944– WWT–17
Buzzell, Edward 1897– .... WWasWT
Buzzi, Ruth 1936– CTFT–72
   Earlier sketches in CTFT–3, 19, 32
Buzzington, Ezra CTFT–67
   Earlier sketch in CTFT–30
Byerley, Vivienne WWT–17
Byers, (Bobbie) Catherine CTFT–1
Byers, Ralph CTFT–30
Byford, Roy 1873–1939 .... WWasWT
Byggdin, Doug CTFT–65
   Earlier sketch in CTFT–29
Byington, Spring 1893–1971 .... WWasWT
Byner, John 1938– CTFT–33
   Earlier sketch in CTFT–7
Bynes, Amanda 1986– CTFT–64
Byng, Douglas 1893– WWT–16
Byng, George W. .... WWasWT
Byrd, Anne Gee 1938– CTFT–56
Byrd, Dan 1986(?)– CTFT–60
Byrd, David CTFT–15
   Earlier sketch in CTFT–8
Byrd, Eugene 1975– CTFT–44
Byrd, Sam 1908–1955 .... WWasWT
Byrd, Thomas Jefferson 1941(?)– CTFT–68
Byrne, Cecily .... WWasWT
Byrne, David 1952– CTFT–53
   Earlier sketches in CTFT–6, 15, 25
Byrne, Gabriel 1950– CTFT–72
   Earlier sketches in CTFT–6, 13, 22, 32
Byrne, Jenna 1970– CTFT–43
Byrne, John 1940– WWT–17
Byrne, Martha 1969– CTFT–62
Byrne, Michael 1943– CTFT–52
Byrne, Patsy 1933– WWT–17
Byrne, Peter 1928– WWT–17
Byrne, Rose 1979– CTFT–59
Byrnes, Jim 1948– CTFT–52
   Earlier sketches in CTFT–15, 25
Byron, Arthur 1872–1943 .... WWasWT
Byron, Jeffrey 1955– CTFT–58

Byron, John 1912– .... WWasWT
Byron, Kathleen 1923– CTFT–43
B–Zar
   See .... Getty, Balthazar

C

Caan, James 1940(?)– CTFT–54
   Earlier sketches in CTFT–7, 16, 26
Caan, Scott 1976– CTFT–67
   Earlier sketch in CTFT–30
Cabalero, Roxann
   See .... Dawson, Roxann
Cabot, Eliot 1899–1938 .... WWasWT
Cabot, Sebastian 1918–1977 .... CTFT–23
Cabot, Susan 1937–1986 .... CTFT–4
Cabrera, Santiago 1978– CTFT–76
Cacaci, Joe CTFT–33
   Earlier sketch in CTFT–6
Caceres, Kurt 1976– CTFT–74
Cacoyannis, Michael 1922– CTFT–11
   Earlier sketch in CTFT–1
Cadeau, Lally 1948– CTFT–28
Cadell, Jean 1884–1967 .... WWasWT
Cadell, Simon 1950–1996 .... CTFT–18
   Earlier sketches in CTFT–2, 9
Cadiff, Andy CTFT–40
Cadman, Ethel 1886– .... WWasWT
Cadorette, Mary CTFT–5
Cady, Frank 1915– CTFT–9
Caesar, Adolph 1934–1986 .... CTFT–3
Caesar, Irving 1895– WWT–17
Caesar, Sid 1922– CTFT–35
   Earlier sketches in CTFT–1, 9; WWT–17
Cafferty, Jack 1942– CTFT–75
Caffrey, Sean CTFT–34
Caffrey, Stephen 1961– CTFT–30
Cage, Nicolas 1964(?)– CTFT–69
   Earlier sketches in CTFT–5, 12, 21, 31
   Brief Entry in CTFT–2
Cagney, James 1899–1986 .... CTFT–3
   Earlier sketch in WWT–10
Cagney, Jeanne 1919– .... WWasWT
Cahill, Eddie 1978– CTFT–73
Cahill, Lily 1886–1955 .... WWasWT
Cahill, Marie 1870–1933 .... WWasWT
Cahill, Steve 1964– CTFT–79
Cahn, Sammy 1913–1993 .... CTFT–12
   Earlier sketch in WWT–17
Cain, Christopher 1943– CTFT–38
   Earlier sketch in CTFT–15
Cain, Dean 1966– CTFT–39
Cain, Henri 1857–? .... WWasWT
Cain, William 1931– CTFT–9
   Earlier sketch in CTFT–1
Caine, Derwent Hall 1892– .... WWasWT
Caine, Hall 1853–1931 .... WWasWT
Caine, Henry 1888–1914 .... WWasWT
Caine, Michael 1933– CTFT–72
   Earlier sketches in CTFT–6, 13, 22, 33
Caird, John 1948– CTFT–23
   Earlier sketch in CTFT–12
Cairncross, James 1915– WWT–17
Cairney, John 1930– WWT–17
Cairns, Tom 1952– CTFT–9
Cake, Jonathan 1967– CTFT–68
Calabresi, Oreste 1857–? .... WWasWT
Calabretta, Tony 1961– CTFT–67
   Earlier sketch in CTFT–30

Calabro, Thomas 1959– CTFT–30
   Earlier sketches in CTFT–21, 31
Calder, David CTFT–34
Calderisi, David 1940– WWT–17
Calder–Marshall, Anna 1947– WWT–17
Calderon, Paul CTFT–53
Caldicot, Richard 1908– WWT–17
Caldwell, Anne 1876–1936 .... WWasWT
Caldwell, L. Scott 1954(?)– CTFT–74
   Earlier sketches in CTFT–8, 33
Caldwell, Marianne ?–1933 .... WWasWT
Caldwell, Sandra CTFT–78
Caldwell, Zoe 1933– CTFT–53
   Earlier sketches in CTFT–1, 10, 18; WWT–17
Cale, Paula 1970– CTFT–62
   Earlier sketch in CTFT–28
Calhern, Louis 1895–1956 .... WWasWT
Calhoun, Monica 1971(?)– CTFT–46
Calhoun, Rory 1922–1999 .... CTFT–9
   Obituary in CTFT–32
Cali, Joseph 1950– CTFT–57
Call, R. D. CTFT–62
   Earlier sketch in CTFT–28
Callahan, E. J. CTFT–42
Callahan, Eva LaRue
   See .... LaRue, Eva
Callahan, Gene 1923(?)–1990 .... CTFT–10
Callahan, James T. 1930– CTFT–30
   Earlier sketches in CTFT–3, 19
Callahan, John 1953– CTFT–21
Callan, K 1942– CTFT–59
   Earlier sketch in CTFT–1
Callan, Michael 1935– CTFT–53
Callaway, Claire Malis
   See .... Malis, Claire
Callaway, Liz 1961– CTFT–61
   Earlier sketch in CTFT–28
Callaway, Mark 1962– CTFT–44
Calleia, Joseph 1897–1975 .... WWasWT
Callen, Bryan 1971– CTFT–58
Callis, James 1971– CTFT–65
Callison, Frank 1942– CTFT–32
Callous, Mean Mark
   See .... Callaway, Mark
Callow, Simon 1949– CTFT–53
   Earlier sketches in CTFT–8, 15, 25; WWT–17
Calloway, Cab 1907– WWT–17
Calloway, Vanessa Bell 1957– CTFT–38
Calmour, Alfred C. 1857?–1912 .... WWasWT
Calthrop, Dion Clayton 1878–1937 .... WWasWT
Calthrop, Donald 1888–1940 .... WWasWT
Calthrop, Gladys E. .... WWasWT
Calvello, Jessica CTFT–49
Calvert, Catherine 1890–1971 .... WWasWT
Calvert, Cecil G. 1871–? .... WWasWT
Calvert, Mrs. Charles 1837–1921 .... WWasWT
Calvert, Jennifer 1963– CTFT–65
Calvert, Louis 1859–1923 .... WWasWT
Calvert, Patricia 1908– .... WWasWT
Calvert, Phyllis 1915– WWT–17
Camacho, Mark 1964(?)– CTFT–50
Camargo, Christian 1970– CTFT–68
Cambern, Donn CTFT–22
   Earlier sketch in CTFT–11
Cameron, Candace
   See .... Bure, Candace Cameron
Cameron, Dean 1962– CTFT–41
Cameron, Donald 1889–1955 .... WWasWT
Cameron, J. Smith
   See .... Smith–Cameron, J.
Cameron, James 1954– CTFT–64
   Earlier sketches in CTFT–10, 17, 29
   Brief Entry in CTFT–3

Cameron, John CTFT–46
Cameron, John 1944– CTFT–27
   Earlier sketch in CTFT–23
Cameron, Kirk 1970(?)– CTFT–40
   Earlier sketches in CTFT–10, 18
   Brief Entry in CTFT–5
Cameron, Violet 1862–1919 .... WWasWT
Camp, Bill CTFT–76
   Earlier sketch in CTFT–32
Camp, Colleen 1953– CTFT–64
   Earlier sketches in CTFT–10, 18, 29
Camp, Hamilton 1934– CTFT–34
   Earlier sketch in CTFT–6
Camp, Joe 1939– CTFT–7
Campanella, Joseph 1927– CTFT–75
   Earlier sketches in CTFT–6, 33
Campanella, Roy II CTFT–36
Campbell, Alan 1957– CTFT–48
   Earlier sketch in CTFT–11
Campbell, Amelia CTFT–37
Campbell, Beverly
   See .... Garland, Beverly
Campbell, Bill 1959– CTFT–62
   Earlier sketch in CTFT–28
Campbell, Bruce 1958– CTFT–72
   Earlier sketches in CTFT–13, 22, 32
Campbell, Cheryl 1951– CTFT–8
Campbell, Christian 1972– CTFT–75
   Earlier sketch in CTFT–34
Campbell, Colin 1968– CTFT–68
Campbell, Douglas 1922– CTFT–6
   Earlier sketch in WWT–17
Campbell, Glen 1938– CTFT–1
Campbell, Graeme 1954– CTFT–79
   Earlier sketch in CTFT–36
Campbell, J. Kenneth CTFT–62
Campbell, Jessica 1982– CTFT–64
   Earlier sketch in CTFT–29
Campbell, Judy 1916– WWT–17
Campbell, Julia 1963– CTFT–49
Campbell, Ken 1941– CTFT–38
   Earlier sketch in WWT–17
Campbell, Ken Hudson 1963– CTFT–79
Campbell, Margaret 1894– .... WWasWT
Campbell, Martin 1958– CTFT–39
   Earlier sketch in CTFT–16
Campbell, Mrs. Patrick 1865–1940 .... WWasWT
Campbell, Naomi 1970– CTFT–71
   Earlier sketches in CTFT–20, 31
Campbell, Neve 1973– CTFT–54
   Earlier sketches on CTFT–16, 26
Campbell, Nicholas 1952– CTFT–79
   Earlier sketch in CTFT–36
Campbell, Patton 1926– WWT–17
Campbell, Scott Allan 1959– CTFT–44
Campbell, Scott Michael CTFT–59
   Earlier sketch in CTFT–27
Campbell, Stella Patrick 1886–1940 ...... WWasWT
Campbell, Tisha 1968– CTFT–62
   Earlier sketch in CTFT–17
Campbell, Violet 1892–1970 .... WWasWT
Campbell, William
   See .... Campbell, Bill
Campbell–Martin, Tisha
   See .... Campbell, Tisha
Campenella, Joe
   See .... Campanella, Joseph
Campion, Clifford 1949– CTFT–4
Campion, Cyril 1894–1961 .... WWasWT
Campion, Jane 1954(?)– CTFT–29
   Earlier sketches in CTFT–10, 18
Campos, Bruno 1973– CTFT–67
Campton, David 1924– WWT–17

Camroux, Ken CTFT–39
Canada, Ron CTFT–46
Canals, Maria 1966– CTFT–73
Canary, David 1938– CTFT–25
Canby, Vincent 1924– CTFT–4
Candelier, Isabelle CTFT–34
Candler, Peter 1926– CTFT–1
Candy, John 1950–1994 .... CTFT–5
   Obituary in CTFT–12
   Brief Entry in CTFT–2
Canerday, Natalie 1962– CTFT–59
   Earlier sketch in CTFT–27
Canet, Guillaume 1973– CTFT–30
Canfield, Gene CTFT–65
Canfield, Mark
   See .... Zanuck, Darryl F.
Caniparoli, Val 1951– CTFT–13
Cannan, Denis 1919– WWT–17
Cannan, Gilbert 1884–1955 .... WWasWT
Cannavale, Bobby 1971– CTFT–46
Cannell, Stephen J. 1941– CTFT–39
   Earlier sketches in CTFT–7, 15
Cannistraci, Jay CTFT–32
Cannon, Dyan 1937– CTFT–72
   Earlier sketches in CTFT–3, 12, 22, 32
Cannon, Joey
   See .... Pesci, Joe
Cannon, Katherine 1953– CTFT–60
Cannon, Wanda CTFT–49
Canonero, Milena CTFT–79
   Earlier sketches in CTFT–9, 35
Canova, Diana 1952(?)– CTFT–22
   Earlier sketches in CTFT–1, 12
Canton, Mark 1949– CTFT–37
   Earlier sketch in CTFT–12
Cantor, Arthur 1920– CTFT–7
   Earlier sketch in WWT–17
Cantor, Eddie 1892–1964 .... WWasWT
Capalbo, Carmen 1925– CTFT–1
Capecce, Victor CTFT–3
Capek, Karel 1890–1938 .... WWasWT
Capers, Virginia 1925– CTFT–41
   Earlier sketches in CTFT–12, 20
Caplan, Lizzy 1982– CTFT–70
Caplin, Jeremy O. 1955– CTFT–3
Caplin, Twink CTFT–66
Capodice, John 1938– CTFT–62
   Earlier sketch in CTFT–29
Capra, Francis 1983– CTFT–78
Capra, Frank 1897–1991 .... CTFT–9
Capra, Frank, Jr. CTFT–3
Capri, Mark 1951– CTFT–4
Capshaw, Jessica 1976– CTFT–49
Capshaw, Kate 1953– CTFT–41
   Earlier sketches in CTFT–5, 12, 20
   Brief Entry in CTFT–2
Captain Kangaroo
   See .... Keeshan, Robert J.
Capucine 1935(?)–1990 .... CTFT–9
Capus, Alfred 1858–1922 .... WWasWT
Cara, Irene 1959– CTFT–5
   Brief Entry in CTFT–2
Carafotes, Paul 1963– CTFT–78
Carambo, Cristobal 1950– CTFT–1
Carbonell, Nestor 1967– CTFT–64
   Earlier sketches in CTFT–17, 29
Cardellini, Linda 1975– CTFT–72
   Earlier sketch in CTFT–32
Carden, William 1947– CTFT–4
Cardiff, Jack 1914– CTFT–47
   Earlier sketch in CTFT–10
Cardinal, Tantoo 1950(?)– CTFT–54
   Earlier sketches in CTFT–16, 26

Cardinale, Claudia 1938–......................... CTFT–34
    Earlier sketch in CTFT–4
Carell, Steve 1963– CTFT–64
Carew, James 1876–1938 .... WWasWT
Carew, Topper 1943– CTFT–13
Carey, Claire 1967– CTFT–64
Carey, Denis 1909–1986 .... CTFT–4
    Earlier sketch in WWT–17
Carey, Drew 1958– CTFT–57
    Earlier sketches in CTFT–17, 27
Carey, Harry, Jr. 1921– CTFT–18
    Earlier sketches in CTFT–1, 8
Carey, Joyce 1898–................................. WWT–17
Carey, MacDonald 1913–1994................. CTFT–8
    Obituary in CTFT–13
Carey, Mariah 1970–............................... CTFT–40
Carey, Matthew 1980– CTFT–44
Carey, Philip 1925–................................ CTFT–62
Carey, Ron 1935–................................... CTFT–18
    Earlier sketch in CTFT–8
Carfax, Bruce 1905–1970..................... WWasWT
Cargill, Patrick 1918–............................. WWT–17
Carhart, Timothy 1953–.......................... CTFT–38
Carides, Gia 1964– CTFT–59
    Earlier sketch in CTFT–27
Caridi, Carmine 1933–............................ CTFT–44
Cariou, Len 1939–.................................. CTFT–64
    Earlier sketches in CTFT–1, 3, 19, 29
Carle, Cynthia CTFT–1
Carle, Richard 1871–1941..................... WWasWT
Carleton, Claire 1913– .... WWasWT
Carlier, Madeleine .... WWasWT
Carlin, George 1937–.............................. CTFT–51
    Earlier sketches in CTFT–7, 15, 25
Carlin, Lynn 1938–.................................. CTFT–1
Carlisle, Alexandra 1886–1936 .... WWasWT
Carlisle, Jodi 1960–............................... CTFT–52
Carlisle, Kevin 1935–.............................. CTFT–18
    Earlier sketch in CTFT–2
Carlisle, Kitty 1914– CTFT–3
    Earlier sketch in WWT–17
Carlisle, Margaret 1905–...................... WWasWT
Carlisle, Sybil 1871–? .... WWasWT
Carlos, Walter
    See .... Carlos, Wendy
Carlos, Wendy 1939–.............................. CTFT–25
Carlsen, John A. 1915–......................... WWasWT
Carlson, Len CTFT–52
Carlson, Leslie 1933– CTFT–64
Carlson, Lillian CTFT–62
Carlson, Linda 1945– CTFT–48
Carlton (Arthur Carlton Philps)
    1880–? .... WWasWT
Carlton, Bob 1950–................................. CTFT–8
Carlton, Mark 1945–............................... CTFT–64
Carlyle, Robert 1961– CTFT–67
    Earlier sketches in CTFT–19, 30
Carmack, Chris 1980–............................ CTFT–74
Carme, Pamela 1902– .... WWasWT
Carmel, Roger C. 1932–1986 .... CTFT–4
Carmello, Carolee CTFT–60
    Earlier sketch in CTFT–27
Carmichael, Ian 1920– CTFT–6
    Earlier sketch in WWT–17
Carminati, Tullio 1894–1971 .... WWasWT
Carmines, Al 1936–................................ WWT–17
Carne, Judy 1939–.................................. CTFT–3
Carner, Charles Robert 1957–................. CTFT–66
Carney, Art 1918– CTFT–4
    Earlier sketch in WWT–17
Carney, George 1887–1947 .... WWasWT
Carney, Kate 1870–1950 .... WWasWT
Carney, Kay 1933– CTFT–1

Carnovsky, Morris 1897–....................... WWT–17
Caro, Warren 1907–............................... WWT–17
Carola, Adam
    See.. Carolla, Adam
Caroll, Eddie
    See................................... Carroll, Eddie
Carolla, Adam 1964– CTFT–69
Caron, Cecile.. WWasWT
Caron, Glenn Gordon CTFT–37
    Earlier sketch in CTFT–12
Caron, Leslie 1931– CTFT–33
    Earlier sketches in CTFT–3; WWasWT
Caron, Marguerite .... WWasWT
Carpenter, Carleton 1926–.................... WWT–17
Carpenter, Charisma 1970– CTFT–58
    Earlier sketch in CTFT–27
Carpenter, Constance 1906–.................. WWT–17
Carpenter, Edward Childs 1872–1950..... WWasWT
Carpenter, Freddie 1908–1989 .... CTFT–8
    Earlier sketch in WWT–17
Carpenter, John 1948–............................ CTFT–53
    Earlier sketches in CTFT–1, 8, 15, 25
Carpenter, Maud ?–1967........................ WWasWT
Carpenter, Russell 1950–........................ CTFT–41
    Earlier sketch in CTFT–20
Carpenter, Willie C................................. CTFT–54
Carr, Alexander 1878–1946................... WWasWT
Carr, Allan 1941– CTFT–3
Carr, Darleen 1950–............................... CTFT–55
    Earlier sketches in CTFT–8, 19
Carr, F. Osmond 1858–1916.................. WWasWT
Carr, George ?–1962 .... WWasWT
Carr, Georgia
    See .... Carides, Gia
Carr, Howard 1880–1960..................... WWasWT
Carr, Jane 1909–1957 .... WWasWT
Carr, Jane 1950–.................................... CTFT–72
    Earlier sketches in CTFT–5, 33
Carr, Joseph W. Comyns 1849–1916..... WWasWT
Carr, Lawrence 1916–1969.................... WWasWT
Carr, Martin 1932–................................. CTFT–2
Carr, Paul 1934–.................................... CTFT–56
Carr, Philip 1874–1957......................... WWasWT
Carr, Terry
    See .... Garr, Teri
Carradine, David 1936–.......................... CTFT–72
    Earlier sketches in CTFT–4, 11, 22, 32
Carradine, Ever 1974–............................ CTFT–44
Carradine, John 1906–1988 .... CTFT–7
    Earlier sketches in CTFT–4; WWT–17
Carradine, Keith 1949– CTFT–64
    Earlier sketches in CTFT–1, 10, 18, 29
Carradine, Marina
    See.. D'Este, Coco
Carradine, Robert 1954–........................ CTFT–70
    Earlier sketches in CTFT–3, 20, 31
Carrasco, Carlos CTFT–51
Carr–Cook, Madge 1856–1933............. WWasWT
Carre, Fabrice 1855–?........................... WWasWT
Carre, Michel 1865–? .... WWasWT
Carrera, Barbara 1945–.......................... CTFT–33
    Earlier sketches in CTFT–1, 6
Carrere, Tia 1967–................................. CTFT–732
    Earlier sketches in CTFT–11, 22, 32
Carrey, Jim 1962–.................................. CTFT–72
    Earlier sketches in CTFT–13, 22, 32
Carrick, Edward 1905–......................... WWasWT
Carrick, Hartley 1881–1929 .... WWasWT
Carriere, Jean–Claude 1931–................. CTFT–53
    Earlier sketches in CTFT–8, 15, 25
Carrillo, Elpidia 1963(?)–....................... CTFT–76
    Earlier sketch in CTFT–34
Carrillo, Leo 1880–1961....................... WWasWT

Carrington, Debbie Lee 1959– CTFT–43
Carrington, Ethel 1889–1962 .... WWasWT
Carrington, Murray 1885–1941 .... WWasWT
Carrion, Lizette 1972–............................ CTFT–73
Carro, Luciana...................................... CTFT–76
Carrol, Ronn CTFT–38
Carroll, David–James 1950–1992 .... CTFT–11
    Earlier sketch in CTFT–1
Carroll, Diahann 1935–.......................... CTFT–72
    Earlier sketches in CTFT–3, 20, 32
Carroll, Earl 1893–1948 .... WWasWT
Carroll, Eddie CTFT–69
Carroll, Helena CTFT–1
Carroll, J. Winston CTFT–56
Carroll, Janet 1940– CTFT–48
    Earlier sketch in CTFT–23
Carroll, Leo G. 1892–1972 .... WWasWT
Carroll, Leo M. WWT–14
Carroll, Madeleine 1906–1987 .... WWasWT
Carroll, Nancy 1906–1965 .... WWasWT
Carroll, Pat 1927– CTFT–71
    Earlier sketches in CTFT–3, 19, 31
Carroll, Paul Vincent 1900–1968 .... WWasWT
Carroll, Rocky CTFT–46
Carroll, Sydney W. 1877–1958.............. WWasWT
Carroll, Vinnette CTFT–5
    Earlier sketch in WWT–17
Carroll, Willard 1955–............................ CTFT–77
Carrot Top 1967– CTFT–42
Carry, Julius 1952–................................ CTFT–41
Carsey, Marcy 1944–.............................. CTFT–37
    Earlier sketch in CTFT–13
Carson, Charles 1885–1977 .... WWT–16
Carson, Mrs. Charles L. ?–1919 .... WWasWT
Carson, David CTFT–50
Carson, Doris 1910–............................. WWasWT
Carson, Frances 1895– .... WWasWT
Carson, Jeannie 1929–........................... WWT–17
Carson, John David CTFT–8
Carson, Johnny 1925– CTFT–3
Carson, Kelly 1976–............................... CTFT–74
Carson, Kris
    See................................... Kristofferson, Kris
Carson, Lionel 1873–1937 .... WWasWT
Carson, Lisa Nicole 1969– CTFT–47
    Earlier sketch in CTFT–23
Carson, Murray 1865–1917 .... WWasWT
Carson, Rachel CTFT–73
Carson, T. C. 1958–............................... CTFT–65
    Earlier sketches in CTFT–17, 29
Carte, Mrs. D'Oyly ?–1948.................... WWasWT
Carte, Rupert D'Oyly
    See.............................. D'Oyly Carte, Rupert
Carten, Audrey 1900– .... WWasWT
Carter, Alan CTFT–47
Carter, Alex... CTFT–46
Carter, Chris 1956–................................ CTFT–57
    Earlier sketches in CTFT–16, 26
Carter, Desmond ?–1939 .... WWasWT
Carter, Dixie 1939–................................ CTFT–75
    Earlier sketches in CTFT–5, 33
Carter, Finn 1960– CTFT–61
Carter, Frederick 1900–1970 .... WWasWT
Carter, Helena Bonham
    See .... Bonham Carter, Helena
Carter, Hubert ?–1934........................... WWasWT
Carter, Jack 1923– CTFT–36
    Earlier sketch in CTFT–11
Carter, James L. CTFT–64
Carter, Jason 1960– CTFT–39
Carter, Jesse
    See .... Jacott, Carlos

Carter, Jim... CTFT–73
   Earlier sketch in CTFT–32
Carter, Joelle.. CTFT–72
   Earlier sketch in CTFT–32
Carter, June
   See..................................... Cash, June Carter
Carter, Kristopher 1972–.......................... CTFT–55
Carter, Mrs. Leslie 1862–1937 .... WWasWT
Carter, Leslie
   See .... Zemeckis, Leslie Harter
Carter, Lonnie 1942–................................. CTFT–1
Carter, Lynda 1951– CTFT–70
   Earlier sketches in CTFT–5, 19, 31
   Brief Entry in CTFT–2
Carter, Margaret..................................... WWasWT
Carter, Mell 1894–1965 .... WWasWT
Carter, Nell 1948–2003 .... CTFT–37
   Obituary in CTFT–48
   Earlier sketches in CTFT–3, 13
Carter, Richard... CTFT–35
Carter, Rick 1952–................................... CTFT–79
Carter, T. K. 1956–.................................. CTFT–38
   Earlier sketches in CTFT–4, 15
Carter, Thomas CTFT–79
   Earlier sketches in CTFT–9, 35
Carter–Edwards, James 1840–1930........... WWasWT
Carteret, Anna 1942– CTFT–5
   Earlier sketch in WWT–17
Cartlidge, Katrin 1961–2002 .... CTFT–35
   Obituary in CTFT–49
   Earlier sketch in CTFT–6
Carton, R. C. 1853–1938....................... WWasWT
Cartwright, Angela CTFT–29
Cartwright, Charles 1855–1916 .... WWasWT
Cartwright, Jim 1958– CTFT–38
   Earlier sketch in CTFT–14
Cartwright, Nancy 1959– CTFT–70
   Earlier sketches in CTFT–19, 31
Cartwright, Peggy 1912– .... WWasWT
Cartwright, Veronica 1950(?)– CTFT–67
   Earlier sketches in CTFT–6, 18, 30
   Brief Entry in CTFT–2
Carus, Emma 1879–1927 .... WWasWT
Caruso, David 1956– CTFT–43
   Earlier sketches in CTFT–13, 22
Carvalho, Betty... CTFT–50
Carvell, Marium CTFT–62
Carver, Brent 1951(?)–.............................. CTFT–72
   Earlier sketches in CTFT–20, 32
Carver, Caroline....................................... CTFT–65
   Earlier sketch in CTFT–29
Carver, James C. 1932– CTFT–3
Carver, Mary... CTFT–1
Carver, Steven 1945–............................... CTFT–12
   Earlier sketch in CTFT–1
Carvey, Dana 1955– CTFT–65
   Earlier sketches in CTFT–10, 18, 29
Cary, Falkland 1897–1989......................... CTFT–8
   Earlier sketch in WWT–17
Caryll, Ivan 1861–1921 .... WWasWT
Casados, Eloy CTFT–66
Casady, Cort 1947– CTFT–3
Casartelli, Gabrielle 1910– .... WWasWT
Cascio, Michael 1950–............................ CTFT–46
Cascone, Nicholas.................................... CTFT–40
Casella, Max 1967–.................................. CTFT–67
   Earlier sketch in CTFT–30
Casey, Bernie 1939–................................. CTFT–78
   Earlier sketches in CTFT–7, 35
Casey, Elizabeth
   See .... Banks, Elizabeth
Cash, Dylan 1994–................................... CTFT–78
Cash, Jim.. CTFT–22

Cash, Johnny 1932– CTFT–19
Cash, June Carter 1929–.......................... CTFT–20
Cash, Morny .... WWasWT
Cash, Rita CTFT–50
Cash, Rosalind 1938–1995...................... CTFT–4
   Obituary in CTFT–15
   Earlier sketch in WWT–17
Casnoff, Philip 1955–.............................. CTFT–53
Caso, Alan CTFT–39
Cason, Barbara 1933–................................ CTFT–8
Cass, David S., Sr. CTFT–70
Cass, Henry 1902–1989 .... WWT–17
Cass, Peggy 1926(?)–1999 .... CTFT–3
   Obituary in CTFT–32
   Earlier sketch in WWT–17
Cass, Ronald 1923–................................... CTFT–5
   Earlier sketch in WWT–17
Cassar, Jon 1958–.................................... CTFT–40
Cassaro, Nancy 1959– CTFT–53
Cassavetes, John 1929–1989 .... CTFT–7
   Earlier sketch in CTFT–3
Cassavetes, Nick 1959–........................... CTFT–76
   Earlier sketches in CTFT–22, 32
Cassel, Seymour 1935– CTFT–76
   Earlier sketches in CTFT–9, 34
Cassel, Vincent 1966–.............................. CTFT–47
   Earlier sketch in CTFT–23
Casseus, Gabriel 1963–............................ CTFT–65
Cassidy, David 1950–............................... CTFT–37
   Earlier sketch in CTFT–8
Casseus, Gabriel CTFT–29
Cassidy, Jack 1927–1976......................... WWT–16
Cassidy, Joanna 1944– CTFT–72
   Earlier sketches in CTFT–6, 22, 32
Cassidy, Patrick 1962–............................. CTFT–74
   Earlier sketches in CTFT–8, 33
Cassidy, Shaun 1958–.............................. CTFT–39
   Earlier sketches in CTFT–3, 16
Cassini, John... CTFT–61
Casson, Ann 1915–1990 .... WWasWT
Casson, Christopher 1912–.................... WWasWT
Casson, John 1909–................................ WWasWT
Casson, Lewis T. 1875–1969 .... WWasWT
Casson, Mary 1914–............................... WWasWT
Cassutt, Michael 1954– CTFT–51
   Earlier sketches in CTFT–3, 16
Castang, Veronica.................................... CTFT–1
Castellaneta, Dan 1958– CTFT–38
   Earlier sketches in CTFT–6, 13
Castellano, Richard 1933–1988 .... CTFT–7
Castellucci, Teddy CTFT–65
Castillo, Helen 1955–................................ CTFT–4
Castle, John 1940– WWT–17
Castle, Nick 1947–................................... CTFT–37
   Earlier sketch in CTFT–12
Catalano, Laura CTFT–58
Cates, Gilbert 1934– CTFT–79
   Earlier sketches in CTFT–10, 36
Cates, Joseph 1924–1998 .... CTFT–12
   Obituary in CTFT–32
Cates, Madelyn CTFT–8
Cates, Phoebe 1963(?)– CTFT–18
   Earlier sketch in CTFT–10
   Brief Entry in CTFT–5
Cathcart, Claire CTFT–34
Cathey, Reg E. 1958– CTFT–41
Catillon, Brigitte CTFT–38
Catlett, Mary Jo 1938– CTFT–74
   Earlier sketches in CTFT–2, 33
Catlett, Walter 1889–1960.................... WWasWT
Catling, Thomas 1838–1920................. WWasWT
Caton–Jones, Michael 1957–.................. CTFT–36
   Earlier sketch in CTFT–10

Catrini, Robert 1950–.............................. CTFT–59
Cattley, Cyril 1876–1937 .... WWasWT
Cattrall, Kim 1956–.................................. CTFT–51
   Earlier sketches in CTFT–8, 15, 25
Cauble, Lisa
   See............................... Whelchel, Lisa
Caudell, Toran 1982–............................... CTFT–67
   Earlier sketch in CTFT–30
Cauffiel, Jessica 1976–............................. CTFT–69
Caulfield, Emma 1973(?)–........................ CTFT–65
Caulfield, Maxwell 1959–......................... CTFT–79
   Earlier sketches in CTFT–10, 36
   Brief Entry in CTFT–3
Caute, David 1936–.................................. CTFT–12
Cavadini, Cathy.. CTFT–52
Cavalier, Jason CTFT–52
Cavan, Susan.. CTFT–41
Cavanagh, Thomas 1963(?)–..................... CTFT–75
   Earlier sketch in CTFT–34
Cavanaugh, Christine CTFT–57
   Earlier sketch in CTFT–26
Cavanagh, Lilian ?–1932 .... WWasWT
Cavanagh, Megan CTFT–44
Cavanagh, Paul 1895–1960................... WWasWT
Cavanaugh, Michael 1942–...................... CTFT–78
   Earlier sketches in CTFT–9, 35
Cavani, Liliana 1936(?)–........................... CTFT–33
   Earlier sketch in CTFT–8
Cavett, Dick 1936– CTFT–48
   Earlier sketches in CTFT–1, 8, 15
Caviezel, Jim 1968–................................. CTFT–67
   Earlier sketch in CTFT–30
Cawthorn, Joseph 1867–1949 .... WWasWT
Cayer, D. M.
   See................................. Duffy, Maureen
Cazale, John 1936–1978 .... CTFT–26
Cazenove, Christopher 1945– CTFT–78
   Earlier sketches in CTFT–4, 35; WWT–17
Cease, Jonathan
   See.................................... Osser, Jonathan
Cecchetti, Enrico 1847–1928 .... WWasWT
Cecere, Fulvio CTFT–42
Cecil, Henry 1902–1976 .... WWT–16
Cecil, Jonathan 1939– WWT–17
Cecil, Sylvia 1906– .... WWasWT
Cedar, Larry 1955–........................... [fl–rt]CTFT–65
   Earlier sketch in CTFT–29
Ceder, Elayne Barbara 1946– CTFT–23
   Earlier sketch in CTFT–11
Cedric The Entertainer 1964(?)– CTFT–63
Celedonio, Maria...................................... CTFT–34
Celenatno, Jeff 1960–.............................. CTFT–74
Celestin, Jack 1894–.............................. WWasWT
Celli, Faith 1888–1942 .... WWasWT
Cellier, Antoinette 1913–...................... WWasWT
Cellier, Frank 1884–1948 .... WWasWT
Cera, Michael 1988–................................ CTFT–64
Cerasoli, Lisa 1969–................................. CTFT–30
Cerito, Ada .... WWasWT
Cerny, Berthe... WWasWT
Cervantes, Carlos...................................... CTFT–57
Cervantes, Gary CTFT–56
Cervera, Jorge, Jr. CTFT–50
Cerveris, Michael 1960– CTFT–43
   Earlier sketch in CTFT–22
Cesario, Juliet CTFT–39
Chaback, J. J.
   See.................................... Jenkins, Jane
Chabert, Lacey 1982– CTFT–69
   Earlier sketches in CTFT–19, 31
Chabrol, Claude 1930–............................ CTFT–26
   Earlier sketches in CTFT–8, 16
Chacksfield, Frank CTFT–2

Chadbon, Tom 1946–.............................. CTFT–5
  Earlier sketch in WWT–17
Chadwick, Aimee–Lynn 1984–.............. CTFT–75
Chaffey, Don 1917–............................... CTFT–11
Chagrin, Julian 1940–............................ WWT–17
Chaikin, Joseph 1935– CTFT–7
  Earlier sketch in WWT–17
Chaikin, Shami 1931– CTFT–1
Chaine, Pierre .... WWasWT
Chaken, Maury
  See .... Chaykin, Maury
Chakiris, George 1934–......................... CTFT–51
  Earlier sketch in CTFT–12
Chalfant, Kathleen 1945–...................... CTFT–49
  Earlier sketch in CTFT–24
Chalk, Gary CTFT–42
Chalke, Sarah 1977(?)–......................... CTFT–46
Challenor, (James) Bromley
  1884–1935 .... WWasWT
Chalzel, Leo 1901–1953 .... WWasWT
Chamberlain, George 1891– .... WWasWT
Chamberlain, Richard 1934–................. CTFT–76
  Earlier sketches in CTFT–1, 5, 34; WWT–17
Chamberlin, Kevin 1963–...................... CTFT–79
  Earlier sketch in CTFT–36
Chamberlin, Lee 1938–......................... CTFT–62
  Earlier sketch in CTFT–4
Chambers, Charles Haddon
  1860–1921 .... WWasWT
Chambers, Emma 1969– CTFT–59
  Earlier sketches in CTFT–27; WWasWT
Chambers, H. Kellett 1867–1935 .... WWasWT
Chambers, Justin 1970–........................ CTFT–66
Champion, Gower 1920–1980.............. WWT–17
Champion, Harry 1866–1942 .... WWasWT
Champion, Marge 1919–........................ CTFT–1
Champlin, Donna Lynne CTFT–60
Chan, Jackie 1954(?)–........................... CTFT–55
  Earlier sketches in CTFT–9, 16, 26
Chan, Kim CTFT–48
Chan, Michael Paul............................... CTFT–38
Chance, James T.
  See .... Carpenter, John
Chance, John T.
  See .... Carpenter, John
Chancellor, Betty .... WWasWT
Chancellor, John 1927–.......................... CTFT–7
Chancellor, Joyce 1906–...................... WWasWT
Chandler, Helen 1909–1965................. WWasWT
Chandler, Jeffrey Alan CTFT–2
Chandler, Kyle 1966(?)–....................... CTFT–65
  Earlier sketches in CTFT–17, CTFT–29
Chandler, Simon CTFT–38
Chaney, Jon
  See .... Williams, Jimmy
Chaney, Stewart 1910–1969................. WWasWT
Chang, Doug
  See .... Chiang, Doug
Chang, Gary 1953–............................... CTFT–79
  Earlier sketches in CTFT–10, 36
Chang, Christina 1969–......................... CTFT–75
Chang, Tisa 1941–................................. CTFT–1
Changwei, Gu 1957–............................ CTFT–39
  Earlier sketch in CTFT–13
Channing, Carol 1921– CTFT–70
  Earlier sketches in CTFT–3, 19, 31; WWT–17
Channing, Marvin 1944–........................ CTFT–4
Channing, Stockard 1944– CTFT–56
  Earlier sketches in CTFT–1, 7, 16, 26
Chansky, Dorothy 1951–........................ CTFT–1
Chao, Rosalind 1959(?)–....................... CTFT–69
  Earlier sketches in CTFT–20, 31
Chapa, Damian 1963– CTFT–48

Chapin, Harold 1886–1915 .... WWasWT
Chapin, Louis Le Bourgeois
  1918–... WWT–17
Chapin, Miles 1954–............................... CTFT–1
Chaplin, Alexander 1971–...................... CTFT–39
  Earlier sketch in CTFT–17
Chaplin, Ben 1970– CTFT–56
  Earlier sketch in CTFT–26
Chaplin, Charles Spencer 1889–1977..... WWasWT
Chaplin, Geraldine 1944–...................... CTFT–39
  Earlier sketches in CTFT–3, 9, 16
Chapman, Andi CTFT–39
Chapman, Constance 1912– WWT–17
Chapman, David 1938–........................... CTFT–7
  Earlier sketch in WWT–17
Chapman, Edward 1901–1986 .... WWasWT
Chapman, Graham 1941–1989 .... CTFT–8
Chapman, John R. 1927– CTFT–6
  Earlier sketch in WWT–17
Chapman, Judith.................................... CTFT–53
Chapman, Kevin CTFT–72
Chapman, Lonny 1920(?)–...................... CTFT–56
  Earlier sketches in CTFT–4, 26
Chapman, Michael 1935– CTFT–53
  Earlier sketches in CTFT–8, 15, 25
Chapman, Sean CTFT–66
  Earlier sketch in CTFT–30
Chappell, William 1908– WWT–17
Chappelle, Dave 1973(?)– CTFT–59
  Earlier sketch in CTFT–27
Chappelle, Frederick W. 1895–............. WWasWT
Chappelle, Joe 1961–............................. CTFT–55
Charback, J. J.
  See .... Jenkins, Jane
Charbonneau, Patricia 1958(?)–.............. CTFT–55
  Earlier sketches in CTFT–8, 15, 25
Charby, Jay
  See .... Ellison, Harlan
Charell, Erik 1895–.............................. WWasWT
Charendoff–Strong, Tara
  See .... Strong, Tara
Charest, Micheline 1953(?)–................... CTFT–41
Charisse, Cyd 1921– CTFT–51
  Earlier sketch in CTFT–12
Charles, Josh 1971–.............................. CTFT–47
  Earlier sketches in CTFT–11, 23
Charles, Maria 1929–............................ CTFT–39
  Earlier sketches in CTFT–13; WWT–17
Charles, Melissa CTFT–52
Charles, Pamela 1932–.......................... WWT–17
Charles, RuPaul
  See .... RuPaul
Charles, Tom
  Fahn, Tom CTFT–74
Charles, Walter 1945–............................ CTFT–1
Charleson, Ian 1949–1990...................... CTFT–11
  Earlier sketches in CTFT–1, 4; WWT–17
Charleson, Leslie 1945– CTFT–58
Charleston, Jim CTFT–39
Charney, Jordan 1937–.......................... CTFT–53
Charnin, Martin 1934–.......................... CTFT–32
  Earlier sketches in CTFT–2, 10, 19; WWT–17
Charo 1941(?)–..................................... CTFT–73
Charret, Christian CTFT–46
Chart, Henry Nye 1868–1934 .... WWasWT
Charters, Rodney CTFT–40
Chartoff, Melanie 1955–........................ CTFT–59
  Earlier sketch in CTFT–1
Chartoff, Robert 1933–.......................... CTFT–23
  Earlier sketches in CTFT–3, 12
Charts, Adele
  See .... Loring, Lisa
Charvay, Robert 1858–?........................ WWasWT

Chase, Bailey 1972–.............................. CTFT–47
Chase, Chevy 1943– CTFT–56
  Earlier sketches in CTFT–3, 9, 16, 26
Chase, Daveigh 1990–.......................... CTFT–64
Chase, David 1945–.............................. CTFT–47
Chase, Heather 1978–.......................... CTFT–75
Chase, Ilka 1905–1978......................... WWT–16
Chase, Mary 1907–1981 .... WWT–17
Chase, Pauline 1885–1962 .... WWasWT
Chasen, Heather 1927–.......................... CTFT–6
  Earlier sketch in WWT–17
Chatelain, Christine CTFT–66
Chater, Geoffrey 1921– WWT–17
Chatterton, Ruth 1893–1961 .... WWasWT
Chatwin, Justin 1982–........................... CTFT–68
Chatwin, Margaret ?–1937 .... WWasWT
Chau, Francois 1959–............................ CTFT–71
Chauvaud, Christian CTFT–38
Chauvin, Lilyan 1925(?)–....................... CTFT–54
Chaves, Richard 1951–............................ CTFT–8
Chavira, Ricardo Antonio 1971– CTFT–74
Chayefsky, Paddy 1923–1981.................. CTFT–1
  Earlier sketch in WWT–17
Chaykin, Maury 1949–........................... CTFT–72
  Earlier sketches in CTFT–7, 33
Cheadle, Don 1964–............................. CTFT–72
  Earlier sketches in CTFT–22, 32
Cheatham, Maree 1942–....................... CTFT–57
Cheek, Molly CTFT–43
  Earlier sketch in CTFT–20
Cheese, Jack
  See .... Goldthwait, Bob
Cheeseman, Ken 1954–......................... CTFT–72
  Earlier sketch in CTFT–32
Cheeseman, Peter 1932–....................... WWT–17
Chekhov, Michael 1891–1955.............. WWasWT
Chelsom, Peter 1956–............................ CTFT–36
  Earlier sketches in CTFT–3, 11
Chelton, Nick 1946–............................... CTFT–5
  Earlier sketch in WWT–17
Chen, Joan 1961–.................................. CTFT–39
  Earlier sketch in CTFT–13
Chen, Kaige 1952–................................ CTFT–48
Chen, Ng Yu
  See .... Woo, John
Chen, Terry.. CTFT–62
Cheney, Sheldon 1886–1980................ WWasWT
Cheng, Long
  See .... Chan, Jackie
Chenoweth, Kristin 1968–..................... CTFT–60
  Earlier sketch in CTFT–27
Cheong, George Lee
  See........................... Cheung, George
Chepovetsky, Dmitry CTFT–66
Cher 1946–.. CTFT–66
  Earlier sketches in CTFT–3, 9, 18, 30
  Brief Entry in CTFT–2
Chereau, Patrice 1944–.......................... CTFT–26
Cherkasov, Nikolai 1903–1966.............. WWasWT
Cherones, Tom CTFT–49
Cherrell, Gwen 1926–.......................... WWT–17
Cherry, Charles 1872–1931 .... WWasWT
Cherry, Elizabeth CTFT–60
Cherry, Helen 1915– .... WWasWT
Cherry, Wal 1932–1986 .... WWT–17
Cheskin, Irving W. 1915– WWT–17
Chesne, Steven 1960–........................... CTFT–47
  Earlier sketches in CTFT–12, 23
Chesney, Arthur 1882–1949 .... WWasWT
Chester, Betty 1895–1943 .... WWasWT
Chester, Nora....................................... CTFT–19
  Earlier sketch in CTFT–2
Chestnut, Morris 1969–......................... CTFT–53

Chetham–Strode, Warren 1897– .... WWasWT
Chetwyn, Robert 1933– WWT–17
Chetwynd, Lionel 1940– CTFT–38
  Earlier sketch in CTFT–14
Cheung, George CTFT–53
Cheung, Leslie 1956– CTFT–31
  Earlier sketch in CTFT–19
Cheung, Maggie 1964– CTFT–48
  Earlier sketch in CTFT–24
Chevalier, Albert 1861–1923 .... WWasWT
Chevalier, Marcelle .... WWasWT
Chevalier, Maurice 1888–1972 .... WWasWT
Chevolleau, Richard CTFT–40
Chew, Lee CTFT–3
Chew, Richard CTFT–56
  Earlier sketches in CTFT–11, 23
Cheylov, Milan CTFT–40
Chi
  See .... McBride, Chi
Chianese, Dominic 1934(?)– CTFT–46
Chiang, Doug 1962– CTFT–46
  Earlier sketch in CTFT–23
Chieffo, Michael CTFT–49
Chiklis, Michael 1963– CTFT–57
Child, Harold Hannyngton
  1869–1945 .... WWasWT
Childress, Alice 1920(?)–1994 .... CTFT–10
  Obituary in CTFT–13
Childs, Gilbert ?–1931 .... WWasWT
Chiles, Linden CTFT–9
Chiles, Lois 1947– CTFT–72
  Earlier sketches in CTFT–7, 33
Chill
  See .... Mitchell, Daryl
Chin, Tsai 1937– CTFT–48
  Earlier sketch in CTFT–24
Chin, Wellson
  See .... Chan, Jackie
Chinlund, Nick 1961– CTFT–66
  Earlier sketch in CTFT–30
Chinn, Jeanne CTFT–49
Chinoy, Helen Krich 1922– CTFT–1
Chinyamurindi, Michael CTFT–66
Chioran, Juan 1963– CTFT–78
Chirgwin, George H. 1854–1922 .... WWasWT
Chisholm, Anthony CTFT–66
  Earlier sketch in CTFT–30
Chisholm, Robert 1898–1960 .... WWasWT
Chlumsky, Anna 1980– CTFT–38
  Earlier sketch in CTFT–15
Cho, John CTFT–52
Cho, Margaret 1968– CTFT–65
  Earlier sketches in CTFT–17, CTFT–29
Choate, Tim 1954– CTFT–39
  Earlier sketches in CTFT–1, 17
Chodorov, Edward 1914–1988 .... CTFT–7
  Earlier sketches in WWT–17; WWasWT
Chodorov, Jerome 1911– WWT–17
Chomsky, Marvin J. 1929– CTFT–6
Chong, Marcus 1967– CTFT–48
Chong, Rae Dawn 1961– CTFT–45
  Earlier sketches in CTFT–7, 14, 23
Chong, Tommy 1938– CTFT–40
  Earlier sketches in CTFT–5, 18
  Brief Entry in CTFT–2
Chorpenning, Ruth 1905– .... WWasWT
Chorvat, Scarlett CTFT–78
Chou Jun–fa
  See .... Chow Yun–Fat
Choudhury, Sarita 1966– CTFT–69
  Earlier sketches in CTFT–20, 31
Chow Yun–Fat 1955– CTFT–67
  Earlier sketches in CTFT–19, 30

Chow, Ho 1957– CTFT–76
  Earlier sketch in CTFT–32
Chressanthis, James 1953– CTFT–42
Chriqui, Emmanuelle 1977– CTFT–75
Chris, Marilyn 1938– CTFT–54
Christensen, Erika 1982– CTFT–54
Christensen, Hayden 1981– CTFT–67
Christian, Claudia 1965– CTFT–45
  Earlier sketch in CTFT–23
Christian, Shawn 1965– CTFT–53
Christians, Mady 1900–1951 .... WWasWT
Christianson, Catherine 1957– CTFT–5
Christie, Agatha 1890–1976 .... WWT–16
Christie, Audrey 1912–1989 .... WWT–17
Christie, Campbell 1893–1963 .... WWasWT
Christie, Dorothy 1896– .... WWasWT
Christie, George 1873–1949 .... WWasWT
Christie, Julie 1941– CTFT–45
  Earlier sketches in CTFT–3, 9, 23
Christine, Virginia 1920–1996 .... CTFT–1
  Obituary in CTFT–16
Christmas, Eric 1916– CTFT–20
Christofferson, Debra CTFT–75
  Earlier sketch in CTFT–34
Christopher, Dennis 1955– CTFT–72
  Earlier sketches in CTFT–3, 33
Christopher, Dyllan 1991– CTFT–68
Christopher, Eva Longoria
  See .... Longoria, Eva
Christopher, Roy CTFT–47
  Earlier sketches in CTFT–11, 23
Christopher, Scott 1967– CTFT–75
Christopher, Thom 1940– CTFT–72
  Earlier sketches in CTFT–22, 32
Christopher, Tyler 1972– CTFT–62
Christy, Donald CTFT–2
Chuang, Susan CTFT–79
Chucklestein, Shecky
  See .... Oswalt, Patton
Chuck–Yiu, Clara Law
  See .... Law, Clara
Chud, Bud T.
  See .... Graham, Gerrit
Chudleigh, Arthur 1858–1932 .... WWasWT
Chuipka, Chip CTFT–41
Chula, Babs 1946– CTFT–52
Chulack, Christopher CTFT–56
Chun, Charles CTFT–60
Chung Ling Soo .... WWasWT
Chung, Connie 1946– CTFT–41
  Earlier sketches in CTFT–9, 18
Chung, Ewan 1974(?)– CTFT–68
Chung, George
  See .... Cheung, George
Church, Esme 1893–1972 .... WWasWT
Church, Thomas Haden 1961– CTFT–72
  Earlier sketches in CTFT–22, 32
Church, Tony 1930– CTFT–6
  Earlier sketch in WWT–17
Churchill, Berton 1876–1940 .... WWasWT
Churchill, Caryl 1938– CTFT–19
  Earlier sketches in CTFT–3, 10; WWT–17
Churchill, Diana (Josephine)
  1913– .... WWasWT
Churchill, Marguerite 1910– .... WWasWT
Churchill, Sarah 1914–1982 .... WWT–17
Churchill, Winston 1871–1947 .... WWasWT
Churgin, Lisa Zeno 1955– CTFT–65
  Earlier sketch in CTFT–29
Churikova, Inna 1943– CTFT–23
  Earlier sketch in CTFT–12
Chyna
  See .... Laurer, Joanie

Cialini, Julie Lynn
  See .... McCarthy, Jenny
Ciani, Suzanne 1946– CTFT–38
  Earlier sketch in CTFT–12
Cibrian, Eddie 1973– CTFT–48
Cicchini, Robert 1966– CTFT–72
  Earlier sketch in CTFT–32
Ciccolella, Jude CTFT–48
Ciccone, Madonna Louise
  See .... Madonna
Ciccoritti, Jerry CTFT–37
Ciding, Paul
  See .... Eiding, Paul
Cigliuti, Natalia 1978– CTFT–46
Cilento, Diane 1933– CTFT–5
  Earlier sketch in WWT–17
Cimino, Leonardo CTFT–42
Cimino, Michael 1952– CTFT–18
  Earlier sketches in CTFT–2, 6
Cimmet, Brian CTFT–60
Cinquevalli, Paul 1859–1918 .... WWasWT
Cioffi, Charles 1935– CTFT–50
Cipes, Greg CTFT–55
Cipriano, Joe 1954– CTFT–75
Cistaro, Anthony 1963– CTFT–52
Cizmar, Paula 1949– CTFT–1
Claflin, Scott CTFT–75
Clair, Mavis 1916– .... WWasWT
Claire, Helen 1911–1974 .... WWasWT
Claire, Ina 1895–1985 .... WWasWT
Claire, Ludi 1927– CTFT–1
Claman, Barbara S. 1939– CTFT–1
Clami, Jean–Pierre CTFT–36
Clancy, Deidre 1943– CTFT–5
  Earlier sketch in WWT–17
Clancy, Jim CTFT–76
Clancy, Tom 1947– CTFT–51
  Earlier sketch in CTFT–25
Clanton, Ralph 1914– WWT–17
Clap, Eric
  See .... Clapton, Eric
Clapp, Eric Patrick
  See .... Clapton, Eric
Clapp, Gordon 1948– CTFT–69
  Earlier sketches in CTFT–20, 31
Clapton, Eric 1945– CTFT–39
  Earlier sketch in CTFT–16
Clare, Mary 1894–1970 .... WWasWT
Clare, Tom 1876–? .... WWasWT
Clarence, O. B. 1870–1955 .... WWasWT
Claridge, Norman 1903– WWT–17
Clark, Alfred .... WWasWT
Clark, Anthony 1964– CTFT–39
  Earlier sketch in CTFT–17
Clark, B. D. 1945– CTFT–3
Clark, Barrett H. 1890–1953 .... WWasWT
Clark, Benjamin
  See .... Clark, Bob
Clark, Blake CTFT–42
Clark, Bob 1941– CTFT–72
  Earlier sketches in CTFT–7, 33
Clark, Bobby 1888–1960 .... WWasWT
Clark, Brian 1932– CTFT–4
  Earlier sketch in WWT–17
Clark, Candy 1947 .... CTFT–42
  Earlier sketch in CTFT–1
Clark, China CTFT–2
Clark, Curt
  See .... Westlake, Donald E.
Clark, Dick 1929– CTFT–75
  Earlier sketches in CTFT–3, 33
Clark, Duane CTFT–43
Clark, E. Holman 1864–1925 .... WWasWT

Clark, Ernest 1912– WWT–17
Clark, Eugene CTFT–42
Clark, Fred 1914–1968 .... WWasWT
Clark, Ian D... CTFT–59
Clark, Jim 1931– CTFT–36
   Earlier sketch in CTFT–10
Clark, John Pepper 1935– WWT–17
Clark, John Richard 1932– WWT–17
Clark, Kyle A. CTFT–69
Clark, Mara 1930– CTFT–5
Clark, Marguerite 1887–1940 .... WWasWT
Clark, Marjory 1900– .... WWasWT
Clark, Matt 1936– CTFT–55
   Earlier sketches in CTFT–8, 15, 25
Clark, Oliver 1939–................................. CTFT–69
Clark, Peggy 1915– WWT–17
Clark, Perceval
   See .... Perceval–Clark, P.
Clark, Roy 1933– CTFT–7
Clark, Spencer Treat 1987– CTFT–77
   Earlier sketch in CTFT–34
Clark, Susan 1944– CTFT–3
Clark, Tom CTFT–37
Clark, Vandi
   See.. Clark, Candy
Clark, Wallis 1888–1961 .... WWasWT
Clarke, Brian Patrick 1952(?)– CTFT–60
Clarke, Caitlin 1952– CTFT–38
   Earlier sketches in CTFT–8, 15
Clarke, Cam 1957– CTFT–36
Clarke, Cuthbert 1869–1953 .... WWasWT
Clarke, Dameon CTFT–65
Clarke, David 1908– CTFT–1
Clarke, George 1886–1946 .... WWasWT
Clarke, John.. CTFT–17
Clarke, Lenny 1953– CTFT–65
   Earlier sketches in CTFT–17, 29
Clarke, Mae 1907– .... WWasWT
Clarke, Michael Duncan
   See......................... Duncan, Michael Clarke
Clarke, Mindy.. CTFT–41
Clarke, Nigel 1895– .... WWasWT
Clarke, Richard 1930–.............................. CTFT–5
Clarke, Robert 1920– CTFT–63
Clarke, Rupert 1865–1926 .... WWasWT
Clarke, Sarah 1972– CTFT–68
Clarke, Stanley 1951– CTFT–36
   Earlier sketch in CTFT–11
Clarke–Smith, Douglas A.
   1888–1959 .... WWasWT
Clarkson, Joan 1903– .... WWasWT
Clarkson, Patricia 1959– CTFT–59
   Earlier sketch in CTFT–27
Clarkson, Paul CTFT–25
Clarkson, Willie 1861–1934 .... WWasWT
Clary, Robert 1926–.................................. CTFT–1
Clash, Kevin 1960– CTFT–49
Clatterbuck, Tamara CTFT–38
Claudel, Paul 1868–1955 .... WWasWT
Claughton, Susan .... WWasWT
Clausen, Alf 1941– CTFT–38
   Earlier sketch in CTFT–12
Clavell, James 1925–1994...................... CTFT–17
   Earlier sketch in CTFT–1
Clavell, Kira... CTFT–66
Claver, Bob 1928–.................................... CTFT–2
Claverie, Charles
   See.. Rocket, Charles
Clay, Andrew Dice 1957–........................ CTFT–36
   Earlier sketch in CTFT–11
Claybourne, Doug 1947–......................... CTFT–56
   Earlier sketch in CTFT–23

Clayburgh, Jill 1944–.............................. CTFT–64
   Earlier sketches in CTFT–2, 5, 18, 29
Clayton, Adam 1960– CTFT–40
Clayton, Gina CTFT–56
Clayton, Herbert 1876–1931 .... WWasWT
Clayton, Jack 1921–1995 .... CTFT–5
   Obituary in CTFT–14
Clayton, Tony 1935– CTFT–4
Cleage, Pearl 1948– CTFT–13
Cleather, Gordon 1872–? .... WWasWT
Cleave, Arthur 1884–? .... WWasWT
Cleese, John 1939– CTFT–57
   Earlier sketches in CTFT–4, 14, 27
Clegg, Allegra CTFT–64
   Earlier sketch in CTFT–29
Cleghorne, Ellen 1965– CTFT–38
Clemens, Le Roy 1889–? .... WWasWT
Clemenson, Christian 1959– CTFT–59
   Earlier sketch in CTFT–27
Clement, Clay 1888–1956 .... WWasWT
Clement, Elfrida .... WWasWT
Clement, Shawn K. 1968– CTFT–40
Clement–Scott, Joan 1907–1969 .... WWasWT
Clement–Scott, Margaret
   See .... Scott, Margaret Clement
Clements, John 1910–1988 .... CTFT–6
   Earlier sketch in WWT–17
Clements, Miriam .... WWasWT
Clements, Ronald 1953– CTFT–22
Clendenin, Bob 1964– CTFT–59
   Earlier sketch in CTFT–27
Clennon, David 1943– CTFT–53
   Earlier sketches in CTFT–8, 15, 25
Cleverson, Scott 1969–............................ CTFT–58
Cliche, Karen 1976–................................ CTFT–61
Cliff, Laddie 1891–1937 .... WWasWT
Cliffe, H. Cooper 1862–1939 .... WWasWT
Clifford, Camille .... WWasWT
Clifford, Graeme 1942–........................... CTFT–54
Clifford, Kathleen 1887–1962 .... WWasWT
Clifford, Richard CTFT–34
Clift, Ernest Paul 1881–1963 .... WWasWT
Clift, Montgomery 1920–1966............... WWasWT
Clifton, Bernard 1902–1970 .... WWasWT
Climenhaga, Joel 1922– CTFT–4
Cline, Carrie "CeCe" 1985– CTFT–68
Clinger, Bijou 1955–................................. CTFT–4
Clive, Colin 1900–1937 .... WWasWT
Clive, Vincent ?–1943 .... WWasWT
Clohessy, Robert 1958– CTFT–58
Cloke, Kristen 1968–............................... CTFT–50
Clokey, Art 1921–................................... CTFT–23
Clooney, George 1961–............................ CTFT–51
   Earlier sketches in CTFT–15, 25
Clore, Leon 1919(?)–1992 .... CTFT–12
Close, Eric 1967– CTFT–64
   Earlier sketches in CTFT–17, 29
Close, Glenn 1947– CTFT–56
   Earlier sketches in CTFT–3, 9, 16, 26
Closser, Louise 1872–?........................... WWasWT
Clotworthy, Robert.................................. CTFT–39
Clover, Andrew.. CTFT–73
   Earlier sketch in CTFT–32
Clowes, Richard 1900– .... WWasWT
Clunes, Alec S. 1912– .... WWasWT
Clunes, Martin 1961–.............................. CTFT–732
   Earlier sketch in CTFT–32
Clurman, Harold 1901–1980 .... WWT–17
Clyde, Craig CTFT–68
Clyde, Jeremy 1941(?)–............................ CTFT–34
   Earlier sketch in CTFT–8
Clyde, K. C. 1980–.................................. CTFT–67
Cmiral, Elia 1957–................................... CTFT–47

Coakley, Marion .... WWasWT
Coates, Anne V. 1925–............................ CTFT–47
   Earlier sketches in CTFT–11, 23
Coates, Carolyn CTFT–3
   Earlier sketch in WWT–17
Coates, Kim 1958(?)–.............................. CTFT–44
Coates, Nelson CTFT–48
Cobb, Julie 1947– CTFT–60
Cobb, Kimberly
   See.. Criswell, Kim
Cobb, Lee J. 1911–1976 .... WWasWT
Cobb, Randall "Tex" 1950–.................... CTFT–33
   Earlier sketch in CTFT–7
Cobbald, Jonathan
   See... Barker, Ronnie
Cobbs, Bill 1935–.................................... CTFT–69
   Earlier sketches in CTFT–21, 31
Cobert, Bob 1924–.................................. CTFT–51
   Earlier sketch in CTFT–12
Coborn, Charles 1852–1945.................. WWasWT
Cobould, Chris
   See .... Corbould, Chris
Coburn, Charles (Douville)
   1877–1961 .... WWasWT
Coburn, David.. CTFT–52
Coburn, D(onald) L. 1938– CTFT–1
Coburn, James 1928–2002 .... CTFT–26
   Obituary in CTFT–48
   Earlier sketches in CTFT–3, 16
Coca, Imogene 1908– CTFT–18
   Earlier sketches in CTFT–2, 9; WWT–17
Cocea, Alice 1899– .... WWasWT
Cochran, Charles (Blake) 1872–1951 .... WWasWT
Cochrane, Frank 1882–1962 .... WWasWT
Cochrane, Rory 1972– CTFT–77
   Earlier sketch in CTFT–34
Coco, James 1929–1987 .... CTFT–3
   Earlier sketches in CTFT–1; WWT–17
Cocteau, Jean 1889–1963 .... WWasWT
Codrington, Ann 1895– .... WWasWT
Codron, Michael 1930– CTFT–30
   Earlier sketches in CTFT–2, 19; WWT–17
Cody, Iron Eyes 1904(?)–1999 .... CTFT–9
   Obituary in CTFT–24
Coe, Fred H. 1914–1979........................ WWT–16
Coe, George CTFT–74
Coe, Peter 1929–1987.............................. CTFT–3
   Obituary in CTFT–5
   Earlier sketch in WWT–17
Coe, Richard L. 1914–1995 .... CTFT–1
   Obituary in CTFT–15
Coe, Tucker
   See .... Westlake, Donald E.
Coen, Ethan 1957–.................................. CTFT–51
   Earlier sketches in CTFT–7, 15, 25
Coen, Joel 1953(?)–................................. CTFT–51
   Earlier sketches in CTFT–7, 15, 25
Coeur, Paul.. CTFT–69
Coffey, Brian
   See .... Koontz, Dean R.
Coffey, Denise 1936–.............................. CTFT–34
   Earlier sketch in WWT–17
Coffey, Scott 1967– CTFT–30
Coffin, C. Hayden 1862–1935............... WWasWT
Coffin, Frederick (D.) 1943–..................... CTFT–1
Cogan, David J. 1923–.............................. CTFT–1
Coghill, Nevill 1899–1980 .... WWT–17
Coghlan, Gertrude 1879–1952 .... WWasWT
Coghlan, Rose 1850–1932 .... WWasWT
Cohan, Charles 1886–........................... WWasWT
Cohan, George M. 1878–1942 .... WWasWT
Cohan, Georgette 1900–........................ WWasWT

Cohen, Alexander H. 1920– CTFT–24
Earlier sketches in CTFT–1, 15; WWT–17
Cohen, Edward M. 1936– CTFT–9
Earlier sketch in CTFT–1
Cohen, Eric.. CTFT–51
Cohen, Harry I. 1891–1987.................... WWasWT
Cohen, Jeri Lynn..................................... CTFT–51
Cohen, Larry 1947–................................. CTFT–7
Cohen, Lynn CTFT–50
Cohen, Rob 1949– CTFT–47
Earlier sketch in CTFT–23
Cohen, Scott 1964–................................. CTFT–44
Cohenour, Patti 1952–............................ CTFT–18
Earlier sketch in CTFT–2
Cohn, Mindy 1966– CTFT–72
Earlier sketches in CTFT–22, 32
Cohon, Peter
See .... Coyote, Peter
Coke, Peter (John) 1913– .... WWasWT
Colantoni, Enrico 1963–......................... CTFT–67
Earlier sketches in CTFT–19, 30
Colbert, Claudette 1905(?)–1996 .... CTFT–2
Obituary in CTFT–16
Earlier sketch WWT–17
Colbert, Stephen 1964–............................ CTFT–67
Earlier sketch in CTFT–30
Colbin, Rod 1923– CTFT–2
Colbourne, Maurice 1894–1965........... WWasWT
Colbron, Grace Isabel ?–1943 .... WWasWT
Colchart, Thomas
See .... Coppola, Francis Ford
Cole, Dennis CTFT–4
Cole, Edith 1870–1927 .... WWasWT
Cole, Elizabeth
See.. Ashley, Elizabeth
Cole, Eric Michael 1976–....................... CTFT–64
Earlier sketch in CTFT–29
Cole, Gary 1956– CTFT–54
Earlier sketches in CTFT–8, 16, 26
Cole, George 1925– CTFT–34
Earlier sketch in CTFT–9; WWT–17
Cole, Janis 1954– CTFT–36
Cole, Kay 1948– CTFT–4
Cole, Michael 1968– CTFT–46
Cole, Natalie 1950– CTFT–60
Cole, Nora 1953–.................................... CTFT–31
Earlier sketches in CTFT–2, 18
Cole, Olivia 1942– CTFT–8
Cole, Stephanie 1941– CTFT–34
Cole, Ted CTFT–48
Coleby, Wilfred T. 1865–? .... WWasWT
Coleman, Beth Toussaint
See.. Toussaint, Beth
Coleman, Cy 1929– CTFT–37
Earlier sketches in CTFT–3, 11; WWT–17
Coleman, Dabney 1932– CTFT–64
Earlier sketches in CTFT–3, 10, 18, 29
Coleman, Fanny 1840–1919 .... WWasWT
Coleman, Gary 1968– CTFT–75
Earlier sketches in CTFT–3, 33
Coleman, Graeme CTFT–69
Coleman, Jack 1958– CTFT–74
Earlier sketches in CTFT–8, 33
Coleman, Nancy 1917– CTFT–1
Coleman, Robert 1900–.......................... WWasWT
Coleman, Signy CTFT–34
Coleman, Townsend CTFT–42
Coleridge, Ethel 1883–?......................... WWasWT
Coleridge, Sylvia 1909– WWT–17
Coles, Kim 1966–.................................... CTFT–64
Earlier sketches in CTFT–17, 29
Colgate, William....................................... CTFT–42

Colicos, John 1928–................................. CTFT–8
Earlier sketch in WWT–16
Colin, Georges.. WWasWT
Colin, Jean 1905–1989 .... WWasWT
Colin, Margaret 1957(?)–......................... CTFT–59
Earlier sketches in CTFT–7, 27
Colitti, Tony... CTFT–77
Earlier sketch in CTFT–34
Coll, Ivonne.. CTFT–60
Collamore, Jerome 1891–........................ CTFT–1
Colleano, Bonar 1923–1958.................... WWasWT
Collet, Richard 1885–1946..................... WWasWT
Collette, Charles 1842–1924 .... WWasWT
Collette, Toni 1972–................................ CTFT–65
Earlier sketches in CTFT–17, 29
Colley, Kenneth 1937–............................. CTFT–34
Earlier sketch in CTFT–9
Collier, Constance 1878–1955............... WWasWT
Collier, Gaylan Jane 1924–...................... CTFT–2
Collier, Patience 1910–1987 .... CTFT–5
Earlier sketch in WWT–17
Collier, William 1866–1944 .... WWasWT
Collinge, Patricia 1894–1974 .... WWasWT
Collings, David 1940–............................. CTFT–34
Collingwood, Peter CTFT–40
Collins, A. Greville 1896–...................... WWasWT
Collins, Arthur 1863–1932 .... WWasWT
Collins, Barry 1941–................................ CTFT–5
Earlier sketch in WWT–17
Collins, Charles 1904–1964 .... WWasWT
Collins, Christina CTFT–62
Collins, Clifton, Jr. CTFT–38
Collins, Frank 1878–1957 .... WWasWT
Collins, Gary 1938– CTFT–62
Earlier sketch in CTFT–6
Collins, Greg CTFT–37
Collins, Horace 1875–1964.................... WWasWT
Collins, Jessica 1971– CTFT–64
Collins, Joan 1933– CTFT–51
Earlier sketches in CTFT–2, 8, 15, 25
Collins, Jose 1887–1958....................... WWasWT
Collins, Kathleen
See .... Derek, Bo
Collins, Lynn 1979– CTFT–74
Collins, Paul 1937– CTFT–44
Collins, Pauline 1940– CTFT–35
Earlier sketches in CTFT–8; WWT–17
Collins, Phil 1951–.................................. CTFT–60
Earlier sketch in CTFT–27
Collins, Rickey D'Shon 1983– CTFT–73
Collins, Robert 1930–.............................. CTFT–1
Collins, Russell 1897–1965 .... WWasWT
Collins, Sewell 1876–1934..................... WWasWT
Collins, Shanna CTFT–76
Collins, Stephen 1947– CTFT–77
Earlier sketches in CTFT–3, 34
Collins, Tom
See... Cipriano, Joe
Collins, Winnie 1896–............................. WWasWT
Collison, David 1937– CTFT–5
Earlier sketch in WWT–17
Collison, Frank 1950–.............................. CTFT–56
Collison, Wilson 1892–1941 .... WWasWT
Collister, Peter Lyons 1956– CTFT–69
Colman, Booth 1923– CTFT–63
Colman, Henry CTFT–8
Colman, Ronald 1891–1958................... WWasWT
Colombier, Michel 1939–........................ CTFT–53
Colomby, Scott 1952–............................. CTFT–24
Colon, Mercedes CTFT–69
Colon, Miriam 1936(?)–.......................... CTFT–75
Earlier sketches in CTFT–5, 33; WWT–17
Colonna, Jerry 1904–1986 .... CTFT–4

Colosimo, Vince CTFT–78
Earlier sketch in CTFT–34
Colt, Alvin 1916–.................................... CTFT–6
Earlier sketch in WWT–17
Colton, John B. 1889–1946 .... WWasWT
Coltrane, Robbie 1950– CTFT–48
Earlier sketches in CTFT–12, 23
Columbu, Franco.................................... CTFT–4
Columbus, Chris 1959–........................... CTFT–10
Brief Entry in CTFT–5
Colvey, Catherine CTFT–68
Colvin, Eric.. CTFT–62
Comber, Bobbie 1886–1942.................... WWasWT
Combermere, Edward 1888–................... WWasWT
Combs, Holly Marie 1973–...................... CTFT–42
Combs, Jeffrey 1954– CTFT–39
Comden, Betty 1919–.............................. CTFT–39
Earlier sketches in CTFT–2, 10; WWT–17
Comden, Danny CTFT–78
Comenici, Luigi 1916–............................ CTFT–9
Comer, Anjanette 1939(?)– CTFT–60
Commire, Anne CTFT–1
Como, Perry 1913– CTFT–20
Earlier sketch in CTFT–12
Company of Four.................................... WWasWT
Compte, Maurice CTFT–74
Compton, Edward 1854–1918 .... WWasWT
Compton, Mrs. Edward 1853–1940....... WWasWT
Compton, Fay 1894–1978 .... WWasWT
Compton, Katherine 1858–1928........... WWasWT
Compton, Madge ?–1970 .... WWasWT
Compton, O'Neal 1951–.......................... CTFT–40
Compton, Richard CTFT–36
Compton, Viola 1886–1971 .... WWasWT
Comstock, F. Ray 1880–1949 .... WWasWT
Comstock, Nanette 1873–1942 .... WWasWT
Conaway, Cristi CTFT–40
Conaway, Jeff 1950–............................... CTFT–54
Earlier sketches in CTFT–5, 16, 26
Brief Entry in CTFT–2
Concannon, John N. 1946–...................... CTFT–1
Conchita, Maria
See .... Alonso, Maria Conchita
Conde, Nicholas
See .... Nathan, Robert
Condon, Bill 1956(?)–.............................. CTFT–47
Earlier sketch in CTFT–23
Condon, Daniel Sunjata
See .... Sunjata, Daniel
Condra, Julie 1970– CTFT–58
Conklin, Peggy 1912– .... WWasWT
Conlan, Joseph CTFT–41
Conley, Darlene...................................... CTFT–23
Earlier sketch in CTFT–12
Conley, Jack... CTFT–49
Conley, Joe 1928–................................... CTFT–54
Conn, Didi 1951– CTFT–41
Earlier sketch in CTFT–9
Connell, David CTFT–40
Connell, F. Norreys 1874–1948............. WWasWT
Connell, Jane 1925–................................ CTFT–3
Earlier sketch in WWT–17
Connell, Kelly 1956–............................... CTFT–56
Connelly, Christopher 1941–1988............ CTFT–7
Connelly, Edward J. 1855–1928 .... WWasWT
Connelly, Jennifer 1970–......................... CTFT–72
Earlier sketches in CTFT–13, 22, 32
Connelly, Marc 1890–1980..................... WWT–17
Conners, Barry 1883–1933 .... WWasWT
Connery, Jason 1963–.............................. CTFT–41
Connery, Sean 1930– CTFT–62
Earlier sketches in CTFT–3, 10, 17, 28

Connick, Harry, Jr. 1967– CTFT–47
    Earlier sketches in CTFT–11, 23
Connolly, Billy 1942– CTFT–48
    Earlier sketches in CTFT–11, 23
Connolly, John G. CTFT–79
Connolly, Michael 1947– CTFT–1
Connolly, Walter 1887–1940 .... WWasWT
Connor, Kevin 1937(?)– CTFT–54
Connor, Whitfield 1916–1988 .... CTFT–1
Connors, Chuck 1921–1992 .... CTFT–6
    Obituary in CTFT–11
Connors, Mike 1925– CTFT–77
    Earlier sketches in CTFT–9, 34
Conquest, Arthur 1875–1945 .... WWasWT
Conquest, Fred 1870–1941 .... WWasWT
Conquest, George 1858–1926 .... WWasWT
Conquest, Ida 1876–1937 .... WWasWT
Conrad, Chris 1971– CTFT–41
Conrad, Con 1891–1938 .... WWasWT
Conrad, David 1967– CTFT–65
    Earlier sketches in CTFT–17, 29
Conrad, Michael 1925–1983 .... CTFT–2
Conrad, Robert 1935– CTFT–58
    Earlier sketches in CTFT–3, 15, 26
Conrad, William 1920–1994 .... CTFT–5
    Obituary in CTFT–13
    Earlier sketch in CTFT–2
Conreid, Hans 1917–1980 .... CTFT–2
    Earlier sketch in WWT–17
Conroy, Frances 1953– CTFT–51
    Earlier sketches in CTFT–12, 23
Conroy, Frank 1890–1964 .... WWasWT
Conroy, Jack CTFT–56
Conroy, Kevin 1955– CTFT–41
    Earlier sketch in CTFT–1
Conroy, Pat 1945– CTFT–12
Conroy, Ruaidhri 1979(?)– CTFT–48
    Earlier sketch in CTFT–24
Considine, Charlotte
    See .... Stewart, Charlotte
Considine, John 1938– CTFT–34
    Earlier sketch in CTFT–8
Constanduros, Mabel ?–1957 .... WWasWT
Constantine, Michael 1927– CTFT–46
    Earlier sketch in CTFT–17
Conte, John 1915– .... WWasWT
Conti, Bill 1942– CTFT–47
    Earlier sketches in CTFT–4, 12, 23
Conti, Italia 1874–1946 .... WWasWT
Conti, Tom 1941– CTFT–41
    Earlier sketches in CTFT–3, 10, 18; WWT–17
Contner, James A. CTFT–40
Converse, Frank 1938– CTFT–41
    Earlier sketches in CTFT–3, 9, 19
Converse–Roberts, William CTFT–59
    Earlier sketches in CTFT–7, 27
Convertino, Michael CTFT–41
Conville, David 1929– WWT–17
Convy, Bert 1934–1991 .... CTFT–1
    Obituary in CTFT–10
    Earlier sketch in WWT–17
Conway, Blade Stanhope
    See .... Cummings, Bob
Conway, Gary CTFT–2
Conway, Gerry 1952– CTFT–42
Conway, Harold 1906– .... WWasWT
Conway, Jackie 1922– CTFT–2
Conway, James L. 1950– CTFT–40
Conway, Kevin 1942– CTFT–42
    Earlier sketches in CTFT–2, 6, 18; WWT–17
Conway, Tim 1933– CTFT–76
    Earlier sketches in CTFT–3, 33
Conyngham, Fred 1909– .... WWasWT

Cooder, Ry 1947– CTFT–57
    Earlier sketches in CTFT–8, 16, 26
Coogan, Jackie 1914–1984 .... CTFT–1
Coogan, Keith 1970– CTFT–41
    Earlier sketches in CTFT–10, 18
Coogan, Rif
    See .... Rifkin, Adam
Cook, A. J. 1978– CTFT–64
Cook, Barbara 1927– CTFT–3
    Earlier sketch in WWT–17
Cook, Carole CTFT–60
Cook, Donald 1901–1961 .... WWasWT
Cook, Douglas S. CTFT–28
Cook, Elisha, Jr. 1906(?)–1995 .... CTFT–8
    Obituary in CTFT–14
    Earlier sketch in WWasWT
Cook, James 1937– CTFT–3
Cook, Joe 1890–1959 .... WWasWT
Cook, Linda CTFT–3
Cook, Peter 1937–1995 .... CTFT–4
    Obituary in CTFT–14
    Earlier sketch in WWT–17
Cook, Rachel Leigh 1979– CTFT–48
    Earlier sketch in CTFT–24
Cook, Roderick 1932–1990 .... CTFT–1
Cook, Ron CTFT–34
Cook, "Sir" Eddie
    See .... Rourke, Mickey
Cook, T. S. 1947– CTFT–27
    Earlier sketch in CTFT–3
Cook, Tracey CTFT–39
    Earlier sketch in CTFT–17
Cooke, Alistair 1908– CTFT–8
Cooke, Keith 1959– CTFT–75
Cooke, Stanley 1869–1931 .... WWasWT
Cookman, Anthony Victor
    1894–1962 .... WWasWT
Cooksey, Danny 1975– CTFT–44
Cookson, Georgina .... WWasWT
Cookson, Peter 1913–1990 .... CTFT–9
Cool, Oliver
    See .... Mordente, Tony
Coolidge, Jennifer 1963– CTFT–67
    Earlier sketch in CTFT–30
Coolidge, Martha 1946– CTFT–75
    Earlier sketches in CTFT–8, 33
Coolio 1963– CTFT–68
    Earlier sketches in CTFT–19, 30
Coolus, Romain 1868–1952 .... WWasWT
Coombe, Carol 1911–1966 .... WWasWT
Cooney, Dennis 1938– CTFT–4
Cooney, Kevin 1945– CTFT–52
Cooney, Ray 1932– CTFT–49
    Earlier sketches in CTFT–14; WWT–17
Cooper, Anderson 1967– CTFT–65
Cooper, Anthony Kemble
    1908– .... WWasWT
Cooper, Bradley 1975– CTFT–68
Cooper, Chris 1951– CTFT–38
    Earlier sketches in CTFT–7, 14
Cooper, Chuck 1954– CTFT–70
    Earlier sketches in CTFT–20, 31
Cooper, Daley 1872–? .... WWasWT
Cooper, Darin 1966– CTFT–77
    Earlier sketch in CTFT–34
Cooper, Enid 1902– .... WWasWT
Cooper, Frank Kemble 1857–1918 .... WWasWT
Cooper, Frederick 1890–1945 .... WWasWT
Cooper, Gary 1901–1961 .... CTFT–19
Cooper, Giles 1918–1966 .... WWasWT
Cooper, Gladys 1888–1971 .... WWasWT
Cooper, Greta Kemble .... WWasWT

Cooper, Hal 1923– CTFT–6
    Earlier sketch in CTFT–1
Cooper, Jackie 1922(?)– CTFT–18
    Earlier sketches in CTFT–2, 8
Cooper, Jeanne 1928– CTFT–60
Cooper, Lillian Kemble 1891– .... WWasWT
Cooper, Margaret Gernon .... WWasWT
Cooper, Melville 1896–1973 .... WWasWT
Cooper, Paul W. CTFT–69
Cooper, Richard 1893–1947 .... WWasWT
Cooper, Susan 1935– CTFT–2
Cooper, T. G. 1939– CTFT–3
Cooper, Violet Kemble 1889–1961 .... WWasWT
Coote, Bert 1868–1938 .... WWasWT
Coote, Robert 1909–1982 .... WWT–17
Copeau, Jacques 1878–1949 .... WWasWT
Copeland, Joan 1922– CTFT–33
    Earlier sketches in CTFT–7; WWT–17
Copeland, Maurice 1911– CTFT–1
Copeland, Stewart 1952– CTFT–76
    Earlier sketches in CTFT–5, 33
Copeman, Michael CTFT–68
Copley, Paul 1944– WWT–17
Copley, Peter 1915– WWT–17
Copp, Rick CTFT–44
Coppel, Alec 1910–1972 .... WWasWT
Copperfield, David 1956– CTFT–50
    Earlier sketches in CTFT–7, 15, 24
Coppola, Alicia 1968– CTFT–46
Coppola, Carmine 1910–1991 .... CTFT–7
    Obituary in CTFT–10
Coppola, Chris CTFT–76
Coppola, Christopher 1962– CTFT–76
Coppola, Francis Ford 1939– CTFT–51
    Earlier sketches in CTFT–1, 6, 13, 24
Coppola, Nicolas
    See .... Cage, Nicolas
Coppola, Roman 1965– CTFT–77
Coppola, Sam 1935– CTFT–65
    Earlier sketch in CTFT–29
Coppola, Sofia 1971– CTFT–67
    Earlier sketch in CTFT–30
Coppola, Talia
    See .... Shire, Talia
Coquelin, Jean 1865–1944 .... WWasWT
Coram 1883–? .... WWasWT
Corazza, Vince 1972– CTFT–52
Corbett, Glenn 1930(?)–1993 .... CTFT–17
    Earlier sketch in CTFT–9
Corbett, Gretchen 1947– CTFT–5
    Earlier sketch in WWT–17
Corbett, Harry H. 1925–? WWT–17
Corbett, John 1962– CTFT–72
    Earlier sketches in CTFT–22, 32
Corbett, Leonora 1908–1960 .... WWasWT
Corbett, Thalberg 1864–? .... WWasWT
Corbin, Barry 1940– CTFT–65
    Earlier sketches in CTFT–10, 18, 29
Corbin, John 1870–1959 .... WWasWT
Corbould, Chris CTFT–63
    Earlier sketch in CTFT–28
Corbould, Neil CTFT–38
Corby, Ellen 1913–1999 .... CTFT–9
    Obituary in CTFT–32
Corcoran, Bill CTFT–36
Corcoran, Jane .... WWasWT
Cord, Alex 1933(?)– CTFT–9
    Earlier sketch in CTFT–1
Corddry, Rob 1971– CTFT–78
Cordell, Cathleen 1916– .... WWasWT
Corden, Henry CTFT–46
Cordery, Richard CTFT–34
Cordes, Jim 1932– CTFT–4

Cordier, Gilbert
  See .... Rohmer, Eric
Cordray, Gail Mancuso
  See .... Mancuso, Gail
Corduner, Allan 1951(?)– CTFT–60
  Earlier sketch in CTFT–28
Corenblith, Michael CTFT–55
  Earlier sketch in CTFT–25
Corey, Jeff 1914– CTFT–8
Corey, Wendell 1914–1968 .... WWasWT
Corfman, Caris 1955– CTFT–1
Corigliano, John 1938– CTFT–51
  Earlier sketch in CTFT–12
Corlan, Anthony
  See .... Higgins, Anthony
Corlett, Ian James 1962– CTFT–42
Corlett, William 1938– CTFT–30
  Earlier sketches in CTFT–2, 18
Corley, Annie CTFT–39
Corley, Pat 1930– CTFT–39
  Earlier sketch in CTFT–13
Corliss, Richard Nelson 1944– CTFT–15
Cormack, Danielle CTFT–79
  Earlier sketch in CTFT–36
Cormack, Lynne CTFT–50
Corman, Gene 1927– CTFT–9
  Earlier sketch in CTFT–1
Corman, Roger 1926– CTFT–58
  Earlier sketches in CTFT–2, 7, 15, 26
Cormier, Gerald
  See .... Rudolph, Alan
Cornell, Katharine 1898–1974 .... WWasWT
Cornfeld, Stuart CTFT–63
Cornthwaite, Robert 1917– CTFT–1
Cornwell, Charlotte 1949– CTFT–59
Cornwell, Judy 1942(?)– CTFT–47
  Earlier sketch in CTFT–23; WWT–17
Corone, Antoni CTFT–58
Correia, Don 1951– CTFT–7
Correll, Charles CTFT–40
Corri, Adrienne 1933– CTFT–28
Corri, Charles Montague 1861–? .... WWasWT
Corri, Nick
  See .... Garcia, Jsu
Corrigan, David Andriole
  See .... Andriole, David
Corrigan, Emmett 1871–1932 .... WWasWT
Corrigan, Kevin 1969– CTFT–47
  Earlier sketch in CTFT–23
Corsaro, Frank 1924– CTFT–7
  Earlier sketch in WWT–17
Corson, Richard WWT–17
Cort, Bud 1950– CTFT–38
  Earlier sketches in CTFT–1, 12
Cortese, Dan 1967– CTFT–43
  Earlier sketch in CTFT–21
Cortese, Genevieve 1981– CTFT–76
Cortese, Joseph 1949– CTFT–51
Cortez, Stanley 1908–1997 .... CTFT–13
  Obituary in CTFT–19
Corti, Jesse CTFT–73
Corwin, Betty 1920– CTFT–2
Corwin, Hank CTFT–29
Corwin, Norman 1910– CTFT–1
Corzatte, Clayton CTFT–4
Cosby, Bill 1937– CTFT–75
  Earlier sketches in CTFT–3, 9, 34
Cosell, Howard 1920– CTFT–6
Cosgrave, Peggy CTFT–8
Cosgrove, Daniel 1970– CTFT–54
Cosgrove, Miranda 1993– CTFT–76
Cosmo, James 1948– CTFT–68
  Earlier sketch in CTFT–30

Cossart, Ernest 1876–1951 .... WWasWT
Cossart, Valerie 1910– .... WWasWT
Cossette, Pierre CTFT–56
  Earlier sketch in CTFT–20
Cossins, James 1933– WWT–17
Costabile, Richard 1947– CTFT–3
Costa–Gavras 1933– CTFT–25
  Earlier sketch in CTFT–6
Costanzo, Paulo 1978– CTFT–67
Costanzo, Robert CTFT–36
Costas, Bob 1952– CTFT–45
  Earlier sketches in CTFT–12, 23
Costello, Elvis 1954– CTFT–54
  Earlier sketch in CTFT–26
Costello, Lou 1906–1959 .... CTFT–16
Costello, Mariclare CTFT–60
Costello, Tom 1863–1945 .... WWasWT
Coster, Nicolas 1934– CTFT–53
Costigan, Ken 1934– CTFT–9
  Earlier sketch in CTFT–1
Costner, Kevin 1955– CTFT–56
  Earlier sketches in CTFT–9, 16, 26
  Brief Entry in CTFT–5
Costo, Oscar L. 1953– CTFT–79
  Earlier sketch in CTFT–36
Cotes, Peter 1912–1998 .... WWT–17
  Obituary in CTFT–24
Cotsirilos, Stephanie 1947– CTFT–1
Cotsworth, Staats 1908–1979 .... WWT–16
Cotten, Joseph 1905–1994 .... CTFT–4
  Obituary in CTFT–13
  Earlier sketch in WWT–17
Cottens, Victor de 1862–? .... WWasWT
Cottet, Mia 1968– CTFT–61
Cottle, Matthew CTFT–34
Cotton, Oliver 1944– CTFT–35
  Earlier sketches in CTFT–9; WWT–17
Cotton, Wilfred 1873–? .... WWasWT
Cottrell, Cherry 1909– .... WWasWT[
Cottrell, Richard 1936– CTFT–6
  Earlier sketch in WWT–17
Coufey, Richard
  See .... Jonze, Spike
Couffe, Richard
  See .... Jonze, Spike
Coughlan, Marisa 1973(?)– CTFT–60
  Earlier sketch in CTFT–28
Coulier, Dave 1959– CTFT–50
Coullet, Rhonda 1945– CTFT–19
  Earlier sketch in CTFT–2
Coulouris, George 1903–1989 .... CTFT–8
  Earlier sketch in WWT–17
Coulter, Michael 1952– CTFT–57
  Earlier sketch in CTFT–26
Council, Richard 1947– CTFT–54
Counsell, John 1905–1987 .... WWT–17
Countryman, Michael 1955– CTFT–78
  Earlier sketches in CTFT–9, 35
Couper, Barbara 1903– .... WWasWT
Courage, Alexander 1919– CTFT–36
  Earlier sketch in CTFT–10
Couric, Katie 1957– CTFT–47
  Earlier sketches in CTFT–11, 23
Court, Alyson 1973– CTFT–50
Court, Dorothy .... WWasWT
Courteline, Georges 1860–1929 .... WWasWT
Courtenay, Margaret 1923– WWT–17
Courtenay, Tom 1937– CTFT–76
  Earlier sketches in CTFT–1, 5, 33; WWT–17
Courtenay, William 1875–1933 .... WWasWT
Courtleigh, William 1869–1930 .... WWasWT
Courtneidge, Cicely 1893–1980 .... WWT–17
Courtneidge, Robert 1859–1939 .... WWasWT

Courtneidge, Rosaline 1903–1926 .... WWasWT
Courtney, Gordon 1895–1964 .... WWasWT
Courtney, Maud 1884–? .... WWasWT
Courtney, Richard 1927– CTFT–5
  Earlier sketch in WWT–17
Courtney, Robert
  See .... Ellison, Harlan
Courtney, William Leonard
  1850–1928 .... WWasWT
Cousin Bubba
  See .... Emmons, Wayne
Cousins, Christopher 1960– CTFT–67
Cousteau, Jacques–Yves 1910–1997 .... CTFT–18
Coutard, Raoul 1924–1993 .... CTFT–28
Cove, Martin
  See .... Kove, Martin
Cover, Franklin 1928– CTFT–8
Covert, Allen CTFT–43
Covington, Julie CTFT–4
  Earlier sketch in WWT–17
Cowan, Edie CTFT–1
Cowan, Maurice A. 1891– .... WWasWT
Coward, Noel 1899–1973 .... WWasWT
Cowell, Simon 1959– CTFT–65
Cowen, Laurence 1865–1942 .... WWasWT
Cowen, Ron 1944– CTFT–17
Cowie, Laura 1892–1969 .... WWasWT
Cowl, Jane 1890–1950 .... WWasWT
Cowles, Matthew 1944– CTFT–59
  Earlier sketch in CTFT–27
Cowley, Eric 1886–1948 .... WWasWT
Cox, Alan 1970– CTFT–34
  Earlier sketch in CTFT–6
Cox, Alex 1954– CTFT–75
  Earlier sketches in CTFT–10, 33
  Brief Entry in CTFT–5
Cox, Betsy CTFT–38
Cox, Brian 1946– CTFT–58
  Earlier sketches in CTFT–9, 16, 26; WWT–17
Cox, Christina 1971– CTFT–79
  Earlier sketch in CTFT–46
Cox, Constance 1915– WWT–17
Cox, Courteney 1964– CTFT–48
  Earlier sketches in CTFT–7, 15, 24
Cox, Jennifer Elise 1969– CTFT–75
Cox, Joe Anthony
  See .... Cox, Tony
Cox, Joshua 1965– CTFT–73
Cox, Maryellen CTFT–48
Cox, Nikki 1978– CTFT–68
  Earlier sketch in CTFT–30
Cox, Paul 1940– CTFT–47
  Earlier sketches in CTFT–11, 23
Cox, Richard 1948– CTFT–38
Cox, Richard Ian 1973– CTFT–68
Cox, Ronny 1938– CTFT–72
  Earlier sketches in CTFT–1, 4, 13, 22, 32
Cox, Tony CTFT–38
Cox, Veanne 1963– CTFT–69
  Earlier sketch in CTFT–30
Coyle, Brendan CTFT–38
Coyle, J. J. 1928– CTFT–1
Coyne, Joseph 1867–1941 .... WWasWT
Coyote, Peter 1942– CTFT–26
  Earlier sketches in CTFT–6, 15, 26
Cozart, Cylk 1957– CTFT–65
  Earlier sketch in CTFT–29
Crabe, James 1931–1989 .... CTFT–19
  Earlier sketch in CTFT–2
Cracknell, Ruth 1925– WWT–17
Cragg, Stephen 1950– CTFT–42
Craggs, The .... WWasWT

Craig, Carl 1954– CTFT–53
   Earlier sketches in CTFT–2, 18
Craig, Clyde L.
   See.. Clyde, Craig
Craig, Daniel 1968– CTFT–47
   Earlier sketch in CTFT–23
Craig, Edith 1869–1947 .... WWasWT
Craig, Edward Gordon 1872–1966........ WWasWT
Craig, Helen 1912–1986 .... WWT–17
Craig, Michael 1928– WWT–17
Craig, Stuart 1942– CTFT–38
   Earlier sketch in CTFT–12
Craig, Wendy 1934– WWT–17
Cramer, Rick 1958– CTFT–37
Crampton, Barbara 1962– CTFT–58
Crane, Chilton CTFT–63
Crane, Richard 1944– CTFT–6
   Earlier sketch in WWT–17
Crane, Simon.. CTFT–68
   Earlier sketch in CTFT–30
Crane, W. H. 1845–1928 .... WWasWT
Cranham, Kenneth 1944– CTFT–47
   Earlier sketches in CTFT–11, 23; WWT–17
Cranshaw, Patrick CTFT–32
Cranston, Bryan 1956– CTFT–43
Crauford, J. R. 1847–1930 .... WWasWT
Craven, Arthur Scott 1875–1971 .... WWasWT
Craven, Elise 1898– .... WWasWT
Craven, Frank 1880–1945 .... WWasWT
Craven, Gemma 1950– CTFT–41
   Earlier sketches in CTFT–2, 19; WWT–17
Craven, Matt 1956– CTFT–47
   Earlier sketch in CTFT–23
Craven, Tom 1868–1919 .... WWasWT
Craven, Wes 1939– CTFT–57
   Earlier sketches in CTFT–6, 15, 26
Crawford, Alice 1882– .... WWasWT
Crawford, Anne 1920–1956 .... WWasWT
Crawford, Cheryl 1902–1986 .... CTFT–4
   Earlier sketch in WWT–17
Crawford, Cindy 1966– CTFT–48
   Earlier sketches in CTFT–15, 24
Crawford, Ellen CTFT–72
   Earlier sketches in CTFT–32, 65
Crawford, Joanna 1942– CTFT–4
Crawford, Michael 1942– CTFT–36
   Earlier sketches in CTFT–3, 11; WWT–17
Crawford, Mimi ?–1966 .... WWasWT
Crawley, Amos 1981– CTFT–65
Crawley, Tom 1940– CTFT–2
Creaghan, Dennis 1942– CTFT–65
Creedon, Dennis 1880–? .... WWasWT
Creel, Gavin 1976– CTFT–62
Creel, Leanna 1970– CTFT–50
Creel, Monica 1970– CTFT–74
Cregan, David 1931– CTFT–6
   Earlier sketch in WWT–17
Crenna, Richard 1927–2003 .... CTFT–26
   Obituary in CTFT–48
   Earlier sketches in CTFT–3, 16
Cressall, Maud 1886–1962 .... WWasWT
Cressida, Kathryn CTFT–73
Cresswell, Helen 1934– CTFT–15
Crews, Laura Hope 1880–1942 .... WWasWT
Crews, Terry 1968– CTFT–68
Crewson, Wendy 1959– CTFT–60
   Earlier sketch in CTFT–28
Cribbins, Bernard 1928– CTFT–6
   Earlier sketch in WWT–17
Crichton, Charles 1910– CTFT–8
Crichton, Madge 1881–? .... WWasWT
Crichton, Michael 1942– CTFT–44
   Earlier sketches in CTFT–5, 13, 22

Crider, Missy 1974– CTFT–61
Crier, Catherin 1955(?)– CTFT–41
Crinkley, Richmond 1940–1989 .... CTFT–8
   Earlier sketch in WWT–17
Crisham, Walter .... WWasWT
Crisp, Quentin 1908– CTFT–6
Crispi, Ida .... WWasWT
Crist, Judith 1922– CTFT–1
Crist, Myndy 1975– CTFT–63
Cristina, Ines 1875–? .... WWasWT
Cristofer, Michael 1945– CTFT–33
   Earlier sketches in CTFT–3; WWT–17
Criswell, Kim 1957– CTFT–62
Critchlow, Roark 1963– CTFT–65
   Earlier sketches in CTFT–17, 29
Critt, C. J. 1954– CTFT–1
Crivello, Anthony 1955– CTFT–65
   Earlier sketch in CTFT–29
Croce, Arlene 1934– CTFT–15
Crofoot, Leonard J. CTFT–1
Croft, Anne 1896–1959 .... WWasWT
Croft, Michael 1922–1986 .... WWT–17
Croft, Nita 1902– .... WWasWT
Croft, Paddy CTFT–52
   Earlier sketches in CTFT–10; WWT–17
Croisset, Francis de 1877–1937............. WWasWT
Croke, Wentworth 1871–1930 .... WWasWT
Croker, T. F. Dillon 1831–1912 .... WWasWT
Croker–King, C. H. 1873–1951 .... WWasWT
Crommelynck, Fernand 1885–1970 ...... WWasWT
Cromwell, James 1940– CTFT–65
   Earlier sketches in CTFT–17, 29
Cromwell, John 1887–1979 .... WWT–17
Cronenberg, David 1943– CTFT–53
   Earlier sketches in CTFT–6, 14, 25
Cronenberg, Denise.............................. CTFT–53
   Earlier sketch in CTFT–25
Cronenweth, Jordan 1935–1996............. CTFT–22
Cronin, Jane 1936– CTFT–3
Cronin, Jeanette CTFT–75
   Earlier sketch in CTFT–32
Cronin, Michael CTFT–38
Cronin, Patrick CTFT–75
Cronkite, Walter 1916– CTFT–76
   Earlier sketches in CTFT–6, 33
Cronyn, Hume 1911– CTFT–28
   Earlier sketches in CTFT–1, 7, 17; WWT–17
Cronyn, Tandy 1945– CTFT–9
   Earlier sketch in CTFT–1
Crook, John ?–1922 .... WWasWT
Crook, Leland CTFT–58
Cropper, Anna 1938– WWT–17
Cropper, Roy 1898–1954....................... WWasWT
Crosbie, Annette 1934– CTFT–74
   Earlier sketch in CTFT–32
Crosby, Bing 1901–1977 .... CTFT–26
Crosby, Cathy Lee 1944– CTFT–24
   Earlier sketches in CTFT–15, 26
Crosby, Denise 1957– CTFT–75
   Earlier sketches in CTFT–8, 33
Crosby, Gary 1933–1995....................... CTFT–7
   Obituary in CTFT–15
Crosby, Joan 1934– CTFT–23
   Earlier sketch in CTFT–12
Crosby, Mary 1959– CTFT–41
   Earlier sketches in CTFT–5, 18
   Brief Entry in CTFT–2
Crosby, Norm 1927– CTFT–61
Crosman, Henrietta 1865–1944............. WWasWT
Cross, Ben 1947– CTFT–77
   Earlier sketches in CTFT–6, 34

Cross, Beverley 1931–1998..................... CTFT–6
   Obituary in CTFT–24
   Earlier sketch in WWT–17
Cross, David 1964– CTFT–76
   Earlier sketch in CTFT–33
Cross, Julian 1851–1925 .... WWasWT
Cross, Marcia 1962– CTFT–68
   Earlier sketches in CTFT–19, 30
Cross, Rebecca CTFT–28
Cross, Roger R. CTFT–46
Crossman, Melville
   See.............................. Zanuck, Darryl F.
Croswell, Anne CTFT–1
Crothers, Rachel 1878–1958 .... WWasWT
Crothers, Scatman 1910–1986 .... CTFT–3
Crouch, J. H. 1918– CTFT–1
Crouse, Lindsay 1948– CTFT–72
   Earlier sketches in CTFT–4, 33
Crouse, Russel 1893–1966 .... WWasWT
Crow, Ashley 1960– CTFT–63
Crow, Laura 1945– CTFT–5
Crowden, Graham 1922– CTFT–34
   Earlier sketches in CTFT–9; WWT–17
Crowden, Sarah.................................... CTFT–34
Crowder, Jack
   See.............................. Rasulala, Thalmus
Crowe, Cameron 1957– CTFT–72
   Earlier sketches in CTFT–13, 22, 32
Crowe, Christopher 1948– CTFT–23
   Earlier sketches in CTFT–4, 14
Crowe, Russell 1964– CTFT–57
   Earlier sketches in CTFT–16, 26
Crowley, Bob 1953(?)– CTFT–43
Crowley, Dermot CTFT–38
Crowley, Mart 1935– WWT–17
Crowley, Pat 1929(?)– CTFT–58
   Earlier sketch in CTFT–8
Crowther, Leslie 1933– WWT–17
Croxton, Arthur 1868–? .... WWasWT
Croze, Marie–Josee 1970– CTFT–34
Crudup, Billy 1968– CTFT–61
   Earlier sketches in CTFT–17, 28
Cruickshank, Andrew 1907–1988 .... CTFT–7
   Earlier sketch in WWT–17
Cruickshank, Gladys 1902– .... WWasWT
Cruikshank, A. Stewart 1877–1949 .... WWasWT
Cruikshank, Stewart 1908–1966 .... WWasWT
Cruikshanks, Charles 1844–1928 .... WWasWT
Cruise, Tom 1962– CTFT–57
   Earlier sketches in CTFT–3, 9, 16, 26
   Brief Entry in CTFT–2
Cruse, Doug
   See................................... Kruse, Doug
Crust, Arnold
   See............................... Winner, Michael
Crutchley, Rosalie 1921–1997.................. CTFT–8
   Obituary in CTFT–18
   Earlier sketch in WWasWT
Cruttwell, Hugh 1918– WWT–17
Cruz, Alexis 1974– CTFT–38
Cruz, Penelope 1974– CTFT–51
   Earlier sketch in CTFT–24
Cruz, Raymond CTFT–52
Cruz, Wilson 1973– CTFT–43
   Earlier sketch in CTFT–20
Cruze, Josh CTFT–73
Cryer, Barry 1935– CTFT–34
Cryer, David 1936– WWT–17
Cryer, Gretchen 1935– CTFT–4
   Earlier sketch in WWT–17
Cryer, Jon 1965– CTFT–56
   Earlier sketches in CTFT–4, 16, 26

Cryer, Suzanne 1967(?)– CTFT–75
  Earlier sketch in CTFT–34
Crystal, Billy 1947(?)– CTFT–65
  Earlier sketches in CTFT–3, 10, 18, 29
Crystal, Jennifer 1973– CTFT–76
  Earlier sketch in CTFT–34
Csokas, Marton 1966– CTFT–37
Cuaco, Kaley
  See .... Cuoco, Kaley
Cubitt, David 1965(?)– CTFT–63
Cuccioli, Robert 1958– CTFT–50
  Earlier sketch in CTFT–24
Cucinotta, Maria Grazia 1969– CTFT–62
  Earlier sketch in CTFT–28
Cudlitz, Michael 1965– CTFT–59
Cudney, Roger CTFT–64
Cujo, Frank
  See .... Van Damme, Jean–Claude
Cuka, Frances 1936– CTFT–6
  Earlier sketch in WWT–17
Cukor, George 1899–1983 .... CTFT–1
Culea, Melinda 1955– CTFT–36
Culhane, Shamus 1908– CTFT–10
Culkin, Kieran 1982– CTFT–51
  Earlier sketch in CTFT–24
Culkin, Macaulay 1980(?)– CTFT–47
  Earlier sketch in CTFT–10
Culkin, Michael CTFT–36
Culkin, Rory 1989– CTFT–59
Cullen, Brett 1956– CTFT–73
  Earlier sketch in CTFT–32
Cullen, David 1942– CTFT–23
  Earlier sketches in CTFT–6, 14
Cullen, Max CTFT–34
Cullen, Peter CTFT–36
Culley, Frederick 1879–1942 .... WWasWT
Culliton, Joseph 1948– CTFT–19
  Earlier sketch in CTFT–2
Culliton, Patrick CTFT–24
Culliver, Karen 1959– CTFT–18
  Earlier sketch in CTFT–2
Cullum, J. D. 1966– CTFT–54
Cullum, John 1930– CTFT–39
  Earlier sketches in CTFT–4, 13; WWT–17
Culp, Robert 1930– CTFT–38
  Earlier sketches in CTFT–3, 14
Culp, Steven CTFT–44
Culver, Michael 1938– CTFT–69
Culver, Roland 1900–1984 .... WWT–17
Culver, Timothy J.
  See .... Westlake, Donald E.
Cumberland, Gerald 1879–1926 .... WWasWT
Cumberland, John 1880–? .... WWasWT
Cumming, Alan 1965– CTFT–47
  Earlier sketch in CTFT–23
Cummings, Bob 1910(?)–1990 .... CTFT–17
  Earlier sketch in CTFT–1
Cummings, Brian CTFT–53
Cummings, Constance 1910– CTFT–4
  Earlier sketch in WWT–17
Cummings, Irving 1888–1959 .... CTFT–29
Cummings, Jim 1953– CTFT–36
Cummings, Robert
  See .... Zombie, Rob
Cummings, Vicki 1913–1969 .... WWasWT
Cummins, Gregory Scott CTFT–63
Cummins, Martin 1969– CTFT–67
  Earlier sketch in CTFT–30
Cummins, Peggy 1925– .... WWasWT
Cumpsty, Michael 1960(?)– CTFT–51
  Earlier sketch in CTFT–24
Cunati, Edwige Caroline
  See .... Feuillere, Edwige

Cundey, Dean 1946(?)– CTFT–48
  Earlier sketches in CTFT–11, 23
Cundieff, Rusty 1965(?)– CTFT–23
Cuningham, Philip 1865–? .... WWasWT
Cunliffe, Whit .... WWasWT
Cunningham, Colin 1966– CTFT–75
  Earlier sketch in CTFT–33
Cunningham, J. Morgan
  See .... Westlake, Donald E.
Cunningham, John 1932– CTFT–60
  Earlier sketches in CTFT–10, 27
Cunningham, Merce 1919– CTFT–20
Cunningham, Robert 1866–? .... WWasWT
Cunningham, Sarah 1919–1986 .... CTFT–3
Cunningham, Sean S. 1941– CTFT–61
Cuoco, Kaley 1985– CTFT–62
Cuomo, Douglas J. CTFT–61
Cupito, Suzanne
  See .... Brittany, Morgan
Curel, Viscomte Francois de
  1854–1928 .... WWasWT
Currah, Brian Mason 1929– WWT–17
Curran, Leigh 1943– CTFT–5
Curran, Lynette 1945– CTFT–76
  Earlier sketch in CTFT–33
Curreri, Lee 1961– CTFT–61
Currie, Clive 1877–1935 .... WWasWT
Currie, Finlay 1878–1968 .... WWasWT
Currie, Glenne 1926– CTFT–1
Currie, Michael CTFT–53
Currie, Sondra 1952– CTFT–59
Currier, Terrence CTFT–38
Curry, Ann 1956– CTFT–40
Curry, Christopher CTFT–38
Curry, Julian 1937– CTFT–49
  Earlier sketches in CTFT–11; WWT–17
Curry, Mark 1964– CTFT–38
Curry, Tim 1946– CTFT–58
  Earlier sketches in CTFT–7, 17, 27
Curteis, Ian 1935– CTFT–10
Curtin, Jane 1947– CTFT–56
  Earlier sketches in CTFT–3, 16, 26
Curtin, Valerie 1945(?)– CTFT–41
  Earlier sketches in CTFT–7, 18
Curtis, Anthony
  See .... Curtis, Tony
Curtis, Cliff 1968– CTFT–66
  Earlier sketch in CTFT–29
Curtis, Dan 1928– CTFT–54
  Earlier sketch in CTFT–10
Curtis, James
  See .... Curtis, Tony
Curtis, Jamie Lee 1958– CTFT–73
  Earlier sketches in CTFT–6, 13, 22, 32
Curtis, Jed CTFT–40
Curtis, Keene 1923(?)– CTFT–30
  Earlier sketches in CTFT–2, 19; WWT–17
Curtis, Ken 1916–1991 .... CTFT–10
Curtis, Price
  See .... Ellison, Harlan
Curtis, Richard 1956– CTFT–57
  Earlier sketches in CTFT–15, 26
Curtis, Simon 1960– CTFT–66
  Earlier sketch in CTFT–30
Curtis, Thomas 1991– CTFT–68
Curtis, Tony 1925– CTFT–35
  Earlier sketches in CTFT–3, 9
Curtis–Brown, Robert 1956– CTFT–49
Curtis–Hall, Vondie 1956– CTFT–65
  Earlier sketches in CTFT–17, 29
Curwen, Patric 1884–1949 .... WWasWT
Curzon, Aria Noelle 1987– CTFT–60
Curzon, Frank 1868–1927 .... WWasWT

Curzon, George 1898– .... WWasWT
Cusack, Ann 1961– CTFT–59
  Earlier sketches in CTFT–17, 27
Cusack, Cyril 1910– CTFT–7
  Earlier sketch in WWT–17
Cusack, Dick CTFT–51
Cusack, Joan 1962– CTFT–55
  Earlier sketches in CTFT–7, 15, 26
Cusack, John 1966– CTFT–55
  Earlier sketches in CTFT–8, 15, 26
Cusack, Niamh 1959– CTFT–76
  Earlier sketch in CTFT–33
Cusack, Sinead 1948– CTFT–41
  Earlier sketches in CTFT–2, 18; WWT–17
Cushing, Catherine Chisholm
  1874–1952 .... WWasWT
Cushing, Peter 1913–1994 .... CTFT–4
  Obituary in CTFT–13
  Earlier sketch in WWT–17
Cushing, Tom 1879–1941 .... WWasWT
Cushman, Robert 1943– WWT–17
Cutell, Lou CTFT–61
Cuthbert, Elisha 1982– CTFT–56
Cuthbert, Jon CTFT–59
Cuthbert, Neil 1951– CTFT–6
  Earlier sketch in CTFT–1
Cuthbertson, Allan 1920–1988 .... CTFT–6
  Earlier sketch in WWT–17
Cuthbertson, Iain 1930– CTFT–33
  Earlier sketches in CTFT–2; WWT–17
Cutler, Kate 1870–1955 .... WWasWT
Cutrona, Ryan CTFT–63
Cutter, Lise CTFT–4
Cuvillier, Charles 1879–1955 .... WWasWT
Cypher, Jon 1932– CTFT–35
  Earlier sketch in CTFT–9
Cyphers, Charles 1939– CTFT–56
Cypress, Tawny 1976– CTFT–76
Cyr, Myriam 1960– CTFT–51
Cyrus, Billy Ray 1961– CTFT–41
Czerny, Henry 1959– CTFT–54
  Earlier sketches in CTFT–16, 26
Czuchry, Matt 1977– CTFT–73

D

Dabdoub, Jack 1925– CTFT–2
Dabney, Augusta 1918– CTFT–53
  Earlier sketch in CTFT–1
D'Abo, Maryam 1961(?)– CTFT–38
  Earlier sketches in CTFT–7, 14
D'Abo, Olivia 1969(?)– CTFT–65
  Earlier sketches in CTFT–17, 29
Dacascos, Mark 1964– CTFT–50
da Costa, Joao Benard
  See .... de Almeida, Duarte
da Costa, Liz 1955– CTFT–6
Da Costa, Morton 1914–1989 .... CTFT–6
  Earlier sketch in WWT–17
Daddo, Cameron 1965– CTFT–72
Daemer, Will
  See .... Wade, Robert (Allison)
Dafoe, Willem 1955– CTFT–61
  Earlier sketches in CTFT–7, 17, 28
Daggs, Percy III 1982– CTFT–77
Dagnall, Ells 1868–1935 .... WWasWT
Dagnall, Thomas C. ?–1926 .... WWasWT
Dahl, Arlene 1928(?)– CTFT–55
  Earlier sketch in CTFT–2

Dahl, John 1956– CTFT–28
    Earlier sketch in CTFT–17
Dahl, Roald 1916– CTFT–6
Dahlgren, Tom CTFT–36
Daigle, Suzette CTFT–39
Dailey, Dan 1915–1978 .... WWT–16
Dailey, Irene 1920– CTFT–3
    Earlier sketch in WWT–17
Daily, Bill 1928– CTFT–48
    Earlier sketch in CTFT–9
Daily, Elizabeth 1962– CTFT–50
    Earlier sketch in CTFT–24
Dainard, Neil CTFT–46
Daindridge, Dorothy
    See .... Dandridge, Dorothy
Dainton, Marie 1881–1938 .... WWasWT
Daises, Anthony
    See .... Margheriti, Antonio
Daisies, Anthony
    See .... Margheriti, Antonio
Dajani, Nadia CTFT–39
    Earlier sketch in CTFT–17
Dakota, Alan
    See .... Baltes, Alan
D'Albert, George 1870–1949 .... WWasWT
Daldry, Stephen 1961(?)– CTFT–54
    Earlier sketches in CTFT–16, 26
Dale, Alan 1861–1928 .... WWasWT
Dale, Alan 1947– CTFT–54
Dale, Esther
    See .... May, Elaine
Dale, Grover 1935– CTFT–5
    Earlier sketch in WWT–17
Dale, Holly 1953– CTFT–79
    Earlier sketch in CTFT–36
Dale, James Badge 1978– CTFT–73
Dale, James Littlewood 1886– .... WWasWT
Dale, Jennifer 1955– CTFT–55
Dale, Jim 1935– CTFT–3
    Earlier sketches in CTFT–1; WWT–17
Dale, Margaret 1880–1972 .... WWasWT
Dale, Margaret 1922– .... WWasWT
Dallas, J. J. 1853–1915 .... WWasWT
Dallas, Keith 1978(?)– CTFT–79
Dallas, Meredith Eugene 1916– CTFT–1
Dallesandro, Joe 1948– CTFT–30
Dalmatoff, B. 1862–? .... WWasWT
D'Almeida, Duarte
    See .... de Almeida, Duarte
D'Alroy, Evelyn ?–1915 .... WWasWT
Dalrymple, Jean 1910– WWT–17
Dalton, Abby 1935– CTFT–7
Dalton, Charles 1864–1942 .... WWasWT
Dalton, Doris 1910– .... WWasWT
Dalton, Dorothy 1893–1972 .... WWasWT
Dalton, Jessie
    See .... Quigley, Linnea
Dalton, Kristen CTFT–63
Dalton, Timothy 1944(?)– CTFT–72
    Earlier sketches in CTFT–7, 33
Daltrey, Roger 1944– CTFT–77
    Earlier sketches in CTFT–6, 34
Dalva, Robert 1942– CTFT–1
Daly, Arnold 1875–1927 .... WWasWT
Daly, Blyth 1902– .... WWasWT
Daly, Bob 1936– CTFT–10
Daly, Carson 1973– CTFT–67
    Earlier sketch in CTFT–30
Daly, Dutch 1848–? .... WWasWT
Daly, James 1918–1978 .... WWT–16
Daly, Jane 1948– CTFT–69
Daly, John 1937– CTFT–49
    Earlier sketch in CTFT–11

Daly, John Charles 1914–1991 .... CTFT–13
Daly, Mark 1887–1957 .... WWasWT
Daly, Timothy 1956– CTFT–51
    Earlier sketches in CTFT–8, 15, 25
Daly, Tyne 1946– CTFT–50
    Earlier sketches in CTFT–6, 13, 24
D'Amato, Paul CTFT–33
D'Amboise, Charlotte 1965(?)– CTFT–51
    Earlier sketches in CTFT–11, 23
Dames, Rob 1944– CTFT–4
Damon, John
    See .... McCook, John
Damon, Mark 1933– CTFT–38
    Earlier sketch in CTFT–14
Damon, Matt 1970– CTFT–70
    Earlier sketches in CTFT–20, 31
Damon, Stuart 1937– CTFT–59
    Earlier sketches in CTFT–5; WWT–17
Damski, Mel 1946– CTFT–48
    Earlier sketches in CTFT–11, 23
Damus, Mike 1979– CTFT–30
Dana, Bill 1924– CTFT–9
Dana, F. Mitchell 1942– CTFT–19
    Earlier sketches in CTFT–2; WWT–17
Dana, Henry 1855–1921 .... WWasWT
Dana, Leora 1923– WWT–17
Dance, Charles 1946– CTFT–67
    Earlier sketches in CTFT–2, 4, 11, 18, 30
Dance, George 1865–1932 .... WWasWT
Dandridge, Dorothy 1922–1965 .... CTFT–27
Dane, Clemence 1888–1965 .... WWasWT
Dane, Eric 1972(?)– CTFT–67
Dane, Ethel .... WWasWT
Dane, Marjorie 1898– .... WWasWT
Daneman, Paul 1925– WWT–17
Danes, Claire 1979– CTFT–51
    Earlier sketches in CTFT–15, 25
Danforth, William 1867–1941 .... WWasWT
Dang, Tim CTFT–20
D'Angelo, Beverly 1953(?)– CTFT–67
    Earlier sketches in CTFT–2, 5, 18, 30
Dangerfield, Dick
    See .... Compton, Richard
Dangerfield, Rodney 1922(?)– CTFT–48
    Earlier sketches in CTFT–3, 14, 24
Daniel, Brittany 1976– CTFT–69
Daniel, Gregg CTFT–54
Daniel, Rod CTFT–36
Daniel, Sean 1951– CTFT–41
Daniel, T. 1945– CTFT–1
Daniele, Graciela 1939– CTFT–37
    Earlier sketch in CTFT–10
Danielewski, Tad CTFT–3
Daniell, Henry 1894–1963 .... WWasWT
Danielovitch, Issur
    See .... Douglas, Kirk
Daniels, Anthony 1946– CTFT–40
Daniels, Beata Pozniak
    See .... Pozniak, Beata
Daniels, Bebe 1901–1971 .... WWasWT
Daniels, Danny
    See .... Giagni, D. J.
Daniels, Danny 1924– CTFT–3
Daniels, Faith 1958(?)– CTFT–14
Daniels, Frank 1860–1935 .... WWasWT
Daniels, J. D. 1980– CTFT–44
Daniels, Jake
    See .... Martin, Dan
Daniels, Jeff 1955– CTFT–45
    Earlier sketches in CTFT–4, 11, 23
Daniels, John
    Billingslea, Beau CTFT–74
Daniels, Marc c. 1912–1989 .... CTFT–8

Daniels, Phil 1958– CTFT–62
    Earlier sketches in CTFT–17, 28
Daniels, Ron 1942– CTFT–5
    Earlier sketch in WWT–17
Daniels, William 1927– CTFT–49
    Earlier sketches in CTFT–3, 9
Danilova, Alexandra 1907– .... WWasWT
Danker, Eli CTFT–67
    Earlier sketch in CTFT–30
Danna, Jeff CTFT–41
Danna, Mychael 1958– CTFT–65
    Earlier sketch in CTFT–29
Danner, Blythe 1944(?)– CTFT–65
    Earlier sketches in CTFT–1, 5, 12, 20, 29;
    WWT–17
Danning, Sybil CTFT–39
    Earlier sketches in CTFT–7, 16
Danninger, Sybille
    See .... Danning, Sy
Dano, Linda 1943– .... CTFT
    Earlier sketches in CTFT–17, 27
Dano, Royal 1922–1994 .... CTFT-
    Obituary in CTFT–13
Danova, Cesare 1926–1992 .... CTFT–29
Dansey, Herbert 1870–1917 .... WWasWT
Danshaw, Jeff
    See .... Dashnaw, Jeffrey J.
Danson, Randy CTFT–32
Danson, Ted 1947– CTFT–45
    Earlier sketches in CTFT–1, 4, 11, 23
Dante, Joe 1946– CTFT–74
    Earlier sketches in CTFT–7, 33
Dante, Maria
    See .... Winters, David
Dante, Nicholas 1941–1991 .... CTFT–11
Dantes, Edmond
    See .... Hughes, John
Danton, Ray 1931–1992 .... CTFT–11
Danvers, Johnny 1870–1939 .... WWasWT
Danza, Tony 1951– CTFT–68
    Earlier sketches in CTFT–5, 19, 30
    Brief Entry in CTFT–2
Dapkunaite, Ingeborga 1963– CTFT–54
    Earlier sketch in CTFT–26
D'Aquino, John 1958– CTFT–69
Darabont, Frank 1959– CTFT–62
    Earlier sketch in CTFT–28
D'Arbanville, Patti 1951– CTFT–38
    Earlier sketches in CTFT–7, 14
D'Arbanville–Quinn, Patti
    See .... D'Arbanville, Patti
Darbo, Patrika 1948– CTFT–38
Darby, Jonathan CTFT–30
Darby, Ken 1909–1992 .... CTFT–11
Darby, Kim 1948– CTFT–3
Darbyshire, Iris 1905– .... WWasWT
Darden, Severn 1929–1995 .... CTFT–8
    Obituary in CTFT–14
DaRe, Aldo
    See .... Ray, Aldo
Dare, Daphne WWT–17
Dare, Phyllis 1890–1975 .... WWasWT
Dare, Zena 1887–1975 .... WWasWT
Darewski, Herman 1883–1929 .... WWasWT
Darga, Christopher CTFT–42
Dark, Sidney 1874–1947 .... WWasWT
Darke, Nick 1948– CTFT–12
Darley, Herbert .... WWasWT
Darling, Jennifer 1946– CTFT–39
Darling, T. H.
    See .... Harris, Thomas Walter
Darlington, William Aubrey
    1890–1979 .... WWT–16

Darlow, Cynthia 1949– CTFT–1
Darr, Lisa 1963– CTFT–58
Darragh, Miss ?–1917 .... WWasWT
Darrell, Maisie 1901– .... WWasWT
Darren, James 1936– CTFT–33
  Earlier sketch in CTFT–3
Darrow, Henry 1933– CTFT–47
Darst, Danny CTFT–30
Darthy, Gilda .... WWasWT
Darvas, Lili 1906–1974 .... WWasWT
D'Arville, Camille 1863–1932 .... WWasWT
Dash, Stacey 1966– CTFT–67
Dashnaw, Jeffrey J. CTFT–42
Da Silva, Howard 1909–1986 .... CTFT–5
  Earlier sketch in WWT–17
Dassanowsky, Elfi
  See .... Von Dassanowsky, Elfi
Dastor, Sam CTFT–72
  Earlier sketch in CTFT–32
Datas 1876–? .... WWasWT
Daubeny, Peter 1921–1975 .... WWasWT
Daunt, William 1893–1938 .... WWasWT
Dauphin, Claude 1903–1978 .... WWT–17
Davenport, Harry 1866–1949 .... WWasWT
Davenport, Jack 1973(?)– CTFT–56
Davenport, Nigel 1928– CTFT–33
  Earlier sketches in CTFT–3; WWT–17
Davey, Bruce CTFT–40
Davey, Nuna 1902– .... WWasWT
Davey, Peter 1857–1946 .... WWasWT
Davi, Robert 1952(?)– CTFT–54
  Earlier sketches in CTFT–9, 16, 26
Daviau, Allen 1942– CTFT–10
David, Clifford 1932– CTFT–59
David, Hal 1921– CTFT–51
  Earlier sketch in CTFT–12
David, Joanna 1947– CTFT–68
  Earlier sketches in CTFT–2, 19, 30
David, Keith 1956(?)– CTFT–66
  Earlier sketches in CTFT–8, 15
David, Larry 1947– CTFT–47
  Earlier sketch in CTFT–23
David, Worton ?–1940 .... WWasWT
Davidovich, Lolita 1961– CTFT–65
  Earlier sketches in CTFT–10, 18, 29
Davidson, Amy 1979– CTFT–74
Davidson, Boaz 1943– CTFT–36
Davidson, Eileen 1959– CTFT–27
  Earlier sketch in CTFT–17
Davidson, Gordon 1933– WWT–17
Davidson, Jack CTFT–36
Davidson, John 1941– CTFT–15
  Earlier sketch in CTFT–7
Davidson, Martin 1939– CTFT–36
  Earlier sketch in CTFT–10
Davidson, Richard M. 1940– CTFT–2
Davidson, Tommy 1963(?)– CTFT–47
  Earlier sketch in CTFT–23
Davidson, Tonja Walker
  See .... Walker, Tonja
Davidtz, Embeth 1966– CTFT–54
  Earlier sketches in CTFT–16, 26
Davies, Acton 1870–1916 .... WWasWT
Davies, Ben 1858–1943 .... WWasWT
Davies, Betty–Ann 1910–1955 .... WWasWT
Davies, Edna 1905– .... WWasWT
Davies, Gareth CTFT–42
Davies, Geraint Wyn 1957– CTFT–70
  Earlier sketches in CTFT–21, 31
Davies, Glynis CTFT–69
Davies, Harry Parr 1914–1955 .... WWasWT
Davies, Howard 1945(?)– CTFT–49
  Earlier sketch in CTFT–9

Davies, Hubert Henry 1869–1932 .... WWasWT
Davies, Jackson CTFT–54
Davies, Jeremy 1969– CTFT–48
  Earlier sketch in CTFT–23
Davies, John Rhys
  See .... Rhys–Davies, John
Davies, Kimberley 1973– CTFT–79
Davies, Lane 1950– CTFT–38
Davies, Marion 1897–1961 .... WWasWT
Davies, Robertson 1913– CTFT–4
  Earlier sketch in WWT–17
Davies, Siobhan 1950– CTFT–11
Davies, Tamara CTFT–58
Davies, Terence 1945– CTFT–15
Davies, Valentine 1905–1961 .... CTFT–21
Daviot, Gordon 1897–1952 .... WWasWT
Davis, Allan 1913– WWT–17
Davis, Allen III 1929– CTFT–4
  Earlier sketch in CTFT–1
Davis, Andrew 1947– CTFT–40
Davis, Ann B. 1926– CTFT–3
Davis, Ariel 1912– CTFT–1
Davis, B. J. CTFT–65
Davis, Bette 1908–1989 .... CTFT–8
  Earlier sketches in CTFT–1; WWT–17
Davis, Bill
  See .... Davis, William B.
Davis, Boyd 1885–1963 .... WWasWT
Davis, Brad 1949–1991 .... CTFT–5
  Obituary in CTFT–10
Davis, Bud CTFT–66
  Earlier sketch in CTFT–36
Davis, Carl 1936– CTFT–35
  Earlier sketches in CTFT–9; WWT–17
Davis, Carole 1953– CTFT–61
Davis, Clayton 1948– CTFT–3
Davis, Clifton 1945– CTFT–62
  Earlier sketch in CTFT–6
Davis, Dana 1978– CTFT–76
Davis, Dane A. 1957(?)– CTFT–51
Davis, Daniel 1945 .... CTFT–39
  Earlier sketch in CTFT–17
Davis, Don 1957– CTFT–53
  Earlier sketch in CTFT–25
Davis, Don S. 1942– CTFT–79
Davis, Donald 1928–1998 .... CTFT–10
  Obituary in CTFT–22
Davis, Duane CTFT–53
Davis, Fay 1872–1945 .... WWasWT
Davis, Geena 1957(?)– CTFT–41
  Earlier sketches in CTFT–10, 18
  Brief Entry in CTFT–5
Davis, Gene CTFT–65
Davis, George "Bud"
  See .... Davis, Bud
Davis, Gilbert 1899– .... WWasWT
Davis, Hal 1950– CTFT–6
Davis, Hope 1964– CTFT–44
  Earlier sketch in CTFT–15
Davis, Jeff 1950– CTFT–49
  Earlier sketches in CTFT–1, 9
Davis, Joan 1906–1961 .... WWasWT
Davis, Joe 1912–1984 .... WWT–17
Davis, John CTFT–43
Davis, Judy 1955– CTFT–60
  Earlier sketches in CTFT–7, 14, 27
Davis, Kevin 1945– CTFT–4
Davis, Kristin 1965– CTFT–44
Davis, Luther 1921– CTFT–3
Davis, Mac 1942– CTFT–34
  Earlier sketch in CTFT–3
Davis, Martin Sandford 1927– CTFT–12
Davis, Matthew 1978– CTFT–66

Davis, Michael 1936– CTFT–55
  Earlier sketches in CTFT–2, 19
Davis, Nathan 1917– CTFT–56
Davis, Nathaniel Newnham
  See .... Newnham–Davis, Nathaniel
Davis, Ossie 1917– CTFT–29
  Earlier sketches in CTFT–2, 9, 18; WWT–17
Davis, Owen 1874–1956 .... WWasWT
Davis, Owen 1907–1949 .... WWasWT
Davis, Phoebe 1865–? .... WWasWT
Davis, R. G. 1933– CTFT–2
Davis, Ray C. CTFT–6
  Earlier sketch in WWT–17
Davis, Richard Harding 1864–1916 ...... WWasWT
Davis, Sammi 1964– CTFT–38
Davis, Sammy, Jr. 1925–1990 .... CTFT–11
  Earlier sketches in CTFT–4; WWT–17
Davis, Tom Buffen 1867–1931 .... WWasWT
Davis, Ty
  See .... Davis, B. J.
Davis, Viola CTFT–38
Davis, Viveka CTFT–30
Davis, Warwick 1970– CTFT–45
Davis, Wendy CTFT–45
  Earlier sketch in CTFT–17
Davis, William B. 1938– CTFT–66
  Earlier sketches in CTFT–18, 29
Davis, William Boyd 1885–? .... WWasWT
Davison, Bruce 1946– CTFT–49
  Earlier sketch in CTFT–4
Davison, Jon 1949– CTFT–48
  Earlier sketch in CTFT–10
Davison, Peter 1951– CTFT–35
  Earlier sketch in CTFT–8
Davis–Voss, Sammi
  See .... Davis, Sammi
Davys, Edmund 1947– CTFT–7
Dawber, Pam 1954– CTFT–4
  Earlier sketch in CTFT–1
Dawe, Thomas F. 1881–1928 .... WWasWT
Dawn, Hazel 1891–1988 .... WWasWT
Dawn, Jeff CTFT–36
Dawson, Anna CTFT–5
  Earlier sketch in WWT–17
Dawson, Anthony M.
  See .... Margheriti, Antonio
Dawson, Beatrice 1908–1976 .... WWT–16
Dawson, Forbes 1860–? .... WWasWT
Dawson, Joseph J. CTFT–44
Dawson, Kamala
  See .... Lopez–Dawson, Kamala
Dawson, Portia CTFT–73
Dawson, Richard 1932– CTFT–8
Dawson, Rosario 1979– CTFT–66
Dawson, Roxann 1964– CTFT–39
  Earlier sketches in CTFT–5, 16
Day, Doris 1924– CTFT–7
Day, Edith 1896–1971 .... WWasWT
Day, Frances 1908– .... WWasWT
Day, Laraine 1920– CTFT–27
Day, Larry 1963– CTFT–38
Day, Linda 1938– CTFT–7
Day, Lynda
  See .... George, Lynda Day
Day, Marjorie 1889– .... WWasWT
Day, Matt 1971(?)– CTFT–56
  Earlier sketch in CTFT–26
Day, Richard Digby 1940– WWT–17
Day, Robert 1922– CTFT–11
Day, Simon CTFT–38
Day, Wendee
  See .... Lee, Wendee

Day–Lewis, Daniel 1957– CTFT–56
    Earlier sketches in CTFT–9, 16
    Brief Entry in CTFT–6
Dazey, Charles Turner 1853–1938......... WWasWT
Dazie, Mdlle. 1882–1952 .... WWasWT
Deacon, Brian 1949– CTFT–4
Deacon, Richard 1923–1984 .... CTFT–2
Deakin, Julia CTFT–34
Deakins, Roger 1949– CTFT–45
de Almeida, Duarte CTFT–38
de Almeida, Joaquim 1957– CTFT–43
Dean, Basil 1888–1978 .... WWasWT
Dean, Erica
    See .... Burstyn, Ellen
Dean, Isabel WWT–17
Dean, James 1931–1955 .... CTFT–20
Dean, Julia 1880–1952 .... WWasWT
Dean, Laura 1963– CTFT–3
Dean, Loren 1969– CTFT–48
    Earlier sketches in CTFT–11, 23
Dean, Ron CTFT–79
Deane, Barbara 1886–? .... WWasWT
Deane, Tessa .... WWasWT
De Angelis, Jefferson 1859–1933 .... WWasWT
De Angelis, Rosemary 1933– CTFT–33
    Earlier sketch in CTFT–5
Deans, F. Harris 1886–1961 .... WWasWT
Dearden, Harold 1882–1962 .... WWasWT
Dearden, James 1949– CTFT–10
Dearden, Robin CTFT–56
Dearing, Peter 1912– .... WWasWT
Dearly, Max 1875–1943 .... WWasWT
Dearth, Harry 1876–1933 .... WWasWT
Deas, Justin 1948– CTFT–61
De Baer, Jean CTFT–53
De Bankole, Isaach CTFT–38
de Banzi, Lois CTFT–1
De Banzie, Brenda 1915– .... WWasWT
De Basil, Wassily ?–1951 .... WWasWT
Debatin, Jackie 1972– CTFT–73
De Bear, Archibald 1889–1970 .... WWasWT
De Belleville, Frederic 1857–1923 .... WWasWT
DeBello, James 1980– CTFT–73
Debenham, Cicely 1891–1955 .... WWasWT
Debney, John 1957– CTFT–62
    Earlier sketch in CTFT–28
de Boer, Nicole 1970– CTFT–39
DeBonis, Marcia CTFT–73
De Bont, Jan 1943– CTFT–36
    Earlier sketch in CTFT–11
De Bray, Henry 1889–1965 .... WWasWT
De Burgh, Aimee ?–1946....................... WWasWT
Debuskey, Merle 1923– CTFT–4
DeCarlo, Mark 1962– CTFT–65
    Earlier sketch in CTFT–29
De Carlo, Yvonne 1924–2007 .... CTFT–24
    Obituary in CTFT–75
    Earlier sketch in CTFT–7
De Casalis, Jeanne 1897–1966 .... WWasWT
Deckert, Blue CTFT–43
De Coguel, Constantin
    See .... Gregory, Constantine
de Coppet, Theodosia
    See .... Bara, Theda
De Cordoba, Pedro 1881–1950 .... WWasWT
De Cordova, Frederick 1910– CTFT–7
    Earlier sketch in CTFT–1
De Cordova, Rudolph 1860–1941 .... WWasWT
Decourcelle, Pierre 1856–1926 .... WWasWT
De Courville, Albert P. 1887–1960 .... WWasWT
Decter, Ed 1959– CTFT–41
Dedio, Joey 1966– CTFT–54
DeDomenico, Richard 1936– CTFT–2

Dedrick, Christopher 1947– CTFT–41
Dee, George
    See .... Chakiris, George
Dee, Ruby 1924(?)– CTFT–35
    Earlier sketches in CTFT–1, 9; WWT–17
Dee, Sandra 1942– CTFT–21
Deeley, Michael 1932– CTFT–12
Deer, Don
    See .... Murray, Don
Deering, Olive 1919–1986 .... CTFT–3
    Earlier sketch in WWT–17
Deezen, Eddie 1958– CTFT–53
De Felitta, Raymond CTFT–36
De Fina, Barbara 1949– CTFT–44
De Foe, Louis Vincent 1869–1922 .... WWasWT
De Fontenoy, Diane 1878–? .... WWasWT
De Fore, Don 1919–1993 .... CTFT–4
    Obituary in CTFT–13
De Frece, Lauri 1880–1921 .... WWasWT
De Frece, Walter 1870–? .... WWasWT
DeGeneres, Ellen 1958– CTFT–60
    Earlier sketches in CTFT–17, 28
De Gogeul, Constantin
    See .... Gregory, Constantine
De Groot, Walter 1896– .... WWasWT
de haas, Darius 1968– CTFT–60
De Hartog, Jan 1914– CTFT–2
Dehaven, Gloria 1925(?)– CTFT–61
de Havilland, Olivia 1916– CTFT–6
Dehelly, Emile 1871–? .... WWasWT
Dehn, Paul 1912–1976 .... WWT–16
Dehner, John 1915–1992 .... CTFT–7
    Obituary in CTFT–10
Deitch, Donna 1945– CTFT–40
De Jesus, Wanda 1960– CTFT–59
DeKay, Tim CTFT–53
Dekker, Albert 1905–1962 .... WWasWT
Dekker, Thomas 1987– CTFT–59
DeKoven, Reginald 1859–1920 .... WWasWT
Delafield, E.M. 1890–1943 .... WWasWT
de la Fuente, Cristian 1974(?)– CTFT–63
De La Garza, Alana 1976– CTFT–74
de la Giroday, Francois
    See .... Giroday, Francois
de la Haye, Ina 1906– .... WWasWT
de Lancie, John 1948– CTFT–54
Delaney, Kim 1961– CTFT–55
    Earlier sketches in CTFT–7, 16, 26
Delaney, Shelagh 1939– CTFT–6
    Earlier sketch in WWT–17
DeLange, Herman 1851–1929 .... WWasWT
Delano, Diane 1957– CTFT–58
Delany, Dana 1956– CTFT–65
    Earlier sketches in CTFT–10, 18, 29
de la Pasture, Mrs. Henry 1866–1945 .... WWasWT
DeLappe, Gemze 1922– CTFT–3
DeLaria, Lea 1958– CTFT–56
    Earlier sketch in CTFT–26
de la Roche, Elisa 1949– CTFT–4
Delarosa, Yvonne CTFT–69
De La Tour, Frances 1944– CTFT–23
    Earlier sketches in CTFT–11; WWT–17
Delaunay, Louis 1854–? .... WWasWT
De Laurentiis, Dino 1919(?)– CTFT–38
    Earlier sketches in CTFT–1, 7, 14
Delderfield, R. F. 1912–1972 .... WWasWT
De Legh, Kitty 1887–? .... WWasWT
De Leon, Jack 1897–1956 .... WWasWT
DeLeon, Idalis 1966– CTFT–74
Delerue, Georges 1924–1992 .... CTFT–7
    Obituary in CTFT–11
Delevines .... WWasWT
Delfino, Majandra 1981– CTFT–54

Delfont, Bernard 1909– WWT–17
Delgado, Henry
    See .... Darrow, Henry
Del Grande, Louis CTFT–64
Del Hoyo, George CTFT–56
D'Elia, Bill CTFT–53
de Liagre, Alfred 1904–1987 .... CTFT–5
    Earlier sketch in WWT–17
de Lint, Derek 1950– CTFT–66
    Earlier sketch in CTFT–29
Delisle, Grey CTFT–38
DeLizia, Cara CTFT–63
Delk, Denny CTFT–38
Dell'Agnese, Norma CTFT–50
Dell, Charlie CTFT–43
Dell, Floyd 1887–1969 .... WWasWT
Dell, Gabriel 1919–1988 .... CTFT–7
    Earlier sketch in WWT–17
Dell, Jeffrey 1899– .... WWasWT
Delli Colli, Tonino 1923– CTFT–28
Dellums, Erik Todd 1964– CTFT–56
    Earlier sketch in CTFT–26
Del Mar, Maria 1964– CTFT–75
Delon, Alain 1935– CTFT–38
    Earlier sketch in CTFT–14
De Longis, Anthony 1950– CTFT–41
Delorenzo, Michael 1962(?)– CTFT–38
    Earlier sketch in CTFT–14
Delorme, Hugues .... WWasWT
De Los Reyes, Kamar 1967– CTFT–54
Deloy, George
    See .... Del Hoyo, George
Deloy, George 1953– CTFT–4
Delpy, Julie 1969– CTFT–44
    Earlier sketch in CTFT–15
del Rio, Dolores 1905–1983 .... CTFT–20
del Rivero, Conchita
    See .... Rivera, Chita
Delroy, Irene 1898– .... WWasWT
Del Ruth, Thomas 1943(?)– CTFT–44
    Earlier sketch in CTFT–15
del Toro, Benicio 1967– CTFT–65
    Earlier sketches in CTFT–18, 29
Del Toro, Guillermo 1964– CTFT–60
    Earlier sketch in CTFT–27
De Luca, Michael 1965– CTFT–64
    Earlier sketch in CTFT–29
DeLuise, Carol 1935– CTFT–46
DeLuise, David 1971– CTFT–59
    Earlier sketch in CTFT–27
DeLuise, Dom 1933– CTFT–65
    Earlier sketches in CTFT–2, 9, 18, 29
DeLuise, Michael 1970– CTFT–44
DeLuise, Peter 1966– CTFT–46
De Lungo, Tony 1892– .... WWasWT
Delysia, Alice 1889– .... WWasWT
Demarest, William 1892–1983 .... CTFT–2
De Marney, Derrick 1906–1971 .... WWasWT
De Marney, Terence 1909–1971 .... WWasWT
De Matteo, Drea 1973– CTFT–53
DeMay, Tim
    See .... DeKay, Tim
de Medeiros, Maria 1965– CTFT–38
Demeger, Robert CTFT–30
de Mille, Agnes 1905–1993 .... CTFT–3
    Obituary in CTFT–12
    Earlier sketch in WWT–17
de Mille, Cecil B. 1881–1959 .... WWasWT
de Mille, William C. 1878–1955 .... WWasWT
Deming, Peter 1957– CTFT–53
Demita, John 1956(?)– CTFT–79

Demme, Jonathan 1944–........................ CTFT–43
  Earlier sketches in CTFT–5, 14
Demme, Ted 1963–2002 .... CTFT–30
  Obituary in CTFT–49
De Montherlant, Henry 1896– .... WWasWT
De Mornay, Rebecca 1961(?)–................ CTFT–64
  Earlier sketches in CTFT–3, 11, 18, 29
  Brief Entry in CTFT2
Dempsey, Michael CTFT–36
Dempsey, Patrick 1966–........................ CTFT–45
  Earlier sketches in CTFT–7, 14
Dempster, Hugh 1900–1987................. WWasWT
De Munn, Jeffrey 1947– CTFT–77
  Earlier sketches in CTFT–7, 34
Demy, Jacques 1931–1990 .... CTFT–9
  Obituary in CTFT–10
Dench, Judi 1934– CTFT–72
  Earlier sketches in CTFT–4, 11, 22, 32;
  WWT–17
Denes, Oscar 1893–.............................. WWasWT
Deneuve, Catherine 1943–...................... CTFT–50
  Earlier sketches in CTFT–2, 4, 14, 24
Denham, Isolde 1920– .... WWasWT
Denham, Maurice 1909– CTFT–3
  Earlier sketch in WWT–17
Denham, Reginald 1894–...................... WWT–17
Denier, Lydie 1964–............................... CTFT–59
De Niro, Drena CTFT–53
De Niro, Robert 1943–.......................... CTFT–64
  Earlier sketches in CTFT–1, 4, 10, 18, 29
Denis, Claire 1948– CTFT–31
  Earlier sketch in CTFT–20
Denis, Neil 1987–................................. CTFT–71
Denisof, Alexis 1966– CTFT–42
Denison, Anthony John 1950– CTFT–48
Denison, Michael 1915–1998 .... CTFT–4
  Obituary in CTFT–22
  Earlier sketch in WWT–17
Denker, Henry 1912–............................... CTFT–6
  Earlier sketch in WWT–17
Denkner, Eli
  See.................................... Danker, Eli
Denman, Tony 1979–.............................. CTFT–71
Dennehy, Brian 1938–........................... CTFT–71
  Earlier sketches in CTFT–4, 11, 20, 31
Dennehy, Elizabeth.............................. CTFT–53
Dennen, Barry 1938– CTFT–69
Dennis, Alfred CTFT–64
Dennis, Neil
  See.................................... Denis, Neil
Dennis, Peter 1933–.............................. CTFT–41
Dennis, Sandy 1937–1992 .... CTFT–10
  Earlier sketches in CTFT–1; WWT–17
Dennison, Sally 1941– CTFT–3
Denny, Ernest 1862–1943..................... WWasWT
Denny, Reginald 1891–1967 .... WWasWT
Denny, Simon Baker
  See.................................... Baker, Simon
Denny, William Henry 1853–1915........ WWasWT
Denoff, Sam 1928– CTFT–4
Densham, Pen 1947–............................ CTFT–56
  Earlier sketches in CTFT–12, 22
Dent, Alan 1905–1978.......................... WWT–16
Dent, Catherine CTFT–54
Dent–Cox, Tom 1945–........................... CTFT–45
  Earlier sketch in CTFT–17
Denton, Frank 1878–1945 .... WWasWT
Denton, Jamie 1963– CTFT–53
Dentzer, Susan 1955–............................ CTFT–42
Denver, Bob 1935– CTFT–57
  Earlier sketch in CTFT–7

Denver, John 1943–1997...................... CTFT–15
  Obituary in CTFT–19
  Earlier sketch in CTFT–8
Denville, Alfred J. P. 1876–1955 .... WWasWT
de Oliveira, Manoel 1908– CTFT–26
De Palma, Brian 1940–.......................... CTFT–51
  Earlier sketches in CTFT–1, 6, 13, 24
Depardieu, Gerard 1948– CTFT–45
  Earlier sketches in CTFT–8, 15
DePatie, David H. 1930–....................... CTFT–10
Depp, Johnny 1963– CTFT–65
  Earlier sketches in CTFT–10, 18, 29
Depre, Ernest 1854–?............................ WWasWT
de Prume, Cathryn CTFT–72
  Earlier sketch in CTFT–33
De Ravin, Emilie 1981– CTFT–69
Derek, Bo 1956–................................... CTFT–72
  Earlier sketches in CTFT–3, 33
Derek, John 1926–1998 .... CTFT–3
  Obituary in CTFT–21
De Reyes, Consuelo 1893–1948 .... WWasWT
Dermot, John
  See.................................... Neill, Sam
Dern, Bruce 1936–................................ CTFT–70
  Earlier sketches in CTFT–3, 18, 31
Dern, Laura 1967–................................ CTFT–66
  Earlier sketches in CTFT–10, 18, 29
  Brief Entry in CTFT–3
de Rossi, Portia 1973–........................... CTFT–56
  Earlier sketch in CTFT–26
Derr, Richard 1917–.............................. WWasWT
Derrah, Thomas CTFT–75
  Earlier sketch in CTFT–32
Derricks, Cleavant 1953–...................... CTFT–42
  Earlier sketches in CTFT–6, 18
Derryberry, Debi CTFT–38
Derwent, Clarence 1884–1959............. WWasWT
Derwin, Mark 1960–............................. CTFT–75
De Sanctis, Alfredo .... WWasWT
Desando, Anthony 1965–....................... CTFT–79
  Earlier sketch in CTFT–36
De Santis, Joe 1909–1989 .... CTFT–1
De Santis, Tony CTFT–62
Desantis, Stanley CTFT–41
DeSanto, Daniel 1980(?)–....................... CTFT–74
DeSanto, Susie CTFT–65
Des Barres, Michael 1948– CTFT–48
Desborough, Philip 1883–? .... WWasWT
Descaves, Lucien 1861–1949 .... WWasWT
DeScenna, Linda 1949– CTFT–79
  Earlier sketches in CTFT–10, 36
Deschanel, Caleb 1944– CTFT–48
  Earlier sketches in CTFT–8, 24
Deschanel, Emily 1978–........................ CTFT–68
Deschanel, Zooey 1980– CTFT–68
De Selincourt, Hugh 1878–1951 .... WWasWT
Desert, Alex 1968–................................ CTFT–56
  Earlier sketch in CTFT–26
Desfontaines, Henri 1876–?.................. WWasWT
De Shields, Andre 1946– CTFT–39
  Earlier sketches in CTFT–7; WWT–17
De Sica, Vittorio 1902(?)–1974................ CTFT–24
Desiderio, Robert 1951– CTFT–33
  Earlier sketch in CTFT–6
De Silva, N. 1868–1949 .... WWasWT
Desjardins, Maxime .... WWasWT
Deslys, Gaby 1884–1920 .... WWasWT
Desmond, Dan 1944–........................... CTFT–5
Desmond, Florence 1905– .... WWasWT
DeSoto, Rosana 1950(?)–........................ CTFT–33
  Earlier sketch in CTFT–7
De Sousa, May 1887–1948 .... WWasWT
De Sousa, Melissa CTFT–36

de Souza, Steven E. 1948(?)–.................. CTFT–40
Desplechin, Arnaud 1960–..................... CTFT–28
Despotovich, Nada 1967–...................... CTFT–68
Despres, Loraine.................................. CTFT–6
Despres, Suzanne 1875–1951 .... WWasWT
Desprez, Frank 1853–1916 .... WWasWT
D'Este, Coco 1952–.............................. CTFT–74
Destefano, Ron CTFT–62
Destry, John B..................................... CTFT–39
Desvallieres, Maurice 1857–1926 .... WWasWT
De Sylva B. G. 1895–1950 .... WWasWT
Detmer, Amanda 1971– CTFT–61
Detmers, Maruschka 1962–.................... CTFT–59
  Earlier sketch in CTFT–27
De Torrebruna, Riccardo CTFT–33
De Toth, Andre 1913–........................... CTFT–15
Deutch, Howard................................... CTFT–43
  Earlier sketches in CTFT–12, 22
Deutsch, Benoit–Leon 1892–............... WWasWT
Deutsch, Helen 1906– CTFT–4
Deutsch, Stephen
  See.................................... Simon, Stephen
De Vahl, Anders 1869–? .... WWasWT
Deval, Jacques 1895–1972 .... WWasWT
De Valentina, Rudolpho
  See.................................... Valentino, Rudolph
De Valois, Ninette 1898– .... WWasWT
Devally Piazza, Dana............................. CTFT–65
Devane, William 1937(?)–...................... CTFT–72
  Earlier sketches in CTFT–3, 33
Devant, David 1863–? .... WWasWT
Devarona, Joanna
  See.................................... Kerns, Joanna
Devarona, Joanne
  See.................................... Kerns, Joanna
Deveau, Marie–Sylvie 1963(?)– CTFT–58
  Earlier sketch in CTFT–27
DeVeaux, Nathaniel CTFT–54
Dever, Seamus 1976–............................ CTFT–68
Devereaux, Terry
  See.................................... Torme, Tracy
Deverell, John W. 1880–1965 .... WWasWT
Devereux, William ?–1945 .... WWasWT
Devers, Claire...................................... CTFT–29
Devine, Aidan CTFT–62
Devine, Andy 1905–1977 .... CTFT–21
Devine, George 1910–1966 .... WWasWT
Devine, Loretta 1949(?) CTFT–36
  Earlier sketch in CTFT–10
  Brief Entry in CTFT–3
DeVine, Lawrence 1935– CTFT–1
DeVito, Danny 1944– CTFT–48
  Earlier sketches in CTFT–6, 13, 24
Devlin, Alan CTFT–53
Devlin, Dean 1962–.............................. CTFT–68
  Earlier sketches in CTFT–4, 18, 25, 30
Devlin, Jay 1929–................................. CTFT–1
Devlin, Ryan 1980–.............................. CTFT–78
Devlin, William 1911–1987 .... WWasWT
Devon, Mari
  See.................................... Alan, Jane
Devon, Tony 1951–.............................. CTFT–53
Devore, Gaston 1859–? .... WWasWT
DeVore, Cain 1960–.............................. CTFT–6
De Vries, Henry .... WWasWT
De Vries, Peter 1910–............................ CTFT–1
deVry, William CTFT–40
De Warfaz, George 1889–1966............. WWasWT
Dewell, Michael 1931–.......................... CTFT–5
  Earlier sketch in WWT–17
Dewhurst, Colleen 1924–1991 .... CTFT–11
  Earlier sketches in CTFT–4; WWT–17

Dewhurst, Keith 1931–............................. CTFT–7
  Earlier sketch in WWT–17
De Winton, Alice.................................. WWasWT
De Witt, Joyce 1949–............................ CTFT–41
  Earlier sketch in CTFT–9
De Wolfe, Billy 1907–1974................... WWasWT
De Wolfe, Elsie 1865–1950 .... WWasWT
Dews, Peter 1929–1997 .... CTFT–6
  Obituary in CTFT–18
  Earlier sketch in WWT–17
Dexter, Aubrey 1898–1958................... WWasWT
Dexter, John 1925(?)–1990 .... CTFT–10
  Earlier sketch in WWT–17
Dexter, L. T.
  See............................. Poindexter, Larry
Dey, Susan 1952–................................. CTFT–44
  Earlier sketches in CTFT–5, 12, 22
  Brief Entry in CTFT–2
De Young, Cliff 1946(?)– CTFT–48
  Earlier sketches in CTFT–4, 12, 23
De Zarn, Tim 1952–.............................. CTFT–46
D'Gard, Mike
  See................................. Gregory, Michael
D'Gord, Mike
  See................................. Gregory, Michael
Diaghileff, Serge 1872–1929 .... WWasWT
Diakun, Alex CTFT–65
Diamond Dallas Page
  See.................................. Falkinburg, Page
Diamond, Dustin 1977–......................... CTFT–39
  Earlier sketch in CTFT–17
Diamond, Elizabeth
  See.. Diamond, Liz
Diamond, I. A. L. 1920–1988.................. CTFT–7
  Earlier sketch in CTFT–1
Diamond, Liz CTFT–26
Diamond, Margaret 1916– WWT–17
Diamond, Matthew 1951– CTFT–64
Diamond, Neil 1941– CTFT–53
  Earlier sketch in CTFT–25
Diamond, Reed 1964(?)–........................ CTFT–48
  Earlier sketch in CTFT–24
Diamond, Selma 1921–1985.................... CTFT–2
Diamond, Sheryl Lee
  See...................................... Lee, Sheryl
Diamont, Don 1962– CTFT–38
Dianard, Neil
  See...................................... Dainard, Neil
Diaquino, John
  See.................................. D'Aquino, John
Diaz, Arnold 1949–.............................. CTFT–42
  Earlier sketch in CTFT–17
Diaz, Cameron 1972– CTFT–60
  Earlier sketches in CTFT–17, 28
Diaz, Guillermo CTFT–65
  Earlier sketch in CTFT–29
Di Bianco, Louis.................................. CTFT–75
DiCaprio, Leonardo 1974(?)– CTFT–48
  Earlier sketches in CTFT–14, 24
Dicenta, Joaquin 1860–? .... WWasWT
DiCenzo, George.................................. CTFT–55
  Earlier sketch in CTFT–8
DiCillo, Tom 1954–.............................. CTFT–65
  Earlier sketch in CTFT–29
Dick, Andy 1965–................................ CTFT–73
  Earlier sketches in CTFT–20, 32
Dick, Philip K. 1928–1982 .... CTFT–23
Dickens, C. Stafford 1896–1967 .... WWasWT
Dickens, Kim CTFT–48
Dickerson, Ernest 1952–........................ CTFT–43
  Earlier sketches in CTFT–11, 22
Dickerson, George................................ CTFT–6
Dickey, Paul 1884–1933 .... WWasWT

Dickinson, Angie 1931–......................... CTFT–51
  Earlier sketches in CTFT–2, 6, 13, 24
Dickinson, Janice 1955(?)–..................... CTFT–69
Dickson, Barbara 1948–......................... CTFT–25
Dickson, Dorothy 1896– .... WWasWT
Dickson, Neil CTFT–61
Dickson, Ngila CTFT–43
Didring, Ernst 1868–1931 .... WWasWT
Diehl, John 1958(?)–............................. CTFT–77
  Earlier sketch in CTFT–34
Diener, Joan 1934–.............................. CTFT–4
  Earlier sketch in WWT–17
Diesel, Vin 1967–................................ CTFT–53
  Earlier sketch in CTFT–25
Dietrich, Dena 1928–........................... CTFT–62
  Earlier sketch in CTFT–1
Dietrich, Marlene 1901(?)–1992 .... CTFT–10
  Earlier sketch in WWT–17
Dietz, Howard 1896–1983...................... WWT–17
Dietz, Michael 1971–........................... CTFT–63
Digaetano, Joe 1952–........................... CTFT–42
Digges, Dudley 1879–1947 .... WWasWT
Diggs, Elizabeth 1939–......................... CTFT–3
Diggs, Taye 1972(?)–............................ CTFT–52
  Earlier sketch in CTFT–25
Dighton, John 1909–............................ WWT–16
Dignam, Arthur 1939– CTFT–40
Dignam, Mark 1909–1989 .... CTFT–10
  Earlier sketch in WWT–17
DiLauro, Stephen 1950–......................... CTFT–11
Dill, Deena.. CTFT–69
Dillahunt, Garret 1964– CTFT–54
Dillane, Stephen 1957–......................... CTFT–54
  Earlier sketch in CTFT–26
Dillard, Victoria 1969–.......................... CTFT–62
  Earlier sketches in CTFT–17, 28
Diller, Barry 1942–.............................. CTFT–3
Diller, Phyllis 1917–............................. CTFT–63
  Earlier sketch in CTFT–1
Dilley, Leslie..................................... CTFT–44
  Earlier sketches in CTFT–11, 22
Dillingham, Charles B. 1868–1934 .... WWasWT
Dillman, Bradford 1930–........................ CTFT–18
  Earlier sketch in CTFT–3, 10
Dillon, Denny 1951– CTFT–53
  Earlier sketch in CTFT–25
Dillon, Frances ?–1947 .... WWasWT
Dillon, John 1945–.............................. CTFT–1
Dillon, Kevin 1965(?)–........................... CTFT–54
  Earlier sketches in CTFT–8, 15, 26
Dillon, Matt 1964–.............................. CTFT–54
  Earlier sketches in CTFT–5, 15, 26
  Brief Entry in CTFT–2
Dillon, Melinda 1939–........................... CTFT–41
  Earlier sketches in CTFT–3, 10, 19
Dillon, Mia CTFT–4
  Earlier sketch in CTFT–1
Dillon, Paul CTFT–54
Dillon, Stephen
  See............................... Dillane, Stephen
Di Maggio, John 1968– CTFT–69
Dimbort, Danny CTFT–43
Dimopolous, Stephen CTFT–63
Dinallo, Gregory S. 1941– CTFT–8
Dinehart, Alan 1890–1944 .... WWasWT
Dingo, Ernie 1956–.............................. CTFT–29
Dini, Paul 1957–................................ CTFT–64
Dinicol, Joe 1983–.............................. CTFT–67
Dinklage, Peter 1969–.......................... CTFT–66
Dinner, William CTFT–4
Di Novi, Denise 1956–.......................... CTFT–48
Dinsdale, Reece 1959– CTFT–48
  Earlier sketch in CTFT–9

Dinsmore, Bruce CTFT–61
Diol, Susan 1964–............................... CTFT–53
Dion, Celine 1968–.............................. CTFT–30
Dion, Peter
  See .... Chetwynd, Lionel
Dionisi, Stefano 1966– CTFT–30
Di Pego, Gerald CTFT–48
Diphusa, Patty
  See .... Almodovar, Pedro
Disher, Catherine CTFT–39
Disher, Maurice Willson 1893–1969 ..... WWasWT
Dishy, Bob CTFT–5
  Earlier sketch in WWT–17
Disney, Melissa................................... CTFT–76
Disney, Roy 1930– CTFT–50
  Earlier sketches in CTFT–14, 24
Disney, Walt 1901–1966 .... CTFT–20
Dispenza, Joe 1961– CTFT–7
Diss, Eileen 1931–............................... CTFT–48
  Earlier sketch in CTFT–14
Ditrichstein, Leo 1865–1928 .... WWasWT
DiTutto, Ray
  See .... Williams, Robin
Divine 1945–1988 .... CTFT–7
DiVito, Joanne 1941– CTFT–3
Divoff, Andrew 1955–........................... CTFT–44
Dix, Beulah Marie 1876–1970 .... WWasWT
Dix, Dorothy 1892–1970 .... WWasWT
Dixey, Henry E. 1859–1943 .... WWasWT
Dixon, Adele 1908– .... WWasWT
Dixon, Campbell 1895–1960 .... WWasWT
Dixon, Donna 1957– CTFT–13
  Earlier sketch in CTFT–6
Dixon, George
  See .... Willis, Ted
Dixon, Ivan 1931– CTFT–8
Dixon, Jean 1896–1981......................... WWasWT
Dixon, Leslie CTFT–67
Dixon, MacIntyre 1931– CTFT–64
  Earlier sketch in CTFT–8
Dixon, Neil
  See .... Dickson, Neil
Dixon, Will.. CTFT–59
Djimon
  See .... Hounsou, Djimon
Djola, Badja CTFT–10
D'Lugoff, Art 1924– CTFT–2
D'Lyn, Shae 1963–.............................. CTFT–51
  Earlier sketch in CTFT–24
Dmytryk, Edward 1908–1999................... CTFT–28
Dobbs, Lou 1945– CTFT–67
Dobie, Alan 1932–.............................. CTFT–6
  Earlier sketch in WWT–17
Doble, Frances 1902–1967 .... WWasWT
Dobson, Anita 1949– CTFT–34
Dobson, Kevin 1943–............................ CTFT–76
  Earlier sketches in CTFT–3, 12, 22, 32
Dobson, Michael.................................. CTFT–43
Dobson, Paul CTFT–43
Dobson, Peter 1964–............................ CTFT–49
Dobtcheff, Vernon 1934–....................... CTFT–60
  Earlier sketch in CTFT–27
Dr. Drew
  See.. Pinsky, Drew
Dr. Gonzo
  See............................... Thompson, Hunter S.
Dr. Laura
  See............................... Schlessinger, Laura
Dodd, Ken 1929–................................ WWT–17
Dodd, Lee Wilson 1879–1933............... WWasWT
Dodds, Jamieson 1884–1942................. WWasWT
Dodds, Megan 1970–............................ CTFT–64
Dodds, William CTFT–1

Dodge, Henry Irving 1861–1934 .... WWasWT
Dodimead, David 1919– WWT–17
Dodson, Jack 1931–1994 .... CTFT–8
    Obituary in CTFT–13
    Earlier sketch in CTFT–1
Dodson, John E. 1857–1931 .... WWasWT
Doe, John 1954– CTFT–53
    Earlier sketch in CTFT–25
Doggs, Joe
    See .... Pesci, Joe
Doherty, Shannen 1971– CTFT–45
    Earlier sketches in CTFT–13, 23
Dohring, Jason 1982– CTFT–78
Doig, Lexa 1973– CTFT–38
Dolan, CarolAnne CTFT–48
Dolenz, Ami 1969– CTFT–54
Dolenz, Micky 1945– CTFT–70
    Earlier sketches in CTFT–21, 70
Dolin, Anton 1904–1983 .... WWasWT
Dolly, Jennie 1892–1941 .... WWasWT
Dolly, Rosie 1892–1970 .... WWasWT
Dolman, Richard 1895– .... WWasWT
Doman, John 1945– CTFT–62
    Earlier sketch in CTFT–28
Dombasle, Arielle 1957– CTFT–6
Dominczyk, Dagmara 1976– CTFT–71
Dominczyk, Marika 1980– CTFT–78
Domingo, Placido 1941– CTFT–51
    Earlier sketches in CTFT–14, 24
Dominguez, Rachel
    See .... Morrison, Shelley
Domino
    See .... Coppola, Sofia
Dommartin, Solveig CTFT–29
Donahue, Elinor 1937– CTFT–58
    Earlier sketch in CTFT–7
Donahue, Jack 1892?–1930 .... WWasWT
Donahue, Heather 1974– CTFT–54
Donahue, Phil 1935– CTFT–62
    Earlier sketch in CTFT–6
Donahue, Troy 1936– CTFT–33
    Earlier sketch in CTFT–8
Donald, James 1917– .... WWasWT
Donaldson, Roger 1945– CTFT–10
Donaldson, Sam 1934– CTFT–43
    Earlier sketches in CTFT–12, 22
Donat, Peter 1928– CTFT–36
    Earlier sketches in CTFT–1, 9
Donat, Robert 1905–1958 .... WWasWT
Donath, Ludwig 1907–1967 .... WWasWT
Donato, Marc 1989– CTFT–79
    Earlier sketch in CTFT–36
Donavan, Dave
    See .... Cipriano, Joe
Doncheff, Len CTFT–40
Donehue, Vincent J. 1920–1966 .... WWasWT
Donen, Stanley 1924– CTFT–24
Donenberg, Benjamin 1957– CTFT–2
Donfeld CTFT–11
Doniger, Walter CTFT–2
Donisthorpe, G. Sheila 1898–1946 .... WWasWT
Donlan, Yolande WWT–17
Donleavy, J. P. 1926– WWT–17
Donlevy, Brian 1903–1972 .... WWasWT
Donnay, Maurice 1859–? .... WWasWT
Donnell, Jeff 1921–1988 .... CTFT–1
Donnell, Patrick 1916– WWT–17
Donnellan, Declan 1953– CTFT–23
Donnelly, Candice 1954– CTFT–39
    Earlier sketches in CTFT–8, 15
Donnelly, Donal 1931– CTFT–14
    Earlier sketches in CTFT–3; WWT–17

Donnelly, Dorothy Agnes 1880–1928 ..... WWasWT
Donner, Clive 1926– CTFT–6
    Earlier sketch in WWT–17
Donner, Richard 1930– CTFT–73
    Earlier sketch in CTFT–57
Donner, Richard 1939(?)– CTFT–32
    Earlier sketches in CTFT–5, 12, 22
D'Onofrio, Vincent 1959– CTFT–72
    Earlier sketches in CTFT–12, 22, 32
Donohoe, Amanda 1962– CTFT–32
    Earlier sketches in CTFT–11, 22
Donohue, Jack 1912–1984 .... CTFT–2
    Earlier sketch in WWT–17
Donovan, Arlene CTFT–5
Donovan, Brian CTFT–63
Donovan, Elisa 1971– CTFT–79
    Earlier sketch in CTFT–36
Donovan, Jason 1968– CTFT–75
    Earlier sketch in CTFT–33
Donovan, Jeffrey 1968– CTFT–79
    Earlier sketch in CTFT–36
Donovan, Martin 1957– CTFT–54
    Earlier sketch in CTFT–26
Donovan, Michael CTFT–44
Donovan, Tate 1963– CTFT–44
Doohan, James 1920– CTFT–30
    Earlier sketches in CTFT–8, 18
Dooley, James Michael 1976– CTFT–62
Dooley, Paul 1928– CTFT–66
    Earlier sketches in CTFT–3, 18, 30
Dooley, Rae 1896–1984 .... WWasWT
Dooley, Ray 1952–1984 .... CTFT–1
Dopud, Mike 1969(?)– CTFT–55
Doran, Charles 1877–1964 .... WWasWT
Doran, Matt 1976– CTFT–65
    Earlier sketch in CTFT–29
Doran, Takayo
    See .... Fischer, Takayo
Dore, Alexander 1923– WWT–17
Dorena, Elfi
    See .... Von Dassanowsky, Elfi
Dorff, Stephen 1973– CTFT–72
    Earlier sketches in CTFT–22, 32
Dorff, Steve 1949– CTFT–74
Dorgere, Arlette .... WWasWT
Doria, Diogo CTFT–36
Dorleac, Catherine
    See .... Deneuve, Catherine
Dorleac, Jean–Pierre 1963– CTFT–36
    Earlier sketch in CTFT–11
D'Orme, Aileen 1877–1939 .... WWasWT
Dormer, Daisy 1889– .... WWasWT
Dorn, Cynthia CTFT–51
Dorn, Dolores CTFT–1
Dorn, Harding 1923–1987 .... CTFT–3
Dorn, Michael 1952– CTFT–71
    Earlier sketches in CTFT–20, 31
Dornay, Jules .... WWasWT
Doro, Marie 1882–1956 .... WWasWT
Dorr, Dorothy 1867–? .... WWasWT
D'Orsay, Lawrance 1853–1931 .... WWasWT
Dorval, Adrien CTFT–49
Dorwart, David A. 1948– CTFT–2
Dorziat, Gabrielle .... WWasWT
Dossor, Alan 1941– WWT–17
Dotchin, Angela Marie 1974– CTFT–70
Dotrice, Roy 1925– CTFT–78
    Earlier sketches in CTFT–3, 35; WWT–17
Doucet, Catherine Calhoun
    1875–1958 .... WWasWT
Doucette, Jeff CTFT–46
Doug, Doug E. 1970– CTFT–53

Douglas, Ashanti
    See .... Ashanti
Douglas, Brandon 1968– CTFT–56
Douglas, D. C. 1966– CTFT–72
Douglas, Diana 1923– CTFT–1
Douglas, Eric 1962– CTFT–6
Douglas, Felicity WWT–17
Douglas, Gordon 1907–1993 .... CTFT–2
    Obituary in CTFT–12
Douglas, Illeana 1965– CTFT–70
    Earlier sketches in CTFT–20, 31
Douglas, Julie Condra
    See .... Condra, Julie
Douglas, Juliet 1962– CTFT–8
Douglas, Kenneth ?–1923 .... WWasWT
Douglas, Kirk 1916– CTFT–38
    Earlier sketches in CTFT–1, 7, 14
Douglas, Marc
    See .... Mordente, Tony
Douglas, Melvyn 1901–1980 .... CTFT–1
    Earlier sketch in WWT–17
Douglas, Michael
    See .... Crichton, Michael
Douglas, Michael 1944– CTFT–72
    Earlier sketches in CTFT–1, 4, 11, 22, 32
Douglas, Mike 1925– CTFT–6
Douglas, Robert 1909–1999 .... WWasWT
    Obituary in CTFT–24
Douglas, Sarah 1952– CTFT–78
    Earlier sketches in CTFT–4, 35
Douglas, Shirley 1934– CTFT–63
Douglas, Suzzanne 1957– CTFT–47
    Earlier sketch in CTFT–23
Douglas, Tom 1903– .... WWasWT
Douglas, Torrington ?–1986 .... WWT–17
Douglas, Wallace 1911– WWT–17
Douglass, Albert 1864–1940 .... WWasWT
Douglass, R. H. .... WWasWT
Douglass, Stephen 1921– WWT–17
Douglass, Vincent 1900–1926 .... WWasWT
Dourdan, Gary 1966– CTFT–54
    Earlier sketch in CTFT–26
Dourif, Brad 1950– CTFT–62
    Earlier sketches in CTFT–7, 17, 28
Dovey, Alice 1885–1969 .... WWasWT
Dow, Bill CTFT–77
    Earlier sketch in CTFT–34
Dow, Clara 1883–1969 .... WWasWT
Dow, Ellen Albertini 1918– CTFT–53
    Earlier sketch in CTFT–25
Dow, Tony 1945– CTFT–30
    Earlier sketches in CTFT–2, 18
Dowd, Ann CTFT–59
    Earlier sketch in CTFT–27
Dowd, M'el CTFT–5
    Earlier sketch in WWT–17
Dowd, Ned 1950– CTFT–67
Dowdy, Mrs. Regera
    See .... Gorey, Edward
Dowling, Eddie 1894–1976 .... WWasWT
Dowling, Joan 1928–1954 .... WWasWT
Dowling, Kevin CTFT–53
Dowling, Vincent 1929– CTFT–11
    Earlier sketch in CTFT–2
Down, Angela 1943– WWT–17
Down, Lesley–Anne 1954– CTFT–54
    Earlier sketches in CTFT–5, 15, 26
Downey, Robert CTFT–8
Downey, Robert, Jr. 1965– CTFT–45
    Earlier sketches in CTFT–7, 14, 23
Downey, Roma 1960– CTFT–45
    Earlier sketch in CTFT–17

Downie, Penny.. CTFT–35
　　　Earlier sketch in CTFT–9
Downs, Hugh 1921–................................... CTFT–51
　　　Earlier sketches in CTFT–5, 24
Downs, Jane... WWT–17
Dowse, Denise Y. 1958–........................... CTFT–38
Doyal, Richard
　　　See .... Doyle, Richard
Doyle, Arthur Conan 1859–1930 .... WWasWT
Doyle, Christopher CTFT–41
Doyle, Christopher 1952– CTFT–53
　　　Earlier sketch in CTFT–25
Doyle, David 1925–1997 .... CTFT–7
　　　Obituary in CTFT–17
Doyle, Gerard T.
　　　See .... Doyle, Jerry
Doyle, Jerry 1956–.................................... CTFT–39
Doyle, Jill 1965– CTFT–4
Doyle, Kathleen CTFT–53
Doyle, Patrick 1953– CTFT–48
Doyle, Richard CTFT–53
Doyle, Shawn 1968–................................. CTFT–68
Doyle, Tracey A. CTFT–43
Doyle–Murray, Brian 1945– CTFT–47
　　　Earlier sketch in CTFT–23
D'Oyly Carte, Rupert 1876–? .... WWasWT
Dozier, William 1908–1991 .... CTFT–10
Drago, Billy 1949–.................................... CTFT–77
　　　Earlier sketch in CTFT–34
Dragoti, Stan(ley G.) 1932–..................... CTFT–1
Drake, Alfred 1914–.................................. WWT–17
Drake, Darleen
　　　See .... Carr, Darleen
Drake, Ellen
　　　See... Blake, Ellen
Drake, Fabia 1904–1990 .... CTFT–8
　　　Earlier sketch in WWasWT
Drake, Larry 1949(?)– CTFT–43
　　　Earlier sketches in CTFT–11, 22
Drake, William A. 1899–1965............... WWasWT
Drano, Jane
　　　See .... Wiedlin, Jane
Draper, Courtnee 1985–.......................... CTFT–59
Draper, Polly 1956– CTFT–38
　　　Earlier sketches in CTFT–8, 15
Draper, Ruth 1889–1956 .... WWasWT
Draycott, Wilfred 1848–?....................... WWasWT
Drayton, Alfred 1881–1949................... WWasWT
Dreiser, Theodore 1871–1945 .... WWasWT
Drescher, Fran 1957–............................... CTFT–70
　　　Earlier sketches in CTFT–20, 31
Dresdal, Sonia 1909–1976 .... WWT–16
Dresser, Louise 1882–1965................... WWasWT
Dressler, Eric 1900–.............................. WWasWT
Dressler, Marie 1869–1934................... WWasWT
Dretzin, Julie CTFT–75
Drever, Constance ?–1948..................... WWasWT
Drew, John 1853–1927.......................... WWasWT
Drew, Rick CTFT–79
Drewitt, Stanley 1878–?........................ WWasWT
Drewitz, Devin Douglas 1989–............... CTFT–63
Drexler, Rosalyn CTFT–1
Dreyer, Fred
　　　See... Dryer, Fred
Dreyfus, James 1964–.............................. CTFT–62
　　　Earlier sketch in CTFT–28
Dreyfuss, Henry 1904–1972 .... WWasWT
Dreyfuss, Richard 1947– CTFT–43
　　　Earlier sketches in CTFT–1, 5, 12, 22;
　　　WWT–17
Drinkwater, Albert Edwin
　　　?–1923 .... WWasWT
Drinkwater, John 1882–1937................. WWasWT

Driscoll, Eddie CTFT–53
Drivas, Robert 1938–1986 .... CTFT–2
　　　Earlier sketch in WWT–17
Driver, Donald 1923?–1988 .... CTFT–7
　　　Earlier sketch in WWT–17
Driver, John 1947–................................... CTFT–6
Driver, Minnie 1970(?)–........................... CTFT–57
　　　Earlier sketches in CTFT–15, 26
Droomgoole, Patrick 1930–................... WWT–17
Drouet, Robert 1870–1914 .... WWasWT
Druce, Hubert 1870–1931 .... WWasWT
Drulie, Sylvia CTFT–1
Drummond, Alice 1929–......................... CTFT–79
　　　Earlier sketches in CTFT–1, 3, 35
Drummond, Brian 1969–.......................... CTFT–47
Drummond, Dolores 1834–1926........... WWasWT
Drury, Alan 1949–.................................... CTFT–5
　　　Earlier sketch in WWT–17
Drury, James 1934–.................................. CTFT–26
Drury, William Price 1861–1949........... WWasWT
Dryburgh, Stuart 1952– CTFT–58
　　　Earlier sketch in CTFT–27
Dryden, Vaughan 1875–? .... WWasWT
Dryer, Fred 1946– CTFT–39
　　　Earlier sketches in CTFT–7, 17
Dryer, John F.
　　　See... Dryer, Fred
Drymon, Derek 1965– CTFT–72
Drynan, Jeanie.. CTFT–33
Du, Kefeng
　　　See .... Doyle, Christopher
Dubar, Stan
　　　See .... Suplee, Ethan
Duberman, Martin Bauml
　　　1930–.. CTFT–1
Duberstein, Helen 1926–......................... CTFT–4
Dubin, Charles S. 1919–.......................... CTFT–11
DuBois, Ja'net 1945(?)–........................... CTFT–46
DuBois, Marta CTFT–69
Du Bois, Raoul Pene 1914–................... WWT–17
Duca, Joseph Lo
　　　See .... LoDuca, Joseph
Ducey, John CTFT–65
　　　Earlier sketch in CTFT–29
Duchene, Deborah 1962–........................ CTFT–37
Duchin, Peter 1937–................................. CTFT–1
Duchovny, David 1960– CTFT–50
　　　Earlier sketches in CTFT–14, 24
Duclow, Geraldine 1946–........................ CTFT–4
Ducommun, Rick 1956(?)–....................... CTFT–74
Dudgeon, Neil... CTFT–79
　　　Earlier sketch in CTFT–36
Dudikoff, Michael 1954– CTFT–39
　　　Earlier sketch in CTFT–13
Dudley, Anne 1956–................................ CTFT–72
　　　Earlier sketches in CTFT–20, 32
Dudley, Bide 1877–1944 .... WWasWT
Dudley, Carol L. 1949–........................... CTFT–31
　　　Earlier sketches in CTFT–2, 19
Dudley, William 1947–............................ CTFT–5
　　　Earlier sketch in WWT–17
Duell, William 1923–............................... CTFT–75
　　　Earlier sketches in CTFT–3, 33
Duff, Denice.. CTFT–54
Duff, Haylie 1985–................................... CTFT–73
Duff, Hilary 1987–.................................... CTFT–55
Duff, Howard 1917–1990 .... CTFT–6
Duff, James 1955–.................................... CTFT–73
Duffield, Kenneth 1885–?...................... WWasWT
Duffy, Julia 1951–.................................... CTFT–47
　　　Earlier sketch in CTFT–4
Duffy, Karen 1962– CTFT–26
Duffy, Maureen 1933–............................. CTFT–12

Duffy, Patrick 1949–................................ CTFT–36
　　　Earlier sketches in CTFT–3, 11
Duffy, Thomas F.. CTFT–77
　　　Earlier sketch in CTFT–34
Duflos, Raphael ?–1946 .... WWasWT
Dufour, Val 1927–.................................... CTFT–1
Dugan, Dennis 1946–.............................. CTFT–67
　　　Earlier sketches in CTFT–8, 18, 30
Dugan, Sean 1974–.................................. CTFT–76
　　　Earlier sketch in CTFT–32
Dugan, Tom CTFT–54
Duggan, Andrew 1923–1988 .... CTFT–7
Duggan, Michael....................................... CTFT–41
Duggan, P. G.
　　　See.................................... Malahide, Patrick
Duguay, Christian 1947(?)–...................... CTFT–65
　　　Earlier sketch in CTFT–29
Duhamel, Josh 1972–............................... CTFT–69
Duigan, John 1949–................................. CTFT–62
　　　Earlier sketches in CTFT–17, 28
Dukakis, Olympia 1931–......................... CTFT–57
　　　Earlier sketches in CTFT–1, 7, 15, 26
Duke, Anna Marie
　　　See.. Duke, Patty
Duke, Bill 1943–....................................... CTFT–36
　　　Earlier sketch in CTFT–10
Duke, Daryl... CTFT–12
Duke, Ivy 1896–...................................... WWasWT
Duke, Patty 1946–.................................... CTFT–77
　　　Earlier sketches in CTFT–3, 35
Duke, Vernon 1903–1969 .... WWasWT
Duke–Pearce, Anna
　　　See.. Duke, Patty
Dukes, Ashley 1885–1959..................... WWasWT
Dukes, David 1945– CTFT–30
　　　Earlier sketches in CTFT–2, 7, 18
Du Kore, Lawrence 1933– CTFT–5
Dulce Vida, Julian
　　　See .... Vida, Julian Dulce
Dullea, Keir 1936–................................... CTFT–74
　　　Earlier sketches in CTFT–4, 33; WWT–17
Dullin, Charles 1885–1949 .... WWasWT
Dullzell, Paul 1879–1961...................... WWasWT
Du Maurier, Daphne 1907–1989........... WWasWT
du Maurier, Gerald 1873–1934 .... WWasWT
Dunaway, Faye 1941–.............................. CTFT–61
　　　Earlier sketches in CTFT–1, 7, 17, 28;
　　　WWT–17
Dunbar, Rockmond 1974– CTFT–68
Dunard, David CTFT–56
Duncan, Alastair CTFT–58
Duncan, Augustin 1873–1954.............. WWasWT
Duncan, Christopher B............................. CTFT–56
Duncan, Fiona... CTFT–4
Duncan, Isadora 1880–1927 .... WWasWT
Duncan, Lindsay 1950–............................ CTFT–38
　　　Earlier sketches in CTFT–7, 14
Duncan, Malcolm 1881–1942.............. WWasWT
Duncan, Mary 1903– .... WWasWT
Duncan, Michael Clarke 1957– CTFT–59
　　　Earlier sketch in CTFT–28
Duncan, Patrick Sheane 1947(?)–......... CTFT–16
Duncan, Robert CTFT–78
Duncan, Ronald 1914–............................ WWT–17
Duncan, Rosetta 1900–1959 .... WWasWT
Duncan, Sandy 1946–.............................. CTFT–48
　　　Earlier sketches in CTFT–2, 7, 14; WWT–17
Duncan, Todd 1900–.............................. WWasWT
Duncan, Vivian 1899–1986................... WWasWT
Duncan, William Cary 1874–1945........ WWasWT
Duncan–Petley, Stella 1975–................... CTFT–4
Dunfee, Jack 1901–................................ WWasWT
Dungey, Merrin CTFT–40

Dunham, Joanna 1936– CTFT–6
  Earlier sketch in WWT–17
Dunham, Katherine 1910– WWT–17
Dunkels, Dorothy 1907– .... WWasWT
Dunkels, Marjorie 1916– .... WWasWT
Dunlap, Pamela CTFT–64
  Earlier sketch in CTFT–29
Dunlap, Robert 1942– CTFT–11
Dunlop, Frank 1927– CTFT–21
  Earlier sketches in CTFT–12; WWT–17
Dunlop, Vic, Jr. CTFT–4
Dunn, Andrew CTFT–65
Dunn, Carolyn CTFT–41
Dunn, Conrad
  See .... Jenesky, George
Dunn, Emma 1875–1966 .... WWasWT
Dunn, Geoffrey 1903– WWT–17
Dunn, Jim CTFT–43
Dunn, Joe
  See .... Dunne, Joe
Dunn, Kevin 1956– CTFT–70
  Earlier sketches in CTFT–20, 31
Dunn, Linwood G. 1904–1998 .... CTFT–25
Dunn, Nora 1952– CTFT–43
  Earlier sketches in CTFT–11, 22
Dunn, Thomas G. 1950– CTFT–1
Dunne, Dominick 1925(?)– CTFT–26
  Earlier sketches in CTFT–9, 16
Dunne, Griffin 1955– CTFT–38
  Earlier sketches in CTFT–4, 14
Dunne, Irene 1901(?)–1990 .... CTFT–10
  Earlier sketch in WWasWT
Dunne, Joe CTFT–36
Dunne, Philip 1908–1992 .... CTFT–23
Dunne, Robin 1976– CTFT–51
Dunn–Hill, John CTFT–65
Dunning, Philip 1890–1957 .... WWasWT
Dunning, Nick CTFT–36
Dunning, Ruth 1911– WWT–17
Dunnock, Mildred 1900(?)–1991 .... CTFT–8
  Obituary in CTFT–10
  Earlier sketch in WWT–17
Dunsany, Lord 1878–1957 .... WWasWT
Dunsmore, Rosemary 1953– CTFT–49
Dunst, Kirsten 1982– CTFT–55
  Earlier sketches in CTFT–15, 26
Dupont, Phil CTFT–30
Dupree, Minnie 1875–1947 .... WWasWT
Duprez, Fred 1884–1938 .... WWasWT
Duprez, June 1918– .... WWasWT
Dupuis, Roy 1963– CTFT–41
  Earlier sketch in CTFT–20
Duquesne, Edmond 1855–? .... WWasWT
Duquet, Michelle CTFT–65
du Rand, le Clanche 1941– CTFT–1
Durand, Charles 1912– CTFT–1
Durand, Kevin 1974– CTFT–74
Durang, Christopher 1949– CTFT–38
  Earlier sketches in CTFT–1, 3, 14; WWT–17
Durante, Jimmy 1893–1980 .... WWasWT
Duras, Marguerite 1914– CTFT–4
  Earlier sketch in WWT–17
Durden, Richard CTFT–34
Durmaz, Ercan CTFT–34
Durnham, Charles
  See .... Durning, Charles
Durning, Charles 1923– CTFT–38
  Earlier sketches in CTFT–5, 14
Durrell, Jane
  See .... Wyman, Jane
Durrell, Michael 1943– CTFT–61
Durrenmatt, Friedrich 1921– WWT–17
Dury, Ian 1942– CTFT–9

Du Sautoy, Carmen 1950– CTFT–5
  Earlier sketch in WWT–17
Dusay, Marj 1936– CTFT–67
  Earlier sketch in CTFT–30
Duse, Eleonora 1858–1924 .... WWasWT
Dusenberry, Ann CTFT–8
Dushku, Eliza 1980– CTFT–72
  Earlier sketch in CTFT–33
Dushku, Nate 1977– CTFT–71
Du Souchet, H. A. 1852–1922 .... WWasWT
Dussault, Nancy 1936– CTFT–62
  Earlier sketches in CTFT–4; WWT–17
d'Usseau, Arnaud 1916–1990 .... CTFT–9
  Earlier sketch in WWasWT
Dutronc, Jacques 1943– CTFT–34
Dutt, Sanjay 1959– CTFT–34
Duttine, John 1949– CTFT–73
  Earlier sketches in CTFT–2, 19, 32
Dutton, Charles S. 1951– CTFT–54
  Earlier sketches in CTFT–3, 9, 16, 26
Dutton, Tim CTFT–63
Duval, Georges 1847–1919 .... WWasWT
Duval, James 1972(?)– CTFT–48
  Earlier sketch in CTFT–23
DuVall, Clea 1977– CTFT–59
  Earlier sketch in CTFT–27
Duvall, Robert 1931– CTFT–54
  Earlier sketches in CTFT–1, 7, 15, 26
Duvall, Shelley 1949– CTFT–30
  Earlier sketches in CTFT–3, 18
Duvall, Wayne CTFT–72
  Earlier sketch in CTFT–33
Dux, Emilienne 1874–? .... WWasWT
Duxbury, Elspeth 1909–1967 .... WWasWT
Dwyer, Ada ?–1952 .... WWasWT
Dwyer, David CTFT–41
Dwyer, Deanna
  See .... Koontz, Dean R.
Dwyer, K. R.
  See .... Koontz, Dean R.
Dwyer, Leslie 1906–1986 .... WWasWT
Dyall, Frank 1874–1950 .... WWasWT
Dyall, Valentine 1908–1985 .... WWT–17
Dye, Cameron 1967– CTFT–49
Dye, Dale 1944– CTFT–43
Dye, John 1963– CTFT–41
Dyer, Charles 1928– CTFT–6
  Earlier sketch in WWT–17
Dyer, Christopher 1947– WWT–17
Dyer, Raymond
  See .... Dyer, Charles
Dykstra, John 1947– CTFT–42
  Earlier sketches in CTFT–8, 18
Dylan, Bob 1941– CTFT–31
  Earlier sketch in CTFT–20
Dynamite, Napoleon
  See .... Costello, Elvis
Dyrenforth, James .... WWasWT
Dysart, Richard A. 1929– CTFT–51
  Earlier sketches in CTFT–4, 24; WWT–17
Dziena, Alexis 1984– CTFT–68
Dzundza, George 1945– CTFT–54
  Earlier sketches in CTFT–6, 16, 26

E

Eadie, Dennis 1869–1928 .... WWasWT
Eads, George 1967– CTFT–36
Eagels, Jeanne 1894–1929 .... WWasWT
Eagles, Greg CTFT–47

Eaker, Ira 1922– CTFT–1
Eakes, Bobbie 1961– CTFT–62
Eames, Clare 1896–1930 .... WWasWT
Earle, Virginia 1875–1937 .... WWasWT
Eason, Mules 1915–1977 .... WWT–16
Easterbrook, Leslie CTFT–7
Eastin, Steve CTFT–47
Eastman, Allan CTFT–36
Eastman, Frederick 1859–1920 .... WWasWT
Easton, Michael 1967– CTFT–58
Easton, Richard 1933– CTFT–39
  Earlier sketches in CTFT–5; WWT–17
Easton, Robert 1930– CTFT–63
Easton, Sheena 1959– CTFT–76
  Earlier sketches in CTFT–21, 32
Eastwood, Alison 1972– CTFT–46
Eastwood, Clint 1930– CTFT–45
  Earlier sketches in CTFT–1, 6, 13, 23
Eastwood, Jayne CTFT–62
Eaton, Mary 1902–1948 .... WWasWT
Eaton, Wallas 1917– WWT–17
Eaton, Walter Prichard 1878–1957 .... WWasWT
Eaves, Hilary 1914– .... WWasWT
Ebb, Fred 1936(?)– CTFT–39
  Earlier sketches in CTFT–5, 13; WWT–17
Ebersol, Dick CTFT–14
Ebersole, Christine 1953– CTFT–38
  Earlier sketches in CTFT–2, 5, 14
Ebert, Joyce 1933–1997 .... CTFT–5
  Obituary in CTFT–18
  Earlier sketch in WWT–17
Ebert, Roger 1942– CTFT–35
  Earlier sketch in CTFT–9
Ebrel, Luke
  See .... Elliott, Lucas
Ebsen, Buddy 1908–2003 .... CTFT–3
  Obituary in CTFT–51
Eccles, Donald 1908–1986 .... WWT–17
Eccles, Janet 1895–1966 .... WWasWT
Eccleston, Christopher 1964– CTFT–67
  Earlier sketch in CTFT–30
Echegaray, Miguel 1848–1927 .... WWasWT
Echevarria, Rene CTFT–49
Echevarria, Rocky
  See .... Bauer, Steven
Echikunwoke, Megalyn 1983– CTFT–70
Eck, Scott 1957– CTFT–6
Eckart, Jean 1921– CTFT–3
  Earlier sketch in WWT–17
Eckart, William J. 1920– CTFT–4
  Earlier sketch in WWT–17
Eckhart, Aaaron 1968(?)– CTFT–66
  Earlier sketch in CTFT–30
Eckholdt, Steven 1960– CTFT–38
Eckhouse, James 1955– CTFT–59
  Earlier sketch in CTFT–27
Eckland, Michael
  See .... Eklund, Michael
Eckstein, George 1928– CTFT–2
Eda–Young, Barbara 1945– CTFT–5
  Earlier sketch in WWT–17
Eddinger, Wallace 1881–1929 .... WWasWT
Eddington, Paul 1927–1995 .... CTFT–14
  Obituary in CTFT–15
  Earlier sketches in CTFT–6; WWT–17
Eddison, Robert 1908– WWT–17
Eddy, Nelson 1901–1967 .... WWasWT
Eddy, Teddy Jack
  See .... Busey, Gary
Ede, George 1931– CTFT–1
Edel, Uli 1947– CTFT–61
Edelman, Gregg 1958– CTFT–41
  Earlier sketch in CTFT–9

Edelman, Herbert 1933–1996 .... CTFT–6
  Obituary in CTFT–16
  Earlier sketch in CTFT–1
Edelman, Randy 1947(?)– CTFT–70
  Earlier sketches in CTFT–12, 21, 31
Edelson, Kenneth CTFT–70
  Earlier sketch in CTFT–31
Edelstein, Lisa 1967– CTFT–60
  Earlier sketches in CTFT–17, 28
Eden, Barbara 1934– CTFT–36
  Earlier sketches in CTFT–3, 9
Eden, Diana CTFT–62
Eden, Richard 1956– CTFT–42
Eden, Sidney 1936– CTFT–2
Eder, Linda 1961– CTFT–37
Edeson, Arthur 1891–1970 .... CTFT–26
Edeson, Robert 1868–1931 .... WWasWT
Edgar, David 1948– CTFT–6
  Earlier sketch in WWT–17
Edgar, Marriott 1880–1951 .... WWasWT
Edgar–Bruce, Tonie
  See .... Bruce, Tonie Edgar
Edgerton, Joel 1974– CTFT–49
Edgett, Edwin Francis 1867–1946......... WWasWT
Edgeworth, Jane 1922– WWT–17
Edginton, May ?–1957 .... WWasWT
Edgley, Michael 1943– CTFT–5
  Earlier sketch in WWT–17
Ediss, Connie 1871–1934 .... WWasWT
Edlin, Tubby (Henry) 1882–? .... WWasWT
Edlund, Richard 1940– CTFT–41
  Earlier sketch in CTFT–9
Edmead, Wendy CTFT–1
Edmiston, Walker CTFT–53
Edmonson, Wallace
  See .... Ellison, Harlan
Edmondson, Adrian 1957– CTFT–59
  Earlier sketch in CTFT–27
Edner, Ashley 1990– CTFT–67
  Earlier sketch in CTFT–30
Edner, Bobby 1988– CTFT–59
Edney, Florence 1879–1950 .... WWasWT
Edouin, Rose 1844–1925...................... WWasWT
Edson, Richard 1954– CTFT–67
  Earlier sketch in CTFT–30
Edwardes, Felix ?–1954 .... WWasWT
Edwardes, George 1852–1915.............. WWasWT
Edwardes, Olga 1917– .... WWasWT
Edwardes, Paula .... WWasWT
Edwards, Anthony 1962– CTFT–47
  Earlier sketches in CTFT–6, 14, 23
Edwards, Ben 1916– CTFT–9
  Earlier sketch in WWT–17
Edwards, Blake 1922– CTFT–49
  Earlier sketches in CTFT–1, 6, 15
Edwards, Burt 1928– CTFT–2
Edwards, Edward CTFT–58
Edwards, Eric Alan 1953–.................... CTFT–54
  Earlier sketches in CTFT–15, 26
Edwards, G. Spencer ?–1916 .... WWasWT
Edwards, Henry 1883–1952 .... WWasWT
Edwards, Hilton 1903– WWT–17
Edwards, Julie
  See .... Andrews, Julie
Edwards, Maurice 1922– CTFT–1
Edwards, Monique................................ CTFT–59
Edwards, Osman 1864–1936................. WWasWT
Edwards, Ralph...................................... CTFT–3
Edwards, Rob 1963–............................. CTFT–11
Edwards, Sherman 1919–1981 .... WWT–17
Edwards, Stacy 1965– CTFT–70
  Earlier sketches in CTFT–20, 31
Edwards, Stephen CTFT–58

Edwards, Tom 1880–?........................... WWasWT
Edwards, Vince 1928–1996..................... CTFT–7
  Obituary in CTFT–16
Efron, Zac 1987–.................................... CTFT–74
Egan, Kim CTFT–48
Egan, Maggie CTFT–53
Egan, Michael 1895–1956 .... WWasWT
Egan, Michael 1926– CTFT–19
  Earlier sketch in CTFT–2
Egan, Peter 1946– CTFT–73
  Earlier sketches in CTFT–5, 33; WWT–17
Egan, Susan 1970– CTFT–72
  Earlier sketches in CTFT–20, 32
Egbert, Brothers (Seth and Albert) .... WWasWT
Egerton, George 1860–1945 .... WWasWT
Eggar, Jack 1904– .... WWasWT
Eggar, Samantha 1939– CTFT–73
  Earlier sketches in CTFT–1, 8, 33
Eggby, David 1950– CTFT–55
Eggert, Nicole 1972– CTFT–47
  Earlier sketches in CTFT–4, 14, 23
Eggerth, Marta 1916– CTFT–1
  Earlier sketch in WWasWT
Egoyan, Atom 1960– CTFT–48
  Earlier sketches in CTFT–15, 24
Ehle, Jennifer 1969– CTFT–43
  Earlier sketch in CTFT–22
Ehrlich, Ken CTFT–36
  Earlier sketch in CTFT–11
Eichelberger, Ethyl 1945–1990 .... CTFT–9
Eichhorn, Lisa 1952– CTFT–46
  Earlier sketches in CTFT–6, 13, 23
Eick, David 1968– CTFT–65
Eidelman, Cliff 1967– CTFT–43
  Earlier sketches in CTFT–11, 22
Eiding, Paul CTFT–37
Eigeman, Christopher 1965– CTFT–47
  Earlier sketch in CTFT–23
Eigenburg, David 1964–....................... CTFT–61
Eigsti, Karl 1938– CTFT–5
  Earlier sketch in WWT–17
Eikenberry, Jill 1947(?)– CTFT–46
  Earlier sketches in CTFT–5, 14, 23
Eilbacher, Lisa CTFT–6
Einbinder, Chad 1963(?)–...................... CTFT–74
Einstein, Albert
  See.. Brooks, Albert
Einstein, Bob CTFT–36
Eisele, Robert 1948–............................ CTFT–4
Eisenberg, Ned 1957–.......................... CTFT–53
Eisenstein, Sergei 1898–1948 .... CTFT–29
Eisinger, Irene 1906– .... WWasWT
Eisner, David CTFT–62
Eisner, Michael D. 1942– CTFT–53
  Earlier sketches in CTFT–1, 10, 18
Ejogo, Carmen 1974–........................... CTFT–36
Ekberg, Anita 1931–............................. CTFT–18
  Earlier sketch in CTFT–7
Ekland, Britt 1942–............................... CTFT–53
  Earlier sketches in CTFT–7, 18
Eklund, Michael CTFT–65
Elam, Jack 1916– CTFT–6
  Earlier sketch in CTFT–2
Elcar, Dana 1927–................................ CTFT–6
Eldard, Ron 1965–................................ CTFT–64
  Earlier sketches in CTFT–17, 29
Elder, Eldon 1924– WWT–17
Elder, Lonne III 1931– CTFT–7
  Earlier sketch in WWT–17
Eldred, Arthur ?–1942 .... WWasWT
Eldridge, Craig...................................... CTFT–56
Eldridge, Florence 1901–1988............... WWasWT

Electra, Carmen 1972–.......................... CTFT–67
  Earlier sketch in CTFT–30
Elejalde, Karra 1960–............................ CTFT–35
Elen, Gus 1862–1940 .... WWasWT
Eleniak, Erika 1969–.............................. CTFT–60
  Earlier sketch in CTFT–28
El Fadil, Siddig
  See............................... Siddig, Alexander
Elfman, Bodhi 1968–............................ CTFT–43
Elfman, Danny 1953–............................ CTFT–64
  Earlier sketches in CTFT–10, 18, 29
Elfman, Jenna 1971– CTFT–45
  Earlier sketch in CTFT–23
Elg, Taina 1930–................................... CTFT–1
Elgar, Avril 1932–................................. CTFT–5
  Earlier sketch in WWT–17
Elias, Hector WWT–17
Elias, Jeannie CTFT–38
Elias, Jonathan CTFT–48
Elias, Michael 1940–............................ CTFT–4
Eliasberg, Jan 1954–............................ CTFT–1
Elias–Fahn, Dorothy
  See .... Melendrez, Dorothy
Eliason, Joyce 1934– CTFT–68
Elikann, Larry 1923– CTFT–21
  Earlier sketches in CTFT–2, 12
Eliot, T. S. (Thomas Stearns)
  1888–1965 .... WWasWT
Eliscu, Fernanda 1882–1968 .... WWasWT
Elise, Christine 1965–........................... CTFT–59
  Earlier sketch in CTFT–27
Elise, Kimberly 1971–........................... CTFT–61
Eliza, Adrienne
  See.................................. Bailon, Adrienne
Elizabeth, Shannon 1973–...................... CTFT–67
  Earlier sketch in CTFT–30
Elizondo, Hector 1936– CTFT–47
  Earlier sketches in CTFT–2, 7, 14, 23;
    WWT–17
Elkin, Ilona 1976– CTFT–65
Elkins, Hillard 1929–............................ WWT–17
Ellenshaw, Peter 1913–........................ CTFT–9
Ellenstein, Robert 1923–...................... CTFT–1
Ellerbe, Harry 1906– CTFT–1
Ellerbee, Linda 1944–........................... CTFT–41
  Earlier sketch in CTFT–6
Ellinger, Desiree 1893–1951................. WWasWT
Ellingson, Evan 1988–.......................... CTFT–73
Elliot, Jane 1947–................................. CTFT–62
Elliot, Samuel B.
  See.................................... Page, Samuel
Elliott, Alice 1946–............................... CTFT–4
Elliott, Alison 1970–............................. CTFT–39
  Earlier sketch in CTFT–17
Elliott, Brennan CTFT–74
Elliott, Chris 1960–............................... CTFT–70
  Earlier sketches in CTFT–12, 21, 31
Elliott, David James 1960– CTFT–60
  Earlier sketches in CTFT–17, 28
Elliott, Denholm 1922–1992 .... CTFT–11
  Earlier sketches in CTFT–4; WWT–17
Elliott, George 1899–............................ WWasWT
Elliott, George H. 1884–? .... WWasWT
Elliott, Gertrude 1874–1950 .... WWasWT
Elliott, Lucas 1986–.............................. CTFT–76
Elliott, Madge 1898–1955 .... WWasWT
Elliott, Maxine 1871–1932 .... WWasWT
Elliott, Michael (Allwyn) 1936–................ CTFT–1
Elliott, Michael 1931–1984 .... WWT–17
Elliott, Patricia 1942– CTFT–54
  Earlier sketch in WWT–17
Elliott, Paul 1941–................................ WWT–17

Elliott, Sam 1944– CTFT–44
   Earlier sketches in CTFT–3, 11, 22
Elliott, Scott 1963(?)– CTFT–29
Elliott, Stephen 1945– WWT–17
Elliott, Sumner Locke 1917–1991 .... CTFT–1
   Obituary in CTFT–10
Elliott, Ted CTFT–55
Elliott, Tom
   See .... Jane, Thomas
Elliott, William 1885–1932 .... WWasWT
Ellis, Anita 1920– CTFT–3
Ellis, Anthony L. ?–1944 .... WWasWT
Ellis, Aunjanue 1969– CTFT–64
Ellis, Chris 1956– CTFT–75
   Earlier sketch in CTFT–33
Ellis, Edith 1876–1960 .... WWasWT
Ellis, Edward 1872–1952 .... WWasWT
Ellis, Greg 1968– CTFT–55
Ellis, Landon
   See .... Ellison, Harlan
Ellis, Larry
   See .... Mordente, Tony
Ellis, Leslie 1962– CTFT–5
Ellis, Mary 1900– WWT–17
Ellis, Peter CTFT–45
Ellis, Scott 1957– CTFT–47
   Earlier sketch in CTFT–23
Ellis, Vivian WWT–17
Ellis, Walter 1874–1956 .... WWasWT
Ellison, Harlan 1934– CTFT–36
Elliston, Daisy 1894– .... WWasWT
Elliston, Grace 1881–1950 .... WWasWT
Ellroy, James 1948– CTFT–43
   Earlier sketch in CTFT–22
Ellsworth, Kiko 1973– CTFT–75
Ellwand, Greg CTFT–62
Elmaleh, Gad CTFT–34
Elmes, Frederick CTFT–70
   Earlier sketches in CTFT–19, 31
Elsen, John 1964– CTFT–79
   Earlier sketch in CTFT–36
Elsie, Lily 1886–1962 .... WWasWT
Elso, Pascal CTFT–36
Elsom, Isobel 1893– .... WWasWT
Elsom, John 1934– WWT–17
Elson, Anita 1898– .... WWasWT
Elston, Robert 1934–1987 .... CTFT–1
Elswit, Robert CTFT–64
   Earlier sketch in CTFT–29
Eltinge, Julian 1883–1941 .... WWasWT
Elton, George 1875–1942 .... WWasWT
Elvey, Maurice 1887–1967 .... WWasWT
Elvin, Joe 1862–1935 .... WWasWT
Elvin, Violetta 1925– .... WWasWT
Elvira
   See .... Peterson, Cassandra
Elwes, Cary 1962– CTFT–38
   Earlier sketches in CTFT–7, 14
Ely, Ron 1938– CTFT–27
Embry, Ethan 1978– CTFT–48
Emerald, Connie ?–1959 .... WWasWT
Emerson, Faye 1917–1983 .... WWasWT
Emerson, John 1874–1956 .... WWasWT
Emerton, Roy 1892–1944 .... WWasWT
Emery, Gilbert 1875–1945 .... WWasWT
Emery, John 1905–1964 .... WWasWT
Emery, Julie Ann CTFT–67
Emery, Katherine 1908– .... WWasWT
Emery, Lisa CTFT–59
   Earlier sketch in CTFT–27
Emery, Pollie 1875–1958 .... WWasWT
Emery, Winifred 1862–1924 .... WWasWT
Emhardt, Robert 1901?– .... WWasWT

Emick, Jarrod 1969– CTFT–22
Emmerich, Noah 1965– CTFT–46
Emmerich, Roland 1955– CTFT–69
   Earlier sketches in CTFT–19, 31
Emmet, Alfred 1908– WWT–17
Emmett, Robert 1921– CTFT–11
Emmons, Beverly 1943– CTFT–2
Emmons, Wayne CTFT–4
Emney, Fred 1865–1917 .... WWasWT
Emney, Fred 1900– WWT–17
Emney, Joan Fred .... WWasWT
Emonts, Ann 1952– CTFT–1
Emshwiller, Susan CTFT–58
Enberg, Alexander 1972– CTFT–67
Enberg, Dick 1935– CTFT–56
   Earlier sketches in CTFT–14, 23
Encinas, Javier
   See .... Bardem, Javier
Endelman, Stephen CTFT–58
Ender, Peter CTFT–36
Endoso, Kenny CTFT–42
Endre, Toth
   See .... De Toth, Andre
Enfield, Harry 1961– CTFT–34
Engar, Keith M. 1923– WWT–17
Engel, Georgia 1948– CTFT–41
   Earlier sketches in CTFT–2, 19
Engel, Lehman 1910–1982 .... CTFT–2
Engel, Stephen CTFT–66
Engel, Susan 1935– CTFT–3
   Earlier sketch in WWT–17
Engelbach, David CTFT–4
England, Paul 1893–1968 .... WWasWT
Englander, Ludwig 1853–1914 .... WWasWT
Engle, Debra 1953– CTFT–7
English Stage Company Ltd, The .... WWasWT
English, Diane 1948– CTFT–50
   Earlier sketch in CTFT–11
Englund, Robert 1949(?)– CTFT–48
   Earlier sketches in CTFT–8, 15, 24
Eno, Terry 1948– CTFT–20
   Earlier sketch in CTFT–2
Enriquez, Rene 1933–1990 .... CTFT–7
   Earlier sketch in CTFT–2
Ensign, Michael 1944– CTFT–78
   Earlier sketch in CTFT–35
Enthoven, Gabrielle 1868–1950 .... WWasWT
Epcar, Richard 1955– CTFT–49
Ephraim, Lee 1877–1953 .... WWasWT
Ephron, Nora 1941– CTFT–48
   Earlier sketches in CTFT–8, 15, 24
Eplin, Tom 1960– CTFT–17
Eppolito, Louis CTFT–30
Epps, Jack, Jr. 1949– CTFT–53
   Earlier sketch in CTFT–16
Epps, Mike 1970– CTFT–77
Epps, Omar 1973– CTFT–77
   Earlier sketch in CTFT–34
Epps, Sheldon 1952– CTFT–75
   Earlier sketches in CTFT–3, 33
Epstein, Alvin 1925– CTFT–49
   Earlier sketches in CTFT–9; WWT–17
Epstein, Pierre 1930– CTFT–4
   Earlier sketch in WWT–17
Erbe, Kathryn 1966– CTFT–60
   Earlier sketch in CTFT–28
Erbe, Mickey CTFT–4
Erdman, Jean 1916– CTFT–4
Eric, Fred 1874–1935 .... WWasWT
Erickson, Ethan 1973– CTFT–74
Erickson, Jim CTFT–64
   Earlier sketch in CTFT–29
Erickson, Mitchell 1927– CTFT–2

Eriksen, Kaj–Erik 1979– CTFT–61
Eriksson, Buntel
   See .... Bergman, Ingmar
Eriksson, Buntel
   See .... Josephson, Erland
Erlanger, Abraham L. 1860–1930 .... WWasWT
Erman, John 1935– CTFT–42
   Earlier sketches in CTFT–1, 10, 18
Ermey, R. Lee 1944– CTFT–69
   Earlier sketches in CTFT–19, 31
Erne, Vincent 1884–? .... WWasWT
Ernotte, Andre Gilbert 1943–1999 .... CTFT–1
   Obituary in CTFT–32
Errico, Melissa 1970– CTFT–43
   Earlier sketch in CTFT–22
Errol, Leon, 1881–1951 .... WWasWT
Erskine, Chester 1903–1986 .... WWasWT
Erskine, Howard (Weir) 1926– CTFT–1
Ertmanis, Victor CTFT–56
Ervine, St. John Greer 1883–1971 .... WWasWT
Erwin, Bill 1914– CTFT–77
Erwin, Mike 1978– CTFT–75
Escandon, Fernando CTFT–40
Escargot, Maurice
   See .... Oldman, Gary
Escoffier, Jean–Yves CTFT–27
Esmond, Annie 1873–1945 .... WWasWT
Esmond, Carl 1905– .... WWasWT
Esmond, Henry V. 1869–1922 .... WWasWT
Esmond, Jill 1908–1990 .... WWasWT
Esparza, Raul 1970(?)– CTFT–49
Espenson, Jane CTFT–49
Espinosa, Edouard 1872–1950 .... WWasWT
Esposito, Giancarlo 1958– CTFT–69
   Earlier sketches in CTFT–21, 31
Esposito, Jennifer 1973(?)– CTFT–53
   Earlier sketch in CTFT–25
Essex, David 1947– CTFT–39
   Earlier sketches in CTFT–3, 13; WWT–17
Esslin, Martin 1918– WWT–17
Estabrook, Christine CTFT–75
   Earlier sketches in CTFT–6, 33
Estabrook, Howard 1884–? .... WWasWT
Estefan, Gloria 1957– CTFT–40
Esten, Charles 1965– CTFT–43
Esterman, Laura 1945– CTFT–49
   Earlier sketches in CTFT–1, 11
Estes, Rob 1963– CTFT–69
   Earlier sketches in CTFT–19, 31
Estes, Will 1978– CTFT–68
Estevez, Emilio 1962– CTFT–64
   Earlier sketches in CTFT–3, 10, 19, 29
   Brief Entry in CTFT–2
Estevez, Ramon G.
   See .... Sheen, Martin
Estevez, Renee 1967– CTFT–45
Estrada, Erik 1949– CTFT–69
   Earlier sketches in CTFT–3, 19, 31
Eszterhas, Joe 1944(?)– CTFT–38
   Earlier sketches in CTFT–7, 14
Etherington, James 1902–1948 .... WWasWT
Etic, Stan
   See .... Hoffman, Dustin
Etienne, Treva CTFT–71
Ett, Alan 1952– CTFT–72
   Earlier sketches in CTFT–12, 21, 32
Etting, Ruth 1907–1978 .... WWasWT
Ettinger, Cynthia CTFT–58
Eubanks, Bob 1937(?)– CTFT–54
Eurythmics
   See .... Stewart, David A.
Eustrel, Antony 1904– .... WWasWT
Evangelista, Daniella 1982– CTFT–56

Evans, Andrea 1957– CTFT–54
Evans, Bruce A. 1946– CTFT–53
   Earlier sketch in CTFT–10
Evans, Caradoc 1878–1945 .... WWasWT
Evans, Chris 1966– CTFT–69
   Earlier sketch in CTFT–30
Evans, Chris 1981– CTFT–67
Evans, Clifford 1912– .... WWasWT
Evans, Damon 1950– CTFT–10
Evans, David
   See .... Evans, Dillon
Evans, David M. 1962– CTFT–70
Evans, Dillon 1921– CTFT–6
   Earlier sketch in WWT–17
Evans, Don 1938– CTFT–1
Evans, Edith 1888–1976 .... WWT–16
Evans, Jessie 1918– WWT–17
Evans, Josh Ryan 1982– CTFT–30
Evans, Judi
   See .... Luciano, Judi Evans
Evans, Lee 1964– CTFT–46
Evans, Linda 1942– CTFT–3
Evans, Madge 1909–1981 .... WWasWT
Evans, Maurice 1901–1989 .... CTFT–7
   Earlier sketch in WWT–17
Evans, Michael 1922– .... WWasWT
Evans, Michael Jonas 1949– CTFT–3
Evans, Nancy 1915– .... WWasWT
Evans, Ray 1915– CTFT–1
Evans, Robert 1930– CTFT–35
   Earlier sketch in CTFT–6
Evans, Serena CTFT–34
Evans, Tenniel 1926– WWT–17
Evans, Troy 1948– CTFT–64
   Earlier sketch in CTFT–29
Evans, Will 1873–1931 .... WWasWT
Evans, Winifred 1890– .... WWasWT
Eve 1978– CTFT–65
Eve, Trevor 1951– CTFT–79
   Earlier sketches in CTFT–9, 35
Eveling, (Harry) Stanley 1925– WWT–17
Evelyn, Clara 1886–? .... WWasWT
Evelyn, Judith 1913–1967 .... WWasWT
Evennett, Wallace 1888–? .... WWasWT
Everage, Dame Edna
   See .... Humphries, Barry
Everest, Barbara 1890–1968 .... WWasWT
Everett, Chad 1936(?)– CTFT–67
   Earlier sketches in CTFT–3, 19, 30
Everett, Rupert 1959– CTFT–65
   Earlier sketches in CTFT–8, 19, 29
Everett, Tom CTFT–37
Everhard, Nancy 1957– CTFT–69
Everhart, Angie 1969– CTFT–65
   Earlier sketches in CTFT–19, 29
Everhart, Rex 1920– WWT–17
Everson, William K. 1929– CTFT–17
Evert, Chris 1954– CTFT–45
Everton, Deborah CTFT–56
Evett, Robert 1874–1949 .... WWasWT
Evigan, Greg 1953– CTFT–51
   Earlier sketches in CTFT–7, 15, 24
Ewart, Stephen T. 1869–? .... WWasWT
Ewell, Tom 1909–1994 .... CTFT–4
   Obituary in CTFT–13
   Earlier sketch in WWT–17
Ewen, Lesley CTFT–54
Ewing, Blake McIver 1985– CTFT–71
Ewing, Nicole CTFT–49
Eyen, Jerome
   See .... Eyen, Tom

Eyen, Tom 1941–1991 .... CTFT–3
   Obituary in CTFT–10
   Earlier sketches in CTFT–1; WWT–17
Eyre, Laurence 1881–1959 .... WWasWT
Eyre, Peter 1942– CTFT–79
   Earlier sketches in CTFT–36; WWT–17
Eyre, Richard 1943– CTFT–42
   Earlier sketches in CTFT–12, 21; WWT–17
Eyre, Ronald 1929– CTFT–6
   Earlier sketch in WWT–17
Eysselinck, Walter 1931– WWT–17
Eythe, William 1918–1957 .... WWasWT
Eyton, Frank 1894– .... WWasWT

F

Faat, Jau Yun
   See .... Chow Yun–Fat
Fabares, Shelley 1944(?)– CTFT–27
   Earlier sketches in CTFT–6, 14
Faber, Beryl ?–1912 .... WWasWT
Faber, Leslie 1879–1929 .... WWasWT
Faber, Mrs. Leslie 1880–? .... WWasWT
Faber, Ron 1933– CTFT–5
   Earlier sketch in WWT–17
Fabian, Madge 1880–? .... WWasWT
Fabian, Patrick CTFT–63
Fabiani, Joel 1936– CTFT–56
   Earlier sketch in CTFT–22
Fabio 1959– CTFT–42
   Earlier sketch in CTFT–20
Fabray, Nanette CTFT–4
   Earlier sketch in WWT–17
Fabre, Emile 1870–1955 .... WWasWT
Facinelli, Peter 1973– CTFT–46
Fadal, Shannon Elizabeth
   See .... Elizabeth, Shannon
Fagan, James Bernard 1873–1933 .... WWasWT
Fagan, Myron C. .... WWasWT
Fagerbakke, Bill CTFT–61
   Earlier sketches in CTFT–17, 28
Fahey, Jeff 1952– CTFT–65
   Earlier sketches in CTFT–10, 18, 29
Fahlenbock, Megan CTFT–68
Fahn, Dorothy Elias
   See .... Melendrez, Dorothy
Fahn, Melissa
   See .... Charles, Melissa
Fahn, Tom 1962– CTFT–74
Fain, Sammy 1902–1989 .... CTFT–9
Fair, Adrah 1897– .... WWasWT
Fair, Jeff Eden CTFT–54
Fairbanks, Douglas 1883–1939 .... WWasWT
Fairbanks, Douglas, Jr. 1909– CTFT–3
   Earlier sketch in WWT–17
Fairbrother, Sydney 1872–1941 .... WWasWT
Fairchild, Morgan 1950– CTFT–38
   Earlier sketches in CTFT–2, 5, 14
Fairfax, Lance 1899– .... WWasWT
Fairfax, Lettice 1876–1948 .... WWasWT
Fairfax, Marion 1879–? .... WWasWT
Fairlie, Kristin 1986(?)– CTFT–42
Fairman, Austin 1892–1964 .... WWasWT
Fairman, Michael 1934– CTFT–64
Fairservis, Elfie 1957– CTFT–3
Fairweather, David C. 1899– WWT–17
Fairweather, Virginia 1922– WWT–17
Faison, Donald Adeosun 1974– CTFT–36

Faison, Frankie 1949– CTFT–49
   Earlier sketches in CTFT–8, 15, 24
Faison, George 1947– CTFT–8
Faison, Matthew CTFT–39
   Earlier sketch in CTFT–8
Faison, Sandy CTFT–8
Faith, Rosemary CTFT–4
Faithfull, Marianne 1946– WWT–17
Faix, Anna 1930– CTFT–2
Faizon
   See .... Love, Faizon
Falabella, John CTFT–6
Falck, Lionel 1889–1971 .... WWasWT
Falco, Edie 1963(?)– CTFT–72
   Earlier sketch in CTFT–32
Falcon, Ellen CTFT–11
Falconi, Armando .... WWasWT
Falk, Peter 1927– CTFT–50
   Earlier sketches in CTFT–1, 6, 13, 24
Falkinberg, Page
   See .... Page, Dallas
Falkinburg, Page 1956– CTFT–30
Fallon, Jimmy 1974– CTFT–63
Fallon, Richard G. 1923– CTFT–1
Fallon, Siobhan 1972– CTFT–43
   Earlier sketch in CTFT–22
Falls, Gregory A. 1922– CTFT–1
Falls, Robert 1954– CTFT–39
   Earlier sketch in CTFT–15
Falsey, John 1951– CTFT–22
   Earlier sketch in CTFT–11
Faltermeyer, Harold 1952– CTFT–10
Fancourt, Darrell 1888–1953 .... WWasWT
Fancy, Richard CTFT–36
Fann, Al 1925– CTFT–51
Fanning, Dakota 1994– CTFT–63
Fanning, Elle 1998– CTFT–63
Fanning, Tony CTFT–79
Faracy, Stephanie 1952– CTFT–79
   Earlier sketches in CTFT–11, 36
Faraday, Philip Michael 1875–1969 ...... WWasWT
Faragallah, Ramsey CTFT–67
   Earlier sketch in CTFT–30
Farah, Jameel
   See .... Farr, Jamie
Farentino, Debrah 1961– CTFT–55
   Earlier sketch in CTFT–26
Farentino, James 1938– CTFT–29
   Earlier sketches in CTFT–2, 7, 18; WWT–17
Farer, Ronnie 1951– CTFT–7
Fargas, Antonio 1946– CTFT–76
   Earlier sketches in CTFT–1, 8, 33
Farina, Dennis 1944– CTFT–43
   Earlier sketch in CTFT–22
Faris, Anna 1976– CTFT–66
Faris, Sean 1982– CTFT–68
Farjeon, Herbert 1887–1945 .... WWasWT
Farjeon, Joseph Jefferson 1883–1955 .... WWasWT
Farkoa, Maurice 1867–1916 .... WWasWT
Farleigh, Lynn 1942– CTFT–65
   Earlier sketches in CTFT–3, 19, 29; WWT–17
Farley, Chris 1964–1997 .... CTFT–20
Farley, Morgan 1898–1988 .... CTFT–7
   Earlier sketch in WWasWT
Farmer, Bill CTFT–40
Farmer, Gary 1953– CTFT–54
   Earlier sketches in CTFT–16, 26
Farmer, Ken CTFT–43
Farmiga, Vera 1973– CTFT–61
   Earlier sketch in CTFT–28
Farnsworth, Richard 1920– CTFT–29
   Earlier sketches in CTFT–3, 20
Farnum, Dustin 1874–1929 .... WWasWT

Farnum, William 1876–1953 .... WWasWT
Farone, Felicia 1961– CTFT–7
Farquhar, Malcolm 1924– CTFT–5
    Earlier sketch in WWT–17
Farquhar–Bennett, Nigel
    See.. Cleese, John
Farquharson, Robert 1877–1966........... WWasWT
Farr, Derek 1912–1986........................... CTFT–3
    Earlier sketch in WWT–17
Farr, Diane 1973–.................................. CTFT–75
Farr, Florence 1860–1917 .... WWasWT
Farr, Jamie 1934– CTFT–42
    Earlier sketches in CTFT–1, 20
Farr, Shonda CTFT–59
Farrah 1926– CTFT–5
    Earlier sketch in WWT–17
Farrand, Jan 1925– WWT–17
Farrar, Gwen 1899–1944 .... WWasWT
Farrell, Charles 1900(?)–1990 .... CTFT–9
    Earlier sketch in WWT–17
Farrell, Colin 1976– CTFT–62
Farrell, Glenda 1904–1971 .... WWasWT
Farrell, M. J. 1905– .... WWasWT
Farrell, Marty CTFT–49
    Earlier sketch in CTFT–11
Farrell, Mike 1939– CTFT–59
    Earlier sketches in CTFT–1, 4, 27
Farrell, Nicholas CTFT–35
Farrell, Paul 1893– .... WWasWT
Farrell, Shea 1957– CTFT–5
Farrell, Terry 1963– CTFT–54
    Earlier sketch in CTFT–26
Farrell, Tom Riis CTFT–64
    Earlier sketch in CTFT–29
Farrelly, Bobby 1958(?)– CTFT–43
    Earlier sketch in CTFT–22
Farrelly, Peter 1956– CTFT–47
    Earlier sketch in CTFT–23
Farren, Babs 1904– .... WWasWT
Farren, Fred ?–1956 .... WWasWT
Farren, William 1853–1937 .... WWasWT
Farrer, Ann 1916– .... WWasWT
Farrow, Mia 1945– CTFT–36
    Earlier sketches in CTFT–1, 7; WWT–17
Farwell, Jonathan 1932–....................... CTFT–20
    Earlier sketch in CTFT–2
Fasano, John CTFT–61
Faso, Laurie CTFT–54
Fassbinder, Rainer Werner
    1946–1982 .... CTFT–1
Fassler, Ron CTFT–46
Fat, Chow Yuen
    See.. Chow Yun–Fat
Fatone, Joey 1977–............................... CTFT–48
Fauchois, Rene 1882–1962 .... WWasWT
Faulkner, James 1948–........................... CTFT–62
Faustino, David 1974– CTFT–69
    Earlier sketches in CTFT–12, 21, 31
Favart, Edmee ?–1941 .... WWasWT
Faversham, William 1868–1940 .... WWasWT
Favre, Gina .... WWasWT
Favreau, Jon 1966– CTFT–47
    Earlier sketch in CTFT–23
Fawcett, Alan CTFT–46
Fawcett, Charles S. 1855–1922 .... WWasWT
Fawcett, Eric 1904– .... WWasWT
Fawcett, Farrah 1947–............................ CTFT–75
    Earlier sketches in CTFT–1, 4, 34
Fawcett, George 1860–1939.................. WWasWT
Fawcett, L'Estrange .... WWasWT
Fawcett, Marion 1886–1957.................. WWasWT
Fawcett–Majors, Farrah
    See.. Fawcett, Farrah

Fawn, James 1850–1961 .... WWasWT
Fay, Meagen CTFT–61
Fay, William George 1872–1949........... WWasWT
Faye, Alice 1915–1998 .... CTFT–27
Faye, Joey 1910–................................... WWT–17
Faye, Tina
    See .... Fey, Tina
Fayne, Greta .... WWasWT
Fayre, Eleanor 1910– .... WWasWT
Fazan, Eleanor 1930– WWT–17
Fealy, Maude 1883–1971 .... WWasWT
Fearl, Clifford CTFT–1
Fearnley, John 1914–............................... CTFT–1
Fearnley, Neill CTFT–39
Fearon, George Edward 1901– .... WWasWT
Fearon, Ray 1967– CTFT–71
    Earlier sketch in CTFT–32
Feast, Michael 1946– CTFT–44
    Earlier sketches in CTFT–2, 22; WWT–17
Featherston, Vane 1864–1948 .... WWasWT
Featherstone, Angela 1965– CTFT–44
    Earlier sketch in CTFT–20
Febre, Louis CTFT–53
Feder, A. H. 1909–1997 .... CTFT–7
    Obituary in CTFT–17
    Earlier sketch in WWT–17
Federkiewicz, Stefania
    See .... Powers, Stefanie
Feely, Terence 1928– CTFT–6
    Earlier sketch in WWT–17
Feeney, Caroleen CTFT–35
Fega, Russ CTFT–34
Fehr, Brendan 1977– CTFT–61
Fehr, Oded 1970– CTFT–41
Feiffer, Jules 1929– CTFT–1
    Earlier sketch in WWT–17
Feig, Paul CTFT–39
Feingold, Michael 1945–......................... CTFT–3
    Earlier sketch in WWT–17
Feinman, Joshua 1971– CTFT–78
Feinstein, Michael 1956– CTFT–36
    Earlier sketch in CTFT–11
Feirstein, Bruce 1953–............................ CTFT–28
Feist, Gene 1930– CTFT–5
    Earlier sketch in WWT–17
Feldman, Corey 1971– CTFT–49
    Earlier sketches in CTFT–8, 15, 24
Feldman, Edward S. 1929–..................... CTFT–36
    Earlier sketch in CTFT–10
Feldman, Marty 1934–1982 .... CTFT–1
Feldon, Barbara 1941–............................ CTFT–6
Feldshuh, Tovah 1952– CTFT–45
    Earlier sketches in CTFT–1, 11, 22; WWT–17
Felgate, Peter 1919–.............................. WWasWT
Felix, Hugo 1866–1934 .... WWasWT
Fell, Norman 1924–1998 .... CTFT–19
    Obituary in CTFT–24
    Earlier sketch in CTFT–3
Fellini, Federico 1920–1993..................... CTFT–7
    Obituary in CTFT–12
    Earlier sketch in CTFT–1
Fellowes–Robinson, Dora
    ?–1946 .... WWasWT
Felt, Jan Broberg CTFT–75
Felton, Lindsay 1984– CTFT–69
Felton, Tom 1987– CTFT–67
Fenn, Frederick 1868–1924.................. WWasWT
Fenn, Sherilyn 1965– CTFT–64
    Earlier sketches in CTFT–10, 18, 29
Fenton, George 1950–............................. CTFT–50
    Earlier sketches in CTFT–9, 24
Fenwick, Irene 1887–1936 .... WWasWT

Feore, Colm.. CTFT–64
    Earlier sketch in CTFT–29
Feraudy, Jacques de .... WWasWT
Feraudy, Maurice de 1859–.................. WWasWT
Ferber, Edna 1887–1968...................... WWasWT
Ferguson, Catherine 1895–................... WWasWT
Ferguson, Colin 1972– CTFT–53
Ferguson, Craig 1962–............................ CTFT–75
    Earlier sketch in CTFT–33
Ferguson, Elsie 1885–1961 .... WWasWT
Ferguson, J. Don..................................... CTFT–43
    Earlier sketch in CTFT–22
Ferguson, John
    See............................... Pyper–Ferguson, John
Ferguson, Mark 1961–............................ CTFT–43
Ferguson, Sandra 1967– CTFT–56
Ferguson, Stacy 1975– CTFT–68
Ferland, Jodelle 1994– CTFT–61
Fern, Sable 1876–? .... WWasWT
Fernald, Chester Bailey 1869–1938....... WWasWT
Fernald, John 1905–.............................. WWT–17
Fernan Gomez, Fernando 1921– CTFT–33
Fernandez, Bijou 1877–1961 .... WWasWT
Fernandez, James 1835–1915.............. WWasWT
Fernandez, Peter..................................... CTFT–54
Ferocious Fish
    See .... Guttridge, Jim
    See .... Bennett, Daryl
Ferrabee, Gillian CTFT–64
Ferrar, Beatrice ?–1958 .... WWasWT
Ferrara, Abel 1952(?)– CTFT–39
    Earlier sketch in CTFT–13
Ferrare, Cristina 1950– CTFT–20
Ferrari, Isabella 1964–............................ CTFT–34
Ferrell, Conchata 1943– CTFT–51
    Earlier sketches in CTFT–8, 15, 24
Ferrell, Geoffrey
    See....................................... Blake, Geoffrey
Ferrell, Tyra 1962– CTFT–42
Ferrell, Will 1968(?)– CTFT–51
    Earlier sketch in CTFT–25
Ferrer, Jose 1912(?)–1992 .... CTFT–11
    Earlier sketches in CTFT–2; WWT–17
Ferrer, Mel 1917–.................................. CTFT–6
Ferrer, Miguel 1955– CTFT–77
    Earlier sketches in CTFT–9, 35
Ferrera, America 1984–........................... CTFT–77
Ferrera, Georgina
    See .... Ferrera, America
Ferrero, Martin CTFT–31
    Earlier sketch in CTFT–21
Ferrers, Helen ?–1943 .... WWasWT
Ferretti, Dante 1943– CTFT–43
    Earlier sketches in CTFT–11, 22
Ferri, Claudia... CTFT–79
    Earlier sketch in CTFT–35
Ferrier, Noel 1930– WWT–17
Ferrigno, Lou 1952– CTFT–74
    Earlier sketch in CTFT–8
Ferrin, Ingrid... CTFT–49
Ferris, Barbara 1943– CTFT–5
    Earlier sketch in WWT–17
Ferris, Bob
    See .... Barker, Ronnie
Ferris, Michael....................................... CTFT–61
Ferris, Monk
    See... Sharkey, Jack
Ferro, Pat
    See .... Reese, Della
Ferry, April... CTFT–50
Ferry, David CTFT–68
Fessenden, Beverly Lucy
    See....................................... Garland, Beverly

Feuer, Cy WWT–17
Feuerstein, Mark 1971– CTFT–40
Feuillere, Edwige 1907–1998 .... WWasWT
    Obituary in CTFT–24
Fey, Tina 1970– CTFT–62
Ffolkes, David 1912– .... WWasWT
Ffolliott, Gladys ?–1928 .... WWasWT
Ffrangcon–Davies, Gwen 1896– WWT–17
Fiander, Lewis 1938– CTFT–4
    Earlier sketch in WWT–17
Fibich, Felix 1917– CTFT–4
Fichandler, Zelda 1924– WWT–17
Fichtner, William 1956– CTFT–61
    Earlier sketch in CTFT–28
Fiedel, Brad 1951– CTFT–43
Fiedler, John 1925– CTFT–35
    Earlier sketches in CTFT–1, 7
Field, Alexander 1892–1939 .... WWasWT
Field, Arabella 1970– CTFT–42
    Earlier sketch in CTFT–21
Field, Barbara 1935– CTFT–1
Field, Betty 1918–1973 .... WWT–16
Field, Crystal 1940– CTFT–1
Field, David CTFT–73
    Earlier sketch in CTFT–33
Field, Edward Salisbury 1878–1936 ...... WWasWT
Field, Fern 1934– CTFT–4
Field, Jonathan 1912– .... WWasWT
Field, Jules 1919– CTFT–5
Field, Leonard S. 1908– CTFT–4
Field, Ron ?–1989 .... CTFT–5
    Earlier sketch in WWT–17
Field, Sally 1946– CTFT–64
    Earlier sketches in CTFT–3, 10, 18, 29
Field, Sid 1904–1950 .... WWasWT
Field, Sylvia 1901(?)–1998 .... CTFT–25
    Earlier sketch in WWasWT
Field, Ted 1952(?)– CTFT–36
    Earlier sketch in CTFT–10
Field, Todd 1964– CTFT–78
    Earlier sketch in CTFT–35
Field, Virginia 1917– .... WWasWT
Fielding, Emma 1973(?)– CTFT–48
Fielding, Fenella 1934– CTFT–6
    Earlier sketch in WWT–17
Fielding, Harold WWT–17
Fielding, Marjorie 1892–1956 .... WWasWT
Fields, Adam 1965– CTFT–30
Fields, Alexis 1983– CTFT–56
Fields, Dorothy 1905–1974 .... WWasWT
Fields, Freddie 1923– CTFT–5
Fields, Gracie 1898–1979 .... WWasWT
Fields, Herbert 1897–1958 .... WWasWT
Fields, Holly 1976– CTFT–63
Fields, Joseph 1895–1966 .... WWasWT
Fields, Judy CTFT–2
Fields, Kim 1969– CTFT–48
    Earlier sketches in CTFT–14, 24
Fields, Lew 1867–1941 .... WWasWT
Fields, Michael CTFT–51
Fields, W. C. 1879–1946 .... WWasWT
Fiennes, Joseph 1970– CTFT–48
    Earlier sketch in CTFT–23
Fiennes, Ralph 1962– CTFT–43
    Earlier sketches in CTFT–13, 22
Fierstein, Harvey 1954– CTFT–76
    Earlier sketches in CTFT–1, 6, 33
Fifield, Elaine 1930– .... WWasWT
Figgis, Mike 1948(?)– CTFT–67
    Earlier sketch in CTFT–30
Figman, Max 1868–1952 .... WWasWT
Figueroa, Gabriel 1907–1997 .... CTFT–26
Filippi, Rosina 1866–1930 .... WWasWT

Filippo, Fab 1974(?)– CTFT–58
Filkins, Grace ?–1962 .... WWasWT
Fillion, Nathan 1971– CTFT–54
    Earlier sketch in CTFT–26
Filmer, A. E. .... WWasWT
Filpi, Carmen CTFT–51
    Earlier sketch in CTFT–24
Finch, Peter 1916–1977 .... WWasWT
Fincher, David 1963– CTFT–70
    Earlier sketches in CTFT–20, 31
Finck, Herman 1872–? .... WWasWT
Fincke, SueAnn CTFT–51
Findon, B. W. 1859–1943 .... WWasWT
Fine, David CTFT–65
Fine, Travis 1968– CTFT–42
Finerman, Wendy 1957(?)– CTFT–55
    Earlier sketch in CTFT–25
Finestra, Carmen CTFT–36
    Earlier sketch in CTFT–11
Fingerhut, Arden CTFT–6
Fink, Kenneth CTFT–59
Finkel, Fyvush 1923– CTFT–30
Finkelstein, Kinky
    See .... Feldman, Corey
Finkelstein, William M. CTFT–54
Finlay, Frank 1926– CTFT–76
    Earlier sketches in CTFT–5, 33; WWT–17
Finlay–McLennan, Stewart
    1957– CTFT–65
Finley, Cameron 1987– CTFT–51
Finn, Arthur .... WWasWT
Finn, Charlie CTFT–68
Finn, John 1952– CTFT–77
    Earlier sketch in CTFT–34
Finn, Mary CTFT–65
    Earlier sketch in CTFT–29
Finn, Pat CTFT–54
Finn, William 1952– CTFT–49
    Earlier sketch in CTFT–11
Finnegan, Bill 1928– CTFT–1
Finneran, Katie 1971– CTFT–48
Finney, Albert 1936– CTFT–78
    Earlier sketches in CTFT–1, 5, 35; WWT–17
Finnie, Leo V. III CTFT–69
    Earlier sketch in CTFT–30
Fiore, John CTFT–36
Fiorentino, Linda 1960(?)– CTFT–38
    Earlier sketch in CTFT–14
Firestone, Roy 1953– CTFT–41
Firstenberg, Sam 1950– CTFT–41
Firth, Anne 1918– .... WWasWT
Firth, Colin 1960– CTFT–54
    Earlier sketches in CTFT–9, 16, 26
Firth, David 1945– CTFT–4
    Earlier sketches in CTFT–3; WWT–17
Firth, Elizabeth 1884–? .... WWasWT
Firth, Julian CTFT–53
Firth, Peter 1953– CTFT–38
    Earlier sketches in CTFT–7, 14
Firth, Tazeena 1935– WWT–17
Fischer, Alice 1869–1947 .... WWasWT
Fischer, Marc S. CTFT–67
    Earlier sketch in CTFT–30
Fischer, Takayo CTFT–44
    Earlier sketch in CTFT–22
Fischler, Patrick 1969– CTFT–71
Fish, Nancy CTFT–40
Fishburne, Laurence 1961– CTFT–48
    Earlier sketches in CTFT–7, 14, 24
Fishel, Danielle 1981– CTFT–68
Fisher, Carrie 1956– CTFT–57
    Earlier sketches in CTFT–2, 7, 14, 26
Fisher, Dan CTFT–6

Fisher, Douglas 1934– CTFT–1
Fisher, Frances 1952– CTFT–48
    Earlier sketches in CTFT–8, 15, 24
Fisher, Isla 1976– CTFT–67
Fisher, Joely 1965(?)– CTFT–44
    Earlier sketch in CTFT–22
Fisher, Jules 1937– CTFT–38
    Earlier sketches in CTFT–4, 11; WWT–17
Fisher, Linda 1943– CTFT–49
    Earlier sketches in CTFT–1, 9
Fisher, Lola 1896–1926 .... WWasWT
Fisher, Lucy 1949– CTFT–69
Fisher, Noel 1982– CTFT–73
Fisher, Robert CTFT–4
Fisher, Terry Louise 1946(?)– CTFT–11
Fisher, Thomas L. CTFT–36
Fisher, Tom CTFT–63
Fishler, Patrick
    See .... Fischler, Patrick
Fisk, Jack 1934– CTFT–8
Fiske, Harrison Grey 1861–1942 .... WWasWT
Fiske, Minnie Maddern 1865–1932 .... WWasWT
Fiske, Stephen 1840–1916 .... WWasWT
Fiske, Tarleton
    See .... Bloch, Robert
Fitelson, William H. 1905– CTFT–5
Fitts, Rick CTFT–53
Fitz, Paddy
    See .... McGoohan, Patrick
Fitzgerald, Aubrey Whitestone
    1876–? .... WWasWT
Fitzgerald, Barry 1888–1961 .... WWasWT
Fitzgerald, Edward 1876–? .... WWasWT
Fitzgerald, Geraldine 1914– CTFT–8
    Earlier sketches in CTFT–1; WWT–17
Fitzgerlad, Glenn 1972(?)– CTFT–42
Fitzgerald, Neil 1893– WWT–17
Fitzgerald, Percy Hetherington
    1834–1925 .... WWasWT
Fitzgerald, S. J. Adair 1859–1925 .... WWasWT
Fitzgerald, Tara 1967(?)– CTFT–65
    Earlier sketch in CTFT–29
Fitzgerald, Walter 1896– .... WWasWT
Fitzgerald, Wilbur CTFT–53
    Earlier sketch in CTFT–17
Fitzpatrick, Colleen 1970(?)– CTFT–54
Fitzpatrick, Gabrielle CTFT–71
Fitzpatrick, Jim CTFT–41
Fitzpatrick, Richard CTFT–58
Fitzsimmons, Maureen
    See .... O'Hara, Maureen
Fjelde, Rolf 1926– CTFT–1
Flacco
    See .... Livingston, Paul
Flagg, Fannie 1941(?)– CTFT–11
    Earlier sketch in CTFT–1
Flaherty, Joe 1941– CTFT–73
    Earlier sketch in CTFT–32
Flaherty, Lanny 1942– CTFT–42
    Earlier sketches in CTFT–3, 20
Flambe, Mona
    See .... Lauper, Cyndi
Flanagan, Bud 1896–1968 .... WWasWT
Flanagan, Fionnula 1941– CTFT–77
    Earlier sketches in CTFT–8, 33
Flanagan, Hallie 1890–1969 .... WWasWT
Flanagan, Markus 1964– CTFT–78
Flanagan, Pauline 1925– CTFT–1
Flanagan, Richard ?–1917 .... WWasWT
Flanagan, Tommy 1965– CTFT–38
Flanders, Ed 1934–1995 .... CTFT–14
    Earlier sketch in CTFT–6
Flanders, Michael 1922–1975 .... WWasWT

Flanery, Sean Patrick 1965– CTFT–70
   Earlier sketches in CTFT–20, 31
Flanigan, Joe.. CTFT–53
Flannery, Peter 1951–.............................. CTFT–5
   Earlier sketch in WWT–17
Flannery, Susan 1943(?)–........................ CTFT–58
Flannigan, Maureen 1973–........................ CTFT–67
   Earlier sketch in CTFT–30
Flatley, Michael 1958– CTFT–42
   Earlier sketch in CTFT–21
Flatman, Barry CTFT–54
Flatt, Ernest O. 1918–1995...................... CTFT–2
   Obituary in CTFT–14
Flavin, Martin 1883–1967 .... WWasWT
Flea 1962–.. CTFT–48
   Earlier sketch in CTFT–24
Fleet, James CTFT–35
Fleetwood, Susan 1944–1995 .... CTFT–20
   Earlier sketches in CTFT–6; WWT–17
Fleischer, Charles 1950–.......................... CTFT–78
   Earlier sketches in CTFT–9, 35
Fleischer, Max 1883(?)–1972 .... CTFT–20
Fleischer, Richard O. 1916– CTFT–12
   Earlier sketch in CTFT–1
Fleming, Brandon 1889–? .... WWasWT
Fleming, George 1858–1938 .... WWasWT
Fleming, Ian 1888–1969...................... WWasWT
Fleming, Lucy 1947–................................ CTFT–5
   Earlier sketch in WWT–17
Fleming, Peggy 1948–.............................. CTFT–43
Fleming, Shaun 1987–............................. CTFT–71
Fleming, Tom 1927–............................. WWT–17
Flemming, Claude 1884–1952 .... WWasWT
Flemming, Peter 1967– CTFT–54
Flemyng, Jason 1966– CTFT–61
   Earlier sketch in CTFT–28
Flemyng, Robert 1912– WWT–17
Flender, Rodman 1962(?)–....................... CTFT–51
Fleo, Groucho L.
   See .... Priestley, Jason
Flers, P. L. 1867–?.............................. WWasWT
Flers, Robert de 1872–1932 .... WWasWT
Fletcher, Allen 1922– WWT–17
Fletcher, Bramwell 1904–1988................ CTFT–7
   Earlier sketch in WWT–17
Fletcher, Dexter 1966– CTFT–77
   Earlier sketch in CTFT–33
Fletcher, Duane 1922– CTFT–4
Fletcher, Louise 1934–............................. CTFT–58
   Earlier sketches in CTFT–2, 6, 16, 26
Fletcher, Page CTFT–62
Fletcher, Percy 1879–1932 .... WWasWT
Fletcher, Robert 1923– WWT–17
Fleur, Art La
   See .... LaFleur, Art
Fleury, Laura.. CTFT–48
Flex
   See .... Alexander, Flex
Flexner, Anne Crawford 1874–1955 ...... WWasWT
Flick, Stephen Hunter 1949–.................. CTFT–36
   Earlier sketch in CTFT–10
Flicker, Ted 1930– CTFT–1
Flieger, Jean
   See .... St. James, Jean
Flinders, James
   See .... Clarke, Cam
Flint, Katja 1960– CTFT–35
Flint–Shipman, Veronica 1931–.............. WWT–17
Flitter, Josh 1994–.................................. CTFT–79
Flockhart, Calista 1964–.......................... CTFT–70
   Earlier sketches in CTFT–21, 31
Flood, Ann CTFT–3

Florek, Dann 1950– CTFT–51
   Earlier sketch in CTFT–24
Florek, Dave.. CTFT–48
Flores, Tina
   See .... Milian, Christina
Flores, Von 1960– CTFT–40
Flory, Regine 1894–1926......................... WWasWT
Flower, George "Buck" 1937–.................. CTFT–58
Flowers, Wayland 1939–1988 .... CTFT–5
Floyd, Gwendolen ?–1950..................... WWasWT
Floyd, Robert III 1967–........................... CTFT–72
Fluellen, Joel 1908–1990 .... CTFT–9
Flynn, Barbara 1948–.............................. CTFT–39
   Earlier sketches in CTFT–9, 16
Flynn, Colleen 1962–.............................. CTFT–79
   Earlier sketch in CTFT–36
Flynn, Don 1928–.................................... CTFT–1
Flynn, Errol 1909–1959 .... CTFT–20
Flynn, J. Michael CTFT–63
Flynn, Keri
   See.................................. Burstyn, Ellen
Flynn, Leslie
   See .... Flynn, Errol
Flynn, Michael 1944– CTFT–44
Flynn, Miriam CTFT–39
Flynn, Neil 1960(?)– CTFT–62
Flynn, Quinton 1964–.............................. CTFT–46
Flynn, Steven CTFT–36
Fo, Dario 1926–...................................... CTFT–33
   Earlier sketch in CTFT–7
Foan, John
   See .... Bava, Mario
Foch, Nina 1924– CTFT–73
   Earlier sketches in CTFT–4, 33; WWT–17
Fodor, Ladislaus (Lazlo) 1898– .... WWasWT
Fogarty, Jack 1923–................................ CTFT–3
Fogerty, Elsie 1866–1945 .... WWasWT
Foh Shen, Freda CTFT–79
   Earlier sketch in CTFT–36
Fokine, Michel 1880–1942..................... WWasWT
Foley, David 1963–.................................. CTFT–70
   Earlier sketches in CTFT–20, 31
Foley, Ellen 1951–.................................. CTFT–7
Foley, James 1953–................................. CTFT–42
   Earlier sketches in CTFT–12, 21
Foley, Jennifer Crystal
   See .... Crystal, Jennifer
Foley, Scott 1972–.................................. CTFT–67
   Earlier sketch in CTFT–30
Foliart, Dan CTFT–50
Folke, Will
   See.................................... Bloch, Robert
Folland, Alison 1978– CTFT–67
Follows, Megan 1968–............................. CTFT–65
   Earlier sketches in CTFT–7, 18, 29
Folse, Gabriel CTFT–40
Folsey, George, Jr. 1939–........................ CTFT–7
   Earlier sketch in CTFT–1
Fonda, Bridget 1964– CTFT–65
   Earlier sketches in CTFT–10, 18, 29
   Brief Entry in CTFT–8
Fonda, Henry 1905–1982 .... CTFT–1
   Earlier sketch in WWT–17
Fonda, Jane 1937– CTFT–59
   Earlier sketches in CTFT–1, 7, 14, 27;
   WWT–17
Fonda, Peter 1939(?)–............................. CTFT–65
   Earlier sketches in CTFT–2, 19, 29
Fondacaro, Phil 1958– CTFT–50
Foner, Naomi.. CTFT–21
Fontaine, Frank....................................... CTFT–54
Fontaine, Joan 1917– CTFT–24

Fontana, Tom 1951–................................ CTFT–70
   Earlier sketches in CTFT–2, 19, 31
Fontanne, Lynn 1892–1983 .... WWT–16
Fonteyn, Margot 1919–1991 .... CTFT–10
   Earlier sketch in WWasWT
Foote, Hallie 1953–................................. CTFT–75
   Earlier sketches in CTFT–7, 32
Foote, Horton 1916–............................... CTFT–39
   Earlier sketches in CTFT–4, 15; WWT–17
Foray, June 1919–................................... CTFT–35
   Earlier sketch in CTFT–8
Foray, Larry
   See .... Mordente, Tony
Forbes, Brenda 1909– WWT–17
Forbes, Bryan WWT–14
Forbes, Freddie 1895–1952 .... WWasWT
Forbes, James 1871–1938 .... WWasWT
Forbes, Mary 1880–1964...................... WWasWT
Forbes, Meriel 1913– WWT–17
Forbes, Michelle 1967–........................... CTFT–70
   Earlier sketches in CTFT–20, 31
Forbes, Norman 1858–1932 .... WWasWT
Forbes, Ralph 1905–1951 .... WWasWT
Forbes, Tracey CTFT–54
Forbes–Robertson, Beatrice
   1883–1967 .... WWasWT
Forbes–Robertson, Frank 1885–1947..... WWasWT
Forbes–Robertson, Jean 1905–1962....... WWasWT
Forbes–Robertson, Johnstone
   1853–1937 .... WWasWT
Force, Frank
   See .... Nimoy, Leonard
Ford Davies, Oliver CTFT–35
Ford, Audrey.. WWasWT
Ford, Bette 1928–................................... CTFT–63
Ford, Constance 1923(?)–1993 .... CTFT–1
   Obituary in CTFT–11
Ford, D. C. CTFT–36
Ford, Ed E. .... WWasWT
Ford, Faith 1964–.................................... CTFT–36
   Earlier sketch in CTFT–11
Ford, Frances 1939–................................ CTFT–1
Ford, Glenn 1916–2006 .... CTFT–19
   Obituary in CTFT–73
   Earlier sketch in CTFT–3
Ford, Harriet 1868–1949 .... WWasWT
Ford, Harrison 1942– CTFT–48
   Earlier sketches in CTFT–8, 15, 24
Ford, Harry 1877–?................................. WWasWT
Ford, Helen .... WWasWT
Ford, John 1895–1973 .... CTFT–23
Ford, Maria CTFT–30
Ford, Nancy 1935– CTFT–1
Ford, Paul 1901–1976 .... WWT–16
Ford, Ruth 1915– CTFT–7
   Earlier sketch in WWT–17
Ford, Steven 1956– CTFT–37
Ford, Tennessee Ernie 1919–1991 .... CTFT–10
Ford, Thomas Mikal CTFT–61
Ford, Wallace 1898–1966 .... WWasWT
   Earlier sketch in CTFT–9
Forde, Florrie 1876–1940 .... WWasWT
Fordin, Hugh 1935–................................ CTFT–1
Foree, Ken 1941–................................... CTFT–63
Foreman, Amanda 1966–......................... CTFT–54
Foreman, Carl 1914–1984 .... CTFT–2
Foreman, Jamie 1958–............................. CTFT–73
   Earlier sketch in CTFT–33
Foreman, John CTFT–5
Foreman, Richard 1937–.......................... CTFT–14
   Earlier sketch in CTFT–6
Forest, Denis CTFT–41
Forest, Michael 1929–............................. CTFT–54

Forke, Farrah 1967(?)–............................ CTFT–50
Forlani, Claire 1972–.............................. CTFT–73
    Earlier sketches in CTFT–20, 32
Forlow, Ted 1931–................................. CTFT–20
    Earlier sketches in CTFT–2, 6
Forman, Jamie
    See................................ Foreman, Jamie
Forman, Milos 1932–.............................. CTFT–70
    Earlier sketches in CTFT–1, 4, 21, 31
Formby, George 1904–1961 .... WWasWT
Fornes, Maria Irene 1930– CTFT–10
    Earlier sketch in CTFT–1
Forrest, Anne 1897–.............................. WWasWT
Forrest, Frederic 1936–........................... CTFT–65
    Earlier sketches in CTFT–7, 18, 29
Forrest, George 1915–............................ CTFT–10
Forrest, Sam 1870–1944 .... WWasWT
Forrest, Steve 1925–.............................. CTFT–7
Fors, Aaron 1989–................................. CTFT–76
Forster, Robert 1941– CTFT–65
    Earlier sketches in CTFT–2, 19, 29
Forster, Wilfred 1872–1924 .... WWasWT
Forster–Bovill, W. B. 1871–?.................. WWasWT
Forsyth, Bill 1948– CTFT–6
Forsyth, Bruce 1928– CTFT–6
    Earlier sketch in WWT–17
Forsyth, Matthew 1896–1954 .... WWasWT
Forsyth, Neil 1866–1915 .... WWasWT
Forsyth, Rosemary 1943(?)– CTFT–53
Forsythe, Charles CTFT–1
Forsythe, Colin 1961– CTFT–4
Forsythe, Henderson 1917–.................... CTFT–14
    Earlier sketches in CTFT–4; WWT–17
Forsythe, John 1918–............................. CTFT–38
    Earlier sketches in CTFT–1, 7, 14
Forsythe, William 1955– CTFT–62
    Earlier sketches in CTFT–17, 28
Fort, Mary Jane CTFT–65
Forte, Deborah CTFT–55
Forte, Marlene CTFT–44
Fortenberry, John CTFT–40
Fortescus, Miss 1862–1950 .... WWasWT
Fortune, Nadio CTFT–32
Forward, William CTFT–35
Foss, F. A.
    See.......................... Lawrence, Marc
Foss, George R. 1859–1938.................. WWasWT
Fosse, Bob 1927–1987 .... CTFT–1
    Obituary in CTFT–5
    Earlier sketch in WWT–17
Fossey, Brigitte 1946–............................ CTFT–8
Foster, Barry WWT–17
Foster, Basil S. 1882–1959..................... WWasWT
Foster, Ben 1980–................................. CTFT–62
    Earlier sketch in CTFT–28
Foster, Claiborne 1896–........................ WWasWT
Foster, David 1929– CTFT–5
Foster, Edward 1876–1927 .... WWasWT
Foster, Frances 1924–1997 .... CTFT–6
    Obituary in CTFT–18
    Earlier sketch in WWT–17
Foster, Gloria 1936–.............................. CTFT–8
    Earlier sketch in WWT–17
Foster, Jodie 1962–............................... CTFT–51
    Earlier sketches in CTFT–2, 7, 14, 25
Foster, Julia 1942–................................ CTFT–4
    Earlier sketch in WWT–17
Foster, Meg 1948–................................ CTFT–29
    Earlier sketches in CTFT–7, 19
Foster, Norman 1900–1976 .... WWasWT
Foster, Paul 1931–.............................. WWT–17
Foster, Phoebe 1896– .... WWasWT
Foster, Sutton 1975–............................. CTFT–49

Fowlds, Derek 1937–............................. CTFT–41
    Earlier sketch in CTFT–9
Fowler, Beth 1940– CTFT–8
Fowler, Clement 1924– CTFT–10
    Earlier sketch in CTFT–1
Fowler, Keith 1939– CTFT–4
Fox, Bernard 1927–.............................. CTFT–42
    Earlier sketch in CTFT–8
Fox, Charles 1940– CTFT–42
    Earlier sketches in CTFT–12, 21
Fox, Colin.. CTFT–53
Fox, Crystal R. CTFT–61
Fox, Della 1871–1913 .... WWasWT
Fox, Edward 1937–.............................. CTFT–69
    Earlier sketches in CTFT–7, 19, 29
Fox, Emilia 1974– CTFT–70
Fox, Frederick 1910– .... WWasWT
Fox, James 1939–................................. CTFT–69
    Earlier sketches in CTFT–8, 19, 29
Fox, Jorjan 1968–................................. CTFT–71
    Earlier sketch in CTFT–32
Fox, Kerry 1966–................................. CTFT–57
    Earlier sketch in CTFT–26
Fox, Matthew 1966– CTFT–56
    Earlier sketches in CTFT–16, 26
Fox, Megan 1986–................................ CTFT–74
Fox, Michael J. 1961–........................... CTFT–69
    Earlier sketches in CTFT–5, 12, 21, 31
    Brief Entry in CTFT–2
Fox, Rick 1969–................................... CTFT–63
Fox, Robin 1913–1971 .... WWasWT
Fox, Sandy CTFT–42
Fox, Shayna CTFT–67
Fox, Sidney 1910–1942 .... WWasWT
Fox, Terry Curtis 1948– CTFT–1
Fox, Vivica A. 1964–............................. CTFT–44
    Earlier sketch in CTFT–22
Fox, Will H. 1858–? .... WWasWT
Fox, William
    See................................... Fox, James
Fox, William 1911–.............................. WWT–17
Foxworth, Robert 1941– CTFT–60
    Earlier sketches in CTFT–1, 4
Foxworthy, Jeff 1958–........................... CTFT–42
    Earlier sketch in CTFT–20
Foxx, Jamie 1967–................................ CTFT–63
    Earlier sketch in CTFT–28
Foxx, Redd 1922–1991 .... CTFT–10
    Earlier sketch in CTFT–2
Foy, Eddie 1854–1928 .... WWasWT
Foyt, Victoria CTFT–26
Frain, James 1969–............................... CTFT–56
    Earlier sketch in CTFT–26
Fraker, William A. 1923–........................ CTFT–35
    Earlier sketch in CTFT–9
Frakes, Jonathan CTFT–38
    Earlier sketch in CTFT–14
Fraley, Pat 1949–................................. CTFT–37
France, Alexis 1906– .... WWasWT
France, Anatole 1868–1949 .... WWasWT
France, Marie CTFT–42
France, Richard 1938– CTFT–4
France–Ellys....................................... WWasWT
Francine, Anne 1917– CTFT–4
Franciosa, Anthony 1928–...................... CTFT–20
    Earlier sketch in CTFT–3
Francis, Alfred 1909–1985 .... WWT–17
Francis, Andrew CTFT–53
Francis, Anne 1932(?)– CTFT–38
    Earlier sketch in CTFT–14
Francis, Arlene 1908– CTFT–5
    Earlier sketch in WWT–17
Francis, Clive 1946–.............................. WWT–17

Francis, David CTFT–40
Francis, Doris 1903– .... WWasWT
Francis, Freddie 1917–.......................... CTFT–15
    Earlier sketch in CTFT–8
Francis, Genie 1962– CTFT–38
    Earlier sketch in CTFT–14
Francis, Ivor 1917–1986......................... CTFT–4
Francis, Jon
    See.................................... Gries, Jon
Francis, Kay 1905–1968 .... WWasWT
Francis, M. E. 1855–1930...................... WWasWT
Francis–Bruce, Richard 1948–................. CTFT–63
    Earlier sketch in CTFT–28
Franciscus, James 1934–1991 .... CTFT–3
    Obituary in CTFT–10
Francks, Cree Summer
    See.......................... Summer, Cree
Francks, Don 1932– CTFT–70
Francks, Lili CTFT–62
Francks, Rainbow 1979– CTFT–69
Franco, David..................................... CTFT–63
Franco, James 1978–............................. CTFT–72
    Earlier sketch in CTFT–32
Franco, Larry CTFT–62
    Earlier sketch in CTFT–28
Franco, Ramon CTFT–41
Frandsen, Jano CTFT–62
Frank, Bruno 1887–1945 .... WWasWT
Frank, David Michael CTFT–55
Frank, Harriet, Jr. CTFT–11
Frank, Judy 1936– CTFT–7
Frank, Mary K. ?–1988 .... CTFT–1
Frank, Melvin 1913–1988 .... CTFT–23
Frank, Richard 1953–............................ CTFT–8
Frank, Sandy...................................... CTFT–53
Frank, Scott 1960–............................... CTFT–44
    Earlier sketches in CTFT–11, 22
Frankau, Ronald 1894–1951 .... WWasWT
Franke, Christopher 1953– CTFT–60
    Earlier sketch in CTFT–27
Frankel, David 1960–............................. CTFT–61
Frankel, Gene 1923–............................. CTFT–5
    Earlier sketch in WWT–17
Frankel, Kenneth 1941–1998 .... CTFT–9
    Obituary in CTFT–21
    Earlier sketch in CTFT–1
Frankel, Mark 1962–1996 .... CTFT–24
Frankel, Richard 1954– CTFT–49
Franken, Al 1951(?)– CTFT–42
    Earlier sketch in CTFT–21
Franken, Rose 1895–1988 .... WWasWT
Franken, Steve 1932–............................ CTFT–76
Frankenheimer, John 1930–2002............. CTFT–47
    Obituary in CTFT–49
    Earlier sketches in CTFT–5, 23
Frankiss, Betty 1912–........................... WWasWT
Franklin, Bonnie 1944– CTFT–7
    Earlier sketch in CTFT–1
Franklin, Carl 1949–............................. CTFT–48
    Earlier sketches in CTFT–15, 24
Franklin, David................................... CTFT–44
Franklin, Don 1960– CTFT–53
Franklin, Harold B. 1890–1941 .... WWasWT
Franklin, Irene 1876–1941 .... WWasWT
Franklin, Kim Fields
    See.................................... Fields, Kim
Franklin, Pamela 1950–......................... CTFT–8
Franklin, Richard 1948– CTFT–10
Franklyn, Leo 1897–1975...................... WWasWT
Franks, Laurie 1929– CTFT–1
Frann, Mary 1943–1998......................... CTFT–4
    Obituary in CTFT–24

Franz, Dennis 1944– CTFT–48
   Earlier sketches in CTFT–7, 14, 24
Franz, Eduard 1902–1983 .... WWT–16
Franz, Elizabeth 1941– CTFT–79
   Earlier sketch in CTFT–6
Franz, Joy 1945– CTFT–1
Franzese, Daniel 1978– CTFT–71
Frappier, Jill CTFT–54
Fraser, Agnes .... WWasWT
Fraser, Alec 1884–? .... WWasWT
Fraser, Alison 1955– CTFT–5
Fraser, Bill 1908–1987 .... CTFT–5
   Earlier sketch in WWT–17
Fraser, Brendan 1968– CTFT–61
   Earlier sketches in CTFT–16, 28
Fraser, David CTFT–46
Fraser, Hugh CTFT–45
Fraser, John 1931– WWT–17
Fraser, Laura 1976– CTFT–64
   Earlier sketch in CTFT–29
Fraser, Lovat 1903– .... WWasWT
Fraser, Moyra 1923– WWT–17
Fraser, Shelagh WWT–17
Fraser, Winifred 1872–? .... WWasWT
Fraser–Simon, Harold 1878–1944 .... WWasWT
Fratti, Mario 1927– CTFT–2
Frawley, James CTFT–36
   Earlier sketch in CTFT–11
Frawley, William 1893(?)–1966 .... CTFT–16
Frayn, Michael 1933– CTFT–6
   Earlier sketch in WWT–17
Frazee, Harry Herbert 1880–1929 .... WWasWT
Frazer, Rupert 1947– CTFT–42
   Earlier sketches in CTFT–2, 20
Frazier, John 1944– CTFT–37
Frazier, Ronald 1942– CTFT–1
Frears, Stephen 1941– CTFT–48
   Earlier sketches in CTFT–6, 15, 24
Freberg, Stan 1926– CTFT–41
Frechette, Peter 1956(?)– CTFT–59
   Earlier sketch in CTFT–27
Frederick, Pauline 1885–1938 .... WWasWT
Frederick, William
   See .... Knight, William
Fredericks, Neal 1969– CTFT–54
Fredericks, Randy
   See .... Brooks, Randy
Fredrick, Burry 1925– WWT–17
Freear, Louie 1871–1939 .... WWasWT
Freedley, George 1904–1967 .... WWasWT
Freedley, Vinton 1891–1969 .... WWasWT
Freedman, Bill 1929– WWT–17
Freedman, Gerald 1927– CTFT–6
   Earlier sketch in WWT–17
Freedman, Robert L. 1957– CTFT–62
Freek, George 1945– CTFT–1
Freeman, Al, Jr. 1934– CTFT–19
   Earlier sketches in CTFT–7; WWT–17
Freeman, Arny 1908– WWT–17
Freeman, Crispin 1972– CTFT–46
Freeman, Frank 1892–1962 .... WWasWT
Freeman, Harry .... WWasWT
Freeman, J. E. 1946– CTFT–59
   Earlier sketch in CTFT–27
Freeman, Jonathan CTFT–40
Freeman, Jonathan CTFT–40
Freeman, K. Todd CTFT–29
Freeman, Kathleen 1919– CTFT–30
Freeman, Kim Fields
   See .... Fields, Kim
Freeman, Morgan 1937– CTFT–48
   Earlier sketches in CTFT–6, 15, 24; WWT–17

Freeman, Paul 1943– CTFT–76
   Earlier sketch in CTFT–32
Freeman, Rob CTFT–43
Freeman, Stella 1910–1936 .... WWasWT
Freeman, Yvette 1957– CTFT–72
   Earlier sketch in CTFT–32
Frees, Paul 1919–1986 .... CTFT–4
Freleng, Friz 1906–1995 .... CTFT–8
   Obituary in CTFT–14
Frelich, Phyllis 1944– CTFT–41
   Earlier sketches in CTFT–2, 19
French and Saunders
   See .... Saunders, Jennifer
French, Antonia
   See .... Kureishi, Hanif
French, Bruce CTFT–55
French, Elise .... WWasWT
French, Elizabeth .... WWasWT
French, Harold 1900– WWT–17
French, Hermene 1924– .... WWasWT
French, Hugh 1910– .... WWasWT
French, Leslie 1904–1999 .... WWT–17
   Obituary in CTFT–24
French, Stanley J. 1908–1964 .... WWasWT
French, Valerie 1932– CTFT–4
   Earlier sketch in WWT–17
French, Victor 1934–1989 .... CTFT–6
Fresco, Michael CTFT–41
Fresco, Rob CTFT–63
Fresh Prince, The
   See .... Smith, Will
   Earlier sketch in CTFT–13
Fresnay, Pierre 1897–1973 .... WWasWT
Freudenberger, Daniel 1945– WWT–17
Freund, Karl 1890–1969 .... CTFT–30
Frewer, Matt 1958– CTFT–50
   Earlier sketches in CTFT–8, 15, 24
Frewer, Terry CTFT–58
Frey, Leonard 1938–1988 .... WWT–17
Frey, Nathaniel 1913–1970 .... WWasWT
Fricker, Brenda 1945– CTFT–43
   Earlier sketch in CTFT–22
Fridell, Squire 1943– CTFT–1
Fried, Martin 1937– WWT–17
Friedericy, Bonita CTFT–78
Friedkin, William 1935– CTFT–51
   Earlier sketches in CTFT–5, 15, 24
Friedlander, Judah CTFT–64
Friedlander, W. B. ?–1968 .... WWasWT
Friedle, Will 1976– CTFT–62
   Earlier sketches in CTFT–17, 28
Friedman, Bruce Jay 1930– CTFT–3
   Earlier sketches in CTFT–1; WWT–17
Friedman, Jake 1867–? .... WWasWT
Friedman, Lewis 1948– CTFT–4
Friedman, Peter 1949– CTFT–47
   Earlier sketch in CTFT–23
Friedman, Phil 1921–1988 .... CTFT–1
Friedman, Stephen 1937–1996 .... CTFT–4
   Obituary in CTFT–16
Friel, Anna 1976– CTFT–54
   Earlier sketch in CTFT–26
Friel, Brian 1929– CTFT–36
   Earlier sketches in CTFT–10; WWT–17
Friels, Colin 1952– CTFT–54
   Earlier sketches in CTFT–8, 26
Friendly, Ed 1922– CTFT–8
Friendly, Fred 1915–1998 .... CTFT–6
   Obituary in CTFT–21
Frierson, Monte L. 1930– CTFT–4
Fries, Charles CTFT–2
Friesen, Rick 1943– CTFT–1
Friganzi, Trixie 1870–1955 .... WWasWT

Frigon, Miranda 1980– CTFT–74
Friml, Charles Rudolf 1881–1972 .... WWasWT
Frisby, Terence 1932– WWT–17
Frisch, Max 1911– WWT–17
Frith, J. Leslie 1889–1961 .... WWasWT
Frizzell, John CTFT–48
Frizzell, John 1966– CTFT–47
Frohman, Charles 1860–1915 .... WWasWT
Frohman, Daniel 1851–1940 .... WWasWT
Fromage, Marty
   See .... Williams, Robin
Frost, David 1939– CTFT–3
Frost, Lindsay 1962– CTFT–64
Frost, Mark 1953– CTFT–49
   Earlier sketch in CTFT–11
Frost, Roger CTFT–63
Frost, Sadie 1967– CTFT–67
   Earlier sketch in CTFT–30
Froyez, Maurice .... WWasWT
Fruchtman, Milton Allen CTFT–1
Fry, Christopher 1907– WWT–17
Fry, Stephen 1957– CTFT–60
   Earlier sketch in CTFT–27
Frye, Soleil Moon 1976– CTFT–53
   Earlier sketch in CTFT–25
Fryer, Robert 1920– CTFT–2
   Earlier sketch in WWT–17
Fryman, Pamela CTFT–64
Fuchs, Michael J. 1946– CTFT–12
Fudge, Alan 1944– CTFT–42
   Earlier sketch in CTFT–20
Fuentes, Daisy 1966– CTFT–54
   Earlier sketch in CTFT–26
Fugard, Athol 1932– CTFT–51
   Earlier sketches in CTFT–1, 3, 15, 24;
   WWT–17
Fujimoto, Tak CTFT–58
   Earlier sketch in CTFT–27
Fujioka, John CTFT–37
Fulford, Christopher CTFT–35
Fulger, Holly CTFT–49
Fulks, Sarah Jane
   See .... Wyman, Jane
Fuller, Amanda 1984– CTFT–59
Fuller, Benjamin John 1875–? .... WWasWT
Fuller, Bryan 1969– CTFT–76
Fuller, Charles 1939– CTFT–7
Fuller, Drew 1980– CTFT–69
Fuller, Frances 1908– .... WWasWT
Fuller, Janice 1942– CTFT–2
Fuller, John G. 1913– CTFT–1
Fuller, Kurt 1953– CTFT–67
   Earlier sketch in CTFT–30
Fuller, Loie 1862–1928 .... WWasWT
Fuller, Penny 1940– CTFT–39
Fuller, Rosalinde WWT–17
Fuller, Samuel 1912–1997 .... CTFT–8
   Obituary in CTFT–18
Fuller, Simon 1961(?)– CTFT–65
Fullerton, Fiona 1956– CTFT–48
   Earlier sketches in CTFT–8, 15
Fulton, Charles J. 1857–1938 .... WWasWT
Fulton, Maude 1881–1950 .... WWasWT
Fumusa, Dominic 1972– CTFT–74
Funk, Dan 1953– CTFT–66
Funt, Allen 1914– CTFT–9
Fuqua, Lela Rochon
   See .... Rochon, Lela
Furber, Douglas 1885–1961 .... WWasWT
Furguson, Wesley
   See .... Link, William
Furie, Sidney J. 1933– CTFT–69
   Earlier sketches in CTFT–12, 21, 31

Cumulative Index

Furlan, Mira 1955– CTFT–64
    Earlier sketch in CTFT–29
Furlong, Edward 1977– CTFT–51
    Earlier sketches in CTFT–15, 24
Furmann, Benno 1972– CTFT–78
    Earlier sketch in CTFT–35
    See .... Fuermann, Benno
Furniss, Grace Livingston 1864–1938..... WWasWT
Furse, Judith 1912– .... WWasWT
Furse, Roger 1903–1972 .... WWasWT
Furst, Anton 1944(?)–1991 .... CTFT–8
    Obituary in CTFT–10
Furst, Stephen 1955– CTFT–62
    Earlier sketches in CTFT–4, 16, 28
Furth, George 1932– CTFT–3
    Earlier sketch in WWT–17
Fury, David... CTFT–50
Futterman, Dan 1967– CTFT–73
    Earlier sketch in CTFT–33
Fyfe, Jim CTFT–79
    Earlier sketch in CTFT–35
Fyfe, H. Hamilton 1869–1951 .... WWasWT

G

Gabel, Martin 1912–1986 .... CTFT–4
    Earlier sketch in WWT–17
Gaberman, Alexander
    See.................................. Chaplin, Alexander
Gaberman, Sandy
    See.................................. Chaplin, Alexander
Gable, Clark 1901–1960 .... WWasWT
Gable, June 1945– CTFT–36
    Earlier sketches in CTFT–1, 10
Gabor, Eva 1921(?)–1995 .... CTFT–1
    Obituary in CTFT–15
Gabor, Zsa Zsa 1919– CTFT–20
    Earlier sketch in CTFT–3
Gabriel, Gilbert W. 1890–1952 .... WWasWT
Gabriel, Peter 1950– CTFT–60
    Earlier sketch in CTFT–28
Gabrielle, Josefina CTFT–51
Gackle, Kathleen
    See............................... Lloyd, Kathleen
Gadd, Renee 1908– .... WWasWT
Gaffigan, Jim 1966– CTFT–78
    Earlier sketch in CTFT–35
Gaffney, Liam 1911–............................. WWasWT
Gaffney, Mo 1958– CTFT–53
Gage, Patricia CTFT–58
Gagliano, Frank....................................... CTFT–4
    Earlier sketch in WWT–17
Gagnier, Holly 1962–............................ CTFT–41
Gago, Jenny 1953– CTFT–64
Gahagan, Helen 1900– .... WWasWT
Gaige, Crosby 1882–1949..................... WWasWT
Gail, David 1966– CTFT–72
Gail, Max 1943– CTFT–74
    Earlier sketches in CTFT–2, 33
Gail, Zoe .... WWasWT
Gaines, Boyd 1953–............................... CTFT–48
    Earlier sketches in CTFT–8, 15, 24
Gaines, Charles L. 1942– CTFT–3
Gainey, M. C. CTFT–44
Gains, Courtney 1965– CTFT–50
Gainsbourg, Charlotte 1971–.................. CTFT–53
    Earlier sketch in CTFT–25
Galarno, Bill 1938–................................. CTFT–7
Galati, Frank 1943–................................ CTFT–21

Gale, Bob
    See .... Gale, Michael Robert
Gale, John 1929– CTFT–3
    Earlier sketch in WWT–17
Gale, Lorena.. CTFT–53
Gale, Michael Robert 1951– CTFT–13
    Earlier sketch (as Bob Gale) in CTFT–7
Gale, Vincent CTFT–59
Gale, Zona 1874–1938 .... WWasWT
Galecki, Johnny 1975–........................... CTFT–46
Galeotti, Bethany Joy
    See.. Lenz, Joie
Galeota, Michael 1984–.......................... CTFT–68
Galifianakis, Zach 1969– CTFT–64
Galik–Furey, Denise CTFT–64
Galino, Valeria
    See............................... Golino, Valeria
Galipaux, Felix 1860–1931 .... WWasWT
Gallacher, Tom 1934– CTFT–5
    Earlier sketch in WWT–17
Gallagher, Bronagh 1972–....................... CTFT–72
    Earlier sketch in CTFT–32
Gallagher, David 1985– CTFT–67
    Earlier sketch in CTFT–30
Gallagher, Helen 1926– CTFT–5
    Earlier sketch in WWT–17
Gallagher, Mary 1947–........................... CTFT–1
Gallagher, Megan 1960– CTFT–41
    Earlier sketches in CTFT–7, 18
Gallagher, Peter 1955(?)–......................... CTFT–61
    Earlier sketches in CTFT–9, 16, 28
    Brief Entry in CTFT–3
Gallagher, Richard 1900–1955 .... WWasWT
Galland, Bertha 1876–1932 .... WWasWT
Gallant, Felicia
    See.. Dano, Linda
Gallego, Gina 1959–............................... CTFT–56
Gallen, Joel 1957– CTFT–64
Galligan, Zach 1964–............................. CTFT–39
    Earlier sketch in CTFT–13
Gallimore, Florrie 1867–? .... WWasWT
Gallin, Sandy... CTFT–42
Gallini, Matt 1966– CTFT–75
Gallion, Randy
    See............................... Vasquez, Randy
Gallner, Kyle 1986–............................... CTFT–78
Gallo, Paul CTFT–39
    Earlier sketch in CTFT–7
Gallo, Vincent 1961– CTFT–61
    Earlier sketch in CTFT–28
Gallop, Tom CTFT–77
    Earlier sketch in CTFT–34
Galloway, Don 1937– CTFT–2
Galloway, Jane 1950– CTFT–38
    Earlier sketches in CTFT–1, 15
Galsworthy, John 1867–1933 .... WWasWT
Galt, John William 1940– CTFT–54
Galvina, Dino 1890–1960.................... WWasWT
Gam, Rita 1928– CTFT–1
Gamble, Mason 1986–............................ CTFT–57
    Earlier sketch in CTFT–27
Gamble, Tom 1898– .... WWasWT
Gambon, Michael 1940– CTFT–57
    Earlier sketches in CTFT–5, 26; WWT–17
Gammon, James 1940–........................... CTFT–50
    Earlier sketches in CTFT–3, 15, 24
Gance, Abel 1889–1981 .... CTFT–2
Gandolfini, James 1961–......................... CTFT–44
    Earlier sketch in CTFT–22
Gangsta
    See... Eve
Gann, Merrilyn CTFT–56
Gant, David.. CTFT–56

Gant, Richard CTFT–41
Ganz, Bruno 1941–................................ CTFT–50
    Earlier sketches in CTFT–8, 15, 24
Ganz, Lowell 1948– CTFT–45
    Earlier sketch in CTFT–11
Ganz, Tony CTFT–9
Ganzel, Teresa 1957– CTFT–61
Garay, Soo CTFT–59
Garber, Terri 1960– CTFT–64
Garber, Victor 1949– CTFT–57
    Earlier sketches in CTFT–9, 26
Garbo, Greta 1905–1990 .... CTFT–9
Garcia Marquez, Gabriel 1928–............. CTFT–15
Garcia, Adam 1973–.............................. CTFT–62
Garcia, Aimee 1978–............................. CTFT–67
Garcia, Andy 1956– CTFT–49
    Earlier sketches in CTFT–8, 15, 24
Garcia, Damien
    See.................................... Leguizamo, John
Garcia, Joanna 1979–............................. CTFT–46
Garcia, Jorge 1973–............................... CTFT–70
Garcia, Jsu 1963–.................................. CTFT–54
Garcia, Risa Bramon 1957 .... CTFT–26
Garcin, Ginette CTFT–34
Garde, Betty 1905–1989 .... CTFT–9
    Earlier sketch in WWT–17
Gardell, Victor
    See.................................... Gradjeda, Javier
Garden, E. M. 1845–1939 .... WWasWT
Garden, Graeme 1943–........................... CTFT–6
    Earlier sketch in WWT–17
Gardenia, Vincent 1922–1992 .... CTFT–7
    Obituary in CTFT–11
    Earlier sketches in CTFT–2; WWT–17
Gardiner, Cyril 1897–........................... WWasWT
Gardiner, Greg....................................... CTFT–48
Gardiner, Reginald 1903–1980............. WWasWT
Gardner, Ava 1922–1990 .... CTFT–9
    Earlier sketch in CTFT–3
Gardner, Herb 1934– CTFT–39
    Earlier sketch in CTFT–6
Gardner, Jan
    See.................................... Felt, Jan Broberg
Gardner, Shayle 1890–1945 .... WWasWT
Gardner, Will 1879–? .... WWasWT
Gareis, Jennifer 1970–............................ CTFT–68
Garfein, Jack 1930–................................ CTFT–5
Garfield, Allen 1939–............................. CTFT–36
    Earlier sketch in CTFT–10
Garfield, John 1913–1952 .... WWasWT
Garfield, Julie CTFT–1
Gargan, William (Dennis)
    1905–1979 .... WWasWT
Garito, Ken 1968–................................. CTFT–79
    Earlier sketch in CTFT–36
Garity, Troy 1973–................................. CTFT–67
Garland, Beverly 1926– CTFT–60
    Earlier sketch in CTFT–1
Garland, Geoff 1926– CTFT–1
Garland, Judy 1922–1969 .... CTFT–20
Garland, Patrick 1935– CTFT–13
    Earlier sketch in WWT–17
Garland, Robert 1895–1955 .... WWasWT
Garlin, Jeff 1962–.................................. CTFT–64
Garlington, Lee...................................... CTFT–43
Garner, James 1928– CTFT–35
    Earlier sketches in CTFT–3, 9
Garner, Kelli 1984– CTFT–75
Garner, Jay CTFT–30
Garner, Jennifer 1972– CTFT–61
    Earlier sketch in CTFT–28
Garner, Kenneth CTFT–30
Garner, Leonard R., Jr. CTFT–41

Garnett, Edward 1868–1937.................. WWasWT
Garnett, Gale... CTFT–1
Garofalo, Janeane 1964–......................... CTFT–50
Earlier sketches in CTFT–15, 24
Garr, Teri 1949(?)–................................. CTFT–65
Earlier sketches in CTFT–3, 10, 18, 29
Garrett, Arthur 1869–1941 .... WWasWT
Garrett, Betty 1919–............................... CTFT–62
Earlier sketches in CTFT–4; WWT–17
Garrett, Brad 1960–................................ CTFT–44
Earlier sketch in CTFT–22
Garrett, Eliza
See... Roberts, Eliza
Garrett, Hank 1931– CTFT–56
Garrett, Joy... CTFT–1
Garrett, Leif 1961–................................. CTFT–69
Garrett, Spencer 1963– CTFT–44
Garrick, Barbara CTFT–40
Garrick, Gus .... WWasWT
Garrick, John 1902–................................ WWasWT
Garris, Mick 1951– CTFT–50
Garrison, David 1952–............................ CTFT–39
Earlier sketch in CTFT–4
Garrison, Miranda 1950– CTFT–37
Garside, John 1887–1958 .... WWasWT
Garson, Barbara 1941– CTFT–1
Garson, Greer 1903–1996 .... CTFT–8
Obituary in CTFT–16
Earlier sketch in WWasWT
Garson, Willie 1964–.............................. CTFT–59
Earlier sketch in CTFT–27
Garth, Jennie 1972–................................ CTFT–42
Earlier sketch in CTFT–20
Gartin, Christopher................................. CTFT–65
Garver, Kathy 1947–............................... CTFT–44
Earlier sketch in CTFT–22
Gary, Lorraine.. CTFT–7
Gascoigne, Bamber 1935– WWT–17
Gascon, Jean 1921–1988 .... WWT–17
Gaskill, William 1930–........................... CTFT–3
Earlier sketch in WWT–17
Gaspard, Raymond L. 1949–................... CTFT–9
Earlier sketch in CTFT–1
Gass, Kyle 1960– CTFT–76
Gassman, Alessandro 1965– CTFT–51
Earlier sketch in CTFT–25
Gassman, Vittorio 1922–......................... CTFT–8
Gassner, Dennis 1948–........................... CTFT–79
Earlier sketches in CTFT–11, 36
Gassner, John 1903–1967 .... WWasWT
Gast, Leon 1937(?)–............................... CTFT–20
Gasteyer, Ana 1967–.............................. CTFT–38
Gaston, Michael CTFT–48
Gates, Eleanor 1875–1951 .... WWasWT
Gates, Jesse Stuart
See............................... McFadden, Gates
Gates, Larry 1915–................................. WWT–17
Gates, Tucker... CTFT–43
Gateson, Marjorie 1897–1977 .... WWasWT
Gatti, John M. 1872–1929 .... WWasWT
Gaudet, Christie 1957– CTFT–4
Gaul, George 1885–1939 .... WWasWT
Gault, Willie 1960–................................ CTFT–75
Gaunt, William 1937–............................ WWT–17
Gauthier, Chris 1976– CTFT–67
Gauthier, Dan 1963–.............................. CTFT–41
Gautier, Richard 1931– CTFT–54
Gavault, Paul 1867–? .... WWasWT
Gaven, Marcia Mitzman 1959–.............. CTFT–67
Gavin, John 1932– CTFT–2
Gawthorne, Peter A. 1884–1962 .... WWasWT
Gaxton, William 1893–1963 .... WWasWT
Gay, John 1924–..................................... CTFT–9

Gay, Maisie 1883–1945......................... WWasWT
Gay, Noel 1898–1954 .... WWasWT
Gay, Shirley
See .... Brown, Pat Crawford
Gaye, Freda 1907–1986 .... CTFT–4
Earlier sketch in WWasWT
Gaye, Nona 1974–.................................. CTFT–76
Gayheart, Rebecca 1972– CTFT–65
Earlier sketches in CTFT–20, 29
Gaynes, George 1917–............................ CTFT–55
Earlier sketches in CTFT–8; WWT–17
Gaythorne, Pamela 1882–?..................... WWasWT
Gazelle, Wendy...................................... CTFT–67
Gazzara, Ben 1930–............................... CTFT–65
Earlier sketches in CTFT–3, 19, 29; WWT–17
Gazzo, Michael V. 1923–1995 .... CTFT–8
Obituary in CTFT–14
Earlier sketch in CTFT–1
Ge, Chen Kai
See... Chen, Kaige
Gear, Luella 1899–................................. WWasWT
Geary, Anthony 1947– CTFT–18
Earlier sketch in CTFT–6
Brief Entry in CTFT–2
Geddes, David CTFT–49
Gedrick, Jason 1965–............................. CTFT–38
Earlier sketches in CTFT–7, 14
Gee, George 1895–1959 .... WWasWT
Gee, Robbie 1970– CTFT–71
Gee, Shirley 1932–................................. CTFT–12
Geer, Ellen 1941–.................................. CTFT–68
Earlier sketches in CTFT–1, 20, 31
Geer, Kevin.. CTFT–77
Earlier sketch in CTFT–32
Geer, Will 1902–1978............................ WWT–16
Geeson, Judy 1948–............................... CTFT–34
Earlier sketch in CTFT–8
Geffen, David 1943–.............................. CTFT–5
Geidt, Jeremy CTFT–32
Gelb, Arthur 1924–................................ CTFT–1
Gelb, Barbara CTFT–1
Gelbart, Larry 1928–.............................. CTFT–36
Earlier sketches in CTFT–1, 3, 10; WWT–17
Gelber, Jack 1932–................................. CTFT–5
Earlier sketch in WWT–17
Geldof, Bob 1954(?)– CTFT–48
Earlier sketch in CTFT–23
Gelinas, Marc CTFT–34
Gelke, Becky
See .... Baker, Becky Ann
Gellar, Sarah Michelle 1977–................. CTFT–68
Earlier sketches in CTFT–20, 31
Geller, Marc 1959– CTFT–1
Gellman, Yani 1985–.............................. CTFT–68
Gellner, Julius 1899–............................. WWT–17
Gelman, Larry 1930– CTFT–41
Gelman–Waxer, Libby
See .... Rudnick, Paul
Gemier, Firmin 1865–1933.................... WWasWT
Gemignani, Rhoda 1940– CTFT–46
Gemmell, Don 1903– WWT–17
Gems, Pam 1925–................................... CTFT–6
Earlier sketch in WWT–17
Genee, Dame Adeline 1878–1970 .... WWasWT
Genesse, Bryan 1967–............................ CTFT–59
Genest, Edmund CTFT–55
Genet, Jean 1910–1986.......................... CTFT–3
Earlier sketch in WWT–17
Genevie, Michael 1959(?)–..................... CTFT–53
Geniat, Marchell ?–1959 .... WWasWT
Genn, Leo 1905–1978 .... WWT–16
Gennaro, Peter 1919– CTFT–4

Genovese, Mike CTFT–73
Earlier sketch in CTFT–32
Gentile, Denise CTFT–69
George, A. E. 1869–1920 .... WWasWT
George, Brian 1952–.............................. CTFT–77
Earlier sketch in CTFT–34
George, Bud
See .... Davis, Bud
George, Chief Dan 1899–1981 .... CTFT–17
George, Christopher 1929–1983 .... CTFT–21
George, Colin 1929–.............................. CTFT–18
Earlier sketches in CTFT–2; WWT–17
George, Dan
See .... George, Chief Dan
George, Gladys 1904–1954.................... WWasWT
George, Grace 1879–1961 .... WWasWT
George, Jason Winston 1972–................. CTFT–74
George, Lynda Day 1946–...................... CTFT–8
George, Marie 1879–1955 .... WWasWT
George, Melissa 1976–........................... CTFT–62
George, Muriel 1883–1965 .... WWasWT
George, Richard
See.. Epcar, Richard
Gerald, Ara 1900–1957 .... WWasWT
Geraldy, Paul 1885–?............................. WWasWT
Gerard, Gil 1943–.................................. CTFT–6
Gerard, Teddie 1892–1942 .... WWasWT
Geray, Steve 1904–1973......................... WWasWT
Gerber, Ella 1916–................................. CTFT–1
Gerber, Fred CTFT–41
Gerber, Joan 1935– CTFT–54
Gerdes, George 1948–............................ CTFT–73
Earlier sketches in CTFT–4, 33
Gere, Richard 1949–.............................. CTFT–47
Earlier sketches in CTFT–2, 6, 13, 23
Gerety, Peter 1940–................................ CTFT–73
Earlier sketch in CTFT–32
Gerini, Claudia 1971–............................ CTFT–67
Earlier sketch in CTFT–30
German, Edward 1862–1936.................. WWasWT
German, Lauren 1978– CTFT–75
Germann, Greg 1958(?)–......................... CTFT–61
Earlier sketches in CTFT–17, 28
Gerrard, Gene 1892–1971 .... WWasWT
Gerringer, Robert 1926–1989................. CTFT–2
Gerrity, Dan 1958–................................. CTFT–7
Gerroll, Daniel 1951– CTFT–47
Earlier sketches in CTFT–1, 5, 23
Gershon, Gina 1962–............................. CTFT–48
Earlier sketches in CTFT–15, 24
Gershwin, George 1898–1937............... WWasWT
Gershwin, Ira 1896–1983 .... WWasWT
Gerson, Betty Lou 1914–1999............... CTFT–25
Gerson, Carlotta
See .... Mazursky, Paul
Gerstad, John 1924–.............................. WWT–17
Gersten, Bernard 1923– CTFT–5
Earlier sketch in WWT–17
Gertz, Jami 1965–.................................. CTFT–57
Earlier sketches in CTFT–7, 14, 26
Gertz, Paul CTFT–40
Gerussi, Bruno .... WWasWT
Gesner, Zen 1970–................................. CTFT–47
Earlier sketch in CTFT–23
Gest, Morris 1881–1942 .... WWasWT
Gets, Malcolm 1964–............................. CTFT–45
Earlier sketch in CTFT–17
Getty, Balthazar 1975–........................... CTFT–53
Getty, Estelle 1923–............................... CTFT–38
Earlier sketches in CTFT–6, 14
Getz, John 1947– CTFT–46
Getzman, Gary
See .... Goetzman, Gary

Cumulative Index

Geva, Tamara 1907– .... WWasWT
Gevedon, Stephen CTFT–65
Gewe, Raddory
   See .... Gorey, Edward
Gewirtz, Howard....................................... CTFT–65
Gheusi, Pierre B. 1867–? .... WWasWT
Ghini, Massimo 1954– CTFT–30
Ghostley, Alice 1928(?)–........................ CTFT–29
   Earlier sketches in CTFT–2, 19; WWT–17
Gia, Richado
   See .... Gere, Richard
Giacchino, Michael.................................. CTFT–74
Giagni, D. J. 1950– CTFT–4
Giamatti, Marcus 1961– CTFT–44
Giamatti, Paul 1967– CTFT–51
   Earlier sketch in CTFT–25
Giannini, Giancarlo 1942–..................... CTFT–73
   Earlier sketches in CTFT–7, 19, 32
Giannini, Olga... WWasWT
Gibb, Cynthia 1963–............................... CTFT–44
Gibb, Lee
   See..................... Waterhouse, Keith Spencer
Gibbons, Arthur 1871–1935 .... WWasWT
Gibbons, Blake... CTFT–59
Gibbons, Leeza 1957– CTFT–59
   Earlier sketches in CTFT–17, 27
Gibbs, Marla 1931(?)–............................ CTFT–39
   Earlier sketches in CTFT–3, 15
Gibbs, Matyelock CTFT–64
Gibbs, Nancy ?–1956 .... WWasWT
Gibbs, Richard CTFT–65
Gibbs, Timothy 1967–............................. CTFT–55
   Earlier sketch in CTFT–5
Gibney, Susan.. CTFT–44
Gibson, Annabeth 1971– CTFT–61
Gibson, Brenda 1870–? .... WWasWT
Gibson, Chloe 1899– .... WWasWT
Gibson, Deborah 1970– CTFT–51
   Earlier sketch in CTFT–24
Gibson, Henry 1935–............................... CTFT–73
   Earlier sketches in CTFT–3, 19, 32
Gibson, Mel 1956– CTFT–45
   Earlier sketches in CTFT–6, 13, 23
Gibson, Michael 1944– CTFT–5
Gibson, Thomas 1962(?)–........................ CTFT–64
   Earlier sketches in CTFT–17, 29
Gibson, William 1914– CTFT–2
   Earlier sketch in WWT–17
Gibson, William 1948– CTFT–48
   Earlier sketch in CTFT–15
Gibson, Wynne 1905–1987..................... WWasWT
Giddens, George 1845–1920................... WWasWT
Gideon, Melville J. 1884–1933 .... WWasWT
Gidley, Pamela 1965– CTFT–73
   Earlier sketch in CTFT–33
Gielgud, John 1904– CTFT–23
   Earlier sketches in CTFT–1, 7, 14; WWT–17
Gielgud, Val 1900–1981.......................... WWasWT
Gierasch, Stefan 1926– CTFT–36
   Earlier sketch in CTFT–10
Gifaldi, Sam CTFT–74
Giffin, Philip.. CTFT–56
Gifford, Frank 1930– CTFT–22
Gifford, Kathie Lee 1953– CTFT–45
   Earlier sketch in CTFT–22
Gignoux, Regis 1878–?........................... WWasWT
Gil, Arturo 1960–.................................... CTFT–79
   Earlier sketch in CTFT–35
Gilbert, Bruce 1947–............................... CTFT–9
   Earlier sketch in CTFT–1
Gilbert, Jean 1879–1943 .... WWasWT
Gilbert, Lewis 1920– CTFT–41
   Earlier sketch in CTFT–9

Gilbert, Lou 1909–1978 .... WWT–17
Gilbert, Melissa 1964– CTFT–38
   Earlier sketches in CTFT–5, 14
   Brief Entry in CTFT–2
Gilbert, Olive WWT–17
Gilbert, Ronnie 1926–............................ CTFT–18
   Earlier sketch in CTFT–2
Gilbert, Sara 1975– CTFT–39
   Earlier sketch in CTFT–13
Gilbert–Brinkman, Melissa
   See .... Gilbert, Melissa
Gilborn, Steven CTFT–36
Gilder, Rosamond de Kay 1891–1986 .... CTFT–4
   Earlier sketch in WWT–17
Giler, David CTFT–47
Giles, Nancy 1960– CTFT–39
Gilford, Jack 1907(?)–1990 .... CTFT–11
   Earlier sketches in CTFT–2; WWT–17
Gilhooley, Jack 1940– CTFT–1
Gill, Basil 1877–1955 .... WWasWT
Gill, Brendan 1914– WWT–17
Gill, Jack 1955– CTFT–48
Gill, Morgan Brittany
   See .... Brittany, Morgan
Gill, Paul ?–1934 .... WWasWT
Gill, Peter 1939– CTFT–30
   Earlier sketches in CTFT–2, 18; WWT–17
Gill, Tom 1916–1971 .... WWT–16
Gillespie, Dana 1949– CTFT–5
   Earlier sketch in WWT–17
Gillespie, Richard 1878–1952 .... WWasWT
Gillespie, Robert 1933–.......................... CTFT–6
   Earlier sketch in WWT–17
Gillett, Aden 1958–................................ CTFT–57
   Earlier sketch in CTFT–27
Gillett, Eric 1893– .... WWasWT
Gillette, Anita 1936(?)–.......................... CTFT–74
   Earlier sketches in CTFT–4, 33; WWT–17
Gillette, William 1855–1937 .... WWasWT
Gilliam, Terry 1940– CTFT–68
   Earlier sketches in CTFT–5, 12, 21, 31
Gillian, Jerry
   See.. Gilliam, Terry
Gilliard, Carl 1958– CTFT–76
Gilliard, Larry, Jr. CTFT–73
   Earlier sketch in CTFT–33
Gilliatt, Penelope Ann Douglass................. CTFT–1
Gillie, Jean 1915–1949.......................... WWasWT
Gilliland, Helen 1897–1942 .... WWasWT
Gilliland, Richard 1950– CTFT–42
   Earlier sketches in CTFT–12, 21
Gillis, Paulina... CTFT–54
Gillman, Mabelle 1880–? .... WWasWT
Gillmore, Frank 1867–1943 .... WWasWT
Gillmore, Margalo 1897–1986 .... WWasWT
Gillott, Nick CTFT–63
Gillum, Vern CTFT–40
Gilmore, Janette 1905–.......................... WWasWT
Gilmore, Peter 1931– WWT–17
Gilmore, Virginia 1919–1986 .... WWasWT
Gilmore, W. H. .... WWasWT
Gilmour, Brian 1894–1954 .... WWasWT
Gilmour, Ian 1955– CTFT–37
Gilpin, Charles 1878–1930 .... WWasWT
Gilpin, Jack 1951– CTFT–55
   Earlier sketch in CTFT–1
Gilpin, Peri 1961–.................................. CTFT–64
   Earlier sketches in CTFT–18, 29
Gilroy, Frank D. 1925–.......................... CTFT–20
   Earlier sketches in CTFT–3; WWT–17
Gilroy, Tony.. CTFT–67
Gilsig, Jessalyn 1971– CTFT–45
Gilvezan, Dan CTFT–43

Gilyard, Clarence, Jr. 1955– CTFT–57
   Earlier sketch in CTFT–26
Gimbel, Roger 1925–.............................. CTFT–10
Gimpel, Erica 1964– CTFT–46
Gingold, Hermione 1897–1987 .... CTFT–2
   Obituary in CTFT–5
   Earlier sketch in WWT–17
Ginisty, Paul 1858–1932 .... WWasWT
Ginner, Ruby 1886–? .... WWasWT
Ginsbury, Norman 1903–....................... WWT–17
Ginter, Lindsay CTFT–38
Ginty, Robert 1948– CTFT–29
   Earlier sketches in CTFT–2, 18
Gioiello, Bruno 1968–............................ CTFT–60
Giordano, Tony 1939– CTFT–5
Giovanni, Paul 1940–1990 .... CTFT–9
Giovinazzo, Carmine 1973– CTFT–68
Giovinazzo, Rick CTFT–67
   Earlier sketch in CTFT–30
Girard, Francois 1963–........................... CTFT–27
Giraudeau, Philippe 1955– CTFT–4
Giraudoux, Jean 1882–1944 .... WWasWT
Giroday, Francois 1952– CTFT–64
   Earlier sketches in CTFT–2, 19, 29
Gish, Annabeth 1971– CTFT–28
Gish, Dorothy 1898–1968 .... WWasWT
Gish, Lillian 1893–1993 .... CTFT–4
   Obituary in CTFT–11
   Earlier sketch WWT–17
Gisondi, John 1949– CTFT–4
Git, Lei Lin
   See .... Li, Jet
Gitana, Gertie 1887–1957 .... WWasWT
Gittelsohn, Ellen CTFT–50
Giuliana, Donna Hanover
   See .... Hanover, Donna
Giuntoli, Neil CTFT–43
Givens, Robin 1964(?)– CTFT–64
   Earlier sketches in CTFT–10, 18, 29
Gkolino, Baleria
   See .... Golino, Valeria
Glabczynska, Liliana
   See .... Komorowska, Liliana
Glasco, Kimberly CTFT–12
Glaser, Lulu 1874–1958 .... WWasWT
Glaser, Paul Michael 1943– CTFT–42
   Earlier sketches in CTFT–3, 20
Glaspell, Susan 1882–1948 .... WWasWT
Glass, Dee Dee 1948– CTFT–16
Glass, Dudley 1899–.............................. WWasWT
Glass, Joanna McClelland
   1936– CTFT–1
Glass, Montague 1877–1934 .... WWasWT
Glass, Ned 1906–1984............................ CTFT–2
Glass, Philip 1937– CTFT–58
   Earlier sketches in CTFT–6, 26
Glass, Ron 1945– CTFT–68
   Earlier sketches in CTFT–3, 19, 31
Glassco, Bill 1935– CTFT–5
   Earlier sketch in WWT–17
Glasser, Isabel... CTFT–54
Glasser, Phillip 1978–............................ CTFT–65
Glassford, David 1866–1935 .... WWasWT
Glatter, Lesli Linka.................................. CTFT–49
Glau, Summer 1981– CTFT–71
Glaudini, Lola 1972– CTFT–68
   Earlier sketch in CTFT–30
Glave, Karen CTFT–63
Glave, Matthew CTFT–47
   Earlier sketch in CTFT–23
Glaze, Susan 1956– CTFT–4
Glazer, Eugene Robert CTFT–64

Glazer, Mitch 1953– CTFT–56
    Earlier sketch in CTFT–20
Gleason, Jackie 1916–1987 .... CTFT–5
Gleason, James 1886–1959 .... WWasWT
Gleason, Joanna 1950– CTFT–43
    Earlier sketches in CTFT–6, 15
Gleason, John 1941– CTFT–5
    Earlier sketch in WWT–17
Gleason, Mary Pat CTFT–75
Gleason, Paul 1944– CTFT–38
    Earlier sketches in CTFT–7, 14
Gleeson, Brendan 1955(?)– CTFT–66
    Earlier sketch in CTFT–29
Glen, Iain 1961– CTFT–53
    Earlier sketch in CTFT–25
Glendinning, Ernest 1884–1936 .... WWasWT
Glendinning, Ethel 1910– .... WWasWT
Glendinning, John 1857–1916 .... WWasWT
Glenister, Frank 1860–1945 .... WWasWT
Glenn, Scott 1942(?)– CTFT–43
    Earlier sketches in CTFT–4, 11, 22
Glennie, Brian 1912– .... WWasWT
Glennie–Smith, Nick CTFT–56
Glennon, James 1942– CTFT–64
    Earlier sketch in CTFT–29
Glenny, Charles H. 1857–1922 .... WWasWT
Glenville, Peter 1913– WWT–17
Glenville, Shaun 1884–1968 .... WWasWT
Gless, Sharon 1943– CTFT–39
    Earlier sketches in CTFT–6, 13
Glick, Michael S. CTFT–29
Glickman, Jonathan CTFT–38
Glines, John 1933– CTFT–1
Globus, Yoram CTFT–6
Glossop–Harris, Florence
    See .... Harris, Florence Glossop
Glover, Bruce 1932– CTFT–75
Glover, Crispin 1964– CTFT–73
    Earlier sketches in CTFT–6, 33
Glover, Danny 1947– CTFT–70
    Earlier sketches in CTFT–5, 12, 21, 31
Glover, Halcott 1877–1949 .... WWasWT
Glover, James Mackey 1861–? .... WWasWT
Glover, Jamie CTFT–35
Glover, John 1944– CTFT–57
    Earlier sketches in CTFT–4, 26; WWT–17
Glover, Julian 1935– CTFT–39
    Earlier sketches in CTFT–4, 13; WWT–17
Glover, Mrs.
    See .... Blair, Isla
Glover, Savion 1973– CTFT–53
Glover, Susan CTFT–79
    Earlier sketch in CTFT–36
Glover, William 1911– CTFT–3
Glowacki, Janusz 1938– CTFT–15
Gluckman, Leon 1922–1978 .... WWT–16
Glynn, Carlin 1940– CTFT–1
Glynne, Angela 1933– .... WWasWT
Glynne, Mary 1898–1954 .... WWasWT
Gobel, George 1919– CTFT–7
Godard, Jean–Luc 1930– CTFT–31
    Earlier sketches in CTFT–7, 19
Godber, John 1956– CTFT–21
    Earlier sketch in CTFT–12
Goddard, Charles W. 1879–1951 .... WWasWT
Goddard, Paul CTFT–44
Goddard, Paulette 1911(?)–1990 .... CTFT–9
Goddard, Stuart
    See .... Ant, Adam
Goddard, Trevor 1965– CTFT–36
Goddard, Willoughby 1926– WWT–17
Godden, Jimmy 1879–1955 .... WWasWT
Godfrey, Derek 1924– WWT–17

Godfrey, Lynnie CTFT–5
Godfrey, Patrick 1933– CTFT–44
    Earlier sketch in CTFT–22
Godfrey, Peter 1899–1970 .... WWasWT
Godfrey–Turner, L. .... WWasWT
Godin, Maurice CTFT–50
Godreche, Judith 1972– CTFT–54
    Earlier sketch in CTFT–26
Godunov, Alexander 1949–1995 .... CTFT–4
    Obituary in CTFT–14
Goelz, Dave 1946– CTFT–45
Goen, Bob 1954– CTFT–79
Goethals, Angela 1977– CTFT–48
    Earlier sketch in CTFT–13
Goetz, Peter Michael 1941– CTFT–77
    Earlier sketches in CTFT–2, 18, 30
Goetz, Ruth Goodman 1912– WWT–17
Goetzman, Gary 1952– CTFT–60
    Earlier sketch in CTFT–27
Goff, John F. CTFT–59
Goffin, Cora 1902– .... WWasWT
Goffin, Peter 1906– .... WWasWT
Goggin, Dan 1943– CTFT–3
Goggins, Walt CTFT–53
Going, Joanna 1963– CTFT–45
Going, John 1936– CTFT–9
    Earlier sketch in CTFT–1
Goins, Jesse D. CTFT–58
Golan, Menahem 1931(?)– CTFT–35
    Earlier sketch in CTFT–6
Golas, H. G.
    See .... Fondacaro, Phil
Golchan, Frederic 1953– CTFT–12
Gold, Barbara
    See .... Quigley, Linnea
Gold, Ernest 1921–1999 .... CTFT–12
    Obituary in CTFT–32
Gold, Jack 1930– CTFT–49
    Earlier sketch in CTFT–10
Gold, L. Harvey CTFT–54
Gold, Tracey 1969– CTFT–47
    Earlier sketch in CTFT–23
Goldberg, Adam 1970– CTFT–59
    Earlier sketch in CTFT–27
Goldberg, Alan CTFT–48
Goldberg, Amy CTFT–71
Goldberg, Bill 1966– CTFT–68
    Earlier sketch in CTFT–30
Goldberg, Gary David 1944– CTFT–10
Goldberge, Lee CTFT–70
Goldberg, Leonard 1934– CTFT–36
    Earlier sketches in CTFT–3, 11
Goldberg, Whoopi 1955– CTFT–45
    Earlier sketches in CTFT–6, 13, 23
    Brief Entry in CTFT–3
Goldblum, Jeff 1952– CTFT–60
    Earlier sketches in CTFT–6, 16, 27
Golde, Kenny CTFT–47
Goldemberg, Rose Leiman CTFT–1
Golden, Annie 1951– CTFT–48
    Earlier sketch in CTFT–7
Golden, John 1874–1955 .... WWasWT
Golden, Michael 1913– WWT–17
Goldenberg, Billy 1936– CTFT–15
Goldenblatt, Stephen 1945– CTFT–58
    Earlier sketch in CTFT–27
Goldenthal, Elliot 1954– CTFT–51
    Earlier sketch in CTFT–24
Goldie, F. Wyndham 1897–1957 .... WWasWT
Goldie, Hugh 1919– WWT–17
Goldin, Horace .... WWasWT
Goldin, Ricky Paull 1968– CTFT–61
Goldman, Bo 1932– CTFT–8

Goldman, Danny CTFT–66
Goldman, James A. 1927–1998 .... CTFT–8
    Obituary in CTFT–24
    Earlier sketch in WWT–17
Goldman, William 1931– CTFT–39
    Earlier sketches in CTFT–7, 14
Goldner, Charles 1900–1955 .... WWasWT
Goldsman, Akiva CTFT–61
    Earlier sketches in CTFT–16, 28
Goldsmith, Jerry 1929– CTFT–43
    Earlier sketches in CTFT–3, 14
Goldsmith, Merwin 1937– CTFT–4
Goldstein, Harel CTFT–42
Goldstein, Jeffrey L. 1950– CTFT–11
Goldstein, Jenette 1960– CTFT–44
Goldstone, James 1931– CTFT–9
    Earlier sketch in CTFT–1
Goldthwait, Bob 1962– CTFT–60
    Earlier sketches in CTFT–10, 17, 27
    Brief Entry in CTFT–6
Goldwyn, John 1958– CTFT–76
Goldwyn, Samuel 1882(?)–1974 .... CTFT–25
Goldwyn, Samuel, Jr. 1926– CTFT–53
    Earlier sketches in CTFT–8, 18
Goldwyn, Tony 1960– CTFT–44
    Earlier sketches in CTFT–11, 22
Golin, Steve 1955– CTFT–50
Golino, Valeria 1966– CTFT–79
    Earlier sketch in CTFT–35
Gombell, Minna 1893–1973 .... WWasWT
Gomer, Steven CTFT–62
Gomes, Andre CTFT–35
Gomes, Marc 1961(?)– CTFT–59
Gomez, Carlos CTFT–60
Gomez, Carmelo CTFT–35
Gomez, Ian 1964– CTFT–53
    Earlier sketch in CTFT–25
Gomez, Jaime 1965– CTFT–50
Gomez, Nick 1963– CTFT–60
    Earlier sketch in CTFT–27
Gomez, Panchito 1963– CTFT–53
Gomez–Preston, Reagan 1980– CTFT–68
Gondry, Michel 1963(?)– CTFT–68
Gong, Li
    See .... Li, Gong
Gonzalez, Benito
    See .... Bardem, Javier
Gonzalez Gonzalez, Clifton
Gonzalez, Rick 1979– CTFT–67
    See .... Collins, Clifton, Jr.
Gonzalo, Julie 1981– CTFT–74
Gooch, Steve 1945– CTFT–5
    Earlier sketch in WWT–17
Good, Christopher CTFT–75
    Earlier sketch in CTFT–32
Good, Meagan 1981– CTFT–44
Goodall, Caroline 1959– CTFT–50
Goodall, Edyth 1886–1929 .... WWasWT
Gooden, Jack Kelly 1949– CTFT–6
Goodeve, Grant 1952– CTFT–46
Goodhand, Donna CTFT–72
Gooding, Cuba, Jr. 1968– CTFT–38
    Earlier sketch in CTFT–13
Gooding, Omar 1976– CTFT–59
Goodliff, Michael 1914–1976 .... WWT–16
Goodman, Dody 1915– CTFT–55
    Earlier sketches in CTFT–4; WWT–17
Goodman, Henry 1950– CTFT–75
    Earlier sketch in CTFT–32
Goodman, John 1952– CTFT–61
    Earlier sketches in CTFT–9, 16, 28
Goodman, Jules Eckert 1876–1962 .... WWasWT
Goodman, Philip ?–1940 .... WWasWT

Goodner, Carol 1904– .... WWasWT
Goodrich, Arthur 1878–1941 .... WWasWT
Goodrich, Edna 1883–1974 .... WWasWT
Goodrich, Frances 1890–1984 .... CTFT–26
Goodrich, Louis 1865–1945 .... WWasWT
Goodson, Barbara CTFT–38
Goodson, Mark 1915–1992 .... CTFT–3
　Obituary in CTFT–11
Goodwin, Deidre CTFT–59
Goodwin, J. Cheever 1850–1912 .... WWasWT
Goodwin, John 1921– WWT–17
Goodwin, Nat C. 1857–1920 .... WWasWT
Goodwin, Ron 1925– CTFT–12
Goolden, Richard 1895– WWT–17
Goorjian, Michael A. 1971– CTFT–53
Goorwitz, Allen
　See .... Garfield, Allen
Gopal, Ram 1917– .... WWasWT
Gorak, Chris CTFT–65
　Earlier sketch in CTFT–29
Gorcey, Elizabeth 1965– CTFT–5
Gord, Ken CTFT–41
Gordon, Barry 1948– CTFT–54
Gordon, Brian CTFT–69
Gordon, Bryan CTFT–51
Gordon, Burt I. 1922– CTFT–8
Gordon, Charles CTFT–10
Gordon, Charles Kilbourn
　1888–? .... WWasWT
Gordon, Colin 1911–1972 .... WWasWT
Gordon, Douglas 1871–1935 .... WWasWT
Gordon, Eve 1883– CTFT–71
　Earlier sketches in CTFT–19, 31
　Earlier sketch (as Eve Bennett–Gordon) in
　CTFT–2
Gordon, Gale 1906–1995 .... CTFT–9
　Obituary in CTFT–15
　Earlier sketch in CTFT–3
Gordon, Gavin 1901–1970 .... WWasWT
Gordon, Hannah 1941– CTFT–36
　Earlier sketches in CTFT–1, 11
Gordon, Hayes 1920– WWT–17
Gordon, Howard CTFT–42
Gordon, Joyce CTFT–75
Gordon, Keith 1961– CTFT–47
　Earlier sketch in CTFT–7
Gordon, Kitty 1878–1974 .... WWasWT
Gordon, Lawrence 1936– CTFT–54
　Earlier sketches in CTFT–10, 26
Gordon, Leon 1884–1960 .... WWasWT
Gordon, Marjorie 1893– .... WWasWT
Gordon, Mark 1956– CTFT–54
　Earlier sketch in CTFT–26
Gordon, Matt CTFT–79
Gordon, Max 1892–1978 .... WWasWT
Gordon, Michael 1909–1993 .... CTFT–1
　Obituary in CTFT–12
Gordon, Noele 1923– .... WWasWT
Gordon, Pamela 1916– CTFT–37
Gordon, Ruth 1895–1985 .... CTFT–1
　Earlier sketch in WWT–17
Gordon, Serena 1963– CTFT–35
　Earlier sketch in CTFT–9
Gordon, Stuart 1947– CTFT–36
　Earlier sketch in CTFT–11
Gordone, Charles Edward
　1927– WWT–17
Gordon–Lee, Kathleen .... WWasWT
Gordon–Lennox, Cosmo 1869–1921 ..... WWasWT
Gordon–Levitt, Joseph 1981– CTFT–57
　Earlier sketches in CTFT–17, 27
Gordy, Berry, Jr. 1929– CTFT–5

Gore, Aedwyrd
　See .... Gorey, Edward
Gore, Michael 1951– CTFT–21
　Earlier sketch in CTFT–12
Gore–Browne, Robert 1893– .... WWasWT
Gorelik, Mordecai 1899–1990 .... CTFT–9
　Earlier sketch in WWT–17
Gorey, Edward 1925– CTFT–22
Gorham, Christopher 1974– CTFT–56
Goring, Marius 1912–1998 .... CTFT–11
　Obituary in CTFT–24
　Earlier sketch in WWT–17
Gorman, Cliff 1936– CTFT–29
　Earlier sketches in CTFT–2, 7, 18; WWT–17
Gorman, Patrick CTFT–56
Gorme, Eydie 1932(?)– CTFT–49
　Earlier sketch in CTFT–11
Gorney, Karen Lynn CTFT–1
Gorshin, Frank 1934(?)– CTFT–39
　Earlier sketches in CTFT–1, 14
Gorski, Tamara CTFT–37
Gorsse, Henry de 1868–? .... WWasWT
Gosling, Harold 1897– .... WWasWT
Gosling, Ryan 1980– CTFT–41
Goss, Bick 1942– CTFT–4
Goss, Luke 1968– CTFT–48
Gosselaar, Mark–Paul 1974– CTFT–47
　Earlier sketch in CTFT–23
Gossett, Louis, Jr. 1936– CTFT–47
　Earlier sketches in CTFT–6, 13, 23
Gossett, Robert CTFT–49
Gotlieb, Ben 1954– CTFT–1
Goto, Al CTFT–42
Goto, Yukihiro 1954– CTFT–22
Gott, Barbara ?–1944 .... WWasWT
Gottfried, Gilbert 1955– CTFT–50
　Earlier sketches in CTFT–15, 24
Gottfried, Martin 1933– WWT–17
Gottlieb, Carl 1938– CTFT–26
　Earlier sketches in CTFT–1, 6
Gottlieb, Morton 1921– CTFT–5
　Earlier sketch in WWT–17
Gottschalk, Ferdinand 1858–1944 .... WWasWT
Gough, Alfred CTFT–74
Gough, Michael 1916(?)– CTFT–55
　Earlier sketches in CTFT–6, 26; WWT–17
Gould, Diana 1913– .... WWasWT
Gould, Elliott 1938– CTFT–50
　Earlier sketches in CTFT–2, 6, 13, 24;
　WWT–17
Gould, Harold 1923– CTFT–65
　Earlier sketches in CTFT–1, 8, 18, 29
Gould, John
　See .... Gold, Jack
Gould, John 1940– CTFT–5
　Earlier sketch in WWT–17
Gould, Morton 1913–1996 .... CTFT–12
　Obituary in CTFT–16
　Earlier sketch in CTFT–1
Goulding, Edmund 1891–1959 .... WWasWT
Goulem, Alain CTFT–40
Goulet, Robert 1933– CTFT–45
　Earlier sketches in CTFT–4; WWT–17
Gow, James 1907–1952 .... WWasWT
Gow, Ronald 1897– WWT–17
Gowers, Bruce CTFT–65
Goyer, David S. 1966– CTFT–62
　Earlier sketches in CTFT–16, 28
Grabiak, Marita CTFT–63
Grable, Betty 1916–1973 .... WWasWT
Grace, April 1962– CTFT–73
　Earlier sketch in CTFT–33
Grace, Maggie 1983– CTFT–70

Grace, Nickolas 1949– CTFT–6
　Earlier sketch in WWT–17
Grace, Topher 1978– CTFT–68
Grace, Wayne CTFT–45
Gracen, Elizabeth 1960– CTFT–42
　Earlier sketch in CTFT–21
Grade, Lew, Lord 1906–1998 .... CTFT–6
　Obituary in CTFT–24
　Earlier sketch in WWT–17
Grady, Don 1944– CTFT–2
Graef, Vicki CTFT–39
Graff, Ilene 1949– CTFT–48
　Earlier sketch in CTFT–9
Graff, Randy 1955– CTFT–56
　Earlier sketches in CTFT–9, 26
Graff, Todd 1959– CTFT–48
　Earlier sketches in CTFT–7, 14
Graff, Vicki
　See .... Graef, Vicki
Graham Browne, W.
　See .... Browne, W. Graham
Graham, Aimee 1975– CTFT–68
　Earlier sketch in CTFT–30
Graham, Charlotte Akwyoe
　1959– CTFT–4
Graham, Currie 1967– CTFT–71
Graham, Gary 1960– CTFT–41
Graham, Gerrit 1949– CTFT–46
Graham, Harry 1874–1936 .... WWasWT
Graham, Heather 1970– CTFT–65
　Earlier sketches in CTFT–20, 29
Graham, Lauren 1967– CTFT–53
　Earlier sketch in CTFT–25
Graham, Martha 1894–1991 .... CTFT–11
　Earlier sketch in WWasWT
Graham, Morland 1891–1949 .... WWasWT
Graham, Ronny 1919– CTFT–7
　Earlier sketch in WWT–17
Graham, Violet 1890–1967 .... WWasWT
Graham, William A. 1930(?)– CTFT–36
　Earlier sketch in CTFT–10
Graham, Samaria CTFT–63
Grahame, Margot 1911– .... WWasWT
Grahn, Nancy 1958– CTFT–30
Grainer, Ron 1922– WWT–17
Grainger, Gawn 1937(?)– CTFT–77
　Earlier sketches in CTFT–5, 33; WWT–17
Grajeda, Javier CTFT–56
Gramatica, Emma 1874–1965 .... WWasWT
Gramatica, Irma 1873–1962 .... WWasWT
Grammer, Kelsey 1955– CTFT–51
　Earlier sketches in CTFT–7, 14, 25
Granat, Cary CTFT–41
Grandberry, Omarion 1984– CTFT–74
Grandison, Pippa 1970– CTFT–76
　Earlier sketch in CTFT–33
Granger, Farley 1925– CTFT–55
　Earlier sketches in CTFT–3, 19
Granger, Percy 1945– CTFT–4
　Earlier sketch in CTFT–1
Granger, Philip CTFT–62
Granger, Stewart 1913–1993 .... CTFT–8
　Obituary in CTFT–12
　Earlier sketch in WWasWT
Granick, Harry 1898– CTFT–4
Granier, Jeanne ?–1939 .... WWasWT
Grant, Amy 1960– CTFT–45
Grant, Beth 1949– CTFT–38
Grant, Bob 1932– WWT–17
Grant, Cary 1904–1986 .... CTFT–4
　Earlier sketch in CTFT–3

Grant, David Marshall 1955– CTFT–36
  Earlier sketch in CTFT–10
  Brief Entry in CTFT–3
Grant, Faye 1957– CTFT–46
Grant, Hugh 1960– CTFT–50
  Earlier sketches in CTFT–8, 15, 24
Grant, Jennifer 1966– CTFT–73
Grant, Johnny 1923– CTFT–65
Grant, Joyce 1924– CTFT–2
  Earlier sketch in WWT–17
Grant, Lee 1927– CTFT–65
  Earlier sketches in CTFT–1, 8, 18, 29
Grant, Micki WWT–17
Grant, Neil 1882–? .... WWasWT
Grant, Pauline WWT–17
Grant, Richard E. 1957– CTFT–38
  Earlier sketches in CTFT–6, 13
Grant, Rodney A. 1959– CTFT–37
Grant, Tiffany 1968– CTFT–45
Grant, Vince 1961– CTFT–56
Grantham, Leslie 1947– CTFT–76
  Earlier sketch in CTFT–33
Grantham, Wilfrid 1898– .... WWasWT
Granveildt, Brian
  See .... Greenfield, Matt
Granville, Bernard 1886–1936 .... WWasWT
Granville, Charlotte 1863–1942 .... WWasWT
Granville, Sydney ?–1959 .... WWasWT
Granville–Barker, Harley 1877–1946..... WWasWT
Granville–Barker, Helen ?–1950 .... WWasWT
Grassle, Karen 1944– CTFT–19
  Earlier sketch in CTFT–3
Grasso, Giovanni 1875–1930 .... WWasWT
Grate, Gail CTFT–32
Grattan, Harry 1867–1951 .... WWasWT
Gratton, Fred 1894–1966 .... WWasWT
Grauer, Ona CTFT–73
Graves, Clotilde Inez Mary
  1863–1932 .... WWasWT
Graves, George 1876–1949................... WWasWT
Graves, Peter 1911–1994 .... CTFT–2
  Obituary in CTFT–13
  Earlier sketch in WWT–17
Graves, Peter 1926– CTFT–50
  Earlier sketches in CTFT–1, 24
Graves, Rupert 1963– CTFT–49
  Earlier sketches in CTFT–8, 15, 24
Gray, Amlin 1946– CTFT–1
Gray, Barry 1916–1996 .... CTFT–2
  Obituary in CTFT–16
Gray, Bruce CTFT–38
Gray, Charles 1928– CTFT–8
  Earlier sketch in WWT–17
Gray, Charles W. 1949– CTFT–60
Gray, Dolores 1924– CTFT–4
  Earlier sketch in WWT–17
Gray, Dulcie 1919– CTFT–13
  Earlier sketches in CTFT–5; WWT–17
Gray, Elspet 1929– WWT–17
Gray, Erin 1950– CTFT–57
Gray, Eve 1904– .... WWasWT
Gray, F. Gary 1969(?)– CTFT–57
  Earlier sketch in CTFT–26
Gray, Gary LeRoi 1985–......................... CTFT–62
Gray, Jennifer 1916–1962...................... WWasWT
Gray, Linda 1940–.................................. CTFT–76
  Earlier sketches in CTFT–2, 33
Gray, Linda 1910–.................................. WWT–17
Gray, Mackenzie 1957– CTFT–49
Gray, Nicholas Stuart 1919–.................. WWT–17
Gray, Oliver
  See... Gray, Charles
Gray, Richard 1896–.............................. WWasWT

Gray, Sam 1923–..................................... CTFT–1
Gray, Simon 1936–................................ CTFT–18
  Earlier sketches in CTFT–2, 6; WWT–17
Gray, Spalding 1941–............................ CTFT–49
  Earlier sketches in CTFT–7, 15, 24
Gray, Terence 1895–.............................. WWasWT
Gray–Cabey, Noah 1995– CTFT–76
Grayden, Sprague................................... CTFT–74
Graydon, J. L. 1844–? .... WWasWT
Graysmark, John CTFT–49
  Earlier sketch in CTFT–11
Grayson, Kathryn 1924–.......................... CTFT–1
Grayson, Richard 1925–.......................... CTFT–4
Gray–Stanford, Jason CTFT–39
Grazer, Brian 1951– CTFT–57
  Earlier sketches in CTFT–10, 17, 27
Graziano, Stephen 1954– CTFT–41
Great, Don 1951– CTFT–21
  Earlier sketch in CTFT–12
Great Gonzo, The
  See .... Goelz, Dave
Greaza, Walter N. 1900–1973 .... WWasWT
Green, Abel 1900–1973 .... WWasWT
Green, Adolph 1915–............................. CTFT–38
  Earlier sketches in CTFT–2, 10
Green, Benny 1927–1998 .... CTFT–12
  Obituary in CTFT–22
Green, Brian Austin 1973– CTFT–42
  Earlier sketch in CTFT–20
Green, Bruce Seth CTFT–41
Green, Carlito
  See.. Coolio
Green, Dorothy 1886–1961 .... WWasWT
Green, Guy 1913 .... CTFT–26
  Earlier sketch in CTFT–1
Green, Harry 1892–1958 .... WWasWT
Green, Hilton 1929– CTFT–1
Green, Jack N. 1946–............................. CTFT–42
  Earlier sketch in CTFT–20
Green, Janet 1914–................................ WWasWT
Green, Jenna Leigh 1977–...................... CTFT–66
  Earlier sketch in CTFT–17
Green, Joann 1955– CTFT–1
Green, Johnny 1908–1989 .... CTFT–3
Green, Kim Morgan
  See .... Greene, Kim Morgan
Green, Mabel 1890– .... WWasWT
Green, Marion 1890–1956 .... WWasWT
Green, Martyn 1899–1975 .... WWT–16
Green, Michelle
  See.................................... Greene, Michele
Green, Mitzi 1920–1968 .... WWasWT
Green, Patricia CTFT–36
  Earlier sketch in CTFT–10
Green, Paul 1894–1981 .... WWT–17
Green, Seth 1974– CTFT–55
  Earlier sketch in CTFT–26
Green, Stanley 1923–.............................. CTFT–1
Green, Tom 1971– CTFT–60
  Earlier sketch in CTFT–27
Green, Walon 1936–............................... CTFT–42
Green, William 1926–.............................. CTFT–1
Green, Yvonne DeLarosa
  See.................................... Delarosa, Yvonne
Greenaway, Peter 1942– CTFT–71
  Earlier sketches in CTFT–10, 20, 31
Greenbaum, Hyam 1910– .... WWasWT
Greenberg, Adam CTFT–47
  Earlier sketch in CTFT–23
Greenberg, Drew Z. CTFT–74
Greenberg, Edward M. 1924– CTFT–9
  Earlier sketch in CTFT–1

Greenberg, Jerry CTFT–36
  Earlier sketch in CTFT–11
Greenberg, Paul..................................... CTFT–75
Greenberg, Richard 1958(?)–................. CTFT–57
  Earlier sketch in CTFT–25
Greenblatt, William R. 1944–................. CTFT–33
  Earlier sketch in CTFT–7
Greene, Clay M. 1850–1933 .... WWasWT
Greene, Daniel....................................... CTFT–65
Greene, David 1921–............................. CTFT–26
  Earlier sketch in CTFT–1
Greene, Ellen 1950(?)– CTFT–54
  Earlier sketches in CTFT–10, 26
  Brief Entry in CTFT–4
Greene, Evie 1876–1917 .... WWasWT
Greene, Graham 1904–.......................... WWT–17
Greene, Graham 1952–........................... CTFT–50
  Earlier sketches in CTFT–15, 24
Greene, H. Richard CTFT–55
Greene, James 1926– CTFT–36
  Earlier sketches in CTFT–1, 9
Greene, Kim Morgan 1960–................... CTFT–74
Greene, Lorne 1915–1987 .... CTFT–3
  Obituary in CTFT–5
Greene, Lyn 1954(?)– CTFT–42
  Earlier sketches in CTFT–2, 18
Greene, Michael 1933–.......................... CTFT–68
Greene, Michele 1962–.......................... CTFT–71
  Earlier sketches in CTFT–12, 21, 31
Greene, Peter 1964– CTFT–59
  Earlier sketch in CTFT–27
Greene, Richard 1946–............................ CTFT–1
Greener, Dorothy 1917–1971............... WWasWT
Greenfeld, Josh 1928–............................. CTFT–2
Greenfield, Matt CTFT–46
Greenhalgh, Dawn 1934(?)–.................. CTFT–62
Greenhut, Robert 1942(?)– CTFT–79
  Earlier sketches in CTFT–8, 35
Greenlee, David CTFT–21
Greenough, Beverly Sills
  See.. Sills, Beverly
Greenquist, Brad 1959– CTFT–59
Greenstreet, Sydney 1879–1954............ WWasWT
Greenwald, Joseph ?–1938 .... WWasWT
Greenwald, Maggie 1955–...................... CTFT–68
  Earlier sketch in CTFT–30
Greenwald, Robert Mark 1943–............... CTFT–6
  Earlier sketch in CTFT–1
Greenwalt, David 1949–........................ CTFT–49
  Earlier sketch in CTFT–13
Greenwood, Bruce 1956– CTFT–59
  Earlier sketches in CTFT–9, 16, 27
Greenwood, Charlotte 1893–1978 .... WWasWT
Greenwood, Jane 1934–......................... CTFT–36
  Earlier sketches in CTFT–4, 11; WWT–17
Greenwood, Joan 1921–1987 .... CTFT–4
  Earlier sketch in WWT–17
Greenwood, Kathryn 1962– CTFT–78
Greenwood, Walter 1903–1974 .... WWasWT
Greer, Bettejane
  See... Greer, Jane
Greer, Dabbs 1917–............................... CTFT–33
  Earlier sketch in CTFT–8
Greer, Jane 1924–................................... CTFT–8
Greer, Judy 1975– CTFT–40
Greer, Pam
  See.. Grier, Pam
Greet, Clare 1871–1939 .... WWasWT
Greet, Philip (Ben) 1857–1936............. WWasWT
Gregg, Clark CTFT–47
Gregg, Everley 1903–1959 .... WWasWT
Gregg, Hubert 1916– WWT–17
Gregg, Virginia 1916–1986 .... CTFT–2

Gregor, Simon CTFT–34
Gregori, Mercia 1901– .... WWasWT
Gregorio, Rose 1932– CTFT–59
Gregory, Andre 1934– CTFT–33
   Earlier sketches in CTFT–2, 6; WWT–17
Gregory, Constantine 1942– CTFT–64
Gregory, Cynthia 1946– CTFT–23
   Earlier sketch in CTFT–12
Gregory, Don 1934– CTFT–20
   Earlier sketch in CTFT–3
Gregory, Dora 1872–1954 .... WWasWT
Gregory, Dorian 1971– CTFT–69
Gregory, Frank 1884–? .... WWasWT
Gregory, James 1911– CTFT–20
   Earlier sketch in CTFT–3
Gregory, Lady 1859–1932 .... WWasWT
Gregory, Michael 1944– CTFT–65
Gregory, Sara 1921– .... WWasWT
Gregson, James R. 1889– .... WWasWT
Gregson, Joan CTFT–42
Gregson–Williams, Harry CTFT–47
Greif, Leslie CTFT–47
Greig, Joseph CTFT–34
Grein, J. T. 1862–1935 .... WWasWT
Grein, Mrs. J. T.
   See .... Orme, Michael
Greist, Kim 1958– CTFT–33
   Earlier sketch in CTFT–5
Grenfell, Joyce 1910–1979 .... WWT–16
Grenier, Adrian 1976– CTFT–68
   Earlier sketch in CTFT–30
Grenier, Zach 1954(?)– CTFT–74
   Earlier sketches in CTFT–5, 33
Gresac, Madame Fred .... WWasWT
Gresham, Gloria 1946(?)– CTFT–79
   Earlier sketches in CTFT–10, 36
Gress, Googy CTFT–59
   Earlier sketch in CTFT–27
Greth, Roma 1935– CTFT–1
Gretsch, Joel 1963– CTFT–60
Grew, Mary 1902–1971 .... WWasWT
Grey, Anne 1907– .... WWasWT
Grey, Beryl 1927– .... WWasWT
Grey, Brad 1957– CTFT–40
Grey, Clifford 1887–1941 .... WWasWT
Grey, Eve .... WWasWT
Grey, Fettes
   See .... Straczynski, J. Michael
Grey, Jane 1883–1944 .... WWasWT
Grey, Jennifer 1960– CTFT–51
   Earlier sketches in CTFT–7, 15, 24
Grey, Joel 1932– CTFT–54
   Earlier sketches in CTFT–4, 26; WWT–17
Grey, Katherine 1873–1950 .... WWasWT
Grey, Mary .... WWasWT
Grey, Zena 1988– CTFT–74
Greyeyes, Michael 1967– CTFT–54
   Earlier sketch in CTFT–26
Greyson, John 1950– CTFT–27
Gribble, George Dunning
   1882–1956 .... WWasWT
Gribble, Harry Wagstaff 1896–1981 ...... WWasWT
Gribov, Alexel Nikolaevich
   1902– .... WWasWT
Grieco, Richard 1965– CTFT–59
   Earlier sketches in CTFT–10, 17, 27
Grief, Michael CTFT–54
Grier, David Alan 1956(?)– CTFT–70
   Earlier sketches in CTFT–21, 31
Grier, Pam 1949– CTFT–70
   Earlier sketches in CTFT–20, 31
Gries, Jon CTFT–40
Griesemer, John CTFT–29

Grifasi, Joe 1944– CTFT–42
   Earlier sketch in CTFT–1
Griffies, Ethel 1878–1975 .... WWasWT
Griffin, Eddie 1968– CTFT–37
Griffin, Fred 1964– CTFT–71
Griffin, Hayden 1943– WWT–17
Griffin, Jennifer CTFT–62
Griffin, Kathy 1961– CTFT–59
   Earlier sketches in CTFT–17, 27
Griffin, Katie 1974(?)– CTFT–54
Griffin, Lynne 1952– CTFT–75
   Earlier sketches in CTFT–7, 33
Griffin, Merv 1925– CTFT–42
   Earlier sketches in CTFT–3, 20
Griffin, Norman 1887–? .... WWasWT
Griffin, Tim CTFT–79
Griffin, Tom 1946– CTFT–1
Griffis, Rhoda CTFT–54
Griffith, Andy 1926– CTFT–59
   Earlier sketches in CTFT–3, 10, 17, 27
Griffith, David Wark 1880–1948 .... WWasWT
Griffith, Hubert 1896–1953 .... WWasWT
Griffith, Hugh 1912–1980 .... WWT–17
Griffith, Kristin 1953– CTFT–72
   Earlier sketch in CTFT–32
Griffith, Melanie 1957– CTFT–50
   Earlier sketches in CTFT–6, 13, 24
Griffith, Thomas Ian 1960(?)– CTFT–59
Griffith, Tracy 1965– CTFT–51
Griffiths, Derek 1946– WWT–17
Griffiths, Jane 1930–1975 .... WWasWT
Griffiths, Rachel 1968– CTFT–47
   Earlier sketch in CTFT–23
Griffiths, Richard 1947– CTFT–44
   Earlier sketch in CTFT–22
Griffiths, Trevor 1935– CTFT–6
   Earlier sketch in WWT–17
Grifiths, Roger Ashton
   See .... Ashton–Griffiths, Roger
Griggs, William CTFT–37
Grillo, John 1942– CTFT–38
   Earlier sketch in CTFT–12
Grillo–Marxauch, Javier 1969– CTFT–60
Grimaldi, Alberto 1927– CTFT–8
Grimaldi, Marion 1926– WWT–17
Grimes, Scott 1971– CTFT–54
   Earlier sketch in CTFT–26
Grimes, Stephen 1927–1988 .... CTFT–7
Grimes, Tammy 1934– CTFT–49
   Earlier sketches in CTFT–1, 9; WWT–17
Grimshaw, Jim CTFT–42
Grimston, Dorothy May .... WWasWT
Grimwood, Herbert 1875–1929 .... WWasWT
Grinberg, Anouk 1963– CTFT–34
Grint, Rupert 1988– CTFT–67
Grisham, John 1955– CTFT–78
Grisman, Sam H. .... WWasWT
Grismer, Joseph Rhode 1849–1922 .... WWasWT
Griswold, Grace ?–1927 .... WWasWT
Grizzard, George 1928– CTFT–34
   Earlier sketches in CTFT–6; WWT–17
Grodenchik, Max CTFT–55
Grodin, Charles 1935– CTFT–28
   Earlier sketches in CTFT–3, 9, 16; WWT–17
Groenendaal, Cris 1948– CTFT–1
Groener, Harry 1951– CTFT–76
   Earlier sketches in CTFT–8, 33
Groening, Matt 1954– CTFT–27
   Earlier sketches in CTFT–10, 17
Grogg, Sam CTFT–5
Groh, David 1941– CTFT–31
   Earlier sketches in CTFT–3, 20
Groody, Louise 1897–1961 .... WWasWT

Gropman, David CTFT–65
   Earlier sketch in CTFT–29
Gropper, Milton Herbert 1896–1955 ..... WWasWT
Grosbard, Ulu 1929– CTFT–18
   Earlier sketches in CTFT–2; WWT–17
Gross, Ayre 1960– CTFT–49
   Earlier sketches in CTFT–8, 15, 24
Gross, H. Daniel CTFT–69
Gross, Mary 1953– CTFT–42
Gross, Michael 1947– CTFT–38
   Earlier sketches in CTFT–6, 13
Gross, Paul 1959– CTFT–39
   Earlier sketch in CTFT–16
Gross, Richard 1948– CTFT–58
Gross, Shelley 1921– CTFT–4
   Earlier sketch in WWT–17
Grossbart, Jack 1948– CTFT–38
   Earlier sketch in CTFT–13
Grossman, David CTFT–43
Grossman, Gary CTFT–49
Grossman, Gary H. CTFT–50
Grossmith, Ena 1896–1944 .... WWasWT
Grossmith, George 1874–1912 .... WWasWT
Grossmith, Lawrence 1877–1944 .... WWasWT
Grossmith, Weedon 1852–1919 .... WWasWT
Grossvogel, David I. 1925– CTFT–1
Grout, James 1927– CTFT–33
   Earlier sketches in CTFT–6; WWT–17
Grout, Philip 1930– WWT–17
Grove, Barry 1951– CTFT–57
   Earlier sketch in CTFT–4
Grove, Fred 1851–1927 .... WWasWT
Grover, Stanley 1926–1997 .... CTFT–10
   Obituary in CTFT–18
Groves, Charles 1875–1955 .... WWasWT
Groves, Fred 1880–1955 .... WWasWT
Grubba, Eileen CTFT–74
Grubbs, Gary 1949– CTFT–75
   Earlier sketch in CTFT–33
Gruenwald, Thomas 1935– CTFT–1
Gruffudd, Ioan 1973– CTFT–57
   Earlier sketch in CTFT–27
Grun, Bernard 1901–1972 .... WWasWT
Grunberg, Greg 1966– CTFT–73
   Earlier sketch in CTFT–32
Grundy, Lily .... WWasWT
Grundy, Sydney 1848–1914 .... WWasWT
Gruner, Olivier 1960– CTFT–37
Grunig, Tim
   See .... Carhart, Timothy
Grunwald, Ernie CTFT–78
Grusin, Dave 1934– CTFT–27
   Earlier sketches in CTFT–10, 17
Gruska, Jay 1952– CTFT–43
Gruszynski, Alexander 1950– CTFT–56
Guadagni, Nicky CTFT–68
Guardino, Charles CTFT–61
Guardino, Harry 1925–1995 .... CTFT–9
   Obituary in CTFT–15
Guare, John 1938– CTFT–39
   Earlier sketches in CTFT–1, 8; WWT–17
Guastaferro, Vincent CTFT–67
   Earlier sketch in CTFT–30
Guastini, Vincent CTFT–29
Guay, Paul CTFT–51
Guber, Lee 1920–1988 .... CTFT–6
   Earlier sketches in CTFT–4; WWT–17
Guber, Peter 1942– CTFT–53
   Earlier sketches in CTFT–2, 18
Gudegast, Hans
   See .... Braeden, Eric
Guerard Rodgers, Aggie 1943– CTFT–56

Guerra, Castulo 1945– CTFT–75
　　Earlier sketches in CTFT–5, 33
Guerra, Saverio CTFT–45
Guerra, Tonio 1920– CTFT–8
Guerrero, Alvaro CTFT–37
Guerrero, (Maria) 1868–1928 .... WWasWT
Guest, Christopher 1948– CTFT–50
　　Earlier sketches in CTFT–7, 15, 24
Guest, Jean H. 1941– CTFT–5
Guest, Lance 1960– CTFT–48
　　Earlier sketch in CTFT–23
Guest, Nicholas 1955– CTFT–74
Guetary, Georges 1915– CTFT–2
　　Earlier sketch in WWasWT
Guettel, Henry A. 1928– CTFT–1
Guffy, Burnett 1905–1983 .... CTFT–28
Gugino, Carla 1971– CTFT–57
　　Earlier sketches in CTFT–17, 27
Guiches, Gustave 1860–? .... WWasWT
Guilbert, Ann Morgan 1928– CTFT–61
Guilbert, Yvette 1868–1944 .... WWasWT
Guilfoyle, Paul 1955– CTFT–44
　　Earlier sketch in CTFT–22
Guillaume, Robert 1927(?)– CTFT–36
　　Earlier sketches in CTFT–3, 9
Guillem, Sylvie 1965– CTFT–10
Guillemaud, Marcel 1867–? .... WWasWT
Guillen Cuervo, Fernando CTFT–34
Guillory, Bennet CTFT–59
Guillory, Sienna 1975– CTFT–67
Guimera, Angel 1845–1924 .... WWasWT
Guinan, Francis CTFT–71
　　Earlier sketch in CTFT–32
Guinee, Tim CTFT–51
Guinness, Alec 1914– CTFT–24
　　Earlier sketches in CTFT–1, 8, 15; WWT–17
Guinness, Matthew 1942– CTFT–8
Guinon, Albert 1863–1923 .... WWasWT
Guion, Raymond
　　See .... Raymond, Gene
Guiot, Manu
　　See .... Stewart, David A.
Guiry, Tom 1981– CTFT–68
Guitry, Lucien 1860–1925 .... WWasWT
Guitry, Sacha 1885–1957 .... WWasWT
Gulager, Clu 1928– CTFT–33
　　Earlier sketch in CTFT–7
Gullan, Campbell ?–1939 .... WWasWT
Gullette, Sean CTFT–74
　　Earlier sketch in CTFT–33
Gulliver, Charles 1882–1961 .... WWasWT
Gumbel, Bryant 1948– CTFT–42
　　Earlier sketch in CTFT–20
Gummersall, Devon 1978– CTFT–57
　　Earlier sketches in CTFT–17, 27
Gunn, Bill 1934–1989 .... CTFT–8
Gunn, Haidee 1882–1961 .... WWasWT
Gunn, James 1970– CTFT–66
Gunn, Janet 1961– CTFT–37
Gunn, Judy 1914– .... WWasWT
Gunn, Moses 1929–1993 .... CTFT–4
　　Obituary in CTFT–12
　　Earlier sketch in WWT–17
Gunn, Sean CTFT–45
Gunning, Louise 1879–1960 .... WWasWT
Gunston, Norman
　　See .... McDonald, Garry
Gunter, John 1938– CTFT–4
　　Earlier sketch in WWT–17
Gunton, Bob 1945– CTFT–78
　　Earlier sketches in CTFT–1, 6, 35
Gurnee, Hal 1935– CTFT–15

Gurney, A. R., Jr. 1930– CTFT–49
　　Earlier sketches in CTFT–4, 13; WWT–17
Gurney, Claud 1897–1946 .... WWasWT
Gurney, Rachel CTFT–5
　　Earlier sketch in WWT–17
Gurwin, Danny 1972– CTFT–61
Gurwitch, Annabelle 1961– CTFT–59
Guss, Louis 1918– CTFT–65
　　Earlier sketch in CTFT–29
Gussow, Mel 1933– CTFT–12
　　Earlier sketch in WWT–17
Gustafson, Carol 1925– CTFT–1
Gustafson, Karin 1959– CTFT–3
Guthbert, Jon
　　See .... Cuthbert, Jon
Guthior, Chris
　　See .... Gauthier, Chris
Guthrie, Tyrone 1900–1971 .... WWasWT
Gutierrez, Gerald 1952(?)– CTFT–50
　　Earlier sketches in CTFT–1, 4, 15, 24
Guttenberg, Steve 1958– CTFT–61
　　Earlier sketches in CTFT–2, 6, 16, 28
Guttridge, Jim 1965(?)– CTFT–49
Guy, Jasmine 1964– CTFT–36
　　Earlier sketch in CTFT–9
Guy, Joyce CTFT–58
Guyer, Murphy CTFT–56
Guzman, Claudio 1927– CTFT–9
Guzman, Luis 1957(?)– CTFT–56
　　Earlier sketch in CTFT–26
Guzman, Pato 1933(?)–1991 .... CTFT–10
Gwaltney, Jack 1960– CTFT–53
Gwenn, Edmund 1877–1959 .... WWasWT
Gwilym, Mike 1949– CTFT–6
　　Earlier sketch in WWT–17
Gwisdek, Michael 1942– CTFT–34
Gwynn, Michael 1916–1976 .... WWT–16
Gwynne, Fred 1926–1993 .... CTFT–8
　　Obituary in CTFT–12
　　Earlier sketches in CTFT–2; WWT–17
Gwynne, Michael C. 1942– CTFT–36
Gwyther, Geoffrey Matheson
　　1890–1944 .... WWasWT
Gyllenhaal, Jake 1980– CTFT–64
Gyllenhaal, Maggie 1977– CTFT–73
　　Earlier sketch in CTFT–33
Gynt, Greta 1916– .... WWasWT

H

Haas, Belinda CTFT–30
Haas, Charlie 1952– CTFT–2
Haas, Lukas 1976– CTFT–61
　　Earlier sketches in CTFT–8, 16. 28
Haas, Philip CTFT–30
Haber, Alessandro 1947– CTFT–35
Haberle, Stephanie Roth
　　See .... Roth, Stephanie
Hack, Keith 1948– WWT–17
Hack, Olivia 1984– CTFT–55
Hack, Shelley 1952– CTFT–18
　　Earlier sketch in CTFT–7
Hackett, Albert 1900–1995 .... CTFT–23
Hackett, Buddy 1924–2003 .... CTFT–35
　　Obituary in CTFT–51
　　Earlier sketch in CTFT–8
Hackett, James K. 1869–1926 .... WWasWT
Hackett, Joan 1942–1983 .... CTFT–1
Hackett, Martha 1961– CTFT–64

Hackett, Norman Honore 1874–? .... WWasWT
Hackett, Raymond 1902–1958 .... WWasWT
Hackett, Walter 1876–1944 .... WWasWT
Hackford, Taylor 1944– CTFT–38
　　Earlier sketches in CTFT–3, 13
Hackman, Gene 1930– CTFT–70
　　Earlier sketches in CTFT–1, 5, 12, 21, 31
Hackney, Mabel ?–1914 .... WWasWT
Hadary, Jonathan 1948– CTFT–36
　　Earlier sketch in CTFT–10
Haddon, Archibald 1871–1942 .... WWasWT
Haddon, Peter 1898–1962 .... WWasWT
Haddrick, Ron 1929– CTFT–2
　　Earlier sketch in WWT–17
Haden–Guest, Lord
　　See .... Guest, Christopher
Hading, Jane 1859–1933 .... WWasWT
Hadley, Lisa Ann 1970– CTFT–68
　　Earlier sketch in CTFT–30
Haffman, Susannah
　　See .... Hoffman, Susanna
Haffner, Craig CTFT–49
Haft, Linal CTFT–40
Hagan, Anna CTFT–39
Hagan, Molly 1961– CTFT–56
　　Earlier sketch in CTFT–26
Hagen, Daniel CTFT–65
Hagen, Uta 1919– CTFT–2
　　Earlier sketch in WWT–17
Hagerty, Julie 1955– CTFT–73
　　Earlier sketches in CTFT–6, 33
Hagerty, Michael G. 1954– CTFT–66
Haggard, Piers 1939– CTFT–36
　　Earlier sketch in CTFT–11
Haggard, Stephen 1911–1943 .... WWasWT
Haggerty, Dan 1941– CTFT–70
　　Earlier sketches in CTFT–3, 20, 31
Haggerty, Dylan CTFT–68
　　Earlier sketch in CTFT–30
Haggerty, Julie
　　See .... Hagerty, Julie
Haggis, Paul 1953– CTFT–48
　　Earlier sketch in CTFT–13
Hagins, Montrose 1924– CTFT–74
Haglund, Dean 1965– CTFT–39
　　Earlier sketch in CTFT–17
Hagman, Larry 1931– CTFT–39
　　Earlier sketches in CTFT–3, 14
Hagon, Garrick CTFT–43
Hague, Albert 1920– CTFT–4
　　Earlier sketch in WWT–17
Hahn, Don 1955– CTFT–77
Haid, Charles 1943– CTFT–39
　　Earlier sketches in CTFT–7, 14
Haiduk, Stacy 1968– CTFT–37
Haig, Emma 1898–1939 .... WWasWT
Haigh, Kenneth 1931– CTFT–2
　　Earlier sketch in WWT–17
Haight, George 1905– .... WWasWT
Haight, Rip
　　See .... Carpenter, John
Hailey, Arthur 1920– CTFT–6
Hailey, Oliver 1932–1993 .... CTFT–5
　　Obituary in CTFT–11
　　Earlier sketch in WWT–17
Haim, Corey 1971– CTFT–62
　　Earlier sketches in CTFT–8, 16, 28
Haines, Herbert E. 1880–1923 .... WWasWT
Haines, Larry CTFT–1
Haines, Randa 1945– CTFT–48
　　Earlier sketch in CTFT–10
Haines, Robert Terrel 1870–1943 .... WWasWT

Haire, Wilson John 1932– CTFT–6
   Earlier sketch in WWT–17
Hairston, William, Jr. 1928– CTFT–1
Hajos, Mitzi 1891– .... WWasWT
Hakansson, Julia Mathilda
   1853–? .... WWasWT
Hale, Alan, Jr. 1918–1990 .... CTFT–9
Hale, Barbara 1922(?)– CTFT–26
   Earlier sketch in CTFT–7
Hale, Billy 1934– CTFT–10
Hale, Binnie 1899– .... WWasWT
Hale, Fiona 1926– CTFT–1
Hale, Georgina 1943– CTFT–2
   Earlier sketch in WWT–17
Hale, J. Robert 1874–1940 .... WWasWT
Hale, Jennifer CTFT–41
Hale, John 1926– CTFT–6
   Earlier sketch in WWT–17
Hale, Lionel 1909–1977 .... WWT–16
Hale, Louise Closser 1872–1933 .... WWasWT
Hale, Ron 1946– CTFT–66
Hale, S. T. 1899– .... WWasWT
Hale, Sonnie 1902–1959 .... WWasWT
Hale, Tony 1970– CTFT–72
Hales, Jonathan 1937– CTFT–5
   Earlier sketch in WWT–17
Haley, Brian 1963– CTFT–56
   Earlier sketch in CTFT–26
Haley, Jack 1902–1979 .... WWasWT
Haley, Jack, Jr. 1933– CTFT–2
Haley, Jackie Earle 1961– CTFT–74
Halfpenny, Tony 1913– .... WWasWT
Hall, Adrian 1927– CTFT–5
   Earlier sketch in WWT–17
Hall, Albert 1937– CTFT–45
Hall, Anmer 1863–1953 .... WWasWT
Hall, Anthony Michael 1968– CTFT–56
   Earlier sketches in CTFT–7, 14, 26
Hall, Arsenio 1955– CTFT–51
   Earlier sketches in CTFT–7, 14, 25
Hall, Bettina 1906– .... WWasWT
Hall, Brad 1958(?)– CTFT–74
Hall, Caroline CTFT–32
Hall, Conrad L. 1926– CTFT–38
   Earlier sketch in CTFT–13
Hall, David 1929–1953 .... WWasWT
Hall, Davis 1946– CTFT–1
Hall, Deidre 1947– CTFT–46
   Earlier sketch in CTFT–17
Hall, Delores CTFT–1
Hall, Ed 1931–1991 .... CTFT–2
   Obituary in CTFT–10
Hall, Georgine CTFT–32
Hall, Grayson WWT–17
Hall, Irma P. 1936(?)– CTFT–71
   Earlier sketches in CTFT–20, 32
Hall, J. W. .... WWasWT
Hall, Jerry 1956– CTFT–42
   Earlier sketch in CTFT–20
Hall, Kevin Peter 1955(?)–1991 .... CTFT–10
Hall, Laura Nelson 1876–? .... WWasWT
Hall, Lois 1926– CTFT–4
Hall, Monte 1921(?)– CTFT–55
   Earlier sketch in CTFT–4
Hall, Natalie 1904– .... WWasWT
Hall, Pauline 1860–1919 .... WWasWT
Hall, Peter 1930– CTFT–42
   Earlier sketches in CTFT–3, 11, 18; WWT–17
Hall, Phil 1952– CTFT–2
Hall, Philip Baker 1931– CTFT–53
   Earlier sketch in CTFT–25
Hall, Regina 1971– CTFT–61
Hall, Robert David CTFT–40

Hall, Thurston 1882–1958 .... WWasWT
Hall, Traylor
   See .... Howard, Traylor
Hall, Vondie Curtis
   See .... Curtis–Hall, Vondie
Hall, Willis 1929– CTFT–6
   Earlier sketch in WWT–17
Hallahan, Charles 1943–1997 .... CTFT–25
Hallam, Basil 1889–1916 .... WWasWT
Hallam, John 1941– CTFT–74
Hallard, Charles Maitland
   1865–1942 .... WWasWT
Hallatt, Henry 1888–1952 .... WWasWT
Haller, Ernest 1896–1970 .... CTFT–30
Hallett, Jack 1948– CTFT–4
Halliday, John 1880–1947 .... WWasWT
Halliday, Lena ?–1937 .... WWasWT
Halliday, Lynne 1958– CTFT–6
Halliday, Robert 1893– .... WWasWT
Hallie–Foote, Barbara
   See .... Foote, Hallie
Halliwell, David 1936– CTFT–5
   Earlier sketch in WWT–17
Hallowell, Todd CTFT–69
   Earlier sketch in CTFT–30
Hallstroem, Lasse 1946– CTFT–46
   Earlier sketches in CTFT–12, 23
Halmi, Robert 1924– CTFT–45
   Earlier sketch in CTFT–12
Halmi, Robert, Jr. 1957– CTFT–70
Halstan, Margaret 1879–? .... WWasWT
Halsted, Dan 1926– CTFT–41
Halston, Julie 1954– CTFT–75
   Earlier sketches in CTFT–8, 33
Halvorson, Gary CTFT–50
Hambleton, T. Edward 1911– WWT–17
Hambling, Arthur 1888–1952 .... WWasWT
Hambling, Gerry CTFT–36
   Earlier sketch in CTFT–11
Hamburger, Charles
   See .... Rocket, Charles
Hamel, Veronica 1945(?)– CTFT–41
   Earlier sketches in CTFT–7, 18
Hamer, Joseph 1932– CTFT–7
Hamill, Mark 1951– CTFT–35
   Earlier sketches in CTFT–2, 5
Hamilton, Carrie 1963– CTFT–6
Hamilton, Cicely 1872–1952 .... WWasWT
Hamilton, Clayton 1881–1946 .... WWasWT
Hamilton, Cosmo 1872?–1942 .... WWasWT
Hamilton, Diana 1898–1951 .... WWasWT
Hamilton, Dorothy 1897– .... WWasWT
Hamilton, George 1939– CTFT–66
   Earlier sketches in CTFT–3, 18, 29
Hamilton, Guy 1922– CTFT–8
Hamilton, Hale 1880–1942 .... WWasWT
Hamilton, Henry ?–1911 .... WWasWT
Hamilton, Joe 1929–1991 .... CTFT–8
   Obituary in CTFT–10
Hamilton, Josh 1969(?)– CTFT–48
   Earlier sketch in CTFT–23
Hamilton, Kelly 1945– CTFT–1
Hamilton, Linda 1956– CTFT–53
   Earlier sketches in CTFT–7, 14, 25
Hamilton, Lindisfarne 1910– .... WWasWT
Hamilton, Lisa Gay 1964– CTFT–57
   Earlier sketch in CTFT–27
Hamilton, Lynn 1930– CTFT–58
   Earlier sketch in CTFT–1
Hamilton, Margaret 1902–1985 .... CTFT–2
   Earlier sketch in WWT–17
Hamilton, Neil 1899–1984 .... CTFT–2
   Earlier sketch in WWasWT

Hamilton, Patricia CTFT–62
Hamilton, Patrick 1904–1962 .... WWasWT
Hamilton, Richard 1920– CTFT–37
Hamilton, Rose 1874–1955 .... WWasWT
Hamilton, Scott 1958– CTFT–43
Hamilton, Victoria 1971– CTFT–75
   Earlier sketch in CTFT–32
Hamlett, Dilys 1928– CTFT–2
   Earlier sketch in WWT–17
Hamlin, Harry 1951– CTFT–59
   Earlier sketches in CTFT–6, 16, 27
Hamlisch, Marvin 1944– CTFT–39
   Earlier sketches in CTFT–4; WWT–17
Hamm, Virginia
   See .... Fierstein, Harvey
Hammer, Ben CTFT–4
Hammer, Jan 1948– CTFT–39
   Earlier sketches in CTFT–10, 17
Hammersly, Vance
   See .... Odenkirk, Bob
Hammerstein, Arthur 1876–1955 .... WWasWT
Hammerstein, James 1931–1999 .... WWT–17
   Obituary in CTFT–24
Hammerstein, Oscar 1847–1919 .... WWasWT
Hammerstein, Oscar II 1895–1960 .... WWasWT
Hammond, Aubrey 1893–1940 .... WWasWT
Hammond, Bert E. 1880–? .... WWasWT
Hammond, Blake CTFT–30
Hammond, Brandon 1984– CTFT–65
Hammond, Darrell 1960– CTFT–53
   Earlier sketch in CTFT–25
Hammond, David 1948– CTFT–1
Hammond, Dorothy ?–1950 .... WWasWT
Hammond, John
   See .... Billingsea, Beau
Hammond, Kay 1909– .... WWasWT
Hammond, Nicholas CTFT–71
   Earlier sketches in CTFT–8, 19, 31
Hammond, Percy 1873–1936 .... WWasWT
Hammond, Peter 1923– CTFT–20
   Earlier sketch in WWasWT
Hamner, Earl 1923– CTFT–6
Hamori, Andras CTFT–53
   Earlier sketch in CTFT–25
Hampden, Walter 1879–1955 .... WWasWT
Hampshire, Susan 1937(?)– CTFT–39
   Earlier sketches in CTFT–2, 14; WWT–17
Hampton, Christopher 1946– CTFT–74
   Earlier sketches in CTFT–7, 19, 32; WWT–17
Hampton, James 1936– CTFT–34
   Earlier sketch in CTFT–7
Hampton, Louise 1881–1954 .... WWasWT
Hanado, Ohta 1882–? .... WWasWT
Hanauer, Terri CTFT–39
Hancock, Christopher 1928– WWT–17
Hancock, Herbie 1940– CTFT–41
   Earlier sketches in CTFT–8, 18
Hancock, John 1939– CTFT–1
Hancock, Sheila 1933– CTFT–75
   Earlier sketches in CTFT–2, 33; WWT–17
Hancox, Daisy 1898– .... WWasWT
Handl, Irene 1901–1987 .... CTFT–6
   Earlier sketch in WWT–17
Handler, Evan 1961– CTFT–57
   Earlier sketches in CTFT–1, 16, 27
Handman, Wynn 1922– CTFT–4
   Earlier sketch in WWT–17
Hands, Terry 1941– CTFT–13
   Earlier sketches in CTFT–5; WWT–17
Handy, James CTFT–37
Haneke, Michael 1942– CTFT–57
   Earlier sketch in CTFT–27
Hanemann, Michael CTFT–34

Haney, Anne.. CTFT–26
Hanket, Arthur 1954–............................... CTFT–2
Hankin, Larry 1945–................................. CTFT–44
   Earlier sketch in CTFT–22
Hanks, Colin 1977– CTFT–61
Hanks, Jim 1961–..................................... CTFT–37
Hanks, Tom 1956– CTFT–44
   Earlier sketches in CTFT–5, 12
   Brief Entry in CTFT–2
Hanley, William 1931– CTFT–2
   Earlier sketch in WWT–17
Hann, Walter 1838–1922 .... WWasWT
Hanna, Gillian.. CTFT–34
Hanna, William 1910–.............................. CTFT–30
   Earlier sketches in CTFT–8, 18
Hannafin, Daniel 1933–........................... CTFT–5
Hannah, Daryl 1960–................................ CTFT–51
   Earlier sketches in CTFT–6, 13, 24
Hannah, John 1962– CTFT–56
   Earlier sketch in CTFT–26
Hannan, Mary Claire CTFT–62
   Earlier sketch in CTFT–28
Hannen, Hermione 1913–..................... WWasWT
Hannen, Nicholas James 1881–1972 .... WWasWT
Hannigan, Alyson 1974–.......................... CTFT–55
   Earlier sketch in CTFT–26
Hanning, Geraldine 1923–....................... CTFT–1
Hanover, Donna 1950–............................. CTFT–54
Hanray, Lawrence 1874–1947............... WWasWT
Hansberry, Lorraine 1930–1965 .... CTFT–22
Hansen, Gunnar 1947–............................ CTFT–78
Hansen, Nina CTFT–4
Hansen, Peter 1921– CTFT–57
Hansen, Ryan 1981– CTFT–78
Hanson, Curtis 1945–............................... CTFT–72
   Earlier sketches in CTFT–1, 20, 32
Hanson, Gladys 1887–1973 .... WWasWT
Hanson, Harry 1895–.............................. WWasWT
Hanson, John 1922–1998...................... WWT–17
   Obituary in CTFT–24
Hanson, Twiggy
   See .... Twiggy
Hansson, Sigrid Valborg 1874–? .... WWasWT
Harbach, Otto 1873–1963 .... WWasWT
Harben, Hubert 1878–1941 .... WWasWT
Harben, Joan 1909–1953 .... WWasWT
Harbord, Carl .... WWasWT
Harbord, Gordon 1901–.......................... WWasWT
Harbottle, G. Laurence 1924–................. WWT–17
Harbour, Michael N. CTFT–34
Harburg, Edgar Y. 1898–1981 .... WWT–17
Harcourt, Cyril ?–1924 .... WWasWT
Harcourt, James 1873–1951 .... WWasWT
Harcourt, Leslie 1890–............................ WWasWT
Hardacred, John Pitt 1855–1933 .... WWasWT
Harden, Marcia Gay 1959–..................... CTFT–57
   Earlier sketch in CTFT–26
Hardie, Russell 1906–1973 .... WWasWT
Hardiman, Terrence 1937–...................... CTFT–5
   Earlier sketch in WWT–17
Hardin, Jerry CTFT–36
Hardin, Melora 1967–.............................. CTFT–77
   Earlier sketch in CTFT–34
Harding, Ann 1902–1981 .... WWasWT
Harding, D. Lyn 1867–1952 .... WWasWT
Harding, John 1948–................................ CTFT–6
   Earlier sketch in WWT–17
Harding, Rudge .... WWasWT
Hardinge, H. C. M. .... WWasWT
Hardison, Kadeem 1965(?)– CTFT–44
   Earlier sketches in CTFT–11, 22
Hards, Ira 1872–1938............................. WWasWT
Hardwick, Paul 1918–............................. WWT–17

Hardwicke, Cedric 1893–1964.............. WWasWT
Hardwicke, Clarice 1900–.................... WWasWT
Hardwicke, Edward 1932–...................... CTFT–76
   Earlier sketches in CTFT–8, 33; WWT–17
Hardy, Arthur F. 1870–?......................... WWasWT
Hardy, Betty 1904–................................. WWasWT
Hardy, Charisma
   See .... Carpenter, Charisma
Hardy, Jonathan 1940–........................... CTFT–66
   Earlier sketch in CTFT–29
Hardy, Joseph 1929–1990 .... WWT–17
Hardy, Oliver 1892–1957....................... CTFT–16
Hardy, Robert 1925–............................... CTFT–76
   Earlier sketches in CTFT–32; WWT–17, 20
Hare, Betty 1900– .... WWasWT
Hare, David 1947–................................... CTFT–36
   Earlier sketches in CTFT–4, 11; WWT–17
Hare, Doris 1905–................................... WWT–17
Hare, Ernest Dudley 1900– WWT–17
Hare, J. Robertson 1891–1979 .... WWT–16
Hare, John 1844–1921 .... WWasWT
Hare, (John) Gilbert 1869–1951 .... WWasWT
Hare, Will 1919–1997............................. CTFT–26
   Earlier sketch in WWT–17
Hare, Winifred 1875–?............................ WWasWT
Harelik, Mark 1951–............................... CTFT–37
Harewood, Dorian 1950– CTFT–50
   Earlier sketches in CTFT–7, 14, 24
Harford, W. .... WWasWT
Hargitay, Mariska 1964–......................... CTFT–70
   Earlier sketches in CTFT–20, 31
Hargrave, Roy 1908–............................... WWasWT
Hargrove, Dean CTFT–51
   Earlier sketch in CTFT–11
Harik, Jay 1960– CTFT–45
Harjo, Joy 1951–..................................... CTFT–16
Harjola, Lauri
   See .... Harlin, Renny
Harker, Gordon 1885–1967................... WWasWT
Harker, Joseph C. 1855–1927............... WWasWT
Harker, Susannah 1965–......................... CTFT–44
   Earlier sketch in CTFT–22
Harkishin, Jimmi 1965–.......................... CTFT–37
Harlan, Otis 1865–1940 .... WWasWT
Harlin, Renny 1959–............................... CTFT–36
   Earlier sketch in CTFT–10
Harlow, Jean 1911–1937 .... CTFT–22
Harlow, Shalom 1973–............................ CTFT–71
Harman, Barry 1950–.............................. CTFT–6
Harman, Hugh 1903(?)–1982 .... CTFT–21
Harmon, Angie 1972–.............................. CTFT–79
   Earlier sketch in CTFT–36
Harmon, Charlotte................................... CTFT–1
Harmon, Deborah 1951– CTFT–61
Harmon, Lewis 1911–.............................. CTFT–1
Harmon, Mark 1951–.............................. CTFT–51
   Earlier sketches in CTFT–7, 15, 24
Harned, Virginia 1872–1946 .... WWasWT
Harnell, Jess CTFT–37
Harney, Michael CTFT–45
Harnick, Sheldon 1924–......................... CTFT–64
   Earlier sketch in CTFT–1
Harnois, Elisabeth 1979–........................ CTFT–74
Harnos, Christine..................................... CTFT–49
Harper, Frank... CTFT–75
   Earlier sketch in CTFT–33
Harper, Gerald 1929–............................. WWT–17
Harper, Hill 1966(?)–.............................. CTFT–46
   Earlier sketch in CTFT–23
Harper, James CTFT–38
Harper, Jessica 1954–............................. CTFT–6
Harper, Robert 1951–.............................. CTFT–51
Harper, Ron 1936–.................................. CTFT–38

Harper, Tess 1950(?)–............................. CTFT–66
   Earlier sketches in CTFT–7, 18, 29
Harper, Valerie 1940– CTFT–57
   Earlier sketches in CTFT–5, 17, 27
Harras, Patricia....................................... CTFT–53
Harrell, Gordon Lowry 1940– CTFT–1
Harrelson, Woody 1961– CTFT–57
   Earlier sketches in CTFT–10, 17, 27
Harrigan, Nedda
   See .... Logan, Nedda Harrigan
Harrigan, William 1894–1966............... WWasWT
Harring, Laura 1964– CTFT–59
Harrington, Desmond 1976–.................. CTFT–64
Harrington, J. P. 1865–?....................... WWasWT
Harrington, Pat, Jr. 1929–...................... CTFT–76
   Earlier sketches in CTFT–3, 20, 32
Harris, Audrey Sophia 1901–1966 .... WWasWT
Harris, Barbara 1937– CTFT–4
   Earlier sketch in WWT–17
Harris, Barbara Eve 1959–...................... CTFT–64
Harris, Bruklin
   See .... Wright, N'Bushe
Harris, Clare ?–1949 .... WWasWT
Harris, Cynthia 1934– CTFT–55
   Earlier sketch in CTFT–5
Harris, Danielle 1977–............................ CTFT–53
Harris, Ed 1950– CTFT–52
   Earlier sketches in CTFT–2, 6, 14, 25
Harris, Elmer Blaney ?–1966 .... WWasWT
Harris, Estelle 1932– CTFT–44
   Earlier sketch in CTFT–22
Harris, Florence Glossop 1883–1931 .... WWasWT
Harris, George 1949–.............................. CTFT–75
Harris, Harriet Sansom 1955–............... CTFT–33
   Earlier sketch in CTFT–33
Harris, Henry B. 1866–1912 .... WWasWT
Harris, Hyde
   See .... Harris, Timothy
Harris, Jared 1961– CTFT–51
   Earlier sketch in CTFT–25
Harris, Jed 1900–1979........................... WWasWT
Harris, John
   See .... Young, Burt
Harris, Jonathan
   See.................................. Buzzington, Ezra
Harris, Jonathon 1914(?)–....................... CTFT–24
Harris, Julie 1925– CTFT–68
   Earlier sketches in CTFT–2, 8, 18, 30;
   WWT–17
Harris, Laura 1976–................................ CTFT–56
Harris, Lynn CTFT–79
Harris, Margaret F. 1904–...................... WWT–17
Harris, Mel 1957– CTFT–39
   Earlier sketches in CTFT–10, 17
Harris, Michael.. CTFT–17
Harris, Moira CTFT–32
Harris, Neil Patrick 1973–...................... CTFT–73
   Earlier sketches in CTFT–11, 20, 32
Harris, Phil 1904–1995 .... CTFT–24
Harris, Rachel.. CTFT–64
Harris, Richard 1930–2002 .... CTFT–27
   Obituary in CTFT–48
   Earlier sketches in CTFT–9, 16; WWasWT
Harris, Robert 1900–.............................. WWT–17
Harris, Rosemary 1930(?)–...................... CTFT–38
   Earlier sketches in CTFT–3, 13; WWT–17
Harris, Sam H. 1872–1941 .... WWasWT
Harris, Samantha 1973–......................... CTFT–78
Harris, Sherwin David
   See .... Harris, Wood
Harris, Steve 1965– CTFT–44
   Earlier sketch in CTFT–22
Harris, Susan CTFT–13

Harris, Thomas 1940– CTFT–53
 Earlier sketch in CTFT–25
Harris, Thomas Walter 1930– CTFT–16
Harris, Timothy 1946– CTFT–10
Harris, William 1884–1946 .... WWasWT
Harris, Wood 1969– CTFT–79
 Earlier sketch in CTFT–36
Harrison, Austin 1873–1928 .... WWasWT
Harrison, Frederick ?–1926 .... WWasWT
Harrison, George 1943– CTFT–34
 Earlier sketch in CTFT–8
Harrison, Gregory 1950– CTFT–33
 Earlier sketch in CTFT–3
Harrison, Jim CTFT–38
Harrison, Jim 1937– CTFT–13
Harrison, John 1924– CTFT–2
 Earlier sketch in WWT–17
Harrison, Kathleen 1898– WWT–17
Harrison, Michelle CTFT–55
Harrison, Mona ?–1957 .... WWasWT
Harrison, Mya
 See .... Mya
Harrison, Noel CTFT–27
Harrison, Rex 1908–1990 .... CTFT–4
 Obituary in CTFT–9
 Earlier sketch in WWT–17
Harrison, Tony 1937– CTFT–13
Harrold, Jamie CTFT–66
 Earlier sketch in CTFT–29
Harrold, Kathryn 1950– CTFT–68
 Earlier sketches in CTFT–7, 18, 30
Harrow, Lisa CTFT–8
Harry, Deborah 1945– CTFT–68
 Earlier sketches in CTFT–8, 18, 30
Harry, Jackee 1956(?)– CTFT–50
 Earlier sketches in CTFT–10, 17
 Brief Entry in CTFT–5
Harryhausen, Ray 1920– CTFT–8
Harshman, Margo 1986– CTFT–74
Harson, Sley
 See .... Ellison, Harlan
Hart, Bernard 1911–1964 .... WWasWT
Hart, Charles 1961– CTFT–4
Hart, Diane 1926– WWT–17
Hart, Ellis
 See .... Ellison, Harlan
Hart, Emily 1986– CTFT–77
Hart, Harvey 1928–1989 .... CTFT–1
Hart, Ian 1964– CTFT–59
 Earlier sketches in CTFT–16, 27
Hart, Kevin CTFT–75
Hart, Lorenz 1895–1945 .... WWasWT
Hart, Mary 1950– CTFT–45
 Earlier sketch in CTFT–11
Hart, Melissa Joan 1976– CTFT–66
 Earlier sketches in CTFT–18, 29
Hart, Moss 1904–1961 .... WWasWT
Hart, Pamela CTFT–33
Hart, Roxanne 1952– CTFT–60
Hart, Teddy 1897–1971 .... WWasWT
Hart, Vivian .... WWasWT
Hart, William S. 1870–1946 .... WWasWT
Harter, Leslie
 See .... Zemeckis, Leslie Harter
Harth, C. Ernst 1970– CTFT–43
Hartley, Hal 1959– CTFT–44
 Earlier sketch in CTFT–22
Hartley, Mariette 1940– CTFT–73
 Earlier sketches in CTFT–1, 4, 33
Hartley, Richard CTFT–42
Hartley–Milburn, Julie 1904–1949 .... WWasWT

Hartman Black, Lisa 1956– CTFT–62
 Earlier sketches in CTFT–9, 16, 28
 Brief Entry in CTFT–3
Hartman, Butch 1965(?)– CTFT–56
Hartman, David D. 1935– CTFT–56
 Earlier sketches in CTFT–3, 20
Hartman, Jan 1938– CTFT–3
Hartman, Phil 1948– CTFT–14
 Earlier sketch in CTFT–7
Hartnell, William 1908–1975 .... WWasWT
Hartnett, Josh 1978– CTFT–66
 Earlier sketch in CTFT–29
Harty, Patricia 1941– CTFT–61
Harvey
 See .... Weinstein, Harvey
Harvey, Anthony 1931– CTFT–9
 Earlier sketch in CTFT–1
Harvey, Don CTFT–66
 Earlier sketch in CTFT–29
Harvey, Frank 1885–1965 .... WWasWT
Harvey, Frank 1912– WWT–17
Harvey, John Martin 1863–1944 .... WWasWT
Harvey, Laurence 1928–1973 .... WWasWT
Harvey, Morris 1877–1944 .... WWasWT
Harvey, Peter 1933– CTFT–5
 Earlier sketch in WWT–17
Harvey, Rupert 1887–1954 .... WWasWT
Harvey, Steve 1957(?)– CTFT–42
 Earlier sketch in CTFT–21
Harwell, Bobby 1931– CTFT–45
Harwood, Bruce 1963– CTFT–37
Harwood, H. M. 1874–1959 .... WWasWT
Harwood, John 1876–1944 .... WWasWT
Harwood, Ronald 1934– CTFT–8
 Earlier sketch in WWT–17
Haskell, Peter 1934– CTFT–62
 Earlier sketch in CTFT–1
Haskell, Susan 1968– CTFT–44
Haskins, Dennis 1950– CTFT–66
 Earlier sketches in CTFT–18, 29
Hassall, Christopher 1912–1963 .... WWasWT
Hasselhoff, David 1952– CTFT–52
 Earlier sketches in CTFT–7, 14, 25
Hasselquist, Jenny .... WWasWT
Hassler, Patti CTFT–50
Hasso, Signe 1918– WWT–17
Hastings, Basil Macdonald
 1881–1928 .... WWasWT
Hastings, Bob 1925– CTFT–36
Hastings, Edward W. 1931– CTFT–20
 Earlier sketch in CTFT–3
Hastings, Fred .... WWasWT
Hastings, Hugh 1917– CTFT–3
 Earlier sketch in WWT–17
Hastings, Michael 1938– CTFT–2
 Earlier sketch in WWT–17
Hastings, Patrick 1880–1952 .... WWasWT
Haswell, Percy 1871–1945 .... WWasWT
Hatcher, Jeffrey 1958(?)– CTFT–55
Hatcher, Teri 1964– CTFT–43
 Earlier sketch in CTFT–14
Hatfield, Hurd 1920(?)–1998 .... CTFT–10
 Obituary in CTFT–24
Hathaway, Anne 1982– CTFT–76
Hatherton, Arthur ?–1924 .... WWasWT
Hatosy, Shawn 1975– CTFT–66
 Earlier sketch in CTFT–29
Hatton, Fanny 1870–1939 .... WWasWT
Hatton, Frederick 1879–1946 .... WWasWT
Hauer, Rutger 1944– CTFT–52
 Earlier sketches in CTFT–7, 14, 25
Hauff, Thomas CTFT–62
Haun, Lindsey 1984– CTFT–59

Hauptman, William 1942– CTFT–4
Hauptmann, Gerhart 1862–1946 .... WWasWT
Hauser, Cole 1975– CTFT–66
 Earlier sketches in CTFT–18, 29
Hauser, Fay CTFT–61
Hauser, Frank 1922– CTFT–15
 Earlier sketch in WWT–17
Hauser, Wings 1947– CTFT–74
 Earlier sketches in CTFT–8, 33
Havard, Lezley 1944– CTFT–3
Havel, Vaclav 1936– CTFT–39
 Earlier sketches in CTFT–9, 16
Havergal, Giles 1938– CTFT–13
 Earlier sketch in WWT–17
Havers, Nigel 1949– CTFT–76
 Earlier sketches in CTFT–6, 33
Haviland, William 1860–1917 .... WWasWT
Havinga, Nick CTFT–11
Havoc, June 1916– WWT–17
Hawk, Jeremy 1918– WWT–17
Hawke, Ethan 1970– CTFT–43
 Earlier sketch in CTFT–12
Hawkes, John CTFT–37
Hawkes, Terri CTFT–54
Hawkesworth, John 1920– CTFT–8
Hawkins, Iris 1893– .... WWasWT
Hawkins, Jack 1910–1973 .... WWasWT
Hawkins, Stockwell 1874–1927 .... WWasWT
Hawkins, Trish 1945– CTFT–1
Hawks, Howard 1896–1977 .... CTFT–16
Hawn, Goldie 1945– CTFT–71
 Earlier sketches in CTFT–1, 5, 12, 21,31
Haworth, Jill 1945– CTFT–29
Hawthorne, David ?–1942 .... WWasWT
Hawthorne, Elizabeth CTFT–79
 Earlier sketch in CTFT–36
Hawthorne, James
 See .... James, Hawthorne
Hawthorne, Kimberly CTFT–49
Hawthorne, Lil .... WWasWT
Hawthorne, Nigel 1929– CTFT–27
 Earlier sketches in CTFT–2, 10, 17; WWT–17
Hawtrey, Anthony 1909–1954 .... WWasWT
Hawtrey, Charles 1858–1923 .... WWasWT
Hawtrey, Charles 1914–1988 .... WWasWT
Hawtrey, Marjory 1900–1952 .... WWasWT
Hay, Ian 1876–1952 .... WWasWT
Hay, Joan 1894– .... WWasWT
Hay, Mary 1901–1957 .... WWasWT
Hay, Valerie 1910– .... WWasWT
Hayashibara, Megumi 1967– CTFT–41
Hayden, Dennis 1952– CTFT–53
Hayden, Larry 1950– CTFT–5
Hayden, Michael 1963– CTFT–66
 Earlier sketches in CTFT–18, 29
Hayden, Sophie CTFT–5
Hayden, Terese 1921– WWT–17
Haydon, Ethel 1878–1954 .... WWasWT
Haydon, Florence ?–1918 .... WWasWT
Haydon, Julie 1910–1994 .... CTFT–1
 Obituary in CTFT–15
 Earlier sketch in WWasWT
Haydu, Peter 1948– CTFT–4
Haye, Helen 1874–1957 .... WWasWT
Hayek, Salma 1968(?)– CTFT–71
 Earlier sketches in CTFT–20, 32
Hayers, Sidney 1922– CTFT–1
Hayes, Al
 See .... Altman, Robert
Hayes, Catherine Anne 1958– CTFT–4
Hayes, George 1888–1967 .... WWasWT
Hayes, Helen 1900–1993 .... CTFT–11
 Earlier sketch in WWT–17

Hayes, Isaac 1942– CTFT–72
  Earlier sketches in CTFT–20, 32
Hayes, J. Milton 1884–1940 .... WWasWT
Hayes, John Michael 1919– CTFT–23
Hayes, Joseph 1918– CTFT–1
Hayes, Lorraine
  See .... Day, Laraine
Hayes, Patricia 1909–1998 .... CTFT–1
  Obituary in CTFT–24
  Earlier sketch in WWasWT
Hayes, Paul CTFT–58
Hayes, Peter Lind 1915–1998 .... CTFT–1
  Obituary in CTFT–21
Hayes, Phil CTFT–54
Hayes, Sean 1970– CTFT–59
  Earlier sketch in CTFT–27
Hayes, Susan Seaforth 1943– CTFT–38
Hayes, Terri
  See .... Hoyos, Terry
Haygarth, Tony 1945– CTFT–76
  Earlier sketch in CTFT–33
Hayman, Al ?–1917 .... WWasWT
Hayman, David CTFT–36
Hayman, James CTFT–41
Hayman, Lillian 1922– WWT–17
Hayman, Ronald 1932– WWT–17
Haymer, Johnny 1920–1989 .... CTFT–9
Haynes, Tiger 1914– WWT–17
Haynes, Todd 1961– CTFT–12
Haynie, Jim CTFT–66
  Earlier sketch in CTFT–29
Hays, Bill 1938– WWT–17
Hays, David 1930– WWT–17
Hays, Robert 1947– CTFT–75
  Earlier sketches in CTFT–6, 33
Hays, Sanja Milkovic CTFT–40
Haysbert, Dennis 1954(?)– CTFT–57
  Earlier sketch in CTFT–26
Hayter, David 1969– CTFT–54
Hayter, James 1907– WWT–17
Haythorne, Joan 1915– WWT–17
Hayward, Leland 1902–1971 .... WWasWT
Hayward, Rachel CTFT–53
Haywood, Chris 1949– CTFT–75
  Earlier sketch in CTFT–33
Hazell, Hy 1922–1970 .... WWasWT
Hazzard, John E. 1881–1935 .... WWasWT
Head, Anthony 1954– CTFT–71
  Earlier sketches in CTFT–21, 31
Head, Edith 1897–1981 .... CTFT–16
Head, Helaine CTFT–38
  Earlier sketch in CTFT–12
Headley, Heather 1975(?)– CTFT–43
Headly, Glenne 1955(?)– CTFT–61
  Earlier sketches in CTFT–8, 16, 28
Heal, Joan 1922– WWT–17
Heald, Anthony 1944– CTFT–67
  Earlier sketches in CTFT–8, 18, 30
Healy, Christine 1934– CTFT–58
Healy, David 1932–1995 .... CTFT–25
Healy, Mary 1920– CTFT–1
Healy, Pat CTFT–67
  Earlier sketch in CTFT–30
Healy, Tim 1952– CTFT–37
Heap, Douglas 1934– CTFT–9
  Earlier sketch in WWT–17
Heap, Mark CTFT–72
  Earlier sketch in CTFT–32
Heard, John 1945(?)– CTFT–71
  Earlier sketches in CTFT–5, 12, 21, 31
Hearn, George 1934– CTFT–35
  Earlier sketch in CTFT–6
Hearn, Lew 1882–? .... WWasWT

Hearne, Richard 1909– .... WWasWT
Hearst, Rich 1965– CTFT–61
Heath, Eira 1940– WWT–16
Heatherington, Gary
  See .... Hetherington, Gary
Heatherley, Clifford 1888–1937............. WWasWT
Heaton, Patricia 1958– CTFT–59
  Earlier sketches in CTFT–17, 27
Heaton, Tom CTFT–39
Heavy D 1967– CTFT–37
Hebb, Brian R. R. CTFT–37
Heche, Anne 1969– CTFT–58
  Earlier sketches in CTFT–17, 27
Hecht, Ben 1894–1964 .... WWasWT
Hecht, Gina 1953– CTFT–39
Hecht, Jessica 1965– CTFT–72
  Earlier sketches in CTFT–20, 32
Hecht, Paul 1941(?)– CTFT–68
  Earlier sketches in CTFT–1, 8, 18, 30
Heckart, Eileen 1919– CTFT–4
  Earlier sketch in WWT–17
Heckenkamp, Spencer
  See .... Garrett, Spencer
Heckerling, Amy 1955(?)– CTFT–39
  Earlier sketches in CTFT–6, 10, 17
  Brief Entry in CTFT–2
Heckler, Andrew CTFT–67
  Earlier sketch in CTFT–30
Hedaya, Dan 1940– CTFT–59
  Earlier sketches in CTFT–10, 17, 27
Heder, Jon 1977– CTFT–70
Hedison, David 1927(?)– CTFT–67
  Earlier sketches in CTFT–8, 18, 30
Hedley, H. B. ?–1931 .... WWasWT
Hedley, Philip 1938– CTFT–2
  Earlier sketch in WWT–17
Hedman, Martha 1888–? .... WWasWT
Hedren, Tippi 1930(?)– CTFT–76
  Earlier sketches in CTFT–7, 33
Heeley, Desmond WWT–17
Heffernan, John 1934– CTFT–34
  Earlier sketches in CTFT–4; WWT–17
Heffner, Kyle T. CTFT–67
  Earlier sketch in CTFT–30
Hefler, Tricia 1974– CTFT–65
Heflin, Frances 1924– CTFT–1
  Earlier sketch in WWasWT
Heggie, O. P. 1879–1936 .... WWasWT
Heifner, Jack 1946– CTFT–1
Heighton, Brian CTFT–78
Heigl, Katherine 1978– CTFT–61
Heijermans, Herman 1864–1924 .... WWasWT
Heikin, Nancy 1948– CTFT–18
  Earlier sketch in CTFT–2
Heilbronn, William 1879–? .... WWasWT
Hein, Silvio 1879–1928. .... WWasWT
Heindl, Scott CTFT–43
Heinle, Amelia 1973– CTFT–67
  Earlier sketch in CTFT–30
Heinrichs, Rick CTFT–66
  Earlier sketch in CTFT–29
Heinsohn, Elisa 1962– CTFT–6
Heinz, Gerard 1904–1972..................... WWasWT
Heitmeyer, Jayne 1970– CTFT–67
  Earlier sketch in CTFT–30
Helberg, Simon 1980– CTFT–75
Helburn, Theresa 1887–1959 .... WWasWT
Held, Anna 1873–1918 .... WWasWT
Held, Dan 1948– CTFT–3
Helfgott, Daniel 1952– CTFT–38
  Earlier sketch in CTFT–13
Helgeland, Brian 1961– CTFT–71
  Earlier sketches in CTFT–20, 31

Helgenberger, Marg 1958– CTFT–59
  Earlier sketches in CTFT–10, 17, 27
Heller, Buck CTFT–2
Heller, Paul 1927– CTFT–53
  Earlier sketches in CTFT–1, 9
Hellman, Lillian 1905–1984 .... WWT–17
Hellman, Monte 1932– CTFT–27
Helm, Levon 1943(?)– CTFT–33
  Earlier sketch in CTFT–7
Helmond, Katherine 1934– CTFT–49
  Earlier sketches in CTFT–3, 15, 24
Helmore, Arthur 1859–1941 .... WWasWT
Helmsley, Charles Thomas Hunt
  1865–1940.................................... WWasWT
Helper, Stephen Lloyd 1957– CTFT–2
Helpmann, Robert 1909–1986 .... WWT–17
Hemblen, David CTFT–40
Hemecker, Ralph CTFT–39
Heming, Percy 1885– .... WWasWT
Heming, Violet 1895– .... WWasWT
Hemingway, Alan 1951– CTFT–4
Hemingway, Margaux 1955–1996 .... CTFT–13
  Obituary in CTFT–16
Hemingway, Marie 1893–1939 .... WWasWT
Hemingway, Mariel 1961– CTFT–68
  Earlier sketches in CTFT–3, 12, 21, 31
  Brief Entry in CTFT–2
Hemingway, Polly CTFT–34
Hemion, Dwight 1926– CTFT–8
Hemmerde, Edward George
  1871–1948 .... WWasWT
Hemming, Lindy 1948– CTFT–35
  Earlier sketch in CTFT–9
Hemmings, David 1941– CTFT–49
  Earlier sketches in CTFT–7, 14
Hemsley, Harry May 1877–1951 .... WWasWT
Hemsley, Sherman 1938– CTFT–75
  Earlier sketches in CTFT–3, 33
Hemsley, W. T. 1850–1918 .... WWasWT
Hendershott, Adam 1983– CTFT–78
Henderson, A. J. CTFT–54
Henderson, Alex F. 1866–1933 .... WWasWT
Henderson, Dickie 1922– WWT–17
Henderson, Elvira 1903– .... WWasWT
Henderson, Florence 1934– CTFT–41
  Earlier sketches in CTFT–2, 18; WWT–17
Henderson, Joshua CTFT–30
Henderson, May 1884– .... WWasWT
Henderson, Meredith 1983– CTFT–79
Henderson, Ray 1896–1970 .... WWasWT
Henderson, Robert 1904– WWT–17
Henderson, Roy WWT–11
Henderson, Saffron CTFT–41
Henderson, Shirley 1965– CTFT–67
  Earlier sketch in CTFT–30
Henderson, Stephen 1949– CTFT–68
  Earlier sketch in CTFT–30
Hendler, Lauri 1965– CTFT–61
Hendricks, Christina 1978– CTFT–69
Hendricksen, Lance
  See .... Henriksen, Lance
Hendrie, Ernest 1859–1929 .... WWasWT
Hendrix, Elaine 1970(?)– CTFT–49
Heneker, David 1906– WWT–17
Heney, Joan CTFT–65
Henfrey, Janet CTFT–34
Henig, Andi CTFT–2
Henley, Barry Shabaka 1954– CTFT–68
  Earlier sketch in CTFT–30
Henley, Beth 1952– CTFT–21
  Earlier sketches in CTFT–1, 12
Henley, Herbert James 1882–1937 .... WWasWT
Henley, Joan 1904– .... WWasWT

Hennagin, Michael J.
  See.. Goldsmith, Jerry
Hennah, Dan.. CTFT–43
Hennequin, Maurice ?–1926 .... WWasWT
Henner, Marilu 1952– CTFT–52
  Earlier sketches in CTFT–2, 7, 14, 25
Hennessy, Jill 1968– CTFT–66
  Earlier sketches in CTFT–18, 30
Hennessy, Roland Burke 1870–1939 ..... CTFT–61
Hennesy, Carolyn CTFT–61
Hennigan, Sean CTFT–49
Henniger, Rolf 1925– .... WWasWT
Henning, Linda Kaye 1944– CTFT–3
Henning, Megan 1978– CTFT–74
Hennings, Betty 1850–1939 .... WWasWT
Hennings, David CTFT–65
Hennings, Sam 1961– CTFT–61
Henreid, Paul 1908–1992 .... CTFT–12
Henriksen, Lance 1940(?)– CTFT–58
  Earlier sketches in CTFT–8, 17, 27
Henritze, Bette 1924– CTFT–29
  Earlier sketches in CTFT–2, 10, 18; WWT–17
Henry, (Alexander) Victor
  1943–.. WWasWT
Henry, Buck 1930– CTFT–78
  Earlier sketches in CTFT–1, 9, 35
Henry, Charles 1890–1968 .... WWasWT
Henry, David CTFT–50
Henry, Gregg 1952– CTFT–57
  Earlier sketch in CTFT–26
Henry, John
  See.. Richardson, Jay
Henry, Justin 1971– CTFT–56
  Earlier sketch in CTFT–26
Henry, Lenny 1958– CTFT–57
  Earlier sketch in CTFT–26
Henry, Martha 1938– CTFT–56
  Earlier sketch in CTFT–26
Henry, Martin 1872–1942 .... WWasWT
Henry, Noble
  See... Wynorski, Jim
Henry, Tim.. CTFT–66
Henshall, Ruthie....................................... CTFT–27
Henshaw, Jim 1949– CTFT–42
Hensley, John 1977– CTFT–74
Hensley, Shuler 1967– CTFT–47
Henson, Brian 1963– CTFT–68
  Earlier sketches in CTFT–12, 21, 31
Henson, Elden 1977– CTFT–43
Henson, Gladys 1897– WWT–16
Henson, Jim 1936–1990 .... CTFT–11
  Earlier sketch in CTFT–1
Henson, John 1967– CTFT–30
Henson, Leslie 1891–1957 .... WWasWT
Henson, Nicky 1945– CTFT–34
  Earlier sketches in CTFT–5; WWT–17
Henstridge, Natasha 1974– CTFT–61
  Earlier sketch in CTFT–28
Henton, John 1960– CTFT–27
  Earlier sketch in CTFT–17
Hentsch, Juergen CTFT–34
Hentschel, Irene 1891– .... WWasWT
Hepburn, Audrey 1929–1993.................... CTFT–7
  Obituary in CTFT–11
Hepburn, Katharine 1909–2003 .... CTFT–5
  Obituary in CTFT–51
  Earlier sketches in CTFT–1; WWT–17
Hepple, Jeanne 1936– WWT–17
Hepple, Peter 1927– CTFT–5
  Earlier sketch in WWT–17
Heppner, Rosa ?–1979 .... WWT–16
Hepton, Bernard 1925– WWT–17

Herbe, Katheryn
  See... Erbe, Kathryn
Herbert, Alan Patrick 1890–1971 .... WWasWT
Herbert, Evelyn 1898– .... WWasWT
Herbert, F. Hugh 1897–1958 .... WWasWT
Herbert, Henry 1879–1947 .... WWasWT
Herbert, Jocelyn 1917– CTFT–6
  Earlier sketch in WWT–17
Herbert, Rich 1956– CTFT–3
Herbert, Victor 1859–1924 .... WWasWT
Herbst, Rick
  See... Hearst, Rich
Herd, Richard 1932– CTFT–41
Heredia, Wilson Jermaine 1971(?)– CTFT–27
Herlie, Eileen 1920– WWT–17
Herlihy, James Leo 1927–1993 .... CTFT–1
  Obituary in CTFT–12
Herman, Danny 1960– CTFT–2
Herman, David 1967(?)– CTFT–62
Herman, Jerry 1933– CTFT–43
  Earlier sketches in CTFT–1, 3, 20; WWT–17
Herman, Jimmy CTFT–39
Herman, Mark CTFT–27
Herman, Pee–Wee
  See... Reubens, Paul
Hermant, Abel 1862–1950 .... WWasWT
Hernandez, Jay 1978– CTFT–68
Herndon, Richard G. ?–1958 .... WWasWT
Herne, (Katherine) Chrystal
  1883–1950 .... WWasWT
Heron, Joyce 1916–1980 .... WWT–17
Heros, Eugene .... WWasWT
Herrera, Anthony 1944– CTFT–5
Herring, Laura
  See... Harring, Laura
Herring, Lynn 1958– CTFT–30
Herrmann, Bernard 1911–1975 .... CTFT–29
Herrmann, Edward 1943– CTFT–47
  Earlier sketches in CTFT–1, 6, 23
Herrmann, Karl CTFT–54
Herrmann, Keith 1952– CTFT–1
Hersey, David 1939– CTFT–37
  Earlier sketches in CTFT–3, 11; WWT–17
Hershberger, Gary CTFT–59
Hershberger, Kevin 1973– CTFT–53
Hershey, Barbara 1948– CTFT–61
  Earlier sketches in CTFT–3, 10, 17. 28
Hershlag, Natalie
  See... Portman, Natalie
Herskovitz, Marshall 1952– CTFT–68
  Earlier sketches in CTFT–12, 21, 31
Hertford, Whit 1978– CTFT–78
Hertz, Carl 1859– .... WWasWT
Hertzler, Garman
  See... Hertzler, John
Hertzler, John CTFT–39
Hervey, Grizelda 1901– .... WWasWT
Hervey, Jason 1972– CTFT–30
  Earlier sketches in CTFT–8, 18
Hervieu, Paul 1857–1915 .... WWasWT
Herz, Ralph C. 1878–1921 .... WWasWT
Herzfeld, John CTFT–57
  Earlier sketch in CTFT–21
Herzog, Werner 1942– CTFT–52
  Earlier sketches in CTFT–7, 14, 25
Heslewood, Tom 1868–1959 .... WWasWT
Heslop, Charles 1883–1966 .... WWasWT
Heslov, Grant 1963– CTFT–41
Hess, Sandra CTFT–48
Hesseman, Howard 1940– CTFT–68
  Earlier sketches in CTFT–3, 20, 31
Hessler, Gordon 1930– CTFT–23
  Earlier sketch in CTFT–12

Hester, Eric 1976(?)– CTFT–39
Hestnes, Pedro CTFT–35
Heston, Charlton 1923(?)– CTFT–52
  Earlier sketches in CTFT–1, 3, 15, 24;
  WWT–17
Hestor, George 1877–1925 .... WWasWT
Hetherington, Gary 1941– CTFT–56
Hetrick, Jennifer 1958– CTFT–53
Heuer, John Michael 1941–..................... CTFT–6
Heuring, Lori 1973– CTFT–53
Hewes, Henry 1917– WWT–17
Hewett, Christopher CTFT–6
  Earlier sketch in WWT–17
Hewett, Dorothy 1923– WWT–17
Hewett, Jerry
  See.. Hewitt, Jery
Hewitt, Agnes ?–1924 .... WWasWT
Hewitt, Alan 1915–1986 .... CTFT–4
  Earlier sketches in CTFT–1; WWT–17
Hewitt, Don 1922– CTFT–45
  Earlier sketches in CTFT–12, 21
Hewitt, Frankie 1931– CTFT–21
  Earlier sketch in CTFT–12
Hewitt, Henry 1885–1968 .... WWasWT
Hewitt, Jennifer Love 1979– CTFT–66
  Earlier sketches in CTFT–20, 29
Hewitt, Jery CTFT–33
Hewlett, David 1968– CTFT–36
Hewlett, Maurice 1861–1923 .... WWasWT
Hewson, Paul David
  See.. Bono
Hexum, Jon–Eric 1957–1984 .... CTFT–2
Hey, Virginia CTFT–28
Heydt, Louis Jean 1905–1960 .... WWasWT
Heyman, Barton 1937–1996 .... CTFT–1
  Obituary in CTFT–16
Heyman, David 1961– CTFT–79
Heyward, Andy 1949– CTFT–37
Heyward, Dorothy 1890–1961 .... WWasWT
Heyward, Du Bose 1885–1940 .... WWasWT
Heywood, Chris
  See.. Haywood, Chris
Heywood, Jean 1921– CTFT–75
  Earlier sketch in CTFT–33
Hibbard, Edna 1895?–1942 .... WWasWT
Hibbert, Edward 1955– CTFT–62
Hibbert, Henry George 1862–1924 .... WWasWT
Hichens, Robert Smythe 1864–1950 ..... WWasWT
Hickey, John Benjamin 1963– CTFT–53
Hickey, William 1928–1997..................... CTFT–7
  Obituary in CTFT–17
Hickland, Catherine 1956– CTFT–54
Hicklin, Margery 1904– .... WWasWT
Hickman, Charles WWT–17
Hickman, Darryl 1933– CTFT–5
Hickman, Dwayne 1934– CTFT–26
Hicks, Barbara CTFT–9
Hicks, Betty Seymour 1905– .... WWasWT
Hicks, Catherine 1951– CTFT–41
  Earlier sketches in CTFT–7, 18
Hicks, (Edward) Seymour
  1871–1949 .... WWasWT
Hicks, Julian 1858–1941 .... WWasWT
Hicks, Michele 1973– CTFT–63
Hicks, Scott 1953– CTFT–25
Hickson, Joan 1906– WWT–17
Higgins, Anthony 1947– CTFT–75
  Earlier sketches in CTFT–7, 33
Higgins, Clare 1957– CTFT–69
  Earlier sketch in CTFT–8
Higgins, Colin 1941–1988 .... CTFT–5
  Earlier sketch in CTFT–1

Higgins, David 1961– CTFT–57
   Earlier sketch in CTFT–22
Higgins, James 1932– CTFT–1
Higgins, John Michael 1963– CTFT–76
   Earlier sketch in CTFT–33
Higgins, Jonathan CTFT–79
Higgins, Michael 1921(?)– CTFT–75
   Earlier sketches in CTFT–1, 6, 33
Higgins, Norman 1898– .... WWasWT
Higgins, Paul CTFT–35
Higginson, Torri CTFT–68
Highley, Reginald 1884–? .... WWasWT
Hightower, Marilyn 1923– .... WWasWT
Hightower, Rosella 1920– CTFT–16
Highway, Thomson 1951– CTFT–16
Hignell, Rose 1896– .... WWasWT
Hignett, H. R. 1870–1959 .... WWasWT
Hiken, Gerald 1927– CTFT–7
   Earlier sketch in WWT–17
Hilary, Jennifer 1942– CTFT–5
   Earlier sketch in WWT–17
Hildreth, Mark 1978(?)– CTFT–43
Hilferty, Susan CTFT–42
   Earlier sketch in CTFT–9
Hill, Amy 1953– CTFT–44
   Earlier sketch in CTFT–22
Hill, Ann Stahlman 1921– CTFT–4
Hill, Arthur 1922– CTFT–10
   Earlier sketch in WWT–17
Hill, Benny 1925–1992 .... CTFT–5
   Obituary in CTFT–11
Hill, Bernard 1944– CTFT–68
   Earlier sketches in CTFT–20, 31
Hill, Billie .... WWasWT
Hill, Dana 1964– CTFT–7
Hill, Debra CTFT–5
Hill, Denise Nicholas
   See .... Nicholas, Denise
Hill, Dule 1975– CTFT–72
   Earlier sketch in CTFT–32
Hill, Dwayne CTFT–74
Hill, Erica 1976– CTFT–75
Hill, George Roy 1922– CTFT–6
   Earlier sketches in CTFT–1; WWT–17
Hill, Grant CTFT–48
Hill, John
   See .... Koontz, Dean R.
Hill, John Dunn
   See .... Dunn–Hill, John
Hill, Ken 1937–1995 .... CTFT–5
   Obituary in CTFT–14
   Earlier sketch in WWT–17
Hill, Lauryn 1975– CTFT–47
   Earlier sketch in CTFT–23
Hill, Leonard F. 1947– CTFT–1
Hill, Lucienne WWT–17
Hill, Mars Andrew III 1927– CTFT–1
Hill, Matt 1968– CTFT–42
Hill, Peter Murray 1908– .... WWasWT
Hill, Ronnie 1911– WWT–17
Hill, Rose 1914– WWT–17
Hill, Sinclair 1896–1945 .... WWasWT
Hill, Steven 1922– CTFT–8
Hill, Teresa 1969– CTFT–54
Hill, Walter 1942– CTFT–47
   Earlier sketches in CTFT–5, 12, 23
Hill, William CTFT–69
   Earlier sketch in CTFT–30
Hillary, Ann 1930– CTFT–4
Hille, Anastasia CTFT–35
Hillenburg, Stephen 1961– CTFT–73
Hiller, Arthur 1923– CTFT–76
   Earlier sketches in CTFT–1, 8, 33

Hiller, Wendy 1912– CTFT–6
   Earler sketches in WWT–17
Hillerman, John 1932– CTFT–18
   Earlier sketches in CTFT–3, 8
Hilliard, Harriet
   See .... Nelson, Harriet
Hilliard, Kathlyn 1896–1933 .... WWasWT
Hilliard, Patricia 1916– .... WWasWT
Hilliard, Robert C. 1857–1927 .... WWasWT
Hillman, Michael 1902–1941 .... WWasWT
Hillshafer, Bethany Rooney
   See .... Rooney, Bethany
Hilton, Paris 1981– CTFT–65
Hilton–Jacobs, Lawrence 1953– CTFT–47
Hinden, Nathan
   See .... Bloch, Robert
Hindle, Art 1948(?)– CTFT–44
Hindman, Earl 1942– CTFT–41
   Earlier sketches in CTFT–8, 18
Hinds, Ciaran 1953– CTFT–68
   Earlier sketches in CTFT–20, 31
Hines, Cheryl 1965– CTFT–79
Hines, Elizabeth 1899–1971 .... WWasWT
Hines, Grainger CTFT–54
Hines, Gregory 1946– CTFT–44
   Earlier sketches in CTFT–3, 11, 22
Hines, Patrick 1930– WWT–17
Hingle, Pat 1924(?)– CTFT–62
   Earlier sketches in CTFT–2, 8, 16, 28;
   WWT–17
Hinkle, Marin 1966– CTFT–47
   Earlier sketch in CTFT–23
Hinkle, Vernon 1935– CTFT–1
Hinkley, Brent 1969– CTFT–38
Hinkley, Tommy 1960– CTFT–73
   Earlier sketch in CTFT–33
Hinton, Mary 1896– .... WWasWT
Hipp, Paul 1963– CTFT–36
   Earlier sketch in CTFT–10
Hirabayashi, Keith
   See .... Cooke, Keith
Hird, Thora 1913– WWT–17
Hiroyuki–Tagawa, Cary
   See .... Tagawa, Cary–Hiroyuki
Hirsch, Charles Henry 1870–? .... WWasWT
Hirsch, Janis 1950– CTFT–49
   Earlier sketch in CTFT–11
Hirsch, John Stephan 1930–1989 .... CTFT–6
   Earlier sketch in WWT–17
Hirsch, Judd 1935– CTFT–44
   Earlier sketches in CTFT–1, 4, 11, 22;
   WWT–17
Hirsch, Lou CTFT–55
Hirsch, Louis Achille 1881–1924 .... WWasWT
Hirschfeld, Al 1903– CTFT–1
Hirschfelder, David 1960– CTFT–78
Hirschhorn, Clive 1940– WWT–17
Hirschhorn, Joel 1937– CTFT–13
Hirschmann, Henri 1872–? .... WWasWT
Hirsh, David Julian CTFT–79
Hirsh, Hallee 1987– CTFT–50
Hirson, Alice 1929– CTFT–67
   Earlier sketch in CTFT–30
Hislop, Joseph 1887–? .... WWasWT
Hitchcock, Alfred 1899–1980 .... CTFT–1
Hitchcock, Michael 1958– CTFT–73
   Earlier sketch in CTFT–33
Hitchcock, Raymond 1865–1929 .... WWasWT
Hjejle, Iben 1971– CTFT–32
Ho, Don 1930– CTFT–17
Hoag, Jan CTFT–58
Hoag, Judith 1968(?)– CTFT–61
   Earlier sketch in CTFT–28

Hoare, Douglas 1875–? .... WWasWT
Hobart, Deborah 1950– CTFT–51
Hobart, George V. 1867–1926 .... WWasWT
Hobart, Rose 1906– .... WWasWT
Hobbes, Herbert Halliwell
   1877–1962 .... WWasWT
Hobbs, Carleton 1898– .... WWasWT
Hobbs, Frederick 1880–1942 .... WWasWT
Hobbs, Jack 1893–1968 .... WWasWT
Hobbs, William 1939– WWT–17
Hobgood, Burnet M. 1922– WWT–17
Hoblit, Gregory 1944– CTFT–53
   Earlier sketch in CTFT–25
Hobson, Harold 1904– WWT–17
Hobson, May 1889–? .... WWasWT
Hoch, Danny 1970– CTFT–53
   Earlier sketch in CTFT–25
Hochberg, Victoria 1952– CTFT–54
Hochhuth, Rolf 1931– WWT–17
Hochman, Larry 1953– CTFT–6
Hochwaelder, Fritz 1911–1986 .... CTFT–4
Hocking, Kristen
   See .... Dalton, Kristen
Hockney, David 1937– CTFT–17
   Earlier sketch in CTFT–10
Hockridge, Edmund 1919– .... WWasWT
Hoctor, Harriet 1907–1977 .... WWasWT
Hodder, Kane 1955– CTFT–69
Hodge, Edwin 1985– CTFT–63
Hodge, John 1964– CTFT–30
Hodge, Kate 1966– CTFT–74
Hodge, Merton 1904–1958 .... WWasWT
Hodge, Patricia 1946– CTFT–39
   Earlier sketches in CTFT–8, 17
Hodge, William T. 1874–1932 .... WWasWT
Hodgeman, Edwin 1935– WWT–17
Hodges, Eric "Ty" II 1981– CTFT–62
Hodges, Horace 1865–1951 .... WWasWT
Hodges, Patricia CTFT–8
Hodges, Tom 1965– CTFT–43
Hoehler, Freddy
   See .... Koehler, Frederick
Hoenig, Michael 1952– CTFT–47
   Earlier sketches in CTFT–12, 23
Hoeppner, Mark 1957– CTFT–30
Hoey, Dennis 1893–1960 .... WWasWT
Hoey, Iris 1885–? .... WWasWT
Hofert, Earl
   See .... Letterman, David
Hoffe, Barbara .... WWasWT
Hoffe, Monckton 1880–1951 .... WWasWT
Hoffman, Aaron 1880–1924 .... WWasWT
Hoffman, Avi 1958– CTFT–11
Hoffman, Basil 1938– CTFT–5
Hoffman, Bridget
   See .... Marlowe, Ruby
Hoffman, Dustin 1937– CTFT–52
   Earlier sketches in CTFT–1, 7, 14, 24;
   WWT–17
Hoffman, Jane 1911– CTFT–4
   Earlier sketch in WWT–17
Hoffman, Jenna
   See .... Byrne, Jenna
Hoffman, Maud .... WWasWT
Hoffman, Philip Seymour
   1967– CTFT–53
   Earlier sketch in CTFT–25
Hoffman, Rick CTFT–37
Hoffman, Susannah 1963(?)– CTFT–74
Hoffman, William M. 1939– CTFT–4
   Earlier sketch in WWT–17
Hoffmann, Gaby 1982– CTFT–57
   Earlier sketch in CTFT–26

Hofheimer, Charlie 1981– CTFT–36
Hofmann, Isabella 1957– CTFT–39
    Earlier sketch in CTFT–16
Hofsiss, Jack 1950– WWT–17
Hogan, Chris CTFT–41
Hogan, Gabriel 1973– CTFT–67
Hogan, Hulk 1953– CTFT–38
    Earlier sketch in CTFT–13
Hogan, Jonathon 1951– CTFT–66
    Earlier sketch in CTFT–29
Hogan, Michael CTFT–65
Hogan, Michael 1898– .... WWasWT
Hogan, P. J. 1964(?)– CTFT–23
Hogan, Paul 1939(?)– CTFT–52
    Earlier sketches in CTFT–7, 14, 25
Hogan, Robert 1936– CTFT–54
Hogan, Siobhan Fallon
    See .... Fallon, Siobhan
Hogan, Susan CTFT–66
Hogan, Terry "Hulk"
    See .... Hogan, Hulk
Hogarth, Emmett
    See .... Polonsky, Abraham (Lincoln)
Hogestyn, Drake CTFT–18
Hogg, Ian 1937– CTFT–75
    Earlier sketches in CTFT–32; WWT–17
Holbrook, Anna Kathryn CTFT–41
    Earlier sketch in CTFT–18
Holbrook, Hal 1925– CTFT–50
    Earlier sketches in CTFT–1, 7, 15, 24;
    WWT–17
Holbrook, Louise .... WWasWT
Holcomb, Rod CTFT–38
    Earlier sketch in CTFT–12
Hold, John
    See .... Bava, Mario
Holden, Alexandra 1977(?)– CTFT–53
Holden, Arthur CTFT–40
Holden, Gina 1975– CTFT–79
Holden, Jan 1931– WWT–17
Holden, Larry 1969– CTFT–35
Holden, Laurie 1972(?)– CTFT–79
    Earlier sketch in CTFT–36
Holden, Marjean CTFT–49
Holden, Michael CTFT–53
Holden, William 1918–1981 .... CTFT–16
Holden–Reid, Kristen CTFT–68
Holder, Donald CTFT–55
Holder, Geoffrey 1930(?)– CTFT–36
    Earlier sketches in CTFT–10; WWT–17
Holder, Owen 1921– WWT–17
Holdgrive, David 1958– CTFT–4
Holdridge, Lee 1944– CTFT–61
    Earlier sketches in CTFT–8, 16, 28
Hole, John 1939– WWT–17
Holgate, Ron 1937– WWT–17
Holland, Agnieszka 1948– CTFT–47
    Earlier sketches in CTFT–12, 23
Holland, Anthony 1912–1988 .... WWT–17
Holland, Antony CTFT–65
Holland, C. J.
    See .... Hurley, Maurice
Holland, Edmund Milton 1848–1913 .... WWasWT
Holland, Endesha Ida Mae
    1944– CTFT–11
Holland, Jeffrey 1946– CTFT–8
Holland, Josh 1974– CTFT–58
Holland, Mildred 1869–1944 .... WWasWT
Holland, Reece 1956– CTFT–11
Holland, Richard CTFT–62
    Earlier sketch in CTFT–28
Holland, Savage Steve 1960– CTFT–62
Holland, Tom 1943– CTFT–4

Holles, Antony 1901–1950 .... WWasWT
Holles, William 1867–1947 .... WWasWT
Holliday, Jennifer 1960– CTFT–35
    Earlier sketch in CTFT–6
Holliday, Judy 1923–1965 .... WWasWT
Holliday, Kene 1949– CTFT–38
    Earlier sketch in CTFT–12
Holliday, Polly 1937– CTFT–34
    Earlier sketches in CTFT–7
Holliman, Earl 1928– CTFT–31
    Earlier sketches in CTFT–3, 19
Hollis, Stephen 1941– WWT–17
Hollister, Lindsay 1977– CTFT–75
Holloman, Laurel CTFT–37
Holloway, Baliol 1883–1967 .... WWasWT
Holloway, Josh 1969– CTFT–70
Holloway, Julian 1944– WWT–17
Holloway, Stanley 1890–1982 .... WWT–17
Holloway, Sterling 1904– CTFT–5
Holloway, W. E. 1885–1952 .... WWasWT
Holly, Ellen 1931– CTFT–10
Holly, Lauren 1963– CTFT–50
    Earlier sketches in CTFT–15, 24
Holm, Celeste 1919– CTFT–37
    Earlier sketches in CTFT–1, 11; WWT–17
Holm, Hanya WWT–17
Holm, Ian 1931– CTFT–67
    Earlier sketch in CTFT–30
    Earlier sketches in CTFT–2, 9, 19; WWT–17
Holm, John Cecil 1904–1981 .... WWT–17
Holman, Clare CTFT–35
Holman, Libby 1906–1971 .... WWasWT
Holme, Stanford 1904– .... WWasWT
Holme, Thea 1907– WWT–17
Holmes, David 1969– CTFT–79
Holmes, Helen ?–1950 .... WWasWT
Holmes, Katie 1978– CTFT–52
    Earlier sketch in CTFT–25
Holmes, Robert 1899–1945 .... WWasWT
Holmes, Rupert 1947– CTFT–13
Holmes, Taylor 1878–1959 .... WWasWT
Holmes, Tina CTFT–75
Holmes–Gore, Dorothy 1896–1915 ...... WWasWT
Holt, Andrew
    See .... Anhalt, Edward
Holt, Fritz 1940–1987 .... CTFT–1
    Obituary in CTFT–5
Holt, Lester 1959– CTFT–71
Holt, Lorri CTFT–30
Holt, Samuel
    See .... Westlake, Donald E.
Holt, Sandrine 1972– CTFT–77
    Earlier sketch in CTFT–34
Holt, Thelma 1933– WWT–17
Holt, Will 1929– WWT–17
Holtz, Lou 1898– .... WWasWT
Holtzman, Robert CTFT–62
    Earlier sketch in CTFT–28
Holubova, Eva 1959– CTFT–35
Holzer, Adela WWT–17
Homan, David 1907– .... WWasWT
Home, William Douglas 1912– WWT–17
Homeier, Skip 1930– CTFT–8
Homfrey, Gladys ?–1932 .... WWasWT
Homolka, Oscar 1898–1978 .... WWasWT
Hone, Mary 1904– .... WWasWT
Honer, Mary 1914– .... WWasWT
Honey, Fluffer
    See .... Grenier, Adrian
Hong, Chin–pao
    See .... Kam–Bo, Sammo Hung
Hong, James
    See .... Kam–Bo, Sammo Hung

Hong, James 1929– CTFT–63
    Earlier sketches in CTFT–9, 16, 28
Hong, Jinbao
    See .... Kam–Bo, Sammo Hung
Hong, Wilson S. 1934– CTFT–5
Honri, Percy 1874–1953 .... WWasWT
Hood, Basil 1864–1917 .... WWasWT
Hood, Morag 1942– CTFT–2
    Earlier sketch in WWT–17
Hooks, Bobbie Dean
    See .... Hooks, Robert
Hooks, Brian 1973– CTFT–78
Hooks, Jan 1957– CTFT–40
Hooks, Kevin 1958– CTFT–63
    Earlier sketches in CTFT–9, 16, 28
Hooks, Robert 1937– CTFT–35
    Earlier sketch in CTFT–5; WWT–17
Hool, Lance CTFT–34
    Earlier sketch in CTFT–6
Hooper, Ewan 1935– WWT–17
Hooper, Nicholas CTFT–79
Hooper, Tobe 1943– CTFT–50
    Earlier sketches in CTFT–7, 15, 24
Hootkins, William 1948– CTFT–35
Hoover, Richard 1947– CTFT–65
    Earlier sketch in CTFT–29
Hope, Anthony 1863–1933 .... WWasWT
Hope, Barclay 1958– CTFT–60
Hope, Bob 1903– CTFT–42
    Earlier sketches in CTFT–3, 20; WWasWT
Hope, Evelyn ?–1966 .... WWasWT
Hope, Leslie CTFT–41
Hope, Maidie 1881–1937 .... WWasWT
Hope, Nicholas CTFT–34
Hope, Teri
    See .... Garr, Teri
Hope, Vida 1918–1963 .... WWasWT
Hope, William CTFT–47
Hope–Wallace, Philip A. 1911–1979 ..... WWT–16
Hopkins, Anthony 1937– CTFT–43
    Earlier sketches in CTFT–1, 8, 16; WWT–17
Hopkins, Arthur 1878–1950 .... WWasWT
Hopkins, Bo 1942– CTFT–67
    Earlier sketches in CTFT–3, 19, 30
Hopkins, Bruce 1955– CTFT–69
Hopkins, Charles 1884–1953 .... WWasWT
Hopkins, Joan 1915– .... WWasWT
Hopkins, John 1931–1998 .... WWT–17
    Obituary in CTFT–24
Hopkins, Josh 1970– CTFT–73
    Earlier sketch in CTFT–33
Hopkins, Kaitlin 1964– CTFT–72
Hopkins, Miriam 1902–1972 .... WWasWT
Hopkins, Shirley Knight
    See .... Knight, Shirley
Hopkins, Stephen 1958(?)– CTFT–50
    Earlier sketch in CTFT–24
Hopkins, Telma 1948– CTFT–75
    Earlier sketches in CTFT–6, 33
Hopper, De Wolf 1858–1935 .... WWasWT
Hopper, Dennis 1936– CTFT–51
    Earlier sketches in CTFT–4, 13, 24
Hopper, Edna Wallace 1864–1959 .... WWasWT
Hopper, Tim CTFT–73
    Earlier sketch in CTFT–32
Hopper, Victoria 1909– .... WWasWT
Hopwood, Avery 1882–1928 .... WWasWT
Horan, Edward 1898– .... WWasWT
Horan, James 1954– CTFT–41
Horberg, William CTFT–65
    Earlier sketch in CTFT–29
Hordern, Michael 1911–1995 .... CTFT–14
    Earlier sketches in CTFT–6; WWT–17

Horn, Mary 1916– .... WWasWT
Horn, Michelle 1987– CTFT–70
Hornby, Leslie
    See .... Twiggy
Horne, A. P. .... WWasWT
Horne, David 1893–1970..................... WWasWT
Horne, Kenneth 1900– .... WWasWT
Horne, Lena 1917– CTFT–6
Horneff, Wil 1979– CTFT–69
Horner, James 1953– CTFT–61
    Earlier sketches in CTFT–10, 17, 28
Horner, Richard 1920– CTFT–19
    Earlier sketches in CTFT–3; WWT–17
Horniman, Annie Elizabeth Fredericka
    1860–1937 .... WWasWT
Horniman, Roy 1872–1930 .... WWasWT
Hornsby, David CTFT–68
Hornsby, Leslie
    See .... Twiggy
Hornsby, Nancy 1910–1958 .... WWasWT
Hornsby, Russell CTFT–67
    Earlier sketch in CTFT–30
Horovitch, David 1945– CTFT–75
    Earlier sketches in CTFT–6, 33; WWT–17
Horovitz, Israel 1939– CTFT–41
    Earlier sketches in CTFT–3, 19; WWT–17
Horrigan, Sam 1981– CTFT–75
Horrocks, Jane 1964– CTFT–44
    Earlier sketch in CTFT–22
Horsdal, Chelah 1973– CTFT–79
Horse, Michael 1951– CTFT–61
    Earlier sketches in CTFT–17, 28
Horsford, Anna Maria 1949(?)– CTFT–37
    Earlier sketches in CTFT–1, 10
Horsley, Lee 1955– CTFT–41
    Earlier sketches in CTFT–3, 19
Horsnell, Horace 1883–1949 .... WWasWT
Horton, Edward Everett 1886–1970....... WWasWT
Horton, John.. CTFT–54
Horton, Michael CTFT–50
Horton, Peter 1953– CTFT–67
    Earlier sketches in CTFT–8, 18, 30
Horton, Robert 1870–? .... WWasWT
Horvitz, Louis J. 1947– CTFT–49
Horvitz, Richard Steven 1947–............. CTFT–41
Horwitz, Murray 1949– CTFT–3
Hose, Tushka
    See .... Bergen, Tushka
Hosea, Bobby.. CTFT–38
Hoskins, Bob 1942– CTFT–61
    Earlier sketches in CTFT–3, 10, 17, 28;
    WWT–17
Hossack, Allison 1965– CTFT–61
Hostetter, John CTFT–52
Hotchkis, Joan 1927– CTFT–7
Hoty, Dee 1952– CTFT–48
    Earlier sketch in CTFT–10
Hou, Hsiao–hsien 1947–........................ CTFT–27
Houdini, Harry 1873–1926 .... WWasWT
Hough, John 1941– CTFT–2
Houghton, Katharine CTFT–1
Houghton, Norris 1909– WWT–17
Hould–Ward, Ann 1954– CTFT–38
Hounsou, Djimon 1964–......................... CTFT–71
    Earlier sketches in CTFT–21, 31
House, Dakota 1974(?)–......................... CTFT–39
    Earlier sketch in CTFT–17
House, Eric WWT–17
Houseman, John 1902–1988.................... CTFT–2
    Obituary in CTFT–7
    Earlier sketch in WWT–17
Houser, Jerry 1952– CTFT–55
Housman, Laurence 1865–1959............ WWasWT

Houston, Donald 1923–....................... WWT–17
Houston, Jane .... WWasWT
Houston, Josephine 1911–................... WWasWT
Houston, Kent CTFT–65
    Earlier sketch in CTFT–29
Houston, Marques 1981– CTFT–56
Houston, Renee 1902–1980 .... WWT–17
Houston, Whitney 1963– CTFT–47
    Earlier sketches in CTFT–12, 23
Hove, Anders 1956– CTFT–30
Howard, Alan 1937–.............................. CTFT–41
    Earlier sketches in CTFT–6, 16; WWT–17
Howard, Anne Marie 1960(?)– CTFT–59
Howard, Andree 1910–1968 .... WWasWT
Howard, Arliss 1954– CTFT–71
    Earlier sketch in CTFT–32
Howard, Bart 1915–................................. CTFT–3
Howard, Bryce Dallas 1981– CTFT–69
Howard, Clint 1959–.............................. CTFT–50
    Earlier sketches in CTFT–7, 15, 24
Howard, Eugene 1880–1965 .... WWasWT
Howard, J. Bannister 1867–1946.......... WWasWT
Howard, James Newton 1951– CTFT–46
    Earlier sketches in CTFT–12, 23
Howard, Jean Speegle 1928– CTFT–28
    Earlier sketch in CTFT–16
Howard, Jeremy 1981– CTFT–69
Howard, Joseph
    See .... Rudnick, Paul
Howard, Keble 1875–1928 .... WWasWT
Howard, Ken 1944–............................... CTFT–75
    Earlier sketches in CTFT–4, 34; WWT–17
Howard, Kyle 1978–.............................. CTFT–76
    Earlier sketch in CTFT–34
Howard, Leslie 1893–1943 .... WWasWT
Howard, Lisa 1963–............................... CTFT–40
Howard, Norah 1901–1968 .... WWasWT
Howard, Pamela 1939–........................... CTFT–6
    Earlier sketch in WWT–17
Howard, Peter CTFT–53
Howard, Rance 1928– CTFT–52
    Earlier sketch in CTFT–24
Howard, Roger 1938– WWT–17
Howard, Ron 1954– CTFT–44
    Earlier sketches in CTFT–1, 4, 11, 22
Howard, Shawn Michael 1969–............. CTFT–66
    Earlier sketches in CTFT–18, 29
Howard, Sherman 1949– CTFT–51
Howard, Sidney 1891–1939 .... WWasWT
Howard, Sydney 1885–1946 .... WWasWT
Howard, Terrence Dashon....................... CTFT–54
Howard, Traylor 1966(?)–....................... CTFT–58
    Earlier sketch in CTFT–26
Howard, Trevor 1916–1988 .... CTFT–4
    Earlier sketch in WWT–17
Howard, Walter 1866–1922 .... WWasWT
Howard, Willie 1883–1949 .... WWasWT
Howarth, Donald 1931– WWT–17
Howe, Bette
    See.. Henritze, Bette
Howe, George 1900–............................ WWT–17
Howe, James Wong 1899–1976............. CTFT–26
Howe, Tina 1937–.................................. CTFT–15
    Earlier sketch in CTFT–7
Howell, C. Thomas 1966– CTFT–58
    Earlier sketches in CTFT–8, 16, 27
Howell, Chris CTFT–54
Howell, Jane WWT–17
Howell, John 1888–1928 .... WWasWT
Howell, Judy Ruskin
    See... Ruskin, Judy L.
Howell, Tom
    See................................. Howell, C. Thomas

Howells, Ursula 1922–........................... CTFT–41
    Earlier sketches in CTFT–9; WWT–17
Howerd, Frankie 1921– CTFT–2
    Earlier sketch in WWT–17
Howes, Basil 1901–............................... WWasWT
Howes, Bobby 1895–1972 .... WWasWT
Howes, Sally Ann.................................... CTFT–5
    Earlier sketch in WWT–17
Howland, Beth 1941– CTFT–62
    Earlier sketch in CTFT–3
Howland, Jobyna 1880–1936 .... WWasWT
Howlett, Noel 1901–1984..................... WWT–17
Hoy, Maysie CTFT–58
    Earlier sketch in CTFT–26
Hoyes, Charles CTFT–76
    Earlier sketch in CTFT–34
Hoyle, Derek
    See... Dobson, Peter
Hoyos, Terry CTFT–67
Hoyt, John 1905–1991 .... CTFT–27
Hrebejk, Jan 1967– CTFT–34
Hry
    See .... Havel, Vaclav
Hsian–Fei, Wu
    See .... Woo, John
Hsiung, Shih I. 1902–........................... WWasWT
Hu, Kelly 1968–..................................... CTFT–59
    Earlier sketch in CTFT–27
Huban, Eileen 1895–1935 .... WWasWT
Huband, David....................................... CTFT–38
Hubar, Janine
    See .... Temime, Jany
Hubbard, Erica 1979– CTFT–74
Hubbard, Lorna 1910–1954 .... WWasWT
Hubbell, Raymond 1879–1954 .... WWasWT
Huber, Gusti 1914–............................... WWasWT
Huber, Kathleen 1947–........................... CTFT–7
Hubert–Whitten, Janet 1956–............... CTFT–41
    Earlier sketches in CTFT–2, 18
Hubley, Season CTFT–4
Hubley, Whip 1958– CTFT–53
Huby, Roberta .... WWasWT
Huckabee, Cooper 1951– CTFT–65
Hudd, Roy 1936–................................... CTFT–76
    Earlier sketches in CTFT–34; WWT–17
Hudd, Walter 1898–1963 .... WWasWT
Huddleston, David 1930– CTFT–49
    Earlier sketches in CTFT–7, 24
Hudec, M. Leigh
    See... Barrett, Majel
Hudis, Norman 1922– CTFT–4
Hudlin, Reginald 1961– CTFT–79
    Earlier sketches in CTFT–11, 36
Hudlin, Warrington 1953– CTFT–49
    Earlier sketch in CTFT–11
Hudolin, Wendy
    See .... Partridge, Wendy
Hudson, Bill 1949– CTFT–8
Hudson, Ernie 1945–............................. CTFT–59
    Earlier sketches in CTFT–8, 16, 27
Hudson, Gary CTFT–41
Hudson, Hugh.. CTFT–10
Hudson, Jeffery
    See..................................... Crichton, Michael
Hudson, Kate 1979– CTFT–39
Hudson, Oliver 1976–............................ CTFT–71
Hudson, Rock 1925–1985..................... CTFT–2
Hudson, Ruben
    See........................... Santiago–Hudson, Ruben
Hudson, Ruben–Santiago
    See........................... Santiago–Hudson, Ruben
Hudson, Verity 1923–1988.................... WWT–17
Huertas, Jon 1976(?)– CTFT–43

Hues, Matthias 1959– CTFT–63
Huff, Brent 1961–................................ CTFT–37
Huffman, Cady 1965–.......................... CTFT–50
Huffman, Felicity 1962–........................ CTFT–72
    Earlier sketches in CTFT–7, 32
Huffman, Rosanna.................................. CTFT–51
Hufnail, Mark...................................... CTFT–49
Huggett, David
    See .... Barker, Ronnie
Huggins, Erica CTFT–52
    Earlier sketch in CTFT–25
Hugh Kelly, Daniel 1952(?)–.................. CTFT–59
    Earlier sketches in CTFT–25, 53
Hughes, Albert 1972– CTFT–51
    Earlier sketch in CTFT–24
Hughes, Allen 1972–............................ CTFT–51
    Earlier sketch in CTFT–24
Hughes, Allen Lee CTFT–11
Hughes, Annie 1869–1954 .... WWasWT
Hughes, Barnard 1915–........................ CTFT–59
    Earlier sketches in CTFT–1, 7; WWT–17
Hughes, Del 1909–1985 .... CTFT–1
Hughes, Dusty 1947–............................ WWT–17
Hughes, Finola 1960– CTFT–66
    Earlier sketch in CTFT–30
Hughes, Hatcher 1883–1945................ WWasWT
Hughes, Hazel 1913–............................ WWasWT
Hughes, Helen CTFT–68
Hughes, John 1950–.............................. CTFT–46
    Earlier sketches in CTFT–5, 12, 23
Hughes, Langston 1902–1967 .... CTFT–21
Hughes, Laura 1959–............................ CTFT–1
Hughes, Mick 1938–.............................. WWT–17
Hughes, Miko 1986–.............................. CTFT–48
Hughes, Roddy 1891–............................ WWasWT
Hughes, Rupert 1872–1956 .... WWasWT
Hughes, Terry CTFT–50
    Earlier sketch in CTFT–11
Hughes, Tom E. .... WWasWT
Hughes, Wendy CTFT–7
Hughley, D. L. 1963–............................ CTFT–58
    Earlier sketch in CTFT–26
Hugo, Laurence 1927–1994 .... CTFT–1
    Obituary in CTFT–13
Huguenet, Felix 1858–1926 .... WWasWT
Hulbert, Claude 1900–1964 .... WWasWT
Hulbert, Jack 1892–1978 .... WWT–16
Hulce, Thomas 1953–............................ CTFT–48
    Earlier sketch in CTFT–9
    Brief Entry in CTFT–3
Hules, Endre.. CTFT–56
Hull, Henry 1890–1977 .... WWasWT
Hull, Josephine 1886–1957 .... WWasWT
Hulsey, James G. 1927–........................ CTFT–38
    Earlier sketch in CTFT–12
Hume, Benita 1906–1968 .... WWasWT
Humes, Mary–Margaret CTFT–43
Humphrey, Cavada................................ WWT–17
Humphrey, Renee.................................. CTFT–51
Humphreys, Alf CTFT–62
Humphreys, Cecil 1883–1947 .... WWasWT
Humphries, Barry 1934– CTFT–76
    Earlier sketches in CTFT–34; WWT–17
Humphries, John 1895–1927................ WWasWT
Humphris, Gordon 1921– .... WWasWT
Hung, Kam–po
    See .... Kam–Bo, Sammo Hung
Hung, Sammo
    See .... Kam–Bo, Sammo Hung
Hunkins, Lee 1930–.............................. CTFT–1
Hunley, Leann 1955–............................ CTFT–43
Hunnicutt, Gayle 1943(?)– CTFT–16

Hunt, Barbara Leigh
    See .... Leigh–Hunt, Barbara
Hunt, Bob
    See .... Kouf, Jim
Hunt, Bonnie 1964(?)– CTFT–69
    Earlier sketches in CTFT–20, 31
Hunt, Charles W. 1943–1989.................. CTFT–5
Hunt, Helen 1963– CTFT–58
    Earlier sketches in CTFT–8, 16, 27
Hunt, Hugh 1911–................................ WWT–17
Hunt, Linda 1945– CTFT–45
    Earlier sketches in CTFT–3, 9, 23
Hunt, Marsha 1917– CTFT–9
    Earlier sketch in WWasWT
Hunt, Martita 1900–1969 .... WWasWT
Hunt, Peter 1938–................................ CTFT–1
    Earlier sketch in WWT–17
Hunter, Bill 1940–................................ CTFT–33
Hunter, George W. 1851–? .... WWasWT
Hunter, Glenn 1896–1945 .... WWasWT
Hunter, Holly 1958–.............................. CTFT–48
    Earlier sketches in CTFT–6, 13, 24
Hunter, Ian 1900–1975 .... WWasWT
Hunter, Jeffrey 1926–1969...................... CTFT–16
Hunter, Kenneth 1882–? .... WWasWT
Hunter, Kim 1922–2002 .... CTFT–29
    Obituary in CTFT–49
    Earlier sketches in CTFT–3, 19; WWT–17
Hunter, Marian 1944– CTFT–5
Hunter, Norman C. 1908–1971 .... WWasWT
Hunter, Rachel 1969–............................ CTFT–68
Hunter, Ross 1926–1996 .... CTFT–12
    Obituary in CTFT–16
Hunter, Victor William 1910– WWT–17
Huntley, G. P. 1868–1927 .... WWasWT
Huntley, G. P. 1904–............................ WWasWT
Huntley, Noah 1974–............................ CTFT–63
Huntley, Raymond 1904–1990.............. CTFT–10
    Earlier sketch in WWT–17
Huntley, Tim 1904– .... WWasWT
Huntley–Wright, Betty 1911–................ WWasWT
Huntley–Wright, Jose 1918–.................. WWasWT
Hupp, Jana Marie CTFT–34
Huppert, Isabelle 1955(?)–...................... CTFT–34
    Earlier sketch in CTFT–7
Hurd, Gale Anne 1955–.......................... CTFT–46
    Earlier sketches in CTFT–9, 23
Hurd, Michelle 1966– CTFT–61
    Earlier sketch in CTFT–28
Hurgon, Austen A. ?–1942 .... WWasWT
Hurlbut, W. J. 1883–?............................ WWasWT
Hurley, Elizabeth 1965– CTFT–52
    Earlier sketches in CTFT–15, 25
Hurley, Kathy 1947–.............................. CTFT–1
Hurley, Maurice 1939–.......................... CTFT–49
Hurndall, Richard 1910–........................ WWT–17
Hurok, Sol 1888–1974 .... WWasWT
Hurran, Dick 1911–.............................. WWT–17
Hurry, Leslie 1909–1978 .... WWT–16
Hursey, Sherry 1940–............................ CTFT–41
    Earlier sketches in CTFT–3, 19
Hurst, Fannie 1889–1968 .... WWasWT
Hurst, Gregory S. 1947–........................ CTFT–2
Hurst, Michael 1957–............................ CTFT–26
Hurst, Ryan 1976–................................ CTFT–43
Hurt, John 1940–.................................. CTFT–44
    Earlier sketches in CTFT–1, 3, 11, 22; WWT–17
Hurt, Mary Beth 1946(?)– CTFT–38
    Earlier sketches in CTFT–1, 4, 13; WWT–17
Hurt, William 1950– CTFT–45
    Earlier sketches in CTFT–1, 5, 12, 23
Husain, Jory.. CTFT–4

Husmann, Ron 1937– WWT–17
Huss, Toby CTFT–38
Hussein, Waris 1938– CTFT–36
    Earlier sketch in CTFT–11
Hussey, Jimmy 1891–1930 .... WWasWT
Hussey, Olivia 1951–............................ CTFT–38
    Earlier sketches in CTFT–7, 15
Hussey, Ruth 1914–.............................. WWasWT
Huston, Anjelica 1951–.......................... CTFT–44
    Earlier sketches in CTFT–4, 11, 22
Huston, Danny 1962–............................ CTFT–66
    Earlier sketch in CTFT–30
Huston, John 1909–1987 .... CTFT–2
    Obituary in CTFT–5
Huston, Walter 1884–1950 .... WWasWT
Hutchens, Brice
    See .... Cummings, Bob
Hutcherson, Josh 1992– CTFT–78
Hutcheson, David 1905–1976 .... WWT–16
Hutchinson, Harry 1892–1980 .... WWT–16
Hutchinson, Josephine 1904–................ WWasWT
Hutchinson Scott, Jay 1924– .... WWasWT
Hutchison, Doug 1960– CTFT–61
    Earlier sketch in CTFT–28
Hutchison, Emma ?–1965 .... WWasWT
Hutchison, Kieren 1974–........................ CTFT–76
Hutchison, Muriel 1915–1975 .... WWasWT
Hutchison, Percy 1875–1945 .... WWasWT
Huth, Harold 1892–1967 .... WWasWT
Hutman, Jon CTFT–37
Hutt, William 1920–.............................. WWT–17
Hutton, Geoffrey 1909– WWT–17
Hutton, Lauren 1943(?)–........................ CTFT–30
    Earlier sketches in CTFT–3, 18
Hutton, Rif CTFT–44
Hutton, Robert 1920–1994...................... CTFT–9
    Obituary in CTFT–13
Hutton, Timothy 1960– CTFT–44
    Earlier sketches in CTFT–2, 6, 13, 22
Hutzler, Brody 1971–............................ CTFT–69
Hwang, David Henry 1957– CTFT–52
    Earlier sketches in CTFT–5, 12
Hyams, Peter 1943– CTFT–38
    Earlier sketches in CTFT–5, 12
Hyde, James 1962– CTFT–74
Hyde, Jonathan 1947–.......................... CTFT–66
    Earlier sketch in CTFT–29
Hyde, R.
    See .... Ebert, Roger
Hyde–Pierce, David
    See .... Pierce, David Hyde
Hyde–White, Alex 1959– CTFT–77
    Earlier sketches in CTFT–5, 34
Hyde–White, Wilfrid 1903–1991............ CTFT–11
    Earlier sketch in WWT–17
Hyem, Constance Ethel ?–1928 .... WWasWT
Hyland, Frances 1927– WWT–17
Hyland, Sarah 1990–............................ CTFT–61
Hylands, Scott 1943– CTFT–39
    Earlier sketch in CTFT–16
Hylton, Jack 1892–1965 .... WWasWT
Hylton, Millie 1868–1920 .... WWasWT
Hylton, Richard 1920–1962 .... WWasWT
Hyman, Dick 1927–.............................. CTFT–10
Hyman, Earle 1926–.............................. CTFT–36
    Earlier sketches in CTFT–3, 11; WWT–17
Hyman, Joseph M. 1901–1977.............. WWasWT
Hyman, Prudence .... WWasWT
Hymer, John B. ?–1953 .... WWasWT
Hynes, Jessica
    See .... Stevenson, Jessica
Hyson, Dorothy 1915–.......................... WWasWT

Hytner, Nicholas 1956– CTFT–41
    Earlier sketch in CTFT–9
Hytner, Steve CTFT–53

I

Ibbetson, Arthur 1922– CTFT–9
Ibu, Masato 1949– CTFT–34
Ice Cube 1969– CTFT–44
    Earlier sketches in CTFT–13, 22
Ice–T 1958– CTFT–49
    Earlier sketches in CTFT–12, 24
Idalis
    See .... DeLeon, Idalis
Ide, Patrick 1916– WWT–17
Iden, Rosalind 1911– .... WWasWT
Idle, Eric 1943– CTFT–77
    Earlier sketches in CTFT–5, 34
Idlette, Patricia CTFT–74
Idol, Billy 1955– CTFT–43
Idziak, Slawomir Andrzej 1945– CTFT–45
    Earlier sketch in CTFT–16
Idzikowski, Stanislas ?–1977 .... WWasWT
Ifans, Rhys 1968– CTFT–58
    Earlier sketch in CTFT–26
Iger, Robert 1951– CTFT–12
Illing, Peter 1905–1966 .... WWasWT
Illington, Margaret 1881–1934 .... WWasWT
Illington, Marie ?–1927 .... WWasWT
Ilyin, Vladimir 1947– CTFT–34
Imada, Jeff 1955– CTFT–49
Imes–Jackson, Mo'Nique 1967– CTFT–60
Imi, Tony 1937– CTFT–76
    Earlier sketches in CTFT–9, 34
Immerman, William J. 1937– CTFT–1
Imperato, Carlo 1963– CTFT–4
Imperioli, Michael 1966(?)– CTFT–62
    Earlier sketch in CTFT–28
Imrie, Celia 1952– CTFT–61
    Earlier sketch in CTFT–28
Indigo 1984– CTFT–77
Inescort, Elaine ?–1964 .... WWasWT
Inescort, Frieda 1901–1976 .... WWasWT
Ingalls, John F. CTFT–54
Inge, William 1913–1973 .... WWasWT
Ingels, Marty 1936– CTFT–62
    Earlier sketch in CTFT–5
Ingham, Barrie CTFT–5
    Earlier sketch in WWT–17
Ingham, Robert E. 1934– CTFT–1
Ingle, John 1928– CTFT–62
Ingledew, Rosalind
    See .... Allen, Rosalind
Inglesby, Mona 1918– .... WWasWT
Ingram, Rex 1895–1969 .... WWasWT
Ingram, Terry CTFT–62
Innaurato, Albert 1948– CTFT–4
    Earlier sketch in WWT–17
Innes, Angus Mac
    See .... MacInnes, Angus
Innes, Laura 1959(?)– CTFT–59
    Earlier sketches in CTFT–16, 27
Innes, Scott 1966– CTFT–78
Innocent, Harold 1935(?)–1993 .... CTFT–6
    Obituary in CTFT–12
    Earlier sketch in WWT–17
Insana, Tino 1948– CTFT–40

Ionesco, Eugene 1912(?)–1994 .... CTFT–4
    Obituary in CTFT–13
    Earlier sketch in WWT–17
Ireland, Anthony 1902–1957 .... WWasWT
Ireland, Jill 1941–1990 .... CTFT–6
    Obituary in CTFT–9
Ireland, John 1916– CTFT–8
    Earlier sketch in CTFT–1
Ireland, Kathy 1963– CTFT–44
Ireland, Kenneth 1920– CTFT–5
    Earlier sketch in WWT–17
Irish, Annie 1865–1947 .... WWasWT
Irizarry, Vincent 1959– CTFT–26
Irons, Jeremy 1948– CTFT–52
    Earlier sketches in CTFT–2, 7, 14, 25
Ironside, Michael 1950– CTFT–51
    Earlier sketches in CTFT–7, 14, 24
Irrera, Dom 1947– CTFT–55
Irvin, John 1940– CTFT–39
    Earlier sketches in CTFT–8, 16
Irvine, Robin 1901–1933 .... WWasWT
Irving, Amy 1953– CTFT–44
    Earlier sketches in CTFT–1, 4, 11, 22
Irving, Daisy ?–1938 .... WWasWT
Irving, Elizabeth 1904– .... WWasWT
Irving, Ellis 1902– WWT–16
Irving, Ethel 1869–1963 .... WWasWT
Irving, George S. 1922– CTFT–4
    Earlier sketch in WWT–17
Irving, H. B. 1870–1919 .... WWasWT
Irving, Isabel 1871–1944 .... WWasWT
Irving, Jules 1925– WWT–17
Irving, K. Ernest 1878–1953 .... WWasWT
Irving, Laurence Henry Forster
    1897–1914 .... WWasWT
Irving, Laurence Sidney 1871–1914 ...... WWasWT
Irwin, Bill 1950– CTFT–76
    Earlier sketches in CTFT–7, 34
Irwin, Edward 1867–1937 .... WWasWT
Irwin, May 1862–1938 .... WWasWT
Irwin, Steve 1962–2006 .... CTFT–26
    Obituary in CTFT–73
Irwin, Tom 1956– CTFT–63
    Earlier sketch in CTFT–28
Isaacks, Levie CTFT–56
Isaacs, Edith J. R. 1878–1956 .... WWasWT
Isaacs, Jason 1963– CTFT–44
    Earlier sketch in CTFT–22
Isaak, Chris 1956– CTFT–53
    Earlier sketches in CTFT–15, 25
Isabelle, Katharine 1982– CTFT–65
Iscove, Robert 1947– CTFT–63
    Earlier sketch in CTFT–28
Isham, Gyles (Bart) 1903–1976 .... WWasWT
Isham, Mark 1951– CTFT–78
    Earlier sketches in CTFT–4, 35
Isherwood, Christopher 1904–1986 .... WWasWT
Ishibashi, Ryo 1956(?)– CTFT–76
    Earlier sketch in CTFT–34
Ishida, Jim CTFT–38
Ishii, Sogo 1957– CTFT–35
Isler, Seth CTFT–58
Israel, Neal 1945(?)– CTFT–41
    Earlier sketch in CTFT–9
Issyanov, Ravil CTFT–37
Istomina, Maria
    See .... Charisse, Cyd
Italiano, Anne
    See .... Bancroft, Anne
Itami, Juzo 1933–1997 .... CTFT–21
Ito, Robert 1931– CTFT–30
    Earlier sketches in CTFT–7, 18

Itzin, Gregory CTFT–66
    Earlier sketch in CTFT–29
Ivanek, Zeljko 1957– CTFT–72
    Earlier sketches in CTFT–5, 32
    Brief Entry in CTFT–2
Ivanir, Mark 1968– CTFT–75
Ivar, Stan... CTFT–64
Ives, Burl 1909–1995 .... CTFT–3
    Obituary in CTFT–18
    Earlier sketch in WWT–17
Ivey, Dana 1942(?)– CTFT–66
    Earlier sketches in CTFT–2, 5, 18, 29
Ivey, Judith 1951– CTFT–59
    Earlier sketches in CTFT–1, 8, 16, 27
Ivor, Frances .... WWasWT
Ivory, James 1928– CTFT–48
    Earlier sketches in CTFT–1, 6, 13
Iwamatsu, Mako
    See .... Mako
Izenour, George C. 1912– WWT–17
Izzard, Eddie 1962– CTFT–53
    Earlier sketch in CTFT–25

J

J. J.
    See .... Jones, John Marshall
Jablonski, Carl 1937– CTFT–3
Jablonsky, Steve...................................... CTFT–77
Jace, Michael 1965– CTFT–52
Jack and Evelyn 1886?–?/1888–? .... WWasWT
Jackee
    See .... Harry, Jackee
Jacker, Corinne 1933– WWT–17
Jackman, Hugh 1968– CTFT–62
    Earlier sketch in CTFT–28
Jackness, Andrew 1952– CTFT–75
    Earlier sketches in CTFT–4, 33
Jacks, James... CTFT–41
Jacks, John
    See..................................... Jackson, John M.
Jackson, Andrew 1962– CTFT–40
Jackson, Anne 1926(?)– CTFT–30
    Earlier sketches in CTFT–1, 7, 18; WWT–17
Jackson, Barry Vincent 1879–1961 .... WWasWT
Jackson, David CTFT–39
Jackson, Doug CTFT–38
Jackson, Douglas 1940– CTFT–38
    Earlier sketch in CTFT–13
Jackson, Ernestine CTFT–10
Jackson, Ethel 1877–1957 .... WWasWT
Jackson, Freda 1909– WWT–17
Jackson, Frederic 1886–1953 .... WWasWT
Jackson, Gildart CTFT–78
Jackson, Glenda 1936– CTFT–4
    Earlier sketch in WWT–17
Jackson, Gordon 1923–1990................... CTFT–9
    Earlier sketches in CTFT–5; WWT–17
Jackson, Janet 1966– CTFT–42
    Earlier sketch in CTFT–20
Jackson, Jeanine CTFT–56
Jackson, John M. 1950– CTFT–40
    Earlier sketch in CTFT–17
Jackson, Jonathan 1982– CTFT–61
    Earlier sketch in CTFT–28
Jackson, Joshua 1978–............................ CTFT–52
    Earlier sketch in CTFT–25
Jackson, Kate 1949(?)–............................ CTFT–67
    Earlier sketches in CTFT–3, 19, 30

Jackson, Mel CTFT–61
Jackson, Michael 1958– CTFT–42
    Earlier sketch in CTFT–20
Jackson, Nagle 1936– CTFT–9
    Earlier sketch in CTFT–1
Jackson, Nelson 1870–? .... WWasWT
Jackson, Peter 1961– CTFT–60
    Earlier sketch in CTFT–16, 27
Jackson, Randy 1956– CTFT–65
Jackson, Roger L. CTFT–40
Jackson, Samuel L. 1948(?)– CTFT–61
    Earlier sketches in CTFT–10, 17, 28
Jackson, Sherry 1942– CTFT–8
Jackson, Stoney 1960– CTFT–59
Jackson, Tom 1948(?)– CTFT–40
    Earlier sketch in CTFT–17
Jackson, Victoria 1959– CTFT–40
Jacob, Abe J. 1944– CTFT–6
    Earlier sketch in CTFT–2
Jacob, Irene 1966– CTFT–44
    Earlier sketches in CTFT–11, 22
Jacob, Naomi 1889–1964 .... WWasWT
Jacobi, Derek 1938– CTFT–52
    Earlier sketches in CTFT–1, 7, 14, 25;
    WWT–17
Jacobi, Lou 1913– CTFT–7
    Earlier sketch in WWT–17
Jacobs, David 1939– CTFT–37
    Earlier sketch in CTFT–10
Jacobs, Gideon 1990– CTFT–75
Jacobs, Jim 1942– CTFT–1
Jacobs, Lawrence–Hilton
    See .... Hilton–Jacobs, Lawrence
Jacobs, Matthew 1956– CTFT–38
Jacobs, Rusty 1967– CTFT–1
Jacobs, Sally 1932– CTFT–5
    Earlier sketch in WWT–17
Jacobs, William Wymark 1863–1943 .... WWasWT
Jacobson, Peter CTFT–69
    Earlier sketch in CTFT–30
Jacobson, Peter Marc 1957– CTFT–71
Jacobson, Rick CTFT–37
Jacoby, Billy
    See .... Jayne, Billy
Jacoby, Bobby 1973– CTFT–48
Jacoby, Mark 1947– CTFT–43
Jacot, Christopher 1979– CTFT–68
Jacott, Carlos CTFT–41
Jacques, Hattie 1924–1980 .... WWT–17
Jaeck, Scott CTFT–37
Jaeckel, Richard 1926–1997 .... CTFT–5
    Obituary in CTFT–18
Jaenicke, Hannes 1960– CTFT–42
Jaffe, Herb 1921(?)–1991 .... CTFT–5
    Obituary in CTFT–10
Jaffe, Michael 1945– CTFT–75
    Earlier sketches in CTFT–4, 33
Jaffe, Sam 1893–1984 .... CTFT–1
    Earlier sketch in WWT–17
Jaffe, Stanley R. 1940– CTFT–40
    Earlier sketches in CTFT–10, 17
Jaffe, Susan CTFT–13
Jaffer, Melissa 1936– CTFT–76
    Earlier sketch in CTFT–33
Jaffrey, Saeed 1929– CTFT–78
    Earlier sketches in CTFT–8, 35
Jaffrey, Sakina CTFT–76
Jagger, Dean 1903(?)–1991 .... CTFT–11
    Earlier sketch in WWasWT
Jagger, Mick 1943– CTFT–71
    Earlier sketches in CTFT–20, 31
Jaglom, Henry 1943– CTFT–1
Jago, Raphael Bryan 1931– WWT–17

Jaid, Ildiko
    See .... Barrymore, Jaid
Jakobson, Maggie
    See .... Wheeler, Maggie
Jakub, Lisa 1978– CTFT–38
Jalland, Henry 1861–1928 .... WWasWT
James, Bob 1939– CTFT–12
James, Brian 1920– WWT–17
James, Brian d'Arcy CTFT–39
James, Brion 1945– CTFT–25
James, Charity CTFT–56
James, Clifton 1921– CTFT–55
    Earlier sketches in CTFT–1, 3, 19
James, Colton 1988– CTFT–70
James, Daisy .... WWasWT
James, Dorothy Dorian 1930– CTFT–7
James, Emrys 1930–1989 .... CTFT–5
    Earlier sketch in WWT–17
James, Francis 1907– .... WWasWT
James, Fred
    See .... Allen, Fred
James, Gerald 1917– WWT–17
James, Geraldine 1950– CTFT–76
    Earlier sketches in CTFT–8, 34
James, Hawthorne CTFT–51
James, Jesse 1989– CTFT–71
    Earlier sketches in CTFT–21, 31
James, Jessica 1931(?)–1990 .... CTFT–9
    Earlier sketch in CTFT–2
James, John 1956– CTFT–8
James, Julia 1890–1964 .... WWasWT
James, Ken CTFT–49
James, Kevin 1965– CTFT–44
James, Lennie 1965– CTFT–62
James, Pell 1977– CTFT–70
James, Peter 1940– CTFT–13
    Earlier sketches in CTFT–5; WWT–17
James, Peter Francis 1956– CTFT–79
James, Polly 1941– CTFT–5
    Earlier sketch in WWT–17
James, Sid 1913–1976 .... CTFT–25
James, Steve 1954– CTFT–56
    Earlier sketch in CTFT–20
James, Wilson 1872–? .... WWasWT
Jameson, Jerry CTFT–36
    Earlier sketch in CTFT–11
Jameson, Nick CTFT–37
Jameson, Pauline 1920– WWT–17
Jampolis, Neil Peter 1943– CTFT–5
    Earlier sketch in WWT–17
Jan, Tomas
    See .... Forman, Milos
Jane, Esmeralda Belle
    See .... Chabert, Lacey
Jane, Thomas 1969– CTFT–43
Janger, Lane CTFT–29
Janis, Conrad 1928– CTFT–35
    Earlier sketches in CTFT–4; WWT–17
Janis, Elsie (Bierbower) 1889–1956 .... WWasWT
Jankovskij, Oleg
    See .... Yankovsky, Oleg
Janner, Brigitte CTFT–35
Janney, Allison 1960(?)– CTFT–43
    Earlier sketch in CTFT–22
Janney, Russell 1884–1963 .... WWasWT
Jansen, Jim CTFT–50
Janssen, Famke 1964– CTFT–61
    Earlier sketch in CTFT–28
January, Pepper
    See .... Rivers, Joan
Janus, Hugh
    See .... Stevens, Andrew
Janzen, Naomi CTFT–46

Janzurova, Iva 1941– CTFT–34
Jao, Radmar Agana 1966– CTFT–42
    Earlier sketch in CTFT–20
Jarchow, Bruce CTFT–40
Jardine, Betty ?–1945 .... WWasWT
Jarman, Derek 1942–1994 .... CTFT–9
    Obituary in CTFT–13
Jarman, Herbert 1871–1919 .... WWasWT
Jarmusch, Jim 1953– CTFT–60
    Earlier sketches in CTFT–9, 16, 27
    Brief Entry in CTFT–3
Jarre, Kevin CTFT–26
Jarre, Maurice 1924– CTFT–52
    Earlier sketches in CTFT–5, 12, 25
Jarrett, Phillip CTFT–63
Jarrico, Paul 1915–1997 .... CTFT–24
Jarriel, Tom 1934– CTFT–13
Jarrott, Charles 1927– CTFT–38
    Earlier sketches in CTFT–2, 12
Jarvis, E. K.
    See .... Bloch, Robert
Jarvis, Graham 1930– CTFT–1
Jarvis, Martin 1941– CTFT–74
    Earlier sketches in CTFT–4, 33; WWT–17
Jashni, Jon J. CTFT–76
Jason, David 1940– CTFT–1
Jason, Harvey 1940– CTFT–37
Jason, Peter CTFT–37
Jau Yun Faat
    See .... Chow Yun–fat
Jaud, Janyse CTFT–55
Jay, Dorothy 1897– .... WWasWT
Jay, Ernest 1893–1957 .... WWasWT
Jay, Harriett 1863–1932 .... WWasWT
Jay, Isabel 1879–1927 .... WWasWT
Jay, John Herbert 1871–1942 .... WWasWT
Jay, Ricky 1948– CTFT–55
    Earlier sketches in CTFT–14, 26
Jay, Tony 1933(?)– CTFT–52
    Earlier sketch in CTFT–25
Jayce
    See .... Bartok, Jayce
Jayne, Billy 1969– CTFT–58
Jayne, Tara CTFT–46
Jayne, Robert
    See .... Jacoby, Bobby
Jaynes, Roderick
    See .... Coen, Ethan and Coen, Joel
Jayston, Michael 1935– CTFT–50
    Earlier sketches in CTFT–5; WWT–17
Jbara, Gregory 1961– CTFT–59
    Earlier sketches in CTFT–16, 27
Jeakins, Dorothy 1914–1995 .... CTFT–10
    Obituary in CTFT–15
    Earlier sketch in CTFT–1
Jean–Baptiste, Marianne 1967– CTFT–71
    Earlier sketches in CTFT–20, 31
Jean–Thomas, David
    See .... Thomas, David Jean
Jeannin, Marcel CTFT–66
Jeans, Isabel 1891– WWT–17
Jeans, Michael CTFT–4
Jeans, Ronald 1887–? .... WWasWT
Jeans, Ursula 1906– .... WWasWT
Jeayes, Allan 1885–1963 .... WWasWT
Jecko, Timothy 1938– CTFT–4
Jecks, Clara ?–1951 .... WWasWT
Jeffcoat, Don 1975– CTFT–54
Jefferies, Douglas 1884–1959 .... WWasWT
Jeffers, E.
    See .... Eve
Jefferson, Arthur Stanley
    See .... Laurel, Stan

Jefferson, Brenden 1986– CTFT–71
Jefferson, Paris CTFT–46
Jefford, Barbara 1930– CTFT–33
    Earlier sketches in CTFT–6; WWT–17
Jeffrey, Carl
    See .... Jablonski, Carl
Jeffrey, Myles 1990– CTFT–49
Jeffrey, Peter 1929– CTFT–6
    Earlier sketch in WWT–17
Jeffreys, Anne 1923– CTFT–57
    Earlier sketch in WWT–17
Jeffreys, Ellis 1872–1943 .... WWasWT
Jeffries, Lionel 1926– CTFT–49
    Earlier sketch in CTFT–9
Jeffries, Lynn CTFT–55
Jeffries, Maud 1869–1946 .... WWasWT
Jellicoe, Ann 1927– CTFT–2
    Earlier sketch in WWT–17
Jemison, Eddie CTFT–74
Jenesky, George CTFT–37
Jenkins, David 1937– CTFT–42
    Earlier sketches in CTFT–9; WWT–17
Jenkins, George 1908– CTFT–10
    Earlier sketch in WWT–17
Jenkins, Hugh 1908– WWT–17
Jenkins, Jane 1943– CTFT–26
    Earlier sketch in CTFT–14
Jenkins, Jolie CTFT–74
Jenkins, Ken 1940– CTFT–46
Jenkins, Megs 1917– WWT–17
Jenkins, Paul CTFT–79
Jenkins, R. Claud 1878–1967 .... WWasWT
Jenkins, Rebecca 1960– CTFT–71
    Earlier sketches in CTFT–20, 31
Jenkins, Richard 1947– CTFT–48
Jenkins, Sam 1966– CTFT–75
Jenkins, Tamara 1963(?)– CTFT–25
Jenkins, Warren WWT–17
Jenn, Myvanwy 1928– WWT–17
Jenner, Barry CTFT–39
Jenner, Caryl 1917– .... WWasWT
Jenney, Lucinda CTFT–43
Jennings, Alex 1957– CTFT–53
    Earlier sketches in CTFT–14, 25
Jennings, Benton CTFT–60
Jennings, Brent CTFT–58
Jennings, Byron CTFT–40
Jennings, Gertrude E. 1877(?)–1958 .... WWasWT
Jennings, Juanita CTFT–55
Jennings, Ken CTFT–1
Jennings, Peter 1938– CTFT–53
    Earlier sketches in CTFT–6, 25
Jenoure, Aida .... WWasWT
Jenrette, Rita CTFT–4
Jens, Salome 1935– CTFT–34
    Earlier sketches in CTFT–5; WWT–17
Jensen, Brian CTFT–38
Jensen, Erik CTFT–74
Jensen, John 1933– CTFT–1
Jensen, Shelley CTFT–62
Jensen, Todd CTFT–43
Jerald, Penny Johnson
    See .... Johnson, Penny
Jerkew, Abe
    See .... Weber, Jake
Jerome, Daisy 1881–? .... WWasWT
Jerome, Helen 1883–? .... WWasWT
Jerome, Howard CTFT–63
Jerome, Jerome Klapka 1859–1927 .... WWasWT
Jerome, Rowena 1890– .... WWasWT
Jerome, Sadie 1876–1950 .... WWasWT
Jerome, Timothy 1943– CTFT–37
    Earlier sketch in CTFT–10

Jerrold, Mary 1877–1955 .... WWasWT
Jesmer, Chalane
    See .... Newmar, Julie
Jess, Jazzy
    See .... Stevenson, Jessica
Jesse, F. Tennyson 1889–1958 .... WWasWT
Jesse, Stella 1897– .... WWasWT
Jessel, George 1898–1981 .... WWT–17
Jessel, Patricia 1920–1968 .... WWasWT
Jessop, Jack CTFT–60
Jeter, Michael 1952– CTFT–44
    Earlier sketches in CTFT–11, 22
Jett, Joan 1958(?)– CTFT–34
    Earlier sketch in CTFT–4
Jetton, Lisbeth 1962– CTFT–4
Jeung Gwok Wing
    See .... Cheung, Leslie
Jewel 1974– CTFT–61
    Earlier sketch in CTFT–28
Jewel, Jimmy 1912– WWT–17
Jewell, Izetta 1883–? .... WWasWT
Jewison, Norman 1926– CTFT–78
    Earlier sketches in CTFT–1, 6, 35
Jhabvala, Ruth Prawer 1927– CTFT–48
    Earlier sketches in CTFT–1, 6, 13
Jiawei, Wang
    See .... Wong, Kar–Wai
Jie, Li Lian
    See .... Li, Jet
Jiler, John 1946– CTFT–14
Jillette, Penn 1955– CTFT–53
    Earlier sketch in CTFT–25
Jillian
    See .... McWhirter, Jillian
Jillian, Ann 1950– CTFT–57
    Earlier sketches in CTFT–1, 4
Jimenez, Gladis CTFT–61
Jimenez, Neal 1960– CTFT–24
    Earlier sketch in CTFT–12
Jimmy Boy L.
    See .... Ferrara, Abel
Jinaro, Jossara 1978– CTFT–61
Jines, Courtney 1992– CTFT–78
J–Lo
    See .... Lopez, Jennifer
Joachim, Suzy CTFT–43
Joanou, Phil 1961– CTFT–38
    Earlier sketch in CTFT–13
Job, Thomas 1900–1947 .... WWasWT
Jobrani, Maz 1972– CTFT–74
Joel, Clara 1890– .... WWasWT
Joffe, Charles H. 1929– CTFT–34
    Earlier sketch in CTFT–9
Joffe, Roland 1945– CTFT–42
    Earlier sketches in CTFT–5, 12, 21
Joffin, Jon 1963– CTFT–54
Johann, Zita 1904– .... WWasWT
Johansen, Aud 1930– .... WWasWT
Johansen, David 1950(?)– CTFT–39
    Earlier sketch in CTFT–14
Johansson, Paul 1964– CTFT–56
Johansson, Scarlett 1984– CTFT–69
    Earlier sketches in CTFT–21, 31
John, Elton 1947– CTFT–52
    Earlier sketch in CTFT–24
John, Evan 1901–1953 .... WWasWT
John, Graham 1887–? .... WWasWT
John, Rosamund 1913–1998 .... WWasWT
    Obituary in CTFT–24
Johns, Andrew 1935– CTFT–19
    Earlier sketch in CTFT–2
Johns, Eric 1907– .... WWasWT

Johns, Glynis 1923– CTFT–12
    Earlier sketches in CTFT–5; WWT–17
Johns, Mervyn 1899– WWT–17
Johns, Stratford 1925– CTFT–6
    Earlier sketch in CTFT–1
Johnson, Adrienne–Joi CTFT–47
Johnson, Alan CTFT–9
Johnson, Amy Jo 1970– CTFT–56
    Earlier sketch in CTFT–26
Johnson, Anne–Marie 1960– CTFT–53
    Earlier sketches in CTFT–15, 25
Johnson, Arte 1934(?)– CTFT–31
    Earlier sketches in CTFT–3, 19
Johnson, Ashley 1983– CTFT–40
Johnson, Bart CTFT–77
Johnson, Ben 1918–1996 .... CTFT–19
    Earlier sketch in CTFT–3
Johnson, Bill 1918–1957 .... WWasWT
Johnson, Bjorn 1957– CTFT–6
Johnson, Brad 1959– CTFT–66
Johnson, Bryce 1977– CTFT–58
Johnson, Carl 1965– CTFT–40
Johnson, Celia 1908–1982 .... WWT–17
Johnson, Chas. Floyd CTFT–41
    Earlier sketches in CTFT–8, 18
Johnson, Chic 1891–1962 .... WWasWT
Johnson, Clark 1954– CTFT–64
    Earlier sketches in CTFT–16, 28
Johnson, David CTFT–66
    Earlier sketch in CTFT–29
Johnson, Don 1949– CTFT–22
    Earlier sketches in CTFT–6, 13
Johnson, Dwayne 1972– CTFT–43
Johnson, Eric 1979– CTFT–44
Johnson, Gary 1945– CTFT–51
    Earlier sketch in CTFT–12
Johnson, Georgann CTFT–57
Johnson, J. Kenneth 1977– CTFT–74
Johnson, Janet 1915– .... WWasWT
Johnson, Jazz Voyd
    See .... Johnson, Chas. Floyd
Johnson, Kathie Lee
    See .... Gifford, Kathie Lee
Johnson, Kay 1904–1975 .... WWasWT
Johnson, Kenneth 1942– CTFT–36
    Earlier sketch in CTFT–11
Johnson, Kenny CTFT–59
Johnson, Kristen
    See .... Johnston, Kristen
Johnson, Lamont 1922– CTFT–10
Johnson, Laraine
    See .... Day, Laraine
Johnson, Laura 1957– CTFT–47
Johnson, Linda Lee CTFT–1
Johnson, Mark CTFT–29
Johnson, Mark 1945– CTFT–44
    Earlier sketches in CTFT–11, 22
Johnson, Mark Steven 1964– CTFT–61
    Earlier sketch in CTFT–28
Johnson, Mary Lea 1926– CTFT–10
    Earlier sketch in CTFT–1
Johnson, Michelle 1965– CTFT–45
Johnson, Mike
    See .... Sharkey, Jack
Johnson, Molly 1903– .... WWasWT
Johnson, Orrin 1865–1943 .... WWasWT
Johnson, Penny CTFT–44
Johnson, Philip 1900– .... WWasWT
Johnson, Richard 1927– CTFT–39
    Earlier sketches in CTFT–5, 15; WWT–17
Johnson, Rodney Van 1961– CTFT–74
Johnson, Shelly CTFT–38
Johnson, Terry 1955– CTFT–12

Johnson, Van 1917– CTFT–4
    Earlier sketch in WWT–17
Johnson, Willow 1975– CTFT–55
Johnston, Andrew CTFT–55
Johnston, Denis 1901–1984 .... WWT–17
    Earlier sketch in WWasWT
Johnston, Joanna.................................. CTFT–65
Johnston, John Denis CTFT–51
Johnston, Justine CTFT–1
Johnston, Kristen 1967– CTFT–65
    Earlier sketches in CTFT–18, 29
Johnston, Margaret 1918– WWT–17
Johnston, Moffat 1886–1935 .... WWasWT
Johnstone, Anna Hill 1913– CTFT–1
Johnstone, Iain 1943– CTFT–10
Johnstone, Justine 1899– .... WWasWT
Johnstone, Keith CTFT–12
Jo–Jo 1990– CTFT–79
Jokovic, Mirjana 1967– CTFT–49
    Earlier sketch in CTFT–24
Joles, Bob 1959– CTFT–69
Jolicoeur, Paul
    See .... Coeur, Paul
Jolie, Angelina 1975– CTFT–58
    Earlier sketches in CTFT–16, 27
Jolivet, Rita 1894– .... WWasWT
Jolly, Peter 1951– CTFT–1
Jolson, Al 1886–1950 .... WWasWT
Jones, Allan 1907–1992 .... CTFT–6
    Obituary in CTFT–11
Jones, Angus T. 1993– CTFT–74
Jones, Barry 1893– .... WWasWT
Jones, Brooks 1934– CTFT–1
Jones, Carolyn 1929–1983 .... CTFT–26
Jones, Catherine Zeta
    See .... Zeta–Jones, Catherine
Jones, Cherry 1956– CTFT–37
    Earlier sketch in CTFT–10
Jones, Christine.................................... CTFT–66
Jones, Chuck 1912– CTFT–6
Jones, David 1934– CTFT–5
    Earlier sketch in WWT–17
Jones, Davie
    See................................. Bowie, David
Jones, Davy 1945– CTFT–49
    Earlier sketch in CTFT–9
Jones, Deacon 1938– CTFT–28
Jones, Dean 1931(?)– CTFT–44
    Earlier sketches in CTFT–3, 19
Jones, Disley 1926–.............................. WWT–17
Jones, Doug 1960– CTFT–65
Jones, Dudley 1914– WWT–17
Jones, Eddie 1955– CTFT–79
    Earlier sketches in CTFT–7, 34
Jones, Edward ?–1917 .... WWasWT
Jones, Emrys 1915–1972 .... WWasWT
Jones, Felicity CTFT–42
Jones, Freddie 1927– CTFT–34
    Earlier sketch in CTFT–7
Jones, Gary CTFT–40
Jones, Gary 1958–................................ CTFT–38
Jones, Gemma 1942– CTFT–53
    Earlier sketches in CTFT–15, 25; WWT–17
Jones, Grace 1952(?)–........................... CTFT–39
    Earlier sketches in CTFT–7, 14
Jones, Griff Rhys
    See .... Rhys Jones, Griffith
Jones, Griffith 1910– WWT–17
Jones, Hazel 1896–1974 .... WWasWT
Jones, Henry 1912–.............................. CTFT–6
Jones, Henry Arthur 1851–1929 .... WWasWT
Jones, James Earl 1931– CTFT–43
    Earlier sketches in CTFT–4, 11, 22; WWT–17

Jones, Jamison CTFT–68
Jones, Janet 1961– CTFT–13
Jones, Jeffrey 1947– CTFT–25
    Earlier sketches in CTFT–2, 8, 15
Jones, John 1917– CTFT–2
Jones, John Christopher CTFT–40
Jones, John Marshall 1962–............. CTFT–48
Jones, L. Q. 1927– CTFT–26
    Earlier sketch in CTFT–1
Jones, Laura CTFT–29
Jones, Leslie Julian 1910– .... WWasWT
Jones, Margo 1913–1955 .... WWasWT
Jones, Mark Lewis CTFT–59
Jones, Mary WWT–17
Jones, Mickey 1941– CTFT–41
Jones, Nicholas 1946–..................... CTFT–75
    Earlier sketch in CTFT–32
Jones, Nora Rosamund
    See .... John, Rosamund
Jones, O–Lan 1950– CTFT–62
Jones, Orlando CTFT–61
    Earlier sketch in CTFT–28
Jones, Paul 1942–............................ CTFT–5
    Earlier sketch in WWT–17
Jones, Peter 1920–........................... WWT–17
Jones, Quincy 1933– CTFT–52
    Earlier sketches in CTFT–8, 15, 25
Jones, Rashida 1976– CTFT–63
Jones, Renee CTFT–18
Jones, Richard CTFT–23
Jones, Richard T. 1972– CTFT–69
    Earlier sketches in CTFT–20, 31
Jones, Rick...................................... CTFT–56
Jones, Robert Edmond 1887–1954 .... WWasWT
Jones, Rupert Penry
    See................... Penry–Jones, Rupert
Jones, Sam 1954– CTFT–57
    Earlier sketches in CTFT–7, 26
Jones, Samuel Major ?–1952 .... WWasWT
Jones, Shirley 1934–......................... CTFT–44
    Earlier sketches in CTFT–6, 22
Jones, Sidney 1869–1946 .... WWasWT
Jones, Simon 1950– CTFT–36
Jones, Tamala 1974– CTFT–41
    Earlier sketch in CTFT–18
Jones, Terry 1942– CTFT–65
    Earlier sketches in CTFT–7, 18, 29
Jones, Toby 1964(?)–......................... CTFT–44
Jones, Tom
    See......................... Bowie, David
Jones, Tom 1928– CTFT–6
    Earlier sketch in WWT–17
Jones, Tommy Lee 1946– CTFT–52
    Earlier sketches in CTFT–1, 6, 13, 25
Jones, Trefor 1902–1965 .... WWasWT
Jones, Trevor 1949– CTFT–47
    Earlier sketch in CTFT–23
Jones, Tyler Patrick 1994– CTFT–74
Jones, Vinnie 1965– CTFT–73
    Earlier sketch in CTFT–33
Jones, Volcano
    See......................... Mitchell, Adrian
Jones, Whitworth 1873–? .... WWasWT
Jones, William James 1975– CTFT–69
    Earlier sketches in CTFT–18, 29
Jongejans, George
    See......................... Gaynes, George
Jonze, Spike 1969–.......................... CTFT–61
    Earlier sketch in CTFT–28
Jooss, Kurt 1901–1979..................... WWasWT
Joosten, Kathryn 1940(?)–................ CTFT–45
Jordan, Claudia 1973–..................... CTFT–79
Jordan, Derwin CTFT–68

Jordan, Dorothy 1908– .... WWasWT
Jordan, Glenn 1936– CTFT–34
    Earlier sketches in CTFT–2, 9
Jordan, Larry
    See .... Williams, Jordan
Jordan, Michael 1963–................... CTFT–4220
    Earlier sketch in CTFT–20
Jordan, Neil 1950–......................... CTFT–55
    Earlier sketches in CTFT–6, 15, 25
Jordan, Richard 1937(?)–1993 .... CTFT–6
    Obituary in CTFT–12
Jorgensen, Robert 1903–................ WWasWT
Jory, Victor 1902–1982 .... CTFT–2
    Earlier sketch in WWT–17
Joselovitz, Ernest A. 1942– CTFT–1
Joseph, Kimberley 1973–................ CTFT–70
Josephs, Wilfred 1927–................... CTFT–8
Josephson, Erland 1923– CTFT–33
    Earlier sketch in CTFT–8
Joshua, James
    See.......................... Bridges, Jimmy
Joshua, Larry.................................. CTFT–45
Joslyn, Allyn 1905–1981 .... WWasWT
Joslyn, Betsy 1954– CTFT–1
Jost, Jon 1943– CTFT–63
    Earlier sketch in CTFT–28
Joubert, Beverly 1957(?)–................ CTFT–15
Joubert, Dereck 1956– CTFT–15
Joudry, Patricia 1921– CTFT–19
    Earlier sketch in CTFT–2
Jourdan, Louis 1920– CTFT–6
Jourden, Tom CTFT–58
Jouvet, Louis 1887–1951 .... WWasWT
Jovovich, Milla 1975– CTFT–69
    Earlier sketches in CTFT–20, 31
Joy, Helene CTFT–69
Joy, Mark CTFT–51
Joy, Nicholas 1889–1964................ WWasWT
Joy, Robert 1951– CTFT–37
    Earlier sketch in CTFT–10
    Brief Entry in CTFT–3
Joyce, Ella CTFT–38
    Earlier sketch in CTFT–15
Joyce, Kiya Ann 1956–.................... CTFT–6
Joyce, Stephen 1931–..................... CTFT–5
    Earlier sketch in WWT–17
Joyner, Michelle............................. CTFT–34
Jubinville, Kevin 1967– CTFT–47
Judd, Ashley 1968–........................ CTFT–58
    Earlier sketches in CTFT–16, 27
Judge, Christopher 1967–............... CTFT–54
Judge, Ian 1946– CTFT–15
Judge, Mike 1962– CTFT–58
    Earlier sketch in CTFT–26
Judy, James CTFT–32
Jue, Francis 1963–.......................... CTFT–55
    Earlier sketch in CTFT–20
Juergens, Stefan 1962– CTFT–34
Julia, Raul 1940–1994.................... CTFT–13
    Earlier sketches in CTFT–1, 3; WWT–17
Julian, Pat 1947–........................... CTFT–5
Juliani, Alessandro CTFT–65
Jullien, Jean 1854–1919 .... WWasWT
Jump, Gordon 1932–....................... CTFT–41
    Earlier sketches in CTFT–3, 19
June 1901– .... WWasWT
Jun–Fa, Chou CTFT–67
    See Chow Yun–Fat
Junger, Gil CTFT–50
Jungmann, Eric 1981–.................... CTFT–42
Jurasas, Jonas R. 1936– CTFT–2

Jurasik, Peter 1950–............................ CTFT–44
   Earlier sketch in CTFT–22
Justin, John 1917– WWT–17

K

Kaczmarek, Jane 1955–......................... CTFT–65
   Earlier sketches in CTFT–7, 18, 29
Kaczorowski, Peter CTFT–55
Kael, Pauline 1919– CTFT–20
   Earlier sketch in CTFT–3
Kaelred, Katharine 1882–? .... WWasWT
Kagan, Diane 1943–.............................. CTFT–20
   Earlier sketch in CTFT–3
Kagan, Elaine.. CTFT–38
   Earlier sketch in CTFT–15
Kagan, Jeremy 1945– CTFT–53
   Earlier sketches in CTFT–15, 25
Kahali, Simbi
   See .... Khali, Simbi
Kahan, Steve... CTFT–49
Kahn, Florence 1878–1951 .... WWasWT
Kahn, Madeline 1942–1999 .... CTFT–25
   Obituary in CTFT–32
   Earlier sketches in CTFT–3, 8, 15
Kahn, Michael CTFT–57
   Earlier sketches in CTFT–2, 12, 21; WWT–17
Kahn, Michael 1935–............................ CTFT–76
   Earlier sketches in CTFT–13, 21, 32
Kaige, Chen 1952–................................ CTFT–13
Kaikkonen, Gus 1951–.......................... CTFT–1
Kain, Amber 1975–............................... CTFT–7
Kain, Karen 1951–................................ CTFT–21
   Earlier sketch in CTFT–12
Kain, Khalil... CTFT–46
Kaiser, Georg 1878–1945 .... WWasWT
Kaiser, Suki 1967–................................ CTFT–47
Kalcheim, Lee 1938–............................. CTFT–1
Kalember, Patricia 1956(?)– CTFT–59
   Earlier sketches in CTFT–4, 16, 27
Kalfus, Renee Ehrlich............................ CTFT–66
Kalfin, Robert 1933– CTFT–5
   Earlier sketch in WWT–17
Kalfus, Renee Ehrlich............................ CTFT–29
Kalich, Bertha 1874–1939 .... WWasWT
Kalman, Emmerich 1882–1953 .... WWasWT
Kalmar, Bert 1884–1947 .... WWasWT
Kam–Bo, Sammo Hung 1952(?)–........... CTFT–47
   Earlier sketch in CTFT–23
Kambon, Camara.................................... CTFT–78
Kamel, Stanley...................................... CTFT–43
Kamen, Michael 1948– CTFT–47
   Earlier sketch in CTFT–23
Kamen, Robert Mark CTFT–65
Kamin, Daniel Tucker 1947–.................. CTFT–43
Kaminska, Ida 1899–1980 .... WWT–16
Kaminski, Janusz 1959– CTFT–44
   Earlier sketch in CTFT–22
Kanagawa, Hiro..................................... CTFT–45
Kanakaredes, Melina 1967– CTFT–55
   Earlier sketch in CTFT–25
Kanaly, Steve 1946–.............................. CTFT–67
   Earlier sketches in CTFT–3, 19, 30
Kanan, Sean 1966– CTFT–38
Kandel, Paul CTFT–56
Kander, John 1927–............................... CTFT–38
   Earlier sketches in CTFT–5, 13; WWT–17
Kane, Carol 1952– CTFT–55
   Earlier sketches in CTFT–2, 6, 14, 25

Kane, Christian 1974– CTFT–48
Kane, Gail 1887–1966 .... WWasWT
Kane, J. R.
   See .... Carter, James L.
Kane, Paul
   See .... Simon, Paul
Kane, Richard 1938–............................. CTFT–6
   Earlier sketch in WWT–17
Kane, Tom CTFT–37
Kane, Whitford 1881–1956 .... WWasWT
Kane, Wilson
   See .... Bloch, Robert
Kanin, Fay CTFT–4
Kanin, Garson 1912–1999 .... CTFT–2
   Obituary in CTFT–32
   Earlier sketch in WWT–17
Kanin, Michael 1910–1993 .... CTFT–9
   Obituary in CTFT–11
   Earlier sketch in CTFT–1
Kann, Lilly 1898– .... WWasWT
Kanner, Alexis 1942–............................ WWT–17
Kanter, Hal 1918– CTFT–49
   Earlier sketch in CTFT–2
Kanter, Marin 1960–............................. CTFT–5
Kapelos, John 1956– CTFT–39
Kapitas, Tamara
   See .... Davis, Carole
Kaplan, Gabe 1945– CTFT–3
Kaplan, Jonathan 1947– CTFT–57
   Earlier sketch in CTFT–5
Kaplan, Martin 1950–............................ CTFT–11
Kaplan, Michael CTFT–48
Kaplan, Mike 1943–.............................. CTFT–14
Kaplan, Richard 1925–.......................... CTFT–12
Kapoor, Shashi 1938–........................... CTFT–7
Kapoor, Shekar
   See .... Kapur, Shekhar
Kapture Donahue, Mitzi 1964– CTFT–74
Kapur, Shekhar 1951(?)–........................ CTFT–52
   Earlier sketch in CTFT–25
Kar Wei Wong
   See .... Wong, Kar–Wai
Karaszewski, Larry CTFT–66
   Earlier sketch in CTFT–29
Karen, James 1923–.............................. CTFT–34
   Earlier sketch in CTFT–8
Karina, Anna 1940– CTFT–8
Karkalits, Patti
   See .... Karr, Patti
Karlen, John 1933–............................... CTFT–9
Karlin, Fred 1936–................................ CTFT–9
Karlin, Miriam 1925– CTFT–38
   Earlier sketches in CTFT–13; WWT–17
Karloff, Boris 1887–1969...................... WWasWT
Karlweis, Oscar 1859–1956 .... WWasWT
Karn, Richard 1956– CTFT–59
   Earlier sketches in CTFT–16, 27
Karnilova, Maria 1920–......................... WWT–17
Karno, Fred 1866–1941 .... WWasWT
Karpf, Merrill H. 1940–......................... CTFT–62
   Earlier sketch in CTFT–4
Karpluk, Erin.. CTFT–63
Karpman, Laura 1959–.......................... CTFT–78
Karr, Patti 1932–.................................. CTFT–10
Karras, Alex 1935–................................ CTFT–6
   Earlier sketch in CTFT–1
Karsavina, Tamara 1885–1978............... WWasWT
Kartheiser, Vincent 1979–..................... CTFT–39
Karyo, Tcheky 1953–............................. CTFT–58
   Earlier sketch in CTFT–26
Kasanoff, Lawrence 1959– CTFT–38
   Earlier sketch in CTFT–12

Kasarda, John 1943– CTFT–69
   Earlier sketches in CTFT–3, 20, 31
Kasch, Max 1985–................................. CTFT–74
Kasdan, Lawrence 1949– CTFT–42
   Earlier sketches in CTFT–5, 12, 21
Kasdorf, Lenore 1948–.......................... CTFT–38
Kasem, Casey 1932–............................. CTFT–78
   Earlier sketches in CTFT–6, 35
Kash, Linda 1967(?)– CTFT–47
Kasha, Al 1937–.................................... CTFT–12
Kasha, Lawrence N. 1933– CTFT–4
   Earlier sketch in WWT–17
Kask, Daniel 1959–............................... CTFT–46
Kasper, Gary 1958–............................... CTFT–40
Kass, Jerome 1937–............................... CTFT–1
Kassar, Mario 1951–............................. CTFT–42
   Earlier sketches in CTFT–12, 21
Kassin, Michael B. 1947–...................... CTFT–1
Kassir, John 1962(?)–............................. CTFT–38
Kassovitz, Mathieu 1967– CTFT–68
   Earlier sketch in CTFT–30
Kastner, Daphna 1961–......................... CTFT–30
Kasznar, Kurt S. 1913–1979 .... WWT–17
Katims, Robert 1927–........................... CTFT–66
   Earlier sketches in CTFT–18, 29
Katleman, Michael CTFT–55
Katselas, Milton 1933–......................... WWT–17
Katsulas, Andreas CTFT–37
Katt, Bill
   See.. Katt, William
Katt, Nicky 1970–................................. CTFT–68
   Earlier sketch in CTFT–30
Katt, William 1951(?)–........................... CTFT–68
   Earlier sketches in CTFT–3, 19, 30
Kattan, Chris 1970–.............................. CTFT–26
Katz, Cindy... CTFT–42
Katz, Clark
   See .... Proval, David
Katz, Gail CTFT–55
Katz, Judah CTFT–54
Katz, Marty 1947–................................ CTFT–38
   Earlier sketch in CTFT–12
Katz, Natasha CTFT–41
Katz, Tania Raymonde
   See .... Raymonde, Tania
Katzenberg, Jeffrey 1950–..................... CTFT–63
   Earlier sketches in CTFT–10, 17, 28
Katzin, Lee H. 1935– CTFT–12
Katzka, Grabriel 1931–1990 .... CTFT–9
Katzman, Leonard (S.) 1927(?)–1996 .... CTFT–17
   Obituary in CTFT–16
   Earlier sketch in CTFT–10
Katzman, Sam 1901–1973 .... CTFT–21
Kauffman, Stanley L.
   See .... Kaufman, Lloyd
Kaufman, Adam (II) CTFT–70
Kaufman, Andy 1949–1984.................... CTFT–2
Kaufman, Boris 1906–1980 .... CTFT–26
Kaufman, Charlie 1958–........................ CTFT–50
Kaufman, David CTFT–62
Kaufman, George S. 1889–1961............ WWasWT
Kaufman, Lloyd 1945– CTFT–78
   Earlier sketches in CTFT–7, 35
Kaufman, Philip 1936–.......................... CTFT–6
Kaufman, Robert 1931–1991 .... CTFT–11
Kaufman, Victor 1943–.......................... CTFT–8
Kaur, Sat Siri
   See .... Cauffiel, Jessica
Kava, Caroline...................................... CTFT–66
   Earlier sketch in CTFT–29
Kavanaugh, John CTFT–75
Kavelaars, Ingrid 1971–......................... CTFT–69

Kavner, Julie 1951– CTFT–69
    Earlier sketches in CTFT–5, 12, 21, 31
    Brief Entry in CTFT–2
Kavovit, Andrew 1971– CTFT–26
Kawalek, Nancy CTFT–4
Kay, Barnaby CTFT–75
    Earlier sketch in CTFT–32
Kay, Beatrice 1907–1986...................... CTFT–4
Kay, Billy 1984– CTFT–65
Kay, Charles 1930– CTFT–5
    Earlier sketch in WWT–17
Kay, Hadley CTFT–47
Kay, Richard 1937– WWT–17
Kay, Stephen T. CTFT–79
Kayden, William 1929–1987 .... CTFT–1
Kaye, Albert Patrick 1878–1946 .... WWasWT
Kaye, Danny 1913–1987 .... CTFT–3
    Earlier sketch in WWT–17
Kaye, David 1964– CTFT–40
Kaye, Frederick .... WWasWT
Kaye, Judy 1948– CTFT–43
    Earlier sketches in CTFT–1, 9
Kaye, Norman 1927– CTFT–40
Kaye, Stubby 1918– WWT–17
Kaye, Thorsten 1966–......................... CTFT–54
Kayso, Dick
    See.. Kaysoe, Dick
Kaysoe, Dick, 1947– CTFT–35
Kazan, Elia 1909– CTFT–3
    Earlier sketch in WWasWT
Kazan, Lainie 1940(?)–........................ CTFT–73
    Earlier sketches in CTFT–4, 33
Kazan, Nicholas CTFT–37
    Earlier sketch in CTFT–10
Kazann, Zitto CTFT–43
Kazurinsky, Tim 1950– CTFT–6
Keach, James 1947(?)–......................... CTFT–76
    Earlier sketches in CTFT–6, 34
Keach, Stacy 1941– CTFT–52
    Earlier sketches in CTFT–4, 14, 25; WWT–17
Keagy, Grace CTFT–1
Keal, Anita................................... CTFT–20
    Earlier sketch in CTFT–3
Kealy, Thomas J. 1874–1949 .... WWasWT
Kean, Greg 1962– CTFT–63
Kean, Jane 1928– CTFT–1
Kean, Marie 1922–............................. CTFT–6
    Earlier sketch in WWT–17
Kean, Norman 1934–1988 .... CTFT–6
    Earlier sketch in WWT–17
Keanan, Staci 1975–........................... CTFT–38
    Earlier sketch in CTFT–13
Keane, Doris 1881–1945 .... WWasWT
Keane, James 1952– CTFT–62
Keane, John B. 1928–.......................... WWT–17
Keane, Robert Emmett 1883–? .... WWasWT
Kearns, Allen 1893–1956 .... WWasWT
Keating, Charles 1941– CTFT–76
    Earlier sketches in CTFT–5, 34; WWT–17
Keating, Dominic CTFT–46
Keating, Fred 1949– CTFT–73
    Earlier sketch in CTFT–33
Keaton, Buster 1895–1966 .... CTFT–20
Keaton, Diane 1946– CTFT–49
    Earlier sketches in CTFT–1, 6, 13, 24
Keaton, Josh 1979– CTFT–65
Keaton, Michael 1951– CTFT–38
    Earlier sketches in CTFT–6, 13
    Brief Entry in CTFT–2
Keats, Viola 1911–............................ WWT–17
Kebbel, Arielle 1985–......................... CTFT–78
Keck, Michael 1946– CTFT–8

Kee, George
    See.. Cheung, George
Keeffe, Barrie 1945–.......................... CTFT–12
Keegan, Andrew 1979–......................... CTFT–39
Keegan, Donna CTFT–4
Keel, Howard 1919– WWT–17
Keeler, Ruby 1909– WWT–17
Keeley, David 1961– CTFT–50
Keen, Geoffrey 1916–.......................... WWT–17
Keen, Malcolm 1887–1970 .... WWasWT
Keen, Pat CTFT–73
    Earlier sketch in CTFT–32
Keena, Monica 1980– CTFT–26
Keenan, Frank 1858–1929 .... WWasWT
Keene, Elodie 1948–.......................... CTFT–54
Keener, Catherine 1960– CTFT–55
    Earlier sketch in CTFT–26
Keeper, Tina 1988–............................ CTFT–67
    Earlier sketch in CTFT–17
Keeshan, Robert J. 1927– CTFT–4
Keeslar, Matt 1972–........................... CTFT–74
    Earlier sketch in CTFT–33
Kehler, Jack.................................. CTFT–44
    Earlier sketch in CTFT–22
Keiber, Robert John 1946–.................... CTFT–6
Keightley, Cyril 1875–1929 .... WWasWT
Keil, Richard
    See.. Kiel, Richard
Keim, Adelaide 1880–?........................ WWasWT
Keitel, Harvey 1939–.......................... CTFT–46
    Earlier sketches in CTFT–5, 12, 23
Keith, Brian 1921–1997 .... CTFT–9
    Obituary in CTFT–18
    Earlier sketches in CTFT–2; WWT–17
Keith, David 1954– CTFT–43
    Earlier sketches in CTFT–4, 24
Keith, Ian 1899–1960 .... WWasWT
Keith, Larry 1931–............................ CTFT–23
Keith, Marilyn
    See.. Bergman, Marilyn
Keith, Paul 1944–............................. CTFT–1
Keith, Penelope 1939(?)–...................... CTFT–42
    Earlier sketches in CTFT–3, 20; WWT–17
Keith, Robert 1898–1966...................... WWasWT
Keith–Johnston, Colin 1896–................. WWasWT
Kelada, Asaad................................ CTFT–49
Kelamis, Peter................................ CTFT–39
Kelcey, Herbert 1856–1917 .... WWasWT
Kelham, Avice 1892–.......................... WWasWT
Kelker–Kelly, Robert 1964– CTFT–41
    Earlier sketch in CTFT–18
Kell, Joseph 1960– CTFT–58
Kelleher, Tim CTFT–38
Keller, Frederick King 1954– CTFT–40
Keller, Inge 1923– CTFT–33
Keller, Joel S. CTFT–68
Keller, Marthe 1945–.......................... CTFT–44
    Earlier sketches in CTFT–6, 22
Keller, Max A. 1943–.......................... CTFT–2
Keller, Micheline 1948–....................... CTFT–18
    Earlier sketch in CTFT–2
Kellerman, Sally 1937(?)–..................... CTFT–78
    Earlier sketches in CTFT–5, 35
Kellermann, Annette 1888–1975 .... WWasWT
Kelley, David E. 1956–........................ CTFT–63
    Earlier sketch in CTFT–28
Kelley, DeForest 1920–1999.................... CTFT–8
    Obituary in CTFT–32
    Earlier sketch in CTFT–3
Kelley, Sheila 1964(?)–........................ CTFT–74
    Earlier sketch in CTFT–33
Kelley, William 1929–......................... CTFT–7
Kellin, Mike 1922–............................ WWT–17

Kellman, Barnet 1947–......................... CTFT–66
    Earlier sketches in CTFT–2, 18, 29
Kellner, Catherine 1970–...................... CTFT–55
    Earlier sketch in CTFT–26
Kellner, Deborah 1977– CTFT–74
Kellogg, Shirley 1888–? .... WWasWT
Kelly, Andrew
    See........................... Walker, Andrew Kevin
Kelly, Brendan 1964–.......................... CTFT–79
Kelly, Brian 1956–............................ CTFT–1
Kelly, Darragh................................ CTFT–76
    Earlier sketch in CTFT–34
Kelly, David Patrick 1952–.................... CTFT–50
Kelly, E. H. .... WWasWT
Kelly, Eva 1880–1948 .... WWasWT
Kelly, Gene 1912–1996 .... CTFT–3
    Obituary in CTFT–16
    Earlier sketch in WWasWT
Kelly, George 1890–1974 .... WWasWT
Kelly, Jean Louisa 1972– CTFT–63
    Earlier sketch in CTFT–28
Kelly, Joanne 1980–........................... CTFT–79
Kelly, Judy 1913–............................. WWasWT
Kelly, Kevin 1934– CTFT–1
Kelly, Lisa Robin 1975– CTFT–45
Kelly, Marguerite 1959– CTFT–7
Kelly, Michael 1968–.......................... CTFT–68
Kelly, Moira 1968–............................ CTFT–55
    Earlier sketches in CTFT–15, 26
Kelly, Nancy 1921–............................ WWT–17
Kelly, Patsy 1910–1981 .... WWT–17
Kelly, Paul 1899–1956......................... WWasWT
Kelly, Peter CTFT–35
Kelly, Rae’ven 1985–.......................... CTFT–51
Kelly, Renee 1888–1965 .... WWasWT
Kelly, Sean 1943–............................. CTFT–35
Kelly, Terence CTFT–54
Kelly, Tim 1937–.............................. CTFT–1
Kelly, Vivian 1922– CTFT–4
Kelly, W. W. 1853–1933 .... WWasWT
Kelly, Walter C. 1873–1939................... WWasWT
Kelly–Young, Leonard 1948–................... CTFT–58
Kelsch, Ken CTFT–39
Kelsey, Linda 1946–.......................... CTFT–7
Kelso, Vernon 1893–.......................... WWasWT
Kemp, Barry 1949– CTFT–48
    Earlier sketch in CTFT–13
Kemp, Elizabeth 1957– CTFT–8
Kemp, Gary 1959–............................. CTFT–68
    Earlier sketch in CTFT–30
Kemp, George
    See.. Argento, Dario
Kemp, Jeremy 1935–........................... CTFT–35
    Earlier sketches in CTFT–2, 8; WWT–17
Kemp, Martin 1961–........................... CTFT–68
    Earlier sketch in CTFT–30
Kemp, T. C. 1891–1955........................ WWasWT
Kempe, Will 1963– CTFT–71
Kemper, Collin 1870–1955.................... WWasWT
Kemper, Steven CTFT–63
    Earlier sketch in CTFT–28
Kemper, Victor J. 1927–...................... CTFT–48
    Earlier sketches in CTFT–4, 13
Kempinski, Tom 1938–......................... CTFT–12
Kempson, Rachel 1910–........................ CTFT–7
    Earlier sketch in WWT–17
Kemp–Welch, Joan WWT–17
Kendal, Doris .... WWasWT
Kendal, Felicity 1946–........................ CTFT–39
    Earlier sketches in CTFT–3, 14; WWT–17
Kendal, Madge (Margaret)
    1848–1935 .... WWasWT
Kendal, William Hunter 1843–1917 ...... WWasWT

Kendall, Henry 1897–1962 .... WWasWT
Kendall, John 1869–? .... WWasWT
Kendall, William 1903– WWT–16
Kendrick, Alfred 1869–? .... WWasWT
Kennedy, Adrienne 1931– CTFT–13
Kennedy, Arthur 1914–1990 .... CTFT–10
   Earlier sketches in CTFT–3; WWT–17
Kennedy, Bill 1908–1997 .... CTFT–16
Kennedy, Burt 1922– CTFT–6
Kennedy, Charles
   See .... Rocket, Charles
Kennedy, Charles Rann 1871–1950 .... WWasWT
Kennedy, Cheryl 1947– CTFT–5
   Earlier sketch in WWT–17
Kennedy, Edmund 1873–? .... WWasWT
Kennedy, George 1925(?)– CTFT–76
   Earlier sketches in CTFT–1, 6, 34
Kennedy, Harold J. 1914–1988 .... CTFT–6
   Earlier sketch in WWT–17
Kennedy, J. Arthur
   See .... Kennedy, Arthur
Kennedy, Jamie 1970– CTFT–69
   Earlier sketches in CTFT–21, 31
Kennedy, John
   See .... Kennedy, Arthur
Kennedy, Joyce 1898–1943 .... WWasWT
Kennedy, Kathleen 1954– CTFT–49
   Earlier sketches in CTFT–5, 12, 24
Kennedy, Laurie CTFT–1
Kennedy, Madge 1892–1987 .... WWasWT
Kennedy, Margaret 1896–1967 .... WWasWT
Kennedy, Mary 1908– .... WWasWT
Kennedy, Mimi 1948(?)– CTFT–41
   Earlier sketches in CTFT–8, 18
Kennedy, Patrica 1917– WWT–17
Kennell, Ron 1970– CTFT–46
Kennerly, Mel
   See .... Harris, Mel
Kenney, Heather North
   See .... North, Heather
Kenney, James 1930– WWT–16
Kenney, Kerri 1970– CTFT–69
Kenny, Francis CTFT–43
Kenny, Jack 1958– CTFT–7
Kenny, Sean 1932–1973 .... WWasWT
Kenny, Shannon CTFT–46
Kenny, Tom CTFT–37
Kensit, Patsy 1968– CTFT–59
   Earlier sketches in CTFT–9, 16, 27
Kent, Arthur 1955(?)– CTFT–50
Kent, Barry 1932– WWT–17
Kent, Heather Paige 1969– CTFT–78
Kent, Jean 1921– WWT–17
Kent, John B. 1939– CTFT–5
Kent, Keneth 1892–1963 .... WWasWT
Kent, Paul CTFT–58
Kent, Rolfe 1963(?)– CTFT–42
Kent, William 1886–1945 .... WWasWT
Kentish, Agatha 1897– .... WWasWT
Kenton, Godfrey 1902– WWT–17
Kenton, Maxwell
   See .... Southern, Terry
Kenworthy, Duncan 1949– CTFT–55
   Earlier sketch in CTFT–26
Kenwright, Bill 1945– CTFT–38
   Earlier sketches in CTFT–13; WWT–17
Kenyon, Charles 1878–1961 .... WWasWT
Kenyon, Doris 1897– .... WWasWT
Kenyon, Neil ?–1946 .... WWasWT
Kenzle, Leila 1960(?)– CTFT–66
   Earlier sketches in CTFT–18, 29
Keogh, Danny CTFT–76
Keoghan, Phil 1967– CTFT–78

Keown, Eric 1904–1963 .... WWasWT
Kepros, Nicholas 1932– CTFT–1
Kerbosch, Roeland 1940– CTFT–3
Kercheval, Ken 1935– CTFT–62
   Earlier sketch in CTFT–1
Kerin, Nora 1883–? .... WWasWT
Kerker, Gustave Adolph 1857–1923 ...... WWasWT
Kerman, Sheppard 1928– CTFT–4
Kern, Jerome David 1885–1945 .... WWasWT
Kern, Richard
   See .... Karn, Richard
Kernan, David 1939– WWT–17
Kerner, Jordan CTFT–37
Kernochan, Sarah M. 1947– CTFT–51
   Earlier sketch in CTFT–12
Kerns, Joanna 1953– CTFT–66
   Earlier sketches in CTFT–8, 18, 29
Kerr, Bill WWT–17
Kerr, Deborah 1921– CTFT–4
   Earlier sketch in WWT–17
Kerr, E. Katherine 1942– CTFT–34
   Earlier sketches in CTFT–1, 6
Kerr, Edward 1966– CTFT–63
   Earlier sketch in CTFT–28
Kerr, Elaine
   See .... Kerr, E. Katherine
Kerr, Frederick 1858–1933 .... WWasWT
Kerr, Geoffrey 1895– .... WWasWT
Kerr, Jean 1923– CTFT–1
   Earlier sketch in WWT–17
Kerr, Katherine
   See .... Kerr, E. Katherine
Kerr, Molly 1904– .... WWasWT
Kerr, Walter 1913–1996 .... CTFT–4
   Obituary in CTFT–16
   Earlier sketch in WWT–17
Kerridge, Mary 1914– WWT–17
Kerrigan, J. M. 1885–1964 .... WWasWT
Kerris, George
   See .... Chakiris, George
Kerry, Anne 1958– CTFT–1
Kershaw, Willette 1890–1960 .... WWasWT
Kershner, Irvin 1923– CTFT–37
   Earlier sketch in CTFT–10
Kert, Larry 1930(?)–1991 .... CTFT–4
   Obituary in CTFT–10
   Earlier sketch in WWT–17
Kerwin, Brian 1949– CTFT–68
   Earlier sketches in CTFT–8, 19, 30
Kesdekian, Mesrop 1920– CTFT–2
Keshawarz, Donnie 1969– CTFT–71
Kesselring, Joseph O. 1902–1967 .... WWasWT
Kestelman, Sara 1944– CTFT–34
   Earlier sketches in CTFT–5; WWT–17
Kester, Paul 1870–1933 .... WWasWT
Kestner, Boyd 1964– CTFT–54
Ketron, Larry 1947– CTFT–4
   Earlier sketch in CTFT–1
Keyloun, Mark Anthony 1960– CTFT–1
Keymah, T'Keyah Crystal 1962– CTFT–52
   Earlier sketches in CTFT–14, 25
Keys, Nelson 1886–1939 .... WWasWT
Keysar, Franklin 1939–1999 .... CTFT–20
   Obituary in CTFT–24
   Earlier sketch in CTFT–3
Keyser, Christopher 1960– CTFT–65
Khaleed, Thomas Leon
   See .... Thomas, Khleo
Khali, Simbi 1971– CTFT–41
   Earlier sketch in CTFT–18
Khan, Michelle
   See .... Yeoh, Michelle

Khanjian, Arsinee CTFT–68
   Earlier sketch in CTFT–30
Kheel, Lee 1918– CTFT–4
Khondji, Darius 1955– CTFT–51
   Earlier sketch in CTFT–24
Khouri, Callie 1958(?)– CTFT–11
Khursor
   See .... Wandmacher, Michael
Kiarostami, Abbas 1940– CTFT–31
   Earlier sketch in CTFT–20
Kiberlain, Sandrine 1968– CTFT–34
Kidd, Michael 1919– CTFT–10
   Earlier sketch in WWT–17
Kidd, Robert 1943–1980 .... WWT–17
Kidder, Janet CTFT–54
Kidder, Kathryn 1867–1939 .... WWasWT
Kidder, Margot 1948– CTFT–78
   Earlier sketches in CTFT–1, 6, 35
Kidman, Nicole 1967– CTFT–62
   Earlier sketches in CTFT–10, 17, 28
Kidnie, James CTFT–54
Kieferle, Kirsten CTFT–62
Kiel, Richard 1939– CTFT–49
   Earlier sketch in CTFT–9
Kiepura, Jan 1902–1966 .... WWasWT
Kier, Udo 1944– CTFT–47
   Earlier sketch in CTFT–23
Kierney, Tyde CTFT–29
Kieser, Ellwood E. 1929– CTFT–10
Kieslowski, Krzysztof 1941–1996 .... CTFT–11
   Obituary in CTFT–16
Kiesser, Jan CTFT–59
Kightlinger, Laura 1969– CTFT–64
Kihlstedt, Rya 1970(?)– CTFT–31
   Earlier sketch in CTFT–21
Kilborn, Craig 1962– CTFT–45
Kilbride, Percy 1888–1964 .... CTFT–28
Kilcher, Jewel
   See .... Jewel
Kiley, Richard 1922–1999 .... CTFT–6
   Obituary in CTFT–32
   Earlier sketches in CTFT–1; WWT–17
Kilik, Jon 1956– CTFT–59
Killeen, Sheelagh 1940– WWT–17
Killick, C. Egerton 1891–1967 .... WWasWT
Kilmer, Val 1959– CTFT–45
   Earlier sketches in CTFT–7, 14
Kilner, Kevin 1958– CTFT–71
   Earlier sketches in CTFT–21, 31
Kilpatrick, Patrick CTFT–59
   Earlier sketch in CTFT–27
Kilroy, Thomas 1934– CTFT–12
KilroySilk, Robert 1942– CTFT–13
Kilty, Jerome 1922– CTFT–20
   Earlier sketches in CTFT–3; WWT–17
Kim, Daniel Dae CTFT–49
Kim, Derek CTFT–38
Kim, Jacqueline CTFT–67
Kim, Willa CTFT–9
Kim, Yoon-jin 1973– CTFT–70
Kimball, Grace 1870–? .... WWasWT
Kimball, Jeffrey L. 1943– CTFT–38
   Earlier sketch in CTFT–13
Kimball, Louis 1889–1936 .... WWasWT
Kimbrough, Charles 1936– CTFT–37
   Earlier sketch in CTFT–13
Kimmins, Anthony 1901–1964 .... WWasWT
Kimmins, Kenneth 1941– CTFT–59
   Earlier sketch in CTFT–5
Kinberg, Judy 1948– CTFT–7
Kind, Richard 1956– CTFT–61
   Earlier sketches in CTFT–17, 28
Kindler, Andy CTFT–64

Kindler, Damian CTFT–60
Kindley, Jeffrey 1945– CTFT–1
Kiner, Kevin CTFT–42
King, Ada ?–1940 .... WWasWT
King, Alan 1927– CTFT–41
    Earlier sketches in CTFT–3, 19
King, Allan 1930– CTFT–57
King, Cecil ?–1958 .... WWasWT
King, Charles 1889–1944 .... WWasWT
King, Claude 1876–1941 .... WWasWT
King, Cleo 1960– CTFT–75
King, Dennis 1897–1971 .... WWasWT
King, Edith 1896– .... WWasWT
King, Erik CTFT–65
King, Jaime 1979– CTFT–67
King, John Michael 1926– WWT–17
King, Kenneth
    See .... King, Perry
King, Kent Masters 1974– CTFT–58
King, Kip 1937(?)– CTFT–56
King, Larry 1933– CTFT–63
    Earlier sketches in CTFT–10, 17, 28
King, Larry L. 1929– CTFT–10
King, Mabel CTFT–9
King, Melanie Nichols
    See .... Nicholls–King, Melanie
King, Perry 1948– CTFT–59
    Earlier sketches in CTFT–2, 9, 16, 27
King, Philip 1904–1979 .... WWT–16
King, R. Timothy
    See .... Kring, Tim
King, Regina 1971– CTFT–44
    Earlier sketch in CTFT–22
King, Rowena CTFT–74
King, Stephen 1947– CTFT–63
    Earlier sketches in CTFT–8, 17, 28
King, Walter Woolf 1899– .... WWasWT
King, William
    See .... Judge, Mike
King, Woodie, Jr. 1937– CTFT–8
    Earlier sketch in WWT–17
King, Zalman 1941– CTFT–36
    Earlier sketch in CTFT–11
King–Hall, Stephen 1893–1966 .... WWasWT
Kingsley, Ben 1943– CTFT–44
    Earlier sketches in CTFT–1, 4, 11, 22;
    WWT–17
Kingsley, Sidney 1906– WWT–17
Kingston, Alex 1963– CTFT–71
    Earlier sketch in CTFT–32
Kingston, Gertrude 1866–1937 .... WWasWT
Kingston, Mark 1934– WWT–17
Kinison, Sam 1953–1992 .... CTFT–14
Kinmont, Kathleen 1965– CTFT–49
Kinnear, Greg 1963– CTFT–55
    Earlier sketches in CTFT–15, 26
Kinnear, Roy 1934–1988 .... CTFT–7
    Earlier sketch in WWT–17
Kinney, Kathy 1954– CTFT–59
    Earlier sketches in CTFT–17, 27
Kinney, Terry 1954– CTFT–57
    Earlier sketches in CTFT–5, 15, 26
Kinsey, Lance 1960– CTFT–37
    Earlier sketch in CTFT–11
Kinski, Klaus 1926(?)–1991 .... CTFT–5
    Obituary in CTFT–10
Kinski, Nastassja 1961(?)– CTFT–44
    Earlier sketches in CTFT–1, 6, 22
Kinzer, Craig 1953– CTFT–3
Kipness, Joseph WWT–17
Kippax, H. G. 1920– WWT–17
Kipphardt, Heinar 1922– WWT–17

Kirby, Bruno 1949–2006 .... CTFT–37
    Obituary in CTFT–75
    Earlier sketches in CTFT–6, 13
Kirby, John 1894– .... WWasWT
Kirchenbauer, Bill 1953– CTFT–35
    Earlier sketch in CTFT–8
Kirk, Lisa WWT–17
Kirk, Robert CTFT–48
Kirkland, Alexander .... WWasWT
Kirkland, Jack 1902–1969 .... WWasWT
Kirkland, James R. III 1947– CTFT–1
Kirkland, Muriel 1903–1971 .... WWasWT
Kirkland, Patricia 1925– .... WWasWT
Kirkland, Sally 1944– CTFT–44
    Earlier sketches in CTFT–7, 14; WWT–17
Kirkpatrick, David CTFT–55
    Earlier sketch in CTFT–26
Kirkwood, James 1930–1989 .... CTFT–5
    Earlier sketch in WWT–17
Kirkwood, Pat 1921– WWT–17
Kirsch, Stan 1968– CTFT–41
Kirschbaum, Bruce CTFT–49
Kirschner, David CTFT–37
Kirshner, Mia 1976– CTFT–44
    Earlier sketch in CTFT–22
Kirtland, Lousie 1910– WWT–17
Kirwan, Patrick ?–1929 .... WWasWT
Kiser, Terry 1939– CTFT–47
Kishibe, Ittoku 1947– CTFT–34
Kistemaeckers, Henry 1872–1938 .... WWasWT
Kistler, Darci 1964– CTFT–24
    Earlier sketch in CTFT–12
Kita, Candace CTFT–74
Kitano, Takeshi 1948– CTFT–28
Kitay, David CTFT–62
Kitchen, Michael 1948– CTFT–34
    Earlier sketch in CTFT–8
Kitchin, Laurence 1913– WWT–17
Kitt, Eartha 1927– CTFT–41
    Earlier sketches in CTFT–3, 19; WWT–17
Klace, Scott CTFT–71
Klapisch, Cedric 1961– CTFT–55
    Earlier sketch in CTFT–26
Klar, Gary 1947– CTFT–1
Klaris, Harvey J. 1939– CTFT–1
Klassen, Terry CTFT–40
Klauber, Adolph 1879–1933 .... WWasWT
Klausen, Ray 1939– CTFT–37
    Earlier sketch in CTFT–10
Klaw, Marc 1858–1936 .... WWasWT
Klein, Bob
    See .... Klein, Robert
Klein, Charles 1867–1915 .... WWasWT
Klein, Chris 1979– CTFT–68
    Earlier sketch in CTFT–30
Klein, David CTFT–55
    Earlier sketch in CTFT–26
Klein, Linda CTFT–79
Klein, Robert 1942– CTFT–68
    Earlier sketches in CTFT–3, 19, 30; WWT–17
Kleiner, Harry 1916– CTFT–4
Kleiser, Randal 1946– CTFT–44
    Earlier sketches in CTFT–1, 22
Klemperer, Werner 1920– CTFT–15
    Earlier sketch in CTFT–6
Kleyla, Brandon CTFT–23
Kliban, Ken 1943– CTFT–1
Kliesch, Kevin 1970– CTFT–71
Kliewer, Julie
    See .... Maddalena, Julie
Kliewer, Warren 1931– CTFT–1

Kline, Kevin 1947– CTFT–58
    Earlier sketches in CTFT–1, 3, 10, 17, 27;
    WWT–17
Kline, Martin A. CTFT–29
Kline, Richard 1944– CTFT–60
Kloes, Scott
    See .... Klace, Scott
Klotz, Florence 1920– CTFT–11
    Earlier sketches in CTFT–2; WWT–17
Kloser, Harald CTFT–61
Kloves, Steve 1960– CTFT–79
Klugman, Brian CTFT–70
Klugman, Jack 1922(?)– CTFT–41
    Earlier sketches in CTFT–1, 3, 19; WWT–17
Klum, Heidi 1973– CTFT–63
Klunis, Tom 1930– CTFT–1
Klyn, Vincent CTFT–39
Kmeck, George 1949– CTFT–19
    Earlier sketch in CTFT–2
Knapp, Eleanore CTFT–1
Kneale, Nigel 1922– CTFT–9
Kneale, Patricia 1925– WWT–17
Kneece, Dan 1956– CTFT–48
    Earlier sketch in CTFT–13
Knepper, Robert 1959– CTFT–75
    Earlier sketch in CTFT–33
Knight, Arthur 1916–1991 .... CTFT–11
Knight, Christopher 1957– CTFT–63
    Earlier sketch in CTFT–28
Knight, David 1927– WWT–17
Knight, Esmond 1906–1987 .... WWT–17
Knight, Gladys 1944– CTFT–47
Knight, Joan 1924– WWT–17
Knight, Julius 1863–1941 .... WWasWT
Knight, June 1911–1987 .... WWasWT
Knight, Keith CTFT–77
Knight, Keshia CTFT–62
Knight, Lily 1949– CTFT–59
Knight, Michael E. 1959– CTFT–57
    Earlier sketch in CTFT–21
Knight, Shirley 1936(?)– CTFT–68
    Earlier sketches in CTFT–3, 19, 30; WWT–17
Knight, T. R. 1973– CTFT–72
Knight, Ted 1923–1986 .... CTFT–1
Knight, Tuesday CTFT–34
Knight, Wayne 1955– CTFT–71
    Earlier sketches in CTFT–20, 31
Knight, William CTFT–77
Knightley, Keira 1983– CTFT–38
Knighton, Nan CTFT–20
Knight–Pulliam, Keshia
    See .... Pulliam, Keshia Knight
Knobeloch, Jim 1950– CTFT–31
    Earlier sketches in CTFT–1, 19
Knoblock, Edward 1874–1945 .... WWasWT
Knopfler, Mark 1949– CTFT–44
    Earlier sketches in CTFT–8, 22
Knott, Frederick 1916– CTFT–1
Knott, Robert CTFT–37
Knott, Roselle 1870–1948 .... WWasWT
Knotts, Don 1924–2006 .... CTFT–68
    Obituary in CTFT–70
    Earlier sketches in CTFT–3, 19, 30, 68
Knowles, Alex 1850–1917 .... WWasWT
Knowles, Beyonce 1981– CTFT–46
Knowles, Solange 1986– CTFT–78
Knox, Alexander 1907– WWT–17
Knox, Mark "Flex"
    See .... Alexander, Flex
Knox, Terence 1951(?)– CTFT–38
    Earlier sketches in CTFT–7, 15
Kobart, Ruth 1924– WWT–17
Kober, Jeff CTFT–37

Koch, Douglas...CTFT–55
    Earlier sketch in CTFT–26
Koch, Howard W. 1916–........................... CTFT–1
Koch, Howard W., Jr. 1945–.................CTFT–39
    Earlier sketches in CTFT–1, 16
Kodet, Jiri CTFT–34
Kodjoe, Boris 1973–.............................CTFT–78
Koechner, David.....................................CTFT–68
    Earlier sketch in CTFT–30
Koehler, Frederick 1975–.......................CTFT–78
    Earlier sketch in CTFT–34
Koenekamp, Fred J. 1922– CTFT–26
Koenig, Andrew 1968–...........................CTFT–79
Koenig, Joshua
    See .... Koenig, Andrew
Koenig, Walter 1936–............................CTFT–78
    Earlier sketches in CTFT–5, 35
Koepp, David 1963– CTFT–55
    Earlier sketches in CTFT–14, 25
Kohan, Buz 1933–..................................CTFT–51
    Earlier sketch in CTFT–11
Kohler, Estelle WWT–17
Kohn, Gary CTFT–78
Kolb, Mina CTFT–57
Kolb, Therese 1856–1935 ....WWasWT
Kolbe, Winrich CTFT–55
Kolber, Lynne
    See .... Halliday, Lynne
Kolker, Henry 1874–1947.....................WWasWT
Kollmar, Richard 1910–1971 ....WWasWT
Koltai, Lajos 1946–................................CTFT–40
Koltai, Ralph 1924–...............................CTFT–13
    Earlier sketch in WWT–17
Komack, James 1930–1997 ....CTFT–7
    Obituary in CTFT–19
Komarov, Shelley 1949–..........................CTFT–34
    Earlier sketch in CTFT–4
Komisarjevsky, Theodore 1882–1954 .... WWasWT
Komorowska, Liliana CTFT–54
Konchalovsky, Andrei 1937–..................CTFT–34
    Earlier sketch in CTFT–8
Kondan, Karen CTFT–34
Kondazian, Karen 1950–.........................CTFT–34
    Earlier sketch in CTFT–4
Kondrashoff, Kim...................................CTFT–56
Konigsberg, Frank 1933–........................CTFT–35
    Earlier sketch in CTFT–2
Konner, Lawrence...................................CTFT–46
Konrad, Cathy CTFT–61
    Earlier sketch in CTFT–28
Konstam, Anna 1914– ....WWasWT
Konstam, Phyllis 1907– ....WWasWT
Konwicki, Tadeusz 1926–.......................CTFT–13
Koontz, Dean R. 1945–..........................CTFT–55
Kopache, Thomas 1945–.........................CTFT–66
    Earlier sketches in CTFT–2, 18, 29
Kopell, Bernie 1933–.............................CTFT–78
    Earlier sketches in CTFT–6, 35
Kopelson, Arnold 1935–.........................CTFT–61
    Earlier sketches in CTFT–10, 17, 28
Kopit, Arthur 1937–..............................CTFT–4
    Earlier sketch in WWT–17
Koplovitz, Kay 1945–.............................CTFT–23
    Earlier sketch in CTFT–12
Koppel, Ted 1940– CTFT–44
    Earlier sketches in CTFT–12, 22
Kopple, Barbara 1946–...........................CTFT–59
    Earlier sketch in CTFT–27
Kops, Bernard 1926–..............................WWT–17
Kopsa, Mike 1956–.................................CTFT–65
Kopyc, Frank 1948–...............................CTFT–1
Korbich, Eddie 1960–.............................CTFT–34
Korf, Geoff...CTFT–53

Korf, Mia 1965–....................................CTFT–54
Korine, Harmony 1974–.........................CTFT–27
Korittke, Oliver......................................CTFT–35
Korkes, Jon CTFT–79
Korman, Harvey 1927–...........................CTFT–69
    Earlier sketches in CTFT–3, 19, 30
Korman, Lindsay 1978–..........................CTFT–74
Kornfeld, Robert 1919–..........................CTFT–4
Kornman, Cam 1949–.............................CTFT–5
Korologos, Paula
    See .... Cale, Paula
Koromzay, Alix 1971–............................CTFT–66
Korot, Alla 1970–..................................CTFT–69
Korsmo, Charlie 1978–...........................CTFT–24
Korty, John Van Cleave 1936–................CTFT–38
    Earlier sketches in CTFT–1, 12
Korvin, Charles 1907–1998.....................CTFT–24
    Earlier sketch in CTFT–3
Korvin, Geza
    See .... Korvin, Charles
Korzen, Annie...CTFT–74
Kosinski, Jerzy 1933– CTFT–1
Kossoff, David 1919– WWT–17
Kosta, Tessa 1893– ....WWasWT
Kosterman, Mitchell 1958– CTFT–64
Kotcheff, Ted 1931– CTFT–37
    Earlier sketch in CTFT–10
Kotcheff, William T.
    See...Kotcheff, Ted
Koteas, Elias 1961– CTFT–67
    Earlier sketches in CTFT–20, 30
Kotkin, David
    See .... Copperfield, David
Kotlowitz, Dan 1957–............................CTFT–19
    Earlier sketch in CTFT–3
Kotto, Yaphet 1944(?)–..........................CTFT–29
    Earlier sketches in CTFT–5, 17
Kouf, Jim 1951–....................................CTFT–56
Koufey, Richard
    See...Jonze, Spike
Koun, Karolos 1908–1987 ....WWasWT
Kovacs, Ernie 1919–1962 ....CTFT–20
Kovacs, Laszlo 1933(?)–.........................CTFT–57
    Earlier sketches in CTFT–3, 13, 26
Kovacs, Leslie
    See .... Kovacs, Laszlo
Kove, Kenneth 1893– ....WWasWT
Kove, Martin 1946–...............................CTFT–66
    Earlier sketches in CTFT–3, 19, 30
Kovens, Ed 1934–..................................CTFT–2
Kowalski, Bernard L. 1929– CTFT–26
Kozak, Harley Jane 1957–......................CTFT–57
    Earlier sketches in CTFT–12, 22
Kozlowski, Linda 1958–..........................CTFT–14
Krabbe, Jeroen 1944–.............................CTFT–44
    Earlier sketches in CTFT–4, 11, 22
Kraemer, Joe CTFT–70
Krakowski, Jane 1968–...........................CTFT–61
    Earlier sketch in CTFT–28
Kramer, Bert 1934–...............................CTFT–35
    Earlier sketch in CTFT–4
Kramer, Clare 1974–..............................CTFT–47
Kramer, Eric Allan...................................CTFT–57
    Earlier sketch in CTFT–26
Kramer, Joel...CTFT–48
Kramer, Larry 1935–..............................CTFT–13
    Earlier sketch in CTFT–5
Kramer, Marsha 1945– CTFT–35
    Earlier sketch in CTFT–4
Kramer, Stanley E. 1913–.......................CTFT–4
    Earlier sketch in CTFT–1
Kramer, Steve...CTFT–69
    Earlier sketch in CTFT–30

Kramm, Joseph 1907–............................WWT–16
Krane, David CTFT–50
Krane, Jonathan D. 1952–......................CTFT–51
    Earlier sketches in CTFT–12, 24
Krantz, Judith 1928–.............................CTFT–14
Krantz, Steve 1923–..............................CTFT–11
Kraselchik, R.
    See .... Dyer, Charles
Krasna, Norman 1909–1984 ....WWT–17
Krasner, Milton 1904–1988 ....CTFT–7
Krasny, Paul 1935–................................CTFT–11
Krause, Brian 1969–...............................CTFT–66
    Earlier sketch in CTFT–29
Krause, Peter 1965–...............................CTFT–61
    Earlier sketch in CTFT–28
Krauss, Marvin A. 1928–........................CTFT–1
Krauss, Werner 1884–1959 ....WWasWT
Krebs, Susan CTFT–67
    Earlier sketch in CTFT–30
Kremer, Theodore 1873–?......................WWasWT
Kren, Mikulas CTFT–35
Kretchmer, John T. CTFT–43
Kretschmann, Thomas 1962– CTFT–47
Kretzmer, Herbert 1925–.......................WWT–17
Kreuk, Kristin 1982–.............................CTFT–74
Kriegel, David CTFT–51
Krieger, Henry 1945– CTFT–23
Krige, Alice 1954–.................................CTFT–66
    Earlier sketches in CTFT–7, 19, 30
Krimmer, Wortham CTFT–54
Kring, Tim CTFT–69
Kristel, Sylvia 1952–..............................CTFT–34
    Earlier sketch in CTFT–8
Kristofferson, Kris 1936–........................CTFT–53
    Earlier sketches in CTFT–5, 14, 25
Kroeger, Gary 1957– CTFT–5
Kroeker, Allan...CTFT–30
Kroft, Steve 1945–.................................CTFT–27
Krol, Joachim 1957–..............................CTFT–34
Kronenberger, Louis 1904–1980.............WWT–16
Kroopf, Scott..CTFT–58
    Earlier sketch in CTFT–27
Kroopnick, Stephen CTFT–51
Kruger, Alma 1871–1960 ....WWasWT
Kruger, Diane 1976– CTFT–67
Kruger, Otto 1885–1974 ....WWasWT
Krull, Suzanne 1966–.............................CTFT–66
    Earlier sketch in CTFT–30
Krumholtz, David 1978– CTFT–44
    Earlier sketch in CTFT–22
Krupa, Olek CTFT–71
    Earlier sketches in CTFT–21, 31
Krupska, Danya 1923–...........................WWT–17
Kruschen, Jack 1922–............................CTFT–6
Kruse, Doug CTFT–75
Krusiec, Michelle....................................CTFT–56
Krutch, Joseph Wood 1893–1970 ....WWasWT
Krutonog, Boris Lee 1962(?)–.................CTFT–65
Kruzan, Michael CTFT–44
Kubik, Alex...CTFT–4
Kubrick, Stanley 1928–1999 ....CTFT–31
    Earlier sketches in CTFT–1, 7, 19
Kudisch, Marc 1966– CTFT–40
Kudoh, Youki 1971–..............................CTFT–64
    Earlier sketch in CTFT–28
Kudrow, Lisa 1963–...............................CTFT–55
    Earlier sketches in CTFT–15, 26
Kuhn, Judy 1958–..................................CTFT–43
Kulich, Vladimir 1956–..........................CTFT–62
Kulik, Buzz 1923–1999..........................CTFT–12
    Obituary in CTFT–24
Kulp, Nancy 1921–1991 ....CTFT–3
    Obituary in CTFT–10

Kulukundis, Eddie 1932– WWT–17
Kumar, Anil 1969– CTFT–69
Kumchachi, Madame 1843–? .... WWasWT
Kummer, Clare 1888–1958.................... WWasWT
Kummer, Frederic Arnold 1873–1943 ..... WWasWT
Kun, Magda 1912–1945 .... WWasWT
Kunis, Mila 1983– CTFT–66
    Earlier sketch in CTFT–30
Kunneke, Eduard 1885–1953 .... WWasWT
Kuralt, Charles 1934–1997 .... CTFT–15
    Obituary in CTFT–18
    Earlier sketch in CTFT–5
Kureishi, Hanif 1954(?)– CTFT–40
    Earlier sketches in CTFT–10, 17
    Brief Entry in CTFT–5
Kurland, Jeffrey CTFT–48
Kurnitz, Julie 1942– CTFT–4
Kuroda, Emily 1952– CTFT–70
    Earlier sketches in CTFT–20, 31
Kurosawa, Akira 1910–1998 .... CTFT–13
    Obituary in CTFT–24
    Earlier sketch in CTFT–6
Kurth, Juliette 1960– CTFT–4
Kurtis, Bill 1940– CTFT–58
    Earlier sketch in CTFT–26
Kurton, Peggy .... WWasWT
Kurty, Hella ?–1954 .... WWasWT
Kurtz, Gary 1940– CTFT–68
    Earlier sketch in CTFT–6
Kurtz, Swoosie 1944– CTFT–57
    Earlier sketches in CTFT–1, 4, 15, 26
Kurup, Shishir 1961– CTFT–70
    Earlier sketches in CTFT–20, 31
Kurys, Diane 1949– CTFT–8
Kusatsu, Clyde 1948– CTFT–39
    Earlier sketch in CTFT–14
Kushner, Tony 1956(?)– CTFT–13
Kustow, Michael 1939– CTFT–6
    Earlier sketch in WWT–17
Kusturica, Emir 1955(?)– CTFT–39
    Earlier sketch in CTFT–15
Kutcher, Ashton 1978– CTFT–39
Kuzyk, Mimi CTFT–47
Kwabe, Jere
    See .... Weber, Jake
Kwan, Michelle 1980– CTFT–45
Kwan, Nancy 1939– CTFT–7
Kwanten, Ryan 1976– CTFT–72
Kwapis, Ken CTFT–55
Kwouk, Burt 1930– CTFT–55
Kyasht, Lydia 1886–? .... WWasWT
Kyle, Barry 1947– CTFT–5
    Earlier sketch in WWT–17

L

La La
    See .... Vasquez, La La
La Placa, Alison 1959– CTFT–77
La Plante, Laura 1904– .... WWasWT
LaBelle, Patti 1944– CTFT–51
    Earlier sketches in CTFT–12, 24
LaBelle, Rob CTFT–46
LaBeouf, Shia 1986– CTFT–62
Labine, Kyle 1983– CTFT–68
Labine, Tyler 1978– CTFT–68
Labiosa, David CTFT–71
Lablache, Luigi ?–1914 .... WWasWT

Lablanc, Sadie
    See .... Leblanc, Sadie
Laborteaux, Patrick
    See .... Labyorteaux, Patrick
LaBute, Neil 1963– CTFT–47
    Earlier sketch in CTFT–23
Labyorteaux, Patrick 1965(?)– CTFT–40
    Earlier sketch in CTFT–17
Lacamara, Carlos 1958– CTFT–64
Lacey, Catherine 1904–1979 .... WWT–16
Lacey, Ingrid CTFT–34
Lacey, Monica
    See .... Creel, Monica
Lacey, William J. 1931– CTFT–2
Lachman, Edward 1946– CTFT–37
    Earlier sketch in CTFT–13
Lachman, Morton 1918– CTFT–1
Lack, Simon 1917– WWT–17
Lackaye, Wilton 1862–1932 .... WWasWT
Lackey, Elizabeth 1971– CTFT–76
Lacy, Frank 1867–1937 .... WWasWT
Lacy, George 1904– .... WWasWT
Lacy, Monica
    See .... Creel, Monica
Lacy–Thompson, Charles Robert
    1922– WWT–17
Ladd, Alan, Jr. 1937– CTFT–38
    Earlier sketch in CTFT–12
Ladd, Cheryl 1951– CTFT–66
    Earlier sketches in CTFT–2, 6, 18, 30
Ladd, David Alan 1947– CTFT–2
Ladd, Diane 1939– CTFT–43
    Earlier sketches in CTFT–1, 7, 14
Ladd, Jordan 1975– CTFT–40
Lafayette, John CTFT–60
Laffan, Pat CTFT–75
    Earlier sketch in CTFT–33
Laffan, Patricia 1919– .... WWasWT
Lafferty, James 1985– CTFT–74
Lafferty, Sandra Ellis CTFT–57
Laffran, Kevin Barry 1922– WWT–17
LaFleur, Art 1943– CTFT–71
    Earlier sketch in CTFT–32
LaFleur, C. D.
    See .... Flower, George "Buck"
LaFontaine, Don 1940– CTFT–56
LaFosse, Robert 1959– CTFT–22
    Earlier sketch in CTFT–11
La Frenais, Ian 1937– CTFT–52
    Earlier sketch in CTFT–12
Lage, Jordan 1963– CTFT–51
Lageson, Lincoln CTFT–70
Lagerfelt, Caroline 1947– CTFT–66
    Earlier sketches in CTFT–2, 18, 29
Lagravenese, Richard 1959(?)– CTFT–40
La Grua, Tom CTFT–62
Lahr, Bert 1895–1967 .... WWasWT
Lahr, John 1941– WWT–17
Lahti, Christine 1950– CTFT–44
    Earlier sketches in CTFT–1, 4, 11, 22
Lai, Francis 1932– CTFT–54
    Earlier sketches in CTFT–2, 12
Laidler, Francis 1870–1955 .... WWasWT
Lail, Leah 1970– CTFT–67
Laine, Cleo 1927– CTFT–48
    Earlier sketches in CTFT–3, 14
Laine, Jimmy
    See .... Ferrara, Abel
Laing, Peggie 1899– .... WWasWT
Laird, Jack 1923–1991 .... CTFT–1
    Obituary in CTFT–10
Laird, Jenny 1917– WWT–17

Lake, Don 1956– CTFT–76
    Earlier sketch in CTFT–33
Lake, Harriette
    See .... Sothern, Ann
Lake, Lew ?–1939 .... WWasWT
Lake, Ricki 1968– CTFT–59
    Earlier sketches in CTFT–9, 17, 27
Lalaine, 1987– CTFT–70
Lally, Gwen ?–1963 .... WWasWT
LaLoggia, Frank CTFT–4
Lalor, Frank 1869–1932 .... WWasWT
Lam, Ling–Tung
    See .... Lam, Ringo
Lam, Ringo 1954– CTFT–27
Lamarche, Maurice 1958– CTFT–37
LaMarr, Phil 1967– CTFT–71
Lamas, Lorenzo 1958– CTFT–78
    Earlier sketches in CTFT–5, 34
Lamb, Beatrice 1866–? .... WWasWT
Lamb, Larry CTFT–35
Lambelet, Napoleon 1864–1932 .... WWasWT
Lamberg, Adam 1984– CTFT–62
Lambert, Christopher 1957– CTFT–67
    Earlier sketches in CTFT–3, 19, 30
Lambert, Constant 1905–1951 .... WWasWT
Lambert, J. W. 1917– WWT–17
Lambert, Jack 1899–1976 .... WWT–16
Lambert, Jerry CTFT–30
Lambert, Lawson 1870–1944 .... WWasWT
Lambert, Robert 1960– CTFT–11
Lambert, Robert K. CTFT–37
Lamia, Jenna CTFT–79
La Milo .... WWasWT
Lamont, Peter 1929– CTFT–60
    Earlier sketch in CTFT–28
LaMorte, Robia 1970– CTFT–47
Lamos, Mark 1946– CTFT–43
    Earlier sketches in CTFT–1, 9
Lamour, Dorothy 1914–1996 .... CTFT–11
    Obituary in CTFT–16
L'Amour, Louis 1908–1988 .... CTFT–28
Lampert, Zohra 1937– CTFT–4
    Earlier sketch in CTFT–1
Lampkin, Charles 1913–1989 .... CTFT–8
Lampley, Oni Faida 1959(?)– CTFT–54
Lan, David 1952– CTFT–5
    Earlier sketch in WWT–17
La Nasa, Katherine 1966– CTFT–74
    Earlier sketch in CTFT–40
Lancaster, Burt 1913–1994 .... CTFT–6
    Obituary in CTFT–14
    Earlier sketch in CTFT–1
Lancaster, Nora 1882–? .... WWasWT
Lancaster, Sarah 1980– CTFT–75
Lanchester, Elsa 1902–1986 .... CTFT–3
    Obituary in CTFT–4
    Earlier sketch in WWasWT
Lanchester, Robert 1941– CTFT–2
Land, David 1920– WWT–17
Landau, David 1878–1935 .... WWasWT
Landau, Jon 1960– CTFT–42
    Earlier sketch in CTFT–21
Landau, Juliet 1965– CTFT–49
Landau, Les CTFT–50
Landau, Martin 1931(?)– CTFT–55
    Earlier sketches in CTFT–1, 7, 14, 25
Landau, Tina CTFT–32
Landau, Vivien CTFT–3
Landeau, Cecil 1906– .... WWasWT
Landeck, Ben 1864–1928 .... WWasWT
Landen, Dinsdale 1932– CTFT–5
    Earlier sketch in WWT–17
Lander, David L. 1947– CTFT–55

Landers, Audrey 1959– CTFT–55
 Earlier sketch in CTFT–4
Landers, Hal 1928–1991 .... CTFT–11
Landers, Harry 1921– CTFT–9
Landers, Judy CTFT–4
Landes, Michael 1972– CTFT–41
Landes, William–Alan 1945– CTFT–2
Landesberg, Steve 1945– CTFT–51
 Earlier sketches in CTFT–3, 24
Landesman, Heidi CTFT–9
Landey, Clayton CTFT–56
Landi, Elisa 1904–1948 .... WWasWT
Landis, Jerry
 See .... Simon, Paul
Landis, Jessie Royce 1904–1972 .... WWasWT
Landis, John 1950– CTFT–52
 Earlier sketches in CTFT–1, 7, 14, 25
Landis, William 1921– CTFT–3
Lando, Joe 1961– CTFT–60
 Earlier sketches in CTFT–17, 27
Landon, Avice 1908–1976 .... WWT–16
Landon, Michael 1936–1991 .... CTFT–7
 Obituary in CTFT–10
Landor, Rosalyn 1958– CTFT–69
Landry, Ali 1973– CTFT–60
Landry, Karen 1950– CTFT–78
Landsburg, Alan 1933– CTFT–37
 Earlier sketch in CTFT–10
Landsburg, Valerie 1958– CTFT–4
Landstone, Charles 1891– .... WWasWT
Lane, Barbara CTFT–50
Lane, Burton 1912– WWT–17
Lane, Campbell CTFT–69
Lane, Charles 1905– CTFT–9
Lane, Diane 1965– CTFT–51
 Earlier sketches in CTFT–5, 12, 24
 Brief Entry in CTFT–2
Lane, Dorothy 1890– .... WWasWT
Lane, Frederic
 See .... Lehne, Fredric
Lane, Genette 1940– CTFT–4
Lane, Grace 1876–1956 .... WWasWT
Lane, Horace 1880–? .... WWasWT
Lane, Lupino 1892–1959 .... WWasWT
Lane, Nathan 1956– CTFT–60
 Earlier sketches in CTFT–10, 17, 27
Lane, Stewart F. 1951– CTFT–66
 Earlier sketches in CTFT–3, 19, 30
Laneuville, Eric 1952– CTFT–78
 Earlier sketches in CTFT–6, 34
Lang, Alexis CTFT–41
Lang, Andre 1893–1986 .... CTFT–4
Lang, Belinda 1953– CTFT–8
Lang, Charles 1902–1998 .... CTFT–9
 Obituary in CTFT–21
Lang, Charley 1955– CTFT–1
Lang, Fritz 1890–1976 .... CTFT–28
Lang, Harold WWT–17
Lang, Howard 1876–1941 .... WWasWT
Lang, Matheson 1879–1948 .... WWasWT
Lang, Pearl 1922– CTFT–1
Lang, Perry 1959– CTFT–52
Lang, Philip J. 1911–1986 .... CTFT–1
Lang, Robert 1934– CTFT–35
 Earlier sketches in CTFT–5; WWT–17
Lang, Stephen 1952– CTFT–78
 Earlier sketches in CTFT–5, 35
Lang, Walter Alexis
 See .... Lang, Alexis
Langdon, Sue Ann 1936– CTFT–6
Lange, Artie 1967– CTFT–61
 Earlier sketch in CTFT–28
Lange, Hope 1933– CTFT–5

Lange, Jessica 1949– CTFT–45
 Earlier sketches in CTFT–2, 6, 13, 23
Lange, Jim 1933– CTFT–67
Lange, John
 See .... Crichton, Michael
Lange, Michael CTFT–51
Lange, Ted 1947(?)– CTFT–66
 Earlier sketches in CTFT–3, 19, 30
Langella, Frank 1940(?)– CTFT–60
 Earlier sketches in CTFT–1, 9, 17, 27;
 WWT–17
Langer, A. J. 1974– CTFT–42
 Earlier sketch in CTFT–20
Langham, Michael 1919– CTFT–6
 Earlier sketch in WWT–17
Langham, Wallace 1965– CTFT–66
 Earlier sketches in CTFT–20, 30
Langley, Noel 1911– .... WWasWT
Langmann, Claude
 See .... Berri, Claude
Langner, Lawrence 1890–1962 .... WWasWT
Langner, Philip 1926– WWT–17
Langton, Basil 1912– CTFT–2
 Earlier sketch in WWasWT
Langton, Brooke 1970– CTFT–73
 Earlier sketch in CTFT–32
Langtry, Lillie 1852–1929 .... WWasWT
Lannom, Les CTFT–34
Lansbury, Angela 1925– CTFT–53
 Earlier sketches in CTFT–1, 7, 14, 25;
 WWT–17
Lansbury, Bruce 1930– CTFT–13
Lansbury, Edgar 1930– WWT–17
Lansing, Robert 1928–1994 .... CTFT–10
 Obituary in CTFT–14
 Earlier sketch in CTFT–3
Lansing, Sherry 1944– CTFT–1
Lanter, Matt 1983– CTFT–76
Lantieri, Michael CTFT–38
Lantos, Robert 1949– CTFT–55
 Earlier sketch in CTFT–26
Lantz, Robert 1914– CTFT–1
Lantz, Walter 1900–1994 .... CTFT–12
Lanyer, Charles 1942– CTFT–38
 Earlier sketch in CTFT–12
Lanzmann, Claude 1925– CTFT–37
 Earlier sketch in CTFT–13
Lanzoni, Fabio
 See .... Fabio
LaPaglia, Anthony 1959– CTFT–60
 Earlier sketches in CTFT–10, 17, 28
LaPaglia, Jonathan 1969– CTFT–74
Lapaine, Daniel 1970(?)– CTFT–49
Laparcerie, Cora .... WWasWT
Lapine, James 1949– CTFT–40
 Earlier sketch in CTFT–7
Lapis, Peter CTFT–4
La Plante, Lynda 1946(?)– CTFT–78
Lapotaire, Jane 1944– CTFT–37
 Earlier sketches in CTFT–3, 13; WWT–17
Lara, Joe 1962– CTFT–37
Lara, Madame 1876–? .... WWasWT
Lardner, Ring, Jr. 1915– CTFT–5
Laresca, Vincent 1974– CTFT–66
Larimore, Earle 1899–1974 .... WWasWT
Larkin, Linda 1970– CTFT–66
 Earlier sketch in CTFT–29
Larkin, Peter 1926– WWT–17
Larkin, Sheena CTFT–62
Larra, Mariano .... WWasWT
Larrimore, Francine 1898–1975 .... WWasWT
Larroquette, John 1947– CTFT–52
 Earlier sketches in CTFT–3, 14, 25

Larson, Darrell 1950(?)– CTFT–49
Larson, Glen A. 1937(?)– CTFT–39
 Earlier sketches in CTFT–7, 14
Larson, Jack 1933– CTFT–9
Larson, Jill 1947– CTFT–67
 Earlier sketch in CTFT–30
Larson, Jonathan 1960–1996 .... CTFT–21
Larter, Ali 1976– CTFT–60
 Earlier sketch in CTFT–28
La Rue, Danny CTFT–2
LaRue, Eva 1966– CTFT–72
 Earlier sketches in CTFT–21, 32
La Rue, Grace 1882–1956 .... WWasWT
LaRusso, Louis II 1935– WWT–17
La Salle, Eriq 1962– CTFT–55
 Earlier sketches in CTFT–15, 26
LaSardo, Robert CTFT–43
Lascher, David 1972– CTFT–42
LaSelva, Anita CTFT–40
Lashly, James CTFT–54
Lashwood, George ?–1942 .... WWasWT
Lasker, Lawrence 1949– CTFT–11
Laskin, Larissa CTFT–42
Laskin, Michael CTFT–53
Laskus, Jacek 1951– CTFT–51
 Earlier sketches in CTFT–12, 24
Lassally, Walter 1926– CTFT–10
Lasser, Abe
 See .... Wyner, Tom
Lasser, Louise 1939(?)– CTFT–69
 Earlier sketches in CTFT–3, 19, 30
Lasseter, John 1957– CTFT–53
 Earlier sketch in CTFT–25
Lassez, Sarah CTFT–79
Lassick, Sydney 1922– CTFT–1
Laszlo, Andrew 1926– CTFT–1
Laszlo, Ernest 1905(?)–1984 .... CTFT–26
Latessa, Dick 1930(?)– CTFT–54
Latham, Frederick G. ?–1943 .... WWasWT
Latham, Louise CTFT–47
Lathan, Bobbi Jo 1951– CTFT–8
Lathan, Sanaa 1971(?)– CTFT–48
Lathan, Stanley 1945– CTFT–6
Lathbury, Stanley 1873–? .... WWasWT
Lathom, Earl of
 See .... Wilbraham, Edward
Lathrop, Philip 1916– CTFT–12
Latimer, Edyth .... WWasWT
Latimer, Hugh 1913– WWT–17
Latimer, Sally 1910– .... WWasWT
Latona, Jen 1881–? .... WWasWT
La Trobe, Charles 1879–1967 .... WWasWT
Latshaw, Steve 1959– CTFT–74
Lau, Laurence 1954– CTFT–54
Lauchlan, Agnes 1905– WWT–17
Lauder, Harry 1870–1950 .... WWasWT
Lauer, Andrew 1963(?)– CTFT–41
 Earlier sketch in CTFT–18
Lauer, Matt 1957– CTFT–43
Laughlin, John CTFT–54
Laughlin, Sharon 1949– CTFT–1
Laughlin, Tom 1938– CTFT–5
Laughton, Charles 1899–1962 .... WWasWT
Lauper, Cyndi 1953– CTFT–76
 Earlier sketch in CTFT–33
Laurance, Matthew 1950– CTFT–35
 Earlier sketch in CTFT–8
Laurance, Mitchell 1950– CTFT–51
Laurel, Stan 1890–1965 .... CTFT–17
Lauren, Greg CTFT–51
Lauren, Veronica 1980– CTFT–55
Laurence, Ashley 1971– CTFT–68
Laurence, Paula WWT–17

Laurents, Arthur 1918(?)– CTFT–49
    Earlier sketches in CTFT–2, 9; WWT–17
Laurer, Joanie 1970–.............................. CTFT–43
Lauria, Dan 1947– CTFT–69
    Earlier sketches in CTFT–7, 19, 30
Laurie, Hugh 1959– CTFT–47
    Earlier sketch in CTFT–23
Laurie, John 1897–1980 .... WWT–17
Laurie, Piper 1932– CTFT–66
    Earlier sketches in CTFT–3, 10, 17, 29
Laurier, Jay 1879–1969......................... WWasWT
Laurillard, Edward 1870–1936 .... WWasWT
Lauro, Shirley 1933– CTFT–1
Laustsen, Dan CTFT–61
    Earlier sketch in CTFT–28
Lauter, Ed 1940–.................................. CTFT–78
    Earlier sketches in CTFT–5, 35
Lauterman, Peter CTFT–40
    Earlier sketch in CTFT–17
Lautrec, Pete
    See .... Paxton, Bill
Lavalliere, Eve 1866–1929 .... WWasWT
Lavedan, Henri 1859–1940 .... WWasWT
Laver, James 1899–1975 .... WWasWT
Laverick, Beryl 1919– .... WWasWT
La Verne, Lucille 1872–1945................ WWasWT
Lavery, Bryony 1947–............................ CTFT–12
Lavin, Linda 1937–................................ CTFT–41
    Earlier sketches in CTFT–3, 19; WWT–17
Lavorgna, Adam 1981– CTFT–74
Law, Arthur 1844–1913 .... WWasWT
Law, Cheuk–yiu
    See .... Law, Clara
Law, Clara 1957– CTFT–35
Law, John Phillip 1937– CTFT–78
    Earlier sketches in CTFT–7, 34
Law, Jude 1972– CTFT–47
    Earlier sketch in CTFT–23
Law, Mary 1891– .... WWasWT
Law, Moulon 1922– CTFT–2
Law, Phyllida 1932– CTFT–70
    Earlier sketches in CTFT–21, 31
Lawford, Betty 1910–1960 .... WWasWT
Lawford, Christopher 1955– CTFT–61
    Earlier sketch in CTFT–28
Lawford, Ernest ?–1940......................... WWasWT
Lawford, Peter 1923–1984 .... CTFT–2
Lawless, Lucy 1968– CTFT–63
    Earlier sketches in CTFT–17, 28
Lawlor, Charles CTFT–42
Lawlor, Mary....................................... WWasWT
Lawrence, Andrew 1988(?)– CTFT–71
Lawrence, Boyle 1869–1951 .... WWasWT
Lawrence, Carol 1932(?)–....................... CTFT–50
    Earlier sketches in CTFT–4; WWT–17
Lawrence, Carolyn CTFT–74
Lawrence, Charles 1896– .... WWasWT
Lawrence, Colin CTFT–69
Lawrence, D. H. 1885–1930 .... WWasWT
Lawrence, Darrie CTFT–4
Lawrence, Eddie 1921– CTFT–1
Lawrence, Gerald 1873–1957 .... WWasWT
Lawrence, Gertrude 1898–1952 .... WWasWT
Lawrence, Jerome 1915–......................... CTFT–5
    Earlier sketch in WWT–17
Lawrence, Joey 1976–............................ CTFT–51
    Earlier sketches in CTFT–13, 24
Lawrence, Lawrence Shubert, Jr.
    1916–.. CTFT–4
Lawrence, Marc 1910–........................... CTFT–34
    Earlier sketch in CTFT–9
Lawrence, Margaret 1889–1929 .... WWasWT

Lawrence, Mark Christopher
    1964–.. CTFT–79
Lawrence, Martin 1965– CTFT–50
    Earlier sketches in CTFT–13, 24
Lawrence, Matthew 1980–...................... CTFT–71
    Earlier sketches in CTFT–20, 31
Lawrence, Scott CTFT–45
Lawrence, Sharon 1961(?)– CTFT–65
    Earlier sketches in CTFT–18, 29
Lawrence, Shawn CTFT–62
Lawrence, Steve 1935– CTFT–36
    Earlier sketch in CTFT–11
Lawrence, Steven Anthony
    1990–.. CTFT–42
Lawrence, Vicki 1949– CTFT–71
    Earlier sketches in CTFT–1, 19,31
Lawrence, Vincent 1896– .... WWasWT
Lawrence, Vincent S. 1890–1946 .... WWasWT
Lawrence, William John 1862–1940 ..... WWasWT
Lawson, Bianca 1979–............................ CTFT–51
Lawson, Denis 1947– CTFT–78
    Earlier sketches in CTFT–9, 34
Lawson, John 1865–1920 .... WWasWT
Lawson, John Howard 1895–1977 .... WWasWT
Lawson, Leigh 1943– CTFT–41
    Earlier sketch in CTFT–9
Lawson, Maggie 1980– CTFT–52
Lawson, Mary 1910–1941 .... WWasWT
Lawson, Richard 1947– CTFT–78
    Earlier sketches in CTFT–9, 35
Lawson, Twiggy
    See .... Twiggy
Lawson, Wilfrid 1900–1966 .... WWasWT
Lawson, Winifred 1894–1961 .... WWasWT
Lawton, Frank 1904–1969..................... WWasWT
Lawton, Leslie 1942– WWT–17
Lawton, Thais 1881–1956 .... WWasWT
Laye, Dilys 1934– CTFT–37
    Earlier sketches in CTFT–13; WWT–17
Laye, Evelyn 1900– WWT–17
Layton, Joe 1931–1994 .... CTFT–5
    Obituary in CTFT–13
    Earlier sketch in WWT–17
Lazar, Andrew 1966(?)–.......................... CTFT–59
Lazar, Paul... CTFT–63
    Earlier sketch in CTFT–28
Lazarev, Yevgeni.................................... CTFT–64
Lazaridis, Stefanos 1944– CTFT–4
Lazarus, Paul 1954– CTFT–34
    Earlier sketch in CTFT–4
Lazenby, George 1939–........................... CTFT–77
    Earlier sketches in CTFT–2, 34
Lazzarini, Rick 1960(?)– CTFT–63
    Earlier sketch in CTFT–28
Lazzaro, Sofia
    See .... Loren, Sophia
Lea, Nicholas 1962– CTFT–63
    Earlier sketches in CTFT–17, 28
Lea, Ron CTFT–46
Leabo, Loi 1935– CTFT–3
Leach, Robin 1941– CTFT–35
    Earlier sketch in CTFT–5
Leach, Rosemary 1935– CTFT–75
    Earlier sketches in CTFT–8, 32
Leach, Wilford 1929–1988...................... CTFT–6
Leachman, Cloris 1930(?)– CTFT–44
    Earlier sketches in CTFT–1, 4, 22
Leacock, Philip 1917–1990.................... CTFT–10
Leadlay, Edward O. ?–1951 .... WWasWT
Leaf, Richard CTFT–77
Leahy, Eugene 1883–1967.................... WWasWT
Leamore, Tom 1865–1939.................... WWasWT
Lean, Cecil 1878–1935 .... WWasWT

Lean, David 1908–1991 .... CTFT–6
    Obituary in CTFT–10
Lear, Norman 1922– CTFT–73
    Earlier sketches in CTFT–1, 8, 19, 32
Learned, Michael 1939–.......................... CTFT–78
    Earlier sketches in CTFT–1, 6, 35
Leary, David 1939– CTFT–44
    Earlier sketches in CTFT–3, 22
Leary, Denis 1957–................................ CTFT–57
    Earlier sketches in CTFT–15, 26
Leavenworth, Scotty 1990– CTFT–48
Leaver, Philip 1904– .... WWasWT
Leaves, Jane
    See .... Leeves, Jane
Le Bargy, Charles Gustave Auguste
    1858–1936 .... WWasWT
Le Baron, William 1883–1958.............. WWasWT
Lebeau, Pierre CTFT–35
Leblanc, Georgette 1876–1941............. WWasWT
Le Blanc, Lisa
    See .... Kane, Carol
LeBlanc, Matt 1967– CTFT–41
    Earlier sketch in CTFT–18
Leblanc, Sadie 1977–............................. CTFT–68
LeBlanc, Tina 1967(?)–........................... CTFT–12
Le Bow, Will... CTFT–34
Lebowsky, Stanley 1926–1986 .... CTFT–4
Le Breton, Flora 1898– .... WWasWT
Le Brock, Kelly 1960–............................ CTFT–15
Leconte, Marie..................................... WWasWT
Lecoq, Jacques 1921–1999 .... CTFT–24
Leder, Mimi 1952–................................ CTFT–44
    Earlier sketches in CTFT–11, 22
Lederer, Francis 1899– CTFT–1
Lederer, George W. 1861–1938.............. WWasWT
Ledford, Brandy 1969–........................... CTFT–65
Ledford, John CTFT–46
Ledger, Heath 1979–.............................. CTFT–63
    Earlier sketch in CTFT–28
LeDoux, Trish CTFT–46
Ledoyen, Virginie 1976–......................... CTFT–50
    Earlier sketch in CTFT–24
Lee, Alexondra 1975– CTFT–41
Lee, Amanda Winn
    See .... Winn, Amanda
Lee, Ang 1954– CTFT–55
    Earlier sketches in CTFT–15, 26
Lee, Anna 1913– CTFT–1
Lee, Auriol 1880–1941 .... WWasWT
Lee, Bernard 1908–1981 .... WWT–17
Lee, Bert 1880–1946 .... WWasWT
Lee, Bill 1928– CTFT–11
Lee, Bobby
    See .... Ross, Neil
Lee, Brandon 1965–1993 .... CTFT–13
Lee, Bruce 1940–1973 .... CTFT–15
Lee, Canada 1907–1952 .... WWasWT
Lee, Christopher 1922– CTFT–44
    Earlier sketch in CTFT–6
Lee, Damian.. CTFT–37
Lee, Dana CTFT–78
    Earlier sketch in CTFT–35
Lee, Eugene 1939– CTFT–5
    Earlier sketch in WWT–17
Lee, Fran 1910– CTFT–5
Lee, Franne 1941–................................. CTFT–5
    Earlier sketch in WWT–17
Lee, Gypsy Rose 1913–1970 .... WWasWT
Lee, Heather CTFT–71
Lee, Irving Allen 1948– CTFT–3
Lee, Jack 1929– CTFT–1
Lee, James Kyson CTFT–74
Lee, Jason 1968– CTFT–55

Lee, Jason 1970– CTFT–41
    Earlier sketch in CTFT–20
Lee, Jason Scott 1966– CTFT–55
    Earlier sketch in CTFT–20
Lee, Jennie ?–1930 .... WWasWT
Lee, Jet
    See .... Li, Jet
Lee, Joie 1968(?)– CTFT–37
    Earlier sketch in CTFT–13
Lee, Lance 1942– CTFT–1
Lee, Leslie, 1935– CTFT–10
Lee, Marvin
    See .... Fahn, Tom
Lee, Michele 1942– CTFT–40
    Earlier sketch in CTFT–1
Lee, Miko 1965– CTFT–21
Lee, Ming Cho 1930– CTFT–4
    Earlier sketch in WWT–17
Lee, Mushond 1967– CTFT–70
Lee, Pamela Anderson
    See .... Anderson, Pamela
Lee, Robert E. 1918– CTFT–4
    Earlier sketch in WWT–17
Lee, Robert Terry 1957– CTFT–21
Lee, Robinne 1974– CTFT–74
Lee, RonReaco CTFT–57
Lee, Sheryl 1967(?)– CTFT–71
    Earlier sketches in CTFT–19, 31
Lee, Sophie 1968– CTFT–68
    Earlier sketch in CTFT–30
Lee, Spike 1956(?)– CTFT–45
    Earlier sketches in CTFT–6, 13, 23
Lee, Stan 1922– CTFT–46
Lee, Stephen 1951– CTFT–36
Lee, Thomas
    See .... Hill, Walter
Lee, Vanessa 1920– WWT–17
Lee, Wendee CTFT–41
Lee, Will Yun 1975– CTFT–76
Lee, William
    See .... Burroughs, William S.
Lee, Willy
    See .... Burroughs, William S.
Leech, Richard 1922– CTFT–6
    Earlier sketch in WWT–17
Leeds, Phil CTFT–9
Leekley, John CTFT–43
Leerhsen, Erica 1976– CTFT–71
Lees, Nathaniel CTFT–41
Leeves, Jane 1961– CTFT–65
    Earlier sketches in CTFT–18, 29
Lefeaux, Charles 1909– .... WWasWT
Le Feuvre, Guy 1883–1950 .... WWasWT
LeFevre, Adam 1950– CTFT–69
    Earlier sketch in CTFT–1
Lefevre, Maurice .... WWasWT
Lefevre, Rachelle CTFT–62
LeFrak, Francine 1950– CTFT–4
    Earlier sketch in WWT–17
Le Fre, Albert 1870–? .... WWasWT
Leftwich, Alexander 1884–1947 .... WWasWT
Le Gallienne, Eva 1899–1991 .... CTFT–1
    Obituary in CTFT–10
    Earlier sketch in WWT–17
Legarde, Millie .... WWasWT
LeGault, Lance CTFT–7
Leggatt, Alison (Joy) 1904–1990 .... WWT–17
Legge, Michael CTFT–46
Leggio, Jerry 1935– CTFT–66
Leggs, Johnny
    See .... Leguizamo, John
Legrand, Michel 1932 .... CTFT–35
    Earlier sketch in CTFT–9

Le Grand, Phyllis .... WWasWT
LeGros, James 1962– CTFT–43
Leguizamo, John 1965(?)– CTFT–44
    Earlier sketches in CTFT–11, 22
Lehar, Franz 1870–1948 .... WWasWT
Le Hay, Daisy 1883–? .... WWasWT
Le Hay, John 1854–1926 .... WWasWT
Lehman, Ernest 1915(?)– CTFT–22
Lehman, Kristin CTFT–52
Lehman, Lillian 1947– CTFT–74
Lehmann, Beatrix 1903–1979 .... WWT–17
Lehmann, Carla 1917– .... WWasWT
Lehmann, Michael 1957– CTFT–63
Lehne, Fredric CTFT–78
    Earlier sketch in CTFT–35
Lehrer, Jim 1934– CTFT–39
    Earlier sketch in CTFT–15
Lei, Mei–Kei
    See .... Q, Maggie
Leiber, Fritz 1883–1949 .... WWasWT
Leibman, Ron 1937– CTFT–71
    Earlier sketches in CTFT–2, 7, 19, 31;
    WWT–17
Leicester, Ernest 1866–1939 .... WWasWT
Leick, Hudson 1969– CTFT–51
    Earlier sketch in CTFT–24
Leider, Jerry 1931– CTFT–41
    Earlier sketches in CTFT–1, 9
Leifer, Carol 1956– CTFT–42
    Earlier sketch in CTFT–21
Leigh, Andrew George 1887–1957 .... WWasWT
Leigh, Cassandra
    See .... Boyle, Lisa
Leigh, Charlotte 1907– .... WWasWT
Leigh, Chyler 1982– CTFT–47
Leigh, Dan CTFT–42
Leigh, Dorma 1893– .... WWasWT
Leigh, Gracie ?–1950 .... WWasWT
Leigh, Janet 1927– CTFT–41
    Earlier sketches in CTFT–3, 19
Leigh, Jenna
    See .... Green, Jenna Leigh
Leigh, Jennifer Jason 1962– CTFT–52
    Earlier sketches in CTFT–12, 24
Leigh, Katie 1958– CTFT–55
Leigh, Mary 1904–1943 .... WWasWT
Leigh, Mike 1943– CTFT–53
    Earlier sketches in CTFT–6, 14, 25; WWT–17
Leigh, Mitch 1928– CTFT–1
Leigh, Rowland 1902–1963 .... WWasWT
Leigh, Vivien 1913–1967 .... WWasWT
Leigh, Walter 1905– .... WWasWT
Leigheb, Claudio 1848–? .... WWasWT
Leigh–Hunt, Barbara 1935– CTFT–40
    Earlier sketches in CTFT–10, 17; WWT–17
Leighton, Frank 1908–1962 .... WWasWT
Leighton, Laura 1968– CTFT–72
Leighton, Margaret 1922–1976 .... WWT–16
Leighton, Queenie 1872–1943 .... WWasWT
Leiner, Danny CTFT–56
Leister, Frederick 1885–1970 .... WWasWT
Leisure, David 1950– CTFT–38
    Earlier sketch in CTFT–10
    Brief Entry in CTFT–7
Leitch, Christopher CTFT–50
Leitch, Ione Skye
    See .... Skye, Ione
Leitch, Megan 1965– CTFT–34
Leiterman, Richard 1935– CTFT–57
Leland, David 1947– CTFT–17
Lelliott, jeremy 1982– CTFT–48
Le Loka, Tsidii CTFT–69

Lelouch, Claude 1937– CTFT–35
    Earlier sketch in CTFT–8
Lely, Madeline .... WWasWT
Lemaitre, Jules 1853–1914 .... WWasWT
Le Massena, William 1916– WWT–17
Le Mat, Paul 1952(?)– CTFT–59
    Earlier sketch in CTFT–7
Lemay, Harding 1922– CTFT–1
Lembeck, Michael 1948– CTFT–48
    Earlier sketch in CTFT–23
Lemche, Kris
Lemelin, Stephanie 1979– CTFT–79
Lemmon, Chris 1954– CTFT–41
    Earlier sketches in CTFT–7, 19
Lemmon, Jack 1925– CTFT–24
    Earlier sketches in CTFT–2, 7, 14
Lemmons, Kasi 1961(?)– CTFT–43
    Earlier sketch in CTFT–21
Le Moyne, Sarah Cowell 1859–1915 .... WWasWT
Lemper, Ute 1963– CTFT–51
    Earlier sketch in CTFT–24
Lena, Lily 1879–? .... WWasWT
Lenard, Mark 1927–1996 .... CTFT–9
    Obituary in CTFT–16
Lender, Marcelle .... WWasWT
Lenehan, Nancy CTFT–54
Leng, Cheng
    See .... Chan, Jackie
Lenihan, Winifred 1898–1964 .... WWasWT
Lenk, Tom 1976– CTFT–70
Lenkov, Peter M. CTFT–62
Lennard, Arthur 1867–1954 .... WWasWT
Lennertz, Christopher 1972– CTFT–62
Lenney, Dinah CTFT–50
Lennix, Harry J. 1965(?)– CTFT–50
    Earlier sketch in CTFT–24
Lennon, Jarrett 1982– CTFT–45
Lennon, John 1940–1980 .... CTFT–21
Lennon, Thomas 1970– CTFT–79
Lennon, Thomas F. 1951– CTFT–79
    Earlier sketch in CTFT–21
Lennox, Doug CTFT–54
Lennox, Kai CTFT–50
Lennox, Vera 1904– .... WWasWT
Leno, Jay 1950– CTFT–78
    Earlier sketches in CTFT–6, 34
LeNoire, Rosetta 1911– CTFT–37
    Earlier sketches in CTFT–13; WWT–17
Lenormand, Henri-Rene 1882–1951 ..... WWasWT
Lenthall, Franklyn 1919– CTFT–1
Lenya, Lotte 1900–1981 .... WWT–17
Lenz, Joie 1981– CTFT–70
Lenz, Kay 1953– CTFT–39
    Earlier sketches in CTFT–5, 12
Leo, Frank 1874–? .... WWasWT
Leo, Melissa 1960– CTFT–46
    Earlier sketch in CTFT–23
Leon, Anne 1925– .... WWasWT
Leon, Idalis
    See .... DeLeon, Idalis
Leon, Kenny 1957(?)– CTFT–48
Leonard, Billy 1892– .... WWasWT
Leonard, Elmore 1925– CTFT–63
    Earlier sketches in CTFT–10, 17, 28
Leonard, Hugh 1926– CTFT–6
    Earlier sketch in WWT–17
Leonard, Joshua 1975– CTFT–52
Leonard, Lu 1932– CTFT–1
Leonard, Patricia 1916– .... WWasWT
Leonard, Robert ?–1948 .... WWasWT
Leonard, Robert Sean 1969– CTFT–50
    Earlier sketches in CTFT–5, 13, 24

Leonard, Sheldon 1907–1997 .... CTFT–3
  Obituary in CTFT–17
Leonard–Boyne, Eva 1885–1960 .... WWasWT
Leonardi, Marco 1971(?)–...................... CTFT–68
  Earlier sketch in CTFT–30
Leone, Natasha
  See .... Lyonne, Natasha
Leone, Sergio 1929–1989.................... CTFT–5
Leonetti, John R. CTFT–74
Leonetti, Matthew F. 1941– CTFT–74
Leong, Page CTFT–53
Leoni, Tea 1966–.................................. CTFT–69
  Earlier sketches in CTFT–19, 31
Leontovich, Eugenie 1900– WWT–17
Lepage, Robert 1957– CTFT–37
  Earlier sketch in CTFT–13
Leopardi, Chauncey 1981– CTFT–62
Leopold, Stratton 1943– CTFT–40
Lera, Chete CTFT–34
Lerner, Alan Jay 1918–1986 .... CTFT–3
  Earlier sketch in WWT–17
Lerner, Avi CTFT–43
Lerner, Danny CTFT–43
Lerner, Ken CTFT–47
Lerner, Michael 1941(?)–...................... CTFT–44
  Earlier sketches in CTFT–11, 22
Le Roux, Hugues 1860–? .... WWasWT
Leroy, Mervyn 1900–1987.................... CTFT–24
Le Roy, Servais.................................... WWasWT
Le Sage, Stanley 1880–1932................ WWasWT
Leslie, Don 1948–................................ CTFT–1
Leslie, Enid 1888–? .... WWasWT
Leslie, Fred 1881–1945 .... WWasWT
Leslie, Joan 1925– CTFT–5
Leslie, Lew 1886–1963......................... WWasWT
Leslie, Marguerite 1884–1958 .... WWasWT
Leslie, Sylvia 1900– .... WWasWT
Leslie–Stuart, May................................ WWasWT
Lesnie, Andrew 1956–.......................... CTFT–43
Lessac, Michael CTFT–37
Lesser, Len 1922–................................ CTFT–43
  Earlier sketch in CTFT–21
Lesser, Robert CTFT–45
Lessing, Madge .... WWasWT
Lester, Adrian 1968–............................ CTFT–69
  Earlier sketches in CTFT–21, 31
Lester, Alfred 1874–1925...................... WWasWT
Lester, David V. 1945– CTFT–29
Lester, Loren CTFT–72
Lester, Mark 1876–? .... WWasWT
Lester, Mark L. 1946– CTFT–1
Lester, Richard 1932–.......................... CTFT–41
  Earlier sketches in CTFT–3, 19
Lester, Ron 1975–................................ CTFT–71
Lester, Terry CTFT–4
Lester, Vicki
  See .... Kaufman, Lloyd
Lestocq, William ?–1920 .... WWasWT
L'Estrange, Julian 1878–1918 .... WWasWT
Lesure, James 1975–............................ CTFT–69
Lethbridge, J. W. .... WWasWT
Letherman, Lindze 1988–...................... CTFT–75
Leto, Jared 1971– CTFT–47
  Earlier sketch in CTFT–23
LeTrek, Peter
  See .... Paxton, Bill
Letscher, Matt 1970–........................... CTFT–53
  Earlier sketch in CTFT–25
Letterman, David 1947–........................ CTFT–48
  Earlier sketches in CTFT–7, 14, 24
Letts, Dennis....................................... CTFT–54
Letts, Pauline 1917–............................ WWT–17
Leung, Ken CTFT–55

Leung, Tony... CTFT–37
Levant, Brian 1952–............................. CTFT–68
  Earlier sketch in CTFT–30
Leveaux, David 1958– CTFT–26
Leveaux, Montagu V. 1875–?................ WWasWT
Leven, Boris 1908–1986........................ CTFT–4
  Earlier sketch in CTFT–2
Levene, Sam 1905–1980 .... WWT–17
Leventhal, Susan E. CTFT–50
Leventon, Annabel 1942– CTFT–5
  Earlier sketch in WWT–17
Leverick, Beryl..................................... WWT–9
Levering, Kate CTFT–50
Levesque, Joanna
  See .... Jo–Jo
Levesque, Jojo
  See .... Jo–Jo
Levey, Adele .... WWasWT
Levey, Carlotta .... WWasWT
Levey, Ethel 1881–1955........................ WWasWT
Levi, Alan J. CTFT–56
Levi, Shawn CTFT–62
Levi, Zachary 1980–............................. CTFT–74
Le Vien, Jack 1918– CTFT–1
Levin, Charles CTFT–32
Levin, Gerald M. 1939–......................... CTFT–11
Levin, Herman 1907–............................ WWT–17
Levin, Ira 1929– CTFT–9
  Earlier sketches in CTFT–2; WWT–17
Levin, Lloyd CTFT–63
Levin, Peter CTFT–38
  Earlier sketches in CTFT–3, 12
Levine, Catherine Beaumont
  See .... Beaumont, Kathryn
Levine, Dan CTFT–49
LeVine, David 1933–............................. CTFT–5
Levine, Floyd CTFT–78
Levine, Ilana 1963–.............................. CTFT–57
  Earlier sketch in CTFT–26
Levine, James 1943– CTFT–37
  Earlier sketch in CTFT–13
Levine, Jerry 1957–.............................. CTFT–76
Levine, Joseph E. 1905–1987 .... CTFT–5
Levine, Ken 1950– CTFT–49
Levine, Michael 1952–.......................... CTFT–4
Levine, Samm 1982–............................ CTFT–76
Levine, Ted 1957– CTFT–69
  Earlier sketches in CTFT–20, 31
Levinsohn, Gary 1960(?)–...................... CTFT–57
  Earlier sketch in CTFT–26
Levinson, Barry 1942–.......................... CTFT–44
  Earlier sketches in CTFT–11, 22
Levinson, Larry CTFT–70
Levinson, Richard 1934–1987................. CTFT–5
Levison, Charles
  See... Lane, Charles
Levit, Ben 1949– CTFT–4
Levitan, Steven CTFT–66
Leviton, Stewart 1939–........................ WWT–17
Levitt, Ruby R. 1907–1992 .... CTFT–11
Levy, Benn W. 1900–1973 .... WWasWT
Levy, Dani 1957–................................. CTFT–33
Levy, David 1913– CTFT–6
  Earlier sketch in CTFT–3
Levy, Eugene 1946–.............................. CTFT–51
  Earlier sketches in CTFT–7, 14, 24
Levy, Jacques 1935–............................. WWT–17
Levy, Jefery 1958– CTFT–37
Levy, Jonathan 1935–........................... CTFT–7
  Earlier sketch in CTFT–3
Levy, Jose G. 1884–1936...................... WWasWT
Levy, Peter CTFT–54
Levy, Robert L..................................... CTFT–43

Levy, Stephen
  See .... Young, Stephen
Lew, James 1952–................................ CTFT–54
Lewenstein, Oscar 1917– WWT–17
Lewes, Miriam .... WWasWT
Lewey, Todd 1958– CTFT–2
Lewine, Richard 1910– CTFT–1
Lewis, Ada 1875–1925 .... WWasWT
Lewis, Al 1910– CTFT–26
Lewis, Al 1923– CTFT–8
Lewis, Ananda 1973– CTFT–72
Lewis, Arthur 1846–1930 .... WWasWT
Lewis, Arthur 1916– WWT–17
Lewis, Bertha 1887–1931 .... WWasWT
Lewis, Clea 1965– CTFT–53
  Earlier sketch in CTFT–25
Lewis, Curigwen .... WWasWT
Lewis, Daniel E. 1944– CTFT–3
Lewis, David CTFT–69
Lewis, Dawnn 1960– CTFT–47
Lewis, Edmund 1959– CTFT–8
Lewis, Emmanuel 1971– CTFT–7
Lewis, Eric 1855–1935 .... WWasWT
Lewis, Fred 1850–1927 .... WWasWT
Lewis, Frederick G. 1873–1946.............. WWasWT
Lewis, Gary 1958– CTFT–76
  Earlier sketch in CTFT–33
Lewis, Geoffrey 1935– CTFT–66
  Earlier sketches in CTFT–2, 18, 29
Lewis, Jean
  See .... Brent, Eve
Lewis, Jenny 1977(?)–........................... CTFT–34
  Earlier sketch in CTFT–4
Lewis, Jerry 1926– CTFT–63
  Earlier sketch in CTFT–5
Lewis, Joseph H. 1900(?)– CTFT–10
Lewis, Juliette 1973– CTFT–44
  Earlier sketches in CTFT–11, 22
Lewis, Mabel Terry–
  See .... Terry–Lewis, Mabel
Lewis, Marcia 1938– CTFT–22
  Earlier sketches in CTFT–1, 5
Lewis, Martin 1888–1970...................... WWasWT
Lewis, Mary Rio 1922– CTFT–4
Lewis, Matthew 1989– CTFT–76
Lewis, Phill 1968– CTFT–43
Lewis, Richard 1947(?)– CTFT–63
  Earlier sketches in CTFT–10, 17, 28
Lewis, Robert 1909– WWT–17
Lewis, Robert Michael 1934–................. CTFT–50
  Earlier sketch in CTFT–11
Lewis, Shari 1934–1998 .... CTFT–19
  Obituary in CTFT–22
  Earlier sketch in CTFT–3
Lewis, Ted CTFT–42
Lewis, Vicki 1960– CTFT–57
  Earlier sketch in CTFT–26
Lewisohn, Victor Max 1897–1934......... WWasWT
Lewman, Lance 1960– CTFT–45
  Earlier sketch in CTFT–2
LeXLang
  See .... Lang, Alexis
Lexy, Edward 1897– .... WWasWT
Leyden, Leo 1929– CTFT–4
Leyel, Carl F. 1875–1925....................... WWasWT
Leyton, George 1864–? .... WWasWT
Lhermitte, Thierry 1952– CTFT–35
Li, Gong 1965– CTFT–40
  Earlier sketch in CTFT–17
Li, Jet 1963– CTFT–63
  Earlier sketch in CTFT–28
Li, Meiqi
  See .... Q, Maggie

Liberace 1919–1987 .... CTFT–3
Liberatore, Lou 1959– CTFT–5
Libertini, Richard 1933(?)– CTFT–78
    Earlier sketches in CTFT–6, 35
Libin, Paul 1930– CTFT–19
    Earlier sketches in CTFT–2; WWT–17
Libman, Andrea 1984– CTFT–56
Lichine, David 1909–1972 .... WWasWT
Licht, Jeremy 1971– CTFT–8
Lichterman, Victoria 1940– CTFT–4
Licon, Jeffrey 1985– CTFT–61
Liddy, G. Gordon 1930– CTFT–40
Lieber, Mimi CTFT–76
Lieberman, Robert 1947– CTFT–37
    Earlier sketch in CTFT–13
Liebman, Marvin 1923– WWT–16
Lien, Jennifer 1974– CTFT–57
    Earlier sketch in CTFT–26
Lieven, Albert 1906–1971 .... WWasWT
Lieven, Tatiana 1910– .... WWasWT
Lifar, Serge 1905–1986 .... CTFT–4
    Earlier sketch in WWasWT
Lifford, Tina CTFT–64
Light, John CTFT–56
Light, Judith 1949– CTFT–46
    Earlier sketches in CTFT–10, 17
    Brief Entry in CTFT–3
Lightner, Winnie 1901–1971 .... WWasWT
Ligon, Tom 1945– CTFT–79
Lihani, Rob CTFT–48
Lillard, Matthew 1970– CTFT–57
    Earlier sketch in CTFT–26
Lillie, Beatrice 1898–1989 .... WWT–16
Lillies, Leonard 1860–1923 .... WWasWT
Lillis, Rachael 1978– CTFT–42
Lilly, Evangeline 1979– CTFT–70
Lim, Kwan Hi 1931– CTFT–23
Lim, Paul Stephen 1944– CTFT–1
Lima, Kevin 1962(?)– CTFT–66
    Earlier sketch in CTFT–29
Liman, Doug 1965(?)– CTFT–51
    Earlier sketch in CTFT–24
Limbert, Roy 1893–1954 .... WWasWT
Limerick, Mona .... WWasWT
Limon, Iyari 1979– CTFT–70
Limpus, Alban Brownlow 1878–1941 .... WWasWT
Lin, Carol CTFT–76
Lin, Lucy CTFT–59
Linares–Rivas, Manuel 1867–1938 .... WWasWT
Linari, Nancy CTFT–77
Lincoln, Andrew 1973– CTFT–34
Lincoln, Geoffrey
    See .... Mortimer, John
Lincoln, Patrick
    See .... St. Espirit, Patrick
Lind, Gillian 1904– WWT–16
Lind, Letty 1862–1923 .... WWasWT
Lindberg, August 1846–1916 .... WWasWT
Lindberg, Chad 1976– CTFT–59
Lindbjerg, Lalainia CTFT–56
Linde, Betty CTFT–41
Linden, Eric 1909– .... WWasWT
Linden, Hal 1931– CTFT–68
    Earlier sketches in CTFT–3, 19, 30; WWT–17
Linden, Marie 1862–? .... WWasWT
Lindenlaub, Karl Walter CTFT–38
Lindfors, Viveca 1920–1995 .... CTFT–1
    Obituary in CTFT–15
    Earlier sketch in WWT–17
Lindley, Audra 1918–1997 .... CTFT–3
    Obituary in CTFT–19
    Earlier sketch in WWasWT

Lindley, John 1952– CTFT–63
    Earlier sketches in CTFT–17, 28
Lindo, Delroy 1952– CTFT–63
    Earlier sketches in CTFT–17, 28
Lindo, Olga 1898–1968 .... WWasWT
Lindon, Millie 1878–? .... WWasWT
Lindsay, Delia CTFT–34
Lindsay, Howard 1889–1968 .... WWasWT
Lindsay, James 1869–1928 .... WWasWT
Lindsay, Lesley
    See .... Zemeckis, Leslie Harter
Lindsay, Robert 1949(?)– CTFT–44
    Earlier sketches in CTFT–11, 22
    Brief Entry in CTFT–5
Lindsay, Vera 1911– .... WWasWT
Lindsay–Hogg, Michael 1940– CTFT–21
    Earlier sketch in CTFT–2
Lindstrom, Jon 1957– CTFT–69
    Earlier sketch in CTFT–15
Lineback, Richard CTFT–68
    Earlier sketch in CTFT–30
Lineham, Hardee T. CTFT–68
Ling, Bai 1970– CTFT–63
    Earlier sketch in CTFT–28
Ling, Lisa 1973– CTFT–78
Ling, Van CTFT–45
Link, Peter 1944– CTFT–5
    Earlier sketch in WWT–17
Link, Ron 1944– CTFT–13
    Earlier sketch in CTFT–6
Link, William 1933– CTFT–6
Linke, Paul 1948– CTFT–60
Linklater, Richard 1960(?)– CTFT–46
    Earlier sketch in CTFT–23
Linkletter, Art 1912– CTFT–3
Linley, Betty 1890–1951 .... WWasWT
Linley, Cody 1989– CTFT–78
Linn, Bambi 1926– CTFT–1
    Earlier sketch in WWasWT
Linn, Rex 1956– CTFT–38
Linn–Baker, Mark 1954– CTFT–42
    Earlier sketches in CTFT–5, 19
    Brief Entry in CTFT–2
Linnea
    See .... Quigley, Linnea
Linnet & Dunfree Ltd. WWT–16
Linney, Laura 1964– CTFT–71
    Earlier sketches in CTFT–19, 31
Linney, Romulus 1930– CTFT–10
    Earlier sketch in WWT–17
Linnit, S. E. ?–1956 .... WWasWT
Linson, Art 1942(?)– CTFT–38
    Earlier sketch in CTFT–10
Linville, Joanne CTFT–8
Linville, Larry 1939–2000 .... CTFT–31
    Earlier sketches in CTFT–3, 19
Linz, Alex D. 1989– CTFT–71
    Earlier sketches in CTFT–21, 31
Lipper, David CTFT–78
Lion, John 1944– CTFT–2
Lion, Leon M. 1879–1947 .... WWasWT
Lion, Margo 1944– CTFT–55
Liotta, Ray 1955(?)– CTFT–51
    Earlier sketches in CTFT–7, 14, 24
Lipinski, Tara 1982– CTFT–45
Lipman, Clara 1869–1952 .... WWasWT
Lipman, Daniel 1950– CTFT–17
Lipman, Maureen 1946– CTFT–37
    Earlier sketches in CTFT–5, 13; WWT–17
Lipnicki, Jonathan 1990– CTFT–66
    Earlier sketches in CTFT–18, 29
Lippman, Amy CTFT–64
    Earlier sketch in CTFT–28

Lipps, Roslyn 1925– CTFT–2
Lipscomb, Dennis 1942– CTFT–42
    Earlier sketch in CTFT–9
Lipscomb, William Percy 1887–1958 ..... WWasWT
Lipstadt, Aaron 1952– CTFT–41
Lipton, Celia 1923– .... WWasWT
Lipton, Dina CTFT–66
    Earlier sketch in CTFT–29
Lipton, James 1926– CTFT–65
Lipton, Peggy 1947(?)– CTFT–79
    Earlier sketches in CTFT–9, 35
Lipton, Robert 1943– CTFT–79
Lisi, Joe 1950– CTFT–76
    Earlier sketch in CTFT–33
Lisle, Lucille .... WWasWT
Lissauer, Trevor 1973– CTFT–78
Lister, Eve 1918– .... WWasWT
Lister, Francis 1899–1951 .... WWasWT
Lister, Frank 1868–1917 .... WWasWT
Lister, Lance 1901– .... WWasWT
Lister, Laurier 1907– WWT–17
Lister, Moira 1923– WWT–17
Lister, Tom "Tiny" CTFT–58
    Earlier sketch in CTFT–26
Lithgow, John 1945– CTFT–44
    Earlier sketches in CTFT–1, 4, 11, 22
Littell, Robert 1896–1963 .... WWasWT
Litter, Kitty
    See .... Fierstein, Harvey
Little, Cleavon 1939– CTFT–4
    Earlier sketch in WWT–17
Little, Natasha 1970– CTFT–35
Little, Rich 1938– CTFT–63
    Earlier sketches in CTFT–3, 5
Little, Stuart W. 1921– CTFT–4
Littlefield, Catherine 1904–1951 .... WWasWT
Littleford, Beth 1968– CTFT–66
    Earlier sketch in CTFT–30
Littler, Blanche 1899– .... WWasWT
Littler, Emile 1903– WWT–17
Littler, Prince 1901– .... WWasWT
Littleton, Carol 1942– CTFT–37
Littlewood, Joan CTFT–4
    Earlier sketch in WWT–17
Littlewood, Samuel Robinson
    1875–1963 .... WWasWT
Liu, Lucy 1968– CTFT–56
    Earlier sketch in CTFT–26
Lively, Eric 1981– CTFT–77
Lively, Ernie 1947– CTFT–77
Lively, Robyn 1972– CTFT–76
    Earlier sketch in CTFT–34
Lively, Sarah
    See .... Clarke, Sarah
Liveright, Horace B. 1886–1933 .... WWasWT
Livesay, Roger 1906–1976 .... WWT–16
Livesey, Barrie 1904– .... WWasWT
Livesey, E. Carter .... WWasWT
Livesey, Jack 1901–1961 .... WWasWT
Livesey, Sam 1873–1936 .... WWasWT
Livings, Henry 1929– WWT–17
Livingston, Barry 1953– CTFT–69
Livingston, David CTFT–49
Livingston, Harold 1924– CTFT–1
Livingston, Jay 1915– CTFT–1
Livingston, Mary 1906–1983 .... CTFT–21
Livingston, Paul CTFT–33
Livingston, Robert H. 1934– CTFT–2
Livingston, Ron 1968– CTFT–66
    Earlier sketch in CTFT–29
Livingston, Ruth 1927– CTFT–4
Livingstone, Sydney CTFT–35

Livinryte, Wings
See .... Hauser, Wings
LL Cool J 1968– CTFT–45
Llewellyn, Fewlass 1866–1941 .... WWasWT
Llewelyn, Desmond 1914–1999.............. CTFT–22
Obituary in CTFT–32
Lloyd Pack, Roger 1944– CTFT–4
Lloyd Webber, Andrew 1948–................. CTFT–51
Lloyd, Alice 1873–1949 .... WWasWT
Lloyd, Christopher 1938–....................... CTFT–44
Earlier sketches in CTFT–1, 4, 11, 22
Lloyd, David............................... CTFT–55
Earlier sketch in CTFT–11
Lloyd, Doris 1900–1968 .... WWasWT
Lloyd, Emily 1970– CTFT–46
Earlier sketches in CTFT–11, 23
Brief Entry in CTFT–7
Lloyd, Eric 1986– CTFT–49
Lloyd, Florence 1876–? .... WWasWT
Lloyd, Frederick William 1880–1949 .... WWasWT
Lloyd, Gabriel
See .... Kaufman, Lloyd
Lloyd, Harold 1893–1971 .... CTFT–20
Lloyd, Jake 1989–.................................. CTFT–51
Earlier sketch in CTFT–24
Lloyd, Kathleen CTFT–48
Lloyd, Marie 1870–1922 .... WWasWT
Lloyd, Michael 1948– CTFT–47
Earlier sketch in CTFT–10
Lloyd, Norman 1914– CTFT–79
Earlier sketches in CTFT–6, 35
Lloyd, Rosie 1879–1944 .... WWasWT
Lloyd, Sabrina CTFT–61
Earlier sketches in CTFT–17, 28
Lloyd, Sam CTFT–68
Lloyd, Sam Sr. 1925–.............................. CTFT–68
Lloyd, Sharon CTFT–4
Lloyd, Violet 1879–? .... WWasWT
Earlier sketches in CTFT–1, 6, 13, 24;
WWT–17
Loach, Ken 1936– CTFT–52
Earlier sketches in CTFT–12, 24
Loader, A. Mcleod 1869–? .... WWasWT
Loader, Rosa .... WWasWT
Lobel, Adrianne CTFT–11
Earlier sketch in CTFT–1
LoBianco, Tony 1936–........................... CTFT–45
Earlier sketches in CTFT–3, 11, 22
Lobl, Victor... CTFT–53
Locane, Amy 1971– CTFT–48
Lochhead, Liz 1947– CTFT–11
Locke, Edward 1869–1945 .... WWasWT
Locke, Katherine 1910–......................... WWasWT
Locke, Philip 1928– CTFT–6
Earlier sketch in WWT–17
Locke, Sam 1917–1998........................... CTFT–2
Obituary in CTFT–24
Locke, Sondra 1947–.............................. CTFT–5
Locke, Tembi CTFT–72
Locke, William John 1863–1930 .... WWasWT
Lockhart, Gene 1891–1957 .... WWasWT
Lockhart, June 1925– CTFT–36
Earlier sketches in CTFT–1, 9
Locklear, Heather 1961– CTFT–52
Earlier sketches in CTFT–6, 13, 24
Brief Entry in CTFT–2
Lockridge, Richard 1898–1982.............. WWasWT
Lockton, Joan 1901–............................. WWasWT
Lockwood, Gary 1937–........................... CTFT–7
Lockwood, Margaret 1916–1990........... WWT–17
Lockyer, Thomas.................................... CTFT–54
Loco, Tony
See .... Tone–Loc

Loder, Anne Marie 1969–....................... CTFT–46
Loder, Basil 1885–?................................ WWasWT
Loder, Kurt 1945– CTFT–66
LoDuca, Joseph CTFT–45
Loeb, Lisa 1968– CTFT–46
Earlier sketch in CTFT–23
Loeb, Philip 1894–1955 .... WWasWT
Loehr, Bret 1993–.................................. CTFT–75
Loesser, Frank 1910–1969 .... WWasWT
Loewe, Frederick 1901–1988 .... CTFT–6
Earlier sketch in WWT–17
Loewenstern, Tara CTFT–1
Loftin, Lennie CTFT–76
Earlier sketch in CTFT–34
Loftus, Kitty 1867–1927 .... WWasWT
Loftus, Marie 1857–1940....................... WWasWT
Loftus, (Marie) Cecilia 1876–1943......... WWasWT
Logan, Ella 1910–1969 .... WWasWT
Logan, John 1963– CTFT–64
Earlier sketch in CTFT–28
Logan, Joshua 1908–1988 .... CTFT–4
Earlier sketch in WWT–17
Logan, Nedda Harrigan 1900–1989 .... CTFT–8
Logan, Stanley 1885–1953 .... WWasWT
Loggia, Robert 1930– CTFT–44
Earlier sketches in CTFT–1, 4, 11, 22
Logue, Donal 1965(?)– CTFT–47
Earlier sketch in CTFT–23
Lohan, Lindsay 1986– CTFT–55
Lohman, Alison 1979– CTFT–54
Lohr, Aaron 1976–................................ CTFT–74
Lohr, Marie 1890–1975 .... WWasWT
Loken, Kristanna 1979–......................... CTFT–48
Lola
See .... Rieffel, Lisa
Lollobrigida, Gina CTFT–5
Lom, Herbert 1917–............................... WWT–17
Earlier sketches in CTFT–8; WWasWT
Lomas, Herbert 1887–1961 .... WWasWT
Lomax, Pearl Cleage
See .... Cleage, Pearl
Lombard, Karina 1969–.......................... CTFT–71
Earlier sketches in CTFT–19, 31
Lombard, Michael 1934– CTFT–46
Lombardi, Louis 1968–........................... CTFT–71
Lombardozzi, Domenick 1976– CTFT–79
London, Chuck 1946–............................ CTFT–4
London, Jason 1972– CTFT–55
Earlier sketches in CTFT–15, 26
London, Jeremy 1972– CTFT–53
Earlier sketches in CTFT–15, 25
London, Jerri Lynn
See .... Manthey, Jerri
London, Jerry 1937–.............................. CTFT–37
Earlier sketches in CTFT–2, 12
London, Roy 1943–1993 .... CTFT–1
Obituary in CTFT–12
Lone, John 1952– CTFT–6
Loney, Glenn 1928–............................... CTFT–1
Long, Avon 1910–1984 .... WWT–17
Long, Jodi 1958(?)–................................ CTFT–37
Earlier sketches in CTFT–1, 13
Long, John Luther 1861–1927 .... WWasWT
Long, Justin 1978–................................. CTFT–63
Long, Lisa CTFT–78
Long, Mary 1951– CTFT–62
Long, Nia 1970–.................................... CTFT–40
Long, Shelley 1949– CTFT–78
Earlier sketches in CTFT–5, 35
Long, William Ivey CTFT–35
Earlier sketch in CTFT–8
Longbaugh, Harry
See .... Goldman, William

Longden, John 1900– .... WWasWT
Longdon, Terence 1922–........................ WWT–17
Longenecker, John 1947– CTFT–1
Longford, Earl of (Edward Arthur Henry Pakenham)
1902–1961 .... WWasWT
Longo, Tony 1961–................................ CTFT–67
Earlier sketch in CTFT–30
Longoria, Eva 1975–.............................. CTFT–67
Lonnen, Jessie 1886–? .... WWasWT
Lonnen, Nellie 1887–? .... WWasWT
Lonnon, Alice 1872–?............................ WWasWT
Lonsdale, Frederick 1881–1954 .... WWasWT
Lonsdale, Gordon.................................. CTFT–56
Lonsdale, Michel 1931–......................... CTFT–34
Earlier sketch in CTFT–8
Lookinland, Mike 1960– CTFT–63
Earlier sketch in CTFT–28
Loonin, Larry 1941–.............................. CTFT–2
Loos, Anita 1893–1981 .... WWT–17
Lopez, Charlotte
See .... Ayanna, Charlotte
Lopez, Charo 1943–............................... CTFT–35
Lopez, Constance Marie
See............................... Marie, Constance
Lopez, George 1961– CTFT–54
Lopez, Irene Olga CTFT–48
Lopez, Jennifer 1970–........................... CTFT–70
Earlier sketches in CTFT–19, 31
Lopez, Mario 1973–............................... CTFT–71
Earlier sketches in CTFT–19,31
Lopez, Priscilla 1948– CTFT–70
Earlier sketches in CTFT–3, 19, 31
Lopez, Sal, Jr. 1954–............................. CTFT–58
Lopez, Sergi... CTFT–33
Lopez–Dawson, Kamala CTFT–72
Lopokova, Lydia 1892–1981 .... WWasWT
Loquasto, Santo 1944–.......................... CTFT–47
Earlier sketches in CTFT–6, 13, 23; WWT–17
Loraine, Robert 1876–1935 .... WWasWT
Loraine, Violet 1886–1956 .... WWasWT
Lord, Basil 1913–1979 .... WWT–17
Lord, Jack 1920–1998 .... CTFT–1
Obituary in CTFT–21
Lord, Jean–Claude 1943– CTFT–36
Earlier sketch in CTFT–11
Lord, Pauline 1890–1950 .... WWasWT
Lord, Peter 1953–.................................. CTFT–76
Earlier sketch in CTFT–33
Lord, Robert 1945– CTFT–4
Lorde, Andre de 1871–? .... WWasWT
Loren, Bernice 1951– CTFT–1
Loren, Sophia 1934– CTFT–43
Earlier sketches in CTFT–3, 20
Lorenzo, Tina di 1872–1930 .... WWasWT
Lorimer, Jack 1883–? .... WWasWT
Loring, Gloria 1946–............................. CTFT–19
Earlier sketch in CTFT–3
Loring, Lisa 1958–................................ CTFT–21
Loring, Norman 1888–1967 .... WWasWT
Lorit, Jean–Pierre CTFT–33
Lorne, Constance 1914–........................ WWT–16
Lorne, Marion 1888–1968..................... WWasWT
Lorraine, Irma 1885–?............................ WWasWT
Lorraine, Lilian 1892–1955 .... WWasWT
Lortel, Lucille 1905(?)– CTFT–5
Obituary in CTFT–32
Earlier sketch in WWT–17
Losch, Tilly 1907–1975 .... WWasWT
Lotinga, Ernest 1876–1951 .... WWasWT
Lotta 1847–1924 .... WWasWT
Loudon, Dorothy 1933–......................... CTFT–4
Earlier sketches in CTFT–1; WWT–17

Loughlin, Lori 1964– CTFT–57
    Earlier sketches in CTFT–8, 15, 26
Loughlin, Terry CTFT–51
Louis, Barbara CTFT–4
Louis, Justin CTFT–36
Louis, Tobi CTFT–3
Louis–Dreyfus, Julia 1961– CTFT–46
    Earlier sketches in CTFT–13, 23
Louise, Tina 1938(?)– CTFT–42
    Earlier sketches in CTFT–3, 20
Louiso, Todd 1970– CTFT–73
    Earlier sketch in CTFT–32
Lou–Tellegen 1881–1934 .... WWasWT
Lovat, Nancie 1900–1946 .... WWasWT
Love, Bessie ?–1986 .... WWT–17
Love, Courtney 1964– CTFT–61
    Earlier sketches in CTFT–17, 28
Love, Edward CTFT–6
Love, Faizon 1968– CTFT–72
    Earlier sketch in CTFT–32
Love, Mabel 1874–1953 .... WWasWT
Love, Montagu 1877–1943 .... WWasWT
Love, Staci
    See .... Keanan, Staci
Love, Victor 1967– CTFT–53
Lovejoy, Deirdre CTFT–36
Lovejoy, Robin 1923– WWT–17
Lovell, Dyson 1940– CTFT–35
    Earlier sketch in CTFT–2
Lovell, Raymond 1900–1953 .... WWasWT
Lovell, W. T. 1884–? .... WWasWT
Loveman, Michael
    See .... Pataki, Michael
Lovett, Lyle 1957(?)– CTFT–57
    Earlier sketch in CTFT–26
Lovitz, Jon 1957– CTFT–51
    Earlier sketches in CTFT–7, 14, 24
Low, Jason CTFT–67
Lowdell, Amelia CTFT–76
    Earlier sketch in CTFT–34
Lowe, Arthur 1915– WWT–17
Lowe, Chad 1968– CTFT–70
    Earlier sketches in CTFT–7, 19, 31
Lowe, Douglas 1882–? .... WWasWT
Lowe, Edmund 1892–1971 .... WWasWT
Lowe, Enid 1908– .... WWasWT
Lowe, Rachel 1876–? .... WWasWT
Lowe, Rob 1964– CTFT–45
    Earlier sketches in CTFT–6, 13, 23
    Brief Entry in CTFT–2
Lowe, Stephen 1947– CTFT–12
Lowell, Carey 1961– CTFT–61
    Earlier sketches in CTFT–17, 28
Lowell, Helen 1866–1937 .... WWasWT
Lowell, Mollie .... WWasWT
Lower, Geoffrey CTFT–63
    Earlier sketches in CTFT–17, 28
Lowne, Charles Macready
    ?–1941 .... WWasWT
Lowry, Dick M. CTFT–44
    Earlier sketches in CTFT–11, 22
Lowry, Jane 1937– CTFT–1
Lowry, Sam
    See .... Soderbergh, Steven
Lowry, W. McNeil 1913–1993 .... CTFT–1
    Obituary in CTFT–12
Loxley, Violet 1914– .... WWasWT
Loy, Myrna 1905–1993 .... CTFT–3
    Obituary in CTFT–12
Lubatti, Henri CTFT–58
Lubezki, Emmanuel 1964(?)– CTFT–63
    Earlier sketch in CTFT–28
Lubliner, Sheldon R. 1950– CTFT–2

Lucas, Byron CTFT–65
Lucas, Craig 1951(?)– CTFT–47
    Earlier sketch in CTFT–10
Lucas, David CTFT–42
Lucas, George 1944– CTFT–44
    Earlier sketches in CTFT–1, 4, 11, 22
Lucas, Hans
    See .... Godard, Jean–Luc
Lucas, J. Frank 1920– CTFT–7
Lucas, Jessica 1980– CTFT–75
Lucas, Jonathan 1936– CTFT–20
    Earlier sketch in CTFT–2
Lucas, Josh 1971– CTFT–76
    Earlier sketch in CTFT–34
Lucas, Laurent CTFT–34
Lucas, Phil 1942– CTFT–17
Lucchesi, Gary 1955– CTFT–40
    Earlier sketch in CTFT–17
Lucci, Susan 1947– CTFT–59
    Earlier sketches in CTFT–7, 15, 27
Luce, Clare Boothe– 1903–1987 .... WWT–17
Luce, Polly 1905– .... WWasWT
Lucia, Charles CTFT–54
Luciano, Judi Evans CTFT–17
Lucie, Doug 1953– CTFT–12
Luck, Coleman CTFT–53
    Earlier sketch in CTFT–17
Luckham, Cyril 1907–1989 .... CTFT–8
    Earlier sketch in WWT–17
Luckinbill, Laurence 1934(?)– CTFT–19
    Earlier sketches in CTFT–1, 8; WWT–17
Luckinbill, Thad 1975– CTFT–75
Lucking, William 1941– CTFT–56
Luders, Gustav 1866–1913 .... WWasWT
Ludivine
    See .... Sagnier, Ludvine
Ludlam, Charles 1943–1987 .... CTFT–5
    Earlier sketches in CTFT–3; WWT–17
Ludlow, Ian
    See .... Goldberg, Lee
Ludlow, Patrick 1903– WWT–17
Ludwig, Salem 1915– WWT–17
Luecke, Mary
    See .... Frann, Mary
Luedtke, Kurt 1939– CTFT–5
Luetgert, Bailey
    See .... Chase, Bailey
Luft, Lorna 1952– CTFT–42
    Earlier sketch in CTFT–9
Luftig, Aaron
    See .... Lustig, Aaron
Lugg, Alfred 1889– .... WWasWT
Lugg, William 1852–1940 .... WWasWT
Lugne–Poe, A. E. 1870–1940 .... WWasWT
Lugosi, Bela 1888–1956 .... WWasWT
Luguet, Andre 1892– .... WWasWT
Luhrmann, Baz 1962– CTFT–43
    Earlier sketch in CTFT–21
Luis, Rui CTFT–34
Lukas, Paul 1895–1971 .... WWasWT
Luke, Keye 1904–1991 .... CTFT–19
    Earlier sketch in CTFT–8
Luke, Peter 1919– WWT–17
Luker, Rebecca 1961– CTFT–37
Lukyanov, Sergei Vladimirovich
    1910– .... WWasWT
Lumbly, Carl 1952– CTFT–60
    Earlier sketches in CTFT–7, 15, 27
Lumet, Sidney 1924– CTFT–61
    Earlier sketches in CTFT–1, 6, 15, 28
Lumley, Joanna 1946– CTFT–44
    Earlier sketches in CTFT–11, 22
Luna, Barbara 1939– CTFT–54

Luna, Diego 1979– CTFT–63
Lund, Art 1920– WWT–17
Lund, Jordan 1957– CTFT–51
Lundel, Kert Fritjof 1936– WWT–17
Lunden, Joan 1950(?)– CTFT–40
    Earlier sketches in CTFT–10, 17
Lundgren, Dolph 1959– CTFT–78
    Earlier sketches in CTFT–9, 35
Lundy, Jessica 1966– CTFT–52
Luner, Jamie 1971– CTFT–52
    Earlier sketch in CTFT–24
Lung, Chan Yuan
    See .... Chan, Jackie
Lung, Cheng
    See .... Chan, Jackie
Lunghi, Cherie 1953– CTFT–35
    Earlier sketch in CTFT–8
Lunt, Alfred 1892–1977 .... WWT–16
Luo, Zhuoyao
    See .... Law, Clara
Lupino, Stanley 1894–1942 .... WWasWT
Lupino, Wallace 1897–1961 .... WWasWT
LuPone, Patti 1949– CTFT–50
    Earlier sketches in CTFT–1, 5, 12, 24;
    WWT–17
LuPone, Robert 1946– CTFT–44
    Earlier sketches in CTFT–7, 22
Lupus, Peter 1943– CTFT–1
Lurie, John 1952– CTFT–79
Luscombe, Tim 1960– CTFT–8
Lusha, Masiela 1985– CTFT–71
Lusitana, Donna E. CTFT–50
Lustig, Aaron 1956– CTFT–54
Lutes, Eric 1962– CTFT–40
    Earlier sketch in CTFT–17
Luttrell, Rachel CTFT–69
Lutz, Mark CTFT–49
Lutz, Matt 1978– CTFT–68
Lux, Danny CTFT–42
Lyel, Viola 1900–1972 .... WWasWT
Lyle, Lauren
    See .... Adams, Joey Lauren
Lyle, Lyston ?–1920 .... WWasWT
Lyles, Leslie CTFT–69
Lyman, Dorothy 1947– CTFT–42
    Earlier sketches in CTFT–1, 9
Lyman, Will 1948– CTFT–35
    Earlier sketch in CTFT–7
Lyn, Nicole 1978– CTFT–72
Lynch, Barry CTFT–76
Lynch, Brian 1954– CTFT–4
Lynch, David 1946– CTFT–71
    Earlier sketches in CTFT–5, 12, 21, 31
Lynch, Jane 1960– CTFT–64
Lynch, John 1961– CTFT–52
    Earlier sketch in CTFT–24
Lunch, John Carroll 1963(?)– CTFT–45
Lynch, Kelly 1959– CTFT–48
    Earlier sketches in CTFT–11, 23
Lynch, Paul 1946– CTFT–41
Lynch, Richard 1940– CTFT–76
    Earlier sketches in CTFT–5, 33
Lynch, Susan CTFT–35
Lynd, Rosa 1884–1922 .... WWasWT
Lynde, Janice 1948– CTFT–54
Lynde, Paul 1926–1982 .... CTFT–2
Lyndeck, Edmund CTFT–1
Lyndon, Barre 1896– .... WWasWT
Lyndon, Simon CTFT–35
Lyne, Adrian CTFT–7
Lynley, Carol 1942– CTFT–5
Lynn, Jonathan 1943– CTFT–5
    Earlier sketch in WWT–17

Lynn, Matthew
    See .... Lillard, Matthew
Lynn, Meredith Scott CTFT–64
Lynn, Ralph 1882–1962 .... WWasWT
Lynn, Sherry CTFT–40
Lynne, Carole 1918– .... WWasWT
Lynne, Gillian 1926–.................................. CTFT–7
    Earlier sketches in CTFT–4; WWT–17
Lynskey, Melanie 1977– CTFT–61
    Earlier sketch in CTFT–28
Lynton, Mayne 1885–? .... WWasWT
Lyon, Ben 1901–1979 .... WWasWT
Lyon, Milton 1923–1995 .... CTFT–2
    Obituary in CTFT–15
Lyon, Rick CTFT–46
Lyon, Wanda 1897– .... WWasWT
Lyonne, Natasha 1979–............................. CTFT–47
    Earlier sketch in CTFT–23
Lyons, A. Neil 1880–1940 .... WWasWT
Lyons, Phyllis 1960–................................. CTFT–40
Lyons, Stuart 1928–.................................. CTFT–5
Lytell, Bert 1885–1954 .... WWasWT
Lythgoe, Nigel 1949– CTFT–65
Lyttelton, Edith 1870–1948 .... WWasWT
Lytton, Doris 1893–1953 .... WWasWT
Lytton, Henry 1904–1965 .... WWasWT
Lytton, Henry A. 1867–1936 .... WWasWT
Lytton, Ruth .... WWasWT

M

Maberly, Kate 1982– CTFT–78
Mabius, Eric 1971– CTFT–67
    Earlier sketch in CTFT–30
Mabley, Edward 1906–.............................. CTFT–1
Mac, Bernie 1957(?)– CTFT–45
MacAdam, Will 1943– CTFT–2
MacArthur, Charles 1895–1956 .... WWasWT
MacArthur, James 1937– CTFT–19
    Earlier sketch in CTFT–3
Macat, Julio CTFT–68
Macaulay, Joseph ?–1967 .... WWasWT
Macaulay, Marc... CTFT–62
Macaulay, Pauline CTFT–4
Macbeth, Helen... WWasWT
MacBridge, Aeneas
    See .... Mackay, Fulton
MacCaffrey, George 1870–1939............. WWasWT
MacCarthy, Desmond 1877–1952 .... WWasWT
Macchio, Ralph 1962–.............................. CTFT–10
    Earlier sketch in CTFT–3
MacCorkindale, Simon 1952–................. CTFT–35
    Earlier sketch in CTFT–4
MacDermot, Galt WWT–17
MacDermot, Robert 1910–1964 .... WWasWT
Macdermott, Norman 1889–?................ WWasWT
MacDevitt, Brian 1956– CTFT–44
    Earlier sketch in CTFT–5
Macdona, Charles ?–1946 .... WWasWT
MacDonald, Adam 1977–.......................... CTFT–61
MacDonald, Bill CTFT–75
    Earlier sketch in CTFT–33
MacDonald, Bruce
    See .... McDonald, Bruce
MacDonald, Christopher
    See .... McDonald, Christopher
Macdonald, Donald 1898–1959............. WWasWT
MacDonald, Jeanette 1907–1965 .... WWasWT

MacDonald, Karen CTFT–76
    Earlier sketch in CTFT–32
MacDonald, Kelly 1976– CTFT–67
    Earlier sketch in CTFT–30
MacDonald, Mac
    See .... McDonald, Mac
MacDonald, Murray 1899–...................... WWT–17
MacDonald, Norm 1963– CTFT–57
    Earlier sketch in CTFT–26
MacDonald, Scott.. CTFT–61
    Earlier sketch in CTFT–28
Macdonald, Wallace 1891–1978 .... CTFT–21
MacDonald, William CTFT–62
MacDonell, Kathleen 1890–? .... WWasWT
Macdonnell, James
    See .... McDonnell, James
Macdonnell, Leslie A. 1903–.................. WWasWT
Macdonough, Glen 1870–1924............. WWasWT
MacDougall, Roger 1910– WWT–17
MacDowell, Andie 1958– CTFT–61
    Earlier sketches in CTFT–9, 17, 28
Maceda, Jim CTFT–43
Macfadyen, Angus 1963–......................... CTFT–46
MacFadyen, Matthew CTFT–35
Macfarlane, Bruce 1910–1967 .... WWasWT
Macfarlane, Elsa 1899– .... WWasWT
MacFarlane, Seth 1973–............................ CTFT–77
MacGill, Moyna 1895–1975 .... WWasWT
MacGinnis, Niall 1913– .... WWasWT
Macgowan, Kenneth 1888–1963 .... WWasWT
MacGowran, Jack 1918–1973 .... WWasWT
MacGrath, Leueen 1914–.......................... WWT–17
MacGraw, Ali 1939– CTFT–5
MacGregor–Scott, Peter CTFT–41
Machacek, Jiri CTFT–35
Machado, Justina 1972–........................... CTFT–52
Machiz, Herbert 1923–1976 .... WWT–16
Machlis, Neil A. CTFT–40
Macht, Gabriel 1972– CTFT–43
Macht, Stephen 1942– CTFT–45
MacHugh, Augustin 1887–1928............. WWasWT
MacInnes, Angus 1947–............................ CTFT–76
MacIntosh, Joan 1945–............................. CTFT–8
MacIntyre, Marguerite CTFT–47
MacIvor, Daniel 1962– CTFT–46
Mack, Allison 1982– CTFT–45
Mack, Andrew 1863–1931 .... WWasWT
Mack, Billy
    See .... Nighy, Bill
Mack, Carol K. CTFT–1
Mack, Willard 1878–1934...................... WWasWT
Mackay, Barry 1906–................................ WWasWT
MacKay, Don CTFT–63
Mackay, Elsie 1894– .... WWasWT
Mackay, Fulton 1922–1987 .... CTFT–5
    Earlier sketch in WWT–17
Mackay, J. L. 1867–?................................ WWasWT
Mackay, John 1924–.................................. CTFT–5
MacKay, Lizbeth 1951(?)–........................ CTFT–76
    Earlier sketches in CTFT–1, 6, 34
Mackay, Ruth .... WWasWT
Mackaye, Percy 1875–1956 .... WWasWT
Mackeller, Helen 1895– .... WWasWT
Mackenna, Kenneth 1899–1962........... WWasWT
Mackenzie, Andy CTFT–60
Mackenzie, J. C. CTFT–40
Mackenzie, John 1932–............................. CTFT–39
    Earlier sketch in CTFT–15
Mackenzie, Mary 1922–1966 .... WWasWT
MacKenzie, Philip Charles CTFT–76
    Earlier sketches in CTFT–8, 34
MacKenzie, Will 1938–............................. CTFT–44
    Earlier sketches in CTFT–11, 22

Mackey, Paul
    See .... Molina, Jacinto
Mackie, Bob 1940–.................................... CTFT–48
Mackinder, Lionel ?–1915..................... WWasWT
Mackinlay, Jean Sterling 1882–1958...... WWasWT
Mackintosh, Cameron 1946– CTFT–49
    Earlier sketches in CTFT–1, 9, 24
Mackintosh, Steven 1967(?)–.................. CTFT–71
    Earlier sketches in CTFT–19,31
Mackintosh, William 1855–1929.......... WWasWT
Macklin, Albert 1958–............................... CTFT–1
MacLachlan, Kyle 1959(?)– CTFT–40
    Earlier sketches in CTFT–9, 17
MacLaine, Shirley 1934–.......................... CTFT–44
    Earlier sketches in CTFT–1, 4, 11, 22
Maclaren, Ian 1879–?.............................. WWasWT
MacLean, R. D. 1859–1948 .... WWasWT
MacLeish, Archibald 1892–1982........... WWT–17
MacLeod, Doug... CTFT–40
    Earlier sketch in CTFT–17
MacLeod, Gavin 1931(?)– CTFT–40
    Earlier sketches in CTFT–1, 10, 17
Macleod, W. Angus 1874–1962 .... WWasWT
Macliammoir, Michael 1899–1978......... WWT–16
MacMahon, Aline 1899–1991 .... CTFT–11
    Earlier sketch in WWT–17
MacManus, Clive ?–1953 .... WWasWT
MacMartin, John
    See.. McMartin, John
MacMillan, Kenneth 1929–1992 .... CTFT–13
MacMurray, Fred 1908–1991 .... CTFT–3
    Obituary in CTFT–10
MacNaughton, Alan 1920– WWT–17
Macnee, Patrick 1922–.............................. CTFT–39
    Earlier sketches in CTFT–1, 7, 14
MacNeil, Robert 1931–.............................. CTFT–41
    Earlier sketch in CTFT–14
MacNeill, Peter CTFT–60
MacNeille, Tress CTFT–37
MacNicol, Peter 1954(?)– CTFT–49
    Earlier sketches in CTFT–7, 14, 24
MacOwan, Michael 1906–....................... WWT–17
MacOwan, Norman 1877–1961........... WWasWT
Macpherson, Elle 1963(?)– CTFT–63
    Earlier sketches in CTFT–17, 28
MacQuarrie, Stuart
    See .... McQuarrie, Stuart
Macqueen–Pope, W. J. 1888–1960 .... WWasWT
Macquoid, Percy 1852–1925.................. WWasWT
Macrae, Arthur 1908–1962 .... WWasWT
Macrae, Duncan 1905–1967 .... WWasWT
MacRae, Gordon 1921–1986 .... CTFT–3
MacRae, Michael 1949– CTFT–52
Macy, Bill 1922–.. CTFT–35
    Earlier sketches in CTFT–1, 4
Macy, William H. 1950–........................... CTFT–61
    Earlier sketches in CTFT–17, 28
Maday, Charlie CTFT–52
Maddalena, Julie CTFT–48
Maddalena, Marianne CTFT–47
Madden, Cecil (Charles) 1902–1987 ..... WWasWT
Madden, Ciaran 1945–............................. CTFT–5
    Earlier sketch in WWT–17
Madden, David 1955– CTFT–61
    Earlier sketches in CTFT–15, 28
Madden, Donald 1933–............................. WWT–17
Madden, John 1936–.................................. CTFT–68
Madden, John 1949–.................................. CTFT–67
    Earlier sketch in CTFT–30
Maddern, Alan
    See .... Ellison, Harlan
Maddin, Guy 1956–................................... CTFT–61
    Earlier sketch in CTFT–28

Madeira, Marcia 1945– CTFT–1
Madigan, Amy 1950(?)– CTFT–61
    Earlier sketches in CTFT–5, 15, 28
Madio, James 1975– CTFT–70
Madonna 1958(?)– CTFT–63
    Earlier sketches in CTFT–9, 17, 28
    Brief Entry in CTFT–3
Madsen, Michael 1958(?)– CTFT–47
    Earlier sketches in CTFT–13, 23
Madsen, Virginia 1961(?)– CTFT–53
    Earlier sketches in CTFT–7, 14, 25
Maeterlinck, Maurice 1862–1949 .... WWasWT
Maffett, Debbie CTFT–3
Maffia, Roma 1958– CTFT–57
    Earlier sketch in CTFT–26
Maffin, Neil 1959– CTFT–71
    Earlier sketch in CTFT–32
Maganini, Elena CTFT–29
Magee, Patrick ?–1982 .... WWT–17
Maggart, Brandon 1933– CTFT–33
    Earlier sketch in CTFT–8
Maggio, Michael 1951– CTFT–21
    Earlier sketch in CTFT–12
Magnier, Pierre 1869–? .... WWasWT
Magnuson, Ann 1956– CTFT–57
    Earlier sketches in CTFT–7, 14, 26
Magoondi, Yahoots
    See .... Thompson, Brian
Maguelon, Pierre CTFT–33
Maguire, Anna CTFT–65
Maguire, Mickey
    See .... Rooney, Mickey
Maguire, Tobey 1975– CTFT–70
    Earlier sketches in CTFT–19, 31
Mahaffey, Valerie CTFT–1
Maharis, George 1938– CTFT–17
    Earlier sketch in CTFT–10
Maher, Bill 1956– CTFT–63
    Earlier sketches in CTFT–15, 28
Maher, Joseph 1933– CTFT–15
    Earlier sketches in CTFT–1, 8
Maher, Sean 1975– CTFT–74
Mahon, John CTFT–38
Mahoney, John 1940– CTFT–57
    Earlier sketches in CTFT–6, 14, 26
Mahoney, Will 1896–1967 .... WWasWT
Maibaum, Richard 1909–1991 .... CTFT–16
Mailer, Stephen 1966– CTFT–38
    Earlier sketch in CTFT–15
Mailhouse, Robert 1962– CTFT–52
Main, Marjorie 1890–1975 .... CTFT–25
Mainwaring, Ernest 1876–1941 .... WWasWT
Mair, George Herbert 1887–1926 .... WWasWT
Mais, Stuart Petre Brodie 1885–? .... WWasWT
Maitland, Lauderdale ?–1929 .... WWasWT
Maitland, Ruth 1880–1961 .... WWasWT
Maivia, Rocky
    See .... Johnson, Dwayne
Major, Bessie .... WWasWT
Major, Grant 1955(?)– CTFT–68
Major, Leon 1933– CTFT–13
Majorino, Tina 1985(?)– CTFT–25
    Earlier sketch in CTFT–15
Majors, Lee 1940(?)– CTFT–53
    Earlier sketches in CTFT–3, 15, 25
Makaj, Steve CTFT–39
    Earlier sketch in CTFT–38
Makarova, Natalia 1940– CTFT–9
Makatsch, Heike 1971– CTFT–75
    Earlier sketch in CTFT–33
Makavejev, Dusan 1932– CTFT–8
Makeham, Eliot 1882–1956 .... WWasWT
Makepeace, Chris 1964– CTFT–4

Makhnalbaf, Mohsen 1951– CTFT–28
Makichuk, Jim CTFT–46
Makise, Riho 1971– CTFT–34
Makita, Les
    See .... Mykytiuk, Lubomir
Makkena, Wendy CTFT–43
    Earlier sketch in CTFT–21
Mako 1933–2006 .... CTFT–53
    Obituary in CTFT–72
    Earlier sketches in CTFT–8, 15, 25
Malahide, Patrick 1945– CTFT–34
    Earlier sketch in CTFT–4
Malanowski, Tony 1957– CTFT–12
Malas, Spiro 1935(?)– CTFT–50
    Earlier sketch in CTFT–11
Malden, Herbert John 1882–1966 .... WWasWT
Malden, Karl 1914(?)– CTFT–49
    Earlier sketches in CTFT–1, 6, 14
Maleki, Christopher CTFT–74
Maliani, Mike
    See .... Heyward, Andy
Malick, Terrence 1943– CTFT–34
    Earlier sketches in CTFT–1, 6
Malick, Wendie 1950– CTFT–53
    Earlier sketches in CTFT–15, 25
Malicki–Sanchez, Keram 1974– CTFT–59
Malik, Art 1952– CTFT–34
    Earlier sketch in CTFT–7
Malil, Shelley 1964– CTFT–64
Malin, Mary CTFT–49
Malina, Joshua 1966– CTFT–47
Malina, Judith 1926– WWT–17
Malina, Rolondo
    See .... Molina, Rolando
Malinger, Ross 1984– CTFT–52
Malis, Claire 1943– CTFT–55
Malkovich, John 1953– CTFT–71
    Earlier sketches in CTFT–5, 12, 21,31
Mallalieu, Aubrey 1873–1948 .... WWasWT
Malle, Louis 1932–1995 .... CTFT–13
    Obituary in CTFT–15
    Earlier sketches in CTFT–1, 6
Malleson, Miles 1888–1969 .... WWasWT
Mallow, Dave 1948– CTFT–45
Malloy, Matt CTFT–71
    Earlier sketches in CTFT–20, 31
Mallsnerd, Olga
    See .... Bergen, Candice
Malm, Mia 1962– CTFT–4
Malmuth, Bruce 1934– CTFT–2
Malo, Gina 1909–1963 .... WWasWT
Malone, Dorothy 1925– CTFT–5
Malone, J. A. E. ?–1929 .... WWasWT
Malone, Jena 1984– CTFT–71
    Earlier sketches in CTFT–20, 31
Malone, Nancy 1935– CTFT–54
Malone, Patricia 1899– .... WWasWT
Malone, Patrick CTFT–32
Malone, Victor
    See .... Cameron, John
Maloney, Michael 1957– CTFT–34
Maloney, Peter CTFT–36
    Earlier sketch in CTFT–8
Maltby, Henry Francis 1880–1963 .... WWasWT
Maltby, Richard, Jr. 1937– CTFT–22
    Earlier sketches in CTFT–4, 11; WWT–17
Maltin, Leonard 1950– CTFT–44
    Earlier sketches in CTFT–11, 22
Maltz, Albert 1908–1985 .... CTFT–1
Mamabolo, Barbara CTFT–65
Mamet, David 1947– CTFT–60
    Earlier sketches in CTFT–2, 8, 16, 27;
    WWT–17

Mammone, Robert CTFT–61
Mamoulian, Rouben 1897–1987 .... CTFT–6
    Earlier sketch in WWasWT
Manahan, Anna 1924– CTFT–44
    Earlier sketch in CTFT–22
Manasseri, Michael 1974– CTFT–59
Manchen, Klaus 1936– CTFT–33
Manchester, Joe 1932– CTFT–3
Mancina, Mark CTFT–66
    Earlier sketch in CTFT–29
Mancini, Henry 1924–1994 .... CTFT–10
    Obituary in CTFT–13
    Earlier sketch in CTFT–1
Mancuso, Frank G. 1933– CTFT–38
    Earlier sketch in CTFT–11
Mancuso, Frank, Jr. 1958– CTFT–37
Mancuso, Gail CTFT–64
Mancuso, Nick 1948(?)– CTFT–39
    Earlier sketches in CTFT–7, 14
Mandah
    See .... Moore, Mandy
Mandel, Babaloo 1949– CTFT–47
    Earlier sketches in CTFT–11, 23
Mandel, Frank 1884–1958 .... WWasWT
Mandel, Howie 1955– CTFT–36
    Earlier sketch in CTFT–9
    Brief Entry in CTFT–3
Mandelker, Philip ?–1984 .... CTFT–1
Mander, Raymond Josiah Gale
    1917– WWT–17
Mandvi, Aasif 1967(?)– CTFT–62
Mandylor, Costas 1965– CTFT–53
    Earlier sketches in CTFT–15, 25
Mandylor, Louis 1966– CTFT–48
Mane, Tyler CTFT–72
Manesh, Marshall 1950– CTFT–77
    Earlier sketch in CTFT–34
Manetti, Larry 1947– CTFT–46
    Earlier sketch in CTFT–23
Manfredi, Harry 1943– CTFT–62
Manfredi, Nino 1921– CTFT–35
    Earlier sketch in CTFT–8
Mangano, Silvana 1930–1989 .... CTFT–5
Mangold, James 1964– CTFT–66
    Earlier sketch in CTFT–29
Manheim, Camryn 1961– CTFT–46
    Earlier sketch in CTFT–23
Manheim, Michael 1928– CTFT–38
    Earlier sketch in CTFT–12
Manilow, Barry 1943(?)– CTFT–37
Mankiewicz, Don 1922– CTFT–4
Mankiewicz, Herman J. 1897–1953 .... CTFT–23
Mankiewicz, Joseph L. 1909–1993 .... CTFT–5
    Obituary in CTFT–11
Mankiewicz, Tom 1942– CTFT–5
Mankofsky, Isidore 1931– CTFT–13
    Earlier sketch in CTFT–3
Mankowitz, Wolf 1924–1998 .... CTFT–11
    Obituary in CTFT–22
    Earlier sketch in WWT–17
Mankuma, Blu CTFT–41
Mann, Abby 1927– CTFT–5
Mann, Byron 1967(?)– CTFT–65
Mann, Charlton 1876–1958 .... WWasWT
Mann, Christopher 1903– .... WWasWT
Mann, Daniel 1912–1991 .... CTFT–11
Mann, Danny CTFT–49
Mann, Delbert 1920– CTFT–12
    Earlier sketch in CTFT–1
Mann, Emily 1952– CTFT–43
    Earlier sketches in CTFT–1, 12, 21
Mann, Gabriel 1975– CTFT–63

Mann, Leslie 1972– CTFT–67
    Earlier sketch in CTFT–30
Mann, Louis 1865–1931 .... WWasWT
Mann, Michael 1943– CTFT–45
    Earlier sketches in CTFT–5, 12, 23
Mann, Stanley CTFT–11
Mann, Terrence 1951– CTFT–73
    Earlier sketch in CTFT–6
Mann, Theodore 1924– CTFT–24
    Earlier sketches in CTFT–2; WWT–17
Mannering, Dore Lewin 1879–1932 ...... WWasWT
Mannering, Mary 1876–1953 .... WWasWT
Mannering, Moya 1888–? .... WWasWT
Manners, David 1905–1998 .... WWasWT
    Obituary in CTFT–24
Manners, John Hartley 1870–1928 .... WWasWT
Mannheim, Lucie 1905– .... WWasWT
Manning, Ambrose ?–1940 .... WWasWT
Manning, Hugh Gardner 1920– WWT–17
Manning, Irene 1917– .... WWasWT
Manning, Taryn 1978– CTFT–69
Mannion, Tom CTFT–34
Mannix, Bobbie CTFT–28
Mannock, Patrick L. 1887–? .... WWasWT
Manoff, Dinah 1958– CTFT–39
    Earlier sketches in CTFT–3, 14
Manojlovic, Miki 1950– CTFT–33
Manoux, J. P. 1969– CTFT–54
Manquina, Manuel CTFT–34
Mansfield, Alice ?–1938 .... WWasWT
Mansfield, David 1956– CTFT–53
Mansfield, Jayne 1933–1967 .... CTFT–20
Mansfield, John CTFT–55
Manson, Ted CTFT–68
Mantegna, Joe 1947– CTFT–63
    Earlier sketches in CTFT–3, 10, 17, 28
Mantel, Bronwen CTFT–64
Mantell, Michael CTFT–79
    Earlier sketch in CTFT–34
Mantell, Robert Bruce 1854–1928 .... WWasWT
Mantello, Joe 1962– CTFT–53
    Earlier sketch in CTFT–25
Manthey, Jerry 1970– CTFT–70
Mantle, Burns 1873–1948 .... WWasWT
Mantle, Clive 1957– CTFT–57
    Earlier sketch in CTFT–26
Mantooth, Randolph 1945– CTFT–66
Manulis, John Bard 1956– CTFT–1
Manulis, Martin 1915– CTFT–1
Manus, Willard 1930– CTFT–1
Manyu, Zhang
    See .... Cheung, Maggie
Mapa, Alec 1965– CTFT–42
Mapes, Victor 1870–1943 .... WWasWT
Maples, Marla 1963– CTFT–54
Mapother, William 1965– CTFT–62
Mara, Mary CTFT–40
Marasco, Robert 1936–1998 .... WWT–17
    Obituary in CTFT–24
Maravan, Lila ?–1950 .... WWasWT
Marber, Patrick 1964– CTFT–34
Marceau, Marcel 1923– CTFT–23
Marceau, Sophie 1966– CTFT–55
    Earlier sketch in CTFT–25
March, Elspeth CTFT–6
    Earlier sketch in WWT–17
March, Frederic 1897–1975 .... WWasWT
March, Marvin CTFT–37
March, Nadine 1898–1944 .... WWasWT
March, Stephanie 1974– CTFT–79
Marchal, Lynda
    See .... La Plante, Lynda

Marchand, Nancy 1928– CTFT–7
    Earlier sketches in CTFT–1; WWT–17
Marchant, Tony 1959– CTFT–38
    Earlier sketch in CTFT–12
Marciano, David 1960– CTFT–50
Marcil, Vanessa 1969– CTFT–53
Marcille, Eva 1984– CTFT–77
Marcin, Max 1879–1948 .... WWasWT
Marck, Nick CTFT–43
Marcoux, Ted CTFT–55
Marcovicci, Andrea 1948– CTFT–50
    Earlier sketches in CTFT–6, 13
    Brief Entry in CTFT–2
Marcum, Kevin 1955–1987 .... CTFT–19
    Earlier sketch in CTFT–2
Marcus, Donald 1946– CTFT–2
Marcus, Frank 1928– WWT–17
Marcus, Jeff 1960– CTFT–55
    Earlier sketches in CTFT–2, 20
Marcus, Jonathan
    See .... Pesci, Joe
Marcus, Lawrence 1925– CTFT–4
Marcus, Louis 1936– CTFT–5
Marcus, Richard 1937(?)– CTFT–76
Marcus, Stephen 1962– CTFT–75
    Earlier sketch in CTFT–33
Mardirosian, Tom 1947– CTFT–52
    Earlier sketches in CTFT–12, 24
Marescotti, Ivano 1946– CTFT–34
Margetson, Arthur 1897–1951 .... WWasWT
Margheriti, Antonio 1930– CTFT–30
Margo 1918– .... WWasWT
Margolin, Arnold CTFT–79
Margolin, Janet 1943–1993 .... CTFT–5
    Obituary in CTFT–13
Margolin, Stuart 1940– CTFT–44
    Earlier sketches in CTFT–6, 22
Margolis, Jeff CTFT–44
    Earlier sketches in CTFT–11, 22
Margolis, Mark 1939– CTFT–76
    Earlier sketches in CTFT–1, 33
Margolis, Morgan H. CTFT–75
Margolyes, Miriam 1941– CTFT–53
    Earlier sketches in CTFT–6, 14, 25
Margueritte, Victor 1866–1942 .... WWasWT
Margulies, David 1937– CTFT–63
    Earlier sketches in CTFT–1, 10, 17, 28
Margulies, Julianna 1968(?)– CTFT–69
    Earlier sketches in CTFT–19, 31
Margulies, Stan 1920– CTFT–7
Mariani–Zampieri, Terseina
    1871–? .... WWasWT
Mariano, John CTFT–66
    Earlier sketch in CTFT–29
Marie, Baby Rose
    See .... Rose Marie
Marie, Constance 1969– CTFT–46
Marie, Lisa 1968(?)– CTFT–63
    Earlier sketch in CTFT–28
Marienthal, Eli 1986– CTFT–70
Marin, Cheech 1946– CTFT–45
    Earlier sketches in CTFT–6, 13, 23
    Brief Entry in CTFT–2
Marina, Ivana
    See .... Milicevic, Ivana
Marinaro, Ed 1951(?)– CTFT–69
    Earlier sketches in CTFT–7, 19, 31
Marinker, Peter CTFT–65
Marino, John CTFT–30
Marino, Ken 1968– CTFT–52
Marinoff, Fania 1890–1971 .... WWasWT
Mario, Emilio .... WWasWT
Marion, George, Jr. ?–1968 .... WWasWT

Marion, Joan 1908–1945 .... WWasWT
Mariye, Lily 1956– CTFT–49
Mark, Judy CTFT–4
Mark, Laurence CTFT–46
    Earlier sketch in CTFT–23
Mark, Marky
    See .... Wahlberg, Mark
Markel, Heidi Jo CTFT–34
Markey, Enid WWT–16
Markham, Daisy WWT–5
Markham, David 1913– WWT–17
Markham, Kika CTFT–34
Markham, Monte 1935– CTFT–39
    Earlier sketches in CTFT–1, 7
Markinson, Brian CTFT–68
    Earlier sketch in CTFT–30
Markinson, Martin 1931– CTFT–1
Markle, Christopher 1954– CTFT–20
    Earlier sketch in CTFT–2
Markle, Peter 1952(?)– CTFT–56
Markle, Stephen CTFT–55
Markoe, Gerald Jay 1941– CTFT–2
Markova, Alicia 1910– .... WWasWT
Markowitz, Robert 1935– CTFT–38
    Earlier sketch in CTFT–12
Marks, Alfred 1921– WWT–17
Marks, Arthur 1927– CTFT–7
Marks, Jack R. 1935– CTFT–3
Marks, Richard 1943– CTFT–38
    Earlier sketch in CTFT–10
Marlett, Maysie Hoy
    See .... Hoy, Maysie
Marley, John ?–1984 .... CTFT–1
Marlow, Jean CTFT–34
Marlowe, Andrew W. CTFT–28
Marlowe, Anthony 1913– WWT–16
Marlowe, Charles
    See .... Jay, Harriet
Marlowe, Hugh 1911–1982 .... WWT–17
Marlowe, Joan 1920– CTFT–1
Marlowe, Julia 1866–1950 .... WWasWT
Marlowe, Ruby CTFT–47
Marlowe, Theresa 1957– CTFT–8
Marmel, Steve CTFT–56
Marmont, Percy 1883–? .... WWasWT
Marnac, Jane .... WWasWT
Marno, Anne
    See .... Bancroft, Anne
Maropis, Adoni CTFT–59
Marot, Gaston ?–1916 .... WWasWT
Marowitz, Charles 1934– CTFT–5
    Earlier sketch in WWT–17
Marquand, Richard 1937–1987 .... CTFT–2
Marquet, Mary 1895– .... WWasWT
Marquette, Chris 1984– CTFT–75
    Earlier sketch in CTFT–33
Marquette, Sean 1988– CTFT–64
Marquez, Gabriel Garcia
    See .... Garcia Marquez, Gabriel
Marquez, Vanessa CTFT–50
Marquez, William CTFT–55
Marquis, Don 1878–1937 .... WWasWT
Marr, Paula .... WWasWT
Marr, Phil La
    See .... LaMarr, Phillip
Marre, Albert 1925– WWT–17
Marriott, Anthony 1931– CTFT–1
Marriott, B. Rodney 1938–1990 .... CTFT–1
Marriott, Raymond Bowler
    1911– WWT–17
Marriott–Watson, Nan 1899– .... WWasWT
Marrocco, Gino CTFT–62

Mars, Kenneth 1935(?)– CTFT–63
　　Earlier sketches in CTFT–7, 14, 28
Mars, Marjorie 1903–1915 .... WWasWT
Marsala, Melissa CTFT–75
Marsalis, Branford 1960– CTFT–52
　　Earlier sketches in CTFT–12, 24
Marsden, Betty 1919– CTFT–13
　　Earlier sketch in WWT–17
Marsden, James 1973– CTFT–58
　　Earlier sketch in CTFT–27
Marsden, Jason 1975– CTFT–47
Marsden, Les 1957– CTFT–4
Marsden, Roy 1941– CTFT–7
Marsh, Anthony CTFT–33
Marsh, Garry 1902– .... WWasWT
Marsh, Jean 1934– CTFT–58
　　Earlier sketches in CTFT–3, 11, 22
Marsh, Matthew CTFT–34
Marsh, Terence CTFT–44
　　Earlier sketches in CTFT–11, 22
Marsh, Walter CTFT–65
Marshall, Alan
　　See .... Westlake, Donald E.
Marshall, Alan Peter 1938– CTFT–5
Marshall, Amelia 1958– CTFT–55
Marshall, Armina 1900– WWT–17
Marshall, Carole Simpson
　　See .... Simpson, Carole
Marshall, E. G. 1910– CTFT–16
　　Earlier sketches in CTFT–3; WWT–17
Marshall, Everett 1901– .... WWasWT
Marshall, Frank 1946– CTFT–55
　　Earlier sketches in CTFT–7, 14, 26
Marshall, Garry 1934– CTFT–37
　　Earlier sketches in CTFT–1, 6, 13
Marshall, Herbert 1890–1966 .... WWasWT
Marshall, Kathleen 1961– CTFT–38
Marshall, Mona CTFT–45
Marshall, Norman 1901– WWT–17
Marshall, Paula 1964– CTFT–53
　　Earlier sketch in CTFT–25
Marshall, Penny 1943(?)– CTFT–48
　　Earlier sketches in CTFT–1, 6, 13, 23
Marshall, Peter 1930– CTFT–55
Marshall, Phil CTFT–59
Marshall, Rob 1960– CTFT–52
　　Earlier sketch in CTFT–23
Marshall, Tully 1864–1943 .... WWasWT
Marshall, Vanessa 1970– CTFT–76
Marshall, William 1924– CTFT–8
Marson, Aileen, 1912–1939 .... WWasWT
Marsters, James 1962– CTFT–68
　　Earlier sketch in CTFT–30
Marta, Lynne 1946– CTFT–48
Martell, Gillian 1936– WWT–17
Marthold, Jules de 1842–1927 .... WWasWT
Martin, Andrea 1947– CTFT–71
　　Earlier sketches in CTFT–7, 19, 32
Martin, Barney CTFT–37
　　Earlier sketch in CTFT–10
Martin, Chris 1975– CTFT–58
Martin, Christopher 1942– CTFT–5
　　Earlier sketch in WWT–17
Martin, Dan CTFT–66
Martin, Dean 1917–1995 .... CTFT–8
　　Obituary in CTFT–15
Martin, Duane 1970– CTFT–70
　　Earlier sketches in CTFT–20, 31
Martin, Edie 1880–1964 .... WWasWT
Martin, Elliot 1924– CTFT–20
　　Earlier sketches in CTFT–2; WWT–17
Martin, Ernest H. 1919– WWT–17

Martin, George 1926– CTFT–34
　　Earlier sketch in CTFT–8
Martin, Grek
　　See .... Taylor, Jack
Martin, Helen CTFT–8
Martin, Ivan CTFT–79
Martin, Jake
　　See .... Martin, Dan
Martin, John CTFT–55
Martin, Kellie 1975– CTFT–60
　　Earlier sketches in CTFT–16, 27
Martin, Kiel 1945– CTFT–7
Martin, Leila 1936– CTFT–10
Martin, Mary 1913(?)–1990 .... CTFT–11
　　Earlier sketch in WWT–17
Martin, Millicent 1934– CTFT–35
　　Earlier sketches in CTFT–7; WWT–17
Martin, Nan 1927– CTFT–35
Martin, Pamela Sue 1953– CTFT–6
　　Brief Entry in CTFT–2
Martin, Quinn 1922–1987 .... CTFT–5
Martin, Richard 1956– CTFT–45
Martin, Rickey 1971– CTFT–39
Martin, Rudolf 1967– CTFT–57
Martin, Steve 1945– CTFT–46
　　Earlier sketches in CTFT–5, 12, 23
Martin, Strother 1919–1980 .... CTFT–16
Martin, Tantoo
　　See .... Cardinal, Tantoo
Martin, Tisha Campbell
　　See .... Campbell, Tisha
Martin, Vivian 1893–1987 .... WWasWT
Martin, Vivienne 1936–1987 .... WWT–17
Martin, William 1937– CTFT–4
Martin–Cardinal, Tantoo
　　See .... Cardinal, Tantoo
Martindale, Margo 1951– CTFT–68
　　Earlier sketch in CTFT–30
Martindale, Wink 1934– CTFT–55
Martinek, Lisa CTFT–34
Martinetti, Paul 1851–? .... WWasWT
Martinez, A. 1948– CTFT–52
　　Earlier sketches in CTFT–6, 12, 24
Martinez, Cliff 1954– CTFT–66
Martinez, Fele 1976– CTFT–34
Martinez, Olivier 1966– CTFT–34
Martin–Harvey, John
　　See .... Harvey, John Martin–
Martin–Harvey, Muriel 1891–1988 .... WWasWT
Martini, Max 1969– CTFT–48
Martinot, Sadie 1861–1923 .... WWasWT
Martlew, Mary 1919– .... WWasWT
Marton, Andrew 1904–1992 .... CTFT–16
Marton, Pierre
　　See .... Stone, Peter H.
Marvenga, Ilse .... WWasWT
Marvin, Lee 1924–1987 .... CTFT–3
　　Obituary in CTFT–5
Marvin, Mel 1941– CTFT–4
Marvin, Richard CTFT–65
Marx, Arthur 1921– CTFT–1
Marx, Chico 1891–1961 .... CTFT–19
Marx, Groucho 1890(?)–1977 .... CTFT–19
Marx, Gummo 1892(?)–1977 .... CTFT–19
Marx, Harpo 1893(?)–1964 .... CTFT–19
Marx, Zeppo 1901–1979 .... CTFT–19
Mary, Jules 1851–1922 .... WWasWT
Maryan, Charles 1934– CTFT–2
Marzello, Vincent CTFT–34
Masak, Ron 1936– CTFT–46
　　Earlier sketches in CTFT–1, 23
Maschwitz, Eric 1901–1969 .... WWasWT
Masefield, John 1878–1967 .... WWasWT

Mashkov, Vladimir 1963– CTFT–43
Mashton, F. Gary Gray
　　See .... Gray, F. Gary
Masina, Giulietta 1921–1994 .... CTFT–8
　　Obituary in CTFT–13
Mask, Ace 1948– CTFT–67
Maskelyne, John Nevil 1839–? .... WWasWT
Maslansky, Paul 1933– CTFT–13
Mason, Alfred Edward Woodley
　　1865–1948 .... WWasWT
Mason, Beryl 1921– WWT–17
Mason, Brewster 1922–1987 .... CTFT–5
　　Earlier sketch in WWT–17
Mason, Elliot C. 1897–1949 .... WWasWT
Mason, Ethelmae CTFT–3
Mason, Gladys 1886–? .... WWasWT
Mason, Herbert 1891–1960 .... WWasWT
Mason, Jackie 1931– CTFT–6
Mason, James 1909–1984 .... CTFT–1
　　Earlier sketch in WWasWT
Mason, John B. 1857–1919 .... WWasWT
Mason, Kitty 1882–? .... WWasWT
Mason, Madison CTFT–38
Mason, Marsha 1942– CTFT–57
　　Earlier sketches in CTFT–2, 7, 14, 26
Mason, Marshall W. 1940– CTFT–20
　　Earlier sketches in CTFT–1, 3; WWT–17
Mason, Pamela 1918–1996 .... CTFT–1
　　Obituary in CTFT–16
Mason, Reginald 1882–1962 .... WWasWT
Mason, Tom CTFT–41
Massary, Fritzi 1882–1969 .... WWasWT
Massee, Michael CTFT–61
　　Earlier sketch in CTFT–28
Masset, Andrew CTFT–54
Massey, Andrea Evans
　　See .... Evans, Andrea
Massey, Anna 1937– CTFT–57
　　Earlier sketches in CTFT–4, 14, 26; WWT–17
Massey, Daniel 1933–1998 .... CTFT–14
　　Obituary in CTFT–21
　　Earlier sketches in CTFT–6; WWT–17
Massey, Michael
　　See .... Massee, Michael
Massey, Raymond 1896–1983 .... WWT–17
Massi, Bernice WWT–17
Massine, Leonide 1896–1979 .... WWasWT
Massingham, Dorothy 1889–1933 .... WWasWT
Masters, Ben 1947– CTFT–41
　　Earlier sketch in CTFT–9
Masters–King, Kent
　　See .... King, Kent Masters
Masterson, Chase 1963– CTFT–45
Masterson, Christopher 1980– CTFT–68
　　Earlier sketch in CTFT–30
Masterson, Danny 1976– CTFT–46
　　Earlier sketch in CTFT–23
Masterson, Fay 1974– CTFT–73
　　Earlier sketch in CTFT–33
Masterson, Mary Stuart 1966– CTFT–52
　　Earlier sketches in CTFT–7, 14, 25
Masterson, Peter 1934– CTFT–1
Masterson, Sean CTFT–43
Masterson, Whit
　　See .... Wade, Robert (Allison)
Mastrantonio, Mary Elizabeth
　　1958– CTFT–44
　　Earlier sketches in CTFT–1, 4, 11, 22
Mastroianni, Armand 1948– CTFT–41
Mastroianni, Chiara 1972– CTFT–53
　　Earlier sketch in CTFT–25

Mastroianni, Marcello 1924–1996........... CTFT–12
    Obituary in CTFT–16
    Earlier sketch in CTFT–5
Mastrosimone, William 1947–.................. CTFT–8
Masur, Richard 1948– CTFT–44
    Earlier sketches in CTFT–6, 13, 22
Matacena, Orestes.................................. CTFT–41
Matalon, Vivian 1929–........................... CTFT–10
    Earlier sketch in WWT–17
Matamoros, Diego CTFT–35
Matarazzo, Heather 1982–..................... CTFT–60
    Earlier sketch in CTFT–27
Matchett, Kari 1970–.............................. CTFT–68
Matenopoulos, Debbie 1974– CTFT–79
Mather, Aubrey 1885–1958 .... WWasWT
Mather, Donald 1900–.......................... WWasWT
Mathers, Jerry 1948– CTFT–42
    Earlier sketch in CTFT–9
Matheson, Hans 1975– CTFT–50
    Earlier sketch in CTFT–24
Matheson, Murray 1912–1985 .... CTFT–1
Matheson, Richard 1926– CTFT–73
    Earlier sketches in CTFT–1, 6, 33
Matheson, Tim 1947(?)–......................... CTFT–60
    Earlier sketches in CTFT–3, 16, 27
Mathew, Sue CTFT–65
Mathews, Carmen 1914– WWT–17
Mathews, Frances Aymar 1865?–1925.... WWasWT
Mathews, George 1911–......................... WWT–16
Mathews, Hrothgar 1964–...................... CTFT–41
Mathews, James W. ?–1920 .... WWasWT
Mathews, Sheila
    See.................................... Allen, Sheila
Mathias, Sean 1956–.............................. CTFT–15
Mathieson, John CTFT–72
Mathieson, Tim
    See........................... Matheson, Tim
Mathis, Samantha 1970– CTFT–48
Mathison, Cameron 1969–...................... CTFT–68
    Earlier sketch in CTFT–30
Mathison, Melissa 1950(?)–..................... CTFT–16
Matlin, Marlee 1965–.............................. CTFT–60
    Earlier sketches in CTFT–9, 17, 27
    Brief Entry in CTFT–6
Matsusaka, Tom..................................... CTFT–20
    Earlier sketch in CTFT–2
Matteson, Ruth 1909–1975 .... WWasWT
Matthau, Walter 1920–........................... CTFT–26
    Earlier sketches in CTFT–7, 14; WWT–17
Matthews, A. E. 1869–1960 .... WWasWT
Matthews, Adelaide 1886–1948 .... WWasWT
Matthews, Brander 1852–1929 .... WWasWT
Matthews, Chris 1945–........................... CTFT–77
Matthews, Dakin CTFT–37
Matthews, DeLane 1961–........................ CTFT–40
    Earlier sketch in CTFT–17
Matthews, Ethel 1870–?......................... WWasWT
Matthews, Francis 1927–......................... CTFT–1
Matthews, Gina CTFT–71
Matthews, Jessie 1907–1981 .... WWT–17
Matthews, Lester 1900–1975 .... WWasWT
Matthieson, Tim
    See........................... Matheson, Tim
Matthison, Edith Wynne 1875–1955 ..... WWasWT
Mattson, Robin 1956–............................ CTFT–19
Matura, Mustapha 1939– WWT–17
Mature, Victor 1915(?)–1999 .... CTFT–28
Maturin, Eric 1883–1957 .... WWasWT
Matuschanskavasky, Walter
    See.................................. Matthau, Walter
Matz, Peter 1928–.................................. CTFT–24
    Earlier sketch in CTFT–12

Mauceri, John 1945–.............................. CTFT–19
    Earlier sketch in CTFT–3
Mauceri, Patricia 1950– CTFT–55
Maude, Charles Raymond
    ?–1943 .... WWasWT
Maude, Cyril 1862–1951...................... WWasWT
Maude, Elizabeth (Betty) 1912–........... WWasWT
Maude, Gillian .... WWasWT
Maude, Joan 1908–.............................. WWasWT
Maude, Margery 1889–1979 .... WWT–16
Maude–Roxbury, Roddy 1930– WWT–17
Maugham, W. Somerset 1874–1965...... WWasWT
Maule, Annabel 1922–.......................... WWT–17
Maule, Donovan 1899–......................... WWT–16
Maule, Robin 1924–1942 .... WWasWT
Maura, Carmen 1945–........................... CTFT–34
Maurey, Max ?–1947 .... WWasWT
Maurice, Edmund ?–1928 .... WWasWT
Maus, Rodger CTFT–37
Max, Edouard Alexandre de
    1869–1925 .... WWasWT
Maxey, Dawn CTFT–65
Maxfield, James 1939–.......................... CTFT–8
Maxwell, Daphne
    See .... Maxwell–Reid, Daphne
Maxwell, Gerald 1862–1930................ WWasWT
Maxwell, Jan CTFT–42
Maxwell, Lois 1927–............................. CTFT–8
Maxwell, Roberta 1944(?)–.................... CTFT–39
Maxwell, Ronald F. 1947–...................... CTFT–1
Maxwell, Walter 1877–?........................ WWasWT
Maxwell, Wayne F., Jr. CTFT–3
Maxwell–Reid, Daphne 1948–............... CTFT–37
    Earlier sketch in CTFT–13
May, Ada 1900–.................................... WWasWT
May, Akerman 1869–1933 .... WWasWT
May, Beverly 1927–............................... CTFT–1
May, Bradford CTFT–40
May, Deborah CTFT–64
May, Edna 1878–1948.......................... WWasWT
May, Elaine 1932–................................ CTFT–44
    Earlier sketches in CTFT–5, 22; WWT–17
May, Hans 1891–1959 .... WWasWT
May, Jack 1922–.................................... WWT–17
May, Jane.. WWasWT
May, Jodhi 1975– CTFT–35
May, Mathilda 1965– CTFT–43
    Earlier sketch in CTFT–21
May, Mona CTFT–62
May, Pamela 1917– .... WWasWT
May, Val 1927–..................................... WWT–17
May, Winston 1937–............................. CTFT–4
Mayall, Rik 1958–................................. CTFT–57
    Earlier sketch in CTFT–26
Mayberry, Mariann CTFT–76
    Earlier sketch in CTFT–32
Mayer, Billy 1902–1959 .... WWasWT
Mayer, Daniel 1856–1928.................... WWasWT
Mayer, Edwin Justus 1896–1960........... WWasWT
Mayer, Gaston 1869–1923 .... WWasWT
Mayer, Henry ?–1941 .... WWasWT
Mayer, Michael 1961(?)–....................... CTFT–48
    Earlier sketch in CTFT–23
Mayer, Renee 1900–............................. WWasWT
Mayes, Lee R. CTFT–69
    Earlier sketch in CTFT–30
Mayes, Sally CTFT–42
Mayes, Wendell 1919–1992.................. CTFT–10
Mayeur, E. F. 1866–?............................ WWasWT
Mayfield, Cleo 1897–1954 .... WWasWT
Mayfield, Les CTFT–42
Mayhew, Charles 1908– .... WWasWT
Maynard, Ted CTFT–67

Mayne, Ernie .... WWasWT
Mayne, Ferdy 1920– WWT–17
Mayo, Jim
    See................................. L'Amour, Louis
Mayo, Lucille
    See................................ Lortel, Lucille
Mayo, Margaret 1882–1951 .... WWasWT
Mayo, Sam 1881–1938 .... WWasWT
Mayo, Virginia 1920–............................ CTFT–1
Mayron, Melanie 1952–......................... CTFT–40
    Earlier sketches in CTFT–1, 10, 17
Mays, Jayma 1979–................................ CTFT–76
Maysles, Albert 1926(?)– CTFT–40
    Earlier sketch in CTFT–17
Maysles, David 1933–1987 .... CTFT–4
Mazar, Debi 1964–................................. CTFT–48
    Earlier sketch in CTFT–23
Mazerolle, Arlene................................... CTFT–68
Mazur, Monet 1976–............................. CTFT–66
Mazurki, Mike 1909–............................. CTFT–9
Mazursky, Paul 1930–............................ CTFT–55
    Earlier sketches in CTFT–1, 6, 14, 26
Mazzarella, Marcello CTFT–35
Mazzarino, Joseph CTFT–52
Mazzello, Joseph 1983(?)–..................... CTFT–57
    Earlier sketch in CTFT–23
Mazzie, Marin 1960–............................. CTFT–44
    Earlier sketch in CTFT–22
Mazzola, John W. 1928–........................ CTFT–1
MC Bones
    See...................................... Green, Tom
McAdams, Rachel 1976– CTFT–70
McAfee, Anndi 1979–............................ CTFT–50
McAlister, Scarlett 1977–....................... CTFT–77
McAlphine, Donald 1934–..................... CTFT–40
McAnally, Ray 1926–1989 .... CTFT–7
    Earlier sketch in WWT–17
McAnuff, Des 1952–.............................. CTFT–33
    Earlier sketch in CTFT–6
McArdle, Andrea 1963–......................... CTFT–39
    Earlier sketch in CTFT–6
McArdle, J. F. .... WWasWT
McArdle, John 1949–............................. CTFT–73
    Earlier sketch in CTFT–33
McArthur, Alex 1957–............................ CTFT–37
McArthur, Molly 1900– .... WWasWT
McAssey, Michael 1955–........................ CTFT–2
McAvoy, James 1979–............................ CTFT–70
McBain, Diane 1941–............................ CTFT–1
McBeath, Tom CTFT–38
McBride, Chi 1961–............................... CTFT–78
    Earlier sketch in CTFT–35
McBride, Jim 1941– CTFT–38
    Earlier sketches in CTFT–8, 15
McBurney, Simon CTFT–44
    Earlier sketch in CTFT–22
McCabe, Eugene 1930– CTFT–15
McCabe, Ruth CTFT–73
    Earlier sketch in CTFT–33
McCaffrey, James 1960–......................... CTFT–74
    Earlier sketch in CTFT–33
McCall, Kathleen CTFT–4
McCall, Mitzi CTFT–47
McCall, Nancy 1948– CTFT–1
McCallany, Holt 1964– CTFT–68
    Earlier sketch in CTFT–30
McCallin, Clement 1913–1977 .... WWT–17
McCallum, David 1933–......................... CTFT–57
    Earlier sketches in CTFT–1, 7, 14, 26
McCallum, Joanna.................................. CTFT–8
McCallum, John 1918– CTFT–8
    Earlier sketch in WWT–17

McCallum, Rick 1952–........................... CTFT–52
    Earlier sketch in CTFT–24
McCambridge, Mercedes 1918–................ CTFT–5
McCamus, Tom CTFT–40
McCann, Chuck 1934– CTFT–45
McCann, Donal.................................... CTFT–7
McCann, Mary B. CTFT–71
    Earlier sketch CTFT–32
McCann, Sean CTFT–37
McCardle, John
    See .... McArdle, John
McCarter, Charles CTFT–46
McCarthy, Andrew 1962(?)–................... CTFT–37
    Earlier sketches in CTFT–6, 13
McCarthy, Christine
    See .... Elise, Christine
McCarthy, Daniel 1869–? .... WWasWT
McCarthy, Dennis................................. CTFT–41
McCarthy, Frank 1912–1986 .... CTFT–4
McCarthy, Jenny 1972– CTFT–71
    Earlier sketches in CTFT–19, 31
McCarthy, John 1961–.......................... CTFT–56
McCarthy, Julianna CTFT–38
McCarthy, Justin Huntly 1860–1936...... WWasWT
McCarthy, Kevin 1914–......................... CTFT–35
    Earlier sketches in CTFT–4; WWT–17
McCarthy, Lillah 1875–1960 .... WWasWT
McCarthy, Mary 1910–1989.................... CTFT–1
McCarthy, Melissa 1969– CTFT–56
McCarthy, Nobu 1934– CTFT–42
    Earlier sketch in CTFT–20
McCarthy, Shelia 1956(?)–...................... CTFT–42
McCarthy, Thomas CTFT–46
McCartney, Jesse 1987–......................... CTFT–74
McCartney, Linda 1941–1998 .... CTFT–27
McCartney, Paul 1942– CTFT–42
    Earlier sketch in CTFT–17
McCarty, Mary 1923–1980..................... WWT–17
McCarty, Michael CTFT–52
McCaul, Neil...................................... CTFT–75
    Earlier sketch in CTFT–32
McCay, Peggy 1930–............................ CTFT–38
McClain, Cady 1969– CTFT–680
    Earlier sketch in CTFT–30
McClain, Katie
    See......................... McClain, Cady
McClanahan, Rue 1934(?)– CTFT–59
    Earlier sketches in CTFT–4, 16, 27; WWT–17
McClelland, Allan 1917–1989 .... CTFT–8
    Earlier sketch in WWT–17
McClendon, Reiley 1990–...................... CTFT–63
McClintic, Guthrie 1893–1961 .... WWasWT
McClintock, Eddie 1967–...................... CTFT–67
McClory, Sean 1924– CTFT–4
McCloskey, Leigh 1955– CTFT–52
    Earlier sketches in CTFT–15, 25
McClure, Doug 1935–1995..................... CTFT–5
    Obituary in CTFT–14
McClure, Kandyse 1980– CTFT–65
McClure, Marc 1957– CTFT–62
McClure, Michael 1932–........................ CTFT–1
McClurg, Edie 1951– CTFT–60
    Earlier sketches in CTFT–8, 16, 27
McCole–Bartusiak, Sky
    See .... Bartusiak, Skye McCole
McComas, Carroll 1891–1962............... WWasWT
McComb, Heather 1977–....................... CTFT–55
    Earlier sketch in CTFT–26
McConaughey, Matthew 1969–............... CTFT–61
    Earlier sketches in CTFT–17, 28
McConnell, Jean 1928(?)– CTFT–16
McConnell, Judith 1944– CTFT–55
McConnohie, Michael............................ CTFT–49

McCook, John 1945– CTFT–59
    Earlier sketch in CTFT–5
McCord, Nancy .... WWasWT
McCorkle, Kevin.................................. CTFT–66
McCorkle, Mark CTFT–71
McCormack, Catherine 1972–................ CTFT–60
    Earlier sketch in CTFT–27
McCormack, Dan CTFT–28
McCormack, Eric 1963–........................ CTFT–47
    Earlier sketch in CTFT–23
McCormack, J. Patrick CTFT–38
McCormack, Mary 1969–....................... CTFT–59
    Earlier sketch in CTFT–27
McCormack, Patrick KJ.
    See .... McCormack, J. Patrick
McCormack, Patty 1945– CTFT–41
    Earlier sketches in CTFT–8, 19
McCormick, Arthur Langdon
    ?–1954 .... WWasWT
McCormick, Carolyn 1959– CTFT–61
    Earlier sketches in CTFT–17, 28
McCormick, Larry 1933–2004 .... CTFT–61
McCormick, Maureen 1956–.................. CTFT–45
McCormick, Myron 1907–1962 .... WWasWT
McCouch, Grayson 1968– CTFT–74
McCourt, Malachy 1931–...................... CTFT–55
McCowen, Alec 1925–.......................... CTFT–39
    Earlier sketches in CTFT–2, 8, 16
McCoy, Cathy Rigby
    See .... Rigby, Cathy
McCoy, Matt 1958–............................. CTFT–64
McCoy, Sylvester 1943–........................ CTFT–35
McCracken, Esther (Helen)
    1902–................................. WWasWT
McCracken, Jeff CTFT–6
    Earlier sketch in CTFT–1
McCracken, Joan 1922–1961 .... WWasWT
McCrane, Paul 1961–........................... CTFT–71
    Earlier sketches in CTFT–1, 4,32
McCrary, Darius 1976– CTFT–40
McCrary, Joel..................................... CTFT–76
McCuistion, Michael CTFT–56
McCulley, Mark
    See .... Macaulay, Marc
McCulloch, Bruce 1961– CTFT–46
McCulloch, John Tyler
    See .... Burroughs, Edgar Rice
McCullough, Kim 1978– CTFT–66
McCullough, Paul 1883–1936............ WWasWT
McCusker, Stella CTFT–35
McCutcheon, Bill CTFT–7
McDaniel, James 1958– CTFT–71
    Earlier sketches in CTFT–19, 31
McDermott, Dean 1966– CTFT–46
McDermott, Dylan 1962(?)– CTFT–71
    Earlier sketches in CTFT–19, 31
McDermott, Hugh (Patrick)
    1908–1972 .... WWasWT
McDermott, Keith 1953–....................... CTFT–4
McDermott, Shiva Rose 1969(?)– CTFT–70
McDermott, Tom 1912–1996 .... CTFT–2
    Obituary in CTFT–16
McDevitt, Ruth 1895–1976................... WWT–16
McDiarmid, Ian 1947–......................... CTFT–35
    Earlier sketch in CTFT–9
McDonald, Adam
    See .... MacDonald, Adam
McDonald, Audra 1970–........................ CTFT–51
    Earlier sketch in CTFT–24
McDonald, Bruce 1959–........................ CTFT–58
McDonald, Christie 1875–1962 .... WWasWT
McDonald, Christopher 1955(?)–............. CTFT–60
    Earlier sketch in CTFT–27

McDonald, Daniel 1960–....................... CTFT–43
    Earlier sketch in CTFT–21
McDonald, Garry 1948–........................ CTFT–76
    Earlier sketch in CTFT–33
McDonald, Kevin 1961–........................ CTFT–46
McDonald, Mac CTFT–35
McDonald, Tanny 1940–......................... CTFT–1
McDonnell, James CTFT–56
McDonnell, Mary 1952–........................ CTFT–60
    Earlier sketches in CTFT–9, 16, 27
McDonough, Jerome 1946– CTFT–1
McDonough, Mary Beth 1961–.............. CTFT–47
McDonough, Neal 1966–....................... CTFT–55
    Earlier sketch in CTFT–26
McDormand, Frances 1957–................... CTFT–55
    Earlier sketches in CTFT–7, 14, 26
McDougall, Gordon 1941– CTFT–5
    Earlier sketch in WWT–17
McDowall, Roddy 1928–1998 .... CTFT–16
    Obituary in CTFT–32
    Earlier sketches in CTFT–2, 8; WWT–17
McDowell, Alex CTFT–67
    Earlier sketch in CTFT–29
McDowell, Malcolm 1943– CTFT–44
    Earlier sketches in CTFT–5, 16
McEachin, James 1930–........................ CTFT–25
McElhone, Natascha 1971–.................... CTFT–53
    Earlier sketch in CTFT–25
McElwee, Ross 1947(?)– CTFT–15
McEnery, John 1943– CTFT–57
    Earlier sketches in CTFT–14, 26
McEnery, Peter 1940–........................... CTFT–5
    Earlier sketch in WWT–17
McEnroe, John 1959– CTFT–49
McEntire, Reba 1955(?)–....................... CTFT–36
McEveety, Vincent CTFT–38
    Earlier sketch in CTFT–12
McEvoy, Charles 1879–1929 .... WWasWT
McEvoy, J. P. 1897–1958 .... WWasWT
McEwan, Geraldine 1932–..................... CTFT–44
    Earlier sketches in CTFT–6, 22; WWT–17
McEwan, Ian 1948– CTFT–14
MC Face
    See .... Green, Tom
McFadden, Cheryl
    See .... McFadden, Gates
McFadden, Cynthia 1956– CTFT–41
McFadden, Gates 1949– CTFT–59
    Earlier sketches in CTFT–8, 16, 27
McFarland, Rebecca CTFT–79
McFarland, Robert 1931–....................... CTFT–2
McFee, Bruce CTFT–58
McFee, Dwight.................................... CTFT–54
McFerrin, Bobby 1950–......................... CTFT–38
    Earlier sketch in CTFT–12
McGann, Paul 1959– CTFT–50
McGaughey, Nicholas CTFT–35
McGavin, Darren 1922–2006 .... CTFT–23
    Obituary in CTFT–70
    Earlier sketch in CTFT–5
McGee, Bobby CTFT–61
McGee, Jack...................................... CTFT–68
    Earlier sketch in CTFT–30
McGee, Vonetta................................... CTFT–12
McGibbon, Josann................................ CTFT–28
McGill, Bruce 1950–............................ CTFT–57
    Earlier sketches in CTFT–7, 14, 26
McGill, Everett Charles III
    1945–................................... CTFT–1
McGillin, Howard 1953– CTFT–35
    Earlier sketch in CTFT–6
McGillion, Paul 1969–.......................... CTFT–69

McGillis, Kelly 1957(?)– CTFT–35
   Earlier sketch in CTFT–9
   Brief Entry in CTFT–3
McGinley, John C. 1959– CTFT–55
   Earlier sketches in CTFT–14, 26
McGinley, Sean 1956– CTFT–75
   Earlier sketch in CTFT–33
McGinley, Ted 1958– CTFT–51
   Earlier sketches in CTFT–14, 24
McGinnis, Scott 1958– CTFT–7
McGiver, John 1913–1975 .... WWT–16
McGlone, Mike 1972(?)– CTFT–55
   Earlier sketch in CTFT–25
McGlynn, Frank 1866–1951 .... WWasWT
McGonagle, Richard 1946– CTFT–56
McGoohan, Patrick 1928– CTFT–34
   Earlier sketches in CTFT–5; WWasWT
McGough, Roger 1937– CTFT–15
McGovern, Elizabeth 1961– CTFT–44
   Earlier sketches in CTFT–3, 6, 13, 22
   Brief Entry in CTFT–2
McGovern, Maureen 1949– CTFT–37
   Earlier sketches in CTFT–6, 13
McGovern, Terence 1942– CTFT–56
McGowan, John W. .... WWasWT
McGowan, Rose 1973(?)– CTFT–55
   Earlier sketches in CTFT–26
McGowan, Tom 1958– CTFT–52
McGrady, Michael CTFT–61
   Earlier sketch in CTFT–28
McGrath, Derek CTFT–47
McGrath, Douglas 1958– CTFT–55
   Earlier sketch in CTFT–25
McGrath, John 1935– WWT–17
McGrath, Paul 1904–1978 .... WWT–16
McGrath, Tom 1940– CTFT–12
McGraw, Melinda 1963– CTFT–62
McGregor, Ewan 1971– CTFT–58
   Earlier sketches in CTFT–17, 27
McGregor, Jane 1983– CTFT–72
McGregor–Stewart, Kate CTFT–40
McGuane, Thomas 1939– CTFT–8
McGuinness, Frank 1953– CTFT–38
   Earlier sketch in CTFT–12
McGuire, Biff 1926– WWT–17
McGuire, Don 1919–1979 .... CTFT–26
McGuire, Dorothy 1918– CTFT–20
   Earlier sketches in CTFT–3; WWT–17
McGuire, Maeve CTFT–55
McGuire, Michael 1934– CTFT–55
McGuire, Mickey
   See .... Rooney, Mickey
McGuire, Mitch 1936– CTFT–1
McGuire, William Anthony
   1885–1940 .... WWasWT
McHale, Rosemary 1944– CTFT–5
   Earlier sketch in WWT–17
McHattie, Stephen 1947– CTFT–37
   Earlier sketches in CTFT–6, 13
McHenry, Don 1908– CTFT–1
McHenry, Doug 1958(?)– CTFT–39
   Earlier sketch in CTFT–14
McHugh, Florence 1906– .... WWasWT
McHugh, Therese .... WWasWT
McInerney, Bernie 1936– CTFT–57
   Earlier sketch in CTFT–1
McInnerny, Lizzy 1961– CTFT–74
   Earlier sketch in CTFT–32
McInnerny, Tim CTFT–47
McInnis, Angus
   See .... MacInnes, Angus
McIntire, John 1907–1991 .... CTFT–15
McIntosh, Madge 1875–1950 .... WWasWT

McIntosh, Marcia CTFT–4
McIntosh, Tammy 1970– CTFT–45
Mcintosh, Yanna CTFT–54
McIntyre, Dennis 1943(?)–1990 .... CTFT–9
McIntyre, Frank 1879–1949 .... WWasWT
McIntyre, Joseph 1972– CTFT–64
McIntyre, Marilyn 1949– CTFT–78
   Earlier sketches in CTFT–2, 34
McIver Ewing, Blake
   See .... Ewing, Blake McIver
McKay, Don
   See .... MacKay, Don
McKay, Peggy
   See .... McCay, Peggy
McKay, Scott 1915–1987 .... WWT–17
McKayle, Donald 1930– CTFT–1
McKean, Michael 1947– CTFT–51
   Earlier sketches in CTFT–3, 14, 24
McKechnie, Donna 1940(?)– CTFT–64
   Earlier sketches in CTFT–7; WWT–17
McKee, Clive R. 1883–? .... WWasWT
McKee, Gina 1961(?)– CTFT–680
   Earlier sketch in CTFT–30
McKee, Lonette 1954(?)– CTFT–51
   Earlier sketches in CTFT–6, 14, 24
McKellar, Danica 1975– CTFT–50
   Earlier sketch in CTFT–24
McKellar, Don 1963– CTFT–57
   Earlier sketch in CTFT–26
McKellen, Ian 1939– CTFT–44
   Earlier sketches in CTFT–1, 4, 11, 22;
   WWT–17
McKenna, David, 1949– CTFT–4
McKenna, Keith
   See .... Sergei, Ivan
McKenna, Siobhan 1923–1986 .... CTFT–4
   Earlier sketch in WWT–17
McKenna, T. P. 1929– WWT–17
McKenna, Virginia 1931– CTFT–6
   Earlier sketch in WWT–17
McKenzie, Barry
   See .... Humphries, Barry
McKenzie, Benjamin 1978– CTFT–74
McKenzie, Jacqueline 1967– CTFT–59
McKenzie, James B. 1926– WWT–17
McKenzie, Julia 1941– CTFT–50
   Earlier sketches in CTFT–1, 11
McKenzie, Kevin Patrick 1954– CTFT–52
   Earlier sketch in CTFT–12
McKenzie, Mark CTFT–48
McKeon, Doug 1966– CTFT–77
   Earlier sketches in CTFT–4, 34
McKeon, Nancy 1966(?)– CTFT–38
   Earlier sketches in CTFT–8, 15
McKeown, Allan 1946– CTFT–51
   Earlier sketch in CTFT–12
McKeown, Bob CTFT–43
McKeown, Charles CTFT–24
McKern, Abigail 1957– CTFT–57
   Earlier sketch in CTFT–26
McKern, Leo 1920– CTFT–16
   Earlier sketches in CTFT–2, 8; WWT–17
McKillip, Britt 1991– CTFT–63
McKinnel, Norman 1870–1932 .... WWasWT
McKinney, Bill 1931– CTFT–78
   Earlier sketches in CTFT–8, 34
McKinney, Mark 1959– CTFT–57
   Earlier sketch in CTFT–25
McKinnon, Joel
   See .... Miller, Joel McKinnon
McKinnon, Ray 1961(?)– CTFT–76
   Earlier sketch in CTFT–33

McKiou, Patricia
   See .... Latshaw, Steve
Mcknight, David CTFT–54
McLain, John CTFT–2
McLaughlin, Emily 1928–1991 .... CTFT–3
   Obituary in CTFT–10
McLaughlin, John
   See .... Laughlin, John
McLaughlin, John 1927– CTFT–41
McLean, Seaton CTFT–38
McLellan, C. M. S. 1865–1916 .... WWasWT
McLennan, Stewart
   See .... Finlay–McLennan, Stewart
McLennan, Stuart
   See .... Finlay–McLennan, Stewart
McLeod, Gavin
   See .... MacLeod, Gavin
McLeod, Mary E. CTFT–69
McLerie, Allyn Ann 1926– CTFT–5
   Earlier sketch in WWT–17
McLoughlin, Nancy 1960– CTFT–74
McLoughlin, Tom 1950– CTFT–75
MC Lyte 1971– CTFT–74
McMahon, Ed 1923– CTFT–71
   Earlier sketches in CTFT–1, 19, 31
McMahon, Julian 1968– CTFT–42
   Earlier sketch in CTFT–20
McMahon, Vince 1945– CTFT–49
McMains, Cody 1985– CTFT–75
McManus, Declan
   See .... Costello, Elvis
McManus, Don CTFT–54
McManus, Jim CTFT–79
McMartin, John 1959– CTFT–49
   Earlier sketches in CTFT–4, 23; WWT–17
McMaster, Anew 1894–1962 .... WWasWT
McMillan, Dawn CTFT–34
McMillan, Kenneth 1932–1989 .... CTFT–6
   Earlier sketch in CTFT–1
McMillan, Richard CTFT–64
McMillan, Roddy 1923–1979 .... WWT–16
McMoyler, Dave CTFT–37
McMurray, Sam 1952– CTFT–53
   Earlier sketches in CTFT–7, 15, 25
McMurtrey, Joan CTFT–65
McMurtry, Larry 1936– CTFT–22
   Earlier sketch in CTFT–11
McNab, Mercedes 1980– CTFT–56
McNabb, Barry 1960– CTFT–6
McNairy, Scoot CTFT–79
McNally, Kevin 1956– CTFT–78
   Earlier sketch in CTFT–34
McNally, Terence 1939– CTFT–4
   Earlier sketches in CTFT–1; WWT–17
McNamara, Brooks 1937– WWT–17
McNamara, Dermot 1925– CTFT–4
McNamara, William 1965– CTFT–38
   Earlier sketch in CTFT–15
McNaughton, Gus 1884–1969 .... WWasWT
McNaughton, Stephen CTFT–1
McNaughton, Tom 1867–1923 .... WWasWT
McNaughtons, The .... WWasWT
McNeely, Joel CTFT–47
McNeice, Ian 1950– CTFT–66
McNeil, Claudia 1917– WWT–17
McNeil, Kate CTFT–78
   Earlier sketch in CTFT–34
Mcneil, Scott CTFT–37
McNeil, Tress
   See .... MacNeille, Tress
McNeill, Robert Duncan 1964– CTFT–45
   Earlier sketch in CTFT–22
McNichol, James CTFT–3

McNichol, Kristy 1962– CTFT–19
  Earlier sketch in CTFT–3
McNulty, Kevin.................................... CTFT–54
McNutt, Stephen CTFT–54
McPhail, Marnie 1966–......................... CTFT–77
  Earlier sketch in CTFT–34
McPherson, Conor 1970(?)– CTFT–60
  Earlier sketch in CTFT–27
McPherson, Mervyn 1892–.................... WWasWT
McQuade, Kris CTFT–34
McQuarrie, Stuart................................. CTFT–34
McQueen, Armelia 1952–...................... CTFT–38
McQueen, Butterfly 1911– WWT–17
McQueen, Justice Ellis
  See................................ Jones, L. Q.
McQueen, Steve 1930–1980................. CTFT–16
  Earlier sketch in CTFT–1
McQuiggan, John A. 1935–................... CTFT–4
McRae, Bruce 1867–1927 .... WWasWT
McRae, Ellen
  See................................ Burstyn, Ellen
McRae, Frank 1942– CTFT–64
McRae, Glory CTFT–4
McRaney, Gerald 1947(?)– CTFT–60
  Earlier sketches in CTFT–8, 16, 27
McRobbie, Peter 1943–........................ CTFT–68
  Earlier sketches in CTFT–4, 30
McShane, Ian 1942– CTFT–78
  Earlier sketches in CTFT–2, 34; WWT–17
McShane, Jamie.................................... CTFT–71
McShane, Michael 1957(?)– CTFT–46
McTeer, Janet 1961– CTFT–35
  Earlier sketch in CTFT–9
McTiernan, John 1951–........................ CTFT–45
  Earlier sketches in CTFT–11, 22
McVerry, Maureen CTFT–32
McVicar, Daniel 1958–......................... CTFT–59
McWade, Robert 1882–1938................ WWasWT
McWhinnie, Donald 1920–1987............ WWT–17
McWhirter, Jillian CTFT–62
Meacham, Anne 1925– CTFT–3
  Earlier sketch in WWT–17
Meacham, Paul 1939– CTFT–1
Mead, Courtland 1987– CTFT–50
Meade, Julia 1928– CTFT–19
  Earlier sketch in CTFT–3
Meader, George 1888–1963 .... WWasWT
Meadow, Lynne 1946– CTFT–55
  Earlier sketches in CTFT–4; WWT–17
Meadows, Audrey 1925–1996 .... CTFT–2
  Obituary in CTFT–16
Meadows, Jayne 1920(?)–..................... CTFT–61
Meadows, Tim 1961–........................... CTFT–55
  Earlier sketch in CTFT–26
Meaney, Colm 1953– CTFT–53
  Earlier sketches in CTFT–8, 15, 25
Meaney, Kevin 1957–........................... CTFT–76
Means, Russell 1939–........................... CTFT–39
  Earlier sketch in CTFT–15
Meara, Anne 1929–.............................. CTFT–50
  Earlier sketches in CTFT–1, 14, 24
Mears, Michael.................................... CTFT–28
Measor, Adela 1860–1933.................... WWasWT
Measor, Beryl 1908–1965 .... WWasWT
Meat Loaf 1951(?)–.............................. CTFT–51
  Earlier sketch in CTFT–24
Mechoso, Julio Oscar CTFT–38
Medak, Peter 1937– CTFT–2
Medavoy, Mike 1941–.......................... CTFT–10
Medford, Kay 1920–1980 .... WWT–17
Medoff, Mark 1940–............................ CTFT–38
  Earlier sketches in CTFT–4, 12; WWT–17

Medrano, Frank 1954– CTFT–66
  Earlier sketch in CTFT–29
Medwin, Michael 1923– CTFT–49
  Earlier sketch in CTFT–14
Mee, Charles L., Jr. 1938– CTFT–13
Meek, Barbara CTFT–5
Meek, Donald 1880–1946..................... WWasWT
Meeker, Ralph 1920–1988 .... CTFT–7
  Earlier sketch in WWT–17
Meester, Leighton 1986– CTFT–74
Megahey, Leslie 1944–.......................... CTFT–39
  Earlier sketch in CTFT–14
Megard, Andree 1869–? .... WWasWT
Megill, Sheelah CTFT–56
Megrue, Roi Cooper 1883–1927 .... WWasWT
Mehler, Tobias CTFT–69
Mei, Wu Jun
  See................................ Wu, Vivian
Meier, Shane 1977–.............................. CTFT–63
Meighan, Thomas 1879–1936 .... WWasWT
Meiser, Edith 1898–............................. WWT–17
Meisle, Kathryn CTFT–79
  Earlier sketch in CTFT–34
Meister, Brian 1948– CTFT–2
Meistrich, Larry 1967– CTFT–56
Mekka, Eddie 1952–............................ CTFT–43
  Earlier sketches in CTFT–2, 21
Meldrum, Wendel 1958– CTFT–61
  Earlier sketch in CTFT–28
Melendez, Bill 1916–............................ CTFT–45
  Earlier sketch in CTFT–6
Melendez, Ron 1972–........................... CTFT–67
Melendrez, Dorothy CTFT–54
Melfi, Leonard 1935–............................ WWT–17
Melford, Austin 1884–? .... WWasWT
Melford, Jack 1899–............................. WWasWT
Melford, Jill 1934– WWT–17
Melia, Joe CTFT–13
  Earlier sketch in WWT–17
Melissis, Tom CTFT–43
Mell, Randle 1951–.............................. CTFT–64
Mellish, Fuller 1865–1936.................... WWasWT
Mello, Tamara 1977(?)–........................ CTFT–48
Mellor, William C. 1904–1963 .... CTFT–27
Melly, Andree 1932–............................ WWT–17
Melman, Jeffrey CTFT–50
Melnick, Daniel 1932–.......................... CTFT–55
  Earlier sketches in CTFT–3, 19
Melnotte, Violet 1852–1935................. WWasWT
Meloni, Christopher 1961– CTFT–60
  Earlier sketch in CTFT–27
Meltzer, Charles Henry 1852–1936....... WWasWT
Melville, Alan 1910–1984..................... WWT–17
Melville, Andrew 1912– .... WWasWT
Melville, Frederick 1876–1938............. WWasWT
Melville, June 1915–1970 .... WWasWT
Melville, Rose 1873–1946 .... WWasWT
Melville, Walter 1875–1937 .... WWasWT
Melville, Winnie ?–1937...................... WWasWT
Melvin, Duncan 1913–.......................... WWasWT
Melvin, Murray 1932–........................... CTFT–34
  Earlier sketches in CTFT–6; WWT–17
Mendel .... WWasWT
Mendelsohn, Ben 1969– CTFT–37
Mendelson, Lee 1933– CTFT–37
  Earlier sketch in CTFT–12
Mendeluk, George CTFT–45
Mendes, Eva 1974(?)–.......................... CTFT–75
Mendes, Sam 1965–............................. CTFT–51
  Earlier sketches in CTFT–14, 24
Mendillo, Stephen W. 1942–................. CTFT–54
  Earlier sketch in CTFT–1

Meneses, Alex 1965– CTFT–69
  Earlier sketch in CTFT–30
Menges, Chris 1940(?)– CTFT–34
  Earlier sketch in CTFT–7
Menges, Herbert 1902–1972 .... WWasWT
Menke, Sally....................................... CTFT–59
  Earlier sketch in CTFT–27
Menken, Alan 1949–............................ CTFT–45
  Earlier sketches in CTFT–11, 22
Menken, Helen 1901–1966 .... WWasWT
Menosky, Joe CTFT–49
Menshikov, Oleg 1960– CTFT–34
Menville, Scott 1971– CTFT–56
Menzel, Jiri 1938–............................... CTFT–37
  Earlier sketch in CTFT–12
Menzies, Archie 1904–......................... WWasWT
Menzies, Peter, Jr................................ CTFT–59
  Earlier sketch in CTFT–27
Meoli, Christian J. CTFT–46
Meppen, Adrian Joseph 1940– CTFT–3
Merande, Doro 1935– .... WWasWT
Mercer, Beryl 1882–1939 .... WWasWT
Mercer, David 1928–1980..................... WWT–17
Mercer, Johnny 1909–1976 .... WWT–16
Mercer, Marian 1935–.......................... CTFT–62
  Earlier sketches in CTFT–7; WWT–17
Merchant, Ismail 1936–........................ CTFT–37
  Earlier sketches in CTFT–1, 6, 13
Merchant, Paul
  See................................ Ellison, Harlan
Merchant, Vivien 1929–1982 .... WWT–17
Mercouri, Melina 1925–1994................. CTFT–5
  Obituary in CTFT–13
Mercure, Monique 1930–...................... CTFT–57
  Earlier sketches in CTFT–11, 22
Mercurio, Micole CTFT–61
  Earlier sketch in CTFT–28
Mere, Charles 1883–? .... WWasWT
Meredith, Burgess 1909(?)–1997.............. CTFT–4
  Obituary in CTFT–17
  Earlier sketch in WWT–17
Meredith, Don 1938–........................... CTFT–19
  Earlier sketch in CTFT–1
Merendino, James 1967–....................... CTFT–34
Merivale 1882–1939 .... WWasWT
Merivale, Philip 1886–1946 .... WWasWT
Meriwether, Lee 1935–......................... CTFT–2
Merkel, Una 1903–1986 .... WWasWT
Merkerson, S. Epatha 1952–.................. CTFT–59
  Earlier sketches in CTFT–16, 27
Merlin, Joanna 1931–........................... CTFT–37
  Earlier sketch in CTFT–10
Merman, Ethel 1909–1984 .... CTFT–1
  Earlier sketch in WWT–17
Merrall, Mary 1890–1973..................... WWasWT
Merriam, Eve 1916– CTFT–1
Merrick, David 1912– CTFT–6
  Earlier sketch in WWT–17
Merrick, Leonard 1864–1939 .... WWasWT
Merrill, Beth .... WWasWT
Merrill, Bob 1920– WWT–17
Merrill, Dina 1925–............................. CTFT–40
  Earlier sketches in CTFT–1, 8, 15
Merrill, Gary 1915–1990....................... CTFT–1
Merrill–Hartley, Dina
  See................................ Merrill, Dina
Merriman, Ryan 1983–......................... CTFT–39
Merrison, Clive 1945–.......................... CTFT–76
  Earlier sketch in CTFT–33
Merritt, Courtney CTFT–60
Merritt, Grace 1881–?.......................... WWasWT
Merritt, Theresa 1922– CTFT–8
Merson, Billy 1881–1947 .... WWasWT

Mery, Andree .... WWasWT
Merz, Jesse 1973– CTFT–42
Mesa, William CTFT–37
Mese, John 1963– CTFT–78
    Earlier sketch in CTFT–34
Meskimen, Jim 1959–............................. CTFT–68
    Earlier sketch in CTFT–30
Messager, Andre 1853–1929 .... WWasWT
Messick, Don 1926– CTFT–9
    Earlier sketch in CTFT–3
Messina, Chris CTFT–52
Messing, Debra CTFT–71
    Earlier sketches in CTFT–20, 31
Meszaros, Marta 1931–.......................... CTFT–37
    Earlier sketch in CTFT–12
Metaxa, Georges 1899–1950................. WWasWT
Metcalf, Laurie 1955– CTFT–45
    Earlier sketches in CTFT–7, 15
Metcalf, Mark 1946– CTFT–45
    Earlier sketches in CTFT–8, 22
Metcalfe, James Stetson 1858–1927 ...... WWasWT
Metcalfe, Stephen 1953–........................ CTFT–54
    Earlier sketches in CTFT–7, 17
Metchik, Aaron Michael 1980–.............. CTFT–56
Metenier, Oscar 1859–1913 .... WWasWT
Metheny, Pat 1954–................................ CTFT–37
    Earlier sketch in CTFT–12
Methven, Eleanor CTFT–34
Metrano, Art 1937(?)–............................. CTFT–55
    Earlier sketch in CTFT–5
Metzler, Jim 1951–................................. CTFT–61
    Earlier sketch in CTFT–28
Mewes, Jason 1974– CTFT–61
    Earlier sketch in CTFT–28
Meyer, Bertie Alexander 1877–1967 ..... WWasWT
Meyer, Bess CTFT–63
Meyer, Breckin 1974– CTFT–52
    Earlier sketch in CTFT–25
Meyer, Dina 1969–.................................. CTFT–45
    Earlier sketch in CTFT–22
Meyer, Louis 1871–1915 .... WWasWT
Meyer, Nicholas 1945– CTFT–52
    Earlier sketches in CTFT–1, 14, 24
Meyers, Ari 1969–................................... CTFT–33
    Earlier sketch in CTFT–4
Meyers, Jonathan Rhys
    See........................... Rhys–Meyers, Jonathan
Meyers, Kim
    See... Myers, Kim
Meyers, Michael
    See.. Myers, Mike
Meyers, Nancy 1949– CTFT–24
Meyers, Rusty 1957–............................... CTFT–78
    Earlier sketch in CTFT–34
Meyers, Timothy 1945–1989.................... CTFT–1
Meynell, Clyde 1867–1934 .... WWasWT
Miano, Robert 1942– CTFT–45
Miceli, Justine 1959–.............................. CTFT–74
Michael, Christopher CTFT–40
Michael, Gertrude 1910–1965 .... WWasWT
Michael, Kathleen 1917– WWT–17
Michael, Kenn
    See .... Blank, Kenny
Michael, Ralph 1907–............................. WWT–17
Michaele, Michael 1966–......................... CTFT–32
Michaelis, Robert 1884–1965............... WWasWT
Michaels, Joel B. CTFT–54
Michaels, Lorne 1944–............................ CTFT–71
    Earlier sketches in CTFT–2, 9, 20, 31
Michaels, Marilyn 1943–......................... CTFT–8
Michaels, Richard 1936–......................... CTFT–10
    Earlier sketch in CTFT–1
Michaels, Susan...................................... CTFT–48

Michaelson, Knut 1846–........................ WWasWT
Michaely, Joel CTFT–65
Micheaux, Nicki 1971(?)– CTFT–56
Michele, Michael 1966– CTFT–73
Michell, Keith 1928(?)–.......................... CTFT–19
    Earlier sketches in CTFT–2, 8; WWT–17
Michell, Roger 1957–............................. CTFT–59
    Earlier sketch in CTFT–27
Michos, Anastas N. CTFT–66
    Earlier sketch in CTFT–29
Mick, Gabriel
    See .... Mann, Gabriel
Micol, Christina
    See .... Mercurio, Micole
Middendorf, Tracy 1970(?)–................... CTFT–77
    Earlier sketch in CTFT–34
Middlemass, Frank 1919– CTFT–33
    Earlier sketch in CTFT–8
Middleton, Edgar 1894–1939 .... WWasWT
Middleton, George 1880–1967.............. WWasWT
Middleton, Guy 1907–1973 .... WWasWT
Middleton, Josephine 1883–1971 .... WWasWT
Middleton, Ray 1907–1984 .... WWT–17
Midgley, Robin 1934– WWT–17
Midkiff, Dale 1959– CTFT–42
Midler, Bette 1945– CTFT–71
    Earlier sketches in CTFT–4, 11, 21, 31;
    WWT–17
Mifune, Toshiro 1920–1997 .... CTFT–5
    Obituary in CTFT–19
Migden, Chester L. 1921–....................... CTFT–11
Mignona, Andrew James
    See .... Lawrence, Andrew
Mignot, Flore .... WWasWT
Mihok, Dash 1974–................................. CTFT–69
    Earlier sketches in CTFT–20, 30
Mikhalkov, Nikita 1945– CTFT–35
Milano, Alyssa 1972– CTFT–50
    Earlier sketches in CTFT–4, 14, 24
Milch, David 1945– CTFT–52
    Earlier sketch in CTFT–24
Milchan, Arnon 1944– CTFT–51
    Earlier sketches in CTFT–12, 24
Milder, Andy.. CTFT–47
Miler, Claude
    See.. Miller, Claude
Miles, Bernard 1907–............................. WWT–17
Miles, Joanna 1940–............................... CTFT–65
    Earlier sketch in CTFT–1
Miles, Julia CTFT–12
    Earlier sketch in CTFT–1
Miles, Sarah 1941–................................. CTFT–55
    Earlier sketches in CTFT–3, 19; WWT–17
Miles, Sylvia 1932–................................ CTFT–7
    Earlier sketch in CTFT–1
Miles, Vera 1930– CTFT–5
Milford, Gene 1903–1992 .... CTFT–11
Milgrim, Lynn 1940– CTFT–1
Milhoan, Michael CTFT–38
Milian, Christina 1981–........................... CTFT–61
Milian, Tomas 1937–.............................. CTFT–35
Milicevic, Ivana 1978–............................ CTFT–45
Milio, Jim CTFT–49
Militello, Anne E. 1957– CTFT–20
    Earlier sketch in CTFT–3
Milius, John 1944– CTFT–59
    Earlier sketches in CTFT–8, 16, 27
Milkis, Edward Kenneth 1931–1996.......... CTFT–3
    Obituary in CTFT–16
Milland, Ray 1905–1986 .... CTFT–3
Millar, Douglas 1875–1943 .... WWasWT
Millar, Gertie 1879–1952 .... WWasWT
Millar, Mary.. WWT–17

Millar, Miles CTFT–75
Millar, Robins 1889–1968 .... WWasWT
Millar, Ronald 1919– WWT–17
Millard, Evelyn 1869–1941 .... WWasWT
Millard, Ursula 1901– .... WWasWT
Miller, Agnes.. WWasWT
Miller, Allan 1929–................................. CTFT–55
Miller, Ann 1919– CTFT–4
    Earlier sketch in WWT–17
Miller, Annette....................................... CTFT–32
Miller, Arthur 1915– CTFT–31
    Earlier sketches in CTFT–1, 11, 21; WWT–17
Miller, Barry 1958–................................. CTFT–40
    Earlier sketches in CTFT–2, 10, 17
Miller, Bruce CTFT–46
Miller, Buzz 1923– CTFT–1
Miller, Christa 1964–.............................. CTFT–52
    Earlier sketch in CTFT–24
Miller, Claude 1942–.............................. CTFT–56
    Earlier sketch in CTFT–26
Miller, David 1871–1933....................... WWasWT
Miller, David 1909– CTFT–2
Miller, Dennis 1953–.............................. CTFT–61
    Earlier sketches in CTFT–10, 17, 28
Miller, Dick 1928– CTFT–59
    Earlier sketches in CTFT–8, 16, 27
Miller, Gabrielle 1975– CTFT–68
Miller, George 1945– CTFT–68
    Earlier sketches in CTFT–7, 15, 67
Miller, Gilbert Heron 1884–1969 .... WWasWT
Miller, Haley CTFT–32
Miller, Harry M. 1934–........................... WWT–17
Miller, Henry 1860–1926 .... WWasWT
Miller, Hugh (Lorimer) 1889–?.............. WWasWT
Miller, J. P. 1919–................................... CTFT–7
Miller, Jason
    See .... Patric, Jason
Miller, Jason 1939–................................. CTFT–33
    Earlier sketches in CTFT–4; WWT–17
Miller, Joan 1910–1988 .... CTFT–7
    Earlier sketch in WWT–17
Miller, Joel McKinnon CTFT–78
    Earlier sketch in CTFT–34
Miller, Jonny Lee 1972– CTFT–51
    Earlier sketch in CTFT–24
Miller, Jonathan 1934–........................... CTFT–49
    Earlier sketches in CTFT–5, 12, 23; WWT–17
Miller, June 1934–.................................. CTFT–4
Miller, Kristen 1977–.............................. CTFT–73
Miller, Larry 1953– CTFT–76
    Earlier sketch in CTFT–33
Miller, Marilynn 1898–1936.................. WWasWT
Miller, Mark Jeffrey 1953–...................... CTFT–63
Miller, Martin (Rudolf) 1899–1969 .... WWasWT
Miller, Matt K. CTFT–48
Miller, Maxine CTFT–40
Miller, Nolan 1935– CTFT–8
Miller, Paul c. 1949– CTFT–49
Miller, Penelope Ann 1964–.................... CTFT–59
    Earlier sketches in CTFT–2, 10, 17, 27
Miller, Richard 1930–............................. CTFT–3
Miller, Robert Ellis 1932– CTFT–12
Miller, Ruby 1889–1976........................ WWasWT
Miller, Sherry CTFT–61
Miller, Sienna 1981– CTFT–70
Miller, Stephen E. CTFT–62
Miller, Susan 1944–................................ CTFT–1
Miller, Tangi 1974– CTFT–58
Miller, Thomas L. 1940–......................... CTFT–3
Miller, Troy CTFT–70
Miller, Wade
    See........................... Wade, Robert (Allison)
Miller, Walter C. CTFT–50

Miller, Wentworth 1972–........................... CTFT–70
Millett, Maude 1867–1920 .... WWasWT
Millett, Tim 1954–.................................. CTFT–2
Millian, Andra CTFT–5
Millican, Jane 1902– .... WWasWT
Milliet, Paul 1858–?............................. WWasWT
Milligan, Spike 1918–............................ CTFT–36
　　Earlier sketches in CTFT–6; WWT–17
Milligan, Tuck.. CTFT–1
Millington, Rodney 1905–1990.............. WWT–17
Millo, Aprile 1958–............................... CTFT–13
Mills, A. J. 1872–?................................ WWasWT
Mills, Alley 1951–.................................. CTFT–61
　　Earlier sketches in CTFT–10, 17, 28
Mills, Mrs. Clifford ?–1933 .... WWasWT
Mills, Donna 1945(?)–............................ CTFT–72
　　Earlier sketches in CTFT–3, 19, 32
Mills, Florence 1901–........................... WWasWT
Mills, Frank 1870–1921 .... WWasWT
Mills, Hayley 1946–............................... CTFT–71
　　Earlier sketches in CTFT–3, 19, 31; WWT–17
Mills, Horace 1864–1941 .... WWasWT
Mills, John 1908–.................................. CTFT–43
　　Earlier sketches in CTFT–11, 21; WWT–17
Mills, Judson 1969–............................... CTFT–77
　　Earlier sketch in CTFT–34
Mills, Juliet 1941– CTFT–31
　　Earlier sketches in CTFT–3, 19; WWT–17
Mills, Keith
　　See .... Torme, Tracy
Millward 1861–1932 .... WWasWT
Milne, Alan Alexander 1882–1956........ WWasWT
Milne, Paula 1947–............................... CTFT–30
Milner, Martin 1931–.............................. CTFT–7
Milner, Ron 1938–................................ CTFT–10
Milo, Candi CTFT–41
Milos, Sofia CTFT–70
Milsome, Douglas CTFT–56
Milstead, Harris Glenn
　　See.. Divine
Miltern, John E. 1870–1937.................. WWasWT
Milton, Billy 1905–1989........................ WWasWT
Milton, David Scott 1934– CTFT–1
Milton, Ernest 1890–1974 .... WWasWT
Milton, Harry 1900–1965 .... WWasWT
Milton, Maud 1859–1945 .... WWasWT
Milton, Robert ?–1956 .... WWasWT
Milward, Dawson 1870–1926 .... WWasWT
Milward, Kristin CTFT–5
Mimieux, Yvette 1944–........................... CTFT–5
Mina, Mina E... CTFT–56
Minear, Tim 1963–................................ CTFT–49
Mineo, John 1942–.................................. CTFT–2
Mineo, Sal 1939–1976 .... CTFT–2
Miner, Jan 1917–.................................... CTFT–4
　　Earlier sketch in WWT–17
Miner, Rachel 1980–.............................. CTFT–76
Miner, Steve 1951–................................ CTFT–36
　　Earlier sketch in CTFT–9
Miner, Worthington C. 1900–1982 .... WWasWT
Minetti, Maria....................................... WWasWT
Mingenbach, Louise CTFT–65
Minghella, Anthony 1954–..................... CTFT–61
　　Earlier sketches in CTFT–10, 17, 28
Ming–Na 1963– CTFT–45
Minil, Renee du 1868–? .... WWasWT
Mink, Charlotte 1975– CTFT–59
Minkoff, Rob CTFT–28
Minkus, Barbara 1943–........................... CTFT–1
Minnelli, Liza 1946–............................. CTFT–59
　　Earlier sketches in CTFT–1, 8, 16, 27;
　　WWT–17
Minnelli, Vincente 1903–1986 .... CTFT–1

Minney, Rubeigh James 1895– .... WWasWT
Minnillo, Vanessa 1980–........................ CTFT–65
Minogue, Kylie 1968–............................ CTFT–40
Minor, Bob CTFT–54
Minor, Jerry 1969–................................ CTFT–64
Minsky, Charles CTFT–57
Minster, Jack 1901–1966 .... WWasWT
Minter, Kristin 1967(?)–......................... CTFT–53
　　Earlier sketch in CTFT–25
Minter, Mary Miles 1902– .... WWasWT
Minto, Dorothy 1891–........................... WWasWT
Miou–Miou 1950– CTFT–39
　　Earlier sketches in CTFT–8, 16
Miramova, Elena .... WWasWT
Miranda, Michael A. CTFT–64
Miranda, Robert CTFT–74
Mirande, Yves .... WWasWT
Mirbeau, Octave 1848–1917 .... WWasWT
Mirisch, Walter 1921–.............................. CTFT–8
Mirman, Brad 1953–............................. CTFT–57
Mirojnick, Ellen 1949– CTFT–43
　　Earlier sketches in CTFT–11, 21
Mirren, Helen 1945(?)– CTFT–61
　　Earlier sketches in CTFT–2, 10, 17, 28;
　　WWT–17
Mischer, Don... CTFT–1
Misiano, Chris CTFT–56
Mr. T 1952–.. CTFT–50
　　Earlier sketches in CTFT–5, 24
Mistinguett 1875–1956.......................... WWasWT
Mitchelhill, J. P. 1879–1966 .... WWasWT
Mitchell, Adrian 1932–.......................... CTFT–12
Mitchell, Andrea 1946–.......................... CTFT–41
Mitchell, Arthur 1934–.......................... CTFT–12
Mitchell, Beverly 1981– CTFT–67
　　Earlier sketch in CTFT–30
Mitchell, Brian Stokes 1957(?)– CTFT–45
　　Earlier sketch in CTFT–22
Mitchell, Cameron 1918–1994................. CTFT–5
　　Obituary in CTFT–13
Mitchell, Daryl "Chill" 1969– CTFT–70
　　Earlier sketches in CTFT–19, 31
Mitchell, David 1932–............................. CTFT–4
　　Earlier sketch in WWT–17
Mitchell, Dodson 1868–1939................ WWasWT
Mitchell, Donna CTFT–68
Mitchell, Elizabeth 1970–...................... CTFT–51
Mitchell, Elizabeth Maresal
　　See .... Banks, Elizabeth
Mitchell, Grant 1874–1957 .... WWasWT
Mitchell, Gregory 1951– CTFT–8
Mitchell, Herb CTFT–62
Mitchell, Iain CTFT–34
Mitchell, James 1920–............................. CTFT–1
Mitchell, Jerry CTFT–40
Mitchell, Jim CTFT–63
　　Earlier sketch in CTFT–28
Mitchell, John H. 1918–1988.................. CTFT–4
Mitchell, Julian 1935–............................. CTFT–1
Mitchell, Julien 1888–1954 .... WWasWT
Mitchell, Katie 1964–............................ CTFT–15
Mitchell, Keith
　　See.. Coogan, Keith
Mitchell, Kel 1978(?)– CTFT–5124
　　Earlier sketch in CTFT–24
Mitchell, Langdon Elwyn 1862–1935 .... WWasWT
Mitchell, Lauren 1957–............................ CTFT–1
Mitchell, Martha.................................... CTFT–42
Mitchell, Pat 1943–............................... CTFT–24
Mitchell, Radha 1973–........................... CTFT–67
　　Earlier sketch in CTFT–30
Mitchell, Ruth 1919–............................. WWT–17

Mitchell, Sasha 1967–........................... CTFT–38
　　Earlier sketch in CTFT–15
Mitchell, Shareen CTFT–34
Mitchell, Silas Weir CTFT–78
　　Earlier sketch in CTFT–34
Mitchell, Stephen 1907– WWT–17
Mitchell, Thomas 1895–1962 .... WWasWT
Mitchell, Warren 1926–......................... CTFT–33
　　Earlier sketches in CTFT–2; WWT–17
Mitchell, Yvonne 1925–1979 .... WWT–16
Mitchenson, Joe.................................... WWT–17
Mitchum, Robert 1917–1997 .... CTFT–3
　　Obituary in CTFT–18
Mitra, Rhona 1976–............................... CTFT–71
　　Earlier sketch in CTFT–32
Mitzi–Dalty, Mlle. .... WWasWT
Miyazaki, Hayao 1941–.......................... CTFT–35
Miyori, Kim CTFT–38
　　Earlier sketches in CTFT–8, 15
Mizrahi, Isaac 1961–.............................. CTFT–67
　　Earlier sketch in CTFT–30
Mladeck, Kyra CTFT–33
Mobley, Mary Ann 1939(?)–................... CTFT–19
　　Earlier sketch in CTFT–3
Mochrie, Volin 1957–............................ CTFT–35
Mocky, Jean–Pierre 1929–...................... CTFT–35
Moder, Julia
　　See .... Roberts, Julia
Modine, Matthew 1959–........................ CTFT–45
　　Earlier sketches in CTFT–6, 13, 22
　　Brief Entry in CTFT–2
Moeller, Philip 1880–1958 .... WWasWT
Moeller, Ralph 1959–............................ CTFT–45
Moffat, Donald 1930–............................ CTFT–51
　　Earlier sketches in CTFT–4, 14, 24; WWT–17
Moffat, Graham 1866–1951 .... WWasWT
Moffat, Mrs. Graham 1873–1943 .... WWasWT
Moffat, Kate .... WWasWT
Moffat, Margaret 1882–1942 .... WWasWT
Moffat, Winifred 1899– .... WWasWT
Moffatt, Alice 1890–............................. WWasWT
Moffatt, John 1922–................................ CTFT–6
　　Earlier sketch in WWT–17
Moffatt, Joyce Anne 1936–.................... CTFT–12
Moffet, Harold 1892–1938 .... WWasWT
Moffett, D. W. 1954–............................. CTFT–51
　　Earlier sketches in CTFT–1, 24
Mohan, Peter CTFT–41
Mohr, Jay 1970–.................................... CTFT–69
　　Earlier sketches in CTFT–20, 31
Mohyeddin, Zia 1933–........................... WWT–17
Moiseiwitsch, Tanya 1914– WWT–17
Mokae, Zakes 1935–.............................. CTFT–53
　　Earlier sketches in CTFT–2, 7
Moko, L. E.
　　See .... Shaye, Robert
Mokri, Amir 1956(?)– CTFT–38
　　Earlier sketch in CTFT–15
Mol, Gretchen 1972–............................. CTFT–51
　　Earlier sketch in CTFT–24
Molen, Gerald R. 1935–......................... CTFT–38
Molesworth, Ida ?–1951 .... WWasWT
Molin, James
　　See .... Molina, Jacinto
Molina, Alfred 1953– CTFT–44
　　Earlier sketches in CTFT–8, 15
Molina, Armando CTFT–53
Molina, Jacinto 1934–........................... CTFT–35
Molina, Rolando 1971–.......................... CTFT–66
　　Earlier sketch in CTFT–29
Molinaro, Al 1919–................................. CTFT–8
Molinaro, Edouard 1928–....................... CTFT–33
　　Earlier sketch in CTFT–8

Moll, Richard 1943– CTFT–45
   Earlier sketches in CTFT–4, 15
Molla, Jordi 1968– CTFT–67
   Earlier sketch in CTFT–30
Mollen, Jenny 1979– CTFT–70
Mollin, Fred.............................. CTFT–42
Mollin, Larry.............................. CTFT–40
Mollison, Clifford 1897–1986 .... WWT–17
Mollison, Henry 1905– .... WWasWT
Mollison, William 1893–1955 .... WWasWT
Mollo, John 1931– CTFT–48
   Earlier sketches in CTFT–12, 23
Molloy, Dearbhla.............................. CTFT–35
Molnar, Ferencz 1878–1952 .... WWasWT
Molnar, Robert 1927– CTFT–1
Moloney, Janel 1969– CTFT–73
   Earlier sketch in CTFT–32
Moloney, Paddy 1938– CTFT–20
Moloney, Robert.............................. CTFT–59
Molva, David
   See .... Molina, Jacinto
Molyneux, Eileen 1893–1962 .... WWasWT
Momoa, Jason 1979– CTFT–70
Momsen, Taylor 1993– CTFT–70
Monaghan, Cameron 1993– CTFT–74
Monaghan, Dominic 1976– CTFT–43
Monaghan, Michelle 1977– CTFT–63
Monash, Paul 1917– CTFT–33
   Earlier sketch in CTFT–5
Monck, Nugent 1877–1958.................. WWasWT
Monckton, Lionel 1862–1924 .... WWasWT
Moncrieff, Gladys 1893– .... WWasWT
Mondy, Bill CTFT–63
Monet, Daniella 1989– CTFT–79
Monette, Richard 1944– CTFT–21
Monger, Christopher 1950– CTFT–38
   Earlier sketch in CTFT–15
Mo'nique
   See .... Imes–Jackson, Mo'Nique
Monk, Debra 1949– CTFT–43
   Earlier sketch in CTFT–21
Monk, Isabell 1952– CTFT–42
   Earlier sketches in CTFT–2, 20
Monk, Meredith 1942– CTFT–31
   Earlier sketches in CTFT–3, 19
Monkhouse, Allan 1858–1936 .... WWasWT
Monkman, Phyllis 1892– .... WWasWT
Monks, Michael.............................. CTFT–56
Monna–Delza, Mdlle. ?–1921 .... WWasWT
Monoson, Lawrence 1964– CTFT–72
Monroe, Marilyn 1926–1962 .... CTFT–19
Monroe, Meredith 1977– CTFT–43
Monroe, Steve CTFT–54
Montagu, Elizabeth 1909– .... WWasWT
Montague, Bertram 1892– .... WWasWT
Montague, Charles Edward
   1867–1928 .... WWasWT
Montague, Harold 1874–? .... WWasWT
Montague, Lee 1927– CTFT–7
   Earlier sketch in WWT–17
Montalban, Ricardo 1920– CTFT–41
   Earlier sketches in CTFT–3, 19
Montand, Yves 1921–1991 .... CTFT–6
   Obituary in CTFT–10
Montefiore, David 1944– CTFT–3
Montefiore, Eade 1866–1944 .... WWasWT
Montesi, Jorge CTFT–45
Montevecchi, Liliane 1933– CTFT–50
   Earlier sketch in CTFT–11
Montgomery, Anthony CTFT–55
Montgomery, Belinda J. 1950– CTFT–40
   Earlier sketches in CTFT–10, 17
Montgomery, Douglass 1909–1966 .... WWasWT

Montgomery, Earl 1921–1987 .... WWT–17
Montgomery, Elizabeth 1902– WWT–17
Montgomery, Elizabeth 1933–1995 .... CTFT–14
   Earlier sketch in CTFT–3
Montgomery, James 1882–1966 .... WWasWT
Montgomery, Poppy 1972(?)– CTFT–48
Montgomery, Robert 1903–1981 .... WWasWT
Montgomery, Robert 1946– CTFT–1
Montgommery, David Craig
   1870–1917 .... WWasWT
Monticello, Roberto 1954– CTFT–35
   Earlier sketch in CTFT–5
Montrose, Muriel .... WWasWT
Monty Python
   See .... Chapman, Graham
   See .... Cleese, John
   See .... Gilliam, Terry
   See .... Idle, Eric
   See .... Jones, Terry
   See .... Palin, Michael
Monty, Gloria 1921(?)– CTFT–53
   Earlier sketches in CTFT–10, 17
Moody, Lynne.............................. CTFT–49
Moody, Ron 1924– CTFT–41
   Earlier sketches in CTFT–2, 8, 19; WWT–17
Moon, Amy CTFT–70
Moon, Lilakoi
   See .... Bonet, Lisa
Moon, Liliquois
   See .... Bonet, Lisa
Moon, Philip CTFT–41
Moonblood, Q.
   See.............................. Stallone, Sylvester
Mooney, Debra 1947– CTFT–77
   Earlier sketches in CTFT–4, 34
Mooney, William 1936– CTFT–1
Moor, Bill 1931– CTFT–1
Moor, Cherie
   See.............................. Ladd, Cheryl
Moore, A. P. 1906– .... WWasWT
Moore, Alvy 1925–1997 .... CTFT–9
   Obituary in CTFT–17
Moore, Amanda
   See.............................. Moore, Mandy
Moore, Brian 1921–1999 .... CTFT–25
Moore, Cameron 1972– CTFT–65
Moore, Carrie 1883–1956 .... WWasWT
Moore, Cherie
   See.............................. Ladd, Cheryl
Moore, Christina 1973– CTFT–68
Moore, Christopher 1952– CTFT–1
Moore, Christopher Liam.............................. CTFT–53
Moore, Decima 1871–1964 .... WWasWT
Moore, Demi 1962– CTFT–66
   Earlier sketches in CTFT–3, 10, 17, 29
   Brief Entry in CTFT–2
Moore, Dudley 1935–2002 .... CTFT–27
   Obituary in CTFT–49
   Earlier sketches in CTFT–1, 8, 16; WWT–17
Moore, Edward James 1935– CTFT–10
Moore, Eva 1870–1955 .... WWasWT
Moore, Florence 1886–1935 .... WWasWT
Moore, Frank CTFT–40
Moore, George 1852–1933 .... WWasWT
Moore, Grace 1901–1947 .... WWasWT
Moore, Hilda ?–1926 .... WWasWT
Moore, Juanita 1922(?)– CTFT–64
Moore, Judith 1944– CTFT–1
Moore, Julianne 1960– CTFT–58
   Earlier sketches in CTFT–16, 27
Moore, Kim 1956– CTFT–20
   Earlier sketch in CTFT–2

Moore, Lisa Bronwyn CTFT–78
   Earlier sketch in CTFT–34
Moore, Mandy 1984– CTFT–65
Moore, Mary 1861–1931 .... WWasWT
Moore, Mary Tyler 1937(?)– CTFT–51
   Earlier sketches in CTFT–2, 6, 14, 24
Moore, Maureen 1952– CTFT–1
Moore, Melba 1945– CTFT–4
Moore, Michael 1954– CTFT–50
   Earlier sketches in CTFT–14, 24
Moore, Robert 1927–1984 .... CTFT–2
   Earlier sketch in WWT–17
Moore, Roger 1927– CTFT–59
   Earlier sketches in CTFT–5, 17, 27
Moore, Ronald D. CTFT–49
Moore, Sheila 1938– CTFT–56
Moore, Shemar 1970– CTFT–67
   Earlier sketch in CTFT–30
Moore, Sonia 1902– CTFT–2
Moore, Stephen 1937– CTFT–37
   Earlier sketches in CTFT–6, 13; WWT–17
Moore, Tom 1943– CTFT–37
   Earlier sketches in CTFT–1, 13
Moore, Victor Frederick 1876–1962 ...... WWasWT
Moorehead, Agnes 1906–1974 .... WWT–16
Moorer, Lana
   See.............................. MC Lyte
Moorer, Lisa "MC Lyte"
   See.............................. MC Lyte
Moorhouse, Jocelyn 1960– CTFT–50
   Earlier sketch in CTFT–16
Moosekian, Duke CTFT–65
Moosekian, Vahan CTFT–41
Mora, Tiriel 1958– CTFT–63
Morahan, Christopher Thomas
   1929– CTFT–13
   Earlier sketches in CTFT–2, 6; WWT–17
Morales, Esai 1962– CTFT–40
   Earlier sketches in CTFT–10, 17
   Brief Entry in CTFT–5
Moran, Julie 1962– CTFT–68
Moran, Lois 1907–1990 .... WWasWT
Moran, Michael CTFT–70
Moran, Nick 1969– CTFT–73
   Earlier sketch in CTFT–33
Moran, Rob 1963– CTFT–67
   Earlier sketch in CTFT–30
Morand, Eugene 1855–1930 .... WWasWT
Morand, Marcellue Raymond
   1860–1922 .... WWasWT
Moranis, Rick 1954– CTFT–39
   Earlier sketches in CTFT–7, 14
Morant, Angela CTFT–35
Mordente, Tony 1933(?)– CTFT–55
More, Julian 1928– CTFT–6
More, Kenneth 1914–1982 .... WWT–17
More, Unity 1894– .... WWasWT
Moreau, Emile 1852–? .... WWasWT
Moreau, Jeanne 1928– CTFT–63
   Earlier sketches in CTFT–8, 16, 28
Moreau, Marguerite 1977– CTFT–45
Morehart, Deborah
   See.............................. Tylo, Hunter
Morehouse, Ward 1899–1966 .... WWasWT
Morell, Andre 1909–1978 .... WWT–16
Moreno, Rita 1931– CTFT–50
   Earlier sketches in CTFT–1, 3, 14, 24;
   WWT–17
Moreton, Ursula 1903– .... WWasWT
Moretti, Nanni 1953– CTFT–28
   Earlier sketch in CTFT–17
Morey, Charles 1947– CTFT–1
Morfogen, George 1933– CTFT–58

Morgan, Charles Langbridge
1894–1958 .... WWasWT
Morgan, Claudia 1912–1974 .... WWasWT
Morgan, Debbi 1956– CTFT–67
Earlier sketch in CTFT–30
Morgan, Diana 1910– WWT–17
Morgan, Donald M. 1942– CTFT–36
Earlier sketch in CTFT–11
Morgan, Frank 1890–1949 .... WWasWT
Morgan, Gareth 1940– CTFT–5
Earlier sketch in WWT–17
Morgan, Glen 1961– CTFT–56
Morgan, Harry 1915– CTFT–56
Earlier sketch in CTFT–3, 20
Morgan, Helen 1900–1941 .... WWasWT
Morgan, Jaye P. 1931– CTFT–79
Morgan, Jeffrey Dean 1966– CTFT–79
Morgan, Joan 1905– WWT–17
Morgan, Ralph 1888–1956 .... WWasWT
Morgan, Roger 1938– WWT–17
Morgan, Sydney 1885–1931 .... WWasWT
Morgan, Trevor 1986– CTFT–59
Earlier sketch in CTFT–27
Morgenstern, S.
See .... Goldman, William
Morgenstern, Stephanie 1965– CTFT–35
Morgenstern, Susan 1954– CTFT–5
Moriarty, Cathy 1960– CTFT–63
Earlier sketches in CTFT–10, 17, 28
Moriarty, Michael 1941– CTFT–44
Earlier sketches in CTFT–1, 4, 13, 22;
WWT–17
Moriarty, P. H. 1939– CTFT–73
Earlier sketch in CTFT–33
Morison, Patricia 1915– .... WWasWT
Morissette, Alanis 1974– CTFT–61
Earlier sketch in CTFT–28
Morita, Pat 1932(?)–2005 .... CTFT–30
Obituary in CTFT–67
Earlier sketches in CTFT–3, 19
Moritz, Neal H. 1959(?)– CTFT–45
Earlier sketch in CTFT–22
Moriyasu, Atsushi 1956– CTFT–1
Morlay, Gaby 1896–1964 .... WWasWT
Morley, Christopher CTFT–5
Earlier sketch in WWT–17
Morley, Malcolm 1890–1966 .... WWasWT
Morley, Robert 1908–1992 .... CTFT–7
Obituary in CTFT–11
Earlier sketch in WWT–17
Morley, Ruth 1926(?)–1991 .... CTFT–11
Morley, Sheridan 1941– WWT–17
Mornel, Ted 1936– CTFT–2
Moroder, Giorgio 1940– CTFT–49
Earlier sketch in CTFT–10
Morosco, Oliver 1876–1945 .... WWasWT
Morricone, Ennio 1928– CTFT–59
Earlier sketches in CTFT–7, 16, 27
Morris, Aldyth 1901– CTFT–1
Morris, Anita 1943–1994 .... CTFT–8
Obituary in CTFT–13
Morris, Chester 1901–1970 .... WWasWT
Morris, Clara 1846–1925 .... WWasWT
Morris, Edmund 1912–1998 .... CTFT–1
Obituary in CTFT–24
Morris, Garrett 1937– CTFT–60
Earlier sketches in CTFT–8, 16, 27
Morris, Greg 1933–1996 .... CTFT–25
Morris, Haviland 1959– CTFT–42
Earlier sketch in CTFT–20
Morris, Howard 1919– CTFT–42
Morris, Jane CTFT–60
Earlier sketch in CTFT–27

Morris, Joan 1943– CTFT–1
Morris, John 1926– CTFT–1
Morris, Kathryn CTFT–38
Morris, Margaret 1891– .... WWasWT
Morris, Mary 1895–1970 .... WWasWT
Morris, Mary 1915–1988 .... CTFT–8
Earlier sketch WWT–17
Morris, McKay 1891–1955 .... WWasWT
Morris, Michael
See .... Wayne, John
Morris, Oswald 1915– CTFT–10
Morris, Phil 1958(?)– CTFT–42
Morris, Phyllis 1894– WWT–17
Morris, Steveland
See .... Wonder, Stevie
Morris, William 1861–1936 .... WWasWT
Morrisey, Bob CTFT–58
Morrison, Ann 1956– CTFT–2
Morrison, Bill 1940– CTFT–12
Morrison, Duke
See .... Wayne, John
Morrison, George E. 1860–1938 .... WWasWT
Morrison, Hobe 1904– WWT–17
Morrison, Jack 1887–1948 .... WWasWT
Morrison, Jack 1912– WWT–17
Morrison, James 1954– CTFT–35
Morrison, Jennifer 1979– CTFT–79
Morrison, Shelley 1936– CTFT–73
Earlier sketch in CTFT–33
Morrison, Steve 1947– CTFT–10
Morrison, Temuera 1961– CTFT–37
Morrissey, David 1964– CTFT–61
Earlier sketch in CTFT–28
Morrissey, Neil 1962– CTFT–35
Morrissey, Paul 1939– CTFT–8
Morritt, Charles 1860–? .... WWasWT
Morrow, Barry 1948– CTFT–50
Earlier sketch in CTFT–11
Morrow, Doretta 1928–1968 .... WWasWT
Morrow, Karen 1936– CTFT–20
Morrow, Kirby 1973– CTFT–46
Morrow, Mari CTFT–41
Morrow, Max 1991– CTFT–76
Morrow, Rob 1962– CTFT–59
Earlier sketches in CTFT–10, 17, 27
Morrow, Vic 1931–1982 .... CTFT–2
Morse, Barry 1919– .... WWasWT
Morse, David 1953– CTFT–45
Earlier sketches in CTFT–7, 15
Morse, Robert 1931– CTFT–40
Earlier sketches in CTFT–7, 15; WWT–17
Morshower, Glenn 1959– CTFT–38
Mortensen, Viggo 1958– CTFT–70
Earlier sketches in CTFT–21, 31
Mortimer, Charles 1885–1964 .... WWasWT
Mortimer, Emily 1971– CTFT–78
Earlier sketch in CTFT–34
Mortimer, John 1923– CTFT–39
Earlier sketches in CTFT–9, 16; WWT–17
Mortlock, Charles Bernard
1888–1967 .... WWasWT
Morton, Amy CTFT–32
Morton, Arthur 1908– CTFT–5
Morton, Billy 1958– CTFT–67
Earlier sketch in CTFT–30
Morton, Clive 1904–1975 .... WWasWT
Morton, Edward ?–1922 .... WWasWT
Morton, Hugh
See .... McLellan, C. M. S.
Morton, Joe 1947– CTFT–45
Earlier sketches in CTFT–7, 15
Morton, Leon 1912– .... WWasWT
Morton, Martha 1870–1925 .... WWasWT

Morton, Michael ?–1931 .... WWasWT
Morton, Rob
See .... Demme, Jonathan
Morton, Samantha 1977– CTFT–67
Earlier sketch in CTFT–30
Morton, William C.
See .... Morton, Billy
Moscovitch, Maurice 1871–1940 .... WWasWT
Moscow, David 1974– CTFT–78
Earlier sketch in CTFT–35
Moseley, Bill 1951– CTFT–58
Mosely, Mark CTFT–69
Moses, Burke 1959(?)– CTFT–55
Moses, Charles Alexander
1923– CTFT–3
Moses, Gilbert III 1942–1995 .... CTFT–5
Obituary in CTFT–14
Earlier sketch in WWT–17
Moses, Mark 1958– CTFT–41
Moses, Montrose J. 1878–1934 .... WWasWT
Moses, Senta 1973– CTFT–57
Moses, William R. 1959– CTFT–50
Earlier sketch in CTFT–24
Mosheim, Grete 1907– .... WWasWT
Mosher, Gregory 1949– CTFT–51
Earlier sketches in CTFT–14, 24
Moshinsky, Elijah 1946– CTFT–48
Earlier sketch in CTFT–13
Mosier, Scott CTFT–44
Earlier sketch in CTFT–22
Mosley, Roger E. 1938(?)– CTFT–48
Mosley, Walter 1952– CTFT–28
Moss, Arnold 1910–1989 .... CTFT–10
Earlier sketch in WWT–17
Moss, Carrie–Ann 1967(?)– CTFT–56
Earlier sketch in CTFT–26
Moss, Elisabeth 1983– CTFT–48
Moss, (Horace) Edward 1854–? .... WWasWT
Moss, Jeffrey B. 1945– CTFT–4
Moss, Jesse CTFT–78
Moss, Paige CTFT–59
Moss, Tegan 1985– CTFT–76
Moss, W. Keith 1892–1935 .... WWasWT
Mosse, Spencer 1945– CTFT–12
Earlier sketch in CTFT–1
Mossetti, Carlotta 1890–? .... WWasWT
Most, Don 1953– CTFT–76
Earlier sketches in CTFT–7, 34
Mostel, Josh 1946– CTFT–61
Earlier sketches in CTFT–1, 8, 16, 28
Mostel, Zero 1915–1977 .... WWT–17
Mothersbaugh, Mark 1950– CTFT–44
Earlier sketch in CTFT–14
Motley WWT–17
Motta, Bess CTFT–4
Mouezy–Eon, Andre 1880–? .... WWasWT
Mouillot, Gertrude ?–1961 .... WWasWT
Moulan, Frank 1875–1939 .... WWasWT
Mould, Raymond Wesley 1905– .... WWasWT
Moulton, Robert 1922– CTFT–1
Mounet, Jean Paul 1847–1922 .... WWasWT
Mounet–Sully, Jean 1841–1916 .... WWasWT
Mount, Anson 1973– CTFT–63
Mount, Peggy 1916– WWT–17
Mount, Thom 1948– CTFT–53
Earlier sketch in CTFT–10
Mowat, David 1943– CTFT–11
Mowling, Panou
See .... Panou
Mowry, Tahj 1987– CTFT–56
Mowry, Tamera 1978– CTFT–56
Mowry, Tia 1978– CTFT–56
Moxley, Gina CTFT–34

Moya, Natalie 1900– .... WWasWT
Moyer, Stephen 1971– CTFT–76
    Earlier sketch in CTFT–34
Moyers, Bill 1934– CTFT–45
    Earlier sketches in CTFT–7, 15
Mozart, George 1864–1947 .... WWasWT
Mrozek, Slawomir 1930– WWT–17
Mudd, Roger 1928– CTFT–5
Mudgeon, Apeman
    See .... Mitchell, Adrian
Mudie, Leonard 1884–1965 .... WWasWT
Mueller, Maureen CTFT–59
Mueller, Robby 1940– CTFT–48
Muellerleile, Marianne 1948– CTFT–78
    Earlier sketches in CTFT–7, 35
Mueller–Stahl, Armin 1930– CTFT–70
    Earlier sketches in CTFT–11, 21, 31
Muhney, Michael 1975– CTFT–74
Mui, Eddie CTFT–64
Muir, Jean 1911– .... WWasWT
Muirhead, Oliver CTFT–59
Mukhamedov, Irek 1960– CTFT–15
Mula, Frank CTFT–15
Mulcaster, G. H. 1891–1964 .... WWasWT
Muldaur, Diana 1938– CTFT–19
    Earlier sketch in CTFT–8
Muldoon, Patrick 1968(?)– CTFT–48
Muldoon, Richard
    See .... Beaver, Jim
Muldoon, Roland 1941– WWT–17
Muldowney, Dominic 1952– CTFT–37
    Earlier sketch in CTFT–13
Mulgrew, Kate 1955– CTFT–66
    Earlier sketches in CTFT–1, 10, 17, 29
Mulhare, Edward 1923–1997 .... CTFT–10
    Obituary in CTFT–17
Mulheren, Michael CTFT–78
    Earlier sketch in CTFT–35
Mulhern, Matt 1960– CTFT–42
    Earlier sketches in CTFT–2, 20
Mulholland, J. B. 1858–1925 .... WWasWT
Mulkey, Chris 1948– CTFT–47
Mull, Martin 1943– CTFT–52
    Earlier sketches in CTFT–3, 15, 25
Mullally, Megan 1958– CTFT–51
    Earlier sketch in CTFT–24
Mullan, Peter 1960– CTFT–67
    Earlier sketch in CTFT–30
Mullavey, Greg 1939– CTFT–40
    Earlier sketches in CTFT–7, 15
Mullen, Barbara 1914–1979 .... WWT–17
Mullen, Larry, Jr. 1961– CTFT–40
Mulligan, Richard 1932– CTFT–13
    Earlier sketches in CTFT–4; WWT–17
Mulligan, Robert 1925– CTFT–17
    Earlier sketch in CTFT–10
Mulligan, Terry David 1942– CTFT–66
Mullowney, Debrah
    See .... Farentino, Debrah
Mulroney, Dermot 1963– CTFT–45
    Earlier sketches in CTFT–13, 22
Mulrooney, Kelsey 1987– CTFT–71
Mumy, Bill 1954– CTFT–66
    Earlier sketches in CTFT–8, 18, 29
Mundin, Herbert 1898–1939 .... WWasWT
Mundt, Karl
    See .... Goodman, John
Mundy, Meg CTFT–1
    Earlier sketch in WWasWT
Mune, Ian 1941– CTFT–43
Muni, Paul 1895–1967 .... WWasWT
Muniz, Frankie 1985– CTFT–67
    Earlier sketch in CTFT–30

Munns, Robert 1937– CTFT–55
Munoz, Gloria 1948– CTFT–35
Munro, C. K. 1889– .... WWasWT
Munro, Lochlyn 1966(?)– CTFT–53
    Earlier sketch in CTFT–25
Munro, Nan 1905– WWT–17
Munroe, Meredith
    See .... Monroe, Meredith
Munson, Ona 1906–1955 .... WWasWT
Munson, Warren CTFT–53
Murata, Takehiro CTFT–33
Murcell, George 1925–1998 .... WWT–17
    Obituary in CTFT–24
Murcelo, Karmin CTFT–59
Murch, Walter 1943– CTFT–42
    Earlier sketch in CTFT–9
Murdoch, Dame 1919–1999 .... CTFT–32
    Obituary in CTFT–32
Murdoch, Iris 1919– CTFT–15
Murdoch, Laurie 1958– CTFT–62
Murdoch, Richard 1907– CTFT–8
    Earlier sketch in WWT–17
Murdoch, Rupert 1931– CTFT–49
    Earlier sketches in CTFT–5, 23
Murdock, Ann 1890– .... WWasWT
Murdock, George 1930– CTFT–64
Muren, Dennis 1946– CTFT–45
    Earlier sketches in CTFT–13, 22
Murfin, Jane ?–1955 .... WWasWT
Murin, David CTFT–2
Murphy, Audie 1924–1971 .... CTFT–25
Murphy, Ben 1942(?)– CTFT–72
    Earlier sketches in CTFT–3, 19, 31
Murphy, Brianne 1938– CTFT–13
Murphy, Brittany 1977– CTFT–61
    Earlier sketch in CTFT–28
Murphy, Cillian 1976– CTFT–76
Murphy, Donn B. 1930– CTFT–4
Murphy, Donna 1958– CTFT–53
    Earlier sketch in CTFT–25
Murphy, Eddie 1961– CTFT–46
    Earlier sketches in CTFT–2, 6, 13, 22
Murphy, Fred CTFT–64
    Earlier sketch in CTFT–28
Murphy, Gerard 1956– CTFT–43
Murphy, Harry S. CTFT–71
    Earlier sketch in CTFT–32
Murphy, Jy CTFT–32
Murphy, Michael 1938– CTFT–69
    Earlier sketches in CTFT–1, 7, 19, 30
Murphy, Rosemary 1927– CTFT–34
    Earlier sketches in CTFT–7; WWT–17
Murphy, Sally CTFT–63
    Earlier sketch in CTFT–28
Murphy, Thomas 1935– CTFT–12
Murray, Abigail CTFT–61
    Earlier sketch in CTFT–28
Murray, Alma 1854–1945 .... WWasWT
Murray, Barbara 1929– WWT–17
Murray, Bill 1950– CTFT–46
    Earlier sketches in CTFT–1, 6, 13, 23
Murray, Braham 1943– WWT–17
Murray, Brian 1937– CTFT–4
    Earlier sketch in WWT–17
Murray, Brian Doyle
    See .... Doyle–Murray, Brian
Murray, Chad Michael 1981– CTFT–56
Murray, Christopher 1957– CTFT–69
Murray, Don 1929– CTFT–40
    Earlier sketches in CTFT–1, 15
Murray, Douglas ?–1936 .... WWasWT
Murray, George Gilbert Aime
    1866–1957 .... WWasWT

Murray, J. Harold 1891–1940 .... WWasWT
Murray, Joel 1963– CTFT–53
    Earlier sketches in CTFT–15, 25
Murray, Katherine
    See .... Isabelle, Katharine
Murray, Mary Gordon 1953– CTFT–1
Murray, Paul 1885–1949 .... WWasWT
Murray, Peg WWT–17
Murray, Peter 1925– .... WWasWT
Murray, Sean CTFT–41
Murray, Sharon CTFT–2
Murray, Stephen 1912– WWT–17
Murray, T. C. 1873–1959 .... WWasWT
Murtaugh, James 1942– CTFT–61
    Earlier sketch in CTFT–28
Musante, Tony 1936– CTFT–67
    Earlier sketches in CTFT–1, 7, 19, 30
Musaphia, Joseph 1935– CTFT–15
Musburger, Brent 1939– CTFT–20
Musetta
    See .... Vander, Musetta
Musgrove, Gertrude 1912– .... WWasWT
Music, Lorenzo 1937– CTFT–8
Musick, Pat CTFT–43
Musker, John CTFT–21
Musky, Jane 1954– CTFT–75
    Earlier sketches in CTFT–4, 33
Mussenden, Isis CTFT–55
Musser, Tharon 1925– CTFT–20
    Earlier sketches in CTFT–2; WWT–17
Mustillo, Louis CTFT–40
Muth, Ellen 1981– CTFT–62
Muti, Ornella 1955– CTFT–67
    Earlier sketch in CTFT–30
"My Fancy" .... WWasWT
Mya 1979(?)– CTFT–67
Myers, Dwight "Heavy D"
    See .... Heavy D
Myers, Jonathan Rhys
    See .... Rhys–Meyers, Jonathan
Myers, Kim 1966– CTFT–75
Myers, Lou 1945– CTFT–40
Myers, Mike 1963– CTFT–72
    Earlier sketches in CTFT–11, 21, 32
Myers, Paul 1917– WWT–17
Myers, Peter 1923–1978 .... WWT–16
Myers, Richard 1901– .... WWasWT
Myers, Ruth CTFT–37
    Earlier sketch in CTFT–10
Myers, Scott 1955– CTFT–40
Myers, Stanley 1933(?)–1993 .... CTFT–21
    Earlier sketch in CTFT–11
Mykytiuk, Lubomir CTFT–68
Myler, Marina
    See .... Black, Marina
Myles, Lynda CTFT–1
Myles, Sophia 1980– CTFT–70
Myrick, Daniel 1964(?)– CTFT–71
Myrin, Arden 1973– CTFT–79
Myrtil, Odette 1898–1978 .... WWasWT

N

Nabors, Jim 1933– CTFT–3
Nadel, Norman 1915– WWT–17
Nadell, Carol L. 1944– CTFT–1
Nader, Michael 1945– CTFT–19
    Earlier sketch in CTFT–8

Tambor, Jeffrey 1944–.............................CTFT–67
  Earlier sketches in CTFT–6, 19, 30
Tamburro, Charles A.............................CTFT–45
Tamiris, Helen 1905–1966 ....WWasWT
Tan, Philip 1960–.................................CTFT–62
Tan, Yen Chi
  See..Yen, Donnie
Tandy, Jessica 1909–1994 ....CTFT–7
  Obituary in CTFT–13
  Earlier sketches in CTFT–1; WWT–17
Tandy, Valerie 1921–1965 ....WWasWT
Tanguay, Eva 1878–1947 ....WWasWT
Tank, Hayden 1992– CTFT–74
Tanner, Alain 1929–.............................CTFT–36
  Earlier sketch in CTFT–8
Tanner, James T. ?–1951 ....WWasWT
Tanner, Jan
  See.....................................Felt, Jan Broberg
Tanner, Kristen
  See.....................................Darling, Jennifer
Tanner, Richard CTFT–74
Tanner, Tony 1932–..............................CTFT–6
  Earlier sketch in WWT–17
Tapert, Robert G. 1955(?)–....................CTFT–36
Taplin, Jonathan Trumbull 1947–...........CTFT–15
Tapping, Alfred B. ?–1928 ....WWasWT
Tapping, Amanda CTFT–39
Tapping, Mrs. A. B. 1852–1926.............WWasWT
Tarantino, Quentin 1963– CTFT–47
  Earlier sketches in CTFT–13, 23
Tarasova, Alla Konstantinovna
  1898–1973 ....WWasWT
Tarbet, Andrew 1971–...........................CTFT–71
Tarbuck, Barbara 1942– CTFT–55
Tariol–Bauge, Anna 1872–? ....WWasWT
Tarkington, Booth 1862–1946 ....WWasWT
Tarkovsky, Andrei 1932–1986 ....CTFT–23
Tarrach, Juergen 1960–..........................CTFT–36
Tarride, Abel 1867–?.............................WWasWT
Tarses, Jay 1939–..................................CTFT–6
Tartikoff, Brandon 1949–1997 ....CTFT–17
  Obituary in CTFT–18
  Earlier sketch in CTFT–10
  Brief Entry in CTFT–5
Tarver, Milt CTFT–58
Tasca, Jules 1938–.................................CTFT–3
Tash, Max CTFT–53
Tashman, Lilyan 1899–1934..................WWasWT
Tata, Joe E. 1936–.................................CTFT–54
Tate, Beth 1890–?.................................WWasWT
Tate, Harry 1872–1940 ....WWasWT
Tate, James W. 1875–1922 ....WWasWT
Tate, Larenz 1975–................................CTFT–44
  Earlier sketch in CTFT–22
Tate, Nick 1942– CTFT–39
Tate, Reginald 1896–1955 ....WWasWT
Tatro, Duane L. 1927–...........................CTFT–12
Tattersall, David....................................CTFT–49
  Earlier sketch in CTFT–24
Tatum, Bill 1947–..................................CTFT–4
Tatum, Bradford CTFT–60
Tauber, Richard 1891–1948 ....WWasWT
Taubman, Howard 1907– ....WWasWT
Tautou, Audrey 1976(?)–........................CTFT–77
Tavel, Ronald 1941–..............................CTFT–5
  Earlier sketch in WWT–17
Tavernier, Bertrand 1941– CTFT–79
  Earlier sketches in CTFT–7, 35
Tavoli, Luciano
  See......................................Tovoli, Luciano
Tavoularis, Dean 1932–.........................CTFT–37
  Earlier sketch in CTFT–10
Tawde, George 1883–? ....WWasWT

Taxier, Arthur.......................................CTFT–64
Tayback, Vic 1930(?)–1990.....................CTFT–9
  Earlier sketch in CTFT–3
Taylor, Bruce A. 1967–..........................CTFT–41
Taylor, Buck 1938–................................CTFT–52
  Earlier sketch in CTFT–24
Taylor, Cannonball
  See...Taylor, Dub
Taylor, Cecil P. 1929–1981 ....WWT–17
Taylor, Christine 1971–..........................CTFT–60
  Earlier sketches in CTFT–16, 27
Taylor, Clarice 1927– CTFT–7
  Earlier sketch in WWT–17
Taylor, Deems 1885–1966 ....WWasWT
Taylor, Dendrie CTFT–67
Taylor, Don 1920–1998 ....CTFT–5
  Obituary in CTFT–24
Taylor, Dub 1907–1994 ....CTFT–28
Taylor, Elizabeth 1932– CTFT–41
  Earlier sketches in CTFT–1, 7, 18
Taylor, Enid Stamp 1904–1946 ....WWasWT
Taylor, Frank Hoyt CTFT–54
Taylor, Gilbert 1914–............................CTFT–25
Taylor, Harry
  See................................Granick, Harry
Taylor, Hiram 1952–..............................CTFT–3
Taylor, Holland 1943–...........................CTFT–57
  Earlier sketches in CTFT–7, 17
Taylor, Jack 1936–.................................CTFT–69
  Earlier sketch in CTFT–30
Taylor, James Arnold 1969–...................CTFT–45
Taylor, Jeri 1938–..................................CTFT–66
  Earlier sketch in CTFT–17
Taylor, John 1960– CTFT–72
  Earlier sketch in CTFT–31
Taylor, John Russell 1935– CTFT–5
  Earlier sketch in WWT–17
Taylor, Josh CTFT–39
Taylor, Jud 1940– CTFT–12
Taylor, Laurette 1884–1946 ....WWasWT
Taylor, Lili 1967–...................................CTFT–66
  Earlier sketch in CTFT–17
Taylor, Mark L. 1954–............................CTFT–49
Taylor, Meshach 1960– CTFT–41
  Earlier sketches in CTFT–8, 18
Taylor, Myra Lucretia 1960–...................CTFT–55
  Earlier sketch in CTFT–25
Taylor, Natascha
  See...........................McElhone, Natascha
Taylor, Nellie 1894–1932 ....WWasWT
Taylor, Noah 1969–................................CTFT–44
  Earlier sketch in CTFT–22
Taylor, Noel 1917–................................WWT–17
Taylor, Pat 1918–..................................WWasWT
Taylor, Paul 1930–.................................CTFT–12
Taylor, Regina 1960–.............................CTFT–47
  Earlier sketches in CTFT–12, 23
Taylor, Renee 1935(?)– CTFT–42
  Earlier sketches in CTFT–3, 19
Taylor, Rip 1934(?)–...............................CTFT–67
  Earlier sketches in CTFT–3, 19, 30
Taylor, Robert U. 1941– CTFT–10
Taylor, Rod 1930–..................................CTFT–6
Taylor, Roderick CTFT–63
Taylor, Russi CTFT–40
Taylor, Samuel 1912–............................WWT–17
Taylor, Tamara 1970–.............................CTFT–72
Taylor, True
  See..Simon, Paul
Taylor, Valerie 1902–1988......................CTFT–8
  Earlier sketch in WWT–17
Taylor, Veronica 1978–...........................CTFT–46

Taylor, William Buchanan
  1877–? ....WWasWT
Taylor–Young, Leigh 1945(?)–.................CTFT–36
  Earlier sketch in CTFT–6
Taymor, Julie 1952(?)–...........................CTFT–43
  Earlier sketches in CTFT–1, 20
Tcherkassky, Marianna 1952–................CTFT–12
Teague, Lewis 1938(?)–..........................CTFT–40
  Earlier sketches in CTFT–7, 14
Teague, Marshall R. 1953–.....................CTFT–39
Tearle, Conway 1878–1938...................WWasWT
Tearle, Godfrey 1884–?..........................WWasWT
Teasdale, Verree 1906–1987.................WWasWT
Tedrow, Irene 1910(?)–1995 ....CTFT–2
  Obituary in CTFT–15
Teed, Jill CTFT–55
Teed, John 1911–1921 ....WWasWT
Teer, Barbara Ann 1937–.......................CTFT–1
Teichmann, Howard Miles
  1916–1987..CTFT–1
Teitel, Carol ?–1986.............................WWT–17
Teitel, Nathan 1910–.............................CTFT–6
Teitler, William 1951–............................CTFT–76
Teixeira de Mattos, Alexander Louis
  1865–1921 ....WWasWT
Telek, April 1975–.................................CTFT–62
Tell, Alma 1892–1937 ....WWasWT
Tell, Olive 1894–1951 ....WWasWT
Tellegen, Lou
  See......................................Lou–Tellegen
Teller 1948–...CTFT–55
  Earlier sketch in CTFT–26
Temime, Jany CTFT–77
Temperley, Stephen 1949–.....................CTFT–4
Tempest, Francis Adolphus Vane
  See............. Vane–Tempest, Francis Adolphus
Tempest, Marie 1864–1942 ....WWasWT
Temple, Helen 1894– ....WWasWT
Temple, Joan ?–1965 ....WWasWT
Temple, Julien 1953–............................CTFT–40
  Earlier sketch in CTFT–16
Temple, Madge ?–1943..........................WWasWT
Temple, Richard 1847–? ....WWasWT
Templeman, Simon CTFT–66
Templeton, Fay 1865–1939 ....WWasWT
Templeton, W. P. 1913–.........................WWasWT
Tench, John CTFT–66
Tennant, Andy CTFT–65
  Earlier sketch in CTFT–28
Tennant, David 1971–............................CTFT–75
  Earlier sketch in CTFT–32
Tennant, Victoria 1950(?)–......................CTFT–37
  Earlier sketches in CTFT–3, 12
Tennent Ltd., H. M. WWT–17
Tennent, Henry M. 1879–1941..............WWasWT
Tenney, Jon 1961–.................................CTFT–50
Tennon, Julius CTFT–67
Tenny, Jon 1961–..................................CTFT–24
Terajima, Susumu 1963– CTFT–36
Ter–Arutunian, Rouben 1920–................CTFT–7
  Earlier sketch in WWT–17
Tergesen, Lee 1965–..............................CTFT–58
Terlesky, John 1961–.............................CTFT–62
Terrell, Cedrik CTFT–46
  Earlier sketch in CTFT–17
Terris, Norma 1904–1989......................WWasWT
Terriss, Ellaline 1871–1971 ....WWasWT
Terriss, Tom 1874–1964 ....WWasWT
Terry, Angela
  See...Angela, June
Terry, Beatrice ....WWasWT
Terry, Edward O'Connor 1844–1912 .....WWasWT
Terry, Ellen Alice 1847–1928.................WWasWT

Terry, Ethelind 1900– .... WWasWT
Terry, Fred 1863–1933 .... WWasWT
Terry, Hazel 1918–1974 .... WWasWT
Terry, J. E. Harold 1885–1939 .... WWasWT
Terry, John CTFT–49
Terry, Kate 1844–1924 .... WWasWT
Terry, Marlon 1856–1930 .... WWasWT
Terry, Megan 1932– CTFT–5
    Earlier sketch in WWT–17
Terry, Minnie 1882–1964 .... WWasWT
Terry, Nigel 1945– CTFT–61
    Earlier sketches in CTFT–8, 16, 28
Terry, Olive 1884–1957 .... WWasWT
Terry–Thomas 1911–1990 .... CTFT–10
Terson, Peter 1932– WWT–17
Terstall, Eddy 1964– CTFT–34
Terzo, Venus 1967– CTFT–46
Tesh, John 1952– CTFT–50
    Earlier sketch in CTFT–11
Tesich, Steve 1942–1996 .... CTFT–5
    Obituary in CTFT–18
Tesori, Janine CTFT–49
Tessier, Christian 1978– CTFT–68
Testa, Mary 1955– CTFT–39
Tester, Desmond 1919– .... WWasWT
Tetley, Dorothy .... WWasWT
Tetley, Glen 1926– CTFT–12
Tetzel, Joan 1921–1977 .... WWT–16
Tewes, Lauren 1953– CTFT–1
Tewkesbury, Joan 1936– CTFT–7
Tewson, Josephine CTFT–5
Texada, Tia 1973– CTFT–67
    Earlier sketch in CTFT–30
Teyte, Maggie 1889–1976 .... WWasWT
Thacker, David 1950– CTFT–40
    Earlier sketches in CTFT–5, 13
Thaddeus, John CTFT–73
Thal, Eric 1965– CTFT–47
Thane, Elswyth .... WWasWT
Tharp, Twyla 1941– CTFT–51
    Earlier sketch in CTFT–12
Thatcher, Heather ?–1987 .... WWasWT
Thatcher, Torin 1905– .... WWasWT
Thaw, John 1942–2002 .... CTFT–36
    Obituary in CTFT–49
    Earlier sketches in CTFT–9; WWT–17
Thaxter, Phyllis 1920– WWT–17
Thayer, Brynn 1949– CTFT–39
Theaker, Deborah 1964– CTFT–74
    Earlier sketch in CTFT–33
Theilade, Nini 1915– .... WWasWT
Theiss, William Ware CTFT–9
Thelen, Jodi 1962– CTFT–8
Theriault, Janine CTFT–76
    Earlier sketch in CTFT–34
Theron, Charlize 1975– CTFT–45
    Earlier sketch in CTFT–22
Theroux, Justin 1971– CTFT–56
Thesiger, Ernest 1879–1961 .... WWasWT
Theus, BJ 1947– CTFT–13
    Earlier sketch in CTFT–3
Thewlis, David 1963– CTFT–60
    Earlier sketches in CTFT–15, 27
Thibeau, Jack CTFT–7
Thicke, Alan 1947– CTFT–52
    Earlier sketches in CTFT–6, 25
Thiessen, Tiffani–Amber 1974– CTFT–58
    Earlier sketches in CTFT–16, 27
Thigpen, Lynne 1948– CTFT–28
    Earlier sketches in CTFT–8, 16
Thigpen, Sandra 1968– CTFT–59
Thimm, Daisy .... WWasWT

Thinnes, Roy 1936(?)– CTFT–45
    Earlier sketch in CTFT–6
Thirloway, Greg 1961– CTFT–71
Thomas, A. E. 1872–1947 .... WWasWT
Thomas, Agnes .... WWasWT
Thomas, Augustus 1857–1934 .... WWasWT
Thomas, Basil 1912–1957 .... WWasWT
Thomas, Betty 1948(?)– CTFT–27
    Earlier sketches in CTFT–7, 15
Thomas, Brandon 1856–1914 .... WWasWT
Thomas, Bruce CTFT–79
Thomas, Danny 1912(?)–1991 .... CTFT–11
    Earlier sketch in CTFT–3
Thomas, Dave 1949– CTFT–40
    Earlier sketches in CTFT–6, 13
Thomas, David Jean CTFT–61
    Earlier sketch in CTFT–28
Thomas, Derek
    See .... Bogdanovich, Peter
Thomas, Dorothy 1882–? .... WWasWT
Thomas, Drew
    See .... Kramer, Steve
Thomas, Eddie Kaye 1980– CTFT–71
    Earlier sketch in CTFT–31
Thomas, Ellen CTFT–74
    Earlier sketch in CTFT–32
Thomas, Evan 1891– .... WWasWT
Thomas, Gerald 1921–1993 .... CTFT–5
    Obituary in CTFT–12
Thomas, Gerrard
    See .... Kempinski, Tom
Thomas, Gwyn 1913– WWT–17
Thomas, Heather 1957– CTFT–7
Thomas, Henry 1971– CTFT–46
    Earlier sketches in CTFT–6, 14
Thomas, Herbert 1868–? .... WWasWT
Thomas, J. Karen CTFT–70
Thomas, Jake 1990– CTFT–62
Thomas, Jay 1948– CTFT–50
    Earlier sketch in CTFT–24
Thomas, Jeremy 1949– CTFT–47
    Earlier sketches in CTFT–12, 23
Thomas, Jonathan Taylor 1981– CTFT–60
    Earlier sketches in CTFT–16, 27
Thomas, Khleo 1989– CTFT–74
Thomas, Kristin Scott 1960– CTFT–67
    Earlier sketches in CTFT–16, 30
Thomas, Marlo 1937– CTFT–45
    Earlier sketches in CTFT–3, 10, 17
Thomas, Melody
    See .... Scott, Melody Thomas
Thomas, Paul
    See .... Anderson, Paul Thomas
Thomas, Philip Michael 1949– CTFT–6
Thomas, Phyllis 1904– .... WWasWT
Thomas, Raymond Anthony CTFT–40
Thomas, Richard 1951– CTFT–43
    Earlier sketches in CTFT–1, 7, 14
Thomas, Rob 1953– CTFT–62
Thomas, Roseanne
    See .... Roseanne
Thomas, Rufus 1917– CTFT–30
Thomas, Sean Patrick 1970– CTFT–47
Thomas, Serena Scott 1961– CTFT–65
    Earlier sketch in CTFT–28
Thomas, Sharon 1946– CTFT–79
Thomas, Sian CTFT–36
Thomas, Terry
    See .... Terry–Thomas
Thomas, Thom 1941– CTFT–4
Thomas, Tony CTFT–40
    Earlier sketch in CTFT–13

Thomas, Wilson
    See .... Miller, Troy
Thomason, Harry 1940(?)– CTFT–48
    Earlier sketch in CTFT–10
Thomason, Marsha 1976– CTFT–64
Thomassin, Jeanne .... WWasWT
Thomerson, Tim CTFT–40
    Earlier sketches in CTFT–8, 36
Thompson Baker, Scott 1961(?)– CTFT–62
Thompson, Alexander M. 1861–1948 .... WWasWT
Thompson, Andrea 1959– CTFT–57
    Earlier sketch in CTFT–26
Thompson, Bobb'e J. 1996– CTFT–72
Thompson, Brian 1959– CTFT–77
    Earlier sketches in CTFT–7, 35
Thompson, Caroline 1956– CTFT–55
    Earlier sketch in CTFT–11
Thompson, Dianne
    See .... Neil, Alexandra
Thompson, Emma 1959– CTFT–36
    Earlier sketch in CTFT–11
Thompson, Eric 1929–1982 .... CTFT–21
    Earlier sketches in CTFT–6; WWT–17
Thompson, Ernest 1949(?)– CTFT–55
Thompson, Evan 1931– CTFT–5
Thompson, Frank 1920–1977 .... WWT–16
Thompson, Fred 1884–1949 .... WWasWT
Thompson, Fred Dalton 1942– CTFT–78
    Earlier sketch in CTFT–13
Thompson, Frederick W. 1872–1919 ..... WWasWT
Thompson, Gerald Marr 1856–1938 ..... WWasWT
Thompson, Hunter S. 1939– CTFT–30
Thompson, J. Lee 1914– .... WWasWT
Thompson, Jack 1940– CTFT–44
    Earlier sketches in CTFT–7, 14
Thompson, John Douglas 1964(?)– CTFT–32
Thompson, Kenan 1978– CTFT–52
    Earlier sketch in CTFT–24
Thompson, Larry A. 1944– CTFT–37
    Earlier sketch in CTFT–12
Thompson, Lea 1961– CTFT–61
    Earlier sketches in CTFT–9, 16, 28
Thompson, Mark 1957– CTFT–37
Thompson, Reece 1988– CTFT–70
Thompson, Robert 1937– CTFT–7
    Earlier sketch in CTFT–1
Thompson, Sada 1929– CTFT–4
    Earlier sketch in WWT–17
Thompson, Sarah 1979– CTFT–55
Thompson, Scott
    See .... Carrot Top
Thompson, Scott 1959– CTFT–28
    Earlier sketch in CTFT–16
Thompson, Sophie 1962– CTFT–46
    Earlier sketch in CTFT–22
Thompson, Susanna 1958– CTFT–66
    Earlier sketch in CTFT–29
Thompson, Tazewell 1954(?)– CTFT–12
Thompson, Tessa 1983– CTFT–76
Thompson, W. H. 1852–1923 .... WWasWT
Thompson, Wesley CTFT–62
Thomsen, Ulrich 1963– CTFT–61
    Earlier sketch in CTFT–28
Thomson Young, Lee
    See .... Young, Lee Thomson
Thomson, Alex 1929– CTFT–25
Thomson, Beatrix 1900–1986 .... WWasWT
Thomson, Gordon 1951– CTFT–8
Thomson, Kim 1960– CTFT–76
Thomson, Patricia Ayame CTFT–55
    Earlier sketch in CTFT–12
Thora
    See .... Birch, Thora

Thorburn, H. M. 1884–1924 .... WWasWT
Thorin, Donald R. CTFT–31
Thorlacius, Greig
  See.. Thirloway, Greg
Thorndike, (Arthur) Russell
  1885–1972 .... WWasWT
Thorndike, Eileen 1891–1954 .... WWasWT
Thorndike, Sybil 1882–1976 .... WWT–16
Thorne, Angela 1939– CTFT–55
  Earlier sketches in CTFT–3, 20
Thorne, Callie 1969– CTFT–73
  Earlier sketch in CTFT–32
Thorne, Ken 1924– CTFT–67
Thorne, Raymond 1933– CTFT–5
Thorne, Thomas 1841–1918 .... WWasWT
Thorne–Smith, Courtney 1967– CTFT–46
  Earlier sketch in CTFT–14
Thornhill, Lisa 1966– CTFT–48
Thornton, Billy Bob 1955(?)– CTFT–56
  Earlier sketch in CTFT–26
Thornton, David 1955(?)– CTFT–46
  Earlier sketch in CTFT–22
Thornton, Frank 1921– CTFT–8
  Earlier sketch in WWT–17
Thornton, John 1944– CTFT–4
Thornton, Kirk CTFT–46
Thornton, Molly
  See .... Norden, Christine
Thornton, Sigrid 1959– CTFT–39
Thorp, Joseph Peter 1873–1962 .... WWasWT
Thorpe, George 1891–1961.................... WWasWT
Thorpe, Richard 1896–1991 .... CTFT–11
Thorpe–Bates, Peggy 1914–1989 .... CTFT–9
  Earlier sketch in WWT–17
Thorson, Linda 1947– CTFT–42
  Earlier sketch in CTFT–9
Threlfall, David 1953– CTFT–78
  Earlier sketches in CTFT–9, 35
Throckmorton, Cleon 1897–1965.......... WWasWT
Throne, Malachi 1928– CTFT–63
  Earlier sketch in CTFT–8
Throne, Zachary 1967– CTFT–79
Thrush, Michelle 1967– CTFT–68
  Earlier sketch in CTFT–17
Thuillier, Emilio .... WWasWT
Thulin, Ingrid 1929–................................ CTFT–9
Thun, Nancy 1952– CTFT–4
Thurburn, Gwynneth 1899– WWT–16
Thurm, Joel CTFT–33
  Earlier sketch in CTFT–2
Thurman, Uma 1970– CTFT–10
Thurston, Ernest Temple 1879–1933...... WWasWT
Thurston, Todd 1956– CTFT–3
Thyne, T. J. 1976(?)–.............................. CTFT–68
Tibbett, Lawrence 1896–1960 .... WWasWT
Tich, Little 1868–? .... WWasWT
Tichenor, Dylan 1968–............................ CTFT–64
  Earlier sketch in CTFT–28
Tickle, Frank 1893–1955 .... WWasWT
Tickner, French CTFT–64
Ticotin, Rachel 1958– CTFT–38
  Earlier sketch in CTFT–10
Tidmarsh, Vivian 1896–1941 .... WWasWT
Tidy, Frank.. CTFT–57
Tidyman, Ernest 1928–1984 .... CTFT–31
Tiefenbach, Dov 1981–........................... CTFT–69
Tiercelin, Louis 1849–? .... WWasWT
Tiernan, Andrew CTFT–42
Tierney, Gene 1920–1991 .... CTFT–11
Tierney, Harry 1894–1965 .... WWasWT
Tierney, Larry 1919–............................... CTFT–6
Tierney, Malcolm..................................... CTFT–67

Tierney, Maura 1965–............................. CTFT–71
  Earlier sketches in CTFT–21, 32
Tiffe, Angelo CTFT–64
Tigar, Kenneth 1942–............................. CTFT–45
  Earlier sketch in CTFT–8
Tiger, Derry
  See.. Ellison, Harlan
Tighe, Kevin 1944–................................ CTFT–40
  Earlier sketches in CTFT–7, 14
Tilbury, Zeffie 1863–1950..................... WWasWT
Till, Eric 1929–..................................... CTFT–40
  Earlier sketch in CTFT–14
Tilley, Vesta 1864–1952 .... WWasWT
Tillinger, John 1939–.............................. CTFT–14
  Earlier sketch in CTFT–5
Tilly, Jennifer 1958(?)–........................... CTFT–60
  Earlier sketches in CTFT–15, 27
Tilly, Meg 1960–.................................... CTFT–15
  Earlier sketch in CTFT–7
  Brief Entry in CTFT–2
Tilton, Charlene 1958– CTFT–74
  Earlier sketches in CTFT–8, 33
Tilton, James F. 1937–1998 .... CTFT–30
  Earlier sketches in CTFT–2, 19; WWT–17
Timberlake, Justin 1981–........................ CTFT–49
Timbrook, Corbin CTFT–57
Timothy, Christopher 1940– CTFT–4
  Earlier sketch in CTFT–1
Tinker, Grant 1926–................................ CTFT–5
Tinker, Jack 1938–................................. WWT–17
Tinker, Mark 1951– CTFT–50
  Earlier sketch in CTFT–11
Tinney, Frank 1878–1940 .... WWasWT
Tiplady, Brittany 1991–........................... CTFT–36
Tippet, Wayne CTFT–48
Tippo, Patti CTFT–77
Tipton, Jennifer 1937–............................ CTFT–43
  Earlier sketch in CTFT–9
Tirelli, Jaime CTFT–79
Tisch, Lawrence 1923–............................ CTFT–5
Tisch, Steve 1949– CTFT–45
  Earlier sketches in CTFT–3, 14
Tisdale, Ashley 1985–............................ CTFT–71
Titheradge 1889–1934........................... WWasWT
Titheradge, George S. 1848–1916 .... WWasWT
Titheradge, Madge 1887–1961 .... WWasWT
Titmus, Phyllis 1900–1946 .... WWasWT
Titterton, William Richard
  1876–1963 .... WWasWT
Titus, Christopher 1966(?)–..................... CTFT–64
To, Ho Fung
  See .... Doyle, Christopher
Toback, James 1944–.............................. CTFT–75
  Earlier sketches in CTFT–7, 33
Tobeck, Joel 1971–................................ CTFT–36
Tobin, Genevieve 1902– .... WWasWT
Tobin, Vivian 1904– .... WWasWT
Tobolowsky, Stephen 1951– CTFT–44
  Earlier sketch in CTFT–14
Tochi, Brian 1964–................................. CTFT–49
Tockar, Lee CTFT–46
Todd, Ann... WWT–17
Todd, Beverly 1946– CTFT–8
Todd, Hallie 1962– CTFT–49
Todd, J. Garrett .... WWasWT
Todd, Michael 1907–1958..................... WWasWT
Todd, Richard 1919–.............................. CTFT–55
  Earlier sketches in CTFT–3, 20; WWT–17
Todd, Tony 1952–................................... CTFT–37
Todoroff, Tom 1957–.............................. CTFT–66
Togo, Jonathan 1977–............................ CTFT–71
Toguri, David... CTFT–7
  Earlier sketch in WWT–17

Toibin, Niall CTFT–30
Toji, Marcus 1984–................................ CTFT–76
Tokofsky, Jerry H. 1936–......................... CTFT–12
Tolan, Michael 1925– CTFT–1
Tolan, Peter 1958– CTFT–55
  Earlier sketch in CTFT–26
Toland, Gregg 1904–1948...................... CTFT–28
Toler, Sidney 1874–1947 .... WWasWT
Toles–Bey, John CTFT–43
Tolkan, James 1931– CTFT–65
  Earlier sketches in CTFT–8, 16, 28
Tolkin, Michael L. 1950–......................... CTFT–57
  Earlier sketches in CTFT–12, 23
Tolkin, Stephen 1954(?)– CTFT–56
Toll, John CTFT–52
  Earlier sketch in CTFT–24
Toller, Ernst 1893–1939 .... WWasWT
Toller, Rosalie 1885–? .... WWasWT
Tollin, Michael 1956(?)–......................... CTFT–77
Tolsky, Susan 1943–.............................. CTFT–76
Tom, David 1978–.................................. CTFT–64
Tom, Heather 1975–.............................. CTFT–62
Tom, Lauren 1961(?)–............................ CTFT–69
  Earlier sketches in CTFT–2, 19, 30
Tom, Steve 1953–.................................. CTFT–72
Tomei, Concetta 1945– CTFT–52
  Earlier sketch in CTFT–24
Tomei, Marisa 1964–.............................. CTFT–46
  Earlier sketches in CTFT–12, 23
Tomita, Tamlyn 1966– CTFT–45
  Earlier sketches in CTFT–10, 17
Tomlin, Blanche 1889–? .... WWasWT
Tomlin, Lily 1939(?)–.............................. CTFT–50
  Earlier sketches in CTFT–2, 6, 13, 24
Tomlinson, David 1917– WWT–17
Tompkins, Angel CTFT–8
Tompkins, Paul F. 1968– CTFT–64
Toms, Carl 1927– CTFT–13
  Earlier sketches in CTFT–6; WWT–17
Tondo, Jerry CTFT–72
Tone, Franchot 1906–1968.................... WWasWT
Tone–Loc 1966(?)– CTFT–41
Toner, Thomas 1928– CTFT–4
Tong, Jacqueline 1951– CTFT–78
  Earlier sketches in CTFT–7, 35
Tonge, Philip 1892–1959........................ WWasWT
Toolan, Rebecca CTFT–36
Toone, Geoffrey 1910–........................... WWT–17
Tootoosis, Gordon CTFT–45
  Earlier sketch in CTFT–17
Toplyn, Joe 1953– CTFT–77
Topol 1935–.. CTFT–49
  Earlier sketch in CTFT–9
Toporkov, Vasily Osipovich
  1889–? .... WWasWT
Tork, Peter 1942– CTFT–47
  Earlier sketch in CTFT–23
Torme, Mel 1925–1999 .... CTFT–24
Torme, Tracy CTFT–72
Tormey, John CTFT–78
  Earlier sketch in CTFT–35
Torn, Angelica 1965(?)–.......................... CTFT–71
  Earlier sketch in CTFT–32
Torn, Rip 1931–..................................... CTFT–61
  Earlier sketches in CTFT–4, 16, 28; WWT–17
Torrence, David 1870–?.......................... WWasWT
Torrence, Ernest 1878–1933 .... WWasWT
Torres, Gina 1969–................................. CTFT–79
  Earlier sketch in CTFT–36
Torres, Liz 1947–................................... CTFT–37
Torry, Guy... CTFT–55
  Earlier sketch in CTFT–25
Torti, Robert 1961–................................ CTFT–45

Toser, David... CTFT–1
Toth, Lazlo
    See... Novello, Don
Totheroh, Dan 1894–............................... WWasWT
Touissaint, Lorraine 1960–....................... CTFT–45
Toumanova, Tamara 1917–...................... WWasWT
Tours, Frank E. 1877–1963 .... WWasWT
Tousey, Sheila CTFT–76
    Earlier sketch in CTFT–34
Toussaint, Beth 1962– CTFT–70
Toutain, Blanche ?–1932 .... WWasWT
Tovah, Mageina 1979–............................. CTFT–64
Tovoli, Luciano CTFT–65
    Earlier sketch in CTFT–28
Towb, Harry 1925– WWT–17
Towers, Constance 1934–......................... CTFT–78
    Earlier sketches in CTFT–3, 20; WWT–17
Towers, Harry P. 1873–? .... WWasWT
Towers, Jonathan CTFT–51
Towles, Tom 1950– CTFT–59
Towne, Katharine CTFT–28
Towne, Robert 1934– CTFT–65
    Earlier sketches in CTFT–8, 16, 28
Towner, John
    See... Williams, John
Townsend, Robert 1957–.......................... CTFT–40
    Earlier sketches in CTFT–3, 13
Townsend, Stanley CTFT–36
Townsend, Stuart 1972– CTFT–64
Townsend, Sue 1946– CTFT–10
Townsend, Tammy 1970–.......................... CTFT–45
Toye, Geoffrey Edward 1889–1942 .... WWasWT
Toye, Wendy 1917– WWT–17
Toyne, Gabriel 1905–1963 .... WWasWT
Toynton, Ian CTFT–40
Toyokawa, Etsushi 1962– CTFT–36
Tracey, Ian 1964–..................................... CTFT–39
Trachtenberg, Michelle 1985– CTFT–43
Tracy, John 1938–..................................... CTFT–7
Tracy, Keegan Connor 1971–.................... CTFT–67
Tracy, Lee 1898–1968............................. WWasWT
Tracy, Spencer 1900–1967....................... WWasWT
Tracy, Steve 1952–1986 .... CTFT–4
Traill, Peter 1896–1968 .... WWasWT
Trainor, Mary Ellen CTFT–46
    Earlier sketch in CTFT–17
Trammell, Sam 1971–............................... CTFT–49
    Earlier sketch in CTFT–24
Trarieux, Gabriel 1870–? .... WWasWT
Traube, Shepard 1907–1983.................... WWT–17
Traux, Sarah... WWT–6
Travanti, Daniel J. 1940–......................... CTFT–49
    Earlier sketches in CTFT–3, 13
Travers, Ben 1886–1980.......................... WWT–17
Travers, Henry 1874–1965 .... WWasWT
Travers, Linden 1913– .... WWasWT
Travilla, William 1920–1990 .... CTFT–11
Travis, Greg CTFT–41
Travis, Nancy 1961–................................. CTFT–36
    Earlier sketch in CTFT–11
Travis, Randy 1959– CTFT–68
    Earlier sketch in CTFT–30
Travis, Stacey CTFT–37
Travolta, Ellen 1940–............................... CTFT–46
Travolta, Joey 1952–................................ CTFT–46
Travolta, John 1954– CTFT–45
    Earlier sketches in CTFT–2, 13, 22
Travolta, Margaret.................................... CTFT–43
Traylor, Susan CTFT–64
Treacher, Bill 1936–................................. CTFT–37
    Earlier sketch in CTFT–12
Treat, Martin 1950–................................. CTFT–4
Trebek, Alex 1940– CTFT–42

Treble, Sepha .... WWasWT
Trebor, Robert 1953–............................... CTFT–64
Treckman, Emma 1909– .... WWasWT
Tree, David 1915–.................................... WWasWT
Tree, Herbert Beerbohm 1853–1917 ..... WWasWT
Tree, Lady 1863–1937 .... WWasWT
Tree, Viola 1884–1938 .... WWasWT
Trejo, Danny 1944–.................................. CTFT–68
    Earlier sketch in CTFT–30
Tremblett, Ken 1965– CTFT–55
Trench, Herbert 1865–1923.................... WWasWT
Trenholme, Helen 1911–1962 .... WWasWT
Trent, Bruce WWT–16
Trentini, Emma 1885?–1959 .... WWasWT
Tresahar, John ?–1936 .... WWasWT
Trese, Adam 1969–................................... CTFT–52
    Earlier sketch in CTFT–25
Tresmand, Ivy 1898– .... WWasWT
Treveiler, Robert C. CTFT–52
Trevelyan, Hilda 1880–1959 .... WWasWT
Treville, Roger 1903–.............................. WWasWT
Trevino, Jesus Salvador 1946–................. CTFT–46
    Earlier sketch in CTFT–14
Trevor, Ann 1918–1970 .... WWasWT
Trevor, Austin 1897–............................... WWasWT
Trevor, Claire 1909–................................ CTFT–9
    Earlier sketch in WWasWT
Trevor, Leo ?–1927.................................. WWasWT
Trevor, Norman 1877–1945..................... WWasWT
Trewin, John Courtenay 1908–1990 .... WWT–17
Treyz, Russell 1940–................................. CTFT–1
Trickey, Paula 1966– CTFT–59
Trifunovich, Neil CTFT–48
Trigger, Sarah CTFT–29
Trikonis, Gus CTFT–23
Trilling, Ossia 1913– WWT–17
Trinder, Tommy 1909–............................. WWT–17
Trintignant, Jean–Louis 1930–................. WWT–17
    Earlier sketch in CTFT–9
Tripp, Paul 1916–.................................... CTFT–2
Tripplehorn, Jeanne 1963– CTFT–60
    Earlier sketches in CTFT–15, 27
Triska, Jan CTFT–37
Troell, Jan 1931–..................................... CTFT–34
    Earlier sketch in CTFT–8
Troisi, Massimo 1953–1994..................... CTFT–17
Troll, Kitty 1950–..................................... CTFT–4
Tromaville Historian
    See... Kaufman, Lloyd
Troobnick, Eugene 1926–......................... CTFT–5
    Earlier sketch in WWT–17
Troost, Ernest CTFT–48
Trott, Karen CTFT–6
Troughton, David 1950–........................... CTFT–71
    Earlier sketch in CTFT–32
Trouncer, Cecil 1898–1953 .... WWasWT
Troutman, Ivy 1883–1979 .... WWasWT
Troy, Louise WWT–17
Troyer, Verne 1969– CTFT–69
    Earlier sketch in CTFT–31
Truax, Sarah 1877–? .... WWasWT
Trucco, Michael 1970–............................. CTFT–48
Trudeau, Garry 1948– CTFT–7
Trudell, John 1946–................................. CTFT–46
    Earlier sketch in CTFT–17
True, Jim CTFT–32
True, Rachel 1966– CTFT–69
    Earlier sketch in CTFT–30
True–Frost, Jim CTFT–71
Trueman, Paula 1907–.............................. WWT–17
Truesdale, Yanic 1970–............................ CTFT–71
Truex, Ernest 1889–1973 .... WWasWT
Truffaut, Francois 1932–1984 .... CTFT–2

Truffier, Jules 1856–? .... WWasWT
Trujillo, Raoul 1955–............................... CTFT–56
Truman, Tim CTFT–43
Trumbull, Douglas 1942–......................... CTFT–10
Trump, Marla Maples
    See... Maples, Marla
Trussell, Fred 1858–1923 .... WWasWT
Trussler, Simon 1942–.............................. CTFT–5
    Earlier sketch in WWT–17
Tryon, Thomas 1926–1991 .... CTFT–5
    Obituary in CTFT–10
Tsai Ming–liang 1957– CTFT–58
    Earlier sketch in CTFT–27
Tsao, Andrew.. CTFT–51
Tse, Elaine CTFT–52
Tsypin, George 1954–.............................. CTFT–10
Tubau, Maria .... WWasWT
Tubb, Barry 1963–.................................... CTFT–63
Tubiola, Nicole 1978–............................. CTFT–77
Tucci, Christine... CTFT–64
Tucci, Maria CTFT–1
    Earlier sketch in WWT–17
Tucci, Michael 1950(?)– CTFT–41
    Earlier sketches in CTFT–7, 18
Tucci, Stanley 1960– CTFT–60
    Earlier sketches in CTFT–16, 27
Tuchner, Michael 1934– CTFT–55
    Earlier sketch in CTFT–12
Tuck, Hilary 1978–................................... CTFT–74
Tuck, Jessica 1963– CTFT–75
    Earlier sketch in CTFT–33
Tucker, Chris 1972–.................................. CTFT–47
    Earlier sketch in CTFT–23
Tucker, Forrest 1919–1986 .... CTFT–4
    Earlier sketch in CTFT–3
Tucker, Jonathan 1982–............................ CTFT–57
Tucker, Lael
    See............................. Wertenbaker, Timberlake
Tucker, Michael 1944–............................. CTFT–69
    Earlier sketches in CTFT–6, 20, 30
Tucker, Nana
    See... Visitor, Nana
Tucker, Sophie 1884–1966 .... WWasWT
Tucker, Tia Nicole
    See... Texada, Tia
Tudor, Anthony 1909–1987 .... WWasWT
Tudor, Valerie 1910–............................... WWasWT
Tufnel, Nigel
    See... Guest, Christopher
Tuggle, Richard 1948–............................. CTFT–4
Tulean, Ingrid
    See... Thulin, Ingrid
Tull, Patrick 1941– CTFT–8
    Earlier sketch in CTFT–2
Tullio Giordana, Marco 1950– CTFT–36
Tully, George F. 1876–1930...................... WWasWT
Tully, Richard Walton 1877–1945 .... WWasWT
Tumarin, Boris 1910–1979 .... WWT–17
Tunbridge, Joseph A. 1886–1961 .... WWasWT
Tune, Tommy 1939–................................. CTFT–51
    Earlier sketches in CTFT–1, 7, 14; WWT–17
Tung, Jennifer 1973– CTFT–42
Tunie, Tamara 1959–................................ CTFT–45
Tunney, Robin 1972(?)–........................... CTFT–49
    Earlier sketch in CTFT–24
Tupou, Manu CTFT–5
    Earlier sketch in WWT–17
Tupper, Reg 1947–................................... CTFT–77
Tupu, Lani John 1964–............................. CTFT–45
Turco, Paige 1969(?)–............................... CTFT–47
    Earlier sketch in CTFT–23
Turell, Saul 1920–1986 .... CTFT–3
Turleigh, Veronica 1903–1971............... WWasWT

Turman, Glynn 1946(?)– CTFT–36
    Earlier sketch in CTFT–11
Turman, Lawrence 1926– CTFT–10
    Earlier sketch in CTFT–1
Turnbull, John 1880–1956 .... WWasWT
Turnbull, Stanley ?–1924 .... WWasWT
Turner, Alfred 1870–1941 .... WWasWT
Turner, Barbara CTFT–56
Turner, Bree 1977– CTFT–45
Turner, Bridget 1939– CTFT–72
    Earlier sketches in CTFT–5, 32; WWT–17
Turner, David 1927– WWT–17
Turner, Dorothy 1895–1969 .... WWasWT
Turner, Douglas
    See .... Ward, Douglas Turner
Turner, Frank C. 1951– CTFT–56
Turner, Harold 1909–1962 .... WWasWT
Turner, Janine 1962– CTFT–41
    Earlier sketches in CTFT–10, 17
Turner, John Hastings 1892–1956 .... WWasWT
Turner, Karri 1966– CTFT–76
Turner, Kathleen 1954– CTFT–50
    Earlier sketches in CTFT–5, 12, 24
Turner, L. Godfrey
    See .... Godfrey–Turner, L.
Turner, Michael 1921– WWT–17
Turner, Ted 1938– CTFT–55
    Earlier sketches in CTFT–5, 25
Turner, Tina 1939– CTFT–40
    Earlier sketch in CTFT–14
Turner, Tyrin 1971– CTFT–74
Turner–Thompson, Bobb'e J.
    See .... Thompson, Bobb'e J.
Turrin, Joseph 1947– CTFT–11
Turton, Kett 1982– CTFT–69
    Earlier sketch in CTFT–31
Turturice, Robert CTFT–49
Turturro, Aida 1962– CTFT–49
Turturro, John 1957– CTFT–61
    Earlier sketches in CTFT–9, 16, 28
Turturro, Nicholas 1962– CTFT–45
    Earlier sketch in CTFT–17
Tushingham, Rita 1940(?)– CTFT–76
    Earlier sketches in CTFT–7, 34; WWT–17
Tutin, Dorothy 1930– CTFT–26
    Earlier sketches in CTFT–5, 15; WWT–17
Twain, Norman 1930– CTFT–1
Tweed, Shannon 1957– CTFT–51
    Earlier sketch in CTFT–24
Twiggy 1949– CTFT–69
    Earlier sketch in CTFT–3
Twohy, David N. 1955– CTFT–63
    Earlier sketches in CTFT–16, 28
Tyars, Frank 1848–1918 .... WWasWT
Tydings, Alexandra 1972– CTFT–37
Tykwer, Tom 1965– CTFT–68
    Earlier sketch in CTFT–30
Tyler, Aisha 1970– CTFT–68
Tyler, Brian CTFT–63
Tyler, George Crouse 1867–1946 .... WWasWT
Tyler, James Michael 1962– CTFT–76
Tyler, Liv 1977– CTFT–63
    Earlier sketches in CTFT–16, 28
Tyler, Odette 1869–1936 .... WWasWT
Tyler, Steven 1948– CTFT–42
Tylo, Hunter 1962– CTFT–57
    Earlier sketch in CTFT–21
Tylo, Michael 1948– CTFT–66
Tylor, Jack
    See .... Taylor, Jack
Tynan, Brandon 1879–1967 .... WWasWT
Tynan, Kenneth 1927–1980 .... WWT–17
Tynan, Tracy CTFT–57

Tyne, T. J.
    See .... Thyne, T. J.
Tyner, Charles 1925– CTFT–8
Tyrrell, Susan 1946– CTFT–33
    Earlier sketch in CTFT–6
Tyson, Barbara 1964– CTFT–71
Tyson, Cicely 1933– CTFT–69
    Earlier sketches in CTFT–1, 20, 31; WWT–17
Tyson, Richard 1961– CTFT–37
Tyzack, Margaret 1931– CTFT–38
    Earlier sketches in CTFT–10; WWT–17

U

Ubach, Alanna 1975– CTFT–52
Udenio, Fabiana 1964– CTFT–45
Udy, Helene 1962(?)– CTFT–57
Uggams, Leslie 1943– CTFT–63
    Earlier sketch in CTFT–6
Uhry, Alfred 1936– CTFT–52
    Earlier sketch in CTFT–10
Ulliel, Gaspard 1984– CTFT–76
Ullman, Ricky 1986– CTFT–74
Ullman, Tracey 1959– CTFT–36
    Earlier sketch in CTFT–9
    Brief Entry in CTFT–4
Ullmann, Liv 1939– CTFT–44
    Earlier sketches in CTFT–1, 3, 20
Ullrick, Sharon 1947– CTFT–2
Ulmar, Geraldine 1862–1932 .... WWasWT
Ulric, Lenore 1892–1970 .... WWasWT
Ulrich, Bob
    See .... Urich, Robert
Ulrich, Kim Johnston 1955(?)– CTFT–58
Ulrich, Skeet 1969(?)– CTFT–40
    Earlier sketch in CTFT–17
Umberger, Andy CTFT–59
Undertaker, The
    See .... Callaway, Mark
Underwood, Blair 1964– CTFT–77
    Earlier sketches in CTFT–9, 35
Underwood, Jay 1968– CTFT–71
Underwood, Ron 1953– CTFT–60
    Earlier sketch in CTFT–27
Unger, Deborah 1953– CTFT–3
Unger, Deborah Kara 1966– CTFT–69
    Earlier sketches in CTFT–20, 30
Unger, Gladys B. 1885–1940 .... WWasWT
Unger, Joe CTFT–54
Unger, Michael CTFT–60
Union, Gabrielle 1972– CTFT–74
    Earlier sketch in CTFT–33
Unkrich, Lee CTFT–28
Unsworth, Geoffrey 1914–1978 .... CTFT–25
Upbin, Shari 1941– CTFT–3
Upton, Leonard 1901– .... WWasWT
Urban, Karl 1972– CTFT–66
Urbaniak, James 1963– CTFT–56
Ure, Mary 1933–1975 .... WWasWT
Urich, Robert 1946–2002 .... CTFT–31
    Obituary in CTFT–49
    Earlier sketches in CTFT–3, 12, 20
Urioste, Frank J. CTFT–37
    Earlier sketch in CTFT–12
Urla, Joe CTFT–45
Urquhart, Molly .... WWasWT
Urquhart, Robert 1922– CTFT–9
Usher
    See .... Raymond, Usher

Ustinov, Peter 1921– CTFT–28
    Earlier sketches in CTFT–1, 8, 16; WWT–17
Utay, William CTFT–39
Utriainen, Ilona
    See .... Elkin, Ilona
Uzzaman, Badi 1939– CTFT–79
    Earlier sketch in CTFT–36

V

V, Dickie
    See .... Vitale, Dick
Vacano, Jost 1940– CTFT–28
Vaccaro, Brenda 1939– CTFT–39
    Earlier sketches in CTFT–2, 7, 15; WWT–17
Vachell, Horace Annesley
    1861–1955 .... WWasWT
Vachlioti, Denny
    See .... Aldredge, Theoni V.
Vachon, Christine 1962– CTFT–26
Vadim, Christian 1963– CTFT–36
Vadim, Roger 1928– CTFT–5
Vaidya, Daya CTFT–73
Vail, Lester 1900–1959 .... WWasWT
Vajda, Ernest 1887–1954 .... WWasWT
Vajna, Andrew 1944– CTFT–37
    Earlier sketch in CTFT–12
Valabregue, Albin .... WWasWT
Valaida .... WWasWT
Valderrama, Wilmer 1980– CTFT–68
Valdes, David 1950– CTFT–64
    Earlier sketch in CTFT–28
Valdez, Luis 1940– CTFT–5
    Earlier sketch in WWT–17
Valen, Nancy 1968(?)– CTFT–39
Valenti, Jack 1921– CTFT–52
    Earlier sketch in CTFT–12
Valentina, Rudolpho
    See .... Valentino, Rudolph
Valentine 1876–? .... WWasWT
Valentine, Grace 1884–1964 .... WWasWT
Valentine, James 1930– CTFT–12
    Earlier sketch in CTFT–1
Valentine, Karen 1947– CTFT–20
    Earlier sketch in CTFT–3
Valentine, Scott 1958– CTFT–74
    Earlier sketches in CTFT–5, 33
Valentine, Steve CTFT–45
Valentine, Sydney 1865–1919 .... WWasWT
Valentino, Rudolph 1895–1926 .... CTFT–22
Valenza, Tasia 1968– CTFT–39
Valesquez, Patricia
    See .... Velasquez, Patricia
Valk, Frederick 1901–1956 .... WWasWT
Vallance, Louise CTFT–49
Valle, Miriam Colon
    See .... Colon, Miriam
Vallelonga, Nick 1959– CTFT–58
Valletta, Amber 1974– CTFT–65
Valley, Mark 1964– CTFT–39
Valli, Valli 1882–1927 .... WWasWT
Vallone, Raf 1916– CTFT–1
Valverde, Balbina .... WWasWT
Valverde, Fernando 1951– CTFT–36
Van, Billy B. 1870–1950 .... WWasWT
Van, Bobby 1930–1980 .... WWT–17
Van Ark, Joan 1943(?)– CTFT–42
    Earlier sketches in CTFT–7, 18

Van Bargen, Daniel
  See .... Von Bargen, Daniel
Van Beers, Stanley 1911–1961 .... WWasWT
Van Biene, Auguste 1850–1913............. WWasWT
Vanbrugh, Irene 1872–1949 .... WWasWT
Vanbrugh, Prudence 1902– .... WWasWT
Vanbrugh, Violet 1867–1942 .... WWasWT
Van Buskirk, June 1882–? .... WWasWT
VanCamp, Emily 1986–........................... CTFT–74
Vance, Charles 1929–............................. CTFT–5
  Earlier sketch in WWT–17
Vance, Courtney B. 1960(?)– CTFT–66
  Earlier sketches in CTFT–8, 16, 29
Vance, Nina ?–1980 .... WWT–17
Vance, Vivian 1913–1979 .... CTFT–16
Vance–Straker, Marilyn CTFT–38
  Earlier sketch in CTFT–10
Van Cleef, Lee 1925–1989 .... CTFT–8
Van Damme, Jean–Claude
  1960– CTFT–36
  Earlier sketch in CTFT–11
Van Der Beek, James 1977– CTFT–49
  Earlier sketch in CTFT–24
Vander, Musetta 1969–........................... CTFT–73
  Earlier sketch in CTFT–33
Vander Pyl, Jean 1919(?)–1999................ CTFT–25
Vandernoot, Alexandra 1965–................. CTFT–42
Vandervoort, Laura 1984– CTFT–79
van de Sande, Theo 1947–..................... CTFT–79
Van Devere, Trish 1943– CTFT–20
  Earlier sketch in CTFT–3
Van Dien, Casper 1968–.......................... CTFT–50
  Earlier sketch in CTFT–24
Van Dien, Catherine
  See............................... Oxenberg, Catherine
Van Druten, John 1901–1957 .... WWasWT
Van Dusen, Granville R. 1944–.............. CTFT–58
Van Dyke, Barry 1951– CTFT–45
Van Dyke, Dick 1925– CTFT–50
  Earlier sketches in CTFT–3, 13, 24
Van Dyke, Jerry 1931(?)–......................... CTFT–48
  Earlier sketches in CTFT–12, 23
Van Dyke, Phillip 1984– CTFT–50
Vane, Richard CTFT–64
  Earlier sketch in CTFT–28
Vane–Tempest, Francis Adolphus
  1863–1932 .... WWasWT
Van Fleet, Jo 1922(?)–1996....................... CTFT–5
  Obituary in CTFT–16
  Earlier sketch in WWT–17
Van Fossen, Diana.................................. CTFT–24
Van Gelder, Holtropp .... WWasWT
Vangelis 1943–....................................... CTFT–57
  Earlier sketch in CTFT–21
Van Gorkum, Harry CTFT–62
Van Griethuysen, Ted 1934– CTFT–5
  Earlier sketch in WWT–17
Van Gyseghem, Andre 1906–1979......... WWT–17
Van Haren Noman, Eric CTFT–54
Van Heijningen, Mattijs 1944–................ CTFT–34
Van Heusen, Jimmy 1913–1990 .... CTFT–11
  Earlier sketch in WWT–17
Van Holt, Brian 1969–............................ CTFT–69
Van Huet, Fedja 1973–........................... CTFT–34
Van Itallie, Jean–Claude 1936–............... CTFT–3
  Earlier sketch in WWT–17
Van Kamp Merete 1961–......................... CTFT–4
Vanloo, Albert ?–1920 .... WWasWT
Vann, Marc 1954–................................... CTFT–70
Vanne, Marda ?–1970 .... WWasWT
Vanocur, Sander 1928– CTFT–23
  Earlier sketch in CTFT–12
Vanoff, Nick 1930(?)–1991 .... CTFT–10

Van Nostrand, Amy 1953–...................... CTFT–57
Van Oostrum, Kees 1963–...................... CTFT–79
Van Outen, Denise 1974–....................... CTFT–69
  Earlier sketch in CTFT–30
Van Patten, Dick 1928–.......................... CTFT–43
  Earlier sketches in CTFT–1, 20
Van Patten, James 1956–........................ CTFT–73
Van Patten, Joyce 1934–......................... CTFT–73
  Earlier sketches in CTFT–4, 33; WWT–17
Van Patten, Timothy 1959–..................... CTFT–49
Van Patten, Vincent 1957–..................... CTFT–59
Van Patton, Jimmy
  See .... Van Patten, James
Van Peebles, Mario 1957–...................... CTFT–45
  Earlier sketches in CTFT–6, 13, 22
Van Peebles, Melvin 1932–..................... CTFT–29
  Earlier sketches in CTFT–7, 18; WWT–17
Van Runkle, Theadora 1940–.................. CTFT–38
  Earlier sketch in CTFT–10
Van Sant, Gus 1952(?)– CTFT–55
  Earlier sketches in CTFT–11, 26
Van Scoyk, Robert 1928–........................ CTFT–12
Vansittart, Robert G. 1881–1957 .... WWasWT
Van Studdiford, Grace 1873–1927 .... WWasWT
Van Thal, Dennis 1909–.......................... WWasWT
Van Uchelen, Marc 1970– CTFT–36
Van Valkenburgh, Bedorah
  1952– CTFT–42
Van Volkenburg, Ellen .... WWasWT
Van Wyck, Jim....................................... CTFT–39
Van Zandt, Billy..................................... CTFT–65
  Earlier sketch in CTFT–28
Varda, Agnes 1928– CTFT–8
Vardalos, Nia 1962–............................... CTFT–48
Varden, Evelyn 1895–1958.................... WWasWT
Vare, Ethlie Ann 1953–.......................... CTFT–39
Varela, Leonor 1972–............................. CTFT–69
  Earlier sketch in CTFT–31
Varesi, Gilda 1887–?.............................. WWasWT
Vargas, Elizabeth 1963– CTFT–43
Vargas, Jacob 1970(?)–............................ CTFT–62
  Earlier sketch in CTFT–28
Vargas, John 1958–................................. CTFT–53
Vargo, Mark CTFT–62
  Earlier sketch in CTFT–28
Varnel, Marcel 1894–1947 .... WWasWT
Varney, Jim 1949– CTFT–11
Vartan, Michael 1968– CTFT–40
Vasquez, Alberto 1955– CTFT–52
Vasquez, La La 1979– CTFT–67
Vasquez, Randy 1961–............................ CTFT–42
Vassey, Liz 1972–................................... CTFT–70
  Earlier sketch in CTFT–31
Vaucaire, Maurice 1865–1918............... WWasWT
Vaughan, Greg 1973–............................. CTFT–42
Vaughan, Hilda 1898–1957.................... WWasWT
Vaughan, Peter 1923– CTFT–45
  Earlier sketch in CTFT–22
Vaughan, Stuart 1925– CTFT–5
  Earlier sketch in WWT–17
Vaughan, Susie 1853–1950 .... WWasWT
Vaughn, Ned 1964– CTFT–57
  Earlier sketch in CTFT–26
Vaughn, Robert 1932–............................ CTFT–66
  Earlier sketches in CTFT–3, 5, 18, 29
Vaughn, Vince 1970–.............................. CTFT–32
  Earlier sketches in CTFT–21
Vaugier, Emmanuelle 1976– CTFT–63
Vaz Dias, Selma 1911–........................... WWasWT
Vazak, P. H.
  See .... Towne, Robert
Vazquez, Yul CTFT–64

Vdsande
  See................................... van de Sande, Theo
Veber, Pierre 1869–1942 .... WWasWT
Vedrenne, John E. 1867–1930 .... WWasWT
Vega, Alexa 1988– CTFT–40
Vega, Jose 1920–.................................... CTFT–1
Veiller, Bayard 1869–1943 .... WWasWT
Velasquez, Patricia 1971– CTFT–69
Velez, Eddie 1958–................................. CTFT–74
  Earlier sketches in CTFT–5, 33
Velez, Lauren 1964–............................... CTFT–79
Velez, Lupe 1909–1944 .... WWasWT
VelJohnson, Reginald 1952–................... CTFT–42
  Earlier sketch in CTFT–9
Veloudos, Spiro CTFT–51
Venable, James L. CTFT–67
Venables, Bruce..................................... CTFT–36
Venables, Clare 1943–............................ CTFT–6
Venation, Bertha
  See.................................... Fierstein, Harvey
Venito, Larry CTFT–70
Venne, Lottie 1852–1928....................... WWasWT
Vennema, John C. 1948–........................ CTFT–2
Vennera, Chick 1952–............................ CTFT–67
  Earlier sketches in CTFT–7, 18, 29
Vennera, Francis CTFT–67
Venning, Una 1893–.............................. WWasWT
Venora, Diane 1952– CTFT–68
  Earlier sketches in CTFT–6, 20, 30
Ventimiglia, Milo 1977–......................... CTFT–71
Ventresca, Vincent 1965–....................... CTFT–72
Venture, Richard 1923– CTFT–64
Venuta, Benay 1911–.............................. WWT–17
Venza, Jac 1926–.................................... CTFT–38
  Earlier sketch in CTFT–12
Vera, Julia CTFT–79
Verbinski, Gore 1964(?)– CTFT–46
  Earlier sketch in CTFT–22
Verchinina, Nina.................................... WWasWT
Verdon, Gwen 1925– CTFT–20
  Earlier sketches in CTFT–3; WWT–17
Verdu, Maribel 1970–............................. CTFT–29
Vereen, Ben 1946–................................. CTFT–60
  Earlier sketches in CTFT–2, 8, 16, 27;
  WWT–17
Verga, Giovanni 1840–1922................... WWasWT
Vergara, Sofia 1972– CTFT–68
Verheyen, Mariann 1950– CTFT–1
Verhoeven, Paul 1938–........................... CTFT–40
  Earlier sketches in CTFT–8, 16
Verica, Tom 1964– CTFT–72
  Earlier sketches in CTFT–21, 32
Verklan, Laura CTFT–50
Verlaque, Robert 1955–.......................... CTFT–8
Vermilyea, Harold 1889–1958................ WWasWT
Vernacchio, Dorian 1953– CTFT–77
  Earlier sketches in CTFT–2, 34
Verneuil, Louis 1893–1952.................... WWasWT
Verno, Jerry 1895–................................. WWasWT
Vernon, Anne 1924–............................... CTFT–1
Vernon, David 1959–.............................. CTFT–2
Vernon, Frank 1875–1940 .... WWasWT
Vernon, Harriet ?–1923.......................... WWasWT
Vernon, Harry M. 1878–? .... WWasWT
Vernon, John 1932–................................ CTFT–39
  Earlier sketches in CTFT–7, 15
Vernon, Kate 1961–................................ CTFT–45
  Earlier sketch in CTFT–17
Vernon, Richard 1925–1997................... CTFT–5
  Obituary in CTFT–22
  Earlier sketch in WWT–17
Vernon, Virginia 1894–........................... WWasWT

Verona, Stephen CTFT–4
Veroni, Craig CTFT–69
Vessey, Tricia 1972– CTFT–36
Vetere, Richard 1952– CTFT–52
    Earlier sketch in CTFT–12
Vezin, Arthur 1878–? .... WWasWT
Viadas, Juan CTFT–36
Vibart, Henry 1863–1939 .... WWasWT
Vibert, Ronan CTFT–70
Vicious, Sid 1957–1979 .... CTFT–31
Vickery, John 1950– CTFT–55
    Earlier sketch in CTFT–7
Victor, Charles 1896–1965 .... WWasWT
Victor, Harry CTFT–77
Victor, Josephine 1885–? .... WWasWT
Victor, Mark CTFT–79
Victor, Paul Ben
    See .... Ben–Victor, Paul
Victoria, Vesta 1873–1951 .... WWasWT
Vida, Julian Dulce 1966– CTFT–67
Vidal, Christina 1981– CTFT–74
Vidal, Gore 1925– CTFT–20
    Earlier sketches in CTFT–3; WWT–17
Vidal, Lisa 1965– CTFT–45
    Earlier sketch in CTFT–17
Vidler, Steven 1960– CTFT–61
Vieluf, Vince 1970– CTFT–68
    Earlier sketch in CTFT–30
Vierny, Sacha 1919– CTFT–25
Viertel, Thomas 1941– CTFT–50
    Earlier sketch in CTFT–7
Vigo, Jean 1905–1934 .... CTFT–29
Vigoda, Abe 1921– CTFT–70
    Earlier sketches in CTFT–3, 20, 31
Vilar, Jean 1912–1971 .... WWasWT
Vilhelmova, Tatiana 1978– CTFT–36
Villaggio, Paolo 1932– CTFT–36
Villalobos, Reynaldo CTFT–40
Villalonga, Marthe CTFT–33
Villard, Tom 1953–1994 .... CTFT–5
    Obituary in CTFT–15
Villechaize, Herve 1943–1993 .... CTFT–5
    Obituary in CTFT–12
Villiers, James 1933–1998 .... CTFT–5
    Obituary in CTFT–21
    Earlier sketch in WWT–17
Vince, Pruitt Taylor 1960– CTFT–44
    Earlier sketch in CTFT–22
Vincent, Cerina 1979– CTFT–74
Vincent, E. Duke CTFT–42
Vincent, Frank 1939– CTFT–65
    Earlier sketch in CTFT–29
Vincent, Jan–Michael 1944– CTFT–35
    Earlier sketch in CTFT–5
Vincent, Madge 1884–? .... WWasWT
Vincent, Ruth 1877–1955 .... WWasWT
Vines, Margaret 1910– .... WWasWT
Vinovich, Steve 1945– CTFT–77
    Earlier sketches in CTFT–8, 34
Vinson, Chuck 1956– CTFT–51
Vinson, Helen 1907– .... WWasWT
Vint, Jesse CTFT–56
Vinton, Will 1947– CTFT–12
Virtue, Tom CTFT–36
Vischer, Lisa CTFT–48
Vischer, Phil 1966– CTFT–46
Visitor, Nana 1957– CTFT–41
    Earlier sketch in CTFT–17
Visnjic, Goran 1972– CTFT–73
    Earlier sketch in CTFT–32
Vitale, Dick 1939– CTFT–68
    Earlier sketch in CTFT–30

Vitamin C
    See .... Fitzpatrick, Colleen
Viterelli, Joe 1941– CTFT–56
    Earlier sketch in CTFT–26
Vivian, Anthony Crespigny Claud
    1906– .... WWasWT
Vivian–Rees, Joan .... WWasWT
Vlahos, Sam CTFT–53
Vlaming, Jeff CTFT–42
Voelpel, Fred WWT–17
Vogel, Darlene 1962– CTFT–57
Vogel, Paula A. 1951– CTFT–2
Vogel, Virgil W. CTFT–12
Vogt, Mary E. CTFT–48
Voight, Angelina Jolie
    See .... Jolie, Angelina
Voight, Jon 1938– CTFT–39
    Earlier sketches in CTFT–2, 7, 17; WWT–17
Voigts, Richard 1934– CTFT–4
Volage, Charlotte CTFT–2
Voland, Herb CTFT–6
Volantino, Rudolph
    See .... Valentino, Rudolph
Vollmer, Lula 1898–1955 .... WWasWT
Volokh, Ilia CTFT–54
Volpe, Frederick 1865–1932 .... WWasWT
Volz, Nedra CTFT–8
Von Bargen, Daniel 1950– CTFT–73
    Earlier sketches in CTFT–21, 32
von Brandenstein, Patrizia CTFT–79
    Earlier sketches in CTFT–11, 35
Von Dassanowsky, Elfi 1924– CTFT–52
    Earlier sketch in CTFT–24
von Detten, Erik 1982– CTFT–65
    Earlier sketch in CTFT–29
Von Dohlen, Lenny 1958(?)– CTFT–73
    Earlier sketches in CTFT–2, 20, 32
Von Franchenstein, Clement
    1944– CTFT–45
Von Furstenberg, Betsy 1931– CTFT–5
    Earlier sketch in WWT–17
Von Mayrhauser, Jennifer 1948– CTFT–4
Vonnegut, Kurt, Jr. 1922– CTFT–6
Von Oostrum, Kees
    See .... Van Oostrum, Kees
von Oy, Jenna 1977– CTFT–60
Von Palleske, Heidi CTFT–62
Von Scherler, Sasha 1939– CTFT–6
    Earlier sketch in WWT–17
Von Stroheim, Erich 1885–1957 .... CTFT–27
Von Sydow, Max 1929– CTFT–52
    Earlier sketches in CTFT–5, 12, 25
Von Trier, Lars 1956– CTFT–31
    Earlier sketch in CTFT–20
von Zerneck, Frank 1940– CTFT–40
    Earlier sketches in CTFT–1, 13
Voorhies, Lark 1974– CTFT–51
Voskovic, George 1905–1981 .... WWT–17
Vosloo, Arnold 1962– CTFT–56
    Earlier sketch in CTFT–26
Vosper, Frank 1899–1937 .... WWasWT
Voss, Stephanie 1936– WWT–17
Vrana, Vlasta CTFT–61
Vulich, John 1960– CTFT–50

W

Wachowski, Andy 1967– CTFT–66
    Earlier sketch in CTFT–29
Wachowski, Larry 1965– CTFT–66
    Earlier sketch in CTFT–29

Wachs, Caitlin 1989– CTFT–43
Waddell, Garry CTFT–36
Waddell, Justine 1976– CTFT–67
Waddington, Patrick 1901–1987 .... WWT–17
Wade, Adam 1935– CTFT–1
Wade, Allan 1881–1955 .... WWasWT
Wade, Robert CTFT–64
Wade, Robert (Allison) 1920– CTFT–28
Wadler, Louise
    See .... Lortel, Lucille
Wadsworth, Gil CTFT–28
Wagenhals, Lincoln A. 1869–1931 .... WWasWT
Wager, Michael 1925– CTFT–5
    Earlier sketch in WWT–17
Wages, William CTFT–43
Waggoner, Lyle 1935– CTFT–7
Wagner, Charles L. ?–1956 .... WWasWT
Wagner, Chuck 1958– CTFT–60
Wagner, Jack 1959– CTFT–73
    Earlier sketches in CTFT–21, 32
Wagner, Jane 1935– CTFT–6
Wagner, Karyn CTFT–62
    Earlier sketch in CTFT–28
Wagner, Lindsay 1949– CTFT–56
    Earlier sketches in CTFT–3, 15, 26
Wagner, Natasha Gregson
    1970– CTFT–46
Wagner, Paula 1946(?)– CTFT–74
Wagner, Robert 1930– CTFT–44
    Earlier sketches in CTFT–3, 14
Wagner, Robin 1933– CTFT–37
    Earlier sketches in CTFT–3, 11; WWT–17
Wahl, Ken 1953– CTFT–15
    Earlier sketch in CTFT–7
Wahlberg, Donnie 1969– CTFT–62
    Earlier sketch in CTFT–28
Wahlberg, Mark 1971– CTFT–71
    Earlier sketches in CTFT–21, 32
Wahlgren, Pernilla
    See .... August, Pernilla
Wai, Tony Leung Chiu 1962– CTFT–37
Wain, David 1969– CTFT–66
Wain, Edward
    See .... Towne, Robert
Wainwright, Loudon III 1946– CTFT–70
    Earlier sketch CTFT–31
Wainwright, Marie 1853–1923 .... WWasWT
Waisbren, Ben CTFT–79
Waissman, Kenneth 1940– CTFT–5
    Earlier sketch in WWT–17
Waite, Ralph 1928(?)– CTFT–40
    Earlier sketches in CTFT–1, 8, 16
Waite, Ric 1933– CTFT–39
    Earlier sketch in CTFT–13
Waites, Thomas G. CTFT–79
Waits, Tom 1949– CTFT–39
    Earlier sketches in CTFT–6, 13
Wajda, Andrzej 1926(?)– CTFT–40
    Earlier sketches in CTFT–2, 8, 16
Wakefield, Douglas 1899–1951 .... WWasWT
Wakefield, Gilbert Edward
    1892–1963 .... WWasWT
Wakefield, Hugh 1888–1971 .... WWasWT
Wakeman, Keith 1866–1933 .... WWasWT
Waker, Jeb E.
    See .... Weber, Jake
Walbrook, Anton 1900–1966 .... WWasWT
Walbrook, Henry Mackinnon
    1863–1941 .... WWasWT
Walch, Hynden 1980– CTFT–71
Walcott, Derek 1930– CTFT–13
    Earlier sketch in CTFT–6
Waldegrave, Lilias .... WWasWT

Cumulative Index

Walden, Robert 1943– CTFT–49
Walden, Stanley 1932– CTFT–2
Walden, W. G. 1951(?)– CTFT–36
   Earlier sketch in CTFT–11
Waldo, Janet 1930– CTFT–49
   Earlier sketch in CTFT–9
Waldron, Charles D. 1874–1946 .... WWasWT
Wales, William
   See .... Ambrose, David
Walford, Ann 1928– .... WWasWT
Walken, Christopher 1943– CTFT–70
   Earlier sketches in CTFT–3, 12, 20, 31;
   WWT–17
Walker, Albertina 1929– CTFT–12
Walker, Ally 1962(?)– CTFT–30
   Earlier sketch in CTFT–20
Walker, Amanda CTFT–36
Walker, Andrew Kevin 1964– CTFT–55
   Earlier sketch in CTFT–25
Walker, Andrew W. 1979– CTFT–74
Walker, Arnetia 1961– CTFT–54
Walker, Charles 1945– CTFT–50
Walker, Charlotte 1878–1958 .... WWasWT
Walker, Eamonn 1970(?)– CTFT–69
Walker, Jimmie 1947– CTFT–63
   Earlier sketch in CTFT–7
Walker, June 1904–1966 .... WWasWT
Walker, Kathryn CTFT–7
Walker, Kerry 1948– CTFT–40
Walker, Lesley CTFT–62
   Earlier sketch in CTFT–28
Walker, Liza 1971– CTFT–75
   Earlier sketch in CTFT–32
Walker, Marcy 1961– CTFT–79
Walker, Martin 1901–1955 .... WWasWT
Walker, Matthew CTFT–76
Walker, Matthew 1942– CTFT–77
Walker, Nancy 1921–1992 .... CTFT–3
   Obituary in CTFT–11
   Earlier sketch in WWT–17
Walker, Nicholas CTFT–56
Walker, Paul 1973– CTFT–62
   Earlier sketch in CTFT–28
Walker, Peggy Walton
   See .... Walton–Walker, Peggy
Walker, Polly 1908– .... WWasWT
Walker, Polly 1966– CTFT–69
   Earlier sketch in CTFT–30
Walker, Rebecca 1969– CTFT–22
Walker, Shirley 1945– CTFT–51
Walker, Stuart 1888–1941 .... WWasWT
Walker, Syd 1886–1945 .... WWasWT
Walker, Sydney 1921– WWT–17
Walker, Tonja 1960– CTFT–57
Walker, Zena 1934– CTFT–5
   Earlier sketch in WWT–17
Walkley, Arthur Bingham 1855–1926 ..... WWasWT
Wall, Harry 1886–1966 .... WWasWT
Wall, Max 1908–1990 .... WWT–17
Wallace, Chris 1947– CTFT–46
   Earlier sketch in CTFT–22
Wallace, Dee
   See .... Stone, Dee Wallace
Wallace, Edgar 1875–1932 .... WWasWT
Wallace, George 1917– CTFT–57
   Earlier sketch in CTFT–1
Wallace, George 1952– CTFT–55
Wallace, Hazel Vincent 1919– WWT–17
Wallace, Jack CTFT–77
Wallace, Lee 1930–1989 .... CTFT–7
   Earlier sketch in CTFT–1
Wallace, Marcia 1942(?)– CTFT–63
   Earlier sketch in CTFT–8

Wallace, Marie 1939– CTFT–57
Wallace, Mike 1918– CTFT–39
   Earlier sketches in CTFT–10, 17
Wallace, Nellie 1882–1948 .... WWasWT
Wallace, Ray 1881–? .... WWasWT
Wallace, Rheagan 1987– CTFT–74
Wallace, Tommy Lee CTFT–41
   Earlier sketch in CTFT–1
Wallach, Eli 1915– CTFT–66
   Earlier sketches in CTFT–1, 7, 18, 29;
   WWT–17
Wallengren, E. F. 1952– CTFT–52
   Earlier sketch in CTFT–12
Waller, David 1920– CTFT–6
   Earlier sketch in WWT–17
Waller, Edmund Lewis 1884–? .... WWasWT
Waller, Jack 1885–1957 .... WWasWT
Waller, Lewis 1860–1915 .... WWasWT
Waller, Mrs. Lewis 1862–1912 .... WWasWT
Wallgren, Pernilla
   See .... August, Pernilla
Wallin, Pamela 1943(?)– CTFT–42
Walling, Camryn 1990– CTFT–45
Wallis, Bertram 1874–1952 .... WWasWT
Wallis, Ellen Lancaster 1856–1940 .... WWasWT
Wallis, Hal 1889–1986 .... CTFT–4
Wallis, Shani 1933– .... WWasWT
Walls, Tom 1883–1949 .... WWasWT
Walmer, Cassie 1888–? .... WWasWT
Walpole, Hugh 1884–1941 .... WWasWT
Walsh, Blanche 1873–1915 .... WWasWT
Walsh, Brigid Conley
   See .... Brannagh, Brigid
Walsh, David M. CTFT–12
Walsh, Dermot 1924– CTFT–11
   Earlier sketch in CTFT–1
Walsh, Dylan 1963– CTFT–43
Walsh, Frances 1961(?)– CTFT–43
Walsh, Gwynyth CTFT–66
Walsh, J. T. 1943(?)–1998 .... CTFT–16
   Obituary in CTFT–21
   Earlier sketch in CTFT–9
Walsh, Jack CTFT–29
Walsh, James 1937– CTFT–1
Walsh, John 1945– CTFT–45
Walsh, Kate CTFT–45
Walsh, M. Emmet 1935– CTFT–41
   Earlier sketches in CTFT–7, 14
Walsh, Martin CTFT–62
   Earlier sketch in CTFT–28
Walsh, Matt 1964– CTFT–77
Walsh, Sam 1877–1920 .... WWasWT
Walston, Ray 1918(?)– CTFT–17
   Earlier sketches in CTFT–3, 10; WWT–17
Walter, Eugene 1874–1941 .... WWasWT
Walter, Harriet 1950– CTFT–73
   Earlier sketch in CTFT–32
Walter, Jessica 1941(?)– CTFT–30
   Earlier sketches in CTFT–1, 7, 18, 29
Walter, Lisa Ann 1963– CTFT–70
Walter, Olive 1898– .... WWasWT
Walter, Susan 1963– CTFT–48
Walter, Tracey 1942– CTFT–42
Walter, Wilfrid 1882–1958 .... WWasWT
Walter–Ellis, Desmond 1914– WWT–17
Walters, Barbara 1931– CTFT–55
   Earlier sketches in CTFT–6, 13, 25
Walters, Ewart James 1950– CTFT–8
Walters, Jerrie
   See .... Withers, Jane
Walters, Julie 1950– CTFT–57
   Earlier sketches in CTFT–7, 15, 26

Walters, Melora 1968– CTFT–67
   Earlier sketch in CTFT–29
Walters, Polly 1910– .... WWasWT
Walters, Thorley 1913–1991 .... CTFT–10
   Earlier sketch in WWT–17
Walthall, Romy
   See .... Windsor, Romy
Walthers, Gretchen 1938– CTFT–5
Walton, Tony 1934– CTFT–37
   Earlier sketches in CTFT–4, 12; WWT–17
Walton–Walker, Peggy CTFT–77
Walz, Ken 1942– CTFT–4
Wanamaker, Sam 1919–1993 .... CTFT–3
   Obituary in CTFT–12
   Earlier sketch in WWT–17
Wanamaker, Zoe 1949– CTFT–49
   Earlier sketch in CTFT–24
Wandmacher, Michael 1967– CTFT–73
Wandor, Michelene 1940– CTFT–12
Wang, Luoyong 1958– CTFT–46
   Earlier sketch in CTFT–22
Wang, Peter CTFT–5
Wang, Wayne 1949– CTFT–44
   Earlier sketches in CTFT–5, 14
Wanshel, Jeff 1947– CTFT–2
Waram, Percy 1881–1961 .... WWasWT
Warburton, Patrick 1964– CTFT–70
   Earlier sketches in CTFT–31
Warbux, O. D.
   See .... MacLeod, Gavin
Warchus, Matthew 1966– CTFT–52
   Earlier sketch in CTFT–24
Ward, B. J. CTFT–45
Ward, Betty .... WWasWT
Ward, Dave "Squatch" CTFT–64
Ward, David S. 1947(?)– CTFT–37
   Earlier sketches in CTFT–1, 12
Ward, Dorothy 1890–1987 .... WWasWT
Ward, Douglas Turner 1930– CTFT–4
   Earlier sketch in WWT–17
Ward, E. D.
   See .... Gorey, Edward
Ward, Elizabeth
   See .... Gracen, Elizabeth
Ward, Fannie 1872–1952 .... WWasWT
Ward, Fred 1942– CTFT–45
   Earlier sketches in CTFT–9, 16
   Brief Entry in CTFT–3
Ward, Genevieve 1837–1922 .... WWasWT
Ward, Geoffrey 1940– CTFT–39
   Earlier sketch in CTFT–13
Ward, Hugh J. 1871–1941 .... WWasWT
Ward, Jay 1920–1989 .... CTFT–8
Ward, Jim CTFT–49
Ward, Jonathan 1970– CTFT–4
Ward, Lyman 1941– CTFT–64
Ward, Mackenzie 1903– .... WWasWT
Ward, Megan 1969– CTFT–50
   Earlier sketch in CTFT–24
Ward, Penelope Dudley 1914– .... WWasWT
Ward, Polly 1909– .... WWasWT
Ward, Rachel 1957– CTFT–74
   Earlier sketches in CTFT–6, 33
Ward, Ronald 1901– .... WWasWT
Ward, Sandy CTFT–48
Ward, Sela 1956– CTFT–45
   Earlier sketch in CTFT–16
Ward, Simon 1941– CTFT–16
   Earlier sketches in CTFT–5; WWT–17
Ward, Sophie 1964– CTFT–67
   Earlier sketch in CTFT–29
Ward, Susan 1976– CTFT–72
   Earlier sketch in CTFT–31

Ward, Wally
See .... Langham, Wallace
Ward, Zack 1973(?)– CTFT–64
Warde, Frederick B. 1851–1935 .... WWasWT
Warde, Willie 1857–1943 .... WWasWT
Wardell, Brandon CTFT–60
Warden, Jack 1920–2006 .... CTFT–45
    Obituary in CTFT–73
    Earlier sketches in CTFT–1, 8, 16
Wardle, (John) Irving 1929– WWT–17
Wardwell, Geoffrey 1900–1955 .... WWasWT
Ware, Helen 1877–1939 .... WWasWT
Ware, Herta CTFT–36
Ware, John
    See.. Mabley, Edward
Wareing, Alfred 1876–1942 .... WWasWT
Wareing, Lesley 1913– .... WWasWT
Warfield, David 1866–1951 .... WWasWT
Warfield, Joe 1937– CTFT–4
Warfield, Marsha 1955(?)– CTFT–63
    Earlier sketch in CTFT–7
Waring, Barbara 1912– .... WWasWT
Waring, Dorothy May Graham
    1895– .... WWasWT
Waring, Herbert 1857–1932 .... WWasWT
Waring, Richard 1912– WWT–16
Warkol, Jordan 1987– CTFT–71
Warlock, Billy 1961– CTFT–77
Warmington, Stanley J. 1884–1941 .... WWasWT
Warner, David 1941– CTFT–71
    Earlier sketches in CTFT–5, 20, 31; WWT–17
Warner, Deborah 1959– CTFT–50
    Earlier sketch in CTFT–11
Warner, Grace 1873–1925 .... WWasWT
Warner, Henry Byron 1876–1958......... WWasWT
Warner, Julie 1965– CTFT–38
    Earlier sketch in CTFT–10
Warner, Malcolm–Jamal 1970– CTFT–38
    Earlier sketch in CTFT–10
    Brief Entry in CTFT–5
Warner, Mark.. CTFT–61
    Earlier sketch in CTFT–28
Warner, Rick CTFT–63
Warre, Michael 1922– CTFT–6
    Earlier sketch in WWT–17
Warren, Betty 1905– .... WWasWT
Warren, C. Denier 1889–1971 .... WWasWT
Warren, Diane 1956– CTFT–47
Warren, Estella 1978– CTFT–69
Warren, Jeff 1921– WWT–17
Warren, Jennifer CTFT–5
Warren, Jennifer Leigh CTFT–33
    Earlier sketch in CTFT–2
Warren, Kenneth J. 1929–1973 .... WWT–16
Warren, Kiersten CTFT–39
Warren, Lesley Ann 1946(?)– CTFT–39
    Earlier sketches in CTFT–1, 6, 13
Warren, Marcia CTFT–57
    Earlier sketch in CTFT–26
Warren, Michael 1946– CTFT–41
    Earlier sketches in CTFT–7, 18
Warren–Gibson, David CTFT–61
Warrender, Harold 1903–1953 .... WWasWT
Warrick, Ruth 1916– CTFT–3
    Earlier sketch in WWT–17
Warrilow, David 1934–1995 .... CTFT–2
    Obituary in CTFT–15
Warriner, Frederic 1916– WWT–17
Warry, Jillian
    See.. Barberie, Jillian
Warshofsky, David CTFT–62
Warwick, Dionne 1940– CTFT–50
Warwick, Ethel 1882–1951 .... WWasWT

Warwick, Robert 1878–1964 .... WWasWT
Wasco, David CTFT–63
    Earlier sketch in CTFT–28
Washbourne, Mona 1903–1988 .... CTFT–8
    Earlier sketch in WWT–17
Washington, Denzel 1954– CTFT–40
    Earlier sketches in CTFT–9, 17
    Brief Entry in CTFT–3
Washington, Isaiah 1963– CTFT–65
    Earlier sketch in CTFT–28
Washington, Kerry 1977(?)– CTFT–62
Washington, Sharon CTFT–57
Wasilewski, Audrey CTFT–60
Wasilewski, Paul CTFT–74
Wass, Ted 1952– CTFT–67
    Earlier sketches in CTFT–7, 18, 29
Wasser, Jane 1957– CTFT–7
Wasserman, Allan 1952– CTFT–62
Wasserman, Dale 1917– CTFT–5
Wasserman, Jerry CTFT–41
Wasserstein, Wendy 1950– CTFT–44
    Earlier sketches in CTFT–1, 8, 21
Wasson, Craig 1954– CTFT–42
    Earlier sketches in CTFT–8, 17
Wasson, Susanne CTFT–2
Wastaferro, John
    See.. West, Jonathan
Watanabe, Gedde 1955– CTFT–73
    Earlier sketches in CTFT–5, 32
Watari, Tetsuya 1941– CTFT–36
Waterhouse, Keith Spencer
    1929– CTFT–5
    Earlier sketch in WWT–17
Waterlow, Marjorie 1888–1921 .... WWasWT
Waterman, Dennis 1948– CTFT–6
    Earlier sketch in WWT–17
Waters, Dina
    See.. Spybey, Dina
Waters, Ethel 1900–1977 .... WWT–16
Waters, James ?–1923 .... WWasWT
Waters, Jan 1937– CTFT–5
    Earlier sketch in WWT–17
Waters, John 1946– CTFT–26
    Earlier sketch in CTFT–10
    Brief Entry in CTFT–5
Waterston, Sam 1940– CTFT–17
    Earlier sketches in CTFT–3, 10; WWT–17
Watford, Gwen 1927–1994 .... CTFT–6
    Obituary in CTFT–13
    Earlier sketch in WWT–17
Watkin, David 1925– CTFT–44
    Earlier sketches in CTFT–1, 7, 14
Watkins, Linda 1908– .... WWasWT
Watkins, Michael W. CTFT–56
Watkins, Nathan
    See... Page, Samuel
Watkins, Peter 1935– CTFT–8
Watkins, Tuc 1966– CTFT–42
Watkyn, Arthur 1907–1965 .... WWasWT
Watling, Dilys 1946– WWT–17
Watling, Jack 1923– WWT–17
Watros, Cynthia 1968– CTFT–64
Watrouse, Jesse
    See... Bradford, Jesse
Watson, Alberta 1955– CTFT–69
Watson, Barry 1974– CTFT–72
    Earlier sketch in CTFT–31
Watson, Betty Jane 1926 .... WWasWT
Watson, Douglass 1921–1989 .... CTFT–8
    Earlier sketch in WWT–17
Watson, Elizabeth ?–1931 .... WWasWT
Watson, Emily 1967– CTFT–46
    Earlier sketch in CTFT–23

Watson, Emma 1990– CTFT–67
Watson, Henrietta 1873–1964 .... WWasWT
Watson, Horace 1867–1934 .... WWasWT
Watson, John CTFT–48
Watson, Lucile 1879–1962 .... WWasWT
Watson, Malcolm 1853–1929 .... WWasWT
Watson, Margaret ?–1940 .... WWasWT
Watson, Minor 1889–1965 .... WWasWT
Watson, Moray 1928– CTFT–6
    Earlier sketch in CTFT–1
Watson, Muse 1948– CTFT–73
    Earlier sketches in CTFT–21, 32
Watson, Susan 1938– CTFT–10
Watson, Vernon 1885–1949 .... WWasWT
Watson, Wylie 1889–1966 .... WWasWT
Watson–Johnson, Vernee CTFT–48
Watt, Douglas 1914– CTFT–1
Watters, Mark CTFT–77
Wattis, Richard 1912– .... WWasWT
Watts, Dodo 1910– .... WWasWT
Watts, John
    See.. Hanson, John
Watts, Naomi 1968– CTFT–64
Watts, Richard, Jr. 1898– WWT–17
Watts, Robert 1938– CTFT–1
Watts, Rolonda 1959– CTFT–57
Watts, Stephen 1910– WWT–17
Watts–Phillips, John Edward
    1894–1960 .... WWasWT
Waxman, Al 1935– CTFT–31
    Earlier sketches in CTFT–3, 20
Wayans, Damien CTFT–70
Wayans, Damon 1960– CTFT–45
    Earlier sketches in CTFT–10, 17
Wayans, Keenen Ivory 1958– CTFT–41
    Earlier sketches in CTFT–10, 17
Wayans, Kim 1961– CTFT–70
Wayans, Marlon 1972– CTFT–60
    Earlier sketch in CTFT–27
Wayans, Shawn 1971– CTFT–68
    Earlier sketch in CTFT–30
Wayburn, Ned 1874–1942 .... WWasWT
Waylett, Jamie 1989– CTFT–77
Waymire, Kellie CTFT–49
Wayne, David 1914–1995 .... CTFT–7
    Obituary in CTFT–14
    Earlier sketch in WWT–17
Wayne, Ethan 1962– CTFT–63
Wayne, John 1907–1979 .... CTFT–19
Wayne, Naunton 1901–1970 .... WWasWT
Wayne, Patrick 1939– CTFT–20
    Earlier sketch in CTFT–3
Wayne, Rollo 1899–1954 .... WWasWT
Weakland, Kevin L. 1963– CTFT–4
Weary, Ogdred
    See... Gorey, Edward
Weatherly, Amelia
    See... Heinle, Amelia
Weatherly, Michael 1968– CTFT–74
    Earlier sketch in CTFT–33
Weathers, Carl 1948– CTFT–45
    Earlier sketches in CTFT–7, 17
Weathers, Philip 1908– CTFT–4
Weaver, Blayne 1976– CTFT–70
Weaver, Brett 1966– CTFT–45
Weaver, Dennis 1924– CTFT–70
    Earlier sketches in CTFT–3, 14, 40
Weaver, Fritz 1926– CTFT–46
    Earlier sketches in CTFT–2, 8, 16; WWT–17
Weaver, Lee 1930– CTFT–55
    Earlier sketch in CTFT–6
Weaver, Sigourney 1949– CTFT–41
    Earlier sketches in CTFT–3, 10, 17

Cumulative Index

Weaver, William 1917– CTFT–1
Weaving, Hugo 1960– CTFT–57
    Earlier sketch in CTFT–26
Webb, Alan 1906– WWT–17
Webb, Chloe 1957(?)– CTFT–45
    Earlier sketches in CTFT–8, 16
Webb, Clifton 1893–1966 .... WWasWT
Webb, Jack 1920–1982 .... CTFT–1
Webb, Jimmy 1946– CTFT–50
    Earlier sketch in CTFT–11
Webb, Lizbeth 1926– .... WWasWT
Webb, Lucy CTFT–4
Webb, Veronica 1965– CTFT–64
Webber, Andrew Lloyd
    See .... Lloyd–Webber, Andrew
Webber, Robert 1924–1989.................... CTFT–7
Weber, Amy 1972– CTFT–58
Weber, Ben 1972–.................................. CTFT–75
Weber, Carl 1925– CTFT–21
    Earlier sketch in CTFT–3
Weber, Charlie 1977–............................ CTFT–71
Weber, Jake 1964– CTFT–69
    Earlier sketch in CTFT–30
Weber, Joseph 1867–1942 .... WWasWT
Weber, L. Lawrence ?–1940................... WWasWT
Weber, Steven 1961–............................. CTFT–71
    Earlier sketches in CTFT–21, 32
Webster, Ben 1864–1947...................... WWasWT
Webster, Derek CTFT–54
Webster, Margaret 1905–1972.............. WWT–16
Webster, Paul.. CTFT–79
Webster, Victor 1973– CTFT–68
Webster–Gleason, Lucile 1888–1947 .... WWasWT
Weck, Peter 1930–................................ CTFT–33
Wedge, Chris 1957(?)– CTFT–74
Wedgeworth, Ann 1935– CTFT–7
Weeden, Bill... CTFT–60
Weeden, Evelyn ?–1961 .... WWasWT
Weege, Reinhold CTFT–4
Weeks, Danielle CTFT–72
Weezer, Lillian
    See.................................... Johnson, Kenneth
Weguelin, Thomas N. 1885–? .... WWasWT
Wehle, Brenda CTFT–51
Wehlen, Emmy 1887–? .... WWasWT
Weidman, Jerome 1913–1998 .... CTFT–6
    Obituary in CTFT–24
    Earlier sketch in WWT–17
Weidman, John 1946–........................... CTFT–42
Weidner, Paul 1934– CTFT–5
    Earlier sketch in WWT–17
Weigel, Helene 1900–1971 .... WWasWT
Weight, Michael 1906– .... WWasWT
Weihl, Chris
    See................................. Wiehl, Christopher
Weil, Liza 1977–.................................... CTFT–72
Weil, Samuel
    See .... Kaufman, Lloyd
Weill, Claudia CTFT–1
Weill, Kurt 1900–1950 .... WWasWT
Wein, Yossi CTFT–43
Weinberg, Gus 1866–1952.................... WWasWT
Weinberg, Matt 1990–........................... CTFT–66
Weinberg, Max 1951–............................ CTFT–45
Weinberg, Mike 1993–........................... CTFT–74
Weinberg, Ronald A. CTFT–42
Weinberg, Shauna
    See.................................. Robertson, Shauna
Weiner, Robert ?–1989 .... CTFT–1
Weiner, Zane 1953–............................... CTFT–79
    Earlier sketches in CTFT–2, 35
Weinger, Scott 1975– CTFT–46
    Earlier sketch in CTFT–23

Weingrod, Herschel A. 1947– CTFT–15
Weinstein, Bob 1956(?)–......................... CTFT–47
    Earlier sketch in CTFT–23
Weinstein, Harvey 1952–....................... CTFT–73
    Earlier sketches in CTFT–21, 32
Weinstein, Paula H. 1945– CTFT–10
Weintraub, Fred 1928–........................... CTFT–8
    Earlier sketch in CTFT–1
Weintraub, Jerry 1937– CTFT–38
    Earlier sketches in CTFT–7, 14
Weir, Peter 1944–.................................. CTFT–49
    Earlier sketches in CTFT–1, 6, 13
Weis, Don 1922– CTFT–7
Weisbarth, Michael L. CTFT–4
Weisberg, David CTFT–28
Weiskopf, Bob CTFT–2
Weisman, Kevin 1970– CTFT–40
Weisman, Sam CTFT–52
Weiss, Joel 1953– CTFT–2
Weiss, Jonathan
    See .... Thomas, Jonathan Taylor
Weiss, Julie CTFT–39
    Earlier sketch in CTFT–13
Weiss, Marc B. CTFT–2
    Earlier sketch in WWT–17
Weiss, Michael T. 1962– CTFT–73
    Earlier sketches in CTFT–21, 32
Weiss, Peter 1916–1982 .... WWT–17
Weiss, Shaun 1978– CTFT–45
Weisser, Norbert CTFT–56
Weissmuller, Donald 1922– CTFT–6
Weisz, Rachel 1971–.............................. CTFT–41
    Earlier sketch in CTFT–16
Weisz, Richard
    See.. Mamet, David
Weitz, Bruce 1943–................................ CTFT–67
    Earlier sketches in CTFT–7, 18, 29
Weitzenhoffer, Max 1939– CTFT–21
    Earlier sketch in CTFT–3
Welch, Bo 1952– CTFT–50
    Earlier sketches in CTFT–11, 24
Welch, Elisabeth 1909–......................... WWT–17
Welch, James 1865–1917 .... WWasWT
Welch, Michael 1987– CTFT–64
Welch, Raquel 1940–............................. CTFT–70
    Earlier sketches in CTFT–3, 19, 31
Welch, Tahnee 1962–............................. CTFT–16
Welchman, Harry 1886–1966 .... WWasWT
Weld, Tuesday 1943– CTFT–18
    Earlier sketch in CTFT–3
Welden, Ben 1901–............................... WWasWT
Weldon, Deborah Morgan
    See .... Morgan, Debbi
Weldon, Duncan C. 1941– CTFT–39
    Earlier sketches in CTFT–5, 13; WWT–17
Weldon, Harry 1882–? .... WWasWT
Welford, Dallas 1874–1946 .... WWasWT
Welk, Lawrence 1903–1992................... CTFT–12
Welker, Frank 1945– CTFT–50
    Earlier sketch in CTFT–24
Welland, Colin 1934– CTFT–7
Weller, Bernard 1870–1943 .... WWasWT
Weller, Fred 1969(?)–............................ CTFT–47
Weller, Michael 1942– CTFT–2
    Earlier sketch in WWT–17
Weller, Peter 1947– CTFT–39
    Earlier sketches in CTFT–7, 15
Weller, Robb 1949– CTFT–50
Welles, Orson 1915–1985....................... CTFT–3
    Earlier sketch in WWasWT
Wellesley, Arthur 1890– .... WWasWT
Welling, Sylvia 1901–............................ WWasWT
Welling, Tom 1977– CTFT–74

welliver, Titus 1961– CTFT–45
Wellman, Wendell 1944–........................ CTFT–2
Wells, David... CTFT–36
Wells, Deering 1896–1961 .... WWasWT
Wells, John 1956–.................................. CTFT–47
    Earlier sketch in CTFT–23
Wells, John Campbell 1936–1998.......... CTFT–23
Wells, Tico CTFT–62
Wells, Vernon 1945– CTFT–45
    Earlier sketch in CTFT–16
Welsh, Jane 1905–................................ WWasWT
Welsh, Jonathan CTFT–36
Welsh, Kenneth CTFT–36
    Earlier sketch in CTFT–7
Welsh, Margaret CTFT–69
Wen, Ming–Na
    See... Ming–Na
Wenders, Wim 1945–............................ CTFT–52
    Earlier sketches in CTFT–5, 14, 24
Wendkos, Paul 1922– CTFT–40
    Earlier sketches in CTFT–8, 16
Wendt, George 1948–............................ CTFT–67
    Earlier sketches in CTFT–7, 18, 29
Wenham, Jane CTFT–6
    Earlier sketch in WWT–17
Wenman, Henry N. 1875–1953 .... WWasWT
Wentworth, Alexandra 1966–................ CTFT–43
Werbe, Susan CTFT–48
Werner, Peter 1947–.............................. CTFT–55
Werner, Roy CTFT–69
Werner, Tom 1950–............................... CTFT–55
    Earlier sketches in CTFT–12, 25
Werntz, Gary CTFT–64
Wert, Doug CTFT–56
Wertenbaker, Timberlake....................... CTFT–10
Wertmueller, Lina
    See .... Wertmuller, Lina
Wertmuller, Lina 1926–......................... CTFT–79
    Earlier sketches in CTFT–1, 6, 35
Weseluck, Cathy CTFT–46
Wesker, Arnold 1932–........................... CTFT–14
    Earlier sketches in CTFT–7; WWT–17
Wesley, John... CTFT–40
Wesley, Paul 1982–............................... CTFT–74
Wesley, Richard 1945– CTFT–5
    Earlier sketch in WWT–17
Wessler, Charles B. CTFT–48
    Earlier sketch in CTFT–23
West, Adam 1928–................................ CTFT–60
    Earlier sketches in CTFT–8, 16, 27
West, Algernon 1886–?........................ WWasWT
West, Billy 1950–................................... CTFT–60
    Earlier sketch in CTFT–27
West, Caryn CTFT–8
West, Chandra 1970–............................ CTFT–78
    Earlier sketch in CTFT–35
West, Con 1891– .... WWasWT
West, Dominic 1970– CTFT–40
West, Edwin
    See .... Westlake, Donald E.
West, Henry St. Barbe 1880–1935 .... WWasWT
West, Joan 1936–.................................. CTFT–4
West, Joel 1975– CTFT–79
West, Jonathan CTFT–55
West, Kevin 1965– CTFT–57
    Earlier sketch in CTFT–25
West, Lockwood 1905–1989................... CTFT–8
    Earlier sketch in WWT–17
West, Mae 1892–1980 .... CTFT–1
    Earlier sketch in WWT–17
West, Nathan 1978–.............................. CTFT–73
West, Owen
    See .... Koontz, Dean R.

West, Red 1936– CTFT–54
West, Samuel 1966–.............................. CTFT–73
   Earlier sketch in CTFT–32
West, Shane 1978–................................ CTFT–77
   Earlier sketches in CTFT–28, 34
West, Simon 1961– CTFT–61
   Earlier sketch in CTFT–28
West, Thomas E. 1954–........................... CTFT–2
West, Timothy 1934– CTFT–57
   Earlier sketches in CTFT–4, 15, 26; WWT–17
West, Will 1867–1922 .... WWasWT
Westaway, Simon 1958– CTFT–61
Westbrook, John 1922–.......................... WWT–17
Westcott, Netta ?–1953......................... WWasWT
Westenberg, Robert 1953– CTFT–7
Wester, Travis.. CTFT–67
Westerman, Carlie 1993–....................... CTFT–74
Westerman, Floyd Red Crow
   1936(?)–.. CTFT–58
   Earlier sketches in CTFT–16, 27
Westlake, Donald E. 1933– CTFT–39
   Earlier sketch in CTFT–13
Westley, Helen 1879–1942 .... WWasWT
Westman, Nydia 1907–1970 .... WWasWT
Westmore, McKenzie 1977– CTFT–74
Westmore, Michael G. 1938– CTFT–42
   Earlier sketch in CTFT–9
Westmoreland, Jeffrey
   See .... Williams, Brandon
Weston, Celia 1951– CTFT–61
   Earlier sketch in CTFT–28
Weston, Dick
   See .... Rogers, Roy
Weston, Jack 1915(?)–1996 .... CTFT–8
   Obituary in CTFT–16
   Earlier sketches in CTFT–2; WWT–17
Weston, Jeff
   See .... Celentano, Jeff
Weston, Michael 1973– CTFT–36
Weston, Robert P. 1878–1936 .... WWasWT
Weston, Ruth 1911– .... WWasWT
Wetherall, Frances ?–1923..................... WWasWT
Wetmore, Joan 1911–1989 .... WWasWT
Wettig, Patricia 1951– CTFT–42
   Earlier sketch in CTFT–9
Wever, Merritt....................................... CTFT–59
Wexler, Haskell 1922(?)–........................ CTFT–49
   Earlier sketches in CTFT–6, 14, 24
Wexler, Norman 1926–1999 .... CTFT–29
Wexler, Peter 1936–................................ CTFT–6
   Earlier sketch in WWT–17
Wexler, Victor Raider
   See .... Raider–Wexler, Victor
Wexley, John 1902–.............................. WWasWT
Weyand, Ron 1929–................................ CTFT–4
Weyer, Marius 1945– CTFT–69
Whale, James 1896–1957..................... WWasWT
Whalen, Sean 1965–.............................. CTFT–41
Whaley, Frank 1963– CTFT–54
   Earlier sketches in CTFT–13, 25
Whaley, Michael CTFT–74
Whalin, Justin 1974–.............................. CTFT–46
   Earlier sketch in CTFT–17
Whalley, Joanne 1964– CTFT–45
   Earlier sketch in CTFT–17
Whalley, Norma ?–1943 .... WWasWT
Whalley–Kilmer, Joanne
   See........................... Whalley, Joanne
Wharmby, Tony CTFT–63
Wharton, Anthony P. 1877–1943 .... WWasWT
Whately, Kevin 1951–............................ CTFT–36
Whatmore, A. R. 1889–1960................. WWasWT
Wheat, Jim 1952– CTFT–58

Wheat, Ken 1950– CTFT–58
Wheatley, Alan 1907–.......................... WWT–17
Wheatley, Jane 1881–1935.................. WWasWT
Wheatley, Thomas CTFT–36
Wheaton, Wil 1972–.............................. CTFT–41
   Earlier sketches in CTFT–10, 17
   Brief Entry in CTFT–5
Whedon, Joss 1964(?)–........................... CTFT–49
   Earlier sketch in CTFT–24
Wheeldon, Christopher 1973– CTFT–50
Wheeler, Hugh 1912–1987 .... CTFT–5
   Earlier sketch in WWT–17
Wheeler, Ira 1920–................................ CTFT–30
   Earlier sketch in CTFT–7
Wheeler, Lois 1922–............................. WWasWT
Wheeler, Maggie 1961– CTFT–49
Wheeler–Nicholson, Dana CTFT–64
Whelan, Albert 1875–1961 .... WWasWT
Whelan, Peter 1931–.............................. CTFT–24
Whelchel, Lisa 1963–.............................. CTFT–21
   Earlier sketch in CTFT–3
Whelen, Frederick 1867–?..................... WWasWT
Whiffin, Blanche 1845–1936................. WWasWT
Whiley, Manning 1915–........................ WWasWT
Whiplash, Sydney
   See .... Francks, Rainbow
Whipp, Joseph 1937–............................. CTFT–56
Whipple, Sidney Beaumont
   1888–1975 .... WWasWT
Whirry, Shannon 1964–.......................... CTFT–71
   Earlier sketch in CTFT–31
Whisp, Kennilworthy
   See .... Rowling, J. K.
Whistler, Rex 1905–1944 .... WWasWT
Whitaker, Duane 1959– CTFT–75
Whitaker, Forest 1961–.......................... CTFT–58
   Earlier sketches in CTFT–8, 16, 27
Whitaker, Johnny 1959–......................... CTFT–77
Whitall, Ted
   See .... Whittall, Ted
Whitby, Arthur 1869–1922 .... WWasWT
Whitby, Gwynne 1903– WWT–17
White, Bernard CTFT–51
White, Betty 1922– CTFT–39
   Earlier sketches in CTFT–3, 13
White, Bradley CTFT–62
   Earlier sketch in CTFT–28
White, Brian J. 1977–............................. CTFT–63
White, David R. A. CTFT–62
White, George 1890–1968 .... WWasWT
White, George C. 1935– CTFT–1
White, J. Fisher 1865–1945 .... WWasWT
White, Jaleel 1976–............................... CTFT–46
   Earlier sketch in CTFT–17
White, James ?–1927 .... WWasWT
White, Jane 1922–................................. WWT–17
White, Jesse 1919–1997 .... CTFT–6
   Obituary in CTFT–17
White, Joan 1909– WWT–17
White, John Patrick 1972– CTFT–73
White, Julie 1962(?)–.............................. CTFT–46
   Earlier sketch in CTFT–17
White, Karen Malina 1965– CTFT–62
White, Lee 1886–1927 .... WWasWT
White, Lillias 1951– CTFT–67
   Earlier sketches in CTFT–19, 30
White, Michael 1936–............................. CTFT–5
   Earlier sketch in WWT–17
White, Michole CTFT–70
   Earlier sketch in CTFT–31
White, Miles 1914– WWT–17
White, Onna WWT–17
White, Persia CTFT–59

White, Peter CTFT–36
White, Ron CTFT–50
White, Steve CTFT–55
White, Valerie 1915–1975 .... WWT–16
White, Vanna 1957–............................... CTFT–79
   Earlier sketch in CTFT–36
White, Wilfrid Hyde 1903– .... WWasWT
White, Willard 1946–............................. CTFT–50
   Earlier sketch in CTFT–16
Whiteford, Jock .... WWasWT
Whitehead, Geoffrey 1939– CTFT–75
   Earlier sketch in CTFT–32
Whitehead, Paxton 1937–....................... CTFT–75
   Earlier sketches in CTFT–1, 4, 33; WWT–17
Whitehead, Robert 1916– CTFT–2
   Earlier sketch in WWT–17
Whitehead, Ted (E. A.) 1933–................. WWT–17
Whitehouse, Paul CTFT–36
Whitelaw, Arthur 1940–......................... CTFT–6
   Earlier sketch in WWT–17
Whitelaw, Billie 1932–........................... CTFT–77
   Earlier sketches in CTFT–2, 34; WWT–17
Whitemore, Hugh 1936–.......................... CTFT–7
Whitesell, John CTFT–37
   Earlier sketch in CTFT–12
Whiteside, Walker 1869–1942 .... WWasWT
Whitfield, Charles Malik....................... CTFT–43
Whitfield, Dondre 1969– CTFT–47
Whitfield, Fredericka CTFT–74
Whitfield, Lynn 1953(?)– CTFT–36
   Earlier sketch in CTFT–11
Whitfield, Mitchell 1969– CTFT–76
Whitford, Bradley 1959–........................ CTFT–57
   Earlier sketches in CTFT–7, 26
Whitford, Peter 1939–............................ CTFT–40
Whiting, Jack 1901–1961 .... WWasWT
Whiting, John 1917–1963 .... WWasWT
Whitley, Clifford 1894– .... WWasWT
Whitley, Kym 1961–.............................. CTFT–60
Whitling, Townsend 1869–1952 .... WWasWT
Whitlock, Albert 1915–.......................... CTFT–10
Whitman, Mae 1988– CTFT–39
Whitman, Stuart 1926(?)–....................... CTFT–42
   Earlier sketch in CTFT–9
Whitmire, Steve 1959– CTFT–46
Whitmore, James 1921–.......................... CTFT–60
   Earlier sketches in CTFT–2, 7, 16, 27;
   WWT–17
Whitmore, James, Jr. 1948–.................... CTFT–47
   Earlier sketch in CTFT–17
Whitney, David
   See .... Malick, Terrence
Whitney, Fred C. ?–1930 .... WWasWT
Whitney, Sewell................................... CTFT–74
Whitrow, Benjamin 1937–...................... CTFT–35
   Earlier sketch in WWT–17
Whittaker, Herbert 1911– WWT–17
Whittaker, Jonathon.............................. CTFT–54
Whittall, Ted.. CTFT–67
Whittemore, Libby................................ CTFT–43
Whittle, Charles R. ?–1947 .... WWasWT
Whitton, Margaret 1950– CTFT–10
   Earlier sketch in CTFT–2
Whitty, May 1865–1948 .... WWasWT
Whitworth, Geoffrey 1883–1951 .... WWasWT
Whitworth, Johnny 1975– CTFT–73
Whorf, Richard 1906–1966 .... WWasWT
Whytal, Mrs. Russ .... WWasWT
Whytal, Russ 1860–1930....................... WWasWT
Whyte, Robert 1874–1916 .... WWasWT
Whyte, Ron ?–1989 .... CTFT–6
   Earlier sketch in CTFT–1
Whyte, Scott 1978–................................ CTFT–73

Wich, Nathan
    See .... Wertmuller, Lina
Wick, Douglas 1955– CTFT–64
    Earlier sketch in CTFT–28
Wickes, Mary 1916–1995 .... CTFT–7
    Obituary in CTFT–15
    Earlier sketches in CTFT–2; WWasWT
Wickham, Glynne 1922– WWT–17
Wickham, Tony 1922–1948 .... WWasWT
Wicks, Robert
    See .... Buchholz, Bob
Wickwire, Nancy 1925–1975 .... WWT–16
Widdoes, James 1953– CTFT–77
    Earlier sketches in CTFT–3, 35
Widdoes, Kathleen 1939– CTFT–35
    Earlier sketches in CTFT–5; WWT–17
Widdows, Connor CTFT–54
Widen, Gregory CTFT–56
Widmark, Richard 1914– CTFT–20
    Earlier sketch in CTFT–3
Wied, Gustav 1858–1914 .... WWasWT
Wiedlin, Jane 1958– CTFT–67
Wiehe, Dagmar .... WWasWT
Wiehl, Christopher 1966– CTFT–58
Wiemer, Robert 1938– CTFT–20
    Earlier sketch in CTFT–3
Wiener, Josh
    See .... Keaton, Josh
Wiener, Sally Dixon 1926– CTFT–1
Wiesenfeld, Joe 1947– CTFT–51
Wiest, Dianne 1948– CTFT–45
    Earlier sketches in CTFT–5, 12, 22
Wigdor, Geoffrey 1982– CTFT–69
Wilborn, Carlton CTFT–69
Wilbraham, Edward 1895–1930 .... WWasWT
Wilbur, Crane 1889–1973 .... WWasWT
Wilbur, Richard 1921– CTFT–3
    Earlier sketch in WWT–17
Wilby, James 1958– CTFT–60
    Earlier sketches in CTFT–8, 16, 27
Wilcox, Barbara 1906– .... WWasWT
Wilcox, Larry 1947– CTFT–34
    Earlier sketch in CTFT–8
Wilcox, Lisa 1964– CTFT–78
Wilcox, Ralph CTFT–54
Wilcox, Robin CTFT–67
Wilcoxon, Henry 1905– .... WWasWT
Wildberg, John J. 1902–1959 .... WWasWT
Wilde, Cornel 1915–1989 .... CTFT–8
Wilde, Olivia 1984– CTFT–78
Wilder, Alan CTFT–73
    Earlier sketch in CTFT–32
Wilder, Billy 1906–2002 .... CTFT–24
    Obituary in CTFT–49
    Earlier sketches in CTFT–1, 4
Wilder, Clinton 1920–1986 .... WWT–17
Wilder, Gene 1935– CTFT–54
    Earlier sketches in CTFT–2, 7, 14, 25
Wilder, James 1948– CTFT–48
Wilder, Thornton N. 1897–1975 .... WWasWT
Wildhorn, Frank 1959– CTFT–62
Wilding, Mark CTFT–79
Wilding, Michael 1912– .... WWasWT
Wildman, Valerie CTFT–39
Wiles, Jason 1970– CTFT–67
    Earlier sketch in CTFT–29
Wiles, Michael Shamus CTFT–39
Wiley, Gerlad
    See .... Barker, Ronnie
Wilford, Isabel .... WWasWT
Wilhelm, C. 1858–1925 .... WWasWT
Wilhoite, Kathleen 1964– CTFT–73
    Earlier sketch in CTFT–32

Wilkie, Allan 1878–1970 .... WWasWT
Wilkinson, Adrienne 1977– CTFT–69
Wilkinson, Charles CTFT–45
Wilkinson, Colm 1944– CTFT–10
Wilkinson, Henry Spenser
    1853–? .... WWasWT
Wilkinson, Marc 1929– WWT–17
Wilkinson, Norman 1882–1934 .... WWasWT
Wilkinson, Tom 1948– CTFT–73
    Earlier sketches in CTFT–21, 32
Wilkof, Lee 1951– CTFT–43
    Earlier sketch in CTFT–1
Willard, Catherine ?–1954 .... WWasWT
Willard, Edmund 1884–1956 .... WWasWT
Willard, Edward Smith 1853–1915 .... WWasWT
Willard, Fred 1939– CTFT–67
    Earlier sketches in CTFT–7, 18, 29
Willard, John 1885–1942 .... WWasWT
Willes, Christine CTFT–77
Willett, Chad 1971– CTFT–42
William, David 1926– WWT–17
William, Warren 1895–1948 .... WWasWT
Williams, Allen CTFT–58
Williams, Andy 1930(?)– CTFT–21
Williams, Ann 1935– CTFT–2
Williams, Anson 1949– CTFT–9
    Earlier sketches in CTFT–9 .... CTFT–42
Williams, Arthur 1844–1915 .... WWasWT
Williams, Barbara 1954(?)– CTFT–41
Williams, Barry 1954– CTFT–63
    Earlier sketch in CTFT–8
Williams, Billy 1929– CTFT–12
Williams, Billy Dee 1937– CTFT–60
    Earlier sketches in CTFT–2, 8, 16, 27;
    WWT–17
Williams, Bradford Cody 1951– CTFT–1
Williams, Brandon 1974– CTFT–45
Williams, Bransby 1870–1961 .... WWasWT
Williams, Campbell 1906– .... WWasWT
Williams, Cara CTFT–3
Williams, Caroline CTFT–54
Williams, Cindy 1947– CTFT–39
    Earlier sketches in CTFT–3, 13
Williams, Clarence III 1939– CTFT–56
    Earlier sketches in CTFT–7, 15, 26; WWT–17
Williams, Clifford 1926– CTFT–16
    Earlier sketches in CTFT–5; WWT–17
Williams, Cole 1981– CTFT–74
Williams, Cress CTFT–73
    Earlier sketch in CTFT–32
Williams, Cynda 1966– CTFT–56
Williams, Darnell 1955– CTFT–69
Williams, David C. CTFT–56
Williams, Dennis 1944– CTFT–4
Williams, Derek 1910– .... WWasWT
Williams, Dick Anthony 1938– CTFT–78
    Earlier sketches in CTFT–5, 35; WWT–17
Williams, Elizabeth CTFT–40
Williams, Ellis 1951– CTFT–63
Williams, Elmo 1913– CTFT–1
Williams, Emlyn 1905–1987 .... CTFT–5
    Earlier sketch in WWT–17
Williams, Florence 1912– .... WWasWT
Williams, Frances 1903–1959 .... WWasWT
Williams, Fritz 1865–1930 .... WWasWT
Williams, Gareth CTFT–62
Williams, Gary Anthony 1976– CTFT–74
Williams, Greg Kean
    See .... Kean, Greg
Williams, Hal 1938– CTFT–6
Williams, Harcourt 1880–1957 .... WWasWT
Williams, Harland 1967(?)– CTFT–40

Williams, Harry Gregson
    See .... Gregson–Williams, Harry
Williams, Hattie 1872–1942 .... WWasWT
Williams, Heathcote 1941– CTFT–54
    Earlier sketches in CTFT–12, 25
Williams, Hope 1901– .... WWasWT
Williams, Hugh 1904–1969 .... WWasWT
Williams, Hugh Steadman
    1935– CTFT–4
Williams, Jeff CTFT–74
Williams, Jessie Lynch 1871–1929 .... WWasWT
Williams, Jim Cody CTFT–54
Williams, Jimmy CTFT–54
Williams, JoBeth 1948(?)– CTFT–39
    Earlier sketches in CTFT–1, 6, 13
Williams, John 1903– WWT–16
Williams, John 1932– CTFT–45
    Earlier sketches in CTFT–3, 10, 17
Williams, John D. ?–1941 .... WWasWT
Williams, Jordan 1955– CTFT–56
Williams, Joseph 1960– CTFT–77
Williams, Joss CTFT–64
    Earlier sketch in CTFT–28
Williams, Kelli 1970– CTFT–41
Williams, Kenneth 1926–1988 .... CTFT–7
    Earlier sketch in WWT–17
Williams, Kimberly 1971– CTFT–41
    Earlier sketch in CTFT–17
Williams, Malinda 1975– CTFT–62
Williams, Mark CTFT–45
Williams, Mason 1938– CTFT–16
Williams, Matthew CTFT–54
Williams, Melora
    See .... Walters, Melora
Williams, Michael 1935– CTFT–5
    Earlier sketch in WWT–17
Williams, Michael C. 1973– CTFT–71
Williams, Michelle 1980– CTFT–43
    Earlier sketch in CTFT–23
Williams, Montel 1956– CTFT–39
Williams, Natashia 1978– CTFT–72
Williams, Nigel 1948– CTFT–52
    Earlier sketch in CTFT–12
Williams, Olivia 1968– CTFT–58
    Earlier sketch in CTFT–26
Williams, Oren 1992– CTFT–74
Williams, Patrick 1939– CTFT–58
    Earlier sketches in CTFT–12, 25
Williams, Paul 1940– CTFT–47
    Earlier sketches in CTFT–3, 4
Williams, Philip CTFT–65
Williams, R. J. 1978– CTFT–71
Williams, Raymond T. 1972– CTFT–77
Williams, Rhys 1897–1969 .... WWasWT
Williams, Richard 1933– CTFT–12
Williams, Robin 1951(?)– CTFT–40
    Earlier sketches in CTFT–3, 10, 17
Williams, Russell II 1952– CTFT–37
    Earlier sketch in CTFT–12
Williams, Samm–Art 1946– CTFT–8
Williams, Sammy 1948– CTFT–10
Williams, Scott
    See .... Winters, Scott William
Williams, Simon 1946– CTFT–46
    Earlier sketch in CTFT–22
Williams, Sonia 1926– .... WWasWT
Williams, Stephen 1900–1957 .... WWasWT
Williams, Steven 1949– CTFT–46
    Earlier sketches in CTFT–7, 17
Williams, Tam CTFT–36
Williams, Tennessee 1911–1983 .... CTFT–1
    Earlier sketch in WWT–17
Williams, Tonya Lee 1967– CTFT–57

Williams, Treat 1951–............................ CTFT–60
  Earlier sketches in CTFT–2, 8, 16, 27
Williams, Tyler James 1992– CTFT–68
Williams, Vanessa L. 1963–.................... CTFT–52
  Earlier sketches in CTFT–14, 25
Williams, Wade Andrew........................ CTFT–59
Williams, Walter 1887–1940 .... WWasWT
Williamson, David 1942–...................... WWT–17
Williamson, Fred 1937(?)–.................... CTFT–67
  Earlier sketches in CTFT–7, 18, 29
Williamson, Hugh Ross 1901– .... WWasWT
Williamson, James Cassius
  1845–1913 .... WWasWT
Williamson, Kevin 1965– CTFT–73
  Earlier sketches in CTFT–21, 32
Williamson, Mykelti 1960– CTFT–71
  Earlier sketch in CTFT–31
Williamson, Nicol 1938– CTFT–8
  Earlier sketches in CTFT–2; WWT–17
Williamson, Scott CTFT–74
  Earlier sketch in CTFT–33
Willingham, Calder 1923–1995 .... CTFT–25
Willingham, Noble CTFT–17
Willis, Bruce 1955–.............................. CTFT–40
  Earlier sketches in CTFT–9, 17
  Brief Entry in CTFT–3
Willis, Gordon 1931–........................... CTFT–14
  Earlier sketch in CTFT–7
Willis, Jack CTFT–75
  Earlier sketch in CTFT–32
Willis, Jerome CTFT–66
Willis, Ted 1918–1992 .... CTFT–7
  Obituary in CTFT–11
  Earlier sketch in WWT–17
Willison, Walter 1947–........................... CTFT–1
Willman, Noel 1918–1988...................... CTFT–8
  Earlier sketch in WWT–17
Willoughby, Hugh 1891– .... WWasWT
Willows, Alec CTFT–46
Willrich, Rudolph CTFT–78
Wills, Brember ?–1948 .... WWasWT
Wills, Drusilla 1884–1951 .... WWasWT
Willson, Meredith 1902–1984................ CTFT–21
Willson, Osmund 1896–....................... WWasWT
Willson, Paul 1945–............................ CTFT–71
  Earlier sketches in CTFT–21, 32
Willy, M. 1859–1931 .... WWasWT
Wilmer, Dale
  See............................ Wade, Robert (Allison)
Wilmer, Douglas 1920–........................ WWT–17
Wilshin, Sunday 1905–........................ WWasWT
Wilson, Albert Edward 1885–1960........ WWasWT
Wilson, Andy...................................... CTFT–42
Wilson, August 1945– CTFT–40
  Earlier sketch in CTFT–10
  Brief Entry in CTFT–5
Wilson, Beatrice ?–1943 .... WWasWT
Wilson, Brian Anthony 1960(?)–.............. CTFT–55
Wilson, Bridgette 1973–........................ CTFT–75
  Earlier sketch in CTFT–34
Wilson, Chandra 1969–......................... CTFT–72
Wilson, Clerow
  See... Wilson, Flip
Wilson, Colleen Camp
  See..................................... Camp, Colleen
Wilson, Dale CTFT–71
Wilson, Debra 1970– CTFT–62
Wilson, Demond 1946–......................... CTFT–70
Wilson, Diana 1897–1937..................... WWasWT
Wilson, Dick 1916– CTFT–28
Wilson, Dorien 1963–........................... CTFT–49
Wilson, Edith .... WWasWT

Wilson, Elizabeth 1921–....................... CTFT–50
  Earlier sketches in CTFT–2, 8; WWT–17
Wilson, Flip 1933–1998 .... CTFT–3
  Obituary in CTFT–24
Wilson, Francis 1854–1935 .... WWasWT
Wilson, Frank 1891–1956 .... WWasWT
Wilson, Grace 1903– .... WWasWT
Wilson, Harry Leon 1867–1939 .... WWasWT
Wilson, Hugh 1943– CTFT–30
  Earlier sketches in CTFT–7, 19
Wilson, Jim CTFT–57
  Earlier sketch in CTFT–22
Wilson, John C. 1899–1961 .... WWasWT
Wilson, Joseph 1858–1940.................... WWasWT
Wilson, Julie 1924(?)–............................ CTFT–9
Wilson, Katherine .... WWasWT
Wilson, Kristen 1969(?)–....................... CTFT–64
Wilson, Lambert 1958– CTFT–77
  Earlier sketches in CTFT–7, 35
Wilson, Lanford 1937–......................... CTFT–52
  Earlier sketches in CTFT–1, 3, 21; WWT–17
Wilson, Lucy WWT–6
Wilson, Luke 1971– CTFT–47
  Earlier sketch in CTFT–23
Wilson, Mara 1987–............................. CTFT–40
  Earlier sketch in CTFT–16
Wilson, Mark CTFT–49
Wilson, Mary 1944–.............................. CTFT–4
Wilson, Mary Louise 1932–................... CTFT–45
Wilson, Michael G. 1942– CTFT–55
  Earlier sketch in CTFT–28
Wilson, Owen 1968– CTFT–54
  Earlier sketch in CTFT–26
Wilson, Patrick 1973– CTFT–76
  Earlier sketch in CTFT–34
Wilson, Perry 1916– .... WWasWT
Wilson, Peta 1970– CTFT–43
  Earlier sketch in CTFT–21
Wilson, Rainn 1968–............................ CTFT–74
Wilson, Rita 1958(?)–........................... CTFT–59
  Earlier sketches in CTFT–16, 27
Wilson, Robert 1941–............................ CTFT–5
  Earlier sketch in WWT–17
Wilson, Rod....................................... CTFT–43
Wilson, Sandy 1924– WWT–17
Wilson, Scott 1942– CTFT–78
  Earlier sketches in CTFT–7, 35
Wilson, Sheree J. 1958– CTFT–67
Wilson, Snoo 1948–.............................. CTFT–7
  Earlier sketch in WWT–17
Wilson, Stuart 1934– CTFT–48
  Earlier sketch in CTFT–23
Wilson, Thomas F. 1959–...................... CTFT–74
Wilson, Trey 1948–1989 .... CTFT–8
Wilson, W. Cronin ?–1934 .... WWasWT
Wilson, William J. ?–1936 .... WWasWT
Wilson–Sampras, Bridgette
  See .... Wilson, Bridgette
Wilstach, Paul 1870–1952.................... WWasWT
Wilton, Penelope 1946–........................ CTFT–35
  Earlier sketch in CTFT–9
Wiltse, David CTFT–6
Wiman, Anna Deere 1924–1963.......... WWasWT
Wiman, Dwight Deere 1895–1951........ WWasWT
Wimmer, Brian 1959– CTFT–46
  Earlier sketches in CTFT–10, 17
Wimperis, Arthur 1874–1953 .... WWasWT
Winant, Bruce 1957– CTFT–58
Winant, Forrest 1888–1928 .... WWasWT
Winbush, Camille 1987(?)– CTFT–48
Winbush, Troy CTFT–67
Wincer, Simon 1943–........................... CTFT–79
  Earlier sketches in CTFT–9, 35

Winchell, April CTFT–39
Winchell, Paul 1922–........................... CTFT–42
  Earlier sketch in CTFT–9
Winchell, Walter 1897–1972................ WWasWT
Wincott, Jeff 1956(?)–.......................... CTFT–41
  Earlier sketch in CTFT–17
Wincott, Michael 1959–........................ CTFT–46
  Earlier sketch in CTFT–17
Windeatt, George (Alan) 1901–1959 ..... WWasWT
Windermere, Charles 1872–1955 .... WWasWT
Windom, William 1923– CTFT–56
  Earlier sketches in CTFT–2, 7, 26
Windon, Stephen F. 1959– CTFT–59
Windsor, Barbara 1937–....................... WWT–17
Windsor, Marie 1921–........................... CTFT–1
Windsor, Romy CTFT–34
Windust, Bretaigne 1906–1960 .... WWasWT
Windust, Penelope CTFT–6
Winer, Harry 1947–............................. CTFT–39
  Earlier sketch in CTFT–15
Winfield, Paul 1941–............................ CTFT–45
  Earlier sketches in CTFT–6, 13, 23
Winfree, Rachel CTFT–36
Winfrey, Oprah 1954–.......................... CTFT–73
  Earlier sketches in CTFT–9, 21, 32
  Brief Entry in CTFT–3
Winger, Debra 1955(?)–......................... CTFT–54
  Earlier sketches in CTFT–6, 13, 25
  Brief Entry in CTFT–2
Wingert, Wally 1961– CTFT–72
Wingfield, Peter 1962– CTFT–74
  Earlier sketch in CTFT–33
Winick, Gary 1961(?)–.......................... CTFT–73
Winkler, Henry 1945–.......................... CTFT–50
  Earlier sketches in CTFT–2, 13, 24
Winkler, Irwin 1931–........................... CTFT–41
  Earlier sketches in CTFT–3, 10, 17
Winn, Amanda CTFT–56
Winn, Anona .... WWasWT
Winn, Godfrey 1906–1971 .... WWasWT
Winn, Kitty 1944– CTFT–8
Winner, Michael 1935–......................... CTFT–36
  Earlier sketches in CTFT–2, 11
Winning, David 1961–.......................... CTFT–37
Winninger, Charles 1884–1969 .... WWasWT
Winningham, Mare 1959–...................... CTFT–67
  Earlier sketches in CTFT–6, 18, 29
  Brief Entry in CTFT–2
Winogradsky, Louis
  See..................................... Grade, Lord Lew
Winokur, Marissa Jaret 1973–............... CTFT–67
  Earlier sketch in CTFT–30
Winslet, Kate 1975–............................ CTFT–58
  Earlier sketches in CTFT–16, 27
Winslow, Michael 1960(?)– CTFT–38
  Earlier sketches in CTFT–7, 14
Winstead, Mary Elizabeth 1984–.............. CTFT–68
Winston, C. Bruce 1879–1946 .... WWasWT
Winston, Hattie 1945– CTFT–55
  Earlier sketch in CTFT–25
Winston, Matt.................................... CTFT–74
Winston, Stan 1946(?)–......................... CTFT–60
  Earlier sketches in CTFT–16, 27
Winstone, Ray 1957– CTFT–67
  Earlier sketch in CTFT–30
Wint, Maurice Dean CTFT–60
Winter, Alex 1965– CTFT–12
Winter, Edward 1937–........................... CTFT–7
Winter, Jessie .... WWasWT
Winter, Keith 1906–............................ WWasWT
Winter, Ralph 1952–............................ CTFT–37
Winter, William 1836–1917 .... WWasWT

Winterbottom, Michael 1961– CTFT–67
    Earlier sketch in CTFT–30
Winters, David 1939– CTFT–51
    Earlier sketch in CTFT–12
Winters, Dean 1964– CTFT–29
Winters, Deborah CTFT–7
Winters, Jonathan 1925– CTFT–67
    Earlier sketches in CTFT–5, 12, 37
Winters, Marian 1924– WWT–17
Winters, Scott William 1965– CTFT–79
Winters, Shelley 1922(?)– CTFT–39
    Earlier sketches in CTFT–4, 13; WWT–17
Winters, Time 1956– CTFT–78
    Earlier sketches in CTFT–5, 35
Winters, Warrington 1909– CTFT–1
Winther, Michael 1962– CTFT–51
    Earlier sketch in CTFT–12
Winton, Colleen CTFT–52
Winwood, Estelle 1883–? .... WWasWT
Wirth, Billy 1962– CTFT–49
Wirth, Bob 1952– CTFT–11
Wisberg, Aubrey 1909(?)–1990 .... CTFT–9
Wisden, Robert CTFT–45
Wisdom, Norman 1925(?)– CTFT–43
    Earlier sketches in CTFT–20; WWT–17
Wisdom, Robert 1953– CTFT–68
    Earlier sketches in CTFT–19, 30
Wise, Greg 1966– CTFT–65
    Earlier sketch in CTFT–28
Wise, Herbert 1924– CTFT–49
    Earlier sketch in WWT–17
Wise, Jim CTFT–43
Wise, Ray 1947– CTFT–61
Wise, Robert E. 1914– CTFT–2
Wise, Scott 1959(?)– CTFT–39
    Earlier sketch in CTFT–13
Wise, Thomas A. 1865–1928 .... WWasWT
Wiseman, Frederick 1930– CTFT–36
    Earlier sketch in CTFT–8
Wiseman, Joseph 1918– CTFT–9
    Earlier sketch in WWT–17
Wishnoff, Steven 1959– CTFT–79
Witcover, Walt 1924– CTFT–4
Withers, Googie 1917– CTFT–9
    Earlier sketch in WWT–17
Withers, Iva 1917– WWT–16
Withers, Jane 1926– CTFT–70
Witherspoon, Cora 1890–1957 .... WWasWT
Witherspoon, John 1942– CTFT–60
    Earlier sketch in CTFT–27
Witherspoon, L.
    See .... Minor, Jerry
Witherspoon, Reese 1976– CTFT–71
    Earlier sketches in CTFT–19, 31
Witt, Alicia 1975– CTFT–41
    Earlier sketch in CTFT–17
Witt, Katarina 1965– CTFT–45
Witt, Paul Junger 1941– CTFT–39
    Earlier sketches in CTFT–3, 13
Wittliff, William D. 1940– CTFT–79
Wittner, Meg CTFT–39
Wittop, Freddy WWT–17
Wittstein, Ed 1929– CTFT–6
    Earlier sketch in WWT–17
Witty, Joann
    See .... Barnes, Priscilla
Wlcek, James 1964– CTFT–25
Wodehouse, Pelham Granville
    1881–1975 .... WWasWT
Wohl, David 1953– CTFT–75
    Earlier sketches in CTFT–7, 33
Woizikovsky, Leon 1897–1922 .... WWasWT
Wojtasik, George 1935– CTFT–2

Woldin, Judd 1925– CTFT–3
Wolf, Dick 1946– CTFT–39
    Earlier sketches in CTFT–4, 13
Wolf, Scott 1968– CTFT–68
    Earlier sketches in CTFT–19, 30
Wolfe, Aaron
    See .... Koontz, Dean R.
Wolfe, George C. 1954– CTFT–38
    Earlier sketch in CTFT–12
Wolfe, Ian 1896–1992 .... CTFT–9
    Obituary in CTFT–10
Wolfe, Robert Hewitt 1964– CTFT–56
Wolff, Jonathan 1958– CTFT–49
Wolff, Pierre 1863–1944 .... WWasWT
Wolff, Ruth 1932– CTFT–2
Wolfit, Donald 1902–1968 .... WWasWT
Wolfman, Marv CTFT–48
Woller, Kirk R.B. CTFT–73
Wollheim, Eric 1879–1948 .... WWasWT
Wolper, David L. 1928– CTFT–39
    Earlier sketches in CTFT–2, 4, 13
Wolsk, Eugene V. 1928– WWT–17
Wolsky, Albert 1930– CTFT–79
    Earlier sketches in CTFT–11, 36
Wolston, Henry 1877–? .... WWasWT
Wolterstorff, Bob 1949– CTFT–12
Wolveridge, Carol 1940– .... WWasWT
Wolvett, Jaimz
    See .... Woolvett, Jaimz
Womark, David CTFT–68
    Earlier sketch in CTFT–30
Wonder, Stevie 1950– CTFT–44
    Earlier sketch in CTFT–21
Wong, Anna May 1907–1961 .... WWasWT
Wong, B. D. 1962(?)– CTFT–41
    Earlier sketches in CTFT–10, 17
    Brief Entry in CTFT–7
Wong, Brenda
    See .... Aoki, Brenda Jean
Wong, James CTFT–56
Wong, Kar-Wai 1958– CTFT–55
    Earlier sketch in CTFT–25
Wong, Russell 1963– CTFT–74
    Earlier sketch in CTFT–33
Wonsek, Paul 1948– CTFT–2
Wontner, Arthur 1875–1960 .... WWasWT
Woo, John 1948(?)– CTFT–52
    Earlier sketches in CTFT–14, 24
Wood, Arthur 1875–1953 .... WWasWT
Wood, Charles 1932– WWT–17
Wood, Daisy 1877–? .... WWasWT
Wood, David 1944– CTFT–21
    Earlier sketch in WWT–17
Wood, Durinda CTFT–62
Wood, Edna 1918– .... WWasWT
Wood, Elijah 1981– CTFT–68
    Earlier sketches in CTFT–19, 30
Wood, Evan Rachel 1987– CTFT–65
    Earlier sketch in CTFT–28
Wood, Florence .... WWasWT
Wood, Frank 1959– CTFT–79
Wood, G. 1919– CTFT–9
Wood, Haydn 1882–1959 .... WWasWT
Wood, Jane 1886–? .... WWasWT
Wood, John 1931(?)– CTFT–46
    Earlier sketches in CTFT–5, 17; WWT–17
Wood, Martin CTFT–79
Wood, Mrs. John 1833–1915 .... WWasWT
Wood, Metcalfe .... WWasWT
Wood, Natalie 1938–1982 .... CTFT–1
Wood, Oliver CTFT–47
Wood, Peggy 1892–1978 .... WWT–16

Wood, Peter 1927(?)– CTFT–10
    Earlier sketch in WWT–17
Wood, Tom 1963– CTFT–52
Wood, Wee Georgie 1897– .... WWasWT
Woodard, Alfre 1952– CTFT–60
    Earlier sketches in CTFT–9, 16, 27
    Brief Entry in CTFT–5
Woodard, Charlayne 1955– CTFT–52
    Earlier sketches in CTFT–12, 25
Woodbine, Bokeem 1973– CTFT–46
    Earlier sketch in CTFT–23
Woodbridge, George 1907– .... WWasWT
Woodbridge, Patricia 1946– CTFT–75
    Earlier sketches in CTFT–2, 34
Woodburn, Danny 1964– CTFT–68
    Earlier sketch in CTFT–30
Woodburn, James 1888–1948 .... WWasWT
Woodeson, Nicholas CTFT–62
    Earlier sketch in CTFT–28
Woodhouse, Vernon 1874–1936 .... WWasWT
Woodland, Lauren 1978– CTFT–47
Woodman, William 1932–1995 .... CTFT–6
    Obituary in CTFT–15
    Earlier sketch in WWT–17
Woodruff, Henry 1870–1916 .... WWasWT
Woods, Albert Herman 1870–1951 .... WWasWT
Woods, Barbara Alyn CTFT–72
Woods, Carol CTFT–40
Woods, Cary CTFT–27
Woods, James 1947– CTFT–47
    Earlier sketches in CTFT–5, 12, 23
Woods, Michael 1957– CTFT–61
    Earlier sketches in CTFT–16, 27
Woods, Richard CTFT–2
Woodside, D. B. CTFT–680
    Earlier sketch in CTFT–30
Woodthorpe, Peter 1931– WWT–17
Woodvine, John 1929– CTFT–42
    Earlier sketches in CTFT–9; WWT–17
Woodward, Charles, Jr. CTFT–5
    Earlier sketch in WWT–17
Woodward, Edward 1930– CTFT–41
    Earlier sketches in CTFT–6, 17; WWT–17
Woodward, Jennifer CTFT–32
Woodward, Joanne 1930– CTFT–42
    Earlier sketches in CTFT–3, 13; WWT–17
Woodward, Peter 1958– CTFT–40
Woodward, Tim 1953– CTFT–40
Woof, Emily 1967– CTFT–36
Wooland, Norman 1905–1989 .... CTFT–8
    Earlier sketch in WWT–17
Wooldridge, Susan CTFT–8
Woolery, Chuck 1941– CTFT–56
Woolf, Edgar Allan ?–1943 .... WWasWT
Woolf, Walter
    See .... King, Walter Woolf
Woolfenden, Guy Anthony
    1937– WWT–17
Woollcott, Alexander 1887–1943 .... WWasWT
Woolley, Monty 1888–1963 .... WWasWT
Woolnough, Jeff CTFT–67
Woolsey, Brent 1958– CTFT–39
Woolsey, Robert 1889–1938 .... WWasWT
Woolvett, Gordon Michael
    1970– CTFT–79
    Earlier sketch in CTFT–36
Woolvett, Jaimz 1967– CTFT–79
    Earlier sketch in CTFT–36
Wootwell, Tom 1865–? .... WWasWT
Wopat, Tom 1951– CTFT–42
    Earlier sketches in CTFT–7, 19
Wordsworth, Richard 1915– WWT–17

Wordsworth, William Derrick
 1912–1988 .... WWasWT
Workman, C. Herbert 1873–1923 .... WWasWT
Worley, Jo Anne 1939(?)– CTFT–63
 Earlier sketch in CTFT–2
Worlock, Frederic G. 1886–1973 .... WWasWT
Worms, Jean 1884–? .... WWasWT
Woronicz, Henry CTFT–32
Woronov, Mary 1943(?)– CTFT–36
 Earlier sketch in CTFT–8
Worrall, Bruce 1960(?)– CTFT–57
Worrall, Lechmere 1875–? .... WWasWT
Worry, Jillian
 See .... Barberie, Jillian
Worshofsky, Dave
 See .... Warshofsky, David
Worsley, Bruce 1899– .... WWasWT
Worster, Howett 1882–? .... WWasWT
Worth, Irene 1916– CTFT–17
 Earlier sketches in CTFT–3, 10; WWT–17
Worth, Marvin 1926(?)–1998 .... CTFT–12
 Obituary in CTFT–21
Worth, Michael 1972(?)– CTFT–60
Worth, Nicholas 1937– CTFT–36
Worthington, Sam 1976– CTFT–79
Worthington, Wendy 1954– CTFT–53
Worthy, Rick CTFT–51
Wouk, Herman 1915– CTFT–1
Wrangler, Greg CTFT–63
Wray, Dean CTFT–55
Wray, Fay 1907– CTFT–8
Wray, John 1888–1940 .... WWasWT
Wray, Maxwell 1898– .... WWasWT
Wrenn, James W. CTFT–70
Wright, Aloma CTFT–67
Wright, Amy 1950– CTFT–42
 Earlier sketch in CTFT–9
Wright, Bonnie 1991– CTFT–77
Wright, Cowley 1889–1923 .... WWasWT
Wright, David 1941– WWT–17
Wright, Fred 1871–1928 .... WWasWT
Wright, Garland CTFT–7
Wright, Haidee 1868–1943 .... WWasWT
Wright, Hugh E. 1879–1940 .... WWasWT
Wright, Huntley 1869–1943 .... WWasWT
Wright, Janet CTFT–48
Wright, Jeffrey 1965(?)– CTFT–67
 Earlier sketch in CTFT–29
Wright, Katie 1981– CTFT–39
Wright, Max 1943(?)– CTFT–78
 Earlier sketches in CTFT–8, 35
Wright, N'Bushe 1970– CTFT–52
 Earlier sketch in CTFT–24
Wright, Nicholas 1940– WWT–17
Wright, Pamela Payton
 See .... Payton–Wright, Pamela
Wright, Robert 1914– CTFT–12
Wright, Robin
 See .... Penn, Robin Wright
Wright, Samuel E. 1946– CTFT–46
 Earlier sketch in CTFT–22
Wright, Steven 1955– CTFT–78
 Earlier sketches in CTFT–9, 35
Wright, Teresa 1918– CTFT–54
 Earlier sketches in CTFT–3, 10, 17; WWT–17
Wright, Mrs. Theodore ?–1922 .... WWasWT
Wright, Thomas J. CTFT–40
Wright, Tom CTFT–62
Wryde, Dogear
 See .... Gorey, Edward
Wrye, Donald CTFT–37
 Earlier sketch in CTFT–12

Wu Jun Mei
 See .... Wu, Vivian
Wu, David CTFT–49
Wu, John
 See .... Woo, John
Wu, Ping CTFT–39
Wu, Vivian 1966– CTFT–44
 Earlier sketch in CTFT–22
Wuhl, Robert 1951– CTFT–46
 Earlier sketches in CTFT–9, 17
Wuhrer, Kari 1967– CTFT–44
 Earlier sketch in CTFT–22
Wunstorf, Peter CTFT–62
Wurman, Alex 1966– CTFT–62
 Earlier sketch in CTFT–28
Wurtzel, Stuart 1940– CTFT–74
 Earlier sketches in CTFT–5, 33
Wyatt, Frank Gunning 1851–1926 .... WWasWT
Wyatt, Jane 1910(?)–2006 .... CTFT–21
 Obituary in CTFT–74
 Earlier sketches in CTFT–3; WWasWT
Wyatt, Marcus
 See .... Chong, Marcus
Wycherly, Margaret 1884–1956 .... WWasWT
Wyckham, John 1926– CTFT–6
 Earlier sketch in WWT–17
Wyckoff, Evelyn 1917– .... WWasWT
Wyle, Noah 1971– CTFT–61
 Earlier sketches in CTFT–16, 27
Wyler, Gretchen 1932– CTFT–6
 Earlier sketch in CTFT–1
Wyler, William 1902–1981 .... CTFT–26
Wylie, Adam 1984– CTFT–60
Wylie, John 1925– CTFT–7
Wylie, Julian 1878–1934 .... WWasWT
Wylie, Lauri 1880–? .... WWasWT
Wyllie, Daniel CTFT–74
 Earlier sketch in CTFT–33
Wyman, J. H. 1967– CTFT–78
Wyman, Jane 1914(?)– CTFT–20
 Earlier sketch in CTFT–3
Wymark, Patrick 1926–1970 .... WWasWT
Wyn, Marjery 1909– .... WWasWT
Wyndham, Charles 1837–1919 .... WWasWT
Wyndham, Dennis 1887–? .... WWasWT
Wyndham, Gwen .... WWasWT
Wyndham, Howard 1865–1947 .... WWasWT
Wyndham, Olive 1886–? .... WWasWT
Wyner, George 1945– CTFT–75
 Earlier sketches in CTFT–7, 34
Wyner, Joel
 See .... Wyman, J. H.
Wyner, Tom CTFT–49
Wynette, Tammy 1942–1998 .... CTFT–23
Wyngarde, Peter WWT–17
Wynn, Ed 1886–1966 .... WWasWT
Wynn, Keenan 1916–1986 .... CTFT–4
Wynn, Tracy Keenan 1945– CTFT–8
 Earlier sketch in CTFT–1
Wynne, Wish 1882–1931 .... WWasWT
Wynorski, Jim 1950– CTFT–37
Wynter, Dana 1930– CTFT–7
Wynter, Sarah 1973– CTFT–68
 Earlier sketch in CTFT–30
Wynyard, Diana 1906–1964 .... WWasWT
Wynyard, John 1915– WWT–16
Wyse, John 1904– WWT–16
Wyss, Amanda 1960– CTFT–42

X

Xanrof, Leon 1867–1953 .... WWasWT
x–sample
 See .... Clapton, Eric

Y

Yablans, Frank 1935– CTFT–8
 Earlier sketch in CTFT–1
Yablans, Irwin 1934– CTFT–8
 Earlier sketch in CTFT–1
Yaffe, Alan
 See .... Yorinks, Arthur
Yager, Missy CTFT–72
Yagher, Jeff 1962– CTFT–62
Yagher, Kevin 1962– CTFT–65
 Earlier sketch in CTFT–28
Yaitanes, Greg 1971– CTFT–63
Yakin, Boaz 1966– CTFT–61
 Earlier sketch in CTFT–27
Yakko, Sada ?–1946 .... WWasWT
Yakovlev, Alexsadr CTFT–34
Yakusho, Koji 1956– CTFT–75
 Earlier sketch in CTFT–32
Yale, Kathleen Betsko 1939– CTFT–2
Yalman, Tunc 1925– CTFT–2
Yancy, Emily 1939– CTFT–76
Yanez, Michael CTFT–3
Yang, Ginny CTFT–4
Yankovic, "Weird Al" 1959– CTFT–71
 Earlier sketches in CTFT–19, 31
Yankovsky, Oleg 1944– CTFT–36
Yankowitz, Susan 1941– CTFT–1
Yannis, Michael 1922– .... WWasWT
Yapp, Cecil CTFT–8
Yarde, Margaret 1878–1944 .... WWasWT
Yared, Gabriel 1949– CTFT–55
 Earlier sketch in CTFT–25
Yarlett, Claire CTFT–72
Yarrow, Duncan 1884–? .... WWasWT
Yasbeck, Amy 1963(?)– CTFT–41
 Earlier sketch in CTFT–17
Yasutake, Patti CTFT–49
Yates, Peter 1929– CTFT–6
 Earlier sketch in CTFT–1
Yavorska, Lydia 1874–1921 .... WWasWT
Yazmania
 See .... Bleeth, Yasmine
Yeager, Biff CTFT–62
Yeamans, Annie 1835–1912 .... WWasWT
Yearsley, Claude Blakesley
 1885–1961 .... WWasWT
Yearwood, Richard CTFT–4
Yeary, Lee
 See .... Majors, L
Yeatman, Hoyt .... CTFT
Yeats, William Butler 1865–1939 .... WWa
Yelchin, Anton 1989– .... CTF
Yelland, David .... CT
 Earlier sketch in CTFT–28
Yellen, Linda 1949– C
 Earlier sketch in CTFT–3
Yen, Donnie 1963– ....
 Earlier sketch in CTFT–33
Yenque, Jose ....

Yensid, Retlaw Elias
　　See .... Disney, Walt
Yeo, Gwendoline.................................... CTFT–57
Yeoh, Michelle 1963–............................. CTFT–44
　　Earlier sketch in CTFT–22
Yeoman, Robert D. CTFT–65
　　Earlier sketch in CTFT–28
Yesso, Don CTFT–67
Yeston, Maury 1945–.............................. CTFT–24
　　Earlier sketches in CTFT–1, 10
Yeung, Chi–King
　　See .... Yeoh, Michelle
Yiasoumi, George CTFT–79
Yniguez, Richard CTFT–74
　　Earlier sketches in CTFT–6, 33
Yoakam, Dwight 1956–........................... CTFT–41
　　Earlier sketch in CTFT–17
Yoba, Malik 1967–.................................. CTFT–46
　　Earlier sketch in CTFT–17
Yohe, May 1869–1938 .... WWasWT
Yohn, Erica CTFT–48
Yokel, Alexander 1887–1947 .... WWasWT
Yoon–Jin, Kim
　　See .... Kim, Yoon–jin
Yordan, Philip 1914–.............................. CTFT–12
Yorinks, Arthur 1953–............................ CTFT–13
York, Dick 1928–1992 .... CTFT–22
York, Francine 1938– CTFT–43
York, John J. 1958–................................ CTFT–58
York, Kathleen CTFT–50
　　Earlier sketch in CTFT–24
York, Michael 1942– CTFT–51
　　Earlier sketches in CTFT–1, 6, 13, 24
York, Rachel 1971– CTFT–42
York, Robert
　　See .... Urich, Robert
York, Susannah 1941– CTFT–5
Yorke, Augustus ?–1939 .... WWasWT
Yorke, Oswald ?–1943 .... WWasWT
Yorker, Jade 1985– CTFT–74
Yorkin, Bud 1926–.................................. CTFT–1
Yoshiyuki, Kazuko CTFT–36
Yoshizaki, Michiyo CTFT–28
Yost, Graham 1959–............................... CTFT–51
Yothers, Tina 1973– CTFT–21
Youmans, James...................................... CTFT–40
　　Earlier sketch in CTFT–14
Youmans, Vincent 1898–1946 .... WWasWT
Youmans, William CTFT–22
Young, Alan 1919–.................................. CTFT–46
Young, Arthur 1898–1959 .... WWasWT
Young, Bellamy CTFT–63
Young, Bertram Alfred 1912– WWT–17
Young, Bill CTFT–36
Young, Bruce A. CTFT–39
Young, ... 1940–.................................. CTFT–79
　　...... sketches in CTFT–5, 35
...... 1971–.. CTFT–35
　　...... ch in CTFT–8
...... 1954(?)–.. CTFT–47
　　...... in CTFT–23

...... ee
　　...................................... Bloch, Robert
　　.. CTFT–56
　　... CTFT–4
　　... CTFT–4
　　... CTFT–39
　　... CTFT–13

.... WWT–16
.... CTFT–43
.... WWasWT
.... WWasWT

Young, Jacob 1979– CTFT–59
Young, Joan 1903–1984 .... WWT–17
Young, Karen 1958– CTFT–74
　　Earlier sketches in CTFT–8, 33
Young, Lee Thomson 1984– CTFT–71
Young, Loretta 1913– CTFT–8
Young, Neil 1945– CTFT–44
　　Earlier sketch in CTFT–21
Young, Nina 1966– CTFT–76
Young, Ric CTFT–67
　　Earlier sketch in CTFT–29
Young, Rida Johnson 1875–1926.......... WWasWT
Young, Robert 1907–.............................. CTFT–7
Young, Robert M. 1924– CTFT–54
　　Earlier sketch in CTFT–9
Young, Roger 1942– CTFT–73
　　Earlier sketches in CTFT–3, 21, 32
Young, Roland 1887–1953 .... WWasWT
Young, Sean 1959–................................. CTFT–50
　　Earlier sketches in CTFT–7, 14, 24
Young, Stark 1881–1963........................ WWasWT
Young, Stephen 1931–............................ CTFT–49
Young, Terence 1915–1994 .... CTFT–7
　　Obituary in CTFT–13
Young, William Allen CTFT–41
Youngman, Henny 1906(?)–1998 .... CTFT–23
Youngs, Jim.. CTFT–7
Yu, Ryun CTFT–78
Yuan, Roger CTFT–49
Yuan, Ron CTFT–49
Yuen, Russell CTFT–54
Yuen Woo Ping 1945– CTFT–29
Yule, Joe, Jr.
　　See................................... Rooney, Mickey
Yulin, Harris 1937– CTFT–72
　　Earlier sketches in CTFT–7, 21, 32
Yune, Rick 1971– CTFT–77
Yurka, Blanche 1887–1974.................... WWasWT
Yusen, Wu
　　See .... Woo, John
Yuuki, Kudou
　　See.. Kudoh, Youki

Z

Zabel, Bryce CTFT–54
Zabelle, Flora 1880–1968 .... WWasWT
Zabka, William 1965–............................. CTFT–67
　　Earlier sketches in CTFT–7, 18, 29
Zabriskie, Grace 1941– CTFT–59
　　Earlier sketches in CTFT–8, 16, 27
Zacapa, Daniel....................................... CTFT–66
Zacconi, Ermete 1857–1948 .... WWasWT
Zada, Ramy 1958– CTFT–78
　　Earlier sketch in CTFT–35
Zadan, Craig... CTFT–1
Zadora, Pia 1956– CTFT–9
Zaentz, Saul 1921– CTFT–54
　　Earlier sketch in CTFT–9
Zagarino, Frank CTFT–43
Zahara, Alex CTFT–49
Zahn, Paula 1956– CTFT–41
Zahn, Steve 1968– CTFT–50
　　Earlier sketch in CTFT–24
Zaillian, Steven 1953(?)– CTFT–24
Zajonc, Robert "Bobby Z"
　　1947–.. CTFT–39
Zakrzewski, Alex CTFT–57

Zaks, Jerry 1946–.................................. CTFT–6
　　Earlier sketch in CTFT–1
Zal, Roxana 1969–.................................. CTFT–78
　　Earlier sketches in CTFT–4, 35
Zaloom, George CTFT–42
Zaloom, Paul 1951–............................... CTFT–1
Zamacois, Miguel 1866–1939 .... WWasWT
Zambello, Francesca 1956– CTFT–50
Zamora, Del CTFT–67
Zampieri, Vittorio 1862–? .... WWasWT
Zamprogna, Dominic 1979– CTFT–74
Zamprogna, Gema 1976– CTFT–67
　　Earlier sketch in CTFT–29
Zane, Billy 1966– CTFT–68
　　Earlier sketches in CTFT–19, 30
Zane, Lisa 1961– CTFT–71
　　Earlier sketch in CTFT–32
Zanetti, Eugenio CTFT–24
Zangwill, Israel 1864–1926 .... WWasWT
Zann, Lenore 1959– CTFT–59
Zanuck, Darryl F. 1902–1979 .... CTFT–22
Zanuck, Lili Fini 1954– CTFT–43
　　Earlier sketch in CTFT–21
Zanuck, Richard D. 1934– CTFT–50
　　Earlier sketches in CTFT–7, 14, 24
Zanussi, Krzysztof 1939–....................... CTFT–8
Zapata, Carmen 1927– CTFT–42
　　Earlier sketch in CTFT–9
Zappa, Ahmet... CTFT–71
　　Earlier sketches in CTFT–21, 32
Zappa, Dweezil 1969– CTFT–43
　　Earlier sketch in CTFT–21
Zappa, Frank 1940–1993 .... CTFT–21
Zappa, Moon Unit 1967–....................... CTFT–57
　　Earlier sketch in CTFT–21
Zappa, William 1948–............................ CTFT–76
　　Earlier sketch in CTFT–34
Zarvos, Marcelo..................................... CTFT–77
Zaslow, Michael 1944–1998 .... CTFT–23
Zayas, David CTFT–79
Zaza, Paul CTFT–69
Zea, Kristi 1948–................................... CTFT–55
　　Earlier sketches in CTFT–10, 26
Zea, Natalie 1975–................................. CTFT–72
Zeff, Lisa CTFT–48
Zeffirelli, Franco 1923–......................... CTFT–33
　　Earlier sketches in CTFT–4; WWT–17
Zegers, Kevin 1984–............................... CTFT–75
　　Earlier sketches in CTFT–21, 32
Zehetner, Nora 1981– CTFT–74
Zellweger, Renee 1969–......................... CTFT–68
　　Earlier sketches CTFT–19, 30
Zem, Roschdy CTFT–33
Zeman, Jacklyn 1953–............................ CTFT–78
　　Earlier sketch in CTFT–5
Zeman, Richard...................................... CTFT–64
Zemeckis, Leslie Harter CTFT–75
Zemeckis, Robert 1952– CTFT–50
　　Earlier sketches in CTFT–7, 14, 24
Zerbe, Anthony 1936– CTFT–78
　　Earlier sketches in CTFT–6, 35
Zeta–Jones, Catherine 1969– CTFT–45
　　Earlier sketch in CTFT–23
Zetterling, Mai 1925–1994 .... WWasWT
　　Obituary in CTFT–13
Zeus
　　See .... Lister, Tom "Tiny"
ZGansta
　　See .... Lister, Tom "Tiny"
Zhang Guorong
　　See .... Cheung, Leslie
Zhang Yimou 1950–............................... CTFT–28
Zhang Yuan 1963– CTFT–28

Zhang, Ziyi 1979– CTFT–77
Zhu, Yuanlong
    See .... Kam–Bo, Sammo Hung
Zicree, Marc Scott 1955– CTFT–74
Zieff, Howard 1943– CTFT–10
Ziegfeld, Florenz 1867–1932 .... WWasWT
Ziegler, Anne 1910– .... WWasWT
Ziegler, Joseph CTFT–54
    Earlier sketch in CTFT–25
Ziegler, Karen
    See .... Black, Karen
Zielinski, Jerzy 1950– CTFT–47
    Earlier sketch in CTFT–23
Ziemba, Karen 1957– CTFT–46
    Earlier sketches in CTFT–3, 22
Zien, Chip 1947– CTFT–56
    Earlier sketches in CTFT–6, 26
Ziering, Ian 1964– CTFT–72
    Earlier sketches in CTFT–19, 31
Ziff, Irwin 1929– CTFT–4
Zima, Madeline 1985– CTFT–74
Zima, Vanessa 1986– CTFT–75
Zima, Yvonne 1989– CTFT–32
Zimbalist, Efrem, Jr. 1923(?)– CTFT–43
    Earlier sketches in CTFT–3, 21
Zimbalist, Stephanie 1956– CTFT–78
    Earlier sketches in CTFT–6, 35
Zimmer, Constance 1970– CTFT–79
    Earlier sketch in CTFT–36
Zimmer, Hans 1957– CTFT–45
    Earlier sketches in CTFT–10, 17
Zimmerman, Don CTFT–65
    Earlier sketch in CTFT–28

Zimmerman, Grace
    See .... Phillips, Grace
Zimmerman, Herman F. 1935– CTFT–56
Zimmerman, Joey 1986– CTFT–79
    Earlier sketch in CTFT–36
Zimmerman, Mark 1952– CTFT–74
    Earlier sketches in CTFT–2, 33
Zimmerman, Paul 1938–1993 .... CTFT–2
    Obituary in CTFT–12
Zinberg, Michael CTFT–36
    Earlier sketch in CTFT–11
Zindel, Paul 1936– CTFT–20
    Earlier sketches in CTFT–3; WWT–17
Zinkeisen, Doris Clare .... WWasWT
Zinnemann, Fred 1907–1997 .... CTFT–7
    Obituary in CTFT–17
    Earlier sketch in CTFT–1
Zinnemann, Tim CTFT–10
Zippel, David CTFT–32
    Earlier sketch in CTFT–21
Zipprodt, Patricia 1925– CTFT–7
    Earlier sketches in CTFT–2; WWT–17
Zisk, Craig CTFT–64
Zisk, Randall CTFT–77
Ziskin, Laura 1950– CTFT–40
    Earlier sketch in CTFT–16
Zito, Chuck 1953– CTFT–79
Zito, Joseph 1946(?)– CTFT–16
Ziyi, Zhang
    See .... Zhang, Ziyi
Zmed, Adrian 1954– CTFT–75
    Earlier sketches in CTFT–8, 33
Zola, Fred .... WWasWT

Zollar, Jawole Willa Jo 1951(?)– CTFT–11
Zollo, Frederick M. 1950– CTFT–1
Zombie, Rob 1965(?)– CTFT–78
Zophres, Mary 1964(?)– CTFT–44
    Earlier sketch in CTFT–22
Zorich, Louis 1924– CTFT–35
    Earlier sketch in CTFT–2
Zorina, Vera 1917– WWT–17
Zsigmond, Vilmos 1930– CTFT–59
    Earlier sketches in CTFT–2, 8, 16, 27
Zuber, Catherine CTFT–41
Zucco, George 1886–1960 .... WWasWT
Zucker, David 1947– CTFT–42
    Earlier sketches in CTFT–1, 9
Zucker, Jerry 1950– CTFT–27
    Earlier sketches in CTFT–8, 16
Zuckerman, Josh 1985– CTFT–76
Zuckerman, Steve CTFT–50
Zuckmayer, Carl 1896–1977 .... WWT–16
Zuniga, Daphne 1962(?)– CTFT–40
    Earlier sketches in CTFT–8, 16
Zuniga, Jose CTFT–75
    Earlier sketches in CTFT–21, 32
Zuvic, Daniella
    See .... Monet, Daniella
Zwar, Charles 1914–1989 .... WWT–17
Zwerdling, Allen 1922– CTFT–4
Zwick, Edward 1952– CTFT–58
    Earlier sketches in CTFT–3, 16, 27
Zwick, Joel 1942– CTFT–42
    Earlier sketch in CTFT–9
Zylberstein, Elsa 1969– CTFT–36

Cumulative Index